SHORTER TWELFTH EDITION

# LITERATURE
## THE HUMAN EXPERIENCE

W9-BXN-769

**RICHARD ABCARIAN**
California State University, Northridge, Emeritus

**MARVIN KLOTZ**
*Late of* California State University, Northridge

**SAMUEL COHEN**
University of Missouri

bedford/st.martin's
Macmillan Learning
Boston | New York

*For Bedford/St. Martin's*

*Vice President, Editorial, Macmillan Learning Humanities:* Edwin Hill
*Senior Program Director for English:* Leasa Burton
*Program Manager:* John E. Sullivan III
*Executive Marketing Manager:* Joy Fisher Williams
*Director of Content Development:* Jane Knetzger
*Developmental Editor:* Alicia Young
*Content Project Manager:* Louis C. Bruno Jr.
*Senior Workflow Manager:* Lisa McDowell
*Production Supervisor:* Robert Cherry
*Associate Marketing Manager:* Sophia Latorre-Zengierski
*Manager of Publishing Services:* Andrea Cava
*Project Management:* Lumina Datamatics, Inc.
*Composition:* Lumina Datamatics, Inc.
*Director of Rights and Permissions:* Hilary Newman
*Photo Researcher:* Charles Morris
*Permissions Manager:* Kalina Ingham
*Senior Art Director:* Anna Palchik
*Text Design:* Joan O'Connor; DeMasi Design and Publishing Services
*Cover Design:* William Boardman
*Cover Art:* Collage Woman #2, © Elizabeth Rosen, 2015/Morgan Gaynin, Inc.
*Printing and Binding:* Edwards Brothers Malloy

Manufactured in the United States of America.

2   1   0   9   8
f   e   d   c   b

*For information, write:* Bedford/St. Martin's, 75 Arlington Street, Boston, MA 02116

ISBN 978-1-319-05471-7

**Acknowledgments**
*Text acknowledgments and copyrights appear at the back of the book on pages 1021–28, which constitute an extension of the copyright page. Art acknowledgments and copyrights appear on the same page as the art selections they cover.*

For Marv

# Preface for Instructors

> We all suffer alone in the real world; true empathy's impossible. But if a piece of fiction can allow us imaginatively to identify with a character's pain, we might then also more easily conceive of others identifying with our own. This is nourishing, redemptive; we become less alone inside. It might just be that simple.
>
> —David Foster Wallace

While committed readers would agree that they read literature because they find it delightful, instructive, or both, many of your students may read literature because it has been assigned to them in a required class. We've prepared every edition of *Literature: The Human Experience* for such students. For them, we choose literature that's entertaining and thought-provoking enough to capture the interest of indifferent or uncommitted readers. We organize that literature to address cradle-to-grave thematic concerns that are compelling and inescapable. Finally, we show students how to connect with what they encounter in the literature through their reading, discussion, and writing. As David Foster Wallace's epigraph suggests, reading literature can forge empathetic links that are consoling, sustaining, and even redemptive. We believe that students' experience of literature in a course should leave them feeling connected, not only to the writing they read and the writers who wrote it, but also to one another—indeed, to the multitudes of others, past and present, whose lives comprise the human experience.

Everything that's new in the twelfth edition furthers these goals. New works by young writers extend our effort to bring students to literature by including writing that speaks, in voices more like theirs, of experiences to which they can connect. New examples of classic literature on timeless themes continue to represent the best that's been thought and said and as well the perennial need for humans to represent their experiences through imaginative work and storytelling. New pairs and clusters of literary works juxtapose classic and recent writing, encouraging critical comparative thinking. New argument-focused questions ask students to engage more actively with selections, pushing them to think critically and write persuasively about literature. Creative new writing topics strengthen the book's emphasis on getting students to see literature—and life—as writers.

## FEATURES

### A THEMATIC ORGANIZATION THAT CONNECTS LITERATURE TO LIFE.
We believe that students are most immediately engaged by works in which

they can see themselves. The ability of students to connect their experiences to those they read about does not mean they should be assigned nothing but literature about students or Americans or Westerners or young people from anywhere; it does mean that the human experience, in its dazzling variety, can be represented in art and that students can respond to it no matter the different circumstances of reader and writer. In gathering these works, we tried to meet students where they live and take them to places they have never seen. The best way to do this is to concentrate on different themes drawn from human experience and to ask students to read divergent perspectives on these themes. Thus, the anthology is organized into five thematic sections: "Innocence and Experience," "Conformity and Rebellion," "Culture and Identity," "Love and Hate," and "Life and Death." Each section opens with a short introductory essay and questions that invite students to reflect on their own experiences with the chapter's theme.

To enhance teaching flexibility, the thematic structure features two subordinate arrangements of the literature. Embedded in each thematic section, the stories, poems, plays, and essays are grouped by genre; within each genre, selections are arranged chronologically by author's birth date. (The date following the title indicates the selection's first appearance in a book. We have not attempted to date traditional ballads.) The dates, together with an appendix containing biographical notes on the authors, provide students with a brief historical context for each work. So whether you teach literature thematically, generically, or historically—or some combination of the three—the organization of *Literature: The Human Experience* accommodates your approach.

The thematic sections are also punctuated with eleven short units that pair or cluster literary works—often classic with contemporary. While promoting comparative critical thinking with their accompanying questions and writing assignments, these compact clusters provide engaging reading for students. For example, "America through Immigrants' Eyes" brings together poets from Phillis Wheatley to Kofi Awoonor, and in "Love Stinks," poems by Catullus and Aphra Behn are grouped with more modern poets in a cluster about the pain that often accompanies love. The new nonfiction pair "Missing Mothers" couples Jonathan Lethem's powerful reflection on adolescence and loss, "13, 1977, 21," with Ruth Margalit's affecting essay "The Unmothered."

**TWO CHAPTERS OFFER SUPPORT FOR READING AND WRITING ABOUT LITERATURE.** Two introductory chapters, "Responding to Literature" and "Writing about Literature," give students the tools to think about and appreciate what they read and to put those thoughts into words. In these chapters, we discuss the formal elements of each genre and provide descriptions and samples of various forms of written response and documentation. Throughout the thematic sections, study questions challenge students to analyze works, to make connections between them, and to write about them in a variety of ways. At the end of the book, the "Glossary of Critical Approaches" and the "Glossary of Literary Terms" provide additional resources for students learning about how to approach literature.

## NEW TO THIS EDITION

### WIDE-RANGING CONTEMPORARY LITERATURE ANCHORED BY A STURDY SELECTION OF CLASSICS

- *Fiction:* "The End of FIRPO in the World" by George Saunders and Camden Joy's "Dum Dum Boys" are new to this Shorter Twelfth Edition, as are the classics "Half a Day" by Naguib Mahfouz and Lu Xun's "Diary of a Madman."

- *Poetry:* Selections from Jonathan Swift, Czeslaw Milosz, Léopold Sédar Senghor, and others are new to the anthology, as are modern voices such as Dilruba Ahmed, Tishani Doshi, and Chris Abani.

- *Drama:* Edward Albee's *The Sandbox* makes its first appearance in this anthology in the "Life and Death" section.

- *Nonfiction:* The new essays represent some of the most stimulating work in this ever-growing genre, from critically acclaimed essays by Eula Biss and Jonathan Lethem to short examples of creative nonfiction from the much-admired online journal *Brevity*.

**MORE SUPPORT FOR MAKING ARGUMENTS ABOUT LITERATURE.** A new section in the introduction shows students the basic building blocks of argument, and new "Making Arguments" questions throughout the thematic chapters ask students to argue critically about—and with—the literature they're reading.

**TWO NEW CASE STUDIES EXPLORE ARGUMENTS WITHIN THE GENRES.** Case studies on debates about Flannery O'Connor (fiction) and the conditions of modern-day revolutions (nonfiction) show students how literature can make arguments about our world and our lives.

## ACKNOWLEDGMENTS

We would like to thank the professors who generously took time to share their ideas about the previous edition of this anthology. They are Amy Amoroso, University of Maine at Augusta; Lauren Angel-Cann, Collin College–Preston Ridge Campus; Leisa Belleau, University of Southern Indiana; Lynn Clarkson, North Shore Community College; Paul Francoeur, University of Massachusetts Lowell; Claire-Marie Hart, North Shore Community College; Nancy Lee-Jones, Endicott College; Shawn Liang, Mohawk Valley Community College; MaryKate McMaster, Anna Maria College; Marge Morian-Boyle, Dean College; David Mulry, College of Coastal Georgia; Debbie Olson, University of Texas at Arlington; Kirsten Patey-Hurd, Quinsigamond Community College; Jill Rossiter, Lewis-Clark State College; Sandra S. McRae Sajbel, Red Rocks Community College; Karen Ryan, Florida Gulf Coast University; Thomas Schaefer, Middlesex Community College; Celeste M. Sherry, SUNY

Rockland Community College; Judy Sneller, South Dakota School of Mines and Technology; Frederick White, Slippery Rock University; and our reviewers who wish to remain anonymous from New Jersey City University and the University of Massachusetts Lowell.

We wish to thank Karissa Lagos, whose precocious writing skills provided us with a superb research paper. We also wish to thank Anita Zubère, who helped untangle some knotty lines of poetry; Roy Merrens for explaining some of the arcane features of the urban London landscape; and Bainbridge Scott, whose knowledge of music made our task easier. Our thanks also go to Mary Lawless for her thoughtful contributions to the introductory chapters on reading and writing and to Michelle McSweeney for her smart and detailed updates to the biographical notes. Experienced and wise people at Bedford/St. Martin's have guided this book along the way. We thank Edwin Hill, Vice President, Editorial, Macmillan Higher Education Humanities. As well, we are grateful to Kalina Ingham, Lenny J. Behnke, and Charles Morris for procuring permissions and to Louis Bruno and Saraswathi Muralidhar for shepherding the book through production. We thank Billy Boardman for his persistence in creating this edition's vibrant new cover and Sophia Latorre-Zengierski for providing expert marketing advice. As ever, we owe many thanks to Karen Henry and Steve Scipione, as well as heaps of gratitude to editor Alicia Young, for her vision, hard work, and endless patience and good humor. This book would simply not be what it is without their contributions—it would not exist at all. Some of this labor (there's certainly enough to go around) must surely be credited to editorial assistant Jennifer Prince, for whose efforts we are very grateful.

Finally, we would like to recognize the passing of Marvin Klotz, who with Dick Abcarian created this book dedicated to teaching and learning literature as a human creation and a record of human experience, and who saw it through four decades of use in classrooms around the country. On behalf of all of the students and teachers his work touched, we want to acknowledge Marv.

*Richard Abcarian*
*Samuel Cohen*

## GET THE MOST OUT OF YOUR COURSE WITH *LITERATURE: THE HUMAN EXPERIENCE*

*Literature: The Human Experience* doesn't stop with a book. Bedford/St. Martin's offers resources that help you and your students get even more out of your book and course. You'll also find convenient instructor resources, and even a nationwide community of teachers. To learn more about or to order any of the following products, contact your Bedford/St. Martin's sales representative, or visit **macmillanlearning.com**.

### *Assign* LaunchPad Solo for Literature *— the online, interactive guide to close reading.*

**launchpadworks.com**

To get the most out of *Literature: The Human Experience*, assign it with *LaunchPad Solo for Literature*, which can be packaged at **a significant discount**. With easy-to-use and easy-to-assign modules, reading comprehension quizzes, and engaging author videos, *LaunchPad Solo for Literature* guides students through three common assignment types: responding to a reading, drawing connections between two or more texts, and instructor-led collaborative close reading. Get all of our great resources and activities in one fully customizable space online; then use our tools with your own content. To learn more about how you can use *LaunchPad Solo for Literature* in your course, please see pages x–xi of this Preface.

### *Package one of our best-selling brief handbooks at a discount.*

Do you need a pocket-sized handbook for your course? Package *Easy Writer* by Andrea Lunsford or *A Pocket Style Manual* by Diana Hacker and Nancy Sommers with this text at a 20% discount. For more information, go to **macmillanlearning.com**.

### *Teach longer works at a nice price.*

Volumes in our literary reprint series — Bedford College Editions, Bedford Cultural Editions, Case Studies in Contemporary Criticism, Case Studies in Critical Controversy, the Bedford Series in History and Culture, and the Bedford Shakespeare Series — can be shrink-wrapped with *Literature: The Human Experience* at a discount. For a complete list of available titles, visit **macmillanlearning.com**.

### *Trade Up and save 50%.*

Add more value and choice to your students' learning experiences by packaging their Bedford/St. Martin's textbook with one of a thousand titles from our sister publishers, including Farrar, Straus and Giroux and St. Martin's Press — at a discount of 50% off the regular price. Visit **macmillanlearning .com/tradeup** for details.

## *Access your instructor resources and get teaching ideas you can use today.*

Are you looking for professional resources for teaching literature and writing? How about some help with planning classroom activities?

**DOWNLOAD YOUR INSTRUCTOR'S MANUAL.** *Editors' Notes for Teaching Literature: The Human Experience* offers teaching ideas for each selection in the anthology as well as additional thematic connections and writing topics. The manual is available online at **macmillanlearning.com**.

**JOIN OUR COMMUNITY.** The Macmillan English Community is home to Bedford/St. Martin's professional resources, featuring content to support the teaching of literature — including our popular blog, *LitBits*, as well as articles, research studies, and testimonials on the importance of literature in our classrooms and in our lives. Community members may also review projects and ideas in the pipeline. Join at **community.macmillan.com**.

**ENGAGE YOUR STUDENTS WITH DIGITAL ASSIGNMENTS.** *Teaching Literature with Digital Technology* is a collection of digital assignments, each created by a contributor in the fields of literature and composition. Edited by Seattle-based scholar and teacher Tim Hetland and available as a print text or e-Book, this resource for instructors invites students to become knowledge-makers as it introduces creative uses of social media, digital tools, podcasts, multimodal assignments, and digital archives to learn about literature. Sample assignments can be viewed in the Professional Resources folder on the Macmillan English Community site. To order the print text, use ISBN 978-1-4576-2948-8; to order the e-Book, use ISBN 978-1-3190-7643-6.

**ORDER CONTENT FOR YOUR COURSE MANAGEMENT SYSTEM.** Content cartridges for the most common course management systems — Blackboard, Canvas, Angel, Moodle, Sakai, and Desire2Learn — allow you to easily download Bedford/St. Martin's digital materials for your course. For more information, visit **macmillanlearning.com**.

**LaunchPad Solo**
macmillan learning

## PAIRING *LITERATURE: THE HUMAN EXPERIENCE* WITH *LAUNCHPAD SOLO FOR LITERATURE* HELPS STUDENTS SUCCEED.

Available at a significant discount when packaged with *Literature: The Human Experience*, LaunchPad Solo for Literature gets to the heart of close reading. It offers a set of online materials that help beginning literature students learn and practice close reading and critical thinking skills in an interactive environment.

To package *LaunchPad Solo for Literature*, use ISBN 978-1-319-18537-4.

### How can *LaunchPad Solo for Literature* enhance your course?

IT HELPS STUDENTS COME PREPARED TO CLASS.    Assign one of almost 500 reading comprehension quizzes on commonly taught stories, poems, plays, and essays to ensure that your students complete and understand their reading. For homework assignments, have students work through close reading modules that will prepare them for lively, informed classroom discussions.

IT GIVES STUDENTS HANDS-ON PRACTICE IN CLOSE READING.    Easy-to-use and easy-to-assign modules based on widely taught literary selections guide students through three common assignment types:

- *Respond to a Reading* Questions in the margins that refer to specific passages in a publisher-provided literary work prompt students to read carefully and think critically about key issues raised by the text.

- *Draw Connections* Students read and compare two or more publisher-provided texts that illuminate each other. Students can download these texts, which have been annotated to highlight key moments and contextual information, and respond in writing to a series of questions that highlight important similarities and differences between and among the texts.

To explore *LaunchPad Solo for Literature*, visit **launchpadworks.com**.

- *Collaborate on a Reading* Instructors can upload their favorite text or choose from over 200 publisher-provided texts to create a customized lesson on close reading. Using the highlighting tools and Notes feature in LaunchPad, the instructor can post notes or questions about specific passages or issues in a text, prompting students to respond with their own comments, questions, or observations. Students can also respond to each other, further collaborating and deepening their understanding of a text.

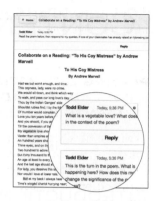

**IT LETS YOU CREATE MULTIMEDIA ASSIGNMENTS ABOUT LITERATURE.** *LaunchPad Solo for Literature* enables you to embed videos, including favorite selections from YouTube, directly into your digital course. Whether you want students to analyze a Shakespearean scene, listen to W. B. Yeats reading his poems, or compare *The Great Gatsby* in print and on film, the tools are at your fingertips. You can annotate these videos for your students, or ask them to leave their own comments directly on the video content itself. Consider some of these assignment suggestions:

- *Create a Dialogue around an Assignment.* Some projects are complicated because they involve many choices and stages. Record yourself explaining the project, and upload the video to the Video Assignment tool. Require students to comment by asking a question or by proposing a topic.
- *Critique a Video as a Group.* Embed a video from YouTube or from another source. In your assignment instructions, provide discussion questions. Require students to add 2–3 comments on the video that respond to the prompt. You may grade this assignment with a rubric.
- *Collaborate on Acting out a Scene from a Play.* Although students most often study plays as written texts, it can be fun and informative to have them act out scenes for their classmates. Assign small groups of students to record themselves acting out their favorite scene from a play and upload the video for the class to watch. You can add your feedback and comments directly on the video.
- *Compare and Share Poems Your Students Read Aloud.* Sound is essential in poetry, and how a poem is read can be as important to understanding as the words themselves. Invite students to record themselves — either using video, or audio only — and share the results with the class. Consider giving each student a "mood" for their reading, so that the class can hear how different tones and interpretations affect their response to the poem.

# CONTENTS

# INNOCENCE AND EXPERIENCE   76

## CONNECTING STORIES: CRUSHES   121

## CASE STUDY IN ARGUMENT
### FINDING GRACE IN FLANNERY O'CONNOR   137

## POETRY   162

# CONFORMITY AND REBELLION   264

## CASE STUDY IN ARGUMENT

# CULTURE AND IDENTITY 428

## CONNECTING POEMS: AMERICA THROUGH IMMIGRANTS' EYES   535

# ALTERNATE CONTENTS

Arranged by genre and alphabetically by the author's last name.

## FICTION

## POETRY

## DRAMA

## NONFICTION

# INTRODUCTION

# RESPONDING TO LITERATURE

There is no Frigate like a Book
To take us Lands away
Nor any Coursers like a Page
Of prancing poetry —

This Traverse may the poorest take
Without oppress of Toll —
How frugal is the Chariot
That bears the Human soul.
    — Emily Dickinson (ca. 1873)

## WHY WE READ LITERATURE

The epigraph from poet Emily Dickinson promotes reading as an escape, a way for us to take a vacation from our lives. If we think about our experiences with literature — and with other forms of entertainment, such as movies and TV shows — that probably sounds about right. Most of us have enjoyed forgetting about the cares of the world with a page-turning thriller or a tear-jerking melodrama. But literature can also help us get closer to life, to understand it in a new way when we get back from our literary journey. We understand what Dickinson means because we can connect to it — we think about our experiences as readers and that helps us understand the poem while, at the same time, the poem clarifies something about how reading makes us feel. The best literature helps us to understand ourselves, one another, and our world in new ways and to make connections that had never occurred to us or that we might have sensed but were unable to express.

Of course, you may not feel this way about reading the kind of literature you expect to find in a textbook. It may be that opening a textbook signals to you that the fun is over. And certainly reading and responding to serious literature requires concentrated attention and is not relaxing in the way that kicking back and watching a TV show might be. But what you may not realize is that you likely respond critically to literature without even realizing that you are doing so. Inevitably, when you encounter any kind of literature, you distinguish good from evil, right from wrong — and you do so based on your own experiences and knowledge of the world. When writers convey cultural ideas about the nature of love, of duty, of heroism — sometimes broadly, sometimes with subtlety — you agree or disagree, are moved or are not. You may not now be moved by the same literature that entranced you when you were a child, or you may have come to appreciate that literature in a fuller, more nuanced way. But you may be surprised, when you turn your attention to "serious" literature, to find how much these works have in common with the books, movies, and TV shows you have turned to for entertainment. Some "popular" authors — Janet Evanovich, Lee Child, John Grisham, Dorothy Sayers, and others — who write spy novels and detective fiction are routinely read in college courses that celebrate literature. Their exciting and suspenseful novels are often made into films, but so, too, are the classic works of William Shakespeare, Jane Austen, Edith Wharton, F. Scott Fitzgerald, and Ernest Hemingway.

Serious literature, no less than popular literature, embodies thrilling adventure. Serious literature is replete with monsters (consider the Old English epic *Beowulf*), ghosts (at the outset of Shakespeare's *Hamlet* and in the middle of *Macbeth*), witches, supernatural spirits, magical transformations, unspeakably brutal wars, terrible murders, and bloody vengeance. Given the close ties between popular and serious literature, scholars, teachers, and readers frequently debate what should be included in textbooks like this one, what literature best represents the "literary canon." Here things get a bit murky. *Canon* is derived from the Latin word meaning "measuring line or rule" and is used in religious discourse to signify "sacred writings admitted to the catalog according to the rule." Early theologians decided which books were the authentic word of God and which were not. But, much like today's literary scholars, they did not always agree. Although it attempts to establish the body of literature that humans need to study and master, the literary canon changes in response to political and social changes. Further, a literary canon is bound to reflect the cultural tradition that produces it. The literary canon of China will differ markedly from the literary canon of the United States. And both will change with the eruptions of history and the demands of fashion.

For example, although American literary history is replete with women writers, they have often been undervalued by the literary canon's guardians. But a century of political struggle — which led, first, to enfranchising women as voters and, later, to a feminist movement that demanded equality for women and their works — has allowed some women authors to gain entry to the canon, forever changing it. Writers like Kate Chopin and Charlotte Perkins Gilman are now routinely included in university courses and women writers are broadly represented in this anthology. Further, the political struggles of Native American, African American, Latino/a, and Asian American citizens have drawn considerable attention to a large and diverse body of writing that was often overlooked by critics who prized European authors. Skillful literary artists from these groups are also represented here.

You might reasonably ask, What difference does broadening the literary canon make? Consider: if you love books and movies, then you know how influential they can be and you'll probably agree that what we read makes a tremendous difference to the world we live in. You learn a great deal about your society from reading — what it values, what it condemns, how it expects you to behave, what constitutes success both economically and morally, what it sees as the very nature of good and evil. If your reading were limited to, say, European works and you were embedded in a non-European social group, you might not discover yourself or your peers in the books you read. Thus, schools and anthologies that project a narrow literary canon would present a world foreign to your experience. The resulting sense of anomie — a rootless lack of purpose, identity, and values — could be terribly damaging. At the same time, ignorance of your neighbors' lifestyles could also seriously impair your life by giving you a skewed, incomplete vision of the world. Conversely, reading widely could help you avoid the baleful consequences of racism, hypernationalism, and ignorance.

The stories, poems, plays, and essays in this textbook have been selected from a diverse array of important authors, some of them very popular, others often most appreciated by scholars and critics. Some of these writers have been read and studied in schools and colleges for centuries while others, especially from historically underrepresented groups, may be entirely new to you. We hope that you enjoy reading the works by the authors and thinkers in this book. We also hope that you find surprising commonalities among these very different writers and between them and you. The units are organized around universal themes and are designed to help you connect your own life and the things you are reading to the many literary traditions that join us to each other, to our collective history, and to the world at large. The literature in this volume will take you out of your comfort zone to "lands away" while giving you new tools for understanding yourself and your immediate world. The only "toll" required is an open mind and an attentive eye.

## READING ACTIVELY AND CRITICALLY

In a well-ordered universe, you would enjoy all your reading — and your delight would derive from your complete absorption in and understanding of what you read. But just as sports require physical conditioning in order for you to perform at your best, you may need to build up your stamina as an effective reader. First of all, pay attention to *how* you read. Can you read fifty pages in one sitting, or do you find your mind wandering after a page or two? If you fall into the latter category, don't worry — we all succumb to the allure of distractions once in a while. But it is up to you to train yourself not to let it diminish your reading experience. If you feel your attention beginning to wander, stop and look back to the place in the text where you began to drift. When you come back to your reading, commit yourself to reading another portion of the passage that's longer than the last one you read. You can hold yourself accountable by writing a short summary — from memory — of what you've read every few sentences, paragraphs, or pages. When you deliberately "train" your mind in this way, your ability to focus and concentrate — and think — will be enhanced, and you will be a better reader for your efforts.

Equally important to reading actively is paying attention to *what* you read. It can be easy to get bogged down by the sheer volume of words on a page, but you can help make sense of them by keeping a pencil in hand and interacting with the page. Mark words you don't recognize and look them up in the dictionary. Note when you feel a protest rising in your throat. Jot down places where the text reminds you of something in your own life or in another work of art — any kind of connection. Active reading takes you beyond the role of an observer, removed and separate from the things you read, and makes you a participant in a conversation with the author or even with the characters. So don't be shy — speak up!

Beyond being an active reader of literature, you must also become a critical reader. Beyond simply perceiving the words on the page, critical reading invites you to question those words in profound, meaningful ways. When we ask you to read critically, we ask that you use the complex set of experiences that define you as a human being — as well as a sense of the cultural imperatives among which you live — to analyze the work you encounter. As a critical reader, you learn to address your biases, enlarge your universe, and test your comfortable convictions. Thus, when you adopt a critical position toward a piece of literature, you need to test and question that position. Ask, What perspective does the author have that led him or her to write this work? What social, cultural, or historical conditions influenced the production of the work? What other ways might the author have presented the ideas or subjects of the work? Are the author's values different from my own? How do my views and experiences affect whether I like or dislike the work? Such questions are stepping stones toward being able to write about literature meaningfully and compellingly (a process that is discussed in greater detail on pp. 32–75).

## READING FICTION

Fiction creates imaginary worlds by telling stories written in *prose* (ordinary, unrhymed language), about realistic characters, set in physical environments, and with sustained attention to descriptive detail.

Works of fiction *narrate*, or tell, stories. Of course, narrative is not specific to fiction or to any other literary genre: telling stories pervades almost every aspect of our daily lives. We learn very early on how to recognize and tell stories, and we rely heavily on narrative to organize and make sense of our experience. For example, when we study history, we mostly study stories of various events. Likewise, an astronomer's account of the universe's origins may take the shape of a narrative. Even in our sleep, we tell ourselves stories in the form of dreams. It is impossible to imagine our lives without these narratives; in fact, every culture uses them to order and make sense of lived experience. Narrative fiction is not meant to recount actual events, of course, though it may refer to real events or real persons. Rather than relate actual experiences, fiction uses narrative to shape imaginary ones.

Works of fiction, however, cannot be reduced to a listing of their narrative events any more than paintings can be replaced by diagrams. Such summaries diminish a work's realism, which is produced by careful description of characters, settings, and actions, as well as its depths of meaning. For example, the emotional impact of James Joyce's "Araby" cannot be captured by summarizing its simple plot. Without suspending critical judgment, readers of fiction have to be willing to suspend disbelief, that is, to enter the imaginary world of the novel or short story.

## The Methods of Fiction

In order to examine the methods of fiction — tone, setting, plot, theme, characterization, point of view, and irony — let us look more closely at James Joyce's "Araby" (p. 121).

**TONE**   One of the things most readers first respond to in a short story is its *tone*. Because it is like a *mood*, tone is difficult to talk about. It can be defined as an author's implicit attitude toward the characters, places, and events in the story and toward the reader of the work. Tone depends for its substance on delicate emotional responses to language and situation. Notice how a distinct tone is established in the language of the opening lines of "Araby":

> North Richmond Street, being blind, was a quiet street except at the hour when the Christian Brothers' School set the boys free. An uninhabited house of two storeys stood at the blind end, detached from its neighbours in a square ground. The other houses of the street, conscious of decent lives within them, gazed at one another with brown imperturbable faces.

Is this scene cheerful? Vital and active? Should we expect this story to celebrate the joys of growing up in Dublin? Negative responses to these questions arise from the tone of the opening description. Notice, for example, that the dead-end street is "blind"; that the school is said to "set the boys free," which makes it sound like a prison; that the uninhabited house is "detached from its neighbours"; and that the other houses, personified, gaze at one another with "brown imperturbable faces" — *brown* being a nondescript color and *imperturbable* reinforcing the still, lifeless, somber quality of the passage as a whole.

**PLOT**   Through the series of events that make up a story's *plot*, an author presents us with a carefully created fictional world. In "Araby," the plot, or the arrangement of a connected sequence of narrative events, can be simply stated. A young boy who lives in a drab but respectable neighborhood develops a crush on his playmate's sister. She asks him if he intends to go to a charity fair that she cannot attend. He resolves to go and purchase a gift for her. He is tormented by the late and drunken arrival of his uncle, who has promised him the money he needs. When the boy finally arrives at the bazaar, he is disappointed by the difference between his expectation and the actuality of the almost deserted fair. He perceives some minor events, overhears some minor conversation, and the climax occurs when he confronts the darkened fair and the banal expression of sexual attraction between two gentlemen and a young woman. This sequence of events prompts the boy to see himself "as a creature driven and derided by vanity."

**CHARACTERIZATION**    One of the obvious differences between short stories and novels is that story writers develop *characters* rapidly and limit the number of developed characters. Many stories have only one fleshed-out, or *round*, character; the other characters are frequently two-dimensional, or *flat*. Rarely does a short story have more than three developed characters.

One feature that distinguishes "Araby" is its *characterization*, or the process by which the characters are rendered to make them seem real to the reader. Characterization, however, cannot easily be separated from the other elements of fiction; that is, it depends heavily on tone, plot, theme, setting, and so on. It is part of the boy's character, for example, that he lives in a brown imperturbable house on North Richmond Street, that he does the things he does (which constitute the plot of the story), and that he learns about what he does (which is the theme). Much of this characterization in "Araby" emerges from Joyce's rich *style*, or the way he uses language and images. Consider how the boy's character is revealed in the following paragraph:

> Her image accompanied me even in places the most hostile to romance. On Saturday evenings when my aunt went marketing I had to go to carry some of the parcels. We walked through the flaring streets, jostled by drunken men and bargaining women, amid the curses of labourers, the shrill litanies of shopboys who stood on guard by the barrels of pigs' cheeks, the nasal chanting of street-singers, who sang a *come-all-you* about O'Donovan Rossa, or a ballad about the troubles in our native land. These noises converged in a single sensation of life for me: I imagined that I bore my chalice safely through a throng of foes. Her name sprang to my lips at moments in strange prayers and praises which I myself did not understand. My eyes were often full of tears (I could not tell why) and at times a flood from my heart seemed to pour itself out into my bosom. I thought little of the future. I did not know whether I would ever speak to her or not or, if I spoke to her, how I could tell her of my confused adoration. But my body was like a harp and her words and gestures were like fingers running upon the wires.

In this passage, character is revealed through *diction*, or choice of words. By using the words *litanies*, *prayers*, and *adoration*, the narrator draws heavily from the distinctive vocabulary of the Roman Catholic Church. (The reference to the harp also reinforces the religious tone of the passage.) *Chalice* and *throng of foes* are related to this tradition as well; a chalice is a cup for the consecrated wine of the Eucharist, and throngs of foes often confronted the Christian martyrs whose deeds are immortalized in religious literature. At the same time, however, these last two phrases call up the world of chivalric romance, which is alluded to in the first line of the paragraph. The narrator's diction casts his awakening sexuality in the mold of high romance on the one hand and Christian devotion on the other. This sense of holy chivalry (reinforced by the earlier reference to the priest who owned a chivalric novel) stands in sharp contrast to the humdrum experience of carrying groceries home from the market.

**SETTING**  Unlike novels, short stories usually work themselves out in a restricted geographical *setting* — in a single place and within a short period of time. Any consideration of setting should include the historical time when a story takes place and the social situation set in the story, as well as the physical location of the events. In "Araby," the dreary details of Dublin are significantly described in the story's very first lines.

**POINT OF VIEW**  A character's or narrator's diction raises important questions about who is narrating the story. What is the narrator like? Is he reliable or unreliable? How can we judge? These questions help us distinguish another element of fiction, *point of view.* "Araby" is a *first-person narrative;* that is, the story is told from the perspective of a narrator who speaks in the first person. Most of the time, first-person narrators use the singular (*I, my*); in "A Rose for Emily" (p. 455), however, Faulkner's narrator uses the first person plural (*we, our*).

*Third-person* point of view — in which the narrator does not appear as a character in the story — is the most common perspective used to tell stories. Using third-person point of view, a narrator tells a story from the outside, referring to the characters as *she, he,* and *they.* A narrator who knows everything, can tell us what the characters are thinking, and can move around in space and time at will is an *omniscient narrator.* Alternatively, a narrator who chooses to focus on the thoughts, feelings, and actions of a single character is called a *limited omniscient narrator.* Generally, the brevity of the short story makes the first-person or limited omniscient narrations the most frequently used points of view for these works, while the lengthy and comparatively complex narrative of novels is more suited to the omniscient point of view.

A less frequently employed point of view is that of the second person, in which the author addresses the action to a character identified as *you.* For example, "You ask the clerk for change; he gives you four quarters. You go outside and wait for the bus." Although it evokes a rare intimacy with the reader, second-person point of view is difficult to sustain even in a short story.

**IRONY**  Authors' decisions about point of view create powerful narrative effects. Throughout "Araby," we sense a gap between the boy's sensibility and that of the more mature narrator, who refers at various times to his "innumerable follies" and "foolish blood." That is, we see the events of "Araby" from the boy's perspective, even though the language is that of an adult. The gap between the boy's knowledge and the narrator's creates *irony*.

There may be more than one level of irony at work in a story. When the narrator calls himself "a creature driven and derided by vanity," whose eyes "burned with anguish and anger," this overstatement is known as *verbal irony*. Some critics have maintained that the romanticized language of the story's conclusion itself invites an ironic reading — that is, we readers may know something about the narrator that he does not know himself — that he idealizes disenchantment as fervently as the boy idealized romance and religion. In short, Joyce may be using *dramatic irony*, encouraging the reader to see things about the first-person narrator that he does not see about himself. Both kinds of irony hinge on differing levels of knowledge and the author's skillful manipulation of narrative perspective.

**THEME**    *Theme* is an underlying idea, a statement that a work makes about its subject. This tiny stretch of experience out of the boy's life introduces him to an awareness of the differences between imagination and reality, between his romantic infatuation and the vulgar reality all about him. The theme of "Araby" emerges from the drab setting and mundane events of the story as a general statement about an intensely idealized and childish love, the shattering recognition of the false sentimentality that occasions it, and the enveloping vulgarity of adult life. By detailing a few events from one boy's life, the story illuminates the painful loss of innocence we all endure. In this case, the *protagonist*, or main character, experiences what Joyce called an *epiphany*, or sudden flash of recognition, that signals the awareness of a set of moral complexities in a world that once seemed uncomplicated and predictable.

We often speak of tone, setting, plot, theme, characterization, and point of view as separate aspects of a story in order to break down a complex narrative into more manageable parts. But this analytic process of identifying various elements is something we have done to the story: the story (if it is a good one) is an integrated whole. The more closely we examine the separate elements, the clearer it becomes that each is integrally related to the others.

In "Araby," Joyce employs the methods of fiction to create a world based on 1895 Dublin and Irish middle-class society. The success or failure of the story depends on Joyce's ability to render that world convincingly and our willingness to enter it imaginatively. We must not refuse to engage that world because the characters do not act as we would have them act or because the events never actually happened. Novelist Henry James urged that readers allow the author to have his or her *donnée*, or "given." When we grant this, the act of reading fiction provides us with much more pleasure and emotional insight.

Here are some questions to ask as you set out to read or write about fiction. Your answers to these questions will help you brainstorm and develop the ideas that form your response to a story.

## QUESTIONS FOR EXPLORING FICTION

**1. WHAT IS THE TONE OF THE STORY?** Does the tone change with the story's events or remain fixed? How does the tone contribute to the effect of the story?

**2. WHAT IS THE PLOT OF THE STORY?** Does the sequence of events that make up the plot emerge logically from the nature of the characters and circumstances? Or does the plot rely on coincidence and arbitrary events?

**3. WHO ARE THE PRINCIPAL CHARACTERS IN THE STORY?** What functions do the minor characters serve? Do any characters change during the course of the story? How and why?

**4. WHAT IS THE SETTING OF THE STORY?** Does it play an important role, or is it simply the place and time where things happen? How would some other setting affect the story?

**5. FROM WHAT POINT OF VIEW IS THE NARRATOR TELLING THE STORY?** Do you trust him or her?

**6. WHAT IS THE THEME OF THE STORY?**

**7. DO YOU FIND AMBIGUITIES IN THE STORY?** Does that ambiguity result in confusion, or does it add to the story's complexity?

**8. DOES THE STORY SEEM TO SUPPORT OR CONFLICT WITH YOUR OWN POLITICAL AND MORAL POSITIONS?**

**9. WHEN WAS THE STORY WRITTEN?** Draw on your knowledge of history and contemporary events as you read the story. Does the story clarify, enhance, or contradict your understanding of history?

**10. CAN YOU CONNECT THE STORY TO ANYTHING ELSE YOU HAVE READ OR SEEN?**

## READING POETRY

Reading poetry is unlike the other reading you do. To appreciate the sounds and meaning of a poem, it is best to start by reading it aloud. Some poems are straightforward, requiring little analysis; others are more dense and complex. Try reading the poem "When I Heard the Learn'd Astronomer" (1865) by Walt Whitman out loud.

When I heard the learn'd astronomer,
When the proofs, the figures, were ranged in columns before me,
When I was shown the charts and diagrams, to add, divide, and measure them,
When I sitting heard the astronomer where he lectured with much
    applause in the lecture-room,
How soon unaccountable I became tired and sick,
Till rising and gliding out I wander'd off by myself,
In the mystical moist night-air, and from time to time,
Look'd up in perfect silence at the stars.

Whitman's distinction between mind (intellectual knowledge) and heart (emotion and feelings) is an old but a useful one. Compelled to analyze, dissect, categorize, and classify, the poem's narrator finally yearns for the simple pleasure of unanalytical enjoyment — to look up "in perfect silence at the stars." You may very well enjoy a poem without recognizing its patterns of imagery or the intricate way its author weaves together the past and the present. But understanding the elements of poetry will allow you to use analysis to enhance your emotional response to a poem — and thereby deepen the pleasure a poem can give you.

Poems have to be read with great intensity but without any sense of urgency. Reading with a relaxed but complete mindfulness, try to slow down, pay attention, and allow the language of the poem to work.

## Word Choice

Once you have listened to the poem, what should you pay attention to next? Start with the words that make up the poem. *Where* a poem takes the reader is inseparable from *how* it takes the reader. Poets pay especially close attention to diction, or their choice of words; every word in a poem counts. In your everyday reading, you encounter unfamiliar words and phrases, and figure out their meanings from the contexts in which they occur. Reading poetry requires even more scrupulous attention to unusual words and phrases. Here, again, making connections will help you get the most out of your reading. Look for words or images that repeat or change as a poem continues. Finding patterns can be the first step in developing an interpretive reading of a poem.

Critics often describe poetry as "heightened language," meaning that the poet strives for precision and richness in the words he or she uses. For the poet, "precision" and "richness" are not contradictory. Words have dictionary, or *denotative*, meanings as well as associative, or *connotative*, meanings; they also have histories and relationships with other words. The English language is rich in synonyms — words whose denotative meanings are roughly the same but whose connotations vary widely (*excite, stimulate, titillate, inflame*; *poor, impoverished, indigent, destitute*). Many words are identical in sound and often in spelling but differ in meaning (*forepaws, four paws*; *lie* ["recline"], *lie* ["fib"]). The meanings of words have changed over time, and the poet may deliberately select a word whose older meaning adds a dimension to the poem.

## Figurative Language

*Figurative language* is the general term we use to describe the many devices of language that allow us to speak nonliterally in order to achieve some special effect. Figurative language makes a comparison between the thing being written about and something else that allows the reader to better picture or understand it. When Robert Burns compares his love to a red rose in his poem "A Red, Red Rose" (p. 646), he abandons literal language because the emotional energy of his thoughts can be expressed more effectively in figurative language.

Figurative language allows us — and the poet — to use *imagery* to transcend both the confinement of the literal and the vagueness of the abstract. The world is revealed to us through our senses — sight, sound, taste, touch, and smell. Through imagery, the poet creates a recognizable world by drawing on this fund of common experiences. The difference between good and bad poetry often turns on the skill with which imagery (or other figurative language) is used. Bad poetry is often bad because the imagery is stale ("golden sunset," "the smiling sun," "the rolling sea") or so skimpy that the poem dissolves into vague and meaningless abstraction.

Consider these familiar old sayings: "The grass is always greener on the other side of the fence"; "A bird in the hand is worth two in the bush"; "The early bird catches the worm." Although these sayings make literal sense (the grass you see from a distance looks greener than the grass under your feet), their meaning to a native speaker of English is clearly not literal. When we use them, we are making general and highly abstract observations about human attitudes and behavior. Yet these generalizations and abstractions are embodied in *concrete* imagery. Try to explain what any of these expressions mean and you will quickly discover that you are using many more words and much vaguer language than the expression itself uses. This is precisely what happens when you try to paraphrase or put into your own words the language of a poem. Like poetry, these sayings rely on the figurative use of language.

**METAPHOR**   Because poetry is an intense and heightened use of language, it relies on more frequent and original use of figurative language than does ordinary speech. One of the most common figurative devices, *metaphor*, in which one thing is compared to something else, occurs frequently in everyday language. "School is a rat race," or "That issue is a minefield for the mayor," we say, and the meaning is vividly clear. When W. H. Auden, commenting on the death of William Butler Yeats, says, "Let the Irish vessel lie/Emptied of his poetry," he pays a complex tribute to the great Irish poet with a metaphor that compels readers to confront not only the loss of a man but also the loss of his poetic voice.

**SIMILE**   *Simile* is closely related to metaphor. But where metaphor says that one thing *is* another, simile says that one thing *is like* another, as in Robert Burns's "O My Luve's like a red, red rose" and Frost's "life is too much like a pathless wood" (p. 646). The distinction between simile and metaphor, while easy enough to make technically, is often difficult to distinguish in terms of effect. Frost establishes a comparison between life and a pathless wood and keeps the two even more fully separated by adding the qualifier "too much." Burns's simile maintains the same separation and, in addition, because it occurs in the opening line of the poem, eliminates any possible confusion the reader might experience if the line were "O My Luve is a red, red rose." You can test the difference in effect by changing a metaphor into a simile or a simile into a metaphor to see if the meaning is in any way altered.

**PERSONIFICATION**    *Personification*, another device of figurative language, attributes human qualities to things or ideas. Personification can make an abstract thing more understandable in terms of human form, emotion, or action. For example, when John Donne, in his poem "Death, Be Not Proud" (p. 895), exclaims "Death, thou shalt die," he transforms the abstraction of death into a human adversary (while also creating a memorable *paradox*).

**ALLUSION**    *Allusion* to other literary works, persons, places, or events enables poets to call up associations and contexts that complicate and enrich their poems. Whether these allusions are obvious or subtle, they draw on knowledge shared by the poet and the reader. In T. S. Eliot's dense and difficult "The Love Song of J. Alfred Prufrock" (p. 513), the speaker says at one point, "I have seen my head (grown slightly bald) brought in upon a platter." A reader familiar with the New Testament might recognize this allusion to John the Baptist's decapitation and better understand Prufrock's sense of spiritual desolation. The association Eliot makes brings an added, intensified layer of meaning to the work.

**SYMBOLS**    A *symbol*, in its broadest sense, is anything that stands for something else. In this sense, most words are symbolic: the word *tree* stands for an object in the real world. When we speak of a symbol in a literary work, however, we mean something more precise. In poetry, a symbol is an object or event that suggests more than itself. It is one of the most common and powerful devices available to the poet, for it allows him or her to convey economically and simply a wide range of meanings.

It is useful to distinguish between two kinds of symbols: *public symbols* and *contextual symbols*. Public symbols are those objects or events that history has invested with rich meanings and associations — for example, national flags or religious objects such as a cross. Yeats uses such a symbol in his poem "Sailing to Byzantium" (p. 903), drawing on the celebrated and enduring art of the ancient Byzantine Empire as a symbol of timelessness.

In contrast to public symbols, contextual symbols are objects or events that are symbolic by virtue of the poet's handling of them in a particular work — that is, by virtue of the context. Consider, for example, the opening lines of Robert Frost's "After Apple-Picking" (p. 905).

> My long two-pointed ladder's sticking through a tree
> Toward heaven still,
> And there's a barrel that I didn't fill
> Beside it, and there may be two or three
> Apples I didn't pick upon some bough.

The apple tree is a literal tree, but it also symbolizes the speaker's life, with a wide range of possible meanings (do the few unpicked apples symbolize the dreams that even the fullest life cannot satisfy?). Contextual symbols tend to present more interpretive difficulties than public symbols do because recognizing them depends on a sensitivity to everything else in the poem.

## The Music of Poetry

A number of terms describe the various sound patterns that project the *music* of poetry. Of these, *rhyme* — the repetition of the final stressed vowel sound and any sounds following — is the best known: *brow, now; debate, relate*; and so on. *Alliteration*, or the repetition of a consonant sound, usually at the beginning of words in close proximity, is also common: "*besiege thy brow.*" Alliteration is frequently used to underscore key words and ideas.

*Rhythm*, created by the relationship between stressed and unstressed syllables, is another way poets can convey meaning. The pattern formed when the lines of a poem follow a recurrent or similar rhythm is the poem's *meter*. The smallest repeated unit in this pattern is called a *foot*. Looking, for example, at the first line of one of Shakespeare's sonnets, we see that the foot consists of an *iamb* — an unstressed syllable followed by a stressed one:

When forty winters shall besiege thy brow.

Because the line consists of five iambs, or sets of unstressed syllables followed by stressed ones, it is called *iambic pentameter*. (If the line had four iambic feet, it would be in iambic tetrameter; if six, iambic hexameter; and so on.)

Other metrical feet include the *trochee, anapest, dactyl,* and *spondee* (all of which are defined in the "Glossary of Literary Terms"); but such terms are the tools of literary study and not its object. Perhaps the most important thing to remember about meter is that it should not be mistaken for the actual rhythm of the poem. Instead, it is best thought of as a kind of ideal rhythm that the poem can play against. Meter suggests certain patterns that invite expectations that may or may not be satisfied. Much of the poet's art consists of crafting variations of sound and rhythm to create specific effects.

Some of these effects are illustrated nicely in the following passage from Alexander Pope's "An Essay on Criticism," in which the definitions of bad and good *verse* are ingeniously supported by the music of the lines.

These[1] equal syllables alone require,
Though oft the ear the open vowels tire;
While expletives their feeble aid do join;
And ten low words oft creep in one dull line;
While they ring round the same unvaried chimes,
With sure returns of still expected rhymes;
Where'er you find "the cooling western breeze,"
In the next line, it "whispers through the trees";

[1] Bad poets.

If crystal streams "with pleasing murmurs creep,"
The reader's threatened (not in vain) with "sleep";
Then, at the last and only couplet fraught
With some unmeaning thing they call a thought,
A needless Alexandrine[2] ends the song
That, like a wounded snake, drags its slow length along.

. . . . .

True ease in writing comes from art, not chance,
As those move easiest who have learned to dance.
'Tis not enough no harshness gives offense,
The sound must seem an echo to the sense:
Soft is the strain when Zephyr gently blows,
And the smooth stream in smoother numbers flows;
But when loud surges lash the sounding shore,
The hoarse, rough verse should like the torrent roar:
When Ajax[3] strives some rock's vast weight to throw,
The line too labors, and the words move slow;
Not so, when swift Camilla[4] scours the plain,
Flies o'er the unbending corn, and skims along the main.

When the speaker condemns the use of ten monosyllables, the line contains ten monosyllables: "And ten low words oft creep in one dull line." When he speaks of the wind, the line is rich in hissing sounds that imitate that wind. When he speaks of Ajax striving, clusters of consonants and stressed syllables combine to slow the line; when he speaks of Camilla's swiftness, the final consonants and initial sounds form liaisons that can be pronounced swiftly.

Analysis of this sort can illuminate and enrich our understanding of poetry, but it does not exhaust the significance of a poem. As the poet Dylan Thomas once remarked,

> You can tear a poem apart to see what makes it technically tick and say to yourself when the works are laid out before you — the vowels, the consonants, the rhymes, and rhythms — "Yes, this is it. This is why the poem moves me so. It is because of the craftsmanship." But you're back where you began. The best craftsmanship always leaves holes and gaps in the works of the poem so that something that is not in the poem can creep, crawl, flash, or thunder in.

A truly fine poem not only repays attention to its formal features but also points beyond its technique to something more sensuous and less domesticated.

Here are some questions to ask when you face the task of reading and writing about poetry.

---

[2] Twelve-syllable line or a line with six rhythmic feet. As in Pope's example, *alexandrines* often follow lines of pentameter, or lines with five metrical feet.
[3] A Greek warrior celebrated for his strength.
[4] A swift-footed queen in Virgil's *Aeneid*.

## QUESTIONS FOR EXPLORING POETRY

**1. WHO IS THE SPEAKER?** What does the poem reveal about the speaker's character? Do you think you can trust this speaker? In some poems the speaker may be nothing more than a voice meditating on a theme, while in others the speaker takes on a specific personality.

**2. IS THE SPEAKER ADDRESSING A PARTICULAR PERSON?** If so, who is that person, and why is the speaker interested in him or her?

**3. DOES THE POEM HAVE A SETTING?** Is the poem occasioned by a particular event?

**4. IS THE THEME OF THE POEM STATED DIRECTLY OR INDIRECTLY?** From what particular lines or words can you identify the theme of the poem?

**5. FROM WHAT PERSPECTIVE IS THE SPEAKER DESCRIBING SPECIFIC EVENTS?** Is the speaker recounting events of the past or events that are occurring in the present? If past events are being recalled, what present meaning do they have for the speaker?

**6. DOES A CLOSE EXAMINATION OF THE FIGURATIVE LANGUAGE OF THE POEM REVEAL ANY PATTERNS?** See p. 1023 and "Glossary of Literary Terms."

**7. WHAT IS THE STRUCTURE OF THE POEM?** Since narrative poems — those that tell stories — reveal a high degree of selectivity, it is useful to ask why the poet has focused on particular details and left out others. Analyzing the structure of a nonnarrative or lyric poem can be more difficult because it does not contain an obvious series of chronologically related events. The structure of the poem will be revealed through an analysis of patterns of images that embody the theme.

**8. WHAT DO SOUND AND METER (SEE "GLOSSARY OF LITERARY TERMS") CONTRIBUTE TO THE POEM?**

**9. WHAT WAS YOUR RESPONSE TO THE POEM ON FIRST READING?** Did your response change after study of the poem or class discussions about it?

## READING DRAMA

Drama is fundamentally different from other literary forms. Unlike fiction, for example, most plays are designed to be performed in public and not read in private. The public nature of drama is reflected in the words we use to discuss it. The word *drama* itself is derived from the Greek word for "action, deed, or performance," and *theater* derives from the Greek word for "sight or contemplation." By their nature, plays are more spectacular than poems or works of fiction. Directors and their staffs pay great attention to costumes, set design, lights, and stage movement; the reader, who doesn't experience these elements, must imagine the action on the basis of words alone. Dramatists use words as starting points for, rather than realizations of, their artistic visions.

Although plays typically lack narration and description — they are designed to show, not tell — they can be considered in terms of setting, plot, theme, characterization, and irony. Indeed, these notions are even more important in drama than in fiction, where narrative style and point of view carry great weight, or in poetry, where diction and imagery are central.

As much as possible, the way to read a play is to imagine that you are its director. In this role you must visualize yourself creating the set and the lighting. You will envision people dressed so that their clothes give support to their words. You will think about timing (how long between events and speeches) and blocking (how the characters move as they interact on stage). Perhaps the best way to confront the literature of the stage, to respond most fully to what is there, is to attempt to produce some scenes either in class or after class. If possible, attend the plays or the rehearsals of plays in production on campus. Nothing will provide better insight into the complexities of the theater than attending a rehearsal where the problems are encountered and solved.

As you read any of the opening speeches of any of the plays in this anthology, imagine yourself the director and make decisions. How should the lines be spoken (quietly, angrily, haltingly)? What should the characters do as they speak (remain stationary, look in some direction, traverse the stage)? How should the stage be lit (partially, brightly, in some color that contributes to the mood of the dialogue and action)? What should the characters who are not speaking do? What possibilities exist for conveying appropriate signals solely through gesture and facial expression — signals not contained in the words you read?

### Stages and Staging

Although staging is more important to spectators than to readers, some knowledge of staging history can enrich your reading of a play. For example, it helps to know that in the Theatre of Dionysus in Athens (below),

© Corbis.

Illustration of the Theatre of Dionysus in Athens.

there was no scene shifting. In Sophocles' *Antigonê* (p. 371), which was staged in an open-air amphitheater seating about 14,000 people, actors entered from the *skene*, or a fixed-stage house, which might have had painted panels to suggest a scene. Important events, especially violent ones, occur offstage, and the audience learns of these events from a messenger, who comes onstage to describe them. This convention was partly a matter of taste, but the conditions of the Greek stage also prevented Sophocles from moving the action to another scene. Later dramatists, writing for a more flexible stage and a more intimate theater, exploited the dramatic possibilities of such violence.

The vast outdoor theater imposed restrictions on acting style. Facial expressions played no role in the actor's craft; in fact, the actors wore large masks, which were probably equipped with some sort of megaphone to amplify speech. As a result, it was difficult to modulate speech to create subtle effects, and the speeches were probably delivered in formal, declamatory style. In addition to these limitations, the Athenian government made available only three principal actors, all male, as the cast (excluding the *chorus*, a group of citizens that commented on the action and characters) for each play. Consequently, there were never more than three players onstage at once, and the roles were designed so that each actor could take several parts, each signified by a different mask.

Shakespeare's stage was altogether different from Sophocles'. Although both theaters were open-air, the enclosure around the Elizabethan stage was much smaller than the Greek amphitheater, and the theater's capacity was limited

The Granger Collection, New York.

London: Swan Theatre. Johannes De Witt's
drawing of the Swan Theatre, London, c. 1596.

© Corbis.

Hypothetical reconstruction of the interior of the Globe Theatre in the days of Shakespeare.

to between 2,000 and 3,000 spectators. As in classical drama, men played all the roles, but they no longer wore masks. The stage protruded into the audience, allowing for more intimacy and a greater range of speech, gesture, and expression. Even so, and despite Hamlet's advice to the troupe "to hold as 't were, the mirror up to nature," Shakespearean *tragedy* did not lend itself to a modern realistic style. Those great speeches are written in verse; they are frequently meant to augment the meager set design with verbal imagery; and they are much denser in texture, image, and import than is ordinary speech. Most of the important action was played out on the uncurtained main platform, jutting into the audience and surrounded on three sides by spectators. The swiftly moving scenes followed each other without interruption, doubtless using different areas of the stage to signify different locations. There was some sort of terrace or balcony one story above the main stage, and there was an area at the back of the main protruding stage that could be curtained off when not in use. Although Shakespeare's plays are usually divided into five separate acts in printed versions, they were played straight through, without intermission, much like a modern motion picture. These characteristics distinguish the Shakespearean stage from the familiar realism of most contemporary theater.

Much current theater uses a *box stage* — essentially a box with one wall removed so that the audience can see into the playing area. The box stage lends itself to realistic settings. It can easily be furnished to look like a room;

© Corbis.

Spectators at a seventeenth-century French box stage.

or, if outdoor scenes are required, painted backdrops and angled sets provide perspective. Shortly after the introduction of the box stage, the possibilities for scenic design produced great set designers and increasingly sophisticated stage machinery. These new possibilities, in turn, freed the dramatist from the physical limitations imposed by earlier stages.

By the late nineteenth century, the versatility of the box stage enabled playwrights such as Henrik Ibsen to write detailed stage settings for the various locations in which the drama unfolds. Further, the furnishing of the stage in Ibsen's plays sometimes functions symbolically to visually reinforce the claustrophobic quality of the bourgeois life depicted in his plays. Later dramatists have relied on realistic settings to convey meaning and to serve symbolic functions. The modern production may take place in a theater that is simply a large empty room (with provisions for technical flexibility in the matter of lighting) that can be rearranged to suit the requirements of specific productions. This ideal of a "theater space" that can be freely manipulated has become increasingly attractive since it frees the dramatist and the performance from limitations built into permanent stage design.

## The Elements of Drama

**CHARACTERS**   Plays usually consist of narratives with plots, settings, themes, characters, and irony, and most plays have no narrators as such. In Greek drama, the chorus functions as a kind of narrator. In Shakespearean drama, the *soliloquy*, in which an actor speaks thoughts aloud, allows the audience to hear what a character is thinking. But in most plays, the story unfolds before our eyes without the intervention of an authorial voice or point of view.

Without a narrator to tell us what a character is thinking, we usually infer a character's thoughts by his or her actions and demeanor, and by *dialogue*, or the words a character speaks to others. Characterization, in plays as in fiction, is a process by which the author establishes the personality of a character, revealed through what the particular character does and says, and by what other characters say. The main character, the hero or *protagonist*, is the center of our attention. He or she is often opposed by another major character, the *antagonist*, whose opposition creates the central conflict of the drama. The protagonist and the antagonist, as well as other characters of major significance in the drama, have a vital interest in the outcome of the action, and grow and develop as the action progresses and are therefore described as *rounded* characters. Those characters who are peripheral to the action, who often supply the kind of exposition a third-person narrator does in fiction, are minor, or *flat*, characters.

**DRAMATIC IRONY**   *Dramatic irony* allows the audience to know more than the characters do about their own circumstances by letting the audience hear more than the characters hear. Shakespeare's *Othello* (p. 672) provides an excellent illustration of the uses of dramatic irony. At the end of act II, Cassio, who has lost his position as Othello's lieutenant, asks Iago for advice on how to regain favor. Iago, who, unknown to Cassio, had engineered Cassio's disgrace, advises him to ask Desdemona, Othello's adored wife, to intervene. Actually this is good advice; ordinarily the tactic would succeed, so much does Othello love his wife and wish to please her. But Iago explains, in a soliloquy to the audience, that he is laying groundwork for the ruin of all the objects of his envy and hatred — Cassio, Desdemona, and Othello:

> . . . for while this honest fool
> Plies Desdemona to repair his fortunes,
> And she for him pleads strongly to the Moor,
> I'll pour this pestilence into his ear
> That she repeals him for her body's lust;
> And, by how much she strives to do him good,
> She shall undo her credit with the Moor.
> So will I turn her virtue into pitch,
> And out of her goodness make the net
> That shall enmesh them all.

Of course, Desdemona, Cassio, and Othello are ignorant of Iago's enmity. Worse, all of them consider Iago a loyal friend. But the audience knows Iago's design, and that knowledge provides the chilling dramatic irony of act III, scene 3.

All the emotional tautness in the audience results from irony, from knowing what the victims do not know. But dramatic irony is the special tool of the dramatist, well suited to produce an electric tension in a live audience that watches and overhears the action onstage.

**PLOT AND CONFLICT** Plays often portray oppositions between characters or groups or even between two aspects of a character's personality. This opposition often takes the form of a *conflict* that drives the plot. In *Othello*, for example, a variety of conflicts shapes the action of the play. Most obviously, Iago's scheming puts Othello in conflict with Cassio, and turns him against Desdemona. But conflicts can be less literal: Othello and Desdemona's marriage puts them at odds with Venetian society, raising larger questions about race and culture. And conflicts can be within a single character: Othello's jealousy triggers conflicting emotions about himself and about his wife.

Understanding the methods of drama can help us analyze a play and its various effects. But such analysis only gestures at the emotional experience produced by successful drama. More than other forms of literature, plays give physical expression to the social and psychological conflicts that define us individually and collectively. As in *Othello*, a play may torment its audience by imposing on admirable characters unfair circumstances that will result in tragic deaths. Or, as in Susan Glaspell's *Trifles* (p. 761), a play may mock prevalent attitudes and compel an audience to reexamine its values. By giving expression to human impulses and conflicts, plays enact our most persistent concerns with the greatest possible intensity.

A traditional and still useful way of looking at the plot of a play is to see it in five parts: exposition, rising action, climax, falling action, and denouement. *Exposition* provides the audience with information about background matters important to the play. The first part of the plot also includes *rising action*, as the plot progresses toward complexity and conflict, which reaches a crisis, or *climax*, of some sort. This is the turning point of the play, when the protagonist must act decisively or make a critical choice from which there is no turning back. This in turn leads to the *falling action*, as the protagonist confronts the inexorable consequences of his or her act or decision. The play ends with the *denouement* (French for "untying or unraveling"), with the conflict resolved or the mystery solved. Although this template cannot be applied to every play, it comes close enough in describing the structure of many plays to make it a useful tool for analyzing much drama.

Here are some more specific questions to ask when you begin to read or write about drama. Write out your answers to check your understanding of a play or to begin collecting ideas for an essay assignment.

## QUESTIONS FOR EXPLORING DRAMA

1. **HOW DOES THE PLAY BEGIN?** Is the exposition presented dramatically as characters interact, novelistically through long speeches that convey a lot of information, or through some device such as a messenger who delivers long letters or lengthy reports?

2. **HOW DOES THE INFORMATION CONVEYED IN EXPOSITION ESTABLISH THE BASIS FOR DRAMATIC IRONY?** Does the audience know more than the characters do? How does that irony create tension in the audience?

3. **WHO ARE THE PRINCIPAL CHARACTERS?** How are the distinctive qualities of each dramatically conveyed? How do they change as the play proceeds? Are they sympathetic? What function do the minor characters serve?

4. **WHERE IS THE PLAY SET?** Why does it matter that it is set there? Does the setting play a significant role in the drama, or is it merely a place, any place?

5. **WHAT IS THE CENTRAL CONFLICT IN THE PLAY?** Is the central conflict between characters, between groups, or even between two parts of a character's personality? How is it resolved? Is the resolution satisfying?

6. **WHAT IS THE CONTEXT FOR THE PLAY?** Do you need to know the historical circumstances out of which the play emerged or something of the life of the author to appreciate the play fully? If so, how does the information enhance your understanding?

7. **WHAT VISUAL AND AUDITORY ELEMENTS OF THE PLAY EFFECT YOUR RESPONSE TO THE PLAY?** Since plays are usually written to be performed rather than read, place yourself in the position of the director and the actors to respond to this aspect of drama if you are reading a text.

8. **WHAT IS THE PLAY'S THEME?** How does the dramatic action embody that theme?

9. **HOW DOES THE PLAY END?** How does the ending connect to the beginning — or any other specific points — of the play?

10. **HAS THE PLAY BEEN MADE INTO A FILM?** In the adaptation, what has been added and what has been deleted? How does this production compare with your reading of the play?

## READING NONFICTION

Essays differ from fiction in that they generally do not create imaginary worlds inhabited by fictional characters. For instance, Langston Hughes describes the real-life experience of attending his Auntie Reed's church as an adolescent in "Salvation" (p. 251), just as George Orwell recounts his own experience of shooting an elephant in Burma in "Shooting an Elephant" (p. 564). And although we cannot independently verify these personal experiences, both works exhibit the formal nonfictional qualities of essays rather than the imagined worlds of short stories.

Writers turn to the essay form when they wish to confront their readers directly with an idea, a problem (often with a proposed solution), an illuminating experience, an important definition, or some flaw (or virtue) in the social system. Usually, the essay is relatively short, and almost always embodies the writer's personal viewpoint. And although the essay may share many elements with other literary forms, it generally speaks with the voice of a real person about the real world. The term *essay* derives from the French verb *essayer* — "try, attempt." That verb, in turn, derives from the Latin verb *exigere* — "weigh out, examine."

While the French term calls attention to the personal perspective that characterizes the essay, the Latin verb suggests that an essay can not only examine personal experiences but can also explore and clarify ideas by arguing for or against a position.

As you read an essay, you need to ask yourself, What is the central argument or idea? Sometimes the answer is obvious, sometimes less so. In some cases, essays do not argue for one thing in particular, but rather meditate on human experience and address the inner lives of their readers. John Donne's "Meditation XVII" (p. 938), for example, does not attack or justify anything. Rather, it reminds us to be aware of our mortality and thereby to alter our interactions with or perceptions of the people around us.

## Types of Nonfiction

If you have taken a composition course, you may have read and written narrative, descriptive, expository, and argumentative essays. While reviewing the characteristics of each of these types, keep in mind that in the real world, authors of essays are more interested in effectiveness than in purity of form, and frequently combine features of different formal types.

**NARRATIVE NONFICTION** Narrative essays recount a sequence of related events and are often autobiographical. But those events are chosen because they suggest or illustrate some larger insight or problem. In "Shooting an Elephant" (p. 564), for example, George Orwell narrates an episode from his life that led him to an important insight about imperialism. In Maxine Hong Kingston's "No Name Woman" (p. 777) the narrator's reflections on the significance of her aunt's suicide in China many years ago, a tragic family secret that still haunts her, powerfully illustrate the deep connection between past and present and the troubling idea that family and culture can oppress. In these narrative essays, the writers discover in their own experiences the evidence for generalizations about themselves and their societies.

**DESCRIPTIVE NONFICTION** Descriptive essays depict sensory observations in words. They evoke in the reader's imagination the sights and sounds, perhaps even the smells, that transport the reader to such places as George

Orwell's Burma. The descriptive essay, like the narrative essay, often addresses complex issues that trouble our lives, but it does so by appealing primarily to sensory awareness — sight, sound, touch, taste, smell — rather than to intellect. The power of description is so great that narrative and expository essays often use lengthy descriptive passages to communicate forcefully.

**EXPOSITORY NONFICTION**   Expository essays attempt to explain and elucidate, to organize and provide information. Often they embody an extended definition of a complex conception such as love or patriotism; other times, they describe a process — how to do something. This book's coverage of essays, for example, is clearly not narrative because it doesn't depend for its form on a chronological sequence of meaningful events. It is not descriptive in the pure sense of that type because it does not depend on conveying sensory impressions. It is, in fact, expository. It acquaints its readers with the techniques and types of essays and provides some tips to help students read essays both analytically and pleasurably. Many of these approaches involve making some kind of connection. You may recognize a number of rhetorical strategies from writing courses you may have taken. We *classify* essays by type; we *compare and contrast* them; we use *definition*; we give *examples* to make a point; we imply that there is a *cause-and-effect* relationship between what readers bring to an essay and the pleasure they derive from it. Similarly, the essayists represented in this book use a variety of such rhetorical strategies to achieve their aims.

**ARGUMENTATIVE NONFICTION**   Although Orwell's "Shooting an Elephant" can be categorized as a narrative essay, we might reasonably assert that it is also argumentative because it is designed to convince readers that imperialism is as destructive to the oppressors as to the oppressed. The argumentative essay wishes to persuade its readers. Thus, it usually deals with controversial ideas, marshals arguments and evidence to support a view, and anticipates and answers opposing arguments. Jonathan Swift accomplishes all these ends in "A Modest Proposal" (p. 403), with an approach complicated by his reliance on irony and satire.

## Analyzing Nonfiction

**THE THESIS**   The best way to begin analyzing an essay is to ask, What is the point of this piece of writing — what is the author trying to show, attack, defend, or prove? If you can answer that question satisfactorily and succinctly, then the analysis of the essay's elements (i.e., its rhetorical strategies, structure, style, tone, and language) becomes easier. Jonathan Swift's "A Modest Proposal" (p. 403), for example, projects a clear thesis. On the other hand, a much more complex and ambitious essay, such as Virginia Woolf's "What If Shakespeare Had Had a Sister?" (p. 556), does not yield up its thesis quite so easily. We might say that Woolf's examination of the historical record leads her to argue that women did not write during the Elizabethan period because literary talent could not flourish in a social system that made women the ill-educated property of men. This formulation of the essay's thesis, as you will see when you read the essay, leaves a good deal out — notably the exhortation to action with which Woolf concludes the piece.

**STRUCTURE AND DETAIL**   Read carefully the first and last paragraphs of a number of essays. Note the writers' strategy for engaging you at the outset with an irresistible proposition:

> In Moulmein, in lower Burma, I was hated by large numbers of people — the only time in my life that I have been important enough for this to happen to me.

> If I speak in the tongues of men and of angels, but have not love, I am a noisy gong or a clanging cymbal.

> I was saved from sin when I was going on thirteen.

These opening sentences are startling, hooking readers so that they will eagerly read on to find out what it was that made Orwell so hated in Burma, why love is so important to Paul, how Langston Hughes was saved from sin. You will find that the opening lines of most well-wrought essays instantly capture your attention.

Endings, too, are critical. And if you examine the concluding lines of any of the essays in this collection, you will find forceful assertions that sharply focus the matter that precedes them. Essayists, unsurprisingly, systematically use gripping beginnings and forceful endings.

What come between those beginnings and endings are often abstract issues — the nature of love, the inevitability of death, the evils of imperialism. Though such abstractions do significantly influence our lives, as subject matter for reading they seem impersonal and distant. Reading about great ideas becomes a sort of academic task, relegated to some intellectual sphere, separate from the pain and passion of our own humanity. The accomplished essay writer, however, entices us to confront such issues by converting abstract ideas into concrete and illustrative detail.

**STYLE AND TONE**   The word *style* refers to all the writing skills that contribute to the effect of any piece of literature. And *tone* — the attitude conveyed by the language a writer chooses — is a particularly significant aspect of writing style. As an illustration of the effect of tone, consider these opening lines of two essays — Jonathan Swift's "A Modest Proposal" and Langston Hughes's "Salvation":

> It is a melancholy object to those who walk through this great town or travel in the country, when they see the streets, the roads, and cabin doors, crowded with

beggars of the female sex, followed by three, four, or six children, all in rags and importuning every passenger for an alms. These mothers, instead of being able to work for their honest livelihood, are forced to employ all their time in strolling to beg sustenance for their helpless infants, who, as they grow up, either turn thieves for want of work, or leave their dear native country to fight for the Pretender in Spain, or sell themselves to the Barbados.

I was saved from sin when I was going on thirteen. But not really saved. It happened like this. There was a big revival at my Auntie Reed's church. Every night for weeks there had been much preaching, singing, praying, and shouting, and some very hardened sinners had been brought to Christ, and the membership of the church had grown by leaps and bounds. Then just before the revival ended, they held a special meeting for children, "to bring the young lambs to the fold."

Both accounts use provocative openings, immediately hooking the reader. Swift's tone, however, is formal; consider the complexity of his syntax ("It is a melancholy object to those who walk through this great town or travel in the country, when they see the streets, the roads, and cabin doors, crowded with beggars of the female sex, followed by three, four, or six children, all in rags and importuning every passenger for an alms") and the sophistication of his diction ("melancholy," "employ," "sustenance").

Hughes's tone, in his first-person account, is personal and informal. He uses colloquial diction ("It happened like this," "leaps and bounds") and a sardonic wit ("some very hardened sinners had been brought to Christ"). Although a reminiscing adult describes the event, the writer creates the voice of a child by using simple grammar and a child's vocabulary.

The tone a writer creates contributes substantially to the message he or she conveys. Jonathan Swift might have written a sound, academic essay about the economic diseases of Ireland and how to cure them — but his invention of the speaker of "A Modest Proposal," who ironically and sardonically proposes the establishment of a human-baby meat-exporting industry, jars the readers in ways no scholarly essay could. The high seriousness of Donne's tone in "Meditation XVII" perfectly suits his contemplation of the relationship among the living, the dying, and the dead.

Style is a more difficult quality to define than tone is. Dictionaries define *style* as both "a manner of expression in language" and "excellence in expression." Certainly it is easier to distinguish between various *manners* of expression than it is to describe just what constitutes *excellence* in expression. For example, the manners of expression of John Donne in "Meditation XVII" (p. 938) and of Judith Ortiz Cofer in "American History" (p. 254) clearly differ. The first muses about death, God, alienation, and community in a style characterized by formality and complex extended images. The second uses the conversational style of a memoirist to evoke a particular moment in her life that has larger resonance in the story of twentieth-century America. Although Cofer considers some of the same broad themes that Donne does, her perspective, focus, and conclusions are entirely different, and this difference is reflected in the tone and style of the piece.

Despite their vast differences, we can describe the excellence of each style. Donne, an Anglican priest, meditates on the community of all living humans and the promise of eternal life in the face of physical death. He evokes a remarkable image when he states that "all mankind is of one author." Not so remarkable, you might argue; God is often called the "author of mankind." But why? This image is powerful not just because it is an apt metaphor but because it is an apt metaphor that famously appears in the opening lines of the Gospel according to John in the Bible, which tells us that "[i]n the beginning was the Word, . . . and the Word was God." Donne develops this idea, further insisting on the intimate relationship among all people because humankind "is one volume." Then he extends this metaphor by arguing that "when one man dies, one chapter is not torn out of the book, but translated into a better language." The vivid image is further extended. "God," Donne tells us, "employs several translators; some pieces are translated by age, some by sickness, some by war, some by justice." By alluding to the actual making of a book by the bookbinder, Donne elaborates on the central image and reestablishes the idea of community: "God's hand is in every translation, and his hand shall bind up all our scattered leaves again for that library where every book shall lie open to one another." Donne alludes to the Bible repeatedly throughout the essay, adding layers to the significance of the "holy book" image and further demonstrating his own faith by showing the depths of his biblical knowledge. The complexity and aptness of Donne's figurative characterization of death is a remarkable stylistic achievement, and one need not share his beliefs to be impressed by his mastery of his medium.

By contrast, Judith Ortiz Cofer's very specific examination of some apparently irreparable rifts in the "human volume" opens with a reference to *Ripley's Believe It or Not*, hardly an exalted cultural allusion and one whose words suggest anything but faith. While Donne argues — in language some readers might find alienating — that we are all connected by God, Cofer attempts a more earthly connection, using everyday language and popular references that she expects contemporary American readers to recognize and grasp immediately. For many of her readers, the Kennedy assassination became the ultimate where-were-you-when-you-heard moment, and the emotional resonance of the reference is as historically specific as Donne's references are not. While Donne's imagery seems intended to convey timeless religious truths, Cofer's brings to mind worldly divisions: even their shared grief over President Kennedy cannot bridge the various cultural divides between the young narrator and her neighbors. Her Catholicism implicitly separates her from white Protestant America and connects her to the martyred Kennedy, yet teenage heartache is more meaningful to the narrator than the death of Kennedy or any comfort or meaning that faith might provide. Indeed, looking toward heaven for answers is registered as a kind of denial in Cofer's essay: even as the girl looks up into the falling snow, she cannot keep from her mind the knowledge that it will get dirty the minute it touches her urban backyard. The "veil" of snow evokes nuns or even the Virgin Mary's traditional cloak, but Cofer tells us, once one looks around and sees the whole picture, one cannot avoid noticing the dirt of urban life turning that white snow grey. Although these essays have some surprising connections—like many essayists, both authors are struggling with questions about their mortality and their place in the world—their larger points, and thus their styles, are starkly different. Particularly in their uses of allusion—the kinds of works they refer to and why—the two pieces could hardly have less in common. Yet what they do share is that the style of each is ideally suited to its subject matter and position, and reinforces some larger truth about each piece. These writers exhibit distinctive manners of expression and distinctive varieties of excellence; in short, they have distinctive styles.

Your principal concern, when reading an essay, must always be to discover its central thesis. What does the writer wish you to understand about his or her experience, the world, or yourself? Once you have understood the essay's thesis, you can enhance your understanding by examining the means the author used to convey it and, perhaps, recognize techniques that will enhance the quality of your own writing. To that end, you ought to examine the essay's structure and the rhetorical strategies that shape it. How does it begin and end? What type is it—narrative, descriptive, expository, argumentative? How do rhetorical strategies—definition, cause and effect, classification, exemplification, comparison and contrast—function to serve the author's purposes? Then analyze the sources of the essay's effectiveness by closely analyzing the language of the essay. Watch the author energize abstract ideas with details and moving experience; consider the uses of figurative language—the metaphors and similes that create both physical and emotional landscapes in the prose; respond to the tone of voice and the stylistic choices that create it. When you have done all this successfully, when you have discovered not only *what* the author has said but also *how* the author moved you to his or her point of view—then you will have understood the essay.

Here are some questions to ask when you face the task of reading and writing about essays.

## QUESTIONS FOR EXPLORING NONFICTION

**1. WHAT IS THE AUTHOR'S THESIS?** What evidence or arguments does the author advance to support the thesis? Is the thesis convincing? If not, why not? Does the author rely on any basic but unstated assumptions?

**2. WHAT IS THE AUTHOR'S TONE?** Select for analysis a passage you consider illustrative of the author's tone. Does the author maintain that tone consistently throughout the essay?

**3. HOW WOULD YOU CHARACTERIZE THE AUTHOR'S STYLE?** For example, are the syntax, length of sentences, and diction elevated and formal or familiar and informal?

**4. WHAT RHETORICAL STRATEGIES DOES THE AUTHOR USE?** For example, can you identify the effective use of narration, description, classification, comparison and contrast, analogy, cause and effect, or definition? Note that one of these rhetorical strategies may constitute the unifying idea of the essay or the means of structuring it.

**5. WHAT ARE THE MAJOR DIVISIONS IN THE ESSAY?** How are they set off? Are the transitions between the divisions effective and easy to follow?

**6. HOW DOES THE AUTHOR BEGIN THE ESSAY?** Does the opening paragraph effectively gain the reader's attention? Does it clearly state the essay's thesis? If it does not, at what point do the author's thesis and purpose become clear? How does the essay's concluding paragraph connect to the opening paragraph?

# WRITING ABOUT LITERATURE

If reading literature offers a way to listen to the surprisingly alive voices of the past, writing about literature affords the opportunity to respond to these voices. Depending on how complicated the piece is or how foreign its world is to your own experiences, your initial responses might be just a jumble of vague impressions. Classroom discussion can help to clarify your thoughts, but the best ideas do not usually come together until you sit down and write. The act of composition often generates a line of thinking. Writing about literature is an invitation to organize your impressions and to check those impressions against the work that prompted them. When you accept this invitation, you undertake a process that helps make sense of the literary work and helps you understand your reactions to it. It is important to remember that your reactions can take the form of arguments — arguments about a work and arguments with it, or arguments with what you take a writer to be saying about the world. Such thoughts can sometimes be difficult to formulate, so the opportunity to write them down and see where they take you is especially valuable.

## RESPONDING TO YOUR READING

As you know from experience, complete essays do not pop into your head immediately after you read a work of literature. The process starts with an impression here, a fragment there, or a question about something that catches your attention, which is why it is important to read actively and annotate while you read.

### Annotating While You Read

Each of the discussions of the four literary genres concludes with "Questions for Exploring," a series of questions that you might bring to the reading of any text. As an active and critical reader, you must attempt to answer those questions as you read — and note your responses as you do. Look at the considerations we raise for readers of poetry (p. 17). We asked some students to apply this questioning and annotating technique to Shakespeare's Sonnet 29, a moderately difficult poem. Here is a composite of what they produced:

All in all, the annotations to this sonnet are quite good. The students grasped the poet's design, largely overcame the difficulties created by somewhat archaic language, and recognized the poet's aim to both flatter his love and express the saving grace that love provides.

But curious things happen with language. The deconstructionist critics (see "Glossary of Critical Approaches," p. 960) have argued that because each reader brings a different set of experiences and assumptions to texts, it is difficult (some say impossible) to confidently understand any text. Put another way, different readers will interpret the same text in vastly different ways. For example, some readers, at the crucial moment when the poet remarks, "Haply I think on thee" (l. 10), might interpret the pronoun not as an *allusion* to a friend or lover but as an allusion to God. In this interpretation the sonnet resolves, not with the saving grace of a love that sets all things right, but with the ineffable saving grace of God that, with the promise of heaven, makes human pain and misery insignificant. Is such a religious reading of the poem simply wrong? And if so, what evidence could we use to show that it is wrong? Are the students who agree that the poet's girlfriend is the agent of his lifted spirits quite right? These are difficult questions, not the least because Shakespeare's sonnets seriously trouble scholars to this day.

At this point (moving away from the formalist critical approach used above — see "Glossary of Critical Approaches"), history comes into play. The edition of Shakespeare's 154 sonnets, published without his permission by Thomas Thorpe roughly ten to eleven years after they were written, was dedicated to "the only Begetter of These Insuing Sonnets Mr. W. H." Alas, we are not sure who Mr. W. H. was. Furthermore, we cannot be certain that the dedication was written by Shakespeare, rather than by Thorpe. Next, we cannot find among Shakespeare's sonnets any others that celebrate God, as some readers might suggest this sonnet does. Also, the sonnets just before and after Sonnet 29 lament that the poet suffers from the separation from his "friend." But that friend is quite possibly a man, not the girlfriend our first group of students found in the text. Literary historians would argue that interpreting this sonnet as a poem praising the restorative power of God cannot be defended given the body of work in which it resides. They would also argue that, although later sonnets (see Sonnet 130, p. 638) clearly are addressed to a woman, this one is more likely addressed to a man. But whether addressed to a woman or a man, the sonnet celebrates love's triumph over the mundane human despair that afflicts us all from time to time. And the modern reader can confidently address it to his or her beloved without being misunderstood.

Here, printed with enough space for your comments, is a dramatic monologue by the British novelist and poet Thomas Hardy (1840–1928). Try annotating it. You will discover that your first notions may have to be modified as you read through the poem. No problem — if this happens, just go back and correct your initial responses. Then compare your annotations to the composite annotations on pages 35–36.

### The Man He Killed

"Had he and I but met

By some old ancient inn,

We should have sat us down to wet

Right many a nipperkin!

"But ranged as infantry,

And staring face to face,

I shot at him as he at me,

And killed him in his place.

"I shot him dead because —

Because he was my foe,

Just so: my foe of course he was:

That's clear enough; although

"He thought he'd 'list, perhaps,

Off-hand-like — just as I —,

Was out of work — had sold his traps —

No other reason why.

"Yes; quaint and curious war is!

You shoot a fellow down

You'd treat, if met where any bar is,

Or help to half-a-crown."

### The Man He Killed

"Had he and I but met   *instead of on the battlefield?*

By some old ancient inn,

We should have sat us down to wet   *We would have shared a meal instead of shooting at each other.*

Right many a nipperkin!

  *napkin?*

"But ranged as infantry,   *Repeated words connect the two soldiers.*

And staring face to face,

I shot at him as he at me,   *They are at odds but doing the same thing.*

And killed him in his place.   *Missing pronoun "I" — did a little bit of the speaker get killed, too?*

"I shot him dead because —   *He's hesitating. Why did he kill him?*

Because he was my foe,

Just so: my foe of course he was:   *Is he trying to convince himself?*

That's clear enough; although   *Is it really that clear?*

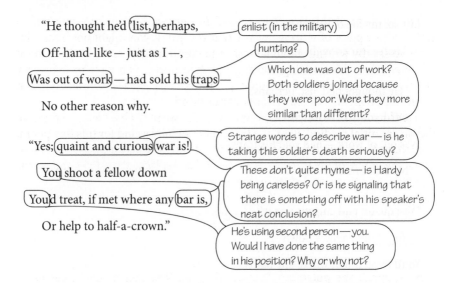

"He thought he'd list, perhaps,

enlist (in the military)

Off-hand-like — just as I —,

hunting?

Was out of work — had sold his traps —

No other reason why.

Which one was out of work? Both soldiers joined because they were poor. Were they more similar than different?

"Yes; quaint and curious war is!

Strange words to describe war — is he taking this soldier's death seriously?

You shoot a fellow down

You'd treat, if met where any bar is,

These don't quite rhyme — is Hardy being careless? Or is he signaling that there is something off with his speaker's neat conclusion?

Or help to half-a-crown."

He's using second person — you. Would I have done the same thing in his position? Why or why not?

Observe how these composite annotations engage with the poem and ask questions of Hardy's poetic structure and language. How do your own annotations compare to these composite annotations? Was there a certain point that you interpreted differently than the composite showed? Can you see how something might be read differently by different people? One of the qualities of literature that makes it so engaging is its openness to interpretation, discussion, and argumentation. Only by asking questions of a piece of literature will it be able to answer you — and the answers it provides are where the process of writing about literature begins.

## Freewriting

Another way to ask questions of a piece of writing is to read it and then write a spontaneous response separately from the piece. Imagine this scenario. Your teacher asks you to write an essay about one of the works you've read, and you don't have a clue about where to start. Consider the following very short poem, "The Span of Life" (1936), by Robert Frost:

The old dog barks backward without getting up.
I can remember when he was a pup.

Set yourself a limit of five minutes to write a response to the poem. Don't worry about style or grammatical correctness, or even whether your observations necessarily make logical sense — just start writing anything that comes to mind. You may be able to write very little at first. What is there to say? The poem seems to need no explanation; its words are familiar, and the dog image unambiguous. How could someone write even a short essay about this piece? Is this a joke?

The purpose of this practice — called *freewriting* — is to force yourself to respond to a piece of writing, even when you think you might not have anything to say. By writing spontaneously and continuously for a certain amount of time, even when writing about a two-line poem, you have to look very closely at the piece — and in doing so, hitherto-unrealized connections can often work their way to the surface of your mind.

If we look again closely at "The Span of Life," we may observe more than we did on an initial reading. First, the title seems awfully grand for this tiny poem. Somehow, these two lines and sixteen words are to make a poetic statement about the nature of life itself. Perhaps we had better look at the lines and words carefully. As a first step, let's scan the poem:

The old dog barks backward without getting up.

I can remember when he was a pup.

Now, speak the poem aloud. Note that the first half of line 1 seems to move slowly, while line 2 seems to prance. That series of four stressed syllables in line 1 "slows" the line. Further, it seems that the words are hard to say quickly — perhaps because the last letter of each stressed syllable has to be finished before you can speak the first letter of the following word: "old *dog barks* backwar*d* without." The *meter* and the sound patterns that describe the dog, old and tired as he is, contribute to the lethargy described in line 1. But is this poem about a mere dog's life or, perhaps, life in general?

In the second line, the lilting *anapestic meter* dances across the page. (An *anapest* is a metrical foot consisting of two unaccented syllables followed by an accented syllable. See *Meter* in the "Glossary of Literary Terms.") The final *n* of "can" slides easily into the initial *r* of "remember"; the easy movements between words and in the sound sequences that follow all contribute to the quickness of the line. Thus, the joyful playfulness of a puppy, suggested by the bounding anapestic meter, is reinforced by the sound patterns embodied in the words chosen to evoke the old dog's youth. Since the title of the poem invites the reader to generalize, we could assume that human life spans, like the old dog's, move from the energetic exuberance of youth to the fatigued immobility of advanced age.

Now the title makes sense — and the *poetic* quality of the sixteen-word *couplet* (two consecutive rhyming lines) emerges from the rhythm and the sounds that reinforce the meaning of the words.

Reread your five-minute freewrite. Did you note any of these matters? Did you wonder about the poem's title? Do you have an alternative reading to suggest? After this discussion, could you now write a short essay on Frost's poem? These first jottings do not require that you bring any special knowledge to this poem, just that you attend to what's there on the page — a puzzling title, an unusual variation of metrical patterns, and the sounds that embody the poem.

Writing about literature challenges you to teach yourself. Every element in a literary work has been deliberately put there by the author — the description of the *setting*, the events that form the *plot*, the *dialogue*, the *imagery*. E. M. Forster, a literary critic and novelist, had one of his characters say, "only connect." This notion is a good one to follow when trying to write an essay that analyzes literature. Does what you are reading remind you of anything in your own life? Of anything else you have read? When you slow down and read even more carefully, you will notice connections between words and images that can help you find the key to interpreting the work of literature at hand. Readers experience a mysterious intellectual and emotional event as a result of the writer's purposeful manipulation of language. When you write about what you've read, you confront not only your response to a work but also the elements within the work that cause your response.

Think about a short story or novel that you have read or a movie you have seen recently. Did you like or dislike the story? Try to list the reasons for your general reaction and evaluation: the characters were interesting or dull and lifeless; the ending satisfied expectations or, perhaps, was surprising; the story was easy to understand; it offered new insights about people, or places, or a different society; you couldn't wait to see what would happen next (or found the story so boring that you had trouble finishing it). Your personal impressions, as you jot them down, represent your response to the work.

When you write about literature, you begin with your response to the work. Then you need to consider the writer's purpose. This is not easy; in fact, some critics argue that the reader can never fully recover the writer's purpose. But you can explore the text, try to discover how the plot, setting, *characterizations* — the very words (sometimes *symbolic*) — all conspire to generate the *theme*, and, finally, work on your feelings so that you have some response.

To write about literature is, in one way or another, an attempt to discover and describe how the writer's art created the reader's response. In other words, whatever your assignment, the fundamental task is to answer two questions: How do I respond to this piece? How has the author brought about my response?

## Keeping a Journal

Your instructor may require you to keep a journal — a day-by-day account of your reactions to and reflections on your reading. Even if a journal is not required, you might want to keep one for a variety of reasons. From a purely practical perspective, writing in a journal regularly is excellent practice at conquering the blank page and generating ideas. You need not construct grammatical sentences, write cohesive paragraphs, develop your ideas, or even make sense. In a journal you are free to comment on only one aspect of a work or on a personal recollection that something in the work triggered. You are recording your reactions, ideas, feelings, questions. Jotting down personal connections — for example, if a character reminds you of a friend or teacher — can be helpful even if they don't make it in into your essay. If you are conscientious about keeping your journal, you may come to find writing in it a pleasant activity.

A journal's helpfulness extends beyond its use as a place for reflection. When the time comes to write a full-length essay for your class, the journal can provide many possible topics. Use your journal to express in writing the pleasure (or pain) of each reading assignment. Jot down unfamiliar words (which you should then, of course, look up in your dictionary). Note your reactions to characters — that some are nasty, others too saintly, some realistically rendered, still others unbelievable. Some of your journal entries may be confessions of confusion, posing open-ended questions about a reading. Others may be a record of personal feelings and recollections triggered by a work; thinking critically about such reactions might generate an essay that examines the conflict between your own moral values and those embodied in a particular work.

Finally, remember that — unless your instructor has specific guidelines for journal keeping — your journal will be the one place where you can write as much or as little as you please, as often or infrequently as you wish, with care and deliberation or careless speed. Its only purpose is to serve your needs. But if you write fairly regularly, you will probably be surprised not only at how much easier the act of writing becomes but also at how many ideas suddenly pop into your head in the act of writing. Henry Adams was surely right when he observed, "The habit of expression leads to the search for something to express."

## Exploring and Planning

**THINKING CRITICALLY**   Thinking critically about literature doesn't mean being critical of literature, that is, thinking about it negatively. Instead it means thinking like a literary critic, thinking about what lies beneath the obvious surface of a work of literature. Critical thinking more generally means not simply accepting everything you see or hear or read; thinking critically about literature means not taking literary works at face value. Instead, you should question everything: what the author seems to want to do, how she or he goes about doing it, what she or he seems to assume, what he or she concludes, and whether the work has a *point of view* or message. Ask yourself whether the work succeeds or does something else, what the effects are of how the author crafted the piece, and whether you agree with his or her assumptions and conclusions. Certainly judgment is involved: you will sometimes end up concluding that an author has succeeded or failed or even said something with which you cannot agree. The claim you end up making about a particular work of literature depends on this process of identifying what a work of literature does and how it does it and then thinking critically about those things.

**ASKING GOOD QUESTIONS**   Often the best ideas for paper topics begin as questions (possibly from a freewrite) or as responses (perhaps from a journal) that can be turned into questions. In reading James Joyce's "Araby" (p. 121), for example, you may notice that the *narrator* makes a big deal out of carrying the groceries home. This observation can be converted into a question: Why the big deal about carrying the groceries home? Or, to focus the question a bit, Why and how does the boy idealize these everyday situations? Note that these questions do not lead to a single irrefutable answer. When you write responses to literature, your goal is to pose a good question, answer it clearly, and support the answer with evidence from the work.

While it is important to clear up basic questions — for example, what a word or phrase means, or who did what, or how the characters are related to one another — successful papers usually take up questions that are less easily settled; in other words, they make a claim that can be argued and supported. For example, you would probably not want to ask whether it was a mistake for Shakespeare's Othello to trust Iago, or whether the *tragedy* could have been avoided if he had acted otherwise. Questions such as these do not lend themselves to sustained discussion. Questions of personal taste are not immediately useful for the same reason; if you say you like a particular work, there is little anyone can say to the contrary. Sometimes such assertions can be usefully converted, especially if you begin to ask why you like or dislike a work. In general, however, you should strive to explore open-ended interpretative and thematic questions rather than rehash the facts or declare personal preferences.

**ESTABLISHING A WORKING THESIS**  Early in the writing process, as you gather ideas about what to write, you should formulate a tentative *working thesis* that states your topic and the point or argument you wish to make about the topic. Although your working thesis will probably change as you collect information, articulating it will help you focus your thoughts and further research. Make your working thesis as specific as possible to limit your topic and keep the scope of the essay manageable. Consider the audience appeal of your working thesis as well.

A *thesis* states the main claim you'll make in your final essay. In your opening paragraph, a clear thesis statement should both state the claim you intend to make and prepare your reader for what follows. The thesis statement should be accompanied by some indication of the *scope* of your argument — the several issues you intend to explore.

For example, generating ideas for an essay about *Othello*, you may be struck by a line Othello utters before the Duke in act I: "Rude I am in my speech, / and little blessed with the soft phrase of peace." Despite this line, you notice that Othello's speech is admirably measured and eloquent. Is he being falsely modest? Is he tailoring his rhetoric to his noble audience? Is there a genuine note of insecurity being sounded? Whatever your preliminary answer, it is the beginning of your working thesis. The next step is to reexamine Othello's speeches to see if you can find evidence to support and refine the claim of your working thesis.

**GATHERING INFORMATION**  Once you have chosen your topic and articulated a working thesis, consider what additional information you will need to explore the issue. This may mean identifying examples from the text of the literary work you are analyzing to support your thesis or gathering information from other sources. The library is likely to be the principal source of additional information, though online research is becoming increasingly reliable.

If you use an electronic source, it is often a simple matter to print online information. If you use print sources in a library, you will need to make a photocopy or take notes. In any case, be sure to indicate on your printout or your note cards the exact publication and location information for all your sources so that you can properly document your sources in the final essay. Even if you are using just one source, you will need to provide information crediting that source in your list of works cited. For more information about documenting sources and creating a Works Cited page, see page 70.

**ORGANIZING INFORMATION**   Writing an essay would be a much quicker and more straightforward process if you could somehow magically know what you wanted to write about before you began your research and then whipped up a succinct thesis followed by a structured outline in which arguments I, II, and III were supported by points A, B, and C. In the real world, writers research a preliminary topic and then impose order on the information they have amassed. Think about how best to group or organize your points so that they will be persuasive to your readers.

One general approach to organizing an essay requires you to complete this statement: "My claim in this essay is X. To demonstrate X, I will support it with arguments A, B, and C." In an essay on *Othello*, for example, you might write, "My claim in this essay is that Othello's fall is a logical consequence of his situation and his character. To demonstrate this thesis, I will examine his age and race, his military life, and his inexperience with European women."

Once you've nailed down the thesis and scope of the essay, you can, in your draft, add layers to support your claim:

> Many writers have argued that the rapid fall of the noble Moor Othello is unbelievable. But consider his situation. He is a black man in a white country; he is much older than his beautiful wife. As a military man, he self-consciously lacks social grace. And his inexperience with European women contributes to the emotional insecurity that finally destroys him.

Where you cite other writers' arguments — as in the first sentence — you must offer documentation for your sources.

The next several paragraphs would follow the organization set up by the opening. First might be a paragraph on Othello's race and age and the attitudes toward him established in act I, followed by a paragraph on Othello's self-conscious unfamiliarity with the behavior of European women. The next paragraph might argue that he sees himself as unappealing to women from his adopted city. Each of these assertions should be supported with dialogue from the play. A conclusion would follow: Othello was never quite as noble as some have suggested and, under the circumstances, was doomed from the start.

One of the intellectual hurdles you'll face as a student of literature is learning to distinguish between a *summary* that recounts events and details and an *analysis* that interprets what events and details might mean. Of course an analysis should provide enough plot summary so that your reader has the context to understand what you are talking about. In fact, if you are confused about the plot of a liter- ary work — what happened, in what order — then writing a summary may help to clear up your confusion. Moreover, writing a summary is often a first step to writing an analysis and offering an interpretation. As you describe what happens in a work of literature, you begin to ask questions about why those events hap- pened. In choosing the details and events to include in your summary, you are making decisions about which details and events are worth attending to when you try to ascribe meaning to them in the context of analysis and interpretation.

The following summary of Shakespeare's *Othello* reduces the play to its major plot elements. Notice that it does not interpret or make arguments about the play, focusing on particular details and explaining what they mean. (Notice also that it is narrated in the present tense, a conventional practice when you summarize.) This is in contrast to the later analysis of *Othello* in this chapter that answers questions of why things happened in the play and what these events might mean to us as readers.

### A Summary of *Othello*

Set in Venice and then Cyprus, *Othello* opens with a scene of the vil- lainous Iago and his henchman Roderigo hatching a vengeful plot against Iago's commanding general Othello, who has passed him over to promote the handsome Michael Cassio to be his Lieutenant. Iago first tries to under- mine Othello by anonymously revealing to the father of Othello's new wife that his daughter is now married to a person of a different race (Othello is a Moor — an African). The father, a nobleman named Brabantio, is appalled that his daughter, Desdemona, is married to a Moor, but when he takes his argument to the Duke of Venice, the Duke, who desires Othello's services to protect Venice from an invasion from Cyprus, judges that Othello and Desdemona truly love each other, and approves their wedding. Thwarted in his first attempts at vengeance, Iago contrives to draw Cassio into a drunken street brawl that leads to Othello stripping Cassio of his new rank.

Iago then advances his vengeance by leading Othello to believe Desdemona has betrayed him with Cassio. Exploiting his loving wife Emilia, Iago uses a handkerchief that Emilia obtains from Desdemona to fool Othello into believing Desdemona is involved with Cassio. Succumbing to Iago's lies, Othello grows mad with jealousy and asks Iago to help him kill Cassio and Desdemona. Iago continues to weave a series of lies and schemes that ultimately trick Othello into murdering his guiltless wife Desdemona. Believing himself a cuckold, Othello ignores Desdemona's protestations of innocence and strangles her in her bed. Then he discovers through Emilia how he has been duped by Iago. Confronted with Iago's betrayal and the enormity of his own crime against an innocent woman who loved him, Othello chooses to commit suicide rather than try to exculpate himself and live knowing his folly. Iago's vengeance is complete, but his crimes, which include the murder of Roderigo and Emilia, have come to light and he is arrested. Still he vows neither to repent nor ever to speak again of his crimes, even in the face of torture and death.

## DRAFTING THE ESSAY

It is important to start writing even if you are unsure about the exact shape or direction of your argument since frequently your ideas develop and become more focused as you proceed. In working through a draft essay on *Othello*, you may initially find yourself interested in, on the one hand, how eloquent you found Othello's address to the court of the Duke of Venice and, on the other hand, his self-characterization as plainspoken, even ill-spoken. Does Othello really believe he is a "rude" speaker? Is he perhaps manipulating his audience? But as you write your first draft and your thoughts evolve, you may find yourself moving from a thesis that Othello has crafty control of his language to something quite different. Keep writing and stay flexible. A first draft does not have to be perfect. It's a stage for making discoveries and clarifying your ideas.

### Opening with an Argument

Once the draft is done and you have a clear idea of your thesis and the passages in the work that best support it, you can begin to shape and refine the essay. In doing so, pay special attention to the introductory paragraph, which should introduce the topic and lead directly to a clear, arguable thesis. While there is no surefire formula for a first paragraph, some strategies are better than others. Avoid the following types of opening sentences:

> Ever since the dawn of time, people have been fascinated by the fall of great men.

> Insecurity is a feeling that can prove harmful in even the most accomplished people.

This kind of throat-clearing generalization is common and even helpful at the draft stage, but it gets the essay off to a slow start. If the working thesis is that Othello is undone not only by treachery but also because of the insecurities that lurk beneath his formidable bearing, a direct approach is more effective:

> In Othello's first speech at the court of the Duke, he presents himself as a simple soldier awkwardly attempting to explain how he won the hand of the beautiful Desdemona. In fact his "rude" words are highly eloquent, and a reader may judge that the proud general is using false modesty to advance his case. Such a judgment ignores a more central issue than Othello's pride and eloquence. His words hint at the insecurities — as a military man short on civilian social graces, an older man with a young wife, a black African in a white European culture — that will cloud his judgment and ultimately prove his undoing.

Note that this opening paragraph introduces the topic and moves directly toward an explicit and arguable claim. By doing so, it lets the reader — and the writer — know where the essay is going. That is, once a clear thesis is in place, both writer and reader can use it as a road map for the rest of the essay.

## Supporting Your Thesis

The body of the essay will be devoted to supporting the thesis. The best way to establish a claim is to cite and analyze carefully selected passages from the text that relate directly to it. The following paragraph focuses on lines that support our sample claim directly:

> As indicated by the preceding examples, numerous passages reveal Othello's various insecurities. But in the following passage, his language manifests them all:

> Haply, for I am black,
>
> And have not those soft parts of conversation
>
> That chamberers have, or for I am decline'd,
>
> Into the vale of years — yet that's not much — (3.3 263–66)

> Here Othello catalogs his self-perceived flaws: His Africanness ("for I am black"), his rough manners ("I... have not those soft parts of conversation"), and his age ("declin'd / Into the vale of years"). He is now tormented by the very qualities and achievements that once set him proudly apart from others in European culture.

The first part of the paragraph tells the reader what to look for in the cited lines, and the subsequent analysis underscores their relevance to the overall argument clearly and convincingly.

If you offer a claim, support it with an analysis of the relevant passages, and consider different interpretations of those passages, you have completed the main task in much writing about literature. Concluding paragraphs can move toward closure by reviewing the claim and its significance, which you should be careful not to overstate. In the essay on *Othello*, for example, it would not be effective to conclude with a sweeping claim that the Moor's insecurities represent Shakespeare's indictment of European culture in his era. Your readers will find your claims more convincing if you do not exaggerate their importance.

## REVISING THE ESSAY

After you've completed your draft, it is time to look at the essay more critically, paying special attention to revision. Revision involves taking a fresh look at your essay's thesis and support, as well as its organization and language. Reading your essay aloud, or asking someone else to read it, will help you catch many problems. Revision is most effective if begun well before the paper is due. Start writing early so that you have time to review your decisions, ask for feedback from others, and revise accordingly. Because you cannot always anticipate audience reaction, a preliminary reading of your writing by a friend, a teaching assistant, a tutor, or an instructor can highlight the areas that need attention or additional revision.

The basic guidelines for good style are not mysterious; in fact, you use them every day in conversation. In conversation and in writing, we all rely heavily on cooperation to make sense of exchanges, and a polished practical style makes cooperation easier. Writers develop such a style by acknowledging that readers expect the same things that listeners expect in conversation: clarity, relevance, and proportion. If you listen to someone who is not clear, who cannot stay on the topic, or who offers too much or too little information, you will quickly lose interest in the conversation. Writers, too, need to be clear, stay on the topic, and give information appropriately. In fact, this attention to audience and appropriateness may be even more important in writing than in conversation because writing does not permit the nonverbal communication and immediate feedback that are part of conversation. As writers, we have to anticipate the absent reader's response; in effect, we have to imagine both halves of a virtual conversation.

Begin by evaluating your essay's thesis. Is it clear? Vagueness or tentativeness here may mean problems later in the essay, so make sure your thesis is crystal clear. Second, is the evidence you present relevant to each major point? While it is tempting and sometimes productive to go off on tangents while drafting a paper, in the final essay if the evidence doesn't fit the claim, tinker with the claim, or go back to the early exploratory writing you did and to your sources to look for better evidence. Are there any points that need to be clarified? Check all your quotations, paraphrases, and summaries for their citations and for accuracy.

Next, can you tighten the organization of your draft? Are your claims and evidence unified? Put yourself in your reader's place, and clarify ambiguities. Each detail or piece of evidence in a paragraph should relate back to the claim it supports in the topic sentence of that paragraph. At the same time, avoid oversupporting some points with too much discussion or detail.

Finally, ask yourself if the general proportions of your essay are suitable. A five-page paper should not use three of those pages to introduce the topic or recount a work's plot. If the essay is too short, the trouble might be an unarguable thesis or insufficient evidence. If it is running too long, eliminate or compress the parts that do not bear directly on the main claim, or limit the claim to something more manageable.

### Editing Your Draft

After you have evaluated and revised your draft and determined the format for your paper, you are ready to edit it carefully, paying close attention to each sentence and paragraph. These guidelines will help you focus on some common trouble spots.

**SELECTING STRONG VERBS**    Careful selection of lively, active verbs will make your writing more interesting to your audience. Consider the main verb in the following sentence:

> Three conflicts, all of which play crucial roles in the plot, are evident in
>
> *Othello.*

The core assertion of this sentence is that "[t]hree conflicts . . . are evident." Notice that nothing actually happens in this sentence. To stir things up, borrow the verb *play* from another part of the sentence:

> Three conflicts play crucial roles in the plot of *Othello*.

The revision is better, but the sentence can be made even more concise using *drive*:

> Three conflicts drive the plot of *Othello*.

The revised sentence more clearly gets to the point, an effect that is rarely lost on an audience. It also permits a more direct move to the topic — namely, the conflicts. Finally, in an economical seven words rather than a verbose fifteen, it neither belabors nor omits anything of importance in the first sentence.

Writing that relies too heavily on *be* verbs often produces wordiness and unnecessary abstraction:

> There <u>was</u> opposition to interracial marriage among most of the citizens
>
> of Venice.

Deleting the *be* verb (*was*) and converting the abstract noun *opposition* into a verb make the sentence more active:

> Most Venetians <u>opposed</u> interracial marriage.

This clearer sentence lets the verb do the major work. Of course, a good verb does not always present itself as an abstract noun in an early draft. Sometimes you'll need to consult a thesaurus or a dictionary to find just the right word.

Search your draft for weak verbs and insignificant words and for sentences that begin *There is, There are, It is.* Often, a few words later, a *that, which,* or *who* will appear. Overuse of *There is* and *There are* produces sentences that bury the action. Edit these sentences by deleting the weak verb constructions and replacing them with strong, precise verbs. For example, change "*There is* a destiny *that* controls the fate of Sam*"* to "Destiny controls Sam's fate." 

Finally, check your draft for passive constructions (the ball *was thrown*), and replace them when possible with active verbs. Passive sentences are often wordier and dull the action of a sentence. For example, change "The essay was read by the class" to "The class read the essay."

**ELIMINATING UNNECESSARY MODIFIERS** When choosing or revising a verb, you are also choosing the sentence elements that necessarily accompany it. These other sentence elements are called *complements* because they complete the meaning of the verb. In the following sentences the complements are underlined:

> Iago betrays <u>Othello</u>.
>
> The boy idealized <u>his situation</u>.

Iago cannot just betray; he has to betray something. Likewise, *his situation* completes the meaning of the verb *idealized*. Almost everything else added to these sentences will be *modifiers* — additional elements that will modify, rather than complete, the meaning of the sentences. A writer can add any number of modifiers to a sentence:

> Iago betrayed Othello cold-bloodedly, with a malignity beyond measure,
>
> a malignity that Coleridge characterized as "motiveless."

From a grammatical standpoint, these modifiers are optional; without them the sentence still expresses a complete thought. Unnecessary modifiers can make your writing heavy and murky:

> Basically, the Greeks invented a rather innovative and distinctive form
>
> of government known as democracy.

Eliminating the modifiers and making a few other snips result in the following:

> The Greeks invented democracy.

The clearer sentence does not lose much in the way of content. Of course, being able to eliminate modifiers does not mean that you should; sometimes modifiers are the most significant parts of a sentence. You can always use modifiers for nuance or emphasis, but you must ruthlessly trim unnecessary modifiers from wordy, unclear sentences.

**GRAMMATICAL CONNECTIONS** Make sure your sentences and paragraphs are firmly linked by using explicit transitional phrases such as *however, although, likewise, for example, therefore,* and so on. Note in this sample opening paragraph how the underlined transitional phrases indicate the relationships between the sentences:

> In his speech before the Duke's court, Othello speaks disarmingly
>
> to the assembled nobles. He flatteringly describes his audience as being
>
> potent, grave, and reverend. He modestly describes himself as being a
>
> blunt-spoken soldier hardly qualified to talk of anything but the wars
>
> that he has seen and fought. However, Othello's modesty is belied by
>
> the deeds of which he speaks. In particular he boldly admits to having
>
> won both the love of Desdemona and many battles, dating from when he

was but a child. The court is looking for a conqueror, and in his guise of

modesty Othello presents himself as that man.

The appearance of *however* halfway through the paragraph signals the contrast between Othello's professed modesty and his powerful deeds. The transitional phrase *in particular* in the next sentence signals that we are narrowing the preceding point and focusing our discussion. Experienced readers look for such transitional phrases that suggest an interpretive path through an argument.

Note that the third sentence of the paragraph repeats a key word from the second one (*describes*); so does the first and fourth sentence (*speaks*). The repetition helps keep the spotlight on Othello's rhetoric, an important notion in the paragraph. Note also the use of *modestly* and *modesty*. By repeating key terms, sometimes with slight variation, you can powerfully illuminate the main idea of a paragraph.

After checking for explicit connections within paragraphs, make sure that the progression of ideas from one paragraph to another is clear. Here again, transitional phrases are useful. A simple transition such as *nevertheless, furthermore,* or *on the other hand* is often adequate. Sometimes the entire opening sentence of a paragraph may provide the transition, including key words, pronouns, or other references to the previous paragraph.

### Proofreading Your Draft

Print out, type, or (if your instructor allows it) neatly write in ink the final copy of your essay for submission to your instructor, taking care to follow any special instructions about format that you have been given. Don't rush; be meticulous. When you have finished, proofread the final copy carefully, looking for spelling or punctuation errors, omitted words, disagreement between subjects and verbs or between pronouns and antecedents, and typographical errors that will detract from the essay you have worked hard to write.

For additional advice on checking your use of sources and documenting in your final essay, see "Some Matters of Form and Documentation" (p. 71). Finally, use "A Checklist for Writing about Literature" (p. 75) to help with a quick review of your final draft.

## SOME COMMON WRITING ASSIGNMENTS

A writing assignment for a literature course may require any of a variety of kinds of writing. You might be called on to compare and contrast literary works, to analyze the language of a work, to discuss the interaction of a work's parts, to discuss a work's theme, or to articulate your own responses to the work. Sometimes an instructor may ask simply that you write an essay on one of the pieces you have read. This type of assignment requires you to create your own boundaries — to find a specific focus that both suits the piece you choose and is manageable within a paper of the assigned length. Sometimes you may be asked to simply summarize a complex literary work. The summary of *Othello* (pp. 42–43) would be adequate if the assignment was this straightforward. Other times, you may be asked to respond creatively, to come up with original work that reimagines a poem or story from your own point of view and in your own words. However, in many literature courses, assigned essays tend to fall into one of three modes — explication, analysis, and comparison and contrast — or some combination of these. Familiarity with these three kinds of writing about literature will help you not only with full-length essay assignments but also with exams and other in-class writing.

## Explication

In an explication essay, you examine a work in much detail. Line by line, *stanza by stanza*, scene by scene, you explain each part as fully as you can and show how the author's techniques produce your response. An *explication* is essentially a demonstration of your thorough understanding of a work.

Here is a sample essay that explicates a relatively difficult poem, Dylan Thomas's "Do Not Go Gentle into That Good Night" (p. 911).

Dylan Thomas's villanelle "Do Not Go Gentle into That Good Night" is addressed to his aged father. The poem is remarkable in a number of ways, most notably in that contrary to most common poetic treatments of the inevitability of death, which argue for serenity or celebrate the peace that death provides, this poem urges resistance and rage in the face of death. It justifies that unusual attitude by describing the rage and resistance to death of four kinds of men, who each can summon up the image of a complete and satisfying life that is denied to him by death.

The first tercet of the intricately rhymed villanelle opens with an arresting line. The adjective *gentle* appears where we would expect the adverb *gently*. The strange diction suggests that *gentle* may describe both the going (i.e., gently dying) and the person (i.e., gentleman) who confronts death. Further, the speaker characterizes "night," here clearly a figure for death, as "good." Yet in the next line, the speaker urges that the aged should violently resist death, characterized as the "close of day" and "the dying of the light." In effect, the first three lines argue that however good death may be, the aged should refuse to die gently, should passionately rave and rage against death.

In the second tercet, the speaker turns to a description of the way the first of four types of men confronts death (which is figuratively defined throughout the poem as "that good night" and "the dying of the light"). These are the "wise men," the scholars, the philosophers, those who understand the inevitability of death, men who "know dark is right." But they do not acquiesce in death "because their words had forked no lightning," because their published wisdom failed to bring them to that sense of completeness and fulfillment that can accept death. Therefore, wise as they are, they reject the theoretical "rightness" of death and refuse to "go gentle."

The second sort of men — "good men," the moralists, the social reformers, those who attempt to better the world through action as the wise men attempt to better it through "words" — also rage against death. Their deeds are, after all, "frail." With sea imagery, the speaker suggests that these men might have accomplished fine and fertile things — their deeds "might have danced in a green bay." But with the "last wave" gone, they see only the frailty, the impermanence of their acts, and so they, too, rage against the death that deprives them of the opportunity to leave a meaningful legacy.

The "wild men," the poets who "sang" the loveliness and vitality of nature, also learn as they approach death that the sensuous joys of human existence wane. As the life-giving sun moves toward dusk, as death approaches, their singing turns to grieving, and they refuse to surrender gently, to leave willingly the warmth, pleasure, and beauty that life can give.

Finally, with a pun suggestive of death, the "grave men," those who go through life with such high seriousness as never to experience gaiety and pleasure, see all the joyous possibilities that they were blind to in life. And they, too, rage against the dying of a light that they had never properly seen before.

The speaker then calls on his aged father to join these men raging against death. Only in this final stanza do we discover that the entire poem is addressed to the speaker's father and that, despite the generalized statements about old age and the focus on types of men, the poem is a personal lyric. The edge of death becomes a "sad height," the summit of wisdom and experience old age attains includes the sad knowledge of life's failure to satisfy the vision we all pursue. The depth and complexity of the speaker's sadness is startlingly given in the second line, when he calls on his father to both curse and bless him. These opposites richly suggest several related possibilities: "Curse me for not living up to your expectations. Curse me for remaining alive as you die. Bless me with forgiveness for my failings. Bless me for teaching you to rage against death." And the curses and blessings are contained in the "fierce tears" — fierce because you will burn and rave and rage against death. As the poem closes by bringing together the two powerful refrains, the speaker himself seems to rage because his father's death will cut off a relationship that is incomplete.

This explication deals with the entire poem by coming to grips with each element in it.

You can learn a great deal about the technique of drama by selecting a short, self-contained scene and writing a careful description of it. The length of plays will probably require that you focus on a single segment — a scene, for example — rather than the entire play. This method of explication will force you to confront every speech and stage direction and to come to some conclusion regarding its function. Why is the set furnished as it is? Why does a character speak the words he or she does or remain silent? What do we learn of characters from the interchanges among them? Assume that everything that occurs in the play, whether on the printed page or on the stage, is put there for a purpose. Seek to discover the purpose, and you will, at the same time, discover the distinctive nature of drama.

Fiction, too, can be treated effectively in a formal explication. As with drama, it will be necessary to limit the text: you will not be able to explicate a ten-page story in a 1,000-word essay. Choose a key passage — a half page that reflects the form and content of the overall story, if possible. Often the first half page of a story, where the author, like the playwright, must supply information to the reader, will make a fine text for an explication. Although the explication will deal principally with only an excerpt, feel free to range across the story and show how the introductory material foreshadows what is to come. Or perhaps you can explicate the climax of the story — the half page that most pointedly establishes the story's theme — and subject it to a close line-by-line reading that illuminates the whole story.

## Analysis

Breaking down a literary work into its elements is only the first step in literary analysis. When you are assigned an analysis essay, you are expected to focus on one of the elements that contributes to the complex compound of a work. This process requires you to extricate the element you plan to explore from the other elements that you can identify, to study this element — not only in isolation but also in relation to the other elements and the work as a whole — and, using the insights you have gained from your special perspective, to make an informed statement about it.

This process may sound complicated, but if you approach it methodically, each stage follows naturally from the stage that precedes it. If, for example, you are to write an analysis essay on characterization in *Othello*, you would begin by thinking about each character in the play. You would then select the character whose development you would like to explore and reread carefully those speeches that help to establish his or her substance. Exploring a character's development in this way involves a good deal of explication: in order to identify the "building blocks" that Shakespeare uses to create a three-dimensional role, you must comb very carefully through that character's speeches and actions. You must also be sensitive to the ways in which other characters respond to these speeches and actions. When you have completed this investigation, you will probably have a good understanding of why you intuitively responded to the character as you did when you first read the play. You will also probably be prepared to make a statement about the character's development: "From a realistic perspective, it is hard to believe that a man of Othello's position could be so gullible; however, Shakespeare develops the role with such craft that we accept the Moor as flesh and blood." At this point, you have moved from the broad *subject* of "characterization in *Othello*" to a thesis, a statement that you must prove. As you formulate your thesis, think of it as a position that you intend to *argue* for with a reader you need to persuade. This approach is useful in any essay that requires a thesis, where you move beyond simple explication and commit yourself to a stand. Note that our sample thesis is *argumentative* on two counts; "characterization in *Othello*" is not remotely argumentative. Further, you have more than enough material to write a well-documented essay of 1,000 words supporting your proposition; you cannot write a well-documented 1,000-word essay on the general subject of characterization in *Othello* without being superficial.

You may be one among the many writers who have trouble finding a starting point. For example, you have been assigned an analysis essay on a very broad subject, such as imagery in love poetry. A few poems come to mind, but you don't know where to begin. You read these poems and underline all the images that you can find. You look at these images over and over, finding no relation among them. You read some more poems, again underlining the images, but you still do not have even the germ of a thesis.

The technique of freewriting might help to overcome your block. You have read and reread the poems you intend to write about. Now, put the assignment temporarily out of your mind, and start writing about one or two of the poems without organizing your ideas, without trying to reach a point. Write down what you like about a poem, what you dislike about it, what sort of person the speaker is, which images seemed striking to you — anything at all about the work. If you do this for perhaps ten minutes, you will probably discover that you are voicing opinions. Pick one that interests you or seems the most promising to explore.

The basic form of the analysis assignment has a few variations. Your instructor might narrow the subject in a specific assignment: analyze the development of Othello's character in act I. This sort of assignment limits the amount of text you will have to study, but the process from this point on is no different from the process you would employ to address a broader subject. Sometimes instructors will supply you with a thesis, and you will have to work backward from the thesis to find supporting material. Again, careful analysis of the text is required. The problem you will have to address when writing an analytical essay remains the same regardless of the literary genre you are asked to discuss. You must find an arguable thesis that deals with the sources of your response to the work.

Suppose your instructor has made the following assignment: write an analysis of Harlan Ellison's story "'Repent, Harlequin!' Said the Ticktockman" (p. 322), in which you discuss the theme of the story in terms of the characters and the setting. Now consider the following opening (taken from a student paper):

> "'Repent, Harlequin!' Said the Ticktockman" is a story depicting a society in which time governs one's life. The setting is the United States, the time approximately 2400 CE somewhere in the heart of the country. Business deals, work shifts, and school lessons are started and finished with exacting precision. Tardiness is intolerable as this would hinder the system. In a society of order, precision, and punctuality, there is no room for likes, dislikes, scruples, or morals. Thus, personalities in people no longer exist. As these "personless" people know no good or bad, they very happily follow in the course of activities that their society has dictated.

At the outset, can you locate a thesis statement? The only sentences that would seem to qualify are the last three in the paragraph. But notice that, although those sentences are not unreasonable responses to the story, they do not establish a thesis that is *responsive to the assignment.* Because the assignment calls for a discussion of theme in terms of character and setting, a thesis statement should argue how character and setting embody the theme. Here is another opening paragraph on the same assignment (also taken from a student paper):

> Harlan Ellison's "'Repent, Harlequin!' Said the Ticktockman" opens with a quotation from Thoreau's essay "Civil Disobedience," which establishes the story's theme. Thoreau's observations about three varieties of men — those who serve the state as machines, those who serve it with their heads, and those who serve it with their consciences — are dramatized in Ellison's story, which takes place about 400 years in the future in a setting characterized by machinelike order. The interaction among the three characters, each of whom represents one of Thoreau's types, results in a telling restatement of his observation that "heroes, patriots, martyrs, reformers in the great sense, and men . . . necessarily resist [the state] and . . . are commonly treated as enemies by it."

Compare these two opening paragraphs sentence by sentence for their responsiveness to the assignment. The first sentence of the first opening does not refer to the theme of the story (or to its setting or characterization). In the second sentence, the discussion of the setting ignores the most important aspect — that the story is set in a machine- and time-dominated future. The last three sentences deal obliquely with character, but they are imprecise and do not establish a thesis. The second opening, on the other hand, immediately states the theme of the story. It goes on to emphasize the relevant aspects of the futuristic setting and then refers to the three characters who animate the story in terms of their reactions to the setting. The last sentence addresses the assignment directly and also serves as a thesis statement for the paper. It states the proposition that will be developed and supported in the rest of the paper. The reader of the second opening will expect the next paragraph of the paper to discuss the setting of the story and subsequent paragraphs to discuss the response to the setting of the three principal characters.

The middles of essays are largely determined by their opening paragraphs. However long the middle of any essay may be, each of its paragraphs ought to be responsive to some explicit statement made at the beginning of the essay.

Note that it is practically impossible to predict what the paragraph following the first opening will address. Here is the first half of that next paragraph as the first student wrote it:

> The Harlequin is a man in the society with no sense of time. His having a personality enables him to have a sense of moral values and a mind of his own. The Harlequin thinks that it is obscene and wrong to let time totally govern the lives of people. So he sets out to disrupt the time schedule with ridiculous antics such as showering people with jelly beans to try to break up the military fashion in which they are used to doing things.

The paragraph then goes on to discuss the Ticktockman, the capture and brainwashing of the Harlequin, and the resulting lateness of the Ticktockman.

Note that nothing in the opening of this student's paper prepared readers for the introduction of the Harlequin. In fact, the opening concluded rather inaccurately that the people within the story "happily follow in the course of activities that their society has dictated." Hence, the description of the Harlequin in the second paragraph is wholly unexpected. Further, because the student has not dealt with the theme of the story (as the assignment asked), the comments about the Harlequin's antics remain disconnected from any clear purpose. They are essentially devoted to what teachers constantly warn against: a mere plot summary. The student has obviously begun to write before analyzing the story sufficiently to understand its theme. With further thought, the student would have perceived that the central thematic issue is resistance to an oppressive state — the issue stated in the epigraph from Thoreau. On the other hand, because the second opening makes that thematic point clearly, we can expect it to be followed by a discussion of the environment (that is, the setting) in which the action occurs. Here is such a paragraph taken from the second student's paper:

> Ellison creates a society that reflects one possible future development of the modern American passion for productivity and efficiency. The setting is in perfect keeping with the time-conscious people who inhabit the city. It is pictured as a neat, colorless, and mechanized city. No mention is made of nature: grass, flowers, trees, and birds do not appear. The buildings are in a "Mondrian arrangement," stark and geometrical. The cold steel sidewalks, slowstrips, and expresstrips move with precision.

> Like a chorus line, people move in unison to board the movers without a
> wasted motion. Doors close silently and lock themselves automatically.
> An ideal efficiency so dominates the social system that any "wasted time"
> is deducted from the life of an inefficient citizen.

Once the setting has been established, the writer turns to the characters,
linking those characters to thematic considerations, beginning with a short
transitional paragraph that shapes the remainder of the middle of the essay:

> Into this smoothly functioning but coldly mechanized soci-
> ety, Ellison introduces three characters: Pretty Alice, one of Thoreau's
> machinelike creatures; the Ticktockman, one of those who "serve the
> state chiefly with their heads, and, as they rarely make any moral
> distinctions, they are as likely to serve the Devil, without intending it,
> as God"; and Everett C. Marm, the Harlequin, whose conscience forces
> him to resist the oppressive state.

Following a logical organization, the essay then includes a paragraph devoted
to each of the three characters:

> Pretty Alice is, probably, very pretty. (Everett didn't fall in love
> with her brains.) In the brief section in which we meet her, we find her
> hopelessly ordinary in her attitudes. She is upset that Marm finds it
> necessary to go about "annoying people." She finds him ridiculous and
> wishes only that he would stay home, as other people do. Clearly, she has
> no understanding of what Everett is struggling against. Though her anger
> finally leads her to betray him, Everett himself can't believe that she has
> done so. His own loyal and understanding nature colors his view of her
> so thoroughly that he cannot imagine the treachery that must have been
> so simple and satisfying for Pretty Alice, whose only desire is to be like
> everybody else.
>
> The Ticktockman is more complex. He sees himself as a servant
> of the state, and he performs his duties with resolution and competence.

He skillfully supports a System he has never questioned. The System exists; it must be good. His conscience is simply not involved in the performance of his duty. He is one of those who follow orders and expect others to follow orders. As a result, the behavior of the Harlequin is more than just an irritant or a rebellion against authority. It is unnerving. The Ticktockman wishes to understand that behavior, and with Everett's time-card in his hand, he muses that he has the name of "*what* he is, not *who* he is. . . . Before I can exercise proper revocation, I have to know *who* this *what* is." And when he confronts Everett, he does not just liquidate him. He insists that Everett repent. He tries to convince Everett that the System is sound, and when he cannot win the argument, he dutifully reconditions Everett, since he is, after all, more interested in justifying the System than in destroying its enemies. It is easy to see this man as a competent servant of the devil who thinks he is serving God.

But only Everett C. Marm truly serves the state because his con-science requires him to resist. He is certainly not physically heroic. His very name suggests weak conformity. Though he loves his Pretty Alice, he can-not resign from the rebellious campaign on which his conscience insists. So without violence, and mainly with the weapon of laughter, he attacks the mechanical precision of the System and succeeds in breaking it down simply by making people late. He is himself, as Pretty Alice points out, always late, and the delays that his antics produce seriously threaten the well-being of the smooth but mindless System he hates. He is captured and refuses, even then, to submit, and so his personality is destroyed by the authorities that fear him. The Ticktockman is too strong for him.

An appropriate ending emerges naturally from this student's treatment of the assignment. Having established that the story presents characters who deal in different ways with the oppressive quality of life in a time- and machine-obsessed society, the student concludes with a comment on the author's criti-cisms of such a society:

Harlequin is defeated, but Ellison, finally, leaves us with an optimistic note. The idea of rebellion against the System will linger in the minds of others. There will be more Harlequins and more disruption of this System. Many rebels will be defeated, but any System that suppresses individualism will give birth to resistance. And Harlequin's defeat is by no means total. The story ends with the Ticktockman himself arriving for work three minutes late.

## Comparison and Contrast

An essay in comparison and contrast shows how two works are similar to and different from each other. It almost always starts with a recognition of similarities, often of subject matter. Sometimes you may be asked to connect what you have read with something in your own life, creating an original comparison, for example, between Peter Meinke's "Advice to My Son" (p. 190) and advice you have been given by an adult in your own life. Most comparison-and-contrast assignments involve two works of the same genre. While it is possible to compare *any* two works, the best comparison-and-contrast essays emerge from the analysis of two works similar enough to illuminate each other. Two works about love, or death, or conformity, or innocence, or identity give you something to begin with. The groupings in this book will suggest some ways you might read certain works together. For example, both Emily Dickinson's "Apparently with no surprise" (p. 900) and Robert Frost's "Design" (p. 909) are about death, and they both use remarkably similar events as the occasion for their poems. Starting with these similarities, you would soon find yourself noting the contrasts (in tone, for example, and theme) between nineteenth-century and twentieth-century views of the nature of God.

Before you begin writing a comparison-and-contrast essay, it is especially important to have clearly in mind the points of comparison and contrast you wish to discuss and the order in which you can most effectively discuss them. You will need to give careful thought to the best way to organize your paper, jotting down the plan your comparison will follow. As a general rule, it is best to avoid dividing the essay into separate discussions of each work. That method tends to produce two separate, loosely joined analysis essays. The successful comparison-and-contrast essay treats some point of similarity or contrast between the two works, then moves on to succeeding points, and ends with an evaluation of the comparative merits of the works.

Like any essay that goes beyond simple explication, a comparison-and-contrast essay requires a strong thesis statement. However, a comparison-and-contrast thesis is generally not difficult to formulate: you must identify the works under consideration and state clearly your reasons for making the comparison.

Here is a student paper that compares and contrasts Dylan Thomas's "Do Not Go Gentle into That Good Night" with the poetic response it triggered from a poet with different views:

Dylan Thomas's "Do Not Go Gentle into That Good Night" and Catherine Davis's "After a Time" demand comparison: Davis's poem was written in deliberate response to Thomas's. Davis assumes the reader's familiarity with "Do Not Go Gentle," which she uses to articulate her contrasting ideas. "After a Time," although it is a literary work in its own right, might even be thought of as serious parody — perhaps the greatest compliment one writer can pay another.

"Do Not Go Gentle into That Good Night" was written by a young man of thirty-eight who addresses it to his old and ailing father. Perhaps because Thomas had very little of his own self-destructive life left as he was composing this piece, he seems to have more insight into the subject of death than most people his age. He advocates raging and fighting against it, not giving in and accepting it.

"After a Time" was written by Davis at about the same age and is addressed to no one in particular. Davis has a different philosophy about death. She "answers" Thomas's poem and presents her differing views using the same poetic form — a villanelle. Evidently, she felt it necessary to present a contrasting point of view eight years after Thomas's death.

While "Do Not Go Gentle" protests and rages against death, Davis's poem suggests a quiet resignation and acquiescence. She seems to feel that raging against death is useless and profitless. She argues that we will eventually become tame, anyway, after the raging is done.

Thomas talks about different types of men and why they rage against death. "Wise men" desire immortality. They rage against death occurring before they've made their mark on history. "Good men" lament the frailty of their deeds. Given more time, they might have accomplished great things. "Wild men" regret their constant hedonistic pursuits. With more time they could prove their worth. "Grave men" are quite the opposite and regret they never took time for the pleasures in life. Now it is too late. They rage against death because they are not ready for it.

His father's death is painful to Thomas because he sees himself lying in that bed; his father's dying reminds him of his own inevitable death. The passion of the last stanza, in which the poet asks his father to bless and curse him, suggests that he has doubts about his relationship with his father. He may feel that he has not been a good enough son. He put off doing things with and for his father because he always felt there would be time later. Now time has run out and he feels cheated.

Catherine Davis advocates a calm submission, a peaceful acquiescence. She feels raging is useless and says that those of us who rage will finally "go tame / When what we have we can no longer use." When she says "One more thing lost is one thing less to lose," the reader can come to terms with the loss of different aspects of the mind and body, such as strength, eyesight, hearing, and intellect. Once one of these is lost, it's one thing less to worry about losing. After a time, everything will be lost, and we'll accept that, too, because we'll be ready for it.

Thomas's imagery is vivid and powerful. His various men not only rage and rave, they *burn*. Their words "forked no lightning," their deeds might have "danced in a green bay," they "sang the sun in flight," and they see that "blind eyes could blaze like meteors." Davis's images are quiet and generally abstract, without much sensory suggestiveness, as in "things lost," a "reassuring ruse," and "all losses are the same." Her most powerful image — "And we go stripped at last the way we came" — makes its point with none of the excitement of Thomas's rage. And yet, I prefer the quiet intelligence of Davis to the high energy of Thomas.

"And we go stripped at last the way we came" can give strange comfort and solace to those of us who always envied those in high places. People are not all created equal at birth, not by a long shot. But we will all be equal when we die. All wealth, power, and trappings will be left behind, and we will all ultimately be equal. So why rage? It won't do us any good.

## THE RESEARCH PAPER

Research papers depend on secondary sources (the primary source is, of course, the work, the historical event, or the literary theory you are studying). Research assignments send you to the library, to the Web, or to any source of information that bears on your project. Whether you are researching to discover the varied responses to a work, to gain some insight into the author's life and times, or to identify relevant critical principles, you will synthesize what you have read *about* the work into a well-organized paper and provide *proper documentation*. But a research paper is not a mindless recitation of what your secondary sources have said. Nor does it require you to suspend your own critical judgment. By the time you settle into writing your paper, you will have learned some things you didn't know before. You have earned — and ought to exercise — the right to make your own claims based on other arguments you have read and the information you have synthesized. An assigned research topic will probably ask you to come to some conclusions. If you choose your own topic, you must discover in your research support for a clear, focused thesis before you begin to write.

Here is a sample student research paper that illustrates the technique. The marginal notes call attention to some of the details that make this a successful effort. In general, notice that the author has done research, but the paper is not weighed down with it. The opening paragraph provides a historical context for the subject of the paper, Kate Chopin's short story "The Storm" (p. 587). The writer has a point of view about the story, or thesis, stated in the second paragraph. While that thesis is developed throughout, the writer makes interesting observations on such matters as the relationship of other Chopin works to the story, the names of characters, local color, and a notable change in American moral attitudes. Note how the writer concludes with two paragraphs that resolve the issues raised in the opening two paragraphs. The sample paper employs the Modern Language Association's (MLA) standard documentation and footnote form. The section that follows the research paper provides further samples that will help you manage formal matters and documentation. It concludes with a checklist that you might want to consult both before you begin writing your paper and before you submit your final draft.

## An Annotated Student Research Paper

Lagos 1

Krissa Lagos

Professor Richard Abcarian

English 255

### Sex and Sensibility
### in Kate Chopin's "The Storm"

Kate Chopin's openly erotic depictions of marital infidelity in her literary works separate her from all other American female writers of her time. The adulterous affair of a strong independent woman depicted in her novel *The Awakening* (1899) created a public scandal. And, though she "never flouted convention as strongly as did her fictitious heroine, she did exhibit an individuality and strength remarkable for upper-middle-class women of the time" (Moon). Her honest and direct portrayal of the sexuality of her female characters was rejected until well into the 1900s, when the minds of readers caught up to her advanced thinking (Skaggs 5). Works such as "The Storm" — once shunned (especially by the male community) because of their focus on sexual exploration — are now celebrated as serious literature. In fact, when Chopin wrote "The Storm" in 1898, she knew that no magazine would ever publish such an uninhibited and uncritical account of an adulterous encounter, and so never attempted to have it published (Toth 206).

*[Margin annotations:]*

Writer's name and page number.

Use MLA standard style or follow instructor's criteria.

Center title.

First paragraph establishes context.

Documents an Internet source with no page number (see Works Cited).

Documents a book in Works Cited and gives page number.

Lagos 2

States the
elements of the
paper's thesis.

In "The Storm," Chopin utilizes the irony characteristic of her writing to give the story a light, easy feel. She also uses diction and imagery to draw the reader into the emotions of her characters. She ignores the usual implications of unfaithfulness to a spouse, and instead focuses on the pleasure inspired by the instant gratification of physical desire.

Provides
important
context for the
story's events.

"The Storm" is in fact a sequel to another short story, "At the 'Cadian Ball." In the first tale, which takes place in Louisiana, a favorite setting for Chopin,[1] a farmer named Bobinôt is captivated with spirited, Spanish-blooded Calixta. Calixta, however, has her eyes on a handsome local planter, Alcée Laballière, who is charmed by her attractive features and openly sexual attitude. At the end of the night, however, Clarisse, a woman who is Alcée's social equal (and also happens to be his cousin), suddenly appears and agrees to marry him. Calixta, deserted by Alcée, is "deemed lucky to get anyone, even stodgy Bobinôt" (Ewell 77).

Discusses the
significance of
setting.

By setting "The Storm" in Louisiana, Chopin is able to take advantage of the unstable, muggy weather of the region to help build up to the story's climax. The events of the tale occur because of the weather: the storm strands Bobinôt and his son Bibi at a store while wife and mother Calixta is at home, and Alcée is driven into Bobinôt and Calixta's house by the

Uses concrete
examples to
bolster
assertions.

approaching rain. More subtle events, nearly all of which carry sensual undercurrents, are also inspired by the weather conditions.

Lagos 3

For instance, when Calixta is first mentioned, she is sewing, and Chopin immediately introduces an indirect sexual undertone to her movements: ". . . she felt very warm and often stopped to mop her face on which the perspiration gathered in beads. She unfastened her white sacque at the throat" (Chopin, "The Storm" 861). Except for what follows, there would be no reason at all to interpret this minor event. However, when Alcée arrives, the loosened collar eventually leads to more than one would imagine possible. First, Calixta is driven into his arms by the lightning crashing all around the house. Alcée attempts to ease her fears while at the same time fighting the desire for her that has been reawakened by contact with her body. Her unbuttoned collar is part of what defeats his battle against his desires:

> He pushed her hair back from her face that was
> warm and steaming. Her lips were as red and moist
> as pomegranate seed. Her white neck and a glimpse
> of her full firm bosom disturbed him powerfully. As
> she glanced up at him the fear in her liquid blue
> eyes had given place to a drowsy gleam that
> unconsciously betrayed a sensuous desire. (Chopin,
> "The Storm" 589)

Obviously the sole reason for Calixta and Alcée succumbing to their passions is not that she unbuttoned her shirt collar. However, the accumulation of this and other details — their shared climax with the storm, the correspondence between them lying contented afterward while the storm departs softly — make

*Ellipses indicate omission in a direct quote.*

*Identifies the specific work from the Works Cited list when there is more than one work by the same author.*

*Shows how Chopin uses details to advance the plot.*

this story a powerful work of art. Chopin crafts her sentences to enhance her narrative's power.

The French Louisiana setting of "The Storm" is typical of many of her writings (Ewell 52). The detailed local color is reflected by the French names of the characters. Calixta, Bobinôt, and Bibi speak the 'Cadian dialect of Louisiana, which in Calixta's case occasionally includes a small smattering of French (Ewell 77). Alcée, in contrast, speaks impeccable English, reflective of his better education. Chopin inserts a significant detail at the beginning of the story when Bobinôt purchases "a can of shrimps, of which Calixta was very fond" (Chopin, "The Storm" 587). The small gesture reveals Bobinôt's affectionate appreciation of his wife.

Discusses Chopin's view of the rights of women.

In "The Storm," Chopin conveys the theme of autonomy, something familiar to her female characters, especially in "The Story of an Hour."[2] Both Calixta and Clarisse are happiest in "The Storm" when they are separated from their husbands and free to do as they wish.

> As for Clarisse, she was charmed upon receiving her husband's letter. She and the babies were doing well. The society was agreeable; many of her old friends seemed to restore the pleasant liberty of her maiden days. Devoted as she was to her husband, their intimate conjugal life was something which she was more than willing to forego for a while. (Chopin, "The Storm" 591)

Therefore Clarisse, though far from the actual storm, benefits from its effects. She feels unfettered, pleased at being given space for the first time since she has been married to Alcée. For Calixta, the short time she spends with Alcée during the storm is enough to make her lift "her pretty chin in the air" and laugh with delight (Chopin, "The Storm" 590).

In "At the 'Cadian Ball," the two couples are paired together at the end of the night due to Alcée's notion of honor and propriety (Ewell 77). As Chopin explains in "The Storm," he never intended to marry Calixta, but he did want more from her than what he took in the story's prequel at the ball: "If she was not an immaculate dove in those days, she was still inviolate; a passionate creature whose very defenselessness had made her defense, against which his honor forbade him to prevail" (Chopin, "The Storm" 589). When the ball ended, only Calixta was left unsatisfied, but by the time "The Storm" takes place, only Bobinôt is still utterly content.

Earlier story is used to establish Alcée's character.

The fact that Calixta is now married somehow frees Alcée from his previous restraints, and he is able to satisfy his craving for her at last. As a result, Alcée is also more content with his wife away, which leads him to write the letter to her urging her to prolong her stay in Biloxi. Bobinôt is the most easily pleased of all. He reaches home cringing at what his wife will say to Bibi and him when she notices how dirty they are. Luckily for the father and son, she is still glowing from her brief interlude with Alcée, and "they laughed much and so loud that anyone might have heard them as far away as Laballière's" (Chopin, "The Storm" 590).

Lagos 6

Chopin's irony shines through "The Storm" in many parts of the story. One of these moments occurs when she addresses the issue of natural right while Calixta and Alcée are making love: "Her firm, elastic flesh that was knowing for the first time its birthright, was like a creamy lily that the sun invites to contribute its breath and perfume to the undying life of the world" (Chopin, "The Storm" 589). Chopin goes further than condoning the affair between Calixta and Alcée by describing it as something completely natural, an event that was meant to occur.

What would have been most shocking to audiences in the nineteenth century was the fact that when the storm ended, there were no repercussions. Alcée "turned and smiled" at Calixta "with a beaming face" and rode away, Calixta showed "nothing but satisfaction" when her husband and son returned home, Bobinôt and Bibi "began to relax and enjoy themselves" when they saw that Calixta was in good spirits, and Clarisse stayed in Biloxi, enjoying herself. For such severe sins to be committed and go unpunished was unheard of in Chopin's time, and "even today some readers find that conclusion unforgivable" (Skaggs 62).

In truth, this very conclusion elevates "The Storm" to the high level it resides on. Through adultery, deception, and self-indulgence, the characters achieve happiness, a surprise ending that Chopin adopted from Guy de Maupassant.[3] This ironic twist makes the story a unique departure from the norm, even today, and "The Storm" ends on a comic note, the reader left as contented as the story's characters.

Asserts the proven thesis stated in the second paragraph.

## Notes

[1]Chopin set many of her stories in the Cane River country of Louisiana; her husband, Oscar, was raised in Louisiana, and they lived there together for twelve years (Toth 92).

[2]In Chopin's "The Story of an Hour," the main character discovers that she prizes individual freedom over all else — even the life and love of her husband.

[3]Guy de Maupassant (1850–1893) was a French writer whose short stories often featured surprise endings.

## Works Cited

Abcarian, Richard, et al., editors. *Literature: The Human Experience.* Shorter 12th ed., Bedford/St. Martin's, 2018.

Chopin, Kate. "At the 'Cadian Ball." *The Complete Works of Kate Chopin.* Edited by Per Seyersted, Louisiana State UP, 1969, pp. 219–27.

---. "The Storm." Abcarian et al., pp. 587–91.

Ewell, Barbara C. *Kate Chopin.* Ungar Publishing, 1986.

Moon, Jennifer. "ClassicNote on Kate Chopin." *GradeSaver,* 30 Mar. 2000, gradesaver.com/classicnotes/kate-chopin.

Skaggs, Peggy. *Kate Chopin.* Twayne Publishers, 1985.

Toth, Emily. *Unveiling Kate Chopin.* UP of Mississippi, 1999.

## SOME MATTERS OF FORM AND DOCUMENTATION

After you have worked hard to draft, revise, and edit an essay, check to be sure you have documented your sources accurately and fairly. A consistent, well-documented essay allows readers to focus on your argument rather than on your document.

### Titles

When included in the body of your essay, the first word and all main words of titles are capitalized. Ordinarily (unless they are the first or last word), articles (*a, an,* and *the*), prepositions (*in, on, of, with, about,* and so on), conjunctions (*and, but, or,* and so on), and the *to* in an infinitive ("A Good Man Is Hard to Find") are not capitalized.

The titles of short stories, poems, articles, essays, songs, episodes of television programs, and parts of larger collections are enclosed in quotation marks.

The titles of plays, books, movies, periodicals, operas, television series, recordings, paintings, and newspapers are italicized. If your word-processing program does not produce italic type that is easily distinguishable from non-italic type, use underlining.

The title you give your essay is neither placed in quotation marks nor italicized. However, the title of a literary work used as a part of your title would be either placed in quotation marks or italicized, depending on the type of work it is.

### Quotations

Quotation marks indicate that you are transcribing someone else's words; those words must, therefore, appear *exactly* as they do in your source.

As a general rule, quotations of not more than four lines of prose or two lines of poetry are placed between quotation marks and incorporated into your own text:

> Near the end of "Young Goodman Brown," the narrator asks, "Had Good-
>
> man Brown fallen asleep in the forest and only dreamed a wild dream
>
> of a witch-meeting?" (88).

If you are quoting two or three lines of verse in your text, indicate the division between lines with a slash. Leave a space before and after the slash:

> Prufrock hears the dilettantish talk in a room where "the women come
>
> and go / Talking of Michelangelo."

Longer quotations are indented half an inch from the left margin and are double-spaced. They are not enclosed in quotation marks, since the indention signals a quotation.

**BRACKETS AND ELLIPSES**    If you insert anything into a quotation — even a word — the inserted material must be placed within brackets. If you wish to omit some material from a passage in quotation marks, the omission must be indicated with ellipsis points — three equally spaced periods. When an ellipsis occurs between complete sentences or at the end of a sentence, a fourth period, indicating the end of the sentence, should be inserted.

Here is an example of a full quotation from an original source:

> As one critic puts it, "Richard Wright, like Dostoevsky before him, sends
>
> his hero underground to discover the truth about the upper world, a
>
> world that has forced him to confess to a crime he has not committed."

Here is the quotation with insertion and omissions:

> As one critic puts it, "Richard Wright . . . sends his hero [Fred Daniels]
>
> underground to discover the truth about the upper world. . . ."

Use a full line of spaced periods to indicate the omission of a line or more of poetry:

> For I have known them all already, known them all —
>
> Have known the evenings, mornings, afternoons,
>
> I have measured out my life with coffee spoons;
>
> .  .  .  .  .  .  .  .  .  .  .  .  .  .  .  .  .  .  .  .  .  .  .  .  .  .  .
>
> And I have known the eyes already, known them all —
>
> The eyes that fix you in a formulated phrase.

**QUOTATION MARKS AND OTHER PUNCTUATION**    Periods and commas are placed *inside* quotation marks:

> In "The Lesson," the narrator describes Miss Moore as someone "who
>
> always looked like she was going to church, though she never did."

Other punctuation marks such as colons or semicolons go outside the concluding quotation marks unless they are part of the material being quoted:

> Bartleby repeatedly insists that he "would prefer not to"; eventually
>
> these words become haunting.

For poetry quotations, provide the line number or numbers in parentheses immediately following the quotation:

With ironic detachment, Prufrock declares that he is "no prophet" (653).

## Documentation

You must acknowledge sources for the ideas you paraphrase or summarize and material you quote. Such acknowledgments are extremely important, for even an unintentional failure to give formal credit to others for their words or ideas can leave you open to an accusation of *plagiarism* — that is, the presentation of someone else's ideas as your own.

In the body of your essay, use parenthetical citations to document those works that you quote, paraphrase, or summarize. A list of your sources should be the last page of your essay, the Works Cited page. If you use other kinds of sources not listed here, consult the *MLA Handbook*, Eighth Edition (2016), or online at style.mla.org/.

This whimsical paragraph demonstrates the use of parenthetical citations.

> Leslie Fiedler's view of the relationship between Jim and Huck
>
> (669–70) uses a method often discussed by other critics (Abcarian
>
> et al. 6–9). Cooper's 1971 study (180) raises similar issues, although
>
> such methods are not useful when dealing with such a line as "North
>
> Richmond Street, being blind, was a quiet street except at the hour
>
> when the Christian Brothers' School set the boys free" (Joyce,
>
> "Araby" 121). But when Joyce refers to the weather (*Dubliners* 224),
>
> the issue becomes clouded.

The first citation gives only the page reference, which is all that is necessary because the author's name is given in the text and only one work by that author appears in the list of works cited. The second citation gives the name of the first editor followed by "et al." to signify that there are two or more authors and thus identifies the work being cited. It then indicates the appropriate pages. The third citation, because the author's name is mentioned in the text, gives only a page reference. The fourth citation must provide the author's name *and* the work cited, because two works by the same author appear in the list of works cited. The last citation, because it refers to an author with two works in the list of works cited, gives the name of the work and the page where the reference can be found.

In short, your parenthetical acknowledgment should contain (1) the *minimum* information required to lead the reader to the appropriate work in the list of works cited and (2) the location within the work to which you refer. Citations give credit whenever it is due and enable your reader to go directly to your sources as quickly and easily as possible.

Works Cited

Abcarian, Richard, et al., editors. *Literature: The Human Experience.*

Shorter 12th ed., Bedford/St. Martin's, 2018.

Cooper, Wendy. *Hair, Sex, Society, Symbolism.* Stein and Day, 1971.

Fiedler, Leslie. "Come Back to the Raft Ag'in, Huck Honey." *Partisan*

*Review*, vol. 15, no. 6, June 1948, pp. 664–71.

Joyce, James. "Araby." Abcarian et al., pp. 121–25.

---. *Dubliners.* Edited by Robert Scholes and A. Walton Litz.

Penguin Books, 1976.

The first of these citations is for this book. Note that the first editor's name is presented surname first, though when there is a second editor or author, that name is presented with the surname last. In this case, since there are more than two editors, the first editor's name is followed by "et al." The second entry illustrates the form for citing a book with one author. The third gives the form for an article published in a periodical (note that the title of the article is in quotes and the title of the journal is italicized). The fourth entry shows how to cite a work included in an anthology. The fifth citation, because it is by the same author as the fourth, begins with three hyphens in place of the author's name.

**DOCUMENTING ONLINE SOURCES** Until recently, there were few standards governing the citation of electronic sources. However, it has become increasingly common to employ at least some online tools while conducting research. The form suggested below will probably serve for most citations to online books, articles, databases, and other kinds of sites. Keep in mind, however, that if it does not, you will have to decide for yourself the best way to include additional information. The most important thing is that you accurately cite every single source you consult whether that source is a Web site or a more traditional source like a book or an encyclopedia.

1. Author's name
2. Title of the work in quotation marks
3. Title of the Web site (italicized)
4. Date of publication or most recent update

**5.** URL of the Web site, without http://

**6.** Date of access, if there is no date of publication provided

> Samuelson, Scott. "Why I Teach Plato to Plumbers." *The Atlantic,*
>
> 29 Apr. 2014, theatlantic.com/education/archive/2014/04/plato
>
> -to-plumbers/361373/.

## A CHECKLIST FOR WRITING ABOUT LITERATURE

**1.** Is my essay clearly responsive to the assignment?

**2.** Does my essay put forward a clearly defined thesis at the outset?

**3.** Does each paragraph have an identifiable topic sentence?

**4.** Have I marshaled my paragraphs logically and provided appropriate transitions?

**5.** Do I support my assertions with evidence?

**6.** Have I used direct quotations appropriately, and have I transcribed them accurately?

**7.** Do I document the sources of other people's ideas and the direct quotations I use? Is the documentation in appropriate form?

**8.** Have I written syntactically correct sentences (no run-ons and no fragments except by design)?

**9.** Have I eliminated as many passive constructions and forms of the verb *to be* as possible?

**10.** Have I avoided long sequences (say, three or more) of prepositional phrases?

**11.** Can I feel good about this essay? Does it embody serious thinking in attractive form (free of typos and other errors)? Can I put my name on the essay with pride?

# INNOCENCE AND EXPERIENCE

*The Veteran*, 1878 (oil on canvas). Gaetano Chierici (1838–1920).

Humans strive to give order and meaning to their lives, to reduce the mystery and unpredictability that constantly threaten them. Life is infinitely more complex and surprising than we imagine, and the categories we establish to give it order and meaning are, for the most part, "a momentary stay against confusion" to borrow Robert Frost's description of poetry. At any time the equilibrium of our lives, the comfortable image of ourselves and the world around us, may be disrupted by something new, forcing us into painful reevaluation. These disruptions create pain, anxiety, and terror but also wisdom and awareness.

The works in this section deal generally with the movement of a central character from moral simplicities and certainties into a more complex and problematic world. Though these works frequently deal with awareness, even wisdom, their central figures rarely act decisively. The main character or protagonist is more often a passive figure who learns the difference between the ideal world he or she imagines and the injurious real world. If the protagonist survives the ordeal, he or she often becomes a better human — better able to wrest some satisfaction from a bleak and threatening world. Many of the works here deal with the passage from childhood to adulthood, the time that certainty gives way to uncertainty.

Almost universally, innocence is associated with childhood and youth, as experience is with age. We teach the young about an ideal world, without explaining that it has not yet been and may never be achieved. As innocents, children are terribly vulnerable to falsehood, to intrusive sexuality, and to the machinations of the wicked, who often triumph.

But the terms *innocence* and *experience* range widely in meaning, and that range is reflected here. Innocence may be social — the innocence of Brown in Nathaniel Hawthorne's "Young Goodman Brown." Or innocence may be seen as the child's ignorance of his or her own mortality, as in Gerard Manley Hopkins's "Spring and Fall." In such works as Nathaniel Hawthorne's "Young Goodman Brown" and Robert Browning's "My Last Duchess," one discovers the tragic consequences of an innocence that is blind.

77

The contrast between what we thought in our youth and what we have come to know, painfully, as adults stands as an emblem of the passage from innocence to experience. Yet all of us remain, to one degree or another, innocent throughout life, since we never — except with death — stop learning from experience. Looked at in this way, experience is the ceaseless assault life makes on our innocence, moving us to a greater wisdom about ourselves and the world around us.

## QUESTIONS FOR THINKING AND WRITING

As you read the selections in this section, consider the following questions. You may want to write out your thoughts informally in a journal or notebook as a way of preparing to respond to the selections, or you may wish to make one of these questions the basis for a formal essay.

**1.** Innocence is often associated with childhood; responsibility, with adulthood. Were you happier or more contented as a preteen than you are now? Why? Which particular aspects of your childhood do you remember with pleasure? Which with pain? Do you look forward to the future with pleasurable anticipation or with dread? Why?

**2.** Do you know any adults who seem to be innocents? On what do you base your judgment? Do you know any preteens who seem to be particularly "adult" in their behavior (beyond politeness and good manners — they may, for example, have to cope with severe family difficulties)? On what do you base your judgment?

**3.** Have you spent your life under the authority of others, such as parents, teachers, and employers? How do you deal with authorities you resent? Do you look forward to exercising authority over others (your own children, your own students, employees under your supervision)? How will your experiences affect your behavior as an authority figure?

**4.** How does the growth from innocence to experience affect one's sexual behavior? Social behavior? Political behavior?

# FICTION

## NATHANIEL HAWTHORNE (1804–1864)

## YOUNG GOODMAN BROWN   1846

Young Goodman[1] Brown came forth at sunset into the street at Salem village; but put his head back, after crossing the threshold, to exchange a parting kiss with his young wife. And Faith, as the wife was aptly named, thrust her own pretty head into the street, letting the wind play with the pink ribbons of her cap while she called to Goodman Brown.

"Dearest heart," whispered she, softly and rather sadly, when her lips were close to his ear, "prithee put off your journey until sunrise and sleep in your own bed to-night. A lone woman is troubled with such dreams and such thoughts that she's afeared of herself sometimes. Pray tarry with me this night, dear husband, of all nights in the year."

"My love and my Faith," replied young Goodman Brown, "of all nights in the year, this one night must I tarry away from thee. My journey, as thou callest it, forth and back again, must needs be done 'twixt now and sunrise. What, my sweet, pretty wife, dost thou doubt me already, and we but three months married?"

"Then God bless you!" said Faith, with the pink ribbons; "and may you find all well when you come back."

"Amen!" cried Goodman Brown. "Say thy prayers, dear Faith, and go to bed   5 at dusk, and no harm will come to thee."

So they parted; and the young man pursued his way until, being about to turn the corner by the meeting-house, he looked back and saw the head of Faith still peeping after him with a melancholy air, in spite of her pink ribbons.

"Poor little Faith!" thought he, for his heart smote him. "What a wretch am I to leave her on such an errand! She talks of dreams, too. Methought as she spoke there was trouble in her face, as if a dream had warned her what work is to be done to-night. But no, no; 'twould kill her to think it. Well, she's a blessed angel on earth; and after this one night I'll cling to her skirts and follow her to heaven."

---

[1] Equivalent to *Mr.*, a title given to a man below the rank of gentleman.

With this excellent resolve for the future, Goodman Brown felt himself justified in making more haste on his present evil purpose. He had taken a dreary road, darkened by all the gloomiest trees of the forest, which barely stood aside to let the narrow path creep through, and closed immediately behind. It was all as lonely as could be; and there is this peculiarity in such a solitude, that the traveller knows not who may be concealed by the innumerable trunks and the thick boughs overhead; so that with lonely footsteps he may yet be passing through an unseen multitude.

"There may be a devilish Indian behind every tree," said Goodman Brown to himself; and he glanced fearfully behind him as he added, "What if the devil himself should be at my very elbow!"

His head being turned back, he passed a crook of the road, and, looking 10 forward again, beheld the figure of a man, in grave and decent attire, seated at the foot of an old tree. He arose at Goodman Brown's approach and walked onward side by side with him.

"You are late, Goodman Brown," said he. "The clock of the Old South[2] was striking as I came through Boston, and that is full fifteen minutes agone."

"Faith kept me back a while," replied the young man, with a tremor in his voice, caused by the sudden appearance of his companion, though not wholly unexpected.

It was now deep dusk in the forest, and deepest in that part of it where these two were journeying. As nearly as could be discerned, the second traveller was about fifty years old, apparently in the same rank of life as Goodman Brown, and bearing a considerable resemblance to him, though perhaps more in expression than features. Still they might have been taken for father and son. And yet, though the elder person was as simply clad as the younger, and as simple in manner too, he had an indescribable air of one who knew the world, and who would not have felt abashed at the governor's dinner table or in King William's[3] court, were it possible that his affairs should call him thither. But the only thing about him that could be fixed upon as remarkable was his staff, which bore the likeness of a great black snake, so curiously wrought that it might almost be seen to twist and wriggle itself like a living serpent. This, of course, must have been an ocular deception, assisted by the uncertain light.

"Come, Goodman Brown," cried his fellow-traveller, "this is a dull pace for the beginning of a journey. Take my staff, if you are so soon weary."

"Friend," said the other, exchanging his slow pace for a full stop, "having 15 kept covenant by meeting thee here, it is my purpose now to return whence I came. I have scruples touching the matter thou wot'st of."

"Sayest thou so?" replied he of the serpent, smiling apart. "Let us walk on, nevertheless, reasoning as we go; and if I convince thee not thou shalt turn back. We are but a little way in the forest yet."

---

[2] A church in Boston.
[3] Ruler of England from 1689 to 1702.

"Too far! too far!" exclaimed the goodman, unconsciously resuming his walk. "My father never went into the woods on such an errand, nor his father before him. We have been a race of honest men and good Christians since the days of the martyrs;[4] and shall I be the first of the name of Brown that ever took this path and kept —"

"Such company, thou wouldst say," observed the elder person, interpreting his pause. "Well said, Goodman Brown! I have been as well acquainted with your family as with ever a one among the Puritans; and that's no trifle to say. I helped your grandfather, the constable, when he lashed the Quaker woman so smartly through the streets of Salem; and it was I that brought your father a pitch-pine knot, kindled at my own hearth, to set fire to an Indian village, in King Philip's war.[5] They were my good friends, both; and many a pleasant walk have we had along this path, and returned merrily after midnight. I would fain be friends with you for their sake."

"If it be as thou sayest," replied Goodman Brown, "I marvel they never spoke of these matters; or, verily, I marvel not, seeing that the least rumor of the sort would have driven them from New England. We are a people of prayer, and good works to boot, and abide no such wickedness."

"Wickedness or not," said the traveller, with the twisted staff, "I have a very 20 general acquaintance here in New England. The deacons of many a church have drunk the communion wine with me; the selectmen of divers towns make me their chairman; and a majority of the Great and General Court[6] are firm supporters of my interest. The governor and I, too — But these are state secrets."

"Can this be so?" cried Goodman Brown, with a stare of amazement at his undisturbed companion. "Howbeit, I have nothing to do with the governor and council; they have their own ways, and are no rule for a simple husband-man[7] like me. But, were I to go on with thee, how should I meet the eye of that good old man, our minister, at Salem village? Oh, his voice would make me tremble both Sabbath day and lecture day."

Thus far the elder traveller had listened with due gravity; but now burst into a fit of irrepressible mirth, shaking himself so violently that his snake-like staff actually seemed to wriggle in sympathy.

"Ha! ha! ha!" shouted he again and again; then composing himself, "Well, go on, Goodman Brown, go on; but, prithee, don't kill me with laughing."

"Well, then, to end the matter at once," said Goodman Brown, considerably nettled, "there is my wife, Faith. It would break her dear little heart; and I'd rather break my own."

---

[4] A reference to the persecution of Protestants in England (1553–1558) by the Catholic monarch Mary Tudor.

[5] War waged (1675–1676) against the colonists of New England by the Indian chief Metacomet, also known as "King Philip."

[6] The Puritan legislature.

[7] An ordinary person.

"Nay, if that be the case," answered the other, "e'en go thy ways, Goodman  25
Brown. I would not for twenty old women like the one hobbling before us that
Faith should come to any harm."

As he spoke he pointed his staff at a female figure on the path, in whom
Goodman Brown recognized a very pious and exemplary dame, who had taught
him his catechism in youth, and was still his moral and spiritual adviser, jointly
with the minister and Deacon Gookin.

"A marvel, truly, that Goody[8] Cloyse should be so far in the wilderness at
nightfall," said he. "But with your leave, friend, I shall take a cut through the
woods until we have left this Christian woman behind. Being a stranger to you,
she might ask whom I was consorting with and whither I was going."

"Be it so," said his fellow-traveller. "Betake you to the woods, and let me keep
the path."

Accordingly the young man turned aside, but took care to watch his companion, who advanced softly along the road until he had come within a staff's
length of the old dame. She, meanwhile, was making the best of her way, with
singular speed for so aged a woman, and mumbling some indistinct words — a
prayer, doubtless — as she went. The traveller put forth his staff and touched
her withered neck with what seemed the serpent's tail.

"The devil!" screamed the pious old lady.                                     30

"Then Goody Cloyse knows her old friend?" observed the traveller, con-
fronting her and leaning on his writhing stick.

"Ah, forsooth, and is it your worship indeed?" cried the good dame. "Yea,
truly is it, and in the very image of my old gossip, Goodman Brown, the
grandfather of the silly fellow that now is. But — would your worship believe
it? — my broomstick hath strangely disappeared, stolen, as I suspect, by that
unhanged witch, Goody Cory, and that, too, when I was all anointed with the
juice of smallage and cinquefoil and wolf's bane —"[9]

"Mingled with fine wheat and the fat of a new-born babe," said the shape of
old Goodman Brown.

"Ah, your worship knows the recipe," cried the old lady, cackling aloud. "So,
as I was saying, being all ready for the meeting, and no horse to ride on, I made
up my mind to foot it; for they tell me there is a nice young man to be taken
into communion to-night. But now your good worship will lend me your arm,
and we shall be there in a twinkling."

"That can hardly be," answered her friend. "I may not spare you my arm,     35
Goody Cloyse; but here is my staff, if you will."

So saying, he threw it down at her feet, where, perhaps, it assumed life, being
one of the rods which its owner had formerly lent to the Egyptian magi.[10] Of
this fact, however, Goodman Brown could not take cognizance. He had cast
up his eyes in astonishment, and, looking down again, beheld neither Goody

---

[8] A polite title for a wife of humble rank.
[9] All these plants were associated with magic and witchcraft.
[10] Allusion to the biblical magicians who turned their rods into serpents (Exodus 7:11–12).

Cloyse nor the serpentine staff, but his fellow-traveller alone, who waited for him as calmly as if nothing had happened.

"That old woman taught me my catechism," said the young man; and there was a world of meaning in this simple comment.

They continued to walk onward, while the elder traveller exhorted his companion to make good speed and persevere in the path, discoursing so aptly that his arguments seemed rather to spring up in the bosom of his auditor than to be suggested by himself. As they went, he plucked a branch of maple to serve for a walking stick, and began to strip it of the twigs and little boughs, which were wet with evening dew. The moment his fingers touched them they became strangely withered and dried up as with a week's sunshine. Thus the pair proceeded, at a good free pace, until suddenly, in a gloomy hollow of the road, Goodman Brown sat himself down on the stump of a tree and refused to go any farther.

"Friend," said he, stubbornly, "my mind is made up. Not another step will I budge on this errand. What if a wretched old woman do choose to go to the devil when I thought she was going to heaven: is that any reason why I should quit my dear Faith and go after her?"

"You will think better of this by and by," said his acquaintance, composedly. 40 "Sit here and rest yourself a while; and when you feel like moving again, there is my staff to help you along."

Without more words, he threw his companion the maple stick, and was as speedily out of sight as if he had vanished into the deepening gloom. The young man sat a few moments by the roadside, applauding himself greatly, and thinking with how clear a conscience he should meet the minister in his morning walk, nor shrink from the eye of good old Deacon Gookin. And what calm sleep would be his that very night, which was to have been spent so wickedly, but so purely and sweetly now, in the arms of Faith! Amidst these pleasant and praiseworthy meditations, Goodman Brown heard the tramp of horses along the road, and deemed it advisable to conceal himself within the verge of the forest, conscious of the guilty purpose that had brought him thither, though now so happily turned from it.

On came the hoof tramps and the voices of the riders, two grave old voices, conversing soberly as they drew near. These mingled sounds appeared to pass along the road, within a few yards of the young man's hiding-place; but, owing doubtless to the depth of the gloom at that particular spot, neither the travellers nor their steeds were visible. Though their figures brushed the small boughs by the wayside, it could not be seen that they intercepted, even for a moment, the faint gleam from the strip of bright sky athwart which they must have passed. Goodman Brown alternately crouched and stood on tiptoe, pulling aside the branches and thrusting forth his head as far as he durst without discerning so much as a shadow. It vexed him the more, because he could have sworn, were such a thing possible, that he recognized the voices of the minister and Deacon Gookin, jogging along quietly, as they were wont to do, when bound to some ordination or ecclesiastical council. While yet within hearing, one of the riders stopped to pluck a switch.

"Of the two, reverend sir," said the voice like the deacon's, "I had rather miss an ordination dinner than to-night's meeting. They tell me that some of our community are to be here from Falmouth[11] and beyond, and others from Connecticut and Rhode Island, besides several of the Indian powwows,[12] who, after their fashion, know almost as much deviltry as the best of us. Moreover, there is a goodly young woman to be taken into communion."

"Mighty well, Deacon Gookin!" replied the solemn old tones of the minister. "Spur up, or we shall be late. Nothing can be done, you know, until I get on the ground."

The hoofs clattered again; and the voices, talking so strangely in the empty    45
air, passed on through the forest, where no church had ever been gathered, nor solitary Christian prayed. Whither, then, could these holy men be journeying so deep into the heathen wilderness? Young Goodman Brown caught hold of a tree for support, being ready to sink down on the ground, faint and overburdened with the heavy sickness of his heart. He looked up to the sky, doubting whether there really was a heaven above him. Yet there was the blue arch, and the stars brightening in it.

"With heaven above and Faith below, I will yet stand firm against the devil!" cried Goodman Brown.

While he still gazed upward into the deep arch of the firmament and had lifted his hands to pray, a cloud, though no wind was stirring, hurried across the zenith and hid the brightening stars. The blue sky was still visible, except directly overhead, where this black mass of cloud was sweeping swiftly northward. Aloft in the air, as if from the depths of the cloud, came a confused and doubtful sound of voices. Once the listener fancied that he could distinguish the accents of towns-people of his own, men and women, both pious and ungodly, many of whom he had met at the communion table, and had seen others rioting at the tavern. The next moment, so indistinct were the sounds, he doubted whether he had heard aught but the murmur of the old forest, whispering without a wind. Then came a stronger swell of those familiar tones, heard daily in the sunshine at Salem village, but never until now from a cloud of night. There was one voice, of a young woman, uttering lamentations, yet with an uncertain sorrow, and entreating for some favor, which, perhaps, it would grieve her to obtain; and all the unseen multitude, both saints and sinners, seemed to encourage her onward.

"Faith!" shouted Goodman Brown, in a voice of agony and desperation; and the echoes of the forest mocked him, crying, "Faith! Faith!" as if bewildered wretches were seeking her all through the wilderness.

The cry of grief, rage, and terror was yet piercing the night, when the unhappy husband held his breath for a response. There was a scream, drowned immediately in a louder murmur of voices, fading into far-off laughter, as

[11] A town near Salem, Massachusetts.
[12] Medicine men.

the dark cloud swept away, leaving the clear and silent sky above Goodman Brown. But something fluttered lightly down through the air and caught on the branch of a tree. The young man seized it, and beheld a pink ribbon.

"My Faith is gone!" cried he, after one stupefied moment. "There is no good on earth; and sin is but a name. Come, devil; for to thee is this world given."

And, maddened with despair, so that he laughed loud and long, did Goodman Brown grasp his staff and set forth again, at such a rate that he seemed to fly along the forest path rather than to walk or run. The road grew wilder and drearier and more faintly traced, and vanished at length, leaving him in the heart of the dark wilderness, still rushing onward with the instinct that guides mortal man to evil. The whole forest was peopled with frightful sounds — the creaking of the trees, the howling of wild beasts, and the yell of Indians; while sometimes the wind tolled like a distant church bell, and sometimes gave a broad roar around the traveller, as if all Nature were laughing him to scorn. But he was himself the chief horror of the scene, and shrank not from its other horrors.

"Ha! ha! ha!" roared Goodman Brown when the wind laughed at him. "Let us hear which will laugh loudest. Think not to frighten me with your deviltry. Come witch, come wizard, come Indian powwow, come devil himself, and here comes Goodman Brown. You may as well fear him as he fears you."

In truth, all through the haunted forest there could be nothing more frightful than the figure of Goodman Brown. On he flew among the black pines, brandishing his staff with frenzied gestures, now giving vent to an inspiration of horrid blasphemy, and now shouting forth such laughter as set all the echoes of the forest laughing like demons around him. The fiend in his own shape is less hideous than when he rages in the breast of man. Thus sped the demoniac on his course, until, quivering among the trees, he saw a red light before him, as when the felled trunks and branches of a clearing have been set on fire, and throw up their lurid blaze against the sky, at the hour of midnight. He paused, in a lull of the tempest that had driven him onward, and heard the swell of what seemed a hymn, rolling solemnly from a distance with the weight of many voices. He knew the tune; it was a familiar one in the choir of the village meeting-house. The verse died heavily away, and was lengthened by a chorus, not of human voices, but of all the sounds of the benighted wilderness pealing in awful harmony together. Goodman Brown cried out, and his cry was lost to his own ear by its unison with the cry of the desert.

In the interval of silence he stole forward until the light glared full upon his eyes. At one extremity of an open space, hemmed in by the dark wall of the forest, arose a rock, bearing some rude, natural resemblance either to an altar or a pulpit, and surrounded by four blazing pines, their tops aflame, their stems untouched, like candles at an evening meeting. The mass of foliage that had overgrown the summit of the rock was all on fire, blazing high into the night and fitfully illuminating the whole field. Each pendent twig and leafy festoon was in a blaze. As the red light arose and fell, a numerous congregation alternately shone forth, then disappeared in shadow, and again grew, as it were, out of the darkness, peopling the heart of the solitary woods at once.

"A grave and dark-clad company," quoth Goodman Brown.                                        55

In truth they were such. Among them, quivering to and fro between gloom and splendor, appeared faces that would be seen next day at the council board of the province, and others which, Sabbath after Sabbath, looked devoutly heavenward, and benignantly over the crowded pews, from the holiest pulpits in the land. Some affirm that the lady of the governor was there. At least there were high dames well known to her, and wives of honored husbands, and widows, a great multitude, and ancient maidens, all of excellent repute, and fair young girls, who trembled lest their mothers should espy them. Either the sudden gleams of light flashing over the obscure field bedazzled Goodman Brown, or he recognized a score of the church members of Salem village famous for their especial sanctity. Good old Deacon Gookin had arrived, and waited at the skirts of that venerable saint, his revered pastor. But, irreverently consorting with these grave, reputable, and pious people, these elders of the church, these chaste dames and dewy virgins, there were men of dissolute lives and women of spotted fame, wretches given over to all mean and filthy vice, and suspected even of horrid crimes. It was strange to see that the good shrank not from the wicked, nor were the sinners abashed by the saints. Scattered also among their pale-faced enemies were the Indian priests, or powwows, who had often scared their native forest with more hideous incantations than any known to English witchcraft.

"But where is Faith?" thought Goodman Brown; and, as hope came into his heart, he trembled.

Another verse of the hymn arose, a slow and mournful strain, such as the pious love, but joined to words which expressed all that our nature can conceive of sin, and darkly hinted at far more. Unfathomable to mere mortals is the lore of fiends. Verse after verse was sung; and still the chorus of the desert swelled between like the deepest tone of a mighty organ; and with the final peal of that dreadful anthem there came a sound, as if the roaring wind, the rushing streams, the howling beasts, and every other voice of the unconcerted wilderness were mingling and according with the voice of guilty man in homage to the prince of all. The four blazing pines threw up a loftier flame, and obscurely discovered shapes and visages of horror on the smoke wreaths above the impious assembly. At the same moment the fire on the rock shot redly forth and formed a glowing arch above its base, where now appeared a figure. With reverence be it spoken, the figure bore no slight similitude, both in garb and manner, to some grave divine of the New England churches.

"Bring forth the converts!" cried a voice that echoed through the field and rolled into the forest.

At the word, Goodman Brown stepped forth from the shadow of the trees     60 and approached the congregation, with whom he felt a loathful brotherhood by the sympathy of all that was wicked in his heart. He could have well-nigh sworn that the shape of his own dead father beckoned him to advance, looking downward from a smoke wreath, while a woman, with dim features of despair, threw out her hand to warn him back. Was it his mother? But he had no power to retreat one step, nor to resist, even in thought, when the minister and good old Deacon Gookin seized his arms and led him to the blazing rock. Thither came also the slender form of a veiled female, led between Goody Cloyse, that pious teacher of the catechism, and Martha Carrier,[13] who had received the devil's promise to be queen of hell. A rampant hag was she. And there stood the proselytes beneath the canopy of fire.

"Welcome, my children," said the dark figure, "to the communion of your race. Ye have found thus young your nature and your destiny. My children, look behind you!"

They turned; and flashing forth, as it were, in a sheet of flame, the fiend worshippers were seen; the smile of welcome gleamed darkly on every visage.

"There," resumed the sable form, "are all whom ye have reverenced from youth. Ye deemed them holier than yourselves, and shrank from your own sin, contrasting it with their lives of righteousness and prayerful aspirations heavenward. Yet here are they all in my worshipping assembly. This night it shall be granted you to know their secret deeds: how hoary-bearded elders of the church have whispered wanton words to the young maids of their households; how many a woman, eager for widows' weeds, has given her husband a drink at bedtime and let him sleep his last sleep in her bosom; how beardless youths have made haste to inherit their fathers' wealth; and how fair damsels — blush not, sweet ones — have dug little graves in the garden, and bidden me, the sole guest, to an infant's funeral. By the sympathy of your human hearts for sin ye shall scent out all the places — whether in church, bed-chamber, street, field, or forest — where crime has been committed, and shall exult to behold the whole earth one stain of guilt, one mighty blood spot. Far more than this. It shall be yours to penetrate, in every bosom, the deep mystery of sin, the fountain of all wicked arts, and which inexhaustibly supplies more evil impulses than human power — than my power at its utmost — can make manifest in deeds. And now, my children, look upon each other."

They did so; and, by the blaze of the hell-kindled torches, the wretched man beheld his Faith, and the wife her husband, trembling before that unhallowed altar.

"Lo, there ye stand, my children," said the figure, in a deep and solemn tone, 65 almost sad with its despairing awfulness, as if his once angelic nature could yet mourn for our miserable race. "Depending upon one another's hearts, ye had still hoped that virtue were not all a dream. Now are ye undeceived. Evil is the nature of mankind. Evil must be your only happiness. Welcome again, my children, to the communion of your race."

"Welcome," repeated the fiend worshippers, in one cry of despair and triumph.

---

[13] One of the women hanged in Salem in 1697 for witchcraft.

And there they stood, the only pair, as it seemed, who were yet hesitating on the verge of wickedness in this dark world. A basin was hollowed, naturally, in the rock. Did it contain water, reddened by the lurid light? or was it blood? or, perchance, a liquid flame? Herein did the shape of evil dip his hand and prepare to lay the mark of baptism upon their foreheads, that they might be partakers of the mystery of sin, more conscious of the secret guilt of others, both in deed and thought, than they could now be of their own. The husband cast one look at his pale wife, and Faith at him. What polluted wretches would the next glance show them to each other, shuddering alike at what they disclosed and what they saw!

"Faith! Faith!" cried the husband, "look up to heaven, and resist the wicked one."

Whether Faith obeyed he knew not. Hardly had he spoken when he found himself amid calm night and solitude, listening to a roar of the wind which died heavily away through the forest. He staggered against the rock, and felt it chill and damp; while a hanging twig, that had been all on fire, besprinkled his cheek with the coldest dew.

The next morning young Goodman Brown came slowly into the street of 70 Salem village, staring around him like a bewildered man. The good old minister was taking a walk along the graveyard to get an appetite for breakfast and meditate his sermon, and bestowed a blessing, as he passed, on Goodman Brown. He shrank from the venerable saint as if to avoid an anathema. Old Deacon Gookin was at domestic worship, and the holy words of his prayer were heard through the open window. "What God doth the wizard pray to?" quoth Goodman Brown. Goody Cloyse, that excellent old Christian, stood in the early sunshine at her own lattice, catechizing a little girl who had brought her a pint of morning's milk. Goodman Brown snatched away the child as from the grasp of the fiend himself. Turning the corner by the meeting-house, he spied the head of Faith, with the pink ribbons, gazing anxiously forth, and bursting into such joy at sight of him that she skipped along the street and almost kissed her husband before the whole village. But Goodman Brown looked sternly and sadly into her face, and passed on without a greeting.

Had Goodman Brown fallen asleep in the forest and only dreamed a wild dream of a witch-meeting?

Be it so if you will; but, alas! it was a dream of evil omen for young Goodman Brown. A stern, a sad, a darkly meditative, a distrustful, if not a desperate man did he become from the night of that fearful dream. On the Sabbath day, when the congregation were singing a holy psalm, he could not listen because an anthem of sin rushed loudly upon his ear and drowned all the blessed strain. When the minister spoke from the pulpit with power and fervid eloquence, and, with his hand on the open Bible, of the sacred truths of our religion, and of saint-like lives and triumphant deaths, and of future bliss or misery unutterable, then did Goodman Brown turn pale, dreading lest the roof should thunder down upon the gray blasphemer and his hearers. Often, awakening suddenly at midnight, he shrank from the bosom of Faith; and at morning or eventide, when the family knelt down at prayer, he scowled and muttered to himself, and gazed sternly at his wife, and turned away. And when he had lived long, and was borne to his grave a hoary corpse, followed by Faith, an aged woman, and children and grandchildren, a goodly procession, besides neighbors not a few, they carved no hopeful verse upon his tombstone, for his dying hour was gloom.

## FOR ANALYSIS

1. At the end of the story, the **narrator** asks, "Had Goodman Brown fallen asleep in the forest and only dreamed a wild dream of a witch-meeting?" Why, instead of answering the question, does he say, "Be it so if you will"?

2. Examine the seemingly supernatural events Brown experiences as he penetrates ever deeper into the forest. Can the reader determine whether those events are really taking place? If not, what purpose does the **ambiguity** serve?

3. What attitude does this story express toward the church of Puritan New England?

4. What elements of the story can be described as **allegorical** or **symbolic**?

5. What is the "guilty purpose" (para. 41) that has drawn Brown to the forest?

## MAKING ARGUMENTS

1. Write an essay in which you argue for or against the proposition that the "truth" Brown discovers during his night in the forest justifies his gloom and withdrawal.

2. Ignore the narrator's suggestion not to worry about the nature of what happened to Young Goodman Brown in the forest. Instead, worry, and make an argument for one side or the other.

## WRITING TOPIC

Write out a paraphrase of Satan's sermon.

## MAKING CONNECTIONS

1. Both this story and Herman Melville's "Bartleby, the Scrivener" (p. 267) deal with **protagonists** who withdraw from life. What similarities and differences do you find in the reasons for their withdrawal, the ways in which they withdraw, and the consequences of their withdrawal?

2. Both Hawthorne's "Young Goodman Brown" and Ralph Ellison's "'Repent, Harlequin!' Said the Ticktockman" (p. 322) rely on fantasy. What advantages does the use of fantasy give the authors?

## Naguib Mahfouz  (1911–2006)

# Half a Day  1989

I proceeded alongside my father, clutching his right hand, running to keep up with the long strides he was taking. All my clothes were new: the black shoes, the green school uniform, and the red tarboosh.[1] My delight in my new clothes, however, was not altogether unmarred, for this was no feast day but the day on which I was to be cast into school for the first time.

My mother stood at the window watching our progress, and I would turn toward her from time to time, as though appealing for help. We walked along a street lined with gardens; on both sides were extensive fields planted with crops, prickly pears, henna trees, and a few date palms.

"Why school?" I challenged my father openly. "I shall never do anything to annoy you."

"I'm not punishing you," he said, laughing. "School's not a punishment. It's the factory that makes useful men out of boys. Don't you want to be like your father and brothers?"

I was not convinced. I did not believe there was really any good to be had 5 in tearing me away from the intimacy of my home and throwing me into this building that stood at the end of the road like some huge, high-walled fortress, exceedingly stern and grim.

When we arrived at the gate we could see the courtyard, vast and crammed full of boys and girls. "Go in by yourself," said my father, "and join them. Put a smile on your face and be a good example to others."

I hesitated and clung to his hand, but he gently pushed me from him. "Be a man," he said. "Today you truly begin life. You will find me waiting for you when it's time to leave."

I took a few steps, then stopped and looked but saw nothing. Then the faces of boys and girls came into view. I did not know a single one of them, and none of them knew me. I felt I was a stranger who had lost his way. But glances of curiosity were directed toward me, and one boy approached and asked, "Who brought you?"

"My father," I whispered.

"My father's dead," he said quite simply. 10

I did not know what to say. The gate was closed, letting out a pitiable screech. Some of the children burst into tears. The bell rang. A lady came along, followed by a group of men. The men began sorting us into ranks. We were formed into an intricate pattern in the great courtyard surrounded on three

[1] A brimless felt hat similar to a fez worn by Muslim men.

sides by high buildings of several floors; from each floor we were overlooked by a long balcony roofed in wood.

"This is your new home," said the woman. "Here too there are mothers and fathers. Here there is everything that is enjoyable and beneficial to knowledge and religion. Dry your tears and face life joyfully."

We submitted to the facts, and this submission brought a sort of contentment. Living beings were drawn to other living beings, and from the first moments my heart made friends with such boys as were to be my friends and fell in love with such girls as I was to be in love with, so that it seemed my misgivings had had no basis. I had never imagined school would have this rich variety. We played all sorts of different games: swings, the vaulting horse, ball games. In the music room we chanted our first songs. We also had our first introduction to language. We saw a globe of the Earth, which revolved and showed the various continents and countries. We started learning the numbers. The story of the Creator of the universe was read to us, we were told of His present world and of His Hereafter, and we heard examples of what He said. We ate delicious food, took a little nap, and woke up to go on with friendship and love, play and learning.

As our path revealed itself to us, however, we did not find it as totally sweet and unclouded as we had presumed. Dust-laden winds and unexpected accidents came about suddenly, so we had to be watchful, at the ready, and very patient. It was not all a matter of playing and fooling around. Rivalries could bring about pain and hatred or give rise to fighting. And while the lady would sometimes smile, she would often scowl and scold. Even more frequently she would resort to physical punishment.

In addition, the time for changing one's mind was over and gone and there was no question of ever returning to the paradise of home. Nothing lay ahead of us but exertion, struggle, and perseverance. Those who were able took advantage of the opportunities for success and happiness that presented themselves amid the worries.

The bell rang announcing the passing of the day and the end of work. The throngs of children rushed toward the gate, which was opened again. I bade farewell to friends and sweethearts and passed through the gate. I peered around but found no trace of my father, who had promised to be there. I stepped aside to wait. When I had waited for a long time without avail, I decided to return home on my own. After I had taken a few steps, a middle-aged man passed by, and I realized at once that I knew him. He came toward me, smiling, and shook me by the hand, saying, "It's a long time since we last met — how are you?"

With a nod of my head, I agreed with him and in turn asked, "And you, how are you?"

"As you can see, not all that good, the Almighty be praised!"

Again he shook me by the hand and went off. I proceeded a few steps, then came to a startled halt. Good Lord! Where was the street lined with gardens? Where had it disappeared to? When did all these vehicles invade it? And when did all these hordes of humanity come to rest upon its surface? How did these hills of refuse come to cover its sides? And where were the fields that bordered it? High buildings had taken over, the street surged with children, and disturbing noises shook the air. At various points stood conjurers showing off their tricks and making snakes appear from baskets. Then there was a band announcing the opening of a circus, with clowns and weight lifters walking in front. A line of trucks carrying central security troops crawled majestically by. The siren of a fire engine shrieked, and it was not clear how the vehicle would cleave its way to reach the blazing fire. A battle raged between a taxi driver and his passenger, while the passenger's wife called out for help and no one answered. Good God! I was in a daze. My head spun. I almost went crazy. How could all this have happened in half a day, between early morning and sunset? I would find the answer at home with my father. But where was my home? I could see only tall buildings and hordes of people. I hastened on to the crossroads between the gardens and Abu Khoda. I had to cross Abu Khoda to reach my house, but the stream of cars would not let up. The fire engine's siren was shrieking at full pitch as it moved at a snail's pace, and I said to myself, "Let the fire take its pleasure in what it consumes." Extremely irritated, I wondered when I would be able to cross. I stood there a long time, until the young lad employed at the ironing shop on the corner came up to me. He stretched out his arm and said gallantly, "Grandpa, let me take you across."

## FOR ANALYSIS

**1.** What is significant about this day for the **narrator**?

**2.** What ages are the different male **characters**? Why are their ages important to the story?

**3.** How would you describe the differences in the **setting** and **mood** of the story at its beginning and at its end? Why do you think the author might have decided to have the story begin and end this way?

## MAKING ARGUMENTS

**1.** While this story is about several things, it is certainly about education. Outline the arguments on both sides of the question, Is this story pro-education or anti-education? (You can also include a third outline that combines both sides of the argument.)

**2.** "Half a Day" could be read as a timeless story about life or as a story whose setting and historical details are central to its meaning. Find some information about its author, his concerns, and the time and place where he lived and wrote; with that information, make the argument for the story being the latter kind.

## WRITING TOPICS

**1.** This story is narrated by a very young boy, so his knowledge of the world and ability to form judgments about it is limited. When writing this kind of story, authors have to strike a balance between the child's innocence and their own (and their readers') experience, providing material for advanced reflection without ascribing perceptions and thoughts to someone too young to have them. Argue that Mahfouz succeeds or fails here by describing his attempt to do so.

**2.** Imagine this experience as an essay or sermon. What might it look like? What kinds of ideas, lessons, or truths might it contain? Rewrite this story as an essay or sermon, or an outline of it.

## MAKING CONNECTIONS

Both "Half a Day" and Toni Cade Bambara's "The Lesson" (p. 100) are in some ways about school, yet both stories are about much more than that. How do the other things that the stories are about appear? What are those things?

## John Updike (1932–2009)

# A & P 1961

In walks these three girls in nothing but bathing suits. I'm in the third check-out slot, with my back to the door, so I don't see them until they're over by the bread. The one that caught my eye first was the one in the plaid green two-piece. She was a chunky kid, with a good tan and a sweet broad soft-looking can with those two crescents of white just under it, where the sun never seems to hit, at the top of the backs of her legs. I stood there with my hand on a box of HiHo crackers trying to remember if I rang it up or not. I ring it up again and the customer starts giving me hell. She's one of these cash-register-watchers, a witch about fifty with rouge on her cheekbones and no eyebrows, and I know it made her day to trip me up. She'd been watching cash registers for fifty years and probably never seen a mistake before.

By the time I got her feathers smoothed and her goodies into a bag — she gives me a little snort in passing, if she'd been born at the right time they would have burned her over in Salem — by the time I get her on her way the girls had circled around the bread and were coming back, without a pushcart, back my way along the counters, in the aisle between the checkouts and the Special bins. They didn't even have shoes on. There was this chunky one, with the two-piece — it was bright green and the seams on the bra were still sharp and her belly was still pretty pale so I guessed she just got it (the suit) — there was this one, with one of those chubby berry-faces, the lips all bunched together under her nose, this one, and a tall one, with black hair that hadn't quite frizzed right, and one of these sunburns right across under the eyes, and a chin that was too long — you know, the kind of girl other girls think is very "striking" and "attractive" but never quite makes it, as they very well know, which is why they like her so much — and then the third one, that wasn't quite so tall. She was the queen. She kind of led them, the other two peeking around and making their shoulders round. She didn't look around, not this queen, she just walked straight on slowly, on these long white prima-donna legs. She came down a little hard on her heels, as if she didn't walk in her bare feet that much, putting down her heels and then letting the weight move along to her toes as if she was testing the floor with every step, putting a little deliberate extra action into it. You never know for sure how girls' minds work (do you really think it's a mind in there or just a little buzz like a bee in a glass jar?) but you got the idea she had talked the other two into coming in here with her, and now she was show-ing them how to do it, walk slow and hold yourself straight.

She had on a kind of dirty-pink — beige maybe, I don't know — bathing suit with a little nubble all over it, and what got me, the straps were down. They were off her shoulders looped loose around the cool tops of her arms, and I guess as a result the suit had slipped a little on her, so all around the top of the cloth there was this shining rim. If it hadn't been there you wouldn't have known there could have been anything whiter than those shoulders. With the straps pushed off, there was nothing between the top of the suit and the top of her head except just *her*, this clean bare plane of the top of her chest down from the shoulder bones like a dented sheet of metal tilted in the light. I mean, it was more than pretty.

She had sort of oaky hair that the sun and salt had bleached, done up in a bun that was unravelling, and a kind of prim face. Walking into the A & P with your straps down, I suppose it's the only kind of face you *can* have. She held her head so high her neck, coming up out of those white shoulders, looked kind of stretched, but I didn't mind. The longer her neck was, the more of her there was.

She must have felt in the corner of her eye me and over my shoulder Stokesie 5 in the second slot watching, but she didn't tip. Not this queen. She kept her eyes moving across the racks, and stopped, and turned so slow it made my stomach rub the inside of my apron, and buzzed to the other two, who kind of huddled against her for relief, and then they all three of them went up the cat-and-dog-food-breakfast-cereal-macaroni-rice-raisins-seasonings-spreads-spaghetti-soft-drinks-crackers-and-cookies aisle. From the third slot I look straight up this aisle to the meat counter, and I watched them all the way. The fat one with the tan sort of fumbled with the cookies, but on second thought she put the package back. The sheep pushing their carts down the aisle — the girls were walking against the usual traffic (not that we have one-way signs or anything) — were pretty hilarious. You could see them, when Queenie's white shoulders dawned on them, kind of jerk, or hop, or hiccup, but their eyes snapped back to their own baskets and on they pushed. I bet you could set off dynamite in an A & P and the people would by and large keep reaching and checking oatmeal off their lists and muttering "Let me see, there was a third thing, began with A, asparagus, no, ah, yes, applesauce!" or whatever it is they do mutter. But there was no doubt, this jiggled them. A few houseslaves in pin curlers even looked around after pushing their carts past to make sure what they had seen was correct.

You know, it's one thing to have a girl in a bathing suit down on the beach, where what with the glare nobody can look at each other much anyway, and another thing in the cool of the A & P, under the fluorescent lights, against all those stacked packages, with her feet paddling along naked over our check-board green-and-cream rubber-tile floor.

"Oh Daddy," Stokesie said beside me. "I feel so faint."

"Darling," I said. "Hold me tight." Stokesie's married, with two babies chalked up on his fuselage already, but as far as I can tell that's the only differ-ence. He's twenty-two, and I was nineteen this April.

"Is it done?" he asks, the responsible married man finding his voice. I forgot to say he thinks he's going to be manager some sunny day, maybe in 1990 when it's called the Great Alexandrov and Petrooshki Tea Company or something.

What he meant was, our town is five miles from a beach, with a big summer colony out on the Point, but we're right in the middle of town, and the women generally put on a shirt or shorts or something before they get out of the car into the street. And anyway these are usually women with six children and varicose veins mapping their legs and nobody, including them, could care less. As I say, we're right in the middle of town, and if you stand at our front doors you can see two banks and the Congregational church and the newspaper store and three real-estate offices and about twenty-seven old freeloaders tearing up Central Street because the sewer broke again. It's not as if we're on the Cape; we're north of Boston and there's people in this town haven't seen the ocean for twenty years.

The girls had reached the meat counter and were asking McMahon something. He pointed, they pointed, and they shuffled out of sight behind a pyramid of Diet Delight peaches. All that was left for us to see was old McMahon patting his mouth and looking after them sizing up their joints. Poor kids, I began to feel sorry for them, they couldn't help it.

Now here comes the sad part of the story, at least my family says it's sad, but I don't think it's so sad myself. The store's pretty empty, it being Thursday afternoon, so there was nothing much to do except lean on the register and wait for the girls to show up again. The whole store was like a pinball machine and I didn't know which tunnel they'd come out of. After a while they come around out of the far aisle, around the light bulbs, records at discount of the Caribbean Six or Tony Martin Sings or some such gunk you wonder they waste the wax on, sixpacks of candy bars, and plastic toys done up in cellophane that fall apart when a kid looks at them anyway. Around they come, Queenie still leading the way, and holding a little gray jar in her hand. Slots Three through Seven are unmanned and I could see her wondering between Stokes and me, but Stokesie with his usual luck draws an old party in baggy gray pants who stumbles up with four giant cans of pineapple juice (what do these bums *do* with all that pineapple juice? I've often asked myself) so the girls come to me. Queenie puts down the jar and I take it into my fingers icy cold. Kingfish Fancy Herring Snacks in Pure Sour Cream: 49¢. Now her hands are empty, not a ring or a bracelet, bare as God made them, and I wonder where the money's coming from. Still with that prim look she lifts a folded dollar bill out of the hollow at the center of her nubbled pink top. The jar went heavy in my hand. Really, I thought that was so cute.

Then everybody's luck begins to run out. Lengel comes in from haggling with a truck full of cabbages on the lot and is about to scuttle into that door marked MANAGER behind which he hides all day when the girls touch his eye. Lengel's pretty dreary, teaches Sunday school and the rest, but he doesn't miss that much. He comes over and says, "Girls, this isn't the beach."

Queenie blushes, though maybe it's just a brush of sunburn I was noticing for the first time, now that she was so close. "My mother asked me to pick up a jar of herring snacks." Her voice kind of startled me, the way voices do when you see the people first, coming out so flat and dumb yet kind of tony, too, the way it ticked over "pick up" and "snacks." All of a sudden I slid right down her voice into her living room. Her father and the other men were standing around in ice-cream coats and bow ties and the women were in sandals picking up herring snacks on toothpicks off a big glass plate and they were all holding drinks the color of water with olives and sprigs of mint in them. When my parents have somebody over they get lemonade and if it's a real racy affair Schlitz in tall glasses with "They'll Do It Every Time" cartoons stencilled on.

"That's all right," Lengel said. "But this isn't the beach." His repeating this 15 struck me as funny, as if it had just occurred to him, and he had been thinking all these years the A & P was a great big sand dune and he was the head lifeguard. He didn't like my smiling — as I say he doesn't miss much — but he concentrates on giving the girls that sad Sunday-school–superintendent stare.

Queenie's blush is no sunburn now, and the plump one in plaid, that I liked better from the back — a really sweet can — pipes up, "We weren't doing any shopping. We just came in for the one thing."

"That makes no difference," Lengel tells her, and I could see from the way his eyes went that he hadn't noticed she was wearing a two-piece before. "We want you decently dressed when you come in here."

"We *are* decent," Queenie says suddenly, her lower lip pushing, getting sore now that she remembers her place, a place from which the crowd that runs the A & P must look pretty crummy. Fancy Herring Snacks flashed in her very blue eyes.

"Girls, I don't want to argue with you. After this come in here with your shoulders covered. It's our policy." He turns his back. That's policy for you. Policy is what the kingpins want. What the others want is juvenile delinquency.

All this while, the customers had been showing up with their carts but, you 20 know, sheep, seeing a scene, they had all bunched up on Stokesie, who shook open a paper bag as gently as peeling a peach, not wanting to miss a word. I could feel in the silence everybody getting nervous, most of all Lengel, who asks me, "Sammy, have you rung up their purchase?"

I thought and said "No" but it wasn't about that I was thinking. I go through the punches, 4, 9, groc, tot — it's more complicated than you think, and after you do it often enough, it begins to make a little song, that you hear words to, in my case "Hello (*bing*) there, you (*gung*) hap-py pee-pul (*splat*)!" — the *splat* being the drawer flying out. I uncrease the bill, tenderly as you may imagine, it just having come from between the two smoothest scoops of vanilla I had ever known were there, and pass a half and a penny into her narrow pink palm, and nestle the herrings in a bag and twist its neck and hand it over, all the time thinking.

The girls, and who'd blame them, are in a hurry to get out, so I say "I quit" to Lengel [loud] enough for them to hear, hoping they'll stop and watch me, their unsuspected hero. They keep right on going, into the electric eye; the door flies open and they flicker across the lot to their car, Queenie and Plaid and Big Tall Goony-Goony (not that as raw material she was so bad), leaving me with Lengel and a kink in his eyebrow.

"Did you say something, Sammy?"

"I said I quit."

"I thought you did."                                                        25

"You didn't have to embarrass them."

"It was they who were embarrassing us."

I started to say something that came out "Fiddle-de-doo." It's a saying of my grandmother's, and I know she would have been pleased.

"I don't think you know what you're saying," Lengel said.

"I know you don't," I said. "But I do." I pull the bow at the back of my apron 30 and start shrugging it off my shoulders. A couple customers that had been heading for my slot begin to knock against each other, like scared pigs in a chute.

Lengel sighs and begins to look very patient and old and gray. He's been a friend of my parents for years. "Sammy, you don't want to do this to your Mom and Dad," he tells me. It's true, I don't. But it seems to me that once you begin a gesture it's fatal not to go through with it. I fold the apron, "Sammy" stitched in red on the pocket, and put it on the counter, and drop the bow tie on top of it. The bow tie is theirs, if you've ever wondered. "You'll feel this for the rest of your life," Lengel says, and I know that's true, too, but remembering how he made that pretty girl blush makes me so scrunchy inside I punch the No Sale tab and the machine whirs "pee-pul" and the drawer splats out. One advantage to this scene taking place in summer, I can follow this up with a clean exit, there's no fumbling around getting your coat and galoshes, I just saunter into the electric eye in my white shirt that my mother ironed the night before, and the door heaves itself open, and outside the sunshine is skating around on the asphalt.

I look around for my girls, but they're gone, of course. There wasn't anybody but some young married screaming with her children about some candy they didn't get by the door of a powder-blue Falcon station wagon. Looking back in the big windows, over the bags of peat moss and aluminum lawn furniture stacked on the pavement, I could see Lengel in my place in the slot, checking the sheep through. His face was dark gray and his back stiff, as if he'd just had an injection of iron, and my stomach kind of fell as I felt how hard the world was going to be to me hereafter.

### FOR ANALYSIS

**1.** Describe Sammy's voice as he tells the story. How does Updike's choice to have him **narrate** help us get a sense of Sammy as a **character**? Is he understandable? Is he likable? Can readers sympathize with him?

**2.** What about "Queenie" is most attractive to Sammy? Is it just her appearance? What else figures in?

**3.** At the very end of the story, Updike has Sammy describe his customers **figuratively** as pigs and sheep. Why do you think he does this? What does this choice reveal about Sammy's attitude toward them, and toward the adult ways of living he is on the verge of?

**4.** Sammy describes his quitting as a gesture. For whom is the gesture made — for one audience, or for multiple audiences? What does it say to each audience?

### MAKING ARGUMENTS

Take up the proposition that Sammy's gesture is futile and empty. Make an argument supporting or refuting this claim.

## WRITING TOPIC

Retell the story with Lengel as **narrator**, showing how that change might affect **point of view**, voice, and meaning.

## MAKING CONNECTIONS

**1.** Compare the connections made between work and identity in "A & P" and in Jamaica Kincaid's "Girl" (p. 107).

**2.** Reread the passage in which Sammy imagines the scene in "Queenie's" parents' living room. Compare to the passage in Toni Cade Bambara's "The Lesson" (p. 100) in which Miss Moore asks about the children's desks at home. What does each moment say about the pictures of the social divisions embedded in each story?

## Toni Cade Bambara   (1939–1995)

# The Lesson   1972

Back in the days when everyone was old and stupid or young and foolish and me and Sugar were the only ones just right, this lady moved on our block with nappy hair and proper speech and no makeup. And quite naturally we laughed at her, laughed the way we did at the junk man who went about his business like he was some big-time president and his sorry-ass horse his secretary. And we kinda hated her too, hated the way we did the winos who cluttered up our parks and pissed on our handball walls and stank up our hallways and stairs so you couldn't halfway play hide-and-seek without a goddamn gas mask. Miss Moore was her name. The only woman on the block with no first name. And she was black as hell, cept for her feet, which were fish-white and spooky. And she was always planning these boring-ass things for us to do, us being my cousin, mostly, who lived on the block cause we all moved North the same time and to the same apartment then spread out gradual to breathe. And our parents would yank our heads into some kinda shape and crisp up our clothes so we'd be presentable for travel with Miss Moore, who always looked like she was going to church, though she never did. Which is just one of the things the grownups talked about when they talked behind her back like a dog. But when she came calling with some sachet she'd sewed up or some gingerbread she'd made or some book, why then they'd all be too embarrassed to turn her down and we'd get handed over all spruced up. She'd been to college and said it was only right that she should take responsibility for the young ones' education, and she not even related by marriage or blood. So they'd go for it. Specially Aunt Gretchen. She was the main gofer in the family. You got some old dumb shit foolishness you want somebody to go for, you send for Aunt Gretchen. She been screwed into the go-along for so long, it's a blood-deep natural thing with her. Which is how she got saddled with me and Sugar and Junior in the first place while our mothers were in a la-de-da apartment up the block having a good ole time.

So this one day Miss Moore rounds us all up at the mailbox and it's puredee hot and she's knockin herself out about arithmetic. And school suppose to let up in summer I heard, but she don't never let up. And the starch in my pinafore scratching the shit outta me and I'm really hating this nappy-head bitch and her goddamn college degree. I'd much rather go to the pool or to the show where it's cool. So me and Sugar leaning on the mailbox being surly, which is a Miss Moore word. And Flyboy checking out what everybody brought for lunch. And Fat Butt already wasting his peanut-butter-and-jelly sandwich like the pig he is. And Junebug punchin on Q.T.'s arm for potato chips. And Rosie Giraffe shifting from one hip to the other waiting for somebody to step on her foot or ask her if she from Georgia so she can kick ass, preferably Mercedes'. And Miss Moore asking us do we know what money is, like we a bunch of retards. I mean real money, she say, like it's only poker chips or monopoly papers we lay on the grocer. So right away I'm tired of this and say so. And would much rather snatch Sugar and go to the Sunset and terrorize the West Indian kids and take their hair ribbons and their money too. And Miss Moore files that remark away for next week's lesson on brotherhood, I can tell. And finally I say we oughta get to the subway cause it's cooler and besides we might meet some cute boys. Sugar done swiped her mama's lipstick, so we ready.

So we heading down the street and she's boring us silly about what things cost and what our parents make and how much goes for rent and how money ain't divided up right in this country. And then she gets to the part about we all poor and live in the slums, which I don't feature. And I'm ready to speak on that, but she steps out in the street and hails two cabs just like that. Then she hustles half the crew in with her and hands me a five-dollar bill and tells me to calculate 10 percent tip for the driver. And we're off. Me and Sugar and Junebug and Flyboy hangin out the window and hollering to everybody, putting lipstick on each other cause Flyboy a faggot anyway, and making farts with our sweaty armpits. But I'm mostly trying to figure how to spend this money. But they all fascinated with the meter ticking and Junebug starts laying bets as to how much it'll read when Flyboy can't hold his breath no more. Then Sugar lays bets as to how much it'll be when we get there. So I'm stuck. Don't nobody want to go for my plan, which is to jump out at the next light and run off to the first bar-b-que we can find. Then the driver tells us to get the hell out cause we there already. And the meter reads eighty-five cents. And I'm stalling to figure out the tip and Sugar say give him a dime. And I decide he don't need it bad as I do, so later for him. But then he tries to take off with Junebug foot still in the door so we talk about his mama something ferocious. Then we check out that we on Fifth Avenue and everybody dressed up in stockings. One lady in a fur coat, hot as it is. White folks crazy.

"This is the place," Miss Moore say, presenting it to us in the voice she uses at the museum. "Let's look in the windows before we go in."

"Can we steal?" Sugar asks very serious like she's getting the ground rules ₅ squared away before she plays. "I beg your pardon," say Miss Moore, and we fall out. So she leads us around the windows of the toy store and me and Sugar screamin, "This is mine, that's mine, I gotta have that, that was made for me, I was born for that," till Big Butt drowns us out.

"Hey, I'm goin to buy that there."

"That there? You don't even know what it is, stupid."

"I do so," he say punchin on Rosie Giraffe. "It's a microscope."

"Whatcha gonna do with a microscope, fool?"

"Look at things." ₁₀

"Like what, Ronald?" ask Miss Moore. And Big Butt ain't got the first notion. So here go Miss Moore gabbing about the thousands of bacteria in a drop of water and the somethinorother in a speck of blood and the million and one living things in the air around us is invisible to the naked eye. And what she say that for? Junebug go to town on that "naked" and we rolling. Then Miss Moore ask what it cost. So we all jam into the window smudgin it up and the price tag say $300. So then she ask how long'd take for Big Butt and Junebug to save up their allowances. "Too long," I say. "Yeh," adds Sugar, "outgrown it by that time." And Miss Moore say no, you never outgrow learning instruments. "Why, even medical students and interns and," blah, blah, blah. And we ready to choke Big Butt for bringing it up in the first damn place.

"This here costs four hundred eighty dollars," say Rosie Giraffe. So we pile up all over her to see what she pointin out. My eyes tell me it's a chunk of glass cracked with something heavy, and different-color inks dripped into the splits, then the whole thing put into a oven or something. But for $480 it don't make sense.

"That's a paperweight made of semi-precious stones fused together under tremendous pressure," she explains slowly, with her hands doing the mining and all the factory work.

"So what's a paperweight?" asks Rosie Giraffe.

"To weigh paper with, dumbbell," say Flyboy, the wise man from the East.  15

"Not exactly," say Miss Moore, which is what she say when you warm or way off too. "It's to weigh paper down so it won't scatter and make your desk untidy." So right away me and Sugar curtsy to each other and then to Mercedes who is more the tidy type.

"We don't keep paper on top of the desk in my class," say Junebug, figuring Miss Moore crazy or lyin one.

"At home, then," she say. "Don't you have a calendar and pencil case and a blotter and a letter-opener on your desk at home where you do your homework?" And she know damn well what our homes look like cause she nosys around in them every chance she gets.

"I don't even have a desk," say Junebug. "Do we?"

"No. And I don't get no homework neither," says Big Butt.  20

"And I don't even have a home," say Flyboy like he do at school to keep the white folks off his back and sorry for him. Send this poor kid to camp posters, is his specialty.

"I do," says Mercedes. "I have a box of stationery on my desk and a picture of my cat. My godmother bought the stationery and the desk. There's a big rose on each sheet and the envelopes smell like roses."

"Who wants to know about your smelly-ass stationery," say Rosie Giraffe fore I can get my two cents in.

"It's important to have a work area all your own so that . . ."

"Will you look at this sailboat, please," say Flyboy, cuttin her off and pointin  25 to the thing like it was his. So once again we tumble all over each other to gaze at this magnificent thing in the toy store which is just big enough to maybe sail two kittens across the pond if you strap them to the posts tight. We all start reciting the price tag like we in assembly. "Handcrafted sailboat of fiberglass at one thousand one hundred ninety-five dollars."

"Unbelievable," I hear myself say and am really stunned. I read it again for myself just in case the group recitation put me in a trance. Same thing. For some reason this pisses me off. We look at Miss Moore and she lookin at us, waiting for I dunno what.

"Who'd pay all that when you can buy a sailboat set for a quarter at Pop's, a tube of glue for a dime, and a ball of string for eight cents? It must have a motor and a whole lot else besides," I say. "My sailboat cost me about fifty cents."

"But will it take water?" say Mercedes with her smart ass.

"Took mine to Alley Pond Park once," say Flyboy. "String broke. Lost it. Pity."

"Sailed mine in Central Park and it keeled over and sank. Had to ask my father for another dollar." 30

"And you got the strap," laugh Big Butt. "The jerk didn't even have a string on it. My old man wailed on his behind."

Little Q.T. was staring hard at the sailboat and you could see he wanted it bad. But he too little and somebody'd just take it from him. So what the hell. "This boat for kids, Miss Moore?"

"Parents silly to buy something like that just to get all broke up," say Rosie Giraffe.

"That much money it should last forever," I figure.

"My father'd buy it for me if I wanted it." 35

"Your father, my ass," say Rosie Giraffe getting a chance to finally push Mercedes.

"Must be rich people shop here," say Q.T.

"You are a very bright boy," say Flyboy. "What was your first clue?" And he rap him on the head with the back of his knuckles, since Q.T. the only one he could get away with. Though Q.T. liable to come up behind you years later and get his licks in when you half expect it.

"What I want to know is," I says to Miss Moore though I never talk to her, I wouldn't give the bitch that satisfaction, "is how much a real boat costs? I figure a thousand'd get you a yacht any day."

"Why don't you check that out," she says, "and report back to the group?" Which really pains my ass. If you gonna mess up a perfectly good swim day least you could do is have some answers. "Let's go in," she say like she got something up her sleeve. Only she don't lead the way. So me and Sugar turn the corner to where the entrance is, but when we get there I kinda hang back. Not that I'm scared, what's there to be afraid of, just a toy store. But I feel funny, shame. But what I got to be shamed about? Got as much right to go in as anybody. But somehow I can't seem to get hold of the door, so I step away for Sugar to lead. But she hangs back too. And I look at her and she looks at me and this is ridiculous. I mean, damn, I have never ever been shy about doing nothing or going nowhere. But then Mercedes steps up and then Rosie Giraffe and Big Butt crowd in behind and shove, and next thing we all stuffed into the doorway with only Mercedes squeezing past us, 40 smoothing out her jumper and walking right down the aisle. Then the rest of us tumble in like a glued-together jigsaw done all wrong. And people lookin at us. And it's like the time me and Sugar crashed into the Catholic church on a dare. But once we got in there and everything so hushed and holy and the candles and the bowin and the handkerchiefs on all the drooping heads, I just couldn't go through with the plan. Which was for me to run up to the altar and do a tap dance while Sugar played the nose flute and messed around in the holy water. And Sugar kept givin me the elbow. Then later teased me so bad I tied her up in the shower and turned it on and locked her in. And she'd be there till this day if Aunt Gretchen hadn't finally figured I was lyin about the boarder takin a shower.

Same thing in the store. We all walkin on tiptoe and hardly touchin the games and puzzles and things. And I watched Miss Moore who is steady watchin us like she waitin for a sign. Like Mama Drewery watches the sky and sniffs the air and takes note of just how much slant is in the bird formation. Then me and Sugar bump smack into each other, so busy gazing at the toys, 'specially the sailboat. But we don't laugh and go into our fat-lady bump-stomach routine. We just stare at that price tag. Then Sugar run a finger over the whole boat. And I'm jealous and want to hit her. Maybe not her, but I sure want to punch somebody in the mouth.

"Watcha bring us here for, Miss Moore?"

"You sound angry, Sylvia. Are you mad about something?" Givin me one of them grins like she tellin a grown-up joke that never turns out to be funny. And she's lookin very closely at me like maybe she planning to do my portrait from memory. I'm mad, but I won't give her that satisfaction. So I slouch around the store bein very bored and say, "Let's go."

Me and Sugar at the back of the train watchin the tracks whizzin by large then small then gettin gobbled up in the dark. I'm thinkin about this tricky toy I saw in the store. A clown that somersaults on a bar then does chin-ups just cause you yank lightly at his leg. Cost $35. I could see me askin my mother for a $35 birthday clown. "You wanna who that costs what?" she'd say, cocking her head to the side to get a better view of the hole in my head. Thirty-five dollars could buy new bunk beds for Junior and Gretchen's boy. Thirty-five dollars and the whole household could go visit Granddaddy Nelson in the country. Thirty-five dollars would pay for the rent and the piano bill too. Who are these people that spend that much for performing clowns and $1000 for toy sailboats? What kinda work they do and how they live and how come we ain't in on it? Where we are is who we are, Miss Moore always pointin out. But it don't necessarily have to be that way, she always adds then waits for somebody to say that poor people have to wake up and demand their share of the pie and don't none of us know what kind of pie she talking about in the first damn place. But she ain't so smart cause I still got her four dollars from the taxi and she sure ain't gettin it. Messin up my day with this shit. Sugar nudges me in my pocket and winks.

Miss Moore lines us up in front of the mailbox where we started from, seem like years ago, and I got a headache for thinkin so hard. And we lean all over each other 45 so we can hold up under the draggy-ass lecture she always finishes us off with at the end before we thank her for borin us to tears. But she just looks at us like she readin tea leaves. Finally she say, "Well, what did you think of F.A.O. Schwarz?"

Rosie Giraffe mumbles, "White folks crazy."

"I'd like to go there again when I get my birthday money," says Mercedes, and we shove her out the pack so she has to lean on the mailbox by herself.

"I'd like a shower. Tiring day," say Flyboy.

Then Sugar surprises me by sayin, "You know, Miss Moore, I don't think all of us here put together eat in a year what that sailboat costs." And Miss Moore lights up like somebody goosed her. "And?" she say, urging Sugar on. Only I'm standin on her foot so she don't continue.

"Imagine for a minute what kind of society it is in which some people can spend on a toy what it would cost to feed a family of six or seven. What do you think?"

"I think," say Sugar pushing me off her feet like she never done before, cause I whip her ass in a minute, "that this is not much of a democracy if you ask me. Equal chance to pursue happiness means an equal crack at the dough, don't it?" Miss Moore is besides herself and I am disgusted with Sugar's treachery. So I stand on her foot one more time to see if she'll shove me. She shuts up, and Miss Moore looks at me, sorrowfully I'm thinkin. And somethin weird is goin on, I can feel it in my chest.

"Anybody else learn anything today?" lookin dead at me. I walk away and Sugar has to run to catch up and don't even seem to notice when I shrug her arm off my shoulder.

"Well, we got four dollars anyway," she says.

"Uh hunh."

"We could go to Hascombs and get half a chocolate layer and then go to the Sunset and still have plenty money for potato chips and ice cream sodas."

"Un hunh."

"Race you to Hascombs," she say.

We start down the block and she gets ahead which is O.K. by me cause I'm going to the West End and then over to the Drive to think this day through. She can run if she want to and even run faster. But ain't nobody gonna beat me at nuthin.

## FOR ANALYSIS

**1.** What are Sylvia's outstanding traits? How are they reflected in her language and in her description of her neighborhood?

**2.** How is Sylvia's **character** revealed through her relationship with Sugar?

**3.** Describe the lesson Miss Moore tries to teach the children by taking them to visit F.A.O. Schwarz.

**4.** How is Sylvia's assessment of Miss Moore at the beginning of the story borne out by the ending?

**5.** What evidence is there that Sylvia has been changed by the visit to F.A.O. Schwarz?

**MAKING ARGUMENTS**

Write an essay arguing for or against the proposition that "The Lesson" ends optimistically.

**WRITING TOPIC**

In your opinion, is Sylvia a reliable or unreliable **narrator**? Why or why not?

**MAKING CONNECTIONS**

**1.** Compare and contrast the use of the **first-person narrator** in this story with that in Updike's "A & P" (p. 94).

**2.** This story and Joyce's "Araby" (p. 121) deal with a child whose sense of justice is offended. What differences and similarities do you find in the source of the distress and the way the distress is resolved?

## JAMAICA KINCAID   (B. 1949)

# GIRL   1983

Wash the white clothes on Monday and put them on the stone heap; wash the color clothes on Tuesday and put them on the clothesline to dry; don't walk barehead in the hot sun; cook pumpkin fritters in very hot sweet oil; soak your little clothes right after you take them off; when buying cotton to make yourself a nice blouse, be sure that it doesn't have gum on it, because that way it won't hold up well after a wash; soak salt fish overnight before you cook it; is it true that you sing benna[1] in Sunday school?; always eat your food in such a way that it won't turn someone else's stomach; on Sundays try to walk like a lady and not like the slut you are so bent on becoming; don't sing benna in Sunday school; you mustn't speak to wharf-rat boys, not even 10 to give directions; don't eat fruits on the street — flies will follow you; *but I don't sing benna on Sundays at all and never in Sunday school;* this is how to sew on a button; this is how to make a button-hole for the button you have just sewed on; this is how to hem a dress when you see the hem coming down and so to prevent yourself from looking like the slut I know you are so bent on becoming; this is how you iron your father's khaki shirt so that it doesn't have a crease; this is how you iron your father's khaki pants so that they don't have a crease; this is how you grow okra — far from the house, because okra tree harbors red ants; when you are growing dasheen,[2] make sure it gets plenty of water or else it makes your throat itch when you are eating it; this is how you 20 sweep a corner; this is how you sweep a whole house; this is how you sweep a yard; this is how you smile to someone you don't like too much; this is how you set a table for dinner with an important guest; this is how you smile to someone you don't like at all; this is how you smile to someone you like completely; this is how you set a table for tea; this is how you set a table for dinner; this is how you set a table for lunch; this is how you set a table for breakfast; this is how to behave in the presence of men who don't know you very well, and this way they won't recognize immediately the slut I have warned you against becoming; be sure to wash every day, even if it is with your own spit; don't squat down to play marbles — you are not a boy, you know; don't pick peo- 30 ple's flowers — you might catch something; don't throw stones at blackbirds, because it might not be a blackbird at all; this is how to make a bread pudding; this is how to make doukona;[3] this is how to make pepper pot; this is how to make a good medicine for a cold; this is how to make a good medicine to

[1] Calypso music.
[2] Taro root.
[3] Spicy plantain pudding.

throw away a child before it even becomes a child; this is how to catch a fish; this is how to throw back a fish you don't like, and that way something bad won't fall on you; this is how to bully a man; this is how a man bullies you; this is how to love a man, and if this doesn't work there are other ways, and if they don't work don't feel too bad about giving up; this is how to spit up in the air if you feel like it, and this is how to move quick so that it doesn't fall on you; 40 this is how to make ends meet; always squeeze bread to make sure it's fresh; *but what if the baker won't let me feel the bread?*; you mean to say that after all you are really going to be the kind of woman who the baker won't let near the bread?

## FOR ANALYSIS

1. What does the title of this piece suggest?

2. Who is the speaker? To whom is she speaking?

3. What kind of "girl" is the advice intended to produce?

4. What is the speaker's biggest fear?

5. Are the girl's two responses spoken aloud to the speaker, or are they only the girl's thoughts? Explain.

6. What do the girl's two responses suggest about her relationship to the speaker?

## MAKING ARGUMENTS

Try to imagine Kincaid writing "Girl" as a more traditional story, with **exposition** and **plot** and **dialogue**. Then argue that the traditional version would be either more or less effective than the way she actually chose to write it.

## WRITING TOPICS

1. List the advice you received from your parents and other elders, and write a paragraph in imitation of Kincaid's piece.

2. Examine the details that constitute the advice in this story. What kind of society and culture do these details seem to suggest?

## MAKING CONNECTIONS

1. Compare the girl in this story with Sylvia, the **narrator** of Bambara's "The Lesson" (p. 100).

2. Describe the speaker in this story, and then compare the speaker with the father in Peter Meinke's poem "Advice to My Son" (p. 190). How do they differ? Do they share any qualities?

## CAMDEN JOY  (B. 1964)

# DUM DUM BOYS    2002

The thing I remember about Cameron—he would start smiling as soon as you'd start talking to him. Can't remember a single conversation we ever had, just remember him smiling. Don't think he knew he was smiling, it just happened, he couldn't help it, couldn't help but trust you, couldn't help but smile at you just for talking to him, watching you with his perfectly round blue-grey eyes, eyes the color of the Civil War, and when you got mid-sentence those eyes would open wider, momentarily surprised, then go back to watching, patiently waiting out your sarcasm with a disarming smile, slim good looks, a little stoned, leaning back, waiting on you to make him laugh, to earn that smile of his, to send his mouth open with laughter, his mouth with those perfect teeth.

Cameron and I first met when we were thirteen, and he alone remained as my comrade from junior high into high school, whereas my other pals of that time were lost along the way to the marching band or the swim team or the yearbook committee or the drama club. Together Cameron and I avoided the lure of school-sponsored activities. "You're running," we'd smirk at some former friend whom we'd catch training for a track and field event. They'd glance up dazed, their expression flushed, looking near death, sweat-covered, short of breath, their bodies ruddy, almost naked in those trim jerseys and gym shorts. Cameron and I would be warmly dressed as usual, long pants, trench coats preserving a pasty pallor. "What are you running *from*?" He and I distrusted the sudden crop of boring new pals one found following such pursuits. We were the only guys who by ninth grade had advanced to spray painting punk rock graffiti, gouging "Flipper" or "Nervous Gender" into the lacquered tops of school desks while our former buddies were still carving nonsense like "REO Speedwagon" or "Boston" or "The Wall." Eventually we met others who sympathized with our graffiti, who also lacked affiliations with any extra-curricular projects, and these became our new friends.

Cameron wrote a song on the guitar I lent him, the beat-up tomato-red Fender Duo-Sonic I bought off the dentist's son for $25. You can hear that model of guitar a lot nowadays, a toy-sized treble-rich guitar with no sustain. I let that guitar of mine go for almost nothing; starved for cash and desperate to get out of my hometown I, against my better judgment, hauled the Duo-Sonic into the music store, where they pointed at this and that defect and—positive that I was fencing stolen goods—said they could only offer me $60 for it. I took their money, then later heard that the Duo-Sonic was in their window—"a classic antique"—wearing a $490 price tag.

I attempted to teach Cameron to play that guitar in my parent's garage after school, weekdays, tried to turn him into a band member, but frankly he wasn't

**109**

very adept. His interest in guitar technique was quashed after meeting Greg of the Circle Jerks. Greg told him about the "Magic Chord," told him that you need just two fingers, that you finger the roots of the bar chord, pluck those strings together very fast, turn the amplifier to full distortion, and everyone will feel you're plenty talented. Greg had Cameron convinced that the rest of the guitar — the other four strings, the pick-up switches and bass/treble knobs — were made for wussy jazz and that no one who played rock and roll should touch them.

So Cameron wrote a song, sorta like you'd imagine, a fast distorted 4/4 hard-core basher which was played on only two strings, with Cameron just shifting the Magic Chord up and down the frets every half-measure. The song had no melody, no words, no title; we covered it, my band, long after Cameron stopped showing up for our garage rehearsals, and we dubbed it "Cameron's Song" in his honor but I doubt he ever came and saw us and I'm not certain, even if he had, whether he would have recognized the piece.

The thing I remember about giving him guitar lessons is Cameron smiling at me the whole time, nodding enthusiastically with a short "Okay, okay" each time I'd show him something.

"You want to hold your pick —"

"Okay, okay."

"Like this."

"Okay, okay."

We'd take our fake identification cards and together go to shows at the Starwood or the Whisky or the Cuckoo's Nest where the headliners dressed as we dressed, plain jeans, normal tee shirts, short hair, where the singers couldn't be heard above the instruments though they screamed themselves hoarse trying, their bent-up mouths appearing like dark wounds gashed into their pallid faces, features in terrific pain, the musicians brazenly using made-up names like "Jello" and "Smear," "Zoom" and "Crash." Our favorite singer was named Dinah Cancer, our favorite bassist Derf Scratch, our favorite drummer D.J. Bonebrake. Occasionally, Cameron and I would come out having favored different folks on the bill — he'd generally enjoy no-nonsense barrage, I'd prefer stronger melodies, better words. But still, we went to the gigs together, endured them all the way through, and to my mind that was the important part, the part that truly made us friends.

*My mother calls and I'm immediately suspicious. I haven't been home in some time, and I know she's anxious to see me, to draw me back any way she can, to position me there, a permanent cushion between her and my little sister. But this time she doesn't sound that way at all; she just isn't sure I've seen the news. It has been drizzling in my hometown for weeks and now the storms are intensifying. Flash flood warnings have closed down most of the local campgrounds, including one located just a quarter-mile from my parent's house, the house I grew up in. In recent years, maybe due to the campground's proximity to freight tracks and the main highway, this particular site has housed a steady flow of unpaying inhabitants — drifters and runaways, migrant workers and homeless, their belongings in milk-crates, their tents improvised out of painter's tarps, their laundry draped like Christmas ornaments over the oleander. This campground straddles a dry creekbed, a broad sand ditch lined with pepper trees where my friends and I would hunt for fossils on summer afternoons.*

*A few weeks each winter the creekbed fills to capacity with roiling waters, the overflow from mountain dams located high over us in the Condor Sanctuary, rushing thousands of feet down, racing and scurrying and taking along gnarled husks of fallen oak and trunks of pine, turning the logs over and over in haste, momentum growing, a crashing river hiding within its foam so many half-visible scraps of weighty things that standing on the bank you might glimpse the top of a stove or a closet full of clothes or a sheared-off car door drifting by, strewn with uprooted tumbleweeds and greasewood.*

*Mom explains that the sheriff scoured the campground after the flash flood warning and removed all the transients, hauling them to higher ground, to safety. But the sheriff had inadvertently missed an occupant, some deranged man, a homeless guy, who drowned soon after in the middle of the night when the river burst its banks, water inundating the site with such force that trash cans and picnic tables were picked up and carried nearly ten miles downstream, washed almost to the beach.*

*In the obituary my mother was surprised to read that the dead man had actu-* 15 *ally been quite young, was a recent graduate from our local high school. She thought I might have known him because we were the same age, graduated the same year. His name sounds familiar to her. Didn't you know some boy, she asks, named Cam-something, whose last name was Joyce?*

Cameron was the kind of kid who reassured parents, easy-going, amiable, even ingenuous, and mean to no one but himself. It used to offend me when I read of people being warned against punk's amorality and anti-ethics because though I often considered myself passionately bankrupt of values, devoutly bored with manners, wonderfully unimpressed with most any grown-up, still this did not seem true of Cameron, who was another kind of punk altogether, irregular, inconsistent, unreliable, yes, but shy too, always kind, civilized.

I would laugh at those anguished predictions about kids my age when I thought of Cameron, riding his quietly pleasant Vespa scooter around the sun-drenched valley, overdressed in his fishtail Union Jack parka with the fur-lined hood.

Tell Cameron not to do something and he wouldn't, whereas most of the rest of us would out of spite. They'd tell us not to skateboard over the pads in front of the automatic doors at the grocery store, they'd tell us time and again, not realizing the more they told us the more fun it was; but Cameron wouldn't do it, they asked him not to and he abruptly lost interest in it.

And yet Cameron was more complicated than that too, for he came along with us when we sourly stalked the school halls, my few friends and me, and any people we passed whom we didn't like we would nod at, declare "After the revolution . . .," and then draw a finger across our throat. And we liked almost none of them, not teachers, not students, and gradually we amassed detailed plans to kill most every one of them.

Leaning on our favorite wall of combination lockers, close to the edge of  20
campus, some of us crouched, positioned so that the wall supported only our
heads, others standing, one knee bent, we would proudly pass around well-
worn copies of berserk books whose scenarios fit us more comfortably than
high school, although I must point out that in this Cameron was not one of
us, he never ascribed to these bibles of ours. Cameron's rebel status — the reason he sought the company of petty thieves, liars, and braggarts like us — was
more intuitive, less thought-out; he did not internalize, the way some of us did,
the distant romance of anomie-struck youth in holy literature; Cameron in a
sense wrote his own story, which he kept to himself and told none of us, and he
shrugged away the books and essays we'd offer while smiling patiently, tall and
lean, seldom speaking, eventually pushing off from our favorite wall, waving
a small "so long" at us without pulling his hands from the deep pockets of his
parka, and then putt-putt-putting away on his polite white Vespa.

We would drive long distances together, all of us, in order to see any showings of *A Clockwork Orange* or *Quadrophenia*, films we knew every line of
dialogue from. One of us would usually have stolen a half-gallon of alcohol
from the back of some parent's liquor cabinet, that untouched chardonnay
from Christmas long ago, that cognac which a grown-up was reserving for
a special occasion, that fancy malt-something which adults keep for later,
and we'd pass it back and forth during the film, sloppy and more alive there
than anywhere, each of us Alex and each of us Jimmy, cocky, defiant, sexy,
intoxicated, dismissive of authority. It seemed to us these films alone appreciated us. *Never Grow Old*, they insisted, for once mature you would be Jimmy,
heartbroken over his return to Brighton, or Alex, helpless in the hands of
well-meaning, bungling adults.

Stretched out in the theater darkness, warm in the bath of flickering light,
I grew bold enough to reflect on how we boys turned out this way, our hearts
like onions, like stones, and why so lost, why so lonely, got far enough in contemplating these concerns to recognize that such musings should proceed no
further if I wanted us still to retain our camaraderie. So I would simply stop,
suddenly and completely, and seek to forget that I had ever raised such impon-
derables, and maybe ask for the bottle to be passed down my way once more,
and work to be drawn back again into the movie.

*I tell my Mom that it's too bad about Cameron but that I'm doing fine and no,
I won't be coming back for the memorial service. After that, weeks follow when I
cannot quell my thoughts of Cameron. I am summoned home every few minutes
by one memory or another. Every time I step into a hot bath I anticipate drowning. I begin to recognize Cameron's mannerisms in most everyone around me,
every coat I see is a parka, every motorcycle a Vespa. At the video store, I linger
over* A Clockwork Orange, *finally decide to rent it, find I can't watch it anymore.
The front window of my neighborhood record store advertises expensive digital
remasterings from many of the bands we used to see, reissues of Twisted Roots
and the B-People and Middle Class. And one night, digging through my drawers
looking for a set of thumbtacks, I uncover instead the receipt for the Duo-Sonic,*

*the guitar I sold after Cameron gave up on it, and the receipt is just a piece of paper with a date and "$60.00" written on it but it holds my attention for an hour until I sigh, pack my bags. Finally, I drive home.*

I remember being with Cameron the first time he did black beauties. He swallowed three, then insisted I haul him over to the Arastradero, this all-ages disco at a nearby strip mall. There was no liquor allowed inside so Cameron and I first sat out on the concrete block at the head of our parking space, me drinking a shoplifted forty-ounce bumper of beer, Cameron jiggling a foot, sharing very little of what he was experiencing. We were sixteen. Once inside, I danced with this college student to one lame new wave hit after another — "One Step Beyond" then "Planet Claire" then "Pump it Up." I felt like a goddamn martyr, faking my pleasure at these songs solely to have this girl come out to the car with me. I looked across at Cameron, who sat beside the dance floor, nervously tapping on a tabletop, utterly enraptured by the sight of the Arastradero's rotating mirrored ball. "I got a bottle in the car," I told the girl, and impulsively I grabbed her hand. "Let's go outside!"

Just then the start of "Heart of Glass" blasted onto the sound system.  25

"No way!" she shook me off. "And miss *this* song?"

She started her wiggling again so I just walked off, dragged Cameron out with me. He revealed that he was seeing spiderweb bridges and stalactites, asked me whether he was hallucinating, softly requested that we listen to some soothing Muzak on the car radio. We drove to get chili at Bob's Big Boy. Cameron had his teeth gritted, no appetite. He set about methodically crunching the crackers with the tips of his thumbs. He did this for some time, silent, suddenly stopped, looked up, squinted, tried to focus on me.

"I got our band name," he whispered. He couldn't stop blinking. "It's real good."

We were forever working to name our band, spent more time on that than rehearsing. I wasn't even sure that there was any band to name, but still I was interested.

He had this clammy look about him, very pale, sort of stuck. "Memorial  30 Garage," he spoke thickly, wiped his nose, gazed off.

"You alright?"

He shuddered, didn't respond.

"You gonna be sick?"

He shook his head, leaned two slender fingers into his pale neck to check his own pulse.

"Okay," I sighed. "Memorial Garage. Do you think maybe you can explain  35 it?"

He clamped shut his eyes, opened them, once more shook his head. "Just Memorial Garage. That's all." I saw that he had started to cry. "Really you fucking gotta trust me on this, man."

*My sister wears a Walkman to the dinner table, my dad asks for the pepper to please be passed, my mom says she fluffed my pillows and my old room is ready. My dad tells me my sister quit eighth grade flag football, my mom says my sister should be able to do whatever she wants, the Walkman plays Alice in Chains. I can make out the high-end rattle of the percussion leaking out the headphones across the table, can't distinguish the band's voices from its instruments. My dad says of course of course and that's not what he meant, my mom asks who wants another helping of squash, my sister loudly announces she has to go use the phone right now. My dad frowns at my mom, my mom shrugs, they look at me. Alice in Chains ends, Primus starts. I ask if there's some reason they're both looking at me, and they go back to their plates.*

*Once I'm gone I can speak up, I can notice how everything they say misfires, bounces off, I can pinpoint unhealthy patterns, sour dynamics, but when I'm in it, when I'm at their dinner table, everything is a haze, familiar, aching, confused, I can be no one but their disappointing son, I can do nothing else but choke out the few lines I have recited my entire life and shake my head at how little I feel, how little I comprehend this act called dinner with my family.*

*I wonder what the hell they are doing wrong because I personally can't think of a thing and yet the fact is that Cameron went mad for drugs the same way I went mad for girls, the fact is that whether or not it was his and my parents — he and I both went mad. I have to question what else they could have done, what could have been lacking, for when we were small boys our folks were the sort who always endeavored to comfort us, to encourage us, they raised us to appreciate sunsets and exercise, they gave us a chance at churchliness, moved us to suburbs close to the beach (they proudly told us this was once an "alluvial flood plain"), they made us camp out in the backyard to show us meteor showers and point out the North Star, bought us paint sets and bicycles and magazine subscriptions, they taught us to recognize good kite-flying weather and to say thanks and stop at stop signs and read newspapers and enjoy public television, and they worked hard at their jobs — perhaps a little too absent, a little too preoccupied, this is true, but still they worked hard nonetheless.*

*But maybe there was something murderous about this work ethic of theirs,* 40 *maybe that was the source of the problem, for I think of how they would read our adolescent Christmas lists like aggrieved parents reading a ransom note, too proud to admit that they could not afford our teenage demands, confident that they could completely buy us back if they only drove themselves harder, removed themselves a little more, stayed late at work for enough nights. And then something happened where they began to work so hard at times we hardly saw them, and it felt as if we were being purposely kept out of their sight, as if we had already in fact been kidnapped, and our parents confirmed this for they began to behave as if they, in turn, were already set on being blackmailed. All I know is, despite the attention lavished on our early upbringings, by the time we were as old as my little sister we wanted none of it, all any of us hoped for was an early death, a violent early death. Out of all of us happily only one got what he'd hoped for; sadly, that was Cameron.*

Cameron barely graduated, he was forever skipping school to cruise around on his Vespa or hitch-hike down to L.A. I think it can be accurately claimed that as his friends we had more to do with his graduating than he ever did, for I believe that he got out of high school mainly due to the gullibility of teachers who believed the stories we fed them, the endless excuses we gave as to why Cameron didn't show up today or yesterday or the day before or last week either for this or that class. The example I remember is Mrs. Constantine, our literature teacher.

Ever the punk rebel, Cameron had taken to wearing exceedingly normal polo shirts and cardigan sweaters to high school and so we, in turn, took to telling Mrs. Constantine that Cameron's frequent absences were the fault of the school golf team.

"I had never before heard that Cameron golfed with our golf team," she informed us skeptically.

"Of course. Why do you think he wears those dorky polo shirts and stupid cardigans all the time?"

Mrs. Constantine considered this. "I suppose," she said. "I might have heard of it if he were the type of boy who talks. Still, I should have seen his name on these lists that are circulated around, that have the names of all the golfers on them."

"Well naturally. But remember it's Cameron, after all. He doesn't want anyone to find out. You know how he is. He does everything he can to keep it a secret. 'L' Angelo Mysterioso,' all that."

Mrs. Constantine nodded, made a gesture to indicate the secret was safe with her because her lips were locked and she had tossed away the key, and then excused many of Cameron Joyce's absences in her ledger as "Necessary for School Business."

Cameron often took far too many uppers and then requested a lift to the disco. One time he was near to overdosing at the Arastradero on a handful of cross-tops. Two beautiful college girls kept checking us out. Eventually they came over and, with no other prelude, just liking the looks of us I guess, asked for Cameron and I to take them home. We drove them to their condo, followed them inside, watched the girls unceremoniously shrug out of their clothes.

"Oh," said Cameron. "Christ." He was suddenly moving away. He had that clammy look and he was staggering back and back, one hand darting behind him, unsuccessfully groping about for a chair, and then he quietly sank to the carpet, a pile of slouched limbs.

One of the girls giggled.

"Should we be worried?" they asked.

"Nope," I said, untangling Cameron's spindly arms and legs, smoothing him out so that he looked a bit more presentable laying there passed out cold on the condo's floor. "He's like this all the time."

"We should maybe call an ambulance though?"

"Amphetamines," I explained. "He'll wake up, he'll be fine." I made sure his breath was visible in a compact mirror and then I shed my own clothes.

*The ice cream parlor closes at eight-thirty so we have to hurry. The dishwasher is quickly filled, my sister is dragged from the telephone, my dad from the computer. My mom, dad sit in the front of the car like always, my sister, me in back. The town goes by the window and nothing appears any different. My sister and I ignore each other. It's been four hours since I got home. We have yet to speak. Her Walkman and headphones rest in her lap, a threat.*

*At the ice cream counter my parents pretend to be newlyweds. My dad croons along with the music on the loudspeaker, my mom giggles, takes his hand, rests a cheek on his shoulder. My sister and I take our cones, move outside. She leans on the car, notices me watching a homeless guy approach. He is having a tough time of it, stumbling, dropping things.*

*Fuck, she laughs, indicating the homeless guy. It's the first word she's directed towards me. Who's this loser? I laugh with her, nod. Her eyes connect with mine, share something. Too weird, wheezes an unfamiliar voice. It's you, hey man. The homeless guy is speaking. He croaks my name a few times. My sister rolls her eyes, stamps her feet, recrosses her arms, licks her cone. Figures, she snorts.*

*The homeless guy wants me to shake his hand. How have you been, he asks, you heard what happened to our friend? Yeah, I reply. I can't recall this guy's name, but I briefly give him my hand. He looks like someone I might have hated in high school, probably someone we'd planned on killing after the revolution. Yeah, I say again, too bad. Could be it's better off, the guy shrugs, he wasn't well, you knew that. Yeah, I say, guess I did.*

*I think of the party I heard about where, after a few drinks, Cameron made everyone whisper because he insisted the government was listening. Everyone assumed he was joking but they indulged him anyway. A few days later, he attacked a group of Asians on the street, claiming that they had placed electrodes in his brain, that they were monitoring his thoughts for the CIA. No one told me what happened to him subsequently; I caught rumors he'd disappeared somewhere across the country, in Boston or New York, I heard that he was calling himself "Camden Joy," writing on some city's walls or some crazy thing, and I kept setting his smile against East Coast backdrops, I'd imagine him smiling as the New Yorkers spoke, smiling like he couldn't help it, couldn't help but trust them, leaning back, just watching, hands deep in his parka, smiling. I always figured I'd find him eventually, I'd imagine these elaborate schemes in which I'd smoke him out, make him reveal himself, like maybe I'd write under that name "Camden Joy" and he'd track me down as a result, schemes like that, which were far-fetched and spooky in a way I knew he'd like, and then after finding me we'd shake our heads over our impossible past, disputing it like an amnesiac might if awakening to a hoax, we'd mock memories of "the good old days," and he'd smile and smile.*

*Hey man, you really gotta come out and see us, the homeless guy is saying to me.* 60 *I would, I say, but I'm just visiting, I'm leaving soon. Come out to the campground first, the guy encourages me, it's where him and me are staying. You and who, I ask. Him and me, the guy says. I got Camden out there. What, I ask. I got Camden with me out there, he says, man, they cremated his ass, don't you know. I got what's left of him out there with me. You should really see him before you go. I'll try, I say. I'm pressed for time, you understand. The guy fidgets for a long time, studying me. You haven't changed, man, he informs me at last, not at all, and he staggers off.*

Cameron and my other friends and I remained close for a long while, for no other reason than that we simply dreaded explaining ourselves to anyone who didn't already get us, who didn't admire the complex hail of references which comprised our daily chit-chat.

Inevitably, Sex and Drugs got in the way of this friendship, for the intensity and immediacy of their sensate gratification so dwarfed the ordinary pleasure of our camaraderie as to make us entirely question the depth and commitment of our feelings towards one another, made us ask whether we truly knew each other, if we were ever even friends at all or just neighbor boys who had a few tastes in common, similar jokes and mannerisms, liked a couple of the same LPs and movies, nothing more.

What were such similarities in the face of Girls, who quickly meant everything to me, or Speed, which began to mean everything to Cameron? It grew crucial that we dismiss the friendship to pursue these bigger joys, and Cameron accepted — just as I was made to grasp and grudgingly admit — that he would have to make himself better understood in order to obtain access to these higher pleasures, and he began to hang out with agitated speed-freaks who endlessly described things they witnessed which were utterly invisible to the rest of us, and I began devoting myself to girls whom I respected solely for the tautness of their trim calves and the willingness in their open smiles. These were, in some ways, our uneasy attempts to apply for membership to new circles, signaling our willingness to be cheaply belittled and lamely categorized by these new so-called pals so that we might be allowed to drop a hungry hand into their grab-bag and come away having scored some of their goodies.

*I stride down our block of tract homes and across the kiddie park, skirting the shopping center the whole while, then continue over the highway, down and up a tall cement embankment, wading through a field of knee-high green brush, across the railroad tracks, down a row of ditches which irrigate a field of baby's breath. Wild anise sprouts everywhere underfoot like weeds, encouraged by the winter's rains, the gentle morning breezes rippling its feathery leaves, the reek of licorice pouring from its sticky, cane-like stalk.*

*So you came, the homeless guy calls out, I knew you would. Well hey there, I* 65 *say, I was just taking a walk. This is incredibly close to where my parents live, actually. The guy ignores me. I knew you would come, he repeats. We always figured if anyone got to be a household word, it'd be you. But then, you're not a household word, he mumbles dismally, not even you.*

*Not even me, I agree.*

*What's the point anyways, he says. Right? You heard Susan Lucci on the radio the other night. No, I reply. Well, he discloses, I got a radio, I got me Camden's radio set-up . . . Wanna see Camden? Not really, I tell him. You came all this way, he mutters. Wanna see where he lived?*

*Yeah, I concede, okay.*

*The guy motions for me to follow, starts across the campsite. Watch the poison oak, he declares. Leaves don't turn red till summer. The guy leads me around barbecue pits, sacks of trash. So, he says, Susan Lucci has had no easy time of it. And you think, if not Susan Lucci, you know, then who. Because what she deserves . . . that's some incredible talent. And that Emmys thing is so screwed. Too weird. Breaks your heart. Oh, I drily put in, absolutely. You don't care for Susan Lucci, he notices. Okay well, you will. I didn't once upon a time either.*

*He points to the top of a eucalyptus tree. That's it, he says simply. About nine* 70
*feet up, three branches diverge off the frame of the main trunk. A piece of ply-*
*wood rests between the limbs.*

*Cameron lived there, I ask.*

*Camden, he corrects me, yeah. He hasn't been Cameron since high school. But
you know, the guy goes on, Camden always kept talking about you. What did he
say, I ask, do you remember? No, he says, you couldn't always hear him real good.
What's funny, I say, is I can't even remember anything we talked about, just him
smiling all the time, you know? Right, the guy says, I know. I hadn't seen him, I
say, in a long time. You kinda — the guy gesticulates frustratedly — we couldn't
find you, right after Camden got picked up for going off on those Jap dudes.*

*I got real busy, I acknowledge. My career just . . . It took off.*

*Fine, he says.*

*I always heard Cameron went to New York City, I say. Sometimes I'd go there,* 75
*I'd look all over for handwriting on the walls. The guy shakes his head, points up
again at the plywood. He came home, he says. He was at the emergency room,
they were calling him psychotic and all this, got him down on this cot, KO'd him
with Thorazine. I met him up there at the crisis center, they were doing him up
with four and a half milligrams of Haldol three times a day. We just took off
together, man, it was getting wicked.*

*The crisis center was in town here?*

*Near here, he nods, yeah. So we've been here now, this is our third springtime.
The state pays us general relief. Were you here that night, I ask, the night the cops
came to get everyone out of the way of the water. Sure, he says. Well, I ask, where
was . . . why didn't you take Cameron with you?*

*Well, he says, the difference there was, Camden didn't like the cops and so he
went and hid in the river bottom, soon as they showed up. And the stupid fucks,
they never even saw him down there.*

*We smile at each other, proud of our friend's ability to confound the law.*

*You know how he was, the guy murmurs, and we smile again.* 80

*Yeah, I admit, I know how he was. I begin to climb the eucalyptus.*

*Be careful, the guy warns me. Camden used to fall from there all the time. Yes,
I think to myself, I can see why, because only two sides of the plywood have any
sort of branch support, the other two open into thin air. None of his belongings
are up here, just this bare plywood placed in the trees. Is this all there was, I ask.
No, the guy replies, I took everything else, his books and shit I got down here
with me. You wanna see them? You still gotta come down and see Camden, man.
Can't believe you haven't even seen Camden.*

*I'm not really interested, I say. I am laying flat, my belly against the plywood,
gazing off through the acrid haze of fried burgers and fast-food neon, and suddenly I jerk at the sight of something. Did you know, I start to ask, then stop. It's
just a coincidence, it's gotta be. What, the guy asks. Well you can see, from this
perch here, you look right at my parent's garage. Yeah, concurs the guy, where
you guys used to rehearse. Exactly, I say. Yeah, he continues, I was aware of that,
Camden did that on purpose. He did, I say. The guy shrugs. I couldn't tell you why.*

*I have my fingers interlaced, palms down, my head on my hands. So, I think to myself, Cameron was home all this time, delusional in the arms of his eucalyptus, conversing with his memories and watching that stupid garage. I shut my eyes against the sunshine and remember the winter weather, the way it hits here and holds on. I picture this board wobbling in a thundershower, Cameron unable to make out the sounds of the highway or the freight trains when above them both is the storm whistling through the treetops, breaking branches in the blackness, shaking loose water and leaves with a high, relentless whoosh. As a child, I remember falling asleep to the rain pelting our roof, and in my mind the source of the storm was a face as big as the sky, a face with its mouth stuck open, howling, and the face was gruesomely contorted, and it never ran out of breath.*

*I feel those childhood storms howling in the pit of my stomach right now, week-* 85 *long storms which seemed never to go away. And every fear ever imagined sings in my bones, there is the fear of being locked up in my room too long alone, the fear of being devoured by the storm, the dwarfed feeling of being left behind, insignificant, a trifling speck of humanity. I know that as a boy, laying in bed, eyes closed, I regularly fell asleep to this feeling, this absolute certainty that I had been forgotten.*

*I feel the abrupt shudder of plywood beneath me.* Hey, *the homeless guy says, shaking the tree.* Hey. You been up there long enough. Come down now and see him. You gotta see Camden, man. You haven't seen him yet.

*In a minute, I say sleepily. Just give me half a minute. I'll be down.*

## FOR ANALYSIS

**1.** At what time(s) is the story set?

**2.** What do you think the "childhood storms" (para. 85) stand for?

**3.** On his return home, the narrator asks himself, "I wonder what the hell they are doing wrong" (para. 39). Who is the "they" he refers to? Why does he ask this question? Does he answer it?

## MAKING ARGUMENTS

**1.** The **narrator** says that the appeal of the books he and his high school friends read was due to "the distant romance of anomie-struck youth in holy literature" (para. 20). How would you argue that "Dum Dum Boys" belongs in this category? How would you argue that it does not?

**2.** The author often writes about music in his fiction, and has also written rock criticism. Read up on punk music and make the argument that the kind of music the boys listen to is important to the story.

## WRITING TOPICS

**1.** Reflect on the significance of the moment when the narrator hears that Cameron has renamed himself. What is the effect of the particular name the author chooses to give him? Why do you think it is important to the story? (Refer to the author's biography to help you think about this.)

**2.** Describe the structure of the story by first annotating it (if you haven't already) and then by thinking about how it's put together. What kinds of sections are there? How does each kind differ? How are they arranged? What are the effects of this structure, and why do you think Joy chose it?

## MAKING CONNECTIONS

**1.** "Dum-Dum Boys" and Updike's "A & P" (p. 94) both feature young men who are drawn to young women. How might this attraction to girls be said to also be in part about other things?

**2.** Naguib Mahfouz tells a story of innocence's loss in "Half a Day" (p. 90) as experienced by a very young boy whose real awakening to life's realities lies ahead of him. From what temporal perspective does Joy's narrator see innocence's loss? How does this difference in perspective effect what the stories are able to see and say?

## CONNECTING STORIES: CRUSHES

*Crush* is a funny word. Its literal meaning is "romantic attraction that is somewhere short of love" — something short-lived and superficial. But buried in the word's etymology is a somewhat contradictory sense of intensity, of something pressing or grinding (and even a sense of violence if you consider the word's original meaning, which included a loud crashing or cracking sound). As you read these stories, look for the ways in which a crush, while it lasts only a brief while and then is gone, can also be intense and even overwhelming. One of the reasons crushes are rich subjects for literature is that as powerful infatuations they contain contradiction, expressing something of life's deepest feelings as well as life's mutability — the quick-changing quality that often drives artists to try to capture lost, fleeting moments. In the following stories, James Joyce and Rivka Galchen manage to capture two similar — and similarly lost — moments, but in very different ways.

## JAMES JOYCE   (1882–1941)

# ARABY   1914

North Richmond Street, being blind, was a quiet street except at the hour when the Christian Brothers' School set the boys free. An uninhabited house of two storeys stood at the blind end, detached from its neighbours in a square ground. The other houses of the street, conscious of decent lives within them, gazed at one another with brown imperturbable faces.

The former tenant of our house, a priest, had died in the back drawing-room. Air, musty from having been long enclosed, hung in all the rooms, and the waste room behind the kitchen was littered with old useless papers. Among these I found a few paper-covered books, the pages of which were curled and damp: *The Abbot*, by Walter Scott, *The Devout Communicant* and *The Memoirs of Vidocq*. I liked the last best because its leaves were yellow. The wild garden behind the house contained a central apple-tree and a few straggling bushes under one of which I found the late tenant's rusty bicycle pump. He had been a very charitable priest; in his will he had left all his money to institutions and the furniture of his house to his sister.

When the short days of winter came dusk fell before we had well eaten our dinners. When we met in the street the houses had grown sombre. The space of sky above us was the colour of ever-changing violet and towards it the lamps of the street lifted their feeble lanterns. The cold air stung us and we played till our bodies glowed. Our shouts echoed in the silent street. The career of our play brought us through the dark muddy lanes behind the houses where we ran the gauntlet of the rough tribes from the cottages, to the back doors of the dark dripping gardens where odours arose from the ashpits, to the dark odorous stables where a coachman smoothed and combed the horse or shook music from the buckled harness. When we returned to the street, light from the kitchen windows had filled the areas. If my uncle was seen turning the corner we hid in the shadow until we had seen him safely housed. Or if Mangan's sister came out on the doorstep to call her brother in to his tea we watched her from our shadow peer up and down the street. We waited to see whether she would remain or go in and, if she remained, we left our shadow and walked up to Mangan's steps resignedly. She was waiting for us, her figure defined by the light from the half-opened door. Her brother always teased her before he obeyed and I stood by the railings looking at her. Her dress swung as she moved her body and the soft rope of her hair tossed from side to side.

Every morning I lay on the floor in the front parlour watching her door. The blind was pulled down to within an inch of the sash so that I could not be seen. When she came out on the doorstep my heart leaped. I ran to the hall, seized my books and followed her. I kept her brown figure always in my eye and, when we came near the point at which our ways diverged, I quickened my pace and passed her. This happened morning after morning. I had never spoken to her, except for a few casual words, and yet her name was like a summons to all my foolish blood.

Her image accompanied me even in places the most hostile to romance. On Saturday evenings when my aunt went marketing I had to go to carry some of the parcels. We walked through the flaring streets, jostled by drunken men and bargaining women, amid the curses of labourers, the shrill litanies of shop-boys who stood on guard by the barrels of pigs' cheeks, the nasal chanting of street-singers, who sang a *come-all-you*[1] about O'Donovan Rossa, or a ballad about the troubles in our native land. These noises converged in a single sensation of life for me: I imagined that I bore my chalice safely through a throng of foes. Her name sprang to my lips at moments in strange prayers and praises which I myself did not understand. My eyes were often full of tears (I could not tell why) and at times a flood from my heart seemed to pour itself out into my bosom. I thought little of the future. I did not know whether I would ever speak to her or not or, if I spoke to her, how I could tell her of my confused adoration. But my body was like a harp and her words and gestures were like fingers running upon the wires.

One evening I went into the back drawing-room in which the priest had died. It was a dark rainy evening and there was no sound in the house. Through one of the broken panes I heard the rain impinge upon the earth, the fine incessant needles of water playing in the sodden beds. Some distant lamp or lighted window gleamed below me. I was thankful that I could see so little. All my senses seemed to desire to veil themselves and, feeling that I was about to slip from them, I pressed the palms of my hands together until they trembled, murmuring: *"O love! O love!"* many times.

5

---

[1] A street ballad beginning with these words. This one is about Jeremiah Donovan, a nineteenth-century Irish nationalist popularly known as O'Donovan Rossa.

At last she spoke to me. When she addressed the first words to me I was so confused that I did not know what to answer. She asked me was I going to *Araby*. I forgot whether I answered yes or no. It would be a splendid bazaar, she said she would love to go.

"And why can't you?" I asked.

While she spoke she turned a silver bracelet round and round her wrist. She could not go, she said, because there would be a retreat that week in her convent. Her brother and two other boys were fighting for their caps and I was alone at the railings. She held one of the spikes, bowing her head towards me. The light from the lamp opposite our door caught the white curve of her neck, lit up her hair that rested there and, falling, lit up the hand upon the railing. It fell over one side of her dress and caught the white border of a petticoat, just visible as she stood at ease.

"It's well for you," she said.                                                                                                          10

"If I go," I said, "I will bring you something."

What innumerable follies laid waste my waking and sleeping thoughts after that evening! I wished to annihilate the tedious intervening days. I chafed against the work of school. At night in my bedroom and by day in the classroom her image came between me and the page I strove to read. The syllables of the word *Araby* were called to me through the silence in which my soul luxuriated and cast an Eastern enchantment over me. I asked for leave to go to the bazaar on Saturday night. My aunt was surprised and hoped it was not some Freemason affair. I answered few questions in class. I watched my master's face pass from amiability to sternness; he hoped I was not beginning to idle. I could not call my wandering thoughts together. I had hardly any patience with the serious work of life which, now that it stood between me and my desire, seemed to me child's play, ugly monotonous child's play.

On Saturday morning I reminded my uncle that I wished to go to the bazaar in the evening. He was fussing at the hallstand, looking for the hat-brush, and answered me curtly:

"Yes, boy, I know."

As he was in the hall I could not go into the front parlour and lie at the win-   15 dow. I left the house in bad humour and walked slowly towards the school. The air was pitilessly raw and already my heart misgave me.

When I came home to dinner my uncle had not yet been home. Still it was early. I sat staring at the clock for some time and, when its ticking began to irritate me, I left the room. I mounted the staircase and gained the upper part of the house. The high cold empty gloomy rooms liberated me and I went from room to room singing. From the front window I saw my companions playing below in the street. Their cries reached me weakened and indistinct and, leaning my forehead against the cool glass, I looked over at the dark house where she lived. I may have stood there for an hour, seeing nothing but the brown-clad figure cast by my imagination, touched discreetly by the lamplight at the curved neck, at the hand upon the railings and at the border below the dress.

When I came downstairs again I found Mrs. Mercer sitting at the fire. She was an old garrulous woman, a pawnbroker's widow, who collected used stamps for some pious purpose. I had to endure the gossip of the tea-table. The meal was prolonged beyond an hour and still my uncle did not come. Mrs. Mercer stood up to go: she was sorry she couldn't wait any longer, but it was after eight o'clock and she did not like to be out late, as the night air was bad for her. When she had gone I began to walk up and down the room, clenching my fists. My aunt said:

"I'm afraid you may put off your bazaar for this night of Our Lord."

At nine o'clock I heard my uncle's latchkey in the hall door. I heard him talking to himself and heard the hallstand rocking when it had received the weight of his overcoat. I could interpret these signs. When he was midway through his dinner I asked him to give me the money to go to the bazaar. He had forgotten.

"The people are in bed and after their first sleep now," he said.     20

I did not smile. My aunt said to him energetically:

"Can't you give him the money and let him go? You've kept him late enough as it is."

My uncle said he was very sorry he had forgotten. He said he believed in the old saying: "All work and no play makes Jack a dull boy." He asked me where I was going and, when I had told him a second time he asked me did I know *The Arab's Farewell to His Steed*. When I left the kitchen he was about to recite the opening lines of the piece to my aunt.

I held a florin tightly in my hand as I strode down Buckingham Street towards the station. The sight of the streets thronged with buyers and glaring with gas recalled to me the purpose of my journey. I took my seat in a third-class carriage of a deserted train. After an intolerable delay the train moved out of the station slowly. It crept onward among ruinous houses and over the twinkling river. At Westland Row Station a crowd of people pressed to the carriage doors; but the porters moved them back, saying that it was a special train for the bazaar. I remained alone in the bare carriage. In a few minutes the train drew up beside an improvised wooden platform. I passed out on to the road and saw by the lighted dial of a clock that it was ten minutes to ten. In front of me was a large building which displayed the magical name.

I could not find any sixpenny entrance and, fearing that the bazaar would be  25 closed, I passed in quickly through a turnstile, handing a shilling to a weary-looking man. I found myself in a big hall girdled at half its height by a gallery. Nearly all the stalls were closed and the greater part of the hall was in darkness. I recognised a silence like that which pervades a church after a service. I walked into the centre of the bazaar timidly. A few people were gathered about the stalls which were still open. Before a curtain, over which the words *Café Chantant* were written in coloured lamps, two men were counting money on a salver. I listened to the fall of the coins.

Remembering with difficulty why I had come I went over to one of the stalls and examined porcelain vases and flowered tea-sets. At the door of the stall a young lady was talking and laughing with two young gentlemen. I remarked their English accents and listened vaguely to their conversation.

"O, I never said such a thing!"

"O, but you did!"

"O, but I didn't!"

"Didn't she say that?"                                                              30

"Yes. I heard her."

"O, there's a . . . fib!"

Observing me the young lady came over and asked me did I wish to buy anything. The tone of her voice was not encouraging; she seemed to have spoken to me out of a sense of duty. I looked humbly at the great jars that stood like Eastern guards at either side of the dark entrance to the stall and murmured:

"No, thank you."

The young lady changed the position of one of the vases and went back to   35 the two young men. They began to talk of the same subject. Once or twice the young lady glanced at me over her shoulder.

I lingered before her stall, though I knew my stay was useless, to make my interest in her wares seem the more real. Then I turned away slowly and walked down the middle of the bazaar. I allowed the two pennies to fall against the sixpence in my pocket. I heard a voice call from one end of the gallery that the light was out. The upper part of the hall was now completely dark.

Gazing up into the darkness I saw myself as a creature driven and derided by vanity; and my eyes burned with anguish and anger.

## FOR ANALYSIS

**1.** Reread the opening paragraph. How does it set the **tone** for the story?

**2.** Why does the **dialogue** the **narrator** overhears at the bazaar trigger the climax of the story and the insight described in the final paragraph?

## MAKING ARGUMENTS

Make an argument that in the end the narrator is either too hard on himself or not hard enough (or at least not appropriately hard). That is, either argue that he is just another human, with all of our failings, or else that he is a special case.

## WRITING TOPICS

**1.** Write a page describing a romantic infatuation you experienced when you were younger that blinded you to the reality of the person you adored.

**2.** Analyze the **imagery** of light and vision in this story.

## Rivka Galchen (b. 1976)

# Wild Berry Blue 2008

This is a story about my love for Roy, though first I have to say a few words about my dad, who was there with me at the McDonald's every Saturday letting his little girl — I was maybe eight — swig his extra half-and-halfs, stack the shells into messy towers. My dad drank from his bottomless cup of coffee and read the paper while I dipped my McDonaldland cookies in milk and pretended to read the paper. He wore gauzy plaid button-ups with pearline snaps. He had girlish wrists, a broad forehead like a Roman, an absolutely terrifying sneeze.

"How's the coffee?" I'd ask.

"Not good, not bad. How's the milk?"

"Terrific," I'd say. Or maybe, "Exquisite."

My mom was at home cleaning the house; our job there at the McDonald's 5 was to be out of her way.

And that's how it always was on Saturdays. We were Jews, we had our rituals. That's how I think about it. Despite the occasional guiltless cheeseburger, despite being secular Israelis living in the wilds of Oklahoma, the ineluctable Jew part in us still snuck out, like an inherited tic, indulging in habits of repetition. Our form of *davenning*. Our little Shabbat.

Many of the people who worked at the McDonald's were former patients of my dad's: mostly drug addicts and alcoholics in rehab programs. McDonald's hired people no one else would hire; I think it was a policy. And my dad, in effect, was the McDonald's–Psychiatric Institute liaison. The McDonald's manager, a deeply Christian man, would regularly come over and say hello to us, and thank my dad for many things. Once he thanked him for, as a Jew, having kept safe the word of God during all the dark years.

"I'm not sure I've done so much," my dad had answered, not seriously.

"But it's been living there in you," the manager said earnestly. He was basically a nice man, admirably tolerant of the accompanying dramas of his work force, dramas I picked up on peripherally. Absenteeism, petty theft, a worker OD-ing in the bathroom. I had no idea what that meant, to OD, but it sounded spooky. "They slip out from under their own control," I heard the manager say one time, and the phrase stuck with me. I pictured one half of a person lifting up a velvet rope and fleeing the other half.

Sometimes, dipping my McDonaldland cookies — Fryguy, Grimace — I'd hold 10 a cookie in the milk too long and it would saturate and crumble to the bottom of the carton. There, it was something mealy, vulgar. Horrible. I'd lose my appetite. Though the surface of the milk often remained pristine I could feel the cookie's presence down below, lurking. Like some ancient bottom-dwelling fish with both eyes on one side of his head.

I'd tip the carton back in order to see what I dreaded seeing, just to feel that queasiness, and also the pre-queasiness of knowing the main queasiness was coming, the anticipatory ill.

Beautiful/Horrible — I had a running mental list. Cleaning lint from the screen of the dryer — beautiful. Bright glare on glass — horrible. Mealworms — also horrible. The stubbles of shaved hair in a woman's armpit — beautiful.

The Saturday I was to meet Roy, after dropping a cookie in the milk, I looked up at my dad. "Cookie," I squeaked, turning a sour face at the carton.

He pulled out his worn leather wallet, with its inexplicable rust stain ring on the front. He gave me a dollar. My mom never gave me money and my dad always gave me more than I needed. (He also called me the Queen of Sheba sometimes, like when I'd stand up on a dining room chair to see how things looked from there.) The torn corner of the bill he gave me was held on with yellowed Scotch tape. Someone had written over the treasury seal in blue pen, "I love Becky!!!"

I go up to the counter with the Becky dollar to buy my replacement milk, and 15 what I see is a tattoo, most of which I can't see. A starched white long-sleeve shirt covers most of it. But a little blue-black lattice of it I can see — a fragment like ancient elaborate metalwork, that creeps down all the way, past the wrist, to the back of the hand, kinking up and over a very plump vein. The vein is so distended I imagine laying my cheek on it in order to feel the blood pulse and flow, to maybe even hear it. Beautiful. So beautiful. I don't know why but I'm certain this tattoo reaches all the way up to his shoulder. His skin is deeply tanned but the webbing between his fingers sooty pale.

This beautiful feeling. I haven't had it about a person before. Not in this way.

In a trembling moment I shift my gaze up to the engraved nametag. There's a yellow M emblem, then *Roy*.

I place my dollar down on the counter. I put it down like it's a password I'm unsure of, one told to me by an unreliable source. "Milk," I say, quietly.

Roy, whose face I finally look at, is staring off, up, over past my head, like a bored lifeguard. He hasn't heard or noticed me, little me, the only person in line. Roy is biting his lower lip and one of his teeth, one of the canines, is much whiter than the others. Along his cheekbones his skin looks dry and chalky. His eyes are blue, with beautiful bruisy eyelids.

I try again, a little bit louder. "Milk." 20

Still he doesn't hear me; I begin to feel as if maybe I am going to cry because of these accumulated moments of being nothing. That's what it feels like standing so close to this type of beauty — like being nothing.

Resolving to give up if I'm not noticed soon I make one last effort and, leaning over on my tiptoes, I push the dollar further along the counter, far enough that it tickles Roy's thigh, which is leaned up against the counter's edge.

He looks down at me, startled, then laughs abruptly. "Hi little sexy," he says. Then he laughs again, too loud, and the other cashier, who has one arm shrunken and paralyzed, turns and looks and then looks away again.

Suddenly these few seconds are everything that has ever happened to me.

My milk somehow purchased I go back to the table wondering if I am green, 25
or emitting a high-pitched whistling sound, or dead.

I realize back at the table that it's not actually the first time I've seen Roy. With great concentration, I dip my Hamburglar cookie into the cool milk. I think that maybe I've seen Roy — that coarse blond hair — every Saturday, for all my Saturdays. I take a bite from my cookie. I have definitely seen him before. Just somehow not in this way.

My dad appears to be safely immersed in whatever is on the other side of the crossword puzzle and bridge commentary page. I feel — a whole birch tree pressing against my inner walls, its leaves reaching to the top of my throat — the awful sense of wanting some other life. I have thought certain boys in my classes have pretty faces, but I have never before felt like laying my head down on the vein of a man's wrist. (I still think about that vein some-times.) Almost frantically I wonder if Roy can see me there at my table, there with my dad, where I've been seemingly all my Saturdays.

Attempting to rein in my anxiety I try and think: What makes me feel this way? Possessed like this? Is it a smell in the air? It just smells like beefy grease. Which is pleasant enough but nothing new. A little mustard. A small vapor of disinfectant. I wonder obscurely if Roy is Jewish, as if that might make normal this spiraling fated feeling I have. As if really what's struck me is just an unobvious family resemblance. But I know that we're the only Jews in town.

Esther married the gentile king, I think, in a desperate absurd flash.

Since a part of me wants to stay forever I finish my cookies quickly. 30

"Let's go," I say.

"Already?"

"Can't we just leave? Let's leave."

There's the Medieval Fair, I think to myself in consolation all Sunday. It's two weekends away, a Saturday. You're always happy at the Medieval Fair, I say to myself, as I fail to enjoy sorting my stamps, fail to stand expectantly, joy-fully, on the dining room chair. Instead I fantasize about running the French fry fryer in the back of McDonald's. I imagine myself learning to construct Happy Meal boxes in a breath, to fold the papers around the hamburgers *just so*. I envision a stool set out for me to climb atop so that I can reach the apple fritter dispenser; Roy spots me, making sure I don't fall. And I get a tattoo. Of a bird, or a fish, or a ring of birds and fish, around my ankle.

But there is no happiness in these daydreams. Just an overcrowded and 35
feverish empty.

At school on Monday I sit dejectedly in the third row of Mrs. Brown's class, because that is where we are on the weekly seating chart rotation. I suffer through exercises in long division, through bits about Magellan. Since I'm not in the front I'm able to mark most of my time drawing a tremendous maze, one that stretches to the outer edges of the notebook paper. This while the teacher reads to us from something about a girl and her horse. Something. A horse. Who cares! Who cares about a horse! I think, filled, suddenly, with unexpected rage. That extra white tooth. The creeping chain of the tattoo. I try so hard to be dedicated to my maze, pressing my pencil sharply into the paper as if to hold down my focus better.

All superfluous, even my sprawling maze, superfluous. A flurry of pencil shavings from the sharpener — they come out as if in a breath — distracts me. A sudden phantom pain near my elbow consumes my attention.

I crumple up my maze dramatically; do a basketball throw to the wastebasket like the boys do. I miss of course but no one seems to notice, which is the nature of my life at school, where I am only noticed in bland embarrassing ways, like when a substitute teacher can't pronounce my last name. The joylessness of my basketball toss — it makes me look over at my once-crush Josh Deere and feel sad for him, for the smallness of his life.

One day, I think, it will be Saturday again.

But time seemed to move so slowly. I'd lost my appetite for certain details 40 of life.

"Do you know about that guy at McDonald's with the one really white tooth?" I brave this question to my dad. This during a commercial break from *Kojak*.

"Roy's a recovering heroin addict," my dad says, turning to stare at me. He always said things to me other people wouldn't have said to kids. He'd already told me about the Oedipus complex and I had stared dully back at him. He would defend General Rommel to me, though I had no idea who General Rommel was. He'd make complex points about the straits of Bosporus. It was as if he couldn't distinguish ages.

So he said that to me, about Roy, which obviously he shouldn't have said. (Here, years later, I still think about the mystery of that plump vein, which seems a contradiction. Which occasionally makes me wonder if there were two Roys.)

"I don't know what the story with the tooth is," my dad adds. "Maybe it's false?" And then it's back to the mystery of *Kojak*.

I wander into the kitchen feeling unfulfilled and so start interrogating my 45 mom about my Purim costume for the carnival that is still two Sundays, eons, away. The Purim carnival is in Tulsa, over an hour's driving distance; I don't know the kids there, and my costume never measures up. "And the crown," I remind her hollowly. I'm not quite bold enough to bring up that she could buy me one of the beautiful ribbon crowns sold at the Medieval Fair, which we'll be at the day before. "I don't want," I mumble mostly to myself, "one of those paper crowns that everyone has."

Thursday night I am at the Skaggs Alpha Beta grocery with my mom. I am lingering amid all the sugar cereals I know will never come home with me. It's only every minute or so that I am thinking about Roy's hand, about how he called me sexy.

Then I see Roy. He has no cart, no basket. He's holding a gallon of milk and a supersized bag of Twizzlers and he is reaching for, I can't quite see — a big oversized box that looks to be Honeycomb. A beautiful assemblage. Beautiful.

I turn away from Roy but stand still. I feel my whole body, even my ears, blushing. The backs of my hands feel itchy the way they always do in spring. Seeking release I touch the cool metal shelving, run my fingers up and over the plastic slipcovers, over the price labels, hearing every nothing behind me. The price labels make a sandy sliding sound when I push them. He's a monster, Roy. Not looking at him, just feeling that power he has over me, a monster.

My mom in lace-up sandals cruises by the aisle with our shopping cart, unveiling to me my ridiculousness. Able now to turn around I see that Roy is gone. I run after my mom and when finally we're in the car again, back door closed on the groceries — I see celery stalks innocently sticking out of a brown paper bag when I turn around — I feel great relief.

I decide to wash my feet in the sink, this always makes me happy. On my dad's $_{50}$ shaving mirror in the bathroom, old Scotch tape holding it in place, is a yellowed bit of paper, torn from a magazine. For years it's been there, inscrutable, and suddenly I feel certain that it carries a secret. About love maybe. About the possessed feeling I have because of Roy.

It says *And human speech is but a cracked kettle upon which we tap crude rhythms for bears to dance to, while we long to make music that —*

Next to the scrap is a sticker of mine, of a green apple.

I look again at the quote: the bears, the kettle.

Silly, I decide. It's all very silly. I start to dry my feet with a towel.

For the impending McDonald's Saturday I resolve to walk right past my $_{55}$ tattooed crush. I'll have nothing to do with him, with his hi little sexys. This denouncement is actually extraordinarily painful since Roy alone is now my whole world. Everything that came before — my coin collection in the Tupperware, the corrugated cardboard trim on school bulletin boards, the terror of the fire pole — now revealed supremely childish and vain. Without even deciding to, I have left all that and now must leave Roy too. I commit to enduring the burden of the universe alone. The universe with its mysterious General Rommels, its heady straits of Bosporus. I resolve to suffer.

Saturday comes again. My mom has already taken the burner covers off the stove and set them in the sink. I'm anxious, like branches shaking in wind, and I'm trying the think-about-the-Medieval-Fair trick. I picture the ducks at the duck pond, the way they waddle right up and snatch the bread slice right out of my hand. I focus on the fair — knowing that time will move forward in that way, eventually waddle forward to the next weekend.

Buckling myself into the front seat of our yellow Pinto I put an imitation Life Saver under my tongue, a blue one. When my dad walks in front of the car on the way to the driver's side, I notice that he has slouchy shoulders. Horrible. Not his shoulders, but my noticing them.

"I love you," I say to my dad. He laughs and says that's good. I sit there hating myself a little.

I concentrate on my candy, on letting it be there, letting it do its exquisitely slow melt under my tongue. Beautiful. I keep that same candy the whole car ride over, through stop signs, waiting for a kid on a Bigwheel to cross, past the Conoco, with patience during the long wait for the final left turn. In my pocket I have more candies. Most of a roll of wild berry. When I move my tongue just a tiny bit, the flavor, the sugary slur, assaults my sensations. I choke on a little bit of saliva.

When we enter I sense Roy at our left; I walk on the far side of my dad, hoping 60 to hide in his shadow. In a hoarse whisper I tell my dad that I'll go save our table and that he should order me the milk and the cookies.

"Okay," he whispers back, winking, as if this is some spy game I am playing.

At the table I stare straight ahead at the molded plastic bench, summoning all my meager power to keep from looking feverishly around. I think I sense Roy's blond hair off in the distance to my left. I glimpse to the side, but see just a potted plant.

"How's the coffee?" I ask after my dad has settled in across from me.

He shrugs his ritual shrug but no words except the question of how is your milk. Is he mad at me? As I begin dipping my cookies with a kind of anguish, I answer that the milk is delicious.

Why do we say these little things? I wonder. Why do I always want the 65 McDonaldland butter cookies and never the chocolate chip? It seems creepy to me suddenly, all the habits and ways of the heart I have that I didn't choose for myself.

I throw back three half-and-halfs.

"Will you get me some more half-and-halfs?" my dad asks.

He asks nicely. And he is really reading the paper while I am not. Of course I'm going to go get creamers. I'm a kid, I remember. He's my dad. All this comes quickly into focus, lines sharp, like feeling the edges of a sticker on paper.

"I don't feel well," I try.

"Really?"                                                                          70

"I mean I feel fine," I say getting out of the chair.

Roy. Taking a wild berry candy from my pocket I resolve again to focus on a candy under my tongue instead of on him. I head first toward the back wall, darting betwixt and between the tables with their attached swiveling chairs. This is the shiniest cleanest place in town, that's what McDonald's was like back then. Even the corners and crevices are clean. It's strange to me in that way. Our house — even after my mom cleans, it's all still in disarray. I'll unfold a blanket and there'll be a stray sock inside. Behind the toilet there's blue lint. That's what makes a home, I think, its special type of mess.

And then I'm at the front counter. I don't look up.

I stand off to the side since I'm not really ordering anything, just asking for a favor, not paying for milk but asking for creamers. Waiting to be noticed, I stare down at the brushed steel counter with its flattering hazy reflection and then it appears, he appears. I see first his palm, reflected in the steel. Then I see his knuckles, the hairs on the back of his hand, the lattice tattoo, the starched shirt cuff that is the beginning of hiding all the rest of the tattoo that I can't see.

Beautiful.                                                                                      75

A part of me decides I am taking him back into my heart. Even if no room will be left for anything else.

Roy notices me. He leans way down, eyes level with my sweaty curls stuck against my forehead, at the place where I know I have my birthmark — a dark brown mole there above my left eyebrow — and he says, his teeth showing, his strange glowing white canine showing — "D'ya need something?" He taps my nose with his finger.

That candy — I had forgotten about it, and I move my tongue and the flavor — it all comes rushing out, overwhelming, and I drool a little bit as I blurt out, "I'm going to the Medieval Fair next weekend." I wipe my wet lips with the back of my hand and see the wild-berry blue saliva staining there.

"Cool," he says, straightening up, and he interlaces his fingers and pushes them outward and they crack deliciously, and I think about macadamias. I think I see him noticing the blue smeared on my right hand. He then says to me: "I love those puppets they sell there — those real plain wood ones."

I just stare at Roy's blue eyes. I love blue eyes. Still to this day I am always  80
telling myself that I don't like them, that I find them lifeless and dull and that I prefer brown eyes, like mine, like my parents', but it's a lie. It's a whole other wilder type of love that I feel for these blue-eyed people of the world. So I look up at him, at those blue eyes, and I'm thinking about those plain wooden puppets — this is all half a second — then the doors open behind me and that invasive heat enters and the world sinks down, mud and mush and the paste left behind by cookies.

"Oh," I say. "Half-and-half."

He reaches into a tray of much-melted ice and bobbing creamers and he hands three to me. My palm burns where he touched me and my vision is blurry; only the grooves on the half-and-half container keep me from vanishing.

"Are you going to the fair?" I brave. Heat in my face again, the feeling just before a terrible rash. I'm already leaving the counter so as not to see those awful blue eyes and I hear, "Ah I'm workin'" and I don't even turn around.

I read the back of my dad's newspaper. They have found more fossils at the Spiro mounds. There's no explanation for how I feel.

How can I describe the days of the next week? I'd hope to see Roy when I ran  85
out to check the mail. I'd go drink from the hose in our front yard thinking he might walk or drive by, even though I had no reason to believe he might ever come to our neighborhood. I got detention for not turning in my book report of *The Yellow Wallpaper*. I found myself rummaging around in my father's briefcase, as if Roy's files — I imagined the yellow Confidential envelope from Clue — might somehow be there. Maybe I don't need to explain this because

who hasn't been overtaken by this monstrous shade of love? I remember walking home from school very slowly, anxiously, as if through foreign, unpredictable terrain. I wanted to buy Roy a puppet at the Medieval Fair. One of the wooden ones like he'd mentioned. Only in that thought could I rest. All the clutter of my mind was waiting to come closer to that moment of purchasing a puppet.

So I did manage to wake up in the mornings. I did try to go to sleep at night. Though my heart seemed to be racing to its own obscure rhythm, private even from me.

Friday night before the fair, hopeless for sleep — my bedroom seemed alien and lurksome — I pulled my maze workbook from the shelf and went into the brightly lit bathroom. I turned on the overhead fan so that it would become noisy enough to overwhelm the sound in my mind of Roy cracking his knuckles, again and again. The whirring fan noise — it was like a quiet. I sat in the empty tub, set the maze book on the rounded ledge and purposely began on a difficult page. I worked cautiously, tracing ahead with my finger before setting pen to paper. This was pleasing, though out of the corner of my eye I saw the yellowed magazine fragment — *cracked kettle* — and it was like a ghost in the room with me, though its message, I felt sure — almost too sure considering that I didn't understand it — had nothing to do with me.

In the morning my mom found me there in the tub, like some passed-out drunk, my maze book open on my small chest. I felt like crying, didn't even know why. I must have fallen asleep there. I reached up to my face, wondering if something had gone wrong with it.

"Do you have a fever?" my mom asked.

It must have seemed like there had to be an explanation. When she left, 90 assured, somewhat, I tried out those words — *Human speech is like a cracked kettle* — like they were the coded answer to a riddle.

I was always that kind of kid who crawled into bed with her parents, who felt safe only with them. If my mom came into my classroom because I had forgotten my lunch at home, I wasn't ashamed like other kids were, but proud. For a few years of my life, up until then, my desires hadn't chased away from me. I wanted to fall asleep on the sofa while my dad watched *The Twilight Zone* and so I did. I wanted couscous with butter and so I had some. Yes, sometimes shopping with my mom I coveted a pair of overalls or a frosted cookie, but the want would be faint and fade as soon as we'd walked away.

I had always loved the Medieval Fair. A woman would dress up in an elaborate mermaid costume and sit under the bridge that spanned the artificial pond. I thought she was beautiful. People tossed quarters down at her. She'd flap her tail, wave coyly. It wasn't until years later that I realized that she was considered trashy.

Further on there was a stacked hay maze that had already become too easy by late elementary school but I liked looking at it from a distance, from up on the small knoll. I think every turn you might take was fine. Whichever way you went you still made it out. I remember it being upsetting, being spat out so soon.

We had left the house uncleaned when we went to the fair that Saturday. I was thinking about the wooden puppet but I felt obligated to hope for a crown; that's what I was supposed to be pining for. I imagined that my mom would think to buy me a crown for my Queen Esther costume. But maybe, I hoped, she would forget all about the crown. It wasn't unlikely. What seemed like the world to me often revealed itself, through her eyes, to be nothing.

We saw the dress-up beggar with the prosthetic nose and warts. We crossed 95 the bridge, saw the mermaid. A pale teenage boy in stonewashed jeans and a tank top leaned against the bridge's railing, smoking, and looking down at her. Two corseted women farther along sang bawdy ballads in the shade of a willow and while we listened a slouchy man went by with a gigantic foam mallet. The whole world, it seemed, was laughing or fighting or crying or unfolding chairs or blending smoothies and this would go on until time immemorial. Vendors sold wooden flutes, Jacob's ladders. The smell of funnel cakes and sour mystery saturated the air. In an open field two ponies and three sheep were there for the petting and the overseer held a baby pig in his hands. We ate fresh ears of boiled corn, smothered with butter and cracked pepper. My mom didn't mention the price. That really did make it feel like a day in some other me's life.

But I felt so unsettled. Roy's tooth in my mind as I bit into the corn, Roy's fingers on my palm as I thrummed my hand along a low wooden fence. I had so little of Roy and yet he had all of me and the feeling ran deep, deep to the most ancient parts of me. So deep that in some way I felt that my love for Roy shamed my people, whoever my people were, whomever I was queen of, people I had never met, nervous people and sad people and dead people, all clambering for air and space inside of me. I didn't even know what I wanted from Roy. I still don't. All my life love has felt like a croquet mallet to the head. Something absurd, ready for violence. Love.

I remember once years later, in a love fit, stealing cherry Luden's cough drops from a convenience store. I had the money to pay for them but I stole them instead. I wanted a cheap childish cherry flavor on my tongue when I saw my love, who of course isn't my love anymore. That painful pathetic euphoria. Low-quality cough drops. That's how I felt looking around anxiously for the wooden puppet stand, how I felt looking twice at every blond man who passed, wondering if he might somehow be Roy, there for me, even though he'd said he wouldn't be there. Thinking about that puppet for Roy eclipsed all other thoughts, put a slithery veil over the whole day. How much would the puppet cost? I didn't have my own pocket money, an allowance or savings or anything like that. I wasn't in the habit of asking for things. I never asked for toys. I never asked for sugar cereals. I felt to do so was wrong. I had almost cried that one day just whispering to myself about the crown. But all I wanted was that puppet because that puppet was going to solve everything.

At the puppet stand I lingered. I was hoping that one of my parents would take notice of the puppets, pick one up. My dad, standing a few paces away, stood out from the crowd in his button-up shirt. He looked weak, sunbeaten. My mom was at my side, her arms crossed across an emergency orange tank top. It struck me, maybe for the first time, that they came to this fair just for me.

"I've never wanted anything this much in my whole life," I confessed in a rush, my hand on the unfinished wood of one of the puppets. "I want this more than a crown."

My mom laughed at me, or at the puppet. "But it's so ugly," she said, in Hebrew. 100

"That's not true," I whispered furiously, feeling as if everything had fallen silent, as if the ground beneath me was shifting. The vendor must surely have understood my mom, by her tone alone. I looked over at him: a fat bearded man talking to a long-haired barefoot princess. He held an end of her dusty hair distractedly; his other hand he had inside the collar of his shirt. He was sweating.

"*Drek*." My mom shrugged. Junk.

"Grouch," I broke out, like a tree root heaving through soil. "You don't like anything," I almost screamed, there in the bright sun. "You never like anything at all." My mother turned her back to me. I sensed the ugly vendor turn our way.

"I'll get it for you," my dad said, suddenly right with us. There followed an awkward argument between my parents, which seemed only to heighten my dad's pleasure in taking out his rust-stained wallet, in standing his ground, in being, irrevocably, on my side.

His alliance struck me as misguided, pathetic, even childish. I felt like a vil- 105 lain. We bought the puppet.

That dumb puppet — I carried it around in its wrinkly green plastic bag. For some reason I found myself haunted by the word *leprosy*. When we watched the minstrel show in the little outdoor amphitheater I tried to forget the green bag under the bench. We only made it a few steps before my mom noticed it was gone. She went back and fetched it.

At home I noticed that the wood of one of the hands of the puppet was cracked. That wasn't the only reason I couldn't give the puppet to Roy. Looking at that mute piece of wood I saw something. A part of me that I'd never chosen, that I would never control. I went to the bathroom, turned on the loud fan, and cried, feeling angry, useless, silly. An image of Roy came to my mind, particularly of that tooth. I felt my love falling off, dissolving.

He was my first love, my first love in the way that first loves are usually second or third or fourth loves. I still think about a stranger in a green jacket across from me at the waiting room at the DMV. About a blue-eyed man with a singed earlobe whom I saw at a Baskin-Robbins with his daughter. My first that kind of love. I never got over him. I never get over anyone.

## FOR ANALYSIS

**1.** How old is the **narrator** when the events in the story occur? How old is she when she tells this story about them? Is there a difference between how she felt at the time these events happened and how she feels about them at the time she tells the story?

**2.** From where does Galchen get the title for her story? What resonance does it have?

## MAKING ARGUMENTS

In paragraph 55, the narrator resolves to live the rest of her life alone rather than live with the "possessed feeling" she has because of her crush (para. 50). Does the story support or refute the idea that she would be better off alone?

## WRITING TOPICS

1. Write about a memory of your early years. What details stand out — what sensory images, what facts about place and time, what sense of your feelings and thoughts? Are there connections between this memory and how you think of yourself now?

2. Have you ever been to a fair — a county or state fair, a Medieval or Renaissance festival? If so, write an account of it that tries to capture the experience. If not, imagine what the experience might be like. What aspects of the experience stand out? What makes it different from regular daily life? How is it similar?

## MAKING CONNECTIONS

1. Compare the **tone** in "Araby" and "Wild Berry Blue." How would you characterize each in terms of humor? What does the use or lack of humor tell us about the way each story handles the significance that the adult **narrator** attaches to childhood experience?

2. Carefully examine the language of paragraph 5 of "Araby" (p. 122). What **stylistic** devices allow the narrator to transform a simple shopping trip into a chivalric romance? Can you find a passage in "Wild Berry Blue" in which Galchen uses style to transform her equally everyday setting and situation into something seemingly more significant or more grand?

3. Compare the endings of these two stories. How do the two narrators think of themselves? How do you think these pictures of their past selves relate to their sense of themselves in the present?

# CASE STUDY IN ARGUMENT

## FINDING GRACE IN FLANNERY O'CONNOR

The fiction of Flannery O'Connor has become famous to readers for the darkness of its vision, for its vivid picture of the Southern grotesque, for its sharp humor, and for its unyielding religious undergirding. Her fiction has also become famous to critics not only for its excellence and power but also for the critical conundrums it introduces. Those who try to teach or write about O'Connor's work find very quickly that there are tensions in her work that translate into tensions between different arguments about exactly what the work is up to. Readers and critics are further vexed by the fact that O'Connor often offered her own interpretations of her stories (see her comments from *Mystery and Manners* about "A Good Man Is Hard to Find" on p. 137), though this did not always go over smoothly, as the essays in this casebook from Bob Dowell, Hallman B. Bryant, and Michael Clark will attest.

As you read "A Good Man Is Hard to Find," keep in mind the fact that these long-running arguments over O'Connor's stories exist, and that in thinking further after your first reading, you will be well-served to keep your mind open to the possibility of multiple interpretations — and to laughing at what might seem at first like some pretty dark stuff.

## FLANNERY O'CONNOR (1925–1964)

# A GOOD MAN IS HARD TO FIND 1953

The grandmother didn't want to go to Florida. She wanted to visit some of her connections in east Tennessee and she was seizing at every chance to change Bailey's mind. Bailey was the son she lived with, her only boy. He was sitting on the edge of his chair at the table, bent over the orange sports section of the *Journal.* "Now look here, Bailey," she said, "see here, read this," and she stood with one hand on her thin hip and the other rattling the newspaper at his bald head. "Here this fellow that calls himself The Misfit is aloose from the Federal Pen and headed toward Florida and you read here what it says he did to these people. Just you read it. I wouldn't take my children in any direction with a criminal like that aloose in it. I couldn't answer to my conscience if I did."

Bailey didn't look up from his reading so she wheeled around then and faced the children's mother, a young woman in slacks, whose face was as broad and innocent as a cabbage and was tied around with a green headkerchief that had two points on the top like a rabbit's ears. She was sitting on the sofa, feeding the baby his apricots out of a jar. "The children have been to Florida before," the old lady said. "You all ought to take them somewhere else for a change so they would see different parts of the world and be broad. They never have been to east Tennessee."

The children's mother didn't seem to hear her but the eight-year-old boy, John Wesley, a stocky child with glasses, said, "If you don't want to go to Florida, why dontcha stay at home?" He and the little girl, June Star, were reading the funny papers on the floor.

"She wouldn't stay at home to be queen for a day," June Star said without raising her yellow head.

"Yes and what would you do if this fellow, The Misfit, caught you?" the 5 grandmother asked.

"I'd smack his face," John Wesley said.

"She wouldn't stay at home for a million bucks," June Star said. "Afraid she'd miss something. She has to go everywhere we go."

"All right, Miss," the grandmother said. "Just remember that the next time you want me to curl your hair."

June Star said her hair was naturally curly.

The next morning the grandmother was the first one in the car, ready to go. 10 She had her big black valise that looked like the head of a hippopotamus in one corner, and underneath it she was hiding a basket with Pitty Sing, the cat, in it. She didn't intend for the cat to be left alone in the house for three days because he would miss her too much and she was afraid he might brush against one of the gas burners and accidentally asphyxiate himself. Her son, Bailey, didn't like to arrive at a motel with a cat.

She sat in the middle of the back seat with John Wesley and June Star on either side of her. Bailey and the children's mother and the baby sat in front and they left Atlanta at eight forty-five with the mileage on the car at 55890. The grandmother wrote this down because she thought it would be interesting to say how many miles they had been when they got back. It took them twenty minutes to reach the outskirts of the city.

The old lady settled herself comfortably, removing her white cotton gloves and putting them up with her purse on the shelf in front of the back window. The children's mother still had on slacks and still had her head tied up in a green kerchief, but the grandmother had on a navy blue straw sailor hat with a bunch of white violets on the brim and a navy blue dress with a small white dot in the print. Her collars and cuffs were white organdy trimmed with lace and at her neckline she had pinned a purple spray of cloth violets containing a sachet. In case of an accident, anyone seeing her dead on the highway would know at once that she was a lady.

She said she thought it was going to be a good day for driving, neither too hot nor too cold, and she cautioned Bailey that the speed limit was fifty-five miles an hour and that the patrolmen hid themselves behind billboards and small clumps of trees and sped out after you before you had a chance to slow down. She pointed out interesting details of the scenery: Stone Mountain; the blue granite that in some places came up to both sides of the highway; the brilliant red clay banks slightly streaked with purple; and the various crops that made rows of green lace-work on the ground. The trees were full of silver-white sunlight and the meanest of them sparkled. The children were reading comic magazines and their mother had gone back to sleep.

"Let's go through Georgia fast so we won't have to look at it much," John Wesley said.

"If I were a little boy," said the grandmother, "I wouldn't talk about my native 15 state that way. Tennessee has the mountains and Georgia has the hills."

"Tennessee is just a hillbilly dumping ground," John Wesley said, "and Georgia is a lousy state too."

"You said it," June Star said.

"In my time," said the grandmother, folding her thin veined fingers, "children were more respectful of their native states and their parents and everything else. People did right then. Oh look at the cute little pickaninny!" she said and pointed to a Negro child standing in the door of a shack. "Wouldn't that make a picture, now?" she asked and they all turned and looked at the little Negro out of the back window. He waved.

"He didn't have any britches on," June Star said.

"He probably didn't have any," the grandmother explained. "Little niggers in 20 the country don't have things like we do. If I could paint, I'd paint that picture," she said.

The children exchanged comic books.

The grandmother offered to hold the baby and the children's mother passed him over the front seat to her. She set him on her knee and bounced him and told him about the things they were passing. She rolled her eyes and screwed up her mouth and stuck her leathery thin face into his smooth bland one. Occasionally he gave her a faraway smile. They passed a large cotton field with five or six graves fenced in the middle of it, like a small island. "Look at the graveyard!" the grandmother said, pointing it out. "That was the old family burying ground. That belonged to the plantation."

"Where's the plantation?" John Wesley asked.

"Gone With the Wind," said the grandmother. "Ha. Ha."

When the children finished all the comic books they had brought, they 25 opened the lunch and ate it. The grandmother ate a peanut butter sandwich and an olive and would not let the children throw the box and the paper napkins out the window. When there was nothing else to do they played a game by choosing a cloud and making the other two guess what shape it suggested. John Wesley took one the shape of a cow and June Star guessed a cow and John Wesley said, no, an automobile, and June Star said he didn't play fair, and they began to slap each other over the grandmother.

The grandmother said she would tell them a story if they would keep quiet. When she told a story, she rolled her eyes and waved her head and was very dramatic. She said once when she was a maiden lady she had been courted by a Mr. Edgar Atkins Teagarden from Jasper, Georgia. She said he was a very good-looking man and a gentleman and that he brought her a watermelon every Saturday afternoon with his initials cut in it, E.A.T. Well, one Saturday, she said, Mr. Teagarden brought the watermelon and there was nobody at home and he left it on the front porch and returned in his buggy to Jasper, but she never got the watermelon, she said, because a nigger boy ate it when he saw the initials, E.A.T.! This story tickled John Wesley's funny bone and he giggled and giggled but June Star didn't think it was any good. She said she wouldn't marry a man that just brought her a watermelon on Saturday. The grandmother said she would have done well to marry Mr. Teagarden because he was a gentleman and had bought Coca-Cola stock when it first came out and that he had died only a few years ago, a very wealthy man.

They stopped at The Tower for barbecued sandwiches. The Tower was a part stucco and part wood filling station and dance hall set in a clearing outside of Timothy. A fat man named Red Sammy Butts ran it and there were signs stuck here and there on the building and for miles up and down the highway saying, TRY RED SAMMY'S FAMOUS BARBECUE. NONE LIKE FAMOUS RED SAMMY'S! RED SAM! THE FAT BOY WITH THE HAPPY LAUGH. A VETERAN! RED SAMMY'S YOUR MAN!

Red Sammy was lying on the bare ground outside The Tower with his head under a truck while a gray monkey about a foot high, chained to a small chinaberry tree, chattered nearby. The monkey sprang back into the tree and got on the highest limb as soon as he saw the children jump out of the car and run toward him.

Inside, The Tower was a long dark room with a counter at one end and tables at the other and dancing space in the middle. They all sat down at a board table next to the nickelodeon and Red Sam's wife, a tall burnt-brown woman with hair and eyes lighter than her skin, came and took their order. The children's mother put a dime in the machine and played "The Tennessee Waltz," and the grandmother said that tune always made her want to dance. She asked Bailey if he would like to dance but he only glared at her. He didn't have a naturally sunny disposition like she did and trips made him nervous. The grandmother's brown eyes were very bright. She swayed her head from side to side and pretended she was dancing in her chair. June Star said play something she could tap to so the children's mother put in another dime and played a fast number and June Star stepped out onto the dance floor and did her tap routine.

"Ain't she cute?" Red Sam's wife said, leaning over the counter. "Would you like to come be my little girl?"

"No I certainly wouldn't," June Star said. "I wouldn't live in a broken-down place like this for a million bucks!" and she ran back to the table.

"Ain't she cute?" the woman repeated, stretching her mouth politely.

"Aren't you ashamed?" hissed the grandmother.

Red Sam came in and told his wife to quit lounging on the counter and hurry up with these people's order. His khaki trousers reached just to his hip bones and his stomach hung over them like a sack of meal swaying under his shirt. He came over and sat down at a table nearby and let out a combination sigh and yodel. "You can't win," he said. "You can't win," and he wiped his sweating red face off with a gray handkerchief. "These days you don't know who to trust," he said. "Ain't that the truth?"

"People are certainly not nice like they used to be," said the grandmother.     35

"Two fellers come in here last week," Red Sammy said, "driving a Chrysler. It was a old beat-up car but it was a good one and these boys looked all right to me. Said they worked at the mill and you know I let them fellers charge the gas they bought? Now why did I do that?"

"Because you're a good man!" the grandmother said at once.

"Yes'm, I suppose so," Red Sam said as if he were struck with this answer.

His wife brought the orders, carrying the five plates all at once without a tray, two in each hand and one balanced on her arm. "It isn't a soul in this green world of God's that you can trust," she said. "And I don't count nobody out of that, not nobody," she repeated, looking at Red Sammy.

"Did you read about that criminal, The Misfit, that's escaped?" asked the     40 grandmother.

"I wouldn't be a bit surprised if he didn't attack this place right here," said the woman. "If he hears about it being here, I wouldn't be none surprised to see him. If he hears it's two cent in the cash register, I wouldn't be a tall surprised if he. . . ."

"That'll do," Red Sam said. "Go bring these people their Co'-Colas," and the woman went off to get the rest of the order.

"A good man is hard to find," Red Sammy said. "Everything is getting terrible. I remember the day you could go off and leave your screen door unlatched. Not no more."

He and the grandmother discussed better times. The old lady said that in her opinion Europe was entirely to blame for the way things were now. She said the way Europe acted you would think we were made of money and Red Sam said it was no use talking about it, she was exactly right. The children ran outside into the white sunlight and looked at the monkey in the lacy chinaberry tree. He was busy catching fleas on himself and biting each one carefully between his teeth as if it were a delicacy.

They drove off again into the hot afternoon. The grandmother took cat     45 naps and woke up every few minutes with her own snoring. Outside of Toombsboro she woke up and recalled an old plantation that she had visited in this neighborhood once when she was a young lady. She said the house had six white columns across the front and that there was an avenue of oaks leading up to it and two little wooden trellis arbors on either side in front where you sat down with your suitor after a stroll in the garden. She recalled exactly which road to turn off to get to it. She knew that Bailey would not be willing to lose any time looking at an old house, but the more she talked about it, the more she wanted to see it once again and find out if the little twin arbors were still standing. "There was a secret panel in this house," she said craftily, not telling the truth but wishing that she were, "and the story went that all the family silver was hidden in it when Sherman[1] came through but it was never found. . . ."

"Hey!" John Wesley said. "Let's go see it! We'll find it! We'll poke all the woodwork and find it! Who lives there? Where do you turn off at? Hey Pop, can't we turn off there?"

"We never have seen a house with a secret panel!" June Star shrieked. "Let's go to the house with the secret panel! Hey Pop, can't we go see the house with the secret panel!"

"It's not far from here, I know," the grandmother said. "It won't take over twenty minutes."

Bailey was looking straight ahead. His jaw was as rigid as a horseshoe. "No," he said.

The children began to yell and scream that they wanted to see the house 50 with the secret panel. John Wesley kicked the back of the front seat and June Star hung over her mother's shoulder and whined desperately into her ear that they never had any fun even on their vacation, that they could never do what THEY wanted to do. The baby began to scream and John Wesley kicked the back of the seat so hard that his father could feel the blows in his kidney.

"All right!" he shouted and drew the car to a stop at the side of the road. "Will you all shut up? Will you all just shut up for one second? If you don't shut up, we won't go anywhere."

"It would be very educational for them," the grandmother murmured.

"All right," Bailey said, "but get this: this is the only time we're going to stop for anything like this. This is the one and only time."

"The dirt road that you have to turn down is about a mile back," the grandmother directed. "I marked it when we passed."

"A dirt road," Bailey groaned.                                                55

After they had turned around and were headed toward the dirt road, the grandmother recalled other points about the house, the beautiful glass over the front doorway and the candle-lamp in the hall. John Wesley said that the secret panel was probably in the fireplace.

"You can't go inside this house," Bailey said. "You don't know who lives there."

"While you all talk to the people in front, I'll run around behind and get in a window," John Wesley suggested.

"We'll all stay in the car," his mother said.

They turned onto the dirt road and the car raced roughly along in a swirl 60 of pink dust. The grandmother recalled the times when there were no paved roads and thirty miles was a day's journey. The dirt road was hilly and there were sudden washes in it and sharp curves on dangerous embankments. All at once they would be on a hill, looking down over the blue tops of trees for miles around, then the next minute, they would be in a red depression with the dust-coated trees looking down on them.

---

[1] William Tecumseh Sherman (1820–1891) was a Union Army general during the American Civil War.

"This place had better turn up in a minute," Bailey said, "or I'm going to turn around."

The road looked as if no one had traveled on it for months.

"It's not much farther," the grandmother said and just as she said it, a horrible thought came to her. The thought was so embarrassing that she turned red in the face and her eyes dilated and her feet jumped up, upsetting her valise in the corner. The instant the valise moved, the newspaper top she had over the basket under it rose with a snarl and Pitty Sing, the cat, sprang onto Bailey's shoulder.

The children were thrown to the floor and their mother, clutching the baby, was thrown out the door onto the ground; the old lady was thrown into the front seat. The car turned over once and landed right-side-up in a gulch off the side of the road. Bailey remained in the driver's seat with the cat — gray-striped with a broad white face and an orange nose — clinging to his neck like a caterpillar.

As soon as the children saw they could move their arms and legs, they 65 scrambled out of the car, shouting, "We've had an ACCIDENT!" The grandmother was curled up under the dashboard, hoping she was injured so that Bailey's wrath would not come down on her all at once. The horrible thought she had before the accident was that the house she had remembered so vividly was not in Georgia but in Tennessee.

Bailey removed the cat from his neck with both hands and flung it out the window against the side of a pine tree. Then he got out of the car and started looking for the children's mother. She was sitting against the side of the red gutted ditch, holding the screaming baby, but she only had a cut down her face and a broken shoulder. "We've had an ACCIDENT!" the children screamed in a frenzy of delight.

"But nobody's killed," June Star said with disappointment as the grandmother limped out of the car, her hat still pinned to her head but the broken front brim standing up at a jaunty angle and the violet spray hanging off the side. They all sat down in the ditch, except the children, to recover from the shock. They were all shaking.

"Maybe a car will come along," said the children's mother hoarsely.

"I believe I have injured an organ," said the grandmother, pressing her side, but no one answered her. Bailey's teeth were clattering. He had on a yellow sport shirt with bright blue parrots designed in it and his face was as yellow as the shirt. The grandmother decided that she would not mention that the house was in Tennessee.

The road was about ten feet above and they could see only the tops of the trees 70 on the other side of it. Behind the ditch they were sitting in there were more woods, tall and dark and deep. In a few minutes they saw a car some distance away on top of a hill, coming slowly as if the occupants were watching them. The grandmother stood up and waved both arms dramatically to attract their attention. The car continued to come on slowly, disappeared around a bend and appeared again, moving even slower, on top of the hill they had gone over. It was a big black battered hearse-like automobile. There were three men in it.

It came to a stop just over them and for some minutes, the driver looked down with a steady expressionless gaze to where they were sitting, and didn't speak. Then he turned his head and muttered something to the other two and they got out. One was a fat boy in black trousers and a red sweat shirt with a silver stallion embossed on the front of it. He moved around on the right side of them and stood staring, his mouth partly open in a kind of loose grin. The other had on khaki pants and a blue striped coat and a gray hat pulled down very low, hiding most of his face. He came around slowly on the left side. Neither spoke.

The driver got out of the car and stood by the side of it, looking down at them. He was an older man than the other two. His hair was just beginning to gray and he wore silver-rimmed spectacles that gave him a scholarly look. He had a long creased face and didn't have on any shirt or undershirt. He had on blue jeans that were too tight for him and was holding a black hat and a gun. The two boys also had guns.

"We've had an ACCIDENT!" the children screamed.

The grandmother had the peculiar feeling that the bespectacled man was someone she knew. His face was as familiar to her as if she had known him all her life but she could not recall who he was. He moved away from the car and began to come down the embankment, placing his feet carefully so that he wouldn't slip. He had on tan and white shoes and no socks, and his ankles were red and thin. "Good afternoon," he said. "I see you all had you a little spill."

"We turned over twice!" said the grandmother.                                    75

"Oncet," he corrected. "We seen it happen. Try their car and see will it run, Hiram," he said quietly to the boy with the gray hat.

"What you got that gun for?" John Wesley asked. "Whatcha gonna do with that gun?"

"Lady," the man said to the children's mother, "would you mind calling them children to sit down by you? Children make me nervous. I want all you all to sit down right together there where you're at."

"What are you telling US what to do for?" June Star asked.

Behind them the line of woods gaped like a dark open mouth. "Come here,"       80
said their mother.

"Look here now," Bailey said suddenly, "we're in a predicament! We're in. . . ."

The grandmother shrieked. She scrambled to her feet and stood staring. "You're The Misfit!" she said. "I recognized you at once!"

"Yes'm," the man said, smiling slightly as if he were pleased in spite of himself to be known, "but it would have been better for all of you, lady, if you hadn't of reckernized me."

Bailey turned his head sharply and said something to his mother that shocked even the children. The old lady began to cry and The Misfit reddened.

"Lady," he said, "don't you get upset. Sometimes a man says things he don't       85
mean. I don't reckon he meant to talk to you thataway."

"You wouldn't shoot a lady, would you?" the grandmother said and removed a clean handkerchief from her cuff and began to slap at her eyes with it.

The Misfit pointed the toe of his shoe into the ground and made a little hole and then covered it up again. "I would hate to have to," he said.

"Listen," the grandmother almost screamed, "I know you're a good man. You don't look a bit like you have common blood. I know you must come from nice people!"

"Yes mam," he said, "finest people in the world." When he smiled he showed a row of strong white teeth. "God never made a finer woman than my mother and my daddy's heart was pure gold," he said. The boy with the red sweat shirt had come around behind them and was standing with his gun at his hip. The Misfit squatted down on the ground. "Watch them children, Bobby Lee," he said. "You know they make me nervous." He looked at the six of them huddled together in front of him and he seemed to be embarrassed as if he couldn't think of anything to say. "Ain't a cloud in the sky," he remarked, looking up at it. "Don't see no sun but don't see no cloud neither."

"Yes, it's a beautiful day," said the grandmother. "Listen," she said, "you 90 shouldn't call yourself The Misfit because I know you're a good man at heart. I can just look at you and tell."

"Hush!" Bailey yelled. "Hush! Everybody shut up and let me handle this!" He was squatting in the position of a runner about to sprint forward but he didn't move.

"I pre-chate that, lady," The Misfit said and drew a little circle in the ground with the butt of his gun.

"It'll take a half a hour to fix this here car," Hiram called, looking over the raised hood of it.

"Well, first you and Bobby Lee get him and that little boy to step over yonder with you," The Misfit said, pointing to Bailey and John Wesley. "The boys want to ast you something," he said to Bailey. "Would you mind stepping back in them woods there with them?"

"Listen," Bailey began, "we're in a terrible predicament! Nobody realizes 95 what this is," and his voice cracked. His eyes were as blue and intense as the parrots in his shirt and he remained perfectly still.

The grandmother reached up to adjust her hat brim as if she were going to the woods with him but it came off in her hand. She stood staring at it and after a second she let it fall to the ground. Hiram pulled Bailey up by the arm as if he were assisting an old man. John Wesley caught hold of his father's hand and Bobby Lee followed. They went off toward the woods and just as they reached the dark edge, Bailey turned and supporting himself against a gray naked pine trunk, he shouted, "I'll be back in a minute, Mamma, wait on me!"

"Come back this instant!" his mother shrilled but they all disappeared into the woods.

"Bailey Boy!" the grandmother called in a tragic voice but she found she was looking at The Misfit squatting on the ground in front of her. "I just know you're a good man," she said desperately. "You're not a bit common!"

"Nome, I ain't a good man," The Misfit said after a second as if he had considered her statement carefully, "but I ain't the worst in the world neither. My daddy said I was a different breed of dog from my brothers and sisters. 'You know,' Daddy said, 'it's some that can live their whole life out without asking about it and it's others has to know why it is, and this boy is one of the latters. He's going to be into everything!'" He put on his black hat and looked up suddenly and then away deep into the woods as if he were embarrassed again. "I'm sorry I don't have on a shirt before you ladies," he said, hunching his shoulders slightly. "We buried our clothes that we had on when we escaped and we're just making do until we can get better. We borrowed these from some folks we met," he explained.

"That's perfectly all right," the grandmother said. "Maybe Bailey has an extra shirt in his suitcase." 100

"I'll look and see terrectly," The Misfit said.

"Where are they taking him?" the children's mother screamed.

"Daddy was a card himself," The Misfit said. "You couldn't put anything over on him. He never got in trouble with the Authorities though. Just had the knack of handling them."

"You could be honest too if you'd only try," said the grandmother. "Think how wonderful it would be to settle down and live a comfortable life and not have to think about somebody chasing you all the time."

The Misfit kept scratching in the ground with the butt of his gun as if he were thinking about it. "Yes'm, somebody is always after you," he murmured. 105

The grandmother noticed how thin his shoulder blades were just behind his hat because she was standing up looking down on him. "Do you ever pray?" she asked.

He shook his head. All she saw was the black hat wiggle between his shoulder blades. "Nome," he said.

There was a pistol shot from the woods, followed closely by another. Then silence. The old lady's head jerked around. She could hear the wind move through the tree tops like a long satisfied insuck of breath. "Bailey Boy!" she called.

"I was a gospel singer for a while," The Misfit said. "I been most everything. Been in the arm service, both land and sea, at home and abroad, been twict married, been an undertaker, been with the railroads, plowed Mother Earth, been in a tornado, seen a man burnt alive oncet," and he looked up at the children's mother and the little girl who were sitting close together, their faces white and their eyes glassy; "I even seen a woman flogged," he said.

"Pray, pray," the grandmother began, "pray, pray. . . ." 110

"I never was a bad boy that I remember of," The Misfit said in an almost dreamy voice, "but somewheres along the line I done something wrong and got sent to the penitentiary. I was buried alive," and he looked up and held her attention to him by a steady stare.

"That's when you should have started to pray," she said. "What did you do to get sent to the penitentiary that first time?"

"Turn to the right, it was a wall," The Misfit said, looking up again at the cloudless sky. "Turn to the left, it was a wall. Look up it was a ceiling, look down it was a floor. I forget what I done, lady. I set there and set there, trying to remember what it was I done and I ain't recalled it to this day. Oncet in a while, I would think it was coming to me, but it never come."

"Maybe they put you in by mistake," the old lady said vaguely.

"Nome," he said. "It wasn't no mistake. They had the papers on me."                    115

"You must have stolen something," she said.

The Misfit sneered slightly. "Nobody had nothing I wanted," he said. "It was a head-doctor at the penitentiary said what I had done was kill my daddy but I known that for a lie. My daddy died in nineteen ought nineteen of the epidemic flu and I never had a thing to do with it. He was buried in the Mount Hopewell Baptist churchyard and you can see for yourself."

"If you would pray," the old lady said, "Jesus would help you."

"That's right," The Misfit said.

"Well then, why don't you pray?" she asked trembling with delight suddenly.       120

"I don't want no hep," he said. "I'm doing all right by myself."

Bobby Lee and Hiram came ambling back from the woods. Bobby Lee was dragging a yellow shirt with bright blue parrots in it.

"Throw me that shirt, Bobby Lee," The Misfit said. The shirt came flying at him and landed on his shoulder and he put it on. The grandmother couldn't name what the shirt reminded her of. "No, lady," The Misfit said while he was buttoning it up, "I found out the crime don't matter. You can do one thing or you can do another, kill a man or take a tire off his car, because sooner or later you're going to forget what it was you done and just be punished for it."

The children's mother had begun to make heaving noises as if she couldn't get her breath. "Lady," he asked, "would you and that little girl like to step off yonder with Bobby Lee and Hiram and join your husband?"

"Yes, thank you," the mother said faintly. Her left arm dangled helplessly    125 and she was holding the baby, who had gone to sleep, in the other. "Hep that lady up, Hiram," The Misfit said as she struggled to climb out of the ditch, "and Bobby Lee, you hold onto that little girl's hand."

"I don't want to hold hands with him," June Star said. "He reminds me of a pig."

The fat boy blushed and laughed and caught her by the arm and pulled her off into the woods after Hiram and her mother.

Alone with The Misfit, the grandmother found that she had lost her voice. There was not a cloud in the sky nor any sun. There was nothing around her but woods. She wanted to tell him that he must pray. She opened and closed her mouth several times before anything came out. Finally she found herself saying, "Jesus, Jesus," meaning Jesus will help you, but the way she was saying it, it sounded as if she might be cursing.

"Yes'm," The Misfit said as if he agreed. "Jesus thown everything off balance. It was the same case with Him as with me except He hadn't committed any crime and they could prove I had committed one because they had the papers on me. Of course," he said, "they never shown me my papers. That's why I sign myself now. I said long ago, you get your signature and sign everything you do and keep a copy of it. Then you'll know what you done and you can hold up the crime to the punishment and see do they match and in the end you'll have something to prove you ain't been treated right. I call myself The Misfit," he said, "because I can't make what all I done wrong fit what all I gone through in punishment."

There was a piercing scream from the woods, followed closely by a pis-  130
tol report. "Does it seem right to you, lady, that one is punished a heap and another ain't punished at all?"

"Jesus!" the old lady cried. "You've got good blood! I know you wouldn't shoot a lady! I know you come from nice people! Pray! Jesus, you ought not to shoot a lady. I'll give you all the money I've got!"

"Lady," The Misfit said, looking beyond her far into the woods, "there never was a body that give the undertaker a tip."

There were two more pistol reports and the grandmother raised her head like a parched old turkey hen crying for water and called, "Bailey Boy, Bailey Boy!" as if her heart would break.

"Jesus was the only One that ever raised the dead," The Misfit continued, "and He shouldn't have done it. He thown everything off balance. If He did what He said, then it's nothing for you to do but thow away everything and follow Him, and if He didn't, then it's nothing for you to do but enjoy the few minutes you got left the best way you can — by killing somebody or burning down his house or doing some other meanness to him. No pleasure but mean- ness," he said and his voice had become almost a snarl.

"Maybe He didn't raise the dead," the old lady mumbled, not knowing what  135
she was saying and feeling so dizzy that she sank down in the ditch with her legs twisted under her.

"I wasn't there so I can't say He didn't," The Misfit said. "I wisht I had of been there," he said, hitting the ground with his fist. "It ain't right I wasn't there because if I had of been there I would of known. Listen lady," he said in a high voice, "if I had of been there I would of known and I wouldn't be like I am now." His voice seemed about to crack and the grandmother's head cleared for an instant. She saw the man's face twisted close to her own as if he were going to cry and she murmured, "Why you're one of my babies. You're one of my own children!" She reached out and touched him on the shoulder. The Misfit sprang back as if a snake had bitten him and shot her three times through the chest. Then he put his gun down on the ground and took off his glasses and began to clean them.

Hiram and Bobby Lee returned from the woods and stood over the ditch, looking down at the grandmother who half sat and half lay in a puddle of blood with her legs crossed under her like a child's and her face smiling up at the cloudless sky.

Without his glasses, The Misfit's eyes were red-rimmed and pale and defenseless-looking. "Take her off and thow her where you thown the others," he said, picking up the cat that was rubbing itself against his leg.

"She was a talker, wasn't she?" Bobby Lee said, sliding down the ditch with a yodel.

"She would of been a good woman," The Misfit said, "if it had been some- 140 body there to shoot her every minute of her life."

"Some fun!" Bobby Lee said.

"Shut up, Bobby Lee," The Misfit said. "It's no real pleasure in life."

## FOR ANALYSIS

1. From whose **point of view** is the story told — that is, through whose eyes do we see events unfold? What is the effect of O'Connor's choice of **narrator**?

2. How would you describe the **tone** of this story? Is it uniform, or does it vary? How? Why do you think O'Connor uses tone the way she does?

3. With whom do you identify in this story? One character, or more, or none? How do you think identification works in this story?

4. Describe this story's **setting**. Does it inform the **mood** or tone of the story? How?

## WRITING TOPICS

1. Compare and contrast The Misfit and the grandmother. Do they come to seem more different or more alike over the course of the story? In what ways?

2. The story's last line is The Misfit's: he says, "It's no real pleasure in life" (para. 142). While "A Good Man Is Hard to Find" is a sad, violent story, there is pleasure in reading it. Write about some of these pleasures. How do you reconcile them with the story's darkness?

## MAKING CONNECTIONS

1. Hawthorne's "Young Goodman Brown" (p. 79) and "A Good Man Is Hard to Find" are both in part about religious belief, though they are of course very different stories. In what do the main characters — Brown, The Misfit, and the grandmother — believe, and not believe?

2. An important line in Bambara's "The Lesson" (p. 100) comes near the end: " 'Anybody else learn anything today?' " (para. 52). "The Lesson" is more obviously a story of education, but in what way is "A Good Man Is Hard to Find" also one? What character learns a lesson in the story? What is the lesson? "The Lesson" ends with the **narrator** reflecting on the impact of her lesson. What is the impact of the lesson in O'Connor's story?

# FROM MYSTERY AND MANNERS    1963

It is true that the old lady is a hypocritical old soul; her wits are no match for the Misfit's, nor is her capacity for grace equal to his; yet I think the unprejudiced reader will feel that the Grandmother has a special kind of triumph in this story which instinctively we do not allow to someone altogether bad.

I often ask myself what makes a story work and what makes it hold up as a story, and I have decided that it is probably some action, some gesture of a character that is unlike any other in the story, one which indicates where the real heart of the story lies. This would have to be an action or a gesture which was both totally right and totally unexpected; it would have to be one that was both in character and beyond character; it would have to suggest both the world and eternity. The action or gesture I'm talking about would have to be on the anagogical level, that is, the level which has to do with the Divine life and our participation in it. It would be a gesture that transcended any neat allegory that might have been intended or any pat moral categories a reader could make. It would be a gesture which somehow made contact with mystery.

There is a point in this story where such a gesture occurs. The Grandmother is at last alone, facing the Misfit. Her head clears for an instant and she realizes, even in her limited way, that she is responsible for the man before her and joined to him by ties of kinship which have their roots deep in the mystery she has been merely prattling about so far. And at this point, she does the right thing, she makes the right gesture.

I find that students are often puzzled by what she says and does here, but I think myself that if I took out this gesture and what she says with it, I would have no story. What was left would not be worth your attention. Our age not only does not have a very sharp eye for the almost imperceptible intrusions of grace, it no longer has much feeling for the nature of the violences which precede and follow them. The devil's greatest wile, Baudelaire has said, is to convince us that he does not exist.

I suppose the reasons for the use of so much violence in modern fiction will 5 differ with each writer who uses it, but in my own stories I have found that violence is strangely capable of returning my characters to reality and preparing them to accept their moment of grace. Their heads are so hard that almost nothing else will do the work. This idea, that reality is something to which we must be returned at considerable cost, is one which is seldom understood by the casual reader, but it is one which is implicit in the Christian view of the world.

I don't want to equate the Misfit with the devil. I prefer to think that, however unlikely this may seem, the old lady's gesture, like the mustard-seed, will grow to be a great crow-filled tree in the Misfit's heart and will be enough of a pain to him there to turn him into the prophet he was meant to become. But that's another story.

This story has been called grotesque, but I prefer to call it literal. A good story is literal in the same sense that a child's drawing is literal. When a child draws, he doesn't intend to distort but to set down exactly what he sees, and as his gaze is direct, he sees the lines that create motion. Now the lines of motion that interest the writer are usually invisible. They are lines of spiritual motion. And in this story you should be on the lookout for such things as the action of grace in the Grandmother's soul, and not for the dead bodies.

## MAKING CONNECTIONS

**1.** How do you understand O'Connor's description of the grandmother's "gesture" as being about grace? Does your interpretation of the story change if you read it as being about a literal moment of salvation?

**2.** Do you read the story differently than O'Connor does? Is her interpretation helpful? What does it mean about how literature works that a reader can disagree with a writer about her own work?

**BOB DOWELL**   (B. 1932)

# FROM THE MOMENT OF GRACE IN THE FICTION OF FLANNERY O'CONNOR   1965

Flannery O'Connor revealed, on more than one occasion, her concern about the public's misconstruing of the meaning of her fiction. She was perturbed by certain critics placing her in the School of Southern Degeneracy, and she was insulted by others placing her in the Southern Gothic School. "Degeneracy," she said, "at least can be taken in a moral sense," for it suggests a standard to degenerate from; but "the Gothic is a degeneracy which is not recognized as such" (L).

In a lecture entitled "Some Aspects of the Grotesque in Southern Literature,"[1] delivered at East Texas State University in the fall of 1962, Miss O'Connor seemed to answer misdirected criticism of her fiction by giving a general explanation of what she was attempting as a writer. Although in this lecture Miss O'Connor generally speaks collectively of Southern writers, she seems to be primarily explaining her own "poetics." Commenting on her grotesque characters, she concludes that the public views these protagonists as freaks and, "with its clinical bias invariably approaches them from the standpoint of abnormal psychology" (L). Such a view obviously annoys the author, for her own view of man is unmistakably theological, and in commenting on the milieu from which her characters are drawn she says that "in the South the general conception of man is still, in the main, theological" (L). The South is hardly Christ-centered, she explains, but "it is most certainly Christ-haunted" (L). Needless to say, psychological explanations for the compulsions of her characters will hardly suffice.

A perusal of Miss O'Connor's fiction will reveal that Christ-haunted figures furnish the author her principal subject matter. Through the conflicts, often violent ones, of these protagonists who oscillate between belief and unbelief, between self-will and submission, the author presents her view of reality. This

---

[1] References to this lecture are indicated in the text as follows: (L).

grotesque drama that she presents takes place in a discernible theological framework in which there is an implicit acceptance of the concept of a created universe, "with all that implies of human limitations and human obligations to an all-powerful Creator" (L). Such a view heightens man's every action, for his every action is seen "under the aspect of eternity" (L). Thus, Miss O'Connor's fiction is primarily concerned with man's life-and-death spiritual struggle. The protagonist, rebelling against belief, forces a crisis that reveals to him his haughty and willful misconception of reality, at which time he experiences what Miss O'Connor has called his "moment of grace." Without exception this moment comes at great price.

The grandmother in "A Good Man Is Hard to Find" experiences her moment of grace only seconds before the Misfit murders her by firing three bullets through her chest. "A Good Man Is Hard to Find" was my introduction to Flannery O'Connor, and I must admit that after considerable reflection on the story, I was still somewhat puzzled by the whole thing and particularly by the grandmother's final remark to the Misfit. As if confessing, she says, "Why you're one of my babies. You're one of my own children" [para. 136]. Upon being questioned about this passage, Miss O'Connor explained that this was the grandmother's "moment of grace."

Such an explanation makes sense only in a theological framework. The 5 Misfit's meanness is the result of his inability to believe. If Christ does exist and can raise the dead, says the Misfit, "then it's nothing for you to do but throw away everything and follow Him, and if He didn't, then it's nothing for you to do but enjoy the few minutes you got left the best way you can — by killing somebody or burning down his house or doing some other meanness to him. No pleasure but meanness" [para. 134]. Because he cannot believe, the Misfit commits himself to evil. The grandmother recognizes him as one of her own children because she suddenly realizes that her superficial commitment to good has been meaningless because she lived without faith, that is to say without Christ. By rejecting Christ, man usurps that place for himself, thereby committing the final disobedience to his Creator. In the O'Connor world whether one commits himself to evil deeds or good deeds makes little difference ultimately, for without Christ one's actions only lead to evil.

"A Good Man Is Hard to Find" dramatizes this theological view. Although it is the Misfit who has the grandmother's family killed and then kills the grandmother himself, it is the grandmother who causes the wreck that places the family at the mercy of the Misfit. It is also the grandmother who identifies the Misfit, thus causing him to deem it necessary to do away with the family for his own safety. [. . .]

Though willing to exploit his unwilling antics, Miss O'Connor never loses sight of man as a created being whose soul is precious to his Creator. Despite his ignorance, his rebelliousness, and his tendency toward evil, man still realizes his fullest potential by participating in a supernatural relation with his Creator. This depends upon his recognition of the existence of evil, of his own tendency toward evil, and his ability to triumph over evil through grace, a supernatural gift from God which comes only with man's full realization of his lost condition and his dependence on Christ. With this realization, which constitutes his moment of grace, man's salvation is begun; he can then begin to fulfill the purpose of his existence, which is to reflect the goodness of his Creator and to share the happiness of heaven with Him. This is Miss O'Connor's view of ultimate reality. [. . .]

Miss O'Connor sought to give new life to what she believed to be significant religious truths that were once a living reality but which the modern mind has tended to either distort or reject. Her stories, which are in a sense grotesque parables, dramatize the existence of evil. Satan's greatest triumph, her works seem to suggest, lies in the fact that he has convinced the world that he does not exist. But for Miss O'Connor he does exist. The backwoods fanatics who either believe he exists or at least are preoccupied with the possibility of his existence may seem ludicrously grotesque to most readers. Yet Miss O'Connor gives serious treatment to these grotesques because their concerns are her concerns. In their defense, she has publicly stated that "their fanaticism is a reproach, not simply an eccentricity. Those who, like Amos or Jeremiah, embrace a neglected truth will be seen to be the most grotesque of all" (L). The conflict between grace and evil in the lives of her characters reflects for the author the most significant drama in the realm of human experience.

## MAKING CONNECTIONS

1. With his "Thus" (para. 3), Dowell makes a claim about O'Connor's fiction. Do you find the evidence that leads up to it convincing? What assumptions about what a story means or is concerned with underlie his claim? What differing assumptions might undermine his claim?

2. Dowell cites O'Connor's distinction between theological and psychological explanations for her **characters**' motivations. Reflect on this distinction. Do you think it is helpful? What psychological motivations would you ascribe to the characters in "A Good Man Is Hard to Find"?

## HALLMAN B. BRYANT    (B. 1936)

# READING THE MAP IN "A GOOD MAN IS HARD TO FIND"    1981

Flannery O'Connor, remarking on her most famous short story, "A Good Man Is Hard to Find," issues several caveats to critics. She allows that "a certain amount of what is the significance of this" kind of investigation has to go on in teaching and in literary analysis, but she cautions against reducing a story to "a problem to be solved" so that it becomes "something which you evaporate to get Instant Enlightenment."

Without evaporating too much I will try to shed light on the significance of some small details in "A Good Man Is Hard to Find." Although I do not think an analysis of O'Connor's use of place names in the story will create instant enlightenment, I believe that the towns alluded to along the route which the family travels were chosen for two reasons: first, and most obviously, to foreshadow; and second, to augment the theme of the story. Furthermore, because the numerous places mentioned in the story can actually be found on the map, with only one important exception, it is thus possible to estimate within a few miles the physical distance that the family travels.

The first thing one notices about "A Good Man Is Hard to Find" is that it is set in a real place — in the state of Georgia. The opening scene describes an Atlanta family quarreling about their vacation plans. The grandmother is opposed to going to Florida ostensibly because a convict "that calls himself The Misfit is aloose from the Federal pen and headed toward Florida." (Apparently the Federal penitentiary from which The Misfit has escaped is the one in Atlanta, although it is not specified in the story.) Regardless of the threat posed by The Misfit, the family heads south for Florida instead of east Tennessee where the grandmother had tried to persuade them to take her. We are told that the family left Atlanta at 8:35 in the morning with the mileage on the car at 55890, a fact recorded by the grandmother because she "thought it would be interesting to say how many miles they had been when they got back." From this point on one can literally follow the journey of the family with a road map and take the mileage they put on their car before the wreck and the subsequent meeting with The Misfit and his henchmen.

One odd fact about their route emerges immediately to anyone familiar with Atlanta and its environs. Although the family lives in Atlanta and is headed south, we are told that they pass Stone Mountain along the way. This natural phenomenon and tourist attraction is about fifteen or sixteen miles from Atlanta on the northeast side of the city. At the time the story was written, one had to follow U.S. 78 North to get to Stone Mountain, a highly unlikely road to take out of Atlanta if one is going to Florida.[1]

---

[1] The detour by Stone Mountain was probably due to O'Connor's uncertainty about its exact location; she simply found it a convenient allusion since Stone Mountain was for years Georgia's most famous tourist attraction, but perhaps there is more than meets the eye. In 1915 a project was begun by the United Daughters of the Confederacy which called for Robert E. Lee and his lieutenants to be carved in heroic scale on the vertical face of the mountain. Ironically, the artist commissioned for the job was a Yankee sculptor named Gutzon Borglum who blasted and chiseled on the mountain until 1928 when funds and patience ran out. After expenditure of hundreds of thousands of dollars in a vain effort to impose the heroes of the "Lost Cause" on the side of the mountain, the project was dropped. The scarred carvings, empty catwalks and scaffolds were reminders of a long series of errors and frustrations of the U.D.C. ladies who dreamed of keeping the past alive with a memorial that would be "the perpetuation of a vision." (See *The Story of Stone Mountain* by Willard Neal [Atlanta: Neal and Rogers, 1963], 23–33). Flannery O'Connor was amused by the quixotic qualities of the U.D.C., and Stone Mountain would evoke for Georgians of O'Connor's generation the folly of a sentimental project — a project almost as futile as the grandmother's in the story, whose fascination with past grandeur is congruent with that of the U.D.C.'s and has equally unfortunate results.

Although one of the children urges his father to "go through Georgia fast 5 so we won't have to look at it much," there nevertheless are some interesting details of scenery along the roadside, and the grandmother tells us about many of the things they pass by. She notices "a cute little pickaninny" standing in the door of a shanty that she fancies would make a nice study for a sentimental painting, but the same subject disgusts her granddaughter June Star, who comments acidly, "He didn't have any britches on." More significantly, the grandmother points out a graveyard with five or six graves fenced off in the middle of a large cotton field, which is a rather obvious foreshadowing of the fate that will befall the family.

When the grandmother can no longer hold the children's attention with roadside attractions, she tells them a story of one of her girlhood suitors, Mr. Edgar Atkins Teagarden, who was from Jasper, Georgia, a small north Georgia town located in Pickens County and approximately fifty or sixty miles from the Tennessee state line. Although we are not told just where the grandmother is from, only that she has "connections in east Tennessee," it seems that to be consistent with her tale of Mr. Teagarden's courtship, she would have to have lived somewhere near Jasper, since he drove to her house by buggy every Saturday and gave her a watermelon monogrammed with his initials, E. A. T.

The family's journey is interrupted by a stop for a lunch of barbecued sandwiches at a café called The Tower which is located in "a clearing outside of Timothy." For economic effect this is one of the great scenes in all of Flannery O'Connor's fiction; yet here one cannot plot the location of the place on the map for there is no town of Timothy in Georgia. (If there is, it is such a small community it is not listed in the state atlas.) Since the other references to places in the story are to actual localities in the state, why does she create a fictitious name at this point? My theory is that in this scene, which has strong moral intention, O'Connor selects the name Timothy for the ironic effect it would produce. The allusion here is not geographical but Biblical, and the Timothy alluded to is almost certainly the book in the New Testament which bears the same name. Usually referred to as the Pastoral Letters, this gospel purports to be letters from Paul addressed to his disciples and through them to the Christian community at large. More than any other writing in the New Testament, the letters to Timothy are concerned with Christian orthodoxy. In this gospel Paul deals essentially with three topics: the opposition of false doctrine; the organization of the church and establishment of ecclesiastical regulations; and exhortations which indicate how to be a good citizen and Christian.

It seems to me that the concerns expressed by Paul in his letter to Timothy are very germane to the concerns expressed by Flannery O'Connor in "A Good Man Is Hard to Find," especially the concern with heretics and the advice on how to be a good Christian. One has only to set the family of six from Atlanta and Red Sammy and his wife (as well as The Misfit) — all of whom Flannery O'Connor considers heretics — against certain passages from Timothy to see that O'Connor's allusion ironically tells us just where these modern-day people are in error. For example, these verses seem to apply especially to Bailey. "He [the husband] must manage his own family well and see that his children obey him with proper respect" (I Tim. 3:4–5).

Also the author of the epistle commands good Christians to keep the faith and avoid "vain discussions" and concern with trivial matters and endless wrangling about genealogies (I Tim. 6:3–10). Further, he admonishes women "to dress modestly, with decency and propriety" and "to learn in quietness and full submission . . . and be silent" (I Tim. 2:9–12). This instruction seems to bear most directly on the grandmother, who is vain about her Old South heritage and certainly conscious of her social standing and what is required to be a lady. This is best brought out in her selection of attire for the trip. She is turned out in white gloves, black purse, a navy blue straw sailor hat with white violets on the brim, a navy blue polka dot dress with collar and cuffs of white organdy trimmed with lace, and on her neck she has pinned a purple spray of cloth violets containing a sachet. Her costume has been prepared so that, in the event of an accident, "anyone seeing her dead on the highway would know at once that she was a lady."

The grandmother's superficial conception of values is ironically under- 10 scored in the vain discussions with her grandchildren about what kind of conduct was once expected from children and her trivial remarks about plantation days and old suitors. Nowhere are her ideas more tellingly satirized than in her conversation with Red Sammy in the café where both complain of misplaced trust in their fellow man, which the grandmother sees as an indication of the general lack of manners in the modern world. She tells Red Sammy, "People are certainly not nice like they used to be." Of course, both Red Sammy and the grandmother are conceited enough to think that they are just as good as they ought to be. When Red Sammy complains of a recent theft of some gasoline by men driving a Chrysler and asks in a puzzled way why he had trusted them, he is quickly told by the grandmother that it was "because you're a good man," to which he candidly assents, "Yes'm, I suppose so."

The grandmother's inability to "learn in quietness" is tragically the cause of the deaths of the entire family. Shortly after Bailey overturns the car in a ditch, they are approached by a bespectacled man who the grandmother feels is "someone she knew" and soon she recognizes the stranger as The Misfit whose picture she has seen, and she blurts out this fact, saying, "You're The Misfit . . . I recognized you at once," to which he replies, "but it would have been better for all of you, lady, if you hadn't of reckernized me."

It is generally agreed that in the traumatic moments that follow in which the grandmother witnesses the deaths of her family and anticipates her own she does learn a lesson she has not heeded previously during her life. This lesson is the central message which Paul attempts to convey to Christians through Timothy and that is, "There is one God and one mediator between God and men, the Lord Jesus Christ, who gave himself to save mankind" (I Tim. 2:5). The evidence for assuming that she has come to a belated awareness that her faith has been misplaced in the pursuit of social graces and a concern with manners is limited to The Misfit's remark, "She would of been a good woman . . . if it had been somebody there to shoot her every minute of her life." Furthermore, in death she appears like a child, and her face is "smiling up at the cloudless sky," suggesting that she has found grace at last.

Another passage from Timothy seems especially applicable at this point: "The Spirit clearly says that in later times some will abandon the faith and follow deceiving spirits and things taught by demons. Such teachings come through hypocritical liars, whose consciences have been seared as with hot iron" (I Tim. 4:1–12). Although the whole cast of characters in the story has abandoned the faith and followed the wrong paths, the indictment of these lines would apply most forcibly to The Misfit who wears glasses and has a scholarly look. He has indeed been taught by demons, and from the Christian point of view that O'Connor takes in "A Good Man Is Hard to Find" he is a hypocritical liar who has no faith in a moral purpose in the universe and teaches that "it's nothing for you to do but enjoy the few minutes you got left the best way you can — by killing somebody or burning down his house or doing some other meanness to him." Thus, according to the ethics of this teacher, goodness is a matter of sadistic gratification. "No pleasure but meanness," he says, indicating how completely his conscience has been seared and his vision warped by his hedonistic atheism.

The numerous ways in which the content of this book of the New Testament dovetails with the characters and the theme of "A Good Man Is Hard to Find" could not be a complete accident. It cannot be demonstrated that Flannery O'Connor conceived of the moral of her story in terms of this specific book, but she made no bones about the fact that she wrote "from the standpoint of Christian orthodoxy";[2] and there is no doubt that Paul wrote from a similar standpoint, and his letter to Timothy has the same hortatory, moralizing tone that we find just below the surface in "A Good Man Is Hard to Find." Thus, it seems likely that she put the town of Timothy on the map because she wanted the reader to pick up the allusion and perhaps [review] the contents of the New Testament, but more probably she saw the parallel between her modern-day characters who have left the main road of Christian faith and Paul's warning to the church when he feared it was in danger off into the byways of heresy.

Just as the name of the town where the family stops for lunch is carefully 15 chosen, so is the name of Red Sammy's café. In Christian iconography towers are ambivalent symbols, that is, they speak *in bono* or *in malo*, to use the vocabulary of medieval exegetes, and can represent either good or evil qualities. For example, the Tower of Babel is symbolic of man's pride and stands for misbegotten human enterprises. The fate of the tower and its architects shows the consequences of overconfidence in the pursuit of fanciful ideas. (Interestingly enough, Nimrod, who began the construction of the tower, was also a mighty hunter, and like Red Sammy, a keeper of wild game, if Red Sammy's monkey can be called wild.)

[2] *The Habit of Being: Letters of Flannery O'Connor*, ed. Sally Fitzgerald (New York: Farrar, 1979), 196.

As well as its nugatory meaning, the tower is a traditional symbol of the Virgin Mary and is a token of her purity and powers of transformation. Mary as the "refugee of sinners" according to Catholic doctrine is appropriately represented by the tower, a place associated with safety and sanctuary.

Outside of its Christian meaning the tower in arcane lore is a portent of disaster. In the sixteenth enigma of the Tarot pack of cards, catastrophe is indicated by the image of a tower struck by lightning. Whether O'Connor knew this fact about the meaning of the tower is uncertain, but she could not have been unaware of the former implications of the tower as a symbol, versed as she was in Biblical and church lore. It is appropriate that the conceited owner of this barbecue palace should have called it The Tower; it is ironic that this tower has no capacity to transform or give refuge.

Leaving Timothy and The Tower behind, both in the Biblical and geographical sense, the family [resume] their trip and we are told that just beyond Toombsboro, Georgia, the grandmother awakens from a nap with the recollection, mistaken as it turns out, that there is an old plantation nearby which she had visited as a girl; she even thinks she remembers the road to take to get there and tells Bailey, "It's not far from here, I know. . . . It wouldn't take over twenty minutes." As it so happens there is a Toomsboro (spelled without the "b") on the map and it is only twenty-three miles south of Milledgeville, Flannery O'Connor's home. She surely knew the place and chose to mention it because the name has an ominous ring, and it also would have been a logical terminus for the family's trip in terms of the time and distance they have traveled since leaving Atlanta in the morning. In fact, if one follows the usual route from Atlanta to Milledgeville (Georgia Highway 212), the distance is 93 miles, and if one adds to this the 23 miles further to Toomsboro, plus the estimated 15 or so miles that the detour to the plantation takes, then it can be calculated that the family has come a total of 130 miles. Considering the conditions of Georgia roads in the late 1940s, one had to drive under 50 m.p.h. to keep from knocking the wheels out of line from the numerous potholes that Governor Talmadge's highway people never patched. Thus, if one assumes that Bailey has averaged around 45 m.p.h. and takes account of the lunch stop, they have been on the road four or five hours and their meeting with The Misfit occurs in the early afternoon of a cloudless day with the mileage on the car standing at about 56020 on the meter. Sadly enough, the grandmother will be forever unaware of this "interesting fact," but we as readers should have a better understanding of how carefully O'Connor has used realistic detail for symbolic effects.

In the course of this story, the family's trip takes them from their complacent and smug living room to a confrontation with ultimate evil and ultimate reality as well. They are not prepared for the meeting because, like the heretics who concerned Paul in his epistle to Timothy, they have been occupied with the trivial things and involved in quarrels; and, like the builders of the Tower of Babel, they are preoccupied with vain enterprises.

Flannery O'Connor saw herself as a prophetic writer and her authorial strategy was to shock; her fiction is intended as a rebuke to rationalistic, materialistic, and humanistic thought — the heresies of the twentieth century. She believed that people in the modern world were not following the true path and had to be made to see their condition for what it was — a wandering by the wayside. In "A Good Man Is Hard to Find" the family's wayward lives are given direction in their final moments, and from O'Connor's point of view they are at last on the right road.

## MAKING CONNECTIONS

**1.** Bryant's "Reading the Map in 'A Good Man Is Hard to Find'" argues not simply for the significance of the journey taken in the story but for the significance of the place names, real and imagined. Compare his account of the story as meticulously constructed so as to imbed this significance to O'Connor's own account of a writer's activity as about discovering meaning as she goes along. Are these two kinds of journeys — one carefully planned, with a road atlas, the other a journey of discovery — reconcilable? If so, how?

**2.** Bryant takes "A Good Man Is Hard to Find" very seriously both as a carefully constructed narrative and as a spiritual and moral tale. Do you think it is possible to appreciate the story without reading it in this way? Why or why not?

## MICHAEL CLARK (1946–1999)

# FLANNERY O'CONNOR'S "A GOOD MAN IS HARD TO FIND": THE MOMENT OF GRACE 1991

"A Good Man Is Hard to Find" is one of Flannery O'Connor's most discussed and most problematic short stories. The major difficulty involves the story's climax. Should the grandmother's final act — her touching of The Misfit — be taken as a token of true, divine grace and spiritual insight? Or should the story be interpreted strictly as a naturalistic document? Perhaps the grandmother achieves no spiritual insight. One can find critics on both sides of the argument. Since the issue is central to O'Connor's work at large, it is worth further examination. While this question may ultimately be impossible to resolve with certainty, further light can be shed upon this critical gesture.

In *Mystery and Manners*, O'Connor asserts that the grandmother's final act is a "moment of grace." Critics, though, have not been convinced. While acknowledging Flannery O'Connor's reading, Madison Jones prefers to stress the "realistic explanation" of grace — a "naturalistic" grace which may be "spelled in lower case letters." Stanley Renner is also uncomfortable with the "religious" explanation and describes "the vague touch" on the Misfit's shoulder as "a parental blessing" or "the ceremonial dubbing of knighthood." Thus the grandmother's response not so much reflects divine grace as it "touches her almost instinctive springs of sympathy and human kinship." Leon Driskell and Joan Brittain seem to see the grandmother's final act not as a transcendent spiritual experience but as a "gesture of kinship," which comes from one whose "revelation, though limited, is adequate." And most recently, Kathleen Ochshorn has entered the fray in a most unequivocal manner, insisting that in "A Good Man Is Hard to Find" "a world of propriety and illusion is laid low by wrath, not redeemed by grace." Rather than seeing the grandmother's final act as an embodiment of spirituality, Ochshorn asserts that the touch expresses the grandmother's "final hope that her noblesse can alter her fate," an interpretation that renders the grandmother's final gesture as mundane, selfish, and in every sense unredeeming. These critical responses — especially Ochshorn's — are symptomatic of the reluctance to read the story in light of O'Connor's religious beliefs.

Should O'Connor's interpretation of the story be judged as wrong? Critics have an excellent authority for a subversive reading in D. H. Lawrence's well-known dictum: trust the tale, not the teller of the tale. Unless the tale itself can guide us in our interpretation, we are threatened with being like the people in Plato's cave, very inadequate interpreters of shadows on the wall. But there is another piece of evidence in the story which has been overlooked and which strengthens O'Connor's claim that the tale should be read in a theological context.

In an indispensable article several years ago, Hallman Bryant noted that there is no Timothy, Georgia, the setting for the encounter with Red Sammy. He argues persuasively that O'Connor is alluding to "the book in the New Testament which bears the same name" — that is, Paul's Epistle to Timothy. The evidence that Bryant presents leaves no doubt that O'Connor did indeed have the Bible in mind. As Bryant notes, several of Paul's teachings are especially germane to the story: the role of the husband (a negative judgment of Bailey, the grandmother's son), for example, and strictures against hypocrisy and false religion (which are useful correctives to the family's, especially the grandmother's, attitudes). However, Bryant glosses O'Connor's story only with reference to a single book of the Bible, Timothy I. But Timothy II can help explain the crux of the story, the touching of The Misfit; it provides a subtext for the central and problematic episode of O'Connor's story, the grandmother's moment of grace.

In his Second Epistle, Paul stresses to Timothy that true grace is associated 5 with the charismatic tradition of the "laying on of hands":

> *I keep the memory of thy tears, and long to see thee again, so as to have my fill of joy when I receive fresh proof of thy sincere faith. That faith dwelt in thy grandmother Lois, and in thy mother, Eunice, before thee; I am fully persuaded that it dwells in thee too. That is why I would remind thee to fan the flame of that special grace which God kindled in thee, when my hands were laid upon thee.*

True faith dwelt in Timothy's mother and grandmother and in Timothy too after Paul's hands were laid upon him. When the grandmother of the story touches The Misfit, she replicates Paul's laying on of hands at the very moment she loses her artificiality and realizes that she and The Misfit are spiritual kin. Both events emphasize the grace which accompanies charismatic physical contact. Those critics who argue for a "realistic" interpretation of the story must ultimately acknowledge and account for O'Connor's biblical allusions. The details of the story, particularly the allusion to Timothy, emphasize that the grandmother has undergone a personal experience that is significantly different from her normally artificial and spiritually dead self. Aside from whether God exists, such moments are real, and they have *de facto* been defined through history as "religious."

In a newly discovered and just recently published letter, O'Connor (in referring to *The Violent Bear It Away*) states the issue clearly and definitively: The novel "can only be understood in religious terms." The same is true of "A Good Man Is Hard to Find." God's grace is not limited by one's religious orientation. Even the most tough-minded critic will acknowledge that all human beings — even the self-satisfied grandmother — have the potential to experience epiphanies, moments of psychological clarity, that could save them from the sour and life-denying restrictions that human beings may labor under. These are moments (from the clarifying moment of the ordinary life to the trance of the mystic) that historically we have come to define as religious.

In *Mystery and Manners*, O'Connor tells us quite directly that the inescapable threat of death shatters the grandmother's complaisance and makes her look at the essential: "violence is strangely capable of returning my characters to reality and preparing them to accept their moment of grace." Life is full of such moments — though perhaps rarely on the crucial life-and-death plane of the grandmother's experience. O'Connor believed that such moments come from God. Theology and art are not mutually exclusive. As O'Connor wrote in *Mystery and Manners*, "In the greatest fiction, the writer's moral sense coincides with his dramatic sense."

## MAKING ARGUMENTS

**1.** People, love 'em or hate 'em: argue for or against the claim that O'Connor is a misanthrope.

**2.** Does authorial intent matter? Argue for or against the claim that O'Connor's stories must be read according to what she says is their intended meaning.

**3.** Can literature make religion "believable"? Can it create belief, or bolster it? Make an argument about literature and religious belief.

## MAKING CONNECTIONS

**1.** What is the "further light" (para. 1) that Clark claims he sheds here? Do you find his argument persuasive?

**2.** Clark somewhat quickly raises and dismisses what he calls "subversive readings" in his third paragraph. What is his argument against them? Does it convince you? Regardless of where you stand, make a counterargument that agrees with Lawrence's dictum, "trust the tale, not the teller of the tale," without merely nodding to Lawrence's "authority."

# POETRY

JONATHAN SWIFT   (1667–1745)

## STELLA'S BIRTH-DAY   1724–25

As when a beauteous nymph decays,
We say she's past her dancing days;
So poets lose their feet by time,
And can no longer dance in rhyme.
Your annual bard had rather chose
To celebrate your birth in prose:
Yet merry folks, who want by chance
A pair to make a country dance,
Call the old housekeeper, and get her
To fill a place for want of better:                                  10
While Sheridan is off the hooks,
And friend Delany at his books,
That Stella may avoid disgrace,
Once more the Dean supplies their place.

Beauty and wit, too sad a truth!
Have always been confined to youth;
The god of wit and beauty's queen,
He twenty-one and she fifteen,
No poet ever sweetly sung,
Unless he were, like Phoebus, young;                                  20
Nor ever nymph inspired to rhyme,
Unless, like Venus, in her prime.
At fifty-six, if this be true,
Am I a poet fit for you?
Or, at the age of forty-three,
Are you a subject fit for me?
Adieu! bright wit, and radiant eyes!
You must be grave and I be wise.
Our fate in vain we would oppose:
But I'll be still your friend in prose:                               30
Esteem and friendship to express,
Will not require poetic dress;

And if the Muse deny her aid
To have them sung, they may be said.

But, Stella, say, what evil tongue
Reports you are no longer young;
That Time sits with his scythe to mow
Where erst sat Cupid with his bow;
That half your locks are turn'd to gray?
I'll ne'er believe a word they say.                          40
'Tis true, but let it not be known,
My eyes are somewhat dimmish grown;
For nature, always in the right,
To your decays adapts my sight;
And wrinkles undistinguished pass,
For I'm ashamed to use a glass:
And till I see them with these eyes,
Whoever says you have them, lies.

No length of time can make you quit
Honour and virtue, sense and wit;                            50
Thus you may still be young to me,
While I can better hear than see.
O ne'er may Fortune show her spite,
To make me deaf, and mend my sight!

### FOR ANALYSIS

**1.** What does this poem seem to be saying about aging? How does it correspond to what you think broader cultural attitudes toward aging are?

**2.** What kind of a birthday poem is this? What do you think Swift is trying to say to Stella?

### WRITING TOPIC

Swift, best known as a prose **satirist**, also wrote political pamphlets and poetry. The choice of poetry over **prose** is mentioned in the poem itself. Why does Swift say he wrote this birthday message in poetry? How does he use the various techniques and methods of poetry to do things prose might not be able to?

### WILLIAM BLAKE    (1757–1827)

# THE CHIMNEY SWEEPER    1789

### (SONGS OF INNOCENCE)

When my mother died I was very young,
And my Father sold me while yet my tongue
Could scarcely cry " 'weep! 'weep! 'weep! 'weep!"
So your chimneys I sweep, and in soot I sleep.

There's little Tom Dacre, who cried when his head,
That curled like a lamb's back, was shaved: so I said,
"Hush, Tom! never mind it, for when your head's bare
You know that the soot cannot spoil your white hair."

And so he was quiet and that very night
As Tom was a-sleeping, he had such a sight!                    10
That thousands of sweepers, Dick, Joe, Ned, and Jack,
Were all of them locked up in coffins of black.

And by came an Angel who had a bright key,
And he opened the coffins and set them all free;
Then down a green plain leaping, laughing, they run,
And wash in a river, and shine in the Sun.

Then naked and white, all their bags left behind,
They rise upon clouds and sport in the wind;
And the Angel told Tom, if he'd be a good boy,
He'd have God for his father, and never want joy.             20

And so Tom awoke; and we rose in the dark,
And got with our bags and our brushes to work.
Though the morning was cold, Tom was happy and warm;
So if all do their duty they need not fear harm.


## THE CHIMNEY SWEEPER     1794

### (SONGS OF EXPERIENCE)

A little black thing among the snow,
Crying "'weep! 'weep!" in notes of woe!
"Where are thy father and mother? say?"
"They are both gone up to the church to pray.

Because I was happy upon the heath,
And smil'd among the winter's snow,
They clothed me in the clothes of death,
And taught me to sing the notes of woe.

And because I am happy and dance and sing,
They think they have done me no injury,                       10
And are gone to praise God and his Priest and King,
Who make up a heaven of our misery."

## MAKING CONNECTIONS

How would you characterize this poem's view of religion? How does it compare to the view implied in the *Songs of Innocence* poem of the same name? How does it inform the poem's larger reflection on the lives of the chimney sweeps?

# THE LAMB 1789

   Little Lamb, who made thee?
   Dost thou know who made thee?
Gave thee life, and bid thee feed
By the stream and o'er the mead;
Gave thee clothing of delight,
Softest clothing, wooly, bright;
Gave thee such a tender voice,
Making all the vales rejoice?
   Little Lamb, who made thee?
   Dost thou know who made thee?      10

   Little Lamb, I'll tell thee,
   Little Lamb, I'll tell thee:
He is callèd by thy name,
For he calls himself a Lamb.
He is meek, and he is mild;
He became a little child.
I a child, and thou a lamb,
We are callèd by his name.
   Little Lamb, God bless thee!
   Little Lamb, God bless thee!      20

# THE SHEPHERD 1789

How sweet is the shepherd's sweet lot!
From the morn to the evening he strays;
He shall follow his sheep all the day,
And his tongue shall be filled with praise.

For he hears the lambs' innocent call,
And he hears the ewes' tender reply;
He is watchful while they are in peace,
For they know when their shepherd is nigh.

# THE GARDEN OF LOVE   1793

I went to the Garden of Love,
And saw what I never had seen:
A Chapel was built in the midst,
Where I used to play on the green.

And the gates of this Chapel were shut,
And "Thou shalt not" writ over the door;
So I turn'd to the Garden of Love,
That so many sweet flowers bore,

And I saw it was filled with graves,
And tomb-stones where flowers should be:     10
And Priests in black gowns were walking their rounds,
And binding with briars my joys & desires.

## FOR ANALYSIS

1. What meanings does the word *love* have in this poem?
2. What is Blake's judgment on established religion?
3. Explain the meaning of *Chapel* (l. 3) and *briars* (l. 12).

## MAKING ARGUMENTS

It has been argued, contrary to most readings of the poem, that there is some ironic distance between the speaker and the poet. How might you make this argument? Where might the poem allow the reader to critique the speaker?

## WRITING TOPIC

Read the definition of **irony** in "Glossary of Literary Terms." Write an essay in which you distinguish between the types of irony used in the second "The Chimney Sweeper" and "The Garden of Love."

# LONDON   1794

I wander through each chartered[1] street,
Near where the chartered Thames does flow
And mark in every face I meet
Marks of weakness, marks of woe.

*London*
   [1] Preempted by the state and leased out under royal patent.

In every cry of every man,
In every infant's cry of fear,
In every voice, in every ban,
The mind-forged manacles I hear:

How the chimney-sweeper's cry
Every blackening church appalls,                    10
And the hapless soldier's sigh
Runs in blood down palace-walls.

But most, through midnight streets I hear
How the youthful harlot's curse
Blasts the new-born infant's tear,
And blights with plagues the marriage-hearse.

# THE TYGER   1794

Tyger! Tyger! burning bright
In the forests of the night,
What immortal hand or eye
Could frame thy fearful symmetry?

In what distant deeps or skies
Burnt the fire of thine eyes?
On what wings dare he aspire?
What the hand dare seize the fire?

And what shoulder, & what art,
Could twist the sinews of thy heart?
And when thy heart began to beat,                   10
What dread hand? & what dread feet?

What the hammer? what the chain?
In what furnace was thy brain?
What the anvil? what dread grasp
Dare its deadly terrors clasp?

When the stars threw down their spears,
And water'd heaven with their tears,
Did he smile his work to see?
Did he who made the Lamb make thee?                 20

Tyger! Tyger! burning bright
In the forests of the night,

What immortal hand or eye
Dare frame thy fearful symmetry?

## ROBERT BROWNING   (1812–1889)

# MY LAST DUCHESS   1842

### FERRARA

That's my last Duchess painted on the wall,
Looking as if she were alive. I call
That piece a wonder, now: Frà Pandolf's[1] hands
Worked busily a day, and there she stands.
Will't please you sit and look at her? I said
"Frà Pandolf" by design, for never read
Strangers like you that pictured countenance,
The depth and passion of its earnest glance,
But to myself they turned (since none puts by
The curtain I have drawn for you, but I)                     10
And seemed as they would ask me, if they durst,
How such a glance came there; so, not the first
Are you to turn and ask thus. Sir, 'twas not
Her husband's presence only, called that spot
Of joy into the Duchess' cheek: perhaps
Frà Pandolf chanced to say "Her mantle laps
Over my lady's wrist too much," or "Paint
Must never hope to reproduce the faint
Half-flush that dies along her throat": such stuff
Was courtesy, she thought, and cause enough                  20
For calling up that spot of joy. She had
A heart — how shall I say? — too soon made glad,
Too easily impressed; she liked whate'er
She looked on, and her looks went everywhere.
Sir, 'twas all one! My favor at her breast,
The dropping of the daylight in the West,
The bough of cherries some officious fool
Broke in the orchard for her, the white mule
She rode with round the terrace — all and each
Would draw from her alike the approving speech,             30
Or blush, at least. She thanked men — good! but thanked

---

*My Last Duchess*
  [1] Frà Pandolf and Claus of Innsbruck (who is mentioned in the last line) are fictitious artists.

Somehow — I know not how — as if she ranked
My gift of a nine-hundred-years-old name
With anybody's gift. Who'd stoop to blame
This sort of trifling? Even had you skill
In speech — which I have not — to make your will
Quite clear to such an one, and say, "Just this
Or that in you disgusts me; here you miss,
Or there exceed the mark" — and if she let
Herself be lessoned° so, nor plainly set                           taught   40
Her wits to yours, forsooth, and made excuse,
— E'en then would be some stooping; and I choose
Never to stoop. Oh sir, she smiled, no doubt,
Whene'er I passed her; but who passed without
Much the same smile? This grew; I gave commands;
Then all smiles stopped together. There she stands
As if alive. Will't please you rise? We'll meet
The company below, then. I repeat,
The Count your master's known munificence°                       generosity
Is ample warrant that no just pretense                                       50
Of mine for dowry will be disallowed;
Though his fair daughter's self, as I avowed
At starting, is my object. Nay, we'll go
Together down, sir. Notice Neptune, though,
Taming a sea-horse, thought a rarity,
Which Claus of Innsbruck cast in bronze for me!

## FOR ANALYSIS

**1.** To whom is the duke speaking, and what is the occasion?

**2.** What does a comparison between the duke's feelings about his artwork and his feelings about his last duchess reveal about his **character**?

**3.** Does this poem rely on **irony**? Explain.

## MAKING ARGUMENTS

Write an essay in which you argue that the reader either is or is not meant to sympathize with the duke's **characterization** of his wife.

## WRITING TOPIC

Browning is said to have meant that the "commands" of line 45 are that the duchess be executed or sent to a convent. Write a poem, short piece of prose, or journal entry, from her **point of view**, addressing the painting of the portrait and her relationship with the speaker.

## EMILY DICKINSON   (1830–1886)

# I FELT A FUNERAL, IN MY BRAIN   1861

I felt a Funeral, in my Brain,
And Mourners to and fro
Kept treading — treading — till it seemed
That Sense was breaking through —

And when they all were seated,
A Service, like a Drum —
Kept beating — beating — till I thought
My Mind was going numb —

And then I heard them lift a Box
And creak across my Soul                                        10
With those same Boots of Lead, again,
Then Space — began to toll,

As all the Heavens were a Bell,
And Being, but an Ear,
And I, and Silence, some strange Race
Wrecked, solitary, here —

And then a Plank in Reason, broke,
And I dropped down, and down —
And hit a World, at every plunge,
And Finished knowing — then —                                  20


## THOMAS HARDY   (1840–1928)

# MEN WHO MARCH AWAY   1914

What of the faith and fire within us
Men who march away
Ere the barn-cocks say
Night is growing gray,
Leaving all that here can win us;
What of the faith and fire within us
Men who march away?
Is it a purblind prank, O think you,
Friend with the musing eye,
Who watch us stepping by                                       10
With doubt and dolorous sigh?
Can much pondering so hoodwink you!

170

Is it a purblind prank, O think you,
Friend with the musing eye?
Nay. We well see what we are doing,
Though some may not see —
Dalliers as they be —
England's need are we;
Her distress would leave us rueing:
Nay. We well see what we are doing,                                      20
Though some may not see!
In our heart of hearts believing
Victory crowns the just,
And that braggarts must
Surely bite the dust,
Press we to the field ungrieving,
In our heart of hearts believing
Victory crowns the just.
Hence the faith and fire within us
Men who march away                                                       30
Ere the barn-cocks say
Night is growing gray,
Leaving all that here can win us;
Hence the faith and fire within us
Men who march away.

## FOR ANALYSIS

**1.** What question does the speaker ask at the beginning of "Men Who March Away"?
How does the poem answer it?

**2.** Some versions of this poem bear the subtitle "Song of the Soldiers." What kind of a
song is this? Does *of* mean "about" or "for"?

## WRITING TOPIC

Compose a companion piece, in poetry or **prose**, written by the "friend with the musing eye" (l. 9). What does this "friend" think of what he sees? Does she or he agree or
disagree with the speaker?

## GERARD MANLEY HOPKINS    (1844–1889)

# SPRING AND FALL    1880

## TO A YOUNG CHILD

Márgarét, áre you gríeving
Over Goldengrove unleaving?°                                      losing leaves
Leáves, líke the things of man, you
With your fresh thoughts care for, can you?

Áh! ás the heart grows older
It will come to such sights colder
By and by, nor spare a sigh
Though worlds of wanwood leafmeal¹ lie;
And yet you wíll weep and know why.
Now no matter, child, the name:                                    10
Sórrow's springs áre the same.
Nor mouth had, no nor mind, expressed
What heart heard of, ghost° guessed:                               soul
It ís the blight man was born for,
It is Margaret you mourn for.

## FOR ANALYSIS

**1.** In this poem Margaret grieves over the passing of spring and the coming of fall. What does the coming of fall **symbolize**?

**2.** Why, when Margaret grows older, will she not sigh over the coming of fall?

**3.** What are "Sórrow's springs" (l. 11)?

## A. E. HOUSMAN (1859–1936)

# WHEN I WAS ONE-AND-TWENTY    1896

When I was one-and-twenty
    I heard a wise man say,
"Give crowns and pounds and guineas
    But not your heart away;
Give pearls away and rubies
    But keep your fancy free."
But I was one-and-twenty,
    No use to talk to me.

When I was one-and-twenty
    I heard him say again,                                         10
"The heart out of the bosom
    Was never given in vain;
'Tis paid with sighs a plenty
    And sold for endless rue."
And I am two-and-twenty,
    And oh, 'tis true, 'tis true.

*Spring and Fall*
¹ Pale woods littered with mouldering leaves.

## ROBERT FROST  (1874–1963)

# THE ROAD NOT TAKEN  1915

Two roads diverged in a yellow wood,
And sorry I could not travel both
And be one traveler, long I stood
And looked down one as far as I could
To where it bent in the undergrowth;

Then took the other, as just as fair,
And having perhaps the better claim,
Because it was grassy and wanted wear;
Though as for that the passing there
Had worn them really about the same,                                    10

And both that morning equally lay
In leaves no step had trodden black.
Oh, I kept the first for another day!
Yet knowing how way leads on to way,
I doubted if I should ever come back.

I shall be telling this with a sigh
Somewhere ages and ages hence:
Two roads diverged in a wood, and I —
I took the one less traveled by,
And that has made all the difference.                                    20


# BIRCHES  1916

When I see birches bend to left and right
Across the lines of straighter darker trees,
I like to think some boy's been swinging them.
But swinging doesn't bend them down to stay
As ice-storms do. Often you must have seen them
Loaded with ice a sunny winter morning
After a rain. They click upon themselves
As the breeze rises, and turn many-colored
As the stir cracks and crazes their enamel.
Soon the sun's warmth makes them shed crystal shells                     10
Shattering and avalanching on the snow-crust —
Such heaps of broken glass to sweep away
You'd think the inner dome of heaven had fallen.
They are dragged to the withered bracken by the load,

And they seem not to break; though once they are bowed
So low for long, they never right themselves:
You may see their trunks arching in the woods
Years afterwards, trailing their leaves on the ground
Like girls on hands and knees that throw their hair
Before them over their heads to dry in the sun.                          20
But I was going to say when Truth broke in
With all her matter-of-fact about the ice-storm
I should prefer to have some boy bend them
As he went out and in to fetch the cows —
Some boy too far from town to learn baseball,
Whose only play was what he found himself,
Summer or winter, and could play alone.
One by one he subdued his father's trees
By riding them down over and over again
Until he took the stiffness out of them,                                30
And not one but hung limp, not one was left
For him to conquer. He learned all there was
To learn about not launching out too soon
And so not carrying the tree away
Clear to the ground. He always kept his poise
To the top branches, climbing carefully
With the same pains you use to fill a cup
Up to the brim, and even above the brim.
Then he flung outward, feet first, with a swish,
Kicking his way down through the air to the ground.                      40
So was I once myself a swinger of birches.
And so I dream of going back to be.
It's when I'm weary of considerations,
And life is too much like a pathless wood
Where your face burns and tickles with the cobwebs
Broken across it, and one eye is weeping
From a twig's having lashed across it open.
I'd like to get away from earth awhile
And then come back to it and begin over.
May no fate willfully misunderstand me                                  50
And half grant what I wish and snatch me away
Not to return. Earth's the right place for love:
I don't know where it's likely to go better.
I'd like to go by climbing a birch tree,
And climb black branches up a snow-white trunk
*Toward* heaven, till the tree could bear no more,
But dipped its top and set me down again.
That would be good both going and coming back.
One could do worse than be a swinger of birches.

**E. E. CUMMINGS**   (1894–1962)

# IN JUST-   1923

in Just-
spring   when the world is mud-
luscious the little
lame balloonman

whistles   far   and wee

and eddieandbill come
running from marbles and
piracies and it's
spring

when the world is puddle-wonderful                    10

the queer
old balloonman whistles
far   and   wee
and bettyandisbel come dancing

from hop-scotch and jump-rope and

it's
spring
and
    the

        goat-footed                                   20

balloonMan   whistles
far
and
wee


**STEVIE SMITH**   (1902–1971)

# NOT WAVING BUT DROWNING   1957

Nobody heard him, the dead man,
But still he lay moaning:
I was much further out than you thought
And not waving but drowning.

Poor chap, he always loved larking
And now he's dead
It must have been too cold for him his heart gave way,
They said.

Oh, no no no, it was too cold always
(Still the dead one lay moaning)                    10
I was much too far out all my life
And not waving but drowning.

### FOR ANALYSIS

**1.** Explain the **paradox** in the first and last **stanzas**, where the speaker describes someone dead as moaning. Who do you suppose the *you* of line 3 is? The *They* of line 8?

**2.** Explain the meaning of line 7. Can it be interpreted in more than one way?

**3.** Explain the meanings of *drowning*.

**4.** The only thing we learn about the dead man is that "he always loved larking" (l. 5). Why is this detail significant? What kind of man do you think he was?

**5.** Does the speaker know more about the dead man than the man's friends do? Explain.

### MAKING ARGUMENTS

Stevie Smith suffered from depression; this poem was reportedly written during an especially bad stretch in her life. Make an argument either that the poem must be read with this biographical information in mind or that it should not. Do you read the poem differently in light of this information? Does this information alter your experience of the poem negatively?

### WRITING TOPICS

**1.** Write an essay describing how you or someone you know suffered the experience of "not waving but drowning."

**2.** Write an essay describing how you came to the realization that someone close to you was not the person you thought he or she was.

### COUNTEE CULLEN   (1903–1946)

# INCIDENT   1925

Once riding in old Baltimore,
    Heart-filled, head-filled with glee,
I saw a Baltimorean
    Keep looking straight at me.

Now I was eight and very small,
　And he was no whit bigger,
And so I smiled, but he poked out
　His tongue and called me, "Nigger."

I saw the whole of Baltimore
　From May until December:　　　　　　　　　　　　　　10
Of all the things that happened there
　That's all that I remember.

## LAWRENCE FERLINGHETTI　(B. 1919)

# CONSTANTLY RISKING ABSURDITY　1958

Constantly risking absurdity
　　　　　　　　and death
　　　whenever he performs
　　　　　　　above the heads
　　　　　　　　　　of his audience
the poet like an acrobat
　　　　　climbs on rime
　　　　　　　to a high wire of his own making
and balancing on eyebeams
　　　　　　　above a sea of faces　　　　　10
　　paces his way
　　　　　　to the other side of day
performing entrechats[1]
　　　　　　and sleight-of-foot tricks
and other high theatrics
　　　　　and all without mistaking
　　　any thing
　　　　　for what it may not be

　For he's the super realist
　　　　　　who must perforce perceive　　　20
　　taut truth
　　　　　before the taking of each stance or step
in his supposed advance
　　　　　toward that still higher perch

---

*Constantly Risking Absurdity*
[1] In ballet, a leap straight upward in which the legs are repeatedly crossed or heels struck together.

where Beauty stands and waits
               with gravity
                    to start her death-defying leap

And he
       a little charleychaplin[2] man
              who may or may not catch         30
        her fair eternal form
              spreadeagled in the empty air
        of existence

## PHILIP LARKIN   (1922–1985)

# THIS BE THE VERSE   1974

They fuck you up, your mum and dad.
   They may not mean to, but they do.
They fill you with the faults they had
   And add some extra, just for you.

But they were fucked up in their turn
   By fools in old-style hats and coats,
Who half the time were soppy-stern
   And half at one another's throats.

Man hands on misery to man.
   It deepens like a coastal shelf.
Get out as early as you can,         10
   And don't have any kids yourself.

## AUDRE LORDE   (1934–1992)

# HANGING FIRE   1978

I am fourteen
and my skin has betrayed me
the boy I cannot live without
still sucks his thumb

---

*Constantly Risking Absurdity*
  [2] Charles Spencer Chaplin (1889–1977) was cinema's most celebrated comedian of the silent-film era. His trademark was the mustachioed Little Tramp, whose pathos and comedy were accompanied by extraordinary acrobatic skills.

in secret
how come my knees are
always so ashy
what if I die
before morning
and momma's in the bedroom                               10
with the door closed.

I have to learn how to dance
in time for the next party
my room is small for me
suppose I die before graduation
they will sing sad melodies
but finally
tell the truth about me
There is nothing I want to do
and too much                                               20
that has to be done
and momma's in the bedroom
with the door closed.

Nobody even stops to think
about my side of it
I should have been on Math Team
my marks were better than his
why do I have to be
the one
wearing braces                                            30
I have nothing to wear tomorrow
will I live long enough
to grow up
and momma's in the bedroom
with the door closed.

## FOR ANALYSIS

**1.** How do you think the speaker's skin has "betrayed" her (l. 2)?

**2.** What does the expression *hang fire* mean? In what ways is the speaker hanging fire?

## MAKING ARGUMENTS

What is "the truth" (l. 18) about the speaker? Is it something specific alluded to in the poem? Is it something specific unnamed in the poem? Or, is it something general to speakers like her or to everyone? Make an argument for one of these options.

## WRITING TOPICS

**1.** Look up the origins of the phrase used in the poem's title. Where does it come from? Is there anything about this original meaning that might add to the poem's meaning?

**2.** Analyze the structure of the poem — how it is divided into parts, how certain lines and images and feelings are repeated. How does the structure enrich the poem's meaning?

## MAKING CONNECTIONS

Compare the speaker's repeated statements about her fear of death in "Hanging Fire" to Margaret in Hopkins's "Spring and Fall" (p. 171). What is different about the attitudes expressed — toward life, toward death, toward growing up — in these two poems?

## ALICIA OSTRIKER   (B. 1937)

# THE DOGS AT LIVE OAK BEACH, SANTA CRUZ   1998

As if there could be a world
Of absolute innocence
In which we forget ourselves

The owners throw sticks
And half-bald tennis balls
Toward the surf
And the happy dogs leap after them
As if catapulted —

Black dogs, tan dogs,
Tubes of glorious muscle —                                    10

Pursuing pleasure
More than obedience
They race, skid to a halt in the wet sand,
Sometimes they'll plunge straight into
The foaming breakers

Like diving birds, letting the green turbulence
Toss them, until they snap and sink

Teeth into floating wood
Then bound back to their owners
Shining wet, with passionate speed                              20
For nothing,
For absolutely nothing but joy.

## LOUISE GLÜCK    (B. 1943)

# THE SCHOOL CHILDREN    1975

The children go forward with their little satchels.
And all morning the mothers have labored
to gather the late apples, red and gold,
like words of another language.

And on the other shore
are those who wait behind great desks
to receive these offerings.

How orderly they are — the nails
on which the children hang
their overcoats of blue or yellow wool.                         10

And the teachers shall instruct them in silence
and the mothers shall scour the orchards for a way out,
drawing to themselves the gray limbs of the fruit trees
bearing so little ammunition.

# THE MYTH OF INNOCENCE    2006

One summer she goes into the field as usual
stopping for a bit at the pool where she often
looks at herself, to see
if she detects any changes. She sees
the same person, the horrible mantle
of daughterliness still clinging to her.

The sun seems, in the water, very close.
That's my uncle spying again, she thinks —
everything in nature is in some way her relative.
*I am never alone*, she thinks,                                 10
turning the thought into a prayer.
Then death appears, like the answer to a prayer.

No one understands anymore
how beautiful he was. But Persephone remembers.
Also that he embraced her, right there,
with her uncle watching. She remembers
sunlight flashing on his bare arms.

This is the last moment she remembers clearly.
Then the dark god bore her away.

She also remembers, less clearly,                                    20
the chilling insight that from this moment
she couldn't live without him again.

The girl who disappears from the pool
will never return. A woman will return,
looking for the girl she was.

She stands by the pool saying, from time to time,
*I was abducted*, but it sounds
wrong to her, nothing like what she felt.
Then she says, *I was not abducted*.                                30
Then she says, *I offered myself, I wanted
to escape my body*. Even, sometimes,
*I willed this*. But ignorance

cannot will knowledge. Ignorance
wills something imagined, which it believes exists.

All the different nouns—
she says them in rotation.
*Death, husband, god, stranger.*
Everything sounds so simple, so conventional.
I must have been, she thinks, a simple girl.

She can't remember herself as that person                           40
but she keeps thinking the pool will remember
and explain to her the meaning of her prayer
so she can understand
whether it was answered or not.

### FOR ANALYSIS

**1.** If you are not familiar with the story of Persephone, read up on it. Reread "The Myth of Innocence" in light of Persephone's tale.

**2.** To what thing or things does the title of the poem refer?

**3.** Of what was the speaker innocent? What has experience taught her?

**WRITING TOPIC**

Glück writes, "But ignorance / cannot will knowledge. Ignorance / wills something imagined, which it believes exists" (ll. 32–34). Write a reflection on a moment in your own life when you wanted to experience something and found when you did that it was not what you thought it would be.

**ALAN FELDMAN**   (B. 1945)

## MY CENTURY   2001

The year I was born the atomic bomb went off.
Here I'd just begun, and someone
found the switch to turn off the world.

In the furnace-light, in the central solar fire
of that heat lamp, the future got very finite,
and it was possible to imagine time-travelers

failing to arrive, because there was no future.
Inside the great dark clock in the hall,
heavy brass cylinders descended.

Tick-tock, the chimes changed their tune                                      10
one phrase at a time. The bomb became
a film star, its glamorous globe of smoke

searing the faces of men in beach chairs.
Someone threw up every day at school.
No time to worry about collective death,

when life itself was permeated by ordeals.
And so we grew up, beneath an umbrella of acceptance.
In bio we learned there were particles

cruising through us like whales through archipelagoes,
and in civics that if Hitler had gotten the bomb                               20
he'd have used it on the inferior races,

and all this time love was etching its scars
on our skins like maps. The heavens
remained pure, except for little white slits

on the perfect blue skin that planes cut
in the icy upper air, like needles sewing.
From one, a tiny seed might fall

that would make a sun on earth.
And so the century passed, with me still in it,
books waiting on the shelves to become cinders,                    30

what we felt locked up inside, waiting to be read,
down the long corridor of time. I was born
the year the bomb exploded. Twice

whole cities were charred like cities in the Bible,
but we didn't look back. We went on thinking
we could go on, our shapes the same,

darkened now against a background lit by fire.
Forgive me for doubting you're there,
Citizens, on your holodecks with earth wallpaper —

a shadow-toned ancestor with poorly pressed pants,               40
protected like a child from knowing the future.

## FOR ANALYSIS

**1.** What kinds of **images** appear in this poem? Natural? Man-made? Large? Small? Why do you think Feldman chose the combination of images that he did?

**2.** What sense of time does this poem have? What might it be trying to express?

**3.** What is this poem's central **paradox**? Where is it first named?

## MAKING ARGUMENTS

Alan Feldman was born in 1945, the year the atomic bomb was used, and this poem was written in 2001. Does the future look as fragile to people born fifty years later than Feldman? How would you argue that it does? How would you argue that it does not?

## WRITING TOPIC

Find a significant historical event that occurred in the year of your birth. In a poem, a short story, or an essay, reflect on the event's significance to you, or to humankind, or simply to the people to whom it happened.

## SANDRA CISNEROS  (B. 1954)

# MY WICKED WICKED WAYS    1987

This is my father.
See? He is young.
He looks like Errol Flynn.[1]

He is wearing a hat
that tips over one eye,
a suit that fits him good,
and baggy pants.

He is also wearing
those awful shoes,
the two-toned ones                                          10
my mother hates.

Here is my mother.
She is not crying.
She cannot look into the lens
because the sun is bright.
The woman,
the one my father knows,
is not here.
She does not come till later.

My mother will get very mad.                                20
Her face will turn red
and she will throw one shoe.
My father will say nothing.
After a while everyone
will forget it.
Years and years will pass.
My mother will stop mentioning it.

This is me she is carrying.
I am a baby.
She does not know                                           30
I will turn out bad.

---

[1] Errol Flynn (1909–1959) was a handsome leading man in many Hollywood movies during the
1930s and 1940s.

## FOR ANALYSIS

1. Why does the speaker tell us that her mother "is not crying" (l. 13)?

2. What will the speaker's mother "get very mad" about (l. 20)?

3. What is the connection between the last four lines and the rest of the poem?

## WRITING TOPIC

Discuss the meaning of the final line of the poem. What does the speaker mean by *bad*?

## SANDRA M. CASTILLO  (B. 1962)

# CHRISTMAS, 1970   2002

We assemble the silver tree,
our translated lives,
its luminous branches,
numbered to fit into its body.
place its metallic roots
to decorate our first Christmas.
Mother finds herself
opening, closing the Red Cross box
she will carry into 1976
like an unwanted door prize,                                    10
a timepiece, a stubborn fact,
an emblem of exile measuring our days,
marked by the moment of our departure,
our lives no longer arranged.

Somewhere,
there is a photograph,
a Polaroid Mother cannot remember was ever taken:
I am sitting under Tia Tere's Christmas tree,
her first apartment in this, our new world:
my sisters by my side,                                         20
I wear a white dress, black boots,
an eight-year-old's resignation;
Mae and Mitzy, age four,
wear red and white snowflake sweaters and identical smiles,
on this, our first Christmas,
away from ourselves.

The future unreal, unmade,
Mother will cry into the new year

with Lidia and Emerito,
our elderly downstairs neighbors,                                          30
who realize what we are too young to understand:
Even a map cannot show you
the way back to a place
that no longer exists.

## FOR ANALYSIS

**1.** How is the tree described in "Christmas, 1970"? Why do you think it is described in this way?

**2.** This poem includes a number of details about time, such as dates and ages and references to the past and the future, and about place, such as the different **settings** and the mention of a map. How do place and time intersect in this poem? Why are they important?

**3.** How does Castillo use verb tense in this poem? How does it change? What do you think it means that it does?

## WRITING TOPIC

Recall a significant moment from your childhood when you were "too young to understand" something. What makes you able to understand it now?

## EVELYN LAU   (B. 1971)

# SOLIPSISM    1994

I spend days at the gym enclosed by four mirrors,
a silver pole balanced on my shoulders.
I slide keys out of the machines, slot them lower
to lift my weights with increased strain,
to pump the last reps in my personal program.

I watch on television a show that is being taped
in the studio across the hall. It is shown simultaneously
in the green room but will not be broadcast publicly
until next week. I feel very special
yet out of step with the rest of the viewing world.          10

In aerobics class we lie on our backs and pump our hips
repetitively towards the ceiling. Soon lovers will come
to smother us with their bodies, pumping equally.
Now there are only our midriffs rising and lowering,
our shapes contained in lycra and cotton.

I break cold medication out of its blister wrap
in the green room, I swallow sedatives in soothing colours.
The makeup person touches my face with gentle fingers.
She covers me in a smock the colour of roses
and together we watch the changes in the mirror.                    20

The faces around me are glazed with perspiration,
their bodies are lovely and plain by turns.
I take my position at the exercise bar between two bodies.
I resume the process of making myself perfect
as they both are, yet not like them, uniquely myself.

I see my body in four funhouse mirrors.
It is shaped exactly like an upended couch.
The gym is a marvel of bodies in motion,
lineups are polite at the popular machines,
active minds are occupied with weight goals, diet instructions.    30

The audience would wave if the camera glanced their way.
It would stampede to the nearest exit in case of fire
or planted bomb, crushing members of its own sex and race.
I am very calm. I have rehearsed my instructions,
not once do I stray from the script or structure.

Journalists declare there are weather and wars
happening outside the fitness-club doors,
but I hear only music and the splash of water fountains.
I only notice how others have tied back their hair.
Rarely do I look outside, for something other or more.            40

## For Analysis

**1.** Look up *solipsism* in the dictionary. Is it an appropriate title for this poem? Explain.

**2.** Consider the first three lines of the last **stanza**. How do they relate to the central issue of this poem?

**3.** How might you define *perfect* as it is used in line 24? Can the speaker make herself perfect in the fitness club? Explain.

## Making Arguments

Who is the speaker in this poem? Is she actually a television personality? Make an argument for who she is based on your reading of the poem.

## WRITING TOPICS

**1.** Describe the circumstances that would allow you to feel that nothing exists or is real but yourself.

**2.** Using someone you know — or know of — as a model, describe the behavior of a solipsistic person. Do you believe that solipsism is a desirable or an undesirable trait? Explain.

## CONNECTING POEMS: VOICES OF EXPERIENCE

The poems in this unit explore the role parents, or parental figures, play in guiding children through the innocence of childhood into the world of experience. The poems also address the contradictions and inconsistencies inherent in this role and in the world of human experience. As you read, pay attention not only to the ways the experienced try to guide the innocent — and the difficulties they have doing it — but also to the texture of their voices. How have the poets personalized these voices? How does the way they speak relate to what they have to say? What do the innocent have to say about the advice they are being given, and how does the way the poets have them express their thoughts relate to how we hear them?

## LANGSTON HUGHES    (1902–1967)

# MOTHER TO SON    1926

Well, son, I'll tell you:
Life for me ain't been no crystal stair.
It's had tacks in it,
And splinters,
And boards torn up,
And places with no carpet on the floor —
Bare.
But all the time
I'se been a-climbin' on,
And reachin' landin's,                                                    10
And turnin' corners,
And sometimes goin' in the dark
Where there ain't been no light.
So boy, don't you turn back.
Don't you set down on the steps
'Cause you finds it's kinder hard.

Don't you fall now —
For I'se still goin', honey,
I'se still climbin',
And life for me ain't been no crystal stair.                    20

## FOR ANALYSIS

**1.** What are the two kinds of stairs in this poem? What do they stand for?

**2.** Analyze the structure of the poem. What are the functions of the various instances of repetition?

## MAKING ARGUMENTS

Over the years, readers have argued about the use of African American vernacular in literature. What do you think about it? Make an argument for or against its use.

## WRITING TOPIC

Write a poem, "Son to Mother," in response to Hughes's poem. It should be about the same topic but have a different **point of view**, perhaps with a different **tone** or sense.

## PETER MEINKE    (B. 1932)

# ADVICE TO MY SON    1965

## —FOR TIM

The trick is, to live your days
as if each one may be your last
(for they go fast, and young men lose their lives
in strange and unimaginable ways)
but at the same time, plan long range
(for they go slow: if you survive
the shattered windshield and the bursting shell
you will arrive
at our approximation here below
of heaven or hell).                                          10

To be specific, between the peony and the rose
plant squash and spinach, turnips and tomatoes;
beauty is nectar
and nectar, in a desert, saves —
but the stomach craves stronger sustenance
than the honied vine.
Therefore, marry a pretty girl

after seeing her mother;
speak truth to one man,
work with another;                                          20
and always serve bread with your wine.

But, son,
always serve wine.

### FOR ANALYSIS

**1.** Explain how the advice of lines 17–21 is logically related to the preceding lines.

**2.** What do the final two lines tell the reader about the speaker?

### MAKING ARGUMENTS

"Advice to my Son" could be read as one in a long line of poems about seizing the day and/or "plan[ning] long range," in the poem's words (l. 5). Does it make more sense to read the poem as an act of giving sensible advice or as a commentary on the long history of poems mentioned above? Make an argument one way or the other.

### WRITING TOPIC

The advice of the first **stanza** seems contradictory. In what ways does the second stanza attempt to resolve the contradiction or explain the "trick" (l. 1)? What do the various plants and the bread and wine **symbolize**?

### ROBERT MEZEY   (B. 1935)

## MY MOTHER   1970

My mother writes from Trenton,
a comedian to the bone
but underneath, serious
and all heart. "Honey," she says,
"be a mensch[1] and Mary too,
it's no good to worry, you
are doing the best you can
your Dad and everyone
thinks you turned out very well
as long as you pay your bills                               10
nobody can say a word
you can tell them to drop dead
so save a dollar it can't

*My Mother*
  [1] A person of integrity and honor.

hurt — remember Frank you went
to highschool with? he still lives
with his wife's mother, his wife
works while he writes his books and
did he ever sell a one
the four kids run around naked
36 and he's never had,                                          20
you'll forgive my expression
even a pot to piss in
or a window to throw it,
such a smart boy he couldn't
read the footprints on the wall
honey you think you know all
the answers you don't, please try
to put some money away
believe me it wouldn't hurt
artist shmartist life's too short                               30
for that kind of, forgive me,
horseshit, I know what you want
better than you, all that counts
is to make a good living
and the best of everything,
as Sholem Aleichem[2] said
he was a great writer did
you ever read his books dear,
you should make what he makes a year
anyway he says some place                                       40
Poverty is no disgrace
but it's no honor either
that's what I say,
          love,
            Mother"

## GARY SOTO   (B. 1952)

# BEHIND GRANDMA'S HOUSE   1985

At ten I wanted fame. I had a comb
And two Coke bottles, a tube of Bryl-creem.
I borrowed a dog, one with
Mismatched eyes and a happy tongue,

[2] Pen name of the Jewish author Sholem Naumovich Rabinovich (1859–1916).

And wanted to prove I was tough
In the alley, kicking over trash cans,
A dull chime of tuna cans falling.
I hurled light bulbs like grenades
And men teachers held their heads,
Fingers of blood lengthening                                    10
On the ground. I flicked rocks at cats,
Their goofy faces spurred with foxtails.
I kicked fences. I shooed pigeons.
I broke a branch from a flowering peach
And frightened ants with a stream of piss.
I said "Shit," "Fuck you," and "No way
Daddy-O" to an imaginary priest
Until grandma came into the alley,
Her apron flapping in a breeze,
Her hair mussed, and said, "Let me help you,"          20
And punched me between the eyes.

## FOR ANALYSIS

**1.** What word appears more than any other in this poem? What might it mean that it appears so often?

**2.** Who gets the "last word" in this poem? Of what does this last word consist?

**3.** What is the actual last word in the poem? Is there a pun involved?

## MAKING ARGUMENTS

Argue with "Behind Grandma's House" by focusing not on the act that ends the poem but at the activity prior to the poem that consists of the ten years of the speaker's life up to that moment. Instead of looking at the punch that may have straightened him out, what acts or conditions might have inclined him to act the way he does in the poem?

## WRITING TOPIC

Describe the effect of the poem's account of the speaker's actions. What feeling comes across from the **rhythms** and sounds and **images**? What moral judgment do you make of the actions they describe? Do these two sets of reactions go together? If not, what is the effect of their being seemingly mismatched?

## MAKING CONNECTIONS

**1.** Compare the **tone** of the advice given in Meinke's "Advice to My Son" (p. 190) with that given in Mezey's "My Mother" (p. 191).

**2.** While only one of these poems is explicitly about school, all are in some way about education. How is each of these about teaching and learning? Is there only one way to teach?

**3.** The voices of experience in two of these poems are explicitly ethnic. What effects do the poems get from quoting, directly or indirectly, the ethnic **dialects** of their experienced voices?

# DRAMA

**HENRIK IBSEN**   (1828–1906)

## A DOLL'S HOUSE[1]   1879

CHARACTERS

Torvald Helmer, a lawyer

Nora, his wife

Dr. Rank

Mrs. Linde

Krogstad

The Helmers' three small
   children

Anne, the children's nurse

A Maid

A Porter

## ACT I

**Scene**

*A room furnished comfortably and tastefully, but not extravagantly. At the back, a door to the right leads to the entrance hall, another to the left leads to Helmer's study. Between the doors stands a piano. In the middle of the left-hand wall is a door, and beyond it a window. Near the window are a round table, armchairs and a small sofa. In the right-hand wall, at the farther end, another door; and on the same side, nearer the footlights, a stove, two easy chairs and a rocking-chair; between the stove and the door, a small table. Engravings on the walls; a cabinet with china and other small objects; a small bookcase with well-bound books. The floors are carpeted, and a fire burns in the stove. It is winter.*

*A bell rings in the hall; shortly afterwards the door is heard to open. Enter Nora, humming a tune and in high spirits. She is in outdoor dress and carries a number of parcels; these she lays on the table to the right. She leaves the outer door open after her, and through it is seen a Porter who is carrying a Christmas tree and a basket, which he gives to the Maid who has opened the door.*

**Nora.**  Hide the Christmas tree carefully, Helen. Be sure the children do not see it till this evening, when it is dressed. *(To the Porter, taking out her purse.)* How much?

**Porter.**  Sixpence.

---

[1] Translated by R. Farquharson Sharp.

194

**Nora.** There is a shilling. No, keep the change. *(The Porter thanks her, and goes out. Nora shuts the door. She is laughing to herself, as she takes off her hat and coat. She takes a packet of macaroons from her pocket and eats one or two; then goes cautiously to her husband's door and listens.)* Yes, he is in.

*(Still humming, she goes to the table on the right.)*

**Helmer** *(calls out from his room).* Is that my little lark twittering out there?
**Nora** *(busy opening some of the parcels).* Yes, it is!
**Helmer.** Is it my little squirrel bustling about?
**Nora.** Yes!
**Helmer.** When did my squirrel come home?
**Nora.** Just now. *(Puts the bag of macaroons into her pocket and wipes her mouth.)* Come in here, Torvald, and see what I have bought.
**Helmer.** Don't disturb me. *(A little later, he opens the door and looks into the room, pen in hand.)* Bought, did you say? All these things? Has my little spendthrift been wasting money again?
**Nora.** Yes, but, Torvald, this year we really can let ourselves go a little. This is the first Christmas that we have not needed to economise.
**Helmer.** Still, you know, we can't spend money recklessly.
**Nora.** Yes, Torvald, we may be a wee bit more reckless now, mayn't we? Just a tiny wee bit! You are going to have a big salary and earn lots and lots of money.
**Helmer.** Yes, after the New Year; but then it will be a whole quarter before the salary is due.
**Nora.** Pooh! we can borrow till then.
**Helmer.** Nora! *(Goes up to her and takes her playfully by the ear.)* The same little featherhead! Suppose, now, that I borrowed fifty pounds to-day, and you spent it all in the Christmas week, and then on New Year's Eve a slate fell on my head and killed me, and ——
**Nora** *(putting her hands over his mouth).* Oh! don't say such horrid things.
**Helmer.** Still, suppose that happened, — what then?
**Nora.** If that were to happen, I don't suppose I should care whether I owed money or not.
**Helmer.** Yes, but what about the people who had lent it?
**Nora.** They? Who would bother about them? I should not know who they were.
**Helmer.** That is like a woman! But seriously, Nora, you know what I think about that. No debt, no borrowing. There can be no freedom or beauty about a home life that depends on borrowing and debt. We two have kept bravely on the straight road so far, and we will go on the same way for the short time longer that there need be any struggle.
**Nora** *(moving towards the stove).* As you please, Torvald.
**Helmer** *(following her).* Come, come, my little skylark must not droop her wings. What is this! Is my little squirrel out of temper? *(Taking out his purse.)* Nora, what do you think I have got here?
**Nora** *(turning round quickly).* Money!

**Helmer.** There you are. *(Gives her some money.)* Do you think I don't know what a lot is wanted for house-keeping at Christmas-time?

**Nora** *(counting).* Ten shillings — a pound — two pounds! Thank you, thank you, Torvald; that will keep me going for a long time.

**Helmer.** Indeed it must.

**Nora.** Yes, yes, it will. But come here and let me show you what I have bought. And all so cheap! Look, here is a new suit for Ivar, and a sword; and a horse and a trumpet for Bob; and a doll and dolly's bedstead for Emmy, — they are very plain, but anyway she will soon break them in pieces. And here are dress-lengths and handkerchiefs for the maids; old Anne ought really to have something better.

**Helmer.** And what is in this parcel?

**Nora** *(crying out).* No, no! you mustn't see that till this evening.

**Helmer.** Very well. But now tell me something reasonable that you would particularly like to have.

**Nora.** No, I really can't think of anything — unless, Torvald ——

**Helmer.** Well?

**Nora** *(playing with his coat buttons, and without raising her eyes to his).* If you really want to give me something, you might — you might ——

**Helmer.** Well, out with it!

**Nora** *(speaking quickly).* You might give me money, Torvald. Only just as much as you can afford; and then one of these days I will buy something with it.

**Helmer.** But, Nora ——

**Nora.** Oh, do! dear Torvald; please, please do! Then I will wrap it up in beautiful gilt paper and hang it on the Christmas tree. Wouldn't that be fun?

**Helmer.** What are little people called that are always wasting money?

**Nora.** Spendthrifts — I know. Let us do as you suggest, Torvald, and then I shall have time to think what I am most in want of. That is a very sensible plan, isn't it?

**Helmer** *(smiling).* Indeed it is — that is to say, if you were really to save out of the money I give you, and then really buy something for yourself. But if you spend it all on the housekeeping and any number of unnecessary things, then I merely have to pay up again.

**Nora.** Oh but, Torvald ——

**Helmer.** You can't deny it, my dear little Nora. *(Puts his arm round her waist.)* It's a sweet little spendthrift, but she uses up a deal of money. One would hardly believe how expensive such little persons are!

**Nora.** It's a shame to say that. I do really save all I can.

**Helmer** *(laughing).* That's very true, — all you can. But you can't save anything!

**Nora** *(smiling quietly and happily).* You haven't any idea how many expenses we skylarks and squirrels have, Torvald.

**Helmer.** You are an odd little soul. Very like your father. You always find some new way of wheedling money out of me, and, as soon as you have got it, it seems to melt in your hands. You never know where it has gone. Still, one must take you as you are. It is in the blood; for indeed it is true that you can inherit these things, Nora.

**Nora.** Ah, I wish I had inherited many of papa's qualities.

**Helmer.** And I would not wish you to be anything but just what you are, my sweet little skylark. But, do you know, it strikes me that you are looking rather — what shall I say — rather uneasy to-day?

**Nora.** Do I?

**Helmer.** You do, really. Look straight at me.

**Nora** *(looks at him).* Well?

**Helmer** *(wagging his finger at her).* Hasn't Miss Sweet-Tooth been breaking rules in town to-day?

**Nora.** No; what makes you think that?

**Helmer.** Hasn't she paid a visit to the confectioner's?

**Nora.** No, I assure you, Torvald ——

**Helmer.** Not been nibbling sweets?

**Nora.** No, certainly not.

**Helmer.** Not even taken a bite at a macaroon or two?

**Nora.** No, Torvald, I assure you really ——

**Helmer.** There, there, of course I was only joking.

**Nora** *(going to the table on the right).* I should not think of going against your wishes.

**Helmer.** No, I am sure of that! Besides, you gave me your word —— *(Going up to her.)* Keep your little Christmas secrets to yourself, my darling. They will all be revealed to-night when the Christmas tree is lit, no doubt.

**Nora.** Did you remember to invite Doctor Rank?

**Helmer.** No. But there is no need; as a matter of course he will come to dinner with us. However, I will ask him, when he comes in this morning. I have ordered some good wine. Nora, you can't think how I am looking forward to this evening.

**Nora.** So am I! And how the children will enjoy themselves, Torvald!

**Helmer.** It is splendid to feel that one has a perfectly safe appointment, and a big enough income. It's delightful to think of, isn't it?

**Nora.** It's wonderful!

**Helmer.** Do you remember last Christmas? For a full three weeks beforehand you shut yourself up every evening till long after midnight, making ornaments for the Christmas tree and all the other fine things that were to be a surprise to us. It was the dullest three weeks I ever spent!

**Nora.** I didn't find it dull.

**Helmer** *(smiling).* But there was precious little result, Nora.

**Nora.** Oh, you shouldn't tease me about that again. How could I help the cat's going in and tearing everything to pieces?

**Helmer.** Of course you couldn't, poor little girl. You had the best of intentions to please us all, and that's the main thing. But it is a good thing that our hard times are over.

**Nora.** Yes, it is really wonderful.

**Helmer.** This time I needn't sit here and be dull all alone, and you needn't ruin your dear eyes and your pretty little hands ——

**Nora** *(clapping her hands).* No, Torvald, I needn't any longer, need I! It's wonderfully lovely to hear you say so! *(Taking his arm.)* Now I will tell you how I have been thinking we ought to arrange things, Torvald. As soon as Christmas is over —— (*A bell rings in the hall.*) There's the bell. (*She tidies the room a little.*) There's someone at the door. What a nuisance!

**Helmer.** If it is a caller, remember I am not at home.

**Maid** (*in the doorway*). A lady to see you, ma'am, — a stranger.

**Nora.** Ask her to come in.

**Maid** (*to Helmer*). The doctor came at the same time, sir.

**Helmer.** Did he go straight into my room?

**Maid.** Yes, sir.

(*Helmer goes into his room. The Maid ushers in Mrs. Linde, who is in traveling dress, and shuts the door.*)

**Mrs. Linde** (*in a dejected and timid voice*). How do you do, Nora?

**Nora** (*doubtfully*). How do you do ——

**Mrs. Linde.** You don't recognise me, I suppose.

**Nora.** No, I don't know — yes, to be sure, I seem to —— (*Suddenly.*) Yes! Christine! Is it really you?

**Mrs. Linde.** Yes, it is I.

**Nora.** Christine! To think of my not recognising you! And yet how could I —— (*In a gentle voice.*) How you have altered, Christine!

**Mrs. Linde.** Yes, I have indeed. In nine, ten long years ——

**Nora.** Is it so long since we met? I suppose it is. The last eight years have been a happy time for me, I can tell you. And so now you have come into the town, and have taken this long journey in winter — that was plucky of you.

**Mrs. Linde.** I arrived by steamer this morning.

**Nora.** To have some fun at Christmas-time, of course. How delightful! We will have such fun together! But take off your things. You are not cold, I hope. (*Helps her.*) Now we will sit down by the stove, and be cosy. No, take this arm-chair; I will sit here in the rocking-chair. (*Takes her hands.*) Now you look like your old self again; it was only the first moment —— You are a little paler, Christine, and perhaps a little thinner.

**Mrs. Linde.** And much, much older, Nora.

**Nora.** Perhaps a little older; very, very little; certainly not much. (*Stops suddenly and speaks seriously.*) What a thoughtless creature I am, chattering away like this. My poor, dear Christine, do forgive me.

**Mrs. Linde.** What do you mean, Nora?

**Nora** (*gently*). Poor Christine, you are a widow.

**Mrs. Linde.** Yes; it is three years ago now.

**Nora.** Yes, I knew; I saw it in the papers. I assure you, Christine, I meant ever so often to write to you at the time, but I always put it off and something always prevented me.

**Mrs. Linde.** I quite understand, dear.

**Nora.** It was very bad of me, Christine. Poor thing, how you must have suffered. And he left you nothing?

**Mrs. Linde.** No.

**Nora.** And no children?

**Mrs. Linde.** No.

**Nora.** Nothing at all, then?

**Mrs. Linde.** Not even any sorrow or grief to live upon.

**Nora** *(looking incredulously at her).* But, Christine, is that possible?

**Mrs. Linde** *(smiles sadly and strokes her hair).* It sometimes happens, Nora.

**Nora.** So you are quite alone. How dreadfully sad that must be. I have three lovely children. You can't see them just now, for they are out with their nurse. But now you must tell me all about it.

**Mrs. Linde.** No, no; I want to hear you.

**Nora.** No, you must begin. I mustn't be selfish to-day, to-day I must only think of your affairs. But there is one thing I must tell you. Do you know we have just had a great piece of good luck?

**Mrs. Linde.** No, what is it?

**Nora.** Just fancy, my husband has been made manager of the Bank!

**Mrs. Linde.** Your husband? What good luck!

**Nora.** Yes, tremendous! A barrister's profession is such an uncertain thing, especially if he won't undertake unsavoury cases; and naturally Torvald has never been willing to do that, and I quite agree with him. You may imagine how pleased we are! He is to take up his work in the Bank at the New Year, and then he will have a big salary and lots of commissions. For the future we can live quite differently — we can do just as we like. I feel so relieved and so happy, Christine! It will be splendid to have heaps of money and not need to have any anxiety, won't it?

**Mrs. Linde.** Yes, anyhow I think it would be delightful to have what one needs.

**Nora.** No, not only what one needs, but heaps and heaps of money.

**Mrs. Linde** *(smiling).* Nora, Nora, haven't you learnt sense yet? In our schooldays you were a great spendthrift.

**Nora** *(laughing).* Yes, that is what Torvald says now. *(Wags her finger at her.)* But "Nora, Nora" is not so silly as you think. We have not been in a position for me to waste money. We have both had to work.

**Mrs. Linde.** You too?

**Nora.** Yes; odds and ends, needlework, crochet-work, embroidery, and that kind of thing. *(Dropping her voice.)* And other things as well. You know Torvald left his office when we were married? There was no prospect of promotion there, and he had to try and earn more than before. But during the first year he overworked himself dreadfully. You see, he had to make money every way he could, and he worked early and late; but he couldn't stand it, and fell dreadfully ill, and the doctors said it was necessary for him to go south.

**Mrs. Linde.** You spent a whole year in Italy, didn't you?

**Nora.** Yes. It was no easy matter to get away, I can tell you. It was just after Ivar was born; but naturally we had to go. It was a wonderfully beautiful journey, and it saved Torvald's life. But it cost a tremendous lot of money, Christine.

**Mrs. Linde.** So I should think.

**Nora.** It cost about two hundred and fifty pounds. That's a lot, isn't it?

**Mrs. Linde.** Yes, and in emergencies like that it is lucky to have the money.

**Nora.** I ought to tell you that we had it from papa.

**Mrs. Linde.** Oh, I see. It was just about that time that he died, wasn't it?

**Nora.** Yes; and, just think of it, I couldn't go and nurse him. I was expecting little Ivar's birth every day and I had my poor sick Torvald to look after. My dear, kind father — I never saw him again, Christine. That was the saddest time I have known since our marriage.

**Mrs. Linde.** And your husband came back quite well?

**Nora.** As sound as a bell!

**Mrs. Linde.** But — the doctor?

**Nora.** What doctor?

**Mrs. Linde.** I thought your maid said the gentleman who arrived here just as I did was the doctor?

**Nora.** Yes, that was Doctor Rank, but he doesn't come here professionally. He is our greatest friend, and comes in at least once every day. No, Torvald has not had an hour's illness since then, and our children are strong and healthy and so am I. *(Jumps up and claps her hands.)* Christine! Christine! it's good to be alive and happy! —— But how horrid of me; I am talking of nothing but my own affairs. *(Sits on a stool near her, and rests her arms on her knees.)* You mustn't be angry with me. Tell me, is it really true that you did not love your husband? Why did you marry him?

**Mrs. Linde.** My mother was alive then, and was bedridden and helpless, and I had to provide for my two younger brothers; so I did not think I was justified in refusing his offer.

**Nora.** No, perhaps you were quite right. He was rich at that time, then?

**Mrs. Linde.** I believe he was quite well off. But his business was a precarious one; and, when he died, it all went to pieces and there was nothing left.

**Nora.** And then? ——

**Mrs. Linde.** Well, I had to turn my hand to anything I could find — first a small shop, then a small school, and so on. The last three years have seemed like one long working-day, with no rest. Now it is at an end, Nora. My poor mother needs me no more, for she is gone; and the boys do not need me either; they have got situations and can shift for themselves.

**Nora.** What a relief you must feel it ——

**Mrs. Linde.** No, indeed; I only feel my life unspeakably empty. No one to live for any more. *(Gets up restlessly.)* That was why I could not stand the life in my little backwater any longer. I hope it may be easier here to find something which will busy me and occupy my thoughts. If only I could have the good luck to get some regular work — office work of some kind ——

**Nora.** But, Christine, that is so frightfully tiring, and you look tired out now. You had far better go away to some watering-place.

**Mrs. Linde** *(walking to the window)*. I have no father to give me money for a journey, Nora.

**Nora** *(rising)*. Oh, don't be angry with me.

**Mrs. Linde** *(going up to her)*. It is you that must not be angry with me, dear. The worst of a position like mine is that it makes one so bitter. No one to work for, and yet obliged to be always on the look-out for chances. One must live, and so one becomes selfish. When you told me of the happy turn your fortunes have taken — you will hardly believe it — I was delighted not so much on your account as on my own.

**Nora.** How do you mean? — Oh, I understand. You mean that perhaps Torvald could get you something to do.

**Mrs. Linde.** Yes, that was what I was thinking of.

**Nora.** He must, Christine. Just leave it to me; I will broach the subject very cleverly — I will think of something that will please him very much. It will make me so happy to be of some use to you.

**Mrs. Linde.** How kind you are, Nora, to be so anxious to help me! It is doubly kind in you, for you know so little of the burdens and troubles of life.

**Nora.** I ——? I know so little of them?

**Mrs. Linde** *(smiling)*. My dear! Small household cares and that sort of thing! — You are a child, Nora.

**Nora** *(tosses her head and crosses the stage)*. You ought not to be so superior.

**Mrs. Linde.** No?

**Nora.** You are just like the others. They all think that I am incapable of anything really serious ——

**Mrs. Linde.** Come, come ——

**Nora.** — that I have gone through nothing in this world of cares.

**Mrs. Linde.** But, my dear Nora, you have just told me all your troubles.

**Nora.** Pooh! — those were trifles. *(Lowering her voice.)* I have not told you the important thing.

**Mrs. Linde.** The important thing? What do you mean?

**Nora.** You look down upon me altogether, Christine — but you ought not to. You are proud, aren't you, of having worked so hard and so long for your mother?

**Mrs. Linde.** Indeed, I don't look down on any one. But it is true that I am both proud and glad to think that I was privileged to make the end of my mother's life almost free from care.

**Nora.** And you are proud to think of what you have done for your brothers.

**Mrs. Linde.** I think I have the right to be.

**Nora.** I think so, too. But now, listen to this; I too have something to be proud and glad of.

**Mrs. Linde.** I have no doubt you have. But what do you refer to?

**Nora.** Speak low. Suppose Torvald were to hear! He mustn't on any account — no one in the world must know, Christine, except you.

**Mrs. Linde.** But what is it?

**Nora.** Come here. *(Pulls her down on the sofa beside her.)* Now I will show you that I too have something to be proud and glad of. It was I who saved Torvald's life.

**Mrs. Linde.** "Saved"? How?

**Nora.** I told you about our trip to Italy. Torvald would never have recovered if he had not gone there ——

**Mrs. Linde.** Yes, but your father gave you the necessary funds.

**Nora** *(smiling)*. Yes, that is what Torvald and all the others think, but ——

**Mrs. Linde.** But ——

**Nora.** Papa didn't give us a shilling. It was I who procured the money.

**Mrs. Linde.** You? All that large sum?

**Nora.** Two hundred and fifty pounds. What do you think of that?

**Mrs. Linde.** But, Nora, how could you possibly do it? Did you win a prize in the Lottery?

**Nora** (*contemptuously*). In the Lottery? There would have been no credit in that.

**Mrs. Linde.** But where did you get it from, then?

**Nora** (*humming and smiling with an air of mystery*). Hm, hm! Aha!

**Mrs. Linde.** Because you couldn't have borrowed it.

**Nora.** Couldn't I? Why not?

**Mrs. Linde.** No, a wife cannot borrow without her husband's consent.

**Nora** (*tossing her head*). Oh, if it is a wife who has any head for business — a wife who has the wit to be a little bit clever ——

**Mrs. Linde.** I don't understand it at all, Nora.

**Nora.** There is no need you should. I never said I had borrowed the money. I may have got it some other way. (*Lies back on the sofa.*) Perhaps I got it from some other admirer. When anyone is as attractive as I am ——

**Mrs. Linde.** You are a mad creature.

**Nora.** Now, you know you're full of curiosity, Christine.

**Mrs. Linde.** Listen to me, Nora dear. Haven't you been a little bit imprudent?

**Nora** (*sits up straight*). Is it imprudent to save your husband's life?

**Mrs. Linde.** It seems to me imprudent, without his knowledge, to ——

**Nora.** But it was absolutely necessary that he should not know! My goodness, can't you understand that? It was necessary he should have no idea what a dangerous condition he was in. It was to me that the doctors came and said that his life was in danger, and that the only thing to save him was to live in the south. Do you suppose I didn't try, first of all, to get what I wanted as if it were for myself? I told him how much I should love to travel abroad like other young wives; I tried tears and entreaties with him; I told him that he ought to remember the condition I was in, and that he ought to be kind and indulgent to me; I even hinted that he might raise a loan. That nearly made him angry, Christine. He said I was thoughtless, and that it was his duty as my husband not to indulge me in my whims and caprices — as I believe he called them. Very well I thought, you must be saved — and that was how I came to devise a way out of the difficulty ——

**Mrs. Linde.** And did your husband never get to know from your father that the money had not come from him?

**Nora.** No, never. Papa died just at that time. I had meant to let him into the secret and beg him never to reveal it. But he was so ill then — alas, there never was any need to tell him.

**Mrs. Linde.** And since then have you never told your secret to your husband?

**Nora.** Good Heavens, no! How could you think so? A man who has such strong opinions about these things! And besides, how painful and humiliating it would be for Torvald, with his manly independence, to know that he owed me anything! It would upset our mutual relations altogether; our beautiful happy home would no longer be what it is now.

**Mrs. Linde.** Do you mean never to tell him about it?

**Nora** *(meditatively, and with a half smile).* Yes—some day, perhaps, after many years, when I am no longer as nice-looking as I am now. Don't laugh at me! I mean, of course, when Torvald is no longer as devoted to me as he is now; when my dancing and dressing-up and reciting have palled on him; then it may be a good thing to have something in reserve——*(Breaking off.)* What nonsense! That time will never come. Now, what do you think of my great secret, Christine? Do you still think I am of no use? I can tell you, too, that this affair has caused me a lot of worry. It has been by no means easy for me to meet my engagements punctually. I may tell you that there is something that is called, in business, quarterly interest, and another thing called payment in instalments, and it is always so dreadfully difficult to manage them. I have had to save a little here and there, where I could, you understand. I have not been able to put aside much from my housekeeping money, for Torvald must have a good table. I couldn't let my children be shabbily dressed; I have felt obliged to use up all he gave me for them, the sweet little darlings!

**Mrs. Linde.** So it has all had to come out of your own necessaries of life, poor Nora?

**Nora.** Of course. Besides, I was the one responsible for it. Whenever Torvald has given me money for new dresses and such things, I have never spent more than half of it; I have always bought the simplest and cheapest things. Thank Heaven, any clothes look well on me, and so Torvald has never noticed it. But it was often very hard on me, Christine—because it is delightful to be really well dressed, isn't it?

**Mrs. Linde.** Quite so.

**Nora.** Well, then I have found other ways of earning money. Last winter I was lucky enough to get a lot of copying to do; so I locked myself up and sat writing every evening until quite late at night. Many a time I was desperately tired; but all the same it was a tremendous pleasure to sit there working and earning money. It was like being a man.

**Mrs. Linde.** How much have you been able to pay off in that way?

**Nora.** I can't tell you exactly. You see, it is very difficult to keep an account of a business matter of that kind. I only know that I have paid every penny that I could scrape together. Many a time I was at my wits' end. *(Smiles.)* Then I used to sit here and imagine that a rich old gentleman had fallen in love with me——

**Mrs. Linde.** What! Who was it?

**Nora.** Be quiet!—that he had died; and that when his will was opened it contained, written in big letters, the instruction: "The lovely Mrs. Nora Helmer is to have all I possess paid over to her at once in cash."

**Mrs. Linde.** But, my dear Nora—who could the man be?

**Nora.** Good gracious, can't you understand? There was no old gentleman at all; it was only something that I used to sit here and imagine, when I couldn't think of any way of procuring money. But it's all the same now; the tiresome old person can stay where he is, as far as I am concerned; I don't care about him or his will either, for I am free from care now. *(Jumps up.)* My goodness, it's delightful to think of, Christine! Free from care! To be able to be free from care, quite free from care; to be able to play and romp with the children; to be able to keep the house beautifully and have everything just as Torvald likes it! And, think of it, soon the spring will come and the big blue sky! Perhaps we shall be able to take a little trip — perhaps I shall see the sea again! Oh, it's a wonderful thing to be alive and be happy. (*A bell is heard in the hall.*)

**Mrs. Linde** (*rising*).  There is the bell; perhaps I had better go.

**Nora.**  No, don't go; no one will come in here; it is sure to be for Torvald.

**Servant** (*at the hall door*).  Excuse me, ma'am — there is a gentleman to see the master, and as the doctor is with him ——

**Nora.**  Who is it?

**Krogstad** (*at the door*).  It is I, Mrs. Helmer. (*Mrs. Linde starts, trembles, and turns to the window.*)

**Nora** (*takes a step towards him, and speaks in a strained, low voice*).  You? What is it? What do you want to see my husband about?

**Krogstad.**  Bank business — in a way. I have a small post in the Bank, and I hear your husband is to be our chief now ——

**Nora.**  Then it is ——

**Krogstad.**  Nothing but dry business matters, Mrs. Helmer; absolutely nothing else.

**Nora.**  Be so good as to go into the study, then. (*She bows indifferently to him and shuts the door into the hall; then comes back and makes up the fire in the stove.*)

**Mrs. Linde.**  Nora — who was that man?

**Nora.**  A lawyer, of the name of Krogstad.

**Mrs. Linde.**  Then it really was he.

**Nora.**  Do you know the man?

**Mrs. Linde.**  I used to — many years ago. At one time he was a solicitor's clerk in our town.

**Nora.**  Yes, he was.

**Mrs. Linde.**  He is greatly altered.

**Nora.**  He made a very unhappy marriage.

**Mrs. Linde.**  He is a widower now, isn't he?

**Nora.**  With several children. There now, it is burning up.

(*Shuts the door of the stove and moves the rocking-chair aside.*)

**Mrs. Linde.**  They say he carries on various kinds of business.

**Nora.**  Really! Perhaps he does; I don't know anything about it. But don't let us think of business; it is so tiresome.

**Doctor Rank** (*comes out of Helmer's study. Before he shuts the door he calls to him*).  No, my dear fellow, I won't disturb you; I would rather go in to your wife for a little while. (*Shuts the door and sees Mrs. Linde.*) I beg your pardon; I am afraid I am disturbing you too.

**Nora.**  No, not at all. (*Introducing him.*) Doctor Rank, Mrs. Linde.

**Rank.**  I have often heard Mrs. Linde's name mentioned here. I think I passed you on the stairs when I arrived, Mrs. Linde?

**Mrs. Linde.** Yes, I go up very slowly; I can't manage stairs well.

**Rank.** Ah! some slight internal weakness?

**Mrs. Linde.** No, the fact is I have been overworking myself.

**Rank.** Nothing more than that? Then I suppose you have come to town to amuse yourself with our entertainments?

**Mrs. Linde.** I have come to look for work.

**Rank.** Is that a good cure for overwork?

**Mrs. Linde.** One must live, Doctor Rank.

**Rank.** Yes, the general opinion seems to be that it is necessary.

**Nora.** Look here, Doctor Rank — you know you want to live.

**Rank.** Certainly. However wretched I may feel, I want to prolong the agony as long as possible. All my patients are like that. And so are those who are morally diseased; one of them, and a bad case too, is at this very moment with Helmer——

**Mrs. Linde** *(sadly).* Ah!

**Nora.** Whom do you mean?

**Rank.** A lawyer of the name of Krogstad, a fellow you don't know at all. He suffers from a diseased moral character, Mrs. Helmer; but even he began talking of its being highly important that he should live.

**Nora.** Did he? What did he want to speak to Torvald about?

**Rank.** I have no idea; I only heard that it was something about the Bank.

**Nora.** I didn't know this — what's his name — Krogstad had anything to do with the Bank.

**Rank.** Yes, he has some sort of appointment there. *(To Mrs. Linde.)* I don't know whether you find also in your part of the world that there are certain people who go zealously snuffing about to smell out moral corruption, and, as soon as they have found some, put the person concerned into some lucrative position where they can keep their eye on him. Healthy natures are left out in the cold.

**Mrs. Linde.** Still I think the sick are those who most need taking care of.

**Rank** *(shrugging his shoulders).* Yes, there you are. That is the sentiment that is turning Society into a sickhouse.

*(Nora, who has been absorbed in her thoughts, breaks out into smothered laughter and claps her hands.)*

**Rank.** Why do you laugh at that? Have you any notion what Society really is?

**Nora.** What do I care about tiresome Society? I am laughing at something quite different, something extremely amusing. Tell me, Doctor Rank, are all the people who are employed in the Bank dependent on Torvald now?

**Rank.** Is that what you find so extremely amusing?

**Nora** *(smiling and humming).* That's my affair! *(Walking about the room.)* It's perfectly glorious to think that we have — that Torvald has so much power over so many people. *(Takes the packet from her pocket.)* Doctor Rank, what do you say to a macaroon?

**Rank.** What, macaroons? I thought they were forbidden here.

**Nora.** Yes, but these are some Christine gave me.

**Mrs. Linde.** What! I? —

**Nora.** Oh, well, don't be alarmed! You couldn't know that Torvald had forbidden them. I must tell you that he is afraid they will spoil my teeth. But, bah! — once in a way —— That's so, isn't it, Doctor Rank? By your leave? *(Puts a macaroon into his mouth.)* You must have one too, Christine. And I shall have one, just a little one — or at most two. *(Walking about.)* I am tremendously happy. There is just one thing in the world now that I should dearly love to do.

**Rank.** Well, what is that?

**Nora.** It's something I should dearly love to say, if Torvald could hear me.

**Rank.** Well, why can't you say it?

**Nora.** No, I daren't; it's so shocking.

**Mrs. Linde.** Shocking?

**Rank.** Well, I should not advise you to say it. Still, with us you might. What is it you would so much like to say if Torvald could hear you?

**Nora.** I should just love to say — Well, I'm damned!

**Rank.** Are you mad?

**Mrs. Linde.** Nora, dear ——!

**Rank.** Say it, here he is!

**Nora** *(hiding the packet).* Hush! Hush! Hush!

*(Helmer comes out of his room, with his coat over his arm and his hat in his hand.)*

**Nora.** Well, Torvald dear, have you got rid of him?

**Helmer.** Yes, he has just gone.

**Nora.** Let me introduce you — this is Christine, who has come to town.

**Helmer.** Christine ——? Excuse me, but I don't know ——

**Nora.** Mrs. Linde, dear; Christine Linde.

**Helmer.** Of course. A school friend of my wife's, I presume?

**Mrs. Linde.** Yes, we have known each other since then.

**Nora.** And just think, she has taken a long journey in order to see you.

**Helmer.** What do you mean?

**Mrs. Linde.** No, really, I ——

**Nora.** Christine is tremendously clever at book-keeping, and she is frightfully anxious to work under some clever man, so as to perfect herself ——

**Helmer.** Very sensible, Mrs. Linde.

**Nora.** And when she heard you had been appointed manager of the Bank — the news was telegraphed, you know — she travelled here as quick as she could. Torvald, I am sure you will be able to do something for Christine, for my sake, won't you?

**Helmer.** Well, it is not altogether impossible. I presume you are a widow, Mrs. Linde?

**Mrs. Linde.** Yes.

**Helmer.** And have had some experience of book-keeping?

**Mrs. Linde.** Yes, a fair amount.

**Helmer.** Ah! well, it's very likely I may be able to find something for you ——

**Nora** *(clapping her hands)*. What did I tell you? What did I tell you?

**Helmer.** You have just come at a fortunate moment, Mrs. Linde.

**Mrs. Linde.** How am I to thank you?

**Helmer.** There is no need. *(Puts on his coat.)* But to-day you must excuse me ——

**Rank.** Wait a minute; I will come with you.

*(Brings his fur coat from the hall and warms it at the fire.)*

**Nora.** Don't be long away, Torvald dear.

**Helmer.** About an hour, not more.

**Nora.** Are you going too, Christine?

**Mrs. Linde** *(putting on her cloak)*. Yes, I must go and look for a room.

**Helmer.** Oh, well then, we can walk down the street together.

**Nora** *(helping her)*. What a pity it is we are so short of space here; I am afraid it is impossible for us ——

**Mrs. Linde.** Please don't think of it! Good-bye, Nora dear, and many thanks.

**Nora.** Good-bye for the present. Of course you will come back this evening. And you too, Dr. Rank. What do you say? If you are well enough? Oh, you must be! Wrap yourself up well.

*(They go to the door all talking together. Children's voices are heard on the staircase.)*

**Nora.** There they are. There they are! *(She runs to open the door. The Nurse comes in with the children.)* Come in! Come in! *(Stoops and kisses them.)* Oh, you sweet blessings! Look at them, Christine! Aren't they darlings?

**Rank.** Don't let us stand here in the draught.

**Helmer.** Come along, Mrs. Linde; the place will only be bearable for a mother now!

*(Rank, Helmer, and Mrs. Linde go downstairs. The Nurse comes forward with the children; Nora shuts the hall door.)*

**Nora.** How fresh and well you look! Such red cheeks! — like apples and roses. *(The children all talk at once while she speaks to them.)* Have you had great fun? That's splendid! What, you pulled both Emmy and Bob along on the sledge? — both at once? — that *was* good. You are a clever boy, Ivar. Let me take her for a little, Anne. My sweet little baby doll! *(Takes the baby from the Maid and dances it up and down.)* Yes, yes, mother will dance with Bob too. What! Have you been snowballing? I wish I had been there too! No, no, I will take their things off, Anne; please let me do it, it is such fun. Go in now, you look half frozen. There is some hot coffee for you on the stove.

*(The Nurse goes into the room on the left. Nora takes off the children's things and throws them about, while they all talk to her at once.)*

**Nora.** Really! Did a big dog run after you? But it didn't bite you? No, dogs don't bite nice little dolly children. You mustn't look at the parcels, Ivar. What are they? Ah, I daresay you would like to know. No, no — it's something nasty! Come, let us have a game! What shall we play at? Hide and Seek? Yes, we'll play Hide and Seek. Bob shall hide first. Must I hide? Very well, I'll hide first.

*(She and the children laugh and shout, and romp in and out of the room; at last Nora hides under the table, the children rush in and look for her, but do not see her; they hear her smothered laughter, run to the table, lift up the cloth and find her. Shouts of laughter. She crawls forward and pretends to frighten them. Fresh laughter. Meanwhile there has been a knock at the hall door, but none of them has noticed it. The door is half opened, and Krogstad appears. He waits a little; the game goes on.)*

**Krogstad.** Excuse me, Mrs. Helmer.

**Nora** *(with a stifled cry, turns round and gets up on to her knees).* Ah! what do you want?

**Krogstad.** Excuse me, the outer door was ajar; I suppose someone forgot to shut it.

**Nora** *(rising).* My husband is out, Mr. Krogstad.

**Krogstad.** I know that.

**Nora.** What do you want here, then?

**Krogstad.** A word with you.

**Nora.** With me? — *(to the children, gently.)* Go in to nurse. What? No, the strange man won't do mother any harm. When he has gone we will have another game. *(She takes the children into the room on the left, and shuts the door after them.)* You want to speak to me?

**Krogstad.** Yes, I do.

**Nora.** To-day? It is not the first of the month yet.

**Krogstad.** No, it is Christmas Eve, and it will depend on yourself what sort of a Christmas you will spend.

**Nora.** What do you want? To-day it is absolutely impossible for me ——

**Krogstad.** We won't talk about that till later on. This is something different. I presume you can give me a moment?

**Nora.** Yes — yes, I can — although ——

**Krogstad.** Good. I was in Olsen's Restaurant and saw your husband going down the street ——

**Nora.** Yes?

**Krogstad.** With a lady.

**Nora.** What then?

**Krogstad.** May I make so bold as to ask if it was a Mrs. Linde?

**Nora.** It was.

**Krogstad.** Just arrived in town?

**Nora.** Yes, to-day.

**Krogstad.** She is a great friend of yours, isn't she?

**Nora.**  She is. But I don't see ——

**Krogstad.**  I knew her too, once upon a time.

**Nora.**  I am aware of that.

**Krogstad.**  Are you? So you know all about it; I thought as much. Then I can ask you, without beating about the bush — is Mrs. Linde to have an appointment in the Bank?

**Nora.**  What right have you to question me, Mr. Krogstad? — You, one of my husband's subordinates! But since you ask, you shall know. Yes, Mrs. Linde *is* to have an appointment. And it was I who pleaded her cause, Mr. Krogstad, let me tell you that.

**Krogstad.**  I was right in what I thought, then.

**Nora** *(walking up and down the stage)*.  Sometimes one has a tiny little bit of influence, I should hope. Because one is a woman, it does not necessarily follow that ——. When anyone is in a subordinate position, Mr. Krogstad, they should really be careful to avoid offending anyone who — who ——

**Krogstad.**  Who has influence?

**Nora.**  Exactly.

**Krogstad** *(changing his tone)*.  Mrs. Helmer, you will be so good as to use your influence on my behalf.

**Nora.**  What? What do you mean?

**Krogstad.**  You will be so kind as to see that I am allowed to keep my subordinate position in the Bank.

**Nora.**  What do you mean by that? Who proposes to take your post away from you?

**Krogstad.**  Oh, there is no necessity to keep up the pretence of ignorance. I can quite understand that your friend is not very anxious to expose herself to the chance of rubbing shoulders with me; and I quite understand, too, whom I have to thank for being turned off.

**Nora.**  But I assure you ——

**Krogstad.**  Very likely; but, to come to the point, the time has come when I should advise you to use your influence to prevent that.

**Nora.**  But, Mr. Krogstad, I *have* no influence.

**Krogstad.**  Haven't you? I thought you said yourself just now ——

**Nora.**  Naturally I did not mean you to put that construction on it. I! What should make you think I have any influence of that kind with my husband?

**Krogstad.**  Oh, I have known your husband from our student days. I don't suppose he is any more unassailable than other husbands.

**Nora.**  If you speak slightingly of my husband, I shall turn you out of the house.

**Krogstad.**  You are bold, Mrs. Helmer.

**Nora.**  I am not afraid of you any longer. As soon as the New Year comes, I shall in a very short time be free of the whole thing.

**Krogstad** *(controlling himself)*.  Listen to me, Mrs. Helmer. If necessary, I am prepared to fight for my small post in the Bank as if I were fighting for my life.

**Nora.**  So it seems.

**Krogstad.**  It is not only for the sake of the money; indeed, that weighs least with me in the matter. There is another reason — well, I may as well tell you. My position is this. I daresay you know, like everybody else, that once, many years ago, I was guilty of an indiscretion.

**Nora.** I think I have heard something of the kind.

**Krogstad.** The matter never came into court; but every way seemed to be closed to me after that. So I took to the business that you know of. I had to do something; and, honestly, I don't think I've been one of the worst. But now I must cut myself free from all that. My sons are growing up; for their sake I must try and win back as much respect as I can in the town. This post in the Bank was like the first step up for me — and now your husband is going to kick me downstairs again into the mud.

**Nora.** But you must believe me, Mr. Krogstad; it is not in my power to help you at all.

**Krogstad.** Then it is because you haven't the will; but I have means to compel you.

**Nora.** You don't mean that you will tell my husband that I owe you money?

**Krogstad.** Hm! — suppose I were to tell him?

**Nora.** It would be perfectly infamous of you. *(Sobbing.)* To think of his learning my secret, which has been my joy and pride, in such an ugly, clumsy way — that he should learn it from you! And it would put me in a horribly disagreeable position ——

**Krogstad.** Only disagreeable?

**Nora** *(impetuously)*. Well, do it, then! — and it will be the worse for you. My husband will see for himself what a blackguard you are, and you certainly won't keep your post then.

**Krogstad.** I asked you if it was only a disagreeable scene at home that you were afraid of?

**Nora.** If my husband does get to know of it, of course he will at once pay you what is still owing, and we shall have nothing more to do with you.

**Krogstad** *(coming a step nearer)*. Listen to me, Mrs. Helmer. Either you have a very bad memory or you know very little of business. I shall be obliged to remind you of a few details.

**Nora.** What do you mean?

**Krogstad.** When your husband was ill, you came to me to borrow two hundred and fifty pounds.

**Nora.** I didn't know anyone else to go to.

**Krogstad.** I promised to get you that amount ——

**Nora.** Yes, and you did so.

**Krogstad.** I promised to get you that amount, on certain conditions. Your mind was so taken up with your husband's illness, and you were so anxious to get the money for your journey, that you seem to have paid no attention to the conditions of our bargain. Therefore it will not be amiss if I remind you of them. Now, I promised to get the money on the security of a bond which I signed.

**Nora.** Yes, and which I signed.

**Krogstad.** Good. But below your signature there were a few lines constituting your father a surety for the money; those lines your father should have signed.

**Nora.** Should? He did sign them.

**Krogstad.** I had left the date blank; that is to say your father should himself have inserted the date on which he signed the paper. Do you remember that?

**Nora.** Yes, I think I remember ——

**Krogstad.** Then I gave you the bond to send by post to your father. Is that not so?

**Nora.** Yes.

**Krogstad.** And you naturally did so at once, because five or six days afterwards you brought me the bond with your father's signature. And then I gave you the money.

**Nora.** Well, haven't I been paying it off regularly?

**Krogstad.** Fairly so, yes. But — to come back to the matter in hand — that must have been a very trying time for you, Mrs. Helmer?

**Nora.** It was, indeed.

**Krogstad.** Your father was very ill, wasn't he?

**Nora.** He was very near his end.

**Krogstad.** And died soon afterwards?

**Nora.** Yes.

**Krogstad.** Tell me, Mrs. Helmer, can you by any chance remember what day your father died? — on what day of the month, I mean.

**Nora.** Papa died on the 29th of September.

**Krogstad.** That is correct; I have ascertained it for myself. And, as that is so, there is a discrepancy *(taking a paper from his pocket)* which I cannot account for.

**Nora.** What discrepancy? I don't know ——

**Krogstad.** The discrepancy consists, Mrs. Helmer, in the fact that your father signed this bond three days after his death.

**Nora.** What do you mean? I don't understand ——

**Krogstad.** Your father died on the 29th of September. But, look here; your father has dated his signature the 2nd of October. It is a discrepancy, isn't it? *(Nora is silent.)* Can you explain it to me? *(Nora is still silent.)* It is a remarkable thing, too, that the words "2nd of October," as well as the year, are not written in your father's handwriting but in one that I think I know. Well, of course it can be explained; your father may have forgotten to date his signature, and someone else may have dated it haphazard before they knew of his death. There is no harm in that. It all depends on the signature of the name; and *that* is genuine, I suppose, Mrs. Helmer? It was your father himself who signed his name here?

**Nora** *(after a short pause, throws her head up and looks defiantly at him).* No, it was not. It was I that wrote papa's name.

**Krogstad.** Are you aware that is a dangerous confession?

**Nora.** In what way? You shall have your money soon.

**Krogstad.** Let me ask you a question; why did you not send the paper to your father?

**Nora.** It was impossible; papa was so ill. If I had asked him for his signature, I should have had to tell him what the money was to be used for; and when he was so ill himself I couldn't tell him that my husband's life was in danger — it was impossible.

**Krogstad.** It would have been better for you if you had given up your trip abroad.

**Nora.** No, that was impossible. That trip was to save my husband's life; I couldn't give that up.

**Krogstad.** But did it never occur to you that you were committing a fraud on me?

**Nora.** I couldn't take that into account; I didn't trouble myself about you at all. I couldn't bear you, because you put so many heartless difficulties in my way, although you knew what a dangerous condition my husband was in.

**Krogstad.** Mrs. Helmer, you evidently do not realise clearly what it is that you have been guilty of. But I can assure you that my one false step, which lost me all my reputation, was nothing more or nothing worse than what you have done.

**Nora.** You? Do you ask me to believe that you were brave enough to run a risk to save your wife's life?

**Krogstad.** The law cares nothing about motives.

**Nora.** Then it must be a very foolish law.

**Krogstad.** Foolish or not, it is the law by which you will be judged, if I produce this paper in court.

**Nora.** I don't believe it. Is a daughter not to be allowed to spare her dying father anxiety and care? Is a wife not to be allowed to save her husband's life? I don't know much about law; but I am certain that there must be laws permitting such things as that. Have you no knowledge of such laws — you who are a lawyer? You must be a very poor lawyer, Mr. Krogstad.

**Krogstad.** Maybe. But matters of business — such business as you and I have had together — do you think I don't understand that? Very well. Do as you please. But let me tell you this — if I lose my position a second time, you shall lose yours with me.

*(He bows, and goes out through the hall.)*

**Nora** *(appears buried in thought for a short time, then tosses her head).* Nonsense! Trying to frighten me like that — I am not so silly as he thinks. *(Begins to busy herself putting the children's things in order.)* And yet ——? No, it's impossible! I did it for love's sake.

**The Children** *(in the doorway on the left).* Mother, the stranger man has gone out through the gate.

**Nora.** Yes, dears, I know. But don't tell anyone about the stranger man. Do you hear? Not even papa.

**Children.** No, mother; but will you come and play again?

**Nora.** No, no, — not now.

**Children.** But, mother, you promised us.

**Nora.** Yes, but I can't now. Run away in; I have such a lot to do. Run away in, my sweet little darlings. *(She gets them into the room by degrees and shuts the door on them; then sits down on the sofa, takes up a piece of needlework and sews a few stitches, but soon stops.)* No! *(Throws down the work, gets up, goes to the hall door and calls out.)* Helen! bring the tree in. *(Goes to the table on the left, opens a drawer, and stops again.)* No, no! it is quite impossible!

**Maid** (*coming in with the tree*).  Where shall I put it, ma'am?

**Nora.**  Here, in the middle of the floor.

**Maid.**  Shall I get you anything else?

**Nora.**  No, thank you. I have all I want.

(*Exit Maid.*)

**Nora** (*begins dressing the tree*).  A candle here — and flowers here ——. The horrible man! It's all nonsense — there's nothing wrong. The tree shall be splendid! I will do everything I can think of to please you, Torvald! — I will sing for you, dance for you — (*Helmer comes in with some papers under his arm.*) Oh! are you back already?

**Helmer.**  Yes. Has anyone been here?

**Nora.**  Here? No.

**Helmer.**  That is strange. I saw Krogstad going out of the gate.

**Nora.**  Did you? Oh yes, I forgot, Krogstad was here for a moment.

**Helmer.**  Nora, I can see from your manner that he has been here begging you to say a good word for him.

**Nora.**  Yes.

**Helmer.**  And you were to appear to do it of your own accord; you were to conceal from me the fact of his having been here; didn't he beg that of you too?

**Nora.**  Yes, Torvald, but ——

**Helmer.**  Nora, Nora, and you would be a party to that sort of thing? To have any talk with a man like that, and give him any sort of promise? And to tell me a lie into the bargain?

**Nora.**  A lie ——?

**Helmer.**  Didn't you tell me no one had been here? (*Shakes his finger at her.*) My little song-bird must never do that again. A song-bird must have a clean beak to chirp with — no false notes! (*Puts his arm round her waist.*) That is so, isn't it? Yes, I am sure it is. (*Lets her go.*) We will say no more about it. (*Sits down by the stove.*) How warm and snug it is here!

(*Turns over his papers.*)

**Nora** (*after a short pause, during which she busies herself with the Christmas tree*).  Torvald!

**Helmer.**  Yes.

**Nora.**  I am looking forward tremendously to the fancy dress ball at the Stenborgs' the day after to-morrow.

**Helmer.**  And I am tremendously curious to see what you are going to surprise me with.

**Nora.**  It was very silly of me to want to do that.

**Helmer.**  What do you mean?

**Nora.**  I can't hit upon anything that will do; everything I think of seems so silly and insignificant.

**Helmer.**  Does my little Nora acknowledge that at last?

**Nora** (*standing behind his chair with her arms on the back of it*).  Are you very busy, Torvald?

**Helmer.** Well ——

**Nora.** What are all those papers?

**Helmer.** Bank business.

**Nora.** Already?

**Helmer.** I have got authority from the retiring manager to undertake the necessary changes in the staff and in the rearrangement of the work; and I must make use of the Christmas week for that, so as to have everything in order for the new year.

**Nora.** Then that was why this poor Krogstad ——

**Helmer.** Hm!

**Nora** *(leans against the back of his chair and strokes his hair).* If you hadn't been so busy I should have asked you a tremendously big favour, Torvald.

**Helmer.** What is that? Tell me.

**Nora.** There is no one has such good taste as you. And I do so want to look nice at the fancy-dress ball. Torvald, couldn't you take me in hand and decide what I shall go as, and what sort of a dress I shall wear?

**Helmer.** Aha! so my obstinate little woman is obliged to get someone to come to her rescue?

**Nora.** Yes, Torvald, I can't get along a bit without your help.

**Helmer.** Very well, I will think it over, we shall manage to hit upon something.

**Nora.** That *is* nice of you. *(Goes to the Christmas tree. A short pause.)* How pretty the red flowers look ——. But, tell me, was it really something very bad that this Krogstad was guilty of?

**Helmer.** He forged someone's name. Have you any idea what that means?

**Nora.** Isn't it possible that he was driven to do it by necessity?

**Helmer.** Yes; or, as in so many cases, by imprudence. I am not so heartless as to condemn a man altogether because of a single false step of that kind.

**Nora.** No you wouldn't, would you, Torvald?

**Helmer.** Many a man has been able to retrieve his character, if he has openly confessed his fault and taken his punishment.

**Nora.** Punishment ——?

**Helmer.** But Krogstad did nothing of that sort; he got himself out of it by a cunning trick, and that is why he has gone under altogether.

**Nora.** But do you think it would ——?

**Helmer.** Just think how a guilty man like that has to lie and play the hypocrite with everyone, how he has to wear a mask in the presence of those near and dear to him, even before his own wife and children. And about the children — that is the most terrible part of it all, Nora.

**Nora.** How?

**Helmer.** Because such an atmosphere of lies infects and poisons the whole life of a home. Each breath the children take in such a house is full of the germs of evil.

**Nora** *(coming nearer him).* Are you sure of that?

**Helmer.** My dear, I have often seen it in the course of my life as a lawyer. Almost everyone who has gone to the bad early in life has had a deceitful mother.

**Nora.** Why do you only say — mother?

**Helmer.** It seems most commonly to be the mother's influence, though naturally a bad father's would have the same result. Every lawyer is familiar with the fact. This Krogstad, now, has been persistently poisoning his own children with lies and dissimulation; that is why I say he has lost all moral character. *(Holds out his hands to her.)* That is why my sweet little Nora must promise me not to plead his cause. Give me your hand on it. Come, come, what is this? Give me your hand. There now, that's settled. I assure you it would be quite impossible for me to work with him; I literally feel physically ill when I am in the company of such people.

**Nora** *(takes her hand out of his and goes to the opposite side of the Christmas tree).* How hot it is in here; and I have such a lot to do.

**Helmer** *(getting up and putting his papers in order).* Yes, and I must try and read through some of these before dinner; and I must think about your costume, too. And it is just possible I may have something ready in gold paper to hang up on the tree. *(Puts his hand on her head.)* My precious little singing-bird!

*(He goes into his room and shuts the door after him.)*

**Nora** *(after a pause, whispers).* No, no — it isn't true. It's impossible; it must be impossible.

*(The Nurse opens the door on the left.)*

**Nurse.** The little ones are begging so hard to be allowed to come in to mamma.

**Nora.** No, no, no! Don't let them come in to me! You stay with them, Anne.

**Nurse.** Very well, ma'am.

*(Shuts the door.)*

**Nora** *(pale with terror).* Deprave my little children? Poison my home? *(A short pause. Then she tosses her head.)* It's not true. It can't possibly be true.

## Act II

**The Same Scene**

*The Christmas tree is in the corner by the piano, stripped of its ornaments and with burnt-down candle-ends on its dishevelled branches. Nora's cloak and hat are lying on the sofa. She is alone in the room, walking about uneasily. She stops by the sofa and takes up her cloak.*

**Nora** *(drops the cloak).* Someone is coming now! *(Goes to the door and listens.)* No — it is no one. Of course, no one will come to-day, Christmas Day — nor tomorrow either. But, perhaps — *(Opens the door and looks out).* No, nothing in the letter-box; it is quite empty. *(Comes forward.)* What rubbish! of course he can't be in earnest about it. Such a thing couldn't happen; it is impossible — I have three little children.

*(Enter the Nurse from the room on the left, carrying a big cardboard box.)*

**Nurse.**  At last I have found the box with the fancy dress.

**Nora.**  Thanks; put it on the table.

**Nurse** *(doing so)*.  But it is very much in want of mending.

**Nora.**  I should like to tear it into a hundred thousand pieces.

**Nurse.**  What an idea! It can easily be put in order — just a little patience.

**Nora.**  Yes, I will go and get Mrs. Linde to come and help me with it.

**Nurse.**  What, out again? In this horrible weather? You will catch cold, ma'am, and make yourself ill.

**Nora.**  Well, worse than that might happen. How are the children?

**Nurse.**  The poor little souls are playing with their Christmas presents, but ——

**Nora.**  Do they ask much for me?

**Nurse.**  You see, they are so accustomed to have their mamma with them.

**Nora.**  Yes, but, nurse, I shall not be able to be so much with them now as I was before.

**Nurse.**  Oh well, young children easily get accustomed to anything.

**Nora.**  Do you think so? Do you think they would forget their mother if she went away altogether?

**Nurse.**  Good heavens! — went away altogether?

**Nora.**  Nurse, I want you to tell me something I have often wondered about — how could you have the heart to put your own child out among strangers?

**Nurse.**  I was obliged to, if I wanted to be little Nora's nurse.

**Nora.**  Yes, but how could you be willing to do it?

**Nurse.**  What, when I was going to get such a good place by it? A poor girl who has got into trouble should be glad to. Besides, that wicked man didn't do a single thing for me.

**Nora.**  But I suppose your daughter has quite forgotten you.

**Nurse.**  No, indeed she hasn't. She wrote to me when she was confirmed, and when she was married.

**Nora** *(putting her arms round her neck)*.  Dear old Anne, you were a good mother to me when I was little.

**Nurse.**  Little Nora, poor dear, had no other mother but me.

**Nora.**  And if my little ones had no other mother, I am sure you would —— What nonsense I am talking! *(Opens the box.)* Go in to them. Now I must ——. You will see to-morrow how charming I shall look.

**Nurse.**  I am sure there will be no one at the ball so charming as you, ma'am.

*(Goes into the room on the left.)*

**Nora** *(begins to unpack the box, but soon pushes it away from her)*.  If only I dared go out. If only no one would come. If only I could be sure nothing would happen here in the meantime. Stuff and nonsense! No one will come. Only I mustn't think about it. I will brush my muff. What lovely, lovely gloves! Out of my thoughts, out of my thoughts! One, two, three, four, five, six —— *(Screams.)* Ah! there is someone coming ——

*(Makes a movement towards the door, but stands irresolute. Enter Mrs. Linde from the hall, where she has taken off her cloak and hat.)*

**Nora.** Oh, it's you, Christine. There is no one else out there, is there? How good of you to come!

**Mrs. Linde.** I heard you were up asking for me.

**Nora.** Yes, I was passing by. As a matter of fact, it is something you could help me with. Let us sit down here on the sofa. Look here. To-morrow evening there is to be a fancy-dress ball at the Stenborgs', who live above us; and Torvald wants me to go as a Neapolitan fisher-girl, and dance the Tarantella that I learnt at Capri.

**Mrs. Linde.** I see; you are going to keep up the character.

**Nora.** Yes, Torvald wants me to. Look, here is the dress; Torvald had it made for me there, but now it is all so torn, and I haven't any idea ——

**Mrs. Linde.** We will easily put that right. It is only some of the trimming come unsewn here and there. Needle and thread? Now then, that's all we want.

**Nora.** It *is* nice of you.

**Mrs. Linde** *(sewing).* So you are going to be dressed up to-morrow, Nora. I will tell you what — I shall come in for a moment and see you in your fine feathers. But I have completely forgotten to thank you for a delightful evening yesterday.

**Nora** *(gets up, and crosses the stage).* Well I don't think yesterday was as pleasant as usual. You ought to have come to town a little earlier, Christine. Certainly Torvald does understand how to make a house dainty and attractive.

**Mrs. Linde.** And so do you, it seems to me; you are not your father's daughter for nothing. But tell me, is Doctor Rank always as depressed as he was yesterday?

**Nora.** No; yesterday it was very noticeable. I must tell you that he suffers from a very dangerous disease. He has consumption of the spine, poor creature. His father was a horrible man who committed all sorts of excesses; and that is why his son was sickly from childhood, do you understand?

**Mrs. Linde** *(dropping her sewing).* But, my dearest Nora, how do you know anything about such things?

**Nora** *(walking about).* Pooh! When you have three children, you get visits now and then from — from married women, who know something of medical matters, and they talk about one thing and another.

**Mrs. Linde** *(goes on sewing. A short silence).* Does Doctor Rank come here every day?

**Nora.** Every day regularly. He is Torvald's most intimate friend, and a great friend of mine too. He is just like one of the family.

**Mrs. Linde.** But tell me this — is he perfectly sincere? I mean, isn't he the kind of man that is very anxious to make himself agreeable?

**Nora.** Not in the least. What makes you think that?

**Mrs. Linde.** When you introduced him to me yesterday, he declared he had often heard my name mentioned in this house; but afterwards I noticed that your husband hadn't the slightest idea who I was. So how could Doctor Rank ——?

**Nora.** That is quite right, Christine. Torvald is so absurdly fond of me that he wants me absolutely to himself, as he says. At first he used to seem almost jealous if I mentioned any of the dear folk at home, so naturally I gave up doing so. But I often talk about such things with Doctor Rank, because he likes hearing about them.

**Mrs. Linde.** Listen to me, Nora. You are still very like a child in many things, and I am older than you in many ways and have a little more experience. Let me tell you this — you ought to make an end of it with Doctor Rank.

**Nora.** What ought I to make an end of?

**Mrs. Linde.** Of two things, I think. Yesterday you talked some nonsense about a rich admirer who was to leave you money ——

**Nora.** An admirer who doesn't exist, unfortunately! But what then?

**Mrs. Linde.** Is Doctor Rank a man of means?

**Nora.** Yes, he is.

**Mrs. Linde.** And has no one to provide for?

**Nora.** No, no one; but ——

**Mrs. Linde.** And comes here every day?

**Nora.** Yes, I told you so.

**Mrs. Linde.** But how can this well-bred man be so tactless?

**Nora.** I don't understand you at all.

**Mrs. Linde.** Don't prevaricate, Nora. Do you suppose I don't guess who lent you the two hundred and fifty pounds?

**Nora.** Are you out of your senses? How can you think of such a thing! A friend of ours, who comes here every day! Do you realise what a horribly painful position that would be?

**Mrs. Linde.** Then it really isn't he?

**Nora.** No, certainly not. It would never have entered into my head for a moment. Besides, he had no money to lend then; he came into his money afterwards.

**Mrs. Linde.** Well, I think that was lucky for you, my dear Nora.

**Nora.** No, it would never have come into my head to ask Doctor Rank. Although I am quite sure that if I had asked him ——

**Mrs. Linde.** But of course you won't.

**Nora.** Of course not. I have no reason to think it could possibly be necessary. But I am quite sure that if I told Doctor Rank ——

**Mrs. Linde.** Behind your husband's back?

**Nora.** I must make an end of it with the other one, and that will be behind his back too. I *must* make an end of it with him.

**Mrs. Linde.** Yes, that is what I told you yesterday, but ——

**Nora** (*walking up and down*). A man can put a thing like that straight much easier than a woman ——

**Mrs. Linde.** One's husband, yes.

**Nora.** Nonsense! (*Standing still.*) When you pay off a debt you get your bond back, don't you?

**Mrs. Linde.** Yes, as a matter of course.

**Nora.** And can tear it into a hundred thousand pieces, and burn it up — the nasty dirty paper!

**Mrs. Linde** *(looks hard at her, lays down her sewing and gets up slowly).*  Nora, you are concealing something from me.

**Nora.**  Do I look as if I were?

**Mrs. Linde.**  Something has happened to you since yesterday morning. Nora, what is it?

**Nora** *(going nearer to her).*  Christine! *(Listens.)* Hush! there's Torvald come home. Do you mind going in to the children for the present? Torvald can't bear to see dressmaking going on. Let Anne help you.

**Mrs. Linde** *(gathering some of the things together).*  Certainly — but I am not going away from here till we have had it out with one another.

*(She goes into the room on the left, as Helmer comes in from the hall.)*

**Nora** *(going up to Helmer).*  I have wanted you so much, Torvald dear.

**Helmer.**  Was that the dressmaker?

**Nora.**  No, it was Christine; she is helping me to put my dress in order. You will see I shall look quite smart.

**Helmer.**  Wasn't that a happy thought of mine, now?

**Nora.**  Splendid! But don't you think it is nice of me, too, to do as you wish?

**Helmer.**  Nice? — because you do as your husband wishes? Well, well, you little rogue, I am sure you did not mean it in that way. But I am not going to disturb you; you will want to be trying on your dress, I expect.

**Nora.**  I suppose you are going to work.

**Helmer.**  Yes. *(Shows her a bundle of papers.)* Look at that. I have just been into the bank.

*(Turns to go into his room.)*

**Nora.**  Torvald.

**Helmer.**  Yes.

**Nora.**  If your little squirrel were to ask you for something very, very prettily ——?

**Helmer.**  What then?

**Nora.**  Would you do it?

**Helmer.**  I should like to hear what it is, first.

**Nora.**  Your squirrel would run about and do all her tricks if you would be nice, and do what she wants.

**Helmer.**  Speak plainly.

**Nora.**  Your skylark would chirp about in every room, with her song rising and falling ——

**Helmer.**  Well, my skylark does that anyhow.

**Nora.**  I would play the fairy and dance for you in the moonlight, Torvald.

**Helmer.**  Nora — you surely don't mean that request you made of me this morning?

**Nora** *(going near him).*  Yes, Torvald, I beg you so earnestly ——

**Helmer.**  Have you really the courage to open up that question again?

**Nora.** Yes, dear, you *must* do as I ask; you *must* let Krogstad keep his post in the Bank.

**Helmer.** My dear Nora, it is his post that I have arranged Mrs. Linde shall have.

**Nora.** Yes, you have been awfully kind about that; but you could just as well dismiss some other clerk instead of Krogstad.

**Helmer.** This simply incredible obstinacy! Because you chose to give him a thoughtless promise that you would speak for him, I am expected to ——

**Nora.** That isn't the reason, Torvald. It is for your own sake. This fellow writes in the most scurrilous newspapers; you have told me so yourself. He can do you an unspeakable amount of harm. I am frightened to death of him ——

**Helmer.** Ah, I understand; it is recollections of the past that scare you.

**Nora.** What do you mean?

**Helmer.** Naturally you are thinking of your father.

**Nora.** Yes—yes, of course. Just recall to your mind what these malicious creatures wrote in the papers about papa, and how horribly they slandered him. I believe they would have procured his dismissal if the Department had not sent you over to inquire into it, and if you had not been so kindly disposed and helpful to him.

**Helmer.** My little Nora, there is an important difference between your father and me. Your father's reputation as a public official was not above suspicion. Mine is, and I hope it will continue to be so, as long as I hold my office.

**Nora.** You never can tell what mischief these men may contrive. We ought to be so well off, so snug and happy here in our peaceful home, and have no cares — you and I and the children, Torvald! That is why I beg of you so earnestly ——

**Helmer.** And it is just by interceding for him that you make it impossible for me to keep him. It is already known at the Bank that I mean to dismiss Krogstad. Is it to get about now that the new manager has changed his mind at his wife's bidding ——

**Nora.** And what if it did?

**Helmer.** Of course! — if only this obstinate little person can get her way! Do you suppose I am going to make myself ridiculous before my whole staff, to let people think that I am a man to be swayed by all sorts of outside influence? I should very soon feel the consequences of it, I can tell you! And besides, there is one thing that makes it quite impossible for me to have Krogstad in the Bank as long as I am manager.

**Nora.** Whatever is that?

**Helmer.** His moral failings I might perhaps have overlooked, if necessary ——

**Nora.** Yes, you could — couldn't you?

**Helmer.** And I hear he is a good worker, too. But I knew him when we were boys. It was one of those rash friendships that so often prove an incubus in after life. I may as well tell you plainly, we were once on very intimate terms with one another. But this tactless fellow lays no restraint on himself when other people are present. On the contrary, he thinks it gives him the right to adopt a familiar tone with me, and every minute it is "I say, Helmer, old fellow!" and that sort of thing. I assure you it is extremely painful for me. He would make my position in the Bank intolerable.

**Nora.** Torvald, I don't believe you mean that.

**Helmer.** Don't you? Why not?

**Nora.** Because it is such a narrow-minded way of looking at things.

**Helmer.** What are you saying? Narrow-minded? Do you think I am narrow-minded?

**Nora.** No, just the opposite, dear — and it is exactly for that reason.

**Helmer.** It's the same thing. You say my point of view is narrow-minded, so I must be so too. Narrow-minded! Very well — I must put an end to this. *(Goes to the hall-door and calls.)* Helen!

**Nora.** What are you going to do?

**Helmer** *(looking among his papers)*. Settle it. *(Enter Maid.)* Look here; take this letter and go downstairs with it at once. Find a messenger and tell him to deliver it, and be quick. The address is on it, and here is the money.

**Maid.** Very well, sir.                              *(Exit with the letter.)*

**Helmer** *(putting his papers together)*. Now then, little Miss Obstinate.

**Nora** *(breathlessly)*. Torvald — what was that letter?

**Helmer.** Krogstad's dismissal.

**Nora.** Call her back, Torvald! There is still time. Oh Torvald, call her back! Do it for my sake — for your own sake — for the children's sake! Do you hear me, Torvald? Call her back! You don't know what that letter can bring upon us.

**Helmer.** It's too late.

**Nora.** Yes, it's too late.

**Helmer.** My dear Nora, I can forgive the anxiety you are in, although really it is an insult to me. It is, indeed. Isn't it an insult to think that I should be afraid of a starving quill-driver's vengeance? But I forgive you nevertheless, because it is such eloquent witness to your great love for me. *(Takes her in his arms.)* And that is as it should be, my darling Nora. Come what will, you may be sure I shall have both courage and strength if they be needed. You will see I am man enough to take everything upon myself.

**Nora** *(in a horror-stricken voice)*. What do you mean by that?

**Helmer.** Everything, I say ——

**Nora** *(recovering herself)*. You will never have to do that.

**Helmer.** That's right. Well, we will share it, Nora, as man and wife should. That is how it shall be. *(Caressing her.)* Are you content now? There! there! — not these frightened dove's eyes! The whole thing is only the wildest fancy! — Now, you must go and play through the Tarantella and practise with your tambourine. I shall go into the inner office and shut the door, and I shall hear nothing; you can make as much noise as you please. *(Turns back at the door.)* And when Rank comes, tell him where he will find me.

*(Nods to her, takes his papers and goes into his room, and shuts the door after him.)*

**Nora** *(bewildered with anxiety, stands as if rooted to the spot, and whispers)*. He was capable of doing it. He will do it. He will do it in spite of everything. — No, not that! Never, never! Anything rather than that! Oh, for some help, some way out of it! *(The door-bell rings.)* Doctor Rank! Anything rather than that — anything, whatever it is!

*(She puts her hands over her face, pulls herself together, goes to the door and opens it. Rank is standing without, hanging up his coat. During the following dialogue it begins to grow dark.)*

**Nora.** Good-day, Doctor Rank. I knew your ring. But you mustn't go in to Torvald now; I think he is busy with something.

**Rank.** And you?

**Nora** *(brings him in and shuts the door after him)*. Oh, you know very well I always have time for you.

**Rank.** Thank you. I shall make use of as much of it as I can.

**Nora.** What do you mean by that? As much of it as you can?

**Rank.** Well, does that alarm you?

**Nora.** It was such a strange way of putting it. Is anything likely to happen?

**Rank.** Nothing but what I have long been prepared for. But certainly didn't expect it to happen so soon.

**Nora** *(gripping him by the arm)*. What have you found out? Doctor Rank, you must tell me.

**Rank** *(sitting down by the stove)*. It is all up with me. And it can't be helped.

**Nora** *(with a sigh of relief)*. Is it about yourself?

**Rank.** Who else? It is no use lying to one's self. I am the most wretched of all my patients, Mrs. Helmer. Lately I have been taking stock of my internal economy. Bankrupt! Probably within a month I shall lie rotting in the churchyard.

**Nora.** What an ugly thing to say!

**Rank.** The thing itself is cursedly ugly, and the worst of it is that I shall have to face so much more that is ugly before that. I shall only make one more examination of myself; when I have done that, I shall know pretty certainly when it will be that the horrors of dissolution will begin. There is something I want to tell you. Helmer's refined nature gives him an unconquerable disgust at everything that is ugly; I won't have him in my sick-room.

**Nora.** Oh, but, Doctor Rank ——

**Rank.** I won't have him there. Not on any account. I bar my door to him. As soon as I am quite certain that the worst has come, I shall send you my card with a black cross on it, and then you will know that the loathsome end has begun.

**Nora.** You are quite absurd to-day. And I wanted you so much to be in a really good humour.

**Rank.** With death stalking beside me? — To have to pay this penalty for another man's sin! Is there any justice in that? And in every single family, in one way or another, some such inexorable retribution is being exacted ——

**Nora** *(putting her hands over her ears)*. Rubbish! Do talk of something cheerful.

**Rank.** Oh, it's a mere laughing matter, the whole thing. My poor innocent spine has to suffer for my father's youthful amusements.

**Nora** (*sitting at the table on the left*).  I suppose you mean that he was too partial to asparagus and pâté de foie gras, don't you.

**Rank.**  Yes, and to truffles.

**Nora.**  Truffles, yes. And oysters too, I suppose?

**Rank.**  Oysters, of course, that goes without saying.

**Nora.**  And heaps of port and champagne. It is sad that all these nice things should take their revenge on our bones.

**Rank.**  Especially that they should revenge themselves on the unlucky bones of those who have not had the satisfaction of enjoying them.

**Nora.**  Yes, that's the saddest part of it all.

**Rank** (*with a searching look at her*).  Hm! ——

**Nora** (*after a short pause*).  Why did you smile?

**Rank.**  No, it was you that laughed.

**Nora.**  No, it was you that smiled, Doctor Rank!

**Rank** (*rising*).  You are a greater rascal than I thought.

**Nora.**  I am in a silly mood to-day.

**Rank.**  So it seems.

**Nora** (*putting her hands on his shoulders*).  Dear, dear Doctor Rank, death mustn't take you away from Torvald and me.

**Rank.**  It is a loss you would easily recover from. Those who are gone are soon forgotten.

**Nora** (*looking at him anxiously*).  Do you believe that?

**Rank.**  People form new ties, and then ——

**Nora.**  Who will form new ties?

**Rank.**  Both you and Helmer, when I am gone. You yourself are already on the high road to it, I think. What did that Mrs. Linde want here last night?

**Nora.**  Oho! — you don't mean to say you are jealous of poor Christine?

**Rank.**  Yes, I am. She will be my successor in this house. When I am done for, this woman will —

**Nora.**  Hush! don't speak so loud. She is in that room.

**Rank.**  To-day again. There, you see.

**Nora.**  She has only come to sew my dress for me. Bless my soul, how unreasonable you are! (*Sits down on the sofa.*) Be nice now, Doctor Rank, and to-morrow you will see how beautifully I shall dance, and you can imagine I am doing it all for you — and for Torvald too, of course. (*Takes various things out of the box.*) Doctor Rank, come and sit down here, and I will show you something.

**Rank** (*sitting down*).  What is it?

**Nora.**  Just look at those!

**Rank.**  Silk stockings.

**Nora.**  Flesh-coloured. Aren't they lovely? It is so dark here now, but to-morrow —. No, no, no! you must only look at the feet. Oh well, you may have leave to look at the legs too.

**Rank.**  Hm! —

**Nora.**  Why are you looking so critical? Don't you think they will fit me?

**Rank.** I have no means of forming an opinion about that.

**Nora** *(looks at him for a moment)*. For shame! *(Hits him lightly on the ear with the stockings.)* That's to punish you. *(Folds them up again.)*

**Rank.** And what other nice things am I to be allowed to see?

**Nora.** Not a single thing more, for being so naughty. *(She looks among the things, humming to herself.)*

**Rank** *(after a short silence)*. When I am sitting here, talking to you as intimately as this, I cannot imagine for a moment what would have become of me if I had never come into this house.

**Nora** *(smiling)*. I believe you do feel thoroughly at home with us.

**Rank** *(in a lower voice, looking straight in front of him)*. And to be obliged to leave it all —

**Nora.** Nonsense, you are not going to leave it.

**Rank** *(as before)*. And not be able to leave behind one the slightest token of one's gratitude, scarcely even a fleeting regret — nothing but an empty place which the first comer can fill as well as any other.

**Nora.** And if I asked you now for a —? No!

**Rank.** For what?

**Nora.** For a big proof of your friendship —

**Rank.** Yes, yes!

**Nora.** I mean a tremendously big favour —

**Rank.** Would you really make me so happy for once?

**Nora.** Ah, but you don't know what it is yet.

**Rank.** No — but tell me.

**Nora.** I really can't, Doctor Rank. It is something out of all reason; it means advice, and help, and a favour —

**Rank.** The bigger a thing it is the better. I can't conceive what it is you mean. Do tell me. Haven't I your confidence?

**Nora.** More than anyone else. I know you are my truest and best friend, and so I will tell you what it is. Well, Doctor Rank, it is something you must help me to prevent. You know how devotedly, how inexpressibly deeply Torvald loves me; he would never for a moment hesitate to give his life for me.

**Rank** *(leaning towards her)*. Nora — do you think he is the only one —?

**Nora** *(with a slight start)*. The only one —?

**Rank.** The only one who would gladly give his life for your sake.

**Nora** *(sadly)*. Is that it?

**Rank.** I was determined you should know it before I went away, and there will never be a better opportunity than this. Now you know it, Nora. And now you know, too, that you can trust me as you would trust no one else.

**Nora** *(rises, deliberately and quietly)*. Let me pass.

**Rank** *(makes room for her to pass him, but sits still)*. Nora!

**Nora** *(at the hall door)*. Helen, bring in the lamp. *(Goes over to the stove.)* Dear Doctor Rank, that was really horrid of you.

**Rank.** To have loved you as much as anyone else does? Was that horrid?

**Nora.** No, but to go and tell me so. There was really no need —

**Rank.** What do you mean? Did you know —? (*Maid enters with lamp, puts it down on the table, and goes out.*) Nora — Mrs. Helmer — tell me, had you any idea of this?

**Nora.** Oh, how do I know whether I had or whether I hadn't? I really can't tell you — To think you could be so clumsy, Doctor Rank! We were getting on so nicely.

**Rank.** Well, at all events you know now that you can command me, body and soul. So won't you speak out?

**Nora** (*looking at him*). After what happened?

**Rank.** I beg you to let me know what it is.

**Nora.** I can't tell you anything now.

**Rank.** Yes, yes. You mustn't punish me in that way. Let me have permission to do for you whatever a man may do.

**Nora.** You can do nothing for me now. Besides, I really don't need any help at all. You will find that the whole thing is merely fancy on my part. It really is so — of course it is! (*Sits down in the rocking-chair, and looks at him with a smile.*) You are a nice sort of man, Doctor Rank! — don't you feel ashamed of yourself, now the lamp has come?

**Rank.** Not a bit. But perhaps I had better go — forever?

**Nora.** No, indeed, you shall not. Of course you must come here just as before. You know very well Torvald can't do without you.

**Rank.** Yes, but you?

**Nora.** Oh, I am always tremendously pleased when you come.

**Rank.** It is just that, that put me on the wrong track. You are a riddle to me. I have often thought that you would almost as soon be in my company as in Helmer's.

**Nora.** Yes — you see there are some people one loves best, and others whom one would almost always rather have as companions.

**Rank.** Yes, there is something in that.

**Nora.** When I was at home, of course I loved papa best. But I always thought it tremendous fun if I could steal down into the maids' room, because they never moralised at all, and talked to each other about such entertaining things.

**Rank.** I see — it is *their* place I have taken.

**Nora** (*jumping up and going to him*). Oh, dear, nice Doctor Rank, I never meant that at all. But surely you can understand that being with Torvald is a little like being with papa ——

(*Enter Maid from the hall.*)

**Maid.** If you please, ma'am. (*Whispers and hands her a card.*)

**Nora** (*glancing at the card*). Oh! (*Puts it in her pocket.*)

**Rank.** Is there anything wrong?

**Nora.** No, no, not in the least. It is only something — it is my new dress ——

**Rank.** What? Your dress is lying there.

**Nora.** Oh, yes, that one; but this is another. I ordered it. Torvald mustn't know about it ——

**Rank.** Oho! Then that was the great secret.

**Nora.** Of course. Just go in to him; he is sitting in the inner room. Keep him as long as ——

**Rank.** Make your mind easy; I won't let him escape. *(Goes into Helmer's room.)*

**Nora** *(to the Maid).* And he is standing waiting in the kitchen?

**Maid.** Yes; he came up the back stairs.

**Nora.** But didn't you tell him no one was in?

**Maid.** Yes, but it was no good.

**Nora.** He won't go away?

**Maid.** No; he says he won't until he has seen you, ma'am.

**Nora.** Well, let him come in — but quietly. Helen, you mustn't say anything about it to anyone. It is a surprise for my husband.

**Maid.** Yes ma'am, I quite understand.                                *(Exit.)*

**Nora.** This dreadful thing is going to happen! It will happen in spite of me! No, no, no, it can't happen — it shan't happen!

*(She bolts the door of Helmer's room. The Maid opens the hall door for Krogstad and shuts it after him. He is wearing a fur coat, high boots, and a fur cap.)*

**Nora** *(advancing towards him).* Speak low — my husband is at home.

**Krogstad.** No matter about that.

**Nora.** What do you want of me?

**Krogstad.** An explanation of something.

**Nora.** Make haste then. What is it?

**Krogstad.** You know, I suppose, that I have got my dismissal.

**Nora.** I couldn't prevent it, Mr. Krogstad. I fought as hard as I could on your side, but it was no good.

**Krogstad.** Does your husband love you so little, then? He knows what I can expose you to, and yet he ventures ——

**Nora.** How can you suppose that he has any knowledge of the sort?

**Krogstad.** I didn't suppose so at all. It would not be the least like our dear Torvald Helmer to show so much courage —

**Nora.** Mr. Krogstad, a little respect for my husband, please.

**Krogstad.** Certainly — all the respect he deserves. But since you have kept the matter so carefully to yourself, I make bold to suppose that you have a little clearer idea, than you had yesterday, of what it actually is that you have done?

**Nora.** More than you could ever teach me.

**Krogstad.** Yes, such a bad lawyer as I am.

**Nora.** What is it you want of me?

**Krogstad.** Only to see how you were, Mrs. Helmer. I have been thinking about you all day long. A mere cashier, a quill-driver, a — well, a man like me — even he has a little of what is called feeling, you know.

**Nora.** Show it, then; think of my little children.

**Krogstad.** Have you and your husband thought of mine? But never mind about that. I only wanted to tell you that you need not take this matter too seriously. In the first place there will be no accusation made on my part.

**Nora.** No, of course not; I was sure of that.

**Krogstad.** The whole thing can be arranged amicably; there is no reason why anyone should know anything about it. It will remain a secret between us three.

**Nora.** My husband must never get to know anything about it.

**Krogstad.** How will you be able to prevent it? Am I to understand that you can pay the balance that is owing?

**Nora.** No, not just at present.

**Krogstad.** Or perhaps that you have some expedient for raising the money soon?

**Nora.** No expedient that I mean to make use of.

**Krogstad.** Well, in any case, it would have been of no use to you now. If you stood there with ever so much money in your hand, I would never part with your bond.

**Nora.** Tell me what purpose you mean to put it to.

**Krogstad.** I shall only preserve it — keep it in my possession. No one who is not concerned in the matter shall have the slightest hint of it. So that if the thought of it has driven you to any desperate resolution ——

**Nora.** It has.

**Krogstad.** If you had it in your mind to run away from your home ——

**Nora.** I had.

**Krogstad.** Or even something worse ——

**Nora.** How could you know that?

**Krogstad.** Give up the idea.

**Nora.** How did you know I had thought of *that*?

**Krogstad.** Most of us think of that at first. I did, too — but I hadn't the courage.

**Nora** (*faintly*). No more had I.

**Krogstad** (*in a tone of relief*). No, that's it, isn't it — you hadn't the courage either?

**Nora.** No, I haven't — I haven't.

**Krogstad.** Besides, it would have been a great piece of folly. Once the first storm at home is over —. I have a letter for your husband in my pocket.

**Nora.** Telling him everything?

**Krogstad.** In as lenient a manner as I possibly could.

**Nora** (*quickly*). He mustn't get the letter. Tear it up. I will find some means of getting money.

**Krogstad.** Excuse me, Mrs. Helmer, but I think I told you just now ——

**Nora.** I am not speaking of what I owe you. Tell me what sum you are asking my husband for, and I will get the money.

**Krogstad.** I am not asking your husband for a penny.

**Nora.** What do you want, then?

**Krogstad.** I will tell you. I want to rehabilitate myself, Mrs. Helmer; I want to get on; and in that your husband must help me. For the last year and a half I have not had a hand in anything dishonourable, and all that time I have been struggling in most restricted circumstances. I was content to work my way up step by step. Now I am turned out, and I am not going to be satisfied with merely being taken into favour again. I want to get on, I tell you. I want to get into the Bank again, in a higher position. Your husband must make a place for me —

**Nora.** That he will never do!

**Krogstad.** He will; I know him; he dare not protest. And as soon as I am in there again with him, then you will see! Within a year I shall be the manager's right hand. It will be Nils Krogstad and not Torvald Helmer who manages the Bank.

**Nora.** That's a thing you will never see!

**Krogstad.** Do you mean that you will ——?

**Nora.** I have courage enough for it now.

**Krogstad.** Oh, you can't frighten me. A fine, spoilt lady like you ——

**Nora.** You will see, you will see.

**Krogstad.** Under the ice, perhaps? Down into the cold, coal-black water? And then, in the spring, to float up to the surface, all horrible and unrecognisable, with your hair fallen out ——

**Nora.** You can't frighten me.

**Krogstad.** Nor you me. People don't do such things, Mrs. Helmer. Besides, what use would it be? I should have him completely in my power all the same.

**Nora.** Afterwards? When I am no longer ——

**Krogstad.** Have you forgotten that it is I who have the keeping of your reputation? *(Nora stands speechlessly looking at him.)* Well, now, I have warned you. Do not do anything foolish. When Helmer has had my letter, I shall expect a message from him. And be sure you remember that it is your husband himself who has forced me into such ways as this again. I will never forgive him for that. Good-bye, Mrs. Helmer. *(Exit through the hall.)*

**Nora** *(goes to the hall door, opens it slightly and listens)*. He is going. He is not putting the letter in the box. Oh no, no! that's impossible! *(Opens the door by degrees.)* He is going. He is standing outside. He is not going downstairs. Is he hesitating? Can he ——

*(A letter drops into the box; then Krogstad's footsteps are heard, till they die away as he goes downstairs. Nora utters a stifled cry and runs across the room to the table by the sofa. A short pause.)*

**Nora.** In the letter-box. *(Steals across to the hall door.)* There it lies — Torvald, Torvald, there is no hope for us now!

*(Mrs. Linde comes in from the room on the left carrying the dress.)*

**Mrs. Linde.** There, I can't see anything more to mend now. Would you like to try it on ——?

**Nora** *(in a hoarse whisper)*. Christine, come here.

**Mrs. Linde** *(throwing the dress down on the sofa)*. What is the matter with you? You look so agitated!

**Nora.** Come here. Do you see that letter? There look — you can see it through the glass in the letter-box.

**Mrs. Linde.** Yes, I see it.

**Nora.** That letter is from Krogstad.

**Mrs. Linde.** Nora — it was Krogstad who lent you the money!

**Nora.** Yes, and now Torvald will know all about it.

**Mrs. Linde.** Believe me, Nora, that's the best thing for both of you.

**Nora.** You don't know all. I forged a name.

**Mrs. Linde.** Good heavens ——!

**Nora.** I only want to say this to you, Christine — you must be my witness.

**Mrs. Linde.** Your witness? What do you mean? What am I to —?

**Nora.** If I should go out of my mind — and it might easily happen ——

**Mrs. Linde.** Nora!

**Nora.** Or if anything else should happen to me — anything, for instance, that might prevent my being here —

**Mrs. Linde.** Nora! Nora! you are quite out of your mind.

**Nora.** And if it should happen that there were someone who wanted to take all the responsibility, all the blame, you understand ——

**Mrs. Linde.** Yes, yes — but how can you suppose —?

**Nora.** Then you must be my witness, that it is not true, Christine. I am not out of my mind at all; I am in my right senses now, and I tell you no one else has known anything about it; I, and I alone, did the whole thing. Remember that.

**Mrs. Linde.** I will, indeed. But I don't understand all this.

**Nora.** How should you understand it? A wonderful thing is going to happen.

**Mrs. Linde.** A wonderful thing?

**Nora.** Yes, a wonderful thing! — But it is so terrible, Christine; it *mustn't* happen, not for all the world.

**Mrs. Linde.** I will go at once and see Krogstad.

**Nora.** Don't go to him; he will do you some harm.

**Mrs. Linde.** There was a time when he would gladly do anything for my sake.

**Nora.** He?

**Mrs. Linde.** Where does he live?

**Nora.** How should I know —? Yes *(feeling in her pocket)* here is his card. But the letter, the letter ——!

**Helmer** *(calls from his room, knocking at the door).* Nora!

**Nora** *(cries out anxiously).* Oh, what's that? What do you want?

**Helmer.** Don't be so frightened. We are not coming in; you have locked the door. Are you trying on your dress?

**Nora.** Yes, that's it. I look so nice, Torvald.

**Mrs. Linde** *(who has read the card).* I see he lives at the corner here.

**Nora.** Yes, but it's no use. It is hopeless. The letter is lying there in the box.

**Mrs. Linde.** And your husband keeps the key?

**Nora.** Yes, always.

**Mrs. Linde.** Krogstad must ask for his letter back unread, he must find some pretence ——

**Nora.** But it is just at this time that Torvald generally ——

**Mrs. Linde.** You must delay him. Go in to him in the meantime. I will come back as soon as I can.

*(She goes out hurriedly through the hall door.)*

**Nora** *(goes to Helmer's door, opens it and peeps in).* Torvald!

**Helmer** *(from the inner room).* Well? May I venture at last to come into my own room again? Come along, Rank, now you will see — *(Halting in the doorway.)* But what is this?

**Nora.** What is what, dear?

**Helmer.** Rank led me to expect a splendid transformation.

**Rank** *(in the doorway).* I understood so, but evidently I was mistaken.

**Nora.** Yes, nobody is to have the chance of admiring me in my dress until tomorrow.

**Helmer.** But, my dear Nora, you look so worn out. Have you been practising too much?

**Nora.** No, I have not practised at all.

**Helmer.** But you will need to —

**Nora.** Yes, indeed I shall, Torvald. But I can't get on a bit without you to help me; I have absolutely forgotten the whole thing.

**Helmer.** Oh, we will soon work it up again.

**Nora.** Yes, help me, Torvald. Promise that you will! I am so nervous about it — all the people —. You must give yourself up to me entirely this evening. Not the tiniest bit of business — you mustn't even take a pen in your hand. Will you promise, Torvald dear?

**Helmer.** I promise. This evening I will be wholly and absolutely at your service, you helpless little mortal. Ah, by the way, first of all I will just ——

*(Goes towards the hall door.)*

**Nora.** What are you going to do there?

**Helmer.** Only see if any letters have come.

**Nora.** No, no! don't do that, Torvald!

**Helmer.** Why not?

**Nora.** Torvald, please don't. There is nothing there.

**Helmer.** Well, let me look. *(Turns to go to the letter-box. Nora at the piano, plays the first bars of the Tarantella. Helmer stops in the doorway.)* Aha!

**Nora.** I can't dance to-morrow if I don't practise with you.

**Helmer** *(going up to her).* Are you really so afraid of it, dear?

**Nora.** Yes, so dreadfully afraid of it. Let me practise at once; there is time now, before we go to dinner. Sit down and play for me, Torvald dear; criticise me, and correct me as you play.

**Helmer.** With great pleasure, if you wish me to.

*(Sits down at the piano.)*

**Nora** *(takes out of the box a tambourine and a long variegated shawl. She hastily drapes the shawl round her. Then she springs to the front of the stage and calls out).* Now play for me! I am going to dance!

*(Helmer plays and Nora dances. Rank stands by the piano behind Helmer and looks on.)*

**Helmer** *(as he plays).* Slower, slower!
**Nora.** I can't do it any other way.
**Helmer.** Not so violently, Nora!
**Nora.** This is the way.
**Helmer** *(stops playing).* No, no — that is not a bit right.
**Nora** *(laughing and swinging the tambourine).* Didn't I tell you so?
**Rank.** Let me play for her.
**Helmer** *(getting up).* Yes, do. I can correct her better then.

*(Rank sits down at the piano and plays. Nora dances more and more wildly. Helmer has taken up a position beside the stove, and during her dance gives her frequent instructions. She does not seem to hear him; her hair comes down and falls over her shoulders; she pays no attention to it, but goes on dancing. Enter Mrs. Linde.)*

**Mrs. Linde** *(standing as if spell-bound in the doorway).* Oh! ——
**Nora** *(as she dances).* Such fun, Christine!
**Helmer.** My dear darling Nora, you are dancing as if your life depended on it.
**Nora.** So it does.
**Helmer.** Stop, Rank; this is sheer madness. Stop, I tell you! *(Rank stops playing, and Nora suddenly stands still. Helmer goes up to her.)* I could never have believed it. You have forgotten everything I taught you.
**Nora** *(throwing away the tambourine).* There, you see.
**Helmer.** You will want a lot of coaching.
**Nora.** Yes, you see how much I need it. You must coach me up to the last minute. Promise me that, Torvald!
**Helmer.** You can depend on me.
**Nora.** You must not think of anything but me, either to-day or to-morrow; you mustn't open a single letter — not even open the letter-box ——
**Helmer.** Ah, you are still afraid of that fellow ——
**Nora.** Yes, indeed I am.
**Helmer.** Nora, I can tell from your looks that there is a letter from him lying there.
**Nora.** I don't know; I think there is; but you must not read anything of that kind now. Nothing horrid must come between us till this is all over.
**Rank** *(whispers to Helmer).* You mustn't contradict her.
**Helmer** *(taking her in his arms).* The child shall have her way. But to-morrow night, after you have danced ——
**Nora.** Then you will be free.

*(The Maid appears in the doorway to the right.)*

**Maid.** Dinner is served, ma'am.

**Nora.** We will have champagne, Helen.

**Maid.** Very good, ma'am. *(Exit.)*

**Helmer.** Hullo! — are we going to have a banquet?

**Nora.** Yes, a champagne banquet till the small hours. *(Calls out.)* And a few maca-roons, Helen — lots, just for once!

**Helmer.** Come, come, don't be so wild and nervous. Be my own little skylark, as you used.

**Nora.** Yes, dear, I will. But go in now and you too, Doctor Rank. Christine, you must help me to do up my hair.

**Rank** *(whispers to Helmer as they go out).* I suppose there is nothing — she is not expecting anything?

**Helmer.** Far from it, my dear fellow; it is simply nothing more than this childish nervousness I was telling you of.

*(They go into the right-hand room.)*

**Nora.** Well!

**Mrs. Linde.** Gone out of town.

**Nora.** I could tell from your face.

**Mrs. Linde.** He is coming home to-morrow evening. I wrote a note for him.

**Nora.** You should have let it alone; you must prevent nothing. After all, it is splen-did to be waiting for a wonderful thing to happen.

**Mrs. Linde.** What is it that you are waiting for?

**Nora.** Oh, you wouldn't understand. Go in to them, I will come in a moment. *(Mrs. Linde goes into the dining-room. Nora stands still for a little while, as if to compose herself. Then she looks at her watch.)* Five o'clock. Seven hours till midnight. Then the Tarantella will be over. Twenty-four and seven? Thirty-one hours to live.

**Helmer** *(from the doorway on the right).* Where's my little skylark?

**Nora** *(going to him with her arms outstretched).* Here she is!

## ACT III

### The Same Scene

*The table has been placed in the middle of the stage, with chairs round it. A lamp is burning on the table. The door into the hall stands open. Dance music is heard in the room above. Mrs. Linde is sitting at the table idly turning over the leaves of a book; she tries to read, but does not seem able to collect her thoughts. Every now and then she listens intently for a sound at the outer door.*

**Mrs. Linde** *(looking at her watch).* Not yet — and the time is nearly up. If only he does not —. *(Listens again.)* Ah, there he is. *(Goes into the hall and opens the outer door carefully. Light footsteps are heard on the stairs. She whispers.)* Come in. There is no one here.

**Krogstad** *(in the doorway).* I found a note from you at home. What does this mean?

**Mrs. Linde.** It is absolutely necessary that I should have a talk with you.

**Krogstad.** Really? And is it absolutely necessary that it should be here?

**Mrs. Linde.** It is impossible where I live; there is no private entrance to my rooms. Come in; we are quite alone. The maid is asleep, and the Helmers are at the dance upstairs.

**Krogstad** *(coming into the room).* Are the Helmers really at a dance to-night?

**Mrs. Linde.** Yes, why not?

**Krogstad.** Certainly — why not?

**Mrs. Linde.** Now, Nils, let us have a talk.

**Krogstad.** Can we two have anything to talk about?

**Mrs. Linde.** We have a great deal to talk about.

**Krogstad.** I shouldn't have thought so.

**Mrs. Linde.** No, you have never properly understood me.

**Krogstad.** Was there anything else to understand except what was obvious to all the world — a heartless woman jilts a man when a more lucrative chance turns up?

**Mrs. Linde.** Do you believe I am as absolutely heartless as all that? And do you believe that I did it with a light heart?

**Krogstad.** Didn't you?

**Mrs. Linde.** Nils, did you really think that?

**Krogstad.** If it were as you say, why did you write to me as you did at the time?

**Mrs. Linde.** I could do nothing else. As I had to break with you, it was my duty also to put an end to all that you felt for me.

**Krogstad** *(wringing his hands).* So that was it. And all this — only for the sake of money!

**Mrs. Linde.** You must not forget that I had a helpless mother and two little brothers. We couldn't wait for you, Nils; your prospects seemed hopeless then.

**Krogstad.** That may be so, but you had no right to throw me over for anyone else's sake.

**Mrs. Linde.** Indeed I don't know. Many a time did I ask myself if I had the right to do it.

**Krogstad** *(more gently).* When I lost you, it was as if all the solid ground went from under my feet. Look at me now — I am a shipwrecked man clinging to a bit of wreckage.

**Mrs. Linde.** But help may be near.

**Krogstad.** It *was* near; but then you came and stood in my way.

**Mrs. Linde.** Unintentionally, Nils. It was only to-day that I learnt it was your place I was going to take in the Bank.

**Krogstad.** I believe you, if you say so. But now that you know it, are you not going to give it up to me?

**Mrs. Linde.** No, because that would not benefit you in the least.

**Krogstad.** Oh, benefit, benefit — I would have done it whether or no.

**Mrs. Linde.** I have learnt to act prudently. Life, and hard, bitter necessity have taught me that.

**Krogstad.** And life has taught me not to believe in fine speeches.

**Mrs. Linde.** Then life has taught you something very reasonable. But deeds you must believe in?

**Krogstad.** What do you mean by that?

**Mrs. Linde.** You said you were like a shipwrecked man clinging to some wreckage.

**Krogstad.** I had good reason to say so.

**Mrs. Linde.** Well, I am like a shipwrecked woman clinging to some wreckage — no one to mourn for, no one to care for.

**Krogstad.** It was your own choice.

**Mrs. Linde.** There was no other choice — then.

**Krogstad.** Well, what now?

**Mrs. Linde.** Nils, how would it be if we two shipwrecked people could join forces?

**Krogstad.** What are you saying?

**Mrs. Linde.** Two on the same piece of wreckage would stand a better chance than each on their own.

**Krogstad.** Christine!

**Mrs. Linde.** What do you suppose brought me to town?

**Krogstad.** Do you mean that you gave me a thought?

**Mrs. Linde.** I could not endure life without work. All my life, as long as I can remember, I have worked, and it has been my greatest and only pleasure. But now I am quite alone in the world — my life is so dreadfully empty and I feel so forsaken. There is not the least pleasure in working for one's self. Nils, give me someone and something to work for.

**Krogstad.** I don't trust that. It is nothing but a woman's overstrained sense of generosity that prompts you to make such an offer of yourself.

**Mrs. Linde.** Have you ever noticed anything of the sort in me?

**Krogstad.** Could you really do it? Tell me — do you know all about my past life?

**Mrs. Linde.** Yes.

**Krogstad.** And do you know what they think of me here?

**Mrs. Linde.** You seemed to me to imply that with me you might have been quite another man.

**Krogstad.** I am certain of it.

**Mrs. Linde.** Is it too late now?

**Krogstad.** Christine, are you saying this deliberately? Yes, I am sure you are. I see it in your face. Have you really the courage then —?

**Mrs. Linde.** I want to be a mother to someone, and your children need a mother. We two need each other. Nils, I have faith in your real character — I can dare anything together with you.

**Krogstad** (*grasps her hands*). Thanks, thanks, Christine! Now I shall find a way to clear myself in the eyes of the world. Ah, but I forgot ——

**Mrs. Linde** (*listening*). Hush! The Tarantella! Go, go!

**Krogstad.** Why? What is it?

**Mrs. Linde.** Do you hear them up there? When that is over, we may expect them back.

**Krogstad.** Yes, yes — I will go. But it is all no use. Of course you are not aware what steps I have taken in the matter of the Helmers.

**Mrs. Linde.** Yes, I know all about that.

**Krogstad.** And in spite of that have you the courage to —?

**Mrs. Linde.** I understand very well to what lengths a man like you might be driven by despair.

**Krogstad.** If I could only undo what I have done!

**Mrs. Linde.** You cannot. Your letter is lying in the letter-box now.

**Krogstad.** Are you sure of that?

**Mrs. Linde.** Quite sure, but ——

**Krogstad** (with a searching look at her). Is that what it all means? — that you want to save your friend at my cost? Tell me frankly. Is that it?

**Mrs. Linde.** Nils, a woman who has once sold herself for another's sake, doesn't do it a second time.

**Krogstad.** I will ask for my letter back.

**Mrs. Linde.** No, no.

**Krogstad.** Yes, of course I will. I will wait here till Helmer comes; I will tell him he must give me my letter back — that it only concerns my dismissal — that he is not to read it ——

**Mrs. Linde.** No, Nils, you must not recall your letter.

**Krogstad.** But, tell me, wasn't it for that very purpose that you asked me to meet you here?

**Mrs. Linde.** In my first moment of fright, it was. But twenty-four hours have elapsed since then, and in that time I have witnessed incredible things in this house. Helmer must know all about it. This unhappy secret must be disclosed; they must have a complete understanding between them, which is impossible with all this concealment and falsehood going on.

**Krogstad.** Very well, if you will take the responsibility. But there is one thing I can do in any case, and I shall do it at once.

**Mrs. Linde** (listening). You must be quick and go! The dance is over; we are not safe a moment longer.

**Krogstad.** I will wait for you below.

**Mrs. Linde.** Yes, do. You must see me back to my door.

**Krogstad.** I have never had such an amazing piece of good fortune in my life.

(Goes out through the outer door. The door between the room and the hall remains open.)

**Mrs. Linde** (tidying up the room and laying her hat and cloak ready). What a difference! what a difference! Someone to work for and live for — a home to bring comfort into. That I will do, indeed. I wish they would be quick and come — (Listens.) Ah, there they are now. I must put on my things.

(Takes up her hat and cloak. Helmer's and Nora's voices are heard outside; a key is turned, and Helmer brings Nora almost by force into the hall. She is in an Italian *costume with a large black shawl round her; he is in evening dress and a black domino² which is flying open.)*

**Nora** *(hanging back in the doorway, and struggling with him).* No, no, no! — don't take me in. I want to go upstairs again; I don't want to leave so early.

**Helmer.** But, my dearest Nora ——

**Nora.** Please, Torvald dear — please, *please* — only an hour more.

**Helmer.** Not a single minute, my sweet Nora. You know that was our agreement. Come along into the room; you are catching cold standing there.

*(He brings her gently into the room, in spite of her resistance.)*

**Mrs. Linde.** Good evening.

**Nora.** Christine!

**Helmer.** You here, so late, Mrs. Linde?

**Mrs. Linde.** Yes, you must excuse me; I was so anxious to see Nora in her dress.

**Nora.** Have you been sitting here waiting for me?

**Mrs. Linde.** Yes, unfortunately I came too late, you had already gone upstairs; and I thought I couldn't go away again without having seen you.

**Helmer** *(taking off Nora's shawl).* Yes, take a good look at her. I think she is worth looking at. Isn't she charming, Mrs. Linde?

**Mrs. Linde.** Yes, indeed she is.

**Helmer.** Doesn't she look remarkably pretty? Everyone thought so at the dance. But she is terribly self-willed, this sweet little person. What are we to do with her? You will hardly believe that I had almost to bring her away by force.

**Nora.** Torvald, you will repent not having let me stay, even if it were only for half an hour.

**Helmer.** Listen to her, Mrs. Linde! She had danced her Tarantella, and it had been a tremendous success, as it deserved — although possibly the performance was a trifle too realistic — a little more so, I mean, than was strictly compatible with the limitations of art. But never mind about that! The chief thing is, she had made a success — she had made a tremendous success. Do you think I was going to let her remain there after that, and spoil the effect? No indeed! I took my charming little Capri maiden — my capricious little Capri maiden, I should say — on my arm; took one quick turn round the room; a curtsey on either side, and, as they say in novels, the beautiful apparition disappeared. An exit ought always to be effective, Mrs. Linde; but that is what I cannot make Nora understand. Pooh! this room is hot. *(Throws his domino on a chair and opens the door of his room.)* Hullo! it's dark in here. Oh, of course — excuse me ——.

*(He goes in and lights some candles.)*

---

² A long, loose, hooded cloak.

**Nora** (*in a hurried and breathless whisper*). Well?

**Mrs. Linde** (*in a low voice*). I have had a talk with him.

**Nora.** Yes, and ——

**Mrs. Linde.** Nora, you must tell your husband all about it.

**Nora** (*in an expressionless voice*). I knew it.

**Mrs. Linde.** You have nothing to be afraid of as far as Krogstad is concerned; but you must tell him.

**Nora.** I won't tell him.

**Mrs. Linde.** Then the letter will.

**Nora.** Thank you, Christine. Now I know what I must do. Hush ——!

**Helmer** (*coming in again*). Well, Mrs. Linde, have you admired her?

**Mrs. Linde.** Yes, and now I will say good-night.

**Helmer.** What, already? Is this yours, this knitting?

**Mrs. Linde** (*taking it*). Yes, thank you, I have very nearly forgotten it.

**Helmer.** So you knit?

**Mrs. Linde.** Of course.

**Helmer.** Do you know, you ought to embroider.

**Mrs. Linde.** Really? Why?

**Helmer.** Yes, it's far more becoming. Let me show you. You hold the embroidery thus in your left hand, and use the needle with the right — like this — with a long, easy sweep. Do you see?

**Mrs. Linde.** Yes, perhaps ——

**Helmer.** But in the case of knitting — that can never be anything but ungraceful; look here — the arms close together, the knitting-needles going up and down — it has a sort of Chinese effect —. That was really excellent champagne they gave us.

**Mrs. Linde.** Well, — good-night, Nora, and don't be self-willed any more.

**Helmer.** That's right, Mrs. Linde.

**Mrs. Linde.** Good-night, Mr. Helmer.

**Helmer** (*accompanying her to the door*). Good-night, good-night. I hope you will get home all right. I should be very happy to — but you haven't any great distance to go. Good-night, good-night. (*She goes out; he shuts the door after her, and comes in again.*) Ah! — at last we have got rid of her. She is a frightful bore, that woman.

**Nora.** Aren't you very tired, Torvald?

**Helmer.** No, not in the least.

**Nora.** Nor sleepy?

**Helmer.** Not a bit. On the contrary, I feel extraordinarily lively. And you? — you really look both tired and sleepy.

**Nora.** Yes, I am very tired. I want to go to sleep at once.

**Helmer.** There, you see it was quite right of me not to let you stay there any longer.

**Nora.** Everything you do is quite right, Torvald.

**Helmer** (*kissing her on the forehead*). Now my little skylark is speaking reasonably. Did you notice what good spirits Rank was in this evening?

**Nora.** Really? Was he? I didn't speak to him at all.

**Helmer.** And I very little, but I have not for a long time seen him in such good form. (*Looks for a while at her and then goes nearer to her.*) It is delightful to be at home by ourselves again, to be all alone with you — you fascinating, charming little darling!

**Nora.** Don't look at me like that, Torvald.

**Helmer.** Why shouldn't I look at my dearest treasure? — at all the beauty that is mine, all my very own?

**Nora** (*going to the other side of the table*). You mustn't say things like that to me to-night.

**Helmer** (*following her*). You have still got the Tarantella in your blood, I see. And it makes you more captivating than ever. Listen — the guests are beginning to go now. (*In a lower voice.*) Nora — soon the whole house will be quiet.

**Nora.** Yes, I hope so.

**Helmer.** Yes, my own darling Nora. Do you know, when I am out at a party with you like this, why I speak so little to you, keep away from you, and only send a stolen glance in your direction now and then? — do you know why I do that? It is because I make believe to myself that we are secretly in love, and you are my secretly promised bride, and that no one suspects there is anything between us.

**Nora.** Yes, yes — I know very well your thoughts are with me all the time.

**Helmer.** And when we are leaving, and I am putting the shawl over your beautiful young shoulders — on your lovely neck — then I imagine that you are my young bride and that we have just come from the wedding, and I am bringing you for the first time into our home — to be alone with you for the first time — quite alone with my shy little darling! All this evening I have longed for nothing but you. When I watched the seductive figures of the Tarantella, my blood was on fire; I could endure it no longer, and that was why I brought you down so early ——

**Nora.** Go away, Torvald! You must let me go. I won't ——

**Helmer.** What's that? You're joking, my little Nora! You won't — you won't? Am I not your husband —?

(*A knock is heard at the outer door.*)

**Nora** (*starting*). Did you hear ——?

**Helmer** (*going into the hall*). Who is it?

**Rank** (*outside*). It is I. May I come in for a moment?

**Helmer** (*in a fretful whisper*). Oh, what does he want now? (*Aloud.*) Wait a minute? (*Unlocks the door.*) Come, that's kind of you not to pass by our door.

**Rank.** I thought I heard your voice, and felt as if I should like to look in. (*With a swift glance round.*) Ah, yes! — these dear familiar rooms. You are very happy and cosy in here, you two.

**Helmer.** It seems to me that you looked after yourself pretty well upstairs too.

**Rank.** Excellently. Why shouldn't I? Why shouldn't one enjoy everything in this world? — at any rate as much as one can, and as long as one can. The wine was capital ——

**Helmer.** Especially the champagne.

**Rank.** So you noticed that too? It is almost incredible how much I managed to put away!

**Nora.** Torvald drank a great deal of champagne to-night, too.

**Rank.** Did he?

**Nora.** Yes, and he is always in such good spirits afterwards.

**Rank.** Well, why should one not enjoy a merry evening after a well-spent day?

**Helmer.** Well spent? I am afraid I can't take credit for that.

**Rank** (*clapping him on the back*). But I can, you know!

**Nora.** Doctor Rank, you must have been occupied with some scientific investigation to-day.

**Rank.** Exactly.

**Helmer.** Just listen — little Nora talking about scientific investigations!

**Nora.** And may I congratulate you on the result?

**Rank.** Indeed you may.

**Nora.** Was it favourable, then?

**Rank.** The best possible, for both doctor and patient — certainty.

**Nora** (*quickly and searchingly*). Certainty?

**Rank.** Absolute certainty. So wasn't I entitled to make a merry evening of it after that?

**Nora.** Yes, you certainly were, Doctor Rank.

**Helmer.** I think so too, so long as you don't have to pay for it in the morning.

**Rank.** Oh well, one can't have anything in this life without paying for it.

**Nora.** Doctor Rank — are you fond of fancy-dress balls?

**Rank.** Yes, if there is a fine lot of pretty costumes.

**Nora.** Tell me — what shall we two wear at the next?

**Helmer.** Little featherbrain! — are you thinking of the next already?

**Rank.** We two? Yes, I can tell you. You shall go as a good fairy ——

**Helmer.** Yes, but what do you suggest as an appropriate costume for that?

**Rank.** Let your wife go dressed just as she is in everyday life.

**Helmer.** That was really very prettily turned. But can't you tell us what you will be?

**Rank.** Yes, my dear friend, I have quite made up my mind about that.

**Helmer.** Well?

**Rank.** At the next fancy dress ball I shall be invisible.

**Helmer.** That's a good joke!

**Rank.** There is a big black hat — have you never heard of hats that make you invisible? If you put one on, no one can see you.

**Helmer** (*suppressing a smile*). Yes, you are quite right.

**Rank.** But I am clean forgetting what I came for. Helmer, give me a cigar — one of the dark Havanas.

**Helmer.** With the greatest pleasure.

(*Offers him his case.*)

**Rank** (*takes a cigar and cuts off the end*). Thanks.

**Nora** (*striking a match*). Let me give you a light.

**Rank.** Thank you. *(She holds the match for him to light his cigar.)* And now good-bye!

**Helmer.** Good-bye, good-bye, dear old man!

**Nora.** Sleep well, Doctor Rank.

**Rank.** Thank you for that wish.

**Nora.** Wish me the same.

**Rank.** You? Well, if you want me to — sleep well! And thanks for the light.

*(He nods to them both and goes out.)*

**Helmer** *(in a subdued voice).* He has drunk more than he ought.

**Nora** *(absently).* Maybe. *(Helmer takes a bunch of keys out of his pocket and goes into the hall.)* Torvald! what are you going to do there?

**Helmer.** Empty the letter-box; it is quite full; there will be no room to put the newspaper in to-morrow morning.

**Nora.** Are you going to work to-night?

**Helmer.** You know quite well I'm not. What is this? Some one has been at the lock.

**Nora.** At the lock —?

**Helmer.** Yes, someone has. What can it mean? I should never have thought the maid —. Here is a broken hairpin. Nora, it is one of yours.

**Nora** *(quickly).* Then it must have been the children —

**Helmer.** Then you must get them out of those ways. There, at last I have got it open. *(Takes out the contents of the letter-box, and calls to the kitchen.)* Helen! — Helen, put out the light over the front door. *(Goes back into the room and shuts the door into the hall. He holds out his hand full of letters.)* Look at that — look what a heap of them there are. *(Turning them over.)* What on earth is that?

**Nora** *(at the window).* The letter — No! Torvald, no!

**Helmer.** Two cards — of Rank's.

**Nora.** Of Doctor Rank's?

**Helmer** *(looking at them).* Doctor Rank. They were on the top. He must have put them in when he went out.

**Nora.** Is there anything written on them?

**Helmer.** There is a black cross over the name. Look there — what an uncomfortable idea! It looks as if he were announcing his own death.

**Nora.** It is just what he is doing.

**Helmer.** What? Do you know anything about it? Has he said anything to you?

**Nora.** Yes. He told me that when the cards came it would be his leave-taking from us. He means to shut himself up and die.

**Helmer.** My poor old friend. Certainly I knew we should not have him very long with us. But so soon! And so he hides himself away like a wounded animal.

**Nora.** If it has to happen, it is best it should be without a word — don't you think so, Torvald?

**Helmer** *(walking up and down).* He had so grown into our lives. I can't think of him as having gone out of them. He, with his sufferings and his loneliness, was like a cloudy background to our sunlit happiness. Well, perhaps it is best so. For him, anyway. (*Standing still.*) And perhaps for us too, Nora. We two are thrown quite upon each other now. (*Puts his arms round her.*) My darling wife, I don't feel as if I could hold you tight enough. Do you know, Nora, I have often wished that you might be threatened by some great danger, so that I might risk my life's blood, and everything, for your sake.

Nora (*disengages herself, and says firmly and decidedly*). Now you must read your letters, Torvald.

Helmer. No, no; not to-night. I want to be with you, my darling wife.

Nora. With the thought of your friend's death ——

Helmer. You are right, it has affected us both. Something ugly has come between us — the thought of the horrors of death. We must try and rid our minds of that. Until then — we will each go to our own room.

Nora (*hanging on his neck*). Good-night, Torvald — Good-night!

Helmer (*kissing her on the forehead*). Good-night, my little singing-bird. Sleep sound, Nora. Now I will read my letters through.

(*He takes his letters and goes into his room, shutting the door after him.*)

Nora (*gropes distractedly about, seizes Helmer's domino, throws it round her, while she says in quick, hoarse, spasmodic whispers*). Never to see him again. Never! Never! (*Puts her shawl over her head.*) Never to see my children again either — never again. Never! Never! — Ah! the icy, black water — the unfathomable depths — If only it were over! He has got it now — now he is reading it. Good-bye, Torvald and my children!

(*She is about to rush out through the hall, when Helmer opens his door hurriedly and stands with an open letter in his hand.*)

Helmer. Nora!

Nora. Ah! ——

Helmer. What is this? Do you know what is in this letter?

Nora. Yes, I know. Let me go! Let me get out!

Helmer (*holding her back*). Where are you going?

Nora (*trying to get free*). You shan't save me, Torvald!

Helmer (*reeling*). True? Is this true, what I read here? Horrible! No, no — it is impossible that it can be true.

Nora. It is true. I have loved you above everything else in the world.

Helmer. Oh, don't let us have any silly excuses.

Nora (*taking a step towards him*). Torvald ——!

Helmer. Miserable creature — what have you done?

Nora. Let me go. You shall not suffer for my sake. You shall not take it upon yourself.

Helmer. No tragedy airs, please. (*Locks the hall door.*) Here you shall stay and give me an explanation. Do you understand what you have done? Answer me! Do you understand what you have done?

**Nora** (*looks steadily at him and says with a growing look of coldness in her face*). Yes, now I am beginning to understand thoroughly.

**Helmer** (*walking about the room*). What a horrible awakening! All these eight years — she who was my joy and pride — a hypocrite, a liar — worse, worse — a criminal! The unutterable ugliness of it all! For shame! For shame! (*Nora is silent and looks steadily at him. He stops in front of her.*) I ought to have suspected that something of the sort would happen. I ought to have foreseen it. All your father's want of principle — be silent! — all your father's want of principle has come out in you. No religion, no morality, no sense of duty —. How I am punished for having winked at what he did! I did it for your sake, and this is how you repay me.

**Nora.** Yes, that's just it.

**Helmer.** Now you have destroyed all my happiness. You have ruined all my future. It is horrible to think of! I am in the power of an unscrupulous man; he can do what he likes with me, ask anything he likes of me, give me any orders he pleases — I dare not refuse. And I must sink to such miserable depths because of a thoughtless woman!

**Nora.** When I am out of the way, you will be free.

**Helmer.** No fine speeches, please. Your father had always plenty of those ready, too. What good would it be to me if you were out of the way, as you say? Not the slightest. He can make the affair known everywhere; and if he does, I may be falsely suspected of having been a party to your criminal action. Very likely people will think I was behind it all — that it was I who prompted you! And I have to thank you for all this — you whom I have cherished during the whole of our married life. Do you understand now what it is you have done for me?

**Nora** (*coldly and quietly*). Yes.

**Helmer.** It is so incredible that I can't take it in. But we must come to some understanding. Take off that shawl. Take it off, I tell you. I must try and appease him some way or another. The matter must be hushed up at any cost. And as for you and me, it must appear as if everything between us were just as before — but naturally only in the eyes of the world. You will still remain in my house, that is a matter of course. But I shall not allow you to bring up the children; I dare not trust them to you. To think that I should be obliged to say so to one whom I have loved so dearly, and whom I still ——. No, that is all over. From this moment happiness is not the question; all that concerns us is to save the remains, the fragments, the appearance ——

(*A ring is heard at the front-door bell.*)

**Helmer** (*with a start*). What is that? So late! Can the worst ——? Can he ——? Hide yourself, Nora. Say you are ill.

(*Nora stands motionless. Helmer goes and unlocks the hall door.*)

**Maid** (*half-dressed, comes to the door*). A letter for the mistress.

**Helmer.** Give it to me. (*Takes the letter, and shuts the door.*) Yes, it is from him. You shall not have it; I will read it myself.

**Nora.** Yes, read it.

**Helmer** *(standing by the lamp).* I scarcely have the courage to do it. It may mean ruin for both of us. No, I must know. *(Tears open the letter, runs his eye over a few lines, looks at a paper enclosed and gives a shout of joy.)* Nora! *(She looks at him questioningly.)* Nora! — No, I must read it once again ——. Yes, it is true! I am saved! Nora, I am saved!

**Nora.** And I?

**Helmer.** You too, of course; we are both saved, both you and I. Look, he sends you your bond back. He says he regrets and repents — that a happy change in his life — never mind what he says! We are saved, Nora! No one can do anything to you. Oh, Nora, Nora! — no, first I must destroy these hateful things. Let me see ——. *(Takes a look at the bond.)* No, no, I won't look at it. The whole thing shall be nothing but a bad dream to me. *(Tears up the bond and both letters, throws them all into the stove, and watches them burn.)* There — now it doesn't exist any longer. He says that since Christmas Eve you ——. These must have been three dreadful days for you, Nora.

**Nora.** I have fought a hard fight these three days.

**Helmer.** And suffered agonies, and seen no way out but ——. No, we won't call any of the horrors to mind. We will only shout with joy, and keep saying, "It's all over! It's all over!" Listen to me, Nora. You don't seem to realise that it is all over. What is this? — such a cold, set face! My poor little Nora, I quite understand; you don't feel as if you could believe that I have forgiven you. But it is true, Nora, I swear it; I have forgiven you everything. I know that what you did, you did out of love for me.

**Nora.** That is true.

**Helmer.** You have loved me as a wife ought to love her husband. Only you had not sufficient knowledge to judge of the means you used. But do you suppose you are any the less dear to me, because you don't understand how to act on your own responsibility? No, no; only lean on me; I will advise you and direct you. I should not be a man if this womanly helplessness did not just give you a double attractiveness in my eyes. You must not think any more about the hard things I said in my first moment of consternation, when I thought everything was going to overwhelm me. I have forgiven you, Nora; I swear to you I have forgiven you.

*(She goes out through the door to the right.)*

**Helmer.** No, don't go ——. *(Looks in.)* What are you doing in there?

**Nora** *(from within).* Taking off my fancy dress.

**Helmer** *(standing at the open door).* Yes, do. Try and calm yourself, and make your mind easy again, my frightened little singing-bird. Be at rest, and feel secure; I have broad wings to shelter you under. *(Walks up and down by the door.)* How warm and cosy our home is, Nora. Here is shelter for you; here I will protect you like a hunted dove that I have saved from a hawk's claws. I will bring peace to your poor beating heart. It will come, little by little, Nora, believe me.

To-morrow morning you will look upon it all quite differently; soon everything will be just as it was before. Very soon you won't need me to assure you that I have forgiven you; you will yourself feel the certainty that I have done so. Can you suppose I should ever think of such a thing as repudiating you, or even reproaching you? You have no idea what a true man's heart is like, Nora. There is something so indescribably sweet and satisfying, to a man, in the knowledge that he has forgiven his wife — forgiven her freely, and with all his heart. It seems as if that had made her, as it were, doubly his own; he has given her a new life, so to speak; and she has in a way become both wife and child to him. So you shall be for me after this, my little scared, helpless darling. Have no anxiety about anything, Nora; only be frank and open with me, and I will serve as will and conscience both to you ——. What is this? Not gone to bed? Have you changed your things?

**Nora** (*in everyday dress*). Yes, Torvald, I have changed my things now.

**Helmer.** But what for? — so late as this.

**Nora.** I shall not sleep to-night.

**Helmer.** But, my dear Nora ——

**Nora** (*looking at her watch*). It is not so very late. Sit down here, Torvald. You and I have much to say to one another.

*(She sits down at one side of the table.)*

**Helmer.** Nora — what is this? — this cold, set face?

**Nora.** Sit down. It will take some time; I have a lot to talk over with you.

**Helmer** (*sits down at the opposite side of the table*). You alarm me, Nora! — and I don't understand you.

**Nora.** No, that is just it. You don't understand me, and I have never understood you either — before to-night. No, you mustn't interrupt me. You must simply listen to what I say. Torvald, this is a settling of accounts.

**Helmer.** What do you mean by that?

**Nora** (*after a short silence*). Isn't there one thing that strikes you as strange in our sitting here like this?

**Helmer.** What is that?

**Nora.** We have been married now eight years. Does it not occur to you that this is the first time we two, you and I, husband and wife, have had a serious conversation?

**Helmer.** What do you mean by serious?

**Nora.** In all these eight years — longer than that — from the very beginning of our acquaintance, we have never exchanged a word on any serious subject.

**Helmer.** Was it likely that I would be continually and for ever telling you about worries that you could not help me to bear?

**Nora.** I am not speaking about business matters. I say that we have never sat down in earnest together to try and get at the bottom of anything.

**Helmer.** But, dearest Nora, would it have been any good to you?

**Nora.** That is just it; you have never understood me. I have been greatly wronged, Torvald — first by papa and then by you.

**Helmer.** What! By us two — by us two, who have loved you better than anyone else in the world?

**Nora** *(shaking her head).* You have never loved me. You have only thought it pleasant to be in love with me.

**Helmer.** Nora, what do I hear you saying?

**Nora.** It is perfectly true, Torvald. When I was at home with papa, he told me his opinion about everything, and so I had the same opinions; and if I differed from him I concealed the fact, because he would not have liked it. He called me his doll-child, and he played with me just as I used to play with my dolls. And when I came to live with you ——

**Helmer.** What sort of an expression is that to use about our marriage?

**Nora** *(undisturbed).* I mean that I was simply transferred from papa's hands into yours. You arranged everything according to your own taste, and so I got the same tastes as you — or else I pretended to, I am really not quite sure which — I think sometimes the one and sometimes the other. When I look back on it, it seems to me as if I had been living here like a poor woman — just from hand to mouth. I have existed merely to perform tricks for you, Torvald. But you would have it so. You and papa have committed a great sin against me. It is your fault that I have made nothing of my life.

**Helmer.** How unreasonable and how ungrateful you are, Nora! Have you not been happy here?

**Nora.** No, I have never been happy. I thought I was, but it has never really been so.

**Helmer.** Not — not happy!

**Nora.** No, only merry. And you have always been so kind to me. But our home has been nothing but a playroom. I have been your doll-wife, just as at home I was papa's doll-child; and here the children have been my dolls. I thought it great fun when you played with me, just as they thought it great fun when I played with them. That is what our marriage has been, Torvald.

**Helmer.** There is some truth in what you say — exaggerated and strained as your view of it is. But for the future it shall be different. Playtime shall be over, and lesson-time shall begin.

**Nora.** Whose lessons? Mine, or the children's?

**Helmer.** Both your and the children's, my darling Nora.

**Nora.** Alas, Torvald, you are not the man to educate me into being a proper wife for you.

**Helmer.** And you can say that!

**Nora.** And I — how am I fitted to bring up the children?

**Helmer.** Nora!

**Nora.** Didn't you say so yourself a little while ago — that you dare not trust me to bring them up?

**Helmer.** In a moment of anger! Why do you pay any heed to that?

**Nora.** Indeed, you were perfectly right. I am not fit for the task. There is another task I must undertake first. I must try and educate myself — you are not the man to help me in that. I must do that for myself. And that is why I am going to leave you now.

**Helmer** *(springing up)*. What do you say?

**Nora.** I must stand quite alone, if I am to understand myself and everything about me. It is for that reason that I cannot remain with you any longer.

**Helmer.** Nora! Nora!

**Nora.** I am going away from here now, at once. I am sure Christine will take me in for the night ——

**Helmer.** You are out of your mind! I won't allow it! I forbid you!

**Nora.** It is no use forbidding me anything any longer. I will take with me what belongs to myself. I will take nothing from you, either now or later.

**Helmer.** What sort of madness is this!

**Nora.** To-morrow I shall go home — I mean, to my old home. It will be easiest for me to find something to do there.

**Helmer.** You blind, foolish woman!

**Nora.** I must try and get some sense, Torvald.

**Helmer.** To desert your home, your husband and your children! And you don't consider what people will say!

**Nora.** I cannot consider that at all. I only know that it is necessary for me.

**Helmer.** It's shocking. This is how you would neglect your most sacred duties.

**Nora.** What do you consider my most sacred duties?

**Helmer.** Do I need to tell you that? Are they not your duties to your husband and your children?

**Nora.** I have other duties just as sacred.

**Helmer.** That you have not. What duties could those be?

**Nora.** Duties to myself.

**Helmer.** Before all else, you are a wife and a mother.

**Nora.** I don't believe that any longer. I believe that before all else I am a reasonable human being, just as you are — or, at all events, that I must try and become one. I know quite well, Torvald, that most people would think you right, and that views of that kind are to be found in books; but I can no longer content myself with what most people say, or with what is found in books. I must think over things for myself and get to understand them.

**Helmer.** Can you not understand your place in your own home? Have you not a reliable guide in such matters as that? — have you no religion?

**Nora.** I am afraid, Torvald, I do not exactly know what religion is.

**Helmer.** What are you saying?

**Nora.** I know nothing but what the clergyman said, when I went to be confirmed. He told us that religion was this, and that, and the other. When I am away from all this, and am alone, I will look into that matter too. I will see if what the clergyman said is true, or at all events if it is true for me.

**Helmer.** This is unheard of in a girl of your age! But if religion cannot lead you aright, let me try and awaken your conscience. I suppose you have some moral sense? Or — answer me — am I to think you have none?

**Nora.** I assure you, Torvald, that is not an easy question to answer. I really don't know. The thing perplexes me altogether. I only know that you and I look at it in quite another light. I am learning, too, that the law is quite another thing from what I supposed; but I find it impossible to convince myself that the law is right. According to it a woman has no right to spare her old dying father, or to save her husband's life. I can't believe that.

**Helmer.** You talk like a child. You don't understand the conditions of the world in which you live.

**Nora.** No, I don't. But now I am going to try. I am going to see if I can make out who is right, the world or I.

**Helmer.** You are ill, Nora; you are delirious; I almost think you are out of your mind.

**Nora.** I have never felt my mind so clear and certain as to-night.

**Helmer.** And is it with a clear and certain mind that you forsake your husband and your children?

**Nora.** Yes, it is.

**Helmer.** Then there is only one possible explanation.

**Nora.** What is that?

**Helmer.** You do not love me any more.

**Nora.** No, that is just it.

**Helmer.** Nora! — and you can say that?

**Nora.** It gives me great pain, Torvald, for you have always been so kind to me, but I cannot help it. I do not love you any more.

**Helmer** (regaining his composure). Is that a clear and certain conviction too?

**Nora.** Yes, absolutely clear and certain. That is the reason why I will not stay here any longer.

**Helmer.** And can you tell me what I have done to forfeit your love?

**Nora.** Yes, indeed I can. It was to-night, when the wonderful thing did not happen; then I saw you were not the man I had thought you.

**Helmer.** Explain yourself better — I don't understand you.

**Nora.** I have waited so patiently for eight years; for, goodness knows, I knew very well that wonderful things don't happen every day. Then this horrible misfortune came upon me; and then I felt quite certain that the wonderful thing was going to happen at last. When Krogstad's letter was lying out there, never for a moment did I imagine that you would consent to accept this man's conditions. I was so absolutely certain that you would say to him: Publish the thing to the whole world. And when that was done ——

**Helmer.** Yes, what then? — when I had exposed my wife to shame and disgrace?

**Nora.** When that was done, I was so absolutely certain, you would come forward and take everything upon yourself, and say: I am the guilty one.

**Helmer.** Nora ——!

**Nora.** You mean that I would never have accepted such a sacrifice on your part? No, of course not. But what would my assurances have been worth against yours? That was the wonderful thing which I hoped for and feared; and it was to prevent that, that I wanted to kill myself.

**Helmer.** I would gladly work night and day for you, Nora — bear sorrow and want for your sake. But no man would sacrifice his honour for the one he loves.

**Nora.** It is a thing hundreds of thousands of women have done.

**Helmer.** Oh, you think and talk like a heedless child.

**Nora.** Maybe. But you neither think nor talk like the man I could bind myself to. As soon as your fear was over — and it was not fear for what threatened me, but for what might happen to you — when the whole thing was past, as far as you were concerned it was exactly as if nothing at all had happened. Exactly as before, I was your little skylark, your doll, which you would in future treat with doubly gentle care, because it was so brittle and fragile. *(Getting up.)* Torvald — it was then it dawned upon me that for eight years I had been living here with a strange man, and had borne him three children ——. Oh, I can't bear to think of it! I could tear myself into little bits!

**Helmer** *(sadly)*. I see, I see. An abyss has opened between us — there is no denying it. But, Nora, would it not be possible to fill it up?

**Nora.** As I am now, I am no wife for you.

**Helmer.** I have it in me to become a different man.

**Nora.** Perhaps — if your doll is taken away from you.

**Helmer.** But to part! — to part from you! No, no, Nora, I can't understand that idea.

**Nora** *(going out to the right)*. That makes it all the more certain that it must be done.

*(She comes back with her cloak and hat and a small bag which she puts on a chair by the table.)*

**Helmer.** Nora, Nora, not now! Wait till to-morrow.

**Nora** *(putting on her cloak)*. I cannot spend the night in a strange man's room.

**Helmer.** But can't we live here like brother and sister ——?

**Nora** *(putting on her hat)*. You know very well that would not last long. *(Puts the shawl round her.)* Good-bye, Torvald. I won't see the little ones. I know they are in better hands than mine. As I am now, I can be of no use to them.

**Helmer.** But some day, Nora — some day?

**Nora.** How can I tell? I have no idea what is going to become of me.

**Helmer.** But you are my wife, whatever becomes of you.

**Nora.** Listen, Torvald. I have heard that when a wife deserts her husband's house, as I am doing now, he is legally freed from all obligations towards her. In any case I set you free from all your obligations. You are not to feel yourself bound in the slightest way, any more than I shall. There must be perfect freedom on both sides. See here is your ring back. Give me mine.

**Helmer.** That too?

**Nora.** That too.

**Helmer.** Here it is.

**Nora.** That's right. Now it is all over. I have put the keys here. The maids know all about everything in the house — better than I do. To-morrow, after I have left her, Christine will come here and pack up my own things that I brought with me from home. I will have them sent after me.

**Helmer.** All over! All over! — Nora, shall you never think of me again?

**Nora.** I know I shall often think of you and the children and this house.

**Helmer.** May I write to you, Nora?

**Nora.** No — never. You must not do that.

**Helmer.** But at least let me send you ——

**Nora.** Nothing — nothing ——

**Helmer.** Let me help you if you are in want.

**Nora.** No. I can receive nothing from a stranger.

**Helmer.** Nora — can I never be anything more than a stranger to you?

**Nora** (*taking her bag*). Ah, Torvald, the most wonderful thing of all would have to happen.

**Helmer.** Tell me what that would be!

**Nora.** Both you and I would have to be so changed that ——. Oh, Torvald, I don't believe any longer in wonderful things happening.

**Helmer.** But I will believe in it. Tell me? So changed that ——?

**Nora.** That our life together would be a real wedlock. Good-bye.

(*She goes out through the hall.*)

Helmer (*sinks down on a chair at the door and buries his face in his hands*). Nora! Nora! (*Looks round, and rises.*) Empty. She is gone. (*A hope flashes across his mind.*) The most wonderful thing of all ——?

(*The sound of a door shutting is heard from below.*)

## FOR ANALYSIS

**1.** What evidence can you find to support the interpretation that this play is not only about the Helmers' marriage but also about the institution of marriage itself?

**2.** What does the first meeting between Nora and Mrs. Linde tell us about Nora's character?

**3.** On a number of occasions, Nora recalls her father. What relevance do these recollections have to the development of the **theme**?

**4.** Is Krogstad presented as a conventional villain, or are we meant to sympathize with him? Explain.

**5.** What function does Dr. Rank serve in the play?

**6.** Examine the stage directions at the beginning of each act. In what ways do they contribute to and reflect the developing action?

**7.** Acts I and II contain early **dialogues** between Nora and Torvald. What changes in Nora does a comparison between the two dialogues reveal?

**8.** At what point in the action does Nora begin to understand the truth of her situation and take responsibility for her life?

**9.** Summarize the various arguments Torvald uses in his attempt to persuade Nora not to leave.

**10.** Is the feminist theme of the play weakened by Ibsen's failure to suggest how Nora could conceivably make it on her own in such a patriarchal society? Explain.

## MAKING ARGUMENTS

*A Doll's House* aroused great controversy in its time. Today, we like to think society has evolved beyond such prejudices. Do you think this play, if it first appeared now, would arouse no controversy? Would some still find it objectionable? Support your argument with reference both to the text and also to the current state of gender relations, legal and social, in the Western world.

## WRITING TOPICS

**1.** Does the fact that Nora abandons her children undermine her otherwise heroic decision to walk out on a hollow marriage? For an 1880 German production, Ibsen — in response to public demand — provided an alternate ending in which Nora, after struggling with her conscience, decides that she cannot abandon her children. Do you think this is a better ending than the original one?

**2.** How does the **subplot** involving the relationship between Mrs. Linde and Krogstad add force to the main **plot** of *A Doll's House*?

**3.** When you were younger, did you ever defy social pressure because the cost of conforming was too high? Describe the source of the pressure, the issues at stake, and the consequences of your refusal. Since then, have you had second thoughts about your actions? Would you act the same way now that you are older?

**4.** Write a brief description of a marriage you are familiar with that endured only out of inertia, economic pressure, or fear.

## MAKING CONNECTIONS

Compare the attitudes toward women revealed in this play with those in Susan Glaspell's *Trifles* (p. 761).

# NONFICTION

<u>**LANGSTON HUGHES**</u>   (1902–1967)

## SALVATION   1940

I was saved from sin when I was going on thirteen. But not really saved. It happened like this. There was a big revival at my Auntie Reed's church. Every night for weeks there had been much preaching, singing, praying, and shouting, and some very hardened sinners had been brought to Christ, and the membership of the church had grown by leaps and bounds. Then just before the revival ended, they held a special meeting for children, "to bring the young lambs to the fold." My aunt spoke of it for days ahead. That night I was escorted to the front row and placed on the mourners' bench with all the other young sinners, who had not yet been brought to Jesus.

My aunt told me that when you were saved you saw a light, and something happened to you inside! And Jesus came into your life! And God was with you from then on! She said you could see and hear and feel Jesus in your soul. I believed her. I had heard a great many old people say the same thing and it seemed to me they ought to know. So I sat there calmly in the hot, crowded church, waiting for Jesus to come to me.

The preacher preached a wonderful rhythmical sermon, all moans and shouts and lonely cries and dire pictures of hell, and then he sang a song about the ninety and nine safe in the fold, but one little lamb was left out in the cold. Then he said: "Won't you come? Won't you come to Jesus? Young lambs, won't you come?" And he held out his arms to all us young sinners there on the mourners' bench. And the little girls cried. And some of them jumped up and went to Jesus right away. But most of us just sat there.

A great many old people came and knelt around us and prayed, old women with jet-black faces and braided hair, old men with work-gnarled hands. And the church sang a song about the lower lights are burning, some poor sinners to be saved. And the whole building rocked with prayer and song.

Still I kept waiting to *see* Jesus.                                                                                          5

Finally all the young people had gone to the altar and were saved, but one boy and me. He was a rounder's son named Westley. Westley and I were surrounded by sisters and deacons praying. It was very hot in the church, and getting late now. Finally Westley said to me in a whisper: "God damn! I'm tired o' sitting here. Let's get up and be saved." So he got up and was saved.

Then I was left all alone on the mourners' bench. My aunt came and knelt at my knees and cried, while prayers and song swirled all around me in the little church. The whole congregation prayed for me alone, in a mighty wail of moans and voices. And I kept waiting serenely for Jesus, waiting, waiting — but he didn't come. I wanted to see him, but nothing happened to me. Nothing! I wanted something to happen to me, but nothing happened.

I heard the songs and the minister saying: "Why don't you come? My dear child, why don't you come to Jesus? Jesus is waiting for you. He wants you. Why don't you come? Sister Reed, what is this child's name?"

"Langston," my aunt sobbed.

"Langston, why don't you come? Why don't you come and be saved? Oh, 10 Lamb of God! Why don't you come?"

Now it was really getting late. I began to be ashamed of myself, holding everything up so long. I began to wonder what God thought about Westley, who certainly hadn't seen Jesus either, but who was now sitting proudly on the platform, swinging his knickerbockered legs and grinning down at me, surrounded by deacons and old women on their knees praying. God had not struck Westley dead for taking his name in vain or for lying in the temple. So I decided that maybe to save further trouble, I'd better lie, too, and say that Jesus had come, and get up and be saved.

So I got up.

Suddenly the whole room broke into a sea of shouting, as they saw me rise. Waves of rejoicing swept the place. Women leaped in the air. My aunt threw her arms around me. The minister took me by the hand and led me to the platform.

When things quieted down, in a hushed silence, punctuated by a few ecstatic "Amens," all the new young lambs were blessed in the name of God. Then joyous singing filled the room.

That night, for the last time in my life but one — for I was a big boy twelve 15 years old — I cried. I cried, in bed alone, and couldn't stop. I buried my head under the quilts, but my aunt heard me. She woke up and told my uncle I was crying because the Holy Ghost had come into my life, and because I had seen Jesus. But I was really crying because I couldn't bear to tell her that I had lied, that I had deceived everybody in the church, that I hadn't seen Jesus, and that now I didn't believe there was a Jesus any more, since he didn't come to help me.

### FOR ANALYSIS

1. Is the **tone** of this essay comic or serious or both? Explain.
2. What role does Westley (para. 6) play in the narrative?
3. Can the word *salvation* as Hughes uses it be construed in more than one way? Explain.

**4.** Discuss how the **point of view** of a **narrator** who looks back on a childhood experience helps define the meaning of the experience.

## MAKING ARGUMENTS

How would you argue that young Langston did the right thing in "Salvation"? What points would you use to argue that he did the wrong thing?

## WRITING TOPIC

Describe an experience in which public pressure forced you either to express an opinion or a belief that you didn't really hold or to act in a way you otherwise would not have.

## MAKING CONNECTIONS

**1.** Compare and contrast Hughes's loss of **innocence** with that of Sylvia in Bambara's "The Lesson" (p. 98).

**2.** Compare and contrast the **narrator's** attitude toward adult authority in this story with Sylvia's in Bambara's "The Lesson" (p. 98).

# JUDITH ORTIZ COFER  (1952–2016)

# AMERICAN HISTORY  1993

I once read in a *Ripley's Believe It or Not* column that Paterson, New Jersey, is the place where the Straight and Narrow (streets) intersect. The Puerto Rican tenement known as El Building was one block up from Straight. It was, in fact, the corner of Straight and Market; not "at" the corner, but *the* corner. At almost any hour of the day, El Building was like a monstrous jukebox, blasting out *salsas* from open windows as the residents, mostly new immigrants just up from the island, tried to drown out whatever they were currently enduring with loud music. But the day President Kennedy was shot, there was a profound silence in El Building, even the abusive tongues of viragoes, the cursing of the unemployed, and the screeching of small children had been somehow muted. President Kennedy was a saint to these people. In fact, soon his photograph would be hung alongside the Sacred Heart and over the spiritist altars that many women kept in their apartments. He would become part of the hierarchy of martyrs they prayed to for favors that only one who had died for a cause would understand.

On the day that President Kennedy was shot, my ninth grade class had been out in the fenced playground of Public School Number 13. We had been given "free" exercise time and had been ordered by our P.E. teacher, Mr. DePalma, to "keep moving." That meant that the girls should jump rope and the boys toss basketballs through a hoop at the far end of the yard. He in the meantime would "keep an eye" on us from just inside the building.

It was a cold gray day in Paterson. The kind that warns of early snow. I was miserable, since I had forgotten my gloves and my knuckles were turning red and raw from the jump rope. I was also taking a lot of abuse from the black girls for not turning the rope hard and fast enough for them.

"Hey, Skinny Bones, pump it, girl. Ain't you got no energy today?" Gail, the biggest of the black girls who had the other end of the rope yelled, "Didn't you eat your rice and beans and pork chops for breakfast today?"

The other girls picked up the "pork chop" and made it into a refrain: "pork 5 chop, pork chop, did you eat your pork chop?" They entered the double ropes in pairs and exited without tripping or missing a beat. I felt a burning on my cheeks, and then my glasses fogged up so that I could not manage to coordinate the jump rope with Gail. The chill was doing to me what it always did, entering my bones, making me cry, humiliating me. I hated the city, especially in winter. I hated Public School Number 13. I hated my skinny flat-chested body, and I envied the black girls who could jump rope so fast that their legs became a blur. They always seemed to be warm while I froze.

There was only one source of beauty and light for me that school year. The only thing I had anticipated at the start of the semester. That was seeing Eugene. In August, Eugene and his family had moved into the only house on the block that had a yard and trees. I could see his place from my window in El Building. In fact, if I sat on the fire escape I was literally suspended above Eugene's backyard. It was my favorite spot to read my library books in the summer. Until that August the house had been occupied by an old Jewish couple. Over the years I had become part of their family, without their knowing it, of course. I had a view of their kitchen and their backyard, and though I could not hear what they said, I knew when they were arguing, when one of them was sick, and many other things. I knew all this by watching them at mealtimes. I could see their kitchen table, the sink and the stove. During good times, he sat at the table and read his newspapers while she fixed the meals. If they argued, he would leave and the old woman would sit and stare at nothing for a long time. When one of them was sick, the other would come and get things from the kitchen and carry them out on a tray. The old man had died in June. The last week of school I had not seen him at the table at all. Then one day I saw that there was a crowd in the kitchen. The old woman had finally emerged from the house on the arm of a stocky middle-aged woman whom I had seen there a few times before, maybe her daughter. Then a man had carried out suitcases. The house had stood empty for weeks. I had had to resist the temptation to climb down into the yard and water the flowers the old lady had taken such good care of.

By the time Eugene's family moved in, the yard was a tangled mass of weeds. The father had spent several days mowing, and when he finished, I didn't see the red, yellow, and purple clusters that meant flowers to me from where I sat. I didn't see this family sit down at the kitchen table together. It was just the mother, a red-headed tall woman who wore a white uniform — a nurse's, I guessed it was; the father was gone before I got up in the morning and was never there at dinner time. I only saw him on weekends when they sometimes sat on lawn chairs under the oak tree, each hidden behind a section of the newspaper; and there was Eugene. He was tall and blond, and he wore glasses. I liked him right away because he sat at the kitchen table and read books for hours. That summer, before we had even spoken one word to each other, I kept him company on my fire escape.

Once school started I looked for him in all my classes, but P.S. 13 was a huge, overpopulated place and it took me days and many discreet questions to discover that Eugene was in honors classes for all his subjects; classes that were not open to me because English was not my first language, though I was a straight A student. After much maneuvering I managed "to run into him" in the hallway where his locker was — on the other side of the building from mine — and in study hall at the library, where he first seemed to notice me but did not speak; and finally, on the way home after school one day when I decided to approach him directly, though my stomach was doing somersaults.

I was ready for rejection, snobbery, the worst. But when I came up to him, practically panting in my nervousness, and blurted out: "You're Eugene. Right?" He smiled, pushed his glasses up on his nose, and nodded. I saw then that he was blushing deeply. Eugene liked me, but he was shy. I did most of the talking that day. He nodded and smiled a lot. In the weeks that followed, we walked home together. He would linger at the corner of El Building for a few minutes then walk down to his two-story house. It was not until Eugene moved into that house that I noticed that El Building blocked most of the sun and that the only spot that got a little sunlight during the day was the tiny square of earth the old woman had planted with flowers.

I did not tell Eugene that I could see inside his kitchen from my bedroom. 10 I felt dishonest, but I liked my secret sharing of his evenings, especially now that I knew what he was reading, since we chose our books together at the school library.

One day my mother came into my room as I was sitting on the window-sill staring out. In her abrupt way she said: "Elena, you are acting 'moony.'" *Enamorada* was what she really said — that is, like a girl stupidly infatuated. Since I had turned fourteen and started menstruating my mother had been more vigilant than ever. She acted as if I was going to go crazy or explode or something if she didn't watch me and nag me all the time about being a señorita now. She kept talking about virtue, morality, and other subjects that did not interest me in the least. My mother was unhappy in Paterson, but my father had a good job at the blue jeans factory in Passaic, and soon, he kept assuring us, we would be moving to our own house there. Every Sunday we drove out to the suburbs of Paterson, Clifton, and Passaic, out to where people mowed grass on Sundays in the summer and where children made snowmen in the winter from pure white snow, not like the gray slush of Paterson, which seemed to fall from the sky in that hue. I had learned to listen to my parents' dreams, which were spoken in Spanish, as fairy tales, like the stories about life in the island paradise of Puerto Rico before I was born. I had been to the Island once as a little girl, to grandmother's funeral, and all I remembered was wailing women in black, my mother becoming hysterical and being given a pill that made her sleep two days, and me feeling lost in a crowd of strangers all claiming to be my aunts, uncles, and cousins. I had actually been glad to return to the city. We had not been back there since then, though my parents talked constantly about buying a house on the beach someday, retiring on the island — that was a common topic among the residents of El Building. As for me, I was going to go to college and become a teacher.

But after meeting Eugene I began to think of the present more than of the future. What I wanted now was to enter that house I had watched for so many years. I wanted to see the other rooms where the old people had lived and where the boy I liked spent his time. Most of all, I wanted to sit at the kitchen table with Eugene like two adults, like the old man and his wife had done, maybe drink some coffee and talk about books. I had started reading *Gone with the Wind*. I was enthralled by it, with the daring and the passion of the beautiful girl living in a mansion, and with her devoted parents and the slaves who did everything for them. I didn't believe such a world had ever really existed, and I wanted to ask Eugene some questions, since he and his parents, he had told me, had come up from Georgia, the same place where the novel was set. His father worked for a company that had transferred him to Paterson. His mother was very unhappy, Eugene said, in his beautiful voice that rose and fell over words in a strange, lilting way. The kids at school called him the Hick and made fun of the way he talked. I knew I was his only friend so far, and I liked that, though I felt sad for him sometimes. Skinny Bones and the Hick, was what they called us at school when we were seen together.

The day Mr. DePalma came out into the cold and asked us to line up in front of him was the day that President Kennedy was shot. Mr. DePalma, a short, muscular man with slicked-down black hair, was the science teacher, P.E. coach, and disciplinarian at P.S. 13. He was the teacher to whose homeroom you got assigned if you were a troublemaker, and the man called out to break up playground fights, and to escort violently angry teenagers to the office. And Mr. DePalma was the man who called your parents in for "a conference."

That day, he stood in front of two rows of mostly black and Puerto Rican kids, brittle from their efforts to "keep moving" on a November day that was turning bitter cold. Mr. DePalma, to our complete shock, was crying. Not just silent adult tears, but really sobbing. There were a few titters from the back of the line where I stood, shivering.

"Listen," Mr. DePalma raised his arms over his head as if he were about to 15 conduct an orchestra. His voice broke, and he covered his face with his hands. His barrel chest was heaving. Someone giggled behind me.

"Listen," he repeated, "something awful has happened." A strange gurgling came from his throat, and he turned around and spit on the cement behind him.

"Gross," someone said, and there was a lot of laughter.

"The president is dead, you idiots. I should have known that wouldn't mean anything to a bunch of losers like you kids. Go home." He was shrieking now. No one moved for a minute or two, but then a big girl let out a "yeah!" and ran to get her books piled up with the others against the brick wall of the school building. The others followed in a mad scramble to get to their things before somebody caught on. It was still an hour to the dismissal bell.

A little scared, I headed for El Building. There was an eerie feeling on the streets. I looked into Mario's drugstore, a favorite hangout for the high school crowd, but there were only a couple of old Jewish men at the soda bar, talking with the short order cook in tones that sounded almost angry, but they were keeping their voices low. Even the traffic on one of the busiest intersections in Paterson — Straight Street and Park Avenue — seemed to be moving slower. There were no horns blasting that day. At El Building, the usual little group of unemployed men were not hanging out on the front stoop, making it difficult for women to enter the front door. No music spilled out from open doors in the hallway. When I walked into our apartment, I found my mother sitting in front of the grainy picture of the television set.

She looked up at me with a tear-streaked face and just said: "Dios mío," turn- 20
ing back to the set as if it were pulling at her eyes. I went into my room.

Though I wanted to feel the right thing about President Kennedy's death, I
could not fight the feeling of elation that stirred in my chest. Today was the day
I was to visit Eugene in his house. He had asked me to come over after school
to study for an American history test with him. We had also planned to walk
to the public library together. I looked down into his yard. The oak tree was
bare of leaves, and the ground looked gray with ice. The light through the large
kitchen window of his house told me that El Building blocked the sun to such
an extent that they had to turn lights on in the middle of the day. I felt ashamed
about it. But the white kitchen table with the lamp hanging just above it looked
cozy and inviting. I would soon sit there, across from Eugene, and I would tell
him about my perch just above his house. Maybe I would.

In the next thirty minutes I changed clothes, put on a little pink lipstick, and
got my books together. Then I went in to tell my mother that I was going to a
friend's house to study. I did not expect her reaction.

"You are going out *today*?" The way she said "today" sounded as if a storm
warning had been issued. It was said in utter disbelief. Before I could answer,
she came toward me and held my elbows as I clutched my books.

"*Hija*, the president has been killed. We must show respect. He was a great
man. Come to church with me tonight."

She tried to embrace me, but my books were in the way. My first impulse 25
was to comfort her, she seemed so distraught, but I had to meet Eugene in
fifteen minutes.

"I have a test to study for, Mama. I will be home by eight."

"You are forgetting who you are, *Niña*. I have seen you staring down at that
boy's house. You are heading for humiliation and pain." My mother said this in
Spanish and in a resigned tone that surprised me, as if she had no intention of
stopping me from "heading for humiliation and pain." I started for the door.
She sat in front of the TV, holding a white handkerchief to her face.

I walked out to the street and around the chain-link fence that separated
El Building from Eugene's house. The yard was neatly edged around the little walk that led to the door. It always amazed me how Paterson, the inner
core of the city, had no apparent logic to its architecture. Small, neat, single
residences like this one could be found right next to huge, dilapidated apartment buildings like El Building. My guess was that the little houses had been
there first, then the immigrants had come in droves, and the monstrosities had
been raised for them — the Italians, the Irish, the Jews, and now us, the Puerto
Ricans, and the blacks. The door was painted a deep green: *verde*, the color of
hope. I had heard my mother say it: *Verde-Esperanza.*

I knocked softly. A few suspenseful moments later the door opened just a
crack. The red, swollen face of a woman appeared. She had a halo of red hair
floating over a delicate ivory face — the face of a doll — with freckles on the
nose. Her smudged eye makeup made her look unreal to me, like a mannequin
seen through a warped store window.

"What do you want?" Her voice was tiny and sweet-sounding, like a little 30 girl's, but her tone was not friendly.

"I'm Eugene's friend. He asked me over. To study." I thrust out my books, a silly gesture that embarrassed me almost immediately.

"You live there?" She pointed up to El Building, which looked particularly ugly, like a gray prison with its many dirty windows and rusty fire escapes. The woman had stepped halfway out, and I could see that she wore a white nurse's uniform with "St. Joseph's Hospital" on the name tag.

"Yes. I do."

She looked intently at me for a couple of heartbeats, then said as if to herself, "I don't know how you people do it." Then directly to me: "Listen. Honey. Eugene doesn't want to study with you. He is a smart boy. Doesn't need help. You understand me. I am truly sorry if he told you you could come over. He cannot study with you. It's nothing personal. You understand? We won't be in this place much longer, no need for him to get close to people — it'll just make it harder for him later. Run back home now."

I couldn't move. I just stood there in shock at hearing these things said to me 35 in such a honey-drenched voice. I had never heard an accent like hers except for Eugene's softer version. It was as if she were singing me a little song.

"What's wrong? Didn't you hear what I said?" She seemed very angry, and I finally snapped out of my trance. I turned away from the green door and heard her close it gently.

Our apartment was empty when I got home. My mother was in someone else's kitchen, seeking the solace she needed. Father would come in from his late shift at midnight. I would hear them talking softly in the kitchen for hours that night. They would not discuss their dreams for the future, or life in Puerto Rico, as they often did; that night they would talk sadly about the young widow and her two children, as if they were family. For the next few days, we would observe *luto* in our apartment; that is, we would practice restraint and silence — no loud music or laughter. Some of the women of El Building would wear black for weeks.

That night, I lay in my bed, trying to feel the right thing for our dead president. But the tears that came up from a deep source inside me were strictly for me. When my mother came to the door, I pretended to be sleeping. Sometime during the night, I saw from my bed the streetlight come on. It had a pink halo around it. I went to my window and pressed my face to the cool glass. Looking up at the light I could see the white snow falling like a lace veil over its face. I did not look down to see it turning gray as it touched the ground below.

## FOR ANALYSIS

**1.** Suggest a reason why the **narrator** spies on the neighbors.

**2.** Why does Elena's mother warn her that "[y]ou are forgetting who you are" and that "[y]ou are heading for humiliation and pain" (para. 27)?

**3.** What does Eugene's mother reveal when she says, "I don't know how you people do it" (para. 34)? Why does she refuse to let Elena study with Eugene?

**4.** How would you describe the **tone** of this essay? Is it bitter? Belligerent? Argumentative? Accepting? Explain.

**5.** Discuss the implications of the essay's title.

## MAKING ARGUMENTS

While we have to assume that Kennedy's assassination and the author's experience at her friend's door did occur on the same day, the essay capitalizes on this fact, putting the events next to each other. It does so, however, not by drawing explicit connections but by leaving that work to the reader. Make the argument that this method is effective; alternatively, argue that spelling things out would be more effective.

## WRITING TOPIC

Explain which event — President Kennedy's death or Eugene's mother's remarks — more significantly shapes the **narrator's** view of American history.

## BRIAN DOYLE   (1956–2017)

# POP ART   2001

In nine years I have been graced with three children and here is what I have
learned about them. They are engines of incalculable joy and agonizing
despair. They are comedy machines. Their language is their own and the order of
their new halting words has never been heard before in the whole history of the
world. They are headlong and hilarious. Their hearts are enormous and sensitive
beyond calculation by man or machine. Their pride is vast. They are cruel, and
move in herds and gaggles and mobs, and woe unto the silent one, the one who
looks funny, the one who speaks awkwardly, the fat one, for she will be shoul-
dered aside, he will never get the ball, she will never be asked to jump rope, he
will not be invited to the pool party, she will weep with confusion and rage, he
will lash out with sharp small fists. Yet they are endlessly kind, kind by nature,
and among them there is often an artless democracy, a linking of arms against the
vast puzzle of the long people. They search for rules and rank, for what is allowed
and what is forbidden, and poke the rules to see which bends and which is steel,
for they wish to know their place in the world, where they might walk, what they
may wear, which shows are allowed, how far they can go, who they are. They rise
early in excitement and return reluctantly to barracks at night for fear of missing a shred of the daily circus. They eat nothing to speak of but grow at stunning
rates that produce mostly leg. They are absorbed by dogs and toast. Mud and jelly
accrue to them. They are at war with wasps. They eat no green things. Once they
learn sarcasm they use it with abandon, slashing here and there without control
and wreaking havoc. When they weep they weep utterly from the marrows of
their lonely bones. They will not speak of death but when it comes, a dark hooded
hawk on the fence, they face it without fear. They are new creatures hourly, and
what you think you know of them is already lost in the river. Their hearts are
dense books no one can read. They speak many languages of the body. To them
you are a stone who has always been and will always be. When they are ill they
shrivel. To father them is not a brief noun but an endless verb that exhausts,
enrages, edifies, elevates, educates; I am a thinner and grayer man than I was; and
closer to joy. They frighten me, for they will make a new world on the bowed back
of the one I love; but they delight me, for to have loved them is to have tasted the
furious love the Maker has for what He made, and fathers still, and always will.

### FOR ANALYSIS

**1.** Why do you think Doyle chose "Pop Art" as his title?

**2.** Describe the **tone** of "Pop Art." Does it have only one, or is it varied? Can you chart
its changes? What effect do these changes have?

## MAKING ARGUMENTS

The final sentence of "Pop Art," in referring to "the Maker," brings up religion, a topic that had not been previously raised. Make an argument about this move; regardless of your own religious beliefs, do you think it is successful? Do you think it is detrimental? Do you think it has little impact either way on the essay?

## WRITING TOPICS

**1.** "Pop Art" first appeared in a creative nonfiction venue called *Brevity*. Write an essay in which you describe the effects "Pop Art" makes with its brevity. Can you imagine it longer? How would it change?

**2.** Write your own short piece, modeled on Doyle's, in which you list descriptions of something or someone in a way that adds up to more than a roster of characteristics and reveals the nature of the subject.

## MAKING CONNECTIONS

**1.** In "Those Winter Sundays," Robert Hayden writes, "What did I know, what did I know / of love's austere and lonely offices?" (p. 664). In what ways could "Pop Art" be seen as a response to Hayden's speaker's innocence of fathering?

**2.** Both "Pop Art" and Galway Kinnell's "After Making Love We Hear Footsteps" (p. 654) examine the relationship between parents and children in ways that move beyond the stereotypical and expected. How does each look at parenthood?

## FURTHER QUESTIONS
## FOR THINKING AND WRITING

**1.** How do the works in this section illustrate Thomas Gray's well-known observation that "where ignorance is bliss, / 'Tis folly to be wise"? **Writing Topic:** Use Gray's observation as the basis for an analysis of Toni Cade Bambara's "The Lesson."

**2.** In poems such as William Blake's "The Garden of Love" and Robert Frost's "Birches," growing up is seen as a growing away from a kind of truth and reality; in other poems, such as Gerard Manley Hopkins's "Spring and Fall," growing up is seen as growing into truth and reality. Do these two groups of poems embody contradictory and mutually exclusive conceptions of childhood? Explain. **Writing Topic:** Select one poem from each of these two groups, and contrast the conception of childhood embodied in each.

**3.** Eighteenth-century novelist Henry Fielding wrote: "Oh Innocence, how glorious and happy a portion art thou to the breast that possesses thee! Thou fearest neither the eyes nor the tongues of men. Truth, the most powerful of all things, is thy strongest friend; and the brighter the light is in which thou art displayed, the more it discovers thy transcendent beauties." Which works in this section support this assessment of innocence? Which works contradict it? How would you characterize the relationship between "truth" and "innocence" in the fiction, drama, and essays presented here? **Writing Topic:** Use this observation as the basis for an analysis of Nathaniel Hawthorne's "Young Goodman Brown" or Toni Cade Bambara's "The Lesson."

**4.** James Joyce's "Araby" and Rivka Galchen's "Wild Berry Blue" deal with some aspect of sexuality as a force that moves the **protagonist** from innocence toward experience. How does the recognition of sexuality function in each of the stories? **Writing Topic:** Discuss the relationship between sexuality and innocence in these stories.

**5.** Which poems in this section depend largely on **irony** for their force? Why do you think irony is a useful device in literature that portrays innocence and experience? **Writing Topic:** Analyze the function of irony in Blake's "The Garden of Love."

**6.** Some authors treat the passage from innocence to experience as **comedy**, while others treat it more seriously, even as **tragedy**. Do you find one or the other treatment more satisfying? Explain. **Writing Topic:** Select one short story, and show how the author achieves either a comic or a serious tone.

# CONFORMITY AND REBELLION

*Golconde*, 1953, by René Magritte (1898–1967).

The works in this section, "Conformity and Rebellion," feature a clash between two well-articulated positions in which a rebel, on principle, confronts and struggles with established authority. Central in these works are powerful external forces — the state, the church, tradition — which sometimes can be obeyed only at the expense of conscience and humanity. At the most general level, these works confront the ages-old dilemma that the very organizations men and women establish to protect and nurture the individual often demand — on pain of economic ruin, social ostracism, even spiritual or physical death — that individuals violate their most deeply cherished beliefs. In these works, some individuals refuse such a demand and translate their awareness of a hostile social order into action against it. In "'Repent, Harlequin!' Said the Ticktockman," Everett C. Marm disrupts a system he doesn't believe in. On a different note, in Melville's "Bartleby, the Scrivener" the crisis arises out of the protagonist's passive refusal to conform to the expectations of society.

Many of the works in this section, particularly the poems, do not treat the theme of conformity and rebellion quite so explicitly and dramatically. Some, like Emily Dickinson's "She rose to His Requirement," reveal the painful injustice of certain traditional values; others, like W. H. Auden's "The Unknown Citizen," tell us that the price exacted for total conformity to the industrial superstate is spiritual death. In "Easter 1916," William Butler Yeats meditates on the awesome meaning of the lives and deaths of political revolutionaries, and in "Harlem," Langston Hughes warns that an inflexible and constricting social order will generate explosion.

While in many of the works the individual is caught up in a crisis that forces him or her into rebellion, in other works the focus may be on the individual's failure to move from awareness into action. For example, the portrait of Auden's unknown citizen affirms the necessity for rebellion by rendering so effectively the hollow life of mindless conformity.

Although diverse in treatment and technique, all the works in this section are about individuals struggling with complex sets of external forces that regulate and define their lives. As social beings, these individuals may recognize that they must be controlled for some larger good; yet they are aware that established social power is often abusive. The institution at its best can act as a conserving force, keeping in check the individual's disruptive impulse to abandon and destroy, without cause, old ways and ideas. At its worst, the power of social institutions is self-serving. It is up to the individual to judge whether power is being abused. Because the power of the individual is often negligible beside that of abusive social forces, it is not surprising that many artists find a fundamental human dignity in the resistance of the individual to organized society.

## QUESTIONS FOR THINKING AND WRITING

Before you begin reading the selections in "Conformity and Rebellion," consider the following questions. Then write out your thoughts informally in a reading journal, if you are keeping one, as a way of preparing to respond to the selections. Or you may wish to make your response to one of these questions the basis for a formal essay.

**1.** How do you define *conformity*? What forms of rebellion are possible for a person in your situation? Do you perceive yourself as a conformist? A rebel? Some combination of the two? Explain.

**2.** How do you define *sanity*? Based on your definition, do you know an insane person? What form does that insanity take? Do you agree or disagree with Emily Dickinson's assertion that "Much Madness is divinest Sense"? Explain.

**3.** Discuss this proposition: governments routinely engage in behavior for which an individual would be imprisoned or institutionalized.

**4.** Freewrite an extended response to each of the following questions: Is war sane? Should one obey an "unjust" law? Should one be guided absolutely by religious principles?

# FICTION

**HERMAN MELVILLE** (1819-1891)

## BARTLEBY, THE SCRIVENER  1853

### A STORY OF WALL STREET

I am a rather elderly man. The nature of my avocations, for the last thirty years, has brought me into more than ordinary contact with what would seem an interesting and somewhat singular set of men, of whom, as yet, nothing, that I know of, has ever been written — I mean, the law-copyists, or scriveners. I have known very many of them, professionally and privately, and, if I pleased, could relate divers histories, at which good-natured gentlemen might smile, and sentimental souls might weep. But I waive the biographies of all other scriveners, for a few passages in the life of Bartleby, who was a scrivener, the strangest I ever saw, or heard of. While, of other law-copyists, I might write the complete life, of Bartleby nothing of that sort can be done. I believe that no materials exist for a full and satisfactory biography of this man. It is an irreparable loss to literature. Bartleby was one of those beings of whom nothing is ascertainable, except from the original sources, and, in his case, those are very small. What my own astonished eyes saw of Bartleby, *that* is all I know of him, except, indeed, one vague report, which will appear in the sequel.

Ere introducing the scrivener, as he first appeared to me, it is fit I make some mention of myself, my employees, my business, my chambers, and general surroundings; because some such description is indispensable to an adequate understanding of the chief character about to be presented. Imprimis: I am a man who, from his youth upwards, has been filled with a profound conviction that the easiest way of life is the best. Hence, though I belong to a profession proverbially energetic and nervous, even to turbulence, at times, yet nothing of that sort have I ever suffered to invade my peace. I am one of those unambitious lawyers who never addresses a jury, or in any way draws down public applause; but, in the cool tranquillity of a snug retreat, do a snug business among rich men's bonds, and mortgages, and title-deeds. All who know me, consider me an eminently *safe* man. The late John Jacob

Astor,[1] a personage little given to poetic enthusiasm, had no hesitation in pronouncing my first grand point to be prudence; my next, method. I do not speak it in vanity, but simply record the fact, that I was not unemployed in my profession by the late John Jacob Astor; a name which, I admit, I love to repeat; for it hath a rounded and orbicular sound to it, and rings like unto bullion. I will freely add, that I was not insensible to the late John Jacob Astor's good opinion.

Some time prior to the period at which this little history begins, my avocations had been largely increased. The good old office, now extinct in the State of New York, of a Master in Chancery,[2] had been conferred upon me. It was not a very arduous office, but very pleasantly remunerative. I seldom lose my temper; much more seldom indulge in dangerous indignation at wrongs and outrages; but, I must be permitted to be rash here, and declare that I consider the sudden and violent abrogation of the office of Master in Chancery, by the new Constitution, as a — premature act; inasmuch as I had counted upon a lifelease of the profits, whereas I only received those of a few short years. But this is by the way.

My chambers were up stairs, at No. —— Wall Street. At one end, they looked upon the white wall of the interior of a spacious sky-light shaft, penetrating the building from top to bottom.

This view might have been considered rather tame than otherwise, deficient in what landscape painters call "life." But, if so, the view from the other end of my chambers offered, at least, a contrast, if nothing more. In that direction, my windows commanded an unobstructed view of a lofty brick wall, black by age and everlasting shade; which wall required no spyglass to bring out its lurking beauties, but, for the benefit of all near-sighted spectators, was pushed up to within ten feet of my window panes. Owing to the great height of the surrounding buildings, and my chambers being on the second floor, the interval between this wall and mine not a little resembled a huge square cistern.

At the period just preceding the advent of Bartleby, I had two persons as copyists in my employment, and a promising lad as an office-boy. First, Turkey; second, Nippers; third, Ginger Nut. These may seem names, the like of which are not usually found in the Directory. In truth, they were nicknames, mutually conferred upon each other by my three clerks, and were deemed expressive of their respective persons or characters. Turkey was a short, pursy Englishman, of about my own age — that is, somewhere not far from sixty. In the morning, one might say, his face was of a fine florid hue, but after twelve o'clock, meridian — his dinner hour — it blazed like a grate full of Christmas coals; and continued blazing — but, as it were, with a gradual wane — till six o'clock P.M., or thereabouts; after which, I saw no more of the proprietor of the face, which, gaining its meridian with the sun, seemed to set with it, to rise, culminate, and decline the following day, with the like regularity and

5

---

[1] A poor immigrant from Germany who became one of the great business tycoons of the nineteenth century.

[2] Courts of Chancery often adjudicated business disputes.

undiminished glory. There are many singular coincidences I have known in the course of my life, not the least among which was the fact, that, exactly when Turkey displayed his fullest beams from his red and radiant countenance, just then, too, at that critical moment, began the daily period when I considered his business capacities as seriously disturbed for the remainder of the twenty-four hours. Not that he was absolutely idle, or averse to business, then; far from it. The difficulty was, he was apt to be altogether too energetic. There was a strange, inflamed, flurried, flighty recklessness of activity about him. He would be incautious in dipping his pen into his inkstand. All his blots upon my documents were dropped there after twelve o'clock meridian. Indeed, not only would he be reckless, and sadly given to making blots in the afternoon, but, some days, he went further, and was rather noisy. At such times, too, his face flamed with augmented blazonry, as if cannel coal had been heaped on anthracite. He made an unpleasant racket with his chair; spilled his sand-box; in mending his pens, impatiently split them all to pieces, and threw them on the floor in a sudden passion; stood up, and leaned over his table, boxing his papers about in a most indecorous manner, very sad to behold in an elderly man like him. Nevertheless, as he was in many ways a most valuable person to me, and all the time before twelve o'clock meridian, was the quickest, steadiest creature, too, accomplishing a great deal of work in a style not easily to be matched — for these reasons, I was willing to overlook his eccentricities, though, indeed, occasionally, I remonstrated with him. I did this very gently, however, because, though the civilest, nay, the blandest and most reverential of men in the morning, yet, in the afternoon, he was disposed, upon provocation, to be slightly rash with his tongue — in fact, insolent. Now, valuing his morning services as I did, and resolved not to lose them — yet, at the same time, made uncomfortable by his inflamed ways after twelve o'clock — and being a man of peace, unwilling by my admonitions to call forth unseemly retorts from him, I took upon me, one Saturday noon (he was always worse on Saturdays) to hint to him, very kindly, that, perhaps, now that he was growing old, it might be well to abridge his labors; in short, he need not come to my chambers after twelve o'clock, but, dinner over, had best go home to his lodgings, and rest himself till tea-time. But no; he insisted upon his afternoon devotions. His countenance became intolerably fervid, as he oratorically assured me — gesticulating with a long ruler at the other end of the room — that if his services in the morning were useful, how indispensable, then, in the afternoon?

"With submission, sir," said Turkey, on this occasion, "I consider myself your right-hand man. In the morning I but marshal and deploy my columns; but in the afternoon I put myself at their head, and gallantly charge the foe, thus" — and he made a violent thrust with the ruler.

"But the blots, Turkey," intimated I.

"True; but, with submission, sir, behold these hairs! I am getting old. Surely, sir, a blot or two of a warm afternoon is not to be severely urged against gray hairs. Old age — even if it blot the page — is honorable. With submission, sir, we *both* are getting old."

This appeal to my fellow-feeling was hardly to be resisted. At all events, 10 I saw that go he would not. So, I made up my mind to let him stay, resolving, nevertheless, to see to it that, during the afternoon, he had to do with my less important papers.

Nippers, the second on my list, was a whiskered, sallow, and, upon the whole, rather piratical-looking young man, of about five and twenty. I always deemed him the victim of two evil powers — ambition and indigestion. The ambition was evinced by a certain impatience of the duties of a mere copyist, an unwarrantable usurpation of strictly professional affairs, such as the original drawing up of legal documents. The indigestion seemed betokened in an occasional nervous testiness and grinning irritability, causing the teeth to audibly grind together over mistakes committed in copying; unnecessary maledictions, hissed, rather than spoken, in the heat of business; and especially by a continual discontent with the height of the table where he worked. Though of a very ingenious, mechanical turn, Nippers could never get this table to suit him. He put chips under it, blocks of various sorts, bits of pasteboard, and at last went so far as to attempt an exquisite adjustment, by final pieces of folded blotting-paper. But no invention would answer. If, for the sake of easing his back, he brought the table-lid at a sharp angle well up towards his chin, and wrote there like a man using the steep roof of a Dutch house for his desk, then he declared that it stopped the circulation in his arms. If now he lowered the table to his waistbands, and stooped over it in writing, then there was a sore aching in his back. In short, the truth of the matter was, Nippers knew not what he wanted. Or, if he wanted anything, it was to be rid of a scrivener's table altogether. Among the manifestations of his diseased ambition was a fondness he had for receiving visits from certain ambiguous-looking fellows in seedy coats, whom he called his clients. Indeed, I was aware that not only was he, at times, considerable of a ward-politician, but he occasionally did a little business at the Justices' courts, and was not unknown on the steps of the Tombs.[3] I have good reason to believe, however, that one individual who called upon him at my chambers, and who, with a grand air, he insisted was his client, was no other than a dun, and the alleged title-deed, a bill. But, with all his failings, and the annoyances he caused me, Nippers, like his compatriot Turkey, was a very useful man to me; wrote a neat, swift hand; and, when he chose, was not deficient in a gentlemanly sort of deportment. Added to this, he always dressed in a gentlemanly sort of way; and so, incidentally, reflected credit upon my chambers. Whereas, with respect to Turkey, I had much ado to keep him from being a reproach to me. His clothes were apt to look oily, and smell of eating houses. He wore his pantaloons very loose and baggy in summer. His coats were execrable, his hat not to be handled. But while the hat was a thing of indifference to me, inasmuch as his natural civility and deference, as a dependent Englishman, always led him to doff it the moment he entered the room, yet his coat was another matter. Concerning his coats,

---

[3] A prison in New York City.

I reasoned with him; but with no effect. The truth was, I suppose, that a man with so small an income could not afford to sport such a lustrous face and a lustrous coat at one and the same time. As Nippers once observed, Turkey's money went chiefly for red ink. One winter day, I presented Turkey with a highly respectable-looking coat of my own — a padded gray coat, of a most comfortable warmth, and which buttoned straight up from the knee to the neck. I thought Turkey would appreciate the favor, and abate his rashness and obstreperousness of afternoons. But no; I verily believe that buttoning himself up in so downy and blanket-like a coat had a pernicious effect upon him — upon the same principle that too much oats are bad for horses. In fact, precisely as a rash, restive horse is said to feel his oats, so Turkey felt his coat. It made him insolent. He was a man whom prosperity harmed.

Though, concerning the self-indulgent habits of Turkey, I had my own private surmises, yet, touching Nippers, I was well persuaded that, whatever might be his faults in other respects, he was, at least, a temperate young man. But, indeed, nature herself seemed to have been his vintner, and, at his birth, charged him so thoroughly with an irritable, brandy-like disposition, that all subsequent potations were needless. When I consider how, amid the stillness of my chambers, Nippers would sometimes impatiently rise from his seat, and stooping over his table, spread his arms wide apart, seize the whole desk, and move it, and jerk it, with a grim, grinding motion on the floor, as if the table were a perverse voluntary agent and vexing him, I plainly perceive that, for Nippers, brandy-and-water were altogether superfluous.

It was fortunate for me that, owing to its peculiar cause — indigestion — the irritability and consequent nervousness of Nippers were mainly observable in the morning, while in the afternoon he was comparatively mild. So that, Turkey's paroxysms only coming on about twelve o'clock, I never had to do with their eccentricities at one time. Their fits relieved each other, like guards. When Nippers's was on, Turkey's was off; and *vice versa*. This was a good natural arrangement, under the circumstances.

Ginger Nut, the third on my list, was a lad, some twelve years old. His father was a car-man, ambitious of seeing his son on the bench instead of a cart, before he died. So he sent him to my office, as student at law, errand-boy, cleaner and sweeper, at the rate of one dollar a week. He had a little desk to himself; but he did not use it much. Upon inspection, the drawer exhibited a great array of shells of various sorts of nuts. Indeed, to this quick-witted youth, the whole noble science of the law was contained in a nutshell. Not the least among the employments of Ginger Nut, as well as one which he discharged with the most alacrity, was his duty as cake and apple purveyor for Turkey and Nippers. Copying law-papers being proverbially a dry, husky sort of business, my two scriveners were fain to moisten their mouths very often with Spitzenbergs,[4] to be had at the numerous stalls nigh the Custom House and Post Office. Also, they sent Ginger Nut very frequently for that peculiar

[4] A variety of apple.

cake — small, flat, round, and very spicy — after which he had been named by them. Of a cold morning, when business was but dull, Turkey would gobble up scores of these cakes, as if they were mere wafers — indeed, they sell them at the rate of six or eight for a penny — the scrape of his pen blending with the crunching of the crisp particles in his mouth. Rashest of all the fiery afternoon blunders and flurried rashnesses of Turkey, was his once moistening a ginger-cake between his lips, and clapping it on to a mortgage, for a seal. I came within an ace of dismissing him then. But he mollified me by making an oriental bow, and saying —

"With submission, sir, it was generous of me to find you in stationery on my own account." 15

Now my original business — that of a conveyancer and title hunter, and drawer-up of recondite documents of all sorts — was considerably increased by receiving the master's office. There was now great work for scriveners. Not only must I push the clerks already with me, but I must have additional help.

In answer to my advertisement, a motionless young man one morning stood upon my office threshold, the door being open, for it was summer. I can see that figure now — pallidly neat, pitiably respectable, incurably forlorn! It was Bartleby.

After a few words touching his qualifications, I engaged him, glad to have among my corps of copyists a man of so singularly sedate an aspect, which I thought might operate beneficially upon the flighty temper of Turkey, and the fiery one of Nippers.

I should have stated before that ground-glass folding-doors divided my premises into two parts, one of which was occupied by my scriveners, the other by myself. According to my humor, I threw open these doors, or closed them. I resolved to assign Bartleby a corner by the folding-doors, but on my side of them, so as to have this quiet man within easy call, in case any trifling thing was to be done. I placed his desk close up to a small side-window in that part of the room, a window which originally had afforded a lateral view of certain grimy backyards and bricks, but which, owing to subsequent erections, commanded at present no view at all, though it gave some light. Within three feet of the panes was a wall, and the light came down from far above, between two lofty buildings, as from a very small opening in a dome. Still further to a satisfactory arrangement, I procured a high green folding screen, which might entirely isolate Bartleby from my sight, though not remove him from my voice. And thus, in a manner, privacy and society were conjoined.

At first, Bartleby did an extraordinary quantity of writing. As if long famishing for something to copy, he seemed to gorge himself on my documents. There was no pause for digestion. He ran a day and night line, copying by sun-light and by candle-light. I should have been quite delighted with his application, had he been cheerfully industrious. But he wrote on silently, palely, mechanically. 20

It is, of course, an indispensable part of a scrivener's business to verify the accuracy of his copy, word by word. Where there are two or more scriveners in an office, they assist each other in this examination, one reading from the copy, the other holding the original. It is a very dull, wearisome, and lethargic affair. I can readily imagine that, to some sanguine temperaments, it would be altogether intolerable. For example, I cannot credit that the mettlesome poet, Byron, would have contentedly sat down with Bartleby to examine a law document of, say five hundred pages, closely written in a crimpy hand.

Now and then, in the haste of business, it had been my habit to assist in comparing some brief document myself, calling Turkey or Nippers for this purpose. One object I had, in placing Bartleby so handy to me behind the screen, was to avail myself of his services on such trivial occasions. It was on the third day, I think, of his being with me, and before any necessity had arisen for having his own writing examined, that, being much hurried to complete a small affair I had in hand, I abruptly called to Bartleby. In my haste and natural expectancy of instant compliance, I sat with my head bent over the original on my desk, and my right hand sideways, and somewhat nervously extended with the copy, so that, immediately upon emerging from his retreat, Bartleby might snatch it and proceed to business without the least delay.

In this very attitude did I sit when I called to him, rapidly stating what it was I wanted him to do — namely, to examine a small paper with me. Imagine my surprise, nay, my consternation, when, without moving from his privacy, Bartleby, in a singularly mild, firm voice, replied, "I would prefer not to."

I sat awhile in perfect silence, rallying my stunned faculties. Immediately it occurred to me that my ears had deceived me, or Bartleby had entirely misunderstood my meaning. I repeated my request in the clearest tone I could assume; but in quite as clear a one came the previous reply, "I would prefer not to."

"Prefer not to," echoed I, rising in high excitement, and crossing the room 25 with a stride. "What do you mean? Are you moon-struck? I want you to help me compare this sheet here — take it," and I thrust it towards him.

"I would prefer not to," said he.

I looked at him steadfastly. His face was leanly composed; his gray eye dimly calm. Not a wrinkle of agitation rippled him. Had there been the least uneasiness, anger, impatience, or impertinence in his manner; in other words, had there been any thing ordinarily human about him, doubtless I should have violently dismissed him from the premises. But as it was, I should have as soon thought of turning my pale plaster-of-paris bust of Cicero out of doors. I stood gazing at him awhile, as he went on with his own writing, and then reseated myself at my desk. This is very strange, thought I. What had one best do? But my business hurried me. I concluded to forget the matter for the present, reserving it for my future leisure. So calling Nippers from the other room, the paper was speedily examined.

A few days after this, Bartleby concluded four lengthy documents, being quadruplicates of a week's testimony taken before me in my High Court of Chancery. It became necessary to examine them. It was an important suit, and great accuracy was imperative. Having all things arranged, I called Turkey, Nippers, and Ginger Nut from the next room, meaning to place the four copies in the hands of my four clerks, while I should read from the original. Accordingly, Turkey, Nippers, and Ginger Nut had taken their seats in a row, each with his document in his hand, when I called to Bartleby to join this interesting group.

"Bartleby! quick, I am waiting."

I heard a slow scrape of his chair legs on the uncarpeted floor, and soon he 30 appeared standing at the entrance of his hermitage.

"What is wanted?" said he, mildly.

"The copies, the copies," said I, hurriedly. "We are going to examine them. There —" and I held towards him the fourth quadruplicate.

"I would prefer not to," he said, and gently disappeared behind the screen.

For a few moments I was turned into a pillar of salt, standing at the head of my seated column of clerks. Recovering myself, I advanced towards the screen, and demanded the reason for such extraordinary conduct.

"*Why* do you refuse?" 35

"I would prefer not to."

With any other man I should have flown outright into a dreadful passion, scorned all further words, and thrust him ignominiously from my presence. But there was something about Bartleby that not only strangely disarmed me, but in a wonderful manner, touched and disconcerted me. I began to reason with him.

"These are your own copies we are about to examine. It is labor saving to you, because one examination will answer for your four papers. It is common usage. Every copyist is bound to help examine his copy. Is it not so? Will you not speak? Answer!"

"I prefer not to," he replied in a flutelike tone. It seemed to me that, while I had been addressing him, he carefully revolved every statement that I made; fully comprehended the meaning; could not gainsay the irresistible conclusion; but, at the same time, some paramount consideration prevailed with him to reply as he did.

"You are decided, then, not to comply with my request — a request made 40 according to common usage and common sense?"

He briefly gave me to understand, that on that point my judgment was sound. Yes: his decision was irreversible.

It is not seldom the case that, when a man is browbeaten in some unprecedented and violently unreasonable way, he begins to stagger in his own plainest faith. He begins, as it were, vaguely to surmise that, wonderful as it may be, all the justice and all the reason is on the other side. Accordingly, if any disinterested persons are present, he turns to them for some reinforcement of his own faltering mind.

"Turkey," said I, "what do you think of this? Am I not right?"

"With submission, sir," said Turkey, in his blandest tone, "I think that you are."

"Nippers," said I, "what do *you* think of it?" 45

"I think I should kick him out of the office."

(The reader, of nice perceptions, will here perceive that, it being morning, Turkey's answer is couched in polite and tranquil terms, but Nippers replies in ill-tempered ones. Or, to repeat a previous sentence, Nippers's ugly mood was on duty, and Turkey's off.)

"Ginger Nut," said I, willing to enlist the smallest suffrage in my behalf, "what do *you* think of it?"

"I think, sir, he's a little *luny*," replied Ginger Nut, with a grin.

"You hear what they say," said I, turning towards the screen, "come forth and do your duty." 50

But he vouchsafed no reply. I pondered a moment in sore perplexity. But once more business hurried me. I determined again to postpone the consideration of this dilemma to my future leisure. With a little trouble we made out to examine the papers without Bartleby, though at every page or two Turkey deferentially dropped his opinion, that this proceeding was quite out of the common; while Nippers, twitching in his chair with a dyspeptic nervousness, ground out, between his set teeth, occasional hissing maledictions against the stubborn oaf behind the screen. And for his (Nippers's) part, this was the first and the last time he would do another man's business without pay.

Meanwhile Bartleby sat in his hermitage, oblivious to everything but his own peculiar business there.

Some days passed, the scrivener being employed upon another lengthy work. His late remarkable conduct led me to regard his ways narrowly. I observed that he never went to dinner; indeed, that he never went anywhere. As yet I had never, of my personal knowledge, known him to be outside of my office. He was a perpetual sentry in the corner. At about eleven o'clock though, in the morning, I noticed that Ginger Nut would advance towards the opening in Bartleby's screen, as if silently beckoned thither by a gesture invisible to me where I sat. The boy would then leave the office, jingling a few pence, and reappear with a handful of ginger-nuts, which he delivered in the hermitage, receiving two of the cakes for his trouble.

He lives, then, on ginger-nuts, thought I; never eats a dinner, properly speaking; he must be a vegetarian, then; but no; he never eats even vegetables; he eats nothing but ginger-nuts. My mind then ran on in reveries concerning the probable effects upon the human constitution of living entirely on ginger-nuts. Ginger-nuts are so called, because they contain ginger as one of their peculiar constituents, and the final flavoring one. Now, what was ginger? A hot, spicy thing. Was Bartleby hot and spicy? Not at all. Ginger, then, had no effect upon Bartleby. Probably he preferred it should have none.

Nothing so aggravates an earnest person as a passive resistance. If the indi- 55 vidual so resisted be of a not inhumane temper, and the resisting one perfectly harmless in his passivity, then, in the better moods of the former, he will endeavor charitably to construe to his imagination what proves impossible to be solved by his judgment. Even so, for the most part, I regarded Bartleby and his ways. Poor fellow! thought I, he means no mischief; it is plain he intends no insolence; his aspect sufficiently evinces that his eccentricities are involuntary. He is useful to me. I can get along with him. If I turn him away, the chances are he will fall in with some less-indulgent employer, and then he will be rudely treated, and perhaps driven forth miserably to starve. Yes. Here I can cheaply purchase a delicious self-approval. To befriend Bartleby; to humor him in his strange willfulness, will cost me little or nothing, while I lay up in my soul what will eventually prove a sweet morsel for my conscience. But this mood was not invariable with me. The passiveness of Bartleby sometimes irritated me. I felt strangely goaded on to encounter him in new opposition — to elicit some angry spark from him answerable to my own. But, indeed, I might as well have essayed to strike fire with my knuckles against a bit of Windsor soap. But one afternoon the evil impulse in me mastered me, and the following little scene ensued:

"Bartleby," said I, "when those papers are all copied, I will compare them with you."

"I would prefer not to."

"How? Surely you do not mean to persist in that mulish vagary?"

No answer.

I threw open the folding-doors near by, and, turning upon Turkey and Nip- 60
pers, exclaimed:

"Bartleby a second time says, he won't examine his papers. What do you think of it, Turkey?"

It was afternoon, be it remembered. Turkey sat glowing like a brass boiler; his bald head steaming; his hands reeling among his blotted papers.

"Think of it?" roared Turkey; "I think I'll just step behind his screen, and black his eyes for him!"

So saying, Turkey rose to his feet and threw his arms into a pugilistic position. He was hurrying away to make good his promise, when I detained him, alarmed at the effect of incautiously rousing Turkey's combativeness after dinner.

"Sit down, Turkey," said I, "and hear what Nippers has to say. What do 65
you think of it, Nippers? Would I not be justified in immediately dismissing Bartleby?"

"Excuse me, that is for you to decide, sir. I think his conduct quite unusual, and, indeed, unjust, as regards Turkey and myself. But it may only be a passing whim."

"Ah," exclaimed I, "you have strangely changed your mind, then — you speak very gently of him now."

"All beer," cried Turkey; "gentleness is effects of beer — Nippers and I dined together to-day. You see how gentle *I* am, sir. Shall I go and black his eyes?"

"You refer to Bartleby, I suppose. No, not to-day, Turkey," I replied; "pray, put up your fists."

I closed the doors, and again advanced towards Bartleby. I felt additional 70
incentives tempting me to my fate. I burned to be rebelled against again. I remembered that Bartleby never left the office.

"Bartleby," said I, "Ginger Nut is away; just step around to the post office, won't you? (it was but a three minutes' walk), and see if there is anything for me."

"I would prefer not to."

"You *will* not?"

"I *prefer* not."

I staggered to my desk, and sat there in a deep study. My blind inveteracy 75 returned. Was there any other thing in which I could procure myself to be ignominiously repulsed by this lean, penniless wight? — my hired clerk? What added thing is there, perfectly reasonable, that he will be sure to refuse to do? "Bartleby!"

No answer.

"Bartleby," in a louder tone.

No answer.

"Bartleby," I roared.

Like a very ghost, agreeably to the laws of magical invocation, at the third 80 summons, he appeared at the entrance of his hermitage.

"Go to the next room, and tell Nippers to come to me."

"I prefer not to," he respectfully and slowly said and mildly disappeared.

"Very good, Bartleby," said I, in a quiet sort of serenely-severe, self-possessed tone, intimating the unalterable purpose of some terrible retribution very close at hand. At the moment I half intended something of the kind. But upon the whole, as it was drawing towards my dinner-hour, I thought it best to put on my hat and walk home for the day, suffering much from perplexity and distress of mind.

Shall I acknowledge it? The conclusion of this whole business was, that it soon became a fixed fact of my chambers, that a pale young scrivener, by the name of Bartleby, had a desk there; that he copied for me at the usual rate of four cents a folio (one hundred words); but he was permanently exempt from examining the work done by him, that duty being transferred to Turkey and Nippers, out of compliment, doubtless, to their superior acuteness; moreover, said Bartleby was never, on any account, to be dispatched on the most trivial errand of any sort; and that even if entreated to take upon him such a matter, it was generally understood that he would "prefer not to" — in other words, he would refuse point blank.

As days passed on, I became considerably reconciled to Bartleby. His steadi- 85 ness, his freedom from all dissipation, his incessant industry (except when he chose to throw himself into a standing revery behind his screen), his great stillness, his unalterableness of demeanor under all circumstances, made him a valuable acquisition. One prime thing was this — *he was always there* — first in the morning, continually through the day, and the last at night. I had a singular confidence in his honesty. I felt my most precious papers perfectly safe in his hands. Sometimes, to be sure, I could not, for the very soul of me, avoid falling into sudden spasmodic passions with him. For it was exceeding difficult to bear in mind all the time those strange peculiarities, privileges, and unheard of exemptions, forming the tacit stipulations on Bartleby's part under which he remained in my office. Now and then, in the eagerness of dispatching pressing business, I would inadvertently summon Bartleby, in a short, rapid tone, to put his finger, say, on the incipient tie of a bit of red tape with which I was about compressing some papers. Of course, from behind the screen the usual answer, "I prefer not to," was sure to come; and then, how could a human creature, with the common infirmities of our nature, refrain from bitterly exclaiming upon such perverseness—such unreasonableness? However, every added repulse of this sort which I received only tended to lessen the probability of my repeating the inadvertence.

Here it must be said, that according to the custom of most legal gentlemen occupying chambers in densely-populated law buildings, there were several keys to my door. One was kept by a woman residing in the attic, which person weekly scrubbed and daily swept and dusted my apartments. Another was kept by Turkey for convenience sake. The third I sometimes carried in my own pocket. The fourth I knew not who had.

Now, one Sunday morning I happened to go to Trinity Church, to hear a celebrated preacher, and finding myself rather early on the ground I thought I would walk round to my chambers for a while. Luckily I had my key with me; but upon applying it to the lock, I found it resisted by something inserted from the inside. Quite surprised, I called out; when to my consternation a key was turned from within; and thrusting his lean visage at me, and holding the door ajar, the apparition of Bartleby appeared, in his shirt sleeves, and otherwise in a strangely tattered *déshabillé*, saying quietly that he was sorry, but he was deeply engaged just then, and—preferred not admitting me at present. In a brief word or two, he moreover added, that perhaps I had better walk around the block two or three times, and by that time he would probably have concluded his affairs.

Now, the utterly unsurmised appearance of Bartleby, tenanting my law-chambers of a Sunday morning, with his cadaverously gentlemanly *nonchalance*, yet withal firm and self-possessed, had such a strange effect upon me, that incontinently I slunk away from my own door, and did as desired. But not without sundry twinges of impotent rebellion against the mild effrontery of this unaccountable scrivener. Indeed, it was his wonderful mildness chiefly, which not only disarmed me, but unmanned me as it were. For I consider that one, for the time, is somehow unmanned when he tranquilly permits his hired clerk to dictate to him, and order him away from his own premises. Furthermore, I was full of uneasiness as to what Bartleby could possibly be doing in my office in his shirt sleeves, and in an otherwise dismantled condition of a Sunday morning. Was anything amiss going on? Nay, that was out of the question. It was not to be thought of for a moment that Bartleby was an immoral person. But what could he be doing there?—copying? Nay again, whatever might be his eccentricities, Bartleby was an eminently decorous person. He would be the last man to sit down to his desk in any state approaching to nudity. Besides, it was Sunday; and there was something about Bartleby that forbade the supposition that he would by any secular occupation violate the proprieties of the day.

Nevertheless, my mind was not pacified; and full of a restless curiosity, at last I returned to the door. Without hindrance I inserted my key, opened it, and entered. Bartleby was not to be seen. I looked round anxiously, peeped behind his screen; but it was very plain that he was gone. Upon more closely examining the place, I surmised that for an indefinite period Bartleby must have eaten, dressed, and slept in my office, and that, too, without plate, mirror, or bed. The cushioned seat of a rickety old sofa in one corner bore the faint impress of a lean, reclining form. Rolled away under his desk, I found a blanket; under the empty grate, a blacking box and brush; on a chair, a tin basin, with soap and a ragged towel; in a newspaper a few crumbs of ginger-nuts and a morsel of cheese. Yes, thought I, it is evident enough that Bartleby has been making his home here, keeping bachelor's hall all by himself. Immediately then the thought came sweeping across me, what miserable friendlessness and loneliness are here revealed! His poverty is great; but his solitude, how horrible! Think of it. Of a Sunday, Wall Street is deserted as Petra;[5] and every night of every day it is an emptiness. This building, too, which of week-days hums with industry and life, at nightfall echoes with sheer vacancy, and all through Sunday is for-lorn. And here Bartleby makes his home; sole spectator of a solitude which he has seen all populous — a sort of innocent and transformed Marius brooding among the ruins of Carthage![6]

For the first time in my life a feeling of over-powering stinging melancholy 90 seized me. Before, I had never experienced aught but a not unpleasing sadness. The bond of a common humanity now drew me irresistibly to gloom. A frater-nal melancholy! For both I and Bartleby were sons of Adam. I remembered the bright silks and sparkling faces I had seen that day, in gala trim, swan-like sailing down the Mississippi of Broadway; and I contrasted them with the pallid copy-ist, and thought to myself, Ah, happiness courts the light, so we deem the world is gay; but misery hides aloof, so we deem that misery there is none. These sad fancyings — chimeras, doubtless, of a sick and silly brain — led on to other and more special thoughts, concerning the eccentricities of Bartleby. Presentiments of strange discoveries hovered round me. The scrivener's pale form appeared to me laid out, among uncaring strangers, in its shivering winding sheet.

Suddenly I was attracted by Bartleby's closed desk, the key in open sight left in the lock.

I mean no mischief, seek the gratification of no heartless curiosity, thought I; besides, the desk is mine, and its contents, too, so I will make bold to look within. Everything was methodically arranged, the papers smoothly placed. The pigeon holes were deep, and removing the files of documents, I groped into their recesses. Presently I felt something there, and dragged it out. It was an old bandanna handkerchief, heavy and knotted. I opened it, and saw it was a saving's bank.

I now recalled all the quiet mysteries which I had noted in the man. I remem-bered that he never spoke but to answer; that, though at intervals he had con-siderable time to himself, yet I had never seen him reading — no, not even a newspaper; that for long periods he would stand looking out, at his pale win-dow behind the screen, upon the dead brick wall; I was quite sure he never visited any refectory or eating house; while his pale face clearly indicated that he never drank beer like Turkey; or tea and coffee even, like other men; that

---

[5] A city in Palestine found by explorers in 1812. It had been deserted and lost for centuries.

[6] Gaius Marius (155–86 BCE), a plebeian general who was forced to flee from Rome. Nineteenth-century democratic literature sometimes pictured him old and alone among the ruins of Carthage.

he never went anywhere in particular that I could learn; never went out for a walk, unless, indeed, that was the case at present; that he had declined telling who he was, or whence he came, or whether he had any relatives in the world; that though so thin and pale, he never complained of ill health. And more than all, I remembered a certain unconscious air of pallid — how shall I call it? — of pallid haughtiness, say, or rather an austere reserve about him, which had positively awed me into my tame compliance with his eccentricities, when I had feared to ask him to do the slightest incidental thing for me, even though I might know, from his long-continued motionlessness, that behind his screen he must be standing in one of those dead-wall reveries of his.

Revolving all these things, and coupling them with the recently discovered fact, that he made my office his constant abiding place and home, and not forgetful of his morbid moodiness; revolving all these things, a prudential feeling began to steal over me. My first emotions had been those of pure melancholy and sincerest pity; but just in proportion as the forlornness of Bartleby grew and grew to my imagination, did that same melancholy merge into fear, that pity into repulsion. So true it is, and so terrible, too, that up to a certain point the thought or sight of misery enlists our best affections; but, in certain special cases, beyond that point it does not. They err who would assert that invariably this is owing to the inherent selfishness of the human heart. It rather proceeds from a certain hopelessness of remedying excessive and organic ill. To a sensitive being, pity is not seldom pain. And when at last it is perceived that such pity cannot lead to effectual succor, common sense bids the soul be rid of it. What I saw that morning persuaded me that the scrivener was the victim of innate and incurable disorder. I might give alms to his body; but his body did not pain him; it was his soul that suffered, and his soul I could not reach.

I did not accomplish the purpose of going to Trinity Church that morning. Somehow, the things I had seen disqualified me for the time from churchgoing. I walked homeward, thinking what I would do with Bartleby. Finally, I resolved upon this — I would put certain calm questions to him the next morning, touching his history, etc., and if he declined to answer them openly and unreservedly (and I supposed he would prefer not), then to give him a twenty dollar bill over and above whatever I might owe him, and tell him his services were no longer required; but that if in any other way I could assist him, I would be happy to do so, especially if he desired to return to his native place, wherever that might be, I would willingly help to defray the expenses. Moreover, if, after reaching home, he found himself at any time in want of aid, a letter from him would be sure of a reply.

The next morning came.

"Bartleby," said I, gently calling to him behind his screen.

No reply.

"Bartleby," said I, in a still gentler tone, "come here; I am not going to ask you to do anything you would prefer not to do — I simply wish to speak to you."

Upon this he noiselessly slid into view. <sup>100</sup>

"Will you tell me, Bartleby, where you were born?"

"I would prefer not to."

"Will you tell me *anything* about yourself?"

"I would prefer not to."

"But what reasonable objection can you have to speak to me? I feel friendly 105 towards you."

He did not look at me while I spoke, but kept his glance fixed upon my bust of Cicero, which, as I then sat, was directly behind me, some six inches above my head.

"What is your answer, Bartleby," said I, after waiting a considerable time for a reply, during which his countenance remained immovable, only there was the faintest conceivable tremor of the white attenuated mouth.

"At present I prefer to give no answer," he said, and retired into his hermitage.

It was rather weak in me I confess, but his manner, on this occasion, nettled me. Not only did there seem to lurk in it a certain calm disdain, but his perverseness seemed ungrateful, considering the undeniable good usage and indulgence he had received from me.

Again I sat ruminating what I should do. Mortified as I was at his behavior, 110 and resolved as I had been to dismiss him when I entered my office, nevertheless I strangely felt something superstitious knocking at my heart, and forbidding me to carry out my purpose, and denouncing me for a villain if I dared to breathe one bitter word against this forlornest of mankind. At last, familiarly drawing my chair behind his screen, I sat down and said: "Bartleby, never mind, then, about revealing your history; but let me entreat you, as a friend, to comply as far as may be with the usages of this office. Say now, you will help to examine papers tomorrow or next day: in short, say now, that in a day or two you will begin to be a little reasonable — say so, Bartleby."

"At present I would prefer not to be a little reasonable," was his mildly cadaverous reply.

Just then the folding-doors opened, and Nippers approached. He seemed suffering from an unusually bad night's rest, induced by severer indigestion than common. He overheard those final words of Bartleby.

"*Prefer not*, eh?" gritted Nippers — "I'd *prefer* him, if I were you, sir," addressing me — "I'd *prefer* him; I'd give him preferences, the stubborn mule! What is it, sir, pray, that he *prefers* not to do now?"

Bartleby moved not a limb.

"Mr. Nippers," said I, "I'd prefer that you would withdraw for the present." 115

Somehow, of late, I had got into the way of involuntarily using this word "prefer" upon all sorts of not exactly suitable occasions. And I trembled to think that my contact with the scrivener had already and seriously affected me in a mental way. And what further and deeper aberration might it not yet produce? This apprehension had not been without efficacy in determining me to summary measures.

As Nippers, looking very sour and sulky, was departing, Turkey blandly and deferentially approached.

"With submission, sir," said he, "yesterday I was thinking about Bartleby here, and I think that if he would but prefer to take a quart of good ale every day, it would do much towards mending him, and enabling him to assist in examining his papers."

"So you have got the word, too," said I, slightly excited.

"With submission, what word, sir," asked Turkey, respectfully crowding 120 himself into the contracted space behind the screen, and by so doing, making me jostle the scrivener. "What word, sir?"

"I would prefer to be left alone here," said Bartleby, as if offended at being mobbed in his privacy.

"*That's* the word, Turkey," said I — "*that's* it."

"Oh, *prefer*? oh yes — queer word. I never use it myself. But, sir, as I was saying, if he would but prefer —"

"Turkey," interrupted I, "you will please withdraw."

"Oh certainly, sir, if you prefer that I should." 125

As he opened the folding-door to retire, Nippers at his desk caught a glimpse of me, and asked whether I would prefer to have a certain paper copied on blue paper or white. He did not in the least roguishly accent the word prefer. It was plain that it involuntarily rolled from his tongue. I thought to myself, surely I must get rid of a demented man, who already has in some degree turned the tongues, if not the heads of myself and clerks. But I thought it prudent not to break the dismission at once.

The next day I noticed that Bartleby did nothing but stand at his window in his dead-wall revery. Upon asking him why he did not write, he said that he had decided upon doing no more writing.

"Why, how now? What next?" exclaimed I, "do no more writing?"

"No more."

"And what is the reason?" 130

"Do you not see the reason for yourself?" he indifferently replied.

I looked steadfastly at him, and perceived that his eyes looked dull and glazed. Instantly it occurred to me, that his unexampled diligence in copying by his dim window for the first few weeks of his stay with me might have temporarily impaired his vision.

I was touched. I said something in condolence with him. I hinted that of course he did wisely in abstaining from writing for a while; and urged him to embrace that opportunity of taking wholesome exercise in the open air. This, however, he did not do. A few days after this, my other clerks being absent, and being in a great hurry to dispatch certain letters by the mail, I thought that, having nothing else earthly to do, Bartleby would surely be less inflexible than usual, and carry these letters to the post office. But he blankly declined. So, much to my inconvenience, I went myself.

Still added days went by. Whether Bartleby's eyes improved or not, I could not say. To all appearance, I thought they did. But when I asked him if they did, he vouchsafed no answer. At all events, he would do no copying. At last, in reply to my urgings, he informed me that he had permanently given up copying.

"What!" exclaimed I; "suppose your eyes should get entirely well — better 135
than ever before — would you not copy then?"

"I have given up copying," he answered, and slid aside.

He remained as ever, a fixture in my chamber. Nay — if that were possible —
he became still more of a fixture than before. What was to be done? He would
do nothing in the office; why should he stay there? In plain fact, he had now
become a millstone to me, not only useless as a necklace, but afflictive to bear.
Yet I was sorry for him. I speak less than truth when I say that, on his own
account, he occasioned me uneasiness. If he would but have named a single relative or friend, I would instantly have written, and urged their taking the poor
fellow away to some convenient retreat. But he seemed alone, absolutely alone
in the universe. A bit of wreck in the mid-Atlantic. At length, necessities connected with my business tyrannized over all other considerations. Decently as
I could, I told Bartleby that in six days time he must unconditionally leave the
office. I warned him to take measures, in the interval, for procuring some other
abode. I offered to assist him in this endeavor, if he himself would but take the
first step towards a removal. "And when you finally quit me, Bartleby," added I,
"I shall see that you go not away entirely unprovided. Six days from this hour,
remember."

At the expiration of that period, I peeped behind the screen, and lo! Bartleby
was there.

I buttoned up my coat, balanced myself; advanced slowly towards him,
touched his shoulder, and said, "The time has come; you must quit this place; I
am sorry for you; here is money; but you must go."

"I would prefer not," he replied, with his back still towards me. 140

"You *must*."

He remained silent.

Now I had an unbounded confidence in this man's common honesty. He
had frequently restored to me sixpences and shillings carelessly dropped upon
the floor, for I am apt to be very reckless in such shirt-button affairs. The proceeding, then, which followed will not be deemed extraordinary.

"Bartleby," said I, "I owe you twelve dollars on account; here are thirty-two, the
odd twenty are yours — Will you take it?" and I handed the bills towards him.

But he made no motion. 145

"I will leave them here, then," putting them under a weight on the table.
Then taking my hat and cane and going to the door, I tranquilly turned and
added — "After you have removed your things from these offices, Bartleby,
you will of course lock the door — since every one is now gone for the day but
you — and if you please, slip your key underneath the mat, so that I may have
it in the morning. I shall not see you again; so good-by to you. If, hereafter, in
your new place of abode, I can be of any service to you, do not fail to advise me
by letter. Good-by, Bartleby, and fare you well."

But he answered not a word; like the last column of some ruined temple, he
remained standing mute and solitary in the middle of the otherwise deserted
room.

As I walked home in a pensive mood, my vanity got the better of my pity. I could not but highly plume myself on my masterly management in getting rid of Bartleby. Masterly I call it, and such it must appear to any dispassionate thinker. The beauty of my procedure seemed to consist in its perfect quietness. There was no vulgar bullying, no bravado of any sort, no choleric hectoring, and striding to and fro across the apartment, jerking out vehement commands for Bartleby to bundle himself off with his beggarly traps. Nothing of the kind. Without loudly bidding Bartleby depart — as an inferior genius might have done — I *assumed* the ground that depart he must; and upon that assumption built all I had to say. The more I thought over my procedure, the more I was charmed with it. Nevertheless, next morning, upon awakening, I had my doubts — I had somehow slept off the fumes of vanity. One of the coolest and wisest hours a man has, is just after he awakes in the morning. My procedure seemed as sagacious as ever — but only in theory. How it would prove in practice — there was the rub. It was truly a beautiful thought to have assumed Bartleby's departure; but, after all, that assumption was simply my own, and none of Bartleby's. The great point was, not whether I had assumed that he would quit me, but whether he would prefer to do so. He was more a man of preferences than assumptions.

After breakfast, I walked down town, arguing the probabilities *pro* and *con*. One moment I thought it would prove a miserable failure, and Bartleby would be found all alive at my office as usual; the next moment it seemed certain that I should find his chair empty. And so I kept veering about. At the corner of Broadway and Canal Street, I saw quite an excited group of people standing in earnest conversation.

"I'll take odds he doesn't," said a voice as I passed.                              150

"Doesn't go? — done!" said I; "put up your money."

I was instinctively putting my hand in my pocket to produce my own, when I remembered that this was an election day. The words I had overheard bore no reference to Bartleby, but to the success or non-success of some candidate for the mayoralty. In my intent frame of mind, I had, as it were, imagined that all Broadway shared in my excitement, and were debating the same question with me. I passed on, very thankful that the uproar of the street screened my momentary absent-mindedness.

As I had intended, I was earlier than usual at my office door. I stood listening for a moment. All was still. He must be gone. I tried the knob. The door was locked. Yes, my procedure had worked to a charm; he indeed must be vanished. Yet a certain melancholy mixed with this: I was almost sorry for my brilliant success. I was fumbling under the door mat for the key, which Bartleby was to have left there for me, when accidentally my knee knocked against a panel, producing a summoning sound, and in response a voice came to me from within — "Not yet; I am occupied."

It was Bartleby.

I was thunderstruck. For an instant I stood like the man who, pipe in mouth,   155 was killed one cloudless afternoon long ago in Virginia, by summer lightning;

at his own warm open window he was killed, and remained leaning out there upon the dreamy afternoon, till some one touched him, when he fell.

"Not gone!" I murmured at last. But again obeying that wondrous ascendancy which the inscrutable scrivener had over me, and from which ascendancy, for all my chafing, I could not completely escape, I slowly went down stairs and out into the street, and while walking round the block, considered what I should next do in this unheard-of perplexity. Turn the man out by an actual thrusting I could not; to drive him away by calling him hard names would not do; calling in the police was an unpleasant idea; and yet, permit him to enjoy his cadaverous triumph over me — this, too, I could not think of. What was to be done? or, if nothing could be done, was there anything further that I could *assume* in the matter? Yes, as before I had prospectively assumed that Bartleby would depart, so now I might retrospectively assume that departed he was. In the legitimate carrying out of this assumption, I might enter my office in a great hurry, and pretending not to see Bartleby at all, walk straight against him as if he were air. Such a proceeding would in a singular degree have the appearance of a home-thrust. It was hardly possible that Bartleby could withstand such an application of the doctrine of assumption. But upon second thoughts the success of the plan seemed rather dubious. I resolved to argue the matter over with him again.

"Bartleby," said I, entering the office, with a quietly severe expression, "I am seriously displeased. I am pained, Bartleby. I had thought better of you. I had imagined you of such a gentlemanly organization, that in any delicate dilemma a slight hint would suffice — in short, an assumption. But it appears I am deceived. Why," I added, unaffectedly starting, "you have not even touched that money yet," pointing to it, just where I had left it the evening previous.

He answered nothing.

"Will you, or will you not, quit me?" I now demanded in a sudden passion, advancing close to him.

"I would prefer *not* to quit you," he replied, gently emphasizing the *not*. 160

"What earthly right have you to stay here? Do you pay any rent? Do you pay my taxes? Or is this property yours?"

He answered nothing.

"Are you ready to go on and write now? Are your eyes recovered? Could you copy a small paper for me this morning? or help examine a few lines? or step round to the post office? In a word, will you do anything at all, to give a coloring to your refusal to depart the premises?"

He silently retired into his hermitage.

I was now in such a state of nervous resentment that I thought it but pru- 165 dent to check myself at present from further demonstrations. Bartleby and I were alone. I remembered the tragedy of the unfortunate Adams and the still more unfortunate Colt in the solitary office of the latter; and how poor Colt, being dreadfully incensed by Adams, and imprudently permitting himself to get wildly excited, was at unawares hurried into his fatal act — an act which certainly no man could possibly deplore more than the actor himself.[7] Often it had occurred to me in my ponderings upon the subject that had that altercation taken place in the public street, or at a private residence, it would not have terminated as it did. It was the circumstance of being alone in a solitary office, up stairs, of a building entirely unhallowed by humanizing domestic associations — an uncarpeted office, doubtless, of a dusty, haggard sort of appearance — this it must have been, which greatly helped to enhance the irritable desperation of the hapless Colt.

But when this old Adam of resentment rose in me and tempted me concerning Bartleby, I grappled him and threw him. How? Why, simply by recalling the divine injunction: "A new commandment give I unto you, that ye love one another." Yes, this it was that saved me. Aside from higher considerations, charity often operates as a vastly wise and prudent principle — a great safeguard to its possessor. Men have committed murder for jealousy's sake, and anger's sake, and hatred's sake, and selfishness' sake, and spiritual pride's sake; but no man, that ever I heard of, ever committed a diabolical murder for sweet charity's sake. Mere self-interest, then, if no better motive can be enlisted, should, especially with high-tempered men, prompt all beings to charity and philanthropy. At any rate, upon the occasion in question, I strove to drown my exasperated feelings towards the scrivener by benevolently construing his conduct. Poor fellow, poor fellow! thought I, he don't mean anything; and besides, he has seen hard times, and ought to be indulged.

I endeavored, also, immediately to occupy myself, and at the same time to comfort my despondency. I tried to fancy, that in the course of the morning, at such time as might prove agreeable to him, Bartleby, of his own free accord, would emerge from his hermitage and take up some decided line of march in the direction of the door. But no. Half-past twelve o'clock came; Turkey began to glow in the face, overturn his inkstand, and become generally obstreperous; Nippers abated down into quietude and courtesy; Ginger Nut munched his noon apple; and Bartleby remained standing at his window in one of his profoundest dead-wall reveries. Will it be credited? Ought I to acknowledge it? That afternoon I left the office without saying one further word to him.

Some days now passed, during which, at leisure intervals I looked a little into "Edwards on the Will," and "Priestley on Necessity."[8] Under the circumstances, those books induced a salutary feeling. Gradually I slid into the persuasion that these troubles of mine, touching the scrivener, had been all predestinated from eternity, and Bartleby was billeted upon me for some mysterious purpose of an all-wise Providence, which it was not for a mere mortal like me to fathom. Yes, Bartleby, stay there behind your screen, thought I; I shall persecute you no more; you are harmless and noiseless as any of these old chairs; in short, I never feel so private as when I know you are here. At last I see it, I feel it; I penetrate

---

[7] A sensational 1841 homicide case in which John C. Colt murdered printer Samuel Adams in a fit of passion.

[8] Jonathan Edwards (1703–1758), American theologian, and Joseph Priestley (1733–1804), English clergyman and chemist, both held that a person's life was predetermined.

to the predestinated purpose of my life. I am content. Others may have loftier parts to enact; but my mission in this world, Bartleby, is to furnish you with office-room for such period as you may see fit to remain.

I believe that this wise and blessed frame of mind would have continued with me, had it not been for the unsolicited and uncharitable remarks obtruded upon me by my professional friends who visited the rooms. But thus it often is, that the constant friction of illiberal minds wears out at last the best resolves of the more generous. Though to be sure, when I reflected upon it, it was not strange that people entering my office should be struck by the peculiar aspect of the unaccountable Bartleby, and so be tempted to throw out some sinister observations concerning him. Sometimes an attorney, having business with me, and calling at my office, and finding no one but the scrivener there, would undertake to obtain some sort of precise information from him touching my whereabouts; but without heeding his idle talk, Bartleby would remain standing immovable in the middle of the room. So after contemplating him in that position for a time, the attorney would depart, no wiser than he came.

Also, when a reference was going on, and the room full of lawyers and witnesses, and business driving fast, some deeply-occupied legal gentleman present, seeing Bartleby wholly unemployed, would request him to run round to his (the legal gentleman's) office and fetch some papers for him. Thereupon, Bartleby would tranquilly decline, and yet remain idle as before. Then the lawyer would give a great stare, and turn to me. And what could I say? At last I was made aware that all through the circle of my professional acquaintance, a whisper of wonder was running round, having reference to the strange creature I kept at my office. This worried me very much. And as the idea came upon me of his possibly turning out a long-lived man, and keep occupying my chambers, and denying my authority; and perplexing my visitors; and scandalizing my professional reputation; and casting a general gloom over the premises; keeping soul and body together to the last upon his savings (for doubtless he spent but half a dime a day), and in the end perhaps outlive me, and claim possession of my office by right of his perpetual occupancy: as all these dark anticipations crowded upon me more and more, and my friends continually intruded their relentless remarks upon the apparition in my room; a great change was wrought in me. I resolved to gather all my faculties together, and forever rid me of this intolerable incubus.

Ere revolving any complicated project, however, adapted to this end, I first simply suggested to Bartleby the propriety of his permanent departure. In a calm and serious tone, I commended the idea to his careful and mature consideration. But, having taken three days to meditate upon it, he apprised me, that his original determination remained the same; in short, that he still preferred to abide with me.

What shall I do? I now said to myself, buttoning up my coat to the last button. What shall I do? what ought I to do? what does conscience say I *should* do with this man, or, rather, ghost. Rid myself of him, I must; go, he shall. But how? You will not thrust him, the poor, pale, passive mortal — you will not thrust such a helpless creature out of your door? you will not dishonor yourself by such cruelty? No, I will not, I cannot do that. Rather would I let him live and die here, and then mason up his remains in the wall. What, then, will you do? For all your coaxing, he will not budge. Bribes he leaves under your own paper-weight on your table; in short, it is quite plain that he prefers to cling to you.

Then something severe, something unusual must be done. What! surely you will not have him collared by a constable, and commit his innocent pallor to the common jail? And upon what ground could you procure such a thing to be done? — a vagrant, is he? What! he a vagrant, a wanderer, who refuses to budge? It is because he will *not* be a vagrant, then, that you seek to count him *as* a vagrant. That is too absurd. No visible means of support: there I have him. Wrong again: for indubitably he *does* support himself, and that is the only unanswerable proof that any man can show of his possessing the means so to do. No more, then. Since he will not quit me, I must quit him. I will change my offices; I will move elsewhere, and give him fair notice, that if I find him in my new premises I will then proceed against him as a common trespasser.

Acting accordingly, next day I thus addressed him: "I find these chambers too far from the City Hall; the air is unwholesome. In a word, I propose to remove my offices next week, and shall no longer require your services. I tell you this now, in order that you may seek another place."

He made no reply, and nothing more was said. 175

On the appointed day I engaged carts and men, proceeded to my chambers, and, having but little furniture, everything was removed in a few hours. Throughout, the scrivener remained standing behind the screen, which I directed to be removed the last thing. It was withdrawn; and, being folded up like a huge folio, left him the motionless occupant of a naked room. I stood in the entry watching him a moment, while something from within me upbraided me.

I re-entered, with my hand in my pocket — and — and my heart in my mouth.

"Good-by, Bartleby; I am going — good-by, and God some way bless you; and take that," slipping something in his hand. But it dropped upon the floor, and then — strange to say — I tore myself from him whom I had so longed to be rid of.

Established in my new quarters, for a day or two I kept the door locked, and started at every footfall in the passages. When I returned to my rooms, after any little absence, I would pause at the threshold for an instant, and attentively listen, ere applying my key. But these fears were needless. Bartleby never came nigh me.

I thought all was going well, when a perturbed-looking stranger visited 180 me, inquiring whether I was the person who had recently occupied rooms at No. ——— Wall Street.

Full of forebodings, I replied that I was.

"Then, sir," said the stranger, who proved a lawyer, "you are responsible for the man you left there. He refuses to do any copying; he refuses to do anything; he says he prefers not to; and he refuses to quit the premises."

"I am very sorry, sir," said I, with assumed tranquillity, but an inward tremor, "but, really, the man you allude to is nothing to me — he is no relation or apprentice of mine, that you should hold me responsible for him."

"In mercy's name, who is he?"

"I certainly cannot inform you. I know nothing about him. Formerly I 185 employed him as a copyist; but he has done nothing for me now for some time past."

"I shall settle him, then — good morning, sir."

Several days passed, and I heard nothing more; and, though I often felt a charitable prompting to call at the place and see poor Bartleby, yet a certain squeamishness, of I know not what, withheld me.

All is over with him, by this time, thought I, at last, when, through another week, no further intelligence reached me. But, coming to my room the day after, I found several persons waiting at my door in a high state of nervous excitement.

"That's the man — here he comes," cried the foremost one, whom I recognized as the lawyer who had previously called upon me alone.

"You must take him away, sir, at once," cried a portly person among them, 190 advancing upon me, and whom I knew to be the landlord of No. —— Wall Street. "These gentlemen, my tenants, cannot stand it any longer; Mr. B——," pointing to the lawyer, "has turned him out of his room, and he now persists in haunting the building generally, sitting upon the banisters of the stairs by day, and sleeping in the entry by night. Everybody is concerned; clients are leaving the offices; some fears are entertained of a mob; something you must do, and that without delay."

Aghast at this torrent, I fell back before it, and would fain have locked myself in my new quarters. In vain I persisted that Bartleby was nothing to me — no more than to any one else. In vain — I was the last person known to have anything to do with him, and they held me to the terrible account. Fearful, then, of being exposed in the papers (as one person present obscurely threatened), I considered the matter, and, at length, said, that if the lawyer would give me a confidential interview with the scrivener, in his (the lawyer's) own room, I would, that afternoon, strive my best to rid them of the nuisance they complained of.

Going up stairs to my old haunt, there was Bartleby silently sitting upon the banister at the landing.

"What are you doing here, Bartleby?" said I.

"Sitting upon the banister," he mildly replied.

I motioned him into the lawyer's room, who then left us. 195

"Bartleby," said I, "are you aware that you are the cause of great tribulation to me, by persisting in occupying the entry after being dismissed from the office?"

No answer.

"Now one of two things must take place. Either you must do something, or something must be done to you. Now what sort of business would you like to engage in? Would you like to re-engage in copying for some one?"

"No; I would prefer not to make any change."

"Would you like a clerkship in a dry-goods store?" 200

"There is too much confinement about that. No, I would not like a clerkship; but I am not particular."

"Too much confinement," I cried, "why, you keep yourself confined all the time!"

"I would prefer not to take a clerkship," he rejoined, as if to settle that little item at once.

"How would a bar-tender's business suit you? There is no trying of the eyesight in that."

"I would not like it at all; though, as I said before, I am not particular." 205

His unwonted wordiness inspirited me. I returned to the charge.

"Well, then, would you like to travel through the country collecting bills for the merchants? That would improve your health."

"No, I would prefer to be doing something else."

"How, then, would going as a companion to Europe, to entertain some young gentleman with your conversation — how would that suit you?"

"Not at all. It does not strike me that there is anything definite about that. I 210 like to be stationary. But I am not particular."

"Stationary you shall be, then," I cried, now losing all patience, and, for the first time in all my exasperating connection with him, fairly flying into a passion. "If you do not go away from these premises before night, I shall feel bound — indeed, I *am* bound — to — to — to quit the premises myself!" I rather absurdly concluded, knowing not with what possible threat to try to frighten his immobility into compliance. Despairing of all further efforts, I was precipitately leaving him, when a final thought occurred to me — one which had not been wholly unindulged before.

"Bartleby," said I, in the kindest tone I could assume under such exciting circumstances, "will you go home with me now — not to my office, but my dwelling — and remain there till we can conclude upon some convenient arrangement for you at our leisure? Come, let us start now, right away."

"No: at present I would prefer not to make any change at all."

I answered nothing; but, effectually dodging every one by the suddenness and rapidity of my flight, rushed from the building, ran up Wall Street towards Broadway, and, jumping into the first omnibus, was soon removed from pursuit. As soon as tranquillity returned, I distinctly perceived that I had now done all that I possibly could, both in respect to the demands of the landlord and his tenants, and with regard to my own desire and sense of duty, to benefit Bartleby, and shield him from rude persecution. I now strove to be entirely care-free and quiescent; and my conscience justified me in the attempt; though, indeed, it was not so successful as I could have wished. So fearful was I of being again hunted out by the incensed landlord and his exasperated tenants, that, surrendering my business to Nippers, for a few days, I drove about the upper part of the town and through the suburbs, in my rockaway; crossed over to Jersey City and Hoboken, and paid fugitive visits to Manhattanville and Astoria. In fact, I almost lived in my rockaway for the time.

When again I entered my office, lo, a note from the landlord lay upon the   215
desk. I opened it with trembling hands. It informed me that the writer had sent
to the police, and had Bartleby removed to the Tombs as a vagrant. Moreover,
since I knew more about him than any one else, he wished me to appear at
that place, and make a suitable statement of the facts. These tidings had a conflicting effect upon me. At first I was indignant; but, at last, almost approved.
The landlord's energetic, summary disposition, had led him to adopt a procedure which I do not think I would have decided upon myself; and yet, as a last
resort, under such peculiar circumstances, it seemed the only plan.

As I afterwards learned, the poor scrivener, when told that he must be conducted to the Tombs, offered not the slightest obstacle, but, in his pale, unmoving way, silently acquiesced.

Some of the compassionate and curious by-standers joined the party; and
headed by one of the constables arm in arm with Bartleby, the silent procession filed its way through all the noise, and heat, and joy of the roaring thor-
oughfares at noon.

The same day I received the note, I went to the Tombs, or, to speak more
properly, the Halls of Justice. Seeking the right officer, I stated the purpose
of my call, and was informed that the individual I described was, indeed,
within. I then assured the functionary that Bartleby was a perfectly honest
man, and greatly to be compassionated, however unaccountably eccentric. I
narrated all I knew, and closed by suggesting the idea of letting him remain
in as indulgent confinement as possible, till something less harsh might be
done — though, indeed, I hardly knew what. At all events, if nothing else
could be decided upon, the alms-house must receive him. I then begged to
have an interview.

Being under no disgraceful charge, and quite serene and harmless in all his
ways, they had permitted him freely to wander about the prison, and, especially, in the inclosed grass-platted yards thereof. And so I found him there,
standing all alone in the quietest of the yards, his face towards a high wall,
while all around, from the narrow slits of the jail windows, I thought I saw
peering out upon him the eyes of murderers and thieves.

"Bartleby!"                                                                   220

"I know you," he said, without looking round — "and I want nothing to say
to you."

"It was not I that brought you here, Bartleby," said I, keenly pained at his
implied suspicion. "And to you, this should not be so vile a place. Nothing
reproachful attaches to you by being here. And see, it is not so sad a place as
one might think. Look, there is the sky, and here is the grass."

"I know where I am," he replied, but would say nothing more, and so I left
him.

As I entered the corridor again, a broad meat-like man, in an apron, accosted
me, and, jerking his thumb over his shoulder, said — "Is that your friend?"

"Yes."                                                                       225

"Does he want to starve? If he does, let him live on the prison fare, that's all."

"Who are you?" asked I, not knowing what to make of such an unofficially speaking person in such a place.

"I am the grub-man. Such gentlemen as have friends here, hire me to provide them with something good to eat."

"Is this so?" said I, turning to the turnkey.

He said it was.                                                          230

"Well, then," said I, slipping some silver into the grub-man's hands (for so they called him), "I want you to give particular attention to my friend there; let him have the best dinner you can get. And you must be as polite to him as possible."

"Introduce me, will you?" said the grub-man, looking at me with an expression which seemed to say he was all impatience for an opportunity to give a specimen of his breeding.

Thinking it would prove of benefit to the scrivener, I acquiesced; and, asking the grub-man his name, went up with him to Bartleby.

"Bartleby, this is a friend; you will find him very useful to you."

"Your sarvant, sir, your sarvant," said the grub-man, making a low salutation    235
behind his apron. "Hope you find it pleasant here, sir; nice grounds — cool apartments — hope you'll stay with us some time — try to make it agreeable. What will you have for dinner to-day?"

"I prefer not to dine to-day," said Bartleby, turning away. "It would disagree with me; I am unused to dinners." So saying, he slowly moved to the other side of the inclosure, and took up a position fronting the deadwall.

"How's this?" said the grub-man, addressing me with a stare of astonishment. "He's odd, ain't he?"

"I think he is a little deranged," said I, sadly.

"Deranged? deranged is it? Well, now, upon my word, I thought that friend of yourn was a gentleman forger; they are always pale and genteel-like, them forgers. I can't help pity 'em — can't help it, sir. Did you know Monroe Edwards?" he added, touchingly, and paused. Then, laying his hand piteously on my shoulder, sighed, "he died of consumption at Sing-Sing.[9] So you weren't acquainted with Monroe?"

"No, I was never socially acquainted with any forgers. But I cannot stop    240
longer. Look to my friend yonder. You will not lose by it. I will see you again."

Some few days after this, I again obtained admission to the Tombs, and went through the corridors in quest of Bartleby; but without finding him.

"I saw him coming from his cell not long ago," said a turnkey, "may be he's gone to loiter in the yards."

So I went in that direction.

"Are you looking for the silent man?" said another turnkey, passing me. "Yonder he lies — sleeping in the yard there. 'Tis not twenty minutes since I saw him lie down."

The yard was entirely quiet. It was not accessible to the common prisoners.    245
The surrounding walls of amazing thickness, kept off all sounds behind them.

[9] The state prison near Ossining, New York.

The Egyptian character of the masonry weighed upon me with its gloom. But a soft imprisoned turf grew under foot. The heart of the eternal pyramids, it seemed, wherein, by some strange magic, through the clefts, grass-seed, dropped by birds, had sprung.

Strangely huddled at the base of the wall, his knees drawn up, and lying on his side, his head touching the cold stones, I saw the wasted Bartleby. But nothing stirred. I paused; then went close up to him; stooped over, and saw that his dim eyes were open; otherwise he seemed profoundly sleeping. Something prompted me to touch him. I felt his hand, when a tingling shiver ran up my arm and down my spine to my feet.

The round face of the grub-man peered upon me now. "His dinner is ready. Won't he dine to-day, either? Or does he live without dining?"

"Lives without dining," said I, and closed the eyes.

"Eh! — He's asleep, ain't he?"

"With kings and counselors," murmured I.

250

There would seem little need for proceeding further in this history. Imagination will readily supply the meagre recital of poor Bartleby's interment. But, ere parting with the reader, let me say, that if this little narrative has sufficiently interested him, to awaken curiosity as to who Bartleby was, and what manner of life he led prior to the present narrator's making his acquaintance, I can only reply, that in such curiosity I fully share, but am wholly unable to gratify it. Yet here I hardly know whether I should divulge one little item of rumor, which came to my ear a few months after the scrivener's decease. Upon what basis it rested, I could never ascertain; and hence, how true it is I cannot now tell. But, inasmuch as this vague report has not been without a certain suggestive interest to me, however said, it may prove the same with some others; and so I will briefly mention it. The report was this: that Bartleby had been a subordinate clerk in the Dead Letter[10] Office at Washington, from which he had been suddenly removed by a change in the administration. When I think over this rumor, hardly can I express the emotions which seize me. Dead letters! does it not sound like dead men? Conceive a man by nature and misfortune prone to a pallid hopelessness, can any business seem more fitted to heighten it than that of continually handling these dead letters, and assorting them for the flames? For by the cartload they are annually burned. Some times from out the folded paper the pale clerk takes a ring — the finger it was meant for, perhaps, moulders in the grave; a bank-note sent in swiftest charity — he whom it would relieve, nor eats nor hungers any more; pardon for those who died despairing; hope for those who died unhoping; good tidings for those who died stifled by unrelieved calamities. On errands of life, these letters speed to death.

Ah, Bartleby! Ah, humanity!

---

[10] A letter that is undeliverable and unreturnable.

## FOR ANALYSIS

**1.** List a half dozen adjectives that describe the **narrator**. Would the narrator agree that these adjectives are accurate?

**2.** What is it about Bartleby that so intrigues and fascinates the narrator? Why does the narrator continue to feel a moral obligation to an employee who refuses to work and curtly rejects kind offers of help?

**3.** What thematic function do Turkey and Nippers serve?

**4.** As the narrator congratulates himself on the cleverness of his scheme to dismiss Bartleby, he becomes fascinated with his "assumptions" about how Bartleby will behave. Examine the passage (paras. 149–56), and show how it advances the narrator's growing awareness of what Bartleby represents.

**5.** Readers differ as to whether this is the story of Bartleby or the lawyer-narrator. What is your view?

**6.** Would it be fair to describe Bartleby as a rebel without a cause, as a young man who refuses to participate in a comfortable and well-ordered business world but fails to offer any alternative way of life? Write a paragraph or two explaining why or why not.

## MAKING ARGUMENTS

Commentators on Occupy Wall Street (OWS) have discussed the movement's connections to Melville's "Bartleby, the Scrivener." Do a little reading on OWS and argue for or against those connections.

## WRITING TOPICS

**1.** About midway through the story (paras. 87–94), the **narrator** discovers that Bartleby has been living in the law offices, and he is profoundly moved when his eyes fall on the scrivener's worldly possessions. Reread those paragraphs, and write an analysis showing how they describe the narrator's growing awareness of who Bartleby is.

**2.** With his final utterance, "Ah, Bartleby! Ah, humanity!" the narrator apparently penetrates the mystery of the silent scrivener. The comment suggests that the narrator sees Bartleby as a representative of humanity. In what sense might the narrator have come to see Bartleby in this light?

**3.** Why does Melville allow the narrator (and the reader) to discover so little about Bartleby and the causes of his behavior? All we learn of Bartleby's past is told in the next-to-last paragraph. What clues does this paragraph give us to the narrator's fascination with Bartleby?

## MAKING CONNECTIONS

Compare and contrast Bartleby's rebellion to that of the **protagonist** in Updike's "A & P" (p. 94). What do we know about the motivations of each? How do we know what we know? How do the stories seem to want us to feel about each of these acts of rebellion and the protagonists who commit them?

## FRANZ KAFKA  (1883–1924)

# A HUNGER ARTIST[1]  1924

In recent decades the public's interest in the art of fasting has suffered a marked decline. While formerly it used to pay very well to stage large exhibitions of this kind under private management, today this is quite impossible. Those were different times. Back then the whole town was engaged with the hunger artist; during his fast, the audience's involvement grew from day to day; everyone wanted to see the hunger artist at least once a day; during the later stages subscribers used to sit in specially reserved seats in front of the small barred cage all day long; there were even exhibitions at night by torchlight to heighten the effect; on fine days his cage was carried out into the open, and that was particularly the time when the hunger artist was shown to children; while for the adults he was often just an entertainment in which they took part because it happened to be in fashion, for the children, who stood open-mouthed, holding each other's hands for safety's sake, watching him as he sat there on the straw spread out for him, even spurning a chair, he was a pale figure in a black leotard with enormously protruding ribs, sometimes nodding politely, answering questions with a forced smile, occasionally even stretching his arm through the bars to let them feel how skinny he was, but then again withdrawing completely into himself, paying attention to no one, not even noticing the striking of the clock, so important for him, the only piece of furniture in his cage, but merely staring into space with his eyes almost shut, taking a sip now and then from a tiny glass of water to moisten his lips.

Besides the changing spectators there were also permanent guards selected by the public — strangely enough, usually butchers — who had the job of watching the hunger artist day and night always three at a time to make sure that he didn't consume any nourishment in some secret manner. But this was no more than a formality introduced to reassure the public, because insiders knew well enough that during his fast, the hunger artist would never, under any circumstances, not even under duress, swallow the smallest crumb; his code of honor as an artist forbade it. Not every watchman, of course, was capable of understanding this; often there were groups of night guards who were very lax in carrying out their duties and deliberately congregated in a far corner and absorbed themselves in a game of cards, obviously intending to give the hunger artist the chance to take a little refreshment, which they assumed he could produce from some secret stash. Nothing was more tormenting to the hunger artist than such watchmen; they made him miserable; they made his fasting seem terribly difficult; sometimes he would overcome his physical

[1] Translated by Ann Charters.

**295**

weakness and sing for as long as he could keep it up during their watch, to show how unfair their suspicions were. But that was of little use; they only marveled at his skill in being able to eat even while singing. He much preferred the guards who sat right up against the bars and who weren't satisfied with the dim night lighting in the hall and so trained on him the beams of the flashlights supplied to them by his manager. The harsh light didn't disturb him at all, since he wasn't able to sleep deeply anyway, whereas he could always doze off a little whatever the light or the hour, even in the overcrowded, noisy hall. He was quite prepared to spend the whole night entirely without sleep with such watchmen; he was prepared to swap jokes with them, to tell them stories about his nomadic life and listen to their stories in turn, anything just to keep them awake, to be able to show them again and again that he had nothing to eat in his cage and that he was fasting like no one of them could fast. But he was happiest when morning came and a lavish breakfast was served to them at his expense, on which they threw themselves with the appetites of healthy men after a weary night's vigil. Of course there were even people who would see this breakfast as an attempt to bribe the guards, but that was really going too far, and when these people were asked if they would be willing to take over the night watch without breakfast, just for the sake of the cause, they slunk away, though they stuck to their suspicions all the same.

But suspicions of this nature were really inseparable from fasting. No one, after all, was capable of spending all his days and nights continuously watching the hunger artist, so no one could be absolutely certain from firsthand knowledge that his fasting had truly been an unbroken and faultless performance; only the hunger artist himself could know that, and only he, therefore, could be at the same time both the performer and the satisfied spectator of his own fasting. Yet there was another reason why he was never satisfied; perhaps it wasn't only his fasting that made him so emaciated that many people, much to their regret, couldn't attend his performances because they couldn't bear the sight of him; perhaps he had become so emaciated from dissatisfaction with himself. For he alone knew something that not even other insiders knew: how easy it was to fast. It was the easiest thing in the world. He made no secret of this, either, though no one believed him; at best some thought him modest, but mostly they regarded him as a publicity seeker or even took him for a fraud, a person for whom fasting was easy because he knew how to make it easy and then also even had the audacity more or less to admit it. He was forced to endure all of this, he'd even grown accustomed to it all in the course of time, but inwardly his own dissatisfaction gnawed at him, yet never after a single fasting period — you had to grant him this much — had he voluntarily left his cage. The manager had set forty days as the maximum period of the fasting; he would never allow a fast to run beyond this limit, not even in the major cities, and for good reason. Experience had shown that the public's interest in any town could be stimulated for about forty days by increasing the advertisements, but then the public lost interest, and a substantial drop in attendance was noted; naturally there were small variations in this matter between the different towns and regions, but as a rule forty days was the limit. So then on the fortieth day the gate of the flower-decorated cage was opened, an enthusiastic crowd of spectators filled the hall, a military band played, two doctors entered the cage to take the hunger artist's vital measurements, the results were announced to the audience through a megaphone, and finally two young ladies came forward, pleased that they had won the lottery for the honor of leading the hunger artist out of the cage and down a few steps toward a small table where a carefully prepared invalid's meal was served. And at this point, the hunger artist always resisted. True, he willingly surrendered his bony arms to the outstretched hands of these solicitous ladies as they bent down to him, but he refused to stand up. Why stop now, after just forty days? He could have kept going for much longer, infinitely longer; why stop now when he was at his best — indeed, when he had not yet even reached his best fasting form? Why did they want to rob him of the glory of fasting longer, not only of being the greatest hunger artist of all time, which he probably already was — but also of surpassing himself to achieve the unimaginable, because he felt that his capacity to fast was limitless. Why had this audience, which pretended to admire him so much, had so little patience with him; if he could endure fasting longer, why couldn't they endure it? Besides, he was tired, he was comfortable sitting in straw, and now he was supposed to stand upright and go to a meal; the thought alone nauseated him to such a point that he was prevented from expressing it with great difficulty, only out of regard for the ladies. And he gazed up into the eyes of the ladies, who appeared so friendly but were actually so cruel, and shook his head, which weighed heavily on his feeble neck. But then what happened was always what happened. The manager came forward, silently raised his arms over the hunger artist — the band music made speech impossible — as if he were calling upon heaven to look down on its handiwork there in the straw; on this pathetic martyr, which the hunger artist certainly was, only in an entirely different sense; he grasped the hunger artist around his emaciated waist with exaggerated care as if to suggest what a feeble object he had to deal with here; and giving him a secret shake or two, so that the hunger artist's legs and upper body wobbled to and fro, he handed him over to the care of the ladies, who had turned deathly pale in the meantime. Now the hunger artist submitted to everything; his head lay on his chest, as if it had rolled there by chance and stopped itself inexplicably; his body was hollowed out; his legs were squeezed tightly together at the knees in some instinct of self-preservation, but his feet were scraping at the ground, as if it weren't the real ground — they were still seeking the real ground; and the entire weight of his body, admittedly very modest, lay on one of the ladies, who — looking around for help, with panting breath — this wasn't how she had pictured her position of honor — first craned her neck back as far as possible, at least to keep her face from touching the hunger artist, then finding this impossible, when her more fortunate companion didn't come to her aid, instead contenting herself with carrying before her the small bundle of bones that was the hunger artist's hand, the first lady burst into tears amid the audience's delighted laughter and had to be replaced by an attendant who had been standing by in readiness. Then came the meal, a little of which the manager spooned into the nearly unconscious, comatose hunger artist to the accompaniment of cheerful patter designed to divert attention away from the hunger artist's condition; then came the toast drunk to the audience, which the hunger artist allegedly whispered to the manager; the band concluded everything with a great fanfare; the crowd melted away, and nobody had any cause to feel dissatisfied with the show, no one, only the hunger artist, always just him alone.

So he lived for many years with regular short periods of rest, in apparent glory honored by the world, yet in spite of that mostly in a dark mood that became even darker because no one took it seriously. And indeed, how could anyone have comforted him? What more could he wish for? And if once in awhile some good natured soul came along and felt sorry for him and tried to explain to him that his depression was probably caused by his fasting, it sometimes happened, especially if his fast were well advanced, that the hunger artist responded with a burst of rage and to everyone's alarm began to shake the bars of his cage like a wild beast. But the manager had a method of punishment that he was fond of using in such cases. He would apologize publicly to the assembled audience for the hunger artist, admitting that his behavior could only be excused as an irritable condition brought on by his fasting, something that well-fed people by no means could easily understand; in this connection, he would go on to speak of the hunger artist's claim that he was able to fast for a much longer time than he did fast; the manager praised the high aspirations, the good will, the great measure of self-denial undoubtedly implicit in this claim; but then he would seek to refute this claim simply enough by producing photographs, which were at the same time offered for sale to the public; for these pictures showed the hunger artist on his fortieth day of fasting, in bed, almost dead from exhaustion. This perversion of the truth, which assuredly was familiar to the hunger artist, always unnerved him anew and was too much for him. Here the result of the premature ending of his fast was presented as its cause! To fight against this lack of understanding, against this world of ignorance, was impossible. Up to that point he always stood clinging to the bars of his cage, listening eagerly to the manager in good faith, but as soon as the photographs appeared he would let go and sink back with a groan onto his straw, and the reassured public could come close again and inspect him.

When the witnesses to such scenes recalled them a few years later, they often ₅ failed to understand them at all. For in the meantime, the previously mentioned decline of the public's interest in fasting had occurred; it seemed to happen almost overnight; there may have been deeper reasons for it, but who cared about digging them up; in any case, the day came when the hunger artist found himself deserted by the pleasure-seeking crowds, who went streaming past him toward other exhibitions. For one last time his manager dragged him across half Europe to see if the old interest might be revived here and there; all in vain, it was as if a repulsion for exhibition fasting had set in everywhere by secret pact. In reality it couldn't have come about so suddenly, of course, and people now belatedly recalled a number of warning signs that had neither been adequately noted nor adequately dealt with in the flush of success, but now it was too late for countermeasures. Of course fasting would surely make a comeback some day, but that was no comfort to the living. What should the hunger artist do now? He who had been applauded by thousands couldn't appear as a sideshow in village fairs, and as for starting a new profession, the hunger artist was not merely too old, but he was also, above all, too fanatically devoted to his fasting. So he took leave of his manager, his companion throughout an unparalleled career, and found an engagement for himself with a large circus; in order to spare his own feelings, he avoided reading the terms of his contract.

A large circus, with its immense number of personnel and animals and apparatus, all constantly replacing and supplementing one another, can always find a use for anyone at any time, even a hunger artist, provided, of course, that his demands are sufficiently modest, and furthermore in this particular case it wasn't just the hunger artist himself who was being booked, but also his long-famous name; indeed, considering the peculiar nature of his art, which doesn't decrease with advancing age, one couldn't even say that he was a super-annuated artist, past his prime, and seeking refuge in a quiet circus job; on the contrary, the hunger artist pledged that he could fast just as well as ever, which was clearly believable; in fact, he even claimed that if they let him have his way, as they readily promised him, he would truly astound the world by setting a new record, a claim that only provoked a smile from the experts, considering the public's current mood, which the hunger artist, in his enthusiasm, was apt to forget.

Basically, however, the hunger artist hadn't lost his sense of the real situation, and he accepted it as self-evident that he and his cage would not be placed as a star attraction in the center ring, but rather would be offered as a sideshow in a readily accessible site near the animal cages. Large, brightly colored posters made a frame for his cage and proclaimed what was to be seen there. When the audience came pouring out during the intermission to look at the animals, they almost inevitably had to pass the hunger artist's cage and stop there for a moment; they would perhaps have stayed longer, if those pressing them from behind in the narrow passageway, who couldn't understand the delay on the path to the animals they were so eager to see, hadn't made a longer, more leisurely contemplation impossible. This was also the reason why the hunger artist, who naturally looked forward to these visiting periods as his purpose in life, trembled at their prospect as well. At first he could hardly wait for the intermissions; he had been delighted watching the crowds come surging toward him, until it was made clear to him only too soon — not even the most obstinate, almost deliberate self-deception could obscure the fact — that most of these people, to judge from their actions, were again and again without exception on their way to the wild animals. And that first sight of them from a distance always remained the best. For as soon as they had reached him, he was immediately deafened by the shouting and cursing from the two contending factions which kept continuously forming — those who wanted to stop and stare at him (and the hunger artist soon found them the more distasteful) out of no real interest but only just as a whim or out of defiance, and those others who only wanted to go straight to the animal cages. Once the first rush was over, then came the stragglers, and these, who had nothing to prevent them from stopping as long as they liked, hurried by with long strides, without hardly even a side glance at him, as they rushed to see the animals in the remaining time. And it was an all too rare stroke of luck when the father of a family came along with his children, pointed to the hunger artist, explained in detail what was happening, told stories about earlier years when he himself had witnessed similar but incomparably more splendid performances, but then the children, since they hadn't been sufficiently prepared by either school or life, remained rather uncomprehending — what was fasting to them? — yet the gleam of their inquisitive eyes suggested something new to come, better and more merciful times. Perhaps, the hunger artist sometimes said to himself, things could become a little better if his cage were located not so close to the animal cages. That made the choice of destination too easy for people, to say nothing of how the stench of the stables, the restlessness of the animals at night, the serving of raw meat to the beasts of prey, and the roars at feeding time constantly offended and depressed him. But he did not dare to complain to the management; after all, he had the animals to thank for the throng of visitors, among them here and there even someone who was there just to see him; and who could tell where they might hide him if he called attention to his existence and thereby to the fact that, strictly speaking, he was no more than an obstacle in the path to the animals.

A small obstacle, to be sure, an obstacle growing smaller all the time. It has become customary nowadays to want to find it strange to call attention to a hunger artist, and in accordance with this custom his fate was sealed. He might fast as much as he could, and indeed he did, but nothing could save him now, people passed him by. Just try to explain the art of fasting to someone! Someone who doesn't feel it cannot be made to understand it. The colorful posters became dirty and illegible, they were torn down and no one thought to replace them; the little signboard tallying the number of days fasted, which at first had been carefully changed every day, had long remained the same, for after the first few weeks the staff had grown tired of even this small task; and so the hunger artist just went on fasting as he had once dreamed of doing, and it was indeed no trouble for him to do so, as he had always predicted, but no one counted the days; no one, not even the hunger artist himself, knew how great his achievement was, and his heart grew heavy. And once in a while, when some casual passer-by stopped, ridiculed the outdated number on the board, and talked about a hoax, that was in its way the stupidest lie ever invented by indifference and inherent malice, since the hunger artist didn't cheat, he was working honestly, but the world was cheating him of his reward.

So again many more days passed and there came an end to that as well. One day a supervisor happened to notice the cage, and he asked the attendants why this perfectly useful cage with the rotten straw in it was left unoccupied; no one knew, until somebody with the help of the signboard remembered the hunger artist. They poked into the straw with sticks and found the hunger artist underneath. "Are you still fasting?" asked the supervisor. "When on earth do you mean to stop?" "Forgive me, everybody," whispered the hunger artist; only the supervisor, who pressed his ear against the bars, understood him. "Certainly," said the supervisor, tapping his finger at the side of his forehead to suggest the hunger artist's condition to the staff, "we forgive you." "I always wanted you to admire my fasting," said the hunger artist. "We do admire it," said the supervisor obligingly. "But you shouldn't admire it," said the hunger artist. "All right, then, we don't admire it," said the supervisor, "but why shouldn't we admire it?" "Because I have to fast, I can't help it," said the hunger artist. "How about that," said the supervisor. "Why can't you help it?" "Because," said the hunger artist, lifting his shriveled head a little, and puckering his lips as if for a kiss, he spoke right into the supervisor's ear, so that nothing would be missed, "because I couldn't find the food I liked. If I had found it, believe me, I shouldn't have made any fuss and stuffed myself just like you and everyone else." These were his last words, but in his dying eyes there remained the firm, if no longer proud, conviction that he was still continuing to fast.

"Now clear this out!" said the supervisor, and they buried the hunger art- 10 ist, straw and all. Then they put a young panther into the cage. Even the most insensitive felt it was refreshing to see this wild creature leaping about in a cage that had been neglected for so long. He lacked for nothing. The food that he liked was brought to him by his keepers without hesitation; he didn't even appear to miss his freedom; that noble body, full to almost bursting with all he needed, seemed to carry freedom itself around with it; it appeared to be placed somewhere in his jaws; and the joy of life streamed with such ardent passion from his throat, that it wasn't easy for the onlookers to withstand it. But they braced themselves, surrounded the cage, and never wanted to move on.

### For Analysis

**1.** Many readers interpret this story as a parable of the artist in the modern world, while others see it as a religious parable. What evidence do you find in the story to support either interpretation?

**2.** Suggest reasons for Kafka's selection of an expert in fasting (rather than a priest or a singer, for example) as the central figure in the story.

**3.** How does Kafka manage to achieve such a bizarre, dreamlike effect with dry and factual **prose**?

**4.** Since his greatest achievements involve inwardness and withdrawal, why does the hunger artist nevertheless seem to need an audience?

## MAKING ARGUMENTS

Should the hunger artist be admired for his passionate and single-minded devotion to his art or condemned for his withdrawal from humanity and his sickness of will? Why? Be sure to discuss the significance of the panther put in the cage after the artist's death.

## WRITING TOPIC

In an essay, compare the hunger artist with Melville's Bartleby. Discuss the origins, rationale, consequences, and significance of their behavior.

## MAKING CONNECTIONS

1. Compare this story with Hawthorne's "Young Goodman Brown" (p. 79) and Melville's "Bartleby, the Scrivener" (p. 267). What similarities do the central figures in the three stories share? What differences do you find? How does the alienation of each of the central figures contribute to each story's **theme**?

2. Describe feelings of isolation and alienation that you have experienced. What caused those feelings? How did you cope with them? How, finally, do you differ from the hunger artist?

## RALPH ELLISON  (1914–1994)

# BATTLE ROYAL  1952

I t goes a long way back, some twenty years. All my life I had been looking
for something, and everywhere I turned someone tried to tell me what it
was. I accepted their answers too, though they were often in contradiction and
even self-contradictory. I was naive. I was looking for myself and asking everyone except myself questions which I, and only I, could answer. It took me a
long time and much painful boomeranging of my expectations to achieve a
realization everyone else appears to have been born with: that I am nobody but
myself. But first I had to discover that I am an invisible man!

And yet I am no freak of nature, nor of history. I was in the cards, other
things having been equal (or unequal) eighty-five years ago. I am not ashamed
of my grandparents for having been slaves. I am only ashamed of myself for
having at one time been ashamed. About eighty-five years ago they were told
that they were free, united with others of our country in everything pertain-
ing to the common good, and, in everything social, separate like the fingers of
the hand. And they believed it. They exulted in it. They stayed in their place,
worked hard, and brought up my father to do the same. But my grandfather is
the one. He was an odd old guy, my grandfather, and I am told I take after him.
It was he who caused the trouble. On his deathbed he called my father to him
and said, "Son, after I'm gone I want you to keep up the good fight. I never told
you, but our life is a war and I have been a traitor all my born days, a spy in the
enemy's country ever since I give up my gun back in the Reconstruction. Live
with your head in the lion's mouth. I want you to overcome 'em with yeses,
undermine 'em with grins, agree 'em to death and destruction, let 'em swoller
you till they vomit or bust wide open." They thought the old man had gone
out of his mind. He had been the meekest of men. The younger children were
rushed from the room, the shades drawn, and the flame of the lamp turned so
low that it sputtered on the wick like the old man's breathing. "Learn it to the
younguns," he whispered fiercely; then he died.

But my folks were more alarmed over his last words than over his dying.
It was as though he had not died at all, his words caused so much anxiety. I
was warned emphatically to forget what he had said and, indeed, this is the
first time it has been mentioned outside the family circle. It had a tremendous
effect upon me, however. I could never be sure of what he meant. Grandfather
had been a quiet old man who never made any trouble, yet on his deathbed
he had called himself a traitor and a spy, and he had spoken of his meekness
as a dangerous activity. It became a constant puzzle which lay unanswered in
the back of my mind. And whenever things went well for me I remembered

my grandfather and felt guilty and uncomfortable. It was as though I was carrying out his advice in spite of myself. And to make it worse, everyone loved me for it. I was praised by the most lily-white men of the town. I was considered an example of desirable conduct — just as my grandfather had been. And what puzzled me was that the old man had defined it as *treachery*. When I was praised for my conduct I felt a guilt that in some way I was doing something that was really against the wishes of the white folks, that if they had understood they would have desired me to act just the opposite, that I should have been sulky and mean, and that that really would have been what they wanted, even though they were fooled and thought they wanted me to act as I did. It made me afraid that some day they would look upon me as a traitor and I would be lost. Still I was more afraid to act any other way because they didn't like that at all. The old man's words were like a curse. On my graduation day I delivered an oration in which I showed that humility was the secret, indeed, the very essence of progress. (Not that I believed this — how could I, remembering my grandfather? — I only believed that it worked.) It was a great success. Everyone praised me and I was invited to give the speech at a gathering of the town's leading white citizens. It was a triumph for our whole community.

It was in the main ballroom of the leading hotel. When I got there I discovered that it was on the occasion of a smoker, and I was told that since I was to be there anyway I might as well take part in the battle royal to be fought by some of my schoolmates as part of the entertainment. The battle royal came first.

All of the town's big shots were there in their tuxedoes, wolfing down the 5 buffet foods, drinking beer and whiskey and smoking black cigars. It was a large room with a high ceiling. Chairs were arranged in neat rows around three sides of a portable boxing ring. The fourth side was clear, revealing a gleaming space of polished floor. I had some misgivings over the battle royal, by the way. Not from a distaste for fighting, but because I didn't care too much for the other fellows who were to take part. They were tough guys who seemed to have no grandfather's curse worrying their minds. No one could mistake their toughness. And besides, I suspected that fighting a battle royal might detract from the dignity of my speech. In those pre-invisible days I visualized myself as a potential Booker T. Washington. But the other fellows didn't care too much for me either, and there were nine of them. I felt superior to them in my way, and I didn't like the manner in which we were all crowded together into the servants' elevator. Nor did they like my being there. In fact, as the warmly lighted floors flashed past the elevator we had words over the fact that I, by taking part in the fight, had knocked one of their friends out of a night's work.

We were led out of the elevator through a rococo hall into an anteroom and told to get into our fighting togs. Each of us was issued a pair of boxing gloves and ushered out into the big mirrored hall, which we entered looking cautiously about us and whispering, lest we might accidentally be heard above the noise of the room. It was foggy with cigar smoke. And already the whiskey was taking effect. I was shocked to see some of the most important men of the town quite tipsy. They were all there — bankers, lawyers, judges, doctors, fire chiefs, teachers, merchants. Even one of the more fashionable pastors. Something we could not see was going on up front. A clarinet was vibrating sensuously and the men were standing up and moving eagerly forward. We were a small tight group, clustered together, our bare upper bodies touching and shining with anticipatory sweat; while up front the big shots were becoming increasingly excited over something we still could not see. Suddenly I heard the school superintendent, who had told me to come, yell, "Bring up the shines, gentlemen! Bring up the little shines!"

We were rushed up to the front of the ballroom, where it smelled even more strongly of tobacco and whiskey. Then we were pushed into place. I almost wet my pants. A sea of faces, some hostile, some amused, ringed around us, and in the center, facing us, stood a magnificent blonde — stark naked. There was dead silence. I felt a blast of cold air chill me. I tried to back away, but they were behind me and around me. Some of the boys stood with lowered heads, trembling. I felt a wave of irrational guilt and fear. My teeth chattered, my skin turned to goose flesh, my knees knocked. Yet I was strongly attracted and looked in spite of myself. Had the price of looking been blindness, I would have looked. The hair was yellow like that of a circus kewpie doll, the face heavily powdered and rouged, as though to form an abstract mask, the eyes hollow and smeared a cool blue, the color of a baboon's butt. I felt a desire to spit upon her as my eyes brushed slowly over her body. Her breasts were firm and round as the domes of East Indian temples, and I stood so close as to see the fine skin texture and beads of pearly perspiration glistening like dew around the pink and erected buds of her nipples. I wanted at one and the same time to run from the room, to sink through the floor, or go to her and cover her from my eyes and the eyes of the others with my body; to feel the soft thighs, to caress her and destroy her, to love her and murder her, to hide from her, and yet to stroke where below the small American flag tattooed upon her belly her thighs formed a capital V. I had a notion that of all in the room she saw only me with her impersonal eyes.

And then she began to dance, a slow sensuous movement; the smoke of a hundred cigars clinging to her like the thinnest of veils. She seemed like a fair bird-girl girdled in veils calling to me from the angry surface of some gray and threatening sea. I was transported. Then I became aware of the clarinet playing and the big shots yelling at us. Some threatened us if we looked and others if we did not. On my right I saw one boy faint. And now a man grabbed a silver pitcher from a table and stepped close as he dashed ice water upon him and stood him up and forced two of us to support him as his head hung and moans issued from his thick bluish lips. Another boy began to plead to go home. He was the largest of the group, wearing dark red fighting trunks much too small to conceal the erection which projected from him as though in answer to the insinuating low-registered moaning of the clarinet. He tried to hide himself with his boxing gloves.

And all the while the blonde continued dancing, smiling faintly at the big shots who watched her with fascination, and faintly smiling at our fear.

I noticed a certain merchant who followed her hungrily, his lips loose and drooling. He was a large man who wore diamond studs in a shirtfront which swelled with the ample paunch underneath, and each time the blonde swayed her undulating hips he ran his hand through the thin hair of his bald head and, with his arms upheld, his posture clumsy like that of an intoxicated panda, wound his belly in a slow and obscene grind. This creature was completely hypnotized. The music had quickened. As the dancer flung herself about with a detached expression on her face, the men began reaching out to touch her. I could see their beefy fingers sink into her soft flesh. Some of the others tried to stop them and she began to move around the floor in graceful circles, as they gave chase, slipping and sliding over the polished floor. It was mad. Chairs went crashing, drinks were spilt, as they ran laughing and howling after her. They caught her just as she reached a door, raised her from the floor, and tossed her as college boys are tossed at a hazing, and above her red fixed-smiling lips I saw the terror and disgust in her eyes, almost like my own terror and that which I saw in some of the other boys. As I watched, they tossed her twice and her soft breasts seemed to flatten against the air and her legs flung wildly as she spun. Some of the more sober ones helped her to escape. And I started off the floor, heading for the anteroom with the rest of the boys.

Some were still crying and in hysteria. But as we tried to leave we were stopped and ordered to get into the ring. There was nothing to do but what we were told. All ten of us climbed under the ropes and allowed ourselves to be blindfolded with broad bands of white cloth. One of the men seemed to feel a bit sympathetic and tried to cheer us up as we stood with our backs against the ropes. Some of us tried to grin. "See that boy over there?" one of the men said. "I want you to run across at the bell and give it to him right in the belly. If you don't get him, I'm going to get you. I don't like his looks." Each of us was told the same. The blindfolds were put on. Yet even then I had been going over my speech. In my mind each word was as bright as flame. I felt the cloth pressed into place, and frowned so that it would be loosened when I relaxed. 10

But now I felt a sudden fit of blind terror. I was unused to darkness. It was as though I had suddenly found myself in a dark room filled with poisonous cottonmouths. I could hear the bleary voices yelling insistently for the battle royal to begin.

"Get going in there!"

"Let me at that big nigger!"

I strained to pick up the school superintendent's voice, as though to squeeze some security out of that slightly more familiar sound.

"Let me at those black sonsabitches!" someone yelled. 15

"No, Jackson, no!" another voice yelled. "Here, somebody, help me hold Jack."

"I want to get at that ginger-colored nigger. Tear him limb from limb," the first voice yelled.

I stood against the ropes trembling. For in those days I was what they called ginger-colored, and he sounded as though he might crunch me between his teeth like a crisp ginger cookie.

Quite a struggle was going on. Chairs were being kicked about and I could hear voices grunting as with a terrific effort. I wanted to see, to see more desperately than ever before. But the blindfold was as tight as a thick skin-puckering scab and when I raised my gloved hands to push the layers of white aside a voice yelled, "Oh, no you don't, black bastard! Leave that alone!"

"Ring the bell before Jackson kills him a coon!" someone boomed in the 20 sudden silence. And I heard the bell clang and the sound of the feet scuffling forward.

A glove smacked against my head. I pivoted, striking out stiffly as some-one went past, and felt the jar ripple along the length of my arm to my shoulder. Then it seemed as though all nine of the boys had turned upon me at once. Blows pounded me from all sides while I struck out as best I could. So many blows landed upon me that I wondered if I were not the only blindfolded fighter in the ring, or if the man called Jackson hadn't succeeded in getting me after all.

Blindfolded, I could no longer control my motions. I had no dignity. I stumbled about like a baby or a drunken man. The smoke had become thicker and with each new blow it seemed to sear and further restrict my lungs. My saliva became like hot bitter glue. A glove connected with my head, filling my mouth with warm blood. It was everywhere. I could not tell if the moisture I felt upon my body was sweat or blood. A blow landed hard against the nape of my neck. I felt myself going over, my head hitting the floor. Streaks of blue light filled the black world behind the blindfold. I lay prone, pretending that I was knocked out, but felt myself seized by hands and yanked to my feet. "Get going, black boy! Mix it up!" My arms were like lead, my head smarting from blows. I managed to feel my way to the ropes and held on, trying to catch my breath. A glove landed in my mid-section and I went over again, feeling as though the smoke had become a knife jabbed into my guts. Pushed this way and that by the legs milling around me, I finally pulled erect and discovered that I could see the black, sweat-washed forms weaving in the smoky-blue atmosphere like drunken dancers weaving to the rapid drum-like thuds of blows.

Everyone fought hysterically. It was complete anarchy. Everybody fought everybody else. No group fought together for long. Two, three, four, fought one, then turned to fight each other, were themselves attacked. Blows landed below the belt and in the kidney, with the gloves open as well as closed, and with my eye partly opened now there was not so much terror. I moved carefully, avoiding blows, although not too many to attract attention, fighting from group to group. The boys groped about like blind, cautious crabs crouching to protect their mid-sections, their heads pulled in short against their shoulders, their arms stretched nervously before them, with their fists testing the smoke-filled air like the knobbed feelers of hypersensitive snails. In one corner I glimpsed a boy violently punching the air and heard him scream in pain as he smashed his hand against a ring post. For a second I saw him bent over holding his hand, then going down as a blow caught his unprotected head. I played one group against the other, slipping in and throwing a punch then stepping out of range while pushing the others into the melee to take the blows blindly aimed at me. The smoke was agonizing and there were no rounds, no bells at three minute intervals to relieve our exhaustion. The room spun round me, a swirl of lights, smoke, sweating bodies surrounded by tense white faces. I bled from both nose and mouth, the blood spattering upon my chest.

The men kept yelling, "Slug him, black boy! Knock his guts out!"

"Uppercut him! Kill him! Kill that big boy!"                                                   25

Taking a fake fall, I saw a boy going down heavily beside me as though we were felled by a single blow, saw a sneaker-clad foot shoot into his groin as the two who had knocked him down stumbled upon him. I rolled out of range, feeling a twinge of nausea.

The harder we fought the more threatening the men became. And yet, I had begun to worry about my speech again. How would it go? Would they recognize my ability? What would they give me?

I was fighting automatically and suddenly I noticed that one after another of the boys was leaving the ring. I was surprised, filled with panic, as though I had been left alone with an unknown danger. Then I understood. The boys had arranged it among themselves. It was the custom for the two men left in the ring to slug it out for the winner's prize. I discovered this too late. When the bell sounded two men in tuxedoes leaped into the ring and removed the blindfold. I found myself facing Tatlock, the biggest of the gang. I felt sick at my stomach. Hardly had the bell stopped ringing in my ears than it clanged again and I saw him moving swiftly toward me. Thinking of nothing else to do I hit him smash on the nose. He kept coming, bringing the rank sharp violence of stale sweat. His face was a black blank of a face, only his eyes alive — with hate of me and aglow with a feverish terror from what had happened to us all. I became anxious. I wanted to deliver my speech and he came at me as though he meant to beat it out of me. I smashed him again and again, taking his blows as they came. Then on a sudden impulse I struck him lightly and as we clinched, I whispered, "Fake like I knocked you out, you can have the prize."

"I'll break your behind," he whispered hoarsely.

"For *them*?"                                                                                   30

"For *me*, sonofabitch!"

They were yelling for us to break it up and Tatlock spun me half around with a blow, and as a joggled camera sweeps in a reeling scene, I saw the howling red faces crouching tense beneath the cloud of blue-gray smoke. For a moment the world wavered, unraveled, flowed, then my head cleared and Tatlock bounced before me. That fluttering shadow before my eyes was his jabbing left hand. Then falling forward, my head against his damp shoulder, I whispered,

"I'll make it five dollars more."

"Go to hell!"

But his muscles relaxed a trifle beneath my pressure and I breathed, "Seven!"   35

"Give it to your ma," he said, ripping me beneath the heart.

And while I still held him I butted him and moved away. I felt myself bombarded with punches. I fought back with hopeless desperation. I wanted to deliver my speech more than anything else in the world, because I felt that only these men could judge truly my ability, and now this stupid clown was ruining my chances. I began fighting carefully now, moving in to punch him and out again with my greater speed. A lucky blow to his chin and I had him going too — until I heard a loud voice yell, "I got my money on the big boy."

Hearing this, I almost dropped my guard. I was confused: Should I try to win against the voice out there? Would not this go against my speech, and was not this a moment for humility, for nonresistance? A blow to my head as I danced about sent my right eye popping like a jack-in-the-box and settled my dilemma. The room went red as I fell. It was a dream fall, my body languid and fastidious as to where to land, until the floor became impatient and smashed up to meet me. A moment later I came to. An hypnotic voice said FIVE emphatically. And I lay there, hazily watching a dark red spot of my own blood shaping itself into a butterfly, glistening and soaking into the soiled gray world of the canvas.

When the voice drawled TEN I was lifted up and dragged to a chair. I sat dazed. My eye pained and swelled with each throb of my pounding heart and I wondered if now I would be allowed to speak. I was wringing wet, my mouth still bleeding. We were grouped along the wall now. The other boys ignored me as they congratulated Tatlock and speculated as to how much they would be paid. One boy whimpered over his smashed hand. Looking up front, I saw attendants in white jackets rolling the portable ring away and placing a small square rug in the vacant space surrounded by chairs. Perhaps, I thought, I will stand on the rug to deliver my speech.

Then the M.C. called to us, "Come on up here boys and get your money." 40

We ran forward to where the men laughed and talked in their chairs, waiting. Everyone seemed friendly now.

"There it is on the rug," the man said. I saw the rug covered with coins of all dimensions and a few crumpled bills. But what excited me, scattered here and there, were the gold pieces.

"Boys, it's all yours," the man said. "You get all you grab."

"That's right, Sambo," a blond man said, winking at me confidentially.

I trembled with excitement, forgetting my pain. I would get the gold and the 45 bills, I thought. I would use both hands. I would throw my body against the boys nearest me to block them from the gold.

"Get down around the rug now," the man commanded, "and don't anyone touch it until I give the signal."

"This ought to be good," I heard.

As told, we got around the square rug on our knees. Slowly the man raised his freckled hand as we followed it upward with our eyes.

I heard, "These niggers look like they're about to pray!"

Then, "Ready," the man said. "Go!" 50

I lunged for a yellow coin lying on the blue design of the carpet, touching it and sending a surprised shriek to join those rising around me. I tried frantically to remove my hand but could not let go. A hot, violent force tore through my body, shaking me like a wet rat. The rug was electrified. The hair bristled up on my head as I shook myself free. My muscles jumped, my nerves jangled, writhed. But I saw that this was not stopping the other boys. Laughing in fear and embarrassment, some were holding back and scooping up the coins knocked off by the painful contortions of the others. The men roared above us as we struggled.

"Pick it up, goddamnit, pick it up!" someone called like a bass-voiced parrot. "Go on, get it!"

I crawled rapidly around the floor, picking up the coins, trying to avoid the coppers and to get greenbacks and the gold. Ignoring the shock by laughing, as I brushed the coins off quickly, I discovered that I could contain the electricity — a contradiction, but it works. Then the men began to push us onto the rug. Laughing embarrassedly, we struggled out of their hands and kept after the coins. We were all wet and slippery and hard to hold. Suddenly I saw a boy lifted into the air, glistening with sweat like a circus seal, and dropped, his wet back landing flush upon the charged rug, heard him yell and saw him literally dance upon his back, his elbows beating a frenzied tatoo upon the floor, his muscles twitching like the flesh of a horse stung by many flies. When he finally rolled off, his face was gray and no one stopped him when he ran from the floor amid booming laughter.

"Get the money," the M.C. called. "That's good hard American cash!"

And we snatched and grabbed, snatched and grabbed. I was careful not to 55 come too close to the rug now, and when I felt the hot whiskey breath descend upon me like a cloud of foul air I reached out and grabbed the leg of a chair. It was occupied and I held on desperately.

"Leggo, nigger! Leggo!"

The huge face wavered down to mine as he tried to push me free. But my body was slippery and he was too drunk. It was Mr. Colcord, who owned a chain of movie houses and "entertainment palaces." Each time he grabbed me I slipped out of his hands. It became a real struggle. I feared the rug more than I did the drunk, so I held on, surprising myself for a moment by trying to topple *him* upon the rug. It was such an enormous idea that I found myself actually carrying it out. I tried not to be obvious, yet when I grabbed his leg, trying to tumble him out of the chair, he raised up roaring with laughter, and, looking at me with soberness dead in the eye, kicked me viciously in the chest. The chair leg flew out of my hand. I felt myself going and rolled. It was as though I had rolled through a bed of hot coals. It seemed a whole century would pass before I would roll free, a century in which I was seared through the deepest levels of my body to the fearful breath within me and the breath seared and heated to the point of explosion. It'll all be over in a flash, I thought as I rolled clear. It'll all be over in a flash.

But not yet, the men on the other side were waiting, red faces swollen as though from apoplexy as they bent forward in their chairs. Seeing their fingers coming toward me I rolled away as a fumbled football rolls off the receiver's fingertips, back into the coals. That time I luckily sent the rug sliding out of place and heard the coins ringing against the floor and the boys scuffling to pick them up and the M.C. calling, "All right, boys, that's all. Go get dressed and get your money."

I was limp as a dish rag. My back felt as though it had been beaten with wires.

When we had dressed the M.C. came in and gave us each five dollars, except 60 Tatlock, who got ten for being last in the ring. Then he told us to leave. I was not to get a chance to deliver my speech, I thought. I was going out into the dim alley in despair when I was stopped and told to go back. I returned to the ballroom, where the men were pushing back their chairs and gathering in groups to talk.

The M.C. knocked on a table for quiet. "Gentlemen," he said, "we almost forgot an important part of the program. A most serious part, gentlemen. This boy was brought here to deliver a speech which he made at his graduation yesterday. . . ."

"Bravo!"

"I'm told that he is the smartest boy we've got out there in Greenwood. I'm told that he knows more big words than a pocket-sized dictionary."

Much applause and laughter.

"So now, gentlemen, I want you to give him your attention." 65

There was still laughter as I faced them, my mouth dry, my eye throbbing. I began slowly, but evidently my throat was tense, because they began shouting, "Louder! Louder!"

"We of the younger generation extol the wisdom of that great leader and educator," I shouted, "who first spoke these flaming words of wisdom: 'A ship lost at sea for many days suddenly sighted a friendly vessel. From the mast of the unfortunate vessel was seen a signal: "Water, water; we die of thirst!" The answer from the friendly vessel came back: "Cast down your bucket where you are." The captain of the distressed vessel, at last heeding the injunction, cast down his bucket, and it came up full of fresh sparkling water from the mouth of the Amazon River.' And like him I say, and in his words, 'To those of my race who depend upon bettering their condition in a foreign land, or who underestimate the importance of cultivating friendly relations with the Southern white man, who is his next-door neighbor, I would say: "Cast down your bucket where you are" — cast it down in making friends in every manly way of the people of all races by whom we are surrounded. . . .'"

I spoke automatically and with such fervor that I did not realize that the men were still talking and laughing until my dry mouth, filling up with blood from the cut, almost strangled me. I coughed, wanting to stop and go to one of the tall brass, sand-filled spittoons to relieve myself, but a few of the men, especially the superintendent, were listening and I was afraid. So I gulped it down, blood, saliva, and all, and continued. (What powers of endurance I had during those days! What enthusiasm! What a belief in the rightness of things!) I spoke even louder in spite of the pain. But still they talked and still they laughed, as though deaf with cotton in dirty ears. So I spoke with greater emotional emphasis. I closed my ears and swallowed blood until I was nauseated.

The speech seemed a hundred times as long as before, but I could not leave out a single word. All had to be said, each memorized nuance considered, rendered. Nor was that all. Whenever I uttered a word of three or more syllables a group of voices would yell for me to repeat it. I used the phrase "social responsibility" and they yelled:

"What's the word you say, boy?"

"Social responsibility," I said. 70

"What?"

"Social . . ."

"Louder."

". . . responsibility."

"More!" 75

"Respon —"

"Repeat!"

" — sibility."

The room filled with the uproar of laughter until, no doubt, distracted by having to gulp down my blood, I made a mistake and yelled a phrase I had often seen denounced in newspaper editorials, heard debated in private.

"Social . . ." 80

"What?" they yelled.

". . . equality —"

The laughter hung smokelike in the sudden stillness. I opened my eyes, puzzled. Sounds of displeasure filled the room. The M.C. rushed forward. They shouted hostile phrases at me. But I did not understand.

A small dry mustached man in the front row blared out, "Say that slowly, son!"

"What sir?" 85

"What you just said!"

"Social responsibility, sir," I said.

"You weren't being smart, were you, boy?" he said, not unkindly.

"No, sir!"

"You sure that about 'equality' was a mistake?" 90

"Oh, yes, sir," I said. "I was swallowing blood."

"Well, you had better speak more slowly so we can understand. We mean to do right by you, but you've got to know your place at all times. All right, now, go on with your speech."

I was afraid. I wanted to leave but I wanted also to speak and I was afraid they'd snatch me down.

"Thank you, sir," I said, beginning where I had left off, and having them ignore me as before.

Yet when I finished there was a thunderous applause. I was surprised to see 95 the superintendent come forth with a package wrapped in white tissue paper, and, gesturing for quiet, address the men.

"Gentlemen, you see that I did not overpraise this boy. He makes a good speech and some day he'll lead his people in the proper paths. And I don't have to tell you that that is important in these days and times. This is a good, smart boy, and so to encourage him in the right direction, in the name of the Board of Education I wish to present him a prize in the form of this . . ."

He paused, removing the tissue paper and revealing a gleaming calfskin brief case.

". . . in the form of this first-class article from Shad Whitmore's shop."

"Boy," he said, addressing me, "take this prize and keep it well. Consider it a badge of office. Prize it. Keep developing as you are and some day it will be filled with important papers that will help shape the destiny of your people."

I was so moved that I could hardly express my thanks. A rope of bloody   100 saliva forming a shape like an undiscovered continent drooled upon the leather and I wiped it quickly away. I felt an importance that I had never dreamed.

"Open it and see what's inside," I was told.

My fingers a-tremble, I complied, smelling the fresh leather and finding an official-looking document inside. It was a scholarship to the state college for Negroes. My eyes filled with tears and I ran awkwardly off the floor.

I was overjoyed; I did not even mind when I discovered that the gold pieces I had scrambled for were brass pocket tokens advertising a certain make of automobile.

When I reached home everyone was excited. Next day the neighbors came to congratulate me. I even felt safe from grandfather, whose deathbed curse usually spoiled my triumphs. I stood beneath his photograph with my brief case in hand and smiled triumphantly into his stolid black peasant's face. It was a face that fascinated me. The eyes seemed to follow everywhere I went.

That night I dreamed I was at a circus with him and that he refused to   105 laugh at the clowns no matter what they did. Then later he told me to open my brief case and read what was inside and I did, finding an official envelope stamped with the state seal; and inside the envelope I found another and another, endlessly, and I thought I would fall of weariness. "Them's years," he said. "Now open that one." And I did and in it I found an engraved document containing a short message in letters of gold. "Read it," my grandfather said. "Out loud."

"To Whom It May Concern," I intoned. "Keep This Nigger-Boy Running."

I awoke with the old man's laughter ringing in my ears.

(It was a dream I was to remember and dream again for many years after. But at the time I had no insight into its meaning. First I had to attend college.)

**FOR ANALYSIS**

**1.** What phrase does the **narrator** inadvertently utter, causing the room to go quiet? Why does it have such an effect?

**2.** Why is it significant that the naked woman in the story is white?

**3.** The meaning of the grandfather's last words, recounted at the story's opening, are ambiguous; the narrator even says, "I could never be sure of what he meant" (para. 3). Does the meaning become clearer by the end of the story? What do you think it is, and how is it revealed?

## MAKING ARGUMENTS

Construct two arguments — one for and one against the plan of action urged on the narrator's father by his grandfather. Was it good advice? Has it been followed? Has it worked?

## WRITING TOPICS

**1.** Write about the **symbolism** in "Battle Royal." For what might the different objects and different activities stand? How do they fit together? Why do you think Ellison has his **protagonist** see and experience these symbolic things?

**2.** Write a reflective personal essay on invisibility. Possible topics for this essay include ways in which you are invisible, ways in which other people you know or see are invisible, and ways in which you are guilty of not seeing others.

## MAKING CONNECTIONS

**1.** There is much more action in "Battle Royal" than in Bambara's "The Lesson" (p. 100). It is more obvious, then, that Bambara's story is about what its main **character** sees and what she learns from it. How, in spite of Ellison's story's differences, is it like Bambara's? Does the main character learn a lesson? How? What is it?

**2.** Read "Battle Royal" in the context of the connections unit "Voices of Experience" (p. 189). What voices of experience speak in this story, including but not limited to the grandfather? What advice do they give? How is it taken? To which of the poems in "Voices of Experience" is "Battle Royal" most similar? To which is it most different?

## SHIRLEY JACKSON   (1916–1965)

# THE LOTTERY   1948

The morning of June 27th was clear and sunny, with the fresh warmth of a full-summer day; the flowers were blossoming profusely and the grass was richly green. The people of the village began to gather in the square, between the post office and the bank, around ten o'clock; in some towns there were so many people that the lottery took two days and had to be started on June 26th, but in this village, where there were only about three hundred people, the whole lottery took less than two hours, so it could begin at ten o'clock in the morning and still be through in time to allow the villagers to get home for noon dinner.

The children assembled first, of course. School was recently over for the summer, and the feeling of liberty sat uneasily on most of them; they tended to gather together quietly for a while before they broke into boisterous play, and their talk was still of the classroom and the teacher, of books and reprimands. Bobby Martin had already stuffed his pockets full of stones, and the other boys soon followed his example, selecting the smoothest and roundest stones; Bobby and Harry Jones and Dickie Delacroix — the villagers pronounced his name "Dellacroy" — eventually made a great pile of stones in one corner of the square and guarded it against the raids of the other boys. The girls stood aside, talking among themselves, looking over their shoulders at the boys, and the very small children rolled in the dust or clung to the hands of their older brothers or sisters.

Soon the men began to gather, surveying their own children, speaking of planting and rain, tractors and taxes. They stood together, away from the pile of stones in the corner, and their jokes were quiet and they smiled rather than laughed. The women, wearing faded house dresses and sweaters, came shortly after their menfolk. They greeted one another and exchanged bits of gossip as they went to join their husbands. Soon the women, standing by their husbands, began to call to their children, and the children came reluctantly, having to be called four or five times. Bobby Martin ducked under his mother's grasping hand and ran, laughingly, back to the pile of stones. His father spoke up sharply, and Bobby came quickly and took his place, between his father and his oldest brother.

The lottery was conducted — as were the square dances, the teenage club, the Halloween program — by Mr. Summers, who had time and energy to devote to civic activities. He was a round-faced, jovial man and he ran the coal business, and people were sorry for him, because he had no children and his wife was a scold. When he arrived in the square, carrying the black wooden box, there was a murmur of conversation among the villagers, and he waved and called

"Little late today, folks." The postmaster, Mr. Graves, followed him, carrying a three-legged stool, and the stool was put in the center of the square and Mr. Summers set the black box down on it. The villagers kept their distance, leaving a space between themselves and the stool, and when Mr. Summers said, "Some of you fellows want to give me a hand?" there was a hesitation before two men, Mr. Martin and his oldest son, Baxter, came forward to hold the box steady on the stool while Mr. Summers stirred up the papers inside it.

The original paraphernalia for the lottery had been lost long ago, and the 5 black box now resting on the stool had been put into use even before Old Man Warner, the oldest man in town, was born. Mr. Summers spoke frequently to the villagers about making a new box, but no one liked to upset even as much tradition as was represented by the black box. There was a story that the present box had been made with some pieces of the box that had preceded it, the one that had been constructed when the first people settled down to make a village here. Every year, after the lottery, Mr. Summers began talking about a new box, but every year the subject was allowed to fade off without anything's being done. The black box grew shabbier each year; by now it was no longer completely black but splintered badly along one side to show the original wood color, and in some places faded and stained.

Mr. Martin and his oldest son, Baxter, held the black box securely on the stool until Mr. Summers had stirred the papers thoroughly with his hand. Because so much of the ritual had been forgotten or discarded, Mr. Summers had been successful in having slips of paper substituted for the chips of wood that had been used for generations. Chips of wood, Mr. Summers had argued, had been all very well when the village was tiny, but now that the population was more than three hundred and likely to keep on growing, it was necessary to use something that would fit more easily into the black box. The night before the lottery, Mr. Summers and Mr. Graves made up the slips of paper and put them in the box, and it was then taken to the safe of Mr. Summers's coal company and locked up until Mr. Summers was ready to take it to the square the next morning. The rest of the year, the box was put away, sometimes one place, sometimes another; it had spent one year in Mr. Graves's barn and another year underfoot in the post office, and sometimes it was set on a shelf in the Martin grocery and left there.

There was a great deal of fussing to be done before Mr. Summers declared the lottery open. There were the lists to make up — of heads of families, heads of households in each family, members of each household in each family. There was the proper swearing-in of Mr. Summers by the postmaster, as the official of the lottery; at one time, some people remembered, there had been a recital of some sort, performed by the official of the lottery, a perfunctory, tuneless chant that had been rattled off duly each year; some people believed that the official of the lottery used to stand just so when he said or sang it, others believed that he was supposed to walk among the people, but years and years ago this part of the ritual had been allowed to lapse. There had been, also, a ritual salute, which the official of the lottery had had to use in addressing each person who came up to draw from the box, but this also had changed with time, until now it was felt necessary only for the official to speak to each person approaching. Mr. Summers was very good at all this; in his clean white shirt and blue jeans, with one hand resting carelessly on the black box, he seemed very proper and important as he talked interminably to Mr. Graves and the Martins.

Just as Mr. Summers finally left off talking and turned to the assembled villagers, Mrs. Hutchinson came hurriedly along the path to the square, her sweater thrown over her shoulders, and slid into place in the back of the crowd. "Clean forgot what day it was," she said to Mrs. Delacroix, who stood next to her, and they both laughed softly. "Thought my old man was out back stacking wood," Mrs. Hutchinson went on, "and then I looked out the window and the kids were gone, and then I remembered it was the twenty-seventh and came a-running." She dried her hands on her apron, and Mrs. Delacroix said, "You're in time, though. They're still talking away up there."

Mrs. Hutchinson craned her neck to see through the crowd and found her husband and children standing near the front. She tapped Mrs. Delacroix on the arm as a farewell and began to make her way through the crowd. The people separated good-humoredly to let her through; two or three people said, in voices just loud enough to be heard across the crowd, "Here comes your Missus, Hutchinson," and "Bill, she made it after all." Mrs. Hutchinson reached her husband, and Mr. Summers, who had been waiting, said cheerfully, "Thought we were going to have to get on without you, Tessie." Mrs. Hutchinson said, grinning, "Wouldn't have me leave m'dishes in the sink, now, would you, Joe?" and soft laughter ran through the crowd as the people stirred back into position after Mrs. Hutchinson's arrival.

"Well, now," Mr. Summers said soberly, "guess we better get started, get this over with, so's we can go back to work. Anybody ain't here?"  10

"Dunbar," several people said. "Dunbar, Dunbar."

Mr. Summers consulted his list. "Clyde Dunbar," he said. "That's right. He's broke his leg, hasn't he? Who's drawing for him?"

"Me, I guess," a woman said, and Mr. Summers turned to look at her. "Wife draws for her husband," Mr. Summers said. "Don't you have a grown boy to do it for you, Janey?" Although Mr. Summers and everyone else in the village knew the answer perfectly well, it was the business of the official of the lottery to ask such questions formally. Mr. Summers waited with an expression of polite interest while Mrs. Dunbar answered.

"Horace's not but sixteen yet," Mrs. Dunbar said regretfully. "Guess I gotta fill in for the old man this year."

"Right," Mr. Summers said. He made a note on the list he was holding. Then  15 he asked, "Watson boy drawing this year?"

A tall boy in the crowd raised his hand. "Here," he said. "I'm drawing for m'mother and me." He blinked his eyes nervously and ducked his head as several voices in the crowd said things like "Good fellow, Jack," and "Glad to see your mother's got a man to do it."

"Well," Mr. Summers said, "guess that's everyone. Old Man Warner make it?"

"Here," a voice said, and Mr. Summers nodded.

. . .

A sudden hush fell on the crowd as Mr. Summers cleared his throat and looked at the list. "All ready?" he called. "Now, I'll read the names—heads of families first—and the men come up and take a paper out of the box. Keep the paper folded in your hand without looking at it until everyone has had a turn. Everything clear?"

The people had done it so many times that they only half listened to the directions; most of them were quiet, wetting their lips, not looking around. Then Mr. Summers raised one hand high and said, "Adams." A man disengaged himself from the crowd and came forward. "Hi, Steve," Mr. Summers said, and Mr. Adams said, "Hi, Joe." They grinned at one another humorlessly and nervously. Then Mr. Adams reached into the black box and took out a folded paper. He held it firmly by one corner as he turned and went hastily back to his place in the crowd, where he stood a little apart from his family, not looking down at his hand.

"Allen." Mr. Summers said. "Anderson. . . . Betham."

"Seems like there's no time at all between lotteries any more," Mrs. Delacroix said to Mrs. Graves in the back row. "Seems like we got through the last one only last week."

"Time sure goes fast," Mrs. Graves said.

"Clark. . . . Delacroix."

"There goes my old man," Mrs. Delacroix said. She held her breath while her husband went forward.

"Dunbar," Mr. Summers said, and Mrs. Dunbar went steadily to the box while one of the women said, "Go on, Janey," and another said, "There she goes."

"We're next," Mrs. Graves said. She watched while Mr. Graves came around from the side of the box, greeted Mr. Summers gravely, and selected a slip of paper from the box. By now, all through the crowd there were men holding the small folded papers in their large hands, turning them over and over nervously. Mrs. Dunbar and her two sons stood together, Mrs. Dunbar holding the slip of paper.

"Harburt. . . . Hutchinson."

"Get up there, Bill," Mrs. Hutchinson said, and the people near her laughed.

"Jones."

"They do say," Mr. Adams said to Old Man Warner, who stood next to him, "that over in the north village they're talking of giving up the lottery."

Old Man Warner snorted. "Pack of crazy fools," he said. "Listening to the young folks, nothing's good enough for *them*. Next thing you know, they'll be wanting to go back to living in caves, nobody work any more, live *that* way for a while. Used to be a saying about 'Lottery in June, corn be heavy soon.' First thing you know, we'd all be eating stewed chickweed and acorns. There's *always* been a lottery," he added petulantly. "Bad enough to see young Joe Summers up there joking with everybody."

"Some places have already quit lotteries," Mrs. Adams said.

"Nothing but trouble in *that*," Old Man Warner said stoutly. "Pack of young fools."

"Martin." And Bobby Martin watched his father go forward. "Overdyke. . . . 35
Percy."

"I wish they'd hurry," Mrs. Dunbar said to her older son. "I wish they'd hurry."

"They're almost through," her son said.

"You get ready to run tell Dad," Mrs. Dunbar said.

Mr. Summers called his own name and then stepped forward precisely and selected a slip from the box. Then he called, "Warner."

"Seventy-seventh year I been in the lottery," Old Man Warner said as he 40
went through the crowd. "Seventy-seventh time."

"Watson." The tall boy came awkwardly through the crowd. Someone said, "Don't be nervous, Jack," and Mr. Summers said, "Take your time, son."

"Zanini."

After that, there was a long pause, a breathless pause, until Mr. Summers, holding his slip of paper in the air, said, "All right fellows." For a minute, no one moved, and then all the slips of paper were opened. Suddenly, all the women began to speak at once, saying, "Who is it?" "Who's got it?" "Is it the Dunbars?" "Is it the Watsons?" Then the voices began to say, "It's Hutchinson. It's Bill," "Bill Hutchinson's got it."

"Go tell your father," Mrs. Dunbar said to her older son.

People began to look around to see the Hutchinsons. Bill Hutchinson 45
was standing quiet, staring down at the paper in his hand. Suddenly, Tessie Hutchinson shouted to Mr. Summers, "You didn't give him time enough to take any paper he wanted. I saw you. It wasn't fair!"

"Be a good sport, Tessie," Mrs. Delacroix called, and Mrs. Graves said, "All of us took the same chance."

"Shut up, Tessie," Bill Hutchinson said.

"Well, everyone," Mr. Summers said, "That was done pretty fast, and now we've got to be hurrying a little more to get it done in time." He consulted his next list. "Bill," he said, "you draw for the Hutchinson family. You got any other households in the Hutchinsons?"

"There's Don and Eva," Mrs. Hutchinson yelled. "Make *them* take their chance!"

"Daughters draw with their husbands' families, Tessie," Mr. Summers said 50
gently. "You know that as well as anyone else."

"It wasn't *fair*," Tessie said.

"I guess not, Joe," Bill Hutchinson said regretfully. "My daughter draws with her husband's family, that's only fair. And I've got no other family except the kids."

"Then, as far as drawing for families is concerned, it's you," Mr. Summers said in explanation, "and as far as drawing for households is concerned, that's you, too. Right?"

"Right," Bill Hutchinson said.

"How many kids, Bill?" Mr. Summers asked formally.                          55

"Three," Bill Hutchinson said. "There's Bill, Jr., and Nancy, and little Dave. And Tessie and me."

"All right then," Mr. Summers said. "Harry, you got their tickets back?"

Mr. Graves nodded and held up the slips of paper. "Put them in the box, then," Mr. Summers directed. "Take Bill's and put it in."

"I think we ought to start over," Mrs. Hutchinson said, as quietly as she could. "I tell you it wasn't *fair*. You didn't give him time enough to choose. *Every*body saw that."

Mr. Graves had selected the five slips and put them in the box, and he dropped all the papers but those onto the ground, where the breeze caught them and lifted them off. 60

"Listen, everybody," Mrs. Hutchinson was saying to the people around her.

"Ready, Bill?" Mr. Summers asked, and Bill Hutchinson, with one quick glance around at his wife and children, nodded.

"Remember," Mr. Summers said, "take the slips and keep them folded until each person has taken one. Harry, you help little Dave." Mr. Graves took the hand of the little boy, who came willingly with him up to the box. "Take a paper out of the box, Davy," Mr. Summers said. Davy put his hand into the box and laughed. "Take just *one* paper," Mr. Summers said. "Harry, you hold it for him." Mr. Graves took the child's hand and removed the folded paper from the tight fist and held it while little Dave stood next to him and looked up at him wonderingly.

"Nancy next," Mr. Summers said. Nancy was twelve, and her school friends breathed heavily as she went forward, switching her skirt, and took a slip daintily from the box. "Bill, Jr.," Mr. Summers said, and Billy, his face red and his feet over-large, nearly knocked the box over as he got a paper out. "Tessie," Mr. Summers said. She hesitated for a minute, looking around defiantly, and then set her lips and went up to the box. She snatched a paper out and held it behind her.

"Bill," Mr. Summers said, and Bill Hutchinson reached into the box and felt around, bringing his hand out at last with the slip of paper in it. 65

The crowd was quiet. A girl whispered, "I hope it's not Nancy," and the sound of the whisper reached the edges of the crowd.

"It's not the way it used to be," Old Man Warner said clearly. "People ain't the way they used to be."

"All right," Mr. Summers said. "Open the papers. Harry, you open little Dave's."

Mr. Graves opened the slip of paper and there was a general sigh through the crowd as he held it up and everyone could see that it was blank. Nancy and Bill, Jr., opened theirs at the same time, and both beamed and laughed, turning around to the crowd and holding their slips of paper above their heads.

"Tessie," Mr. Summers said. There was a pause, and then Mr. Summers looked at Bill Hutchinson, and Bill unfolded his paper and showed it. It was blank. 70

"It's Tessie," Mr. Summers said, and his voice was hushed. "Show us her paper, Bill."

Bill Hutchinson went over to his wife and forced the slip of paper out of her hand. It had a black spot on it, the black spot Mr. Summers had made the night before with the heavy pencil in the coal-company office. Bill Hutchinson held it up, and there was a stir in the crowd.

"All right, folks," Mr. Summers said. "Let's finish quickly."

Although the villagers had forgotten the ritual and lost the original black box, they still remembered to use stones. The pile of stones the boys had made earlier was ready; there were stones on the ground with the blowing scraps of paper that had come out of the box. Mrs. Delacroix selected a stone so large she had to pick it up with both hands and turned to Mrs. Dunbar. "Come on," she said. "Hurry up."

Mrs. Dunbar had small stones in both hands, and she said, gasping for 75 breath, "I can't run at all. You'll have to go ahead and I'll catch up with you."

The children had stones already, and someone gave little Davy Hutchinson a few pebbles.

Tessie Hutchinson was in the center of a cleared space by now, and she held her hands out desperately as the villagers moved in on her. "It isn't fair," she said. A stone hit her on the side of the head.

Old Man Warner was saying, "Come on, come on, everyone." Steve Adams was in the front of the crowd of villagers, with Mrs. Graves beside him.

"It isn't fair, it isn't right," Mrs. Hutchinson screamed, and then they were upon her.

## FOR ANALYSIS

**1.** What evidence in the story suggests that the lottery is a ritualistic ceremony?

**2.** Does the straightforward narrative **style** describing the holiday atmosphere diminish or intensify the horror of the story's conclusion? Explain.

**3.** Might the story be a comment on religious orthodoxy? Explain.

## MAKING ARGUMENTS

After the 1948 publication of "The Lottery," Jackson and the *New Yorker*, which published it, received hundreds of negative letters, often angry ones. Make an argument for the importance to this reaction of the historical climate in which "The Lottery" was written and read, in particular the Cold War; make reference to historical evidence as well as to textual evidence.

## WRITING TOPICS

**1.** Explain the purpose of the lottery, and identify contemporary rituals that exhibit similar purposes.

**2.** Magic and religion differ because magicians can compel change whereas priests can only ask for change. Comment on this distinction. Can you identify magical elements in religion?

## MAKING CONNECTIONS

Compare this story with Leslie Marmon Silko's "The Man to Send Rain Clouds" (p. 873). What similarities do you find? What differences?

## HARLAN ELLISON® (B. 1934)

# "REPENT, HARLEQUIN!" SAID THE TICKTOCKMAN 1965

There are always those who ask, what is it all about? For those who need to ask, for those who need points sharply made, who need to know "where it's at," this:

*The mass of men serve the state thus, not as men mainly, but as machines, with their bodies. They are the standing army, and the militia, jailors, constables, posse comitatus, etc. In most cases there is no free exercise whatever of the judgment or of the moral sense; but they put themselves on a level with wood and earth and stones; and wooden men can perhaps be manufactured that will serve the purpose as well. Such command no more respect than men of straw or a lump of dirt. They have the same sort of worth only as horses and dogs. Yet such as these even are commonly esteemed good citizens. Others — as most legislators, politicians, lawyers, ministers, and officeholders — serve the state chiefly with their heads; and, as they rarely make any moral distinctions, they are as likely to serve the Devil, without intending it, as God. A very few, as heroes, patriots, martyrs, reformers in the great sense, and men, serve the state with their consciences also, and so necessarily resist it for the most part; and they are commonly treated as enemies by it.*

Henry David Thoreau
CIVIL DISOBEDIENCE

That is the heart of it. Now begin in the middle, and later learn the beginning; the end will take care of itself.

But because it was the very world it was, the very world they had allowed it to *become*, for months his activities did not come to the alarmed attention of The Ones Who Kept The Machine Functioning Smoothly, the ones who poured the very best butter over the cams and mainsprings of the culture. Not until it had become obvious that somehow, someway, he had become a notoriety, a celebrity, perhaps even a hero for (what Officialdom inescapably tagged) "an emotionally disturbed segment of the populace," did they turn it over to the Ticktockman and his legal machinery. But by then, because it was the very world it was, and they had no way to predict he would happen — possibly a strain of disease long-defunct, now, suddenly, reborn in a system where immunity had been forgotten, had lapsed — he had been allowed to become too real. Now he had form and substance.

He had become a *personality*, something they had filtered out of the system many decades before. But there it was, and there *he* was, a very definitely imposing personality. In certain circles — middle-class circles — it was thought disgusting. Vulgar ostentation. Anarchistic. Shameful. In others, there was only sniggering: those strata where thought is subjugated to form and ritual, niceties, proprieties. But down below, ah, down below, where the people always needed their saints and sinners, their bread and circuses, their heroes and villains, he was considered a Bolivar; a Napoleon; a Robin Hood; a Dick Bong (Ace of Aces); a Jesus; a Jomo Kenyatta.

And at the top — where, like socially-attuned Shipwreck Kellys, every tremor 5 and vibration threatening to dislodge the wealthy, powerful and titled from their flagpoles — he was considered a menace; a heretic; a rebel; a disgrace; a peril. He was known down the line, to the very heartmeat core, but the important reactions were high above and far below. At the very top, at the very bottom.

So his file was turned over, along with his time-card and his cardioplate, to the office of the Ticktockman.

The Ticktockman: very much over six feet tall, often silent, a soft purring man when things went timewise. The Ticktockman.

Even in the cubicles of the hierarchy, where fear was generated, seldom suffered, he was called the Ticktockman. But no one called him that to his mask.

You don't call a man a hated name, not when that man, behind his mask, is capable of revoking the minutes, the hours, the days and nights, the years of your life. He was called the Master Timekeeper to his mask. It was safer that way.

"This is *what* he is," said the Ticktockman with genuine softness, "but not 10 *who* he is. This time-card I'm holding in my left hand has a name on it, but it is the name of *what* he is, not *who* he is. The cardioplate here in my right hand is also named, but not *whom* named, merely *what* named. Before I can exercise proper revocation, I have to know *who* this *what* is."

To his staff, all the ferrets, all the loggers, all the finks, all the commex, even the mineez, he said, "Who is this Harlequin?"

He was not purring smoothly. Timewise, it was jangle.

However, it *was* the longest speech they had ever heard him utter at one time, the staff, the ferrets, the loggers, the finks, the commex, but not the mineez, who usually weren't around to know, in any case. But even they scurried to find out.

Who is the Harlequin?

High above the third level of the city, he crouched on the humming 15 aluminum-frame platform of the air-boat (foof! air-boat, indeed! swizzleskid is what it was, with a tow-rack jerry-rigged) and he stared down at the neat Mondrian arrangement of the buildings.

Somewhere nearby, he could hear the metronomic left-right-left of the 2:47 PM shift, entering the Timkin roller-bearing plant in their sneakers. A minute later, precisely, he heard the softer right-left-right of the 5:00 AM formation, going home.

An elfin grin spread across his tanned features, and his dimples appeared for a moment. Then, scratching at his thatch of auburn hair, he shrugged within his motley, as though girding himself for what came next, and threw the joy-stick forward, and bent into the wind as the air-boat dropped. He skimmed over a slidewalk, purposely dropping a few feet to crease the tassels of the ladies of fashion, and — inserting thumbs in large ears — he stuck out his tongue, rolled his eyes, and went wugga-wugga-wugga. It was a minor diversion. One pedestrian skittered and tumbled, sending parcels everywhichway, another wet herself, a third keeled slantwise and the walk was stopped automatically by the servitors till she could be resuscitated. It was a minor diversion.

Then he swirled away on a vagrant breeze, and was gone. Hi-ho. As he rounded the cornice of the Time-Motion Study Building, he saw the shift, just boarding the slidewalk. With practiced motion and an absolute conservation of movement, they sidestepped up onto the slow-strip and (in a chorus line reminiscent of a Busby Berkeley film of the antediluvian 1930s) advanced across the strips ostrich-walking till they were lined up on the expresstrip.

Once more, in anticipation, the elfin grin spread, and there was a tooth missing back there on the left side. He dipped, skimmed, and swooped over them; and then, scrunching about on the air-boat, he released the holding pins that fastened shut the ends of the home-made pouring troughs that kept his cargo from dumping prematurely. And as he pulled the trough-pins, the air-boat slid over the factory workers and one hundred and fifty thousand dollars' worth of jelly beans cascaded down on the expresstrip.

Jelly beans! Millions and billions of purples and yellows and greens and 20 licorice and grape and raspberry and mint and round and smooth and crunchy outside and soft-mealy inside and sugary and bouncing jouncing tumbling clittering clattering skittering fell on the heads and shoulders and hardhats and carapaces of the Timkin workers, tinkling on the slidewalk and bouncing away and rolling about underfoot and filling the sky on their way down with all the colors of joy and childhood and holidays, coming down in a steady rain, a solid wash, a torrent of color and sweetness out of the sky from above, and entering a universe of sanity and metronomic order with quite-mad coocoo newness. Jelly beans!

The shift workers howled and laughed and were pelted, and broke ranks, and the jelly beans managed to work their way into the mechanism of the slidewalks after which there was a hideous scraping as the sound of a million fingernails rasped down a quarter of a million blackboards, followed by a coughing and a sputtering, and then the slidewalks all stopped and everyone was dumped thisawayandthataway in a jackstraw tumble, still laughing and popping little jelly bean eggs of childish color into their mouths. It was a holiday, and a jollity, an absolute insanity, a giggle. But . . .

The shift was delayed seven minutes.

They did not get home for seven minutes.

The master schedule was thrown off by seven minutes.

Quotas were delayed by inoperative slidewalks for seven minutes. 25

He had tapped the first domino in the line, and one after another, like chik chik chik, the others had fallen.

The System had been seven minutes' worth of disrupted. It was a tiny matter, one hardly worthy of note, but in a society where the single driving force was order and unity and equality and promptness and clocklike precision and attention to the clock, reverence of the gods of the passage of time, it was a disaster of major importance.

So he was ordered to appear before the Ticktockman. It was broadcast across every channel of the communications web. He was ordered to be *there* at 7:00 dammit on time. And they waited, and they waited, but he didn't show up till almost ten-thirty, at which time he merely sang a little song about moonlight in a place no one had ever heard of, called Vermont, and vanished again. But they had all been waiting since seven, and it wrecked *hell* with their schedules. So the question remained: Who is the Harlequin?

But the *unasked* question (more important of the two) was: how did we get *into* this position, where a laughing, irresponsible japer of jabberwocky and jive could disrupt our entire economic and cultural life with a hundred and fifty thousand dollars' worth of jelly beans . . .

*Jelly* for God's sake *beans*! This is madness! Where did he get the money to 30 buy a hundred and fifty thousand dollars' worth of jelly beans? (They knew it would have cost that much, because they had a team of Situation Analysts pulled off another assignment, and rushed to the slidewalk scene to sweep up and count the candies, and produce findings, which disrupted *their* schedules and threw their entire branch at least a day behind.) Jelly beans! Jelly . . . *beans*? Now wait a second—a second accounted for—no one has manufactured jelly beans for over a hundred years. Where did he get jelly beans?

That's another good question. More than likely it will never be answered to your complete satisfaction. But then, how many questions ever are?

The middle you know. Here is the beginning. How it starts:

A DESK PAD. DAY FOR DAY, AND TURN EACH DAY. 9:00—OPEN THE MAIL. 9:45—APPOINTMENT WITH PLANNING COMMISSION BOARD. 10:30—DISCUSS INSTALLATION PROGRESS CHARTS WITH J.L. 11:45—PRAY FOR RAIN. 12:00—LUNCH. *AND SO IT GOES.*

"I'm sorry, Miss Grant, but the time for interviews was set at 2:30, and it's almost five now. I'm sorry you're late, but those are the rules. You'll have to wait till next year to submit application for this college again." *And so it goes.*

The 10:10 local stops at Cresthaven, Galesville, Tonawanda Junction, Selby, and 35 Farnhurst, but not at Indiana City, Lucasville and Colton, except on Sunday. The 10:35 express stops at Galesville, Selby, and Indiana City, except on Sundays & Holidays, at which time it stops at . . . *and so it goes.*

"I couldn't wait, Fred. I had to be at Pierre Cartain's by 3:00, and you said you'd meet me under the clock in the terminal at 2:45, and you weren't there, so I had to go on. You're always late, Fred. If you'd been there, we could have sewed it up together, but as it was, well, I took the order alone . . ." *And so it goes.*

Dear Mr. and Mrs. Atterley: In reference to your son Gerold's constant tardiness, I am afraid we will have to suspend him from school unless some more reliable method can be instituted guaranteeing he will arrive at his classes on time. Granted he is an exemplary student, and his marks are high, his constant flouting of the schedules of this school makes it impractical to maintain him in a system where the other children seem capable of getting where they are supposed to be on time *and so it goes.*

YOU CANNOT VOTE UNLESS YOU APPEAR AT 8:45 AM.

"I don't care if the script is *good*, I need it Thursday!"

**CHECK-OUT TIME IS 2:00 PM.**                                    40

"You got here late. The job's taken. Sorry."

YOUR SALARY HAS BEEN DOCKED FOR TWENTY MINUTES TIME LOST.

"God, what time is it, I've gotta run!"

And so it goes. And so it goes. And so it goes. And so it goes goes goes goes goes tick tock tick tock tick tock and one day we no longer let time serve us, we serve time and we are slaves of the schedule, worshippers of the sun's passing, bound into a life predicated on restrictions because the system will not function if we don't keep the schedule tight.

Until it becomes more than a minor inconvenience to be late. It becomes a  45 sin. Then a crime. Then a crime punishable by this:

> EFFECTIVE 15 JULY 2389 12:00:00 midnight, the office of the Master Timekeeper will require all citizens to submit their time-cards and cardioplates for processing. In accordance with Statute 555-7-SGH-999 governing the revocation of time per capita, all cardioplates will be keyed to the individual holder and —

What they had done was devise a method of curtailing the amount of life a person could have. If he was ten minutes late, he lost ten minutes of his life. An hour was proportionately worth more revocation. If someone was consistently tardy, he might find himself, on a Sunday night, receiving a communiqué from the Master Timekeeper that his time had run out, and he would be "turned off" at high noon on Monday, please straighten your affairs, sir, madame, or bisex.

And so, by this simple scientific expedient (utilizing a scientific process held dearly secret by the Ticktockman's office) the System was maintained. It was the only expedient thing to do. It was, after all, patriotic. The schedules had to be met. After all, there *was* a war on!

But, wasn't there always?

"Now that is really disgusting," the Harlequin said, when Pretty Alice 50
showed him the wanted poster. "Disgusting and *highly* improbable. After all,
this isn't the Day of the Desperado. A *wanted* poster!"

"You know," Pretty Alice noted, "you speak with a great deal of inflection."

"I'm sorry," said the Harlequin, humbly.

"No need to be sorry. You're always saying 'I'm sorry.' You have such massive
guilt, Everett, it's really very sad."

"I'm sorry," he said again, then pursed his lips so the dimples appeared
momentarily. He hadn't wanted to say that at all. "I have to go out again. I have
to *do* something."

Pretty Alice slammed her coffee-bulb down on the counter. "Oh for God's 55
*sake*, Everett, can't you stay home just *one* night! Must you always be out in that
ghastly clown suit, running around an*noy*ing people?"

"I'm —" He stopped, and clapped the jester's hat onto his auburn thatch with
a tiny tinkling of bells. He rose, rinsed out his coffee-bulb at the spray, and put
it into the dryer for a moment. "I have to go."

She didn't answer. The faxbox was purring, and she pulled a sheet out,
read it, threw it toward him on the counter. "It's about you. Of course. You're
ridiculous."

He read it quickly. It said the Ticktockman was trying to locate him. He
didn't care, he was going out to be late again. At the door, dredging for an exit
line, he hurled back petulantly, "Well, *you* speak with inflection, *too*!"

Pretty Alice rolled her pretty eyes heavenward. "You're ridiculous."

The Harlequin stalked out, slamming the door, which sighed shut softly, 60
and locked itself.

There was a gentle knock, and Pretty Alice got up with an exhalation of
exasperated breath, and opened the door. He stood there. "I'll be back about
ten-thirty, okay?"

She pulled a rueful face. "Why do you tell me that? Why? You *know* you'll be
late! You *know* it! You're *always* late, so why do you tell me these dumb things?"
She closed the door.

On the other side, the Harlequin nodded to himself. *She's right. She's always
right. I'll be late. I'm always late. Why* do *I tell her these dumb things?*

He shrugged again, and went off to be late once more.

He had fired off the firecracker rockets that said: I will attend the 115th 65
annual International Medical Association Invocation at 8:00 PM precisely. I do
hope you will all be able to join me.

The words had burned in the sky, and of course the authorities were there,
lying in wait for him. They assumed, naturally, that he would be late. He
arrived twenty minutes early, while they were setting up the spiderwebs to trap
and hold him. Blowing a large bullhorn, he frightened and unnerved them so,
their own moisturized encirclement webs sucked closed, and they were hauled
up, kicking and shrieking, high above the amphitheater's floor. The Harlequin
laughed and laughed, and apologized profusely. The physicians, gathered in

solemn conclave, roared with laughter, and accepted the Harlequin's apologies with exaggerated bowing and posturing, and a merry time was had by all, who thought the Harlequin was a regular foofaraw in fancy pants; all, that is, but the authorities, who had been sent out by the office of the Ticktockman; they hung there like so much dockside cargo, hauled up above the floor of the amphitheater in a most unseemly fashion.

(In another part of the same city where the Harlequin carried on his "activities," totally unrelated in every way to what concerns us here, save that it illustrates the Ticktockman's power and import, a man named Marshall Delahanty received his turn-off notice from the Ticktockman's office. His wife received the notification from the gray-suited minee who delivered it, with the traditional "look of sorrow" plastered hideously across his face. She knew what it was, even without unsealing it. It was a billet-doux of immediate recognition to everyone these days. She gasped, and held it as though it were a glass slide tinged with botulism, and prayed it was not for her. Let it be for Marsh, she thought, brutally, realistically, or one of the kids, but not for me, please dear God, not for me. And then she opened it, and it *was* for Marsh, and she was at one and the same time horrified and relieved. The next trooper in the line had caught the bullet. "Marshall," she screamed, "Marshall! Termination, Marshall! OhmiGod, Marshall, whattl we do, whattl we do, Marshall omigodmarshall ..." and in their home that night was the sound of tearing paper and fear, and the stink of madness went up the flue and there was nothing, absolutely nothing they could do about it.

(But Marshall Delahanty tried to run. And early the next day, when turn-off time came, he was deep in the Canadian forest two hundred miles away, and the office of the Ticktockman blanked his cardioplate, and Marshall Delahanty keeled over, running, and his heart stopped, and the blood dried up on its way to his brain, and he was dead that's all. One light went out on the sector map in the office of the Master Timekeeper, while notification was entered for fax reproduction, and Georgette Delahanty's name was entered on the dole roles till she could remarry. Which is the end of the footnote, and all the point that need be made, except don't laugh, because that is what would happen to the Harlequin if ever the Ticktockman found out his real name. It isn't funny.)

The shopping level of the city was thronged with the Thursday-colors of the buyers. Women in canary yellow chitons and men in pseudo-Tyrolean outfits that were jade and leather and fit very tightly, save for the balloon pants.

When the Harlequin appeared on the still-being-constructed shell of the new Efficiency Shopping Center, his bullhorn to his elfishly-laughing lips, everyone pointed and stared, and he berated them: 70

"Why let them order you about? Why let them tell you to hurry and scurry like ants or maggots? Take your time! Saunter a while! Enjoy the sunshine, enjoy the breeze, let life carry you at your own pace! Don't be slaves of time, it's a helluva way to die, slowly, by degrees ... down with the Ticktockman!"

Who's the nut? most of the shoppers wanted to know. Who's the nut oh wow I'm gonna be late I gotta run . . .

And the construction gang on the Shopping Center received an urgent order from the office of the Master Timekeeper that the dangerous criminal known as the Harlequin was atop their spire, and their aid was urgently needed in apprehending him. The work crew said no, they would lose time on their construction schedule, but the Ticktockman managed to pull the proper threads of governmental webbing, and they were told to cease work and catch that nitwit up there on the spire; up there with the bullhorn. So a dozen and more burly workers began climbing into their construction platforms, releasing the a-grav plates, and rising toward the Harlequin.

After the debacle (in which, through the Harlequin's attention to personal safety, no one was seriously injured), the workers tried to reassemble, and assault him again, but it was too late. He had vanished. It had attracted quite a crowd, however, and the shopping cycle was thrown off by hours, simply hours. The purchasing needs of the system were therefore falling behind, and so measures were taken to accelerate the cycle for the rest of the day, but it got bogged down and speeded up and they sold too many float-valves and not nearly enough wegglers, which meant that the popli ratio was off, which made it necessary to rush cases and cases of spoiling Smash-O to stores that usually needed a case only every three or four hours. The shipments were bollixed, the transshipments were misrouted, and in the end, even the swizzleskid industries felt it.

"Don't come back till you have him!" the Ticktockman said, very quietly, 75 very sincerely, extremely dangerously.

They used dogs. They used probes. They used cardioplate crossoffs. They used teepers. They used bribery. They used stiktytes. They used intimidation. They used torment. They used torture. They used finks. They used cops. They used search&seizure. They used fallaron. They used betterment incentive. They used fingerprints. They used the Bertillon system. They used cunning. They used guile. They used treachery. They used Raoul Mitgong, but he didn't help much. They used applied physics. They used techniques of criminology.

And what the hell: they caught him.

After all, his name was Everett C. Marm, and he wasn't much to begin with, except a man who had no sense of time.

"Repent, Harlequin!" said the Ticktockman.

"Get stuffed!" the Harlequin replied, sneering.                              80

"You've been late a total of sixty-three years, five months, three weeks, two days, twelve hours, forty-one minutes, fifty-nine seconds, point oh three six one one one microseconds. You've used up everything you can, and more. I'm going to turn you off."

"Scare someone else. I'd rather be dead than live in a dumb world with a bogeyman like you."

"It's my job."

"You're full of it. You're a tyrant. You have no right to order people around and kill them if they show up late."

"You can't adjust. You can't fit in." 85

"Unstrap me, and I'll fit my fist into your mouth."

"You're a nonconformist."

"That didn't used to be a felony."

"It is now. Live in the world around you."

"I hate it. It's a terrible world." 90

"Not everyone thinks so. Most people enjoy order."

"I don't, and most of the people I know don't."

"That's not true. How do you think we caught you?"

"I'm not interested."

"A girl named Pretty Alice told us who you were." 95

"That's a lie."

"It's true. You unnerve her. She wants to belong; she wants to conform; I'm going to turn you off."

"Then do it already, and stop arguing with me."

"I'm not going to turn you off."

"You're an idiot!" 100

"Repent, Harlequin!" said the Ticktockman.

"Get stuffed."

So they sent him to Coventry. And in Coventry they worked him over. It was just like what they did to Winston Smith in NINETEEN EIGHTY-FOUR, which was a book none of them knew about, but the techniques are really quite ancient, and so they did it to Everett C. Marm; and one day, quite a long time later, the Harlequin appeared on the communications web, appearing elfin and dimpled and bright-eyed, and not at all brainwashed, and he said he had been wrong, that it was a good, a very good thing indeed, to belong, to be right on time hip-ho and away we go, and everyone stared up at him on the public screens that covered an entire city block, and they said to themselves, well, you see, he was just a nut after all, and if that's the way the system is run, then let's do it that way, because it doesn't pay to fight city hall, or in this case, the Ticktockman. So Everett C. Marm was destroyed, which was a loss, because of what Thoreau said earlier, but you can't make an omelet without breaking a few eggs, and in every revolution a few die who shouldn't, but they have to, because that's the way it happens, and if you make only a little change, then it seems to be worthwhile. Or, to make the point lucidly:

"Uh, excuse me, sir, I, uh, don't know how to uh, to uh, tell you this, but you were three minutes late. The schedule is a little, uh, bit off."

He grinned sheepishly. 105

"That's ridiculous!" murmured the Ticktockman behind his mask. "Check your watch." And then he went into his office, going *mrmee, mrmee, mrmee, mrmee.*

## FOR ANALYSIS

1. What are the **connotations** of the names *Harlequin* and *Everett C. Marm*? Is the contrast between the names similar to that between, say, *Superman* and *Clark Kent*?

2. What is it about his society that drives Everett C. Marm to rebel?

3. What is Pretty Alice's role in the story?

## MAKING ARGUMENTS

Carefully read the passage (para. 1) taken from Thoreau's "Civil Disobedience." Write an essay explaining why you do or do not agree (in whole or in part) with Thoreau's view of "the state" and with his classification of citizens as those who serve the state with their "bodies," those who serve it with their "heads," and those who serve it with their "consciences." In which group would you place Everett C. Marm?

## WRITING TOPICS

1. Explain the final section of the story (paras. 104–6). Has the Ticktockman triumphed?

2. Characterize Pretty Alice. Why does she turn Everett in?

## MAKING CONNECTIONS

1. Compare the statement this story makes about the human spirit with that made in Updike's "A & P" (p. 94). Do Everett C. Marm and Sammy share any attributes?

2. Compare Everett C. Marm and the narrator in Ellison's "Battle Royal" (p. 303) as rebels. Who is more successful as a rebel? As a conformist? Will the narrator of "Battle Royal" grow up to be like the Harlequin?

## AMY TAN  (B. 1952)

# TWO KINDS   1989

My mother believed you could be anything you wanted to be in America. You could open a restaurant. You could work for the government and get good retirement. You could buy a house with almost no money down. You could become rich. You could become instantly famous.

"Of course you can be prodigy, too," my mother told me when I was nine. "You can be best anything. What does Auntie Lindo know? Her daughter, she is only best tricky."

America was where all my mother's hopes lay. She had come here in 1949 after losing everything in China: her mother and father, her family home, her first husband, and two daughters, twin baby girls. But she never looked back with regret. There were so many ways for things to get better.

We didn't immediately pick the right kind of prodigy. At first my mother thought I could be a Chinese Shirley Temple. We'd watch Shirley's old movies on TV as though they were training films. My mother would poke my arm and say, "*Ni kan*"— You watch. And I would see Shirley tapping her feet, or singing a sailor song, or pursing her lips into a very round O while saying, "Oh my goodness."

"*Ni kan*," said my mother as Shirley's eyes flooded with tears. "You already 5 know how. Don't need talent for crying!"

Soon after my mother got this idea about Shirley Temple, she took me to a beauty training school in the Mission district and put me in the hands of a student who could barely hold the scissors without shaking. Instead of getting big fat curls, I emerged with an uneven mass of crinkly black fuzz. My mother dragged me off to the bathroom and tried to wet down my hair.

"You look like Negro Chinese," she lamented, as if I had done this on purpose.

The instructor of the beauty training school had to lop off these soggy clumps to make my hair even again. "Peter Pan is very popular these days," the instructor assured my mother. I now had hair the length of a boy's, with straight-across bangs that hung at a slant two inches above my eyebrows. I liked the haircut and it made me actually look forward to my future fame.

In fact, in the beginning, I was just as excited as my mother, maybe even more so. I pictured this prodigy part of me as many different images, trying each one on for size. I was a dainty ballerina girl standing by the curtains, waiting to hear the right music that would send me floating on my tiptoes. I was like the Christ child lifted out of the straw manger, crying with holy indignity. I was Cinderella stepping from her pumpkin carriage with sparkly cartoon music filling the air.

In all of my imaginings, I was filled with a sense that I would soon become 10 *perfect*. My mother and father would adore me. I would be beyond reproach. I would never feel the need to sulk for anything.

But sometimes the prodigy in me became impatient. "If you don't hurry up and get me out of here, I'm disappearing for good," it warned. "And then you'll always be nothing."

Every night after dinner, my mother and I would sit at the Formica kitchen table. She would present new tests, taking her examples from stories of amazing children she had read in *Ripley's Believe It or Not*, or *Good Housekeeping, Reader's Digest*, and a dozen other magazines she kept in a pile in our bathroom. My mother got these magazines from people whose houses she cleaned. And since she cleaned many houses each week, we had a great assortment. She would look through them all, searching for stories about remarkable children.

The first night she brought out a story about a three-year-old boy who knew the capitals of all the states and even of most of the European countries. A teacher was quoted as saying the little boy could also pronounce the names of the foreign cities correctly.

"What's the capital of Finland?" my mother asked me, looking at the magazine story.

All I knew was the capital of California, because Sacramento was the name 15 of the street we lived on in Chinatown. "Nairobi!" I guessed, saying the most foreign word I could think of. She checked to see if that was possibly one way to pronounce "Helsinki" before showing me the answer.

The tests got harder — multiplying numbers in my head, finding the queen of hearts in a deck of cards, trying to stand on my head without using my hands, predicting the daily temperatures in Los Angeles, New York, and London.

One night I had to look at a page from the Bible for three minutes and then report everything I could remember. "Now Jehoshaphat had riches and honor in abundance and . . . that's all I remember, Ma," I said.

And after seeing my mother's disappointed face once again, something inside of me began to die. I hated the tests, the raised hopes and failed expectations. Before going to bed that night, I looked in the mirror above the bathroom sink and when I saw only my face staring back — and that it would always be this ordinary face — I began to cry. Such a sad, ugly girl! I made high-pitched noises like a crazed animal, trying to scratch out the face in the mirror.

And then I saw what seemed to be the prodigy side of me — because I had never seen that face before. I looked at my reflection, blinking so I could see more clearly. The girl staring back at me was angry, powerful. This girl and I were the same. I had new thoughts, willful thoughts, or rather thoughts filled with lots of won'ts. I won't let her change me, I promised myself. I won't be what I'm not.

So now on nights when my mother presented her tests, I performed listlessly, 20 my head propped on one arm. I pretended to be bored. And I was. I got so bored I started counting the bellows of the foghorns out on the bay while my mother drilled me in other areas. The sound was comforting and reminded me of the cow jumping over the moon. And the next day, I played a game with myself, seeing if my mother would give up on me before eight bellows. After a while I usually counted only one, maybe two bellows at most. At last she was beginning to give up hope.

Two or three months had gone by without any mention of my being a prodigy again. And then one day my mother was watching *The Ed Sullivan Show* on TV. The TV was old and the sound kept shorting out. Every time my mother got halfway up from the sofa to adjust the set, the sound would come back on and Ed would be talking. As soon as she sat down, Ed would go silent again. She got up, the TV broke into loud piano music. She sat down. Silence. Up and down, back and forth, quiet and loud. It was like a stiff embraceless dance between her and the TV set. Finally she stood by the set with her hand on the sound dial.

She seemed entranced by the music, a little frenzied piano piece with this mesmerizing quality, sort of quick passages and then teasing lilting ones before it returned to the quick playful parts.

"*Ni kan,*" my mother said, calling me over with hurried hand gestures, "Look here."

I could see why my mother was fascinated by the music. It was being pounded out by a little Chinese girl, about nine years old, with a Peter Pan haircut. The girl had the sauciness of a Shirley Temple. She was proudly modest like a proper Chinese child. And she also did a fancy sweep of a curtsy, so that the fluffy skirt of her white dress cascaded slowly to the floor like the petals of a large carnation.

In spite of these warning signs, I wasn't worried. Our family had no piano  25 and we couldn't afford to buy one, let alone reams of sheet music and piano lessons. So I could be generous in my comments when my mother bad-mouthed the little girl on TV.

"Play note right, but doesn't sound good! No singing sound," complained my mother.

"What are you picking on her for?" I said carelessly. "She's pretty good. Maybe she's not the best, but she's trying hard." I knew almost immediately I would be sorry I said that.

"Just like you," she said. "Not the best. Because you not trying." She gave a little huff as she let go of the sound dial and sat down on the sofa.

The little Chinese girl sat down also to play an encore of "Anitra's Dance" by Grieg.[1] I remember the song, because later on I had to learn how to play it.

Three days after watching *The Ed Sullivan Show*, my mother told me what  30 my schedule would be for piano lessons and piano practice. She had talked to Mr. Chong, who lived on the first floor of our apartment building. Mr. Chong was a retired piano teacher, and my mother had traded housecleaning services

[1] From Edvard Grieg's (1843–1907) incidental music composed for Henrik Ibsen's play *Peer Gynt.*

for weekly lessons and a piano for me to practice on every day, two hours a day, from four until six.

When my mother told me this, I felt as though I had been sent to hell. I whined and then kicked my foot a little when I couldn't stand it anymore.

"Why don't you like me the way I am? I'm *not* a genius! I can't play the piano. And even if I could, I wouldn't go on TV if you paid me a million dollars!" I cried.

My mother slapped me. "Who ask you be genius?" she shouted. "Only ask you be your best. For you sake. You think I want you be genius? Hnnh! What for! Who ask you!"

"So ungrateful," I heard her mutter in Chinese. "If she had as much talent as she has temper, she would be famous now."

Mr. Chong, whom I secretly nicknamed Old Chong, was very strange, 35 always tapping his fingers to the silent music of an invisible orchestra. He looked ancient in my eyes. He had lost most of the hair on top of his head and he wore thick glasses and had eyes that always looked tired and sleepy. But he must have been younger than I thought, since he lived with his mother and was not yet married.

I met Old Lady Chong once and that was enough. She had this peculiar smell like a baby that had done something in its pants. And her fingers felt like a dead person's, like an old peach I once found in the back of the refrigerator; the skin just slid off the meat when I picked it up.

I soon found out why Old Chong had retired from teaching piano. He was deaf. "Like Beethoven!" he shouted to me. "We're both listening only in our head!" And he would start to conduct his frantic silent sonatas.

Our lessons went like this. He would open the book and point to different things, explaining their purpose: "Key! Treble! Bass! No sharps or flats! So this is C major! Listen now and play after me!"

And then he would play the C scale a few times, a simple chord, and then, as if inspired by an old unreachable itch, he would gradually add more notes and running trills and a pounding bass until the music was really something quite grand.

I would play after him, the simple scale, the simple chord, and then I just 40 played some nonsense that sounded like a cat running up and down on top of garbage cans. Old Chong smiled and applauded and then said, "Very good! But now you must learn to keep time!"

So that's how I discovered that Old Chong's eyes were too slow to keep up with the wrong notes I was playing. He went through the motions in half-time. To help me keep rhythm, he stood behind me, pushing down on my right shoulder for every beat. He balanced pennies on top of my wrists so I would keep them still as I slowly played scales and arpeggios. He had me curve my hand around an apple and keep that shape when playing chords. He marched stiffly to show me how to make each finger dance up and down, staccato like an obedient little soldier.

He taught me all these things, and that was how I also learned I could be lazy and get away with mistakes, lots of mistakes. If I hit the wrong notes because

I hadn't practiced enough, I never corrected myself. I just kept playing in rhythm. And Old Chong kept conducting his own private reverie.

So maybe I never really gave myself a fair chance. I did pick up the basics pretty quickly, and I might have become a good pianist at that young age. But I was so determined not to try, not to be anybody different that I learned to play only the most ear-splitting preludes, the most discordant hymns.

Over the next year, I practiced like this, dutifully in my own way. And then one day I heard my mother and her friend Lindo Jong both talking in a loud bragging tone of voice so others could hear. It was after church, and I was leaning against the brick wall wearing a dress with stiff white petticoats. Auntie Lindo's daughter, Waverly, who was about my age, was standing farther down the wall about five feet away. We had grown up together and shared all the closeness of two sisters squabbling over crayons and dolls. In other words, for the most part, we hated each other. I thought she was snotty. Waverly Jong had gained a certain amount of fame as "Chinatown's Littlest Chinese Chess Champion."

"She bring home too many trophy," lamented Auntie Lindo that Sunday. "All day she play chess. All day I have no time do nothing but dust off her winnings." She threw a scolding look at Waverly, who pretended not to see her.

"You lucky you don't have this problem," said Auntie Lindo with a sigh to my mother.

And my mother squared her shoulders and bragged: "Our problem worser than yours. If we ask Jing-mei wash dish, she hear nothing but music. It's like you can't stop this natural talent."

And right then I was determined to put a stop to her foolish pride.

A few weeks later, Old Chong and my mother conspired to have me play in a talent show which would be held in the church hall. By then, my parents had saved up enough to buy me a secondhand piano, a black Wurlitzer spinet with a scarred bench. It was the showpiece of our living room.

For the talent show, I was to play a piece called "Pleading Child" from Schumann's *Scenes from Childhood*. It was a simple, moody piece that sounded more difficult than it was. I was supposed to memorize the whole thing, playing the repeat parts twice to make the piece sound longer. But I dawdled over it, playing a few bars and then cheating, looking up to see what notes followed. I never really listened to what I was playing. I daydreamed about being somewhere else, about being someone else.

The part I liked to practice best was the fancy curtsy: right foot out, touch the rose on the carpet with a pointed foot, sweep to the side, left leg bends, look up, and smile.

My parents invited all the couples from the Joy Luck Club to witness my debut. Auntie Lindo and Uncle Tin were there. Waverly and her two older brothers had also come. The first two rows were filled with children both younger and older than I was. The littlest ones got to go first. They recited simple nursery rhymes, squawked out tunes on miniature violins, twirled Hula Hoops, pranced in pink ballet tutus, and when they bowed or curtsied, the audience would sigh in unison, "Awww," and then clap enthusiastically.

When my turn came, I was very confident. I remember my childish excitement. It was as if I knew, without a doubt, that the prodigy side of me really did exist. I had no fear whatsoever, no nervousness. I remember thinking to myself, This is it! This is it! I looked out over the audience, at my mother's blank face, my father's yawn, Auntie Lindo's stiff-lipped smile, Waverly's sulky expression. I had on a white dress, layered with sheets of lace, and a pink bow in my Peter Pan haircut. As I sat down, I envisioned people jumping to their feet and Ed Sullivan rushing up to introduce me to everyone on TV.

And I started to play. It was so beautiful. I was so caught up in how lovely I looked that at first I didn't worry how I would sound. So it was a surprise to me when I hit the first wrong note and I realized something didn't sound quite right. And then I hit another and another followed that. A chill started at the top of my head and began to trickle down. Yet I couldn't stop playing, as though my hands were bewitched. I kept thinking my fingers would adjust themselves back, like a train switching to the right track. I played this strange jumble through two repeats, the sour notes staying with me all the way to the end.

When I stood up, I discovered my legs were shaking. Maybe I had just been 55 nervous and the audience, like Old Chong, had seen me go through the right motions and had not heard anything wrong at all. I swept my right foot out, went down on my knee, looked up and smiled. The room was quiet, except for Old Chong, who was beaming and shouting, "Bravo! Bravo! Well done!" But then I saw my mother's face, her stricken face. The audience clapped weakly, and as I walked back to my chair, with my whole face quivering as I tried not to cry, I heard a little boy whisper loudly to his mother, "That was awful," and the mother whispered, "Well, she certainly tried."

And now I realized how many people were in the audience, the whole world, it seemed. I was aware of eyes burning into my back. I felt the shame of my mother and father as they sat stiffly throughout the rest of the show.

We could have escaped during intermission. Pride and some strange sense of honor must have anchored my parents to their chairs. And so we watched it all: the eighteen-year-old boy with a fake moustache who did a magic show and juggled flaming hoops while riding a unicycle. The breasted girl with white makeup who sang an aria from *Madama Butterfly* and got an honorable mention. And the eleven-year-old boy who won first prize playing a tricky violin song that sounded like a busy bee.

After the show, the Hsus, the Jongs, and the St. Clairs from the Joy Luck Club came up to my mother and father.

"Lots of talented kids," Auntie Lindo said vaguely, smiling broadly.

"That was somethin' else," my father said, and I wondered if he was referring 60 to me in a humorous way, or whether he even remembered what I had done.

Waverly looked at me and shrugged her shoulders. "You aren't a genius like me," she said matter-of-factly. And if I hadn't felt so bad, I would have pulled her braids and punched her stomach.

But my mother's expression was what devastated me: a quiet, blank look that said she had lost everything. I felt the same way, and it seemed as if everybody were now coming up, like gawkers at the scene of an accident, to see what parts were actually missing. When we got on the bus to go home, my father was humming the busy-bee tune and my mother was silent. I kept thinking she wanted to wait until we got home before shouting at me. But when my father unlocked the door to our apartment, my mother walked in and then went to the back, into the bedroom. No accusations. No blame. And in a way, I felt disappointed. I had been waiting for her to start shouting, so I could shout back and cry and blame her for all my misery.

I assumed my talent-show fiasco meant I never had to play the piano again. But two days later, after school, my mother came out of the kitchen and saw me watching TV.

"Four clock," she reminded me as if it were any other day. I was stunned, as though she were asking me to go through the talent-show torture again. I wedged myself more tightly in front of the TV.

"Turn off TV," she called from the kitchen five minutes later.                    65

I didn't budge. And then I decided. I didn't have to do what my mother said anymore. I wasn't her slave. This wasn't China. I had listened to her before, and look what happened. She was the stupid one.

She came out of the kitchen and stood in the arched entryway of the living room. "Four clock," she said once again, louder.

"I'm not going to play anymore," I said nonchalantly. "Why should I? I'm not a genius."

She stood in front of the TV. I saw her chest was heaving up and down in an angry way.

"No!" I said, and I now felt stronger, as if my true self had finally emerged.  70 So this was what had been inside me all along.

"No! I won't!" I screamed.

She yanked me by the arm, pulled me off the floor, snapped off the TV. She was frighteningly strong, half pulling, half carrying me toward the piano as I kicked the throw rugs under my feet. She lifted me up and onto the hard bench. I was sobbing by now, looking at her bitterly. Her chest was heaving even more and her mouth was open, smiling crazily as if she were pleased that I was crying.

"You want me to be someone that I'm not!" I sobbed. "I'll never be the kind of daughter you want me to be!"

"Only two kinds of daughters," she shouted in Chinese. "Those who are obedient and those who follow their own mind! Only one kind of daughter can live in this house. Obedient daughter!"

"Then I wish I weren't your daughter. I wish you weren't my mother," I  75 shouted. As I said these things I got scared. It felt like worms and toads and slimy things crawling out of my chest, but it also felt good, as if this awful side of me had surfaced, at last.

"Too late change this," said my mother shrilly.

And I could sense her anger rising to its breaking point. I wanted to see it spill over. And that's when I remembered the babies she had lost in China, the ones we never talked about. "Then I wish I'd never been born!" I shouted. "I wish I were dead! Like them."

It was as if I had said the magic words. Alakazam! — and her face went blank, her mouth closed, her arms went slack, and she backed out of the room, stunned, as if she were blowing away like a small brown leaf, thin, brittle, lifeless.

It was not the only disappointment my mother felt in me. In the years that followed, I failed her so many times, each time asserting my own will, my right to fall short of expectations. I didn't get straight As. I didn't become class president. I didn't get into Stanford. I dropped out of college.

For unlike my mother, I did not believe I could be anything I wanted to be. I could only be me.   80

And for all those years, we never talked about the disaster at the recital or my terrible accusations afterward at the piano bench. All that remained unchecked, like a betrayal that was now unspeakable. So I never found a way to ask her why she had hoped for something so large that failure was inevitable.

And even worse, I never asked her about what frightened me the most: Why had she given up hope?

For after our struggle at the piano, she never mentioned my playing again. The lessons stopped. The lid to the piano was closed, shutting out the dust, my misery, and her dreams.

So she surprised me. A few years ago, she offered to give me the piano, for my thirtieth birthday. I had not played in all those years. I saw the offer as a sign of forgiveness, a tremendous burden removed.

"Are you sure?" I asked shyly. "I mean, won't you and Dad miss it?"   85

"No, this your piano," she said firmly. "Always your piano. You only one can play."

"Well, I probably can't play anymore," I said. "It's been years."

"You pick up fast," said my mother, as if she knew this was certain. "You have natural talent. You could been genius if you want to."

"No I couldn't."

"You just not trying," said my mother. And she was neither angry nor sad. She said it as if to announce a fact that could never be disproved. "Take it," she said.   90

But I didn't at first. It was enough that she had offered it to me. And after that, every time I saw it in my parents' living room, standing in front of the bay windows, it made me feel proud, as if it were a shiny trophy that I had won back.

Last week I sent a tuner over to my parents' apartment and had the piano reconditioned, for purely sentimental reasons. My mother had died a few months before and I had been getting things in order for my father, a little bit at a time. I put the jewelry in special silk pouches. The sweaters she had knitted in yellow, pink, bright orange — all the colors I hated — I put those in moth-proof boxes. I found some old Chinese silk dresses, the kind with little slits up the sides. I rubbed the old silk against my skin, then wrapped them in tissue and decided to take them home with me.

After I had the piano tuned, I opened the lid and touched the keys. It sounded even richer than I remembered. Really, it was a very good piano. Inside the bench were the same exercise notes with handwritten scales, the same second-hand music books with their covers held together with yellow tape.

I opened up the Schumann book to the dark little piece I had played at the recital. It was on the left-hand page, "Pleading Child." It looked more difficult than I remembered. I played a few bars, surprised at how easily the notes came back to me.

And for the first time, or so it seemed, I noticed the piece on the right-hand 95 side. It was called "Perfectly Contented." I tried to play this one as well. It had a lighter melody but the same flowing rhythm and turned out to be quite easy. "Pleading Child" was shorter but slower; "Perfectly Contented" was longer, but faster. And after I played them both a few times, I realized they were two halves of the same song.

## FOR ANALYSIS

**1.** Do you think the **conflict** between the mother and daughter is unique to this family? To Asian American families? To any group of families? Why or why not?

**2.** What does the mother want for her daughter? What does the daughter want for herself?

**3.** What is the significance of the story's last paragraph?

## MAKING ARGUMENTS

Using evidence from the story as well as drawing on your own experience, support or refute the notion that children should be allowed to choose their own paths.

## WRITING TOPIC

Describe the similarities or the differences between the mother's attempt to influence her daughter's life and your own family's attempt to influence yours.

## MAKING CONNECTIONS

Several of the stories in "Conformity and Rebellion" are driven by tensions between parents and children. Compare "Two Kinds" with stories from elsewhere in this anthology, such as William Faulkner's "A Rose for Emily" (p. 455) or Alice Walker's "Everyday Use" (p. 488). Each of these stories deals with a different culture. What significant similarities do you find among them? What substantive differences?

## GEORGE SAUNDERS (B. 1958)

# THE END OF FIRPO IN THE WORLD 1998

The boy on the bike flew by the Chink's house, and the squatty-body's house, and the house where the dead guy had rotted for five days, remembering that the Chink had once called him nasty, and the squatty-body had once called the cops when he'd hit her cat with a lug nut on a string, and the chick in the dead guy's house had once asked if he, Cody, ever brushed his teeth. Someday when he'd completed the invention of his special miniaturizing ray he would shrink their houses and flush them down the shitter while in tiny voices all three begged for some sophisticated mercy, but he would only say, Sophisticated? When were you ever sophisticated to me? And from the toilet bowl they would say, Well yes, you're right, we were pretty mean, flush us down, we deserve it; but no, at the last minute he would pluck them out and place them in his lunchbox so he could send them on secret missions such as putting hideous boogers of assassination in Lester Finn's thermos if Lester Finn ever again asked him in Civics why his rear smelled like hot cotton with additional crap cling-ons.

It was a beautiful, sunny day and the aerobics class at the Rec had let out and cars were streaming out of the parking lot with sun glinting off their hoods, and he rode along on the sidewalk, racing the cars as they passed.

Here was the low-hanging willow where you had to duck down, here was the place with the tilty sidewalk square that served as a ramp when you jerked hard on the handlebars, which he did, and the crowd went wild, and the announcers in the booth above the willow shook their heads and said, Wow, he takes that jump like there's no tomorrow while them other racers fret about it like tiny crying babies!

Were the Dalmeyers home?

Their gray car was still in the driveway.                                     5

He would need to make another lap.

Yesterday he had picked up a bright-red goalie pad and all three Dalmeyers had screamed at him, Not that pad Cody you dick, we never use those pads in the driveway because they get scuffed, you rectum, those are only for ice, were you born a rectal shitbrain or did you take special rectal shitbrain lessons, in rectal shitbrain lessons did they teach you how to ruin everybody's things?

Well yes, he had ruined a few Dalmeyer things in his life, he had yes pounded a railroad spike in a good new volleyball, he had yes secretly scraped a ski with a nail, he had yes given the Dalmeyer dog Rudy a cut on its leg with a shovel, but that had been an accident, he'd thrown the shovel at a rosebush and stupid Rudy had walked in front of it.

And the Dalmeyers had snatched away the goalie pad and paraded around the driveway making the nosehole sound, and when he tried to laugh to show he was a good sport he made the nosehole sound for real, and they totally cracked up, and Zane Dalmeyer said why didn't he take his trademark nosehole sound on Broadway so thousands could crap their pants laughing? And Eric Dalmeyer said hey if only he had like fifty different-sized noseholes that each made a different sound then he could play songs. And they laughed so hard at the idea of him playing songs on Broadway on his fifty different-sized noseholes that they fell to the driveway thrashing their idiotic Dalmeyer limbs, even Ginnie, the baby Dalmeyer, and ha ha ha that had been a laugh, that had been so funny he had almost gone around one two three four and smashed their cranial cavities with his off-brand gym shoes, which were another puzzling dilemmoid, because why did he have Arroes when every single Dalmeyer, even Ginnie, had the Nikes with the lights in the heel that lit up?

Fewer cars were coming by now from the Rec; the ones that did were going faster, and he no longer tried to race them. 10

Oh, it would be revenge, sweet revenge, when he stuck the lozenge stolen from wood shop up the Dalmeyers' water hose, and the next time they turned the hose on it exploded, and all the Dalmeyers, even Dad Dalmeyer, stood around in their nice tan pants puzzling over it like them guys on "Nova." And the Dalmeyers were so stupid they would conclude that it had been a miracle, and would call some guys from a science lab to confirm the miracle, and one of the lab guys would flip the wooden lozenge into the air and say to Dad Dalmeyer, You know what, a very clever Einstein lives in your neighborhood and I suggest that in the future you lock this hose up, because in all probability this guy cannot be stopped. And he, Cody, would give the lab guy a wink and later, when they were walking away, the lab guy would say, Look, why not come live with us in the experimental space above our lab and help us discover some amazing compounds with the same science brain that thought up this brilliant lozenge, because, frankly, when we lab guys were your age, no way, this lozenge concept was totally beyond us, we were just playing with baby toys and doing baby math, but you, you're really something scientifically special.

And when the Dalmeyers came for a lab tour with a school group they would approach him with their big confident underwater watches and say wow oh boy had they ever missed the boat in terms of him, sorry, they were so very sorry, what was this beaker for, how did this burner work, was it really true that he had built a whole entire *T. Rex* from scratch and energized it by taming the miraculous power of cosmic thunder? And down in the basement the *T. Rex* would rear up its ugly head and want to have a Dalmeyer snack, but using his special system of codes, pounding on a heat pipe a different number of times for each alphabet letter, he would tell the *T. Rex*, No no no, don't eat a single Dalmeyer, although why not lift Eric Dalmeyer up just for the fun of it on the tip of your tremendous green snout and give him a lesson in what kind of power those crushing jaws would have if he, Cody, pounded out on the heat pipe Kill Kill Kill.

Pedalling wildly now, he passed into the strange and dangerous zone of three consecutive MonteVistas, and inside of each lived an old wop in a dago tee, and sometimes in the creepy trees there were menacing gorillas he took potshots at from bikeback, but not today, he was too busy with revenge to think about monkeys, and then he was out, into the light, coasting into a happier zone of forthright and elephantine BuenoVerdes that sat very honestly with the big open eyes that were their second-story windows, and in his mind as he passed he said hello HELLO to the two elephants and they in turn said to him in kind Dumbo voices hey Cody HEY CODY.

The block was shaped something like South America and as he took the tight turn that was Cape Horn he looked across The Field to his small yellow house, which was neither MonteVista nor BuenoVerde, but predated the subdivision and smelled like cat pee and hamburger blood and had recently been christened by Ma's boyfriend Daryl, that dick, The House of FIRPO, FIRPO being the word Daryl used to describe anything he, Cody, did that was bad or dorky. Sometimes Mom and Daryl tried to pretend FIRPO was a lovey-dovey term by tousling his hair when they said it but other times they gave him a poke or pinch and sometimes when they thought he couldn't hear they whispered very darkly and meanly to one another FIRP attack in progress and he would go to his room and make the nosehole sound in his closet, after which they would come in and fine him a quarter for each nosehole sound they thought they had heard him make, which was often many, many more than he had actually really made.

Sometimes at night in his room Mom babied him by stroking his big wide   15 head and saying he didn't have to pay all the quarters he owed for making the nosehole sound, but other times she said if he didn't knock it off and lose a few pounds how was he ever going to get a date in junior high, because who wanted to date a big chubby nosehole snorter, and then he couldn't help it, it made him nervous to think of junior high, and he made the nosehole sound and she said, Very funny I hope you're amusing your own self because you're not amusing my ass one bit.

The Dalmeyer house now came into sight.

The Dalmeyer car was gone.

It was Go Time.

The decisive butt-kicking he was about to give the Dalmeyer hose would constitute the end of FIRPO in the world, and all, including Ma, would have to bow down before him, saying, Wow wow wow, do we ever stand corrected in terms of you, how could someone FIRPO hatch and execute such a daring manly plan?

The crowd was on its feet now, screaming his name, and he passed the Chink's   20 house again, here was the driveway down which he must turn to cross the street to the Dalmeyers', but then oh crap he was going too fast and missed it, and the announcers in the booth above the willow gasped in pleasure at his sudden decisive decision to swerve across the newly sodded lawn of the squatty-body's house. His bike made a trough in the sod and went HUMPF over the curb, and as the white car struck him the boy and the bike flew together in a high comic arc across the street and impacted the oak on the opposite side with such violence that the bike wrapped around the tree and the boy flew back into the street.

Arghh arghh Daryl will be pissed and say Cody why are you bleeding like a stuck pig you little shit. There was something red wrong with his Arroes. At Payless when they bought the Arroes Mom said, If you squirm once more you're gonna be facedown on this carpet with my hand whacking your big fat ass. Daryl will say I buy you a good bike and what do you do, you ruin it. Ma will come up with a dish towel and start swiping at the blood and Daryl will say don't ruin that dish towel, he made his bed let him sleep in it, I'll hose him off in the yard, a little shivering won't kill him, he did the crime let him do the time. Or Ma might throw a fit like the night he slipped and fell in the school play, and Ms. Phillips said, Tell your mother, Cody, how you came to slip and fall during the school play so that everyone in the auditorium was looking at you instead of Julia who was at that time speaking her most important line.

And Mom said, Cody are you deaf?

And Ms. Phillips said, He slipped because when I told him stay out of that mopped spot did he do it? No, he did not, he walked right through it on purpose and then down he went.

Which is exactly what he does at home, Mom said. Sometimes I think he's wired wrong.

And Ms. Phillips said, Well, today, Cody, you learned a valuable lesson  25 which is if someone tells you don't do something, don't do it, because maybe that someone knows something you don't from having lived a longer time than you.

And Daryl said, Or maybe he liked falling on his butt in front of all his friends.

Now a white-haired stickman with no shirt was bending over him, touch touch touching him all over, like looking to see if he was wearing a bulletproof vest, doing some very nervous mouthbreathing, with a silver cross hanging down, and around his nipples were sprigs of white hair.

Oh boy, oh God, said the stickman. Say something, pal, can you talk?

And he tried to talk but nothing came and tried to move but nothing moved.

Oh God, said the stickman, don't go, pal, please say something, stay here  30 with me now, we'll get through this.

What crazy teeth. What a stickman. The stickman's hands flipped around like nervous old-lady hands in movies where the river is rising and the men are away. What a Holy Roller. What a FIRPO. A Holy Roller FIRPO stickman with hairy nips and plus his breath smelled like coffee.

Listen, God loves you, said the stickman. You're going, O.K., I see you're going, but look, please don't go without knowing you are beautiful and loved. O.K.? Do you hear me? You are good, do you know that? God loves you. God loves you. He sent His son to die for you.

Oh the freaking FIRPO, why couldn't he just shut up? If the stickman thought he, Cody, was good he must be FIRPO because he, Cody, wasn't good, he was FIRPO, Mom had said so and Daryl had said so and even Mr. Dean in Science had told him to stop lying the time he tried to tell about seeing the falling star. The announcers in the booth above the willow began weeping as he sat on

Mom's lap and said he was very sorry for having been such a FIRPO son and Mom said, Oh thank you, thank you, Cody, for finally admitting it, that makes it nice, and her smile was so sweet he closed his eyes and felt a certain urge to sort of shake things out and oh Christ dance.

You are beautiful, beautiful, the stickman kept saying, long after the boy had stopped thrashing, God loves you, you are beautiful in His sight.

## FOR ANALYSIS

**1.** What are the two meanings of the title in the story?

**2.** Cody's mother says that he is "wired wrong" (para. 24). Do you agree? How would you describe him?

**3.** What do the Dalmeyers represent to Cody and to the story?

## MAKING ARGUMENTS

When the story first appeared in the *New Yorker*, under the title it said "Cody's last stand." From the observation that this line is an intentional echo of Custer's last stand, make the argument that this echo can help readers understand the story better.

## WRITING TOPICS

**1.** Annotate Saunders's story, marking where the **third-person narration** uses free indirect discourse (FID) — that is, where the narrator's words seem like they could come from Cody's mouth. Analyze Saunders's use of FID and its effectiveness.

**2.** How do you take the last line of the story? How do Cody or the story feel about religion? Describe what you think the fact that the story ends as it does means in terms of religion.

## MAKING CONNECTIONS

Compare Cody's rebellion with that of Everett C. Marm in Harlan Ellison's " 'Repent, Harlequin!' Said the Ticktockman" (p. 322). What is the nature of each? Is there a way to judge whether each succeeds?

# POETRY

### RICHARD CRASHAW  (1613–1649)

## BUT MEN LOVED DARKNESS RATHER THAN LIGHT  1646

> The world's light shines, shine as it will,
> The world will love its darkness still.
> I doubt though when the world's in hell,
> It will not love its darkness half so well.

### FOR ANALYSIS

**1.** Would you characterize this poem as complicated or simple? Think in terms of **rhyme, rhythm, diction,** and **imagery**. How does the complexity — or simplicity — of its form relate to its subject and meaning?

**2.** What is the biblical **allusion** that Crashaw makes here? Use a search engine to find it. Does knowing the lines to which the poem refers help you to better understand it?

### WRITING TOPIC

While Crashaw was writing out of a specifically religious worldview, it's not hard to imagine a way in which this poem could be read more broadly if the idea of hell is not taken literally. To what other situations or phenomena or ideas could this poem apply?

### WILLIAM WORDSWORTH  (1770–1850)

## THE WORLD IS TOO MUCH WITH US  1807

> The world is too much with us; late and soon,
> Getting and spending, we lay waste our powers;
> Little we see in Nature that is ours;
> We have given our hearts away, a sordid boon!
> This Sea that bares her bosom to the moon,
> The winds that will be howling at all hours,
> And are up-gathered now like sleeping flowers,
> For this, for everything, we are out of tune;

It moves us not. — Great God! I'd rather be
A Pagan suckled in a creed outworn; 10
So might I, standing on this pleasant lea,
Have glimpses that would make me less forlorn;
Have sight of Proteus rising from the sea;
Or hear old Triton blow his wreathèd horn.[1]

## FOR ANALYSIS

**1.** What does "world" mean in line 1?

**2.** What does Wordsworth complain of in the first four lines?

**3.** In lines 4–8 Wordsworth tells us what we have lost; in the concluding lines he suggests a remedy. What is that remedy? What do Proteus and Triton **symbolize**?

## MAKING ARGUMENTS

Relying on a little research to establish some key differences between Western life in 1807, the year of this poem's appearance, and today, argue that the world is still too much with us, is with us to a greater degree, or is less with us.

## WRITING TOPIC

In what ways does Wordsworth's use of **images** both define what we have lost and suggest a remedy for this loss?

## ALFRED, LORD TENNYSON    (1809–1892)

# ULYSSES[1]    1833

It little profits that an idle king,
By this still hearth, among these barren crags,
Matched with an agèd wife, I mete and dole
Unequal laws unto a savage race,
That hoard, and sleep, and feed, and know not me.

  I cannot rest from travel; I will drink
Life to the lees. All times I have enjoyed
Greatly, have suffered greatly, both with those
That loved me, and alone; on shore, and when
Through scudding drifts the rainy Hyades[2] 10

*The World Is Too Much with Us*
   [1] Proteus and Triton are both figures from Greek mythology. Proteus had the power to assume different forms; Triton was often represented blowing on a conch shell.

*Ulysses*
   [1] Ulysses, according to Greek legend, was the king of Ithaca and a hero of the Trojan War. Tennyson represents him as eager to resume the life of travel and adventure.
   [2] A group of stars in the constellation Taurus. According to Greek mythology, the rising of these stars with the sun foretold rain.

Vexed the dim sea. I am become a name;
For always roaming with a hungry heart
Much have I seen and known — cities of men
And manners, climates, councils, governments,
Myself not least, but honored of them all —
And drunk delight of battle with my peers,
Far on the ringing plains of windy Troy.
I am a part of all that I have met;
Yet all experience is an arch wherethrough
Gleams that untraveled world whose margin fades          20
Forever and forever when I move.
How dull it is to pause, to make an end,
To rust unburnished, not to shine in use!
As though to breathe were life. Life piled on life
Were all too little, and of one to me
Little remains; but every hour is saved
From that eternal silence, something more,
A bringer of new things; and vile it were
For some three suns to store and hoard myself,
And this gray spirit yearning in desire          30
To follow knowledge like a sinking star,
Beyond the utmost bound of human thought.

    This is my son, mine own Telemachus,
To whom I leave the scepter and the isle —
Well-loved of me, discerning to fulfill
This labor, by slow prudence to make mild
A rugged people, and through soft degrees
Subdue them to the useful and the good.
Most blameless is he, centered in the sphere
Of common duties, decent not to fail          40
In offices of tenderness, and pay
Meet° adoration to my household gods,          proper
When I am gone. He works his work, I mine.

    There lies the port; the vessel puffs her sail;
There gloom the dark, broad seas. My mariners,
Souls that have toiled, and wrought, and thought with me —
That ever with a frolic welcome took
The thunder and the sunshine, and opposed
Free hearts, free foreheads — you and I are old;
Old age hath yet his honor and his toil.          50
Death closes all; but something ere the end,
Some work of noble note, may yet be done,
Not unbecoming men that strove with Gods.

The lights begin to twinkle from the rocks;
The long day wanes; the slow moon climbs; the deep
Moans round with many voices. Come, my friends,
'Tis not too late to seek a newer world.
Push off, and sitting well in order smite
The sounding furrows; for my purpose holds
To sail beyond the sunset, and the baths                    60
Of all the western stars, until I die.
It may be that the gulfs will wash us down;
It may be we shall touch the Happy Isles,[3]
And see the great Achilles, whom we knew.
Though much is taken, much abides; and though
We are not now that strength which in old days
Moved earth and heaven, that which we are, we are —
One equal temper of heroic hearts,
Made weak by time and fate, but strong in will
To strive, to seek, to find, and not to yield.              70

## FOR ANALYSIS

**1.** Is Ulysses' desire to abdicate his duties as king irresponsible?

**2.** Contrast Ulysses with his son Telemachus (see ll. 33–43). Is Telemachus admirable?

**3.** At the conclusion of the poem, Ulysses is determined not to yield. Yield to what?

## MAKING ARGUMENTS

While many readers have for years seen Tennyson as identifying with and being
sympathetic toward the speaker in this poem, others have detected an ironic distance
between the poet and the hero. Make an argument defending the traditional reading
of the poem, or make an argument for a reading in which Ulysses is at least as much
an object of criticism as an object of sympathy.

## EMILY DICKINSON    (1830–1886)

# MUCH MADNESS IS
# DIVINEST SENSE—    1862

Much Madness is divinest Sense —
To a discerning Eye —
Much Sense — the starkest Madness —
'Tis the Majority

*Ulysses*
[3] The Islands of the Blessed (also Elysium), thought to be in the far western oceans, where those
favored by the gods, such as Achilles, enjoyed life after death.

In this, as All, prevail —
Assent — and you are sane —
Demur — you're straightway dangerous —
And handled with a Chain —


# SHE ROSE TO HIS REQUIREMENT   CA. 1863

She rose to His Requirement — dropt
The Playthings of Her Life
To take the honorable Work
Of Woman, and of Wife —

If ought° She missed in Her new Day,                          anything
Of Amplitude, or Awe —
Or first Prospective — Or the Gold
In using, wear away,

It lay unmentioned — as the Sea
Develope Pearl, and Weed,                                           10
But only to Himself — be known
The Fathoms they abide —

## FOR ANALYSIS

**1.** What are the "Playthings" referred to in line 2?

**2.** Why does the poet refer to both "Woman" and "Wife" in line 4, since a wife is also a woman?

**3.** Look up the words *amplitude*, *awe*, and *prospective* in your dictionary, and consider how these words help you to understand the woman's losses.

**4.** What does "It" in the third **stanza** refer to?

**5.** Why is the sea **image** at the end of the poem appropriate? What does the contrast between "Pearl" and "Weed" suggest?

**6.** The last word of the poem, *abide*, has several meanings. Which of them are relevant to the meaning of the poem?

## MAKING ARGUMENTS

Make the contrarian argument that Dickinson's stance on marriage, while informed by observation of the institution in her historical moment, is not based on firsthand knowledge, since she never married. Be creative if you want, but be sure to stick to the text — while also bringing in any outside knowledge or logical arguments you think might support your case.

## WRITING TOPIC

Write an essay describing a woman you know who gave up an important part of herself to be a wife.

## MAKING CONNECTIONS

Compare and contrast the attitudes toward marriage in this poem with those in Glück's "The Myth of Innocence" (p. 181).

## THOMAS HARDY    (1840–1928)

# THE MAN HE KILLED    1902

"Had he and I but met
    By some old ancient inn,
We should have sat us down to wet
    Right many a nipperkin!

"But ranged as infantry,
    And staring face to face,
I shot at him as he at me,
    And killed him in his place.

"I shot him dead because —
    Because he was my foe,                    10
Just so: my foe of course he was:
    That's clear enough; although

"He thought he'd 'list, perhaps,
    Off-hand-like — just as I —
Was out of work — had sold his traps —
    No other reason why.

"Yes; quaint and curious war is!
    You shoot a fellow down
You'd treat, if met where any bar is,
    Or help to half-a-crown."                 20

## WILLIAM BUTLER YEATS  (1865–1939)

# EASTER 1916[1]  1916

I have met them at close of day
Coming with vivid faces
From counter or desk among grey
Eighteenth-century houses.
I have passed with a nod of the head
Or polite meaningless words,
Or have lingered awhile and said
Polite meaningless words,
And thought before I had done
Of a mocking tale or a gibe                    10
To please a companion
Around the fire at the club,
Being certain that they and I
But lived where motley is worn:
All changed, changed utterly:
A terrible beauty is born.

That woman's days were spent
In ignorant good-will,
Her nights in argument
Until her voice grew shrill.                    20
What voice more sweet than hers
When, young and beautiful,
She rode to harriers?[2]
This man had kept a school
And rode our wingéd horse;[3]
This other his helper and friend
Was coming into his force;
He might have won fame in the end,
So sensitive his nature seemed,
So daring and sweet his thought.               30
This other man I had dreamed
A drunken, vainglorious lout.

---

[1] On Easter Monday in 1916, a group of Irish nationalists seized key points in Ireland, including the Dublin Post Office, from which they proclaimed an independent Irish Republic. At first, most of the Irish were indifferent to the nationalists' futile yet heroic gesture, but as the rebellion was crushed and the leaders executed, they became heroes in the eyes of their fellow citizens. Some of those leaders are alluded to in the second stanza and are named in lines 75 and 76.

[2] In the aristocratic sport of hare hunting, a "pack of harriers" refers to the hounds as well as the persons following the chase.

[3] In Greek mythology, a winged horse is associated with poetic inspiration.

He had done most bitter wrong
To some who are near my heart,
Yet I number him in the song;
He, too, has resigned his part
In the casual comedy;
He, too, has been changed in his turn,
Transformed utterly:
A terrible beauty is born.                                        40

Hearts with one purpose alone
Through summer and winter seem
Enchanted to a stone
To trouble the living stream.
The horse that comes from the road,
The rider, the birds that range
From cloud to tumbling cloud,
Minute by minute they change;
A shadow of cloud on the stream
Changes minute by minute;                                        50
A horse-hoof slides on the brim,
And a horse plashes within it;
The long-legged moor-hens dive,
And hens to moor-cocks call;
Minute by minute they live:
The stone's in the midst of all.

Too long a sacrifice
Can make a stone of the heart.
O when may it suffice?
That is Heaven's part, our part                                  60
To murmur name upon name,
As a mother names her child
When sleep at last has come
On limbs that had run wild.
What is it but nightfall?
No, no, not night but death;
Was it needless death after all?
For England may keep faith
For all that is done and said.
We know their dream; enough                                      70
To know they dreamed and are dead;
And what if excess of love
Bewildered them till they died?
I write it out in a verse —
MacDonagh and MacBride

And Connolly and Pearse[4]
Now and in time to be,
Wherever green is worn,
Are changed, changed utterly:
A terrible beauty is born.                                           80

## FOR ANALYSIS

**1.** What is "changed utterly"? In what sense can beauty be "terrible" (ll. 15–16)?

**2.** Who or what does "they" in line 55 refer to? What does the "stone" in lines 43 and 56 **symbolize**? What is Yeats contrasting?

**3.** How does the poet answer the question he asks in line 67?

## MAKING ARGUMENTS

Is Yeats convinced that these sacrifices were worthwhile in the end? While many read the poem as ultimately ambivalent, reject that conclusion for the sake of argument. How would you argue that Yeats is ambivalent? How would you argue that he is not?

## WRITING TOPIC

In the first **stanza**, the attitude of the poet toward the people he is describing is indifferent, even contemptuous. How is that attitude modified in the rest of the poem?

# THE SECOND COMING[1]   1921

Turning and turning in the widening gyre°                           spiral
The falcon cannot hear the falconer;
Things fall apart; the center cannot hold;
Mere anarchy is loosed upon the world,
The blood-dimmed tide is loosed, and everywhere
The ceremony of innocence is drowned;
The best lack all conviction, while the worst
Are full of passionate intensity.

Surely some revelation is at hand;
Surely the Second Coming is at hand;                               10
The Second Coming! Hardly are those words out

---

*Easter 1916*
  [4] Thomas MacDonagh, John MacBride, James Connolly, and Patrick Pearse, shot by a firing squad at Kilmainham Jail in Dublin following the Easter Rising.

*The Second Coming*
  [1] The New Testament (Matthew 24:29–44) describes the Second Coming of Christ as following a period of tribulation to judge the living and the dead and to inaugurate the millennium.

When a vast image out of *Spiritus Mundi*[2]
Troubles my sight: somewhere in sands of the desert
A shape with lion body and the head of a man,
A gaze blank and pitiless as the sun,
Is moving its slow thighs, while all about it
Reel shadows of the indignant desert birds.
The darkness drops again; but now I know
That twenty centuries of stony sleep
Were vexed to nightmare by a rocking cradle,                    20
And what rough beast, its hour come round at last,
Slouches towards Bethlehem to be born?

## CARL SANDBURG    (1878–1967)

# I AM THE PEOPLE, THE MOB    1916

I am the people — the mob — the crowd — the mass.
Do you know that all the great work of the world is done through me?
I am the workingman, the inventor, the maker of the world's food and clothes.
I am the audience that witnesses history. The Napoleons come from me
        and the Lincolns. They die. And then I send forth more Napoleons
        and Lincolns.
I am the seed ground. I am a prairie that will stand for much plowing.
        Terrible storms pass over me. I forget. The best of me is sucked
        out and wasted. I forget. Everything but Death comes to me and
        makes me work and give up what I have. And I forget.          10
Sometimes I growl, shake myself and spatter a few red drops for history to
        remember. Then — I forget.
When I, the People, learn to remember, when I, the People, use the lessons
        of yesterday and no longer forget who robbed me last year, who
        played me for a fool — then there will be no speaker in all the
        world say the name: "The People," with any fleck of a sneer in
        his voice or any far-off smile of derision.
The mob — the crowd — the mass — will arrive then.

## FOR ANALYSIS

**1.** Describe the speaker in this poem. Who is speaking? What is the effect of having this kind of speaker?

**2.** How does the poem change in the last of the lines that begins "I am"?

*The Second Coming*
    [2] The Soul or Spirit of the Universe, which Yeats believed constituted a fund of racial images and memories.

## MAKING ARGUMENTS

To whom do you think Sandburg was addressing this poem? Is his speaker talking to itself — to "the mob" — or to people of a different social class? Make an argument for one or the other, or both, with reference to specific moments in the poem.

## WRITING TOPIC

What political beliefs does this poem implicitly champion? Try to construct a **concrete** political platform out of the more **abstract** ideas expressed here.

## WALLACE STEVENS (1879–1955)

# PETER QUINCE AT THE CLAVIER[1]  1915

### I

Just as my fingers on these keys
Make music, so the self-same sounds
On my spirit make a music too.

Music is feeling then, not sound;
And thus it is that what I feel,
Here in this room, desiring you,

Thinking of your blue-shadowed silk,
Is music. It is like the strain
Waked in the elders by Susanna:[2]

Of a green evening, clear and warm,                                    10
She bathed in her still garden, while
The red-eyed elders, watching, felt

The basses of their being throb
In witching chords, and their thin blood
Pulse pizzicati° of Hosanna.                           a pizzicato note or passage

*Peter Quince at the Clavier*
    [1] Peter Quince is a character from William Shakespeare's *A Midsummer Night's Dream*. He is the playwright and stage manager of "The Most Lamentable Comedy and Most Cruel Death of Pyramus and Thisbe," a comical amateur play performed at Theseus and Hippolyta's wedding. He is the speaker in Stevens's poem.
    [2] In the book of Daniel in the Bible, two village elders spy on a young Hebrew wife named Susanna while she bathes in the garden spring. The elders threaten to accuse her of committing adultery unless she makes love to them. She refuses and they accuse her of infidelity, tarnishing her reputation. However, a cross-examination of the elders later reveals that they fabricated the story, after which the elders are put to death.

## II

In the green water, clear and warm,
Susanna lay.
She searched
The touch of springs,
And found                                                          20
Concealed imaginings.
She sighed
For so much melody.

Upon the bank she stood
In the cool
Of spent emotions.
She felt, among the leaves,
The dew
Of old devotions.

She walked upon the grass,                                        30
Still quavering.
The winds were like her maids,
On timid feet,
Fetching her woven scarves,
Yet wavering.

A breath upon her hand
Muted the night.
She turned —
A cymbal crashed,
And roaring horns.                                                40

## III

Soon, with a noise like tambourines,
Came her attendant Byzantines.

They wondered why Susanna cried
Against the elders by her side:

And as they whispered, the refrain
Was like a willow swept by rain.

Anon, their lamps' uplifted flame
Revealed Susanna and her shame.

And then the simpering Byzantines,
Fled, with a noise like tambourines.                              50

## IV

Beauty is momentary in the mind —
The fitful tracing of a portal;
But in the flesh it is immortal.

The body dies; the body's beauty lives.
So evenings die, in their green going,
A wave, interminably flowing.
So gardens die, their meek breath scenting
The cowl° of Winter, done repenting.                    a hood or long hooded cloak
So maidens die, to the auroral
Celebration of a maiden's choral.                        60

Susanna's music touched the bawdy strings
Of those white elders; but, escaping,
Left only Death's ironic scraping.
Now, in its immortality, it plays
On the clear viol° of her memory,                        a bowed, stringed instrument
And makes a constant sacrament of praise.

### FOR ANALYSIS

**1.** Who is this poem's speaker? What is he or she doing? How does this inform the poem's meaning?

**2.** Who is Susanna? What is she doing? How important is her identity to the poem?

**3.** What things are compared in "Peter Quince at the Clavier"?

**4.** Section IV begins: "Beauty is momentary in the mind — / The fitful tracing of a portal; / But in the flesh it is immortal" (ll. 51–53). What does this mean? How does this idea relate to the poem as a whole?

### MAKING ARGUMENTS

Is poetry the same thing as music? What does this poem have to say on the matter? Make an argument answering these questions.

### WRITING TOPIC

Describe the poem's music, section by section. How does Stevens use the poet's tools to create and vary the sound of the lines? How do the sections differ from one another? How do these differences relate to the poem's meanings?

### MAKING CONNECTIONS

**1.** Connect "Peter Quince at the Clavier" to another art — painting.

**2.** Read Stevens's poem with Blake's "The Garden of Love" (p. 166). What are the points of connection? Are these gardens similar? How about what happens in them?

## CLAUDE MCKAY   (1890–1948)

# IF WE MUST DIE   1922

If we must die, let it not be like hogs
Hunted and penned in an inglorious spot,
While round us bark the mad and hungry dogs,
Making their mock at our accurséd lot.
If we must die, O let us nobly die,
So that our precious blood may not be shed
In vain; then even the monsters we defy
Shall be constrained to honor us though dead!
O kinsmen! we must meet the common foe!
Though far outnumbered let us show us brave,                    10
And for their thousand blows deal one deathblow!
What though before us lies the open grave?
Like men we'll face the murderous, cowardly pack,
Pressed to the wall, dying, but fighting back!


## LANGSTON HUGHES   (1902–1967)

# HARLEM   1951

What happens to a dream deferred?

Does it dry up
like a raisin in the sun?
Or fester like a sore —
And then run?
Does it stink like rotten meat?
Or crust and sugar over —
like a syrupy sweet?

Maybe it just sags
like a heavy load.                    10

*Or does it explode?*

## W. H. AUDEN   (1907–1973)

# THE UNKNOWN CITIZEN   1940

### (TO JS/07/M/378
### THIS MARBLE MONUMENT
### IS ERECTED BY THE STATE)

He was found by the Bureau of Statistics to be
One against whom there was no official complaint,
And all the reports on his conduct agree
That, in the modern sense of an old-fashioned word, he was a saint,
For in everything he did he served the Greater Community.
Except for the War till the day he retired
He worked in a factory and never got fired,
But satisfied his employers, Fudge Motors Inc.
Yet he wasn't a scab or odd in his views,
For his Union reports that he paid his dues,                                    10
(Our report on his Union shows it was sound)
And our Social Psychology workers found
That he was popular with his mates and liked a drink.
The Press are convinced that he bought a paper every day
And that his reactions to advertisements were normal in every way.
Policies taken out in his name prove that he was fully insured,
And his Health-card shows he was once in hospital but left it cured.
Both Producers Research and High-Grade Living declare
He was fully sensible to the advantages of the Installment Plan
And had everything necessary to the Modern Man,                                 20
A phonograph, radio, a car and a frigidaire.
Our researchers into Public Opinion are content
That he held the proper opinions for the time of year;
When there was peace, he was for peace; when there was war, he went.
He was married and added five children to the population,
Which our Eugenist says was the right number for a parent of his generation,
And our teachers report that he never interfered with their education.
Was he free? Was he happy? The question is absurd:
Had anything been wrong, we should certainly have heard.

## DUDLEY RANDALL   (1914–2000)

# BALLAD OF BIRMINGHAM   1969

### (ON THE BOMBING OF A CHURCH IN BIRMINGHAM, ALABAMA, 1963)[1]

"Mother dear, may I go downtown
Instead of out to play,
And march the streets of Birmingham
In a Freedom March today?"

"No, baby, no, you may not go,
For the dogs are fierce and wild,
And clubs and hoses, guns and jails
Aren't good for a little child."

"But, mother, I won't be alone.
Other children will go with me,                                   10
And march the streets of Birmingham
To make our country free."

"No, baby, no, you may not go,
For I fear those guns will fire.
But you may go to church instead
And sing in the children's choir."

She has combed and brushed her night-dark hair,
And bathed rose petal sweet.
And drawn white gloves on her small brown hands,
And white shoes on her feet.                                      20

The mother smiled to know her child
Was in the sacred place,
But that smile was the last smile
To come upon her face.

For when she heard the explosion,
Her eyes grew wet and wild.
She raced through the streets of Birmingham
Calling for her child.

---

[1] This poem commemorates the murder of four young African American girls when a bomb was thrown into the Sixteenth Street Baptist Church in 1963, one of the early and most traumatic events in the modern civil rights movement.

She clawed through bits of glass and brick,
Then lifted out a shoe.                                                    30
"Oh, here's the shoe my baby wore,
But, baby, where are you?"


## GWENDOLYN BROOKS   (1917–2000)

# WE REAL COOL   1959

**THE POOL PLAYERS**

**SEVEN AT THE GOLDEN SHOVEL.**


We real cool. We
Left school. We

Lurk late. We
Strike straight. We

Sing sin. We
Thin gin. We

Jazz June. We
Die soon.


## MARGE PIERCY   (B. 1936)

# THE MARKET ECONOMY   1973

Suppose some peddler offered
you can have a color TV
but your baby will be
born with a crooked spine;
you can have polyvinyl cups
and wash and wear
suits but it will cost
you your left lung
rotted with cancer; suppose
somebody offered you                                                      10
a frozen precooked dinner
every night for ten years
but at the end
your colon dies
and then you do,

slowly and with much pain.
You get a house in the suburbs
but you work in a new plastics
factory and die at fifty-one
when your kidneys turn off.                    20
But where else will you
work? where else can
you rent but Smog City?
The only houses for sale
are under the yellow sky.
You've been out of work for
a year and they're hiring
at the plastics factory.
Don't read the fine
print, there isn't any.                        30

**FOR ANALYSIS**

1. Characterize the **tone** of this poem.

2. Would this still be a poem if it were printed as a paragraph? Compare this poem with Carolyn Forché's "The Colonel" (p. 363), which is written as a paragraph. Which do you find more "poetic"? Explain.

3. What is meant by the last two lines of the poem?

**MAKING ARGUMENTS**

Regardless of your own politics, how would you make the argument that "the market" isn't to blame for the ills Piercy's poem enumerates? What would you propose as an alternative cause?

**CAROLYN FORCHÉ**   (B. 1950)

# THE COLONEL   1981

What you have heard is true. I was in his house. His wife carried a tray of coffee and sugar. His daughter filed her nails, his son went out for the night. There were daily papers, pet dogs, a pistol on the cushion beside him. The moon swung bare on its black cord over the house. On the television was a cop show. It was in English. Broken bottles were embedded in the walls round the house to scoop the kneecaps from a man's legs or cut his hands to lace. On the windows there were gratings like those in liquor stores. We had dinner, rack of lamb, good wine, a gold bell was on the table for calling the maid. The maid brought green mangoes, salt, a type of bread. I was asked how I enjoyed the country. There was a brief commercial in Spanish. His wife took everything away. There  10 was some talk then of how difficult it had become to govern. The parrot said hello on the terrace. The colonel told it to shut up, and pushed himself from the table. My friend said to me with his eyes: say nothing. The colonel returned with a sack used to bring groceries home. He spilled many human ears on the table. They were like dried peach halves. There is no other way to say this. He took one of them in his hands, shook it in our faces, dropped it into a water glass. It came alive there. I am tired of fooling around he said. As for the rights of anyone, tell your people they can go fuck themselves. He swept the ears to the floor with his arm and held the last of his wine in the air. Something for your poetry, no? he said. Some of the ears on the floor caught this scrap of his        20 voice. Some of the ears on the floor were pressed to the ground.

### FOR ANALYSIS

**1.** What is the occasion of this poem? Where is it set? How would you characterize the colonel's family?

**2.** In line 11 the speaker recounts, "There was some talk then of how difficult it had become to govern." Can you suggest why it had become difficult to govern? How does the colonel respond to these difficulties?

**3.** What does the last sentence suggest?

**4.** This piece is printed as if it were **prose**. Does it have any of the formal characteristics of a poem?

### MAKING ARGUMENTS

Poems have often traditionally been classified as public or private. Is "The Colonel" a public poem or a private poem? Make the argument that the idea of a "poetry of witness," a phrase that appeared in the subtitle of Forché's 1993 international anthology *Against Forgetting*, provides a way out of this problem of classification.


### NATASHA TRETHEWEY   (B. 1966)

# FLOUNDER    2000

*Here*, she said, *put this on your head.*
She handed me a hat.
*You 'bout as white as your dad,*
*and you gone stay like that.*

Aunt Sugar rolled her nylons down
around each bony ankle,
and I rolled down my white knee socks
letting my thin legs dangle,

circling them just above water
and silver backs of minnows                                     10
flitting here then there between
the sun spots and the shadows.

*This is how you hold the pole*
*to cast the line out straight.*
*Now put that worm on your hook,*
*throw it out and wait.*

She sat spitting tobacco juice
into a coffee cup.
Hunkered down when she felt the bite,
jerked the pole straight up                                   20

reeling and tugging hard at the fish
that wriggled and tried to fight back.
*A flounder*, she said, and *you can tell*
*'cause one of its sides is black.*

*The other side is white*, she said.
It landed with a thump.
I stood there watching that fish flip-flop,
switch sides with every jump.

## FOR ANALYSIS

**1.** Why does Aunt Sugar want the speaker to put a hat on? Why is it important to her?

**2.** What is the most important physical characteristic of the flounder? What is the most important action it takes?

**3.** What kind of sentence does Aunt Sugar address the speaker with in lines 1, 15, and 16? Why might that be important for the poem's depiction of their relationship and of what the aunt has to say to the speaker?

## MAKING ARGUMENTS

"Flounder" is pretty clear on the speaker's parents' racial identity — one is white, the other black. But what about Aunt Sugar? What things about her, from the way she talks to the attitudes you would have to assume, make the argument that she is white? What things would you have to assume if she is black?

## WRITING TOPIC

Animals are used in literature for as many different reasons as there are different kinds of animals on the planet. Most animal appearances in stories and poems are motivated by something other than a desire to focus on the animals themselves; more often, they are there in the service of a **plot** or as **metaphorical** illustrations about people. Do you think the way we use animals in imaginative literature is significant? What does it mean to you about our relation to the nonhuman animal world?

The poems in this section are all about America the nation and America the idea. None of them celebrates the nation — in its present or in its past — in an uncritical way, but neither do any of them condemn it wholesale. As you read these poems, written in a number of different places and times, pay attention to how they are in some ways quite similar and how in others they diverge in what they have to say about the American present, the American past, and American identity — and in the way they say those things. Also look for connections between what they have to say and how that message is presented through form.

## WALT WHITMAN (1819–1892)

# ONE SONG, AMERICA, BEFORE I GO    1872

One song, America, before I go,
I'd sing, o'er all the rest, with trumpet sound,
For thee — the Future.

I'd sow a seed for thee of endless Nationality;
I'd fashion thy Ensemble, including Body and Soul;
I'd show, away ahead, thy real Union, and how it may be accomplish'd.

(The paths to the House I seek to make,
But leave to those to come, the House itself.)

Belief I sing — and Preparation;
As Life and Nature are not great with reference to the Present only,    10
But greater still from what is yet to come,
Out of that formula for Thee I sing.

### FOR ANALYSIS

**1.** In his poem "America," Whitman **parodies** the patriotic song "My Country 'Tis of Thee" to draw attention to some less positive aspects of American history. What kind of song of America does Whitman sing here?

**2.** Why is the future important here? What is Whitman saying about the present and past of America?

### MAKING ARGUMENTS

Imagine Whitman as a contemporary of yours, writing poetry about America today. Make an argument for what sort of opinions he would hold, what kinds of policies he would support or oppose, even what political party he would identify with.

## LANGSTON HUGHES   (1902–1967)

# I, TOO   1926

I, too, sing America.

I am the darker brother.
They send me to eat in the kitchen
When company comes,
But I laugh,
And eat well,
And grow strong.

Tomorrow,
I'll be at the table
When company comes.                                                    10
Nobody'll dare
Say to me,
"Eat in the kitchen,"
Then.

Besides,
They'll see how beautiful I am
And be ashamed —

I, too, am America.

### FOR ANALYSIS

**1.** The title "I, Too" alludes to Walt Whitman's "I Hear America Singing" (you may find it helpful to look at Whitman's poem online). Why does Hughes add the word "too"? How does it respond to the Whitman poem to which it **alludes**?

**2.** How does this poem's last line relate to the first? What does the difference express?

### MAKING ARGUMENTS

Think about the "they" in "I, Too." Who are "they" in relation to the speaker? Who are they in relation to the audience? Make an argument about the identity of "they," about the identity of the audience, and about how the poem wants its readers to feel about this group.

## ALLEN GINSBERG (1926–1997)

# A SUPERMARKET IN CALIFORNIA 1955

What thoughts I have of you tonight, Walt Whitman, for I walked
down the sidestreets under the trees with a headache self-conscious looking
at the full moon.
In my hungry fatigue, and shopping for images, I went into the neon
fruit supermarket, dreaming of your enumerations!
What peaches and what penumbras! Whole families shopping at
night! Aisles full of husbands! Wives in the avocados, babies in the tomatoes!
—and you, Garcia Lorca, what were you doing down by the watermelons?

I saw you, Walt Whitman, childless, lonely old grubber, poking
among the meats in the refrigerator and eyeing the grocery boys.          10
I heard you asking questions of each: Who killed the pork chops?
What price bananas? Are you my Angel?
I wandered in and out of the brilliant stacks of cans following you,
and followed in my imagination by the store detective.
We strode down the open corridors together in our solitary fancy
tasting artichokes, possessing every frozen delicacy, and never passing the
cashier.

Where are we going, Walt Whitman? The doors close in a hour.
Which way does your beard point tonight?
(I touch your book and dream of our odyssey in the supermarket and          20
feel absurd.)
Will we walk all night through solitary streets? The trees add shade
to shade, lights out in the houses, we'll both be lonely.
Will we stroll dreaming of the lost America of love past blue automobiles
in driveways, home to our silent cottage?
Ah, dear father, graybeard, lonely old courage-teacher, what America
did you have when Charon quit poling his ferry and you got out on a
smoking bank and stood watching the boat disappear on the black waters of
Lethe?

## FOR ANALYSIS

**1.** Why does the speaker address Whitman? What is the poem's relation to him?

**2.** How does the speaker feel about contemporary America? How does he feel about
the America of the past?

## MAKING ARGUMENTS

Imagine an argument between you and Ginsberg over whether America is really
lost, or still lost. How would you make an argument against the poem's idea of a lost
America? Think in terms of the poem and your understanding of both the country's
past and present.

## SHIRLEY GEOK-LIN LIM  (B. 1944)

# LEARNING TO LOVE AMERICA  1998

because it has no pure products

because the Pacific Ocean sweeps along the coastline
because the water of the ocean is cold
and because land is better than ocean

because I say we rather than they

because I live in California
I have eaten fresh artichokes
and jacaranda bloom in April and May

because my senses have caught up with my body
my breath with the air it swallows                                          10
my hunger with my mouth

because I walk barefoot in my house

because I have nursed my son at my breast
because he is a strong American boy
because I have seen his eyes redden when he is asked who he is
because he answers I don't know

because to have a son is to have a country
because my son will bury me here
because countries are in our blood and we bleed them

because it is late and too late to change my mind                          20
because it is time.

## FOR ANALYSIS

**1.** The first line of William Carlos Williams's "To Elsie" refers to "The pure products
of America." What about this line might have made Lim want to invoke it in the first
line of her poem?

**2.** What do the words that follow the repeated "because" explain? Of what are they
the cause?

## MAKING ARGUMENTS

Make an argument about line 19 in "Learning to Love America." Are our countries in
our blood? What does it mean to say this? Is it a good thing? A bad thing? Both?

### MAKING CONNECTIONS

**1.** Each of the poems in this section refers to other, earlier creative works. Are there any parallels in the way they make these references? Why do you think they make them? What's the connection between poetic **allusion** and the way these poems view America?

**2.** Many of these poems reflect on America not simply in general but in relation to personal identity. What are the connections between them in regard to the way national identity takes shape? What kinds of identity are implicitly and explicitly considered?

**3.** What role does love play in these poems? What kinds of love are represented? How are they treated? How does their treatment relate to their poem's **themes**?

**4.** Each of these poems is in some way about process — about being in the middle of something happening, becoming, or being undertaken. Why is this shared trait significant? How are these poems about a process or processes?

# CONFORMITY AND REBELLION

# DRAMA

## SOPHOCLES (496?–406 BCE)

## ANTIGONÊ[1]    CA. 441 BCE

### CHARACTERS

| | |
|---|---|
| Antigonê | Teiresias |
| Ismenê | A Sentry |
| Eurydicê | A Messenger |
| Creon | Chorus |
| Haimon | |

### Scene

*Before the Palace of Creon, King of Thebes. A central double door, and two lateral doors. A platform extends the length of the facade, and from this platform three steps lead down into the "orchestra," or chorus-ground.*

### Time

*Dawn of the day after the repulse of the Argive army from the assault on Thebes.*

### PROLOGUE

*(Antigonê and Ismenê enter from the central door of the Palace.)*

**Antigonê.** Ismenê, dear sister,
   You would think that we had already suffered enough
   For the curse on Oedipus:[2]
   I cannot imagine any grief

---

[1] An English version by Dudley Fitts and Robert Fitzgerald.    [2] Oedipus, a former king of Thebes, unwittingly killed his father and married his own mother, Iocastê. By her he had four children, the sisters Antigonê and Ismenê and the brothers Polyneicês and Eteoclês. When Oedipus realized what he had done, he blinded himself and left Thebes. Eteoclês drove Polyneicês out of Thebes after a quarrel, but Polyneicês returned with an army and laid siege to Thebes. In the ensuing struggle, the brothers killed each other. Creon became king and, as a punishment, decreed that Polyneicês be denied the rites of burial.

That you and I have not gone through. And now —
Have they told you of the new decree of our King Creon?
**Ismenê.** I have heard nothing: I know
That two sisters lost two brothers, a double death
In a single hour; and I know that the Argive army
Fled in the night; but beyond this, nothing.                    10
**Antigonê.** I thought so. And that is why I wanted you
To come out here with me. There is something we must do.
**Ismenê.** Why do you speak so strangely?
**Antigonê.** Listen, Ismenê:
Creon buried our brother Eteoclês
With military honors, gave him a soldier's funeral,
And it was right that he should; but Polyneicês,
Who fought as bravely and died as miserably, —
They say that Creon has sworn
No one shall bury him, no one mourn for him,                    20
But his body must lie in the fields, a sweet treasure
For carrion birds to find as they search for food.
That is what they say, and our good Creon is coming here
To announce it publicly; and the penalty —
Stoning to death in the public square.
                                        There it is,
And now you can prove what you are:
A true sister, or a traitor to your family.
**Ismenê.** Antigonê, you are mad! What could I possibly do?
**Antigonê.** You must decide whether you will help me or not.
**Ismenê.** I do not understand you. Help you in what?          30
**Antigonê.** Ismenê, I am going to bury him. Will you come?
**Ismenê.** Bury him! You have just said the new law forbids it.
**Antigonê.** He is my brother. And he is your brother, too.
**Ismenê.** But think of the danger! Think what Creon will do!
**Antigonê.** Creon is not strong enough to stand in my way.
**Ismenê.** Ah sister!
Oedipus died, everyone hating him
For what his own search brought to light, his eyes
Ripped out by his own hand; and Iocastê died,
His mother and wife at once: she twisted the cords             40
That strangled her life; and our two brothers died,
Each killed by the other's sword. And we are left:
But oh, Antigonê,
Think how much more terrible than these
Our own death would be if we should go against Creon
And do what he has forbidden! We are only women,
We cannot fight with men, Antigonê!
The law is strong, we must give in to the law

In this thing, and in worse. I beg the Dead
To forgive me, but I am helpless: I must yield                                    50
To those in authority. And I think it is dangerous business
To be always meddling.
**Antigonê.**                      If that is what you think,
I should not want you, even if you asked to come.
You have made your choice, you can be what you want to be.
But I will bury him; and if I must die,
I say that this crime is holy: I shall lie down
With him in death, and I shall be as dear
To him as he to me.
                          It is the dead,
Not the living, who make the longest demands:
We die for ever . . .
                          You may do as you like,                               60
Since apparently the laws of the gods mean nothing to you.
**Ismenê.** They mean a great deal to me; but I have no strength
To break laws that were made for the public good.
**Antigonê.** That must be your excuse, I suppose. But as for me,
I will bury the brother I love.
**Ismenê.**                              Antigonê,
I am so afraid for you!
**Antigonê.** You need not be:
You have yourself to consider, after all.
**Ismenê.** But no one must hear of this, you must tell no one!
I will keep it a secret, I promise!
**Antigonê.**                           Oh tell it! Tell everyone!
Think how they'll hate you when it all comes out                                 70
If they learn that you knew about it all the time!
**Ismenê.** So fiery! You should be cold with fear.
**Antigonê.** Perhaps. But I am doing only what I must.
**Ismenê.** But can you do it? I say that you cannot.
**Antigonê.** Very well: when my strength gives out, I shall do no more.
**Ismenê.** Impossible things should not be tried at all.
**Antigonê.** Go away, Ismenê:
I shall be hating you soon, and the dead will too,
For your words are hateful. Leave me my foolish plan:
I am not afraid of the danger; if it means death,                               80
It will not be the worst of deaths — death without honor.
**Ismenê.** Go then, if you feel you must.
You are unwise,
But a loyal friend indeed to those who love you.

*(Exit into the Palace. Antigonê goes off, L. Enter the Chorus.)*

## PÁRODOS³

**Chorus.** Now the long blade of the sun, lying                    *(Strophe 1)*
    Level east to west, touches with glory
    Thebes of the Seven Gates. Open, unlidded
    Eye of golden day! O marching light
    Across the eddy and rush of Dircê's stream,⁴
    Striking the white shields of the enemy
    Thrown headlong backward from the blaze of morning!
**Choragos.**⁵ Polyneicês their commander
    Roused them with windy phrases,
    He the wild eagle screaming                                          10
    Insults above our land,
    His wings their shields of snow,
    His crest their marshalled helms.

**Chorus.** Against our seven gates in a yawning ring          *(Antistrophe 1)*
    The famished spears came onward in the night;
    But before his jaws were sated with our blood,
    Or pinefire took the garland of our towers,
    He was thrown back; and as he turned, great Thebes —
    No tender victim for his noisy power —
    Rose like a dragon behind him, shouting war.                  20
**Choragos.** For God hates utterly
    The bray of bragging tongues;
    And when he beheld their smiling,
    Their swagger of golden helms,
    The frown of his thunder blasted
    Their first man from our walls.

**Chorus.** We heard his shout of triumph high in the air      *(Strophe 2)*
    Turn to a scream; far out in a flaming arc
    He fell with his windy torch, and the earth struck him.
    And others storming in fury no less than his                    30
    Found shock of death in the dusty joy of battle.
**Choragos.** Seven captains at seven gates
    Yielded their clanging arms to the god
    That bends the battle-line and breaks it.
    These two only, brothers in blood,

---

³ The Párodos is the *ode* sung by the Chorus as it entered the theater and moved down the aisles to the playing area. The *strophe*, in Greek tragedy, is the unit of verse the Chorus chanted as it moved to the left in a dance rhythm. The Chorus sang the *antistrophe* as it moved to the right, and the *epode* while standing still.    ⁴ A stream near Thebes.    ⁵ Choragos is the leader of the Chorus.

Face to face in matchless rage,
Mirroring each the other's death,
Clashed in long combat.

**Chorus.** But now in the beautiful morning of victory            *(Antistrophe 2)*
Let Thebes of the many chariots sing for joy!            40
With hearts for dancing we'll take leave of war:
Our temples shall be sweet with hymns of praise,
And the long night shall echo with our chorus.

## SCENE 1

**Choragos.** But now at last our new King is coming:
Creon of Thebes, Menoikeus' son.
In this auspicious dawn of his reign
What are the new complexities
That shifting Fate has woven for him?
What is his counsel? Why has he summoned
The old men to hear him?

*(Enter Creon from the Palace, C. He addresses the Chorus from the top step.)*

**Creon.** Gentlemen: I have the honor to inform you that our Ship of State, which recent storms have threatened to destroy, has come safely to harbor at last, guided by the merciful wisdom of Heaven. I have summoned you here  10 this morning because I know that I can depend upon you: your devotion to King Laïos was absolute; you never hesitated in your duty to our late ruler Oedipus; and when Oedipus died, your loyalty was transferred to his children. Unfortunately, as you know, his two sons, the princes Eteoclês and Polyneicês, have killed each other in battle; and I, as the next in blood, have succeeded to the full power of the throne.

I am aware, of course, that no Ruler can expect complete loyalty from his subjects until he has been tested in office. Nevertheless, I say to you at the very outset that I have nothing but contempt for the kind of Governor who is afraid, for whatever reason, to follow the course that he knows is best for  20 the State; and as for the man who sets private friendship above the public welfare, — I have no use for him, either. I call God to witness that if I saw my country headed for ruin, I should not be afraid to speak out plainly; and I need hardly remind you that I would never have any dealings with an enemy of the people. No one values friendship more highly than I; but we must remember that friends made at the risk of wrecking our Ship are not real friends at all.

These are my principles, at any rate, and that is why I have made the following decision concerning the sons of Oedipus: Eteoclês, who died as a man should die, fighting for his country, is to be buried with full military honors, with all the  30 ceremony that is usual when the greatest heroes die; but his brother Polyneicês, who broke his exile to come back with fire and sword against his native city and the shrines of his fathers' gods, whose one idea was to spill the blood of his blood and sell his own people into slavery — Polyneicês, I say, is to have no burial: no man is to touch him or say the least prayer for him; he shall lie on the plain, unburied; and the birds and the scavenging dogs can do with him whatever they like.

This is my command, and you can see the wisdom behind it. As long as I am King, no traitor is going to be honored with the loyal man. But whoever shows by word and deed that he is on the side of the State, — he shall have my respect 40 while he is living and my reverence when he is dead.

**Choragos.** If that is your will, Creon, son of Menoikeus,
You have the right to enforce it: we are yours.
**Creon.** That is my will. Take care that you do your part.
**Choragos.** We are old men: let the younger ones carry it out.
**Creon.** I do not mean that: the sentries have been appointed.
**Choragos.** Then what is it that you would have us do?
**Creon.** You will give no support to whoever breaks this law.
**Choragos.** Only a crazy man is in love with death!
**Creon.** And death it is; yet money talks, and the wisest
Have sometimes been known to count a few coins too many. 50

*(Enter Sentry from L.)*

**Sentry.** I'll not say that I'm out of breath from running, King, because every time I stopped to think about what I have to tell you, I felt like going back. And all the time a voice kept saying, "You fool, don't you know you're walking straight into trouble?"; and then another voice: "Yes, but if you let somebody else get the news to Creon first, it will be even worse than that for you!" But good sense won out, at least I hope it was good sense, and here I am with a story that makes no sense at all; but I'll tell it anyhow, because, as they say, what's going to happen's going to happen, and—
**Creon.** Come to the point. What have you to say? 60
**Sentry.** I did not do it. I did not see who did it. You must not punish me for what someone else has done.
**Creon.** A comprehensive defense! More effective, perhaps,
If I knew its purpose. Come: what is it?
**Sentry.** A dreadful thing ... I don't know how to put it —
**Creon.** Out with it!
**Sentry.**                Well, then;
The dead man —
              Polyneicês —

*(Pause. The Sentry is overcome, fumbles for words. Creon waits impassively.)*

70

out there —

someone, —

New dust on the slimy flesh!

*(Pause. No sign from Creon.)*

Someone has given it burial that way, and
Gone . . .

*(Long pause. Creon finally speaks with deadly control.)*

**Creon.** And the man who dared do this?
**Sentry.**                                I swear I
Do not know! You must believe me!

                                 Listen:
The ground was dry, not a sign of digging, no,
Not a wheel track in the dust, no trace of anyone.
It was when they relieved us this morning: and one of them,
The corporal, pointed to it.

                          There it was,
The strangest —

            Look:
The body, just mounded over with light dust: you see?
Not buried really, but as if they'd covered it
Just enough for the ghost's peace. And no sign
Of dogs or any wild animal that had been there.

90

And then what a scene there was! Every man of us
Accusing the other: we all proved the other man did it,
We all had proof that we could not have done it.
We were ready to take hot iron in our hands,
Walk through fire, swear by all the gods,
*It was not I!*
*I do not know who it was, but it was not I!*

*(Creon's rage has been mounting steadily, but the Sentry is too intent upon his story to notice it.)*

And then, when this came to nothing, someone said
A thing that silenced us and made us stare
Down at the ground: you had to be told the news,
And one of us had to do it! We threw the dice,
And the bad luck fell to me. So here I am,
No happier to be here than you are to have me:
Nobody likes the man who brings bad news.

90

80

**Choragos.** I have been wondering, King: can it be that the gods have done this?
**Creon** *(furiously).* Stop!

Must you doddering wrecks
Go out of your heads entirely? "The gods!"
Intolerable!
The gods favor this corpse? Why? How had he served them?
Tried to loot their temples, burn their images,                                       100
Yes, and the whole State, and its laws with it!
Is it your senile opinion that the gods love to honor bad men?
A pious thought —
              No, from the very beginning
There have been those who have whispered together,
Stiff-necked anarchists, putting their heads together,
Scheming against me in alleys. These are the men,
And they have bribed my own guard to do this thing.
*(Sententiously.)* Money!
There's nothing in the world so demoralizing as money.                              110
Down go your cities,
Homes gone, men gone, honest hearts corrupted,
Crookedness of all kinds, and all for money!
*(To Sentry.)*                           But you —!
I swear by God and by the throne of God,
The man who has done this thing shall pay for it!
Find that man, bring him here to me, or your death
Will be the least of your problems: I'll string you up
Alive, and there will be certain ways to make you
Discover your employer before you die;                                              120
And the process may teach you a lesson you seem to have missed:
The dearest profit is sometimes all too dear:
That depends on the source. Do you understand me?
A fortune won is often misfortune.

**Sentry.** King, may I speak?
**Creon.**                      Your very voice distresses me.
**Sentry.** Are you sure that it is my voice, and not your conscience?
**Creon.** By God, he wants to analyze me now!
**Sentry.** It is not what I say, but what has been done, that hurts you.
**Creon.** You talk too much.                                                      130
**Sentry.**                   Maybe; but I've done nothing.
**Creon.** Sold your soul for some silver: that's all you've done.
**Sentry.** How dreadful it is when the right judge judges wrong!
**Creon.** Your figures of speech
May entertain you now; but unless you bring me the man,
You will get little profit from them in the end.

*(Exit Creon into the Palace.)*

**Sentry.** "Bring me the man" —!
  I'd like nothing better than bringing him the man!
  But bring him or not, you have seen the last of me here.
  At any rate, I am safe!                                140

*(Exit Sentry.)*

## ODE I

**Chorus.** Numberless are the world's wonders, but none       *(Strophe 1)*
  More wonderful than man; the stormgray sea
  Yields to his prows, the huge crests bear him high;
  Earth, holy and inexhaustible, is graven
  With shining furrows where his plows have gone
  Year after year, the timeless labor of stallions.

  The lightboned birds and beasts that cling to cover,     *(Antistrophe 1)*
  The lithe fish lighting their reaches of dim water,
  All are taken, tamed in the net of his mind;
  The lion on the hill, the wild horse windy-maned,        10
  Resign to him; and his blunt yoke has broken
  The sultry shoulders of the mountain bull.

  Words also, and thought as rapid as air,            *(Strophe 2)*
  He fashions to his good use; statecraft is his,
  And his the skill that deflects the arrows of snow,
  The spears of winter rain: from every wind
  He has made himself secure — from all but one:
  In the late wind of death he cannot stand.

  O clear intelligence, force beyond all measure!     *(Antistrophe 2)*
  O fate of man, working both good and evil!         20
  When the laws are kept, how proudly his city stands!
  When the laws are broken, what of his city then?
  Never may the anarchic man find rest at my hearth,
  Never be it said that my thoughts are his thoughts.

## SCENE 2

*(Re-enter Sentry leading Antigonê.)*

**Choragos.** What does this mean? Surely this captive woman
  Is the Princess, Antigonê. Why should she be taken?
**Sentry.** Here is the one who did it! We caught her
  In the very act of burying him. — Where is Creon?

**Choragos.** Just coming from the house.

*(Enter Creon, C.)*

**Creon.** What has happened?
Why have you come back so soon?
**Sentry** *(expansively).* O King,
A man should never be too sure of anything:
I would have sworn
That you'd not see me here again: your anger
Frightened me so, and the things you threatened me with; 10
But how could I tell then
That I'd be able to solve the case so soon?
No dice-throwing this time: I was only too glad to come!

Here is this woman. She is the guilty one:
We found her trying to bury him.
Take her, then; question her; judge her as you will.
I am through with the whole thing now, and glad of it.
**Creon.** But this is Antigonê! Why have you brought her here?
**Sentry.** She was burying him, I tell you!
**Creon** *(severely).* Is this the truth?
**Sentry.** I saw her with my own eyes. Can I say more? 20
**Creon.** The details: come, tell me quickly!
**Sentry.** It was like this:
After those terrible threats of yours, King,
We went back and brushed the dust away from the body.
The flesh was soft by now, and stinking,
So we sat on a hill to windward and kept guard.
No napping this time! We kept each other awake.
But nothing happened until the white round sun
Whirled in the center of the round sky over us:
Then, suddenly,
A storm of dust roared up from the earth, and the sky 30
Went out, the plain vanished with all its trees
In the stinging dark. We closed our eyes and endured it.
The whirlwind lasted a long time, but it passed;
And then we looked, and there was Antigonê!
I have seen
A mother bird come back to a stripped nest, heard
Her crying bitterly a broken note or two
For the young ones stolen. Just so, when this girl
Found the bare corpse, and all her love's work wasted,
She wept, and cried on heaven to damn the hands 40
That had done this thing.
And then she brought more dust

And sprinkled wine three times for her brother's ghost.
We ran and took her at once. She was not afraid,
Not even when we charged her with what she had done.
She denied nothing.

        And this was a comfort to me,
And some uneasiness: for it is a good thing
To escape from death, but it is no great pleasure
To bring death to a friend.

           Yet I always say
There is nothing so comfortable as your own safe skin!
**Creon** (*slowly, dangerously*). And you, Antigonê,         50
You with your head hanging, — do you confess this thing?
**Antigonê.** I do. I deny nothing.
**Creon** (*to Sentry*).         You may go.

(*Exit Sentry.*)

(*To Antigonê.*) Tell me, tell me briefly:
Had you heard my proclamation touching this matter?
**Antigonê.** It was public. Could I help hearing it?
**Creon.** And yet you dared defy the law.
**Antigonê.**             I dared.
It was not God's proclamation. That final Justice
That rules the world below makes no such laws.

Your edict, King, was strong,
But all your strength is weakness itself against        60
The immortal unrecorded laws of God.
They are not merely now: they were, and shall be,
Operative for ever, beyond man utterly.

I knew I must die, even without your decree:
I am only mortal. And if I must die
Now, before it is my time to die,
Surely this is no hardship: can anyone
Living, as I live, with evil all about me,
Think Death less than a friend? This death of mine
Is of no importance; but if I had left my brother        70
Lying in death unburied, I should have suffered.
Now I do not.

        You smile at me. Ah Creon,
Think me a fool, if you like; but it may well be
That a fool convicts me of folly.
**Choragos.** Like father, like daughter: both headstrong, deaf to reason!
She has never learned to yield.

**Creon.**                    She has much to learn.
  The inflexible heart breaks first, the toughest iron
  Cracks first, and the wildest horses bend their necks
  At the pull of the smallest curb.
                      Pride? In a slave?
  This girl is guilty of a double insolence,                    80
  Breaking the given laws and boasting of it.
  Who is the man here,
  She or I, if this crime goes unpunished?
  Sister's child, or more than sister's child,
  Or closer yet in blood — she and her sister
  Win bitter death for this!
  *(To servants.)*          Go, some of you,
  Arrest Ismenê. I accuse her equally.
  Bring her: you will find her sniffling in the house there.

  Her mind's a traitor: crimes kept in the dark
  Cry for light, and the guardian brain shudders;            90
  But how much worse than this
  Is brazen boasting of barefaced anarchy!
**Antigonê.**  Creon, what more do you want than my death?
**Creon.**                                        Nothing.
  That gives me everything.
**Antigonê.**               Then I beg you: kill me.
  This talking is a great weariness: your words
  Are distasteful to me, and I am sure that mine
  Seem so to you. And yet they should not seem so:
  I should have praise and honor for what I have done.
  All these men here would praise me
  Were their lips not frozen shut with fear of you.            100
  *(Bitterly.)* Ah the good fortune of kings,
  Licensed to say and do whatever they please!
**Creon.**  You are alone here in that opinion.
**Antigonê.**  No, they are with me. But they keep their tongues in leash.
**Creon.**  Maybe. But you are guilty, and they are not.
**Antigonê.**  There is no guilt in reverence for the dead.
**Creon.**  But Eteoclês — was he not your brother too?
**Antigonê.**  My brother too.
**Creon.**                    And you insult his memory?
**Antigonê** *(softly).*  The dead man would not say that I insult it.
**Creon.**  He would: for you honor a traitor as much as him.      110
**Antigonê.**  His own brother, traitor or not, and equal in blood.
**Creon.**  He made war on his country. Eteoclês defended it.
**Antigonê.**  Nevertheless, there are honors due all the dead.
**Creon.**  But not the same for the wicked as for the just.

**Antigonê.** Ah Creon, Creon,
　Which of us can say what the gods hold wicked?
**Creon.** An enemy is an enemy, even dead.
**Antigonê.** It is my nature to join in love, not hate.
**Creon** *(finally losing patience).* Go join them, then; if you must have your
　　love,
　Find it in hell!　　　　　　　　　　　　　　　　　　　　　　120
**Choragos.** But see, Ismenê comes:

*(Enter Ismenê, guarded.)*

　Those tears are sisterly, the cloud
　That shadows her eyes rains down gentle sorrow.
**Creon.** You too, Ismenê,
　Snake in my ordered house, sucking my blood
　Stealthily — and all the time I never knew
　That these two sisters were aiming at my throne!
　　　　　　　　　　　　　　　　　　Ismenê,
　Do you confess your share in this crime, or deny it?
　Answer me.
**Ismenê.** Yes, if she will let me say so. I am guilty.　　　　　130
**Antigonê** *(coldly).* No, Ismenê. You have no right to say so.
　You would not help me, and I will not have you help me.
**Ismenê.** But now I know what you meant; and I am here
　To join you, to take my share of punishment.
**Antigonê.** The dead man and the gods who rule the dead
　Know whose act this was. Words are not friends.
**Ismenê.** Do you refuse me, Antigonê? I want to die with you:
　I too have a duty that I must discharge to the dead.
**Antigonê.** You shall not lessen my death by sharing it.
**Ismenê.** What do I care for life when you are dead?　　　　140
**Antigonê.** Ask Creon. You're always hanging on his opinions.
**Ismenê.** You are laughing at me. Why, Antigonê?
**Antigonê.** It's a joyless laughter, Ismenê.
**Ismenê.**　　　　　　　　　　But can I do nothing?
**Antigonê.** Yes. Save yourself. I shall not envy you.
　There are those who will praise you; I shall have honor, too.
**Ismenê.** But we are equally guilty!
**Antigonê.**　　　　　　　　No more, Ismenê.
　You are alive, but I belong to Death.
**Creon** *(to the Chorus).* Gentlemen, I beg you to observe these girls:
　One has just now lost her mind; the other,
　It seems, has never had a mind at all.　　　　　　　　　150
**Ismenê.** Grief teaches the steadiest minds to waver, King.
**Creon.** Yours certainly did, when you assumed guilt with the guilty!

**Ismenê.** But how could I go on living without her?
**Creon.**                                                     You are.

    She is already dead.
**Ismenê.**                          But your own son's bride!
**Creon.** There are places enough for him to push his plow.

    I want no wicked women for my sons!
**Ismenê.** O dearest Haimon, how your father wrongs you!
**Creon.** I've had enough of your childish talk of marriage!
**Choragos.** Do you really intend to steal this girl from your son?
**Creon.** No; Death will do that for me.
**Choragos.**                                    Then she must die?                          160
**Creon** (*ironically*). You dazzle me.

                 — But enough of this talk!
    (*To Guards.*) You there, take them away and guard them well:
    For they are but women, and even brave men run
    When they see Death coming.


    (*Exeunt Ismenê, Antigonê, and Guards.*)


## ODE II


**Chorus.** Fortunate is the man who has never tasted                          (*Strophe 1*)
    God's vengeance!
Where once the anger of heaven has struck, that house is shaken
For ever: damnation rises behind each child
Like a wave cresting out of the black northeast,
When the long darkness under sea roars up
And bursts drumming death upon the windwhipped sand.


I have seen this gathering sorrow from time long past                          (*Antistrophe I*)
Loom upon Oedipus' children: generation from generation
Takes the compulsive rage of the enemy god.
So lately this last flower of Oedipus' line                          10
Drank the sunlight! but now a passionate word
And a handful of dust have closed up all its beauty.


    What mortal arrogance                          (*Strophe 2*)
    Transcends the wrath of Zeus?
Sleep cannot lull him, nor the effortless long months
Of the timeless gods: but he is young for ever,
And his house is the shining day of high Olympos.
    And that is and shall be,
    And all the past, is his.
No pride on earth is free of the curse of heaven,                          20

The straying dreams of men                                    (*Antistrophe 2*)
  May bring them ghosts of joy:
But as they drowse, the waking embers burn them;
Or they walk with fixed eyes, as blind men walk.
But the ancient wisdom speaks for our own time:
  *Fate works most for woe*
  *With Folly's fairest show.*
Man's little pleasure is the spring of sorrow.

## SCENE 3

**Choragos.**  But here is Haimon, King, the last of all your sons.
  Is it grief for Antigonê that brings him here,
  And bitterness at being robbed of his bride?

*(Enter Haimon.)*

**Creon.**  We shall soon see, and no need of diviners,
                                                          — Son,
  You have heard my final judgment on that girl:
  Have you come here hating me, or have you come
  With deference and with love, whatever I do?
**Haimon.**  I am your son, father. You are my guide.
  You make things clear for me, and I obey you.
  No marriage means more to me than your continuing wisdom.          10
**Creon.**  Good. That is the way to behave: subordinate
  Everything else, my son, to your father's will.
  This is what a man prays for, that he may get
  Sons attentive and dutiful in his house,
  Each one hating his father's enemies,
  Honoring his father's friends. But if his sons
  Fail him, if they turn out unprofitably,
  What has he fathered but trouble for himself
  And amusement for the malicious?
                                  So you are right
  Not to lose your head over this woman.                             20
  Your pleasure with her would soon grow cold, Haimon,
  And then you'd have a hellcat in bed and elsewhere.
  Let her find her husband in Hell!
  Of all the people in this city, only she
  Has had contempt for my law and broken it.

  Do you want me to show myself weak before the people?
  Or to break my sworn word? No, and I will not.

The woman dies.
I suppose she'll plead "family ties." Well, let her.
If I permit my own family to rebel,                                                    30
How shall I earn the world's obedience?
Show me the man who keeps his house in hand,
He's fit for public authority.
                                   I'll have no dealings
With law-breakers, critics of the government:
Whoever is chosen to govern should be obeyed —
Must be obeyed, in all things, great and small,
Just and unjust! O Haimon,
The man who knows how to obey, and that man only,
Knows how to give commands when the time comes.
You can depend on him, no matter how fast                                              40
The spears come: he's a good soldier, he'll stick it out.
Anarchy, anarchy! Show me a greater evil!
This is why cities tumble and the great houses rain down,
This is what scatters armies!


No, no: good lives are made so by discipline.
We keep the laws then, and the lawmakers,
And no woman shall seduce us. If we must lose,
Let's lose to a man, at least! Is a woman stronger than we?
**Choragos.** Unless time has rusted my wits,
What you say, King, is said with point and dignity.                                    50
**Haimon** (*boyishly earnest*). Father:
Reason is God's crowning gift to man, and you are right
To warn me against losing mine. I cannot say —
I hope that I shall never want to say! — that you
Have reasoned badly. Yet there are other men
Who can reason, too; and their opinions might be helpful.
You are not in a position to know everything
That people say or do, or what they feel:
Your temper terrifies them — everyone
Will tell you only what you like to hear.                                              60
But I, at any rate, can listen; and I have heard them
Muttering and whispering in the dark about this girl.
They say no woman has ever, so unreasonably,
Died so shameful a death for a generous act:
"She covered her brother's body. Is this indecent?
She kept him from dogs and vultures. Is this a crime?
Death? — She should have all the honor that we can give her!"


This is the way they talk out there in the city.

You must believe me:
Nothing is closer to me than your happiness.                               70
What could be closer? Must not any son
Value his father's fortune as his father does his?
I beg you, do not be unchangeable:
Do not believe that you alone can be right.
The man who thinks that,
The man who maintains that only he has the power
To reason correctly, the gift to speak, the soul —
A man like that, when you know him, turns out empty.
It is not reason never to yield to reason!

In flood time you can see how some trees bend                               80
And because they bend, even their twigs are safe,
While stubborn trees are torn up, roots and all.
And the same thing happens in sailing:
Make your sheet fast, never slacken — and over you go,
Head over heels and under: and there's your voyage.
Forget you are angry! Let yourself be moved!
I know I am young; but please let me say this:
The ideal condition
Would be, I admit, that men should be right by instinct;
But since we are all too likely to go astray,                              90
The reasonable thing is to learn from those who can teach.

**Choragos.** You will do well to listen to him, King,
If what he says is sensible. And you, Haimon,
Must listen to your father. — Both speak well.

**Creon.** You consider it right for a man of my years and experience
To go to school to a boy?

**Haimon.**                     It is not right
If I am wrong. But if I am young, and right,
What does my age matter?

**Creon.** You think it right to stand up for an anarchist?

**Haimon.** Not at all. I pay no respect to criminals.                      100

**Creon.** Then she is not a criminal?

**Haimon.** The City would deny it, to a man.

**Creon.** And the City proposes to teach me how to rule?

**Haimon.** Ah. Who is it that's talking like a boy now?

**Creon.** My voice is the one voice giving orders in this City!

**Haimon.** It is no City if it takes orders from one voice.

**Creon.** The State is the King!

**Haimon.**                     Yes, if the State is a desert.

*(Pause.)*

**Creon.** This boy, it seems, has sold out to a woman.

**Haimon.** If you are a woman: my concern is only for you.
**Creon.** So? Your "concern"! In a public brawl with your father!     110
**Haimon.** How about you, in a public brawl with justice?
**Creon.** With justice, when all that I do is within my rights?
**Haimon.** You have no right to trample on God's right.
**Creon** (*completely out of control*).    Fool, adolescent fool! Taken in by a
   woman!
**Haimon.** You'll never see me taken in by anything vile.
**Creon.** Every word you say is for her!
**Haimon** (*quietly, darkly*).        And for you.
   And for me. And for the gods under the earth.
**Creon.** You'll never marry her while she lives.
**Haimon.** Then she must die. — But her death will cause another.
**Creon.** Another?     120
   Have you lost your senses? Is this an open threat?
**Haimon.** There is no threat in speaking to emptiness.
**Creon.** I swear you'll regret this superior tone of yours!
   You are the empty one!
**Haimon.**         If you were not my father,
   I'd say you were perverse.
**Creon.** You girlstruck fool, don't play at words with me!
**Haimon.** I am sorry. You prefer silence.
**Creon.**          Now, by God —!
   I swear, by all the gods in heaven above us,
   You'll watch it, I swear you shall!
   (*To the servants.*)       Bring her out!
   Bring the woman out! Let her die before his eyes!     130
   Here, this instant, with her bridegroom beside her!
**Haimon.** Not here, no; she will not die here, King.
   And you will never see my face again.
   Go on raving as long as you've a friend to endure you.

(*Exit Haimon.*)

**Choragos.** Gone, gone.
   Creon, a young man in a rage is dangerous!
**Creon.** Let him do, or dream to do, more than a man can.
   He shall not save these girls from death.
**Choragos.**          These girls?
   You have sentenced them both?
**Creon.**         No, you are right.
   I will not kill the one whose hands are clean.     140
**Choragos.** But Antigonê?
**Creon** (*somberly*). I will carry her far away
   Out there in the wilderness, and lock her
   Living in a vault of stone. She shall have food,

As the custom is, to absolve the State of her death.
And there let her pray to the gods of hell:
They are her only gods:
Perhaps they will show her an escape from death,
Or she may learn
           though late,
That piety shown the dead is pity in vain.         150

*(Exit Creon.)*

## ODE III

**Chorus.**  Love, unconquerable              *(Strophe)*
    Waster of rich men, keeper
    Of warm lights and all-night vigil
    In the soft face of a girl:
    Sea-wanderer, forest-visitor!
    Even the pure Immortals cannot escape you,
    And mortal man, in his one day's dusk,
    Trembles before your glory.

    Surely you swerve upon ruin          *(Antistrophe)*
    The just man's consenting heart,        10
    As here you have made bright anger
    Strike between father and son —
    And none had conquered but Love!
    A girl's glance working the will of heaven:
    Pleasure to her alone who mocks us,
    Merciless Aphroditê.[6]

## SCENE 4

**Choragos** *(as Antigonê enters guarded)*.  But I can no longer stand in awe
    of this,
    Nor, seeing what I see, keep back my tears.
    Here is Antigonê, passing to that chamber
    Where all find sleep at last.

**Antigonê.**  Look upon me, friends, and pity me      *(Strophe 1)*
    Turning back at the night's edge to say
    Good-by to the sun that shines for me no longer;

---

[6] Aphroditê is the goddess of love.

Now sleepy Death
Summons me down to Acheron,[7] that cold shore:
There is no bridesong there, nor any music.          10
**Chorus.** Yet not unpraised, not without a kind of honor,
    You walk at last into the underworld;
    Untouched by sickness, broken by no sword.
    What woman has ever found your way to death?
**Antigonê.** How often I have heard the story of Niobê,[8]          *(Antistrophe 1)*
    Tantalos' wretched daughter, how the stone
    Clung fast about her, ivy-close: and they say
    The rain falls endlessly
    And sifting soft snow; her tears are never done.
    I feel the loneliness of her death in mine.          20
**Chorus.** But she was born of heaven, and you
    Are woman, woman-born. If her death is yours,
    A mortal woman's, is this not for you
    Glory in our world and in the world beyond?

**Antigonê.** You laugh at me. Ah, friends, friends,          *(Strophe 2)*
    Can you not wait until I am dead? O Thebes,
    O men many-charioted, in love with Fortune,
    Dear springs of Dircê, sacred Theban grove,
    Be witnesses for me, denied all pity,
    Unjustly judged! and think a word of love          30
    For her whose path turns
    Under dark earth, where there are no more tears.
**Chorus.** You have passed beyond human daring and come at last
    Into a place of stone where Justice sits.
    I cannot tell
    What shape of your father's guilt appears in this.

**Antigonê.** You have touched it at last: that bridal bed          *(Antistrophe 2)*
    Unspeakable, horror of son and mother mingling:
    Their crime, infection of all our family!
    O Oedipus, father and brother!          40
    Your marriage strikes from the grave to murder mine.
    I have been a stranger here in my own land:
    All my life
    The blasphemy of my birth has followed me.
**Chorus.** Reverence is a virtue, but strength

---

[7] A river of Hades.    [8] Niobê married an ancestor of Oedipus named Amphion. Her fourteen children were killed by Apollo and Artemis after Niobê boasted to their mother, Leto, that her children were superior to them. She wept incessantly and was finally transformed into a rock on Mt. Sipylos, whose streams are her tears.

Lives in established law: that must prevail.
You have made your choice,
Your death is the doing of your conscious hand.

**Antigonê.** Then let me go, since all your words are bitter,      *(Epode)*
   And the very light of the sun is cold to me.          50
   Lead me to my vigil, where I must have
   Neither love nor lamentation; no song, but silence.

*(Creon interrupts impatiently.)*

**Creon.** If dirges and planned lamentations could put off death,
   Men would be singing for ever.
   *(To the servants.)*                 Take her, go!
   You know your orders: take her to the vault
   And leave her alone there. And if she lives or dies,
   That's her affair, not ours: our hands are clean.
**Antigonê.** O tomb, vaulted bride-bed in eternal rock,
   Soon I shall be with my own again
   Where Persephonê[9] welcomes the thin ghosts underground:        60
   And I shall see my father again, and you, mother,
   And dearest Polyneicês —
                     dearest indeed
   To me, since it was my hand
   That washed him clean and poured the ritual wine:
   And my reward is death before my time!

   And yet, as men's hearts know, I have done no wrong,
   I have not sinned before God. Or if I have,
   I shall know the truth in death. But if the guilt
   Lies upon Creon who judged me, then, I pray,
   May his punishment equal my own.
**Choragos.**                    O passionate heart,        70
   Unyielding, tormented still by the same winds!
**Creon.** Her guards shall have good cause to regret their delaying.
**Antigonê.** Ah! That voice is like the voice of death!
**Creon.** I can give you no reason to think you are mistaken.
**Antigonê.** Thebes, and you my fathers' gods,
   And rulers of Thebes, you see me now, the last
   Unhappy daughter of a line of kings,
   Your kings, led away to death. You will remember
   What things I suffer, and at what men's hands,

---

[9] Queen of Hades.

Because I would not transgress the laws of heaven.                              80
*(To the guards, simply.)* Come: let us wait no longer.

*(Exit Antigonê, L., guarded.)*

## ODE IV

**Chorus.** All Danaê's[10] beauty was locked away                    *(Strophe 1)*
    In a brazen cell where the sunlight could not come:
    A small room, still as any grave, enclosed her.
    Yet she was a princess too,
    And Zeus in a rain of gold poured love upon her.
    O child, child,
    No power in wealth or war
    Or tough sea-blackened ships
    Can prevail against untiring Destiny!

    And Dryas' son[11] also, that furious king,         *(Antistrophe 1)*  10
    Bore the god's prisoning anger for his pride:
    Sealed up by Dionysos in deaf stone,
    His madness died among echoes.
    So at the last he learned what dreadful power
    His tongue had mocked:
    For he had profaned the revels,
    And fired the wrath of the nine
    Implacable Sisters[12] that love the sound of the flute.

    And old men tell a half-remembered tale             *(Strophe 2)*
    Of horror where a dark ledge splits the sea           20
    And a double surf beats on the gray shores:
    How a king's new woman,[13] sick
    With hatred for the queen he had imprisoned,
    Ripped out his two sons' eyes with her bloody hands
    While grinning Arês[14] watched the shuttle plunge
    Four times: four blind wounds crying for revenge,

    Crying, tears and blood mingled. — Piteously born,    *(Antistrophe 2)*
    Those sons whose mother was of heavenly birth!

---

[10] Though Danaê, a beautiful princess of Argos, was confined by her father, Zeus visited her in the form of a shower of gold, and she gave birth to Perseus as a result.    [11] Lycurgus, king of Thrace, who was driven mad by Dionysos, the god of wine.    [12] The Muses.    [13] The ode alludes to a story indicating the uselessness of high birth against implacable fate. The king's new woman is Eidothea, the second wife of King Phineus. Though Cleopatra, his first wife, was the daughter of Boreas, the north wind, and Phineus himself was descended from kings, Eidothea, out of hatred for Cleopatra, blinded her two sons.    [14] The god of war.

Her father was the god of the North Wind
And she was cradled by gales,                                              30
She raced with young colts on the glittering hills
And walked untrammeled in the open light:
But in her marriage deathless Fate found means
To build a tomb like yours for all her joy.

## SCENE 5

*(Enter blind Teiresias, led by a boy. The opening speeches of Teiresias should be in singsong contrast to the realistic lines of Creon.)*

**Teiresias.** This is the way the blind man comes, Princes, Princes,
    Lock-step, two heads lit by the eyes of one.
**Creon.** What new thing have you to tell us, old Teiresias?
**Teiresias.** I have much to tell you: listen to the prophet, Creon.
**Creon.** I am not aware that I have ever failed to listen.
**Teiresias.** Then you have done wisely, King, and ruled well.
**Creon.** I admit my debt to you. But what have you to say?
**Teiresias.** This, Creon: you stand once more on the edge of fate.
**Creon.** What do you mean? Your words are a kind of dread.
**Teiresias.** Listen, Creon:                                            10
    I was sitting in my chair of augury, at the place
    Where the birds gather about me. They were all a-chatter,
    As is their habit, when suddenly I heard
    A strange note in their jangling, a scream, a
    Whirring fury; I knew that they were fighting,
    Tearing each other, dying
    In a whirlwind of wings clashing. And I was afraid.
    I began the rites of burnt-offering at the altar,
    But Hephaistos[15] failed me: instead of bright flame,
    There was only the sputtering slime of the fat thigh-flesh     20
    Melting: the entrails dissolved in gray smoke;
    The bare bone burst from the welter. And no blaze!

    This was a sign from heaven. My boy described it,
    Seeing for me as I see for others.

    I tell you, Creon, you yourself have brought
    This new calamity upon us. Our hearths and altars
    Are stained with the corruption of dogs and carrion birds
    That glut themselves on the corpse of Oedipus' son.

---

[15] The god of fire.

The gods are deaf when we pray to them, their fire
Recoils from our offering, their birds of omen                                    30
Have no cry of comfort, for they are gorged
With the thick blood of the dead.
                                        O my son,
These are no trifles! Think: all men make mistakes,
But a good man yields when he knows his course is wrong,
And repairs the evil. The only crime is pride.

Give in to the dead man, then: do not fight with a corpse —
What glory is it to kill a man who is dead?
Think, I beg you:
It is for your own good that I speak as I do.
You should be able to yield for your own good.                                    40
Creon.  It seems that prophets have made me their especial province.
    All my life long
    I have been a kind of butt for the dull arrows
    Of doddering fortune-tellers!
                            No, Teiresias:
    If your birds — if the great eagles of God himself
    Should carry him stinking bit by bit to heaven,
    I would not yield. I am not afraid of pollution:
    No man can defile the gods.
                            Do what you will,
    Go into business, make money, speculate
    In India gold or that synthetic gold from Sardis,                             50
    Get rich otherwise than by my consent to bury him.
    Teiresias, it is a sorry thing when a wise man
    Sells his wisdom, lets out his words for hire!
Teiresias.  Ah Creon! Is there no man left in the world —
Creon.  To do what? — Come, let's have the aphorism!
Teiresias.  No man who knows that wisdom outweighs any wealth?
Creon.  As surely as bribes are baser than any baseness.
Teiresias.  You are sick, Creon! You are deathly sick!
Creon.  As you say: it is not my place to challenge a prophet.
Teiresias.  Yet you have said my prophecy is for sale.                            60
Creon.  The generation of prophets has always loved gold.
Teiresias.  The generation of kings has always loved brass.
Creon.  You forget yourself! You are speaking to your King.
Teiresias.  I know it. You are a king because of me.
Creon.  You have a certain skill; but you have sold out.
Teiresias.  King, you will drive me to words that —
Creon.                                        Say them, say them!
    Only remember: I will not pay you for them.

**Teiresias.**  No, you will find them too costly.
**Creon.**                                    No doubt. Speak:
  Whatever you say, you will not change my will.
**Teiresias.**  Then take this, and take it to heart!                            70
  The time is not far off when you shall pay back
  Corpse for corpse, flesh of your own flesh.
  You have thrust the child of this world into living night,
  You have kept from the gods below the child that is theirs:
  The one in a grave before her death, the other,
  Dead, denied the grave. This is your crime:
  And the Furies and the dark gods of Hell
  Are swift with terrible punishment for you.

  Do you want to buy me now, Creon?
                              Not many days,
  And your house will be full of men and women weeping,            80
  And curses will be hurled at you from far
  Cities grieving for sons unburied, left to rot
  Before the walls of Thebes.
  These are my arrows, Creon: they are all for you.

  *(To boy.)* But come, child: lead me home.
  Let him waste his fine anger upon younger men.
  Maybe he will learn at last
  To control a wiser tongue in a better head.

*(Exit Teiresias.)*

**Choragos.**  The old man has gone, King, but his words
  Remain to plague us. I am old, too,                              90
  But I cannot remember that he was ever false.
**Creon.**  That is true. . . . It troubles me.
  Oh it is hard to give in! but it is worse
  To risk everything for stubborn pride.
**Choragos.**  Creon: take my advice.
**Creon.**                                    What shall I do?
**Choragos.**  Go quickly: free Antigonê from her vault
  And build a tomb for the body of Polyneicês.
**Creon.**  You would have me do this?
**Choragos.**                                    Creon, yes!
  And it must be done at once: God moves                           100
  Swiftly to cancel the folly of stubborn men.
**Creon.**  It is hard to deny the heart! But I
  Will do it: I will not fight with destiny.

**Choragos.** You must go yourself, you cannot leave it to others.
**Creon.** I will go

     — Bring axes, servants:
Come with me to the tomb. I buried her, I
Will set her free.

     Oh quickly!
My mind misgives —
The laws of the gods are mighty, and a man must serve them
To the last days of his life!

*(Exit Creon.)*

## PAEAN[16]

---

**Choragos.** God of many names            *(Strophe 1)*
**Chorus.**          O Iacchos[17]
            Son
 of Kadmeian Sémelê
       O born of the Thunder!
 Guardian of the West
       Regent
 of Eleusis's plain
       O Prince of maenad Thebes
 and the Dragon Field by rippling Ismenos:[18]

**Choragos.** God of many names          *(Antistrophe 1)*
**Chorus.**         the flame of torches
 flares on our hills
       the nymphs of Iacchos
 dance at the spring of Castalia:[19]
 from the vine-close mountain
        come ah come in ivy:
 *Evohé evohé!* sings through the streets of Thebes       10

**Choragos.** God of many names           *(Strophe 2)*
**Chorus.**        Iacchos of Thebes
 heavenly Child
       of Sémelê bride of the Thunderer!
 The shadow of plague is upon us:
         come

---

[16] A hymn.   [17] Iacchos is a name for Dionysos. His mother was Sémelê, daughter of Kadmos, the founder of Thebes. His father was Zeus. The Maenads were priestesses of Dionysos who cry "evohé evohé."   [18] A river of Thebes, sacred to Apollo. Dragon Field refers to the legend that the ancestors of Thebes sprang from the dragon's teeth sown by Kadmos.   [19] A spring on Mt. Parnasos.

with clement feet;
> oh come from Parnasos
down the long slopes
> across the lamenting water

**Choragos.**  Iô Fire! Chorister of the throbbing stars!          *(Antistrophe 2)*
> O purest among the voices of the night!
> Thou son of God, blaze for us!

**Chorus.**  Come with choric rapture of circling Maenads
> *Who cry Iô Iacche!*
> > *God of many names!*                                                          20

# EXODOS

*(Enter Messenger, L.)*

**Messenger.**  Men of the line of Kadmos, you who live
> Near Amphion's[20] citadel:
> > I cannot say
> Of any condition of human life "This is fixed,
> This is clearly good, or bad." Fate raises up,
> And Fate casts down the happy and unhappy alike:
> No man can foretell his Fate.
> > Take the case of Creon:
> Creon was happy once, as I count happiness:
> Victorious in battle, sole governor of the land,
> Fortunate father of children nobly born.
> And now it has all gone from him! Who can say          10
> That a man is still alive when his life's joy fails?
> He is a walking dead man. Grant him rich,
> Let him live like a king in his great house:
> If his pleasure is gone, I would not give
> So much as the shadow of smoke for all he owns.

**Choragos.**  Your words hint at sorrow: what is your news for us?
**Messenger.**  They are dead. The living are guilty of their death.
**Choragos.**  Who is guilty? Who is dead? Speak!
**Messenger.**                                             Haimon.
> Haimon is dead; and the hand that killed him
> Is his own hand.                                                                20
**Choragos.**  His father's? or his own?
**Messenger.**  His own, driven mad by the murder his father had done.

---

[20] A child of Zeus and Antiope. He is noted for building the walls of Thebes by charming the stones into place with a lyre.

**Choragos.** Teiresias, Teiresias, how clearly you saw it all!

**Messenger.** This is my news: you must draw what conclusions you can from it.

**Choragos.** But look: Eurydicê, our Queen:
    Has she overheard us?

*(Enter Eurydicê from the Palace, C.)*

**Eurydicê.** I have heard something, friends:
    As I was unlocking the gate of Pallas'[21] shrine,
    For I needed her help today, I heard a voice
    Telling of some new sorrow. And I fainted          30
    There at the temple with all my maidens about me.
    But speak again: whatever it is, I can bear it:
    Grief and I are no strangers.

**Messenger.**                Dearest lady,
    I will tell you plainly all that I have seen.
    I shall not try to comfort you: what is the use,
    Since comfort could lie only in what is not true?
    The truth is always best.

                    I went with Creon
    To the outer plain where Polyneicês was lying,
    No friend to pity him, his body shredded by dogs.
    We made our prayers in that place to Hecatê[22]       40
    And Pluto,[23] that they would be merciful. And we bathed
    The corpse with holy water, and we brought
    Fresh-broken branches to burn what was left of it,
    And upon the urn we heaped up a towering barrow
    Of the earth of his own land.

                    When we were done, we ran
    To the vault where Antigonê lay on her couch of stone.
    One of the servants had gone ahead,
    And while he was yet far off he heard a voice
    Grieving within the chamber, and he came back
    And told Creon. And as the King went closer,       50
    The air was full of wailing, the words lost,
    And he begged us to make all haste. "Am I a prophet?"
    He said, weeping, "And must I walk this road,
    The saddest of all that I have gone before?
    My son's voice calls me on. Oh quickly, quickly!
    Look through the crevice there, and tell me
    If it Haimon, or some deception of the gods!"

---

[21] Pallas Athene, goddess of wisdom.    [22] Hecatê is often identified with Persephone, a goddess of Hades; generally Hecatê is a goddess of sorcery and witchcraft.    [23] King of Hades and brother of Zeus and Poseidon.

We obeyed; and in the cavern's farthest corner
We saw her lying:
She had made a noose of her fine linen veil            60
And hanged herself. Haimon lay beside her,
His arms about her waist, lamenting her,
His love lost under ground, crying out
That his father had stolen her away from him.

When Creon saw him the tears rushed to his eyes
And he called to him: "What have you done, child? Speak to me.
What are you thinking that makes your eyes so strange?
O my son, my son, I come to you on my knees!"
But Haimon spat in his face. He said not a word,
Staring—
                    And suddenly drew his sword            70
And lunged. Creon shrank back, the blade missed; and the boy,
Desperate against himself, drove it half its length
Into his own side, and fell. And as he died
He gathered Antigonê close in his arms again,
Choking, his blood bright red on her white cheek.
And now he lies dead with the dead, and she is his
At last, his bride in the houses of the dead.

*(Exit Eurydicê into the Palace.)*

**Choragos.** She has left us without a word. What can this mean?
**Messenger.** It troubles me, too; yet she knows what is best,
Her grief is too great for public lamentation,            80
And doubtless she has gone to her chamber to weep
For her dead son, leading her maidens in his dirge.
**Choragos.** It may be so: but I fear this deep silence.

*(Pause.)*

**Messenger.** I will see what she is doing. I will go in.

*(Exit Messenger into the Palace.)*
*(Enter Creon with attendants, bearing Haimon's body.)*

**Choragos.** But here is the King himself: oh look at him,
Bearing his own damnation in his arms.
**Creon.** Nothing you say can touch me any more.
My own blind heart has brought me
From darkness to final darkness. Here you see

The father murdering, the murdered son — 90
And all my civic wisdom!
Haimon my son, so young to die,
I was the fool, not you; and you died for me.
**Choragos.** That is the truth; but you were late in learning it.
**Creon.** This truth is hard to bear. Surely a god
Has crushed me beneath the hugest weight of heaven,
And driven me headlong a barbaric way
To trample out the thing I held most dear.

The pains that men will take to come to pain!

*(Enter Messenger from the Palace.)*

**Messenger.** The burden you carry in your hands is heavy, 100
But it is not all: you will find more in your house.
**Creon.** What burden worse than this shall I find there?
**Messenger.** The Queen is dead.
**Creon.** O port of death, deaf world,
Is there no pity for me? And you, Angel of evil,
I was dead, and your words are death again.
Is it true, boy? Can it be true?
Is my wife dead? Has death bred death?
**Messenger.** You can see for yourself.

*(The doors are opened, and the body of Eurydicê is disclosed within.)*

**Creon.** Oh pity! 110
All true, all true, and more than I can bear!
O my wife, my son!
**Messenger.** She stood before the altar, and her heart
Welcomed the knife her own hand guided,
And a great cry burst from her lips for Megareus[24] dead,
And for Haimon dead, her sons; and her last breath
Was a curse for their father, the murderer of her sons,
And she fell, and the dark flowed in through her closing eyes.
**Creon.** O God, I am sick with fear.
Are there no swords here? Has no one a blow for me? 120
**Messenger.** Her curse is upon you for the deaths of both.
**Creon.** It is right that it should be. I alone am guilty.
I know it, and I say it. Lead me in,
Quickly, friends.
I have neither life nor substance. Lead me in.

[24] Son of Creon who was killed in the attack on Thebes.

**Choragos.** You are right, if there can be right in so much wrong.
   The briefest way is best in a world of sorrow.
**Creon.** Let it come,
   Let death come quickly, and be kind to me.
   I would not ever see the sun again.                                    130
**Choragos.** All that will come when it will; but we, meanwhile,
   Have much to do. Leave the future to itself.
**Creon.** All my heart was in that prayer!
**Choragos.** Then do not pray any more: the sky is deaf.
**Creon.** Lead me away. I have been rash and foolish.
   I have killed my son and my wife.
   I look for comfort; my comfort lies here dead.
   Whatever my hands have touched has come to nothing.
   Fate has brought all my pride to a thought of dust.

*(As Creon is being led into the house, the Choragos advances and speaks directly to the audience.)*

**Choragos.** There is no happiness where there is no wisdom;          140
   No wisdom but in submission to the gods.
   Big words are always punished,
   And proud men in old age learn to be wise.

## For Analysis

**1.** Show how the Prologue establishes the **mood** and **theme** of the play. What does it reveal about the **characters** of the two sisters?

**2.** What evidence is there that Creon would treat Antigonê differently if she were a man?

**3.** Does the character of Antigonê change in the course of the play?

**4.** Does the action of the play prepare us for Creon's sudden realization that he has been wrong?

**5.** Is there any justification for Antigonê's cold refusal to allow Ismenê to share her martyrdom?

**6.** Speculate on why Sophocles never brings Haimon and Antigonê together.

**7.** How does the **chorus** contribute to the dramatic development and tension of the play?

**8.** Analyze the use of **dramatic irony** in the play.

## Making Arguments

Critics are divided on the question of whether Antigonê or Creon is the **protagonist** of the play. How does the answer to this question affect one's interpretation of the play? How would you argue for one or the other?

### WRITING TOPICS

**1.** Summarize the **theme** of this play in a brief paragraph.

**2.** Write a one-page essay using this play and Susan Glaspell's *Trifles* (p. 761) as the basis for defining poetic drama on the one hand and realistic drama on the other.

### MAKING CONNECTIONS

Compare the grounds on which Antigonê makes her argument with those on which Jonathan Swift bases his in "A Modest Proposal" (p. 403). How can you identify them? How do they use them to argue their points?

# NONFICTION

**JONATHAN SWIFT**   (1667–1745)

# A MODEST PROPOSAL   1729

I t is a melancholy object to those who walk through this great town[1] or
travel in the country, when they see the streets, the roads, and cabin doors,
crowded with beggars of the female sex, followed by three, four, or six children,
all in rags and importuning every passenger for an alms. These mothers,
instead of being able to work for their honest livelihood, are forced to employ
all their time in strolling to beg sustenance for their helpless infants, who, as
they grow up, either turn thieves for want of work, or leave their dear native
country to fight for the Pretender in Spain, or sell themselves to the Barbados.[2]

I think it is agreed by all parties that this prodigious number of children
in the arms, or on the backs, or at the heels of their mothers, and frequently
of their fathers, is in the present deplorable state of the kingdom a very great
additional grievance; and therefore whoever could find out a fair, cheap, and
easy method of making these children sound, useful members of the commonwealth would deserve so well of the public as to have his statue set up for a
preserver of the nation.

But my intention is very far from being confined to provide only for the
children of professed beggars; it is of a much greater extent, and shall take in
the whole number of infants at a certain age who are born of parents in effect
as little able to support them as those who demand our charity in the streets.

As to my own part, having turned my thoughts for many years upon this
important subject, and maturely weighed the several schemes of other
projectors,[3] I have always found them grossly mistaken in their computation.
It is true, a child just dropped from its dam may be supported by her milk
for a solar year, with little other nourishment; at most not above the value of

[1] Dublin.
[2] Many Irish men joined the army of the exiled James Stuart (1688–1766), who laid claim to the
British throne. Others exchanged their labor for passage to the British colony of Barbados, in the
Caribbean.
[3] People with projects.

two shillings,[4] which the mother may certainly get, or the value in scraps, by her lawful occupation of begging; and it is exactly at one year that I propose to provide for them in such a manner as instead of being a charge upon their parents or the parish, or wanting food and raiment for the rest of their lives, they shall on the contrary contribute to the feeding, and partly to the clothing, of many thousands.

There is likewise another great advantage in my scheme, that it will prevent those voluntary abortions, and that horrid practice of women murdering their bastard children, alas, too frequent among us, sacrificing the poor innocent babes, I doubt, more to avoid the expense than the shame, which would move tears and pity in the most savage and inhuman breast.

The number of souls in this kingdom being usually reckoned one million and a half, of these I calculate there may be about two hundred thousand couples whose wives are breeders; from which number I subtract thirty thousand couples who are able to maintain their own children, although I apprehend there cannot be so many under the present distress of the kingdom; but this being granted, there will remain an hundred and seventy thousand breeders. I again subtract fifty thousand for those women who miscarry, or whose children die by accident or disease within the year. There only remain an hundred and twenty thousand children of poor parents annually born. The question therefore is, how this number shall be reared and provided for, which, as I have already said, under the present situation of affairs, is utterly impossible by all the methods hitherto proposed. For we can neither employ them in handicraft or agriculture; we neither build houses (I mean in the country) nor cultivate land. They can very seldom pick up a livelihood by stealing till they arrive at six years old except where they are of towardly parts;[5] although I confess they learn the rudiments much earlier, during which time they can however be looked upon only as probationers, as I have been informed by a principal gentleman in the country of Cavan, who protested to me that he never knew above one or two instances under the age of six, even in a part of the kingdom so renowned for the quickest proficiency in that art.

I am assured by our merchants that a boy or a girl before twelve years old is no salable commodity; and even when they come to this age they will not yield above three pounds, or three pounds and half a crown at most on the Exchange;[6] which cannot turn to account either to the parents or the kingdom, the charge of nutriment and rags having been at least four times that value.

I shall now therefore humbly propose my own thoughts, which I hope will not be liable to the least objection.

I have been assured by a very knowing American of my acquaintance in London, that a young healthy child well nursed is at a year old a most delicious,

---

[4] A shilling was worth about twenty-five cents.
[5] Able and eager to learn.
[6] A pound was twenty shillings; a crown, five shillings.

nourishing, and wholesome food, whether stewed, roasted, baked, or boiled; and I make no doubt that it will equally serve in a fricassee or a ragout.

I do therefore humbly offer it to public consideration that of the hundred 10 and twenty thousand children, already computed, twenty thousand may be reserved for breed, whereof only one fourth part to be males, which is more than we allow to sheep, black cattle, or swine; and my reason is that these children are seldom the fruits of marriage, a circumstance not much regarded by our savages, therefore one male will be sufficient to serve four females. That the remaining hundred thousand may at a year old be offered in sale to the persons of quality and fortune through the kingdom, always advising the mother to let them suck plentifully in the last month, so as to render them plump and fat for a good table. A child will make two dishes at an entertainment for friends; and when the family dines alone, the fore or hind quarter will make a reasonable dish, and seasoned with a little pepper or salt will be very good boiled on the fourth day, especially in winter.

I have reckoned upon a medium that a child just born will weigh twelve pounds, and in a solar year if tolerably nursed increaseth to twenty-eight pounds.

I grant this food will be somewhat dear, and therefore very proper for landlords, who, as they have already devoured most of the parents, seem to have the best title to the children.

Infant's flesh will be in season throughout the year, but more plentiful in March, and a little before and after. For we are told by a grave author, an eminent French physician,[7] that fish being a prolific diet, there are more children born in Roman Catholic countries about nine months after Lent than at any other season; therefore, reckoning a year after Lent, the markets will be more glutted than usual, because the number of popish infants is at least three to one in this kingdom; and therefore it will have one other collateral advantage, by lessening the number of Papists among us.

I have already computed the charge of nursing a beggar's child (in which list I reckon all cottagers, laborers, and four-fifths of the farmers) to be about two shillings per annum, rags included; and I believe no gentleman would repine to give ten shillings for the carcass of a good fat child, which, as I have said, will make four dishes of excellent nutritive meat, when he hath only some particular friend or his own family to dine with him. Thus the squire will learn to be a good landlord, and grow popular among the tenants; the mother will have eight shillings net profit, and be fit for work till she produces another child.

Those who are more thrifty (as I must confess the times require) may flay 15 the carcass; the skin of which artificially[8] dressed will make admirable gloves for ladies, and summer boots for fine gentlemen.

As to our city of Dublin, shambles[9] may be appointed for this purpose in the most convenient parts of it, and butchers we may be assured will not be

---

[7] François Rabelais, sixteenth-century French comic writer.
[8] Skillfully.
[9] Slaughterhouses.

wanting; although I rather recommend buying the children alive, and dressing them hot from the knife as we do roasting pigs.

A very worthy person, a true lover of his country, and whose virtues I highly esteem, was lately pleased in discoursing on this matter to offer a refinement upon my scheme. He said that many gentlemen of his kingdom, having of late destroyed their deer, he conceived that the want of venison might be well supplied by the bodies of young lads and maidens, not exceeding fourteen years of age nor under twelve, so great a number of both sexes in every country being now ready to starve for want of work or service; and these to be disposed of by their parents, if alive, or otherwise by their nearest relations. But with due deference to so excellent a friend and so deserving a patriot, I cannot be altogether in his sentiments; for as to the males, my American acquaintance assured me from frequent experience that their flesh was generally tough and lean, like that of our schoolboys, by continual exercise, and their taste disagreeable; and to fatten them would not answer the charge. Then as to the females; it would, I think with humble submission, be a loss to the public, because they soon would become breeders themselves; and besides, it is not improbable that some scrupulous people might be apt to censure such a practice (although indeed very unjustly) as a little bordering upon cruelty; which, I confess, hath always been with me the strongest objection against any project, how well soever intended.

But in order to justify my friend, he confessed that this expedient was put into his head by the famous Psalmanazar,[10] a native of the island Formosa, who came from thence to London above twenty years ago, and in conversation told my friend that in his country when any young person happened to be put to death, the executioner sold the carcass to persons of quality as a prime dainty; and that in his time the body of a plump girl of fifteen, who was crucified for an attempt to poison the emperor, was sold to his Imperial Majesty's prime minister of state, and other great mandarins of the court, in joints from the gibbet, at four hundred crowns. Neither indeed can I deny that if the same use were made of several plump young girls in this town, who without one single groat[11] to their fortunes cannot stir abroad without a chair,[12] and appear at the playhouse and assemblies in foreign fineries which they never will pay for, the kingdom would not be the worse.

Some persons of a desponding spirit are in great concern about the vast number of poor people who are aged, diseased, or maimed, and I have been desired to employ my thoughts what course may be taken to ease the nation of so grievous an encumberance. But I am not in the least pain upon the matter, because it is very well known that they are every day dying and rotting by cold and famine, and filth and vermin, as fast as can be reasonably expected. And

---

[10] George Psalmanazar was a Frenchman who passed himself off as a native of Formosa (the former name for Taiwan).

[11] A coin worth about four cents.

[12] A sedan chair, an enclosed chair carried by poles on the front and back.

as to the younger laborers, they are now in almost as hopeful a condition. They cannot get work, and consequently pine away for want of nourishment to a degree that if any time they are accidently hired to common labor, they have not the strength to perform it; and thus the country and themselves are happily delivered from the evils to come.

I have too long digressed, and therefore I shall return to my subject. I think the advantages by the proposal which I have made are obvious and many, as well as of the highest importance.

For first, I have already observed, it would greatly lessen the number of Papists, with whom we are yearly overrun, being the principal breeders of the nation as well as our most dangerous enemies; and who stay at home on purpose to deliver the kingdom to the Pretender, hoping to take their advantage by the absence of so many good Protestants, who have chose rather to leave their country than to stay at home and pay tithes against their conscience to an Episcopal curate.

Secondly, the poorer tenants will have something valuable of their own, which by law may be made liable to distress,[13] and help to pay their landlord's rent, their corn and cattle being already seized and money a thing unknown.

Thirdly, whereas the maintenance of a hundred thousand children, from two years old and upwards, cannot be computed at less than ten shillings a piece per annum, the nation's stock will be thereby increased fifty thousand pounds per annum, besides the profit of a new dish introduced to the tables of all gentlemen of fortune in the kingdom who have any refinement in taste. And all the money will circulate among ourselves, the goods being entirely of our own growth and manufacture.

Fourthly, the constant breeders, besides the gain of eight shillings sterling per annum by the sale of their children, will be rid of the charge of maintaining them after the first year.

Fifthly, this food would likewise bring great custom to taverns, where the vintners will certainly be so prudent as to procure the best receipts[14] for dressing it to perfection, and consequently have their houses frequented by all the fine gentlemen, who justly value themselves upon their knowledge in good eating; and a skillful cook, who understands how to oblige his guests, will contrive to make it as expensive as they please.

Sixthly, this would be a great inducement to marriage, which all wise nations have either encouraged by rewards or enforced by laws and penalties. It would increase the care and tenderness of mothers towards their children, when they were sure of a settlement for life to the poor babes, provided in some sort by the public, to their annual profit instead of expense. We should see an honest emulation among the married women, which of them could bring the fattest child to the market. Men would become as fond of their wives during the time of their pregnancy as they are now of their mares in foal, their cows in calf, or

---

[13] Seizure for payment of debts.
[14] Recipes.

sows when they are ready to farrow; nor offer to beat or kick them (as is too frequent a practice) for fear of a miscarriage.

Many other advantages might be enumerated. For instance, the addition of some thousand carcasses in our exportation of barreled beef, the propagation of swine's flesh, and improvements in the art of making good bacon, so much wanted among us by the great destruction of pigs, too frequent at our tables, which are no way comparable in taste or magnificence to a well-grown, fat, yearling child, which roasted whole will make a considerable figure at a lord mayor's feast or any other public entertainment. But this and many others I omit, being studious of brevity.

Supposing that one thousand families in this city would be constant customers for infants' flesh, besides others who might have it at merry meetings, particularly weddings and christenings, I compute that Dublin would take off annually about twenty thousand carcasses, and the rest of the kingdom (where probably they will be sold somewhat cheaper) the remaining eighty thousand.

I can think of no one objection that will possibly be raised against this proposal unless it should be urged that the number of people will be thereby much lessened in the kingdom. This I freely own, and it was indeed one principal design in offering it to the world. I desire the reader will observe, that I calculate my remedy for this one individual kingdom of Ireland and for no other that ever was, is, or I think ever can be upon earth. Therefore let no man talk to me of other expedients: of taxing our absentees at five shillings a pound: of using neither clothes nor household furniture except what is of our own growth and manufacture: of utterly rejecting the materials and instruments that promote foreign luxury: of curing the expensiveness of pride, vanity, idleness, and gaming in our women: of introducing a vein of parsimony, prudence, and temperance: of learning to love our country, in the want of which we differ even from Laplanders and the inhabitants of Topinamboo:[15] of quitting our animosities and factions, nor acting any longer like the Jews, who were murdering one another at the very moment their city was taken:[16] of being a little cautious not to sell our country and conscience for nothing: of teaching landlords to have at least one degree of mercy toward their tenants: lastly, of putting a spirit of honesty, industry, and skill into our shopkeepers; who, if a resolution could now be taken to buy only our native goods, would immediately unite to cheat and exact upon us in the price, the measure, and the goodness, nor could ever yet be brought to make one fair proposal of just dealing, though often and earnestly invited to it.

Therefore, I repeat, let no man talk to me of these and the like expedients, 30 till he hath at least some glimpse of hope that there will be some hearty and sincere attempt to put them in practice.

---

[15] A district in Brazil, inhabited in Swift's day by primitive tribes.
[16] While the Roman emperor Titus laid siege to Jerusalem in 70 CE, bloody fighting erupted among factions within the city.

But as to myself, having been wearied out for many years of offering vain, idle, visionary thoughts, and at length utterly despairing of success, I fortunately fell upon this proposal, which, as it is wholly new, so it hath something solid and real, of no expense and little trouble, full in our own power, and whereby we can incur no danger in disobliging England. For this kind of commodity will not bear exportation, the flesh being of too tender a consistence to admit a long continuance in salt, although perhaps I could name a country[17] which would be glad to eat up our whole nation without it.

After all, I am not so violently bent upon my own opinion as to reject any offer proposed by wise men, which shall be found equally innocent, cheap, easy, and effectual. But before something of that kind shall be advanced in contradiction to my scheme, and offering a better, I desire the author or authors will be pleased maturely to consider two points. First, as things now stand, how they will be able to find food and raiment for an hundred thousand useless mouths and backs. And secondly, there being a round million of creatures in human figure throughout this kingdom, whose sole subsistence put into a common stock would leave them in debt two millions of pounds sterling, adding those who are beggars by profession to the bulk of farmers, cottagers, and laborers, with their wives and children who are beggars in effect; I desire those politicians who dislike my overture, and may perhaps be so bold to attempt to answer, that they will first ask the parents of these mortals whether they would not at this day think it a great happiness to have been sold for food at a year old in this manner I prescribe, and thereby have avoided such a perpetual scene of misfortunes as they have since gone through by the oppression of landlords, the impossibility of paying rent without money or trade, the want of common sustenance, with neither house nor clothes to cover them from the inclemencies of the weather, and the most inevitable prospect of entailing the like or greater miseries upon their breed forever.

I profess, in the sincerity of my heart, that I have not the least personal interest in endeavoring to promote this necessary work, having no other motive than the public good of my country, by advancing our trade, providing for infants, relieving the poor, and giving some pleasure to the rich. I have no children by which I can propose to get a single penny; the youngest being nine years old, and my wife past childbearing.

**FOR ANALYSIS**

**1.** What kind of person is the speaker? What does his tone of voice reveal about who he is? Is his voice direct and transparent, or does it seem deliberately created to achieve a specific effect?

**2.** In what sense is the proposal "modest"?

**3.** Where are the major divisions of the essay? What function does each serve?

**4.** What function does paragraph 29 serve?

---

[17] England.

**5.** Explain what Swift means when he says in paragraph 20, "I have too long digressed."

**6.** Whom is Swift addressing in this essay?

## MAKING ARGUMENTS

Rather than making your own argument, write a detailed description of the use of argument in "A Modest Proposal." Pay attention to the use of argument techniques both by the speaker (or "projector") and by Swift himself as author of the essay.

## WRITING TOPICS

**1.** Some background information on Swift's life, as well as familiarity with his other works, would make it clear that in this essay he is being satiric. Without that background — that is, on the basis of this essay alone — would you conclude that Swift is writing **satire**? Explain.

**2.** In one brief paragraph, paraphrase the major arguments Swift uses to support his plan.

## MAKING CONNECTIONS

Two other works in this anthology that use **satire** include W. H. Auden, "The Unknown Citizen" (p. 360), and Harlan Ellison, "'Repent, Harlequin!' Said the Ticktockman" (p. 410). Compare and contrast the use of satire in one of these works with Swift's use of satire.

# CASE STUDY IN ARGUMENT

## MAKING CHANGE

These three essays take on the subject of attempting to make social change through the mobilization of public opinion. Each writer has different ideas about what form such mobilization might take and how opinion, once mobilized, expresses itself and works for change. All three focus on moments when citizens desire a change in the status quo, but each of these essays has its own stance on these moments, its own attitude about what constitutes taking to the streets, and what defines success. As you read, note the differences not only in the opinions of these three writers but also in the ways in which they express those opinions — the way they do (or don't) issue their own invitations to take part in such movements, or to think critically about them.

## BILL McKIBBEN  (B. 1960)

## A CALL TO ARMS: AN INVITATION TO DEMAND ACTION ON CLIMATE CHANGE  2014

This is an invitation, an invitation to come to New York City. An invitation to anyone who'd like to prove to themselves, and to their children, that they give a damn about the biggest crisis our civilization has ever faced.

My guess is people will come by the tens of thousands, and it will be the largest demonstration yet of human resolve in the face of climate change. Sure, some of it will be exciting — who doesn't like the chance to march and sing and carry a clever sign through the canyons of Manhattan? But this is dead-serious business, a signal moment in the gathering fight of human beings to do something about global warming before it's too late to do anything but watch. You'll tell your grandchildren, assuming we win. So circle September 20th and 21st on your calendar, and then I'll explain.

Since Ban Ki-moon runs the United Nations, he's altogether aware that we're making no progress as a planet on slowing climate change. He presided over the collapse of global-climate talks at Copenhagen in 2009, and he knows the prospects are not much better for the "next Copenhagen" in Paris in December 2015. In order to spur those talks along, he's invited the world's leaders to New York in late September for a climate summit.

But the "world's leaders" haven't been leaders on climate change — at least not leaders enough. Like many of us, they've attended to the easy stuff, but they haven't set the world on a fundamentally new course. Barack Obama is

411

the perfect example: Sure, he's imposed new mileage standards for cars, but he's also opened vast swaths of territory to oil drilling and coal mining, which will take us past Saudi Arabia and Russia as the world's biggest petro producer.

Like other world leaders, that is, he's tried, but not nearly hard enough. 5 Consider what he told *The New Yorker* in an interview earlier this year: "At the end of the day, we're part of a long-running story. We just try to get our paragraph right." And "I think we are fortunate at the moment that we do not face a crisis of the scale and scope that Lincoln or FDR faced."

We do, though; we face a crisis as great as any president has ever encountered. Here's how his paragraph looks so far: Since he took office, summer sea ice in the Arctic has mostly disappeared, and at the South Pole, scientists in May made clear that the process of massive melt is now fully under way, with 10 feet of sea-level rise in the offing. Scientists have discovered the depth of changes in ocean chemistry: that seawater is 30 percent more acidic than just four decades ago, and it's already causing trouble for creatures at the bottom of the marine food chain. America has weathered the hottest year in its history, 2012, which saw a drought so deep that the corn harvest largely failed. At the moment, one of the biggest states in Obama's union, California, is caught in a drought deeper than any time since Europeans arrived. Hell, a few blocks south of the U.N. buildings, Hurricane Sandy turned the Lower East Side of New York into a branch of the East River. And that's just the United States. The world's scientists earlier this spring issued a 32-volume report explaining exactly how much worse it's going to get, which is, to summarize, a lot worse even than they'd thought before. It's not that the scientists are alarmists — it's that the science is alarming. Here's how one Princeton scientist summarized the situation for reporters: "We're all sitting ducks."

The gap between "We're all sitting ducks" and "We do not face a crisis" is the gap between halfhearted action and the all-out effort that might make a difference. It's the gap between changing light bulbs and changing the system that's powering our destruction.

In a rational world, no one would need to march. In a rational world, policymakers would have heeded scientists when they first sounded the alarm 25 years ago. But in this world, reason, having won the argument, has so far lost the fight. The fossil-fuel industry, by virtue of being perhaps the richest enterprise in human history, has been able to delay effective action, almost to the point where it's too late.

So in this case taking to the streets is very much necessary. It's not all that's necessary — a sprawling fossil-fuel resistance works on a hundred fronts around the world, from putting up solar panels to forcing colleges to divest their oil stocks to electioneering for truly green candidates. And it's true that marching doesn't always work: At the onset of the war in Iraq, millions marched, to no immediate avail. But there are moments when it's been essential. This is how the Vietnam War was ended, and segregation too — or consider the nuclear-freeze campaign of the early 1980s, when half a million people gathered in New York's Central Park. The rally, and all the campaigning that led to it, set the mood for a planet — even, amazingly, in the Reagan era. By mid-decade, the conservative icon was proposing to Mikhail Gorbachev that they abolish nuclear weapons altogether.

The point is, sometimes you can grab the zeitgeist by the scruff of the neck 10 and shake it a little. At the moment, the overwhelming sense around the world is nothing will happen in time. That's on the verge of becoming a self-fulfilling prophecy — indeed, as I've written in these pages, it's very clear that the fossil-fuel industry has five times as much carbon in its reserves as it would take to break the planet. On current trajectories, the industry will burn it, and governments will make only small whimpering noises about changing the speed at which it happens. A loud movement — one that gives our "leaders" permission to actually lead, and then scares them into doing so — is the only hope of upending that prophecy.

A loud movement is, of necessity, a big movement — and this fossil-fuel resistance draws from every corner of our society. It finds powerful leadership from the environmental-justice community, the poor people, often in communities of color, who have suffered most directly under the reign of fossil fuel. In this country they're survivors of Sandy and Katrina and the BP spill; they're the people whose kids troop off to kindergarten clutching asthma inhalers because they live next to oil refineries, and the people whose reservations become resource colonies. Overseas, they're the ones whose countries are simply disappearing.

Sometimes in the past, trade unionists have fought against environmentalists — but unions in health care, mass transit, higher education, domestic work, and building services are all beginning to organize for September, fully aware that there are no jobs on a dead planet. Energy-sector unions see the jobs potential in massive solar installation and a "just transition" off fossil fuels. Here's a banner I know you'll see in the streets of New York: CLIMATE/JOBS. TWO CRISES, ONE SOLUTION.

There will be clergy and laypeople from synagogues and churches and mosques, now rising in record numbers to say, "If the Bible means anything, it means that we need to care for the world God gave us." And there will, of course, be scientists, saying, "What exactly don't you understand about what we've been telling you for a quarter-century?"

And students will arrive from around the country, because who knows better how to cope with long bus rides and sleeping on floors — and who knows better that their very futures are at stake? They're near the front of this battle right now, getting arrested at Harvard and at Washington University as they fight for fossil-fuel divestment, and shaking up the establishment enough that Stanford, with its $18.7 billion endowment, just agreed to get rid of its coal stocks. Don't worry about "kids today." Kids today know how to organize at least as well as kids in the Sixties.

And then there will be those of us plain old middle-class Americans who 15 may still benefit from our lives of cheap fossil fuel, but who just can't stand to watch the world drift into chaos. We look around and see that the price of solar panels has fallen 90 percent in a few decades; we understand that it won't be easy to shift our economy off coal and gas and oil, but we know that it will be easier than coping with temperatures that no human has ever seen. We may have different proposed solutions — carbon taxes! tidal power! — but we know that none of them will happen unless we open up some space. That's our job: opening up space for change on the scale that physics requires. No more fine words, no more nifty websites. Hard deeds. Now.

You can watch the endgame of the fossil-fuel era with a certain amount of hope. The pieces are in place for real, swift, sudden change, not just slow and grinding linear shifts: If Germany on a sunny day can generate half its power from solar panels, and Texas makes a third of its electricity from wind, then you know technology isn't an impossible obstacle anymore. The pieces are in place, but the pieces won't move themselves. That's where movements come in. They're not subtle; they can't manage all the details of this transition. But they can build up pressure on the system, enough, with luck, to blow out those bags of money that are blocking progress with the force of Typhoon Haiyan on a Filipino hut. Because if our resistance fails, there will be ever-stronger typhoons. The moment to salvage something of the Holocene is passing fast. But it hasn't passed yet, which is why September is so important.

Day to day this resistance is rightly scattered, local and focused on the more mundane: installing a new zoning code, putting in a solar farm, persuading the church board to sell its BP stock. But sometimes it needs to come together and show the world how big it's gotten. That next great moment is late September in New York. See you there.

## FOR ANALYSIS

**1.** What are the effects of climate change that are already apparent? What steps does McKibben claim might avert climate change?

**2.** Why does McKibben argue that the fossil fuel industry bears much of the blame for the climate crisis?

**3.** Analyze McKibben's **style**. As he claims, these arguments are serious business; does McKibben's writing match the seriousness? Characterize his **tone** and **diction**, and what you imagine is the desired effect on readers.

## MAKING ARGUMENTS

McKibben quotes Barack Obama saying, "I think we are fortunate at the moment that we do not face a crisis of the scale and scope that Lincoln or FDR faced" (para. 5). McKibben himself describes climate change as "the biggest crisis our civilization has ever faced" (para. 1). Construct an argument concerning the comparisons Obama suggests, making or refuting the claim that one or the other (or both) are bigger crises than climate change.

## WRITING TOPICS

**1.** Discuss taking to the streets as a political tactic. How does it work? Cite historical examples of successes and failures of street protest.

**2.** What role do governments play in the crisis, according to McKibben? How might they avert it?

# REBECCA SOLNIT  (B. 1961)

# REVOLUTIONS PER MINUTE  2008

When I was a young activist, the '60s were not yet far enough away, and people still talked about "after the revolution." They still believed in some sort of decisive event that would make everything different — an impossible event, because even a change in administration cannot bring a universal change of heart, and the process of changing imagination and culture is plodding, incremental, frustrating, comes complete with backlashes . . . and is wildly exciting if you slow down enough to see the broad spans of time across which change occurs. A lot of people then were waiting for the revolution; a lot of people now have lost faith that there will be one. The overthrow of the United States government seems extremely unlikely at the moment, but the transformation of everything within, around, and despite it has been under way for decades, including radical transformation in the governments of many other countries.

Sex before marriage. Bob and his boyfriend. Madame Speaker. Do those words make your hair stand on end or your eyes widen? Their flatness is the register of successful revolution. Many of the changes are so incremental that you adjust without realizing something has changed until suddenly one day you realize everything is different. I was reading something about food politics recently and thinking it was boring.

Then I realized that these were incredibly exciting ideas — about understanding where your food comes from and who grows it and what its impact on the planet and your body are. Fifteen or twenty years ago, hardly anyone thought about where coffee came from, or milk, or imagined fair-trade coffee. New terms like *food miles*, fairly new words like *organic, sustainable, non-GMO*, and reborn phenomena like farmers' markets are all the result of what it's fair to call the food revolution, and it has been so successful that ideas that were once startling and subversive have become familiar en route to becoming status quo. So my boredom was one register of victory.

Although we typically associate revolution with the sudden overthrow of a regime, the Industrial Revolution was an incremental change in everyday life and production that began a little over two centuries ago and never ended. It's a useful reminder of what else revolution is. Late in 2006, I had the pleasure and honor of meeting Grace Lee Boggs in Detroit, where she's lived and organized radical politics since the 1950s. Grace, who was born to Chinese immigrant parents in 1915, earned a PhD in philosophy in 1935, and married the African-American labor organizer Jimmy Boggs in the early 1950s, has lived long enough to see the whole idea of revolution change. She said to me, "In the first half of this century people never thought revolution involved transforming ourselves, that it required a two-sided transformation. They thought that all we had to do was transform the system, that all the problems were on the other side. It took the splitting of the atom and the Montgomery bus boycott to introduce us to a whole new way of thinking about revolution as tied to evolution." In another interview, she expanded on this rejection of the idea that everything would change suddenly: "In revolutionary struggles throughout the twentieth century, we've seen that state power, viewed as a way to empower workers, ends up disempowering them. So we have to begin thinking differently. The old concept used to be: first we make the political revolution and then the cultural revolution. Now we have to think about how the cultural revolution can empower people differently."

The fantasy of a revolution is that it will make everything different — and regime-changing revolutions generally make a difference, sometimes a significantly positive one — but the making of differences in everyday practices is a more protracted and incremental and ultimately more revolutionary process. Last month, I was asked in public about where the antiglobalization movement now stood. I gulped a little. I'm a slow thinker — I like to have a month to a year to mull something over, which is why I'm a writer. My first thought was that there wasn't anything so dramatic and dynamic and visible as those ten thousand blockaders in the streets of Seattle on November 30 and December 1, 1999. Fortunately, I made the other person go first, and by the time her answer was complete, mine had grown to encompass how the very ideas around corporate globalization had spread, so that what was wild new thinking by radicals or revolutionaries in the streets in 1999 had become a reasonable position for many governments to take by 2003 or so — and even some of the Democratic presidential candidates by 2008.

In recent years, most Latin American nations have turned against the ideology of unfettered markets and trade pacts, and even in countries whose governments have not, most of the citizens have. Immanuel Wallerstein, the left-wing sociologist with a talent for prophecy, wrote an essay earlier this year headed "2008: The Demise of Neoliberal Globalization." In it he said, "The political balance is swinging back. Neoliberal globalization will be written about ten years from now as a cyclical swing in the history of the capitalist world-economy. The real question is not whether this phase is over but whether the swing back will be able, as in the past, to restore a state of relative equilibrium in the world-system. Or has too much damage been done?" Such critiques of globalization have ceased to be inflammatory or extraordinary as the global public has grown increasingly educated in economics and the sinister underside of all those free-trade treaties. Those of us who fought against them won some practical victories and a lot more in the realm of public imagination, but the position ceased to belong exclusively to us as it became a reasonable position for many to take. This is why we need training in slowness, and the long attention span that makes it possible to see the remarkable changes of our time.

There's also the widespread greening of the public imagination, with climate change having finally arrived on center stage. Cities and states across the country are now pushing to regulate emissions (and having to fight the Bush administration's EPA in order to do so). My own state is even looking at regulating commercial airplane emissions. The revolution is here, but it doesn't look like what people expected, and it isn't even visible to those who aren't practiced in the long view.

If the term *revolution* can be used to describe the Industrial Revolution, then perhaps we are launched upon something as profound — a backlash against the industrial revolution that brought us the acceleration of everyday life, the industrialization of time and space, the shrinkage of the contemplative time and space in which to understand ourselves and our lives. That is to say, the revolution is in part against the very speedup that has made us all busy, distracted, anxious, and unable even to perceive the tenor of our own times. So it is a revolution in perception and daily practice, as well as against the concrete institutions that spell the misery of everyday life for too many and the destruction of the Earth for us all.

It may never be finished, but the time to join it is now.

## FOR ANALYSIS

**1.** What does Solnit use food politics as an example of?

**2.** What are the different kinds of revolution Solnit lists? What makes them different? Are they all equally important?

**3.** How would you characterize this essay in terms of the different modes of writing Solnit employs? Where does she describe, or explain, or tell a story, or exhort to action? How does she make it all fit together?

## MAKING ARGUMENTS

Toward the end of her essay, Solnit writes, "The revolution is here, but it doesn't look like what people expected, and it isn't even visible to those who aren't practiced in the long view" (para. 7). Argue against Solnit here, in favor of the short view. Why might it be important to be impatient?

## WRITING TOPICS

**1.** Solnit writes, "Many of the changes are so incremental that you adjust without realizing something has changed until suddenly one day you realize everything is different" (para. 2). Write about something that has changed in the world around you in your lifetime. Did you notice it happening?

**2.** Grace Lee Boggs is quoted as saying, "It took the splitting of the atom and the Montgomery bus boycott to introduce us to a whole new way of thinking about revolution as tied to evolution" (para. 4). How did these events lead to this way of thinking?

**MALCOLM GLADWELL**  (B. 1963)

# Small Change: Why the Revolution Will Not Be Tweeted  2010

At four-thirty in the afternoon on Monday, February 1, 1960, four college students sat down at the lunch counter at the Woolworth's in downtown Greensboro, North Carolina. They were freshmen at North Carolina A. & T., a black college a mile or so away.

"I'd like a cup of coffee, please," one of the four, Ezell Blair, said to the waitress.

"We don't serve Negroes here," she replied.

The Woolworth's lunch counter was a long L-shaped bar that could seat sixty-six people, with a standup snack bar at one end. The seats were for whites. The snack bar was for blacks. Another employee, a black woman who worked at the steam table, approached the students and tried to warn them away. "You're acting stupid, ignorant!" she said. They didn't move. Around five-thirty, the front doors to the store were locked. The four still didn't move. Finally, they left by a side door. Outside, a small crowd had gathered, including a photographer from the Greensboro *Record*. "I'll be back tomorrow with A. & T. College," one of the students said.

By next morning, the protest had grown to twenty-seven men and four 5 women, most from the same dormitory as the original four. The men were dressed in suits and ties. The students had brought their schoolwork, and studied as they sat at the counter. On Wednesday, students from Greensboro's "Negro" secondary school, Dudley High, joined in, and the number of protesters swelled to eighty. By Thursday, the protesters numbered three hundred, including three white women, from the Greensboro campus of the University of North Carolina. By Saturday, the sit-in had reached six hundred. People spilled out onto the street. White teenagers waved Confederate flags. Someone threw a firecracker. At noon, the A. & T. football team arrived. "Here comes the wrecking crew," one of the white students shouted.

By the following Monday, sit-ins had spread to Winston-Salem, twenty-five miles away, and Durham, fifty miles away. The day after that, students at Fayetteville State Teachers College and at Johnson C. Smith College, in Charlotte, joined in, followed on Wednesday by students at St. Augustine's College and Shaw University, in Raleigh. On Thursday and Friday, the protest crossed state lines, surfacing in Hampton and Portsmouth, Virginia, in Rock Hill, South Carolina, and in Chattanooga, Tennessee. By the end of the month, there were sit-ins throughout the South, as far west as Texas. "I asked every student I met what the first day of the sitdowns had been like on his campus," the political theorist Michael Walzer wrote in *Dissent*. "The answer was always the same: 'It was like a fever. Everyone wanted to go.'" Some seventy thousand students eventually took part. Thousands were arrested and untold thousands more radicalized. These events in the early sixties became a civil-rights war that engulfed the South for the rest of the decade — and it happened without e-mail, texting, Facebook, or Twitter.

The world, we are told, is in the midst of a revolution. The new tools of social media have reinvented social activism. With Facebook and Twitter and the like, the traditional relationship between political authority and popular will has been upended, making it easier for the powerless to collaborate, coordinate, and give voice to their concerns. When ten thousand protesters took to the streets in Moldova in the spring of 2009 to protest against their country's Communist government, the action was dubbed the Twitter Revolution, because of the means by which the demonstrators had been brought together. A few months after that, when student protests rocked Tehran, the State Department took the unusual step of asking Twitter to suspend scheduled maintenance of its Web site, because the Administration didn't want such a critical organizing tool out of service at the height of the demonstrations. "Without Twitter the people of Iran would not have felt empowered and confident to stand up for freedom and democracy," Mark Pfeifle, a former national-security adviser, later wrote, calling for Twitter to be nominated for the Nobel Peace Prize. Where activists were once defined by their causes, they are now defined by their tools. Facebook warriors go online to push for change. "You are the best hope for us all," James K. Glassman, a former senior State Department official, told a crowd of cyber activists at a recent conference sponsored by Facebook, A. T. & T., Howcast, MTV, and Google. Sites like Facebook, Glassman said, "give the U.S. a significant competitive advantage over terrorists. Some time ago, I said that Al Qaeda was 'eating our lunch on the Internet.' That is no longer the case. Al Qaeda is stuck in Web 1.0. The Internet is now about interactivity and conversation."

These are strong, and puzzling, claims. Why does it matter who is eating whose lunch on the Internet? Are people who log on to their Facebook page really the best hope for us all? As for Moldova's so-called Twitter Revolution, Evgeny Morozov, a scholar at Stanford who has been the most persistent of digital evangelism's critics, points out that Twitter had scant internal significance in Moldova, a country where very few Twitter accounts exist. Nor does it seem to have been a revolution, not least because the protests — as Anne Applebaum suggested in the *Washington Post* — may well have been a bit of stagecraft cooked up by the government. (In a country paranoid about Romanian revanchism,[1] the protesters flew a Romanian flag over the Parliament building.) In the Iranian case, meanwhile, the people tweeting about the demonstrations were almost all in the West. "It is time to get Twitter's role in the events in Iran right," Golnaz Esfandiari wrote, this past summer, in *Foreign Policy*. "Simply put: There was no Twitter Revolution inside Iran." The cadre of prominent bloggers, like Andrew Sullivan, who championed the role of social media in Iran,

---

[1] A political policy of a nation or an ethnic group, intended to regain lost territory or standing (from the French: *revanche*, "revenge").

Esfandiari continued, misunderstood the situation. "Western journalists who couldn't reach — or didn't bother reaching? — people on the ground in Iran simply scrolled through the English-language tweets post with tag #iranelection," she wrote. "Through it all, no one seemed to wonder why people trying to coordinate protests in Iran would be writing in any language other than Farsi."

Some of this grandiosity is to be expected. Innovators tend to be solipsists. They often want to cram every stray fact and experience into their new model. As the historian Robert Darnton has written, "The marvels of communication technology in the present have produced a false consciousness about the past — even a sense that communication has no history, or had nothing of importance to consider before the days of television and the Internet." But there is something else at work here, in the outsized enthusiasm for social media. Fifty years after one of the most extraordinary episodes of social upheaval in American history, we seem to have forgotten what activism is.

Greensboro in the early nineteen-sixties was the kind of place where racial  10
insubordination was routinely met with violence. The four students who first sat down at the lunch counter were terrified. "I suppose if anyone had come up behind me and yelled 'Boo,' I think I would have fallen off my seat," one of them said later. On the first day, the store manager notified the police chief, who immediately sent two officers to the store. On the third day, a gang of white toughs showed up at the lunch counter and stood ostentatiously behind the protesters, ominously muttering epithets such as "burr-head nigger." A local Ku Klux Klan leader made an appearance. On Saturday, as tensions grew, someone called in a bomb threat, and the entire store had to be evacuated.

The dangers were even clearer in the Mississippi Freedom Summer Project of 1964, another of the sentinel campaigns of the civil-rights movement. The Student Nonviolent Coordinating Committee recruited hundreds of Northern, largely white unpaid volunteers to run Freedom Schools, register black voters, and raise civil-rights awareness in the Deep South. "No one should go *anywhere* alone, but certainly not in an automobile and certainly not at night," they were instructed. Within days of arriving in Mississippi, three volunteers — Michael Schwerner, James Chaney, and Andrew Goodman — were kidnapped and killed, and, during the rest of the summer, thirty-seven black churches were set on fire and dozens of safe houses were bombed; volunteers were beaten, shot at, arrested, and trailed by pickup trucks full of armed men. A quarter of those in the program dropped out. Activism that challenges the status quo — that attacks deeply rooted problems — is not for the faint of heart.

What makes people capable of this kind of activism? The Stanford sociologist Doug McAdam compared the Freedom Summer dropouts with the participants who stayed, and discovered that the key difference wasn't, as might be expected, ideological fervor. "*All* of the applicants — participants and withdrawals alike — emerge as highly committed, articulate supporters of the goals and values of the summer program," he concluded. What mattered more was an applicant's degree of personal connection to the civil-rights movement. All the volunteers were required to provide a list of personal contacts — the people they wanted kept apprised of their activities — and participants were far more likely than dropouts to have close friends who were also going to Mississippi. High-risk activism, McAdam concluded, is a "strong-tie" phenomenon.

This pattern shows up again and again. One study of the Red Brigades, the Italian terrorist group of the nineteen-seventies, found that seventy percent of recruits had at least one good friend already in the organization. The same is true of the men who joined the mujahideen in Afghanistan. Even revolutionary actions that look spontaneous, like the demonstrations in East Germany that led to the fall of the Berlin Wall, are, at core, strong-tie phenomena. The opposition movement in East Germany consisted of several hundred groups, each with roughly a dozen members. Each group was in limited contact with the others: at the time, only thirteen percent of East Germans even had a phone. All they knew was that on Monday nights, outside St. Nicholas Church in downtown Leipzig, people gathered to voice their anger at the state. And the primary determinant of who showed up was "critical friends" — the more friends you had who were critical of the regime the more likely you were to join the protest.

So one crucial fact about the four freshmen at the Greensboro lunch counter — David Richmond, Franklin McCain, Ezell Blair, and Joseph McNeil — was their relationship with one another. McNeil was a roommate of Blair's in A. & T.'s Scott Hall dormitory. Richmond roomed with McCain one floor up, and Blair, Richmond, and McCain had all gone to Dudley High School. The four would smuggle beer into the dorm and talk late into the night in Blair and McNeil's room. They would all have remembered the murder of Emmett Till in 1955, the Montgomery bus boycott that same year, and the showdown in Little Rock in 1957. It was McNeil who brought up the idea of a sit-in at Woolworth's. They'd discussed it for nearly a month. Then McNeil came into the dorm room and asked the others if they were ready. There was a pause, and McCain said, in a way that works only with people who talk late into the night with one another, "Are you guys chicken or not?" Ezell Blair worked up the courage the next day to ask for a cup of coffee because he was flanked by his roommate and two good friends from high school.

The kind of activism associated with social media isn't like this at all. The 15 platforms of social media are built around weak ties. Twitter is a way of following (or being followed by) people you may never have met. Facebook is a tool for efficiently managing your acquaintances, for keeping up with the people you would not otherwise be able to stay in touch with. That's why you can have a thousand "friends" on Facebook, as you never could in real life.

This is in many ways a wonderful thing. There is strength in weak ties, as the sociologist Mark Granovetter has observed. Our acquaintances — not our friends — are our greatest source of new ideas and information. The Internet lets us exploit the power of these kinds of distant connections with marvellous efficiency. It's terrific at the diffusion of innovation, interdisciplinary collaboration, seamlessly matching up buyers and sellers, and the logistical functions of the dating world. But weak ties seldom lead to high-risk activism.

In a new book called *The Dragonfly Effect: Quick, Effective, and Powerful Ways to Use Social Media to Drive Social Change*, the business consultant Andy Smith and the Stanford Business School professor Jennifer Aaker tell the story of Sameer Bhatia, a young Silicon Valley entrepreneur who came down with acute myelogenous leukemia. It's a perfect illustration of social media's strengths. Bhatia needed a bone-marrow transplant, but he could not find a match among his relatives and friends. The odds were best with a donor of his ethnicity, and there were few South Asians in the national bone-marrow database. So Bhatia's business partner sent out an e-mail explaining Bhatia's plight to more than four hundred of their acquaintances, who forwarded the e-mail to their personal contacts; Facebook pages and You-Tube videos were devoted to the Help Sameer campaign. Eventually, nearly twenty-five thousand new people were registered in the bone-marrow database, and Bhatia found a match.

But how did the campaign get so many people to sign up? By not asking too much of them. That's the only way you can get someone you don't really know to do something on your behalf. You can get thousands of people to sign up for a donor registry, because doing so is pretty easy. You have to send in a cheek swab and — in the highly unlikely event that your bone marrow is a good match for someone in need — spend a few hours at the hospital. Donating bone marrow isn't a trivial matter. But it doesn't involve financial or personal risk; it doesn't mean spending a summer being chased by armed men in pickup trucks. It doesn't require that you confront socially entrenched norms and practices. In fact, it's the kind of commitment that will bring only social acknowledgment and praise.

The evangelists of social media don't understand this distinction; they seem to believe that a Facebook friend is the same as a real friend and that signing up for a donor registry in Silicon Valley today is activism in the same sense as sitting at a segregated lunch counter in Greensboro in 1960. "Social networks are particularly effective at increasing motivation," Aaker and Smith write. But that's not true. Social networks are effective at increasing *participation* — by lessening the level of motivation that participation requires. The Facebook page of the Save Darfur Coalition has 1,282,339 members, who have donated an average of nine cents apiece. The next biggest Darfur charity on Facebook has 22,073 members, who have donated an average of thirty-five cents. Help Save Darfur has 2,797 members, who have given, on average, fifteen cents. A spokesperson for the Save Darfur Coalition told *Newsweek*, "We wouldn't necessarily gauge someone's value to the advocacy movement based on what they've given. This is a powerful mechanism to engage this critical population. They inform their community, attend events, volunteer. It's not something you can measure by looking at a ledger." In other words, Facebook activism succeeds not by motivating people to make a real sacrifice but by motivating them to do the things that people do when they are not motivated enough to make a real sacrifice. We are a long way from the lunch counters of Greensboro.

*     *     *

The students who joined the sit-ins across the South during the winter of 20
1960 described the movement as a "fever." But the civil-rights movement was
more like a military campaign than like a contagion. In the late nineteen-fifties,
there had been sixteen sit-ins in various cities throughout the South, fifteen of
which were formally organized by civil-rights organizations like the NAACP
and CORE. Possible locations for activism were scouted. Plans were drawn
up. Movement activists held training sessions and retreats for would-be
protesters. The Greensboro Four were a product of this groundwork: all were
members of the NAACP Youth Council. They had close ties with the head of
the local NAACP chapter. They had been briefed on the earlier wave of sit-ins
in Durham, and had been part of a series of movement meetings in activist
churches. When the sit-in movement spread from Greensboro throughout the
South, it did not spread indiscriminately. It spread to those cities which had
preexisting "movement centers" — a core of dedicated and trained activists
ready to turn the "fever" into action.

The civil-rights movement was high-risk activism. It was also, crucially, strategic activism: a challenge to the establishment mounted with precision and
discipline. The NAACP was a centralized organization, run from New York
according to highly formalized operating procedures. At the Southern Christian Leadership Conference, Martin Luther King, Jr., was the unquestioned
authority. At the center of the movement was the black church, which had,
as Aldon D. Morris points out in his superb 1984 study, "The Origins of the
Civil Rights Movement," a carefully demarcated division of labor, with various
standing committees and disciplined groups. "Each group was task-oriented
and coordinated its activities through authority structures," Morris writes.
"Individuals were held accountable for their assigned duties, and important
conflicts were resolved by the minister, who usually exercised ultimate authority over the congregation."

This is the second crucial distinction between traditional activism and its
online variant: social media are not about this kind of hierarchical organization. Facebook and the like are tools for building *networks*, which are the opposite, in structure and character, of hierarchies. Unlike hierarchies, with their
rules and procedures, networks aren't controlled by a single central authority.
Decisions are made through consensus, and the ties that bind people to the
group are loose.

This structure makes networks enormously resilient and adaptable in low-
risk situations. Wikipedia is a perfect example. It doesn't have an editor, sitting in New York, who directs and corrects each entry. The effort of putting
together each entry is self-organized. If every entry in Wikipedia were to be
erased tomorrow, the content would swiftly be restored, because that's what
happens when a network of thousands spontaneously devote their time to a
task.

There are many things, though, that networks don't do well. Car companies sensibly use a network to organize their hundreds of suppliers, but not
to design their cars. No one believes that the articulation of a coherent design

philosophy is best handled by a sprawling, leaderless organizational system. Because networks don't have a centralized leadership structure and clear lines of authority, they have real difficulty reaching consensus and setting goals. They can't think strategically; they are chronically prone to conflict and error. How do you make difficult choices about tactics or strategy or philosophical direction when everyone has an equal say?

The Palestine Liberation Organization originated as a network, and the 25 international-relations scholars Mette Eilstrup-Sangiovanni and Calvert Jones argue in a recent essay in *International Security* that this is why it ran into such trouble as it grew: "Structural features typical of networks — the absence of central authority, the unchecked autonomy of rival groups, and the inability to arbitrate quarrels through formal mechanisms — made the P.L.O. excessively vulnerable to outside manipulation and internal strife."

In Germany in the nineteen-seventies, they go on, "the far more unified and successful left-wing terrorists tended to organize hierarchically, with professional management and clear divisions of labor. They were concentrated geographically in universities, where they could establish central leadership, trust, and camaraderie through regular, face-to-face meetings." They seldom betrayed their comrades in arms during police interrogations. Their counterparts on the right were organized as decentralized networks, and had no such discipline. These groups were regularly infiltrated, and members, once arrested, easily gave up their comrades. Similarly, Al Qaeda was most dangerous when it was a unified hierarchy. Now that it has dissipated into a network, it has proved far less effective.

The drawbacks of networks scarcely matter if the network isn't interested in systemic change — if it just wants to frighten or humiliate or make a splash — or if it doesn't need to think strategically. But if you're taking on a powerful and organized establishment you have to be a hierarchy. The Montgomery bus boycott required the participation of tens of thousands of people who depended on public transit to get to and from work each day. It lasted a *year*. In order to persuade those people to stay true to the cause, the boycott's organizers tasked each local black church with maintaining morale, and put together a free alternative private carpool service, with forty-eight dispatchers and forty-two pickup stations. Even the White Citizens Council, King later said, conceded that the carpool system moved with "military precision." By the time King came to Birmingham, for the climactic showdown with Police Commissioner Eugene (Bull) Connor, he had a budget of a million dollars, and a hundred full-time staff members on the ground, divided into operational units. The operation itself was divided into steadily escalating phases, mapped out in advance. Support was maintained through consecutive mass meetings rotating from church to church around the city.

Boycotts and sit-ins and nonviolent confrontations — which were the weapons of choice for the civil-rights movement — are high-risk strategies. They leave little room for conflict and error. The moment even one protester deviates from the script and responds to provocation, the moral legitimacy of the entire protest is compromised. Enthusiasts for social media would no doubt have us believe that King's task in Birmingham would have been made infinitely easier had he been able to communicate with his followers through Facebook, and contented himself with tweets from a Birmingham jail. But networks are messy: think of the ceaseless pattern of correction and revision, amendment and debate, that characterizes Wikipedia. If Martin Luther King, Jr., had tried to do a wiki-boycott in Montgomery, he would have been steamrollered by the white power structure. And of what use would a digital communication tool be in a town where ninety-eight percent of the black community could be reached every Sunday morning at church? The things that King needed in Birmingham — discipline and strategy — were things that online social media cannot provide.

The bible of the social-media movement is Clay Shirky's *Here Comes Everybody*. Shirky, who teaches at New York University, sets out to demonstrate the organizing power of the Internet, and he begins with the story of Evan, who worked on Wall Street, and his friend Ivanna, after she left her smart phone, an expensive Sidekick, on the back seat of a New York City taxicab. The telephone company transferred the data on Ivanna's lost phone to a new phone, whereupon she and Evan discovered that the Sidekick was now in the hands of a teenager from Queens, who was using it to take photographs of herself and her friends.

When Evan e-mailed the teenager, Sasha, asking for the phone back, she replied that his "white ass" didn't deserve to have it back. Miffed, he set up a Web page with her picture and a description of what had happened. He forwarded the link to his friends, and they forwarded it to their friends. Someone found the MySpace page of Sasha's boyfriend, and a link to it found its way onto the site. Someone found her address online and took a video of her home while driving by; Evan posted the video on the site. The story was picked up by the news filter Digg. Evan was now up to ten e-mails a minute. He created a bulletin board for his readers to share their stories, but it crashed under the weight of responses. Evan and Ivanna went to the police, but the police filed the report under "lost," rather than "stolen," which essentially closed the case. "By this point millions of readers were watching," Shirky writes, "and dozens of mainstream news outlets had covered the story." Bowing to the pressure, the NYPD reclassified the item as "stolen." Sasha was arrested, and Evan got his friend's Sidekick back.

Shirky's argument is that this is the kind of thing that could never have happened in the pre-Internet age — and he's right. Evan could never have tracked down Sasha. The story of the Sidekick would never have been publicized. An army of people could never have been assembled to wage this fight. The police wouldn't have bowed to the pressure of a lone person who had misplaced something as trivial as a cell phone. The story, to Shirky, illustrates "the ease and speed with which a group can be mobilized for the right kind of cause" in the Internet age.

Shirky considers this model of activism an upgrade. But it is simply a form of organizing which favors the weak-tie connections that give us access to information over the strong-tie connections that help us persevere in the face of danger. It shifts our energies from organizations that promote strategic and disciplined activity and toward those which promote resilience and adaptability. It makes it easier for activists to express themselves, and harder for that expression to have any impact. The instruments of social media are well suited to making the existing social order more efficient. They are not a natural enemy of the status quo. If you are of the opinion that all the world needs is a little buffing around the edges, this should not trouble you. But if you think that there are still lunch counters out there that need integrating it ought to give you pause.

Shirky ends the story of the lost Sidekick by asking, portentously, "What happens next?" — no doubt imagining future waves of digital protesters. But he has already answered the question. What happens next is more of the same. A networked, weak-tie world is good at things like helping Wall Streeters get phones back from teenage girls. *Viva la revolución.*

## FOR ANALYSIS

**1.** Why does Gladwell begin with the story of the lunch counter sit-ins?

**2.** According to Gladwell, what is the difference between a strong tie and a weak tie? What is the significance of that difference for his argument?

**3.** How would you characterize Gladwell's **tone**? List word choices and descriptions that reveal his attitude toward his subject. Do you think his tone helps or hurts his argument?

## MAKING ARGUMENTS

How would you refute Gladwell's argument? List your counterargument points, and try both to respond to his specific arguments and also to make your own.

## WRITING TOPIC

Gladwell finds claims for the importance of the Internet to contemporary social movements "puzzling" (para. 8). How do you feel about it? Have you seen or participated in Internet-related activities that have had social or political effects? Were these positive effects? Write about your experience or observations, and reflect on your feelings about them.

## MAKING CONNECTIONS

**1.** Compare Gladwell's and McKibben's essays: what they argue and how. Compare **tone**, nuance, use of evidence, and use of rhetoric. Do you find one more convincing than the other? How much of that relies on your feelings about the issues and how much on the differences in the way the authors make their arguments about the issues?

**2.** Compare McKibben's and Solnit's essays. How do their views of what revolution is differ? Whose view do you find more accurate or useful? Can both be right, and important?

**3.** For all of the writers in this cluster, what drives change?

## FURTHER QUESTIONS FOR THINKING AND WRITING

**1.** What support do the works in this section offer for Emily Dickinson's assertion that "Much Madness is divinest Sense"? **Writing Topic:** The central characters in Herman Melville's "Bartleby, the Scrivener" and Harlan Ellison's "'Repent, Harlequin!' Said the Ticktockman" are viewed by society as mad. How might it be argued that they exhibit "divinest sense"?

**2.** In a number of these works, a single individual rebels against society and suffers defeat or death. Are these works therefore pessimistic and despairing? If not, what is the purpose of the rebellions, and why do the authors choose to bring their characters to such ends? **Writing Topic:** Compare two works from this section that offer support for the idea that a single individual can have a decisive effect on society.

**3.** Examine some of the representatives of established order — the lawyer in "Bartleby, the Scrivener," the Ticktockman — and discuss what attitudes they share and how effectively they function as spokespeople for law and order. **Writing Topic:** Compare and evaluate the kinds of order that each represents.

**4.** William Butler Yeats's "Easter 1916" and Carolyn Forché's "The Colonel" are poems about political struggle against oppressive rulers. In what ways are the poems similar? In what ways are they different? **Writing Topic:** Select the poem that makes the most powerful and effective case on behalf of the oppressed, and write an argument defending your choice.

**5.** Most of us live out our lives in the ordinary and humdrum world that is rejected in poems such as William Wordsworth's "The World Is Too Much with Us" and W. H. Auden's "The Unknown Citizen." Can these poems be said to be calls to social irresponsibility? **Writing Topic:** Consider whether "we" in Wordsworth's poem and the unknown citizen are simply objects of scorn or whether they deserve sympathy and perhaps even respect.

**6.** Characters in two of the works in this section — the Harlequin in "'Repent, Harlequin!' Said the Ticktockman" and Bartleby in "Bartleby, the Scrivener" — are rebels. What similarities do you find between these rebels? **Writing Topic:** Explain how the attitudes and actions of these characters constitute an attack on the status quo.

**7.** Many works in this section deal explicitly with the relationship between individuals and religion. What similarities do you find among them? What differences? **Writing Topic:** Compare and contrast the way that relationship is perceived in Shirley Jackson's "The Lottery" and Salman Rushdie's "Imagine There's No Heaven."

# CULTURE AND IDENTITY

*This Is Harlem* (detail), 1943, by Jacob Lawrence.

Historically, a group of people bound together by kinship and geography will form a society that exhibits a *culture* — common language, behavioral rules, traditions, skills, mores, religion, and art that define the civilization of that group. Literary works, including folklore and myth, are inseparable from the particular human society from which they emerge.

Until relatively recently, with the invention of trains, automobiles, and airplanes, travel over long distances was difficult. Instant communication — the telephone, the Internet — is an innovation of our time. Originally, information about other societies could be heard only as far away as a human could shout. Letters helped transmit ideas and cultural values over time and distance, but no more quickly than a horse could gallop or a ship could sail. For thousands of years cultures lived in relative isolation from each other, and hence they tended to develop distinctive traits and values. Within China, for instance, there are numerous well-defined cultures: the Uighurs of the northwest, the coastal Chinese of Shanghai, the Tibetan mountain people, the Szechuanese of the southwest. They eat different foods; they practice different religions; they speak different dialects.

Though technological advances have made the world seem smaller and, generally, have ended the geographical isolation of various cultures, these advances have not diminished the powerful cultural distinctions that mark societies all over the world. In fact, modern communication and transport have sometimes served to bring cultures into conflict. The works in this section, varied as they are, share a preoccupation with the connection between culture and identity. Some, such as George Orwell's "Shooting an Elephant," examine the devastating consequences of cultural imperialism. Others, such as Louise Erdrich's "Dear John Wayne," focus on the way dominant cultural stereotypes distort and undermine the sense of self.

The works in this section demonstrate how powerfully culture shapes identity. They reveal the tension generated by interacting cultures, and offer insight into the conflicts that usually emerge. But these works also provide an opportunity for us to step outside the bounds and bonds of our own culture and to experience just how complex, diverse, and interesting the human condition can be.

## QUESTIONS FOR THINKING AND WRITING

As you read the selections in this section, consider the questions that follow. You may want to write out your thoughts informally — in a journal, if you are keeping one — as a way of preparing to respond to the selections. Or you may wish to make one of these questions the basis for a formal essay.

**1.** What cultural tradition(s) do you come from? Describe this tradition as fully as you can. Do you feel that you live in or out of the cultural mainstream? Explain.

**2.** Except for Native Americans, the people of the United States descended from or arrived as citizens of foreign cultures. Is there, nonetheless, an American culture? Explain. The United States was once called a *cultural melting pot*. Now it is sometimes called a *cultural mosaic*. Which **metaphor** strikes you as more apt? Explain.

**3.** Do economic considerations affect culture? Aside from their wealth, are the rich different from the poor? Explain. Does education strengthen or weaken traditional culture? Explain.

**4.** What are some of the positive and negative associations you have with the values of the cultural tradition(s) you come from? Is the preservation of these values a good thing or a bad thing? Explain.

# FICTION

**LU XUN**   (1881–1936)

## DIARY OF A MADMAN[1]   1918

*T*here was once a pair of male siblings whose actual names I beg your
indulgence to withhold. Suffice it to say that we three were boon companions during our school years. Subsequently, circumstances contrived to rend us
asunder so that we were gradually bereft of knowledge regarding each other's
activities.

Not too long ago, however, I chanced to hear that one of them had been hard
afflicted with a dread disease. I obtained this intelligence at a time when I happened to be returning to my native haunts and, hence, made so bold as to detour
somewhat from my normal course in order to visit them. I encountered but one
of the siblings. He apprised me that it had been his younger brother who had suffered the dire illness. By now, however, he had long since become sound and fit
again; in fact he had already repaired to other parts to await a substantive official appointment.[2]

The elder brother apologized for having needlessly put me to the inconvenience
of this visitation, and concluding his disquisition with a hearty smile, showed
me two volumes of diaries which, he assured me, would reveal the nature of his
brother's disorder during those fearful days.

As to the lapsus calami *that occur in the course of the diaries, I have altered
not a word. Nonetheless, I have changed all the names, despite the fact that their
publication would be of no great consequence since they are all humble villagers
unknown to the world at large.*

Recorded this 2nd day in the 7th year of the Republic.[3]

5

---

[1] Translated by William A. Lyell.

[2] When there were too many officials for the number of offices to be filled, a man might well be
appointed to an office that already had an incumbent. The new appointee would proceed to his post
and wait until said office was vacated. Sometimes there would be a number of such appointees waiting
their turns. [Translator's note.]

[3] April 2, 1918. This introduction is written in classical Chinese, while the diary entries that follow
are all in the colloquial language. [Translator's note.]

## 1

Moonlight's really nice tonight. Haven't seen it in over thirty years. Seeing it today, I feel like a new man. I know now that I've been completely out of things for the last three decades or more. But I've still got to be *very* careful. Otherwise, how do you explain those dirty looks the Zhao family's dog gave me?

I've got good reason for my fears.

## 2

No moonlight at all tonight — something's not quite right. When I made my way out the front gate this morning — ever so carefully — there was something funny about the way the Venerable Old Zhao looked at me: seemed as though he was afraid of me and yet, at the same time, looked as though he had it in for me. There were seven or eight other people who had their heads together whispering about me. They were afraid I'd see them too! All up and down the the street people acted the same way. The meanest looking one of all spread his lips out wide and actually *smiled* at me! A shiver ran from the top of my head clear down to the tips of my toes, for I realized that meant they already had their henchmen well deployed, and were ready to strike.

But I wasn't going to let that intimidate *me*. I kept right on walking. There was a group of children up ahead and they were talking about me too. The expressions in their eyes were just like the Venerable Old Zhao's, and their faces were iron gray. I wondered what grudge the children had against me that they were acting this way too. I couldn't contain myself any longer and shouted, "Tell me, tell me!" But they just ran away.

Let's see now, what grudge can there be between me and the Venerable Old Zhao, or the people on the street for that matter? The only thing I can think of is that twenty years ago I trampled the account books kept by Mr. Antiquity, and he was hopping mad about it too. Though the Venerable Old Zhao doesn't know him, he must have gotten wind of it somehow. Probably decided to right the injustice I had done Mr. Antiquity by getting all those people on the street to gang up on me. But the children? Back then they hadn't even come into the world yet. Why should they have given me those funny looks today? Seemed as though they were afraid of me and yet, at the same time, looked as though they would like to do me some harm. That really frightens me. Bewilders me. Hurts me.

I have it! Their fathers and mothers have *taught* them to be like that!

## 3

I can never get to sleep at night. You really have to study something before you can understand it.

Take all those people: some have worn the cangue on the district magistrate's order, some have had their faces slapped by the gentry, some have had their wives ravished by *yamen* clerks,[4] some have had their dads and moms dunned to death by creditors; and yet, right at the time when all those terrible things were taking place, the expressions on their faces were never as frightened, or as savage, as the ones they wore yesterday.

Strangest of all was that woman on the street. She slapped her son and said: "Damn it all, you've got me so riled up I could take a good bite right out of your hide!" She was talking to him, but she was looking at me! I tried, but couldn't conceal a shudder of fright. That's when that ghastly crew of people, with their green faces and protruding fangs, began to roar with laughter. Old Fifth Chen ran up, took me firmly in tow, and dragged me away.

When we got back, the people at home all pretended not to know me. The expressions in their eyes were just like all the others too. After he got me into the study, Old Fifth Chen bolted the door from the outside — just the way you would pen up a chicken or a duck! That made figuring out what was at the bottom of it all harder than ever.

A few days back one of our tenant farmers came in from Wolf Cub Village to report a famine. Told my elder brother the villagers had all ganged up on a "bad" man and beaten him to death. Even gouged out his heart and liver. Fried them up and ate them to bolster their own courage! When I tried to horn in on the conversation, Elder Brother and the tenant farmer both gave me sinister looks. I realized for the first time today that the expression in their eyes was just the same as what I saw in those people on the street.

As I think of it now, a shiver's running from the top of my head clear down to the tips of my toes.

If they're capable of eating people, then who's to say they won't eat *me*?

Don't you see? That woman's words about "taking a good bite," and the laughter of that ghastly crew with their green faces and protruding fangs, and the words of our tenant farmer a few days back — it's perfectly clear to me now that all that talk and all that laughter were really a set of secret signals. Those words were poison! That laughter, a knife! Their teeth are bared and waiting — white and razor sharp! Those people are cannibals!

As I see it myself, though I'm not what you'd call an evil man, still, ever since I trampled the Antiquity family's account books, it's hard to say *what* they'll do. They seem to have something in mind, but I can't begin to guess what. What's more, as soon as they turn against someone, they'll *say* he's evil anyway. I can still remember how it was when Elder Brother was teaching me composition. No matter how good a man was, if I could find a few things wrong with him he would approvingly underline my words; on the other hand, if I made a few allowances for a bad man, he'd say I was "an extraordinary student, an absolute genius." When all is said and done, how can I possibly guess what people like *that* have in mind, especially when they're getting ready for a cannibals' feast?

---

[4] The cangue was a split board, hinged at one end and locked at the other; holes were cut out to accommodate the prisoner's neck and wrists. *Yamen* was the term for local government offices. The petty clerks who worked in them were notorious for relying on their proximity to power in order to bully and abuse the common people. [Translator's note.]

You have to *really* go into something before you can understand it. I seemed to remember, though not too clearly, that from ancient times on people have often been eaten, and so I started leafing through a history book to look it up. There were no dates in this history, but scrawled this way and that across every page were the words BENEVOLENCE, RIGHTEOUSNESS, and MORALITY. Since I couldn't get to sleep anyway, I read that history very carefully for most of the night, and finally I began to make out what was written *between* the lines; the whole volume was filled with a single phrase: EAT PEOPLE!

The words written in the history book, the things the tenant farmer said — all of it began to stare at me with hideous eyes, began to snarl and growl at me from behind bared teeth!

Why sure, *I'm* a person too, and they want to eat *me*!

### 4

In the morning I sat in the study for a while, calm and collected. Old Fifth Chen brought in some food — vegetables and a steamed fish. The fish's eyes were white and hard. Its mouth was wide open, just like the mouths of those people who wanted to eat human flesh. After I'd taken a few bites, the meat felt so smooth and slippery in my mouth that I couldn't tell whether it was fish or human flesh. I vomited.

"Old Fifth," I said, "tell Elder Brother that it's absolutely stifling in here and that I'd like to take a walk in the garden." He left without answering, but sure enough, after a while the door opened. I didn't even budge — just sat there waiting to see what they'd do to me. I *knew* that they wouldn't be willing to set me loose.

Just as I expected! Elder Brother came in with an old man in tow and walked slowly toward me. There was a savage glint in the old man's eyes. He was afraid I'd see it and kept his head tilted toward the floor while stealing sidewise glances at me over the temples of his glasses. "You seem to be fine today," said Elder Brother.

"You bet!" I replied.

"I've asked Dr. He to come and examine your pulse today."

"He's welcome!" I said. But don't think for one moment that I didn't know the old geezer was an executioner in disguise! Taking my pulse was nothing but a ruse; he wanted to feel my flesh and decide if I was fat enough to butcher yet. He'd probably even get a share of the meat for his troubles. I wasn't a *bit* afraid. Even though I don't eat human flesh, I still have a lot more courage than those who do. I thrust both hands out to see how the old buzzard would make his move.[5] Sitting down, he closed his eyes and felt my pulse for a good long while. Then he froze. Just sat there without moving a muscle for another good long while. Finally he opened his spooky eyes and said: "Don't let your thoughts run away with you. Just convalesce in peace and quiet for a few days and you'll be all right."

---

[5] In Chinese medicine the pulse is taken at both wrists. [Translator's note.]

Don't let my thoughts run away with me? Convalesce in peace and quiet? If 30
I convalesce till I'm good and fat, they get more to eat, but what do *I* get out of
it? How can I possibly be *all right*? What a bunch! All they think about is eating human flesh, and then they go sneaking around, thinking up every which
way they can to camouflage their real intentions. They were comical enough
to crack *anybody* up. I couldn't hold it in any longer and let out a good loud
laugh. Now *that* really felt good. I knew in my heart of hearts that my laughter
was *packed* with courage and righteousness. And do you know what? They
were so completely subdued by it that the old man and my elder brother both
went pale!

But the more *courage* I had, the more that made them want to eat me so
that they could get a little of it for free. The old man walked out. Before he had
taken many steps, he lowered his head and told Elder Brother, "To be eaten as
soon as possible!" He nodded understandingly. So, Elder Brother, you're in it
too! Although that discovery seemed unforeseen, it really wasn't, either. My
own elder brother had thrown in with the very people who wanted to eat me!

My elder brother is a cannibal!

I'm brother to a cannibal.

Even though I'm to be the victim of cannibalism, I'm *brother* to a cannibal
all the same!


## 5

During the past few days I've taken a step back in my thinking. Suppos- 35
ing that old man wasn't an executioner in disguise but really was a doctor — well, he'd still be a cannibal just the same. In *Medicinal . . . something or
other* by Li Shizhen, the grandfather of the doctor's trade, it says quite clearly
that human flesh can be eaten, so how can that old man say that *he's* not a
cannibal too?[6]

And as for my own elder brother, I'm not being the least bit unfair to him.
When he was explaining the classics to me, he said with his very own tongue
that it was all right to *exchange children and eat them*. And then there was
another time when he happened to start in on an evil man and said that not
only should the man be killed, but his *flesh should be eaten* and *his skin used as
a sleeping mat* as well.[7]

---

[6] *Taxonomy of Medicinal Herbs*, a gigantic work, was the most important pharmacopoeia in traditional China. Li Shizhen lived from 1518 to 1593. [Translator's note.]

[7] Both italicized expressions are from the *Zuozhuan* (Zuo Commentary [to the *Spring and Autumn
Annals*]), a historical work which dates from the third century B.C. In 448 B.C., an officer who was
exhorting his own side not to surrender is recorded as having said, "When the army of Chu besieged
the capital of Song [in 603 B.C.], the people exchanged their children and ate them, and used the bones
for fuel; and still they would not submit to a covenant at the foot of their walls. For us who have sustained no great loss, to do so is to cast our state away" (Legge 5.817). It is also recorded that in 551 B.C.
an officer boasting of his own prowess before his ruler, pointed to two men whom his ruler considered
brave and said, "As to those two, they are like beasts, whose flesh I will eat, and then sleep upon their
skins" (Legge 5.492). [Translator's note.]

When our tenant farmer came in from Wolf Cub Village a few days back and talked about eating a man's heart and liver, Elder Brother didn't seem to see anything out of the way in that either — just kept nodding his head. You can tell from that alone that his present way of thinking is every bit as malicious as it was when I was a child. If it's all right to exchange *children* and eat them, then *anyone* can be exchanged, anyone can be eaten. Back then I just took what he said as explanation of the classics and let it go at that, but now I realize that while he was explaining, the grease of human flesh was smeared all over his lips, and what's more, his mind was filled with plans for further cannibalism.

## 6

Pitch black out. Can't tell if it's day or night. The Zhao family's dog has started barking again.

Savage as a lion, timid as a rabbit, crafty as a fox . . .

## 7

I'm on to the way they operate. They'll never be willing to come straight out 40 and kill me. Besides, they wouldn't dare. They'd be afraid of all the bad luck it might bring down on them if they did. And so, they've gotten everyone into cahoots with them and have set traps all over the place so that I'll do *myself* in. When I think back on the looks of those men and women on the streets a few days ago, coupled with the things my elder brother's been up to recently, I can figure out eight or nine tenths of it. From their point of view, the best thing of all would be for me to take off my belt, fasten it around a beam, and hang myself. They wouldn't be guilty of murder, and yet they'd still get everything they're after. Why, they'd be so beside themselves with joy, they'd sob with laughter. Or if they couldn't get me to do that, maybe they could torment me until I died of fright and worry. Even though I'd come out a bit leaner that way, they'd still nod their heads in approval.

Their kind only know how to eat dead meat. I remember reading in a book somewhere about something called the *hai-yi-na*. Its general appearance is said to be hideous, and the expression in its eyes particularly ugly and malicious. Often eats carrion, too. Even chews the bones to a pulp and swallows them down. Just thinking about it's enough to frighten a man.

The *hai-yi-na* is kin to the wolf.[8] The wolf's a relative of the dog, and just a few days ago the Zhao family dog gave me a funny look. It's easy to see that he's in on it too. How did that old man expect to fool *me* by staring at the floor?

My elder brother's the most pathetic of the whole lot. Since he's a human being too, how can he manage to be so totally without qualms, and what's more, even gang up with them to eat me? Could it be that he's been used to

---

[8] Three Chinese characters are used here for phonetic value only — that is, *hai yi na* is a transliteration into Chinese of the English word "hyena." [Translator's note.]

this sort of thing all along and sees nothing wrong with it? Or could it be that he's lost all conscience and just goes ahead and does it even though he knows it's wrong?

If I'm going to curse cannibals, I'll have to start with him. And if I'm going to *convert* cannibals, I'll have to start with him too.

### 8

Actually, by now even they should long since have understood the truth of 45 this . . .

Someone came in. Couldn't have been more than twenty or so. I wasn't able to make out what he looked like too clearly, but he was all smiles. He nodded at me. His smile didn't look like the real thing either. And so I asked him, "Is this business of eating people right?"

He just kept right on smiling and said, "Except perhaps in a famine year, how could anyone get eaten?" I knew right off that he was one of them — one of those monsters who devour people!

At that point my own courage increased a hundredfold and I asked him, "Is it right?"

"Why are you talking about this kind of thing anyway? You really know how to . . . uh . . . how to pull a fellow's leg. Nice weather we're having."

"The weather *is* nice. There's a nice moon out, too, but I *still* want to know if 50 it's right."

He seemed quite put out with me and began to mumble, "It's not —"

"Not right? Then how come they're still eating people?"

"No one's eating anyone."

"No one's *eating* anyone? They're eating people in Wolf Cub Village this very minute. And it's written in all the books, too, written in bright red blood!"

His expression changed and his face went gray like a slab of iron. His eyes 55 started out from their sockets as he said, "Maybe they are, but it's always been that way, it's —"

"Just because it's always been that way, does that make it *right*?"

"I'm not going to discuss such things with you. If you insist on talking about that, then *you're* the one who's in the wrong!"

I leaped from my chair, opened my eyes, and looked around — but the fellow was nowhere to be seen. He was far younger than my elder brother, and yet he was actually one of them. It must be because his mom and dad taught him to be that way. And he's probably already passed it on to his own son. No wonder that even the children give me murderous looks.

### 9

They want to eat others and at the same time they're afraid that other people are going to eat them. That's why they're always watching each other with such suspicious looks in their eyes.

But all they'd have to do is give up that way of thinking, and then they could 60
travel about, work, eat, and sleep in perfect security. Think how happy they'd
feel! It's only a threshold, a pass. But what do they do instead? What is it that
these fathers, sons, brothers, husbands, wives, friends, teachers, students, enemies, and even people who don't know each other *really* do? Why they all join
together to hold each other back, and talk each other out of it!

That's it! They'd rather *die* than take that one little step.

## 10

I went to see Elder Brother bright and early. He was standing in the courtyard looking at the sky. I went up behind him so as to cut him off from the
door back into the house. In the calmest and friendliest of tones, I said, "Elder
Brother, there's something I'd like to tell you."

"Go right ahead." He immediately turned and nodded his head.

"It's only a few words, really, but it's hard to get them out. Elder Brother, way
back in the beginning, it's probably the case that primitive peoples *all* ate some
human flesh. But later on, because their ways of thinking changed, some gave up
the practice and tried their level best to improve themselves; they kept on changing until they became human beings, *real* human beings. But the others didn't;
they just kept right on with their cannibalism and stayed at that primitive level.

"You have the same sort of thing with evolution in the animal world. Some 65
reptiles, for instance, changed into fish, and then they evolved into birds, then
into apes, and then into human beings.[9] But the others didn't want to improve
themselves and just kept right on being reptiles down to this very day.

"Think how ashamed those primitive men who have remained cannibals
must feel when they stand before *real* human beings. They must feel even
more ashamed than reptiles do when confronted with their brethren who have
evolved into apes.

"There's an old story from ancient times about Yi Ya boiling his son and
serving him up to Jie Zhou. But if the truth be known, people have *always*
practiced cannibalism, all the way from the time when Pan Gu separated
heaven and earth down to Yi Ya's son, down to Xu Xilin, and on down to the
man they killed in Wolf Cub Village.[10] And just last year when they executed

[9] Darwin's theory of evolution was immensely important to Chinese intellectuals during Lu Xun's
lifetime and the common coin of much discourse. [Translator's note.]

[10] An early philosophical text, *Guan Zi*, reports that the famous cook, Yi Ya, boiled his son and
served him to his ruler, Duke Huan of Qi (685–643 B.C.), because the meat of a human infant was
one of the few delicacies the duke had never tasted. Jie and Zhou were the last evil rulers of the Shang
(1776–1122 B.C.) and Zhou (1122–221 B.C.) dynasties. The madman has mixed up some facts here.

Pan Gu (literally, Coiled-up Antiquity) was born out of an egg. As he stood up he separated heaven
and earth. The world, as we know it, was formed from his body.

Xu Xilin (1873–1907) was from Lu Xun's hometown, Shaoxing. After studies in Japan he returned
to China and served as head of the Anhui Police Academy. When a high Qing official, En Ming, participated in a graduation ceremony at the academy, Xu assassinated him, hoping that this spark would
touch off the revolution. After the assassination, he and some of his students at the academy occupied
the police armory and managed, for a while, to hold off En Ming's troops. When Xu was finally captured, En Ming's personal bodyguards dug out his heart and liver and ate them. [Translator's note.]

a criminal in town, there was even someone with T.B. who dunked a steamed bread roll in his blood and then licked it off.[11]

"When they decided to eat me, by yourself, of course, you couldn't do much to prevent it, but why did you have to go and *join* them? Cannibals are capable of anything! If they're capable of eating me, then they're capable of eating *you* too! Even within their own group, they think nothing of devouring each other. And yet all they'd have to do is turn back—*change*—and then everything would be fine. Even though people may say, 'It's always been like this,' we can still do our best to improve. And we can start today!

"You're going to tell me it can't be done! Elder Brother, I think you're very likely to say that. When that tenant wanted to reduce his rent the day before yesterday, wasn't it you who said it couldn't be done?"

At first he just stood there with a cold smile, but then his eyes took on a murderous gleam. (I had exposed their innermost secrets.) His whole face had gone pale. Some people were standing outside the front gate. The Venerable Old Zhao and his dog were among them. Stealthily peering this way and that, they began to crowd through the open gate. Some I couldn't make out too well—their faces seemed covered with cloth. Some looked the same as ever—smiling green faces with protruding fangs. I could tell at a glance that they all belonged to the same gang, that they were all cannibals. But at the same time I also realized that they didn't all think the same way. Some thought *it's always been like this* and that they really should eat human flesh. Others knew they shouldn't but went right on doing it anyway, always on the lookout for fear someone might give them away. And since that's exactly what I had just done, I knew they must be furious. But they were all *smiling* at me—cold little smiles!

At this point Elder Brother suddenly took on an ugly look and barked, "Get out of here! All of you! What's so funny about a madman?"

Now I'm on to *another* of their tricks: not only are they unwilling to change, but they're already setting me up for their next cannibalistic feast by labeling me a "madman." That way, they'll be able to eat me without getting into the slightest trouble. Some people will even be grateful to them. Wasn't that the very trick used in the case that the tenant reported? Everybody ganged up on a "bad" man and ate him. It's the same old thing.

Old Fifth Chen came in and made straight for me, looking mad as could be. But he wasn't going to shut *me* up! I was going to tell that bunch of cannibals off, and no two ways about it!

"You can change! You can change from the bottom of your hearts! You ought to know that in the future they're not going to allow cannibalism in the world anymore. If you don't change, you're going to devour each other anyway. And even if a lot of you *are* left, a real human being's going to come along and eradicate the lot of you, just like a hunter getting rid of wolves—or reptiles!"

[11] A similar incident is the basis for Lu Xun's story "Medicine." Human blood was believed to be a cure for tuberculosis. [Translator's note.]

Old Fifth Chen chased them all out. I don't know where Elder Brother dis- 75 appeared to. Old Fifth talked me into going back to my room.

It was pitch black inside. The beams and rafters started trembling overhead. They shook for a bit, and then they started getting bigger and bigger. They piled themselves up into a great heap on top of my body!

The weight was incredibly heavy and I couldn't even budge — they were trying to kill me! But I knew their weight was an illusion, and I struggled out from under them, my body bathed in sweat. I was still going to have my say. "Change this minute! Change from the bottom of your hearts! You ought to know that in the future they're not going to allow cannibals in the world anymore . . ."

## 11

The sun doesn't come out. The door doesn't open. It's two meals a day.

I picked up my chopsticks and that got me thinking about Elder Brother. I realized that the reason for my younger sister's death lay entirely with him. I can see her now — such a lovable and helpless little thing, only five at the time. Mother couldn't stop crying, but *he* urged her to stop, probably because he'd eaten sister's flesh himself and hearing mother cry over her like that shamed him! But if he's still capable of feeling shame, then maybe . . .

Younger Sister was eaten by Elder Brother. I have no way of knowing 80 whether Mother knew about it or not.

I think she *did* know, but while she was crying she didn't say anything about it. She probably thought it was all right, too. I can remember once when I was four or five, I was sitting out in the courtyard taking in a cool breeze when Elder Brother told me that when parents are ill, a son, in order to be counted as a really good person, should slice off a piece of his own flesh, boil it, and let them eat it.[12] At the time Mother didn't come out and say there was anything wrong with that. But if it was all right to eat one piece, then there certainly wouldn't be anything wrong with her eating the whole body. And yet when I think back to the way she cried and cried that day, it's enough to break my heart. It's all strange — very, very strange.

## 12

Can't think about it anymore. I just realized today that I too have muddled around for a good many years in a place where they've been continually eating people for four thousand years. Younger Sister happened to die at just the time when Elder Brother was in charge of the house. Who's to say he didn't slip some of her meat into the food we ate?

Who's to say I didn't eat a few pieces of my younger sister's flesh without knowing it? And now it's my turn . . .

---

[12] In traditional literature, stories about such gruesome acts of filial piety were not unusual. [Translator's note.]

Although I wasn't aware of it in the beginning, now that I *know* I'm someone with four thousand years' experience of cannibalism behind me, how hard it is to look real human beings in the eye!

## 13

Maybe there are some children around who still haven't eaten human flesh. 85
Save the children . . .

### FOR ANALYSIS

**1.** How is this story framed? Why do you think the author chose to introduce the story in this way?

**2.** How would you describe the diarist's state of mind? Use words not found in the title. How does the author convey his state to us?

**3.** What might the cannibalism in this story be a **metaphor** for?

### MAKING ARGUMENTS

Build an argument for reading this story as an **allegory**. What does it allegorize? How do you know? Build your argument on textual and historical evidence.

### WRITING TOPICS

**1.** Like Swift's "A Modest Proposal" (p. 403), "Diary of a Madman" employs the figure of eating one's young. In what ways might one think that a society "eats" its young?

**2.** Lu Xun's creation of the diarist's voice is noteworthy in its effectiveness. Keep a log in which you track the subtle and not-so-subtle changes in that voice, noting not what the diarist sees but how he expresses it. Are there any observations you can make about the author's specific techniques? Any generalizations about his method?

### MAKING CONNECTIONS

Read "Diary of a Madman" with Charlotte Perkins Gilman's "The Yellow Wallpaper" (p. 442). How are they similar? How do they differ? What do those differences mean for the way each story reads and for any greater significance you might find in them?

## Charlotte Perkins Gilman (1860–1935)

# The Yellow Wallpaper 1892

It is very seldom that mere ordinary people like John and myself secure ancestral halls for the summer.

A colonial mansion, a hereditary estate, I would say a haunted house and reach the height of romantic felicity — but that would be asking too much of fate!

Still I will proudly declare that there is something queer about it.

Else, why should it be let so cheaply? And why have stood so long untenanted?

John laughs at me, of course, but one expects that. 5

John is practical in the extreme. He has no patience with faith, an intense horror of superstition, and he scoffs openly at any talk of things not to be felt and seen and put down in figures.

John is a physician, and *perhaps* — (I would not say it to a living soul, of course, but this is dead paper and a great relief to my mind) — *perhaps* that is one reason I do not get well faster.

You see, he does not believe I am sick! And what can one do?

If a physician of high standing, and one's own husband, assures friends and relatives that there is really nothing the matter with one but temporary nervous depression — a slight hysterical tendency — what is one to do?

My brother is also a physician, and also of high standing, and he says the 10 same thing.

So I take phosphates or phosphites — whichever it is, and tonics, and air and exercise, and journeys, and am absolutely forbidden to "work" until I am well again.

Personally, I disagree with their ideas.

Personally, I believe that congenial work, with excitement and change, would do me good.

But what is one to do?

I did write for a while in spite of them; but it *does* exhaust me a good 15 deal — having to be so sly about it, or else meet with heavy opposition.

I sometimes fancy that in my condition if I had less opposition and more society and stimulus — but John says the very worst thing I can do is to think about my condition, and I confess it always makes me feel bad.

So I will let it alone and talk about the house.

The most beautiful place! It is quite alone, standing well back from the road, quite three miles from the village. It makes me think of English places that you read about, for there are hedges and walls and gates that lock, and lots of separate little houses for the gardeners and people.

442

There is a *delicious* garden! I never saw such a garden — large and shady, full of box-bordered paths, and lined with long grape-covered arbors with seats under them.

There were greenhouses, too, but they are all broken now.                    20

There was some legal trouble, I believe, something about the heirs and co-heirs; anyhow, the place has been empty for years.

That spoils my ghostliness, I am afraid, but I don't care — there is something strange about the house — I can feel it.

I even said so to John one moonlight evening, but he said what I felt was a draught, and shut the window.

I get unreasonably angry with John sometimes. I'm sure I never used to be so sensitive. I think it is due to this nervous condition.

But John says if I feel so I shall neglect proper self-control; so I take pains to    25
control myself — before him, at least, and that makes me very tired.

I don't like our room a bit. I wanted one downstairs that opened onto the piazza and had roses all over the window, and such pretty old-fashioned chintz hangings! But John would not hear of it.

He said there was only one window and not room for two beds, and no near room for him if he took another.

He is very careful and loving, and hardly lets me stir without special direction.

I have a schedule prescription for each hour in the day; he takes all care from me, and so I feel basely ungrateful not to value it more.

He said we came here solely on my account, that I was to have perfect rest    30
and all the air I could get. "Your exercise depends on your strength, my dear," said he, "and your food somewhat on your appetite; but air you can absorb all the time." So we took the nursery at the top of the house.

It is a big, airy room, the whole floor nearly, with windows that look all ways, and air and sunshine galore. It was a nursery first, and then playroom and gymnasium, I should judge, for the windows are barred for little children, and there are rings and things in the walls.

The paint and paper look as if a boys' school had used it. It is stripped off — the paper — in great patches all around the head of my bed, about as far as I can reach, and in a great place on the other side of the room low down. I never saw a worse paper in my life. One of those sprawling, flamboyant patterns committing every artistic sin.

It is dull enough to confuse the eye in following, pronounced enough constantly to irritate and provoke study, and when you follow the lame uncertain curves for a little distance they suddenly commit suicide — plunge off at outrageous angles, destroy themselves in unheard-of contradictions.

The color is repellent, almost revolting; a smouldering unclean yellow, strangely faded by the slow-turning sunlight. It is a dull yet lurid orange in some places, a sickly sulphur tint in others.

No wonder the children hated it! I should hate it myself if I had to live in this    35
room long.

There comes John, and I must put this away — he hates to have me write a word.

We have been here two weeks, and I haven't felt like writing before, since that first day.

I am sitting by the window now, up in this atrocious nursery, and there is nothing to hinder my writing as much as I please, save lack of strength.

John is away all day, and even some nights when his cases are serious.

I'm glad my case is not serious! 40

But these nervous troubles are dreadfully depressing.

John does not know how much I really suffer. He knows there is no reason to suffer, and that satisfies him.

Of course it is only nervousness. It does weigh on me so not to do my duty in any way!

I meant to be such a help to John, such a real rest and comfort, and here I am a comparative burden already!

Nobody would believe what an effort it is to do what little I am able — to 45 dress and entertain, and order things.

It is fortunate Mary is so good with the baby. Such a dear baby!

And yet I *cannot* be with him, it makes me so nervous.

I suppose John never was nervous in his life. He laughs at me so about this wallpaper!

At first he meant to repaper the room, but afterward he said that I was letting it get the better of me, and that nothing was worse for a nervous patient than to give way to such fancies.

He said that after the wallpaper was changed it would be the heavy bedstead, 50 and then the barred windows, and then that gate at the head of the stairs, and so on.

"You know the place is doing you good," he said, "and really, dear, I don't care to renovate the house just for a three months' rental."

"Then do let us go downstairs," I said. "There are such pretty rooms there."

Then he took me in his arms and called me a blessed little goose, and said he would go down to the cellar, if I wished, and have it whitewashed into the bargain.

But he is right enough about the beds and windows and things.

It is as airy and comfortable a room as anyone need wish, and, of course, 55 I would not be so silly as to make him uncomfortable just for a whim.

I'm really getting quite fond of the big room, all but that horrid paper.

Out of one window I can see the garden — those mysterious deep-shaded arbors, the riotous old-fashioned flowers, and bushes and gnarly trees.

Out of another I get a lovely view of the bay and a little private wharf belonging to the estate. There is a beautiful shaded lane that runs down there from the house. I always fancy I see people walking in these numerous paths and arbors, but John has cautioned me not to give way to fancy in the least. He says that with my imaginative power and habit of story-making, a nervous weakness like mine is sure to lead to all manner of excited fancies, and that I ought to use my will and good sense to check the tendency. So I try.

I think sometimes that if I were only well enough to write a little it would relieve the press of ideas and rest me.

But I find I get pretty tired when I try. 60

It is so discouraging not to have any advice and companionship about my work. When I get really well, John says we will ask Cousin Henry and Julia down for a long visit; but he says he would as soon put fireworks in my pillow-case as to let me have those stimulating people about now.

I wish I could get well faster.

But I must not think about that. This paper looks to me as if it *knew* what a vicious influence it had!

There is a recurrent spot where the pattern lolls like a broken neck and two bulbous eyes stare at you upside down.

I get positively angry with the impertinence of it and the everlastingness. 65 Up and down and sideways they crawl, and those absurd, unblinking eyes are everywhere. There is one place where two breadths didn't match, and the eyes go all up and down the line, one a little higher than the other.

I never saw so much expression in an inanimate thing before, and we all know how much expression they have! I used to lie awake as a child and get more entertainment and terror out of blank walls and plain furniture than most children could find in a toy-store.

I remember what a kindly wink the knobs of our big old bureau used to have, and there was one chair that always seemed like a strong friend.

I used to feel that if any of the other things looked too fierce I could always hop into that chair and be safe.

The furniture in this room is no worse than inharmonious, however, for we had to bring it all from downstairs. I suppose when this was used as a play-room they had to take the nursery things out, and no wonder! I never saw such ravages as the children have made here.

The wallpaper, as I said before, is torn off in spots, and it sticketh closer than 70 a brother — they must have had perseverance as well as hatred.

Then the floor is scratched and gouged and splintered, the plaster itself is dug out here and there, and this great heavy bed, which is all we found in the room, looks as if it had been through the wars.

But I don't mind it a bit — only the paper.

There comes John's sister. Such a dear girl as she is, and so careful of me! I must not let her find me writing.

She is a perfect and enthusiastic housekeeper, and hopes for no better pro-fession. I verily believe she thinks it is the writing which made me sick!

But I can write when she is out, and see her a long way off from these 75 windows.

There is one that commands the road, a lovely shaded winding road, and one that just looks off over the country. A lovely country, too, full of great elms and velvet meadows.

This wallpaper has a kind of sub-pattern in a different shade, a particularly irritating one, for you can only see it in certain lights, and not clearly then.

But in the places where it isn't faded and where the sun is just so — I can see a strange, provoking, formless sort of figure that seems to skulk about behind that silly and conspicuous front design.

There's sister on the stairs!

Well, the Fourth of July is over! The people are all gone and I am tired out. John thought it might do me good to see a little company, so we just had Mother and Nellie and the children down for a week.

Of course I didn't do a thing. Jennie sees to everything now.

But it tired me all the same.

John says if I don't pick up faster he shall send me to Weir Mitchell in the fall.

But I don't want to go there at all. I had a friend who was in his hands once, and she says he is just like John and my brother, only more so!

Besides, it is such an undertaking to go so far.

I don't feel as if it was worthwhile to turn my hand over for anything, and I'm getting dreadfully fretful and querulous.

I cry at nothing, and cry most of the time.

Of course I don't when John is here, or anybody else, but when I am alone.

And I am alone a good deal just now. John is kept in town very often by serious cases, and Jennie is good and lets me alone when I want her to.

So I walk a little in the garden or down that lovely lane, sit on the porch under the roses, and lie down up here a good deal.

I'm getting really fond of the room in spite of the wallpaper. Perhaps *because* of the wallpaper.

It dwells in my mind so!

I lie here on this great immovable bed — it is nailed down, I believe — and follow that pattern about by the hour. It is as good as gymnastics, I assure you. I start, we'll say, at the bottom, down in the corner over there where it has not been touched, and I determine for the thousandth time that I *will* follow that pointless pattern to some sort of a conclusion.

I know a little of the principle of design, and I know this thing was not arranged on any laws of radiation, or alternation, or repetition, or symmetry, or anything else that I ever heard of.

It is repeated, of course, by the breadths, but not otherwise.

Looked at in one way, each breadth stands alone; the bloated curves and flourishes — a kind of "debased Romanesque" with delirium tremens — go waddling up and down in isolated columns of fatuity.

But, on the other hand, they connect diagonally, and the sprawling outlines run off in great slanting waves of optic horror, like a lot of wallowing seaweeds in full chase.

The whole thing goes horizontally, too, at least it seems so, and I exhaust myself in trying to distinguish the order of its going in that direction.

They have used a horizontal breadth for a frieze, and that adds wonderfully to the confusion.

There is one end of the room where it is almost intact, and there, when the  100
crosslights fade and the low sun shines directly upon it, I can almost fancy
radiation after all, — the interminable grotesque seems to form around a common center and rush off in headlong plunges of equal distraction.

It makes me tired to follow it. I will take a nap, I guess.

I don't know why I should write this.

I don't want to.

I don't feel able.

And I know John would think it absurd. But I *must* say what I feel and think  105
in some way — it is such a relief!

But the effort is getting to be greater than the relief.

Half the time now I am awfully lazy, and lie down ever so much. John says
I musn't lose my strength, and has me take cod liver oil and lots of tonics and
things, to say nothing of ale and wine and rare meat.

Dear John! He loves me very dearly, and hates to have me sick. I tried to
have a real earnest reasonable talk with him the other day, and tell him how
I wish he would let me go and make a visit to Cousin Henry and Julia.

But he said I wasn't able to go, nor able to stand it after I got there; and I did
not make out a very good case for myself, for I was crying before I had finished.

It is getting to be a great effort for me to think straight. Just this nervous  110
weakness, I suppose.

And dear John gathered me up in his arms, and just carried me upstairs and
laid me on the bed, and sat by me and read to me till it tired my head.

He said I was his darling and his comfort and all he had, and that I must take
care of myself for his sake, and keep well.

He says no one but myself can help me out of it, that I must use my will and
self-control and not let any silly fancies run away with me.

There's one comfort — the baby is well and happy, and does not have to
occupy this nursery with the horrid wallpaper.

If we had not used it, that blessed child would have! What a fortunate escape!  115
Why, I wouldn't have a child of mine, an impressionable little thing, live in
such a room for worlds.

I never thought of it before, but it is lucky that John kept me here after all;
I can stand it so much easier than a baby, you see.

Of course I never mention it to them any more — I am too wise — but I keep
watch of it all the same.

There are things in that wallpaper that nobody knows but me, or ever will.

Behind that outside pattern the dim shapes get clearer every day.

It is always the same shape, only very numerous.  120

And it is like a woman stooping down and creeping about behind that pattern. I don't like it a bit. I wonder — I begin to think — I wish John would take
me away from here!

It is so hard to talk with John about my case, because he is so wise, and
because he loves me so.

But I tried it last night.

It was moonlight. The moon shines in all around just as the sun does.

I hate to see it sometimes, it creeps so slowly, and always comes in by one 125 window or another.

John was asleep and I hated to waken him, so I kept still and watched the moonlight on that undulating wallpaper till I felt creepy.

The faint figure behind seemed to shake the pattern, just as if she wanted to get out.

I got up softly and went to feel and see if the paper *did* move, and when I came back John was awake.

"What is it, little girl?" he said. "Don't go walking about like that — you'll get cold."

I thought it was a good time to talk, so I told him that I really was not gain- 130 ing here, and that I wished he would take me away.

"Why, darling!" said he, "Our lease will be up in three weeks, and I can't see how to leave before.

"The repairs are not done at home, and I cannot possibly leave town just now. Of course if you were in any danger, I could and would, but you really are better, dear, whether you can see it or not. I am a doctor, dear, and I know. You are gaining flesh and color, your appetite is better, I feel really much easier about you."

"I don't weigh a bit more," said I, "nor as much; and my appetite may be better in the evening when you are here but it is worse in the morning when you are away!"

"Bless her little heart!" said he with a big hug, "She shall be as sick as she pleases! But now let's improve the shining hours by going to sleep, and talk about it in the morning!"

"And you won't go away?" I asked gloomily. 135

"Why, how can I, dear? It is only three weeks more and then we will take a nice little trip of a few days while Jennie is getting the house ready. Really, dear, you are better!"

"Better in body perhaps —" I began, and stopped short, for he sat up straight and looked at me with such a stern, reproachful look that I could not say another word.

"My darling," said he, "I beg of you, for my sake and for our child's sake, as well as for your own, that you will never for one instant let that idea enter your mind! There is nothing so dangerous, so fascinating, to a temperament like yours. It is a false and foolish fancy. Can you trust me as a physician when I tell you so?"

So of course I said no more on that score, and we went to sleep before long. He thought I was asleep first, but I wasn't, and lay there for hours trying to decide whether that front pattern and the back pattern really did move together or separately.

On a pattern like this, by daylight, there is a lack of sequence, a defiance of 140 law, that is a constant irritant to a normal mind.

The color is hideous enough, and unreliable enough, and infuriating enough, but the pattern is torturing.

You think you have mastered it, but just as you get well under way in following, it turns a back-somersault and there you are. It slaps you in the face, knocks you down, and tramples upon you. It is like a bad dream.

The outside pattern is a florid arabesque, reminding one of a fungus. If you can imagine a toadstool in joints, an interminable string of toadstools, budding and sprouting in endless convolutions — why, that is something like it.

That is, sometimes!

There is one marked peculiarity about this paper, a thing nobody seems to notice but myself, and that is that it changes as the light changes. 145

When the sun shoots in through the east window — I always watch for that first long, straight ray — it changes so quickly that I never can quite believe it.

That is why I watch it always.

By moonlight — the moon shines in all night when there is a moon — I wouldn't know it was the same paper.

At night in any kind of light, in twilight, candlelight, lamplight, and worst of all by moonlight, it becomes bars! The outside pattern, I mean, and the woman behind it is as plain as can be.

I didn't realize for a long time what the thing was that showed behind, that dim sub-pattern, but now I am quite sure it is a woman. 150

By daylight she is subdued, quiet. I fancy it is the pattern that keeps her so still. It is so puzzling. It keeps me quiet by the hour.

I lie down ever so much now. John says it is good for me, and to sleep all I can.

Indeed he started the habit by making me lie down for an hour after each meal.

It is a very bad habit, I am convinced, for you see, I don't sleep.

And that cultivates deceit, for I don't tell them I'm awake — oh, no! 155

The fact is I am getting a little afraid of John.

He seems very queer sometimes, and even Jennie has an inexplicable look.

It strikes me occasionally, just as a scientific hypothesis, that perhaps it is the paper!

I have watched John when he did not know I was looking, and come into the room suddenly on the most innocent excuses, and I've caught him several times *looking at the paper!* And Jennie too. I caught Jennie with her hand on it once.

She didn't know I was in the room, and when I asked her in a quiet, a very quiet voice, with the most restrained manner possible, what she was doing with the paper — she turned around as if she had been caught stealing, and looked quite angry — asked me why I should frighten her so! 160

Then she said that the paper stained everything it touched, that she had found yellow smooches on all my clothes and John's and she wished we would be more careful!

Did not that sound innocent? But I know she was studying that pattern, and I am determined that nobody shall find it out but myself!

Life is very much more exciting now than it used to be. You see, I have something more to expect, to look forward to, to watch. I really do eat better, and am more quiet than I was.

John is so pleased to see me improve! He laughed a little the other day, and said I seemed to be flourishing in spite of my wallpaper.

I turned it off with a laugh. I had no intention of telling him it was *because*  165 of the wallpaper — he would make fun of me. He might even want to take me away.

I don't want to leave now until I have found it out. There is a week more, and I think that will be enough.

I'm feeling so much better!

I don't sleep much at night, for it is so interesting to watch developments; but I sleep a good deal in the daytime.

In the daytime it is tiresome and perplexing.

There are always new shoots on the fungus, and new shades of yellow all  170 over it. I cannot keep count of them, though I have tried conscientiously.

It is the strangest yellow, that wallpaper! It makes me think of all the yellow things I ever saw — not beautiful ones like buttercups, but old, foul, bad yellow things.

But there is something else about that paper — the smell! I noticed it the moment we came into the room, but with so much air and sun it was not bad. Now we have had a week of fog and rain, and whether the windows are open or not, the smell is here.

It creeps all over the house.

I find it hovering in the dining-room, skulking in the parlor, hiding in the hall, lying in wait for me on the stairs.

It gets into my hair.                                                                                        175

Even when I go to ride, if I turn my head suddenly and surprise it — there is that smell!

Such a peculiar odor, too! I have spent hours in trying to analyze it, to find what it smelled like.

It is not bad — at first — and very gentle, but quite the subtlest, most enduring odor I ever met.

In this damp weather it is awful. I wake up in the night and find it hanging over me.

It used to disturb me at first. I thought seriously of burning the house — to  180 reach the smell.

But now I am used to it. The only thing I can think of that it is like is the *color* of the paper! A yellow smell.

There is a very funny mark on this wall, low down, near the mopboard. A streak that runs round the room. It goes behind every piece of furniture, except the bed, a long, straight, even *smooch*, as if it had been rubbed over and over.

I wonder how it was done and who did it, and what they did it for. Round and round and round — round and round and round — it makes me dizzy!

I really have discovered something at last.

Through watching so much at night, when it changes so, I have finally found out. 185
The front pattern *does* move — and no wonder! The woman behind shakes it!

Sometimes I think there are a great many women behind, and sometimes only one, and she crawls around fast, and her crawling shakes it all over.

Then in the very bright spots she keeps still, and in the very shady spots she just takes hold of the bars and shakes them hard.

And she is all the time trying to climb through. But nobody could climb through that pattern — it strangles so; I think that is why it has so many heads.

They get through, and then the pattern strangles them off and turns them 190 upside down and makes their eyes white!

If those heads were covered or taken off it would not be half so bad.

I think that woman gets out in the daytime!

And I'll tell you why — privately — I've seen her!

I can see her out of every one of my windows!

It is the same woman, I know, for she is always creeping, and most women 195 do not creep by daylight.

I see her in that long shaded lane, creeping up and down. I see her in those dark grape arbors, creeping all around the garden.

I see her on that long road under the trees, creeping along, and when a carriage comes she hides under the blackberry vines.

I don't blame her a bit. It must be very humiliating to be caught creeping by daylight!

I always lock the door when I creep by daylight. I can't do it at night, for I know John would suspect something at once.

And John is so queer now that I don't want to irritate him. I wish he would 200 take another room! Besides, I don't want anybody to get that woman out at night but myself.

I often wonder if I could see her out of all the windows at once.

But, turn as fast as I can, I can only see out of one at one time.

And though I always see her, she *may* be able to creep faster than I can turn! I have watched her sometimes away off in the open country, creeping as fast as a cloud shadow in a high wind.

If only that top pattern could be gotten off from the under one! I mean to try it, little by little.

I have found out another funny thing, but I shan't tell it this time! It does not 205 do to trust people too much.

There are only two more days to get this paper off, and I believe John is beginning to notice. I don't like the look in his eyes.

And I hear him ask Jennie a lot of professional questions about me. She had a very good report to give.

She said I slept a good deal in the daytime.

John knows I don't sleep very well at night, for all I'm so quiet!

He asked me all sorts of questions, too, and pretended to be very loving and 210 kind.

As if I couldn't see through him!

Still, I don't wonder he acts so, sleeping under this paper for three months.

It only interests me, but I feel sure John and Jennie are secretly affected by it.

Hurrah! This is the last day, but it is enough. John is to stay in town over night, and won't be out until this evening.

Jennie wanted to sleep with me — the sly thing; but I told her I should 215 undoubtedly rest better for a night all alone.

That was clever, for really I wasn't alone a bit! As soon as it was moonlight and that poor thing began to crawl and shake the pattern, I got up and ran to help her.

I pulled and she shook. I shook and she pulled, and before morning we had peeled off yards of that paper.

A strip about as high as my head and half around the room.

And then when the sun came and that awful pattern began to laugh at me, I declared I would finish it to-day!

We go away to-morrow, and they are moving all my furniture down again to 220 leave things as they were before.

Jennie looked at the wall in amazement, but I told her merrily that I did it out of pure spite at the vicious thing.

She laughed and said she wouldn't mind doing it herself, but I must not get tired.

How she betrayed herself that time!

But I am here, and no person touches this paper but Me — not *alive!*

She tried to get me out of the room — it was too patent! But I said it was so 225 quiet and empty and clean now that I believed I would lie down again and sleep all I could, and not to wake me even for dinner — I would call when I woke.

So now she is gone, and the servants are gone, and the things are gone, and there is nothing left but that great bedstead nailed down, with the canvas mattress we found on it.

We shall sleep downstairs to-night, and take the boat home to-morrow.

I quite enjoy the room, now it is bare again.

How those children did tear about here!

This bedstead is fairly gnawed! 230

But I must get to work.

I have locked the door and thrown the key down into the front path.

I don't want to go out, and I don't want to have anybody come in, till John comes.

I want to astonish him.

I've got a rope up here that even Jennie did not find. If that woman does get 235 out, and tries to get away, I can tie her!

But I forgot I could not reach far without anything to stand on!

This bed will *not* move!

I tried to lift and push it until I was lame, and then I got so angry I bit off a little piece at one corner — but it hurt my teeth.

Then I peeled off all the paper I could reach standing on the floor. It sticks horribly and the pattern just enjoys it! All those strangled heads and bulbous eyes and waddling fungus growths just shriek with derision!

I am getting angry enough to do something desperate. To jump out of the 240
window would be admirable exercise, but the bars are too strong even to try.

Besides I wouldn't do it. Of course not. I know well enough that a step like
that is improper and might be misconstrued.

I don't like to *look* out of the windows even — there are so many of those
creeping women, and they creep so fast.

I wonder if they all come out of that wallpaper as I did?

But I am securely fastened now by my well-hidden rope — you don't get *me*
out in the road there!

I suppose I shall have to get back behind the pattern when it comes night, 245
and that is hard!

It is so pleasant to be out in this great room and creep around as I please!

I don't want to go outside. I won't, even if Jennie asks me to.

For outside you have to creep on the ground, and everything is green instead
of yellow.

But here I can creep smoothly on the floor, and my shoulder just fits in that
long smooch around the wall, so I cannot lose my way.

Why, there's John at the door!                                           250

It is no use, young man, you can't open it!

How he does call and pound!

Now he's crying to Jennie for an axe.

It would be a shame to break down that beautiful door!

"John, dear!" said I in the gentlest voice, "The key is down by the front steps, 255
under a plantain leaf!"

That silenced him for a few moments.

Then he said — very quietly indeed, "Open the door, my darling!"

"I can't," said I. "The key is down by the front door under a plantain leaf!"
And then I said it again, several times, very gently and slowly, and said it so
often that he had to go and see, and he got it of course, and came in. He stopped
short by the door.

"What is the matter?" he cried. "For God's sake, what are you doing!"

I kept on creeping just the same, but I looked at him over my shoulder.     260

"I've got out at last," said I, "in spite of you and Jane. And I've pulled off most
of the paper, so you can't put me back!"

Now why should that man have fainted? But he did, and right across my
path by the wall, so that I had to creep over him every time!

## FOR ANALYSIS

**1.** Why have the **narrator** and her husband, John, rented the mansion?

**2.** In the opening paragraphs, what **tone** does the narrator's description of the mansion establish?

**3.** Describe the **character** of John. Does the narrator's view of him change in the course of the story? Explain.

**4.** After telling us that her husband, John, is a physician, the narrator adds that "*perhaps that is one reason I do not get well faster*" (para. 7). What does she mean by this comment?

**5.** How does the narrator's description of what she sees in the outside world reflect her inner state?

**6.** Who is Jennie? What is her function in the story?

**7.** The narrator both accepts her husband's control over her and disobeys him by secretly continuing to write. What effect does writing have on her? Is her husband correct in his judgment that writing will hinder her recovery?

**8.** What evidence does the story provide to explain the narrator's present state?

**9.** In what ways does the wallpaper embody the **theme** of the story?

## MAKING ARGUMENTS

Can it be argued that, on some level, the **narrator** refuses to recover? Explain the logic of your argument and state the evidence you would use. What would it mean for the story that she refused to recover?

## WRITING TOPICS

**1.** Analyze the way **irony** is used in this story.

**2.** Write an essay in which you imaginatively reconstruct the early life of the **narrator**, including her marriage, to explain her illness.

**3.** Write an essay describing the aptness of wallpaper as a **symbol** for the life of the narrator.

**4.** In a paragraph, explain why we never learn the narrator's name.

## MAKING CONNECTIONS

**1.** Compare the marriage relationship in this story with the marriage in Ibsen's play *A Doll's House* (p. 194).

**2.** Compare the wallpaper in this story with the birdcage in Susan Glaspell's play *Trifles* (p. 761) as **symbols**. In what ways are they similar? In what ways different? Which do you find more effective? Explain.

**3.** Considered as a horror story, in what ways is Gilman's narrative similar to Edgar Allan Poe's "The Cask of Amontillado" (p. 803)? In what ways is it different?

## JAMES BALDWIN    (1924–1987)

# SONNY'S BLUES    1957

I read about it in the paper, in the subway, on my way to work. I read it, and I couldn't believe it, and I read it again. Then perhaps I just stared at it, at the newsprint spelling out his name, spelling out the story. I stared at it in the swinging lights of the subway car, and in the faces and bodies of the people, and in my own face, trapped in the darkness which roared outside.

It was not to be believed and I kept telling myself that, as I walked from the subway station to the high school. And at the same time I couldn't doubt it. I was scared, scared for Sonny. He became real to me again. A great block of ice got settled in my belly and kept melting there slowly all day long, while I taught my classes algebra. It was a special kind of ice. It kept melting, sending trickles of ice water all up and down my veins, but it never got less. Sometimes it hardened and seemed to expand until I felt my guts were going to come spilling out or that I was going to choke or scream. This would always be at a moment when I was remembering some specific thing Sonny had once said or done.

When he was about as old as the boys in my classes his face had been bright and open, there was a lot of copper in it; and he'd had wonderfully direct brown eyes, and great gentleness and privacy. I wondered what he looked like now. He had been picked up, the evening before, in a raid on an apartment downtown, for peddling and using heroin.

I couldn't believe it: but what I mean by that is that I couldn't find any room for it anywhere inside me. I had kept it outside me for a long time. I hadn't wanted to know. I had had suspicions, but I didn't name them, I kept putting them away. I told myself that Sonny was wild, but he wasn't crazy. And he'd always been a good boy, he hadn't ever turned hard or evil or disrespectful, the way kids can, so quick, so quick, especially in Harlem. I didn't want to believe that I'd ever see my brother going down, coming to nothing, all that light in his face gone out, in the condition I'd already seen so many others. Yet it had happened and here I was, talking about algebra to a lot of boys who might, every one of them for all I knew, be popping off needles every time they went to the head. Maybe it did more for them than algebra could.

I was sure that the first time Sonny had ever had horse,[1] he couldn't have been much older than these boys were now. These boys, now, were living as we'd been living then, they were growing up with a rush and their heads bumped abruptly against the low ceiling of their actual possibilities. They were filled with rage. All they really knew were two darknesses, the darkness

5

---

[1] Heroin.

of their lives, which was now closing in on them, and the darkness of the movies, which had blinded them to that other darkness, and in which they now, vindictively, dreamed, at once more together than they were at any other time, and more alone.

When the last bell rang, the last class ended, I let out my breath. It seemed I'd been holding it for all that time. My clothes were wet — I may have looked as though I'd been sitting in a steam bath, all dressed up, all afternoon. I sat alone in the classroom a long time. I listened to the boys outside, downstairs, shouting and cursing and laughing. Their laughter struck me for perhaps the first time. It was not the joyous laughter which — God knows why — one associates with children. It was mocking and insular, its intent to denigrate. It was disenchanted, and in this, also, lay the authority of their curses. Perhaps I was listening to them because I was thinking about my brother and in them I heard my brother. And myself.

One boy was whistling a tune, at once very complicated and very simple, it seemed to be pouring out of him as though he were a bird, and it sounded very cool and moving through all that harsh, bright air, only just holding its own through all those other sounds.

I stood up and walked over to the window and looked down into the courtyard. It was the beginning of the spring and the sap was rising in the boys. A teacher passed through them every now and again, quickly, as though he or she couldn't wait to get out of that courtyard, to get those boys out of their sight and off their minds. I started collecting my stuff. I thought I'd better get home and talk to Isabel.

The courtyard was almost deserted by the time I got downstairs. I saw this boy standing in the shadow of a doorway, looking just like Sonny. I almost called his name. Then I saw that it wasn't Sonny, but somebody we used to know, a boy from around our block. He'd been Sonny's friend. He'd never been mine, having been too young for me, and, anyway, I'd never liked him. And now, even though he was a grown-up man, he still hung around that block, still spent hours on the street corners, was always high and raggy. I used to run into him from time to time and he'd often work around to asking me for a quarter or fifty cents. He always had some real good excuse, too, and I always gave it to him. I don't know why.

But now, abruptly, I hated him. I couldn't stand the way he looked at me, 10 partly like a dog, partly like a cunning child. I wanted to ask him what the hell he was doing in the school courtyard.

He sort of shuffled over to me, and he said, "I see you got the papers. So you already know about it."

"You mean about Sonny? Yes, I already know about it. How come they didn't get you?"

He grinned. It made him repulsive and it also brought to mind what he'd looked like as a kid. "I wasn't there. I stay away from them people."

"Good for you." I offered him a cigarette and I watched him through the smoke. "You come all the way down here just to tell me about Sonny?"

"That's right." He was sort of shaking his head and his eyes looked strange, 15
as though they were about to cross. The bright sun deadened his damp dark
brown skin and it made his eyes look yellow and showed up the dirt in his
kinked hair. He smelled funky. I moved a little away from him and I said,
"Well, thanks. But I already know about it and I got to get home."

"I'll walk you a little ways," he said. We started walking. There were a couple
of kids still loitering in the courtyard and one of them said goodnight to me
and looked strangely at the boy beside me.

"What're you going to do?" he asked me. "I mean, about Sonny?"

"Look. I haven't seen Sonny for over a year, I'm not sure I'm going to do anything. Anyway, what the hell *can* I do?"

"That's right," he said quickly, "ain't nothing you can do. Can't much help old
Sonny no more, I guess."

It was what I was thinking and so it seemed to me he had no right to say it. 20

"I'm surprised at Sonny, though," he went on — he had a funny way of talking, he looked straight ahead as though he were talking to himself — "I thought
Sonny was a smart boy, I thought he was too smart to get hung."

"I guess he thought so too," I said sharply, "and that's how he got hung. And
how about you? You're pretty goddamn smart, I bet."

Then he looked directly at me, just for a minute. "I ain't smart," he said. "If I
was smart, I'd have reached for a pistol a long time ago."

"Look. Don't tell *me* your sad story, if it was up to me, I'd give you one." Then
I felt guilty — guilty, probably, for never having supposed that the poor bastard
*had* a story of his own, much less a sad one, and I asked, quickly, "What's going
to happen to him now?"

He didn't answer this. He was off by himself some place. 25

"Funny thing," he said, and from his tone we might have been discussing
the quickest way to get to Brooklyn, "when I saw the papers this morning,
the first thing I asked myself was if I had anything to do with it. I felt sort of
responsible."

I began to listen more carefully. The subway station was on the corner, just
before us, and I stopped. He stopped, too. We were in front of a bar and he
ducked slightly, peering in, but whoever he was looking for didn't seem to be
there. The juke box was blasting away with something black and bouncy and I
half watched the barmaid as she danced her way from the juke box to her place
behind the bar. And I watched her face as she laughingly responded to something someone said to her, still keeping time to the music. When she smiled
one saw the little girl, one sensed the doomed, still-struggling woman beneath
the battered face of the semi-whore.

"I never *give* Sonny nothing," the boy said finally, "but a long time ago I
come to school high and Sonny asked me how it felt." He paused, I couldn't
bear to watch him, I watched the barmaid, and I listened to the music which
seemed to be causing the pavement to shake. "I told him it felt great." The
music stopped, the barmaid paused and watched the juke box until the music
began again. "It did."

All this was carrying me some place I didn't want to go. I certainly didn't want to know how it felt. It filled everything, the people, the houses, the music, the dark, quicksilver barmaid, with menace; and this menace was their reality.

"What's going to happen to him now?" I asked again.

"They'll send him away some place and they'll try to cure him." He shook his head. "Maybe he'll even think he's kicked the habit. Then they'll let him loose" — he gestured, throwing his cigarette into the gutter. "That's all."

"What do you mean, that's *all*?"

But I knew what he meant.

"I *mean*, that's *all*." He turned his head and looked at me, pulling down the corners of his mouth. "Don't you know what I mean?" he asked, softly.

"How the hell *would* I know what you mean?" I almost whispered it, I don't know why.

"That's right," he said to the air, "how would *he* know what I mean?" He turned toward me again, patient and calm, and yet I somehow felt him shaking, shaking as though he were going to fall apart. I felt that ice in my guts again, the dread I'd felt all afternoon; and again I watched the barmaid, moving about the bar, washing glasses, and singing. "Listen. They'll let him out and then it'll just start all over again. That's what I mean."

"You mean — they'll let him out. And then he'll just start working his way back in again. You mean he'll never kick the habit. Is that what you mean?"

"That's right," he said, cheerfully. "*You* see what I mean."

"Tell me," I said at last, "why does he want to die? He must want to die, he's killing himself, why does he want to die?"

He looked at me in surprise. He licked his lips. "He don't want to die. He wants to live. Don't nobody want to die, ever."

Then I wanted to ask him — too many things. He could not have answered, or if he had, I could not have borne the answers. I started walking. "Well, I guess it's none of my business."

"It's going to be rough on old Sonny," he said. We reached the subway station. "This is your station?" he asked. I nodded. I took one step down. "Damn!" he said, suddenly. I looked up at him. He grinned again. "Damn it if I didn't leave all my money home. You ain't got a dollar on you, have you? Just for a couple of days, is all."

All at once something inside gave and threatened to come pouring out of me. I didn't hate him any more. I felt that in another moment I'd start crying like a child.

"Sure," I said. "Don't sweat." I looked in my wallet and didn't have a dollar, I only had a five. "Here," I said. "That hold you?"

He didn't look at it — he didn't want to look at it. A terrible, closed look came over his face, as though he were keeping the number on the bill a secret from him and me. "Thanks," he said, and now he was dying to see me go. "Don't worry about Sonny. Maybe I'll write him or something."

"Sure," I said. "You do that. So long."

"Be seeing you," he said. I went on down the steps.

And I didn't write Sonny or send him anything for a long time. When I finally did, it was just after my little girl died, and he wrote me back a letter which made me feel like a bastard.

Here's what he said:

Dear brother,

You don't know how much I needed to hear from you. I wanted to write you many a time but I dug how much I must have hurt you and so I didn't write. But now I feel like a man who's been trying to climb up out of some deep, real deep and funky hole and just saw the sun up there, outside. I got to get outside.

I can't tell you much about how I got here. I mean I don't know how to tell you. I guess I was afraid of something or I was trying to escape from something and you know I have never been very strong in the head (smile). I'm glad Mama and Daddy are dead and can't see what's happened to their son and I swear if I'd known what I was doing I would never have hurt you so, you and a lot of other fine people who were nice to me and who believed in me.

I don't want you to think it had anything to do with me being a musician. It's more than that. Or maybe less than that. I can't get anything straight in my head down here and I try not to think about what's going to happen to me when I get outside again. Sometime I think I'm going to flip and never get outside and sometime I think I'll come straight back. I tell you one thing, though, I'd rather blow my brains out than go through this again. But that's what they all say, so they tell me. If I tell you when I'm coming to New York and if you could meet me, I sure would appreciate it. Give my love to Isabel and the kids and I was sure sorry to hear about little Gracie. I wish I could be like Mama and say the Lord's will be done, but I don't know it seems to me that trouble is the one thing that never does get stopped and I don't know what good it does to blame it on the Lord. But maybe it does some good if you believe it.

Your brother,
Sonny

Then I kept in constant touch with him and I sent him whatever I could and 50 I went to meet him when he came back to New York. When I saw him many things I thought I had forgotten came flooding back to me. This was because I had begun, finally, to wonder about Sonny, about the life that Sonny lived inside. This life, whatever it was, had made him older and thinner and it had deepened the distant stillness in which he had always moved. He looked very unlike my baby brother. Yet, when he smiled, when we shook hands, the baby brother I'd never known looked out from the depths of his private life, like an animal waiting to be coaxed into the light.

"How you been keeping?" he asked me.

"All right. And you?"

"Just fine." He was smiling all over his face. "It's good to see you again."

"It's good to see you."

The seven years' difference in our ages lay between us like a chasm: I won- 55
dered if these years would ever operate between us as a bridge. I was remembering, and it made it hard to catch my breath, that I had been there when he
was born; and I had heard the first words he had ever spoken. When he started
to walk, he walked from our mother straight to me. I caught him just before he
fell when he took the first steps he ever took in this world.

"How's Isabel?"

"Just fine. She's dying to see you."

"And the boys?"

"They're fine, too. They're anxious to see their uncle."

"Oh, come on. You know they don't remember me." 60

"Are you kidding? Of course they remember you."

He grinned again. We got into a taxi. We had a lot to say to each other, far
too much to know how to begin.

As the taxi began to move, I asked, "You still want to go to India?"

He laughed. "You still remember that. Hell, no. This place is Indian enough
for me."

"It used to belong to them," I said. 65

And he laughed again. "They damn sure knew what they were doing when
they got rid of it."

Years ago, when he was around fourteen, he'd been all hipped on the idea of
going to India. He read books about people sitting on rocks, naked, in all kinds
of weather, but mostly bad, naturally, and walking barefoot through hot coals
and arriving at wisdom. I used to say that it sounded to me as though they
were getting away from wisdom as fast as they could. I think he sort of looked
down on me for that.

"Do you mind," he asked, "if we have the driver drive alongside the park?
On the west side — I haven't seen the city in so long."

"Of course not," I said. I was afraid that I might sound as though I were
humoring him, but I hoped he wouldn't take it that way.

So we drove along, between the green of the park and the stony, lifeless 70
elegance of hotels and apartment buildings, toward the vivid, killing streets
of our childhood. These streets hadn't changed, though housing projects jut-
ted up out of them now like rocks in the middle of a boiling sea. Most of the
houses in which we had grown up had vanished, as had the stores from which
we had stolen, the basements in which we had first tried sex, the rooftops from
which we had hurled tin cans and bricks. But houses exactly like the houses of
our past yet dominated the landscape, boys exactly like the boys we once had
been found themselves smothering in these houses, came down into the streets
for light and air and found themselves encircled by disaster. Some escaped
the trap, most didn't. Those who got out always left something of themselves
behind, as some animals amputate a leg and leave it in the trap. It might be
said, perhaps, that I had escaped, after all, I was a school teacher; or that
Sonny had, he hadn't lived in Harlem for years. Yet, as the cab moved uptown
through streets which seemed, with a rush, to darken with dark people, and as

I covertly studied Sonny's face, it came to me that what we both were seeking through our separate cab windows was that part of ourselves which had been left behind. It's always at the hour of trouble and confrontation that the missing member aches.

We hit 110th Street and started rolling up Lenox Avenue. And I'd known this avenue all my life, but it seemed to me again, as it had seemed on the day I'd first heard about Sonny's trouble, filled with a hidden menace which was its very breath of life.

"We almost there," said Sonny.

"Almost." We were both too nervous to say anything more.

We live in a housing project. It hasn't been up long. A few days after it was up it seemed uninhabitably new, now, of course, it's already rundown. It looks like a parody of the good, clean, faceless life — God knows the people who live in it do their best to make it a parody. The beat-looking grass lying around isn't enough to make their lives green, the hedges will never hold out the streets, and they know it. The big windows fool no one, they aren't big enough to make space out of no space. They don't bother with the windows, they watch the TV screen instead. The playground is most popular with the children who don't play at jacks, or skip rope, or roller skate, or swing, and they can be found in it after dark. We moved in partly because it's not too far from where I teach, and partly for the kids; but it's really just like the houses in which Sonny and I grew up. The same things happen, they'll have the same things to remember. The moment Sonny and I started into the house I had the feeling that I was simply bringing him back into the danger he had almost died trying to escape.

Sonny has never been talkative. So I don't know why I was sure he'd be dying to talk to me when supper was over the first night. Everything went fine, the oldest boy remembered him, and the youngest boy liked him, and Sonny had remembered to bring something for each of them; and Isabel, who is really much nicer than I am, more open and giving, had gone to a lot of trouble about dinner and was genuinely glad to see him. And she's always been able to tease Sonny in a way that I haven't. It was nice to see her face so vivid again and to hear her laugh and watch her make Sonny laugh. She wasn't, or, anyway, she didn't seem to be, at all uneasy or embarrassed. She chatted as though there were no subject which had to be avoided and she got Sonny past his first, faint stiffness. And thank God she was there, for I was filled with that icy dread again. Everything I did seemed awkward to me, and everything I said sounded freighted with hidden meaning. I was trying to remember everything I'd heard about dope addiction and I couldn't help watching Sonny for signs. I wasn't doing it out of malice. I was trying to find out something about my brother. I was dying to hear him tell me he was safe.

"Safe!" my father grunted, whenever Mama suggested trying to move to a neighborhood which might be safer for children. "Safe, hell! Ain't no place safe for kids, nor nobody."

He always went on like this, but he wasn't, ever, really as bad as he sounded, not even on weekends, when he got drunk. As a matter of fact, he was always on the lookout for "something a little better," but he died before he found it. He died suddenly, during a drunken weekend in the middle of the war, when Sonny was fifteen. He and Sonny hadn't ever got on too well. And this was partly because Sonny was the apple of his father's eye. It was because he loved Sonny so much and was frightened for him, that he was always fighting with him. It doesn't do any good to fight with Sonny. Sonny just moves back, inside himself, where he can't be reached. But the principal reason that they never hit it off is that they were so much alike. Daddy was big and rough and loud-talking, just the opposite of Sonny, but they both had — that same privacy.

Mama tried to tell me something about this, just after Daddy died. I was home on leave from the army.

This was the last time I ever saw my mother alive. Just the same, this picture gets all mixed up in my mind with pictures I had of her when she was younger. The way I always see her is the way she used to be on a Sunday afternoon, say, when the old folks were talking after the big Sunday dinner. I always see her wearing pale blue. She'd be sitting on the sofa. And my father would be sitting in the easy chair, not far from her. And the living room would be full of church folks and relatives. There they sit, in chairs all around the living room, and the night is creeping up outside, but nobody knows it yet. You can see the darkness growing against the windowpanes and you hear the street noises every now and again, or maybe the jangling beat of a tambourine from one of the churches close by, but it's real quiet in the room. For a moment nobody's talking, but every face looks darkening, like the sky outside. And my mother rocks a little from the waist, and my father's eyes are closed. Everyone is looking at something a child can't see. For a minute they've forgotten the children. Maybe a kid is lying on the rug, half asleep. Maybe somebody's got a kid in his lap and is absent-mindedly stroking the kid's head. Maybe there's a kid, quiet and big-eyed, curled up in a big chair in the corner. The silence, the darkness coming, and the darkness in the faces frighten the child obscurely. He hopes that the hand which strokes his forehead will never stop — will never die. He hopes that there will never come a time when the old folks won't be sitting around the living room, talking about where they've come from, and what they've seen, and what's happened to them and their kinfolk.

But something deep and watchful in the child knows that this is bound [80] to end, is already ending. In a moment someone will get up and turn on the light. Then the old folks will remember the children and they won't talk any more that day. And when light fills the room, the child is filled with darkness. He knows that every time this happens he's moved just a little closer to that darkness outside. The darkness outside is what the old folks have been talking about. It's what they've come from. It's what they endure. The child knows that they won't talk any more because if he knows too much about what's happened to *them*, he'll know too much too soon, about what's going to happen to *him*.

The last time I talked to my mother, I remember I was restless. I wanted to get out and see Isabel. We weren't married then and we had a lot to straighten out between us.

There Mama sat, in black, by the window. She was humming an old church song, *Lord, you brought me from a long ways off.* Sonny was out somewhere. Mama kept watching the streets.

"I don't know," she said, "if I'll ever see you again, after you go off from here. But I hope you'll remember the things I tried to teach you."

"Don't talk like that," I said, and smiled. "You'll be here a long time yet."

She smiled, too, but she said nothing. She was quiet for a long time. And 85 I said, "Mama, don't you worry about nothing. I'll be writing all the time, and you be getting the checks. . . ."

"I want to talk to you about your brother," she said, suddenly. "If anything happens to me he ain't going to have nobody to look out for him."

"Mama," I said, "ain't nothing going to happen to you *or* Sonny. Sonny's all right. He's a good boy and he's got good sense."

"It ain't a question of his being a good boy," Mama said, "nor of his having good sense. It ain't only the bad ones, nor yet the dumb ones that gets sucked under." She stopped, looking at me. "Your Daddy once had a brother," she said, and she smiled in a way that made me feel she was in pain. "You didn't never know that, did you?"

"No," I said, "I never knew that," and I watched her face.

"Oh, yes," she said, "your Daddy had a brother." She looked out of the win- 90 dow again. "I know you never saw your Daddy cry. But *I* did — many a time, through all these years."

I asked her, "What happened to his brother? How come nobody's ever talked about him?"

This was the first time I ever saw my mother look old.

"His brother got killed," she said, "when he was just a little younger than you are now. I knew him. He was a fine boy. He was maybe a little full of the devil, but he didn't mean nobody no harm."

Then she stopped and the room was silent, exactly as it had sometimes been on those Sunday afternoons. Mama kept looking out into the streets.

"He used to have a job in the mill," she said, "and, like all young folks, he 95 just liked to perform on Saturday nights. Saturday nights, him and your father would drift around to different places, go to dances and things like that, or just sit around with people they knew, and your father's brother would sing, he had a fine voice, and play along with himself on his guitar. Well, this particular Saturday night, him and your father was coming home from some place, and they were both a little drunk and there was a moon that night, it was bright like day. Your father's brother was feeling kind of good, and he was whistling to himself, and he had his guitar slung over his shoulder. They was coming down a hill and beneath them was a road that turned off from the highway. Well, your father's brother, being always kind of frisky, decided to run down this hill, and he did, with that guitar banging and clanging behind him, and he ran across the road, and he was making water behind a tree. And your father was sort of amused at him and he was still coming down the hill, kind of slow. Then he heard a car motor and that same minute his brother stepped from behind the tree, into the road, in the moonlight. And he started to cross the road. And your father started to run down the hill, he says he don't know why. This car was full of white men. They was all drunk, and when they seen your father's brother they let out a great whoop and holler and they aimed the car straight at him. They was having fun, they just wanted to scare him, the way they do sometimes, you know. But they was drunk. And I guess the boy, being drunk, too, and scared, kind of lost his head. By the time he jumped it was too late. Your father says he heard his brother scream when the car rolled over him, and he heard the wood of that guitar when it give, and he heard them strings go flying, and he heard them white men shouting, and the car kept on a-going and it ain't stopped till this day. And, time your father got down the hill, his brother weren't nothing but blood and pulp."

Tears were gleaming on my mother's face. There wasn't anything I could say.

"He never mentioned it," she said, "because I never let him mention it before you children. Your Daddy was like a crazy man that night and for many a night thereafter. He says he never in his life seen anything as dark as that road after the lights of that car had gone away. Weren't nothing, weren't nobody on that road, just your Daddy and his brother and that busted guitar. Oh, yes. Your Daddy never did really get right again. Till the day he died he weren't sure but that every white man he saw was the man that killed his brother."

She stopped and took out her handkerchief and dried her eyes and looked at me.

"I ain't telling you all this," she said, "to make you scared or bitter or to make you hate nobody. I'm telling you this because you got a brother. And the world ain't changed."

I guess I didn't want to believe this. I guess she saw this in my face. She turned away from me, toward the window again, searching those streets. 100

"But I praise my Redeemer," she said at last, "that He called your Daddy home before me. I ain't saying it to throw no flowers at myself, but, I declare, it keeps me from feeling too cast down to know I helped your father get safely through this world. Your father always acted like he was the roughest, strongest man on earth. And everybody took him to be like that. But if he hadn't had me there — to see his tears!"

She was crying again. Still, I couldn't move. I said, "Lord, Lord, Mama, I didn't know it was like that."

"Oh, honey," she said, "there's a lot that you don't know. But you are going to find out." She stood up from the window and came over to me. "You got to hold on to your brother," she said, "and don't let him fall, no matter what it looks like is happening to him and no matter how evil you gets with him. You going to be evil with him many a time. But don't you forget what I told you, you hear?"

"I won't forget," I said. "Don't you worry, I won't forget. I won't let nothing happen to Sonny."

My mother smiled as though she was amused at something she saw in my 105 face. Then, "You may not be able to stop nothing from happening. But you got to let him know you's *there*."

Two days later I was married, and then I was gone. And I had a lot of things on my mind and I pretty well forgot my promise to Mama until I got shipped home on a special furlough for her funeral.

And, after the funeral, with just Sonny and me alone in the empty kitchen, I tried to find out something about him.

"What do you want to do?" I asked him.

"I'm going to be a musician," he said.

For he had graduated, in the time I had been away, from dancing to the juke 110 box to finding out who was playing what, and what they were doing with it, and he had bought himself a set of drums.

"You mean, you want to be a drummer?" I somehow had the feeling that being a drummer might be all right for other people but not for my brother Sonny.

"I don't think," he said, looking at me very gravely, "that I'll ever be a good drummer. But I think I can play a piano."

I frowned. I'd never played the role of the oldest brother quite so seriously before, had scarcely ever, in fact, *asked* Sonny a damn thing. I sensed myself in the presence of something I didn't really know how to handle, didn't understand. So I made my frown a little deeper as I asked: "What kind of musician do you want to be?"

He grinned. "How many kinds do you think there are?"

"Be *serious*," I said. 115

He laughed, throwing his head back, and then looked at me. "I *am* serious."

"Well, then, for Christ's sake, stop kidding around and answer a serious question. I mean, do you want to be a concert pianist, you want to play classical music and all that, or — or what?" Long before I finished he was laughing again. "For Christ's *sake*, Sonny!"

He sobered, but with difficulty. "I'm sorry. But you sound so — *scared!*" and he was off again.

"Well, you may think it's funny now, baby, but it's not going to be so funny when you have to make your living at it, let me tell you *that*." I was furious because I knew he was laughing at me and I didn't know why.

"No," he said, very sober now, and afraid, perhaps, that he'd hurt me, 120 "I don't want to be a classical pianist. That isn't what interests me. I mean" — he paused, looking hard at me, as though his eyes would help me to understand, and then gestured helplessly, as though perhaps his hand would help — "I mean, I'll have a lot of studying to do, and I'll have to study *everything*, but, I mean, I want to play *with* — jazz musicians." He stopped. "I want to play jazz," he said.

Well, the word had never before sounded as heavy, as real, as it sounded that afternoon in Sonny's mouth. I just looked at him and I was probably frowning a real frown by this time. I simply couldn't see why on earth he'd want to spend his time hanging around nightclubs, clowning around on bandstands, while people pushed each other around a dance floor. It seemed — beneath him, somehow. I had never thought about it before, had never been forced to, but I suppose I had always put jazz musicians in a class with what Daddy called "good-time people."

"Are you *serious*?"

"Hell, *yes*, I'm serious."

He looked more helpless than ever, and annoyed, and deeply hurt.

I suggested, helpfully: "You mean — like Louis Armstrong?"[2]                   125

His face closed as though I'd struck him. "No. I'm not talking about none of that old-time, down home crap."

"Well, look, Sonny, I'm sorry, don't get mad. I just don't altogether get it, that's all. Name somebody — you know, a jazz musician you admire."

"Bird."

"Who?"

"Bird! Charlie Parker![3] Don't they teach you nothing in the goddamn army?"   130

I lit a cigarette. I was surprised and then a little amused to discover that I was trembling. "I've been out of touch," I said. "You'll have to be patient with me. Now. Who's this Parker character?"

"He's just one of the greatest jazz musicians alive," said Sonny, sullenly, his hands in his pockets, his back to me. "Maybe *the* greatest," he added, bitterly, "that's probably why *you* never heard of him."

"All right," I said, "I'm ignorant. I'm sorry. I'll go out and buy all the cat's records right away, all right?"

"It don't," said Sonny, with dignity, "make any difference to me. I don't care what you listen to. Don't do me no favors."

I was beginning to realize that I'd never seen him so upset before. With   135 another part of my mind I was thinking that this would probably turn out to be one of those things kids go through and that I shouldn't make it seem important by pushing it too hard. Still, I didn't think it would do any harm to ask: "Doesn't all this take a lot of time? Can you make a living at it?"

He turned back to me and half leaned, half sat, on the kitchen table. "Everything takes time," he said, "and — well, yes, sure, I can make a living at it. But what I don't seem to be able to make you understand is that it's the only thing I want to do."

"Well, Sonny," I said, gently, "you know people can't always do exactly what they *want* to do —"

"*No*, I don't know that," said Sonny, surprising me. "I think people *ought* to do what they want to do, what else are they alive for?"

"You getting to be a big boy," I said desperately, "it's time you started thinking about your future."

---

[2] Louis "Satchmo" Armstrong (1901–1971) played the trumpet and was one of the most innovative and influential figures in the history of jazz.

[3] Charlie "Bird" Parker (1920–1955), a seminal saxophonist, was one of the originators of the bebop style of jazz. Parker was also a heroin addict.

"I'm thinking about my future," said Sonny, grimly. "I think about it all the 140 time."

I gave up. I decided, if he didn't change his mind, that we could always talk about it later. "In the meantime," I said, "you got to finish school." We had already decided that he'd have to move in with Isabel and her folks. I knew this wasn't the ideal arrangement because Isabel's folks are inclined to be dicty[4] and they hadn't especially wanted Isabel to marry me. But I didn't know what else to do. "And we have to get you fixed up at Isabel's."

There was a long silence. He moved from the kitchen table to the window. "That's a terrible idea. You know it yourself."

"Do you have a *better* idea?"

He just walked up and down the kitchen for a minute. He was as tall as I was. He had started to shave. I suddenly had the feeling that I didn't know him at all.

He stopped at the kitchen table and picked up my cigarettes. Looking at me 145 with a kind of mocking, amused defiance, he put one between his lips. "You mind?"

"You smoking already?"

He lit the cigarette and nodded, watching me through the smoke. "I just wanted to see if I'd have the courage to smoke in front of you." He grinned and blew a great cloud of smoke to the ceiling. "It was easy." He looked at my face. "Come on, now. I bet you was smoking at my age, tell the truth."

I didn't say anything but the truth was on my face, and he laughed. But now there was something very strained in his laugh. "Sure. And I bet that ain't all you was doing."

He was frightening me a little. "Cut the crap," I said. "We already decided that you was going to go and live at Isabel's. Now what's got into you all of a sudden?"

"*You* decided it," he pointed out. "*I* didn't decide nothing." He stopped in 150 front of me, leaning against the stove, arms loosely folded. "Look, brother. I don't want to stay in Harlem no more, I really don't." He was very earnest. He looked at me, then over toward the kitchen window. There was something in his eyes I'd never seen before, some thoughtfulness, some worry all his own. He rubbed the muscle of one arm. "It's time I was getting out of here."

"Where do you want to *go*, Sonny?"

"I want to join the army. Or the navy, I don't care. If I say I'm old enough, they'll believe me."

Then I got mad. It was because I was so scared. "You must be crazy. You goddamn fool, what the hell do you want to go and join the *army* for?"

"I just told you. To get out of Harlem."

"Sonny, you haven't even finished *school*. And if you really want to be a 155 musician, how do you expect to study if you're in the *army*?"

He looked at me, trapped, and in anguish. "There's ways. I might be able to work out some kind of deal. Anyway, I'll have the G.I. Bill when I come out."

---

[4] Snobbish.

"*If* you come out." We stared at each other. "Sonny, please. Be reasonable. I know the setup is far from perfect. But we got to do the best we can."

"I ain't learning nothing in school," he said. "Even when I go." He turned away from me and opened the window and threw his cigarette out into the narrow alley. I watched his back. "At least, I ain't learning nothing you'd want me to learn." He slammed the window so hard I thought the glass would fly out, and turned back to me. "And I'm sick of the stink of these garbage cans!"

"Sonny," I said, "I know how you feel. But if you don't finish school now, you're going to be sorry later that you didn't." I grabbed him by the shoulders. "And you only got another year. It ain't so bad. And I'll come back and I swear I'll help you do *whatever* you want to do. Just try to put up with it till I come back. Will you please do that? For me?"

He didn't answer and he wouldn't look at me.          160

"Sonny. You hear me?"

He pulled away. "I hear you. But you never hear anything *I* say."

I didn't know what to say to that. He looked out of the window and then back at me. "OK," he said, and sighed. "I'll try."

Then I said, trying to cheer him up a little, "They got a piano at Isabel's. You can practice on it."

And as a matter of fact, it did cheer him up for a minute. "That's right,"   165 he said to himself. "I forgot that." His face relaxed a little. But the worry, the thoughtfulness, played on it still, the way shadows play on a face which is staring into the fire.

But I thought I'd never hear the end of that piano. At first, Isabel would write me, saying how nice it was that Sonny was so serious about his music and how, as soon as he came in from school, or wherever he had been when he was supposed to be at school, he went straight to that piano and stayed there until suppertime. And, after supper, he went back to that piano and stayed there until everybody went to bed. He was at the piano all day Saturday and all day Sunday. Then he bought a record player and started playing records. He'd play one record over and over again, all day long sometimes, and he'd improvise along with it on the piano. Or he'd play one section of the record, one chord, one change, one progression, then he'd do it on the piano. Then back to the record. Then back to the piano.

Well, I really don't know how they stood it. Isabel finally confessed that it wasn't like living with a person at all, it was like living with sound. And the sound didn't make any sense to her, didn't make any sense to any of them — naturally. They began, in a way, to be afflicted by this presence that was living in their home. It was as though Sonny were some sort of god, or monster. He moved in an atmosphere which wasn't like theirs at all. They fed him and he ate, he washed himself, he walked in and out of their door; he certainly wasn't nasty or unpleasant or rude, Sonny isn't any of those things; but it was as though he were all wrapped up in some cloud, some fire, some vision all his own; and there wasn't any way to reach him.

At the same time, he wasn't really a man yet, he was still a child, and they had to watch out for him in all kinds of ways. They certainly couldn't throw him out. Neither did they dare to make a great scene about that piano because even they dimly sensed, as I sensed, from so many thousands of miles away, that Sonny was at that piano playing for his life.

But he hadn't been going to school. One day a letter came from the school board and Isabel's mother got it—there had, apparently, been other letters but Sonny had torn them up. This day, when Sonny came in, Isabel's mother showed him the letter and asked where he'd been spending his time. And she finally got it out of him that he'd been down in Greenwich Village, with musicians and other characters, in a white girl's apartment. And this scared her and she started to scream at him and what came up, once she began—though she denies it to this day—was what sacrifices they were making to give Sonny a decent home and how little he appreciated it.

Sonny didn't play the piano that day. By evening, Isabel's mother had 170 calmed down but then there was the old man to deal with, and Isabel herself. Isabel says she did her best to be calm but she broke down and started crying. She says she just watched Sonny's face. She could tell, by watching him, what was happening with him. And what was happening was that they penetrated his cloud, they had reached him. Even if their fingers had been a thousand times more gentle than human fingers ever are, he could hardly help feeling that they had stripped him naked and were spitting on that nakedness. For he also had to see that his presence, that music, which was life or death to him, had been torture for them and that they had endured it, not at all for his sake, but only for mine. And Sonny couldn't take that. He can take it a little better today than he could then but he's still not very good at it and, frankly, I don't know anybody who is.

The silence of the next few days must have been louder than the sound of all the music ever played since time began. One morning, before she went to work, Isabel was in his room for something and she suddenly realized that all of his records were gone. And she knew for certain that he was gone. And he was. He went as far as the navy would carry him. He finally sent me a postcard from some place in Greece and that was the first I knew that Sonny was still alive. I didn't see him any more until we were both back in New York and the war had long been over.

He was a man by then, of course, but I wasn't willing to see it. He came by the house from time to time, but we fought almost every time we met. I didn't like the way he carried himself, loose and dreamlike all the time, and I didn't like his friends, and his music seemed to be merely an excuse for the life he led. It sounded just that weird and disordered.

Then we had a fight, a pretty awful fight, and I didn't see him for months. By and by I looked him up, where he was living, in a furnished room in the Village, and I tried to make it up. But there were lots of other people in the room and Sonny just lay on his bed, and he wouldn't come downstairs with me, and he treated these other people as though they were his family and

I weren't. So I got mad and then he got mad, and then I told him that he might just as well be dead as live the way he was living. Then he stood up and he told me not to worry about him any more in life, that he *was* dead as far as I was concerned. Then he pushed me to the door and the other people looked on as though nothing were happening, and he slammed the door behind me. I stood in the hallway, staring at the door. I heard somebody laugh in the room and then the tears came to my eyes. I started down the steps, whistling to keep from crying, I kept whistling to myself, *You going to need me, baby, one of these cold, rainy days.*

I read about Sonny's trouble in the spring. Little Grace died in the fall. She was a beautiful little girl. But she only lived a little over two years. She died of polio and she suffered. She had a slight fever for a couple of days, but it didn't seem like anything and we just kept her in bed. And we would certainly have called the doctor, but the fever dropped, she seemed to be all right. So we thought it had just been a cold. Then, one day, she was up, playing, Isabel was in the kitchen fixing lunch for the two boys when they'd come in from school, and she heard Grace fall down in the living room. When you have a lot of children you don't always start running when one of them falls, unless they start screaming or something. And, this time, Gracie was quiet. Yet, Isabel says that when she heard that *thump* and then that silence, something happened to her to make her afraid. And she ran to the living room and there was little Grace on the floor, all twisted up, and the reason she hadn't screamed was that she couldn't get her breath. And when she did scream, it was the worst sound, Isabel says, that she'd ever heard in all her life, and she still hears it sometimes in her dreams. Isabel will sometimes wake me up with a low, moaning, strangling sound and I have to be quick to awaken her and hold her to me and where Isabel is weeping against me seems a mortal wound.

I think I may have written Sonny the very day that little Grace was buried. I 175 was sitting in the living room in the dark, by myself, and I suddenly thought of Sonny. My trouble made his real.

One Saturday afternoon, when Sonny had been living with us, or, anyway, been in our house, for nearly two weeks, I found myself wandering aimlessly about the living room, drinking from a can of beer, and trying to work up courage to search Sonny's room. He was out, he was usually out whenever I was home, and Isabel had taken the children to see their grandparents. Suddenly I was standing still in front of the living room window, watching Seventh Avenue. The idea of searching Sonny's room made me still. I scarcely dared to admit to myself what I'd be searching for. I didn't know what I'd do if I found it. Or if I didn't.

On the sidewalk across from me, near the entrance to a barbecue joint, some people were holding an old-fashioned revival meeting. The barbecue cook, wearing a dirty white apron, his conked[5] hair reddish and metallic in

---

[5] Straightened and greased.

the pale sun, and a cigarette between his lips, stood in the doorway, watching them. Kids and older people paused in their errands and stood there, along with some older men and a couple of very tough-looking women who watched everything that happened on the avenue, as though they owned it, or were maybe owned by it. Well, they were watching this, too. The revival was being carried on by three sisters in black, and a brother. All they had were their voices and their Bibles and a tambourine. The brother was testifying and while he testified two of the sisters stood together, seeming to say, amen, and the third sister walked around with the tambourine outstretched and a couple of people dropped coins into it. Then the brother's testimony ended and the sister who had been taking up the collection dumped the coins into her palm and transferred them to the pocket of her long black robe. Then she raised both hands, striking the tambourine against the air, and then against one hand, and she started to sing. And the two other sisters and the brother joined in.

It was strange, suddenly, to watch, though I had been seeing these meetings all my life. So, of course, had everybody else down there. Yet, they paused and watched and listened and I stood still at the window. "'*Tis the old ship of Zion*," they sang, and the sister with the tambourine kept a steady, jangling beat, "*it has rescued many a thousand!*" Not a soul under the sound of their voices was hearing this song for the first time, not one of them had been rescued. Nor had they seen much in the way of rescue work being done around them. Neither did they especially believe in the holiness of the three sisters and the brother, they knew too much about them, knew where they lived, and how. The woman with the tambourine, whose voice dominated the air, whose face was bright with joy, was divided by very little from the woman who stood watching her, a cigarette between her heavy, chapped lips, her hair a cuckoo's nest, her face scarred and swollen from many beatings, and her black eyes glittering like coal. Perhaps they both knew this, which was why, when, as rarely, they addressed each other, they addressed each other as Sister. As the singing filled the air the watching, listening faces underwent a change, the eyes focusing on something within; the music seemed to soothe a poison out of them; and time seemed, nearly, to fall away from the sullen, belligerent, battered faces, as though they were fleeing back to their first condition, while dreaming of their last. The barbecue cook half shook his head and smiled, and dropped his cigarette and disappeared into his joint. A man fumbled in his pockets for change and stood holding it in his hand impatiently, as though he had just remembered a pressing appointment further up the avenue. He looked furious. Then I saw Sonny, standing on the edge of the crowd. He was carrying a wide, flat notebook with a green cover, and it made him look, from where I was standing, almost like a schoolboy. The coppery sun brought out the copper in his skin, he was very faintly smiling, standing very still. Then the singing stopped, the tambourine turned into a collection plate again. The furious man dropped in his coins and vanished, so did a couple of the women, and Sonny dropped some change in the plate, looking directly at the woman with a little smile. He started across the avenue, toward the house. He has a slow, loping walk, something like the way Harlem hipsters walk, only he's imposed on this his own half-beat. I had never really noticed it before.

I stayed at the window, both relieved and apprehensive. As Sonny disappeared from my sight, they began singing again. And they were still singing when his key turned in the lock.

"Hey," he said.  180

"Hey, yourself. You want some beer?"

"No. Well, maybe." But he came up to the window and stood beside me, looking out. "What a warm voice," he said.

They were singing *If I could only hear my mother pray again!*

"Yes," I said, "and she can sure beat that tambourine."

"But what a terrible song," he said, and laughed. He dropped his notebook  185
on the sofa and disappeared into the kitchen. "Where's Isabel and the kids?"

"I think they went to see their grandparents. You hungry?"

"No." He came back into the living room with his can of beer. "You want to come some place with me tonight?"

I sensed, I don't know how, that I couldn't possibly say no. "Sure. Where?"

He sat down on the sofa and picked up his notebook and started leafing through it. "I'm going to sit in with some fellows in a joint in the Village."

"You mean, you're going to play, tonight?"  190

"That's right." He took a swallow of his beer and moved back to the window. He gave me a sidelong look. "If you can stand it."

"I'll try," I said.

He smiled to himself and we both watched as the meeting across the way broke up. The three sisters and the brother, heads bowed, were singing *God be with you till we meet again.* The faces around them were very quiet. Then the song ended. The small crowd dispersed. We watched the three women and the lone man walk slowly up the avenue.

"When she was singing before," said Sonny, abruptly, "her voice reminded me for a minute of what heroin feels like sometimes — when it's in your veins. It makes you feel sort of warm and cool at the same time. And distant. And — and sure." He sipped his beer, very deliberately not looking at me. I watched his face. "It makes you feel — in control. Sometimes you've got to have that feeling."

"Do you?" I sat down slowly in the easy chair.  195

"Sometimes." He went to the sofa and picked up his notebook again. "Some people do."

"In order," I asked, "to play?" And my voice was very ugly, full of contempt and anger.

"Well" — he looked at me with great, troubled eyes, as though, in fact, he hoped his eyes would tell me things he could never otherwise say — "they *think* so. And *if* they think so —!"

"And what do *you* think?" I asked.

He sat on the sofa and put his can of beer on the floor. "I don't know," he  200
said, and I couldn't be sure if he were answering my question or pursuing his

thoughts. His face didn't tell me. "It's not so much to *play*. It's to *stand* it, to be able to make it at all. On any level." He frowned and smiled: "In order to keep from shaking to pieces."

"But these friends of yours," I said, "they seem to shake themselves to pieces pretty goddamn fast."

"Maybe." He played with the notebook. And something told me that I should curb my tongue, that Sonny was doing his best to talk, that I should listen. "But of course you only know the ones that've gone to pieces. Some don't — or at least they haven't *yet* and that's just about all *any* of us can say." He paused. "And then there are some who just live, really, in hell, and they know it and they see what's happening and they go right on. I don't know." He sighed, dropped the notebook, folded his arms. "Some guys, you can tell from the way they play, they on something *all* the time. And you can see that, well, it makes something real for them. But of course," he picked up his beer from the floor and sipped it and put the can down again, "they *want* to, too, you've got to see that. Even some of them that say they don't — *some*, not all."

"And what about you?" I asked — I couldn't help it. "What about you? Do *you* want to?"

He stood up and walked to the window and remained silent for a long time. Then he sighed. "Me," he said. Then: "While I was downstairs before, on my way here, listening to that woman sing, it struck me all of a sudden how much suffering she must have had to go through — to sing like that. It's *repulsive* to think you have to suffer that much."

I said: "But there's no way not to suffer — is there, Sonny?" 205

"I believe not," he said and smiled, "but that's never stopped anyone from trying." He looked at me. "Has it?" I realized, with this mocking look, that there stood between us, forever, beyond the power of time or forgiveness, the fact that I had held silence — so long! — when he had needed human speech to help him. He turned back to the window. "No, there's no way not to suffer. But you try all kinds of ways to keep from drowning in it, to keep on top of it, and to make it seem — well, like *you*. Like you did something, all right, and now you're suffering for it. You know?" I said nothing. "Well you know," he said, impatiently, "why *do* people suffer? Maybe it's better to do something to give it a reason, *any* reason."

"But we just agreed," I said, "that there's no way not to suffer. Isn't it better, then, just to — take it?"

"But nobody just takes it," Sonny cried, "that's what I'm telling you! *Everybody* tries not to. You're just hung up on the *way* some people try — it's not *your* way!"

The hair on my face began to itch, my face felt wet. "That's not true," I said, "that's not true. I don't give a damn what other people do, I don't even care how they suffer. I just care how *you* suffer." And he looked at me. "Please believe me," I said, "I don't want to see you — die — trying not to suffer."

"I won't," he said, flatly, "die trying not to suffer. At least, not any faster than 210 anybody else."

"But there's no need," I said, trying to laugh, "is there? in killing yourself."

I wanted to say more, but I couldn't. I wanted to talk about will power and how life could be — well, beautiful. I wanted to say that it was all within; but was it? or, rather, wasn't that exactly the trouble? And I wanted to promise that I would never fail him again. But it would all have sounded — empty words and lies.

So I made the promise to myself and prayed that I would keep it.

"It's terrible sometimes, inside," he said, "that's what's the trouble. You walk these streets, black and funky and cold, and there's not really a living ass to talk to, and there's nothing shaking, and there's no way of getting it out — that storm inside. You can't talk it and you can't make love with it, and when you finally try to get with it and play it, you realize *nobody's* listening. So *you've* got to listen. You got to find a way to listen."

And then he walked away from the window and sat on the sofa again, as 215 though all the wind had suddenly been knocked out of him. "Sometimes you'll do *anything* to play, even cut your mother's throat." He laughed and looked at me. "Or your brother's." Then he sobered. "Or your own." Then: "Don't worry. I'm all right now and I think I'll *be* all right. But I can't forget — where I've been. I don't mean just the physical place I've been, I mean where I've *been*. And *what* I've been."

"What have you been, Sonny?" I asked.

He smiled — but sat sideways on the sofa, his elbow resting on the back, his fingers playing with his mouth and chin, not looking at me. "I've been something I didn't recognize, didn't know I could be. Didn't know anybody could be." He stopped, looking inward, looking helplessly young, looking old. "I'm not talking about it now because I feel *guilty* or anything like that — maybe it would be better if I did, I don't know. Anyway, I can't really talk about it. Not to you, not to anybody," and now he turned and faced me. "Sometimes, you know, and it was actually when I was most *out* of the world, I felt that I was in it, that I was *with* it, really, and I could play or I didn't really have to *play*, it just came out of me, it was there. And I don't know how I played, thinking about it now, but I know I did awful things, those times, sometimes, to people. Or it wasn't that I *did* anything to them — it was that they weren't real." He picked up the beer can; it was empty; he rolled it between his palms: "And other times — well, I needed a fix, I needed to find a place to lean, I needed to clear a space to *listen* — and I couldn't find it, and I — went crazy, I did terrible things to *me*, I was terrible *for* me." He began pressing the beer can between his hands, I watched the metal begin to give. It glittered, as he played with it like a knife, and I was afraid he would cut himself, but I said nothing. "Oh well. I can never tell you. I was all by myself at the bottom of something, stinking and sweating and crying and shaking, and I smelled it, you know? *my* stink, and I thought I'd die if I couldn't get away from it and yet, all the same, I knew that everything I was doing was just locking me in with it. And I didn't know," he paused, still flattening the beer can, "I didn't know, I still *don't* know, something kept telling me that maybe it was good to smell your own stink, but

I didn't think that *that* was what I'd been trying to do—and—who can stand it?" and he abruptly dropped the ruined beer can, looking at me with a small, still smile, and then rose, walking to the window as though it were the lodestone rock. I watched his face, he watched the avenue. "I couldn't tell you when Mama died—but the reason I wanted to leave Harlem so bad was to get away from drugs. And then, when I ran away, that's what I was running from—really. When I came back, nothing had changed, *I* hadn't changed, I was just—older." And he stopped, drumming with his fingers on the windowpane. The sun had vanished, soon darkness would fall. I watched his face. "It can come again," he said, almost as though speaking to himself. Then he turned to me. "It can come again," he repeated. "I just want you to know that."

"All right," I said, at last. "So it can come again. All right."

He smiled, but the smile was sorrowful. "I had to try to tell you," he said.

"Yes," I said. "I understand that." 220

"You're my brother," he said, looking straight at me, and not smiling at all.

"Yes," I repeated, "yes. I understand that."

He turned back to the window, looking out. "All that hatred down there," he said, "all that hatred and misery and love. It's a wonder it doesn't blow the avenue apart."

We went to the only nightclub on a short, dark street, downtown. We squeezed through the narrow, chattering, jampacked bar to the entrance of the big room, where the bandstand was. And we stood there for a moment, for the lights were very dim in this room and we couldn't see. Then, "Hello, boy," said the voice and an enormous black man, much older than Sonny or myself, erupted out of all that atmospheric lighting and put an arm around Sonny's shoulder. "I been sitting right here," he said, "waiting for you."

He had a big voice, too, and heads in the darkness turned toward us. 225

Sonny grinned and pulled a little away, and said, "Creole, this is my brother. I told you about him."

Creole shook my hand. "I'm glad to meet you, son," he said, and it was clear that he was glad to meet me *there*, for Sonny's sake. And he smiled, "You got a real musician in *your* family," and he took his arm from Sonny's shoulder and slapped him, lightly, affectionately, with the back of his hand.

"Well. Now I've heard it all," said a voice behind us. This was another musician, and a friend of Sonny's, a coal-black, cheerful-looking man, built close to the ground. He immediately began confiding to me, at the top of his lungs, the most terrible things about Sonny, his teeth gleaming like a lighthouse and his laugh coming up out of him like the beginning of an earthquake. And it turned out that everyone at the bar knew Sonny, or almost everyone; some were musicians, working there, or nearby, or not working, some were simply hangers-on, and some were there to hear Sonny play. I was introduced to all of them and they were all very polite to me. Yet, it was clear that, for them, I was only Sonny's brother. Here, I was in Sonny's world. Or, rather: his kingdom. Here, it was not even a question that his veins bore royal blood.

They were going to play soon and Creole installed me, by myself, at a table in a dark corner. Then I watched them, Creole, and the little black man, and Sonny, and the others, while they horsed around, standing just below the bandstand. The light from the bandstand spilled just a little short of them and, watching them laughing and gesturing and moving about, I had the feeling that they, nevertheless, were being most careful not to step into that circle of light too suddenly; that if they moved into the light too suddenly, without thinking, they would perish in flame. Then, while I watched, one of them, the small, black man, moved into the light and crossed the bandstand and started fooling around with his drums. Then — being funny and being, also, extremely cere-monious — Creole took Sonny by the arm and led him to the piano. A woman's voice called Sonny's name and a few hands started clapping. And Sonny, also being funny and being ceremonious, and so touched, I think, that he could have cried, but neither hiding it nor showing it, riding it like a man, grinned, and put both hands to his heart and bowed from the waist.

Creole then went to the bass fiddle and a lean, very bright-skinned brown 230 man jumped up on the bandstand and picked up his horn. So there they were, and the atmosphere on the bandstand and in the room began to change and tighten. Someone stepped up to the microphone and announced them. Then there were all kinds of murmurs. Some people at the bar shushed others. The waitress ran around, frantically getting in the last orders, guys and chicks got closer to each other, and the lights on the bandstand, on the quartet, turned to a kind of indigo. Then they all looked different there. Creole looked about him for the last time, as though he were making certain that all his chickens were in the coop, and then he — jumped and struck the fiddle. And there they were.

All I know about music is that not many people ever really hear it. And even then, on the rare occasions when something opens within, and the music enters, what we mainly hear, or hear corroborated, are personal, private, van-ishing evocations. But the man who creates the music is hearing something else, is dealing with the roar rising from the void and imposing order on it as it hits the air. What is evoked in him, then, is of another order, more terrible because it has no words, and triumphant, too, for that same reason. And his triumph, when he triumphs, is ours. I just watched Sonny's face. His face was troubled, he was working hard, but he wasn't with it. And I had the feeling that, in a way, everyone on the bandstand was waiting for him, both waiting for him and pushing him along. But as I began to watch Creole, I realized that it was Creole who held them all back. He had them on a short rein. Up there, keeping the beat with his whole body, wailing on the fiddle, with his eyes half closed, he was listening to everything, but he was listening to Sonny. He was having a dialogue with Sonny. He wanted Sonny to leave the shoreline and strike out for the deep water. He was Sonny's witness that deep water and drowning were not the same thing — he had been there, and he knew. And he wanted Sonny to know. He was waiting for Sonny to do the things on the keys which would let Creole know that Sonny was in the water.

And, while Creole listened, Sonny moved, deep within, exactly like someone in torment. I had never before thought of how awful the relationship must be between the musician and his instrument. He has to fill it, this instrument, with the breath of life, his own. He has to make it do what he wants it to do. And a piano is just a piano. It's made out of so much wood and wires and little hammers and big ones, and ivory. While there's only so much you can do with it, the only way to find this out is to try; to try and make it do everything.

And Sonny hadn't been near a piano for over a year. And he wasn't on much better terms with his life, not the life that stretched before him now. He and the piano stammered, started one way, got scared, stopped; started another way, panicked, marked time, started again; then seemed to have found a direction, panicked again, got stuck. And the face I saw on Sonny I'd never seen before. Everything had been burned out of it, and, at the same time, things usually hidden were being burned in, by the fire and fury of the battle which was occurring in him up there.

Yet, watching Creole's face as they neared the end of the first set, I had the feeling that something had happened, something I hadn't heard. Then they finished, there was scattered applause, and then, without an instant's warning, Creole started into something else, it was almost sardonic, it was *Am I Blue.*[6] And, as though he commanded, Sonny began to play. Something began to happen. And Creole let out the reins. The dry, low, black man said something awful on the drums, Creole answered, and the drums talked back. Then the horn insisted, sweet and high, slightly detached perhaps, and Creole listened, commenting now and then, dry, and driving, beautiful and calm and old. Then they all came together again, and Sonny was part of the family again. I could tell this from his face. He seemed to have found, right there beneath his fingers, a damn brand-new piano. It seemed that he couldn't get over it. Then, for a while, just being happy with Sonny, they seemed to be agreeing with him that brand-new pianos certainly were a gas.

Then Creole stepped forward to remind them that what they were playing 235 was the blues. He hit something in all of them, he hit something in me, myself, and the music tightened and deepened, apprehension began to beat the air. Creole began to tell us what the blues were all about. They were not about anything very new. He and his boys up there were keeping it new, at the risk of ruin, destruction, madness, and death, in order to find new ways to make us listen. For, while the tale of how we suffer, and how we are delighted, and how we may triumph is never new, it always must be heard. There isn't any other tale to tell, it's the only light we've got in all this darkness.

And this tale, according to that face, that body, those strong hands on those strings, has another aspect in every country, and a new depth in every generation. Listen, Creole seemed to be saying, listen. Now these are Sonny's blues. He made the little black man on the drums know it, and the bright, brown

---

[6] One of the standard tunes in the jazz/blues repertoire.

man on the horn. Creole wasn't trying any longer to get Sonny in the water. He was wishing him Godspeed. Then he stepped back, very slowly, filling the air with the immense suggestion that Sonny speak for himself.

Then they all gathered around Sonny and Sonny played. Every now and again one of them seemed to say, amen. Sonny's fingers filled the air with life, his life. But that life contained so many others. And Sonny went all the way back, he really began with the spare, flat statement of the opening phrase of the song. Then he began to make it his. It was very beautiful because it wasn't hurried and it was no longer a lament. I seemed to hear with what burning he had made it his, and what burning we had yet to make it ours, how we could cease lamenting. Freedom lurked around us and I understood, at last, that he could help us to be free if we would listen, that he would never be free until we did. Yet, there was no battle in his face now, I heard what he had gone through, and would continue to go through until he came to rest in earth. He had made it his: that long line, of which we knew only Mama and Daddy. And he was giving it back, as everything must be given back, so that, passing through death, it can live forever. I saw my mother's face again, and felt, for the first time, how the stones of the road she had walked on must have bruised her feet. I saw the moonlit road where my father's brother died. And it brought something else back to me, and carried me past it, I saw my little girl again and felt Isabel's tears again, and I felt my own tears begin to rise. And I was yet aware that this was only a moment, that the world waited outside, as hungry as a tiger, and that trouble stretched above us, longer than the sky.

Then it was over. Creole and Sonny let out their breath, both soaking wet, and grinning. There was a lot of applause and some of it was real. In the dark, the girl came by and I asked her to take drinks to the bandstand. There was a long pause, while they talked up there in the indigo light and after awhile I saw the girl put a Scotch and milk on top of the piano for Sonny. He didn't seem to notice it, but just before they started playing again, he sipped from it and looked toward me, and nodded. Then he put it back on top of the piano. For me, then, as they began to play again, it glowed and shook above my brother's head like the very cup of trembling.[7]

## FOR ANALYSIS

**1.** Explain this story's title.

**2.** What is the relation between the opening events and the end of the story?

**3.** What function does the **narrator's** encounter with Sonny's friend at the beginning of the story (paras. 9–47) serve?

---

[7] See the Old Testament, Isaiah 51:17, 22–23: "Awake, awake, stand up, O Jerusalem, which hast drunk at the hand of the Lord the cup of his fury; thou hast drunken the dregs of the cup of trembling, and wrung them out. . . . Behold, I have taken out of thine hand the cup of trembling, even the dregs of the cup of my fury; thou shalt no more drink it again: But I will put it into the hand of them that afflict thee."

**4.** Does the story offer any explanation for Sonny's addiction? Explain.

**5.** What adjectives would you use to describe the narrator? Does he change in the course of the story? Explain.

**6.** What effects does Baldwin achieve by rearranging the order of events?

**7.** What does the final sentence mean?

## MAKING ARGUMENTS

Make an argument about the relationship between suffering and creativity. Is there something inherent in suffering that enables artists to make great art? As evidence, use "Sonny's Blues" and any other artists or works of art with which you're familiar.

## WRITING TOPICS

**1.** What does this story have to say about the sources of creativity?

**2.** Discuss the significance of the **narrator's** observations on the revival meeting (paras. 177–78) to the **theme** of the story.

## MAKING CONNECTIONS

**1.** Compare and contrast the way racism is portrayed in this story with its portrayal in Bambara's "The Lesson" (p. 100).

**2.** Kafka's "A Hunger Artist" (p. 295) is also about an artist and the process of artistic creation. What similarities or differences do you find between Kafka's story and Baldwin's?

## ALICE WALKER (B. 1944)

# EVERYDAY USE 1973

### FOR YOUR GRANDMAMA

I will wait for her in the yard that Maggie and I made so clean and wavy yesterday afternoon. A yard like this is more comfortable than most people know. It is not just a yard. It is like an extended living room. When the hard clay is swept clean as a floor and the fine sand around the edges lined with tiny, irregular grooves anyone can come and sit and look up into the elm tree and wait for the breezes that never come inside the house.

Maggie will be nervous until after her sister goes: she will stand hopelessly in corners homely and ashamed of the burn scars down her arms and legs, eyeing her sister with a mixture of envy and awe. She thinks her sister has held life always in the palm of one hand, that "no" is a word the world never learned to say to her.

You've no doubt seen those TV shows where the child who has "made it" is confronted, as a surprise, by her own mother and father, tottering in weakly from backstage. (A pleasant surprise, of course: What would they do if parent and child came on the show only to curse out and insult each other?) On TV mother and child embrace and smile into each other's faces. Sometimes the mother and father weep, the child wraps them in her arms and leans across the table to tell how she would not have made it without their help. I have seen these programs.

Sometimes I dream a dream in which Dee and I are suddenly brought together on a TV program of this sort. Out of a dark and soft-seated limousine I am ushered into a bright room filled with many people. There I meet a smiling, gray, sporty man like Johnny Carson who shakes my hand and tells me what a fine girl I have. Then we are on the stage and Dee is embracing me with tears in her eyes. She pins on my dress a large orchid, even though she has told me once that she thinks orchids are tacky flowers.

In real life I am a large, big-boned woman with rough, man-working hands. 5 In the winter I wear flannel nightgowns to bed and overalls during the day. I can kill and clean a hog as mercilessly as a man. My fat keeps me hot in zero weather. I can work outside all day, breaking ice to get water for washing. I can eat pork liver cooked over the open fire minutes after it comes steaming from the hog. One winter I knocked a bull calf straight in the brain between the eyes with a sledge hammer and had the meat hung up to chill before nightfall. But of course all this does not show on television. I am the way my daughter would want me to be: a hundred pounds lighter, my skin like an uncooked barley pancake. My hair glistens in the hot bright lights. Johnny Carson has much to do to keep up with my quick and witty tongue.

But that is a mistake. I know even before I wake up. Who ever knew a Johnson with a quick tongue? Who can even imagine me looking a strange white man in the eye? It seems to me I have talked to them always with one foot raised in flight, with my head turned in whichever way is farthest from them. Dee, though. She would always look anyone in the eye. Hesitation was no part of her nature.

"How do I look, Mama?" Maggie says, showing just enough of her thin body enveloped in pink skirt and red blouse for me to know she's there, almost hidden by the door.

"Come out into the yard," I say.

Have you ever seen a lame animal, perhaps a dog run over by some careless person rich enough to own a car, sidle up to someone who is ignorant enough to be kind to him? That is the way my Maggie walks. She has been like this, chin on chest, eyes on ground, feet in shuffle, ever since the fire that burned the other house to the ground.

Dee is lighter than Maggie, with nicer hair and a fuller figure. She's a woman 10 now, though sometimes I forget. How long ago was it that the other house burned? Ten, twelve years? Sometimes I can still hear the flames and feel Maggie's arms sticking to me, her hair smoking and her dress falling off her in little black papery flakes. Her eyes seemed stretched open, blazed open by the flames reflected in them. And Dee. I see her standing off under the sweet gum tree she used to dig gum out of; a look of concentration on her face as she watched the last dingy gray board of the house fall in toward the red-hot brick chimney. Why don't you do a dance around the ashes? I'd wanted to ask her. She had hated the house that much.

I used to think she hated Maggie, too. But that was before we raised the money, the church and me, to send her to Augusta to school. She used to read to us without pity; forcing words, lies, other folks' habits, whole lives upon us two, sitting trapped and ignorant underneath her voice. She washed us in a river of make-believe, burned us with a lot of knowledge we didn't necessarily need to know. Pressed us to her with the serious way she read, to shove us away at just the moment, like dimwits, we seemed about to understand.

Dee wanted nice things. A yellow organdy dress to wear to her graduation from high school; black pumps to match a green suit she'd made from an old suit somebody gave me. She was determined to stare down any disaster in her efforts. Her eyelids would not flicker for minutes at a time. Often I fought off the temptation to shake her. At sixteen she had a style of her own: and knew what style was.

I never had an education myself. After second grade the school was closed down. Don't ask me why: in 1927 colored asked fewer questions than they do now. Sometimes Maggie reads to me. She stumbles along good-naturedly but can't see well. She knows she is not bright. Like good looks and money, quickness passed her by. She will marry John Thomas (who has mossy teeth in an earnest face) and then I'll be free to sit here and I guess just sing church songs to myself. Although I never was a good singer. Never could carry a tune. I was always better at a man's job. I used to love to milk till I was hoofed in the side in '49. Cows are soothing and slow and don't bother you, unless you try to milk them the wrong way.

I have deliberately turned my back on the house. It is three rooms, just like the one that burned, except the roof is tin; they don't make shingle roofs any more. There are no real windows, just some holes cut in the sides, like the portholes in a ship, but not round and not square, with rawhide holding the shutters up on the outside. This house is in a pasture, too, like the other one. No doubt when Dee sees it she will want to tear it down. She wrote me once that no matter where we "choose" to live, she will manage to come see us. But she will never bring her friends. Maggie and I thought about this and Maggie asked me, "Mama, when did Dee ever *have* any friends?"

She had a few. Furtive boys in pink shirts hanging about on washday after 15 school. Nervous girls who never laughed. Impressed with her they worshiped the well-turned phrase, the cute shape, the scalding humor that erupted like bubbles in lye. She read to them.

When she was courting Jimmy T she didn't have much time to pay to us, but turned all her faultfinding power on him. He *flew* to marry a cheap gal from a family of ignorant flashy people. She hardly had time to recompose herself.

When she comes I will meet — but there they are!

Maggie attempts to make a dash for the house, in her shuffling way, but I stay her with my hand. "Come back here," I say. And she stops and tries to dig a well in the sand with her toe.

It is hard to see them clearly through the strong sun. But even the first glimpse of leg out of the car tells me it is Dee. Her feet were always neat-looking, as if God himself had shaped them with a certain style. From the other side of the car comes a short, stocky man. Hair is all over his head a foot long and hanging from his chin like a kinky mule tail. I hear Maggie suck in her breath. "Uhnnnh," is what it sounds like. Like when you see the wriggling end of a snake just in front of your foot on the road. "Uhnnnh."

Dee next. A dress down to the ground, in this hot weather. A dress so loud 20 it hurts my eyes. There are yellows and oranges enough to throw back the light of the sun. I feel my whole face warming from the heat waves it throws out. Earrings, too, gold and hanging down to her shoulders. Bracelets dangling and making noises when she moves her arm up to shake the folds of the dress out of her armpits. The dress is loose and flows, and as she walks closer, I like it. I hear Maggie go "Uhnnnh" again. It is her sister's hair. It stands straight up like the wool on a sheep. It is black as night and around the edges are two long pigtails that rope about like small lizards disappearing behind her ears.

"Wa-su-zo-Tean-o!" she says, coming on in that gliding way the dress makes her move. The short stocky fellow with the hair to his navel is all grinning and he follows up with "Asalamalakim, my mother and sister!" He moves to hug

Maggie but she falls back, right up against the back of my chair. I feel her trembling there and when I look up I see the perspiration falling off her chin.

"Don't get up," says Dee. Since I am stout it takes something of a push. You can see me trying to move a second or two before I make it. She turns, showing white heels through her sandals, and goes back to the car. Out she peeks next with a Polaroid. She stoops down quickly and lines up picture after picture of me sitting there in front of the house with Maggie cowering behind me. She never takes a shot without making sure the house is included. When a cow comes nibbling around the edge of the yard she snaps it and me and Maggie *and* the house. Then she puts the Polaroid in the back seat of the car, and comes up and kisses me on the forehead.

Meanwhile Asalamalakim is going through motions with Maggie's hand. Maggie's hand is as limp as a fish, and probably as cold, despite the sweat, and she keeps trying to pull it back. It looks like Asalamalakim wants to shake hands but wants to do it fancy. Or maybe he don't know how people shake hands. Anyhow, he soon gives up on Maggie.

"Well," I say. "Dee."

"No, Mama," she says. "Not 'Dee,' Wangero Leewanika Kemanjo!"      25

"What happened to 'Dee'?" I wanted to know.

"She's dead," Wangero said. "I couldn't bear it any longer being named after the people who oppress me."

"You know as well as me you was named after your aunt Dicie," I said. Dicie is my sister. She named Dee. We called her "Big Dee" after Dee was born.

"But who was *she* named after?" asked Wangero.

"I guess after Grandma Dee," I said.      30

"And who was she named after?" asked Wangero.

"Her mother," I said, and saw Wangero was getting tired. "That's about as far back as I can trace it," I said. Though, in fact, I probably could have carried it back beyond the Civil War through the branches.

"Well," said Asalamalakim, "there you are."

"Uhnnnh," I heard Maggie say.

"There I was not," I said, "before 'Dicie' cropped up in our family, so why      35 should I try to trace it that far back?"

He just stood there grinning, looking down on me like somebody inspecting a Model A car. Every once in a while he and Wangero sent eye signals over my head.

"How do you pronounce this name?" I asked.

"You don't have to call me by it if you don't want to," said Wangero.

"Why shouldn't I?" I asked. "If that's what you want us to call you, we'll call you."

"I know it might sound awkward at first," said Wangero.      40

"I'll get used to it," I said. "Ream it out again."

Well, soon we got the name out of the way. Asalamalakim had a name twice as long and three times as hard. After I tripped over it two or three times he told me to just call him Hakim-a-barber. I wanted to ask him was he a barber, but I didn't really think he was, so I didn't ask.

"You must belong to those beef-cattle peoples down the road," I said. They said "Asalamalakim" when they met you, too, but they didn't shake hands. Always too busy: feeding the cattle, fixing the fences, putting up salt-lick shelters, throwing down hay. When the white folks poisoned some of the herd the men stayed up all night with rifles in their hands. I walked a mile and a half just to see the sight.

Hakim-a-barber said, "I accept some of their doctrines, but farming and raising cattle is not my style." (They didn't tell me, and I didn't ask, whether Wangero [Dee] had really gone and married him.)

We sat down to eat and right away he said he didn't eat collards and pork 45 was unclean. Wangero, though, went on through the chitlins and corn bread, the greens and everything else. She talked a blue streak over the sweet potatoes. Everything delighted her. Even the fact that we still used the benches her daddy made for the table when we couldn't afford to buy chairs.

"Oh, Mama!" she cried. Then turned to Hakim-a-barber. "I never knew how lovely these benches are. You can feel the rump prints," she said, running her hands underneath her and along the bench. Then she gave a sigh and her hand closed over Grandma Dee's butter dish. "That's it!" she said. "I knew there was something I wanted to ask you if I could have." She jumped up from the table and went over in the corner where the churn stood, the milk in its clabber by now. She looked at the churn and looked at it.

"This churn top is what I need," she said. "Didn't Uncle Buddy whittle it out of a tree you all used to have?"

"Yes," I said.

"Uh huh," she said happily. "And I want the dasher, too."

"Uncle Buddy whittle that, too?" asked the barber.                                    50

Dee (Wangero) looked up at me.

"Aunt Dee's first husband whittled the dash," said Maggie so low you almost couldn't hear her. "His name was Henry, but they called him Stash."

"Maggie's brain is like an elephant's," Wangero said, laughing. "I can use the churn top as a centerpiece for the alcove table," she said, sliding a plate over the churn, "and I'll think of something artistic to do with the dasher."

When she finished wrapping the dasher the handle stuck out. I took it for a moment in my hands. You didn't even have to look close to see where hands pushing the dasher up and down to make butter had left a kind of sink in the wood. In fact, there were a lot of small sinks; you could see where thumbs and fingers had sunk into the wood. It was beautiful light yellow wood, from a tree that grew in the yard where Big Dee and Stash had lived.

After dinner Dee (Wangero) went to the trunk at the foot of my bed and 55 started rifling through it. Maggie hung back in the kitchen over the dishpan. Out came Wangero with two quilts. They had been pieced by Grandma Dee and then Big Dee and me had hung them on the quilt frames on the front porch and quilted them. One was in the Lone Star pattern. The other was Walk Around the Mountain. In both of them were scraps of dresses Grandma Dee had worn fifty and more years ago. Bits and pieces of Grandpa Jarrell's

Paisley shirts. And one teeny faded blue piece, about the size of a penny matchbox, that was from Great Grandpa Ezra's uniform that he wore in the Civil War.

"Mama," Wangero said sweet as a bird. "Can I have these old quilts?"

I heard something fall in the kitchen, and a minute later the kitchen door slammed.

"Why don't you take one or two of the others?" I asked. "These old things was just done by me and Big Dee from some tops your grandma pieced before she died."

"No," said Wangero. "I don't want those. They are stitched around the borders by machine."

"That'll make them last better," I said.                                            60

"That's not the point," said Wangero. "These are all pieces of dresses Grandma used to wear. She did all this stitching by hand. Imagine!" She held the quilts securely in her arms, stroking them.

"Some of the pieces, like those lavender ones, come from old clothes her mother handed down to her," I said, moving up to touch the quilts. Dee (Wangero) moved back just enough so that I couldn't reach the quilts. They already belonged to her.

"Imagine!" she breathed again, clutching them closely to her bosom.

"The truth is," I said, "I promised to give them quilts to Maggie, for when she marries John Thomas."

She gasped like a bee had stung her.                                                65

"Maggie can't appreciate these quilts!" she said. "She'd probably be backward enough to put them to everyday use."

"I reckon she would," I said. "God knows I been saving 'em for long enough with nobody using 'em. I hope she will!" I didn't want to bring up how I had offered Dee (Wangero) a quilt when she went away to college. Then she had told me they were old-fashioned, out of style.

"But they're *priceless!*" she was saying now, furiously; for she has a temper. "Maggie would put them on the bed and in five years they'd be in rags. Less than that!"

"She can always make some more," I said. "Maggie knows how to quilt."

Dee (Wangero) looked at me with hatred. "You just will not understand. The   70
point is these quilts, *these* quilts!"

"Well," I said, stumped. "What would *you* do with them?"

"Hang them," she said. As if that was the only thing you *could* do with quilts.

Maggie by now was standing in the door. I could almost hear the sound her feet made as they scraped over each other.

"She can have them, Mama," she said, like somebody used to never winning anything, or having anything reserved for her. "I can 'member Grandma Dee without the quilts."

I looked at her hard. She had filled her bottom lip with checkerberry snuff  75
and it gave her face a kind of dopey, hangdog look. It was Grandma Dee and Big Dee who taught her how to quilt herself. She stood there with her scarred

hands hidden in the folds of her skirt. She looked at her sister with something like fear but she wasn't mad at her. This was Maggie's portion. This was the way she knew God to work.

When I looked at her like that something hit me in the top of my head and ran down to the soles of my feet. Just like when I'm in church and the spirit of God touches me and I get happy and shout. I did something I never had done before: hugged Maggie to me, then dragged her on into the room, snatched the quilts out of Miss Wangero's hands and dumped them into Maggie's lap. Maggie just sat there on my bed with her mouth open.

"Take one or two of the others," I said to Dee.

But she turned without a word and went out to Hakim-a-barber.

"You just don't understand," she said, as Maggie and I came out to the car.

"What don't I understand?" I wanted to know.                                      80

"Your heritage," she said. And then she turned to Maggie, kissed her, and said, "You ought to try to make something of yourself, too, Maggie. It's really a new day for us. But from the way you and Mama still live you'd never know it."

She put on some sunglasses that hid everything above the tip of her nose and her chin.

Maggie smiled; maybe at the sunglasses. But a real smile, not scared. After we watched the car dust settle I asked Maggie to bring me a dip of snuff. And then the two of us sat there just enjoying, until it was time to go in the house and go to bed.

## FOR ANALYSIS

**1.** What are the **narrator's** outstanding traits, her weaknesses, and her strengths?

**2.** How would you describe the narrator's feelings about her daughter Dee? About her daughter Maggie?

**3.** How would you describe the narrator's descriptions of herself? Are her actions consistent with the kind of person she says she is? Explain.

**4.** Why does the narrator recall the burning of the house? How does this event from the past help the reader understand the present action?

**5.** What are the sources of the story's humor?

**6.** What does Dee's boyfriend, Asalamalakim, represent?

**7.** Why does the narrator give the quilts to Maggie?

**8.** Explain the title. What is the meaning of the subtitle, "For Your Grandmama"?

## MAKING ARGUMENTS

So much of "Everyday Use" is about the **narrator**, down to her **voice** — the way she describes what she sees and feels and thinks. Make an argument about Walker's choice to write in the first person, arguing either that she could or could not have achieved the same effects if she had written in the third person. How would Walker have let us see things from the narrator's **point of view**?

## WRITING TOPICS

**1.** Analyze the opening two paragraphs of the story, showing how they set the **tone** and establish the tension of the story.

**2.** Write an essay analyzing the **conflict** in the story and the way it is resolved. Is the resolution satisfying? Explain.

## MAKING CONNECTIONS

Compare Dee in this story and Miss Moore in Bambara's "The Lesson" (p. 100) as characters whose intellectual and educational superiority enables them to unsettle the tranquillity of those around them.

SHERMAN ALEXIE   (B. 1966)

# THIS IS WHAT IT MEANS
# TO SAY PHOENIX, ARIZONA   1993

J ust after Victor lost his job at the BIA,[1] he also found out that his father had
died of a heart attack in Phoenix, Arizona. Victor hadn't seen his father in a
few years, only talked to him on the telephone once or twice, but there still was a
genetic pain, which was soon to be pain as real and immediate as a broken bone.

Victor didn't have any money. Who does have money on a reservation, except
the cigarette and fireworks salespeople? His father had a savings account waiting to be claimed, but Victor needed to find a way to get to Phoenix. Victor's
mother was just as poor as he was, and the rest of his family didn't have any use
at all for him. So Victor called the Tribal Council.

"Listen," Victor said. "My father just died. I need some money to get to
Phoenix to make arrangements."

"Now, Victor," the council said. "You know we're having a difficult time
financially."

"But I thought the council had special funds set aside for stuff like this."   5

"Now, Victor, we do have some money available for the proper return of
tribal members' bodies. But I don't think we have enough to bring your father
all the way back from Phoenix."

"Well," Victor said. "It ain't going to cost all that much. He had to be cremated. Things were kind of ugly. He died of a heart attack in his trailer and
nobody found him for a week. It was really hot, too. You get the picture."

"Now, Victor, we're sorry for your loss and the circumstances. But we can
really only afford to give you one hundred dollars."

"That's not even enough for a plane ticket."

"Well, you might consider driving down to Phoenix."   10

"I don't have a car. Besides, I was going to drive my father's pickup back up
here."

"Now, Victor," the council said. "We're sure there is somebody who could drive
you to Phoenix. Or is there somebody who could lend you the rest of the money?"

"You know there ain't nobody around with that kind of money."

"Well, we're sorry, Victor, but that's the best we can do."

Victor accepted the Tribal Council's offer. What else could he do? So he   15
signed the proper papers, picked up his check, and walked over to the Trading
Post to cash it.

[1] The Bureau of Indian Affairs, a division of the U.S. Department of the Interior, oversees the
administration of federal programs for American Indians, Indian tribes, and Alaskan natives.

While Victor stood in line, he watched Thomas Builds-the-Fire standing near the magazine rack, talking to himself. Like he always did. Thomas was a storyteller that nobody wanted to listen to. That's like being a dentist in a town where everybody has false teeth.

Victor and Thomas Builds-the-Fire were the same age, had grown up and played in the dirt together. Ever since Victor could remember, it was Thomas who always had something to say.

Once, when they were seven years old, when Victor's father still lived with the family, Thomas closed his eyes and told Victor this story: "Your father's heart is weak. He is afraid of his own family. He is afraid of you. Late at night he sits in the dark. Watches the television until there's nothing but that white noise. Sometimes he feels like he wants to buy a motorcycle and ride away. He wants to run and hide. He doesn't want to be found."

Thomas Builds-the-Fire had known that Victor's father was going to leave, knew it before anyone. Now Victor stood in the Trading Post with a one-hundred-dollar check in his hand, wondering if Thomas knew that Victor's father was dead, if he knew what was going to happen next.

Just then Thomas looked at Victor, smiled, and walked over to him.    20

"Victor, I'm sorry about your father," Thomas said.

"How did you know about it?" Victor asked.

"I heard it on the wind. I heard it from the birds. I felt it in the sunlight. Also, your mother was just in here crying."

"Oh," Victor said and looked around the Trading Post. All the other Indians stared, surprised that Victor was even talking to Thomas. Nobody talked to Thomas anymore because he told the same damn stories over and over again. Victor was embarrassed, but he thought that Thomas might be able to help him. Victor felt a sudden need for tradition.

"I can lend you the money you need," Thomas said suddenly. "But you have    25 to take me with you."

"I can't take your money," Victor said. "I mean, I haven't hardly talked to you in years. We're not really friends anymore."

"I didn't say we were friends. I said you had to take me with you."

"Let me think about it."

Victor went home with his one hundred dollars and sat at the kitchen table. He held his head in his hands and thought about Thomas Builds-the-Fire, remembered little details, tears and scars, the bicycle they shared for a summer, so many stories.

Thomas Builds-the-Fire sat on the bicycle, waited in Victor's yard. He    30 was ten years old and skinny. His hair was dirty because it was the Fourth of July.

"Victor," Thomas yelled. "Hurry up. We're going to miss the fireworks."

After a few minutes, Victor ran out of his house, jumped the porch railing, and landed gracefully on the sidewalk.

"And the judges award him a 9.95, the highest score of the summer," Thomas said, clapped, laughed.

"That was perfect, cousin," Victor said. "And it's my turn to ride the bike."

Thomas gave up the bike and they headed for the fairgrounds. It was nearly 35 dark and the fireworks were about to start.

"You know," Thomas said. "It's strange how us Indians celebrate the Fourth of July. It ain't like it was *our* independence everybody was fighting for."

"You think about things too much," Victor said. "It's just supposed to be fun. Maybe Junior will be there."

"Which Junior? Everybody on this reservation is named Junior."

And they both laughed.

The fireworks were small, hardly more than a few bottle rockets and a 40 fountain. But it was enough for two Indian boys. Years later, they would need much more.

Afterwards, sitting in the dark, fighting off mosquitoes, Victor turned to Thomas Builds-the-Fire.

"Hey," Victor said. "Tell me a story."

Thomas closed his eyes and told this story: "There were these two Indian boys who wanted to be warriors. But it was too late to be warriors in the old way. All the horses were gone. So the two Indian boys stole a car and drove to the city. They parked the stolen car in front of the police station and then hitchhiked back home to the reservation. When they got back, all their friends cheered and their parents' eyes shone with pride. *You were very brave*, everybody said to the two Indian boys. *Very brave.*"

"Ya-hey," Victor said. "That's a good one. I wish I could be a warrior."

"Me, too," Thomas said.                                                    45

They went home together in the dark, Thomas on the bike now, Victor on foot. They walked through shadows and light from streetlamps.

"We've come a long ways," Thomas said. "We have outdoor lighting."

"All I need is the stars," Victor said. "And besides, you still think about things too much."

They separated then, each headed for home, both laughing all the way.

Victor sat at his kitchen table. He counted his one hundred dollars again and 50 again. He knew he needed more to make it to Phoenix and back. He knew he needed Thomas Builds-the-Fire. So he put his money in his wallet and opened the front door to find Thomas on the porch.

"Ya-hey, Victor," Thomas said. "I knew you'd call me."

Thomas walked into the living room and sat down on Victor's favorite chair.

"I've got some money saved up," Thomas said. "It's enough to get us down there, but you have to get us back."

"I've got this hundred dollars," Victor said. "And my dad had a savings account I'm going to claim."

"How much in your dad's account?"                                          55

"Enough. A few hundred."

"Sounds good. When we leaving?"

When they were fifteen and had long since stopped being friends, Victor and Thomas got into a fistfight. That is, Victor was really drunk and beat Thomas up for no reason at all. All the other Indian boys stood around and watched it happen. Junior was there and so were Lester, Seymour, and a lot of others. The beating might have gone on until Thomas was dead if Norma Many Horses hadn't come along and stopped it.

"Hey, you boys," Norma yelled and jumped out of her car. "Leave him alone."

If it had been someone else, even another man, the Indian boys would've 60 just ignored the warnings. But Norma was a warrior. She was powerful. She could have picked up any two of the boys and smashed their skulls together. But worse than that, she would have dragged them all over to some tipi and made them listen to some elder tell a dusty old story.

The Indian boys scattered, and Norma walked over to Thomas and picked him up.

"Hey, little man, are you okay?" she asked.

Thomas gave her a thumbs up.

"Why they always picking on you?"

Thomas shook his head, closed his eyes, but no stories came to him, no 65 words or music. He just wanted to go home, to lie in his bed and let his dreams tell his stories for him.

Thomas Builds-the-Fire and Victor sat next to each other in the airplane, coach section. A tiny white woman had the window seat. She was busy twisting her body into pretzels. She was flexible.

"I have to ask," Thomas said, and Victor closed his eyes in embarrassment.

"Don't," Victor said.

"Excuse me, miss," Thomas asked. "Are you a gymnast or something?"

"There's no something about it," she said. "I was first alternate on the 1980 70 Olympic team."

"Really?" Thomas asked.

"Really."

"I mean, you used to be a world-class athlete?" Thomas asked.

"My husband still thinks I am."

Thomas Builds-the-Fire smiled. She was a mental gymnast, too. She pulled 75 her leg straight up against her body so that she could've kissed her kneecap.

"I wish I could do that," Thomas said.

Victor was ready to jump out of the plane. Thomas, that crazy Indian storyteller with ratty old braids and broken teeth, was flirting with a beautiful Olympic gymnast. Nobody back home on the reservation would ever believe it.

"Well," the gymnast said. "It's easy. Try it."

Thomas grabbed at his leg and tried to pull it up into the same position as the gymnast. He couldn't even come close, which made Victor and the gymnast laugh.

"Hey," she asked. "You two are Indian, right?" 80

"Full-blood," Victor said.

"Not me," Thomas said. "I'm half magician on my mother's side and half clown on my father's."

They all laughed.

"What are your names?" she asked.

"Victor and Thomas." 85

"Mine is Cathy. Pleased to meet you all."

The three of them talked for the duration of the flight. Cathy the gymnast complained about the government, how they screwed the 1980 Olympic team by boycotting.[2]

"Sounds like you all got a lot in common with Indians," Thomas said.

Nobody laughed.

After the plane landed in Phoenix and they had all found their way to the 90 terminal, Cathy the gymnast smiled and waved good-bye.

"She was really nice," Thomas said.

"Yeah, but everybody talks to everybody on airplanes," Victor said. "It's too bad we can't always be that way."

"You always used to tell me I think too much," Thomas said. "Now it sounds like you do."

"Maybe I caught it from you."

"Yeah." 95

Thomas and Victor rode in a taxi to the trailer where Victor's father died.

"Listen," Victor said as they stopped in front of the trailer. "I never told you I was sorry for beating you up that time."

"Oh, it was nothing. We were just kids and you were drunk."

"Yeah, but I'm still sorry."

"That's all right." 100

Victor paid for the taxi and the two of them stood in the hot Phoenix summer. They could smell the trailer.

"This ain't going to be nice," Victor said. "You don't have to go in."

"You're going to need help."

Victor walked to the front door and opened it. The stink rolled out and made them both gag. Victor's father had lain in that trailer for a week in hundred-degree temperatures before anyone found him. And the only reason anyone found him was because of the smell. They needed dental records to identify him. That's exactly what the coroner said. They needed dental records.

"Oh, man," Victor said. "I don't know if I can do this." 105

"Well, then don't."

---

[2] The United States withdrew from the 1980 Olympics in Moscow to protest the Soviet Union's invasion of Afghanistan in 1979.

"But there might be something valuable in there."

"I thought his money was in the bank."

"It is. I was talking about pictures and letters and stuff like that."

"Oh," Thomas said as he held his breath and followed Victor into the trailer.  110

When Victor was twelve, he stepped into an underground wasp nest. His foot was caught in the hole, and no matter how hard he struggled, Victor couldn't pull free. He might have died there, stung a thousand times, if Thomas Builds-the-Fire had not come by.

"Run," Thomas yelled and pulled Victor's foot from the hole. They ran then, hard as they ever had, faster than Billy Mills, faster than Jim Thorpe, faster than the wasps could fly.

Victor and Thomas ran until they couldn't breathe, ran until it was cold and dark outside, ran until they were lost and it took hours to find their way home. All the way back, Victor counted his stings.

"Seven," Victor said. "My lucky number."

Victor didn't find much to keep in the trailer. Only a photo album and a  115
stereo. Everything else had that smell stuck in it or was useless anyway.

"I guess this is all," Victor said. "It ain't much."

"Better than nothing," Thomas said.

"Yeah, and I do have the pickup."

"Yeah," Thomas said. "It's in good shape."

"Dad was good about that stuff."  120

"Yeah, I remember your dad."

"Really?" Victor asked. "What do you remember?"

Thomas Builds-the-Fire closed his eyes and told this story: "I remember when I had this dream that told me to go to Spokane, to stand by the Falls in the middle of the city and wait for a sign. I knew I had to go there but I didn't have a car. Didn't have a license. I was only thirteen. So I walked all the way, took me all day, and I finally made it to the Falls. I stood there for an hour waiting. Then your dad came walking up. *What the hell are you doing here?* he asked me. I said, *Waiting for a vision.* Then your father said, *All you're going to get here is mugged.* So he drove me over to Denny's, bought me dinner, and then drove me home to the reservation. For a long time I was mad because I thought my dreams had lied to me. But they didn't. Your dad was my vision. *Take care of each other* is what my dreams were saying. *Take care of each other.*"

Victor was quiet for a long time. He searched his mind for memories of his father, found the good ones, found a few bad ones, added it all up, and smiled.

"My father never told me about finding you in Spokane," Victor said.  125

"He said he wouldn't tell anybody. Didn't want me to get in trouble. But he said I had to watch out for you as part of the deal."

"Really?"

"Really. Your father said you would need the help. He was right."

"That's why you came down here with me, isn't it?" Victor asked.

"I came because of your father."                                                    130

Victor and Thomas climbed into the pickup, drove over to the bank, and claimed the three hundred dollars in the savings account.

Thomas Builds-the-Fire could fly.

Once, he jumped off the roof of the tribal school and flapped his arms like a crazy eagle. And he flew. For a second, he hovered, suspended above all the other Indian boys who were too smart or too scared to jump.

"He's flying," Junior yelled, and Seymour was busy looking for the trick wires or mirrors. But it was real. As real as the dirt when Thomas lost altitude and crashed to the ground.

He broke his arm in two places.                                                     135

"He broke his wing," Victor chanted, and the other Indian boys joined in, made it a tribal song.

"He broke his wing, he broke his wing, he broke his wing," all the Indian boys chanted as they ran off, flapping their wings, wishing they could fly, too. They hated Thomas for his courage, his brief moment as a bird. Everybody has dreams about flying. Thomas flew.

One of his dreams came true for just a second, just enough to make it real.

Victor's father, his ashes, fit in one wooden box with enough left over to fill a cardboard box.

"He always was a big man," Thomas said.                                             140

Victor carried part of his father and Thomas carried the rest out to the pickup. They set him down carefully behind the seats, put a cowboy hat on the wooden box and a Dodgers cap on the cardboard box. That's the way it was supposed to be.

"Ready to head back home?" Victor asked.

"It's going to be a long drive."

"Yeah, take a couple days, maybe."

"We can take turns," Thomas said.                                                   145

"Okay," Victor said, but they didn't take turns. Victor drove for sixteen hours straight north, made it halfway up Nevada toward home before he finally pulled over.

"Hey, Thomas," Victor said. "You got to drive for a while."

"Okay."

Thomas Builds-the-Fire slid behind the wheel and started off down the road. All through Nevada, Thomas and Victor had been amazed at the lack of animal life, at the absence of water, of movement.

"Where is everything?" Victor had asked more than once.                            150

Now when Thomas was finally driving they saw the first animal, maybe the only animal in Nevada. It was a long-eared jackrabbit.

"Look," Victor yelled. "It's alive."

Thomas and Victor were busy congratulating themselves on their discovery when the jackrabbit darted out into the road and under the wheels of the pickup.

"Stop the goddamn car," Victor yelled, and Thomas did stop, backed the pickup to the dead jackrabbit.

"Oh, man, he's dead," Victor said as he looked at the squashed animal.   155
"Really dead."

"The only thing alive in this whole state and we just killed it."

"I don't know," Thomas said. "I think it was suicide."

Victor looked around the desert, sniffed the air, felt the emptiness and loneliness, and nodded his head.

"Yeah," Victor said. "It had to be suicide."   160

"I can't believe this," Thomas said. "You drive for a thousand miles and there ain't even any bugs smashed on the windshield. I drive for ten seconds and kill the only living thing in Nevada."

"Yeah," Victor said. "Maybe I should drive."

"Maybe you should."

Thomas Builds-the-Fire walked through the corridors of the tribal school by himself. Nobody wanted to be anywhere near him because of all those stories. Story after story.

Thomas closed his eyes and this story came to him: "We are all given one   165
thing by which our lives are measured, one determination. Mine are the stories which can change or not change the world. It doesn't matter which as long as I continue to tell the stories. My father, he died on Okinawa in World War II, died fighting for this country, which had tried to kill him for years. My mother, she died giving birth to me, died while I was still inside her. She pushed me out into the world with her last breath. I have no brothers or sisters. I have only my stories which came to me before I even had the words to speak. I learned a thousand stories before I took my first thousand steps. They are all I have. It's all I can do."

Thomas Builds-the-Fire told his stories to all those who would stop and listen. He kept telling them long after people had stopped listening.

Victor and Thomas made it back to the reservation just as the sun was rising. It was the beginning of a new day on earth, but the same old shit on the reservation.

"Good morning," Thomas said.

"Good morning."

The tribe was waking up, ready for work, eating breakfast, reading the news-   170
paper, just like everybody else does. Willene LeBret was out in her garden wearing a bathrobe. She waved when Thomas and Victor drove by.

"Crazy Indians made it," she said to herself and went back to her roses.

Victor stopped the pickup in front of Thomas Builds-the-Fire's HUD house.[3] They both yawned, stretched a little, shook dust from their bodies.

---

[3] The Department of Housing and Urban Development, an agency of the U.S. government, provides subsidized housing for low-income persons.

"I'm tired," Victor said.

"Of everything," Thomas added.

They both searched for words to end the journey. Victor needed to thank 175
Thomas for his help, for the money, and make the promise to pay it all back.

"Don't worry about the money," Thomas said. "It don't make any difference
anyhow."

"Probably not, enit?"

"Nope."

Victor knew that Thomas would remain the crazy storyteller who talked
to dogs and cars, who listened to the wind and pine trees. Victor knew that he
couldn't really be friends with Thomas, even after all that had happened. It was
cruel but it was real. As real as the ashes, as Victor's father, sitting behind the seats.

"I know how it is," Thomas said. "I know you ain't going to treat me any 180
better than you did before. I know your friends would give you too much shit
about it."

Victor was ashamed of himself. Whatever happened to the tribal ties, the
sense of community? The only real thing he shared with anybody was a bottle
and broken dreams. He owed Thomas something, anything.

"Listen," Victor said and handed Thomas the cardboard box which contained half of his father. "I want you to have this."

Thomas took the ashes and smiled, closed his eyes, and told this story: "I'm
going to travel to Spokane Falls one last time and toss these ashes into the
water. And your father will rise like a salmon, leap over the bridge, over me,
and find his way home. It will be beautiful. His teeth will shine like silver, like a
rainbow. He will rise, Victor, he will rise."

Victor smiled.

"I was planning on doing the same thing with my half," Victor said. "But I 185
didn't imagine my father looking anything like a salmon. I thought it'd be like
cleaning the attic or something. Like letting things go after they've stopped
having any use."

"Nothing stops, cousin," Thomas said. "Nothing stops."

Thomas Builds-the-Fire got out of the pickup and walked up his driveway.
Victor started the pickup and began the drive home.

"Wait," Thomas yelled suddenly from his porch. "I just got to ask one favor."

Victor stopped the pickup, leaned out the window, and shouted back. "What
do you want?"

"Just one time when I'm telling a story somewhere, why don't you stop and 190
listen?" Thomas asked.

"Just once?"

"Just once."

Victor waved his arms to let Thomas know that the deal was good. It was
a fair trade, and that was all Victor had ever wanted from his whole life. So
Victor drove his father's pickup toward home while Thomas went into his
house, closed the door behind him, and heard a new story come to him in the
silence afterwards.

## FOR ANALYSIS

**1.** Explain the title. What does "This" refer to?

**2.** When they were boys, Victor would chide Thomas for thinking too much. Why did he do so? What does Thomas think about?

**3.** What is the significance of Thomas's conversation with Cathy, the Olympic gymnast, during the plane ride to Phoenix?

**4.** Why has Thomas evoked such dislike and hostility in Victor and others of the tribe?

**5.** Why is Victor drawn to Thomas despite the embarrassment he feels at being seen with the reservation pariah?

**6.** How does Victor change in the course of the story?

**7.** Explain the final sentence.

## MAKING ARGUMENTS

The narrator interrupts the flashback describing the Fourth of July celebration to remark, "Years later, they would need much more" (para. 40). Using evidence from the narrative (which takes place years after this event), make an argument that the story either throws light on the meaning of this comment or does not support it.

## WRITING TOPICS

**1.** This story, taken from Alexie's book *The Lone Ranger and Tonto Fistfight in Heaven*, is the basis for the 1998 movie *Smoke Signals* (available to rent or stream). After viewing the movie, write a paper about how the story was expanded and changed for the film version.

**2.** Analyze the ways in which Alexie creates a comic **tone** in this story.

## MAKING CONNECTIONS

Compare this story and Ernest Hemingway's "Hills Like White Elephants" (p. 594) as stories that rely heavily on **dialogue** rather than narration.

# POETRY

## JONATHAN SWIFT (1667–1745)

## MARKET WOMEN'S CRIES

### APPLES

Come buy my fine wares,
Plums, apples and pears.
A hundred a penny,
In conscience too many:
Come, will you have any?
My children are seven,
I wish them in Heaven;
My husband's a sot,
With his pipe and his pot,
Not a farthen[1] will gain them,          10
And I must maintain them.

### ONIONS

Come, follow me by the smell,
Here are delicate onions to sell;
I promise to use you well.
They make the blood warmer,
You'll feed like a farmer;
For this is every cook's opinion,
No savoury dish without an onion;
But, lest your kissing should be spoiled,
Your onions must be thoroughly boiled:       20
    Or else you may spare
    Your mistress a share,

[1] A former British monetary unit equal to one fourth of a penny.

The secret will never be known:
  She cannot discover
  The breath of her lover,
But think it as sweet as her own.


## HERRINGS

  Be not sparing,
  Leave off swearing.
  Buy my herring
  Fresh from Malahide,                                               30
  Better never was tried.
Come, eat them with pure fresh butter and mustard,
Their bellies are soft, and as white as a custard.
Come, sixpence a dozen, to get me some bread,
Or, like my own herrings, I soon shall be dead.

### FOR ANALYSIS

**1.** What is the scene of this poem? Do you imagine it is a common one for poetry? Why or why not?

**2.** Are these the typical things you would expect someone selling items at a market to say? Do you think Swift ever heard any market women actually say them?

**3.** Characterize the movement in each of the three **stanzas** from their opening to their ending. How do they change? What are the effects?

### MAKING ARGUMENTS

Imagine someone who is critical of Swift's poem for its emphasis on the unhappiness of these women. On what grounds might this critic make this argument? Why is this emphasis a problem? What alternative might Swift have pursued?

### WRITING TOPICS

**1.** Imagine writing a modern "Market Women's Cries." Where would you set it? What would you have them selling? What would they say about their wares and their lives?

**2.** Think about the speakers in this poem in terms of their identity. How do you imagine they are seen — classified, evaluated — by others? How do you think they see themselves? What if anything does the poem have to say about their identity (or identities)?

### MAKING CONNECTIONS

Both "Market Women's Cries" and Sandburg's "I Am the People, the Mob" (p. 355) are about regular people rather than kings, or knights, or princesses. How does each poem treat its subject? What does each have to say about everyday life?

## WALT WHITMAN (1819–1892)

## FROM SONG OF MYSELF 1855

### 1

I celebrate myself, and sing myself,
And what I assume you shall assume,
For every atom belonging to me as good belongs to you.

I loafe and invite my soul,
I lean and loafe at my ease observing a spear of summer grass.

My tongue, every atom of my blood, form'd from this soil, this air,
Born here of parents born here from parents the same, and their parents
      the same,
I, now thirty-seven years old in perfect health begin,
Hoping to cease not till death.

Creeds and schools in abeyance,                      10
Retiring back a while sufficed at what they are, but never forgotten,
I harbor for good or bad, I permit to speak at every hazard,
Nature without check with original energy.

### 6

A child said *What is the grass?* fetching it to me with full hands;
How could I answer the child? I do not know what it is any more than he.

I guess it must be the flag of my disposition, out of hopeful green stuff woven.

Or I guess it is the handkerchief of the Lord,
A scented gift and remembrancer designedly dropt,
Bearing the owner's name someway in the corners, that we may see and
      remark, and say *Whose?*

Or I guess the grass is itself a child, the produced babe of the vegetation.    20

Or I guess it is a uniform hieroglyphic,
And it means, Sprouting alike in broad zones and narrow zones,
Growing among black folks as among white,
Kanuck, Tuckahoe, Congressman, Cuff, I give them the same, I receive them the
      same.

And now it seems to me the beautiful uncut hair of graves.

Tenderly will I use you curling grass,
It may be you transpire from the breasts of young men,
It may be if I had known them I would have loved them,
It may be you are from old people, or from offspring taken soon out of
    their mothers' laps,
And here you are the mothers' laps.              30

This grass is very dark to be from the white heads of old mothers,
Darker than the colorless beards of old men,
Dark to come from under the faint red roofs of mouths.

O I perceive after all so many uttering tongues,
And I perceive they do not come from the roofs of mouths for nothing.

I wish I could translate the hints about the dead young men and women,
And the hints about old men and mothers, and the offspring taken soon out
    of their laps.

What do you think has become of the young and old men?
And what do you think has become of the women and children?

They are alive and well somewhere,              40
The smallest sprout shows there is really no death,
And if ever there was it led forward life, and does not wait at the end to arrest it,
And ceas'd the moment life appear'd.

All goes onward and outward, nothing collapses,
And to die is different from what anyone supposed, and luckier.

## 50

There is that in me — I do not know what it is — but I know it is in me.

Wrench'd and sweaty — calm and cool then my body becomes,
I sleep — I sleep long.

I do not know it — it is without name — it is a word unsaid,
It is not in any dictionary, utterance, symbol.          50

Sometimes it swings on more than the earth I swing on,
To it the creation is the friend whose embracing awakes me.

Perhaps I might tell more. Outlines! I plead for my brothers and sisters.

Do you see O my brothers and sisters?
It is not chaos or death — it is form, union, plan — it is eternal life — it is Happiness.

## 51

The past and present wilt — I have fill'd them, emptied them.
And proceed to fill my next fold of the future.

Listener up there! what have you to confide to me?
Look in my face while I snuff the sidle of evening,
(Talk honestly, no one else hears you, and I stay only a minute longer.)    60

Do I contradict myself?
Very well then I contradict myself.
(I am large, I contain multitudes.)

I concentrate toward them that are nigh, I wait on the door-slab.

Who has done his day's work? who will soonest be through with his supper?
Who wishes to walk with me?

Will you speak before I am gone? will you prove already too late?

## 52

The spotted hawk swoops by and accuses me, he complains of my gab
        and my loitering.

I too am not a bit tamed, I too am untranslatable,
I sound my barbaric yawp over the roofs of the world.    70

The last scud of day holds back for me,
It flings my likeness after the rest and true as any on the shadowed wilds,
It coaxes me to the vapor and the dusk.

I depart as air, I shake my white locks at the runaway sun,
I effuse my flesh in eddies, and drift it in lacy jags.

I bequeath myself to the dirt to grow from the grass I love,
If you want me again look for me under your boot-soles.

You will hardly know who I am or what I mean,
But I shall be good health to you nevertheless,
And filter and fibre your blood.    80

Failing to fetch me at first keep encouraged,
Missing me one place search another,
I stop somewhere waiting for you.

## FOR ANALYSIS

**1.** Who or what is the speaker of this poem? List the lines in which he seems to be an individual speaker. Then make a list of the lines in which he seems to be something more.

**2.** The poem from which these excerpts are drawn is part of a book, *Leaves of Grass*. Why does this poem pay so much attention to grass? What does it mean?

**3.** How does this poem "contain multitudes" (l. 63)?

## MAKING ARGUMENTS

Some critics at the time *Leaves of Grass* was published (and since) have criticized it as self-involved. Make an argument, on the evidence of this excerpt from one of its poems, that refutes this criticism. How is it about more than the poet or speaker? How does it use this personal, singing-of-itself voice to be about more than the poet's interest in himself?

## WRITING TOPICS

**1.** Whitman writes, "You will hardly know who I am or what I mean, / But I shall be good health to you nevertheless" (ll. 78–79). How might this poem be intended to be "good" for its readers?

**2.** "Song of Myself" achieves strong and varied effects. Reread the poem, and keep a log of your reactions — your emotional, intellectual, and hard-to-categorize responses — as you encounter the different parts of the poem. Then write a reflection on this log. Do you see any patterns? As you moved again through "Song of Myself," what did you notice about how it works as a poem and on you as a reader?

## EMILY DICKINSON    (1830–1886)

# I'M NOBODY! WHO ARE YOU?    CA. 1861, 1891

I'm Nobody! Who are you?
Are you — Nobody — Too?
Then there's a pair of us!
Don't tell! they'd advertise — you know!

How dreary — to be — Somebody!
How public — like a Frog —
To tell one's name — the livelong June —
To an admiring Bog!

## JAMES WELDON JOHNSON (1871–1938)

# A POET TO HIS BABY SON 1935

Tiny bit of humanity,
Blessed with your mother's face,
And cursed with your father's mind.

I say cursed with your father's mind,
Because you can lie so long and so quietly on your back,
Playing with the dimpled big toe of your left foot,
And looking away,
Through the ceiling of the room, and beyond.
Can it be that already you are thinking of being a poet?

Why don't you kick and howl,                                            10
And make the neighbors talk about
"That damned baby next door,"
And make up your mind forthwith
To grow up and be a banker
Or a politician or some other sort of go-getter
Or—?—whatever you decide upon,
Rid yourself of these incipient thoughts
About being a poet.

For poets no longer are makers of songs,
Chanters of the gold and purple harvest,                               20
Sayers of the glories of earth and sky,
Of the sweet pain of love
And the keen joy of living;
No longer dreamers of the essential dreams,
And interpreters of the eternal truth,
Through the eternal beauty.
Poets these days are unfortunate fellows.
Baffled in trying to say old things in a new way
Or new things in an old language,
They talk abracadabra                                                  30
In an unknown tongue,
Each one fashioning for himself
A wordy world of shadow problems,
And as a self-imagined Atlas,
Struggling under it with puny legs and arms,
Groaning out incoherent complaints at his load.

My son, this is no time nor place for a poet;
Grow up and join the big, busy crowd
That scrambles for what it thinks it wants
Out of this old world which is — as it is —                              40
And, probably, always will be.

Take the advice of a father who knows:
You cannot begin too young
Not to be a poet.

## FOR ANALYSIS

**1.** What is this poem's **tone**? Does it have more than one?

**2.** What did you expect the poem to be like based on the poem's title and opening lines? How did it meet or not meet your expectations?

**3.** Why does the speaker think his son shouldn't grow up to be a poet?

## MAKING ARGUMENTS

You will hear people say the same things about poets and poetry today that Johnson wrote eighty years ago. Citing his specific claims about poetry in 1935 and applying them to the contemporary scene, argue for or against those claims, using as evidence contemporary poems in this book or that you know from elsewhere and any other support you think relevant.

## WRITING TOPICS

**1.** Many poems are in part about poetry itself. What does this poem have to say specifically about poetry? Paraphrase its thoughts about the state of the genre.

**2.** "A Poet to His Baby Son" would not be what it is without the skillful use of **irony**. List the different ways and moments in which Johnson uses irony. What is the effect on you as you read? How is that effect different than it might be if Johnson's sentiments were expressed more directly?

## T. S. ELIOT  (1888–1965)

# THE LOVE SONG OF
# J. ALFRED PRUFROCK   1917

*S'io credessi che mia risposta fosse*
*a persona che mai tornasse al mondo,*
*questa fiamma staria senza più scosse.*
*Ma per ciò che giammai di questo fondo*

*non tornò vivo alcun, s'i'odo il vero,*
*senza tema d'infamia ti rispondo.*[1]

Let us go then, you and I,
When the evening is spread out against the sky
Like a patient etherized upon a table;
Let us go, through certain half-deserted streets,
The muttering retreats
Of restless nights in one-night cheap hotels
And sawdust restaurants with oyster shells:
Streets that follow like a tedious argument
Of insidious intent
To lead you to an overwhelming question . . .                   10
Oh, do not ask, "What is it?"
Let us go and make our visit.

In the room the women come and go
Talking of Michelangelo.

The yellow fog that rubs its back upon the windowpanes,
The yellow smoke that rubs its muzzle on the windowpanes
Licked its tongue into the corners of the evening,
Lingered upon the pools that stand in drains,
Let fall upon its back the soot that falls from chimneys,
Slipped by the terrace, made a sudden leap,                      20
And seeing that it was a soft October night,
Curled once about the house, and fell asleep.

And indeed there will be time
For the yellow smoke that slides along the street,
Rubbing its back upon the windowpanes;
There will be time, there will be time
To prepare a face to meet the faces that you meet;
There will be time to murder and create,
And time for all the works and days of hands
That lift and drop a question on your plate;                     30
Time for you and time for me,
And time yet for a hundred indecisions,
And for a hundred visions and revisions,
Before the taking of a toast and tea.

---

[1] From Dante, *Inferno*, XXVII, 61–66. The speaker is Guido da Montefeltro, who is imprisoned in a flame in the level of hell reserved for false counselors. He tells Dante and Virgil, "If I thought my answer were given to one who might return to the world, this flame would stay without further movement. But since from this depth none has ever returned alive, if what I hear is true, I answer you without fear of infamy."

In the room the women come and go
Talking of Michelangelo.

And indeed there will be time
To wonder, "Do I dare?" and, "Do I dare?"
Time to turn back and descend the stair,
With a bald spot in the middle of my hair — 40
(They will say: "How his hair is growing thin!")
My morning coat, my collar mounting firmly to the chin,
My necktie rich and modest, but asserted by a simple pin —
(They will say: "But how his arms and legs are thin!")
Do I dare
Disturb the universe?
In a minute there is time
For decisions and revisions which a minute will reverse.

For I have known them all already, known them all —
Have known the evenings, mornings, afternoons, 50
I have measured out my life with coffee spoons;
I know the voices dying with a dying fall
Beneath the music from a farther room.
　　So how should I presume?

And I have known the eyes already, known them all —
The eyes that fix you in a formulated phrase,
And when I am formulated, sprawling on a pin,
When I am pinned and wriggling on the wall,
Then how should I begin
To spit out all the butt-ends of my days and ways? 60
　　And how should I presume?

And I have known the arms already, known them all —
Arms that are braceleted and white and bare
(But in the lamplight, downed with light brown hair!)
Is it perfume from a dress
That makes me so digress?
Arms that lie along a table, or wrap about a shawl.
　　And should I then presume?
　　And how should I begin?

　　　　　　　.　.　.　.

Shall I say, I have gone at dusk through narrow streets 70
And watched the smoke that rises from the pipes
Of lonely men in shirt-sleeves, leaning out of windows? . . .

I should have been a pair of ragged claws
Scuttling across the floors of silent seas.

> . . . .

And the afternoon, the evening, sleeps so peacefully!
Smoothed by long fingers,
Asleep . . . tired . . . or it malingers,
Stretched on the floor, here beside you and me.
Should I, after tea and cakes and ices,
Have the strength to force the moment to its crisis?                          80
But though I have wept and fasted, wept and prayed,
Though I have seen my head (grown slightly bald) brought in upon a platter,[2]
I am no prophet — and here's no great matter;
I have seen the moment of my greatness flicker,
And I have seen the eternal Footman hold my coat, and snicker,
And in short, I was afraid.

And would it have been worth it, after all,
After the cups, the marmalade, the tea,
Among the porcelain, among some talk of you and me,
Would it have been worth while,                                              90
To have bitten off the matter with a smile,
To have squeezed the universe into a ball
To roll it toward some overwhelming question,
To say: "I am Lazarus,[3] come from the dead,
Come back to tell you all, I shall tell you all" —
If one, settling a pillow by her head,
      Should say: "That is not what I meant at all.
      That is not it, at all."

And would it have been worth it, after all,
Would it have been worth while,                                             100
After the sunsets and the dooryards and the sprinkled streets,
After the novels, after the teacups, after the skirts that trail along the floor —
And this, and so much more? —
It is impossible to say just what I mean!
But as if a magic lantern threw the nerves in patterns on a screen:
Would it have been worth while
If one, settling a pillow or throwing off a shawl,
And turning toward the window, should say:
      "That is not it at all,
      That is not what I meant, at all."                                    110

> . . . .

---

[2] Like the head of John the Baptist. See Matthew 14:3–12.
[3] See John 11:1–14 and Luke 16:19–26.

No! I am not Prince Hamlet, nor was meant to be;
Am an attendant lord, one that will do
To swell a progress,° start a scene or two,                              state journey
Advise the prince; no doubt, an easy tool,
Deferential, glad to be of use,
Politic, cautious, and meticulous;
Full of high sentence,° but a bit obtuse;                               sententiousness
At times, indeed, almost ridiculous —
Almost, at times, the Fool.

I grow old . . . I grow old . . .                                        120
I shall wear the bottoms of my trousers rolled.°                        cuffed

Shall I part my hair behind? Do I dare to eat a peach?
I shall wear white flannel trousers, and walk upon the beach.
I have heard the mermaids singing, each to each.

I do not think that they will sing to me.

I have seen them riding seaward on the waves
Combing the white hair of the waves blown back
When the wind blows the water white and black.

We have lingered in the chambers of the sea
By sea-girls wreathed with seaweed red and brown                        130
Till human voices wake us, and we drown.

## FOR ANALYSIS

**1.** This poem may be understood as a **stream of consciousness** passing through the mind of Prufrock. The "you and I" of line 1 may be different aspects of his personality. Or perhaps the "you and I" is parallel to Guido da Montefeltro, who speaks the epigraph, and Dante, to whom he tells the story that resulted in his damnation — hence, "you" is the reader and "I" is Prufrock. The poem is disjointed because it proceeds by psychological rather than logical stages. To what social class does Prufrock belong? How does Prufrock respond to the attitudes and values of his class? Does he change in the course of the poem?

**2.** Line 92 provides a good example of literary **allusion** (see the last stanza of Marvell's "To His Coy Mistress," p. 977). How does an awareness of the allusion contribute to your response?

**3.** What might the song of the mermaids (l. 124) signify, and why does Prufrock think they will not sing to him (l. 125)?

**4.** T. S. Eliot once said that some poetry "can communicate without being understood." Is this such a poem?

**MAKING ARGUMENTS**

Upon the poem's publication, one reviewer wrote, "The fact that these things occurred to the mind of Mr. Eliot is surely of the very smallest importance to anyone, even to himself. They certainly have no relation to poetry." Regardless of whether you agree with this dismissive reviewer, construct an argument for the importance of the things that occurred to Eliot's mind. Make your argument in terms of this poem specifically but also as a defense of poetry in general.

**WRITING TOPIC**

What sort of man is J. Alfred Prufrock? How does the poet establish his characteristics?

## HOWARD NEMEROV    (1920–1991)

# MONEY    1977

*an introductory lecture*

This morning we shall spend a few minutes
Upon the study of symbolism, which is basic
To the nature of money. I show you this nickel.
Icons and cryptograms are written all over
The nickel: one side shows a hunchbacked bison
Bending his head and curling his tail to accommodate
The circular nature of money. Over him arches
UNITED STATES OF AMERICA, and, squinched in
Between that and his rump, E PLURIBUS UNUM,
A Roman reminiscence that appears to mean                                    10
An indeterminately large number of things
All of which are the same. Under the bison
A straight line giving him a ground to stand on
Reads FIVE CENTS. And on the other side of our nickel
There is the profile of a man with long hair
And a couple of feathers in the hair; we know
Somehow that he is an American Indian, and
He wears the number nineteen-thirty-six.
Right in front of his eyes the word LIBERTY, bent
To conform with the curve of the rim, appears                               20
To be falling out of the sky Y first; the Indian
Keeps his eyes downcast and does not notice this;
To notice it, indeed, would be shortsighted of him.
So much for the iconography of one of our nickels,

Which is now becoming a rarity and something of
A collectors' item: for as a matter of fact
There is almost nothing you can buy with a nickel,
The representative American Indian was destroyed
A hundred years or so ago, and his descendants'
Relations with liberty are maintained with reservations,          30
Or primitive concentration camps; while the bison,
Except for a few examples kept in cages,
Is now extinct. Something like that, I think,
Is what Keats must have meant in his celebrated
Ode on a Grecian Urn.
                    Notice, in conclusion,
A number of circumstances sometimes overlooked
Even by experts: (*a*) Indian and bison,
Confined to obverse and reverse of the coin,
Can never see each other; (*b*) they are looking          40
In opposite directions, the bison past
The Indian's feathers, the Indian past
The bison's tail; (*c*) they are upside down
To one another; (*d*) the bison has a human face
Somewhat resembling that of Jupiter Ammon.
I hope that our studies today will have shown you
Something of the import of symbolism
With respect to the understanding of what is symbolized.

## FOR ANALYSIS

**1.** What object is the poem's speaker describing? Why do you think Nemerov chose that object in particular?

**2.** What are the different ways in which **symbolism** is basic to the nature of money?

**3.** What is your "understanding of what is symbolized" (l. 48) in this poem?

## MAKING ARGUMENTS

Regardless of your own feelings, argue against Nemerov's implicit reading of U.S. history. What would such an argument say about the history of European contact, settlement, and displacement? What would it say about the ideals enshrined on U.S. currency?

## WRITING TOPIC

Find another everyday item that can be seen as a **symbol** of larger things and look at it in the way Nemerov's poem looks at the buffalo nickel. What do you see?

## MAKING CONNECTIONS

Explain Nemerov's **allusion** to John Keats's "Ode on a Grecian Urn" (p. 889). What is it that Keats "must have meant"?

## ETHERIDGE KNIGHT (1931–1991)

# HARD ROCK RETURNS TO PRISON FROM THE HOSPITAL FOR THE CRIMINAL INSANE 1968

Hard Rock was "known not to take no shit
From nobody," and he had the scars to prove it:
Split purple lips, lumped ears, welts above
His yellow eyes, and one long scar that cut
Across his temple and plowed through a thick
Canopy of kinky hair.

The WORD was that Hard Rock wasn't a mean nigger
Anymore, that the doctors had bored a hole in his head,
Cut out part of his brain, and shot electricity
Through the rest. When they brought Hard Rock back,          10
Handcuffed and chained, he was turned loose,
Like a freshly gelded stallion, to try his new status.
And we all waited and watched, like Indians at a corral,
To see if the WORD was true.

As we waited we wrapped ourselves in the cloak
Of his exploits: "Man, the last time, it took eight
Screws to put him in the Hole." "Yeah, remember when he
Smacked the captain with his dinner tray?" "He set
The record for time in the Hole — 67 straight days!"
"Ol Hard Rock! man, that's one crazy nigger."                20
And then the jewel of a myth that Hard Rock had once bit
A screw on the thumb and poisoned him with syphilitic spit.

The testing came, to see if Hard Rock was really tame.
A hillbilly called him a black son of a bitch
And didn't lose his teeth, a screw who knew Hard Rock
From before shook him down and barked in his face.
And Hard Rock did nothing. Just grinned and looked silly,
His eyes empty like knot holes in a fence.

And even after we discovered that it took Hard Rock
Exactly 3 minutes to tell you his first name,                30
We told ourselves that he had just wised up,
Was being cool; but we could not fool ourselves for long,
And we turned away, our eyes on the ground. Crushed.

He had been our Destroyer, the doer of things
We dreamed of doing but could not bring ourselves to do,
The fears of years, like a biting whip,
Had cut grooves too deeply across our backs.

# MARGE PIERCY  (B. 1936)

## BARBIE DOLL  1973

This girlchild was born as usual
and presented dolls that did pee-pee
and miniature GE stoves and irons
and wee lipsticks the color of cherry candy.
Then in the magic of puberty, a classmate said:
You have a great big nose and fat legs.

She was healthy, tested intelligent,
possessed strong arms and back,
abundant sexual drive and manual dexterity.
She went to and fro apologizing.                                    10
Everyone saw a fat nose on thick legs.

She was advised to play coy,
exhorted to come on hearty,
exercise, diet, smile and wheedle.
Her good nature wore out
like a fan belt.
So she cut off her nose and her legs
and offered them up.

In the casket displayed on satin she lay
with the undertaker's cosmetics painted on,                         20
a turned-up putty nose,
dressed in a pink and white nightie.
Doesn't she look pretty? everyone said.
Consummation at last.
To every woman a happy ending.

### FOR ANALYSIS

**1.** In what way does this poem have a "happy ending" (l. 25)? Is it really happy?

**2.** List the characteristics attributed to the girl in the poem. Which are judged by others to be important? Which are judged unimportant? Why?

**3.** Why does the girl apologize? Should she?

## MAKING ARGUMENTS

People have long argued over what makes boys and girls conform to society's expectations. Some argue that the differences are genetic: that boys and girls are intrinsically different. Others argue that gendered behavior is socialized: that differences come not from nature but from nurture. Where do you stand on this argument? What evidence could you cite to support your position?

## WRITING TOPIC

Reflect on the turn in line 17. Why is this an unusual moment? What are its effects? Why do you think Piercy chooses to have something like this happen?

## KAY RYAN   (B. 1945)

# ALL SHALL BE RESTORED   1996

The grains shall be collected
from the thousand shores
to which they found their way,
and the boulder restored,
and the boulder itself replaced
in the cliff, and likewise
the cliff shall rise
or subside until the plate of earth
is without fissure. Restoration
knows no half measure. It will                                    10
not stop when the treasured and lost
bronze horse remounts the steps.
Even this horse will founder backward
to coin, cannon, and domestic pots,
which themselves shall bubble and
drain back to green veins in stone.
And every word written shall lift off
letter by letter, the backward text
read ever briefer, ever more antic
in its effort to insist that nothing                             20
shall be lost.

## FOR ANALYSIS

**1.** What process is being reversed in lines 1–9? In lines 10–16? What kind of processes are these? Are they actually reversible?

**2.** What does the last sentence add to the poem's meaning? How is the last clause — "nothing shall be lost" — related to the poem's title?

**3.** Describe the **style** of the poem. What kind of voice does Ryan create? How does she do it?

## MAKING ARGUMENTS

"All Shall Be Restored" focuses on loss. How would you make an argument that life is not a march from birth to death but rather a cycle? How, on the evidence of what you know about the natural world and the social world, could life be read not as tending inexorably toward loss but rather as a never-ending process of change?

## WRITING TOPIC

One of the most important facts of human experience is that it ends — at least in the case of individual life. Many different aspects of human culture can be seen, in part, to be dealing with this eventuality: either accepting this natural process or working against it. What does "All Shall Be Restored" say about the way people deal with death?

## JUAN FELIPE HERRERA    (B. 1948)

# 187 REASONS MEXICANOS CAN'T CROSS THE BORDER (REMIX)    1994

> — *Abutebaris modo subjunctivo denuo.*[1]

Because Lou Dobbs has been misusing the subjunctive again
Because our suitcases are made with biodegradable maguey fibers
Because we still resemble La Malinche
Because multiplication is our favorite sport
Because we'll dig a tunnel to Seattle
Because Mexico needs us to keep the peso from sinking
Because the Berlin Wall is on the way through Veracruz
Because we just learned we are Huichol
Because someone made our IDs out of corn
Because our border thirst is insatiable                                        10
Because we're on peyote & Coca-Cola & Banamex
Because it's Indian land stolen from our mothers
Because we're too emotional when it comes to our mothers
Because we've been doing it for over five hundred years already
Because it's too easy to say "I am from here"
Because Latin American petrochemical juice flows first
Because what would we do in El Norte
Because Nahuatl, Mayan & Chicano will spread to Canada
Because Zedillo & Salinas & Fox are still on vacation
Because the World Bank needs our abuelita's account                            20
Because the CIA trains better with brown targets

---

[1] You've been misusing the subjunctive again.

Because our accent is unable to hide U.S. colonialism
Because what will the Hispanik MBAs do
Because our voice resembles La Llorona's
Because we are still voting
Because the North is really South
Because we can read about it in an ethnic prison
Because Frida beat us to it
Because U.S. & European Corporations would rather visit us first
Because environmental U.S. industrial pollution suits our color          30
Because of a new form of Overnight Mayan Anarchy
Because there are enough farmworkers in California already
Because we're meant to usher a postmodern gloom into Mexico
Because Nabisco, Exxon, & Union Carbide gave us Mal de Ojo
Because every nacho chip can morph into a Mexican Wrestler
Because it's better to be rootless, unconscious, & rapeable
Because we're destined to have the "Go Back to Mexico" Blues
Because of Pancho Villa's hidden treasure in Chihuahua
Because of Bogart's hidden treasure in the Sierra Madre
Because we need more murals honoring our Indian Past          40
Because we are really dark French Creoles in a Cantínflas costume
Because of this Aztec reflex to sacrifice ourselves
Because we couldn't clean up hurricane Katrina
Because of this Spanish penchant to be polite and aggressive
Because we had a vision of Sor Juana in drag
Because we smell of tamales soaked in Tequila
Because we got hooked listening to Indian Jazz in Chiapas
Because we're still waiting to be cosmic
Because our passport says we're out of date
Because our organ donor got lost in a Bingo game          50
Because we got to learn English first & get in line & pay a little fee
Because we're understanding & appreciative of our Capitalist neighbors
Because our 500-year penance was not severe enough
Because we're still running from La Migra
Because we're still kissing the Pope's hand
Because we're still practicing to be Franciscan priests
Because they told us to sit & meditate & chant "Nosotros los Pobres"
Because of the word "Revolución" & the words "Viva Zapata"
Because we rely more on brujas than lawyers
Because we never finished our Ph.D. in Total United Service          60
Because our identity got mixed up with passion
Because we have visions instead of televisions
Because our huaraches are made with Goodyear & Uniroyal
Because the pesticides on our skin are still glowing
Because it's too easy to say "American Citizen" in cholo
Because you can't shrink-wrap enchiladas

Because a Spy in Spanish sounds too much like "Es Pie" in English
Because our comadres are an International Political Party
Because we believe in The Big Chingazo Theory of the Universe
Because we're still holding our breath in the Presidential Palace in                70
    Mexico City
Because every Mexican is a Living Theatre of Rebellion
Because Hollywood needs its subject matter in proper folkloric costume
Because the Grammys & iTunes are finally out in Spanish
Because the Right is writing an epic poem of apology for our proper edification
Because the Alamo really is pronounced "Alamadre"
Because the Mayan concept of zero means "U.S. Out of Mexico"
Because the oldest ceiba in Yucatán is prophetic
Because England is making plans
Because we can have Nicaragua, Honduras, & Panama anyway
Because 125 million Mexicans can be wrong                                           80
Because we'll smuggle an earthquake into New York
Because we'll organize like the Vietnamese in San José
Because we'll organize like the Mixtecos in Fresno
Because East L.A. is sinking
Because the Christian Coalition doesn't cater at César Chávez Parque
Because you can't make mace out of beans
Because the computers can't pronounce our names
Because the National Border Police are addicted to us
Because Africa will follow
Because we're still dressed in black rebozos                                        90
Because we might sing a corrido at any moment
Because our land grants are still up for grabs
Because our tattoos are indecipherable
Because people are hanging milagros on the 2,000 miles of border wire
Because we're locked into Magical Realism
Because Mexican dependence is a form of higher learning
Because making chilaquiles leads to plastic explosives
Because a simple Spanish Fly can mutate into a raging Bird Flu
Because we eat too many carbohydrates
Because we gave enough blood at the Smithfield, Inc., slaughterhouse in            100
    Tar Heel, North Carolina
Because a quinceañera will ruin the concept of American virginity
Because huevos rancheros are now being served at Taco Bell as Wavoritos
Because every Mexican grito undermines English intonation
Because the President has a Mexican maid
Because the Vice President has a Mexican maid
Because it's Rosa López's fault O.J. Simpson was guilty
Because Banda music will take over the White House
Because Aztec sexual aberrations are still in practice
Because our starvation & squalor isn't as glamorous as Somalia's

Because agribusiness will whack us anyway                                    110
Because the information superhighway is not for Chevys & Impalas
Because white men are paranoid of Frida's mustache
Because the term "mariachi" comes from the word "cucarachi"
Because picking grapes is not a British tradition
Because they are still showing *Zoot Suit* in prisons
Because Richie Valens is alive in West Liberty, Iowa
Because ? & the Mysterians cried 97 tears not 96
Because Hoosgow, Riata and Rodeo are Juzgado, Riata and Rodeo
Because Jackson Hole, Wyoming, will blow as soon as we hit Oceanside
Because U.S. narco-business needs us in Nogales                              120
Because the term "Mexican" comes from "Mexicanto"
Because Mexican queers crossed already
Because Mexican lesbians wear Ben Davis pants & sombreros de palma to work
Because VFW halls aren't built to serve cabeza con tripas
Because the National Guard are going international
Because we still bury our feria in the backyard
Because we don't have international broncas for profit
Because we are in love with our sister Rigoberta Menchú
Because California is on the verge of becoming California
Because the PRI is a family affair                                          130
Because we may start a television series called *No Chingues Conmigo*
Because we are too sweet & obedient & confused & (still) full of rage
Because the CIA needs us in a Third World State of mind
Because brown is the color of the future
Because we turned Welfare into El Huero Fèlix
Because we know what the Jews have been through
Because we know what the Blacks have been through
Because the Irish became the San Patricio Corps at the Battle of Churubusco
Because of our taste for Yiddish gospel raps & tardeadas & salsa limericks
Because El Sistema Nos La Pela                                              140
Because you can take the boy outta Mexico but not outta the Boycott
Because the Truckers, Arkies and Okies enjoy our telenovelas
Because we'd rather shop at the flea market than Macy's
Because pan dulce feels sexual, especially conchas & the elotes
Because we'll Xerox tamales in order to survive
Because we'll export salsa to Russia & call it "Pikushki"
Because cilantro aromas follow us wherever we go
Because we'll unionize & sing *De Colores*
Because A Day Without a Mexican is a day away
Because we're in touch with our Boricua camaradas                          150
Because we are the continental majority
Because we'll build a sweat lodge in front of Bank of America
Because we should wait for further instructions from Televisa
Because 125 million Mexicanos are potential Chicanos

Because we'll take over the Organic Foods business with a
    molcajete
Because 2,000 miles of maquiladoras want to promote us
Because the next Olympics will commemorate the Mexico City
    massacre of 1968
Because there is an Aztec temple beneath our Nopales
Because we know how to pronounce all the Japanese corporations
Because the Comadre network is more accurate than CNN       160
Because the Death Squads are having a hard time with Caló
Because the mayor of San Diego likes salsa medium-picante
Because the Navy, Army, Marines like us topless in Tijuana
Because when we see red, white & blue we just see red
Because when we see the numbers 187 we still see red
Because we need to pay a little extra fee to the Border
Because Mexican Human Rights sounds too Mexican
Because Chrysler is putting out a lowrider
Because they found a lost Chicano tribe in Utah
Because harina white flour bag suits don't cut it at graduation    170
Because we'll switch from AT&T & MCI to Y-que, y-que
Because our hand signs aren't registered
Because Freddy Fender wasn't Baldomar Huerta's real name
Because "lotto" is another Chicano word for "pronto"
Because we won't nationalize a State of Immigrant Paranoia
Because the depression of the '30s was our fault
Because "xenophobia" is a politically correct term
Because we shoulda learned from the Chinese Exclusion Act of 1882
Because we shoulda listened to the Federal Immigration Laws of
    1917, '21, '24 & '30
Because we lack a Nordic/Teutonic approach       180
Because Executive Order 9066 of 1942 shudda had us too
Because Operation Wetback took care of us in the '50s
Because Operation Clean Sweep picked up the loose ends in the '70s
Because one more operation will finish us off anyway
Because you can't deport 12 million migrantes in a Greyhound bus
Because we got this thing about walking out of everything
Because we have a heart that sings rancheras and feet that polka

## FOR ANALYSIS

**1.** In 1994, California voters passed a ballot initiative called Proposition 187 that sought to deny "illegal aliens" a variety of social services guaranteed to legal residents, claiming that such services placed an undue financial burden on the state. The measure was later overturned by federal courts. Why do you think Herrera chose 187 for his title? How many lines are in the poem?

**2.** Repetition of a word or phrase at the beginning of a sentence, clause, or line of poetry is called *anaphora*. How does Herrera use anaphora, and to what effect?

## MAKING ARGUMENTS

Immigration remains a major topic of argument in U.S. politics. Summarize the arguments on both sides — of those in favor of loosening rules against illegal immigrants and helping them achieve citizenship and of those in favor of making it harder to enter the country and increasing deportation.

## WRITING TOPICS

**1.** Write a "because" list poem about some issue of interest to you and in which you dispute reasons or motivations.

**2.** Describe the complicated use of **irony** in "187 Reasons Mexicanos Can't Cross the Border."

## MAKING CONNECTIONS

Compare the ways in which Louise Erdrich's "Dear John Wayne" (p. 522) and "187 Reasons Mexicanos Can't Cross the Border" are concerned not just with how minorities are seen by the majority culture but also how minorities see themselves.

## GREGORY DJANIKIAN   (B. 1949)

# SAILING TO AMERICA   1989

*Alexandria, 1956*

The rugs had been rolled up and islands of them
Floated in the centers of every room,
And now, on the bare wood floors,
My sister and I were skimming among them
In the boats we'd made from newspaper,
Sheets of them pinned to each other,
Dhows, gondolas, clippers, arks.
There was a mule outside on the street
Braying under a load of figs, though mostly
There was quiet, a wind from the desert                          10
Was putting the city to sleep,
But we were too far adrift, the air
Was scurfy and wet, the currents tricking
Our bows against reef and coral
And hulls shearing under the weight of cargo.
"Ahoy and belay!" I called to my sister,
"Avast, avast!" she yelled back from her rigging,
And neither of us knew what we were saying

But the words came to us as from a movie,
Cinemascopic, American. "Richard Widmark,"                          20
I said. "Clark Gable, Bogie," she said,
"Yo-ho-ho." We had passed Cyprus
And now there was Crete or Sardinia
Maybe something larger further off.
The horizon was everywhere I turned,
The waters were becoming turgid,
They were roiling, weeks had passed.
"America, America, land-ho!" I yelled directionless.
"Gibraltar," my sister said, "Heave to,"
And signalling a right, her arm straight out,                      30
She turned and bravely set our course
North-by-northwest for the New World.
Did we arrive? Years later, yes.
By plane, suddenly. With suitcases
And something as hazy as a future.
The November sun was pale and far off,
The air was colder than we'd ever felt,
And already these were wonders to us
As much as snow would be or evergreens,
And it would take me a long time                                   40
Before I'd ever remember
Boats made of paper, islands of wool,
And my sister's voice, as in a fog,
Calling out the hazards,
Leading me on, getting us there.


## JUDITH ORTIZ COFER   (1952–2016)

# LATIN WOMEN PRAY   1987

Latin women pray
In incense sweet churches
They pray in Spanish to an Anglo God
With a Jewish heritage.

And this Great White Father
Imperturbable in his marble pedestal
Looks down upon his brown daughters
Votive candles shining like lust
In his all seeing eyes
Unmoved by their persistent prayers.                               10

Yet year after year
Before his image they kneel
Margarita Josefina Maria and Isabel
All fervently hoping
That if not omnipotent
At least he be bilingual.


## LOUISE ERDRICH    (B. 1954)

# DEAR JOHN WAYNE    1984

August and the drive-in picture is packed.
We lounge on the hood of the Pontiac
surrounded by the slow-burning spirals they sell
at the window, to vanquish the hordes of mosquitoes.
Nothing works. They break through the smoke screen for blood.

Always the lookout spots the Indians first,
spread north to south, barring progress.
The Sioux or some other Plains bunch
in spectacular columns, ICBM missiles,
feathers bristling in the meaningful sunset.                          10

The drum breaks. There will be no parlance.
Only the arrows whining, a death-cloud of nerves
swarming down on the settlers
who die beautifully, tumbling like dust weeds
into the history that brought us all here
together: this wide screen beneath the sign of the bear.

The sky fills, acres of blue squint and eye
that the crowd cheers. His face moves over us,
a thick cloud of vengeance, pitted
like the land that was once flesh. Each rut,                          20
each scar makes a promise: *It is
not over, this fight, not as long as you resist.*

*Everything we see belongs to us.*

A few laughing Indians fall over the hood
slipping in the hot spilled butter.
*The eye sees a lot, John, but the heart is so blind.*

*Death makes us owners of nothing.*
He smiles, a horizon of teeth
the credits reel over, and then the white fields
again blowing in the true-to-life dark.                                    30
The dark films over everything.
We get into the car
scratching our mosquito bites, speechless and small
as people are when the movie is done.
We are back in our skins.

How can we help but keep hearing his voice,
the flip side of the sound track, still playing:
*Come on, boys, we got them*
*where we want them, drunk, running.*
*They'll give us what we want, what we need.*                              40
Even his disease was the idea of taking everything.
Those cells, burning, doubling, splitting out of their skins.

## FOR ANALYSIS

**1.** Part of the power of "Dear John Wayne" lies in the difference between its two **settings**, or places. What are they? What are their differences, and why are they significant?

**2.** Describing the "Indians" in the movie, Erdrich calls them "The Sioux or some other Plains bunch" (l. 8). What **ironic** effect is intended by this last phrase? Note other places where Erdrich is being ironic. What are the effects there?

**3.** From its very title onward, Erdrich's poem is concerned with the question of audience. Who are the different audiences implied in this poem, intended and actual? Who are the different speakers? As a reader, which audience are you?

## MAKING ARGUMENTS

Make an argument for the significance of the poem's last two lines. What is "his disease"? To what does "taking everything" refer? How does the rest of the poem resonate in the image of the last line?

## WRITING TOPICS

**1.** Address the issue of this poem's complicated **tone**. What are its various **moods** and attitudes toward its subjects? When and how do they shift, and to what effect?

**2.** Draw a line down the middle of a piece of paper. In the left column, write down everything the white men in the poem see. In the right column, write down everything the Native Americans in the poem see. Compare the two columns in an essay that discusses the issue of power in seeing and being seen.

## MARILYN CHIN  (B. 1955)

# HOW I GOT THAT NAME   1994

### AN ESSAY ON ASSIMILATION

I am Marilyn Mei Ling Chin.
Oh, how I love the resoluteness
of that first person singular
followed by that stalwart indicative
of "be," without the uncertain i-n-g
of "becoming." Of course,
the name had been changed
somewhere between Angel Island and the sea,
when my father the paperson
in the late 1950s                                                    10
obsessed with a bombshell blonde
transliterated "Mei Ling" to "Marilyn."
And nobody dared question
his initial impulse — for we all know
lust drove men to greatness,
not goodness, not decency.
And there I was, a wayward pink baby,
named after some tragic white woman
swollen with gin and Nembutal.
My mother couldn't pronounce the "r."                               20
She dubbed me "Numba one female offshoot"
for brevity: henceforth, she will live and die
in sublime ignorance, flanked
by loving children and the "kitchen deity."
While my father dithers,
a tomcat in Hong Kong trash —
a gambler, a petty thug,
who bought a chain of chopsuey joints
in Piss River, Oregon,
with bootlegged Gucci cash.                                         30
Nobody dared question his integrity given
his nice, devout daughters,
and his bright, industrious sons
as if filial piety were the standard
by which all earthly men were measured.

Oh, how trustworthy our daughters,
how thrifty our sons!

How we've managed to fool the experts
in education, statistics and demography—
We're not very creative but not adverse to rote-learning.                    40
Indeed, they can *use* us.
But the "Model Minority" is a tease.
We know you are watching now,
so we refuse to give you any!
Oh, bamboo shoots, bamboo shoots!
The further west we go, we'll hit east;
the deeper down we dig, we'll find China.
History has turned its stomach
on a black polluted beach—
where life doesn't hinge                                                      50
on that red, red wheelbarrow,
but whether or not our new lover
in the final episode of "Santa Barbara"
will lean over a scented candle
and call us a "bitch."
Oh God, where have we gone wrong?
We have no inner resources!

Then, one redolent spring morning
the Great Patriarch Chin
peered down from his kiosk in heaven                                          60
and saw that his descendants were ugly.
One had a squarish head and a nose without a bridge.
Another's profile—long and knobbed as a gourd.
A third, the sad, brutish one
may never, never marry.
And I, his least favorite—
"not quite boiled, not quite cooked,"
a plump pomfret simmering in my juices—
too listless to fight for my people's destiny.
"To kill without resistance is not slaughter"                                70
says the proverb. So, I wait for imminent death.
The fact that this death is also metaphorical
is testament to my lethargy.

So here lies Marilyn Mei Ling Chin,
married once, twice to so-and-so, a Lee and a Wong,
granddaughter of Jack "the patriarch"
and the brooding Suilin Fong,
daughter of the virtuous Yuet Kuen Wong
and G. G. Chin the infamous,

sister of a dozen, cousin of a million,                                    80
survived by everybody and forgotten by all.
She was neither black nor white,
neither cherished nor vanquished,
just another squatter in her own bamboo grove
minding her poetry —
when one day heaven was unmerciful,
and a chasm opened where she stood.
Like the jowls of a mighty white whale,
or the jaws of a metaphysical Godzilla,
it swallowed her whole.                                                    90
She did not flinch nor writhe,
nor fret about the afterlife,
but stayed! Solid as wood, happily
a little gnawed, tattered, mesmerized
by all that was lavished upon her
and all that was taken away!

### FOR ANALYSIS

**1.** Why does the speaker "love the resoluteness / of that first person singular / followed by that stalwart indicative / of 'be'" (ll. 2–5)?

**2.** Why is how the poet/**persona** got her name so important?

**3.** What is wrong, in the speaker's eyes, with being a "Model Minority" (l. 42)?

### MAKING ARGUMENTS

There have been a number of different models for immigrants to the United States to follow — from the melting pot to multiculturalism. What are the arguments for the desirability of one over the other? Outline the arguments on each side of the spectrum from total assimilation to ethnic pride and preservation of culture of origin.

### WRITING TOPICS

**1.** How is this poem, as its subtitle claims, "An essay on assimilation"? What was "lavished upon her" (l. 95) and what was "taken away" (l. 96)?

**2.** *Assimilation* is usually meant to indicate what happens to immigrants in a new land. Write about a situation in your life when you had to assimilate in a different sense — not as an international immigrant or a child of immigrants but as a person in a new place. What impact did the experience have on your sense of self?

## TASLIMA NASRIN  (B. 1962)

# THINGS CHEAPLY HAD[1]  1991

In the market nothing can be had as cheap as women.
If they get a small bottle of *alta*[2] for their feet
      they spend three nights sleepless for sheer joy.
If they get a few bars of soap to scrub their skin
      and some scented oil for their hair
they become so submissive that they scoop out
      chunks of their flesh
to be sold in the flea market twice a week.
If they get a jewel for their nose
      they lick feet for seventy days or so,       10
a full three and a half months
      if it's a single striped sari.[3]

Even the mangy cur of the house barks now and then,
and over the mouths of women cheaply had
      there's a lock
a golden lock.

## FOR ANALYSIS

**1.** Why is the lock in the final line of the poem "golden"?

**2.** What are the "things" of the title? Do they include more than the items the women "get"?

## MAKING ARGUMENTS

While Nasrin's subject is the treatment of women in a male-dominated culture, her poem does not describe actual specific acts and effects of mistreatment but rather illustrates the situation through poetic **hyperbole**. Make an argument for one or the other side of this question: does her decision to write about this subject in this way result in a more powerful poem than being literal would have created?

---

[1] Translated from the Bengali by Carolyne Wright with Mohammad Nurul Huda and the author.

[2] *Alta*, or lac-dye, is a red liquid with which South Asian women decorate the borders of their feet on ceremonial occasions, such as weddings and dance performances. *Alta* is more in vogue among Hindus, but Bangladeshi women also use it, and it can be seen on the feet of Muslim heroines and harem women in Moghul miniature paintings. [Translator's note.]

[3] An outer garment worn chiefly by women of India and Pakistan, consisting of a length of cloth wrapped around the waist at one end and draped over the shoulder or head at the other.

## OMAR PÉREZ (B. 1964)

## CONTRIBUTIONS TO A RUDIMENTARY CONCEPT OF NATION[1]  1995/2007

On the volatile nights of a winter
nature corroborates with magnanimity
a Cuban is in training for amusement or amnesia,
so often and unfairly assumed as the same,
he brings candy to God, he cultivates the vernacular, he fights off
cirrhosis with fruit poached in syrup, he conducts business;
thus research has shown that The Cuban is resourceful.
In the weighty choreographies of a summer
nature authorizes already with suspicion
a Cuban meets the ocean with offerings and harpoons,                    10
so often and unfairly assumed as the same,
he finger-counts the casualties, he commits an infraction
he slides his hands into his pockets, he avows and commits;
thus analysis has shown that The Cuban is inspired.
Let's attend the improbable territory
where with pasty mouths a Cuban and The Cuban engage in virile
     conversation
we will learn there by what voyage, by what strange condition
     by what exchange
we fall prey to so much ingenuity.                                       20

### FOR ANALYSIS

**1.** What nation is the nation to which the title refers? Why is this important? Could it be any nation?

**2.** What stereotypes about the Cuban people does the poem allude to?

**3.** What is the difference between "a Cuban" and "The Cuban"?

### MAKING ARGUMENTS

Although he did not know it until his mid-twenties, Pérez is the son of Che Guevara. Do a little research into Guevara and make an argument concerning the relevance of the poet's parentage to this poem. Does it change the way you read it? If so, how? If not, why not?

### WRITING TOPICS

Pérez spent a year in an agricultural reeducation camp for signing a manifesto suggesting political changes in Cuba. Reread this poem and try to describe its politics. What does it say about Cuban nationhood and identity? What does it say about Cuban political history?

[1] Translated by Roberto Tejada.

# CHRIS ABANI (B. 1966)

## BLUE 2004

### I

Africans in the hold fold themselves
to make room for hope. In the afternoon's
ferocity, tar, grouting the planks like the glue
of family, melts to the run of a child's licorice stick.

Wet decks crack, testing the wood's mettle.
Distilled from evaporating brine, salt
dusts the floor, tickling with the measure
into time and the thirst trapped below.

### II

The captain's new cargo of Igbos disturbs him.
They stand, computing the swim back to land.                    10
Haitians still say: *Igbo pend'c or'a ya!*
But we do not hang ourselves in cowardice.

### III

Sold six times on the journey to the coast,
once for a gun, then cloth, then iron
manilas, her pride was masticated like husks
of chewing sticks, spat from morning-rank mouths.

Breaking loose, edge of handcuffs held high
like the blade of a vengeful axe, she runs
across the salt scratch of deck,
pain deeper than the blue inside a flame.                        20

### IV

The sound, like the break of bone
could have been the Captain's skull
or the musket shot dropping her
over the side, her chains wrapped
around his neck in dance.

## FOR ANALYSIS

**1.** What is the **setting** of "Blue"?

**2.** Read the poem aloud to yourself. What patterns of sound do you notice (from listening to what you read and from feeling your face move as you read)?

**3.** Describe the poem's shifting focus. What is it at the start of the poem? What is it at the end? What are the effects of this shift?

## MAKING ARGUMENTS

Make an argument for the significance of the poem's mention of the captain. Take into account the context, the history, and the different ethnicities and national origins of the poem's audience.

## WRITING TOPIC

Abani's poem rests on his ability to put himself into the shoes of people whose lives were very different from his. Write or describe a poem of your own in which you try to do a similar thing (with different people). What are the difficulties of such a task? What are the possibilities?

## MAKING CONNECTIONS

Compare this poem to McKay's "If We Must Die" (p. 359). What motivates the speaker in McKay's poem? What motivates the woman in "Blue"? What do they share despite the differences in their circumstances?

## KEVIN YOUNG   (B. 1970)

# NEGATIVE   2005

Wake to find everything black
what was white, all the vice
versa — white maids on TV, black

sitcoms that star white dwarfs
cute as pearl buttons, Black Presidents,
Black Houses, White Horse

candidates. All bleach burns
clothes black. Drive roads
white as you are, white songs

on the radio stolen by black bands                    10
like secret pancake recipes, white back-up
singers, ball-players & boxers all

white as tar. Feathers on chickens
dark as everything, boiling in the pot
that called the kettle honky. Even

whites of the eye turn dark, pupils
clear & changing as a cat's.
Is this what we've wanted

& waited for? to see snow
covering everything black                                    20
as Christmas, dark pages written

white upon? All our eclipses bright,
dark stars shooting across pale
sky, glowing like ash in fire, shower

every skin. Only money keeps
green, still grows & burns like grass
under dark daylight.

## TERRANCE HAYES   (B. 1971)

# ROOT   2006

My parents would have had me believe
there was no such thing as race
there in the wild backyard, our knees black
with store-bought grass and dirt,
black as the soil of pastures or of orchards
grown above graves. We clawed free
the stones and filled their beds with soil
and covered the soil with sod
as if we owned the earth.
We worked into the edge of darkness                          10
and rose in the edge of darkness
until everything came from the dirt.
We clawed free the moss and brambles,
the colonies of crab-weed, the thorns
patrolling stems and I liked it then:
the mute duty that tightened my parents'
backs as if they meant to work
the devil from his den. Rock and spore
and scraps of leaf; wild bouquets withered

in bags by the road, cast from the ground                                      20
we broke. We scrubbed the patio,
we raked the cross hatch of pine needles,
we soaked the ant-cathedrals in gas.
I found an axe blade beneath an untamed hedge,
its edge too dull to sever vine and half expected
to find a jawbone scabbed with mud,
because no one told me what happened
to the whites who'd owned the house.
No one spoke of the color that curled
around our tools or of the neighbors                                           30
who knew our name before we knew theirs.
Sometimes they were almost visible,
clean as fence posts in porch light;
their houses burning with wonder,
their hammocks drunk with wind.
When I dreamed, I dreamed of them
and believed they dreamed of us
and believed we were made of dirt or shadows:
something not held or given, irredeemable, inexact,
all of us asking what it means to be black . . .                               40
I have never wanted another life, but I know the story
of pursuit: the dream of a gate standing open,
a grill and folding chairs, a new yard boxed in light.

## For Analysis

**1.** Does the speaker believe what his parents wanted him to believe? How do you know?

**2.** Who is "them" in line 36? Who is "us" in line 37? What is the nature of their relationship?

**3.** Describe the main action in this poem. Does its significance lie in what it is or in what it stands for? If the latter, why do you think Hayes chooses to dramatize his subject in this way?

## Making Arguments

It has been argued that U.S. society is now "post-racial." Support or refute this claim, using as support a summary of what is meant by the claim, historical evidence, and evidence drawn from the contemporary scene.

## Writing Topic

Imaginative literature often works by indirection — by finding hidden, obscured, or circuitous routes to ideas rather than following well-worn, straight paths to the thing or idea or feeling it wants to represent. From the first line, "Root" works in this way. Write a description of the ways in which Hayes says things in ways other than straight out.

**TISHANI DOSHI**  (B. 1975)

# THE IMMIGRANT'S SONG   2013

Let us not speak of those days
when coffee beans filled the morning
with hope, when our mothers' headscarves
hung like white flags on washing lines.
Let us not speak of the long arms of sky
that used to cradle us at dusk.
And the baobabs — let us not trace
the shape of their leaves in our dreams,
or yearn for the noise of those nameless birds
that sang and died in the church's eaves.                      10
Let us not speak of men,
stolen from their beds at night.
Let us not say the word
                        *disappeared.*
Let us not remember the first smell of rain.
Instead, let us speak of our lives now —
the gates and bridges and stores.
And when we break bread
in cafés and at kitchen tables
with our new brothers,                                        20
let us not burden them with stories
of war or abandonment.
Let us not name our old friends
who are unravelling like fairy tales
in the forests of the dead.
Naming them will not bring them back.
Let us stay here, and wait for the future
to arrive, for grandchildren to speak
in forked tongues about the country
we once came from.                                            30
*Tell us about it*, they might ask.
And you might consider telling them
of the sky and the coffee beans,
the small white houses and dusty streets.
You might set your memory afloat
like a paper boat down a river.
You might pray that the paper
whispers your story to the water,
that the water sings it to the trees,
that the trees howl and howl                                  40
it to the leaves. If you keep still

and do not speak, you might hear
your whole life fill the world
until the wind is the only word.

## FOR ANALYSIS

**1.** What is the situation the speaker recounts? Where is he now? Where has he come from? How specific can you be in your answers? Why is that, and what is the effect when reading the poem?

**2.** Note the repetition of the statements such as those in lines 1 and 5. Where else do statements of this kind appear? How do they change? What is their significance to the poem as a whole?

## MAKING ARGUMENTS

Make an argument for the larger significance of the word *disappeared* in "The Immigrant's Song" (l. 14). What is its first, more obvious meaning? What else might it refer to?

## WRITING TOPIC

Describe a number of alternative poems that could be written under the title "The Immigrant's Song." How could they differ in their attitudes about the lives immigrants lead and the ways they think about them?

## LAMENT—I   2013

When I see the houses in this city,
the electric gates and uniformed men
employed to guard the riches of the rich,
the gilded columns and gardens,
the boats on water, I wonder,
how to describe my home to you:
the short, mud walls,
the whispering roof, the veranda
on which my whole family
used to spread sheets and sleep.                    10

The year I came to find work in the city,
my wife painted our house white
so it would be brighter than the neighbours'.
I beat her for her foolishness.
The children are hungry, I said,
the cow is old,

the money collector is after my blood,
and you steal like a magpie —
half a month's wage — to decorate
your nest like a shiny jewel?                                    20

The monsoon finally arrived the year I left,
dripped through the thatch,
peeled paint off the walls.
The wells grew full and overflowed.
The farmers rejoiced in the fields.
My son sat with his mouth open
catching drops of water like a frog.
My wife clung to the walls and wept.

When I fall asleep on the pavements
in this city, I try to imagine my wife's skin                    30
against mine, the kohl in her eyes,
the white walls, the whole village sky
bearing down upon us
with all the weight of the stars.
I think of returning to that life,
but mostly I try to remember
how the world was once.
I want to open my mouth like my son,
and swallow things whole —
feel water filling all the voids,                                40
until I am shaped back into existence.

## CONNECTING POEMS: AMERICA THROUGH IMMIGRANTS' EYES

The poems in this section are about immigration to America, seen from a
variety of angles and through a number of different lenses. The events about
which these poets write occurred in the mid-eighteenth century, the late
nineteenth century, the early twentieth century, and in our contemporary
moments. The places of origin of the immigrants include Africa and Europe
and the Americas. The motivation for coming to the United States vary as
well: from the search for a better life, to the fleeing of a worsening one, to
the absence of motivation that characterizes being stolen unwillingly from
one's home. Despite these differences, there is much that unites these poems.
As you read and notice all of these differences, keep an eye out for those
connections.

## PHILLIS WHEATLEY  (1753–1784)

# ON BEING BROUGHT FROM AFRICA TO AMERICA  1773

'Twas mercy brought me from my pagan land,
Taught my benighted soul to understand
That there's a God, that there's a Savior too:
Once I redemption neither sought nor knew.
Some view our sable race with scornful eye,
"Their color is a diabolic die.°"                                    dye
Remember, Christians, Negros, black as Cain,
May be refined, and join th' angelic train.

## FOR ANALYSIS

**1.** Wheatley was brought from Senegal or Gambia to the United States and sold as a slave to the Wheatley family in Boston when she was seven or eight years old. What is your response to the poem's first three lines? Why?

**2.** Paraphrase "Negros, black as Cain, / May be refined, and join th' angelic train."

**3.** What historical conditions would perhaps account for the fame of the poet and the extraordinary contemporary wonder at her achievements?

**4.** Can you imagine an African American poet writing a similar poem in the twenty-first century? Explain.

## MAKING ARGUMENTS

Imagine a response to Wheatley that takes issue with the sentiment expressed in the poem's first three lines. Use research into the history of slavery and the slave trade as well as any evidence you may find within the poem.

## WRITING TOPIC

First write a review of this poem based on your perception of eighteenth-century society in Massachusetts; then write a twenty-first-century review.

## EMMA LAZARUS  (1849–1887)

# THE NEW COLOSSUS[1]  1883

Not like the brazen giant of Greek fame,[2]
With conquering limbs astride from land to land;
Here at our sea-washed, sunset gates shall stand
A mighty woman with a torch, whose flame
Is the imprisoned lightning, and her name

---

*The New Colossus*
   [1] This poem was engraved on a bronze plaque and mounted inside the Statue of Liberty in 1903.
   [2] The Colossus of Rhodes, one of the Seven Wonders of the Ancient World.

Mother of Exiles. From her beacon-hand
Glows world-wide welcome; her mild eyes command
The air-bridged harbor that twin cities frame.
"Keep, ancient lands, your storied pomp!" cries she
With silent lips. "Give me your tired, your poor,                    10
Your huddled masses yearning to breathe free,
The wretched refuse of your teeming shore.
Send these, the homeless, tempest-tost to me,
I lift my lamp beside the golden door!"

## FOR ANALYSIS

**1.** What was the Colossus of Rhodes? How does Lazarus describe it in the poem's opening lines?

**2.** To what does "mighty woman with a torch" (l. 4) refer? To what other object in the poem is it compared?

## MAKING ARGUMENTS

Is the United States still a haven for exiles? Was it ever? Answer these questions, using historical evidence to support your argument.

## WRITING TOPICS

Write or imagine a similar poem about a major statue or monument. What could be said about it? How might you say it?

## LÉOPOLD SÉDAR SENGHOR   (1906–2001)

# TO NEW YORK[1]   1998

*(for jazz orchestra and trumpet solo)*

New York! At first I was bewildered by your beauty,
Those huge, long-legged, golden girls.
So shy, at first, before your blue metallic eyes and icy smile,
So shy. And full of despair at the end of skyscraper streets
Raising my owl eyes at the eclipse of the sun.
Your light is sulphurous against the pale towers
Whose heads strike lightning into the sky,
Skyscrapers defying storms with their steel shoulders
And weathered skin of stone.
But two weeks on the naked sidewalks of Manhattan —                10
At the end of the third week the fever
Overtakes you with a jaguar's leap
Two weeks without well water or pasture all birds of the air
Fall suddenly dead under the high, sooty terraces.

---

[1] Translated by Melvin Dixon.

No laugh from a growing child, his hand in my cool hand.
No mother's breast, but nylon legs. Legs and breasts
Without smell or sweat. No tender word, and no lips,
Only artificial hearts paid for in cold cash
And not one book offering wisdom.
The painter's palette yields only coral crystals.                    20
Sleepless nights, O nights of Manhattan!
Stirring with delusions while car horns blare the empty hours
And murky streams carry away hygenic loving
Like rivers overflowing with the corpses of babies.

## II

Now is the time of signs and reckoning, New York!
Now is the time of manna and hyssop.
You have only to listen to God's trombones, to your heart
Beating to the rhythm of blood, your blood.
I saw Harlem teeming with sounds and ritual colors
And outrageous smells —                                             30
At teatime in the home of the drugstore-deliveryman
I saw the festival of Night begin at the retreat of day.
And I proclaim Night more truthful than the day.
It is the pure hour when God brings forth
Life immemorial in the streets,
All the amphibious elements shining like suns.
Harlem, Harlem! Now I've seen Harlem, Harlem!
A green breeze of corn rising from the pavements
Plowed by the Dan dancers' bare feet,
Hips rippling like silk and spearhead breasts,                      40
Ballets of water lilies and fabulous masks
And mangoes of love rolling from the low houses
To the feet of police horses.
And along sidewalks I saw streams of white rum
And streams of black milk in the blue haze of cigars.
And at night I saw cotton flowers snow down
From the sky and the angels' wings and sorcerers' plumes.
Listen, New York! O listen to your bass male voice,
Your vibrant oboe voice, the muted anguish of your tears
Falling in great clots of blood,                                    50
Listen to the distant beating of your nocturnal heart,
The tom-tom's rhythm and blood, tom-tom blood and tom-tom.

## III

New York! I say New York, let black blood flow into your blood.
Let it wash the rust from your steel joints, like an oil of life
Let it give your bridges the curve of hips and supple vines.

Now the ancient age returns, unity is restored,
The reconciliation of the Lion and Bull and Tree
Idea links to action, the ear to the heart, sign to meaning.
See your rivers stirring with musk alligators
And sea cows with mirage eyes. No need to invent the Sirens.          60
Just open your eyes to the April rainbow
And your eyes, especially your ears, to God
Who in one burst of saxophone laughter
Created heaven and earth in six days,
And on the seventh slept a deep Negro sleep.

## FOR ANALYSIS

**1.** Why do you think Senghor describes New York as having "blue metallic eyes" and an "icy smile" (l. 3)? To what is this description contrasted?

**2.** How does the speaker feel about New York?

**3.** Why do you think Senghor divides the poem up as he does? What are the similarities and differences between the three sections? What is the significance of the movement from the first to the second to the third?

## MAKING ARGUMENTS

Senghor was a champion of Négritude, which promoted a pan-African diasporic identity — that is, a belief that there was something essential about people of African descent, regardless of whether they lived in Africa or elsewhere, that united them. Later black writers claimed that this idea paradoxically promoted racism, since it still maintained that there were traits essential to different races. The movement was a response to colonialism and racism. How would you construct the arguments on both sides of this issue?

## WRITING TOPIC

Senghor gives "To New York" faux instructions for instrumental arrangement. Describe the ways in which the poem is musical in the way that it is written and explain why music is important to it thematically.


## KOFI AWOONOR   (1935–2013)

# AMERICA   2014

A name only once
crammed into the child's fitful memory
in malnourished villages,
vast deliriums like the galloping foothills of the Colorado:
of Mohawks and the Chippewa,
horsey penny-movies
brought cheap at the tail of the war
to Africa. Where indeed is the Mississippi panorama
and the girl that played the piano and
kept her hand on her heart          10

as Flanagan drank a quart of moonshine
before the eyes of the town's gentlemen?
What happened to your locomotive in Winter, Walt,
and my ride across the prairies in the trail
of the stage-coach, the gold-rush and the Swanee River?
Where did they bury Geronimo,
heroic chieftain, lonely horseman of this apocalypse
who led his tribesmen across deserts of cholla
and emerald hills
in pursuit of despoilers,                                        20
half-starved immigrants
from a despoiled Europe?
What happened to Archibald's
soul's harvest on this raw earth
of raw hates?
To those that have none
a festival is preparing at graves' ends
where the mockingbird's hymn
closes evening of prayers
and supplication as                                             30
new winds blow from graves
flowered in multi-colored cemeteries even
where they say the races are intact.

## For Analysis

**1.** What is the **setting** of this poem? From whose **point of view** is it seen?

**2.** What history does the poem's speaker recount? What history is he or she part of?

## Making Arguments

While U.S. influence around the globe has been economically and militarily significant, there are some who say its greatest influence has been cultural, in particular through the spread of its films around the world. How would you argue that that influence has been positive? Negative? Mixed?

## Writing Topic

Imagine going to a place you have heard and seen a lot about but never been to. How might it differ from what you expect?

## Making Connections

**1.** Are all of these poems even about immigration? Which are not, and how do they compare to each other and to the "truer" immigration poems?

**2.** Compare these poems' views on immigration to the United States. Is there one experience or many?

# DRAMA

**DAVID HENRY HWANG** (B. 1957)

## TRYING TO FIND CHINATOWN    1996

CHARACTERS

**Benjamin**, Caucasian male, early twenties.
**Ronnie**, Asian American male, mid-twenties.

**Time and Place**
*A street corner on the Lower East Side, New York City. The present.*

**Note on Music**
*Obviously, it would be foolish to require that the actor portraying Ronnie perform the specified violin music live. The score of this play can be played on tape over the house speakers, and the actor can feign playing the violin using a bow treated with soap. However, in order to effect a convincing illusion, it is desirable that the actor possess some familiarity with the violin or another stringed instrument.*

*Darkness. Over the house speakers, sound fades in: Hendrix-like virtuoso rock 'n' roll riffs — heavy feedback, distortion, phase shifting, wah-wah — amplified over a tiny Fender pug-nose.*

*Lights fade up to reveal that the music's being played over a solid-body electric violin by Ronnie, a Chinese American male in his mid-twenties; he is dressed in retro-'60s clothing and has a few requisite '90s body mutilations. He's playing on a sidewalk for money, his violin case open before him; change and a few stray bills have been left by previous passersby.*

*Benjamin enters; he's in his early twenties, blond, blue-eyed, a midwestern tourist in the big city. He holds a scrap of paper in his hands, scanning street signs for an address. He pauses before Ronnie, listens for a while. With a truly bravura run, Ronnie concludes the number and falls to his knees, gasping. Benjamin applauds.*

**Benjamin.** Good. That was really great. *(Pause)* I didn't . . . I mean, a fiddle . . . I mean, I'd heard them at square dances, on country stations and all, but I never . . . wow, this must really be New York City!

*(Benjamin applauds, starts to walk on. Still on his knees, Ronnie clears his throat loudly.)*

Oh, I . . . you're not just doing this for your health, right?

*(Benjamin reaches in his pocket, pulls out a couple of coins. Ronnie clears his throat again.)*

Look, I'm not a millionaire, I'm just . . .

*(Benjamin pulls out his wallet, removes a dollar bill. Ronnie nods his head and gestures toward the violin case as he takes out a pack of cigarettes, lights one.)*

**Ronnie.** And don't call it a "fiddle," OK?

**Benjamin.** Oh. Well, I didn't mean to —

**Ronnie.** You sound like a wuss. A hick. A dipshit.

**Benjamin.** It just slipped out. I didn't really —

**Ronnie.** If this was a fiddle, I'd be sitting here with a cob pipe, stomping my cowboy boots and kicking up hay. Then I'd go home and fuck my cousin.

**Benjamin.** Oh! Well, I don't really think —

**Ronnie.** Do you see a cob pipe? Am I fucking my cousin?

**Benjamin.** Well, no, not at the moment, but —

**Ronnie.** All right. Then this is a violin, now you give me your money, and I ignore the insult. Herein endeth the lesson.

*(Pause.)*

**Benjamin.** Look, a dollar's more than I've ever given to a . . . to someone asking for money.

**Ronnie.** Yeah, well, this is New York. Welcome to the cost of living.

**Benjamin.** What I mean is, maybe in exchange, you could help me —?

**Ronnie.** Jesus Christ! Do you see a sign around my neck reading "Big Apple Fucking Tourist Bureau"?

**Benjamin.** I'm just looking for an address, I don't think it's far from here, maybe you could . . . ?

*(Benjamin holds out his scrap of paper, Ronnie snatches it away.)*

**Ronnie.** You're lucky I'm such a goddamn softy. *(He looks at the paper)* Oh, fuck you. Just suck my dick, you and the cousin you rode in on.

**Benjamin.** I don't get it! What are you —?

**Ronnie.** Eat me. You know exactly what I —

**Benjamin.** I'm just asking for a little —

**Ronnie.** "13 Doyers Street"? Like you don't know where that is?

**Benjamin.** Of course I don't know! That's why I'm asking —

**Ronnie.** C'mon, you trailer-park refugee. You don't know that's Chinatown?

**Benjamin.** Sure I know that's Chinatown.

**Ronnie.** I know you know that's Chinatown.

**Benjamin.** So? That doesn't mean I know where Chinatown —

**Ronnie.** So why is it that you picked *me*, of all the street musicians in the city — to point you in the direction of Chinatown? Lemme guess — is it the earring? No, I don't think so. The Hendrix riffs? Guess again, you fucking moron.

**Benjamin.** Now, wait a minute. I see what you're —

**Ronnie.** What are you gonna ask me next? Where you can find the best dim sum in the city? Whether I can direct you to a genuine opium den? Or do I happen to know how you can meet Miss Saigon for a night of nookie-nookie followed by a good old-fashioned ritual suicide? Now, get your white ass off my sidewalk. One dollar doesn't even begin to make up for all this aggravation. Why don't you go back home and race bullfrogs, or whatever it is you do for —?

**Benjamin.** Brother, I can absolutely relate to your anger. Righteous rage, I suppose, would be a more appropriate term. To be marginalized, as we are, by a white racist patriarchy, to the point where the accomplishments of our people are obliterated from the history books, this is cultural genocide of the first order, leading to the fact that you must do battle with all of Euro-America's emasculating and brutal stereotypes of Asians — the opium den, the sexual objectification of the Asian female, the exoticized image of a tourist's Chinatown which ignores the exploitation of workers, the failure to unionize, the high rate of mental illness and tuberculosis — against these, each day, you rage, no, not as a victim, but as a survivor, yes, brother, a glorious warrior survivor!

*(Silence.)*

**Ronnie.** Say what?

**Benjamin.** So, I hope you can see that my request is not —

**Ronnie.** Wait, wait.

**Benjamin.** — motivated by the sorts of racist assumptions —

**Ronnie.** But, but where . . . how did you learn all that?

**Benjamin.** All what?

**Ronnie.** All that — you know — oppression stuff — tuberculosis . . .

**Benjamin.** It's statistically irrefutable. TB occurs in the community at a rate —

**Ronnie.** Where did *you* learn it?

**Benjamin.** I took Asian American studies. In college.

**Ronnie.** Where did you go to college?

**Benjamin.** University of Wisconsin. Madison.

**Ronnie.** Madison, Wisconsin?

**Benjamin.** That's not where the bridges are, by the way.

**Ronnie.** Huh? Oh, right . . .

**Benjamin.** You wouldn't believe the number of people who —

**Ronnie.** They have Asian American studies in Madison, Wisconsin? Since when?

**Benjamin.** Since the last Third World Unity hunger strike. *(Pause)* Why do you look so surprised? We're down.

**Ronnie.** I dunno. It just never occurred to me, the idea of Asian students in the Midwest going on a hunger strike.

**Benjamin.** Well, a lot of them had midterms that week, so they fasted in shifts. *(Pause)* The administration never figured it out. The Asian students put that "They all look alike" stereotype to good use.

**Ronnie.** OK, so they got Asian American studies. That still doesn't explain —

**Benjamin.** What?

**Ronnie.** Well . . . what *you* were doing taking it?

**Benjamin.** Just like everyone else. I wanted to explore my roots. And, you know, the history of oppression which is my legacy. After a lifetime of assimilation, I wanted to find out who I really am.

*(Pause.)*

**Ronnie.** And did you?

**Benjamin.** Sure. I learned to take pride in my ancestors who built the railroads, my Popo who would make me a hot bowl of jok with thousand-day-old eggs when the white kids chased me home yelling, "Gook! Chink! Slant-eyes!"

**Ronnie.** OK, OK, that's enough!

**Benjamin.** Painful to listen to, isn't it?

**Ronnie.** I don't know what kind of bullshit ethnic studies program they're running over in Wuss-consin, but did they bother to teach you that in order to find your Asian "roots," it's a good idea to first be Asian?

*(Pause.)*

**Benjamin.** Are you speaking metaphorically?

**Ronnie.** No! Literally! Look at your skin!

**Benjamin.** You know, it's very stereotypical to think that all Asian skin tones conform to a single hue.

**Ronnie.** You're white! Is this some kind of redneck joke or something? Am I the first person in the world to tell you this?

**Benjamin.** Oh! Oh! Oh!

**Ronnie.** I know real Asians are scarce in the Midwest, but . . . Jesus!

**Benjamin.** No, of course, I . . . I see where your misunderstanding arises.

**Ronnie.** Yeah. It's called, "You white."

**Benjamin.** It's just that — in my hometown of Tribune, Kansas, and then at school — see, everyone knows me — so this sort of thing never comes up. *(He offers his hand)* Benjamin Wong. I forget that a society wedded to racial constructs constantly forces me to explain my very existence.

**Ronnie.** Ronnie Chang. Otherwise known as "The Bow Man."

**Benjamin.** You see, I was adopted by Chinese American parents at birth. So, clearly, I'm an Asian American —

**Ronnie.** Even though you're blond and blue-eyed.

**Benjamin.** Well, you can't judge my race by my genetic heritage alone.

**Ronnie.** If genes don't determine race, what does?

**Benjamin.** Perhaps you'd prefer that I continue in denial, masquerading as a white man?

**Ronnie.** You can't just wake up and say, "Gee, I *feel* black today."

**Benjamin.** Brother, I'm just trying to find what you've already got.

**Ronnie.** What do I got?

**Benjamin.** A home. With your people. Picketing with the laundry workers. Taking refuge from the daily slights against your masculinity in the noble image of Gwan Gung.

**Ronnie.** Gwan who?

**Benjamin.** C'mon — the Chinese god of warriors and — what do you take me for? There're altars to him up all over the community.

**Ronnie.** I dunno what community you're talking about, but it's sure as hell not mine.

*(Pause.)*

**Benjamin.** What do you mean?

**Ronnie.** I mean, if you wanna call Chinatown *your* community, OK, knock yourself out, learn to use chopsticks, big deal. Go ahead, try and find your "roots" in some dim sum parlor with headless ducks hanging in the window. Those places don't tell you a thing about who *I* am.

**Benjamin.** Oh, I get it.

**Ronnie.** You get what?

**Benjamin.** You're one of those self-hating, *assimilated* Chinese Americans, aren't you?

**Ronnie.** Oh, Jesus.

**Benjamin.** You probably call yourself "Oriental," huh? Look, maybe I can help you. I have some books I can —

**Ronnie.** Hey, I read all those Asian identity books when you were still slathering on industrial-strength sunblock. *(Pause)* Sure, I'm Chinese. But folks like you act like that means something. Like, all of a sudden, you know who I am. You think identity's that simple? That you can wrap it all up in a neat package and say, "I have ethnicity, therefore I am"? All you fucking ethnic fundamentalists. Always settling for easy answers. You say you're looking for identity, but you can't begin to face the real mysteries of the search. So instead, you go skin-deep, and call it a day. *(Pause. He turns away from Benjamin and starts to play his violin — slow and bluesy.)*

**Benjamin.** So what are you? "Just a human being"? That's like saying you *have* no identity. If you asked me to describe my dog, I'd say more than, "He's just a dog."

**Ronnie.** What — you think if I deny the importance of my race, I'm nobody? There're worlds out there, worlds you haven't even begun to understand. Open your eyes. Hear with your ears.

*(Ronnie holds his violin at chest level, but does not attempt to play during the following monologue. As he speaks, rock and jazz violin tracks fade in and out over the house speakers, bringing to life the styles of music he describes.)*

I concede — it was called a fiddle long ago — but that was even before the birth of jazz. When the hollering in the fields, the rank injustice of human bondage, the struggle of God's children against the plagues of the devil's white man, when all these boiled up into that bittersweet brew, called by later generations, the blues. That's when fiddlers like Son Sims held their chin rests at their chests, and sawed away like the hillbillies still do today. And with the coming of ragtime appeared the pioneer Stuff Smith, who sang as he stroked the catgut, with his raspy, Louis Armstrong–voice — gruff and sweet like the timber of horse-hair riding south below the fingerboard — and who finally sailed for Europe to find ears that would hear. Europe — where Stephane Grappelli initiated a magical French violin, to be passed from generation to generation — first he, to Jean-Luc Ponty, then Ponty to Didier Lockwood. Listening to Grappelli play "A Nightingale Sang in Berkeley Square" is to understand not only the song of birds, but also how they learn to fly, fall in love on the wing, and finally falter one day, to wait for darkness beneath a London street lamp. And Ponty — he showed how the modern violin man can accompany the shadow of his own lead lines, which cascade, one over another, into some nether world beyond the range of human hearing. Joe Venuti. Noel Pointer. Sven Asmussen. Even the Kronos Quartet, with their arrangement of "Purple Haze." Now, tell me, could any legacy be more rich, more crowded with mythology and heroes to inspire pride? What can I say if the banging of a gong or the clinking of a pickax on the Transcontinental Railroad fails to move me even as much as one note, played through a violin MIDI controller by Michael Urbaniak? *(He puts his violin to his chin, begins to play a jazz composition of his own invention)* Does it have to sound like Chinese opera before people like you decide I know who I am?

*(Benjamin stands for a long moment, listening to Ronnie play. Then, he drops his dollar into the case, turns and exits right. Ronnie continues to play a long moment. Then Benjamin enters downstage left, illuminated in his own spotlight. He sits on the floor of the stage, his feet dangling off the lip. As he speaks, Ronnie continues playing his tune, which becomes underscoring for Benjamin's monologue. As the music continues, does it slowly begin to reflect the influence of Chinese music?)*

**Benjamin.** When I finally found Doyers Street, I scanned the buildings for Number 13. Walking down an alley where the scent of freshly steamed char siu bao lingered in the air, I felt immediately that I had entered a world where all things were finally familiar. *(Pause)* An old woman bumped me with her shopping bag — screaming to her friend in Cantonese, though they walked no more than a few inches apart. Another man — shouting to a vendor in Sze-Yup. A youth, in white undershirt, perhaps a recent newcomer, bargaining with a grocer in Hokkien. I walked through this ocean of dialects, breathing in the richness with deep gulps, exhilarated by the energy this symphony brought to my step. And when I finally saw the number 13, I nearly wept at my good fortune. An old tenement, paint peeling, inside walls no doubt thick with a century of grease and broken dreams — and yet, to me, a temple — the house where my father was born. I suddenly saw it all: Gung Gung, coming home from his sixteen-hour days pressing shirts he could never afford to own, bringing with him candies for my father, each sweet wrapped in the hope of a better life. When my father left the ghetto, he swore he would never return. But he had, this day, in the thoughts and memories of his son, just six months after his death. And as I sat on the stoop, I pulled a hua-moi from my pocket, sucked on it, and felt his spirit returning. To this place where his ghost, and the dutiful hearts of all his descendants, would always call home. *(He listens for a long moment)* And I felt an ache in my heart for all those lost souls, denied this most important of revelations: to know who they truly are.

*(Benjamin sucks his salted plum and listens to the sounds around him. Ronnie continues to play. The two remain oblivious of one another. Lights fade slowly to black.)*

*End of play*

## FOR ANALYSIS

**1.** Two things about Benjamin are revealed in his first big speech (p. 543). What are they? What two different sets of stereotypes make them surprising?

**2.** Why does Benjamin consider himself Chinese? Why does Ronnie disagree?

**3.** The second-to-last stage direction (not counting "End of play") ends: "As the music continues, does it slowly begin to reflect the influence of Chinese music?" (p. 546). Why might Hwang have written this stage direction? What comment might it be making about the discussion the two **characters** have been having?

## MAKING ARGUMENTS

Ronnie and Benjamin disagree about the importance of ethnic heritage to identity. Make an argument for the view you find more persuasive, using the play and anything else you think supports your argument.

## WRITING TOPIC

Hwang writes **dialogue** in a very particular way for each character. Describe the **style** of each character's lines, and compare them. What does the way in which each talks say about him as a person? What do the similarities and differences between the ways they talk say about the similarities and differences between them as people?

## MAKING CONNECTIONS

Compare this play to Chin's poem "How I Got That Name" (p. 524). How does each work relate Chinese identity to mainstream "white" American identity?

# NONFICTION

**VIRGINIA WOOLF**   (1882–1941)

## WHAT IF SHAKESPEARE HAD HAD A SISTER?[1]   1929

It was disappointing not to have brought back in the evening some important statement, some authentic fact. Women are poorer than men because — this or that. Perhaps now it would be better to give up seeking for the truth, and receiving on one's head an avalanche of opinion hot as lava, discoloured as dish-water. It would be better to draw the curtains; to shut out distractions; to light the lamp; to narrow the enquiry and to ask the historian, who records not opinions but facts, to describe under what conditions women lived, not throughout the ages, but in England, say in the time of Elizabeth.

For it is a perennial puzzle why no woman wrote a word of that extraordinary literature when every other man, it seemed, was capable of song or sonnet. What were the conditions in which women lived, I asked myself; for fiction, imaginative work that is, is not dropped like a pebble upon the ground, as science may be; fiction is like a spider's web, attached ever so lightly perhaps, but still attached to life at all four corners. Often the attachment is scarcely perceptible; Shakespeare's plays, for instance, seem to hang there complete by themselves. But when the web is pulled askew, hooked up at the edge, torn in the middle, one remembers that these webs are not spun in midair by incorporeal creatures, but are the work of suffering human beings, and are attached to grossly material things, like health and money and the houses we live in.

I went, therefore, to the shelf where the histories stand and took down one of the latest, Professor Trevelyan's *History of England*. Once more I looked up

[1] *A Room of One's Own*, from which this essay is taken, is based on two lectures Woolf delivered on women and literature at Newnham College and Girton College, Cambridge University. In the opening chapter, Woolf declares that without "money and a room of her own," a woman cannot write fiction. In the following chapter, she recounts her unsuccessful attempt to turn up information at the British Library on the lives of women. This essay is from Chapter 3, from which a few passages are omitted. The essay ends with the concluding paragraph of the book.

Women, found "position of," and turned to the pages indicated. "Wife-beating," I read, "was a recognized right of man, and was practiced without shame by high as well as low. . . . Similarly," the historian goes on, "the daughter who refused to marry the gentleman of her parents' choice was liable to be locked up, beaten and flung about the room, without any shock being inflicted on public opinion. Marriage was not an affair of personal affection, but of family avarice, particularly in the 'chivalrous' upper classes. . . . Betrothal often took place while one or both of the parties was in the cradle, and marriage when they were scarcely out of the nurses' charge." That was about 1470, soon after Chaucer's time. The next reference to the position of women is some two hundred years later, in the time of the Stuarts. "It was still the exception for women of the upper and middle class to choose their own husbands, and when the husband had been assigned, he was lord and master, so far at least as law and custom could make him. Yet even so," Professor Trevelyan concludes, "neither Shakespeare's women nor those of authentic seventeenth-century memoirs, like the Verneys and the Hutchinsons, seem wanting in personality and character." Certainly, if we consider it, Cleopatra must have had a way with her; Lady Macbeth, one would suppose, had a will of her own; Rosalind, one might conclude, was an attractive girl. Professor Trevelyan is speaking no more than the truth when he remarks that Shakespeare's women do not seem wanting in personality and character. Not being a historian, one might go even further and say that women have burnt like beacons in all the works of all the poets from the beginning of time — Clytemnestra, Antigone, Cleopatra, Lady Macbeth, Phèdre, Cressida, Rosalind, Desdemona, the Duchess of Malfi, among the dramatists; then among the prose writers: Millamant, Clarissa, Becky Sharp, Anna Karenina, Emma Bovary, Madame de Guermantes[2] — the names flock to mind, nor do they recall women "lacking in personality and character." Indeed, if woman had no existence save in the fiction written by men, one would imagine her a person of the utmost importance; very various; heroic and mean; splendid and sordid; infinitely beautiful and hideous in the extreme; as great as a man, some think even greater. But this is woman in fiction. In fact, as Professor Trevelyan points out, she was locked up, beaten and flung about the room.

A very queer, composite being thus emerges. Imaginatively she is of the highest importance; practically she is completely insignificant. She pervades poetry from cover to cover; she is all but absent from history. She dominates the lives of kings and conquerors in fiction; in fact she was the slave of any boy whose parents forced a ring upon her finger. Some of the most inspired words, some of the most profound thoughts in literature fell from her lips; in real life she could hardly read, could scarcely spell, and was the property of her husband.

It was certainly an odd monster that one made up by reading the historians 5 first and the poets afterwards — a worm winged like an eagle; the spirit of life and beauty in a kitchen chopping up suet. But these monsters, however amusing to the imagination, have no existence in fact. What one must do to bring her to

[2] Female characters from great works of literature.

life was to think poetically and prosaically at one and the same moment, thus keeping in touch with fact — that she is Mrs. Martin, aged thirty-six, dressed in blue, wearing a black hat and brown shoes; but not losing sight of fiction either — that she is a vessel in which all sorts of spirits and forces are coursing and flashing perpetually. The moment, however, that one tries this method with the Elizabethan woman, one branch of illumination fails; one is held up by the scarcity of facts. One knows nothing detailed, nothing perfectly true and substantial about her. History scarcely mentions her. And I turned to Professor Trevelyan again to see what history meant to him. I found by looking at his chapter headings that it meant —

"The Manor Court and the Methods of Open-field Agriculture . . . The Cistercians and Sheep-farming . . . The Crusades . . . The University . . . The House of Commons . . . The Hundred Years' War . . . The Wars of the Roses . . . The Renaissance Scholars . . . The Dissolution of the Monasteries . . . Agrarian and Religious Strife . . . The Origin of English Seapower . . . The Armada . . ." and so on. Occasionally an individual woman is mentioned, an Elizabeth, or a Mary; a queen or a great lady. But by no possible means could middle-class women with nothing but brains and character at their command have taken part in any one of the great movements which, brought together, constitute the historian's view of the past. Nor shall we find her in any collection of anecdotes. Aubrey hardly mentions her.[3] She never writes her own life and scarcely keeps a diary; there are only a handful of her letters in existence. She left no plays or poems by which we can judge her . . . Here am I asking why women did not write poetry in the Elizabethan age, and I am not sure how they were educated; whether they were taught to write; whether they had sitting-rooms to themselves; how many women had children before they were twenty-one; what, in short, they did from eight in the morning till eight at night. They had no money evidently; according to Professor Trevelyan they were married whether they liked it or not before they were out of the nursery, at fifteen or sixteen very likely. It would have been extremely odd, even upon this showing, had one of them suddenly written the plays of Shakespeare, I concluded, and I thought of that old gentleman, who is dead now, but was a bishop, I think, who declared that it was impossible for any woman, past, present, or to come, to have the genius of Shakespeare. He wrote to the papers about it. He also told a lady who applied to him for information that cats do not as a matter of fact go to heaven, though they have, he added, souls of a sort. How much thinking those old gentlemen used to save one! How the borders of ignorance shrank back at their approach! Cats do not go to heaven. Women cannot write the plays of Shakespeare.

Be that as it may, I could not help thinking, as I looked at the works of Shakespeare on the shelf, that the bishop was right at least in this; it would have been impossible, completely and entirely, for any woman to have written the plays of Shakespeare in the age of Shakespeare. Let me imagine, since facts are so hard to come by, what would have happened had Shakespeare had

[3] John Aubrey (1626–1697), author of *Brief Lives*, a biographical work.

a wonderfully gifted sister, called Judith, let us say. Shakespeare himself went, very probably — his mother was an heiress — to the grammar school, where he may have learnt Latin — Ovid, Virgil and Horace — and the elements of grammar and logic. He was, it is well known, a wild boy who poached rabbits, perhaps shot a deer, and had, rather sooner than he should have done, to marry a woman in the neighbourhood, who bore him a child rather quicker than was right. That escapade sent him to seek his fortune in London. He had, it seemed, a taste for the theatre; he began by holding horses at the stage door. Very soon he got work in the theatre, became a successful actor, and lived in the hub of the universe, meeting everybody, knowing everybody, practising his art on the boards, exercising his wits in the streets, and even getting access to the palace of the queen. Meanwhile his extraordinarily gifted sister, let us suppose, remained at home. She was as adventurous, as imaginative, as agog to see the world as he was. But she was not sent to school. She had no chance of learning grammar and logic, let alone of reading Horace and Virgil. She picked up a book now and then, one of her brother's perhaps, and read a few pages. But then her parents came in and told her to mend the stockings or mind the stew and not moon about with books and papers. They would have spoken sharply but kindly, for they were substantial people who knew the conditions of life for a woman and loved their daughter — indeed, more likely than not she was the apple of her father's eye. Perhaps she scribbled some pages up in an apple loft on the sly, but was careful to hide them or set fire to them. Soon, however, before she was out of her teens, she was to be betrothed to the son of a neighbouring wool-stapler. She cried out that marriage was hateful to her, and for that she was severely beaten by her father. Then he ceased to scold her. He begged her instead not to hurt him, not to shame him in this matter of her marriage. He would give her a chain of beads or a fine petticoat, he said; and there were tears in his eyes. How could she disobey him? How could she break his heart? The force of her own gift alone drove her to it. She made up a small parcel of her belongings, let herself down by a rope one summer's night and took the road to London. She was not seventeen. The birds that sang in the hedge were not more musical than she was. She had the quickest fancy, a gift like her brother's, for the tune of words. Like him, she had a taste for the theatre. She stood at the stage door; she wanted to act, she said. Men laughed in her face. The manager — a fat, loose-lipped man — guffawed. He bellowed something about poodles dancing and women acting — no woman, he said, could possibly be an actress.[4] He hinted — you can imagine what. She could get no training in her craft. Could she even seek her dinner in a tavern or roam the streets at midnight? Yet her genius was for fiction and lusted to feed abundantly upon the lives of men and women and the study of their ways. At last — for she was very young, oddly like Shakespeare the poet in her face, with the same grey eyes and rounded brows — at last Nick Greene the actor-manager took pity on her; she found herself with child by that gentleman and

---

[4] In Shakespeare's day, women's roles were played by males.

so — who shall measure the heat and violence of the poet's heart when caught and tangled in a woman's body? — killed herself one winter's night and lies buried at some cross-roads where the omnibuses now stop outside the Elephant and Castle.[5]

That, more or less, is how the story would run, I think, if a woman in Shakespeare's day had had Shakespeare's genius. But for my part, I agree with the deceased bishop, if such he was — it is unthinkable that any woman in Shakespeare's day should have had Shakespeare's genius. For genius like Shakespeare's is not born among labouring, uneducated, servile people. It was not born in England among the Saxons and the Britons. It is not born today among the working classes. How, then, could it have been born among women whose work began, according to Professor Trevelyan, almost before they were out of the nursery, who were forced to it by their parents and held to it by all the power of law and custom? Yet genius of a sort must have existed among women as it must have existed among the working classes. Now and again an Emily Brontë or a Robert Burns blazes out and proves its presence.[6] But certainly it never got itself on to paper. When, however, one reads of a witch being ducked, of a woman possessed by devils, of a wise woman selling herbs, or even of a very remarkable man who had a mother, then I think we are on the track of a lost novelist, a suppressed poet, of some mute and inglorious[7] Jane Austen, some Emily Brontë who dashed her brains out on the moor or moped and mowed about the highways crazed with the torture that her gift had put her to. Indeed, I would venture to guess that Anon, who wrote so many poems without signing them, was often a woman. It was a woman Edward Fitzgerald,[8] I think, suggested who made the ballads and the folk-songs, crooning them to her children, beguiling her spinning with them, or the length of the winter's night.

This may be true or it may be false — who can say? — but what is true in it, so it seemed to me, reviewing the story of Shakespeare's sister as I had made it, is that any woman born with a great gift in the sixteenth century would certainly have gone crazed, shot herself, or ended her days in some lonely cottage outside the village, half witch, half wizard, feared and mocked at. For it needs little skill in psychology to be sure that a highly gifted girl who had tried to use her gift for poetry would have been so thwarted and hindered by other people, so tortured and pulled asunder by her own contrary instincts, that she must have lost her health and sanity to a certainty. No girl could have walked to London and stood at a stage door and forced her way into the presence of actor-managers without doing herself a violence and suffering an anguish which may have been irrational — for chastity may be a fetish invented by certain societies for unknown reasons — but were none the less inevitable. Chastity had then, it has even now, a religious importance in a woman's life, and has so

---

[5] A tavern.

[6] Emily Brontë (1818–1848), English novelist, and Robert Burns (1759–1796), Scottish poet.

[7] Thomas Gray's description in "Elegy Written in a Country Churchyard" of a peasant whose underdeveloped poetic genius might be as powerful as the great John Milton's.

[8] Edward FitzGerald (1809–1883), translator and poet.

wrapped itself round with nerves and instincts that to cut it free and bring it to the light of day demands courage of the rarest. To have lived a free life in London in the sixteenth century would have meant for a woman who was poet and playwright a nervous stress and dilemma which might well have killed her. Had she survived, whatever she had written would have been twisted and deformed, issuing from a strained and morbid imagination. And undoubtedly, I thought, looking at the shelf where there are no plays by women, her work would have gone unsigned. That refuge she would have sought certainly. It was the relic of the sense of chastity that dictated anonymity to women even so late as the nineteenth century. Currer Bell, George Eliot, George Sand,[9] all the victims of inner strife as their writings prove, sought ineffectively to veil themselves by using the name of a man. Thus they did homage to the convention, which if not implanted by the other sex was liberally encouraged by them (the chief glory of a woman is not to be talked of, said Pericles,[10] himself a much-talked-of man), that publicity in women is detestable. . . .

That woman, then, who was born with a gift of poetry in the sixteenth century, was an unhappy woman, a woman at strife against herself. All the conditions of her life, all her own instincts, were hostile to the state of mind which is needed to set free whatever is in the brain. But what is the state of mind that is most propitious to the act of creation, I asked? Can one come by any notion of the state that furthers and makes possible that strange activity? Here I opened the volume containing the Tragedies of Shakespeare. What was Shakespeare's state of mind, for instance, when he wrote *Lear* and *Antony and Cleopatra*? It was certainly the state of mind most favourable to poetry that there has ever existed. But Shakespeare himself said nothing about it. We only know casually and by chance that he "never blotted a line."[11] Nothing indeed was ever said by the artist himself about his state of mind until the eighteenth century perhaps. Rousseau[12] perhaps began it. At any rate, by the nineteenth century self-consciousness had developed so far that it was the habit for men of letters to describe their minds in confessions and autobiographies. Their lives also were written, and their letters were printed after their deaths. Thus, though we do not know what Shakespeare went through when he wrote *Lear*, we do know what Carlyle went through when he wrote the *French Revolution*; what Flaubert went through when he wrote *Madame Bovary*; what Keats was going through when he tried to write poetry against the coming of death and the indifference of the world.

And one gathers from this enormous modern literature of confession and self-analysis that to write a work of genius is almost always a feat of prodigious difficulty. Everything is against the likelihood that it will come from the writer's mind whole and entire. Generally material circumstances are against it. Dogs

---

[9] The pseudonyms of Charlotte Brontë (1816–1855) and Mary Ann Evans (1819–1880), English novelists, and Amandine-Aurore-Lucie Dupin (1804–1876), French novelist.

[10] Pericles (ca. 495–429 BCE), Athenian statesman and general.

[11] According to Ben Jonson, Shakespeare's contemporary.

[12] Jean-Jacques Rousseau (1712–1778), French philosopher, author of *The Confessions of Jean-Jacques Rousseau*.

will bark; people will interrupt; money must be made; health will break down. Further, accentuating all these difficulties and making them harder to bear is the world's notorious indifference. It does not ask people to write poems and novels and histories; it does not need them. It does not care whether Flaubert finds the right word or whether Carlyle scrupulously verifies this or that fact. Naturally, it will not pay for what it does not want. And so the writer, Keats, Flaubert, Carlyle, suffers, especially in the creative years of youth, every form of distraction and discouragement. A curse, a cry of agony, rises from those books of analysis and confession. "Mighty poets in their misery dead"[13] — that is the burden of their song. If anything comes through in spite of this, it is a miracle, and probably no book is born entire and uncrippled as it was conceived.

But for women, I thought, looking at the empty shelves, these difficulties were infinitely more formidable. In the first place, to have a room of her own, let alone a quiet room or a sound-proof room, was out of the question, unless her parents were exceptionally rich or very noble, even up to the beginning of the nineteenth century. Since her pin money, which depended on the good will of her father, was only enough to keep her clothed, she was debarred from such alleviations as came even to Keats or Tennyson or Carlyle, all poor men, from a walking tour, a little journey to France, from the separate lodging which, even if it were miserable enough, sheltered them from the claims and tyrannies of their families. Such material difficulties were formidable; but much worse were the immaterial. The indifference of the world which Keats and Flaubert and other men of genius have found so hard to bear was in her case not indifference but hostility. The world did not say to her as it said to them, Write if you choose; it makes no difference to me. The world said with a guffaw, Write? What's the good of your writing? . . .

I told you in the course of this paper that Shakespeare had a sister; but do not look for her in Sir Sidney Lee's life of the poet. She died young — alas, she never wrote a word. She lies buried where the omnibuses now stop, opposite the Elephant and Castle. Now my belief is that this poet who never wrote a word and was buried at the cross-roads still lives. She lives in you and me, and in many other women who are not here tonight, for they are washing up the dishes and putting the children to bed. But she lives; for great poets do not die; they are continuing presences; they need only the opportunity to walk among us in the flesh. This opportunity, as I think, it is now coming within your power to give her. For my belief is that if we live another century or so — I am talking of the common life which is the real life and not of the little separate lives which we live as individuals — and have five hundred a year each of us and rooms of our own; if we have the habit of freedom and the courage to write exactly what we think; if we escape a little from the common sitting-room and see human beings not always in their relation to each other but in relation to reality; and the sky, too, and the trees or whatever it may be in themselves; if we look past

---

[13] From William Wordsworth's poem "Resolution and Independence."

Milton's bogey, for no human being should shut out the view; if we face the fact, for it is a fact, that there is no arm to cling to, but that we go alone and that our relation is to the world of reality and not only to the world of men and women, then the opportunity will come and the dead poet who was Shakespeare's sister will put on the body which she has so often laid down. Drawing her life from the lives of the unknown who were her forerunners, as her brother did before her, she will be born. As for her coming without that preparation, without that effort on our part, without that determination that when she is born again she shall find it possible to live and write her poetry, that we cannot expect, for that would be impossible. But I maintain that she would come if we worked for her, and that so to work, even in poverty and obscurity, is worth while.

## FOR ANALYSIS

**1.** How does Woolf explain the contrast between the women of fact and women as they have been portrayed in fiction?

**2.** What answers do historians provide to the "perennial puzzle" Woolf mentions in the first sentence of paragraph 2? What generalizations might we make about the meaning of "history" on the basis of Woolf's research into the status of women?

**3.** Analyze the effect of Woolf's concluding remarks about the bishop (para. 6): "Cats do not go to heaven. Women cannot write the plays of Shakespeare." Then consider her later comment (para. 8), "I agree with the deceased bishop, if such he was — it is unthinkable that any woman in Shakespeare's day should have had Shakespeare's genius." Does this contradict what she has been saying?

**4.** Explain the link Woolf makes between chastity and the problem of the gifted woman writer (para. 9).

**5.** In what ways does the first part of Woolf's essay prepare the reader to accept her imagined life of Shakespeare's sister?

## MAKING ARGUMENTS

Do you believe that our culture has changed so significantly in its attitudes toward women that Woolf's arguments have lost their relevance? Write an essay arguing why or why not.

## WRITING TOPIC

Speculate on why, while being as economically dependent on men as servants were throughout much of Western history, women were sometimes portrayed in fiction as being "as great as a man, some think even greater" (para. 3).

## MAKING CONNECTIONS

**1.** Among the women who "have burnt like beacons" (para. 3) in the works of great male writers, Woolf cites Desdemona in Shakespeare's *Othello* (p. 664). Do you agree with her assessment? Might Woolf have included Nora in Ibsen's *A Doll's House* (p. 194)? Explain.

**2.** What do you think Woolf would think of Mrs. Peters and Mrs. Hale in Susan Glaspell's *Trifles* (p. 753) and Calixta in Kate Chopin's "The Storm" (p. 579)?

## GEORGE ORWELL  (1903–1950)

# SHOOTING AN ELEPHANT  1936

In Moulmein, in lower Burma, I was hated by large numbers of people — the only time in my life that I have been important enough for this to happen to me. I was sub-divisional police officer of the town, and in an aimless, petty kind of way anti-European feeling was very bitter. No one had the guts to raise a riot, but if a European woman went through the bazaars alone somebody would probably spit betel juice over her dress. As a police officer I was an obvious target and was baited whenever it seemed safe to do so. When a nimble Burman tripped me up on the football field and the referee (another Burman) looked the other way, the crowd yelled with hideous laughter. This happened more than once. In the end the sneering yellow faces of young men that met me everywhere, the insults hooted after me when I was at a safe distance, got badly on my nerves. The young Buddhist priests were the worst of all. There were several thousands of them in the town and none of them seemed to have anything to do except stand on street corners and jeer at Europeans.

All this was perplexing and upsetting. For at that time I had already made up my mind that imperialism was an evil thing and the sooner I chucked up my job and got out of it the better. Theoretically — and secretly, of course — I was all for the Burmese and all against their oppressors, the British. As for the job I was doing, I hated it more bitterly than I can perhaps make clear. In a job like that you see the dirty work of Empire at close quarters. The wretched prisoners huddling in the stinking cages of the lock-ups, the grey, cowed faces of the long-term convicts, the scarred buttocks of the men who had been flogged with bamboos — all these oppressed me with an intolerable sense of guilt. But I could get nothing into perspective. I was young and ill-educated and I had had to think out my problems in the utter silence that is imposed on every Englishman in the East. I did not even know that the British Empire is dying, still less did I know that it is a great deal better than the younger empires that are going to supplant it. All I knew was that I was stuck between my hatred of the empire I served and my rage against the evil-spirited little beasts who tried to make my job impossible. With one part of my mind I thought of the British[1] as an unbreakable tyranny, as something clamped down, *in saecula saeculorum*,[2] upon the will of prostrate peoples; with another part I thought that the greatest joy in the world would be to drive a bayonet into a Buddhist priest's guts. Feelings like these are the normal by-products of imperialism; ask any Anglo-Indian official, if you can catch him off duty.

[1] The imperial British government of India and Burma.
[2] For eternity.

One day something happened which in a roundabout way was enlightening. It was a tiny incident in itself, but it gave me a better glimpse than I had had before of the real nature of imperialism — the real motive for which despotic governments act. Early one morning the sub-inspector at a police station the other end of the town rang me up on the 'phone and said that an elephant was ravaging the bazaar. Would I please come and do something about it? I did not know what I could do, but I wanted to see what was happening and I got on to a pony and started out. I took my rifle, an old .44 Winchester and much too small to kill an elephant, but I thought the noise might be useful *in terrorem*. Various Burmans stopped me on the way and told me about the elephant's doings. It was not, of course, a wild elephant, but a tame one which had gone "must." It had been chained up, as tame elephants always are when their attack of "must" is due, but on the previous night it had broken its chain and escaped. Its mahout,[3] the only person who could manage it when it was in that state, had set out in pursuit, but had taken the wrong direction and was now twelve hours' journey away, and in the morning the elephant had suddenly reappeared in the town. The Burmese population had no weapons and were quite helpless against it. It had already destroyed somebody's bamboo hut, killed a cow and raided some fruit-stalls and devoured the stock; also it had met the municipal rubbish van and, when the driver jumped out and took to his heels, had turned the van over and inflicted violences upon it.

The Burmese sub-inspector and some Indian constables were waiting for me in the quarter where the elephant had been seen. It was a very poor quarter, a labyrinth of squalid bamboo huts, thatched with palm-leaf, winding all over a steep hillside. I remember that it was a cloudy, stuffy morning at the beginning of the rains. We began questioning the people as to where the elephant had gone and, as usual, failed to get any definite information. That is invariably the case in the East; a story always sounds clear enough at a distance, but the nearer you get to the scene of events the vaguer it becomes. Some of the people said that the elephant had gone in one direction, some said that he had gone in another, some professed not even to have heard of any elephant. I had almost made up my mind that the whole story was a pack of lies, when we heard yells a little distance away. There was a loud, scandalized cry of "Go away, child! Go away this instant!" and an old woman with a switch in her hand came round the corner of a hut, violently shooing away a crowd of naked children. Some more women followed, clicking their tongues and exclaiming; evidently there was something that the children ought not to have seen. I rounded the hut and saw a man's dead body sprawling in the mud. He was an Indian, a black Dravidian coolie, almost naked, and he could not have been dead many minutes. The people said that the elephant had come suddenly upon him round the corner of the hut, caught him with its trunk, put its foot on his back and ground him into the earth. This was the rainy season and the ground was soft, and his face had scored a trench a foot deep and a couple of yards long. He was lying on his

---

[3] The keeper and driver of an elephant.

belly with arms crucified and head sharply twisted to one side. His face was coated with mud, the eyes wide open, the teeth bared and grinning with an expression of unendurable agony. (Never tell me, by the way, that the dead look peaceful. Most of the corpses I have seen look devilish.) The friction of the great beast's foot had stripped the skin from his back as neatly as one skins a rabbit. As soon as I saw the dead man I sent an orderly to a friend's house nearby to borrow an elephant rifle. I had already sent back the pony, not wanting it to go mad with fright and throw me if it smelt the elephant.

The orderly came back in a few minutes with a rifle and five cartridges, and meanwhile some Burmans had arrived and told us that the elephant was in the paddy fields below, only a few hundred yards away. As I started forward practically the whole population of the quarter flocked out of the houses and followed me. They had seen the rifle and were all shouting excitedly that I was going to shoot the elephant. They had not shown much interest in the elephant when he was merely ravaging their homes, but it was different now that he was going to be shot. It was a bit of fun to them, as it would be to an English crowd; besides they wanted the meat. It made me vaguely uneasy. I had no intention of shooting the elephant — I had merely sent for the rifle to defend myself if necessary — and it is always unnerving to have a crowd following you. I marched down the hill, looking and feeling a fool, with the rifle over my shoulders and an ever-growing army of people jostling at my heels. At the bottom, when you got away from the huts, there was a metalled road and beyond that a miry waste of paddy fields a thousand yards across, not yet ploughed but soggy from the first rains and dotted with coarse grass. The elephant was standing eight yards from the road, his left side towards us. He took not the slightest notice of the crowd's approach. He was tearing up branches of grass, beating them against his knees to clean them and stuffing them into his mouth.

I had halted on the road. As soon as I saw the elephant I knew with perfect certainty that I ought not to shoot him. It is a serious matter to shoot a working elephant — it is comparable to destroying a huge and costly piece of machinery — and obviously one ought not to do it if it can possibly be avoided. And at that distance, peacefully eating, the elephant looked no more dangerous than a cow. I thought then and I think now that his attack of "must" was already passing off; in which case he would merely wander harmlessly about until the mahout came back and caught him. Moreover, I did not in the least want to shoot him. I decided that I would watch him for a little while to make sure that he did not turn savage again, and then go home.

But at that moment I glanced round at the crowd that had followed me. It was an immense crowd, two thousand at the least and growing every minute. It blocked the road for a long distance on either side. I looked at the sea of yellow faces above the garish clothes — faces all happy and excited over this bit of fun, all certain that the elephant was going to be shot. They were watching me as they would watch a conjurer about to perform a trick. They did not like me, but with the magical rifle in my hands I was momentarily worth watching. And suddenly I realized that I should have to shoot the elephant after all. The people expected it of me and I had got to do it; I could feel their two thousand wills pressing me forward, irresistibly. And it was at this moment, as I stood there with the rifle in my hands, that I first grasped the hollowness, the futility of the white man's dominion in the East. Here was I, the white man with his gun, standing in front of the unarmed native crowd — seemingly the leading actor of the piece; but in reality I was only an absurd puppet pushed to and fro by the will of those yellow faces behind. I perceived in this moment that when the white man turns tyrant it is his own freedoms that he destroys. He becomes a sort of hollow, posing dummy, the conventionalized figure of a sahib. For it is the condition of his rule that he shall spend his life in trying to impress the "natives," and so in every crisis he has got to do what the "natives" expect of him. He wears a mask, and his face grows to fit it. I had got to shoot the elephant. I had committed myself to doing it when I sent for the rifle. A sahib has got to act like a sahib; he has got to appear resolute, to know his own mind and do definite things. To come all that way, rifle in hand, with two thousand people marching at my heels, and then to trail feebly away, having done nothing — no, that was impossible. The crowd would laugh at me. And my whole life, every white man's life in the East, was one long struggle not to be laughed at.

But I did not want to shoot the elephant. I watched him beating his bunch of grass against his knees, with that preoccupied grandmotherly air that elephants have. It seemed to me that it would be murder to shoot him. At that age I was not squeamish about killing animals, but I had never shot an elephant and never wanted to. (Somehow it always seems worse to kill a *large* animal.) Besides, there was the beast's owner to be considered. Alive, the elephant was worth at least a hundred pounds; dead, he would only be worth the value of his tusks, five pounds, possibly. But I had to act quickly. I turned to some experienced-looking Burmans who had been there when we arrived, and asked them how the elephant had been behaving. They all said the same thing: he took no notice of you if you left him alone, but he might charge if you went too close to him.

It was perfectly clear to me what I ought to do. I ought to walk up to within, say, twenty-five yards of the elephant and test his behavior. If he charged, I could shoot; if he took no notice of me, it would be safe to leave him until the mahout came back. But also I knew that I was going to do no such thing. I was a poor shot with a rifle and the ground was soft mud into which one would sink at every step. If the elephant charged and I missed him, I should have about as much chance as a toad under a steam-roller. But even then I was not thinking particularly of my own skin, only of the watchful yellow faces behind. For at that moment, with the crowd watching me, I was not afraid in the ordinary sense, as I would have been if I had been alone. A white man mustn't be frightened in front of "natives"; and so, in general, he isn't frightened. The sole thought in my mind was that if anything went wrong those two thousand Burmans would see me pursued, caught, trampled on and reduced to a grinning corpse like that Indian up the hill. And if that happened it was quite probable that some of them would laugh. That would never do. There was only one alternative. I shoved the cartridges into the magazine and lay down on the road to get a better aim.

The crowd grew very still, and a deep, low, happy sigh, as of people who see the 10 theatre curtain go up at last, breathed from innumerable throats. They were going to have their bit of fun after all. The rifle was a beautiful German thing with cross-hair sights. I did not then know that in shooting an elephant one would shoot to cut an imaginary bar running from ear-hole to ear-hole. I ought, therefore, as the elephant was sideways on, to have aimed straight at his ear-hole; actually I aimed several inches in front of this, thinking the brain would be further forward.

When I pulled the trigger I did not hear the bang or feel the kick — one never does when a shot goes home — but I heard the devilish roar of glee that went up from the crowd. In that instant, in too short a time, one would have thought, even for the bullet to get there, a mysterious, terrible change had come over the elephant. He neither stirred nor fell, but every line of his body had altered. He looked suddenly stricken, shrunken, immensely old, as though the fright-ful impact of the bullet had paralysed him without knocking him down. At last, after what seemed a long time — it might have been five seconds, I dare say — he sagged flabbily to his knees. His mouth slobbered. An enormous senil-ity seemed to have settled upon him. One could have imagined him thousands of years old. I fired again into the same spot. At the second shot he did not col-lapse but climbed with desperate slowness to his feet and stood weakly upright, with legs sagging and head drooping. I fired a third time. That was the shot that did for him. You could see the agony of it jolt his whole body and knock the last remnant of strength from his legs. But in falling he seemed for a moment to rise, for as his hind legs collapsed beneath him he seemed to tower upward like a huge rock toppling, his trunk reaching skywards like a tree. He trumpeted, for the first and only time. And then down he came, his belly towards me, with a crash that seemed to shake the ground even where I lay.

I got up. The Burmans were already racing past me across the mud. It was obvious that the elephant would never rise again, but he was not dead. He was breathing very rhythmically with long rattling gasps, his great mound of a side painfully rising and falling. His mouth was wide open — I could see far down into caverns of pale pink throat. I waited a long time for him to die, but his breathing did not weaken. Finally I fired my two remaining shots into the spot where I thought his heart must be. The thick blood welled out of him like red velvet, but still he did not die. His body did not even jerk when the shots hit him, the tortured breathing continued without a pause. He was dying, very slowly and in great agony, but in some world remote from me where not even a bullet could damage him further. I felt that I had got to put an end to that dreadful noise. It seemed dreadful to see the great beast lying there, powerless to move and yet powerless to die, and not even to be able to finish him. I sent back for my small rifle and poured shot after shot into his heart and down his throat. They seemed to make no impression. The tortured gasps continued as steadily as the ticking of a clock.

In the end I could not stand it any longer and went away. I heard later that it took him half an hour to die. Burmans were bringing dahs[4] and baskets even

[4] Knives.

before I left, and I was told they had stripped his body almost to the bones by the afternoon.

Afterwards, of course, there were endless discussions about the shooting of the elephant. The owner was furious, but he was only an Indian and could do nothing. Besides, legally I had done the right thing, for a mad elephant has to be killed, like a mad dog, if its owner fails to control it. Among the Europeans opinion was divided. The older men said I was right, the younger men said it was a damn shame to shoot an elephant for killing a coolie, because an elephant was worth more than any damn Coringhee coolie. And afterwards I was very glad that the coolie had been killed; it put me legally in the right and it gave me a sufficient pretext for shooting the elephant. I often wondered whether any of the others grasped that I had done it solely to avoid looking a fool.

## FOR ANALYSIS

**1.** Examine carefully paragraphs 11 and 12, in which Orwell describes the death of the elephant. Is the reader meant to take the passage only literally, or can a case be made that the elephant's death is imbued with **symbolic** meaning? Explain.

**2.** Orwell tells us repeatedly that his sympathies are with the Burmese. Yet he describes them as "evil-spirited little beasts" (para. 2). Explain this ambivalence.

**3.** What does the experience described in paragraph 7 teach Orwell?

**4.** What is your reaction to Orwell's final comment: "I was very glad that the coolie had been killed; it put me legally in the right and it gave me a sufficient pretext for shooting the elephant. I often wondered whether any of the others grasped that I had done it solely to avoid looking a fool"?

**5.** Midway through the essay (para. 7), Orwell discloses the significance the event had for him. Why does he disclose it then rather than save it for the conclusion?

## MAKING ARGUMENTS

Do you agree with Orwell's rationalization that under the circumstances he had no choice but "to shoot the elephant" (para. 7)? Build an argument for your answer.

## WRITING TOPICS

**1.** In a brief paragraph, summarize the lesson Orwell learned from his experience.

**2.** What does Orwell conclude about the position of foreign authorities in a hostile country?

**3.** Describe a situation in which you were required to behave in an official capacity in a way that contradicted your personal beliefs.

## MAKING CONNECTIONS

**1.** Compare the techniques and arguments used in this essay to attack imperialism with those used in Swift's "A Modest Proposal" (p. 403).

**2.** While they are dissimilar in subject matter, this story and Bambara's "The Lesson" (p. 100) culminate in climactic events that change the **protagonists**. Compare those events and their effect on the two protagonists.

**EULA BISS** (B. 1977)

# TIME AND DISTANCE OVERCOME 2008

O f what use is such an invention?" *The New York World* asked shortly
after Alexander Graham Bell first demonstrated his telephone in 1876.
The world was not waiting for the telephone.

Bell's financial backers asked him not to work on his new invention anymore because it seemed too dubious an investment. The idea on which the
telephone depended — the idea that every home in the country could be connected with a vast network of wires suspended from poles set an average of one
hundred feet apart — seemed far more unlikely than the idea that the human
voice could be transmitted through a wire.

Even now it is an impossible idea, that we are all connected, all of us.

"At the present time we have a perfect network of gas pipes and water pipes
throughout our large cities," Bell wrote to his business partners, in defense of
his idea. "We have main pipes laid under the streets communicating by side
pipes with the various dwellings. . . . In a similar manner it is conceivable that
cables of telephone wires could be laid under ground, or suspended overhead,
communicating by branch wires with private dwellings, counting houses,
shops, manufactories, etc., uniting them through the main cable. . . ."

Imagine the mind that could imagine this. That could see us all connected 5
through one branching cable. The mind of a man who wanted to invent, more
than the telephone, a machine that would allow the deaf to hear.

For a short time, the telephone was little more than a novelty. For twenty-five
cents you could see it demonstrated by Bell himself, in a church, along with some
singing and recitations by local talent. From a mile away, Bell would receive a
call from "the invisible Mr. Watson." Then the telephone became a plaything of
the rich. A Boston banker paid for a private line between his office and his home
so that he could let his family know exactly when he would be home for dinner.

Mark Twain was among the first to own a telephone, but he wasn't completely
taken with it. "The human voice carries entirely too far as it is," he remarked.

By 1889, *The New York Times* was reporting a "War on Telephone Poles."
Wherever telephone companies were erecting poles, homeowners and business owners were sawing them down, or defending their sidewalks with rifles.

In Red Bank, New Jersey, property owners threatened to tar and feather the
workers putting up telephone poles. One judge granted a group of homeowners an injunction to prevent the telephone company from erecting any new
poles. Another judge found that a man who had cut down a pole because it was
"obnoxious" was not guilty of malicious mischief.

Telephone poles, newspaper editorials complained, were an urban blight. 10
The poles carried a wire for each telephone — sometimes hundreds of wires.

562

And in some places there were also telegraph wires, power lines, and trolley cables. The sky was filled with wires.

The War on Telephone Poles was fueled, in part, by that terribly American concern for private property and a reluctance to surrender it to a shared utility. And then there was a fierce sense of aesthetics, an obsession with purity, a dislike for the way the poles and wires marred a landscape that those other new inventions, skyscrapers and barbed wire, were just beginning to complicate. And then perhaps there was also a fear that distance, as it had always been known and measured, was collapsing.

The city council in Sioux Falls, South Dakota, ordered policemen to cut down all the telephone poles in town. And the Mayor of Oshkosh, Wisconsin, ordered the police chief and the fire department to chop down the telephone poles there. Only one pole was chopped down before the telephone men climbed all the poles along the line, preventing any more chopping. Soon, Bell Telephone Company began stationing a man at the top of each pole as soon as it had been set, until enough poles had been set to string a wire between them, at which point it became a misdemeanor to interfere with the poles. Even so, a constable cut down two poles holding forty or fifty wires. And a homeowner sawed down a recently wired pole then fled from police. The owner of a cannery ordered his workers to throw dirt back into the hole the telephone company was digging in front of his building. His men threw the dirt back in as fast as the telephone workers could dig it out. Then he sent out a team with a load of stones to dump into the hole. Eventually, the pole was erected on the other side of the street.

Despite the War on Telephone Poles, it would take only four years after Bell's first public demonstration of the telephone for every town of over 10,000 people to be wired, although many towns were wired only to themselves. And by the turn of the century, there were more telephones than bathtubs in America.

"Time and dist. overcome," read an early advertisement for the telephone. Rutherford B. Hayes pronounced the installation of a telephone in the White House "one of the greatest events since creation." The telephone, Thomas Edison declared, "annihilated time and space, and brought the human family in closer touch."

In 1898, in Lake Comorant, Mississippi, a black man was hanged from a 15 telephone pole. And in Weir City, Kansas. And in Brook Haven, Mississippi. And in Tulsa, where the hanged man was riddled with bullets. In Pittsburg, Kansas, a black man's throat was slit and his dead body was strung up on a telephone pole. Two black men were hanged from a telephone pole in Lewisburg, West Virginia. And two in Hempstead, Texas, where one man was dragged out of the courtroom by a mob and another was dragged out of jail.

A black man was hanged from a telephone pole in Belleville, Illinois, where a fire was set at the base of the pole and the man was cut down half-alive, covered in coal oil, and burned. While his body was burning, the mob beat it with clubs and nearly cut it to pieces.

Lynching, the first scholar of the subject determined, is an American invention. Lynching from bridges, from arches, from trees standing alone in fields, from trees in front of the county courthouse, from trees used as public billboards, from trees barely able to support the weight of a man, from telephone poles, from street lamps, and from poles erected for that purpose. From the middle of the nineteenth century to the middle of the twentieth century black men were lynched for crimes real and imagined, for "disputing with a white man," for "unpopularity," for "asking a white woman in marriage," for "peeping in a window."

The children's game of "telephone" depends on the fact that a message passed quietly from one ear to another to another will get distorted at some point along the line.

In Pine Bluff, Arkansas, a black man charged with kicking a white girl was hanged from a telephone pole. In Long View, Texas, a black man accused of attacking a white woman was hanged from a telephone pole. In Greenville, Mississippi, a black man accused of attacking a white telephone operator was hanged from a telephone pole. "The negro only asked time to pray." In Purcell, Oklahoma, a black man accused of attacking a white woman was tied to a telephone pole and burned. "Men and women in automobiles stood up to watch him die."

The poles, of course, were not to blame. It was only coincidence that they 20 became convenient as gallows, because they were tall and straight, with a crossbar, and because they stood in public places. And it was only coincidence that the telephone pole so closely resembled a crucifix.

Early telephone calls were full of noise. "Such a jangle of meaningless noises had never been heard by human ears," Herbert Casson wrote in his 1910 *History of the Telephone.* "There were the rustling of leaves, the croaking of frogs, the hissing of steam, the flapping of birds' wings. . . . There were spluttering and bubbling, jerking and rasping, whistling and screaming."

In Shreveport, a black man charged with attacking a white girl was hanged from a telephone pole. "A knife was left sticking in the body." In Cumming, Georgia, a black man accused of assaulting a white girl was shot repeatedly then hanged from a telephone pole. In Waco, Texas, a black man convicted of killing a white woman was taken from the courtroom by a mob and burned, then his charred body was hung from a telephone pole.

A postcard was made from the photo of a burned man hanging from a telephone pole in Texas, his legs broken off below the knee and his arms curled up and blackened. Postcards of lynchings were sent out as greetings and warnings until 1908, when the Postmaster General declared them unmailable. "This is the barbecue we had last night," reads one.

"If we are to die," W. E. B. Du Bois wrote in 1911, "in God's name let us not perish like bales of hay." And "if we must die," Claude McKay wrote ten years later, "let it not be like hogs. . . ."

In Danville, Illinois, a black man was hanged from a telephone pole, cut 25 down, burned, shot, and stoned with bricks. "At first the negro was defiant,"

*The New York Times* reported, "but just before he was hanged he begged hard for his life."

In the photographs, the bodies of the men lynched from telephone poles are silhouetted against the sky. Sometimes two men to a pole, hanging above the buildings of a town. Sometimes three. They hung like flags in still air.

In Cumberland, Maryland, a mob used a telephone pole as a battering ram to break into the jail where a black man charged with the murder of a policeman was being held. They kicked him to death then fired twenty shots into his head. They wanted to burn his body, but a minister asked them not to.

The lynchings happened everywhere, all over the United States. From shortly before the invention of the telephone to long after the first trans-Atlantic call. More in the South, and more in rural areas. In the cities and in the North there were race riots.

Riots in Cincinnati, New Orleans, Memphis, New York, Atlanta, Philadelphia, Houston. . . .

During the race riots that destroyed the black section of Springfield, Ohio, a black man was shot and hanged from a telephone pole. 30

During the race riots that set fire to East St. Louis and forced five hundred black people to flee their homes, a black man was hanged from a telephone pole. The rope broke and his body fell into the gutter. "Negros are lying in the gutters every few feet in some places," read the newspaper account.

In 1921, the year before Bell died, four companies of the National Guard were called out to end a race war in Tulsa that began when a white woman accused a black man of rape. Bell had lived to complete the first call from New York to San Francisco, which required 14,000 miles of copper wire and 130,000 telephone poles.

My grandfather was a lineman. He broke his back when a telephone pole fell. "Smashed him onto the road," my father says.

When I was young, I believed that the arc and swoop of telephone wires along the roadways were beautiful. I believed that the telephone poles, with their glass transformers catching the evening sun, were glorious. I believed my father when he said, "My dad could raise a pole by himself." And I believed that the telephone itself was a miracle.

Now, I tell my sister, these poles, these wires do not look the same to me. 35 Nothing is innocent, my sister reminds me. But nothing, I would like to think, remains unrepentant.

One summer, heavy rains fell in Nebraska and some green telephone poles grew small leafy branches.

## A Note on "Time and Distance Overcome"

I began my research for this essay by searching for every instance of the phrase "telephone pole" in the *New York Times* from 1880 to 1920, which resulted in 370 articles. As I read through these articles, starting with the oldest and working forward in time, I was not prepared to discover, in the process, a litany of lynchings. I had not intended to write an essay about lynching, but I found that, given what my research was yielding, I could not avoid it. After reading an article headlined "Colored Scoundrel Lynched," and then another headlined "Mississippi Negro Lynched," and then another headlined "Texas Negro Lynched," I searched for every instance of the word "lynched" in the *New York Times* from 1880 to 1920, which resulted in 2,354 articles.

I refer, in this essay, to the first scholar of lynching, meaning James E. Cutler, author of the 1905 book *Lynch-Law*, in which he writes, on the first page, "lynching is a criminal practice which is peculiar to the United States." This is debatable, of course, and very possibly not true, but there is good evidence that the Italian Antonio Meucci invented a telephone years before Bell began working on his device, so as long as we are going to lay claim to one invention, we might as well take responsibility for the other.

## FOR ANALYSIS

**1.** When does "Time and Distance Overcome" become about more than the advent and spread of the telephone? Make a list of the additional concerns and historical developments Biss connects to Bell's invention. What unites these things?

**2.** Track some of the ironies in Biss's essay, for example, ways in which earlier statements about the value of the telephone (or the negative value of the pole, to some) can be seen differently later.

**3.** What do you make of the essay's final image?

## MAKING ARGUMENTS

The formal technique of juxtaposition is crucial to the way this essay works. Make an argument, relying on a firm definition of juxtaposition and the evidence of particular textual observations, for why this is so and for how the technique is successful.

## WRITING TOPIC

In her note, Biss writes: "I had not intended to write an essay about lynching, but I found that, given what my research was yielding, I could not avoid it." Try to do something similar by researching the history of something everyday and important like the telephone and seeing what unexpected histories emerge. Keep a log of your attempts: it is unlikely you will succeed on your first try, and a record of your failures may itself be instructive about the ways in which research can lead to planned and unplanned outcomes.

## MAKING CONNECTIONS

Read Biss's essay with Carolyn Forché's "The Colonel" (p. 363). What similarities and/or differences do you see in the way that Biss and Forché represent violence in their works?

There are different ways to feel alien to or excluded from a culture. Many people tend to think of immigrants this way: that they often experience a dislocation that is more than geographical, as their cultural environment changes while individual identity lags behind. But there are also ways in which native-born people can feel as if they do not belong. Sometimes this exclusion is felt as a result of racial or ethnic identity in places where the mainstream culture is defined partly by these things, but it can also be the result of differences in social class. All of these "outsider" positions can give writers a unique vantage point. As you read these essays, think about what the experiences of these authors allow them to see. Do they see things in America that native-born people, or people born to the dominant or majority ethnicity or class, may not? Do they see themselves differently, too?

## BHARATI MUKHERJEE (1940–2017)

# TWO WAYS TO BELONG IN AMERICA 1996

This is a tale of two sisters from Calcutta, Mira and Bharati, who have lived in the United States for some thirty-five years, but who find themselves on different sides in the current debate over the status of immigrants.

I am an American citizen and she is not. I am moved that thousands of long-term residents are finally taking the oath of citizenship. She is not.

Mira arrived in Detroit in 1960 to study child psychology and preschool education. I followed her a year later to study creative writing at the University of Iowa. When we left India, we were almost identical in appearance and attitude. We dressed alike, in saris; we expressed identical views on politics, social issues, love, and marriage in the same Calcutta convent-school accent. We would endure our two years in America, secure our degrees, then return to India to marry the grooms of our father's choosing.

Instead, Mira married an Indian student in 1962 who was getting his business administration degree at Wayne State University. They soon acquired the labor certifications necessary for the green card of hassle-free residence and employment.

Mira still lives in Detroit, works in the Southfield, Michigan, school system, 5 and has become nationally recognized for her contributions in the fields of preschool education and parent-teacher relationships. After thirty-six years as a legal immigrant in this country, she clings passionately to her Indian citizenship and hopes to go home to India when she retires.

In Iowa City in 1963, I married a fellow student, an American of Canadian parentage. Because of the accident of his North Dakota birth, I bypassed labor-certification requirements and the race-related "quota" system that favored the applicant's country of origin over his or her merit. I was prepared for (and even welcomed) the emotional strain that came with marrying outside my ethnic community. In thirty-three years of marriage, we have lived in every part of North America. By choosing a husband who was not my father's selection, I was opting for fluidity, self-invention, blue jeans and T-shirts, and renouncing three thousand years (at least) of caste-observant, "pure culture" marriage in the Mukherjee family. My books have often been read as unapologetic (and in some quarters overenthusiastic) texts for cultural and psychological "mongrelization." It's a word I celebrate.

Mira and I have stayed sisterly close by phone. In our regular Sunday morning conversations, we are unguardedly affectionate. I am her only blood relative on this continent. We expect to see each other through the looming crises of aging and ill health without being asked. Long before Vice President Gore's "Citizenship U.S.A." drive, we'd had our polite arguments over the ethics of retaining an overseas citizenship while expecting the permanent protection and economic benefits that come with living and working in America.

Like well-raised sisters, we never said what was really on our minds, but we probably pitied one another. She, for the lack of structure in my life, the erasure of Indianness, the absence of an unvarying daily core. I, for the narrowness of her perspective, her uninvolvement with the mythic depths or the superficial pop culture of this society. But, now, with the scapegoating of "aliens" (documented or illegal) on the increase, and the targeting of long-term legal immigrants like Mira for new scrutiny and new self-consciousness, she and I find ourselves unable to maintain the same polite discretion. We were always unacknowledged adversaries, and we are now, more than ever, sisters.

"I feel used," Mira raged on the phone the other night. "I feel manipulated and discarded. This is such an unfair way to treat a person who was invited to stay and work here because of her talent. My employer went to the I.N.S. and petitioned for the labor certification. For over thirty years, I've invested my creativity and professional skills into the improvement of this country's preschool system. I've obeyed all the rules, I've paid my taxes, I love my work, I love my students, I love the friends I've made. How dare America now change its rules in midstream? If America wants to make new rules curtailing benefits of legal immigrants, they should apply only to immigrants who arrive after those rules are already in place." To my ears, it sounded like the description of a long-enduring, comfortable yet loveless marriage, without risk or recklessness. Have we the right to demand, and to expect, that we be loved? (That, to me, is the subtext of the arguments by immigration advocates.) My sister is an expatriate, professionally generous and creative, socially courteous and gracious, and that's as far as her Americanization can go. She is here to maintain an identity, not to transform it.

I asked her if she would follow the example of others who have decided to become citizens because of the anti-immigration bills in Congress. And here, 10 she surprised me. "If America wants to play the manipulative game, I'll play it too," she snapped. "I'll become a U.S. citizen for now, then change back to Indian when I'm ready to go home. I feel some kind of irrational attachment to India that I don't to America. Until all this hysteria against legal immigrants, I was totally happy. Having my green card meant I could visit any place in the world I wanted to and then come back to a job that's satisfying and that I do very well."

In one family, from two sisters alike as peas in a pod, there could not be a wider divergence of immigrant experience. America spoke to me — I married it — I embraced the demotion from expatriate aristocrat to immigrant nobody, surrendering those thousands of years of "pure culture," the saris, the delightfully accented English. She retained them all. Which of us is the freak?

Mira's voice, I realize, is the voice not just of the immigrant South Asian community but of an immigrant community of the millions who have stayed rooted in one job, one city, one house, one ancestral culture, one cuisine, for the entirety of their productive years. She speaks for greater numbers than I possibly can. Only the fluency of her English and the anger, rather than fear, born of confidence from her education, differentiate her from the seamstresses, the domestics, the technicians, the shop owners, the millions of hardworking but effectively silenced documented immigrants as well as their less fortunate "illegal" brothers and sisters.

Nearly twenty years ago, when I was living in my husband's ancestral homeland of Canada, I was always well employed but never allowed to feel part of the local Quebec or larger Canadian society. Then, through a Green Paper that invited a national referendum on the unwanted side effects of "nontraditional" immigration, the government officially turned against its immigrant communities, particularly those from South Asia.

I felt then the same sense of betrayal that Mira feels now.

I will never forget the pain of that sudden turning, and the casual racist out- 15 bursts the Green Paper elicited. That sense of betrayal had its desired effect and drove me, and thousands like me, from the country.

Mira and I differ, however, in the ways in which we hope to interact with the country that we have chosen to live in. She is happier to live in America as expatriate Indian than as an immigrant American. I need to feel like a part of the community I have adopted (as I tried to feel in Canada as well). I need to put roots down, to vote and make the difference that I can. The price that the immigrant willingly pays, and that the exile avoids, is the trauma of self-transformation.

**FOR ANALYSIS**

**1.** What does Mukherjee mean by "mongrelization" (para. 6)?

**2.** What is the "trauma of self-transformation" (para. 16)? Are there traumas felt by those who choose to remain faithful to their original identity?

**3.** What are Mukherjee's feelings about the culture she left behind? What does she value? To what does she object?

## MAKING ARGUMENTS

Immigration is a controversial political issue. Where do you stand on it? Should the United States make it easier or harder for immigrants to enter the country, to gain access to social services, to stay without becoming citizens, or to become citizens?

## WRITING TOPIC

Mukherjee's sister describes her attachment to India as "irrational" (para. 10), yet she maintains it. Does Mukherjee agree with her sister? Is she similarly attached to her nation, only her new one rather than her old one? Do you think feeling a deep connection to a nation and culture is irrational?

## LACY M. JOHNSON    (B. 1978)

# WHITE TRASH PRIMER    2009

You live with your mama and daddy, your two sisters, three dogs, two horses and exactly twelve cats on a farm so far from town you barely see the street lights' bright white tossed over the horizon. Your mama grows a garden of fresh green vegetables right outside your back door and you and your sisters pick peas and tomatoes in the afternoon while mama hangs clean white sheets on the clothesline and the hot sun freckles your shoulders with small brown spots. When your daddy comes up to the house all sweating and covered in hayseed you set the table and make sure the silverware's in all the right places or you have to drink water with your dinner instead of tea.

You attend second service every Sunday since the day you are born and Brother Dan or Brother Darrell preach about the glory and grace of Jesus Christ and you accept Him as your Lord and Savior or you burn in hell and this is why you've been baptized twice and saved exactly twenty-seven times. Every week your mama and you and your sisters get real dressed up in the pretty cotton dresses she makes special for wearing to church. Your mama's always made all your clothes special with her own two hands and you are grateful for each hem until the rich kids in your Sunday School don't look at you even when you sit right next to them. Your daddy says vanity's an expensive sin but sometimes your mama drives you and your sisters to Wal-Mart anyway and she buys you underwear and socks and a pair of Lee jeans that are exactly two inches shorter than your legs and she presses her lips real tight together the whole time. One day she stops making pretty cotton dresses but the rich kids still don't look at you. They never look at you.

You and your sisters have always got on real good together. On hot summer days you pack peanut-butter sandwiches in a napkin your sister ties to your belt loop and you spend all day wandering the woods along the farm. Your daddy cuts a path with the brush hog and builds a square fort with sixteen knotty black logs instead of dragging them up to the house for firewood. You stop there every day to eat your lunch and you go skinny dipping in the creek and splash your little sister with the cold cold water and sometimes she tells your daddy and all three of you get spanked. Sometimes at night your sister comes to sleep in your bed and you stay up late talking real soft together with your heads under the covers like two peas in a pod and your daddy has to get on you for staying up past your bedtime. One night after mama and daddy are in bed your sister tells you she's moving to an apartment above the Five and Dime downtown and you pull the covers back to see her face in the dark and she says you can come to her place to see her anytime you like. The next day she takes all of her clothes out of her closet and packs them up in a big black trash bag and carries them over her shoulder out the door. Your mama and daddy holler real loud when they find out your sister is living in sin with a black man and you don't get to see her for some time.

Your daddy lets you drive his pickup truck on the gravel road to your house when he's real tired even if you're not old enough because he says it's something you need to know how to do. When you're driving he turns on the radio and listens to Paul Harvey. Sometimes he disagrees with Paul Harvey and explains to you why he is right instead of resting. Sometimes he listens with his eyes closed and his head leaned back against the window. You know he's worrying over money because when your daddy worries over money his forehead gets to looking like tilled soil, mounded in rows like the creek bottom. He works real hard on the farm but the soybeans aren't selling and neither is the corn and the fence needs repairs and the plow's all busted so you take the truck into town without asking and you apply for a job at the fancy Wal-Mart but they don't call you to come in for an INTERVIEW. You apply six times and when they do call you pack peanut-butter sandwiches every day for lunch and every time you get a paycheck you put it in your daddy's bank and sometimes his eyes get to watering and you think he might be going soft. You save every penny you earn, but disappointment's what you get for dreaming because every penny ain't enough. Your daddy's a proud man and his eyes water the hardest you've ever seen when he signs the papers that sell the farm but this time you don't think it's cause he's soft.

You move into a white house with blue shutters and a yard with exactly 5 thirteen trees on a paved street in town and your daddy tears down all the walls and puts up new ones cause black mold spreads where you can't see. He works at the power plant and drops his yellow hard hat by the front door and your mama waits on rich folks at the restaurant and gets real dressed up for work every night and you don't have to set the table anymore cause you and your sister eat peanut-butter sandwiches for dinner and watch cable television before you go to bed. Sometimes you cut the sandwiches into circles with the mouth of a glass and sometimes you add pink and white candy sprinkles mama keeps in the cupboard for cupcakes and you tell your sister you've made her a SURPRISE. You walk to high school every day and you smoke cigarettes and cough down the peach schnapps your mama keeps hidden in the very back of the highest kitchen cabinet and even though it burns your stomach like hell fire you follow the kids to the one-block downtown and drive your truck in circles cause it's the only thing to do. You make friends with a girl your same age and she lets you spend the night at her place sometimes and you sleep real soundly in the AIR CONDITIONING. Sometimes she sneaks her boyfriend in and they have sex in the bed right next to you. One night he brings his friend over and he kisses you and claws your clothes off and you just want to sleep but his breath is stale and sweet like the beer your daddy drinks and when you try to push him off and tell him to stop he puts a pillow over your face and jams himself right up inside you and you can hardly breathe it burns so bad but there is nothing God will do.

You try real hard to get good grades in college cause you know exactly how much it cost but you work forty hours a week at Wal-Mart and sometimes you're so damn tired you can't read the PSYCHOLOGY open in front of you. Sometimes you don't know the words in front of you but you don't have a dictionary and if you fake it your teachers always know that you are faking. Your mama calls and asks how you're doing and you tell her you're doing great, mama, just great and one day she calls to tell you she has CANCER. Your hands sweat and your knees tremble together with sixteen of your cousins and your aunts and uncles and grandparents on both sides and both of your sisters in your mama's hospital room holding hands around her bed while your daddy asks the good Lord for STRENGTH. You don't even breathe until she's waking up from surgery with her mouth pawing open and each time you look she is weaker and smaller and closer to dying and each time your daddy palms his forehead he leaves tracks like the old creek bottom, but now you know it's not just money he worries over, so you tell him you'll drop out of school just till she's better but you don't plan to go back for some time.

You ask your mama how she feels when she picks you up from your apartment to take you to TACO BELL and she pushes you into the bathroom to show you where her breast used to be and hands you the silicon fist she keeps in her bra. You hold it with both hands. You order food. You sit down and when she's half-way through with her second SOFT TACO SUPREME you show her the pink flower tattoo your older sister bought you for your eighteenth birthday. Your mama doesn't say anything but her lips pressed real tight together tell you she is mad. Before she walks out the door and drives away she meets your eyes with hers and you know exactly what she means.

You hide that you are poor. You save up for a pair of LEVI'S jeans and put shirts on layaway. You take furniture from your neighbor's dumpster and thank your luck that they are wasteful. You fog your apartment for roaches and clean with bleach so they don't come out when you have company. You wash your car in the driveway with a hose and dishsoap. Your sister comes to visit and colors your hair NICE AND EASY 98 LIGHTEST BLONDE and paints your fingernails and toenails FIRE ENGINE RED. You make friends with a girl at work who is the same size as you and she gives you things she doesn't like anymore: a blue dress from the mall, a pair of black pumps, a pretty barrette with fake red crystals for your hair. She sets you up on dates with men and at dinner you order steaks and alcoholic drinks even if you're not old enough to drink. Sometimes you let them take you back to the fancy places where they live and if you have sex with them they take you shopping or to Springfield for the weekend and you thank your luck that they are gullible.

You act real tough but you've got a weak spot for HARLEY DAVIDSON motorcycles and a tall man in a leather coat with a broad chest and long black hair makes you want to ride. He takes you down a blacktop road clear out into nowhere and the whole time you've got that great big machine growling right under you, you're reeling in the smell of pine trees and wide green fields. So your fingers tighten on his arm. And your blond hair blows from underneath your helmet and all you can think about with the wind keeping your eyes closed tight is going and staying gone. When he stops his bike on the side of the road and turns around to hold your face real gentle between his hands you let him kiss you. And he takes you home without asking you for anything.

Your mama puts your picture in the paper when you go back to school. 10 You take classes with black folks and brown folks and yellow folks and make friends with who you like. Your parents take you out to dinner with your sisters and when your daddy is half-way through with his second beer and his cheeks are glowing with the red blood rushing to his face he lifts his glass and says that he is proud of you. When he finishes his third beer he goes out to sleep in the car and your mama gives you three brand new black pens and a pad of PostITs from her purse. You study real damn hard this time cause you know this is your last earthly chance to make something of yourself and you buy a dictionary at a yard sale and think you might learn every word if you have DETERMINATION and RESOLVE. When Wal-Mart doesn't let you off to study for a test you tell them to kiss your poor white ass and you apply for student loans and when they give out credit cards on campus you accept exactly three. Your English professor says you have POTENTIAL and you hold this real close to your heart when you're walking up to get your diploma and sixteen of your cousins and your aunts and uncles and grandparents on both sides and your two sisters are hooting and hollering from the stands and your mama blows an air horn and your daddy yells your name so loud and true it's like he's calling you to come up from the creek bottom. And you hear him calling for some time.

## FOR ANALYSIS

**1.** What significance does the title have? What does Johnson mean by "white trash"? What is a "primer"?

**2.** How would you characterize the **style** of the **prose** with which Johnson writes "White Trash Primer"?

**3.** What **point of view** is this essay written in? What effect does it have on you as you read?

## MAKING ARGUMENTS

Reflect on how you relate to the use of the word *you* in "White Trash Primer." How does it make you feel? Do you feel included by it or excluded by it? Why? Argue for or against Johnson's use of the second-person ("you") **point of view**. Cite specific moments when you feel that it is effective or ineffective, and explain why. If you are arguing against it, try to include an argument for an alternative that attempts to explain why it would have been better.

## WRITING TOPIC

Johnson's essay closes on an emotional note. Going back through the essay, note the different **tones** she creates, and reflect on how she prepares her readers for the feelings evoked by the end of the essay.

## MAKING CONNECTIONS

**1.** Both of these essays are in part about what Mukherjee calls "the trauma of self-transformation" (para. 16). What is the nature of Johnson's transformation? How does Johnson present it? Is it traumatic?

**2.** Mukherjee's essay is about immigration, while Johnson's is not. Yet both are about different ways to be in America — different ways to live, different ways to see yourself and be seen by others. Compare the situations the two essays take as their subjects and the ways the two treat those situations.

**3.** Imagine a conversation between Mukherjee and Johnson on the subject of culture. What might each of them mean by the term? How might their definitions be similar, and how might they be different?

## FURTHER QUESTIONS
## FOR THINKING AND WRITING

**1.** Explain how Virginia Woolf's observations in "What If Shakespeare Had Had a Sister?" illuminate the narrator's situation in Charlotte Perkins Gilman's "The Yellow Wallpaper." **Writing Topic:** In an essay, argue for or against the proposition that women are treated with absolute equality in the United States.

**2.** Marge Piercy's "Barbie Doll" and Taslima Nasrin's "Things Cheaply Had" both address certain culturally determined behavior patterns among women. Describe the behavior depicted in these poems. How do the authors feel about the behavior? What devices reveal the authors' attitudes? **Writing Topic:** Define the social tradition that produced the women in these poems. Either defend that tradition as crucial to the social order, or offer a cultural variation that would give women a different social role.

**3.** The speakers in Marilyn Chin's "How I Got That Name" and T. S. Eliot's "The Love Song of J. Alfred Prufrock" exhibit quite different attitudes about their identities. Describe each speaker's attitude toward his identity, and identify which aspects of the poems define those attitudes. In what sense are the speakers' identities culturally determined? **Writing Topic:** In an imaginative essay, describe each speaker's early life, and suggest what cultural forces shaped each of them.

**4.** Some of the works in this section focus on intergenerational tensions within a culture. Compare such tensions among parents and offspring in Alice Walker's "Everyday Use" and Sherman Alexie's "This Is What It Means to Say Phoenix, Arizona."

**5.** The struggle of women to achieve equality is the subject of many works in this section. **Writing Topic:** Examine some of the feminist works in this section. What, if any, common threads do you find running through them, either in content or in the use of literary devices?

**6.** The author's sister in Bharati Mukherjee's "Two Ways to Belong in America" and Prufrock in T. S. Eliot's "The Love Song of J. Alfred Prufrock" are both, in some sense, cultural outsiders. **Writing Topic:** Compare their positions in the dominant culture, the resulting conflicts or tensions, and the strategies they employ in dealing with their status.

# LOVE AND HATE

*Two Lovers*, 1630, by Riza ʻAbbasi (1565–1635). A.H. 1039/1629–30. Safavid period.
From Iran. Tempera and gold on paper, H. 7⅛ in. × W. 4¹¹⁄₁₆ in. (18.1 × 11.9 cm).
Purchase, Francis M. Weld Gift, 1950 (50.164).

L‍ove and death, it is often noted, are the two great themes of literature. Many of the literary works we have placed in the sections "Innocence and Experience," "Conformity and Rebellion," and "Culture and Identity" speak of love and death as well. But in those works, other thematic interests dominate. In this section, we gather a number of works in which love and hate are thematically central.

The rosy conception of love presented in many popular and sentimental stories does not prepare us for the complicated reality we face. We know that the course of true love never runs smoothly, but in those popular stories the obstacles that hinder the lovers are simple and external. If the young lover can land the high-paying job or convince the beloved's parents that he or she is worthy despite social differences, all will be well. But love in life is rarely that simple. The external obstacles may be insuperable, or the obstacles may lie deep within the personality. The major obstacle may well be an individual's difficult and painful effort to understand that he or she has been deceived by an immature or sentimental conception of love.

In this age of psychological awareness, the claims of the flesh are well recognized. But psychology teaches us, as well, to recognize the aggressive aspect of the human condition. The omnipresent selfishness that civilization attempts to check may be aggressively violent as well as lustful. Thus, on one hand, we have the simple eroticism of Kate Chopin's "The Storm" and, on the other, the more complicated, dangerous attraction of Joyce Carol Oates's "Where Are You Going, Where Have You Been?" And Matthew Arnold in "Dover Beach" finds love the only refuge from a chaotic world in which "ignorant armies clash by night."

The cliché has it that love and hate are closely related, and much evidence supports this proposition. But why should love and hate, seeming opposites, lie so close together in the emotional lives of men and women? We are all egos, separate from each other. And as separate individuals, we develop elaborate behavior mechanisms that defend us from each other. But the erotic love relationship differs from other relationships in that it may be defined as a rejection of separateness. The common metaphor speaks of two lovers as joining, as merging into one. That surrender of the "me" to join in an "us" leaves lovers uniquely vulnerable to psychic injury. In short, the defenses are down, and the self-esteem of each of the lovers depends importantly on the behavior of the other. If the lover is betrayed by the beloved, the emotional consequences are uniquely disastrous — hence the peculiarly close relationship between passionate hatred and erotic love.

Words like *love* and *hate* are so general that poets rarely use them except as one term in a metaphor designed to project sharply some aspect of emotional life. The simple sexuality in poems such as Andrew Marvell's "To His Coy Mistress" and Ben Jonson's "Song, To Celia" may be juxtaposed with the hatred and violence generated in *Othello* by sexual jealousy or with the angry impulses of the spurned speaker in Carolyn Kizer's "Bitch."

Perhaps more than anything, the works in this section celebrate the elemental impulses of men and women that run counter to those rational formulations by which we govern our lives. We pursue Othello's love for Desdemona and Iago's hate for Othello and arrive at an irreducible mystery, for neither Othello's love nor Iago's hate yields satisfactorily to rational explanation. Reason does not tell us why Othello and Desdemona love one another or why Iago hates rather than honors Othello.

Love is an act of faith springing from our deep-seated need to join with another human being not only in physical nakedness but in emotional and spiritual nakedness as well. While hate is a denial of that faith and therefore a retreat into spiritual isolation, love is an attempt to break out of the isolation.

## QUESTIONS FOR THINKING AND WRITING

As you read the selections in this section, consider the following questions. You may want to write out your thoughts informally in a journal or notebook as a way of preparing to respond to the selections, or you may wish to make one of these questions the basis for a formal essay.

1. What is love? What is the source of your definition (literature, personal observation, discussions with those you trust)? Have you ever been in love? How did you know? Do you know someone who is in love? How has it changed that person?

2. Have you ever truly hated someone or something? Describe the circumstances, and characterize your hatred.

3. Do you believe that love and hate are closely related? Have you experienced a change from love to hatred, or do you know someone who has? Explain.

4. There are different kinds of love — love of family, of humankind, of a cause. Describe several different kinds of love, and examine your own motives and behavior in different love relationships. Is it possible that certain kinds of love necessarily generate certain hatreds? Explain.

# FICTION

**KATE CHOPIN**   (1850–1904)

## THE STORM   1898

### I

The leaves were so still that even Bibi thought it was going to rain. Bobinôt, who was accustomed to converse on terms of perfect equality with his little son, called the child's attention to certain sombre clouds that were rolling with sinister intention from the west, accompanied by a sullen, threatening roar. They were at Friedheimer's store and decided to remain there till the storm had passed. They sat within the door on two empty kegs. Bibi was four years old and looked very wise.

"Mama'll be 'fraid, yes," he suggested with blinking eyes.

"She'll shut the house. Maybe she got Sylvie helpin' her this evenin'," Bobinôt responded reassuringly.

"No; she ent got Sylvie. Sylvie was helpin' her yistiday," piped Bibi.

Bobinôt arose and going across to the counter purchased a can of shrimps, 5 of which Calixta was very fond. Then he returned to his perch on the keg and sat stolidly holding the can of shrimps while the storm burst. It shook the wooden store and seemed to be ripping great furrows in the distant field. Bibi laid his little hand on his father's knee and was not afraid.

### II

Calixta, at home, felt no uneasiness for their safety. She sat at a side window sewing furiously on a sewing machine. She was greatly occupied and did not notice the approaching storm. But she felt very warm and often stopped to mop her face on which the perspiration gathered in beads. She unfastened her white sacque at the throat. It began to grow dark, and suddenly realizing the situation she got up hurriedly and went about closing windows and doors.

Out on the small front gallery she had hung Bobinôt's Sunday clothes to air and she hastened out to gather them before the rain fell. As she stepped outside,

Alcée Laballière rode in at the gate. She had not seen him very often since her marriage, and never alone. She stood there with Bobinôt's coat in her hands, and the big rain drops began to fall. Alcée rode his horse under the shelter of a side projection where the chickens had huddled and there were plows and a harrow piled up in the corner.

"May I come and wait on your gallery till the storm is over, Calixta?" he asked.

"Come 'long in, M'sieur Alcée."

His voice and her own startled her as if from a trance, and she seized Bobinôt's 10 vest. Alcée, mounting to the porch, grabbed the trousers and snatched Bibi's braided jacket that was about to be carried away by a sudden gust of wind. He expressed an intention to remain outside, but it was soon apparent that he might as well have been out in the open: the water beat in upon the boards in driving sheets, and he went inside, closing the door after him. It was even necessary to put something beneath the door to keep the water out.

"My! what a rain! It's good two years sence it rain' like that," exclaimed Calixta as she rolled up a piece of bagging and Alcée helped her to thrust it beneath the crack.

She was a little fuller of figure than five years before when she married; but she had lost nothing of her vivacity. Her blue eyes still retained their melting quality; and her yellow hair, dishevelled by the wind and rain, kinked more stubbornly than ever about her ears and temples.

The rain beat upon the low, shingled roof with a force and clatter that threatened to break an entrance and deluge them there. They were in the dining room — the sitting room — the general utility room. Adjoining was her bed room, with Bibi's couch along side her own. The door stood open, and the room with its white, monumental bed, its closed shutters, looked dim and mysterious.

Alcée flung himself into a rocker and Calixta nervously began to gather up from the floor the lengths of a cotton sheet which she had been sewing.

"If this keeps up, *Dieu sait*[1] if the levees goin' to stan' it!" she exclaimed. 15

"What have you got to do with the levees?"

"I got enough to do! An' there's Bobinôt with Bibi out in that storm — if he only didn' left Friedheimer's!"

"Let us hope, Calixta, that Bobinôt's got sense enough to come in out of a cyclone."

She went and stood at the window with a greatly disturbed look on her face. She wiped the frame that was clouded with moisture. It was stiflingly hot. Alcée got up and joined her at the window, looking over her shoulder. The rain was coming down in sheets obscuring the view of far-off cabins and enveloping the distant wood in a gray mist. The playing of the lightning was incessant. A bolt struck a tall chinaberry tree at the edge of the field. It filled all visible space with a blinding glare and the crash seemed to invade the very boards they stood upon.

[1] God knows.

Calixta put her hands to her eyes, and with a cry, staggered backward. 20 Alcée's arm encircled her, and for an instant he drew her close and spasmodically to him.

"*Bonté!*"[2] she cried, releasing herself from his encircling arm and retreating from the window, "the house'll go next! If I only knew w'ere Bibi was!" She would not compose herself; she would not be seated. Alcée clasped her shoulders and looked into her face. The contact of her warm, palpitating body when he had unthinkingly drawn her into his arms, had aroused all the old-time infatuation and desire for her flesh.

"Calixta," he said, "don't be frightened. Nothing can happen. The house is too low to be struck, with so many tall trees standing about. There! aren't you going to be quiet? say, aren't you?" He pushed her hair back from her face that was warm and steaming. Her lips were as red and moist as pomegranate seed. Her white neck and a glimpse of her full, firm bosom disturbed him powerfully. As she glanced up at him the fear in her liquid blue eyes had given place to a drowsy gleam that unconsciously betrayed a sensuous desire. He looked down into her eyes and there was nothing for him to do but to gather her lips in a kiss. It reminded him of Assumption.[3]

"Do you remember — in Assumption, Calixta?" he asked in a low voice broken by passion. Oh! she remembered; for in Assumption he had kissed her and kissed and kissed her; until his senses would well nigh fail, and to save her he would resort to a desperate flight. If she was not an immaculate dove in those days, she was still inviolate; a passionate creature whose very defenselessness had made her defense, against which his honor forbade him to prevail. Now — well, now — her lips seemed in a manner free to be tasted, as well as her round, white throat and her whiter breasts.

They did not heed the crashing torrents, and the roar of the elements made her laugh as she lay in his arms. She was a revelation in that dim, mysterious chamber; as white as the couch she lay upon. Her firm, elastic flesh that was knowing for the first time its birthright, was like a creamy lily that the sun invites to contribute its breath and perfume to the undying life of the world.

The generous abundance of her passion, without guile or trickery, was like a 25 white flame which penetrated and found response in depths of his own sensuous nature that had never yet been reached.

When he touched her breasts they gave themselves up in quivering ecstasy, inviting his lips. Her mouth was a fountain of delight. And when he possessed her, they seemed to swoon together at the very borderland of life's mystery.

He stayed cushioned upon her, breathless, dazed, enervated, with his heart beating like a hammer upon her. With one hand she clasped his head, her lips lightly touching his forehead. The other hand stroked with a soothing rhythm his muscular shoulders.

---

[2] An exclamation: Goodness!

[3] A holiday commemorating the ascent of the Virgin Mary to heaven. Assumption is also the name of a Louisiana parish (county) where Calixta and Alcée had a rendezvous in an earlier story.

The growl of the thunder was distant and passing away. The rain beat softly upon the shingles, inviting them to drowsiness and sleep. But they dared not yield.

The rain was over; and the sun was turning the glistening green world into a palace of gems. Calixta, on the gallery, watched Alcée ride away. He turned and smiled at her with a beaming face; and she lifted her pretty chin in the air and laughed aloud.

## III

Bobinôt and Bibi, trudging home, stopped without at the cistern to make  30 themselves presentable.

"My! Bibi, w'at will yo' mama say! You ought to be ashame'. You oughtn' put on those good pants. Look at 'em! An' that mud on yo' collar! How you got that mud on yo' collar, Bibi? I never saw such a boy!" Bibi was the picture of pathetic resignation. Bobinôt was the embodiment of serious solicitude as he strove to remove from his own person and his son's the signs of their tramp over heavy roads and through wet fields. He scraped the mud off Bibi's bare legs and feet with a stick and carefully removed all traces from his heavy brogans. Then, prepared for the worst — the meeting with an over-scrupulous housewife, they entered cautiously at the back door.

Calixta was preparing supper. She had set the table and was dripping coffee at the hearth. She sprang up as they came in.

"Oh, Bobinôt! You back! My! but I was uneasy. W'ere you been during the rain? An' Bibi? he ain't wet? he ain't hurt?" She had clasped Bibi and was kissing him effusively. Bobinôt's explanations and apologies which he had been composing all along the way, died on his lips as Calixta felt him to see if he were dry, and seemed to express nothing but satisfaction at their safe return.

"I brought you some shrimps, Calixta," offered Bobinôt, hauling the can from his ample side pocket and laying it on the table.

"Shrimps! Oh, Bobinôt! you too good fo' anything!" and she gave him a  35 smacking kiss on the cheek that resounded. "*J'vous réponds*,[4] we'll have a feas' to night! umph-umph!"

Bobinôt and Bibi began to relax and enjoy themselves, and when the three seated themselves at table they laughed much and so loud that anyone might have heard them as far away as Laballière's.

## IV

Alcée Laballière wrote to his wife, Clarisse, that night. It was a loving letter, full of tender solicitude. He told her not to hurry back, but if she and the babies liked it at Biloxi, to stay a month longer. He was getting on nicely; and though

---

[4] I'm telling you.

he missed them, he was willing to bear the separation a while longer — realizing that their health and pleasure were the first things to be considered.

V

As for Clarisse, she was charmed upon receiving her husband's letter. She and the babies were doing well. The society was agreeable; many of her old friends and acquaintances were at the bay. And the first free breath since her marriage seemed to restore the pleasant liberty of her maiden days. Devoted as she was to her husband, their intimate conjugal life was something which she was more than willing to forego for a while.

So the storm passed and everyone was happy.

## FOR ANALYSIS

**1.** Aside from the child Bibi, there are four **characters** in this story — two married couples. How did you respond to each of these characters? What are the sources for your reactions?

**2.** How do the characters in the story feel about themselves? About each other? On what evidence in the story do you base your response?

**3.** Discuss the title of the story.

**4.** During the second half of the nineteenth century, certain American writers, including Kate Chopin, evoked a sense of region in their work. What region of the United States provides the **setting** for this story? How do you know?

**5.** What aspects of this story's **style** contribute to its realism?

## MAKING ARGUMENTS

Chopin is often thought of as a Naturalist writer — that is, as one of the writers of the period who saw human life as determined by forces beyond their control, such as economics, biology, or the environment. Based on the evidence you find in "The Storm," make the argument that Chopin is or is not a Naturalist.

## WRITING TOPICS

**1.** Write an essay on modern marriage, using this story to support your analysis.

**2.** Comment on the story's final line. Is "the storm" literal or **symbolic**? If everyone is "happy," do you believe they have the right to be? Or is such a question irrelevant? Explain.

## MAKING CONNECTIONS

Read this story against Galway Kinnell's "After Making Love We Hear Footsteps" (p. 646). How do the children function in relation to the sex in each work? What does the boy's presence after the act mean in each selection?

## ZORA NEALE HURSTON  (1891–1960)

# SWEAT   1926

## I

It was eleven o'clock of a Spring night in Florida. It was Sunday. Any other night, Delia Jones would have been in bed for two hours by this time. But she was a washwoman, and Monday morning meant a great deal to her. So she collected the soiled clothes on Saturday when she returned the clean things. Sunday night after church, she sorted and put the white things to soak. It saved her almost a half-day's start. A great hamper in the bedroom held the clothes that she brought home. It was so much neater than a number of bundles lying around.

She squatted on the kitchen floor beside the great pile of clothes, sorting them into small heaps according to color, and humming a song in a mournful key, but wondering through it all where Sykes, her husband, had gone with her horse and buckboard.

Just then something long, round, limp, and black fell upon her shoulders and slithered to the floor beside her. A great terror took hold of her. It softened her knees and dried her mouth so that it was a full minute before she could cry out or move. Then she saw that it was the big bull whip her husband liked to carry when he drove.

She lifted her eyes to the door and saw him standing there bent over with laughter at her fright. She screamed at him.

"Sykes, what you throw dat whip on me like dat? You know it would skeer  5
me — looks just like a snake, an' you knows how skeered Ah is of snakes."

"Course Ah knowed it! That's how come Ah done it." He slapped his leg with his hand and almost rolled on the ground in his mirth. "If you such a big fool dat you got to have a fit over a earth worm or a string, Ah don't keer how bad Ah skeer you."

"You ain't got no business doing it. Gawd knows it's a sin. Some day Ah'm gointuh drop dead from some of yo' foolishness. 'Nother thing, where you been wid mah rig? Ah feeds dat pony. He ain't fuh you to be drivin' wid no bull whip."

"You sho' is one aggravatin' nigger woman!" he declared and stepped into the room. She resumed her work and did not answer him at once. "Ah done tole you time and again to keep them white folks' clothes outa dis house."

He picked up the whip and glared at her. Delia went on with her work. She went out into the yard and returned with a galvanized tub and set it on the wash-bench. She saw that Sykes had kicked all of the clothes together again, and now stood in her way truculently, his whole manner hoping, *praying*, for an argument. But she walked calmly around him and commenced to re-sort the things.

"Next time, Ah'm gointer kick 'em outdoors," he threatened as he struck a match along the leg of his corduroy breeches. 10

Delia never looked up from her work, and her thin, stooped shoulders sagged further.

"Ah ain't for no fuss t'night, Sykes. Ah just come from taking sacrament at the church house."

He snorted scornfully. "Yeah, you just come from de church house on a Sunday night, but heah you is gone to work on them clothes. You ain't nothing but a hypocrite. One of them amen-corner Christians — sing, whoop, and shout, then come home and wash white folks' clothes on the Sabbath."

He stepped roughly upon the whitest pile of things, kicking them helter-skelter as he crossed the room. His wife gave a little scream of dismay, and quickly gathered them together again.

"Sykes, you quit grindin' dirt into these clothes! How can Ah git through by Sat'day if Ah don't start on Sunday?" 15

"Ah don't keer if you never git through. Anyhow, Ah done promised Gawd and a couple of other men, Ah ain't gointer have it in mah house. Don't gimme no lip neither, else Ah'll throw 'em out and put mah fist up side yo' head to boot."

Delia's habitual meekness seemed to slip from her shoulders like a blown scarf. She was on her feet; her poor little body, her bare knuckly hands bravely defying the strapping hulk before her.

"Looka heah, Sykes, you done gone too fur. Ah been married to you fur fifteen years, and Ah been takin' in washin' fur fifteen years. Sweat, sweat, sweat! Work and sweat, cry and sweat, pray and sweat!"

"What's that got to do with me?" he asked brutally.

"What's it got to do with you, Sykes? Mah tub of suds is filled yo' belly with vittles more times than yo' hands is filled it. Mah sweat is done paid for this house and Ah reckon Ah kin keep on sweatin' in it." 20

She seized the iron skillet from the stove and struck a defensive pose, which act surprised him greatly, coming from her. It cowed him and he did not strike her as he usually did.

"Naw you won't," she panted, "that ole snaggle-toothed black woman you runnin' with ain't comin' heah to pile up on *mah* sweat and blood. You ain't paid for nothin' on this place, and Ah'm gointer stay right heah till Ah'm toted out foot foremost."

"Well, you better quit gittin' me riled up, else they'll be totin' you out sooner than you expect. Ah'm so tired of you Ah don't know whut to do. Gawd! How Ah hates skinny wimmen!"

A little awed by this new Delia, he sidled out of the door and slammed the back gate after him. He did not say where he had gone, but she knew too well. She knew very well that he would not return until nearly daybreak also. Her work over, she went on to bed but not to sleep at once. Things had come to a pretty pass!

She lay awake, gazing upon the debris that cluttered their matrimonial 25
trail. Not an image left standing along the way. Anything like flowers had
long ago been drowned in the salty stream that had been pressed from her
heart. Her tears, her sweat, her blood. She had brought love to the union and
he had brought a longing after the flesh. Two months after the wedding, he
had given her the first brutal beating. She had the memory of his numerous
trips to Orlando with all of his wages when he had returned to her penniless,
even before the first year had passed. She was young and soft then, but now
she thought of her knotty, muscled limbs, her harsh knuckly hands, and drew
herself up into an unhappy little ball in the middle of the big feather bed. Too
late now to hope for love, even if it were not Bertha it would be someone else.
This case differed from the others only in that she was bolder than the others.
Too late for everything except her little home. She had built it for her old days,
and planted one by one the trees and flowers there. It was lovely to her, lovely.

Somehow, before sleep came, she found herself saying aloud: "Oh well,
whatever goes over the Devil's back, is got to come under his belly. Sometime
or ruther, Sykes, like everybody else, is gointer reap his sowing." After that she
was able to build a spiritual earthworks against her husband. His shells could
no longer reach her. AMEN. She went to sleep and slept until he announced his
presence in bed by kicking her feet and rudely snatching the covers away.

"Gimme some kivah heah, an' git yo' damn foots over on yo' own side! Ah
oughter mash you in yo' mouf fuh drawing dat skillet on me."

Delia went clear to the rail without answering him. A triumphant indifference to all that he was or did.

## II

The week was full of work for Delia as all other weeks, and Saturday found her
behind her little pony, collecting and delivering clothes.

It was a hot, hot day near the end of July. The village men on Joe Clarke's 30
porch even chewed cane listlessly. They did not hurl the cane-knots as usual.
They let them dribble over the edge of the porch. Even conversation had collapsed under the heat.

"Heah come Delia Jones," Jim Merchant said, as the shaggy pony came
'round the bend of the road toward them. The rusty buckboard was heaped
with baskets of crisp, clean laundry.

"Yep," Joe Lindsay agreed. "Hot or col', rain or shine, jes'ez reg'lar ez de weeks
roll roun' Delia carries 'em an' fetches 'em on Sat'day."

"She better if she wanter eat," said Moss. "Syke Jones ain't wuth de shot an'
powder hit would tek tuh kill 'em. Not to *huh* he ain't."

"He sho' ain't," Walter Thomas chimed in. "It's too bad, too, cause she wuz
a right pretty li'l trick when he got huh. Ah'd uh mah'ied huh mahself if he
hadnter beat me to it."

Delia nodded briefly at the men as she drove past. 35

"Too much knockin' will ruin *any* 'oman. He done beat huh 'nough tuh kill three women, let 'lone change they looks," said Elijah Moseley. "How Syke kin stommuck dat big black greasy Mogul he's layin' roun' wid, gits me. Ah swear dat eight-rock couldn't kiss a sardine can Ah done thowed out de back do' 'way las' yeah."

"Aw, she's fat, thass how come. He's allus been crazy 'bout fat women," put in Merchant. "He'd a' been tied up wid one long time ago if he could a' found one tuh have him. Did Ah tell yuh 'bout him come sidlin' roun' *mah* wife — bringin' her a basket uh peecans outa his yard fuh a present? Yessir, mah wife! She tol' him tuh take 'em right straight back home, 'cause Delia works so hard ovah dat washtub she reckon everything on de place taste lak sweat an' soapsuds. Ah jus' wisht Ah'd a' caught 'im roun' dere! Ah'd a' made his hips ketch on fiah down dat shell road."

"Ah know he done it, too. Ah sees 'im grinnin' at every 'oman dat passes," Walter Thomas said. "But even so, he useter eat some mighty big hunks uh humble pie tuh git dat li'l 'oman he got. She wuz ez pretty ez a speckled pup! Dat wuz fifteen years ago. He useter be so skeered uh losin' huh, she could make him do some parts of a husband's duty. Dey never wuz de same in de mind."

"There oughter be a law about him," said Lindsay. "He ain't fit tuh carry guts tuh a bear."

Clarke spoke for the first time. "Tain't no law on earth dat kin make a man 40 be decent if it ain't in 'im. There's plenty men dat takes a wife lak dey do a joint uh sugar-cane. It's round, juicy, an' sweet when dey gits it. But dey squeeze an' grind, squeeze an' grind an' wring tell dey wring every drop uh pleasure dat's in 'em out. When dey's satisfied dat dey is wrung dry, dey treats 'em jes' lak dey do a cane-chew. Dey thows 'em away. Dey knows whut dey is doin' while dey is at it, an' hates theirselves fuh it but they keeps on hangin' after huh tell she's empty. Den dey hates huh fuh bein' a cane-chew an' in de way."

"We oughter take Syke an' dat stray 'oman uh his'n down in Lake Howell swamp an' lay on de rawhide till they cain't say Lawd a' mussy. He allus wuz uh ovahbearin niggah, but since dat white 'oman from up north done teached 'im how to run a automobile, he done got too beggety to live — an' we oughter kill 'im," Old Man Anderson advised.

A grunt of approval went around the porch. But the heat was melting their civic virtue and Elijah Moseley began to bait Joe Clarke.

"Come on, Joe, git a melon outa dere an' slice it up for yo' customers. We'se all sufferin' wid de heat. De bear's done got *me!*"

"Thass right, Joe, a watermelon is jes' whut Ah needs tuh cure de eppizudicks," Walter Thomas joined forces with Moseley. "Come on dere, Joe. We all is steady customers an' you ain't set us up in a long time. Ah chooses dat long, bowlegged Floridy favorite."

"A god, an' be dough. You all gimme twenty cents and slice away," Clarke 45 retorted. "Ah needs a col' slice m'self. Heah, everybody chip in. Ah'll lend y'all mah meat knife."

The money was all quickly subscribed and the huge melon brought forth. At that moment, Sykes and Bertha arrived. A determined silence fell on the porch and the melon was put away again.

Merchant snapped down the blade of his jacknife and moved toward the store door.

"Come on in, Joe, an' gimme a slab uh sow belly an' uh pound uh coffee — almost fuhgot 'twas Sat'day. Got to git on home." Most of the men left also.

Just then Delia drove past on her way home, as Sykes was ordering magnificently for Bertha. It pleased him for Delia to see.

"Git whutsoever yo' heart desires, Honey. Wait a minute, Joe. Give huh two 50 bottles uh strawberry soda-water, uh quart parched ground-peas, an' a block uh chewin' gum."

With all this they left the store, with Sykes reminding Bertha that this was his town and she could have it if she wanted it.

The men returned soon after they left, and held their watermelon feast.

"Where did Syke Jones git da 'oman from nohow?" Lindsay asked.

"Ovah Apopka. Guess dey musta been cleanin' out de town when she lef'. She don't look lak a thing but a hunk uh liver wid hair on it."

"Well, she sho' kin squall," Dave Carter contributed. "When she gits ready 55 tuh laff, she jes' opens huh mouf an' latches it back tuh de las' notch. No ole granpa alligator down in Lake Bell ain't got nothin' on huh."

### III

Bertha had been in town three months now. Sykes was still paying her room-rent at Della Lewis' — the only house in town that would have taken her in. Sykes took her frequently to Winter Park to "stomps." He still assured her that he was the swellest man in the state.

"Sho' you kin have dat li'l ole house soon's Ah git dat 'oman outa dere. Everything b'longs tuh me an' you sho' kin have it. Ah sho' 'bominates uh skinny 'oman. Lawdy, you sho' is got one portly shape on you! You kin git *anything* you wants. Dis is *mah* town an' you sho' kin have it."

Delia's work-worn knees crawled over the earth in Gethsemane[1] and up the rocks of Calvary many, many times during these months. She avoided the villagers and meeting places in her efforts to be blind and deaf. But Bertha nullified this to a degree, by coming to Delia's house to call Sykes out to her at the gate.

Delia and Sykes fought all the time now with no peaceful interludes. They slept and ate in silence. Two or three times Delia had attempted a timid friendliness, but she was repulsed each time. It was plain that the breaches must remain agape.

The sun had burned July to August. The heat streamed down like a mil- 60 lion hot arrows, smiting all things living upon the earth. Grass withered, leaves

---

[1] Gethsemane is the garden where, according to the Bible, Jesus and his disciples prayed the night before Jesus was crucified on Calvary (which is also known as Golgotha, "the place of the skull").

browned, snakes went blind in shedding, and men and dogs went mad. Dog days!

Delia came home one day and found Sykes there before her. She wondered, but started to go on into the house without speaking, even though he was standing in the kitchen door and she must either stoop under his arm or ask him to move. He made no room for her. She noticed a soap box beside the steps, but paid no particular attention to it, knowing that he must have brought it there. As she was stooping to pass under his outstretched arm, he suddenly pushed her backward, laughingly.

"Look in de box dere Delia, Ah done brung yuh somethin'!"

She nearly fell upon the box in her stumbling, and when she saw what it held, she all but fainted outright.

"Syke! Syke, mah Gawd! You take dat rattlesnake 'way from heah! You *got-tuh*. Oh, Jesus, have mussy!"

"Ah ain't got tuh do nuthin' uh de kin' — fact is Ah ain't got tuh do nothin'   65
but die. Tain't no use uh you puttin' on airs makin' out lak you skeered uh dat snake — he's gointer stay right heah tell he die. He wouldn't bite me cause Ah knows how tuh handle 'im. Nohow he wouldn't risk breakin' out his fangs 'gin *yo* skinny laigs."

"Naw, now Syke, don't keep dat thing 'round tryin' tuh skeer me tuh death. You knows Ah'm even feared uh earth worms. Thass de biggest snake Ah evah did se. Kill 'im Syke, please."

"Doan ast me tuh do nothin' fuh yuh. Goin' 'round tryin' tuh be so damn asterperious. Naw, Ah ain't gonna kill it. Ah think uh damn sight mo' uh him dan you! Dat's a nice snake an' anybody doan lak 'im kin jes' hit de grit."

The village soon heard that Sykes had the snake, and came to see and ask questions.

"How de hen-fire did you ketch dat six-foot rattler, Syke?" Thomas asked.

"He's full uh frogs so he cain't hardly move, thass how Ah eased up on 'im.   70
But Ah'm a snake charmer an' knows how tuh handle 'em. Shux, dat ain't nothin'. Ah could ketch one eve'y day if Ah so wanted tuh."

"Whut he needs is a heavy hick'ry club leaned real heavy on his head. Dat's de bes' way tuh charm a rattlesnake."

"Naw, Walt, y'all jes' don't understand dese diamon' backs lak Ah do," said Sykes in a superior tone of voice.

The village agreed with Walter, but the snake stayed on. His box remained by the kitchen door with its screen wire covering. Two or three days later it had digested its meal of frogs and literally came to life. It rattled at every movement in the kitchen or the yard. One day as Delia came down the kitchen steps she saw his chalky-white fangs curved like scimitars hung in the wire meshes. This time she did not run away with averted eyes as usual. She stood for a long time in the doorway in a red fury that grew bloodier for every second that she regarded the creature that was her torment.

That night she broached the subject as soon as Sykes sat down to the table.

"Syke, Ah wants you tuh take dat snake 'way fum heah. You done starved 75
me an' Ah put up widcher, you done beat me an Ah took dat, but you don kilt
all mah insides bringin' dat varmint heah."

Sykes poured out a saucer full of coffee and drank it deliberately before he
answered her.

"A whole lot Ah keer 'bout how you feels inside uh out. Dat snake ain't goin'
no damn wheah till Ah gits ready fuh 'im tuh go. So fur as beatin' is concerned,
yuh ain't took near all dat you gointer take ef yuh stay 'round *me*."

Delia pushed back her plate and got up from the table. "Ah hates you,
Sykes," she said calmly. "Ah hates you tuh de same degree dat Ah useter
love yuh. Ah done took an' took till mah belly is full up tuh mah neck. Dat's
de reason Ah got mah letter fum de church an' moved mah membership
tuh Woodbridge — so Ah don't haftuh take no sacrament wid yuh. Ah don't
wantuh see yuh 'round me atall. Lay 'round wid dat 'oman all yuh wants
tuh, but gwan 'way from me an' mah house. Ah hates yuh lak uh suck-egg
dog."

Sykes almost let the huge wad of corn bread and collard greens he was chewing fall out of his mouth in amazement. He had a hard time whipping himself
up to the proper fury to try to answer Delia.

"Well, Ah'm glad you does hate me. Ah'm sho' tiahed uh you hangin' ontuh 80
me. Ah don't want yuh. Look at yuh stringey ole neck! Yo' rawbony laigs an'
arms is enough tuh cut uh man tuh death. You looks jes' lak de devvul's doll-
baby tuh *me*. You cain't hate me no worse dan Ah hates you. Ah been hatin'
*you* fuh years."

"Yo' ole black hide don't look lak nothin' tuh me, but uh passle uh wrinkled
up rubber, wid yo' big ole yeahs flappin' on each side lak uh paih uh buzzard
wings. Don't think Ah'm gointuh be run 'way fum mah house neither. Ah'm
goin' tuh de white folks 'bout *you*, mah young man, de very nex' time you lay
yo' han's on me. Mah cup is done run ovah." Delia said this with no signs of
fear and Sykes departed from the house, threatening her, but made not the
slightest move to carry out any of them.

That night he did not return at all, and the next day being Sunday, Delia was
glad she did not have to quarrel before she hitched up her pony and drove the
four miles to Woodbridge.

She stayed to the night service — "love feast" — which was very warm and
full of spirit. In the emotional winds her domestic trials were borne far and
wide so that she sang as she drove homeward,

> Jurden water, black an' col
> Chills de body, not de soul
> An'Ah wantah cross Jurden in uh calm time.

She came from the barn to the kitchen door and stopped.

"Whut's de mattah, ol' Satan, you ain't kicken' up yo' racket?" She addressed
the snake's box. Complete silence. She went on into the house with a new hope

in its birth struggles. Perhaps her threat to go to the white folks had frightened Sykes! Perhaps he was sorry! Fifteen years of misery and suppression had
brought Delia to the place where she would hope *anything* that looked towards
a way over or through her wall of inhibitions.

She felt in the match-safe behind the stove at once for a match. There was 85
only one there.

"Dat niggah wouldn't fetch nothin' heah tuh save his rotten neck, but he kin
run thew whut Ah brings quick enough. Now he done toted off nigh on tuh
haff uh box uh matches. He done had dat 'oman heah in mah house, too."

Nobody but a woman could tell how she knew this even before she struck
the match. But she did and it put her into a new fury.

Presently she brought in the tubs to put the white things to soak. This time
she decided she need not bring the hamper out of the bedroom; she would go
in there and do the sorting. She picked up the pot-bellied lamp and went in.
The room was small and the hamper stood hard by the foot of the white iron
bed. She could sit and reach through the bedposts — resting as she worked.

"*Ah wantah cross Jurden in uh calm time.*" She was singing again. The mood
of the "love feast," had returned. She threw back the lid of the basket almost
gaily. Then, moved by both horror and terror, she sprang back toward the
door. *There lay the snake in the basket!* He moved sluggishly at first, but even
as she turned round and round, jumped up and down in an insanity of fear,
he began to stir vigorously. She saw him pouring his awful beauty from the
basket upon the bed, then she seized the lamp and ran as fast as she could to
the kitchen. The wind from the open door blew out the light and the darkness
added to her terror. She sped to the darkness of the yard, slamming the door
after her before she thought to set down the lamp. She did not feel safe even on
the ground, so she climbed up in the hay barn.

There for an hour or more she lay sprawled upon the hay a gibbering wreck. 90

Finally she grew quiet, and after that came coherent thought. With this stalked
through her a cold, bloody rage. Hours of this. A period of introspection, a space
of retrospection, then a mixture of both. Out of this an awful calm.

"Well, Ah done de bes' Ah could. If things ain't right, Gawd knows tain't
mah fault."

She went to sleep — a twitch sleep — and woke up to a faint gray sky. There
was a loud hollow sound below. She peered out. Sykes was at the woodpile,
demolishing a wire-covered box.

He hurried to the kitchen door, but hung outside there some minutes before
he entered, and stood some minutes more inside before he closed it after him.

The gray in the sky was spreading. Delia descended without fear now, and 95
crouched beneath the low bedroom window. The drawn shade shut out the
dawn, shut in the night. But the thin walls held back no sound.

"Dat ol' scratch is woke up now!" She mused at the tremendous whirr inside,
which every woodsman knows, is one of the sound illusions. The rattler is a
ventriloquist. His whirr sounds to the right, to the left, straight ahead, behind,
close under foot — everywhere but where it is. Woe to him who guesses wrong

unless he is prepared to hold up his end of the argument! Sometimes he strikes without rattling at all.

Inside, Sykes heard nothing until he knocked a pot lid off the stove while trying to reach the match-safe in the dark. He had emptied his pockets at Bertha's.

The snake seemed to wake up under the stove and Sykes made a quick leap into the bedroom. In spite of the gin he had had, his head was clearing now.

"Mah Gawd!" he chattered, "ef Ah could on'y strack uh light!"

The rattling ceased for a moment as he stood paralyzed. He waited. It    100
seemed that the snake waited also.

"Oh, fuh de light! Ah thought he'd be too sick" — Sykes was muttering to himself when the whirr began again, closer, right underfoot this time. Long before this, Sykes' ability to think had been flattened down to primitive instinct and he leaped — onto the bed.

Outside Delia heard a cry that might have come from a maddened chimpanzee, a stricken gorilla. All the terror, all the horror, all the rage that man possibly could express, without a recognizable human sound.

A tremendous stir inside there, another series of animal screams, the intermittent whirr of the reptile. The shade torn violently down from the window, letting in the red dawn, a huge brown hand seizing the window stick, great dull blows upon the wooden floor punctuating the gibberish of sound long after the rattle of the snake had abruptly subsided. All this Delia could see and hear from her place beneath the window, and it made her ill. She crept over to the four o'clocks and stretched herself on the cool earth to recover.

She lay there. "Delia, Delia!" She could hear Sykes calling in a most despairing tone as one who expected no answer. The sun crept on up, and he called. Delia could not move — her legs had gone flabby. She never moved, he called, and the sun kept rising.

"Mah Gawd!" She heard him moan, "Mah Gawd fum Heben!" She heard    105
him stumbling about and got up from her flower-bed. The sun was growing warm. As she approached the door she heard him call out hopefully, "Delia, is dat you Ah heah?"

She saw him on his hands and knees as soon as she reached the door. He crept an inch or two toward her — all that he was able, and she saw his horribly swollen neck and his one open eye shining with hope. A surge of pity too strong to support bore her away from that eye that must, could not, fail to see the tubs. He would see the lamp. Orlando with its doctors was too far. She could scarcely reach the chinaberry tree, where she waited in the growing heat while inside she knew the cold river was creeping up and up to extinguish that eye which must know by now that she knew.

## FOR ANALYSIS

1. What purpose do the men on the porch serve in the story? How are we supposed to take their opinions on Delia and Sykes?

**2.** While this story is about an unfortunate situation, the **tone** is not uniformly grave. How does Hurston manipulate tone? What are the effects of her choice to mix it up?

**3.** How do you feel about Delia's actions at the end of the story? Do you blame her? Has her love turned to hate, or does she still hope for love?

## MAKING ARGUMENTS

One of the men on the porch says, "Tain't no law on earth dat kin make a man be decent if it ain't in 'im" (para. 40). Reflect on the nature of decentness, with special attention to its source. Do you think people are or are not inherently decent? Or do you think the circumstances of their lives play a part in shaping their characters? Make an argument one way or the other.

## WRITING TOPIC

Stories are seldom written using dialect anymore. Why do you think that is? What do you think of Hurston's use of dialect?

## MAKING CONNECTIONS

Think about this story in connection to a very different story, O'Connor's "A Good Man Is Hard to Find" (p. 137). Both stories feature religious belief prominently, though in very different ways. How does belief inform each story? How do the characters relate to it?

## ERNEST HEMINGWAY  (1899–1961)

# HILLS LIKE WHITE ELEPHANTS  1927

The hills across the valley of the Ebro were long and white. On this side there was no shade and no trees and the station was between two lines of rails in the sun. Close against the side of the station there was the warm shadow of the building and a curtain, made of strings of bamboo beads, hung across the open door into the bar, to keep out flies. The American and the girl with him sat at a table in the shade, outside the building. It was very hot and the express from Barcelona would come in forty minutes. It stopped at this junction for two minutes and went on to Madrid.

"What should we drink?" the girl asked. She had taken off her hat and put it on the table.

"It's pretty hot," the man said.

"Let's drink beer."

"*Dos cervezas*," the man said into the curtain. 5

"Big ones?" a woman asked from the doorway.

"Yes. Two big ones."

The woman brought two glasses of beer and two felt pads. She put the felt pads and the beer glasses on the table and looked at the man and the girl. The girl was looking off at the line of hills. They were white in the sun and the country was brown and dry.

"They look like white elephants," she said.

"I've never seen one," the man drank his beer. 10

"No, you wouldn't have."

"I might have," the man said. "Just because you say I wouldn't have doesn't prove anything."

The girl looked at the bead curtain. "They've painted something on it," she said. "What does it say?"

"Anis del Toro. It's a drink."

"Could we try it?" 15

The man called "Listen" through the curtain. The woman came out from the bar.

"Four reales."

"We want two Anis del Toro."

"With water?"

"Do you want it with water?" 20

"I don't know," the girl said. "Is it good with water?"

"It's all right."

"You want them with water?" asked the woman.

"Yes, with water."

"It tastes like licorice," the girl said and put the glass down. 25

"That's the way with everything."

"Yes," said the girl. "Everything tastes of licorice. Especially all the things you've waited so long for, like absinthe."

"Oh, cut it out."

"You started it," the girl said. "I was being amused. I was having a fine time."

"Well, let's try and have a fine time."                                                    30

"All right. I was trying. I said the mountains looked like white elephants. Wasn't that bright?"

"That was bright."

"I wanted to try this new drink: that's all we do, isn't it — look at things and try new drinks?"

"I guess so."

The girl looked across at the hills.                                                        35

"They're lovely hills," she said. "They don't really look like white elephants. I just meant the coloring of their skin through the trees."

"Should we have another drink?"

"All right."

The warm wind blew the bead curtain against the table.

"The beer's nice and cool," the man said.                                                   40

"It's lovely," the girl said.

"It's really an awfully simple operation, Jig," the man said. "It's not really an operation at all."

The girl looked at the ground the table legs rested on.

"I know you wouldn't mind it, Jig. It's really not anything. It's just to let the air in."

The girl did not say anything.                                                              45

"I'll go with you and I'll stay with you all the time. They just let the air in and then it's all perfectly natural."

"Then what will we do afterward?"

"We'll be fine afterward. Just like we were before."

"What makes you think so?"

"That's the only thing that bothers us. It's the only thing that's made us 50 unhappy."

The girl looked at the bead curtain, put her hand out, and took hold of two of the strings of beads.

"And you think then we'll be all right and be happy."

"I know we will. You don't have to be afraid. I've known lots of people that have done it."

"So have I," said the girl. "And afterward they were all so happy."

"Well," the man said, "if you don't want to you don't have to. I wouldn't 55 have you do it if you didn't want to. But I know it's perfectly simple."

"And you really want to?"

"I think it's the best thing to do. But I don't want you to do it if you don't really want to."

"And if I do it you'll be happy and things will be like they were and you'll love me?"

"I love you now. You know I love you."

"I know. But if I do it, then it will be nice again if I say things are like white 60 elephants, and you'll like it?"

"I'll love it. I love it now but I just can't think about it. You know how I get when I worry."

"If I do it you won't ever worry?"

"I won't worry about that because it's perfectly simple."

"Then I'll do it. Because I don't care about me."

"What do you mean?" 65

"I don't care about me."

"Well, I care about you."

"Oh, yes. But I don't care about me. And I'll do it and then everything will be fine."

"I don't want you to do it if you feel that way."

The girl stood up and walked to the end of the station. Across, on the other 70 side, were fields of grain and trees along the banks of the Ebro. Far away, beyond the river, were mountains. The shadow of a cloud moved across the field of grain and she saw the river through the trees.

"And we could have all this," she said. "And we could have everything and every day we make it more impossible."

"What did you say?"

"I said we could have everything."

"We can have everything."

"No, we can't." 75

"We can have the whole world."

"No, we can't."

"We can go everywhere."

"No, we can't. It isn't ours any more."

"It's ours." 80

"No, it isn't. And once they take it away, you never get it back."

"But they haven't taken it away."

"We'll wait and see."

"Come on back in the shade," he said. "You mustn't feel that way."

"I don't feel any way," the girl said. "I just know things." 85

"I don't want you to do anything that you don't want to do——"

"Nor that isn't good for me," she said. "I know. Could we have another beer?"

"All right. But you've got to realize——"

"I realize," the girl said. "Can't we maybe stop talking?"

They sat down at the table and the girl looked across at the hills on the dry 90 side of the valley and the man looked at her and at the table.

"You've got to realize," he said, "that I don't want you to do it if you don't want to. I'm perfectly willing to go through with it if it means anything to you."

"Doesn't it mean anything to you? We could get along."

"Of course it does. But I don't want anybody but you. I don't want any one else. And I know it's perfectly simple."

"Yes, you know it's perfectly simple."

"It's all right for you to say that, but I do know it." 95

"Would you do something for me now?"

"I'd do anything for you."

"Would you please please please please please please please stop talking?"

He did not say anything but looked at the bags against the wall of the station. There were labels on them from all the hotels where they had spent nights.

"But I don't want you to," he said, "I don't care anything about it."                   100

"I'll scream," the girl said.

The woman came out through the curtains with two glasses of beer and put them down on the damp felt pads. "The train comes in five minutes," she said.

"What did she say?" asked the girl.

"That the train is coming in five minutes."

The girl smiled brightly at the woman, to thank her.                   105

"I'd better take the bags over to the other side of the station," the man said. She smiled at him.

"All right. Then come back and we'll finish the beer."

He picked up the two heavy bags and carried them around the station to the other tracks. He looked up the tracks but could not see the train. Coming back, he walked through the barroom, where people waiting for the train were drinking. He drank an Anis at the bar and looked at the people. They were all waiting reasonably for the train. He went out through the bead curtain. She was sitting at the table and smiled at him.

"Do you feel better?" he asked.

"I feel fine," she said. "There's nothing wrong with me. I feel fine."                   110

## FOR ANALYSIS

**1.** What is a "white elephant"?

**2.** What do you think the couple is arguing about? Is it more than one thing?

## MAKING ARGUMENTS

How do you think the story will turn out? Is there a happy ending in store for this couple? Make your argument with the support of textual evidence.

## WRITING TOPICS

**1.** How would you characterize Hemingway's **style**? Focus on what he includes and what he leaves out. What are the effects of his stylistic choices?

**2.** Much attention is paid in the story to **setting** — to where the main **characters** are sitting in relation to the things around them. Write an analysis of setting in this story. What might the relations of the characters to their surroundings mean? How might it reinforce certain ideas about their situation?

## MAKING CONNECTIONS

Early in the story, the woman says, "that's all we do, isn't it—look at things and try new drinks?" (para. 33). Compare Hemingway's story to Marge Piercy's "Barbie Doll" (p. 513) or Taslima Nasrin's "Things Cheaply Had" (p. 527). On the spare evidence Hemingway provides, what about this woman's life—the way she spends her time— shapes who she is and how she deals with the situation at the center of this story? How does this compare to the views of women presented in the poems?

## RAYMOND CARVER (1938–1988)

# WHAT WE TALK ABOUT
# WHEN WE TALK ABOUT LOVE    1981

My friend Mel McGinnis was talking. Mel McGinnis is a cardiologist, and sometimes that gives him the right.

The four of us were sitting around his kitchen table drinking gin. Sunlight filled the kitchen from the big window behind the sink. There were Mel and me and his second wife, Teresa — Terri, we called her — and my wife, Laura. We lived in Albuquerque then. But we were all from somewhere else.

There was an ice bucket on the table. The gin and the tonic water kept going around, and we somehow got on the subject of love. Mel thought real love was nothing less than spiritual love. He said he'd spent five years in a seminary before quitting to go to medical school. He said he still looked back on those years in the seminary as the most important years in his life.

Terri said the man she lived with before she lived with Mel loved her so much he tried to kill her. Then Terri said, "He beat me up one night. He dragged me around the living room by my ankles. He kept saying, 'I love you, I love you, you bitch.' He went on dragging me around the living room. My head kept knocking on things." Terri looked around the table. "What do you do with love like that?"

She was a bone-thin woman with a pretty face, dark eyes, and brown hair 5 that hung down her back. She liked necklaces made of turquoise, and long pendant earrings.

"My God, don't be silly. That's not love, and you know it," Mel said. "I don't know what you'd call it, but I sure know you wouldn't call it love."

"Say what you want to, but I know it was," Terri said. "It may sound crazy to you, but it's true just the same. People are different, Mel. Sure, sometimes he may have acted crazy. Okay. But he loved me. In his own way maybe, but he loved me. There was love there, Mel. Don't say there wasn't."

Mel let out his breath. He held his glass and turned to Laura and me. "The man threatened to kill me," Mel said. He finished his drink and reached for the gin bottle. "Terri's a romantic. Terri's of the kick-me-so-I'll-know-you-love-me school. Terri, hon, don't look that way." Mel reached across the table and touched Terri's cheek with his fingers. He grinned at her.

"Now he wants to make up," Terri said.

"Make up what?" Mel said. "What is there to make up? I know what I know. 10 That's all."

"How'd we get started on this subject, anyway?" Terri said. She raised her glass and drank from it. "Mel always has love on his mind," she said. "Don't you, honey?" She smiled, and I thought that was the last of it.

"I just wouldn't call Ed's behavior love. That's all I'm saying, honey," Mel said. "What about you guys?" Mel said to Laura and me. "Does that sound like love to you?"

"I'm the wrong person to ask," I said. "I didn't even know the man. I've only heard his name mentioned in passing. I wouldn't know. You'd have to know the particulars. But I think what you're saying is that love is an absolute."

Mel said, "The kind of love I'm talking about is. The kind of love I'm talking about, you don't try to kill people."

Laura said, "I don't know anything about Ed, or anything about the situa- 15 tion. But who can judge anyone else's situation?"

I touched the back of Laura's hand. She gave me a quick smile. I picked up Laura's hand. It was warm, the nails polished, perfectly manicured. I encircled the broad wrist with my fingers, and I held her.

"When I left, he drank rat poison," Terri said. She clasped her arms with her hands. "They took him to the hospital in Sante Fe. That's where we lived then, about ten miles out. They saved his life. But his gums went crazy from it. I mean they pulled away from his teeth. After that, his teeth stood out like fangs. My God," Terri said. She waited a minute, then let go of her arms and picked up her glass.

"What people won't do!" Laura said.

"He's out of the action now," Mel said. "He's dead."

Mel handed me the saucer of limes. I took a section, squeezed it over my 20 drink, and stirred the ice cubes with my finger.

"It gets worse," Terri said. "He shot himself in the mouth. But he bungled that too. Poor Ed," she said. Terri shook her head.

"Poor Ed nothing," Mel said. "He was dangerous."

Mel was forty-five years old. He was tall and rangy with curly soft hair. His face and arms were brown from the tennis he played. When he was sober, his gestures, all his movements, were precise, very careful.

"He did love me though, Mel. Grant me that," Terri said. "That's all I'm ask-ing. He didn't love me the way you love me. I'm not saying that. But he loved me. You can grant me that, can't you?"

"What do you mean, he bungled it?" I said. 25

Laura leaned forward with her glass. She put her elbows on the table and held her glass in both hands. She glanced from Mel to Terri and waited with a look of bewilderment on her open face, as if amazed that such things hap-pened to people you were friendly with.

"How'd he bungle it when he killed himself?" I said.

"I'll tell you what happened," Mel said. "He took this twenty-two pistol he'd bought to threaten Terri and me with. Oh, I'm serious, the man was always threatening. You should have seen the way we lived in those days. Like fugi-tives. I even bought a gun myself. Can you believe it? A guy like me? But I did. I bought one for self-defense and carried it in the glove compartment. Some-times I'd have to leave the apartment in the middle of the night. To go to the hospital, you know? Terri and I weren't married then, and my first wife had the house and kids, the dog, everything, and Terri and I were living in this apartment here. Sometimes, as I say, I'd get a call in the middle of the night and have to go in to the hospital at two or three in the morning. It'd be dark out there in the parking lot, and I'd break into a sweat before I could even get to my car. I never knew if he was going to come up out of the shrubbery or from behind a car and start shooting. I mean, the man was crazy. He was capable of wiring a bomb, anything. He used to call my service at all hours and say he needed to talk to the doctor, and when I'd return the call, he'd say, 'Son of a bitch, your days are numbered.' Little things like that. It was scary, I'm telling you."

"I still feel sorry for him," Terri said.

"It sounds like a nightmare," Laura said. "But what exactly happened after he 30 shot himself?"

Laura is a legal secretary. We'd met in a professional capacity. Before we knew it, it was a courtship. She's thirty-five, three years younger than I am. In addition to being in love, we like each other and enjoy one another's company. She's easy to be with.

"What happened?" Laura said.

Mel said, "He shot himself in the mouth in his room. Someone heard the shot and told the manager. They came in with a passkey, saw what had happened, and called an ambulance. I happened to be there when they brought him in, alive but past recall. The man lived for three days. His head swelled up to twice the size of a normal head. I'd never seen anything like it, and I hope I never do again. Terri wanted to go in and sit with him when she found out about it. We had a fight over it. I didn't think she should see him like that. I didn't think she should see him, and I still don't."

"Who won the fight?" Laura said.

"I was in the room with him when he died," Terri said. "He never came up 35 out of it. But I sat with him. He didn't have anyone else."

"He was dangerous," Mel said. "If you call that love, you can have it."

"It was love," Terri said. "Sure, it's abnormal in most people's eyes. But he was willing to die for it. He did die for it."

"I sure as hell wouldn't call it love," Mel said. "I mean, no one knows what he did it for. I've seen a lot of suicides, and I couldn't say anyone ever knew what they did it for."

Mel put his hands behind his neck and tilted his chair back. "I'm not interested in that kind of love," he said. "If that's love, you can have it."

Terri said, "We were afraid. Mel even made a will out and wrote to his 40 brother in California who used to be a Green Beret. Mel told him who to look for if something happened to him."

Terri drank from her glass. She said, "But Mel's right — we lived like fugitives. We were afraid. Mel was, weren't you, honey? I even called the police at one point, but they were no help. They said they couldn't do anything until Ed actually did something. Isn't that a laugh?" Terri said.

She poured the last of the gin into her glass and waggled the bottle. Mel got up from the table and went to the cupboard. He took down another bottle.

"Well, Nick and I know what love is," Laura said. "For us, I mean," Laura said. She bumped my knee with her knee. "You're supposed to say something now," Laura said, and turned her smile on me.

For an answer, I took Laura's hand and raised it to my lips. I made a big production out of kissing her hand. Everyone was amused.

"We're lucky," I said.                                                                    45

"You guys," Terri said. "Stop that now. You're making me sick. You're still on the honeymoon, for God's sake. You're still gaga, for crying out loud. Just wait. How long have you been together now? How long has it been? A year? Longer than a year?"

"Going on a year and a half," Laura said, flushed and smiling.

"Oh, now," Terri said. "Wait a while."

She held her drink and gazed at Laura.

"I'm only kidding," Terri said.                                                           50

Mel opened the gin and went around the table with the bottle.

"Here, you guys," he said. "Let's have a toast. I want to propose a toast. A toast to love. To true love," Mel said.

We touched glasses.

"To love," we said.

Outside in the backyard, one of the dogs began to bark. The leaves of the  55
aspen that leaned past the window ticked against the glass. The afternoon sun was like a presence in this room, the spacious light of ease and generosity. We could have been anywhere, somewhere enchanted. We raised our glasses again and grinned at each other like children who had agreed on something forbidden.

"I'll tell you what real love is," Mel said. "I mean, I'll give you a good example. And then you can draw your own conclusions." He poured more gin into his glass. He added an ice cube and a sliver of lime. We waited and sipped our drinks. Laura and I touched knees again. I put a hand on her warm thigh and left it there.

"What do any of us really know about love?" Mel said. "It seems to me we're just beginners at love. We say we love each other and we do, I don't doubt it. I love Terri and Terri loves me, and you guys love each other too. You know the kind of love I'm talking about now. Physical love, that impulse that drives you to someone special, as well as love of the other person's being, his or her essence, as it were. Carnal love and, well, call it sentimental love, the day-to-day caring about the other person. But sometimes I have a hard time accounting for the fact that I must have loved my first wife too. But I did, I know I did. So I suppose I am like Terri in that regard. Terri and Ed." He thought about it and then he went on. "There was a time when I thought I loved my first wife more than life itself. But now I hate her guts. I do. How do you explain that? What happened to that love? What happened to it, is what I'd like to know. I wish someone could tell me. Then there's Ed. Okay, we're back to Ed. He loves Terri so much he tries to kill her and he winds up killing himself." Mel stopped talking and swallowed from his glass. "You guys have been together eighteen months and you love each other. It shows all over you. You glow with it. But you both loved other people before you met each other. You've both been married before, just like us. And you probably loved other people before that too, even. Terri and I have been together five years, been married for four. And the terrible thing, the terrible thing is, but the good thing too, the saving grace, you might say, is that if something happened to one of us — excuse me for saying this — but if something happened to one of us tomorrow I think the other one, the other person, would grieve for a while, you know, but then the surviving party would go out and love again, have someone else soon enough. All this, all of this love we're talking about, it would just be a memory. Maybe not even a memory. Am I wrong? Am I way off base? Because I want you to set me straight if you think I'm wrong. I want to know. I mean, I don't know anything, and I'm the first one to admit it."

"Mel, for God's sake," Terri said. She reached out and took hold of his wrist. "Are you getting drunk? Honey? Are you drunk?"

"Honey, I'm just talking," Mel said. "All right? I don't have to be drunk to say what I think. I mean, we're all just talking, right?" Mel said. He fixed his eyes on her.

"Sweetie, I'm not criticizing," Terri said.                                          60

She picked up her glass.

"I'm not on call today," Mel said. "Let me remind you of that. I am not on call," he said.

"Mel, we love you," Laura said.

Mel looked at Laura. He looked at her as if he could not place her, as if she was not the woman she was.

"Love you too, Laura," Mel said. "And you, Nick, love you too. You know    65 something?" Mel said. "You guys are our pals," Mel said.

He picked up his glass.

Mel said, "I was going to tell you about something. I mean, I was going to prove a point. You see, this happened a few months ago, but it's still going on right now, and it ought to make us feel ashamed when we talk like we know what we're talking about when we talk above love."

"Come on now," Terri said. "Don't talk like you're drunk if you're not drunk."

"Just shut up for once in your life," Mel said very quietly. "Will you do me a favor and do that for a minute? So as I was saying, there's this old couple who had this car wreck out on the interstate. A kid hit them and they were all torn to shit and nobody was giving them much chance to pull through."

Terri looked at us and then back at Mel. She seemed anxious, or maybe that's 70 too strong a word.

Mel was handing the bottle around the table.

"I was on call that night," Mel said. "It was May or maybe it was June. Terri and I had just sat down to dinner when the hospital called. There'd been this thing out on the interstate. Drunk kid, teenager, plowed his dad's pickup into this camper with this old couple in it. They were up in their mid-seventies, that couple. The kid — eighteen, nineteen, something — he was DOA. Taken the steering wheel through his sternum. The old couple, they were alive, you understand. I mean, just barely. But they had everything. Multiple fractures, internal injuries, hemorrhaging, contusions, lacerations, the works, and they each of them had themselves concussions. They were in a bad way, believe me. And, of course, their age was two strikes against them. I'd say she was worse off than he was. Ruptured spleen along with everything else. Both kneecaps broken. But they'd been wearing their seatbelts and, God knows, that's what saved them for the time being."

"Folks, this is an advertisement for the National Safety Council," Terri said. "This is your spokesman, Dr. Melvin R. McGinnis, talking." Terri laughed. "Mel," she said, "sometimes you're just too much. But I love you, hon," she said.

"Honey, I love you," Mel said.

He leaned across the table. Terri met him halfway. They kissed. 75

"Terri's right," Mel said as he settled himself again. "Get those seatbelts on. But seriously, they were in some shape, those oldsters. By the time I got down there, the kid was dead, as I said. He was off in a corner, laid out on a gurney. I took one look at the old couple and told the ER nurse to get me a neurologist and an orthopedic man and a couple of surgeons down there right away."

He drank from his glass. "I'll try to keep this short," he said. "So we took the two of them up to the OR and worked like fuck on them most of the night. They had these incredible reserves, those two. You see that once in a while. So we did everything that could be done, and toward morning we're giving them a fifty-fifty chance, maybe less than that for her. So here they are, still alive the next morning. So, okay, we move them into the ICU, which is where they both kept plugging away at it for two weeks, hitting it better and better on all the scopes. So we transfer them out to their own room."

Mel stopped talking. "Here," he said, "let's drink this cheapo gin the hell up. Then we're going to dinner, right? Terri and I know a new place. That's where we'll go, to this new place we know about. But we're not going until we finish up this cut-rate, lousy gin."

Terri said, "We haven't actually eaten there yet. But it looks good. From the outside, you know."

"I like food," Mel said. "If I had it to do all over again, I'd be a chef, you 80 know? Right, Terri?" Mel said.

He laughed. He fingered the ice in his glass.

"Terri knows," he said. "Terri can tell you. But let me say this. If I could come back again in a different life, a different time and all, you know what? I'd like to come back as a knight. You were pretty safe wearing all that armor. It was all right being a knight until gunpowder and muskets and pistols came along."

"Mel would like to ride a horse and carry a lance," Terri said.

"Carry a woman's scarf with you everywhere," Laura said.

"Or just a woman," Mel said.                                                                              85

"Shame on you," Laura said.

Terri said, "Suppose you came back as a serf. The serfs didn't have it so good in those days," Terri said.

"The serfs never had it good," Mel said. "But I guess even the knights were vessels to someone. Isn't that the way it worked? But then everyone is always a vessel to someone. Isn't that right? Terri? But what I liked about knights, besides their ladies, was that they had that suit of armor, you know, and they couldn't get hurt very easy. No cars in those days, you know? No drunk teen-agers to tear into your ass."

"Vassals," Terri said.

"What?" Mel said.                                                                                          90

"Vassals," Terri said. "They were called vassals, not vessels."

"Vassals, vessels," Mel said, "what the fuck's the difference? You knew what I meant anyway. All right," Mel said. "So I'm not educated. I learned my stuff. I'm a heart surgeon, sure, but I'm just a mechanic. I go in and I fuck around and I fix things. Shit," Mel said.

"Modesty doesn't become you," Terri said.

"He's just a humble sawbones," I said. "But sometimes they suffocated in all that armor, Mel. They'd even have heart attacks if it got too hot and they were too tired and worn out. I read somewhere that they'd fall off their horses and not be able to get up because they were too tired to stand with all that armor on them. They got trampled by their own horses sometimes."

"That's terrible," Mel said. "That's a terrible thing, Nicky. I guess they'd just lay    95
there and wait until somebody came along and made a shish kebab out of them."

"Some other vessel," Terri said.

"That's right," Mel said. "Some vassal would come along and spear the bas-tard in the name of love. Or whatever the fuck it was they fought over in those days."

"Same things we fight over these days," Terri said.

Laura said, "Nothing's changed."

The color was still high in Laura's cheeks. Her eyes were bright. She brought    100
her glass to her lips.

Mel poured himself another drink. He looked at the label closely as if study-ing a long row of numbers. Then he slowly put the bottle down on the table and slowly reached for the tonic water.

"What about the old couple?" Laura said. "You didn't finish that story you started."

Laura was having a hard time lighting her cigarette. Her matches kept going out.

The sunshine inside the room was different now, changing, getting thinner. But the leaves outside the window were still shimmering, and I stared at the pattern they made on the panes and on the Formica counter. They weren't the same patterns, of course.

"What about the old couple?" I said.                                    105

"Older but wiser," Terri said.

Mel stared at her.

Terri said, "Go on with your story, hon. I was only kidding. Then what happened?"

"Terri, sometimes," Mel said.                                          110

"Please, Mel," Terri said. "Don't always be so serious, sweetie. Can't you take a joke?"

"Where's the joke?" Mel said.

He held his glass and gazed steadily at his wife.

"What happened?" Laura said.

Mel fastened his eyes on Laura. He said, "Laura, if I didn't have Terri and if I didn't love her so much, and if Nick wasn't my best friend, I'd fall in love with you, I'd carry you off, honey," he said.

"Tell your story," Terri said. "Then we'll go to that new place, okay?"    115

"Okay," Mel said. "Where was I?" he said. He stared at the table and then he began again.

"I dropped in to see each of them every day, sometimes twice a day if I was up doing other calls anyway. Casts and bandages, head to foot, the both of them. You know, you've seen it in the movies. That's just the way they looked, just like in the movies. Little eye-holes and nose-holes and mouth-holes. And she had to have her legs slung up on top of it. Well, the husband was very depressed for the longest while. Even after he found out that his wife was going to pull through, he was still very depressed. Not about the accident, though. I mean, the accident was one thing, but it wasn't everything. I'd get up to his mouth-hole, you know, and he'd say no, it wasn't the accident exactly but it was because he couldn't see her through his eye-holes. He said that was what was making him feel so bad. Can you imagine? I'm telling you, the man's heart was breaking because he couldn't turn his goddamn head and *see* his goddamn wife."

Mel looked around the table and shook his head at what he was going to say.

"I mean, it was killing the old fart just because he couldn't *look* at the fucking woman."

We all looked at Mel.                                                  120

"Do you see what I'm saying?" he said.

Maybe we were a little drunk by then. I know it was hard keeping things in focus. The light was draining out of the room, going back through the window where it had come from. Yet nobody made a move to get up from the table to turn on the overhead light.

"Listen," Mel said. "Let's finish this fucking gin. There's about enough left here for one shooter all around. Then let's go eat. Let's go to the new place."

"He's depressed," Terri said. "Mel, why don't you take a pill?"

Mel shook his head. "I've taken everything there is." 125

"We all need a pill now and then," I said.

"Some people are born needing them," Terri said.

She was using her finger to rub at something on the table. Then she stopped rubbing.

"I think I want to call my kids," Mel said. "Is that all right with everybody? I'll call my kids," he said.

Terri said, "What if Marjorie answers the phone? You guys, you've heard us 130 on the subject of Marjorie? Honey, you know you don't want to talk to Marjorie. It'll make you feel even worse."

"I don't want to talk to Marjorie," Mel said. "But I want to talk to my kids."

"There isn't a day goes by that Mel doesn't say he wishes she'd get married again. Or else die," Terri said. "For one thing," Terri said, "she's bankrupting us. Mel says it's just to spite him that she won't get married again. She has a boyfriend who lives with her and the kids, so Mel is supporting the boyfriend too."

"She's allergic to bees," Mel said. "If I'm not praying she'll get married again, I'm praying she'll get herself stung to death by a swarm of fucking bees."

"Shame on you," Laura said.

"Bzzzzzzz," Mel said, turning his fingers into bees and buzzing them at 135 Terri's throat. Then he let his hands drop all the way to his sides.

"She's vicious," Mel said. "Sometimes I think I'll go up there dressed like a beekeeper. You know, that hat that's like a helmet with the plate that comes down over your face, the big gloves, and the padded coat? I'll knock on the door and let loose a hive of bees in the house. But first I'd make sure the kids were out, of course."

He crossed one leg over the other. It seemed to take him a lot of time to do it. Then he put both feet on the floor and leaned forward, elbows on the table, his chin cupped in his hands.

"Maybe I won't call the kids, after all. Maybe it isn't such a hot idea. Maybe we'll just go eat. How does that sound?"

"Sounds fine to me," I said. "Eat or not eat. Or keep drinking. I could head right on out into the sunset."

"What does that mean, honey?" Laura said. 140

"It just means what I said," I said. "It means I could just keep going. That's all it means."

"I could eat something myself," Laura said. "I don't think I've ever been so hungry in my life. Is there something to nibble on?"

"I'll put out some cheese and crackers," Terri said.

But Terri just sat there. She did not get up to get anything.

Mel turned his glass over. He spilled it out on the table. 145

"Gin's gone," Mel said.

Terri said, "Now what?"

I could hear my heart beating. I could hear everyone's heart. I could hear the human noise we sat there making, not one of us moving, not even when the room went dark.

## FOR ANALYSIS

**1.** What is your reaction to Mel? Is he likable? What does his profession — a scientist and a cardiologist — represent?

**2.** What is the significance of Mel's account of the old couple injured in the car accident?

**3.** Do Mel's feelings about his ex-wife parallel Ed's feelings about Terri? Explain.

## MAKING ARGUMENTS

Raymond Carver is known for his **style**, sometimes called minimalism, characterized by spare language, attention to description, and an inclination to let elements of a story speak for themselves. As became clear later in his career and after his death, much of that style was the product of the interventions of his editor, Gordon Lish; in fact, many of Carver's early stories were originally much longer and much more expansive. Based on this story but drawing especially on your ideas about how fiction should work and what it should do, argue either that Lish did Carver a favor or that Carver would have been better off without him.

## WRITING TOPIC

In an essay, examine the various relationships in the story: Nick and Laura, Mel and Terri, Terri and Ed, Mel and his ex-wife Marjorie, and the injured old couple. How are they similar, and how are they different? Do they all have anything in common? Conclude your essay with a comment on "what we talk about when we talk about love."

## MAKING CONNECTIONS

Compare the marriages in this story, past and present, to the relationship between Sykes and Delia in Hurston's "Sweat" (p. 584). Think in terms of not only love and hate but also any other terms you can imagine. Are there some that are better or worse? What do "better" and "worse" mean to you, in this context?

## JOYCE CAROL OATES (B. 1938)

# WHERE ARE YOU GOING, WHERE HAVE YOU BEEN? 1970

## FOR BOB DYLAN[1]

Her name was Connie. She was fifteen and she had a quick nervous gig-gling habit of craning her neck to glance into mirrors, or checking other people's faces to make sure her own was all right. Her mother, who noticed everything and knew everything and who hadn't much reason any longer to look at her own face, always scolded Connie about it. "Stop gawking at your-self, who are you? You think you're so pretty?" she would say. Connie would raise her eyebrows at these familiar complaints and look right through her mother, into a shadowy vision of herself as she was right at that moment: she knew she was pretty and that was everything. Her mother had been pretty once too, if you could believe those old snapshots in the album, but now her looks were gone and that was why she was always after Connie.

"Why don't you keep your room clean like your sister? How've you got your hair fixed — what the hell stinks? Hair spray? You don't see your sister using that junk."

Her sister June was twenty-four and still lived at home. She was a secretary in the high school Connie attended, and if that wasn't bad enough — with her in the same building — she was so plain and chunky and steady that Connie had to hear her praised all the time by her mother and her mother's sisters. June did this, June did that, she saved money and helped clean the house and cooked and Connie couldn't do a thing, her mind was all filled with trashy daydreams. Their father was away at work most of the time and when he came home he wanted supper and he read the newspaper at supper and after supper he went to bed. He didn't bother talking much to them, but around his bent head Connie's mother kept picking at her until Connie wished her mother was dead and she herself was dead and it was all over. "She makes me want to throw up sometimes," she complained to her friends. She had a high, breathless, amused voice which made everything she said sound a little forced, whether it was sincere or not.

There was one good thing: June went places with girl friends of hers, girls who were just as plain and steady as she, and so when Connie wanted to do that her mother had no objections. The father of Connie's best girl friend drove the girls the three miles to town and left them off at a shopping plaza, so

---

[1] Bob Dylan (b. 1941) is an influential folk-rock musician and songwriter. Oates has commented that she had in mind Dylan's song "It's All Over Now, Baby Blue" when she wrote this story.

that they could walk through the stores or go to a movie, and when he came to pick them up again at eleven he never bothered to ask what they had done.

They must have been familiar sights, walking around that shopping plaza in their shorts and flat ballerina slippers that always scuffed the sidewalk, with charm bracelets jingling on their thin wrists; they would lean together to whisper and laugh secretly if someone passed by who amused or interested them. Connie had long dark blond hair that drew anyone's eye to it, and she wore part of it pulled up on her head and puffed out and the rest of it she let fall down her back. She wore a pull-over jersey blouse that looked one way when she was at home and another way when she was away from home. Everything about her had two sides to it, one for home and one for anywhere that was not home: her walk that could be childlike and bobbing, or languid enough to make anyone think she was hearing music in her head, her mouth which was pale and smirking most of the time, but bright and pink on these evenings out, her laugh which was cynical and drawling at home — "Ha, ha, very funny" — but high-pitched and nervous anywhere else, like the jingling of the charms on her bracelet.

Sometimes they did go shopping or to a movie, but sometimes they went across the highway, ducking fast across the busy road, to a drive-in restaurant where older kids hung out. The restaurant was shaped like a big bottle, though squatter than a real bottle, and on its cap was a revolving figure of a grinning boy who held a hamburger aloft. One night in mid-summer they ran across, breathless with daring, and right away someone leaned out a car window and invited them over, but it was just a boy from high school they didn't like. It made them feel good to be able to ignore him. They went up through the maze of parked and cruising cars to the bright-lit, fly-infested restaurant, their faces pleased and expectant as if they were entering a sacred building that loomed out of the night to give them what haven and what blessing they yearned for. They sat at the counter and crossed their legs at the ankles, their thin shoulders rigid with excitement, and listened to the music that made everything so good: the music was always in the background like music at a church service, it was something to depend upon.

A boy named Eddie came in to talk with them. He sat backwards on his stool, turning himself jerkily around in semi-circles and then stopping and turning again, and after a while he asked Connie if she would like something to eat. She said she did and so she tapped her friend's arm on her way out — her friend pulled her face up into a brave droll look — and Connie said she would meet her at eleven, across the way. "I just hate to leave her like that," Connie said earnestly, but the boy said that she wouldn't be alone for long. So they went out to his car and on the way Connie couldn't help but let her eyes wander over the windshields and faces all around her, her face gleaming with a joy that had nothing to do with Eddie or even this place; it might have been the music. She drew her shoulders up and sucked in her breath with the pure pleasure of being alive, and just at that moment she happened to glance at a face just a few feet from hers. It was a boy with shaggy black hair, in a convertible jalopy painted gold. He stared at her and then his lips widened into a grin. Connie slit her eyes at him and turned away, but she couldn't help glancing back and there he was still watching her. He wagged a finger and laughed and said, "Gonna get you, baby," and Connie turned away without Eddie noticing anything.

She spent three hours with him, at the restaurant where they ate hamburgers and drank Cokes in wax cups that were always sweating, and then down an alley a mile or so away, and when he left her off at five to eleven only the movie house was still open at the plaza. Her girl friend was there, talking with a boy. When Connie came up the two girls smiled at each other and Connie said, "How was the movie?" and the girl said, "*You* should know." They rode off with the girl's father, sleepy and pleased, and Connie couldn't help but look at the darkened shopping plaza with its big empty parking lot and its signs that were faded and ghostly now, and over at the drive-in restaurant where cars were still circling tirelessly. She couldn't hear the music at this distance.

Next morning June asked her how the movie was and Connie said, "So-so."

She and that girl and occasionally another girl went several times a week    10 that way, and the rest of the time Connie spent around the house — it was summer vacation — getting in her mother's way and thinking, dreaming, about the boys she met. But all the boys fell back and dissolved into a single face that was not even a face, but an idea, a feeling, mixed up with the urgent insistent pounding of the music and the humid night air of July. Connie's mother kept dragging her back to the daylight by finding things for her to do or saying, suddenly, "What's this about the Pettinger girl?"

And Connie would say nervously, "Oh, her. That dope." She always drew thick clear lines between herself and such girls, and her mother was simple and kindly enough to believe her. Her mother was so simple, Connie thought, that it was maybe cruel to fool her so much. Her mother went scuffling around the house in old bedroom slippers and complained over the telephone to one sister about the other, then the other called up and the two of them complained about the third one. If June's name was mentioned her mother's tone was approving, and if Connie's name was mentioned it was disapproving. This did not really mean she disliked Connie and actually Connie thought that her mother preferred her to June because she was prettier, but the two of them kept up a pretense of exasperation, a sense that they were tugging and struggling over something of little value to either of them. Sometimes, over coffee, they were almost friends, but something would come up — some vexation that was like a fly buzzing suddenly around their heads — and their faces went hard with contempt.

One Sunday Connie got up at eleven — none of them bothered with church — and washed her hair so that it could dry all day long, in the sun. Her parents and sister were going to a barbecue at an aunt's house and Connie said no, she wasn't interested, rolling her eyes to let her mother know just what she thought of it. "Stay home alone then," her mother said sharply. Connie sat out back in a lawn chair and watched them drive away, her father quiet and bald, hunched around so that he could back the car out, her mother with a look that was still angry and not at all softened through the windshield, and in the back seat poor old June all dressed up as if she didn't know what a barbecue was, with all the running yelling kids and the flies. Connie sat with her eyes closed in the sun, dreaming and dazed with the warmth about her as if this were a kind of love, the caresses of love, and her mind slipped over onto thoughts of the boy she had been with the night before and how nice he had been, how sweet it always was, not the way someone like June would suppose but sweet, gentle, the way it was in movies and promised in songs; and when she opened her eyes she hardly knew where she was, the back yard ran off into weeds and a fence-line of trees and behind it the sky was perfectly blue and still. The asbestos "ranch house" that was now three years old still startled her — it looked small. She shook her head as if to get awake.

It was too hot. She went inside the house and turned on the radio to drown out the quiet. She sat on the edge of her bed, barefoot, and listened for an hour and a half to a program called XYZ Sunday Jamboree, record after record of hard, fast, shrieking songs she sang along with, interspersed by exclamations from "Bobby King": "An' look here you girls at Napoleon's — Son and Charley want you to pay real close attention to this song coming up!"

And Connie paid close attention herself, bathed in a glow of slow-pulsed joy that seemed to rise mysteriously out of the music itself and lay languidly about the airless little room, breathed in and breathed out with each gentle rise and fall of her chest.

After a while she heard a car coming up the drive. She sat up at once, 15 startled, because it couldn't be her father so soon. The gravel kept crunching all the way in from the road — the driveway was long — and Connie ran to the window. It was a car she didn't know. It was an open jalopy, painted a bright gold that caught the sunlight opaquely. Her heart began to pound and her fingers snatched at her hair, checking it, and she whispered "Christ. Christ," wondering how bad she looked. The car came to a stop at the side door and the horn sounded four short taps as if this were a signal Connie knew.

She went into the kitchen and approached the door slowly, then hung out the screen door, her bare toes curling down off the step. There were two boys in the car and now she recognized the driver: he had shaggy, shabby black hair that looked crazy as a wig and he was grinning at her.

"I ain't late, am I?" he said.

"Who the hell do you think you are?" Connie said.

"Toldja I'd be out, didn't I?"

"I don't even know who you are."                    20

She spoke sullenly, careful to show no interest or pleasure, and he spoke in a fast bright monotone. Connie looked past him to the other boy, taking her time. He had fair brown hair, with a lock that fell onto his forehead. His side-burns gave him a fierce, embarrassed look, but so far he hadn't even bothered to glance at her. Both boys wore sunglasses. The driver's glasses were metallic and mirrored everything in miniature.

"You wanta come for a ride?" he said.

Connie smirked and let her hair fall loose over one shoulder.

"Don'tcha like my car? New paint job," he said. "Hey."

"What?"    25

"You're cute."

She pretended to fidget, chasing flies away from the door.

"Don'tcha believe me, or what?" he said.

"Look, I don't even know who you are," Connie said in disgust.

"Hey, Ellie's got a radio, see. Mine's broke down." He lifted his friend's arm    30
and showed her the little transistor the boy was holding, and now Connie began
to hear the music. It was the same program that was playing inside the house.

"Bobby King?" she said.

"I listen to him all the time. I think he's great."

"He's kind of great," Connie said reluctantly.

"Listen, that guy's *great*. He knows where the action is."

Connie blushed a little, because the glasses made it impossible for her to see    35
just what this boy was looking at. She couldn't decide if she liked him or if he
was just a jerk, and so she dawdled in the doorway and wouldn't come down
or go back inside. She said, "What's all that stuff painted on your car?"

"Can'tcha read it?" He opened the door very carefully, as if he was afraid it
might fall off. He slid out just as carefully, planting his feet firmly on the ground,
the tiny metallic world in his glasses slowing down like gelatine hardening and
in the midst of it Connie's bright green blouse. "This here is my name, to begin
with," he said. ARNOLD FRIEND was written in tarlike black letters on the
side, with a drawing of a round grinning face that reminded Connie of a pumpkin, except it wore sunglasses. "I wanta introduce myself, I'm Arnold Friend
and that's my real name and I'm gonna be your friend, honey, and inside the
car's Ellie Oscar, he's kinda shy." Ellie brought his transistor radio up to his
shoulder and balanced it there. "Now these numbers are a secret code, honey,"
Arnold Friend explained. He read off the numbers 33, 19, 17 and raised his
eyebrows at her to see what she thought of that, but she didn't think much of it.
The left rear fender had been smashed and around it was written on the gleaming gold background: DONE BY CRAZY WOMAN DRIVER. Connie had to
laugh at that. Arnold Friend was pleased at her laughter and looked up at her.
"Around the other side's a lot more — you wanta come and see them?"

"No."

"Why not?"

"Why should I?"

"Don'tcha wanta see what's on the car? Don'tcha wanta go for a ride?"    40

"I don't know."

"Why not?"

"I got things to do."

"Like what?"

"Things."    45

He laughed as if she had said something funny. He slapped his thighs.
He was standing in a strange way, leaning back against the car as if he were

balancing himself. He wasn't tall, only an inch or so taller than she would be if she came down to him. Connie liked the way he was dressed, which was the way all of them dressed: tight faded jeans stuffed into black, scuffed boots, a belt that pulled his waist in and showed how lean he was, and a white pull-over shirt that was a little soiled and showed the hard small muscles of his arms and shoulders. He looked as if he possibly did hard work, lifting and carrying things. Even his neck looked muscular. And his face was a familiar face, somehow: the jaw and chin and cheeks slightly darkened, because he hadn't shaved for a day or two, and the nose long and hawk-like, sniffing as if she were a treat he was going to gobble up and it was all a joke.

"Connie, you ain't telling the truth. This is your day set aside for a ride with me and you know it," he said, still laughing. The way he straightened and recovered from his fit of laughing showed that it had been all fake.

"How do you know what my name is?" she said suspiciously.

"It's Connie."

"Maybe and maybe not."                                                                    50

"I know my Connie," he said, wagging his finger. Now she remembered him even better, back at the restaurant, and her cheeks warmed at the thought of how she sucked in her breath just at the moment she passed him — how she must have looked to him. And he had remembered her. "Ellie and I came out here especially for you," he said. "Ellie can sit in back. How about it?"

"Where?"

"Where what?"

"Where're we going?"

He looked at her. He took off the sunglasses and she saw how pale the skin  55 around his eyes was, like holes that were not in shadow but instead in light. His eyes were chips of broken glass that catch the light in an amiable way. He smiled. It was as if the idea of going for a ride somewhere, to some place, was a new idea to him.

"Just for a ride, Connie sweetheart."

"I never said my name was Connie," she said.

"But I know what it is. I know your name and all about you, lots of things," Arnold Friend said. He had not moved yet but stood still leaning back against the side of his jalopy. "I took a special interest in you, such a pretty girl, and found out all about you like I know your parents and sister are gone somewheres and I know where and how long they're going to be gone, and I know who you were with last night, and your best girl friend's name is Betty. Right?"

He spoke in a simple lilting voice, exactly as if he were reciting the words to a song. His smile assured her that everything was fine. In the car, Ellie turned up the volume on his radio and did not bother to look around at them.

"Ellie can sit in the back seat," Arnold Friend said. He indicated his friend  60 with a casual jerk of his chin, as if Ellie did not count and she should not bother with him.

"How'd you find out all that stuff?" Connie said.

"Listen: Betty Schultz and Tony Fitch and Jimmy Pettinger and Nancy Pettinger," he said, in a chant. "Raymond Stanley and Bob Hutter —"

"Do you know all those kids?"

"I know everybody."

"Look, you're kidding. You're not from around here." 65

"Sure."

"But — how come we never saw you before?"

"Sure you saw me before," he said. He looked down at his boots, as if he were a little offended. "You just don't remember."

"I guess I'd remember you," Connie said.

"Yeah?" He looked up at this, beaming. He was pleased. He began to mark 70 time with the music from Ellie's radio, tapping his fists lightly together. Connie looked away from his smile to the car, which was painted so bright it almost hurt her eyes to look at it. She looked at that name, ARNOLD FRIEND. And up at the front fender was an expression that was familiar — MAN THE FLYING SAUCERS. It was an expression kids had used the year before, but didn't use this year. She looked at it for a while as if the words meant something to her that she did not yet know.

"What're you thinking about? Huh?" Arnold Friend demanded. "Not worried about your hair blowing around in the car, are you?"

"No."

"Think I maybe can't drive good?"

"How do I know?"

"You're a hard girl to handle. How come?" he said. "Don't you know I'm your 75 friend? Didn't you see me put my sign in the air when you walked by?"

"What sign?"

"My sign." And he drew an X in the air, leaning out toward her. They were maybe ten feet apart. After his hand fell back to his side, the X was still in the air, almost visible. Connie let the screen door close and stood perfectly still inside it, listening to the music from her radio and the boy's blend together. She stared at Arnold Friend. He stood there so stiffly relaxed, pretending to be relaxed, with one hand idly on the door handle as if he were keeping himself up that way and had no intention of ever moving again. She recognized most things about him, the tight jeans that showed his thighs and buttocks and the greasy leather boots and the tight shirt, and even that slippery friendly smile of his, that sleepy dreamy smile that all the boys used to get across ideas they didn't want to put into words. She recognized all this and also the singsong way he talked, slightly mocking, kidding, but serious and a little melancholy, and she recognized the way he tapped one fist against the other in homage to the perpetual music behind him. But all these things did not come together.

She said suddenly, "Hey, how old are you?"

His smile faded. She could see then that he wasn't a kid, he was much older — thirty, maybe more. At this knowledge her heart began to pound faster.

"That's a crazy thing to ask. Can'tcha see I'm your own age?" 80

"Like hell you are."

"Or maybe a couple years older, I'm eighteen."

"Eighteen?" she said doubtfully.

He grinned to reassure her and lines appeared at the corners of his mouth. His teeth were big and white. He grinned so broadly his eyes became slits and she saw how thick the lashes were, thick and black as if painted with a black tarlike material. Then he seemed to become embarrassed, abruptly, and looked over his shoulder at Ellie. "*Him*, he's crazy," he said. "Ain't he a riot, he's a nut, a real character." Ellie was still listening to the music. His sunglasses told nothing about what he was thinking. He wore a bright orange shirt unbuttoned halfway to show his chest, which was a pale, bluish chest and not muscular like Arnold Friend's. His shirt collar was turned up all around and the very tips of the collar pointed out past his chin as if they were protecting him. He was pressing the transistor radio up against his ear and sat there in a kind of daze, right in the sun.

"He's kinda strange," Connie said.                                                      85

"Hey, she says you're kinda strange! Kinda strange!" Arnold Friend cried. He pounded on the car to get Ellie's attention. Ellie turned for the first time and Connie saw with shock that he wasn't a kid either — he had a fair, hairless face, cheeks reddened slightly as if the veins grew too close to the surface of his skin, the face of a forty-year-old baby. Connie felt a wave of dizziness rise in her at this sight and she stared at him as if waiting for something to change the shock of the moment, make it all right again. Ellie's lips kept shaping words, mumbling along, with the words blasting in his ear.

"Maybe you two better go away," Connie said faintly.

"What? How come?" Arnold Friend cried. "We come out here to take you for a ride. It's Sunday." He had the voice of the man on the radio now. It was the same voice, Connie thought. "Don'tcha know it's Sunday all day and honey, no matter who you were with last night today you're with Arnold Friend and don't you forget it! — Maybe you better step out here," he said, and this last was in a different voice. It was a little flatter, as if the heat was finally getting to him.

"No. I got things to do."

"Hey."                                                                                  90

"You two better leave."

"We ain't leaving until you come with us."

"Like hell I am —"

"Connie, don't fool around with me. I mean, I mean, don't fool *around*," he said, shaking his head. He laughed incredulously. He placed his sunglasses on top of his head, carefully, as if he were indeed wearing a wig, and brought the stems down behind his ears. Connie stared at him, another wave of dizziness and fear rising in her so that for a moment he wasn't even in focus but was just a blur, standing there against his gold car, and she had the idea that he had driven up the driveway all right but had come from nowhere before that and belonged nowhere and that everything about him and even about the music that was so familiar to her was only half real.

"If my father comes and sees you —"                                                     95

"He ain't coming. He's at the barbecue."

"How do you know that?"

"Aunt Tillie's. Right now they're — uh — they're drinking. Sitting around," he said vaguely, squinting as if he were staring all the way to town and over to Aunt Tillie's backyard. Then the vision seemed to get clear and he nodded energetically. "Yeah. Sitting around. There's your sister in a blue dress, huh? And high heels, the poor sad bitch — nothing like you, sweetheart! And your mother's helping some fat woman with the corn, they're cleaning the corn — husking the corn —"

"What fat woman?" Connie cried.

"How do I know what fat woman. I don't know every goddam fat woman in the world!" Arnold Friend laughed. 100

"Oh, that's Mrs. Hornby. . . . Who invited her?" Connie said. She felt a little light-headed. Her breath was coming quickly.

"She's too fat. I don't like them fat. I like them the way you are, honey," he said, smiling sleepily at her. They stared at each other for awhile, through the screen door. He said softly, "Now what you're going to do is this: you're going to come out that door. You're going to sit up front with me and Ellie's going to sit in the back, the hell with Ellie, right? This isn't Ellie's date. You're my date. I'm your lover, honey."

"What? You're crazy —"

"Yes, I'm your lover. You don't know what that is but you will," he said. "I know that too. I know all about you. But look: it's real nice and you couldn't ask for nobody better than me, or more polite. I always keep my word. I'll tell you how it is, I'm always nice at first, the first time. I'll hold you so tight you won't think you have to try to get away or pretend anything because you'll know you can't. And I'll come inside you where it's all secret and you'll give in to me and you'll love me —"

"Shut up! You're crazy!" Connie said. She backed away from the door. She 105 put her hands against her ears as if she'd heard something terrible, something not meant for her. "People don't talk like that, you're crazy," she muttered. Her heart was almost too big now for her chest and its pumping made sweat break out all over her. She looked out to see Arnold Friend pause and then take a step toward the porch lurching. He almost fell. But, like a clever drunken man, he managed to catch his balance. He wobbled in high boots and grabbed hold of one of the porch posts.

"Honey?" he said. "You still listening?"

"Get the hell out of here!"

"Be nice, honey. Listen."

"I'm going to call the police —"

He wobbled again and out of the side of his mouth came a fast spat curse, 110 an aside not meant for her to hear. But even this "Christ!" sounded forced. Then he began to smile again. She watched this smile come, awkward as if he were smiling from inside a mask. His whole face was a mask, she thought wildly, tanned down onto his throat but then running out as if he had plastered make-up on his face but had forgotten about his throat.

"Honey—? Listen, here's how it is. I always tell the truth and I promise you this: I ain't coming in the house after you."

"You better not! I'm going to call the police if you — if you don't —"

"Honey," he said, talking right through her voice, "honey, I'm not coming in there but you are coming out here. You know why?"

She was panting. The kitchen looked like a place she had never seen before, some room she had run inside but which wasn't good enough, wasn't going to help her. The kitchen window had never had a curtain, after three years, and there were dishes in the sink for her to do—probably—and if you ran your hand across the table you'd probably feel something sticky there.

"You listening, honey? Hey?" 115

" — going to call the police —"

"Soon as you touch the phone I don't need to keep my promise and can come inside. You won't want that."

She rushed forward and tried to lock the door. Her fingers were shaking. "But why lock it," Arnold Friend said gently, talking right into her face. "It's just a screen door. It's just nothing." One of his boots was at a strange angle, as if his foot wasn't in it. It pointed out to the left, bent at the ankle. "I mean, anybody can break through a screen door and glass and wood and iron or anything else he needs to, anybody at all and specially Arnold Friend. If the place got lit up with a fire honey you'd come running out into my arms, right into my arms and safe at home — like you knew I was your lover and'd stopped fooling around. I don't mind a nice shy girl but I don't like no fooling around." Part of those words were spoken with a slight rhythmic lilt, and Connie somehow recognized them — the echo of a song from last year, about a girl rushing into her boy friend's arms and coming home again —

Connie stood barefoot on the linoleum floor, staring at him. "What do you want?" she whispered.

"I want you," he said. 120

"What?"

"Seen you that night and thought, that's the one, yes sir. I never needed to look any more."

"But my father's coming back. He's coming to get me. I had to wash my hair first —" She spoke in a dry, rapid voice, hardly raising it for him to hear.

"No, your daddy is not coming and yes, you had to wash your hair and you washed it for me. It's nice and shining and all for me, I thank you, sweetheart," he said, with a mock bow, but again he almost lost his balance. He had to bend and adjust his boots. Evidently his feet did not go all the way down; the boots must have been stuffed with something so that he would seem taller. Connie stared out at him and behind him Ellie in the car, who seemed to be looking off toward Connie's right, into nothing. This Ellie said, pulling the words out of the air one after another as if he were just discovering them, "You want me to pull out the phone?"

"Shut your mouth and keep it shut," Arnold Friend said, his face red from 125 bending over or maybe from embarrassment because Connie had seen his boots. "This ain't none of your business."

"What — what are you doing? What do you want?" Connie said. "If I call the police they'll get you, they'll arrest you —"

"Promise was not to come in unless you touch that phone, and I'll keep that promise," he said. He resumed his erect position and tried to force his shoulders back. He sounded like a hero in a movie, declaring something important. He spoke too loudly and it was as if he were speaking to someone behind Connie. "I ain't made plans for coming in that house where I don't belong but just for you to come out to me, the way you should. Don't you know who I am?"

"You're crazy," she whispered. She backed away from the door but did not want to go into another part of the house, as if this would give him permission to come through the door. "What do you . . . You're crazy, you . . ."

"Huh? What're you saying, honey?"

Her eyes darted everywhere in the kitchen. She could not remember what it    130 was, this room.

"This is how it is, honey: you come out and we'll drive away, have a nice ride. But if you don't come out we're gonna wait till your people come home and then they're all going to get it."

"You want that telephone pulled out?" Ellie said. He held the radio away from his ear and grimaced, as if without the radio the air was too much for him.

"I toldja shut up, Ellie," Arnold Friend said, "you're deaf, get a hearing aid, right? Fix yourself up. This little girl's no trouble and's gonna be nice to me, so Ellie keep to yourself, this ain't your date — right? Don't hem in on me. Don't hog. Don't crush. Don't bird dog. Don't trail me," he said in a rapid meaningless voice, as if he were running through all the expressions he'd learned but was no longer sure which one of them was in style, then rushing on to new ones, making them up with his eyes closed, "Don't crawl under my fence, don't squeeze in my chipmunk hole, don't sniff my glue, suck my popsicle, keep your own greasy fingers on yourself!" He shaded his eyes and peered in at Connie, who was backed against the kitchen table. "Don't mind him honey he's just a creep. He's a dope. Right? I'm the boy for you and like I said you come out here nice like a lady and give me your hand, and nobody else gets hurt, I mean, your nice old bald-headed daddy and your mummy and your sister in her high heels. Because listen: why bring them in this?"

"Leave me alone," Connie whispered.

"Hey, you know that old woman down the road, the one with the chickens    135 and stuff — you know her?"

"She's dead!"

"Dead? What? You know her?" Arnold Friend said.

"She's dead —"

"Don't you like her?"

"She's dead — she's — she isn't here any more —"    140

"But don't you like her, I mean, you got something against her? Some grudge or something?" Then his voice dipped as if he were conscious of a rudeness. He touched the sunglasses perched on top of his head as if to make sure they were still there. "Now you be a good girl."

"What are you going to do?"

"Just two things, or maybe three," Arnold Friend said. "But I promise it won't last long and you'll like me that way you get to like people you're close to. You will. It's all over for you here, so come on out. You don't want your people in any trouble, do you?"

She turned and bumped against a chair or something, hurting her leg, but she ran into the back room and picked up the telephone. Something roared in her ear, a tiny roaring, and she was so sick with fear that she could do nothing but listen to it — the telephone was clammy and very heavy and her fingers groped down to the dial but were too weak to touch it. She began to scream into the phone, into the roaring. She cried out, she cried for her mother, she felt her breath start jerking back and forth in her lungs as if it were something Arnold Friend were stabbing her with again and again with no tenderness. A noisy sorrowful wailing rose all about her and she was locked inside it the way she was locked inside that house.

After a while she could hear again. She was sitting on the floor with her wet back against the wall. 145

Arnold Friend was saying from the door, "That's a good girl. Put the phone back."

She kicked the phone away from her.

"No, honey. Pick it up. Put it back right."

She picked it up and put it back. The dial tone stopped.

"That's a good girl. Now come outside." 150

She was hollow with what had been fear, but what was now just an emptiness. All that screaming had blasted it out of her. She sat, one leg cramped under her, and deep inside her brain was something like a pinpoint of light that kept going and would not let her relax. She thought, I'm not going to see my mother again. She thought, I'm not going to sleep in my bed again. Her bright green blouse was all wet.

Arnold Friend said, in a gentle-loud voice that was like a stage voice, "The place where you came from ain't there any more, and where you had in mind to go is cancelled out. This place you are now — inside your daddy's house — is nothing but a cardboard box I can knock down any time. You know that and always did know it. You hear me?"

She thought, I have got to think. I have to know what to do.

"We'll go out to a nice field, out in the country here where it smells so nice and it's sunny," Arnold Friend said. "I'll have my arms around you so you won't need to try to get away and I'll show you what love is like, what it does. The hell with this house! It looks solid all right," he said. He ran a fingernail down the screen and the noise did not make Connie shiver, as it would have the day before. "Now put your hand on your heart, honey. Feel that? That feels solid too but we know better, be nice to me, be sweet like you can because what else is there for a girl like you but to be sweet and pretty and give in? — and get away before her people come back?"

She felt her pounding heart. Her hand seemed to enclose it. She thought    155
for the first time in her life that it was nothing that was hers, that belonged to her, but just a pounding, living thing inside this body that wasn't really hers either.

"You don't want them to get hurt," Arnold Friend went on. "Now get up, honey. Get up all by yourself."

She stood up.

"Now turn this way. That's right. Come over here to me — Ellie, put that away, didn't I tell you? You dope. You miserable creepy dope," Arnold said. His words were not angry but only part of an incantation. The incantation was kindly. "Now come out through the kitchen to me honey and let's see a smile, try it, you're a brave sweet little girl and now they're eating corn and hotdogs cooked to bursting over an outdoor fire, and they don't know one thing about you and never did and honey, you're better than them because not a one of them would have done this for you."

Connie felt the linoleum under her feet; it was cool. She brushed her hair back out of her eyes. Arnold Friend let go of the post tentatively and opened his arms for her, his elbows pointing in toward each other and his wrists limp, to show that this was an embarrassed embrace and a little mocking, he didn't want to make her self-conscious.

She put out her hand against the screen. She watched herself push the door    160
slowly open as if she were safe back somewhere in the other doorway, watching this body and this head of long hair moving out into the sunlight where Arnold Friend waited.

"My sweet little blue-eyed girl," he said, in a half-sung sigh that had nothing to do with her brown eyes but was taken up just the same by the vast sunlit reaches of the land behind him and on all sides of him, so much land that Connie had never seen before and did not recognize except to know that she was going to it.

### FOR ANALYSIS

**1.** Describe Connie in your own words. What are the sources of her values? What sort of love experience does she imagine?

**2.** When she agrees to go with Eddie, what do you suppose they did in the "alley a mile or so away" (para. 8)?

**3.** How does Arnold Friend differ from Eddie?

**4.** Why is attention paid in the story to Arnold's boots?

**5.** How does Ellie's repeated proposal that Arnold pull out the phone affect your understanding of Arnold and Ellie's motives?

**6.** Does Connie go to Arnold simply to protect her family from his threats? Explain.

**7.** What is going to happen to Connie? Why?

**8.** The story is told by a **third-person narrator** — yet it is limited, essentially, to Connie's viewpoint. Would multiple viewpoints — her mother's, June's, Eddie's, her friend's, Arnold's — enhance or impair the story's impact?

## MAKING ARGUMENTS

Do you believe that Connie knows what is likely to happen to her when she steps outside her house? Is she simply too naïve to see it? Is one of these alternatives somehow worse than the other? Using evidence from the story, argue that Arnold Friend is an incarnation of the devil or some fairy-tale villain.

## WRITING TOPIC

In your experience, do some women find dangerous and unstable men more attractive than gentle and kind men? Support your arguments with **allusions** to Oates's story and other stories you have read.

## MAKING CONNECTIONS

Compare the situation in this story to that in Galchen's "Wild Berry Blue" (p. 126). Both situations are in some ways dangerous; both are in some ways about innocence. How are they similar in these regards? How are they different?

## LYDIA MILLET   (B. 1968)

# LOVE IN INFANT MONKEYS   2009

Harry Harlow had a general hypothesis: Mothers are useful, in scientific terms. They have an intrinsic value, even beyond their breast milk. Call it their company.

In this hypothesis he was bucking a trend in American psychology. For decades experts on parenting had been advising mothers to show their children as little affection as possible. Too much affection was coddling, and coddling weakened a child. "When you are tempted to pet your child," said a president of the American Psychological Association in a speech, "remember that mother love is a dangerous instrument." This school of thought ran counter to what was believed by those not indebted for their child-rearing strategies to a rigorously monitored testing process. But it was dominant in the scholarship. To refute it, Harlow decided, the value of love would have to be demonstrated in a controlled experimental setting.

He worked long hours, seldom leaving his laboratory. With his experiments he made a name for himself, appearing on television programs and traveling the country on speaking engagements. He was seen as a rebel and an iconoclast. He spoke boldly of mother love, calling it "contact comfort." He stressed its value to emotional health.

But he spoke harshly of his test subjects. "The only thing I care about is whether a monkey will turn out a property I can publish," he said. "I don't have any love for them. I never have. How could you love a monkey?"

To know how love works, a scientist must study its absence. This is simple 5 scientific method; Harry admitted it. The suffering of lesser beings is often the price of knowledge. As he put it, "If my work will save only one million human children, I can't get overly concerned about ten monkeys."

Others were doing bold animal experiments at the same time, in the fifties, when Harry started, and after. Rats were dropped in boiling water, cats pinned down for months until their legs withered, dogs irradiated until their skin crisped, monkeys shot in the heads and stomachs or immobilized to have their spinal cords severed. When it came to the treatment of research animals, Harry was squarely in the mainstream. Only his willingness to speak bluntly was avant-garde.

He gathered disciples around him, young women and men who would continue his work, and decades later he would still be revered by psychology. While acknowledging the problem of what some might call animal cruelty, later scholars would view his collateral damage as a necessary unpleasantness. His chief biographer, a woman journalist, described him as a rose in a cornfield.

He was a high-functioning alcoholic, and there were long periods in his life when he was rarely sober. He had wives — first one, then another, then the first one again. He had two sets of children he never saw.

Harry Frederick Harlow had been born Harry Frederick Israel. Around the time of his doctoral dissertation he had changed his last name, not because he was Jewish — for he was not, in fact, Jewish — but because the name Israel sounded Jewish, and this made it hard to secure a good job. He did not dislike Jews; indeed, he admired them for their intelligence and their education. But others in academia had certain prejudices. A famous professor who was also his first mentor did not wish him to continue to be mistaken for a Jew, so Harry deferred to him.

It was a minor accommodation. 10

One way to prove the hypothesis was to take a newborn monkey away from its mother and never give it back. Put it in a bare box, observe it. Anxiety first, shown in trembling and shaking; then come the screams. Watch it huddle, small limbs clutching. Make careful notations. Next, construct a wire mannequin that holds a milk bottle. See if the baby thinks the mannequin is its mother. When it does not think so, give it a mannequin draped with terry cloth, but no milk. See it cling to this milkless cloth mannequin.

Repeat experiment with numerous infants. Make notations.

Second, place infant monkeys in isolation, with neither monkeys nor human contact save the sight of the researchers' hands entering the box to change bedding or food. Leave them there for thirty days. Make careful notations. When the infants are removed, watch two among them starve themselves till they expire. Notations. Repeat with longer isolation periods. First six months, then a year. If necessary, force-feed upon removal from box. Observe: If left in boxes for twelve months, infants will no longer move. Only life signs: pulse and respiration. Upon removal from box, such damaged infants may have to be reisolated for the duration of their short lives. Notations.

Third, attempt to breed the isolate monkeys to produce needed new experimental subjects. When the monkeys show no inclination to mate, inseminate the females. Observe the birth of infants. Observe that the longest-isolated mothers kill infants by chewing off fingers and toes or crushing heads with their teeth. Notations.

Fourth, create bad-mother surrogates: mothers with spikes, mothers that 15 blast cold wind. Put baby monkeys on them. Observe: Time after time, baby monkeys return. Bad mother is better than none.

Only 8:00 pm, and he was already slurring. He would swing by that party. What the hell. Suomi had said he'd be there.

But first, check the experiments.

Walking along the row of vertical chambers, he gave cursory glances inside — one, two, three subjects in a row had given up trying to climb out of their wells of isolation. The pits were designed, of course, to make it impossible to escape.

One subject scrambled and fell back, a weak young female. She looked up with her great round black eyes. Blink blink. She was afraid, but still plucky. Still game to try to get out, change her situation. The others were abject at the bottom of their separate holes, knew by now they could never climb the sides of the wells. As far as they knew, they were in there for good. Plucky got you nowhere if you were a lab monkey.

Then the boxes where Bill had dosed the subjects with reserpine. These 20 monkeys, too, huddled unmoving. Serotonin had been suppressed; this seemed to equate almost uniformly with complete listlessness, complete passivity. Might be other factors, but still: very interesting.

Back past the so-called pits of despair, where the young female — what had they named her? Minestrone? — was still trying to climb the walls and falling repeatedly. She squeaked at him. Well, not at him, technically. She did not know he was there; she could not see him. She could see no one. She was alone.

Harlow got in the car. Drove. Wasn't far. Hated faculty parties, hardly ever went to them: frivolous. Took him away from his work.

He said this to a new female grad student who met him on the walkway, exclaiming at his presence. She had long curly hair and wore no brassiere.

"Dr. Harlow! I can't believe you actually made it!"

"Work allatime," he said, nodding and shrugging at once. Not as easy as he'd 25 thought it would be. Pulled it together, though. "Lucky. Always have smart wives to help me with it."

She shot him a look of pity: Everyone knew the second smart wife was on her cancer deathbed.

"Some of the faculty," he went on, "these guys don't even work on Sundays. Not serious."

She was looking at him like he was a baby bird fallen from its nest. The free-love ones were maternal. Always acting like everyone's little mommy.

Save it up for the kiddies, he thought. Wasted on me.

These days, Peggy dying like this, maybe he should take a break more 30 often — the depression, for one thing. Felt like the top of his head was weighing him down. Headaches constantly. Chest squashed and nervous stomach. Nothing compared to the chemo, but still. Hair and skin greasy. Plus he was tired, face ached with it. Didn't know if he could have kept his head up if he'd stayed at his desk. Fell asleep with a cigarette in his mouth last night, woke up with a stack of papers smoldering. Something smelled wrong. Burned his eyebrow half off, it turned out.

He patted his pocket for his cigarettes. Full pack. His students were going to be here. Chance to talk to Steve again about the chambers. Steve had said not to call them *dungeons*. Bad for public opinion.

Bullshit, but Steve was good at that side of it. Spade a spade, goddammit.

Saw a garden hose sticking out of a spigot against the side of the house. Turned it on, with some difficulty. Wrestled with the hose till cool water sputtered into his mouth. Cleared his head. Tongue felt less mealy. He wiggled the tongue around in his mouth. Testing it.

"Harry! — I can't believe this — Harry!"

Fat woman from the department, what did she do? Personnel? Payroll? 35 Lumbering.

"Ha, ha," he said, dropping the hose, stepping up onto the stoop and lurching into the doorjamb.

"So you're finally out of your cave! Look who's here! It's *Harry*! Can you guys believe this? Come on in!"

There was the good-looking girl from East Germany who was interested in the nuclear-family experiments, smoking in the corner with Jim. Poor Jim, that plagiarism thing with Peggy. Unfair. But nothing he could do about it. Couldn't get in the middle. He shrugged, itchy.

The jacket: How long had he been wearing it? Felt oily. Maybe it was the shirt. Was it supposed to be white? He could not remember. Gray, beige or white? What color was the shirt to begin with?

"Get you a highball, Harry?" 40

It was a hard-to-breathe night. Humid, filmy. He squinted. Barely see the kids in the corner, but all of them seemed to be looking at him.

The fat payroll said something about gin. He nodded. Headache getting worse. Bands of light spanning his field of vision.

"Harry," said a guy from the right. "Harry Harlow, right? Hey, I read 'Love in Infant Monkeys.' Great paper."

"Huh," grunted Harry, "Seen Suomi?"

"Steve's not here yet," said the guy, either frowning or leering. No idea who it 45 was. Might be the chancellor, for all he knew. Wished he would disappear.

"Huh," Harry muttered. Guy was already veering toward something out the side door, where a fountain was playing. A twinkle of water? Mermaids?

"Lie down a little," he told the payroll woman, hovering with a heavy tumbler. He accepted it gratefully, drank it down and gave it right back. Good to be prompt. Aftertaste was hinky. "Spare daybed, maybe? Dark room? Cot thing?"

"Certainly," said the woman. "There, there. You poor dear." She leaned close and whispered with obscene intimacy: "How's she *doing*?"

Wasn't a baby bird, for Chrissake. No broken wing. Piece of his mind; tell her straight she resembled a water buffalo. Should be roaming the Serengeti with her quadruped friends. "Holding up, holding up," he mumbled. "Brave girl, Peggy." Hadn't seen her for more than five minutes since what, Tuesday? Busy. She knew; she understood perfectly.

He persevered to the room at the back. Secluded. The water buffalo showed 50 him in. Closed the door in her face. "No buffalos," he said, quietly but firmly.

He fell down on the bed and felt a brief satisfaction.

When he woke, the party was over. Brimming ashtrays everywhere. Skinny kid fast asleep on the couch, legs straight, sneakers splayed on the sofa arm. He stood over the kitchen sink, full of squeezed-out lemon halves and olives.

He splashed water on his face and gargled out of a used glass. Didn't see a clean one. Who cared. His mouth was pure alcohol, would neutralize the germs. Made his way out of the bungalow, thirsty as hell. Needed something real to drink.

White light; he blinked on the stoop. It was early morning. Sunday? Legs felt heavy, but he would go to the lab. Still had a faint headache, but bearable now.

Lab was empty. Students must be sitting on their asses this weekend. Pure mediocrity.

Walking the gauntlet of the pits of despair he glanced into Minestrone's 55 setup. Saw the top of her head. She was just sitting there. He kept watching; she did not move. Not a spark animated the creature. Finally given up. Now broken. Her spindly arms hung loose from the sockets, doing nothing. Hunched little figure, staring. Nothing there. It had gone.

Had a flask in a special file cabinet. Headed for it. Deep swig.

In the nightmare, which he'd had in other forms before, he stood beside his beautiful boxes, the boxes of his own design, the boxes that B. F. Skinner himself had admired. He mistook each infant monkey for a beloved soul. In that way the nightmare was confusing. He saw each infant in the heart of its mother, precious, unique, held so close because the mother was willing to die for it. The mother, in the dream, knew what he was doing as he took the infant from her. She was fully aware of what was happening to her and her baby. It was as though she were being forced to watch the infant waste away, left alone in the box — not for the length of its life, perhaps, but for the length of its self, until the self flew out and was forever gone.

In the nightmare it was always the mother monkey he faced, not the infants. The mother, with her wild, desperate eyes. He felt what he could think of only as her passion, like a heat emanating. The mother was crazy with love, mad with a singular devotion. All she wanted was the safety of her infant. She would chew off her feet for it. She would do anything.

But she was trapped, simply trapped. He had put her in a cage, and the cage was too strong for her. When he took the baby from her arms, her panic rose so high it could rise no higher; if she knew how to beg she would beg till the end of the world, scream until her throat split. *Give me my baby back.*

He knew the feeling of loss that would last till she died. He knew it the way 60 he knew a distant country. They had their own customs there.

### FOR ANALYSIS

**1.** What is the nature of the **paradox** concerning the topic of Harry Harlow's research and his feeling about his test subjects?

**2.** Why are the details about Harlow's personal past life important: his drinking, his name change, his relationship with his children? Why do you think Millet includes them?

**3.** What do Harlow's experiments prove?

**4.** What is the significance of Harlow's dream?

## MAKING ARGUMENTS

**1.** What is the deep connection between Harlow's personal life and his experiments? Make an argument to answer this question, using your observations about the text as support.

**2.** Animal experimentation has led to many scientific breakthroughs. At the same time, many see it as cruel and unnecessary. Do some research on the topic and construct an argument against or in defense of the practice.

## WRITING TOPICS

**1.** "Love in Infant Monkeys" is not **didactic** fiction — that is, it does not attempt to teach us the right way to think about something. Can you detect a position nonetheless? What is it? How does the story convey it without being direct?

**2.** Millet makes excellent use of free indirect discourse, or the representation of a **character's** thoughts not between quotation marks or after "He thought that" but in the **narrator's** statements, which slide in and out of observations and verbal formulations that originate with the character. List a few places where she does this, and reflect on the effects of her use of the device. How does it work? What does it do to and for readers?

## MAKING CONNECTIONS

Read this story alongside the "Making Change" case study in the "Conformity and Rebellion" chapter (p. 403). Is there anything in that cluster about effecting social change that connects to "Love in Infant Monkeys"?

# POETRY

### SAPPHO  (CA. 610–CA. 580 BCE)

## WITH HIS VENOM[1]

With his venom

Irresistible
and bittersweet

that loosener
of limbs, Love

reptile-like
strikes me down

### WILLIAM SHAKESPEARE  (1564–1616)

## SONNETS  1609

### 18

Shall I compare thee to a summer's day?
Thou art more lovely and more temperate:
Rough winds do shake the darling buds of May,
And summer's lease hath all too short a date:
Sometime too hot the eye of heaven shines,
And often is his gold complexion dimmed;
And every fair from fair sometimes declines,
By chance or nature's changing course untrimmed;
But thy eternal summer shall not fade,

---

*With His Venom*
  [1] Translated by Mary Barnard.

Nor lose possession of that fair thou ow'st,°  owns  10
Nor shall death brag thou wander'st in his shade,
When in eternal lines to time thou grow'st:
    So long as men can breathe, or eyes can see,
    So long lives this, and this gives life to thee.

## FOR ANALYSIS

**1.** Why does the speaker in the poem argue that "a summer's day" is an inappropriate **metaphor** for his beloved?

**2.** What is "this" in line 14?

## MAKING ARGUMENTS

Line 10's "ow'st" has been read as either "ownest" or "owest" and so as meaning either "owns" or "owes." Argue for one or the other reading. Why do you think one works better than the other? What do you take each to mean?

### 29

When, in disgrace with fortune and men's eyes,
I all alone beweep my outcast state
And trouble deaf heaven with my bootless cries
And look upon myself and curse my fate,
Wishing me like to one more rich in hope,
Featured like him, like him with friends possessed,
Desiring this man's art and that man's scope,
With what I most enjoy contented least;
Yet in these thoughts myself almost despising,
Haply I think on thee, and then my state,  10
Like to the lark at break of day arising
From sullen earth, sings hymns at heaven's gate;
    For thy sweet love remembered such wealth brings
    That then I scorn to change my state with kings.

### 64

When I have seen by Time's fell hand defac'd
The rich-proud cost of outworn buried age;
When sometime lofty towers I see down-raz'd,
And brass eternal slave to mortal rage;
When I have seen the hungry ocean gain
Advantage on the kingdom of the shore,
And the firm soil win of the watery main,
Increasing store with loss, and loss with store;
When I have seen such interchange of state,

Or state itself confounded to decay;                                     10
Ruin hath taught me thus to ruminate —
That Time will come and take my love away.
    This thought is as a death, which cannot choose
    But weep to have that which it fears to lose.

### FOR ANALYSIS

**1.** Why does the **narrator** "weep" in the final line? Does he or she mourn the actual death of a loved one? If not death, then what causes the weeping?

**2.** This poem could have been included in this book's final chapter, "Life and Death." Why do you think it was included in this chapter? Is it simply a poem about death? If not, what does it have to say about love beyond the fear of a loved one's death?

### MAKING ARGUMENTS

This poem is usually read as a recognition of the inevitability of death and the pain it causes. Make the argument that the ruminations at the end of the poem offer something positive from this recognition. Is there some alternative offered to the weeping of line 14?

## 116

Let me not to the marriage of true minds
Admit impediments. Love is not love
Which alters when it alteration finds,
Or bends with the remover to remove:
Oh, no! it is an ever-fixèd mark,
That looks on tempests and is never shaken;
It is the star to every wandering bark,
Whose worth's unknown, although his height be taken.
Love's not Time's fool, though rosy lips and cheeks
Within his bending sickle's compass come;                               10
Love alters not with his brief hours and weeks,
But bears it out even to the edge of doom.
    If this be error and upon me proved,
    I never writ, nor no man ever loved.

## 130

My mistress' eyes are nothing like the sun;
Coral is far more red than her lips' red;
If snow be white, why then her breasts are dun;
If hairs be wires, black wires grow on her head.
I have seen roses damasked,° red and white,                    variegated
But no such roses see I in her cheeks;

And in some perfumes is there more delight
Than in the breath that from my mistress reeks.
I love to hear her speak, yet well I know
That music hath a far more pleasing sound;                               10
I grant I never saw a goddess go;
My mistress, when she walks, treads on the ground.
    And yet, by heaven, I think my love as rare
    As any she belied with false compare.[1]

## For Analysis

**1.** It seems at first like the speaker might be insulting his "mistress." Is he? What evidence supports your answer?

**2.** Annotate the poem so that the **sonnet's rhyme** scheme is clear. Where does the scheme change — that is, where does the pattern of alternating pairs of lines whose last words rhyme (for example, in lines 1–4 "sun," "red," "dun," "head," or ABAB) shift to a different pattern? How does the poem take advantage of this shift to make meaning?

**3.** How do the last two lines echo the first line?

## Making Arguments

Make an argument connecting the attitude Shakespeare **satirizes** in Sonnet 130 to a present-day phenomenon. Do attitudes exist today like those Shakespeare observed in his time?

## Writing Topic

This poem plays off the tradition of **Petrarchan** love poetry, whose conventions include the worshipful idealization of the woman who is the subject of the poem. How does Shakespeare's poem **satirize** this kind of love poetry?

## JOHN DONNE    (1572–1631)

# THE FLEA    1633

Mark but this flea, and mark in this,
How little that which thou deniest me is;
It sucked me first, and now sucks thee,
And in this flea our two bloods mingled be;
Thou know'st that this cannot be said
A sin, nor shame, nor loss of maidenhead,
    Yet this enjoys before it woo,
    And pampered swells with one blood made of two,
    And this, alas, is more than we would do.

---

[1] I.e., as any woman misrepresented with false comparisons.

Oh stay, three lives in one flea spare,                                    10
Where we almost, yea more than married, are.
This flea is you and I, and this
Our marriage bed and marriage temple is;
Though parents grudge, and you, we are met,
And cloistered in these living walls of jet,
  Though use° make you apt to kill me        custom
  Let not to that, self-murder added be,
  And sacrilege, three sins in killing three.

Cruel and sudden, hast thou since
Purpled thy nail, in blood of innocence?                                   20
Wherein could this flea guilty be,
Except in that drop which it sucked from thee?
Yet thou triumph'st, and say'st that thou
Find'st not thy self nor me the weaker now;
  'Tis true, then learn how false fears be;
  Just so much honor, when thou yield'st to me,
  Will waste, as this flea's death took life from thee.

## FOR ANALYSIS

**1.** What does the woman addressed in this poem deny the poet (l. 2)?

**2.** What is the woman about to do at the beginning of the second **stanza**? What argument does the poet use to save the flea?

**3.** How does the poet turn the flea's life and death to his own purposes?

## MAKING ARGUMENTS

While in the poem itself the speaker uses the flea to try to persuade someone to sleep with him, Donne himself is not using the poem in the same way. Make an argument for what you think he *is* doing, using the poem itself and research on Donne's work as support.

## WRITING TOPIC

In a paragraph, discuss your response to Donne's use of a flea to animate a seduction poem.

# A VALEDICTION: FORBIDDING MOURNING   1633

As virtuous men pass mildly away,
 And whisper to their souls to go,
Whilst some of their sad friends do say
 The breath goes now, and some say, No;

So let us melt, and make no noise,
   No tear-floods, nor sigh-tempests move,
'Twere profanation of our joys
   To tell the laity our love.

Moving of th' earth° brings harms and fears,                earthquake
   Men reckon what it did and meant;                        10
But trepidation of the spheres,
   Though greater far, is innocent.[1]

Dull sublunary° lovers' love                        under the moon
   (Whose soul is sense) cannot admit
Absence, because it doth remove
   Those things which elemented it.

But we by a love so much refined
   That our selves know not what it is,
Inter-assuréd of the mind,
   Care less, eyes, lips, and hands to miss.                20

Our two souls therefore, which are one,
   Though I must go, endure not yet
A breach, but an expansion,
   Like gold to airy thinness beat.

If they be two, they are two so
   As stiff twin compasses are two;
Thy soul, the fixed foot, makes no show
   To move, but doth, if th' other do.

And though it in the center sit,
   Yet when the other far doth roam,                    30
It leans and harkens after it,
   And grows erect, as that comes home.

Such wilt thou be to me, who must
   Like th' other foot, obliquely run;
Thy firmness makes my circle just,
   And makes me end where I begun.

---

[1] The movement of the heavenly spheres is harmless.

## FOR ANALYSIS

**1.** Two kinds of love are described in this poem: spiritual and physical. How does the **simile** drawn in the first two **stanzas** help define the differences between them?

**2.** How does the contrast between earthquakes and the movement of the spheres in stanza 3 further develop the contrast between the two types of love?

**3.** Explain the comparison between a drawing compass and the lovers in the last three stanzas.

## MAKING ARGUMENTS

Do some research on **metaphor** so that you understand the difference between two ways of seeing metaphor — as a poetic device or as a fundamental tool of cognition, a way in which we use language to understand the world. Using this research and Donne's poem, make an argument about these ways of thinking about metaphor. Is one more important? Is one more fundamental? Are they not as different as they seem?

## BEN JONSON   (1572–1637)

# SONG, TO CELIA[1]   1616

Drink to me only with thine eyes,
    And I will pledge with mine;
Or leave a kiss but in the cup,
    And I'll not look for wine.
The thirst that from the soul doth rise
    Doth ask a drink divine;
But might I of Jove's nectar sup,
    I would not change for thine.
I sent thee late a rosy wreath,
    Not so much honoring thee        10
As giving it a hope, that there
    It could not withered be.
But thou thereon didst only breathe,
    And sent'st it back to me;
Since when it grows, and smells, I swear,
    Not of itself but thee.

*Song, To Celia*
[1] A widely recorded song.

## ROBERT HERRICK (1591–1674)

# TO THE VIRGINS, TO MAKE MUCH OF TIME 1648

Gather ye rosebuds while ye may,
   Old Time is still a-flying;
And this same flower that smiles today,
   Tomorrow will be dying.

The glorious lamp of heaven, the sun,
   The higher he's a-getting,
The sooner will his race be run,
   And nearer he's to setting.

That age is best which is the first,
   When youth and blood are warmer;                               10
But being spent, the worse, and worst
   Times still succeed the former.

Then be not coy, but use your time;
   And while ye may, go marry:
For having lost but once your prime,
   You may for ever tarry.

## ANNE BRADSTREET (CA. 1612–1672)

# TO MY DEAR AND LOVING HUSBAND 1678

If ever two were one, then surely we.
If ever man were loved by wife, then thee;
If ever wife was happy in a man,
Compare with me ye women if you can.
I prize thy love more than whole mines of gold
Or all the riches that the East doth hold.
My love is such that rivers cannot quench,
Nor ought but love from thee give recompense.
Thy love is such I can no way repay;
The heavens reward thee manifold, I pray.                              10
Then while we live, in love let's so persever,
That when we live no more we may live ever.

## ANDREW MARVELL  (1621–1678)

# TO HIS COY MISTRESS   1681

Had we but world enough, and time,
This coyness, lady, were no crime.
We would sit down, and think which way
To walk, and pass our long love's day.
Thou by the Indian Ganges' side
Shouldst rubies find; I by the tide
Of Humber would complain. I would
Love you ten years before the flood,
And you should, if you please, refuse
Til the conversion of the Jews.                                    10
My vegetable love should grow
Vaster than empires and more slow;
An hundred years should go to praise
Thine eyes, and on thy forehead gaze;
Two hundred to adore each breast,
But thirty thousand to the rest;
An age at least to every part,
And the last age should show your heart.
For, lady, you deserve this state,
Nor would I love at lower rate.                                    20
    But at my back I always hear
Time's wingéd chariot hurrying near;
And yonder all before us lie
Deserts of vast eternity.
Thy beauty shall no more be found,
Nor, in thy marble vault, shall sound
My echoing song; then worms shall try
That long-preserved virginity,
And your quaint honor turn to dust,
And into ashes all my lust:                                        30
The grave's a fine and private place,
But none, I think, do there embrace.
    Now therefore, while the youthful hue
Sits on thy skin like morning dew,
And while thy willing soul transpires
At every pore with instant fires,
Now let us sport us while we may,
And now, like amorous birds of prey,
Rather at once our time devour
Than languish in his slow-chapped° power.          slow-jawed   40
Let us roll our strength and all

Our sweetness up into one ball,
And tear our pleasures with rough strife
Thorough° the iron gates of life:                                    through
Thus, though we cannot make our sun
Stand still, yet we will make him run.

## FOR ANALYSIS

**1.** State the argument of the poem (see ll. 1–2, 21–22, 33–34).

**2.** Compare the figures of speech in lines 1–20 with those in lines 33–46. How do they differ?

**3.** Describe the attitude toward life recommended by the poet.

## MAKING ARGUMENTS

Analyze "To His Coy Mistress" as an argument. How does the speaker press his case? How does he support his claim?

## WILLIAM BLAKE  (1757–1827)

# A POISON TREE  1794

I was angry with my friend:
I told my wrath, my wrath did end.
I was angry with my foe:
I told it not, my wrath did grow.

And I watered it in fears,
Night & morning with my tears;
And I sunnéd it with smiles,
And with soft deceitful wiles.

And it grew both day and night,
Till it bore an apple bright.                                           10
And my foe beheld its shine,
And he knew that it was mine,

And into my garden stole,
When the night had veil'd the pole;
In the morning glad I see
My foe outstretched beneath the tree.

### FOR ANALYSIS

**1.** Is anything gained from the parallel readers might draw between this tree and the tree in the Garden of Eden? Explain.

**2.** Explain what the "poison" is.

**3.** Does your own experience verify the first **stanza** of the poem?

### MAKING ARGUMENTS

Given the workings of identification, what is the reader's reaction to the event discovered in the poem's last line? What do you think it is supposed to be? What would it mean for us to be happy about it, or unhappy? Make an argument for how the poem wants us to react at the poem's end, using evidence from the text and any sense you have from reading other poems by Blake of what he might have wanted.

**ROBERT BURNS**   (1759–1796)

# A RED, RED ROSE    1796

O My Luve's like a red, red rose,
    That's newly sprung in June;
O My Luve's like a melodie
    That's sweetly played in tune.

As fair art thou, my bonnie lass,
    So deep in luve am I;
And I will luve thee still, my dear,
    Til a' the seas gang dry.

Till a' the seas gang dry, my dear,
    And the rocks melt wi' the sun:       10
O I will love thee still, my dear,
    While the sands o' life shall run.

And fare thee weel, my only luve,
    And fare thee weel awhile!
And I will come again, my luve,
    Though it were ten thousand mile.

## MATTHEW ARNOLD   (1822–1888)

# DOVER BEACH   1867

The sea is calm tonight.
The tide is full, the moon lies fair
Upon the straits; on the French coast the light
Gleams and is gone; the cliffs of England stand,
Glimmering and vast, out in the tranquil bay.
Come to the window, sweet is the night-air!
Only, from the long line of spray
Where the sea meets the moon-blanched land,
Listen! you hear the grating roar
Of pebbles which the waves draw back, and fling,                    10
At their return, up the high strand,
Begin, and cease, and then again begin,
With tremulous cadence slow, and bring
The eternal note of sadness in.

Sophocles long ago
Heard it on the Aegean, and it brought
Into his mind the turbid ebb and flow
Of human misery; we
Find also in the sound a thought,
Hearing it by this distant northern sea.                           20

The Sea of Faith
Was once, too, at the full, and round earth's shore
Lay like the folds of a bright girdle furled.
But now I only hear
Its melancholy, long, withdrawing roar,
Retreating, to the breath
Of the night-wind, down the vast edges drear
And naked shingles° of the world.                          pebble beaches

Ah, love, let us be true
To one another! for the world, which seems                         30
To lie before us like a land of dreams,
So various, so beautiful, so new,
Hath really neither joy, nor love, nor light,
Nor certitude, nor peace, nor help for pain;
And we are here as on a darkling plain
Swept with confused alarms of struggle and flight,
Where ignorant armies clash by night.

## ROBERT FROST  (1874–1963)

# FIRE AND ICE  1923

Some say the world will end in fire,
Some say in ice,
From what I've tasted of desire
I hold with those who favor fire.
But if it had to perish twice,
I think I know enough of hate
To say that for destruction ice
Is also great
And would suffice.

## DOROTHY PARKER  (1893–1967)

# ONE PERFECT ROSE  1926

A single flow'r he sent me, since we met.
    All tenderly his messenger he chose;
Deep-hearted, pure, with scented dew still wet —
    One perfect rose.

I knew the language of the floweret;
    "My fragile leaves," it said, "his heart enclose."
Love long has taken for his amulet
    One perfect rose.

Why is it no one ever sent me yet
    One perfect limousine, do you suppose?                    10
Ah no, it's always just my luck to get
    One perfect rose.

## THEODORE ROETHKE  (1908–1963)

# I KNEW A WOMAN  1958

I knew a woman, lovely in her bones,
When small birds sighed, she would sigh back at them;
Ah, when she moved, she moved more ways than one:

The shapes a bright container can contain!
Of her choice virtues only gods should speak,
Or English poets who grew up on Greek
(I'd have them sing in chorus, cheek to cheek).

How well her wishes went! She stroked my chin,
She taught me Turn, and Counter-turn, and Stand;
She taught me Touch, that undulant white skin;                    10
I nibbled meekly from her proffered hand;
She was the sickle; I, poor I, the rake,
Coming behind her for her pretty sake
(But what prodigious mowing we did make).

Love likes a gander, and adores a goose:
Her full lips pursed, the errant note to seize;
She played it quick, she played it light and loose;
My eyes, they dazzled at her flowing knees;
Her several parts could keep a pure repose,
Or one hip quiver with a mobile nose                             20
(She moved in circles, and those circles moved).

Let seed be grass, and grass turn into hay:
I'm martyr to a motion not my own;
What's freedom for? To know eternity.
I swear she cast a shadow white as stone.
But who would count eternity in days?
These old bones live to learn her wanton ways:
(I measure time by how a body sways).

## FOR ANALYSIS

1. What is the **rhyme** scheme of this poem?
2. What does line 3 mean?
3. Describe the two principal **images** in the second **stanza**.

## MAKING ARGUMENTS

Roethke was known in his earlier poems for painstaking attention to the self; with his love poems, he turns to others, the love-objects of the poem. Make an argument about this turn: are these poems still about the self also? When we think about love, talk about it, write about, are *in* it, how much is the self still important? Use as evidence the poem and anything else that might support your notions about love.

## WRITING TOPIC

In an essay, describe the role of motion in this celebration of a woman's beauty.

## ELIZABETH BISHOP   (1911–1979)

## ONE ART   1976

The art of losing isn't hard to master;
so many things seem filled with the intent
to be lost that their loss is no disaster.

Lose something every day. Accept the fluster
of lost door keys, the hour badly spent.
The art of losing isn't hard to master.

Then practice losing farther, losing faster:
places, and names, and where it was you meant
to travel. None of these will bring disaster.

I lost my mother's watch. And look! my last, or          10
next-to-last, of three loved houses went.
The art of losing isn't hard to master.

I lost two cities, lovely ones. And, vaster,
some realms I owned, two rivers, a continent.
I miss them, but it wasn't a disaster.

— Even losing you (the joking voice, a gesture
I love) I shan't have lied. It's evident
the art of losing's not too hard to master
though it may look like (*Write* it!) like disaster.


## LISEL MUELLER   (B. 1924)

## HAPPY AND UNHAPPY FAMILIES I   1996

If all happy families are alike,[1]
then so are the unhappy families,
whose lives we celebrate
because they are motion and heat,
because they are what we think of as *life*.
Someone is lying and someone else
is being lied to. Someone is beaten
and someone else is doing the beating.

*Happy and Unhappy Families I*
  [1] An allusion to the celebrated opening line of Leo Tolstoy's novel *Anna Karenina* (1873–1876).

Someone is praying, or weeps
because she does not know how to pray.                    10
Someone drinks all night;
someone cowers in corners;
someone threatens and someone pleads.
Bitter words at the table,
bitter sobs in the bedroom;
reprisal breathed on the bathroom mirror.
The house crackles with secrets;
everyone draws up a plan of escape.
Somebody shatters without a sound.
Sometimes one of them leaves the house             20
on a stretcher, in terrible silence.
How much energy suffering takes!
It is like a fire that burns and burns
but cannot burn down to extinction.
Unhappy families are never idle;
they are where the action is,
unlike the others, the happy ones,
who never raise their voices
and spit no blood, who do nothing
to deserve their happiness.                         30

## For Analysis

**1.** How does the speaker describe unhappy families? What do you think are the characteristics of happy families?

**2.** Describe the **images** used to identify the sources of unhappiness.

**3.** Describe the conditions that generate happy families (ll. 27–30). Do you agree with the speaker? Explain.

## Making Arguments

In line 22, the speaker laments, "How much energy suffering takes!" Do you agree? How much energy does happiness take? Make an argument about the relative energy required to suffer versus to be happy based both on the words of the poem and other works of literature you have read.

## Writing Topic

Argue for or against the proposition that all happy (or unhappy) families are alike. On what assumptions do you base your argument?

## CAROLYN KIZER (1925–2014)

# BITCH 1984

Now, when he and I meet, after all these years,
I say to the bitch inside me, don't start growling.
He isn't a trespasser anymore,
Just an old acquaintance tipping his hat.
My voice says, "Nice to see you,"
As the bitch starts to bark hysterically.
He isn't an enemy now,
Where are your manners, I say, as I say,
"How are the children? They must be growing up."
At a kind word from him, a look like the old days,                    10
The bitch changes her tone: she begins to whimper.
She wants to snuggle up to him, to cringe.
Down, girl! Keep your distance
Or I'll give you a taste of the choke-chain.
"Fine, I'm just fine," I tell him.
She slobbers and grovels.
After all, I am her mistress. She is basically loyal.
It's just that she remembers how she came running
Each evening, when she heard his step;
How she lay at his feet and looked up adoringly                       20
Though he was absorbed in his paper;
Or, bored with her devotion, ordered her to the kitchen
Until he was ready to play.
But the small careless kindnesses
When he'd had a good day, or a couple of drinks,
Come back to her now, seem more important
Than the casual cruelties, the ultimate dismissal.
"It's nice to know you are doing so well," I say.
He couldn't have taken you with him;
You were too demonstrative, too clumsy,                               30
Not like the well-groomed pets of his new friends.
"Give my regards to your wife," I say. You gag
As I drag you off by the scruff,
Saying, "Goodbye! Goodbye! Nice to have seen you again."

### FOR ANALYSIS

**1.** Who is being addressed in lines 13 and 14?

**2.** In what ways does the title suit the poem? In answering this question, consider the **tone** of "Bitch," as well as the many **connotations** of the word.

**3.** What is "the ultimate dismissal" referred to in line 27?

**4.** How would you describe the speaker's present feelings about her former relationship?

# Afternoon Happiness   2002

**for John**

At a party I spy a handsome psychiatrist,
And wish, as we all do, to get her advice for free.
Doctor, I'll say, I'm supposed to be a poet.
All life's awfulness has been grist to me.
We learn that happiness is a Chinese meal,
While sorrow is a nourishment forever.
My new environment is California Dreamer.
I'm fearful I'm forgetting how to brood.
And, Doctor, another thing has got me worried:
I'm not drinking as much as I should . . .                                10

At home, I want to write a happy poem
On love, or a love poem of happiness.
But they won't do, the tensions of every day,
The rub, the minor abrasions of any two
Who share one space. All, there's no substitute for tragedy!
But in this chapter, tragedy belongs
To that other life, the old life before *us*.
Here is my aphorism of the day:
Happy people are monogamous.
Even in California. So how does the poem play                              20

Without the paraphernalia of betrayal and loss?
I don't have a jealous eye or fear
And neither do you. In truth, I'm fond
Of your ex-mate, whom I name "my wife-in-law."
My former husband, that old disaster, is now just funny,
So laugh we do, in what Cyril Connolly
Has called the endless, nocturnal conversation
Of marriage. Which may be the best part.
Darling, must I love you in light verse
Without the tribute of profoundest art?                                    30

Of course it won't last. You will break my heart
Or I yours, by dying. I could weep over that.
But now it seems forced, here in these heaven hills,
The mourning doves mourning, the squirrels mating,
My old cat warm in my lap, here on our terrace
As from below comes a musical cursing
As you mend my favorite plate. Later of course

I could pick a fight; there is always material in that.
But we don't come from fighting people, those
Who scream out red-hot iambs in their hate.                    40

No, love, the heavy poem will have to come
From *temps perdu*, fertile with pain, or perhaps
Detonated by terrors far beyond this place
Where the world rends itself, and its tainted waters
Rise in the east to erode our safety here.
Much as I want to gather a lifetime thrift
And craft, my cunning skills tied in a knot for you,
There is only this useless happiness as gift.

### FOR ANALYSIS

**1.** Explain the comparison in lines 5 and 6.

**2.** Why does the speaker seem to think that happiness is a problem for poets?

**3.** How is this poem about more than poets? What other concerns surface?

### MAKING ARGUMENTS

Would you say this is a happy poem? A sad poem? Something in between? Make an argument for whichever of these options you believe is the case.

### GALWAY KINNELL    (1927–2014)

## AFTER MAKING LOVE WE HEAR FOOTSTEPS    1980

For I can snore like a bullhorn
or play loud music
or sit up talking with any reasonably sober Irishman
and Fergus will only sink deeper
into his dreamless sleep, which goes by all in one flash,
but let there be that heavy breathing
or a stifled come-cry anywhere in the house
and he will wrench himself awake
and make for it on the run — as now, we lie together,
after making love, quiet, touching along the length of our bodies,    10
familiar touch of the long-married,
and he appears — in his baseball pajamas, it happens,
the neck opening so small
he has to screw them on, which one day may make him wonder
about the mental capacity of baseball players —

and says, "Are you loving and snuggling? May I join?"
He flops down between us and hugs us and snuggles himself to sleep,
his face gleaming with satisfaction at being this very child.

In the half darkness we look at each other
and smile
and touch arms across his little, startlingly muscled body —                    20
this one whom habit of memory propels to the ground of his making,
sleeper only the mortal sounds can sing awake,
this blessing love gives again into our arms.

## FOR ANALYSIS

**1.** What two things appear in this poem that rarely appear together in poems? What
is it like to read about them together? Why?

**2.** What expectation is set up by the event related in lines 6–9? Is it met? Does the
speaker have the reaction to this event that we expect?

**3.** What function might lines 12–15 serve? How do they stand apart from the rest of
the poem, and how do they fit in?

## MAKING ARGUMENTS

There is an important thread running through much of Western culture concerning
how we think about our bodies and sex — that the mind or soul is separate from the
body, that sex is for procreation only, that we should be ashamed of our bodies and of
sex. (See Blake for an alternate thread.) Make the argument that Kinnell's poem can be
read as arguing against this set of ideas. How does it do it? Directly? Indirectly?

## WRITING TOPICS

**1.** Do you believe the explanation in line 22? Do you have to for the poem to work?

**2.** Though it is not explicitly expressed, what might the speaker be said to be discovering in this poem?

## ADRIENNE RICH   (1929–2012)

# LIVING IN SIN   1955

She had thought the studio would keep itself;
no dust upon the furniture of love.
Half heresy, to wish the taps less vocal,
the panes relieved of grime. A plate of pears,
a piano with a Persian shawl, a cat
stalking the picturesque amusing mouse
had risen at his urging.
Not that at five each separate stair would writhe

under the milkman's tramp; that morning light
so coldly would delineate the scraps                                    10
of last night's cheese and three sepulchral bottles;
that on the kitchen shelf among the saucers
a pair of beetle-eyes would fix her own —
Envoy from some village in the moldings . . .
Meanwhile, he, with a yawn,
sounded a dozen notes upon the keyboard,
declared it out of tune, shrugged at the mirror,
rubbed at his beard, went out for cigarettes;
while she, jeered by the minor demons,
pulled back the sheets and made the bed and found          20
a towel to dust the table-top,
and let the coffee-pot boil over on the stove.
By evening she was back in love again,
though not so wholly but throughout the night
she woke sometimes to feel the daylight coming
like a relentless milkman up the stairs.

## SYLVIA PLATH   (1932–1963)

# DADDY   1965

You do not do, you do not do
Any more, black shoe
In which I have lived like a foot
For thirty years, poor and white,
Barely daring to breathe or Achoo.

Daddy, I have had to kill you,
You died before I had time —
Marble-heavy, a bag full of God,
Ghastly statue with one gray toe
Big as a Frisco seal                                                          10

And a head in the freakish Atlantic
Where it pours bean green over blue
In the waters off beautiful Nauset.
I used to pray to recover you.
Ach, du.[1]

*Daddy*
  [1] German for "Oh, you."

In the German tongue, in the Polish town
Scraped flat by the roller
Of wars, wars, wars.
But the name of the town is common.
My Polack friend                                                    20

Says there are a dozen or two.
So I never could tell where you
Put your foot, your root,
I never could talk to you.
The tongue stuck in my jaw.

It stuck in a barb wire snare.
Ich, ich, ich, ich,[2]
I could hardly speak.
I thought every German was you.
And the language obscene                                          30

An engine, an engine
Chuffing me off like a Jew.
A Jew to Dachau, Auschwitz, Belsen.
I began to talk like a Jew.
I think I may well be a Jew.

The snows of the Tyrol, the clear beer of Vienna
Are not very pure or true.
With my gypsy ancestress and my weird luck
And my Taroc pack and my Taroc pack
I may be a bit of a Jew.                                          40

I have always been scared of *you*,
With your Luftwaffe,[3] your gobbledygoo.
And your neat mustache
And your Aryan eye, bright blue.
Panzer-man,[4] panzer-man, O You —

Not God but a swastika
So black no sky could squeak through.
Every woman adores a Fascist,
The boot in the face, the brute
Brute heart of a brute like you.                                 50

[2] German for "I, I, I, I."
[3] Name of the German air force during World War II.
[4] *Panzer* refers to German armored divisions during World War II.

You stand at the blackboard, daddy,
In the picture I have of you,
A cleft in your chin instead of your foot
But no less a devil for that, no not
Any less the black man who

Bit my pretty red heart in two.
I was ten when they buried you.
At twenty I tried to die
And get back, back, back to you.
I thought even the bones would do              60

But they pulled me out of the sack,
And they stuck me together with glue.
And then I knew what to do.
I made a model of you,
A man in black with a Meinkampf⁵ look

And a love of the rack and the screw.
And I said I do, I do.
So daddy, I'm finally through.
The black telephone's off at the root,
The voices just can't worm through.              70

If I've killed one man, I've killed two —
The vampire who said he was you
And drank my blood for a year,
Seven years, if you want to know.
Daddy, you can lie back now.

There's a stake in your fat black heart
And the villagers never liked you.
They are dancing and stamping on you.
They always *knew* it was you.
Daddy, daddy, you bastard, I'm through.              80

## FOR ANALYSIS

**1.** How do the **allusions** to Nazism function in the poem?

**2.** Does the poem exhibit the speaker's love for her father or her hatred of him? Explain.

**3.** What type of man does the speaker marry (see ll. 61–70)?

---

⁵ *My Struggle*, the title of Adolf Hitler's autobiography.

**4.** How does the speaker **characterize** her husband and her father in the last two **stanzas**? Might the "Daddy" of the last line of the poem refer to something more than the speaker's father? Explain.

## MAKING ARGUMENTS

One could imagine someone taking offense at lines 31–35, in which the speaker **alludes** to Nazi camps and identifies with the Jewish people. Argue for or against this position. Why is it offensive? Alternatively, why is it not? Use as support for your argument the evidence of the poem and your knowledge (research can help) of the history of World War II and the Jews of Europe.

## WRITING TOPICS

**1.** What is the effect of the peculiar structure, idiosyncratic **rhyme**, unusual words (such as *achoo, gobbledygoo*), and repetitions in the poem?

**2.** What emotional associations does the title "Daddy" possess? Are those associations reinforced or contradicted by the poem?

## LUCILLE CLIFTON (B. 1936–2010)

# THERE IS A GIRL INSIDE    1977

there is a girl inside.
she is randy as a wolf.
she will not walk away
and leave these bones
to an old woman.

she is a green tree
in a forest of kindling.
she is a green girl
in a used poet.

she has waited                                        10
patient as a nun
for the second coming,
when she can break through gray hairs
into blossom

and her lovers will harvest
honey and thyme
and the woods will be wild
with the damn wonder of it.

## FOR ANALYSIS

**1.** Who is the "girl" of this poem? What is she "inside" of?

**2.** What are the "bones" of the first **stanza**? What does the speaker's statement that she will not defer to an old woman tell us about her?

**3.** Describe the prevailing **metaphor** of the poem.

## MAKING ARGUMENTS

The connection of the ideas of vitality and sexuality runs deep — just think about the fertility rituals and **symbols** that have accompanied spring festivals for centuries. Make an argument about the importance of that connection to "There Is a Girl Inside," using as support the poem and anything relevant you find about the way people think about youth and liveliness and sex.

## WRITING TOPIC

In an essay, discuss the appropriateness of the **images** Clifton uses to make her point.

---

## SEAMUS HEANEY (B. 1939-2013)

# VALEDICTION    1966

Lady with the frilled blouse
And simple tartan skirt,
Since you have left the house
Its emptiness has hurt
All thought. In your presence
Time rode easy, anchored
On a smile; but absence
Rocked love's balance, unmoored
The days. They buck and bound
Across the calendar                                         10
Pitched from the quiet sound
Of your flower-tender
Voice. Need breaks on my strand;
You've gone, I am at sea.
Until you resume command
Self is in mutiny.

## FOR ANALYSIS

**1.** What is the central figure of speech (beginning in the middle of line 5) that animates this poem?

**2.** How are *time*, *love's balance*, and *the days* affected by the "lady's" behavior?

**3.** What sort of voice would a "flower-tender / Voice" (ll. 12–13) be?

## MAKING ARGUMENTS

"All you need is love," John Lennon sang, but is it enough? In "Valediction," the speaker seems to say good-bye not only to his lover but also to himself. Make an argument about love and the need to maintain one's own identity. Is it okay to be at sea when left alone, or is it evidence of having lost oneself? Use the poem, other literature or songs, and/or your own experience to support your argument.

## WRITING TOPIC

Write an essay or a poem, serious or humorous, in which you use an extended **metaphor** to describe a fundamental emotion or experience — for example, how falling in love is like racing a car, or how the anguish of separation is like a visit to a dentist, or how attending classes is like a long hike through a desert.

## WYATT PRUNTY  (B. 1947)

# LEARNING THE BICYCLE  2000

## FOR HEATHER

The older children pedal past
Stable as little gyros, spinning hard
To supper, bath, and bed, until at last
We also quit, silent and tired
Beside the darkening yard where trees
Now shadow up instead of down.
Their predictable lengths can only tease
Her as, head lowered, she walks her bike alone
Somewhere between her wanting to ride
And her certainty she will always fall.                    10

Tomorrow, though I will run behind,
Arms out to catch her, she'll tilt then balance wide
Of my reach, till distance makes her small,
Smaller, beyond the place I stop and know
That to teach her I had to follow
And when she learned to let her go.

## FOR ANALYSIS

**1.** Describe the form and **rhyme** scheme of this poem. How does it differ from a **sonnet**?

**2.** What does the speaker learn from the experience of teaching his daughter to ride a bicycle?

**WRITING TOPIC**

Write an analysis of the poem's formal structure, noting how the poem shifts
somewhat at lines 5, 9, and 11. How does the poem's organization and **rhyme**
scheme mimic a typical **sonnet**?

## DAISY FRIED   (B. 1967)

# ECONO MOTEL, OCEAN CITY   2010

Korean monster movie on the SyFy channel,
lurid *Dora the Explorer* blanket draped tentlike
over Baby's portacrib to shield us from unearned
innocence. The monster slings its carapace
in reverse swan dive up the embankment, triple-jointed bug legs
clattering, bathroom door ajar, exhaust roaring,
both of us naked, monster chomps
fast food stands, all that quilted aluminum, eats through streams
of running people, the promiscuously cheerful guilty American
scientist dies horribly. Grease-dusted ceiling fan                          10
paddles erratically, two spars missing. Sheets whirled
to the polluted rug. I reach under the bed, fish out
somebody else's crunched beer can, my forearm comes out
dirty. Monster brachiates from bridge girders like a gibbon
looping round and around uneven bars, those are your fingers
in my tangles or my fingers, my head hangs
half off the king-size, monster takes tiny child actor
to its bone stash. Pillow's wet. The warped ceiling mirror
makes us look like fat porno dwarfs
in centripetal silver nitrate ripples. My glasses on the side table      20
tipped onto scratchproof lenses, earpieces sticking up
like arms out of disaster rubble. Your feet hooked over my feet. What miasma
lays gold dander down on forms of temporary
survivors wandering the promenade? You pull Dora
back over us — Baby's dead to the world — intrude
your propagandistic intimacy jokes,
unforgiving. "What, in a motel room?" I say.
Purple clouds roll back to reveal Armageddon
a dream in bad digital unreality. Explosions repeat patterns like
fake flames dance on fake fireplace logs. Sad Armageddon               30
of marriage: how pretty much nice
we meant to be, and couldn't make a difference.

No relationship is more primary to the human experience than that between parent and child. The relationship of mother or father to baby is one of complete responsibility and complete dependence, but this changes as both grow older and the emotional terrain becomes more tricky and harder to read. The poems in this unit express just a few of the very different kinds of emotions fathers and their children feel for each other, in the context of some of the many difficulties people encounter in life. As you read, take note of how the poems address the ways in which parents' and children's expectations of each other are or are not met and the ways in which feelings are or are not expressed.

## THEODORE ROETHKE (1908–1963)

# MY PAPA'S WALTZ 1948

The whiskey on your breath
Could make a small boy dizzy;
But I hung on like death:
Such waltzing was not easy.

We romped until the pans
Slid from the kitchen shelf;
My mother's countenance
Could not unfrown itself.

The hand that held my wrist
Was battered on one knuckle;                                    10
At every step you missed
My right ear scraped a buckle.

You beat time on my head
With a palm caked hard by dirt,
Then waltzed me off to bed
Still clinging to your shirt.

## FOR ANALYSIS

1. Why is **iambic trimeter** an appropriate **meter** for this poem?

2. What details reveal the kind of person the father is?

3. How would you describe the boy's feelings about his father? The father's about the boy?

## MAKING ARGUMENTS

Some read this poem as more funny than not, while some read the humor as dark and consider the darkness of the poem to be the overriding **tone**. Make an argument concerning this critical disagreement, paying close attention to individual words and phrases and larger effects of the lines, **stanzas**, and the poem as a whole.

## WRITING TOPIC

Describe this poem's tone. What in the way it describes the events, from the title to the **conceit**, expresses this tone?

## ROBERT HAYDEN   (1913–1980)

# THOSE WINTER SUNDAYS   1975

Sundays too my father got up early
and put his clothes on in the blueblack cold,
then with cracked hands that ached
from labor in the weekday weather made
banked fires blaze. No one ever thanked him.

I'd wake and hear the cold splintering, breaking.
When the rooms were warm, he'd call,
and slowly I would rise and dress,
fearing the chronic angers of that house,

Speaking indifferently to him,                                          10
who had driven out the cold
and polished my good shoes as well.
What did I know, what did I know
of love's austere and lonely offices?

## FOR ANALYSIS

**1.** Why Sundays "too" (l. 1)?

**2.** What does *offices* mean (l. 14) in this poem? Why do you think Hayden chooses this word?

**3.** From when in his life does the speaker describe those winter Sundays? How does his relation to the event color his description?

## MAKING ARGUMENTS

Arguably, the final **couplet** of "Winter Sundays" is (as is often case) the most power-ful moment in the poem. Make the unwinnable (because unprovable, not because demonstrably wrong) argument that the sentiment expressed there — of regret for what past ignorance led one to do or not do — is as powerful as any other you know of.

## WRITING TOPICS

**1.** In the last line of the second **stanza**, the speaker refers to "the chronic angers of that house." How does the anger the speaker fears relate to the "love" of the poem's last line?

**2.** Has there been a time in your life when you neglected to thank someone you should have or to appreciate something you should have? How does the recollection make you feel?

## LI-YOUNG LEE   (B. 1957)

# EATING ALONE   1986

I've pulled the last of the year's young onions.
The garden is bare now. The ground is cold,
brown and old. What is left of the day flames
in the maples at the corner of my
eye. I turn, a cardinal vanishes.
By the cellar door, I wash the onions,
then drink from the icy metal spigot.

Once, years back, I walked beside my father
among the windfall pears. I can't recall
our words. We may have strolled in silence. But          10
I still see him bend that way — left hand braced
on knee, creaky — to lift and hold to my
eye a rotten pear. In it, a hornet
spun crazily, glazed in slow, glistening juice.

It was my father I saw this morning
waving to me from the trees. I almost
called to him, until I came close enough
to see the shovel, leaning where I had
left it, in the flickering, deep green shade.

White rice steaming, almost done. Sweet green peas          20
fried in onions. Shrimp braised in sesame
oil and garlic. And my own loneliness.
What more could I, a young man, want.

## FOR ANALYSIS

**1.** Why is the speaker eating alone?

**2.** How do the repeated references to youth and age, things being finished or almost done, function in the poem?

**3.** Why do you think the poet might have chosen to include the **image** of the hornet?

## MAKING ARGUMENTS

The importance of food to this poem cannot be overstated. The same could be true of its importance to culture. Read up as much as time will allow on the cultural uses and meanings of food (that is, beyond keeping people alive) and, using the evidence of any of the works in this book, make an argument concerning the importance of food in literature specifically (as opposed to in culture, or the way we live, more broadly). If at a loss, consider the usefulness to your argument of the idea that literature is how we think about culture.

## WRITING TOPICS

**1.** Read the last **stanza** closely. What is the effect of the **imagery**? What kind of question is asked in the last line? What do you think Lee was trying to do at the end of his poem?

**2.** Why do you think the poet chooses to write about a son remembering his father through the preparation of a meal? What is the significance of eating?

## MAKING CONNECTIONS

**1.** Violence — actual or possible — is a presence in many of these poems. How do these poems express violence, explicitly and implicitly? Why is it such a presence?

**2.** In these poems, love is expressed in funny ways or goes unexpressed even when it is felt. What are some of the different ways in which these poems represent or hint at love?

**3.** In "Winter Sundays," Hayden alludes to the work parents do outside the home with the phrase "labor in the weekday weather" (1.4). What role does the work providers do outside the home play in these poems? What is its significance?

## CONNECTING POEMS: LOVE STINKS

None of the poems in this cluster professes a romantic view of romantic love — that is, none of these poems assumes the possibility of uncomplicated, cupids-and-angels kind of love in real life. As you read these poems in which love is shown to stink, observe the ways in which it does not. That love sometimes or even often brings pain and misery matters only because it sometimes does not.

## CATULLUS (CA. 84–CA. 54 BCE)

# 70

My woman says that she prefers to be married to no one
than to me, not even if Jupiter himself should seek her.
She says: but what a woman says to her passionate lover,
she ought to write on the wind and swift-flowing water.

### FOR ANALYSIS

1. What does it mean to write something on the wind or on water?

2. What significance does the reference to Jupiter carry?

### MAKING ARGUMENTS

Make an argument about this short poem: Is the **tone** humorous, dark, or both?

### WRITING TOPIC

When have you promised something you had no intention of doing? When have you
promised something you might have meant, sort of, but didn't stick to keeping the
promise? Reflect on that moment, on your motivations, and on how you feel about it
looking back.

## APHRA BEHN (1640–1689)

# LOVE IN FANTASTIQUE TRIUMPH SATT    1684

Love in Fantastique Triumph satt
Whilst Bleeding Hearts a round him flow'd,
For whom fresh paines he did Create,
And strange Tyranick power he show'd;
From thy Bright Eyes he took his fire,
Which round about, in sport he hurl'd;
But 'twas from mine he took desire,
Enough to undo the Amorous World.

From me he took his sighs and tears,
From thee his Pride and Crueltie;                           10
From me his Languishments and Feares,
And every Killing Dart from thee;
Thus thou and I, the God have arm'd,
And sett him up a Deity;
But my poor heart alone is harm'd,
Whilst thine the Victor is, and free.

### FOR ANALYSIS

**1.** Who is the speaker? To whom does she speak?

**2.** What is the background of this poem — that is, what is the relationship between the speaker and the immediate audience, and what has happened between them?

**3.** How has love triumphed in this poem?

### MAKING ARGUMENTS

As Michael Jackson says to Paul McCartney in the song "The Girl Is Mine," "I'm a lover, not a fighter." The opposition of love and war, love and violence, loving and fighting, is an old one. An alternate title under which this poem is often published is "Love Armed," which makes even more plain that Love, **personified** in this poem, *is* a fighter. Using any evidence you wish, from your own life to literature to what you may take as universal human truths, make an argument for the ways in which, to quote a song coincidentally also released in 1982 (one month later), "love is a battlefield."

### WRITING TOPIC

Imagine a response to this poem in which speaker and spoken-to are switched.

### EDNA ST. VINCENT MILLAY (1892–1950)

## I KNOW I AM BUT SUMMER TO YOUR HEART (SONNET XXVII)

I know I am but summer to your heart,
And not the full four seasons of the year;
And you must welcome from another part
Such noble moods as are not mine, my dear.
No gracious weight of golden fruits to sell
Have I, nor any wise and wintry thing;
And I have loved you all too long and well
To carry still the high sweet breast of Spring.
Wherefore I say: O love, as summer goes,
I must be gone, steal forth with silent drums,          10
That you may hail anew the bird and rose
When I come back to you, as summer comes.
Else will you seek, at some not distant time,
Even your summer in another clime.

### FOR ANALYSIS

**1.** What is the speaker *not*, to the person to whom he or she speaks? How are these things/qualities described?

**2.** What *is* the speaker to the person to whom he or she speaks? How are these things/qualities described?

**3.** Describe the **tone** of this poem. Is it angry? Wistful? Accepting? Ultimately, is it despairing or hopeful?

## MAKING ARGUMENTS

The first six lines of the poem contain a number of negative words, variations of *no* and *not*, and the entire poem is filled with negation — with what is not true, not the case, not possessed. Make an argument for why Millay might have chosen to write the poem in this way. What is the effect? How does it fit well with the poem's subject?

## WRITING TOPIC

Imagine a version of this poem in which Millay had done something differently. Maybe she argues that she should be everything to her lover, or that her lover should just leave her, or maybe she frames the poem not in negatives but in positives. Write the poem, if you want, or simply describe it.

## FAIZ AHMED FAIZ   (1911–1984)

# BE NEAR ME   1987

Be near me now,
My tormenter, my love, be near me —
At this hour when night comes down,
When, having drunk from the gash of sunset, darkness comes
With the balm of musk in its hands, its diamond lancets,
When it comes with cries of lamentation,
                  with laughter with songs;
Its blue-gray anklets of pain clinking with every step.
At this hour when hearts, deep in their hiding places,
Have begun to hope once more, when they start their vigil          10
For hands still enfolded in sleeves;
When wine being poured makes the sound
                  of inconsolable children
          who, though you try with all your heart,
                cannot be soothed.
When whatever you want to do cannot be done,
When nothing is of any use;
— At this hour when night comes down,
When night comes, dragging its long face,
                  dressed in mourning,         20
Be with me,
My tormenter, my love, be near me.

**1.** Why does the speaker call his or her lover "my tormenter" (ll. 2 and 22)?

**2.** What is the significance of night in "Be Near Me"?

### MAKING ARGUMENTS

Make an argument about this poem's **tone**. Is it uniform or changing? If the former, what is it, and how is it created? If the latter, what are the different tones and how are each created?

### WRITING TOPIC

Read through the poem again and list all of the ways in which things are described in ways that emphasize pain and violence, from **diction** to **imagery** even to sound. Create an alternate list of ways the poem could have been written to describe a love that brings not pain but pleasure, or calm, or something other than that which is Faiz's subject here.

## ANDREA HOLLANDER   (B. 1947)

# BETRAYAL   2009

They decide finally not to speak
of it, the one blemish in their otherwise
blameless marriage. It happened

as these things do, before the permanence
was set, before the children grew
complicated, before the quench
of loving one another became all
each of them wanted from this life.
Years later the bite

of not knowing (and not wanting          10
to know) still pierces the doer
as much as the one to whom it was done:

the threadbare lying, the insufferable longing,
the inimitable lack of touching, the undoing
undone.

### FOR ANALYSIS

**1.** What is the "one blemish" (l. 2)?

**2.** Where in time, relative to the event that is the poem's subject, is this poem situated? Why is this significant?

## MAKING ARGUMENTS

Hollander chooses not to provide any details of the betrayal in "Betrayal," yet it is so important that it is the title of the poem. Make an argument for why she made this choice, taking into account the poem's subject and form and considering alternative ways she might have written the poem as counterarguments.

## WRITING TOPIC

Reflect on a time when you betrayed someone, in one way or another (it doesn't have to be romantic); or, if you have lived a blameless life, reflect on a time when you were betrayed. How does the event compare to Hollander's account of a betrayal, even one that may not have happened?

# DRAMA

**WILLIAM SHAKESPEARE**   (1564–1616)

# OTHELLO   CA. 1604

## CHARACTERS

**Duke of Venice**
**Brabantio,** a Senator
**Senators**
**Gratiano,** Brother to Brabantio
**Lodovico,** Kinsman to Brabantio
**Othello,** a noble Moor; in the
   service of the Venetian State
**Cassio,** his Lieutenant
**Iago,** his Ancient
**Roderigo,** a Venetian Gentleman

**Montano,** Othello's predecessor
   in the Government of Cyprus
**Clown,** Servant to Othello
**Desdemona,** Daughter to
   Brabantio, and Wife to Othello
**Emilia,** Wife to Iago
**Bianca,** Mistress to Cassio
**Sailor, Officers, Gentlemen,**
   **Messengers, Musicians,**
   **Heralds, Attendants**

## Scene
*For the first Act, in Venice; during the rest of the Play, at a Sea-port in Cyprus*

## ACT I

**Scene 1.**   Venice. A Street.

*(Enter Roderigo and Iago.)*

**Roderigo.**   Tush! Never tell me; I take it much unkindly
   That thou, Iago, who has had my purse
   As if the strings were thine, shouldst know of this.[1]

---

[1] I.e., Othello's successful courtship of Desdemona.

**Iago.**  'Sblood,[2] but you will not hear me:
  If ever I did dream of such a matter,
  Abhor me.
**Roderigo.**  Thou told'st me thou didst hold him[3] in thy hate.
**Iago.**  Despise me if I do not. Three great ones of the city,
  In personal suit to make me his lieutenant,
  Off-capp'd[4] to him; and, by the faith of man,          10
  I know my price, I am worth no worse a place;
  But he, as loving his own pride and purposes,
  Evades them, with a bombast circumstance[5]
  Horribly stuff'd with epithets of war;
  And, in conclusion,
  Nonsuits[6] my mediators;[7] for, 'Certes,'[8] says he,
  'I have already chosen my officer.'
  And what was he?
  Forsooth, a great arithmetician,
  One Michael Cassio, a Florentine,                       20
  A fellow almost damn'd in a fair wife;[9]
  That never set a squadron in the field,
  Nor the division of a battle knows
  More than a spinster; unless[10] the bookish theoric,[11]
  Wherein the togèd consuls can propose
  As masterly as he: mere prattle, without practice,
  Is all his soldiership. But he, sir, had the election;
  And I — of whom his eyes had seen the proof
  At Rhodes, at Cyprus, and on other grounds
  Christian and heathen — must be be-lee'd[12] and calm'd   30
  By debitor and creditor; this counter-caster,[13]
  He, in good time, must his lieutenant be,
  And I — God bless the mark! — his Moorship's ancient.[14]
**Roderigo.**  By heaven, I rather would have been his hangman.
**Iago.**  Why, there's no remedy: 'tis the curse of service,
  Preferment goes by letter and affection,
  Not by the old gradation,[15] where each second
  Stood heir to the first. Now, sir, be judge yourself,
  Whe'r[16] I in any just term am affin'd[17]
  To love the Moor.

---

[2] By God's blood.   [3] I.e., Othello.   [4] Took off their caps.   [5] Pompous wordiness, circumlocution.
[6] Turns down.   [7] Spokesmen.   [8] In truth.   [9] A much debated phrase. In the Italian source the
Captain (i.e., Cassio) was married, and it may be that Shakespeare originally intended Bianca to be Cassio's
wife but later changed his mind and failed to alter the phrase here accordingly. Or perhaps Iago simply
sneers at Cassio as a notorious ladies' man.   [10] Except.   [11] Theory.   [12] Left without wind for my sails.
[13] Bookkeeper (cf. "arithmetician" above).   [14] Ensign (but Iago's position in the play seems to be that of
Othello's aide-de-camp).   [15] Seniority.   [16] Whether.   [17] Obliged.

**Roderigo.**                    I would not follow him then.                    40
**Iago.**  O! sir, content you;
 I follow him to serve my turn upon him;
 We cannot all be masters, nor all masters
 Cannot be truly follow'd. You shall mark
 Many a duteous and knee-crooking knave,
 That, doting on his own obsequious bondage,
 Wears out his time, much like his master's ass,
 For nought but provender, and when he's old, cashier'd;
 Whip me such honest knaves. Others there are
 Who, trimm'd in forms and visages of duty,                    50
 Keep yet their hearts attending on themselves,
 And, throwing but shows of service on their lords,
 Do well thrive by them, and when they have lin'd their coats
 Do themselves homage: these fellows have some soul;
 And such a one do I profess myself. For, sir,
 It is as sure as you are Roderigo,
 Were I the Moor, I would not be Iago:
 In following him, I follow but myself;
 Heaven is my judge, not I for love and duty,
 But seeming so, for my peculiar end:                    60
 For when my outward action doth demonstrate
 The native act and figure of my heart
 In compliment extern,[18] 'tis not long after
 But I will wear my heart upon my sleeve
 For daws to peck at: I am not what I am.
**Roderigo.**  What a full fortune does the thick-lips owe,[19]
 If he can carry 't thus!
**Iago.**                    Call up her father;
 Rouse him, make after him, poison his delight,
 Proclaim him in the streets, incense her kinsmen,
 And, though he in a fertile climate dwell,[20]                    70
 Plague him with flies; though that his joy be joy,
 Yet throw such changes of vexation on 't
 As it may lose some colour.
**Roderigo.**  Here is her father's house; I'll call aloud.
**Iago.**  Do; with like timorous[21] accent and dire yell
 As when, by night and negligence, the fire
 Is spied in populous cities.
**Roderigo.**  What, ho! Brabantio: Signior Brabantio, ho!
**Iago.**  Awake! what, ho! Brabantio! thieves! thieves! thieves!

---

[18] External show.    [19] Own.    [20] I.e., is fortunate.    [21] Frightening.

Look to your house, your daughter, and your bags!    80
Thieves! thieves!

*(Enter Brabantio, above, at a window.)*

**Brabantio.**  What is the reason of this terrible summons?
  What is the matter there?
**Roderigo.**  Signior, is all your family within?
**Iago.**  Are your doors lock'd?
**Brabantio.**                    Why? wherefore ask you this?
**Iago.**  'Zounds![22] sir, you're robb'd; for shame, put on your gown;
  Your heart is burst, you have lost half your soul;
  Even now, now, very now, an old black ram
  Is tupping[23] your white ewe. Arise, arise!
  Awake the snorting[24] citizens with the bell,    90
  Or else the devil will make a grandsire of you.
  Arise, I say.
**Brabantio.**  What! have you lost your wits?
**Roderigo.**  Most reverend signior, do you know my voice?
**Brabantio.**  Not I, what are you?
**Roderigo.**  My name is Roderigo.
**Brabantio.**                    The worser welcome:
  I have charg'd thee not to haunt about my doors:
  In honest plainness thou hast heard me say
  My daughter is not for thee; and now, in madness,
  Being full of supper and distempering draughts,    100
  Upon malicious knavery dost thou come
  To start my quiet.
**Roderigo.**  Sir, sir, sir!
**Brabantio.**                    But thou must needs be sure
  My spirit and my place[25] have in them power
  To make this bitter to thee.
**Roderigo.**                    Patience, good sir.
**Brabantio.**  What tell'st thou me of robbing? this is Venice;
  My house is not a grange.[26]
**Roderigo.**                    Most grave Brabantio,
  In simple and pure soul I come to you.
**Iago.**  'Zounds! sir, you are one of those that will not serve God if the devil bid
  you. Because we come to do you service and you think we are ruffians, you'll
  have your daughter covered with a Barbary horse; you'll have your nephews
  neigh to you; you'll have coursers for cousins and gennets[27] for germans.[28]    112
**Brabantio.**  What profane wretch art thou?

---

[22] By God's wounds.    [23] Copulating.    [24] Snoring.    [25] Position.    [26] Isolated farmhouse.
[27] Spanish horses.    [28] Blood relations.

**Iago.** I am one, sir, that comes to tell you, your daughter and the Moor are now
    making the beast with two backs.

**Brabantio.** Thou art a villain.

**Iago.**                    You are — a senator.

**Brabantio.** This thou shalt answer; I know thee, Roderigo.

**Roderigo.** Sir, I will answer any thing. But, I beseech you,
    If 't be your pleasure and most wise consent, —
    As partly, I find, it is, — that your fair daughter,                120
    At this odd-even[29] and dull watch o' the night,
    Transported with no worse nor better guard
    But with a knave of common hire, a gondolier,
    To the gross clasps of a lascivious Moor, —
    If this be known to you, and your allowance,[30]
    We then have done you bold and saucy wrongs;
    But if you know not this, my manners tell me
    We have your wrong rebuke. Do not believe
    That, from[31] the sense of all civility,
    I thus would play and trifle with your reverence:          130
    Your daughter, if you have not given her leave,
    I say again, hath made a gross revolt;
    Tying her duty, beauty, wit and fortunes
    In[32] an extravagant[33] and wheeling stranger
    Of here and every where. Straight satisfy yourself:
    If she be in her chamber or your house,
    Let loose on me the justice of the state
    For thus deluding you.

**Brabantio.**               Strike on the tinder, ho!
    Give me a taper! call up all my people!
    This accident[34] is not unlike my dream;              140
    Belief of it oppresses me already.
    Light, I say! light!                 *(Exit, from above.)*

**Iago.**              Farewell, for I must leave you:
    It seems not meet nor wholesome to my place
    To be produc'd,[35] as, if I stay, I shall,
    Against the Moor; for I do know the state,
    However this may gall him with some check,[36]
    Cannot with safety cast him; for he's embark'd
    With such loud reason to the Cyprus wars, —
    Which even now stand in act, — that, for their souls,
    Another of his fathom[37] they have none,           150
    To lead their business; in which regard,
    Though I do hate him as I do hell-pains,

---

[29] Between night and morning.    [30] By your approval.    [31] Away from.    [32] To.    [33] Expatriate.
[34] Happening.    [35] I.e., as a witness.    [36] Restraining adversity.    [37] Caliber, ability.

Yet, for necessity of present life,
I must show out a flag and sign of love,
Which is indeed but sign. That you shall surely find him,
Lead to the Sagittary[38] the raised search;
And there will I be with him. So, farewell.                    *(Exit.)*

*(Enter below, Brabantio, and servants with torches.)*

**Brabantio.**  It is too true an evil: gone she is,
And what's to come of my despised time
Is nought but bitterness. Now, Roderigo,                                    160
Where didst thou see her? O, unhappy girl!
With the Moor, sayst thou? Who would be a father!
How didst thou know 'twas she? O, she deceives me
Past thought. What said she to you? Get more tapers!
Raise all my kindred! Are they married, think you?
**Roderigo.**  Truly, I think they are.
**Brabantio.**  O heaven! How got she out? O treason of the blood:
Fathers, from hence trust not your daughters' minds
By what you see them act. Are there not charms
By which the property of youth and maidhood                                  170
May be abus'd? Have you not read, Roderigo,
Of some such thing?
**Roderigo.**              Yes, sir, I have indeed.
**Brabantio.**  Call up my brother. O! that you had had her.
Some one way, some another! Do you know
Where we may apprehend her and the Moor?
**Roderigo.**  I think I can discover him, if you please
To get good guard and go along with me.
**Brabantio.**  Pray you, lead on. At every house I'll call;
I may command at most. Get weapons, ho!
And raise some special officers of night.                                    180
On, good Roderigo; I'll deserve[39] your pains.              *(Exeunt.)*

**Scene 2.**   Another Street.

*(Enter Othello, Iago, and Attendants, with torches.)*

**Iago.**  Though in the trade of war I have slain men,
Yet do I hold it very stuff o' the conscience
To do no contriv'd murder: I lack iniquity
Sometimes to do me service. Nine or ten times
I had thought to have yerk'd[40] him here under the ribs.

---

[38] The name of an inn (?).    [39] I.e., reward.    [40] Stabbed.

**Othello.** 'Tis better as it is.

**Iago.**                              Nay, but he prated,
And spoke such scurvy and provoking terms
Against your honour
That, with the little godliness I have,
I did full hard forbear him. But, I pray, sir,                              10
Are you fast married? Be assur'd of this,
That the magnifico[41] is much belov'd,
And hath in his effect a voice potential
As double[42] as the duke's; he will divorce you,
Or put upon you what restraint and grievance
The law — with all his might to enforce it on —
Will give him cable.[43]

**Othello.**                    Let him do his spite:
My services which I have done the signiory[44]
Shall out-tongue his complaints. 'Tis yet to know,[45]
Which when I know that boasting is an honour                              20
I shall promulgate, I fetch my life and being
From men of royal siege, and my demerits[46]
May speak unbonneted[47] to as proud a fortune
As this[48] that I have reach'd; for know, Iago,
But that I love the gentle Desdemona,
I would not my unhoused[49] free condition
Put into circumscription and confine
For the sea's worth. But, look! what lights come yond?

**Iago.** Those are the raised[50] father and his friends:
You were best[51] go in.

**Othello.**                    Not I; I must be found:                              30
My parts, my title, and my perfect[52] soul
Shall manifest me rightly. Is it they?

**Iago.** By Janus,[53] I think no.

*(Enter Cassio and certain Officers, with torches.)*

**Othello.** The servants of the duke, and my lieutenant.
The goodness of the night upon you, friends!
What is the news?

**Cassio.**                    The duke does greet you, general,
And he requires your haste-post-haste appearance,
Even on the instant.

**Othello.**                    What is the matter, think you?

---

[41] One of the grandees, or rulers, of Venice; here, Brabantio.    [42] Iago means that Brabantio's influence equals that of the Doge's with his double vote.    [43] I.e., scope.    [44] The Venetian government. [45] I.e., the signiory does not as yet know.    [46] Merits.    [47] I.e., as equals.    [48] I.e., that of Desdemona's family.    [49] Unconfined.    [50] Aroused.    [51] Had better.    [52] Untroubled by a bad conscience. [53] The two-faced Roman god of portals and doors and (hence) of beginnings and ends.

**Cassio.**  Something from Cyprus, as I may divine.
    It is a business of some heat;[54] the galleys          40
    Have sent a dozen sequent[55] messengers
    This very night at one another's heels,
    And many of the consuls,[56] rais'd and met,
    Are at the duke's already. You have been hotly call'd for;
    When, being not at your lodging to be found,
    The senate hath sent about three several[57] quests
    To search you out.
**Othello.**          'Tis well I am found by you.
    I will but spend a word here in the house,
    And go with you.                      *(Exit.)*
**Cassio.**        Ancient, what makes he here?
**Iago.**  Faith, he to-night hath boarded a land carrack;[58]    50
    If it prove lawful prize, he's made for ever.
**Cassio.**  I do not understand.
**Iago.**              He's married.
**Cassio.**                  To who?

*(Re-enter Othello.)*

**Iago.**  Marry,[59] to — Come, captain, will you go?
**Othello.**                  Have with you.
**Cassio.**  Here comes another troop to seek for you.
**Iago.**  It is Brabantio. General, be advis'd;
    He comes to bad intent.

*(Enter Brabantio, Roderigo, and Officers, with torches and weapons.)*

**Othello.**             Holla! stand there!
**Roderigo.**  Signior, it is the Moor.
**Brabantio.**             Down with him, thief!

*(They draw on both sides.)*

**Iago.**  You, Roderigo! Come, sir, I am for you.[60]
**Othello.**  Keep up your bright swords, for the dew will rust them.
    Good signior, you shall more command with years    60
    Than with your weapons.
**Brabantio.**  O thou foul thief! where hast thou stow'd my daughter?
    Damn'd as thou art, thou hast enchanted her;
    For I'll refer me to all things of sense,
    If she in chains of magic were not bound,
    Whether a maid so tender, fair, and happy,

---

[54] Urgency.   [55] Following one another.   [56] I.e., senators.   [57] Separate.   [58] Treasure ship.   [59] By the Virgin Mary.   [60] Let you and me fight.

So opposite to marriage that she shunn'd
The wealthy curled darlings of our nation,
Would ever have, to incur a general mock,
Run from her guardage to the sooty bosom                          70
Of such a thing as thou; to fear, not to delight.
Judge me the world, if 'tis not gross in sense[61]
That thou hast practis'd on her with foul charms,
Abus'd her delicate youth with drugs or minerals
That weaken motion:[62] I'll have 't disputed on;
'Tis probable, and palpable to thinking.
I therefore apprehend and do attach[63] thee
For an abuser of the world, a practiser
Of arts inhibited and out of warrant.[64]
Lay hold upon him: if he do resist,                                80
Subdue him at his peril.

**Othello.**                    Hold your hands,
Both you of my inclining,[65] and the rest:
Were it my cue to fight, I should have known it
Without a prompter. Where will you that I go
To answer this your charge?

**Brabantio.**                       To prison; till fit time
Of law and course of direct session[66]
Call thee to answer.

**Othello.**            What if I do obey?
How may the duke be therewith satisfied,
Whose messengers are here about my side,
Upon some present[67] business of the state                        90
To bring me to him?

**Officer.**                ʼTis true, most worthy signior;
The duke's in council, and your noble self,
I am sure, is sent for.

**Brabantio.**              How! the duke in council!
In this time of the night! Bring him away.
Mine's not an idle cause: the duke himself,
Or any of my brothers of the state,[68]
Cannot but feel this wrong as 'twere their own;
For if such actions may have passage free,
Bond-slaves and pagans shall our statesmen be.          *(Exeunt.)*

**Scene 3.**   A Council Chamber.

*(The Duke and Senators sitting at a table. Officers attending.)*

**Duke.**  There is no composition[69] in these news
That gives them credit.

---

[61] Obvious.   [62] Normal reactions.   [63] Arrest.   [64] Prohibited and illegal.   [65] Party.   [66] Normal process of law.   [67] Immediate, pressing.   [68] Fellow senators.   [69] Consistency, agreement.

**First Senator.**                    Indeed, they are disproportion'd;
  My letters say a hundred and seven galleys.
**Duke.**  And mine, a hundred and forty.
**Second Senator.**                         And mine, two hundred:
  But though they jump[70] not on a just[71] account, —
  As in these cases, where the aim[72] reports,
  'Tis oft with difference, — yet do they all confirm
  A Turkish fleet, and bearing up to Cyprus.
**Duke.**  Nay, it is possible enough to judgment:
  I do not so secure me in[73] the error,                                    10
  But the main article[74] I do approve[75]
  In fearful sense.
**Sailor** *(within).*    What, ho! what, ho! what, ho!
**Officer.**  A messenger from the galleys.

*(Enter a Sailor.)*

**Duke.**                              Now, what's the business?
**Sailor.**  The Turkish preparation makes for Rhodes;
  So was I bid report here to the state
  By Signior Angelo.
**Duke.**  How say you by this change?
**First Senator.**                         This cannot be
  By no[76] assay[77] of reason; 'tis a pageant[78]
  To keep us in false gaze.[79] When we consider
  The importancy of Cyprus to the Turk,                                      20
  And let ourselves again but understand,
  That as it more concerns the Turk than Rhodes,
  So may he with more facile question bear[80] it,
  For that it stands not in such warlike brace,[81]
  But altogether lacks the abilities
  That Rhodes is dress'd in: if we make thought of this,
  We must not think the Turk is so unskilful
  To leave that latest which concerns him first,
  Neglecting an attempt of ease and gain,
  To wake and wage a danger profitless.                                      30
**Duke.**  Nay, in all confidence, he's not for Rhodes.
**Officer.**  Here is more news.

*(Enter a Messenger.)*

**Messenger.**  The Ottomites,[82] reverend and gracious,
  Steering with due course toward the isle of Rhodes,
  Have there injointed[83] them with an after fleet.[84]

---

[70] Coincide.    [71] Exact.    [72] Conjecture.    [73] Draw comfort from.    [74] Substance.    [75] Believe.
[76] Any.    [77] Test.    [78] (Deceptive) show.    [79] Looking in the wrong direction.    [80] More easily capture.
[81] State of defense.    [82] Turks.    [83] Joined.    [84] Fleet that followed after.

**First Senator.** Ay, so I thought. How many, as you guess?

**Messenger.** Of thirty sail; and now they do re-stem[85]
    Their backward course, bearing with frank appearance
    Their purposes toward Cyprus. Signior Montano,
    Your trusty and most valiant servitor,                 40
    With his free duty[86] recommends[87] you thus,
    And prays you to believe him.

**Duke.** 'Tis certain then, for Cyprus.
    Marcus Luccicos, is not he in town?

**First Senator.** He's now in Florence.

**Duke.** Write from us to him; post-post-haste dispatch.

**First Senator.** Here comes Brabantio and the valiant Moor.

*(Enter Brabantio, Othello, Iago, Roderigo, and Officers.)*

**Duke.** Valiant Othello, we must straight employ you
    Against the general enemy Ottoman.
    *(To Brabantio.)* I did not see you; welcome, gentle signior;    50
    We lack'd your counsel and your help to-night.

**Brabantio.** So did I yours. Good your Grace, pardon me;
    Neither my place nor aught I heard of business
    Hath rais'd me from my bed, nor doth the general care
    Take hold of me, for my particular grief
    Is of so flood-gate[88] and o'erbearing nature
    That it engluts and swallows other sorrows
    And it is still itself.

**Duke.**               Why, what's the matter?

**Brabantio.** My daughter! O! my daughter.

**Duke.** ⎫
**Senators.** ⎭            Dead?

**Brabantio.**                   Ay, to me;
    She is abus'd, stol'n from me, and corrupted          60
    By spells and medicines bought of mountebanks;
    For nature so preposterously to err,
    Being not deficient, blind, or lame of sense,
    Sans[89] witchcraft could not.

**Duke.** Whoe'er he be that in this foul proceeding
    Hath thus beguil'd your daughter of herself
    And you of her, the bloody book of law
    You shall yourself read in the bitter letter
    After your own sense; yea, though our proper[90] son
    Stood[91] in your action.[92]

**Brabantio.**            Humbly I thank your Grace.    70
    Here is the man, this Moor; whom now, it seems,

---

[85] Steer again.   [86] Unqualified expressions of respect.   [87] Informs.   [88] Torrential.   [89] Without.
[90] Own.   [91] Were accused.   [92] Suit.

Your special mandate for the state affairs
Hath hither brought.

**Duke.** }
**Senators.** } We are very sorry for it.

**Duke** (to Othello). What, in your own part, can you say to this?
**Brabantio.** Nothing, but this is so.
**Othello.** Most potent, grave, and reverend signiors,
My very noble and approv'd[93] good masters,
That I have ta'en away this old man's daughter,
It is most true; true, I have married her:
The very head and front of my offending            80
Hath this extent, no more. Rude am I in my speech,
And little bless'd with the soft phrase of peace;
For since these arms of mine had seven years' pith,[94]
Till now some nine moons wasted,[95] they have us'd
Their dearest action in the tented field;
And little of this great world can I speak,
More than pertains to feats of broil and battle;
And therefore little shall I grace my cause
In speaking for myself. Yet, by your gracious patience,
I will a round[96] unvarnish'd tale deliver            90
Of my whole course of love; what drugs, what charms,
What conjuration, and what mighty magic,
For such proceeding I am charg'd withal,
I won his daughter.
**Brabantio.**            A maiden never bold;
Of spirit so still and quiet, that her motion
Blush'd at herself;[97] and she, in spite of nature,
Of years, of country, credit, every thing,
To fall in love with what she fear'd to look on!
It is a judgment maim'd and most imperfect
That will confess[98] perfection so could err            100
Against all rules of nature, and must be driven
To find out practices of cunning hell,
Why this should be. I therefore vouch again
That with some mixtures powerful o'er the blood,
Or with some dram conjur'd to this effect,
He wrought upon her.
**Duke.**            To vouch this, is no proof,
Without more certain and more overt test
Than these thin habits[99] and poor likelihoods
Of modern[100] seeming do prefer against him.

---

[93] Tested (by past experience).    [94] Strength.    [95] Past.    [96] Blunt.    [97] I.e. (her modesty was such that) she blushed at her own emotions; or: she could not move without blushing.    [98] Assert.    [99] Weak appearances.    [100] Commonplace.

**First Senator.** But, Othello, speak: 110
  Did you by indirect and forced courses
  Subdue and poison this young maid's affections;
  Or came it by request and such fair question[101]
  As soul to soul affordeth?
**Othello.**                I do beseech you;
  Send for the lady to the Sagittary,
  And let her speak of me before her father:
  If you do find me foul in her report,
  The trust, the office I do hold of you,
  Not only take away, but let your sentence
  Even fall upon my life.
**Duke.**                Fetch Desdemona hither. 120
**Othello.** Ancient, conduct them; you best know the place.

*(Exeunt Iago and Attendants.)*

  And, till she come, as truly as to heaven
  I do confess the vices of my blood,
  So justly to your grave ears I'll present
  How I did thrive in this fair lady's love,
  And she in mine.
**Duke.** Say it, Othello.
**Othello.** Her father lov'd me; oft invited me;
  Still[102] question'd me the story of my life
  From year to year, the battles, sieges, fortunes 130
  That I have pass'd.
  I ran it through, even from my boyish days
  To the very moment that he bade me tell it;
  Wherein I spake of most disastrous chances,
  Of moving accidents by flood and field,
  Of hair-breadth 'scapes i' the imminent deadly breach,
  Of being taken by the insolent foe
  And sold to slavery, of my redemption thence
  And portance[103] in my travel's history;
  Wherein of antres[104] vast and deserts idle,[105] 140
  Rough quarries, rocks, and hills whose heads touch heaven,
  It was my hint[106] to speak, such was the process;
  And of the Cannibals that each other eat,
  The Anthropophagi,[107] and men whose heads
  Do grow beneath their shoulders. This to hear
  Would Desdemona seriously incline;
  But still the house-affairs would draw her thence;
  Which ever as she could with haste dispatch,

---

[101] Conversation.    [102] Always, regularly.    [103] Behavior.    [104] Caves.    [105] Empty, sterile.
[106] Opportunity.    [107] Man-eaters.

She'd come again, and with a greedy ear
Devour up my discourse. Which I observing,                    150
Took once a pliant[108] hour, and found good means
To draw from her a prayer of earnest heart
That I would all my pilgrimage dilate,[109]
Whereof by parcels[110] she had something heard,
But not intentively:[111] I did consent;
And often did beguile her of her tears,
When I did speak of some distressful stroke
That my youth suffer'd. My story being done,
She gave me for my pains a world of sighs:
She swore, in faith, 'twas strange, 'twas passing[112] strange;    160
'Twas pitiful, 'twas wondrous pitiful:
She wish'd she had not heard it, yet she wish'd
That heaven had made her[113] such a man; she thank'd me,
And bade me, if I had a friend that lov'd her,
I should but teach him how to tell my story,
And that would woo her. Upon this hint I spake.
She lov'd me for the dangers I had pass'd,
And I lov'd her that she did pity them.
This only is the witchcraft I have us'd:
Here comes the lady; let her witness it.                       170

*(Enter Desdemona, Iago, and Attendants.)*

**Duke.**  I think this tale would win my daughter too.
Good Brabantio,
Take up this mangled matter at the best;
Men do their broken weapons rather use
Than their bare hands.
**Brabantio.**               I pray you, hear her speak:
If she confess that she was half the wooer,
Destruction on my head, if my bad blame
Light on the man! Come hither, gentle mistress:
Do you perceive in all this noble company
Where most you owe obedience?
**Desdemona.**                My noble father,              180
I do perceive here a divided duty:
To you I am bound for life and education;
My life and education both do learn[114] me
How to respect you; you are the lord of duty,
I am hitherto your daughter: but here's my husband;
And so much duty as my mother show'd
To you, preferring you before her father,

---

[108] Suitable.    [109] Relate in full.    [110] Piecemeal.    [111] In sequence.    [112] Surpassing.    [113] Direct object; not "for her."    [114] Teach.

So much I challenge[115] that I may profess
Due to the Moor my lord.

**Brabantio.**                    God be with you! I have done.
Please it your Grace, on to the state affairs;                    190
I had rather to adopt a child than get it.
Come hither, Moor:
I here do give thee that with all my heart
Which, but thou hast[116] already, with all my heart
I would keep from thee. For your sake,[117] jewel,
I am glad at soul I have no other child;
For thy escape would teach me tyranny,
To hang clogs on them. I have done, my lord.

**Duke.**  Let me speak like yourself and lay a sentence,[118]
Which as a grize[119] or step, may help these lovers                    200
Into your favour.
When remedies are past, the griefs are ended
By seeing the worst, which[120] late on hopes depended.
To mourn a mischief that is past and gone
Is the next way to draw new mischief on.
What cannot be preserv'd when Fortune takes,
Patience her injury a mockery makes.[121]
The robb'd that smiles steals something from the thief;
He robs himself that spends a bootless grief.

**Brabantio.**  So let the Turk of Cyprus us beguile;                    210
We lose it not so long as we can smile.
He bears the sentence[122] well that nothing bears
But the free comfort which from thence he hears;
But he bears both the sentence and the sorrow
That, to pay grief, must of poor patience borrow.
These sentences, to sugar, or to gall,
Being strong on both sides, are equivocal:[123]
But words are words: I never yet did hear
That the bruis'd heart was pierced[124] through the ear.
I humbly beseech you, proceed to the affairs of state.                    220

**Duke.**  The Turk with a most mighty preparation makes for Cyprus. Othello, the fortitude[125] of the place is best known to you; and though we have there a substitute of most allowed sufficiency,[126] yet opinion, a sovereign mistress of effects, throws a more safer voice on you:[127] you must therefore be content to slubber[128] the gloss of your new fortunes with this more stubborn[129] and boisterous expedition.

---

[115] Claim as right.    [116] Didn't you have it.    [117] Because of you.    [118] Provide a maxim.    [119] Step.
[120] The antecedent is "griefs."    [121] To suffer an irreparable loss patiently is to make light of injury (i.e., to triumph over adversity).    [122] (1) Verdict, (2) Maxim.    [123] Sententious comfort (like the Duke's trite maxims) can hurt as well as soothe.    [124] (1) Lanced (i.e., cured), (2) Wounded.    [125] Strength.
[126] Admitted competence.    [127] General opinion, which mainly determines action, thinks Cyprus safer with you in command.    [128] Besmear.    [129] Rough.

**Othello.** The tyrant custom, most grave senators,
Hath made the flinty and steel couch of war
My thrice-driven[130] bed of down: I do agnize[131]
A natural and prompt alacrity                                    230
I find in hardness, and do undertake
These present wars against the Ottomites.
Most humbly therefore bending to your state,[132]
I crave fit disposition[133] for my wife,
Due reference of place and exhibition,[134]
With such accommodation and besort[135]
As levels with[136] her breeding.
**Duke.**                              If you please,
Be 't at her father's.
**Brabantio.**              I'll not have it so.
**Othello.** Nor I.
**Desdemona.** Nor I; I would not there reside,          240
To put my father in impatient thoughts
By being in his eye. Most gracious duke,
To my unfolding[137] lend your gracious ear;
And let me find a charter[138] in your voice
To assist my simpleness.
**Duke.** What would you, Desdemona?
**Desdemona.** That I did love the Moor to live with him,
My downright violence and storm of fortunes
May trumpet to the world; my heart's subdu'd
Even to the very quality of my lord;[139]                      250
I saw Othello's visage in his mind,
And to his honours and his valiant parts
Did I my soul and fortunes consecrate.
So that, dear lords, if I be left behind,
A moth of peace, and he go to the war,
The rites[140] for which I love him are bereft me,
And I a heavy interim shall support[141]
By his dear[142] absence. Let me go with him.
**Othello.** Let her have your voices.
Vouch with me, heaven, I therefore beg it not          260
To please the palate of my appetite,
Nor to comply with heat, — the young affects[143]
In me defunct, — and proper satisfaction,
But to be free and bounteous to her mind;

---

[130] Made as soft as possible.  [131] Recognize.  [132] Submitting to your authority.  [133] Disposal.  [134] Provision.  [135] Fitness.  [136] Is proper to.  [137] Explanation.  [138] Permission.
[139] I.e., I have become a soldier, like Othello.  [140] I.e., of marriage, or of war, or of both.  [141] Endure.
[142] Closely concerning (i.e., Desdemona).  [143] The passions of youth (hence, here, *immoderate* sexual passion).

And heaven defend[144] your good souls that you think
I will your serious and great business scant
For[145] she is with me. No, when light-wing'd toys
Of feather'd Cupid seel[146] with wanton dulness
My speculative and offic'd instruments,[147]
That[148] my disports corrupt and taint my business,                   270
Let housewives make a skillet of my helm,
And all indign[149] and base adversities
Make head against my estimation![150]

**Duke.**  Be it as you shall privately determine,
Either for her stay or going. The affair cries haste,
And speed must answer it.

**First Senator.**  You must away to-night.

**Othello.**                               With all my heart.

**Duke.**  At nine i' the morning here we'll meet again.
Othello, leave some officer behind,
And he shall our commission bring to you;                   280
With such things else of quality and respect
As doth import you.[151]

**Othello.**            So please your Grace, my ancient;
A man he is of honesty and trust:
To his conveyance I assign my wife,
With what else needful your good grace shall think
To be sent after me.

**Duke.**            Let it be so.
Good-night to every one. *(To Brabantio.)* And, noble signior,
If virtue no delighted[152] beauty lack,
Your son-in-law is far more fair than black.

**First Senator.**  Adieu, brave Moor! use Desdemona well.                   290

**Brabantio.**  Look to her, Moor, if thou hast eyes to see:
She has deceiv'd her father, and may thee.

*(Exeunt Duke, Senators, Officers, &c.)*

**Othello.**  My life upon her faith! Honest Iago,
My Desdemona must I leave to thee:
I prithee, let thy wife attend on her;
And bring them after in the best advantage.[153]
Come, Desdemona; I have but an hour
Of love, of worldly matters and direction,
To spend with thee: we must obey the time.

*(Exeunt Othello and Desdemona.)*

---

[144] Forbid.    [145] Because.    [146] Blind (v.) by sewing up the eyelids (a term from falconry).    [147] Reflective and executive faculties and organs.    [148] So that.    [149] Shameful.    [150] Reputation.    [151] Concern.    [152] Delightful.    [153] Opportunity.

**Roderigo.** Iago! 300

**Iago.** What sayst thou, noble heart?

**Roderigo.** What will I do, think'st thou?

**Iago.** Why, go to bed, and sleep.

**Roderigo.** I will incontinently[154] drown myself.

**Iago.** Well, if thou dost, I shall never love thee after.
Why, thou silly gentleman!

**Roderigo.** It is silliness to live when to live is torment; and then have we a prescription to die when death is our physician.

**Iago.** O! villainous; I have looked upon the world for four times seven years, and since I could distinguish betwixt a benefit and an injury, I never found man that knew how to love himself. Ere I would say, I would drown myself for the love of a guinea-hen, I would change my humanity with a baboon. 312

**Roderigo.** What should I do? I confess it is my shame to be so fond;[155] but it is not in my virtue[156] to amend it.

**Iago.** Virtue! a fig! 'tis in ourselves that we are thus, or thus. Our bodies are our gardens, to the which our wills are gardeners; so that if we will plant nettles or sow lettuce, set hyssop and weed up thyme, supply it with one gender[157] of herbs or distract it with many, either to have it sterile with idleness or manured with industry, why, the power and corrigible[158] authority of this lies in our wills. If the balance of our lives had not one scale of reason to poise another of sensuality, the blood and baseness of our natures would conduct us to most preposterous conclusions; but we have reason to cool our raging motions, our carnal stings, our unbitted[159] lusts, whereof I take this that you call love to be a sect or scion.[160] 324

**Roderigo.** It cannot be.

**Iago.** It is merely a lust of the blood and a permission of the will. Come, be a man. Drown thyself! drown cats and blind puppies. I have professed me thy friend, and I confess me knit to thy deserving with cables of perdurable toughness; I could never better stead thee than now. Put money in thy purse; follow these wars; defeat thy favour[161] with a usurped[162] beard; I say, put money in thy purse. It cannot be that Desdemona should long continue her love to the Moor, — put money in thy purse, — nor he his to her. It was a violent commencement in her, and thou shalt see an answerable sequestration;[163] put but money in thy purse. These Moors are changeable in their wills; — fill thy purse with money: — the food that to him now is as luscious as locusts,[164] shall be to him shortly as bitter as coloquintida.[165] She must change for youth: when she is sated with his body, she will find the error of her choice. She must have change, she must: therefore put money in thy purse. If thou wilt needs damn thyself, do it a more delicate way than drowning. Make all the money thou canst. If

---

[154] Forthwith.   [155] Infatuated.   [156] Strength.   [157] Kind.   [158] Corrective.   [159] I.e., uncontrolled.   [160] Offshoot.   [161] Change thy appearance (for the worse?).   [162] Assumed.   [163] Estrangement.   [164] Sweet-tasting fruits (perhaps the carob, the edible seedpod of an evergreen tree in the Mediterranean area).   [165] Purgative derived from a bitter apple.

sanctimony and a frail vow betwixt an erring[166] barbarian and a supersubtle[167] Venetian be not too hard for my wits and all the tribe of hell, thou shalt enjoy her; therefore make money. A pox of drowning thyself! it is clean out of the way: seek thou rather to be hanged in compassing thy joy than to be drowned and go without her.                                                                                           344

**Roderigo.** Wilt thou be fast to my hopes, if I depend on the issue?[168]

**Iago.** Thou art sure of me: go, make money. I have told thee often, and I retell thee again and again, I hate the Moor; my cause is hearted; thine hath no less reason. Let us be conjunctive[169] in our revenge against him; if thou canst cuckold him, thou dost thyself a pleasure, me a sport. There are many events in the womb of time which will be delivered. Traverse;[170] go: provide thy money. We will have more of this to-morrow. Adieu.                                                                                   351

**Roderigo.** Where shall we meet i' the morning?

**Iago.** At my lodging.

**Roderigo.** I'll be with thee betimes.

**Iago.** Go to: farewell. Do you hear, Roderigo?

**Roderigo.** What say you?

**Iago.** No more of drowning, do you hear?

**Roderigo.** I am changed. I'll sell all my land.

**Iago.** Go to; farewell! put money enough in your purse.                 *(Exit Roderigo.)*

    Thus do I ever make my fool my purse;                                                      360
    For I mine own gain'd knowledge should profane,
    If I would time expend with such a snipe[171]
    But for my sport and profit. I hate the Moor,
    And it is thought abroad[172] that 'twixt my sheets
    He has done my office: I know not if 't be true,
    But I, for mere suspicion in that kind,
    Will do as if for surety.[173] He holds me well;[174]
    The better shall my purpose work on him.
    Cassio's a proper[175] man; let me see now:
    To get his place; and to plume up[176] my will                                              370
    In double knavery; how, how? Let's see:
    After some time to abuse Othello's ear
    That he[177] is too familiar with his wife:
    He hath a person and a smooth dispose[178]
    To be suspected; framed[179] to make women false,
    The Moor is of a free and open nature,
    That thinks men honest that but seem to be so,
    And will as tenderly be led by the nose
    As asses are.
    I have 't; it is engender'd: hell and night                                                 380
    Must bring this monstrous birth to the world's light.                      *(Exit.)*

---

[166] Vagabond.   [167] Exceedingly refined.   [168] Rely on the outcome.   [169] Allied.   [170] March.
[171] Dupe.   [172] People think.   [173] As if it were certain.   [174] In high regard.   [175] Handsome.
[176] Make ready.   [177] I.e., Cassio.   [178] Bearing.   [179] Designed, apt.

## ACT II

**Scene 1.**   A Sea-port Town in Cyprus. An open place near the Quay.

*(Enter Montano and two Gentlemen.)*

**Montano.**  What from the cape can you discern at sea?
**First Gentleman.**  Nothing at all: it is a high-wrought flood;
  I cannot 'twixt the heaven and the main[180]
  Descry a sail.
**Montano.**  Methinks the wind hath spoke aloud at land;
  A fuller blast ne'er shook our battlements;
  If it hath ruffian'd so upon the sea,
  What ribs of oak, when mountains melt on them,
  Can hold the mortise?[181] What shall we hear of this?
**Second Gentleman.**  A segregation[182] of the Turkish fleet;        10
  For do but stand upon the foaming shore,
  The chidden billow seems to pelt the clouds;
  The wind-shak'd surge, with high and monstrous mane,
  Seems to cast water on the burning bear[183]
  And quench the guards of the ever-fixed pole:[184]
  I never did like[185] molestation view
  On the enchafed[186] flood.
**Montano.**                              If that[187] the Turkish fleet
  Be not enshelter'd and embay'd, they are drown'd;
  It is impossible they bear it out.

*(Enter a Third Gentleman.)*

**Third Gentleman.**  News, lad! our wars are done.        20
  The desperate tempest hath so bang'd the Turks
  That their designment halts;[188] a noble ship of Venice
  Hath seen a grievous wrack and suffrance[189]
  On most part of their fleet.
**Montano.**  How! is this true?
**Third Gentleman.**                      The ship is here put in,
  A Veronesa;[190] Michael Cassio,
  Lieutenant to the warlike Moor Othello,
  Is come on shore: the Moor himself's at sea,
  And is in full commission here for Cyprus.
**Montano.**  I am glad on 't; 'tis a worthy governor.        30
**Third Gentleman.**  But this same Cassio, though he speak of comfort
  Touching the Turkish loss, yet he looks sadly

---

[180] Ocean.    [181] Hold the joints together.    [182] Scattering.    [183] Ursa Minor (the Little Dipper).
[184] Polaris, the North Star, almost directly above the Earth's axis, is part of the constellation of the Little Bear, or Dipper.    [185] Similar.    [186] Agitated.    [187] If.    [188] Plan is stopped.    [189] Damage.    [190] Probably a *type* of ship, rather than a ship from Verona — not only because Verona is an inland city but also because of "a noble ship of Venice" above.

And prays the Moor be safe; for they were parted
With foul and violent tempest.
**Montano.** Pray heaven he be;
For I have serv'd him, and the man commands
Like a full soldier. Let's to the sea-side, ho!
As well to see the vessel that's come in
As to throw out our eyes for brave Othello,
Even till we make the main and the aerial blue
An indistinct regard.[191]                                              40
**Third Gentleman.** Come, let's do so;
For every minute is expectancy
Of more arrivance.

*(Enter Cassio.)*

**Cassio.** Thanks, you the valiant of this warlike isle,
That so approve the Moor. O! let the heavens
Give him defence against the elements,
For I have lost him on a dangerous sea.
**Montano.** Is he well shipp'd?
**Cassio.** His bark is stoutly timber'd, and his pilot
Of very expert and approv'd allowance;[192]                             50
Therefore my hopes, not surfeited to death,[193]
Stand in bold cure.[194]

*(Within, 'A sail! — a sail! — a sail!' Enter a Messenger.)*

**Cassio.** What noise?
**Messenger.** The town is empty; on the brow o' the sea
Stand ranks of people, and they cry 'A sail!'
**Cassio.** My hopes do shape him for the governor.

*(Guns heard.)*

**Second Gentleman.** They do discharge their shot of courtesy;
Our friends at least.
**Cassio.** I pray you, sir, go forth.
And give us truth who 'tis that is arriv'd.
**Second Gentleman.** I shall.                          *(Exit.)*   60
**Montano.** But, good lieutenant, is your general wiv'd?
**Cassio.** Most fortunately: he hath achiev'd a maid
That paragons[195] description and wild fame;
One that excels the quirks[196] of blazoning pens,

---

[191] Till our (straining) eyes can no longer distinguish sea and sky.    [192] Admitted and proven to be expert.    [193] Overindulged.    [194] With good chance of being fulfilled.    [195] Exceeds, surpasses.
[196] Ingenuities.

And in th' essential vesture of creation[197]
Does tire the ingener.[198]

*(Re-enter Second Gentleman.)*

               How now! who has put in?
**Second Gentleman.**  'Tis one Iago, ancient to the general.
**Cassio.**  He has had most favourable and happy speed:
  Tempests themselves, high seas, and howling winds,
  The gutter'd[199] rocks, and congregated sands,          70
  Traitors ensteep'd[200] to clog the guiltless keel,
  As having sense of beauty, do omit
  Their mortal[201] natures, letting go safely by
  The divine Desdemona.
**Montano.**            What is she?
**Cassio.**  She that I spake of, our great captain's captain,
  Left in the conduct of the bold Iago,
  Whose footing[202] here anticipates our thoughts
  A se'nnight's[203] speed. Great Jove, Othello guard,
  And swell his sail with thine own powerful breath,
  That he may bless this bay with his tall[204] ship,      80
  Make love's quick pants in Desdemona's arms,
  Give renew'd fire to our extinct spirits,
  And bring all Cyprus comfort!

*(Enter Desdemona, Emilia, Iago, Roderigo, and Attendants.)*

                   O! behold,
  The riches of the ship is come on shore.
  Ye men of Cyprus, let her have your knees.
  Hail to thee, lady! and the grace of heaven,
  Before, behind thee, and on every hand,
  Enwheel thee round!
**Desdemona.**        I thank you, valiant Cassio.
  What tidings can you tell me of my lord?
**Cassio.**  He is not yet arriv'd; nor know I aught        90
  But that he's well, and will be shortly here.
**Desdemona.**  O! but I fear — How lost you company?
**Cassio.**  The great contention of the sea and skies
  Parted our fellowship. But hark! a sail.

*(Cry within, 'A sail — a sail!' Guns heard.)*

**Second Gentleman.**  They give their greeting to the citadel:
  This likewise is a friend.

---

[197] I.e., just as God made her; or: (even in) the (mere) essence of human nature.   [198] Inventor (i.e., of her praises?).   [199] Jagged; or: submerged.   [200] Submerged.   [201] Deadly.   [202] Landing.   [203] Week's.
[204] Brave.

**Cassio.**                    See for the news!                    *(Exit Gentleman.)*
Good ancient, you are welcome: — *(To Emilia.)* welcome, mistress.
Let it not gall your patience, good Iago,
That I extend my manners; 'tis my breeding
That gives me this bold show of courtesy.                    *(Kissing her.)*   100
**Iago.**   Sir, would she give you so much of her lips
As of her tongue she oft bestows on me,
You'd have enough.
**Desdemona.**         Alas! she has no speech.
**Iago.**   In faith, too much;
I find it still when I have list[205] to sleep:
Marry, before your ladyship, I grant,
She puts her tongue a little in her heart,
And chides with thinking.[206]
**Emilia.**   You have little cause to say so.
**Iago.**   Come on, come on; you are pictures[207] out of doors,                    110
Bells[208] in your parlours, wild cats in your kitchens,
Saints in your injuries, devils being offended,
Players[209] in your housewifery,[210] and housewives[211] in your beds.
**Desdemona.**   O! fie upon thee, slanderer.
**Iago.**   Nay, it is true, or else I am a Turk:
You rise to play and go to bed to work.
**Emilia.**   You shall not write my praise.
**Iago.**                    No, let me not.
**Desdemona.**   What wouldst thou write of me, if thou shouldst praise me?
**Iago.**   O gentle lady, do not put me to 't,
For I am nothing if not critical.                    120
**Desdemona.**   Come on; assay. There's one gone to the harbour?
**Iago.**   Ay, madam.
**Desdemona** *(aside).*   I am not merry, but I do beguile
The thing I am by seeming otherwise.
*(To Iago.)* Come, how wouldst thou praise me?
**Iago.**   I am about it; but indeed my invention
Comes from my pate[212] as birdlime does from frize;[213]
It plucks out brains and all: but my muse labours
And thus she is deliver'd.
If she be fair and wise, fairness and wit,                    130
The one's for use, the other useth it.
**Desdemona.**   Well prais'd! How if she be black and witty?
**Iago.**   If she be black,[214] and thereto have a wit,
She'll find a white that shall her blackness fit.
**Desdemona.**   Worse and worse.

---

[205] Wish.   [206] I.e., without words.   [207] I.e., made up, "painted."   [208] I.e., jangly.   [209] Triflers, wastrels.
[210] Housekeeping.   [211] (1) Hussies, (2) (unduly) frugal with their sexual favors, (3) businesslike, serious.
[212] Head.   [213] Coarse cloth.   [214] Brunette, dark haired.

**Emilia.**  How if fair and foolish?

**Iago.**  She never yet was foolish that was fair,
For even her folly[215] help'd to an heir.

**Desdemona.**  These are old fond[216] paradoxes to make fools laugh i' the alehouse.
What miserable praise has thou for her that's foul and foolish?                    140

**Iago.**  There's none so foul and foolish thereunto,
But does foul pranks which fair and wise ones do.

**Desdemona.**  O heavy ignorance! thou praisest the worst best. But what praise
couldst thou bestow on a deserving woman indeed, one that, in the authority of
her merit, did justly put on the vouch[217] of very malice itself?

**Iago.**  She that was ever fair and never proud,
Had tongue at will and yet was never loud,
Never lack'd gold and yet went never gay,
Fled from her wish and yet said 'Now I may,'
She that being anger'd, her revenge being nigh,                    150
Bade her wrong stay and her displeasure fly,
She that in wisdom never was so frail
To change the cod's head for the salmon's tail,[218]
She that could think and ne'er disclose her mind,
See suitors following and not look behind,
She was a wight, if ever such wight were, —

**Desdemona.**  To do what?

**Iago.**  To suckle fools and chronicle small beer.[219]

**Desdemona.**  O most lame and impotent conclusion! Do not learn of him, Emilia,
though he be thy husband. How say you, Cassio? Is he not a most profane and
liberal[220] counsellor?                    161

**Cassio.**  He speaks home,[221] madam; you may relish him more in the soldier than
in[222] the scholar.

**Iago** *(aside).*  He takes her by the palm: ay, well said, whisper; with as little a web
as this will I ensnare as great a fly as Cassio. Ay, smile upon her, do; I will gyve[223]
thee in thine own courtship. You say true, 'tis so, indeed. If such tricks as these
strip you out of your lieutenantry, it had been better you had not kissed your
three fingers so oft, which now again you are most apt to play the sir[224] in. Very
good; well kissed! an excellent courtesy! 'tis so, indeed. Yet again your fingers
to your lips? would they were clyster-pipes[225] for your sake! *(A trumpet heard.)*
The Moor! I know his trumpet.[226]                    171

**Cassio.**  'Tis truly so.

**Desdemona.**  Let's meet him and receive him.

**Cassio.**  Lo! where he comes.

*(Enter Othello and Attendants.)*

---

[215] Here also, wantonness.    [216] Foolish.    [217] Compel the approval.    [218] To make a foolish
exchange (a bawdy secondary meaning is probable).    [219] I.e., keep petty household accounts.
[220] Free-spoken, licentious.    [221] To the mark, aptly.    [222] As . . . as.    [223] Entangle.    [224] Gentleman.
[225] Syringes, enema pipes.    [226] I.e., Othello's distinctive trumpet call.

**Othello.** O my fair warrior!

**Desdemona.**                    My dear Othello!

**Othello.** It gives me wonder great as my content
  To see you here before me. O my soul's joy!
  If after every tempest come such calms,
  May the winds blow till they have waken'd death!
  And let the labouring bark climb hills of seas          180
  Olympus-high, and duck again as low
  As hell's from heaven! If it were now to die,
  'Twere now to be most happy, for I fear
  My soul hath her content so absolute
  That not another comfort like to this
  Succeeds in unknown fate.

**Desdemona.**                    The heavens forbid
  But that our loves and comforts should increase
  Even as our days do grow!

**Othello.** Amen to that, sweet powers!
  I cannot speak enough of this content;          190
  It stops me here; it is too much of joy:
  And this, and this, the greatest discords be          *(Kissing her.)*
  That e'er our hearts shall make!

**Iago** *(aside).*                    O! you are well tun'd now,
  But I'll set down[227] the pegs that make this music,
  As honest as I am.

**Othello.**          Come, let us to the castle.
  News, friends; our wars are done, the Turks are drown'd.
  How does my old acquaintance of this isle?
  Honey, you shall be well desir'd[228] in Cyprus;
  I have found great love amongst them. O my sweet,
  I prattle out of fashion, and I dote          200
  In mine own comforts. I prithee, good Iago,
  Go to the bay and disembark my coffers.
  Bring thou the master to the citadel;
  He is a good one, and his worthiness
  Does challenge much respect. Come, Desdemona,
  Once more well met at Cyprus.

*(Exeunt all except Iago and Roderigo.)*

**Iago.** Do thou meet me presently at the harbour. Come hither. If thou be'st valiant,
  as they say base men being in love have then a nobility in their natures more
  than is native to them, list[229] me. The lieutenant to-night watches on the court of
  guard:[230] first, I must tell thee this, Desdemona is directly in love with him.          210

**Roderigo.** With him! Why, 'tis not possible.

---

[227] Loosen.     [228] Welcomed.     [229] Listen to.     [230] Guardhouse.

**Iago.** Lay thy finger thus, and let thy soul be instructed. Mark me with what violence she first loved the Moor but for bragging and telling her fantastical lies; and will she love him still for prating? let not thy discreet heart think it. Her eye must be fed; and what delight shall she have to look on the devil? When the blood is made dull with the act of sport, there should be, again to inflame it, and to give satiety a fresh appetite, loveliness in favour, sympathy in years, manners, and beauties; all which the Moor is defective in. Now, for want of these required conveniences, her delicate tenderness will find itself abused, begin to heave the gorge,[231] disrelish and abhor the Moor; very nature will instruct her in it, and compel her to some second choice. Now, sir, this granted, as it is a most pregnant[232] and unforced position, who stands so eminently in the degree of this fortune as Cassio does? a knave very voluble, no further conscionable[233] than in putting on the mere form of civil and humane seeming, for the better compassing of his salt[234] and most hidden loose affection? why, none; why, none: a slipper[235] and subtle knave, a finder-out of occasions, that has an eye can stamp and counterfeit advantages, though true advantage never present itself; a devilish knave! Besides, the knave is handsome, young, and hath all those requisites in him that folly and green minds look after; a pestilent complete knave! and the woman hath found him already.                                                                          231

**Roderigo.** I cannot believe that in her; she is full of most blessed condition.

**Iago.** Blessed fig's end! the wine she drinks is made of grapes;[236] if she had been blessed she would never have loved the Moor; blessed pudding! Didst thou not see her paddle with the palm of his hand? didst not mark that?

**Roderigo.** Yes, that I did; but that was but courtesy.

**Iago.** Lechery, by this hand! an index[237] and obscure prologue to the history of lust and foul thoughts. They met so near with their lips, that their breaths embraced together. Villainous thoughts, Roderigo! when these mutualities so marshal the way, hard at hand comes the master and main exercise, the incorporate[238] conclusion. Pish![239] But, sir, be you ruled by me: I have brought you from Venice. Watch you to-night; for the command, I'll lay 't upon you: Cassio knows you not. I'll not be far from you: do you find some occasion to anger Cassio, either by speaking too loud, or tainting[240] his discipline; or from what other course you please, which the time shall more favourably minister.          245

**Roderigo.** Well.

**Iago.** Sir, he is rash and very sudden in choler, and haply may strike at you: provoke him, that he may; for even out of that will I cause these of Cyprus to mutiny, whose qualification[241] shall come into no true taste again but by the displanting of Cassio. So shall you have a shorter journey to your desires by the means I shall then have to prefer[242] them; and the impediment most profitably removed, without the which there were no expectation of our prosperity.

**Roderigo.** I will do this, if I can bring it to any opportunity.

---

[231] Vomit.    [232] Obvious.    [233] Conscientious.    [234] Lecherous.    [235] Slippery.    [236] I.e., she is only flesh and blood.    [237] Pointer.    [238] Carnal.    [239] Exclamation of disgust.    [240] Disparaging.    [241] Appeasement.    [242] Advance.

**Iago.**  I warrant thee. Meet me by and by at the citadel: I must fetch his necessaries
ashore. Farewell.

**Roderigo.**  Adieu.                                                                     *(Exit.)*

**Iago.**  That Cassio loves her, I do well believe it;
That she loves him, 'tis apt,²⁴³ and of great credit:²⁴⁴
The Moor, howbeit that I endure him not,                                           260
Is of a constant, loving, noble nature;
And I dare think he'll prove to Desdemona
A most dear²⁴⁵ husband. Now, I do love her too;
Not out of absolute lust, — though peradventure²⁴⁶
I stand accountant²⁴⁷ for as great a sin, —
But partly led to diet my revenge,
For that I do suspect the lusty Moor
Hath leap'd into my seat; the thought whereof
Doth like a poisonous mineral gnaw my inwards;
And nothing can or shall content my soul                                           270
Till I am even'd with him, wife for wife;
Or failing so, yet that I put the Moor
At least into a jealousy so strong
That judgment cannot cure. Which thing to do,
If this poor trash²⁴⁸ of Venice, whom I trash²⁴⁹
For his quick hunting, stand the putting-on,²⁵⁰
I'll have our Michael Cassio on the hip;
Abuse him to the Moor in the rank garb,²⁵¹
For I fear Cassio with my night-cap too,
Make the Moor thank me, love me, and reward me                                    280
For making him egregiously an ass
And practising upon his peace and quiet
Even to madness. 'Tis here, but yet confus'd:
Knavery's plain face is never seen till us'd.                                       *(Exit.)*

**Scene 2.**   A Street.

*(Enter a Herald with a proclamation; people following.)*

**Herald.**   It is Othello's pleasure, our noble and valiant general, that, upon certain
tidings now arrived, importing the mere²⁵² perdition of the Turkish fleet, every
man put himself into triumph; some to dance, some to make bonfires, each man
to what sport and revels his addiction leads him; for, besides these beneficial news,
it is the celebration of his nuptial. So much was his pleasure should be proclaimed.
All offices²⁵³ are open, and there is full liberty of feasting from this present hour
of five till the bell have told eleven. Heaven bless the isle of Cyprus and our noble
general Othello!                                                                   *(Exeunt.)*

---

²⁴³ Natural, probable.    ²⁴⁴ Easily believable.    ²⁴⁵ A pun on the word in the sense of expensive.
²⁴⁶ Perchance, perhaps.    ²⁴⁷ Accountable.    ²⁴⁸ I.e., Roderigo.    ²⁴⁹ Check, control.    ²⁵⁰ Inciting.
²⁵¹ Gross manner.    ²⁵² Utter.    ²⁵³ Kitchens and storehouses.

**Scene 3.** A Hall in the Castle.

*(Enter Othello, Desdemona, Cassio, and Attendants.)*

**Othello.** Good Michael, look you to the guard to-night:
Let's teach ourselves that honourable stop,[254]
Not to outsport discretion.
**Cassio.** Iago hath direction what to do:
But, notwithstanding, with my personal[255] eye
Will I look to 't.
**Othello.**          Iago is most honest.
Michael, good-night; to-morrow with your earliest
Let me have speech with you. *(To Desdemona.)* Come, my dear love,
The purchase made, the fruits are to ensue;
That profit's yet to come 'twixt me and you.                    10
Good-night.

*(Exeunt Othello, Desdemona, and Attendants.)*

*(Enter Iago.)*

**Cassio.** Welcome, Iago; we must to the watch.
**Iago.** Not this hour, lieutenant; 'tis not yet ten o' the clock. Our general casts us thus early for the love of his Desdemona, who let us not therefore blame; he hath not yet made wanton the night with her, and she is sport for Jove.
**Cassio.** She's a most exquisite lady.
**Iago.** And, I'll warrant her, full of game.
**Cassio.** Indeed, she is a most fresh and delicate creature.
**Iago.** What an eye she has! methinks it sounds a parley[256] of provocation.
**Cassio.** An inviting eye: and yet methinks right modest.                    20
**Iago.** And when she speaks, is it not an alarum[257] to love?
**Cassio.** She is indeed perfection.
**Iago.** Well, happiness to their sheets! Come, lieutenant, I have a stoup of wine, and here without are a brace[258] of Cyprus gallants that would fain have a measure to the health of black Othello.
**Cassio.** Not to-night, good Iago: I have very poor and unhappy brains for drinking: I could well wish courtesy would invent some other custom of entertainment.
**Iago.** O! they are our friends; but one cup: I'll drink for you.                    29
**Cassio.** I have drunk but one cup to-night, and that was craftily qualified[259] too, and, behold, what innovation[260] it makes here: I am unfortunate in the infirmity, and dare not task my weakness with any more.
**Iago.** What, man! 'tis a night of revels; the gallants desire it.

---

[254] Discipline.   [255] Own.   [256] Conference.   [257] Call-to-arms.   [258] Pair.   [259] Diluted.   [260] Change, revolution.

**Cassio.** Where are they?

**Iago.** Here at the door; I pray you, call them in.

**Cassio.** I'll do 't; but it dislikes me.                                                                              *(Exit.)*

**Iago.** If I can fasten but one cup upon him,
With that which he hath drunk to-night already,
He'll be as full of quarrel and offence
As my young mistress' dog. Now, my sick fool Roderigo,                                    40
Whom love has turn'd almost the wrong side out,
To Desdemona hath to-night carous'd
Potations pottle-deep;[261] and he's to watch.
Three lads of Cyprus, noble swelling spirits,
That hold their honours in a wary distance,[262]
The very elements[263] of this warlike isle,
Have I to-night fluster'd with flowing cups,
And they watch too. Now, 'mongst this flock of drunkards,
Am I to put our Cassio in some action
That may offend the isle. But here they come.                                                   50
If consequence[264] do but approve my dream,
My boat sails freely, both with wind and stream.

*(Re-enter Cassio, with him Montano, and Gentlemen. Servant following with wine.)*

**Cassio.** 'Fore God, they have given me a rouse[265] already.

**Montano.** Good faith, a little one; not past a pint, as I am a soldier.

**Iago.** Some wine, ho!
*(Sings.)* And let me the canakin[266] clink, clink;
And let me the canakin clink:
A soldier's a man;
A life's but a span;
Why then let a soldier drink.                                                                         60
Some wine, boys!

**Cassio.** 'Fore God, an excellent song.

**Iago.** I learned it in England, where indeed they are most potent in potting; your Dane, your German, and your swag-bellied[267] Hollander, — drink ho! — are nothing to your English.

**Cassio.** Is your Englishman so expert in his drinking?

**Iago.** Why, he drinks you[268] with facility your Dane dead drunk; he sweats not to overthrow your Almain;[269] he gives your Hollander a vomit ere the next pottle can be filled.

**Cassio.** To the health of our general!                                                                  70

**Montano.** I am for it, lieutenant; and I'll do you justice.

---

[261] Bottoms-up.    [262] Take offense easily.    [263] Types.    [264] Succeeding events.    [265] Drink.    [266] Small cup.    [267] With a pendulous belly.    [268] The "ethical" dative, i.e., you'll see that he drinks.    [269] German.

**Iago.**  O sweet England!
  (*Sings.*)  King Stephen was a worthy peer,
        His breeches cost him but a crown;
     He held them sixpence all too dear,
        With that he call'd the tailor lown.[270]
     He was a wight of high renown,
        And thou art but of low degree:
     'Tis pride that pulls the country down,
        Then take thine auld cloak about thee.      80
  Some wine, ho!
**Cassio.**  Why, this is a more exquisite song than the other.
**Iago.**  Will you hear 't again?
**Cassio.**  No; for I hold him to be unworthy of his place that does those things. Well, God's above all; and there be souls must be saved, and there be souls must not be saved.
**Iago.**  It's true, good lieutenant.
**Cassio.**  For mine own part, — no offence to the general, nor any man of quality, — I hope to be saved.
**Iago.**  And so do I too, lieutenant.      90
**Cassio.**  Ay; but, by your leave, not before me; the lieutenant is to be saved before the ancient. Let's have no more of this; let's to our affairs. God forgive us our sins! Gentlemen, let's look to our business. Do not think, gentlemen, I am drunk: this is my ancient; this is my right hand, and this is my left hand. I am not drunk now; I can stand well enough, and speak well enough.
**All.**  Excellent well.
**Cassio.**  Why, very well, then; you must not think then that I am drunk.

                                            (*Exit.*)

**Montano.**  To the platform, masters; come, let's set the watch.
**Iago.**  You see this fellow that is gone before;
  He is a soldier fit to stand by Caesar      100
  And give direction; and do but see his vice;
  'Tis to his virtue a just equinox,[271]
  The one as long as the other; 'tis pity of him.
  I fear the trust Othello puts him in,
  On some odd time of his infirmity,
  Will shake this island.
**Montano.**              But is he often thus?
**Iago.**  'Tis evermore the prologue to his sleep;
  He'll watch the horologe a double set,[272]
  If drink rock not his cradle.
**Montano.**                It were well
  The general were put in mind of it.      110
  Perhaps he sees it not; or his good nature

---

[270] Lout, rascal.    [271] Equivalent.    [272] Stand watch twice twelve hours.

Prizes the virtue that appears in Cassio,
And looks not on his evils. Is not this true?

*(Enter Roderigo.)*

**Iago** *(aside to him).*  How now, Roderigo!
　I pray you, after the lieutenant; go.　　　　　　　　　*(Exit Roderigo.)*
**Montano.**  And 'tis great pity that the noble Moor
　Should hazard such a place as his own second
　With one of an ingraft[273] infirmity;
　It were an honest action to say
　So to the Moor.
**Iago.**　　　　　Not I, for this fair island:　　　　　　　120
　I do love Cassio well, and would do much
　To cure him of this evil. But hark! what noise?

*(Cry within, 'Help! Help!' Re-enter Cassio, driving in Roderigo.)*

**Cassio.**  You rogue! you rascal!
**Montano.**　　　　　　　　What's the matter, lieutenant?
**Cassio.**  A knave teach me my duty!
　I'll beat the knave into a twiggen[274] bottle.
**Roderigo.**  Beat me!
**Cassio.**　　　　　Dost thou prate, rogue?

*(Striking Roderigo.)*

**Montano** *(staying him).*  Nay, good lieutenant;
　I pray you, sir, hold your hand.
**Cassio.**　　　　　　　　Let me go, sir,
　Or I'll knock you o'er the mazzard.[275]
**Montano.**　　　　　　　　Come, come; you're drunk.
**Cassio.**  Drunk!　　　　　　　　　　　　　　　　　130

*(They fight.)*

**Iago** *(aside to Roderigo).*  Away, I say! go out, and cry a mutiny.

　　　　　　　　　　　　　　　　　　　　　*(Exit Roderigo.)*

　Nay, good lieutenant! God's will, gentlemen!
　Help, ho! Lieutenant! sir! Montano! sir!
　Help, masters! Here's a goodly watch indeed!

*(Bell rings.)*

　Who's that that rings the bell? Diablo, ho!

---

[273] Ingrained.　　[274] Wicker.　　[275] Head.

The town will rise: God's will! lieutenant, hold!
You will be sham'd for ever.

*(Re-enter Othello and Attendants.)*

**Othello.**               What is the matter here?
**Montano.** 'Zounds! I bleed still; I am hurt to the death.

*(He faints.)*

**Othello.** Hold, for your lives!               140
**Iago.** Hold, ho, lieutenant! Sir! Montano! gentlemen!
  Have you forgot all sense of place and duty?
  Hold! the general speaks to you; hold for shame!
**Othello.** Why, how now, ho! from whence ariseth this?
  Are we turn'd Turks, and to ourselves do that
  Which heaven hath forbid the Ottomites?
  For Christian shame put by this barbarous brawl;
  He that stirs next to carve for his own rage
  Holds his soul light; he dies upon his motion.
  Silence that dreadful bell! it frights the isle     150
  From her propriety. What is the matter, masters?
  Honest Iago, that look'st dead with grieving,
  Speak, who began this? On thy love, I charge thee.
**Iago.** I do not know; friends all but now, even now,
  In quarter[276] and in terms like bride and groom
  Devesting[277] them for bed; and then, but now, —
  As if some planet had unwitted men, —
  Swords out, and tilting one at other's breast,
  In opposition bloody. I cannot speak
  Any beginning to this peevish odds,[278]     160
  And would in action glorious I had lost
  Those legs that brought me to a part of it!
**Othello.** How comes it, Michael, you are thus forgot?
**Cassio.** I pray you, pardon me; I cannot speak.
**Othello.** Worthy Montano, you were wont be civil;
  The gravity and stillness of your youth
  The world hath noted, and your name is great
  In mouths of wisest censure:[279] what's the matter,
  That you unlace[280] your reputation thus
  And spend your rich opinion[281] for the name     170
  Of a night-brawler? give me answer to it.
**Montano.** Worthy Othello, I am hurt to danger;
  Your officer, Iago, can inform you,

---

[276] On duty.    [277] Undressing.    [278] Silly quarrel.    [279] Judgment.    [280] Undo.    [281] High reputation.

While I spare speech, which something now offends[282] me,
Of all that I do know; nor know I aught
By me that's said or done amiss this night,
Unless self-charity be sometimes a vice,
And to defend ourselves it be a sin
When violence assails us.

**Othello.**                    Now, by heaven,
My blood begins my safer guides to rule,                    180
And passion, having my best judgment collied,[283]
Assays to lead the way. If I once stir,
Or do but lift this arm, the best of you
Shall sink in my rebuke. Give me to know
How this foul rout began, who set it on;
And he that is approv'd[284] in this offence,
Though he had twinn'd with me — both at a birth —
Shall lose me. What! in a town of war,
Yet wild, the people's hearts brimful of fear,
To manage private and domestic quarrel,                    190
In night, and on the court and guard of safety!
'Tis monstrous. Iago, who began 't?

**Montano.**  If partially affin'd,[285] or leagu'd in office,
Thou dost deliver more or less than truth,
Thou art not soldier.

**Iago.**                    Touch me not so near;
I had rather[286] have this tongue cut from my mouth
Than it should do offence to Michael Cassio;
Yet, I persuade myself, to speak the truth
Shall nothing wrong him. Thus it is, general.
Montano and myself being in speech,                    200
There comes a fellow crying out for help,
And Cassio following with determin'd sword
To execute upon him. Sir, this gentleman
Steps in to Cassio, and entreats his pause;
Myself the crying fellow did pursue,
Lest by his clamour, as it so fell out,
The town might fall in fright; he, swift of foot,
Outran my purpose, and I return'd the rather
For that I heard the clink and fall of swords,
And Cassio high in oath, which till to-night                    210
I ne'er might say before. When I came back, —
For this was brief, — I found them close together,
At blow and thrust, even as again they were
When you yourself did part them.

---

[282] Pains, harms.    [283] Clouded.    [284] Proved (i.e., guilty).    [285] Favorably biased (by ties of friendship, or as Cassio's fellow officer).    [286] More quickly.

More of this matter can I not report:
But men are men; the best sometimes forget:
Though Cassio did some little wrong to him,
As men in rage strike those that wish them best,
Yet, surely Cassio, I believe, receiv'd
From him that fled some strange indignity, 220
Which patience could not pass.
**Othello.**                                        I know, Iago.
Thy honesty and love doth mince[287] this matter,
Making it light to Cassio. Cassio, I love thee;
But never more be officer of mine.

*(Enter Desdemona, attended.)*

Look! if my gentle love be not rais'd up;
    *(To Cassio.)* I'll make thee an example.
**Desdemona.**                                What's the matter?
**Othello.** All's well now, sweeting; come away to bed.
Sir, for your hurts, myself will be your surgeon.
Lead him off.                                      *(Montano is led off.)*
Iago, look with care about the town, 230
And silence those whom this vile brawl distracted.
Come, Desdemona; 'tis the soldier's life,
To have their balmy slumbers wak'd with strife.

*(Exeunt all but Iago and Cassio.)*

**Iago.** What! are you hurt, lieutenant?
**Cassio.** Ay; past all surgery.
**Iago.** Marry, heaven forbid!
**Cassio.** Reputation, reputation, reputation! O! I have lost my reputation. I have
lost the immortal part of myself, and what remains is bestial. My reputation,
Iago, my reputation!
**Iago.** As I am an honest man, I thought you had received some bodily wound;
there is more offence in that than in reputation. Reputation is an idle and
most false imposition;[288] oft got without merit, and lost without deserving:
you have lost no reputation at all, unless you repute yourself such a loser.
What! man; there are ways to recover the general again; you are but now cast
in his mood,[289] a punishment more in policy[290] than in malice; even so as one
would beat his offenceless dog to affright an imperious lion. Sue to him again,
and he is yours.
**Cassio.** I will rather sue to be despised than to deceive so good a commander with
so slight, so drunken and so indiscreet an officer. Drunk! and speak parrot![291]

---

[287] Tone down.    [288] Something external.    [289] Dismissed because he is angry.    [290] I.e., more for
the sake of the example or to show his fairness.    [291] I.e., without thinking.

and squabble, swagger, swear, and discourse fustian[292] with one's own shadow! O thou invisible spirit of wine! if thou hast no name to be known by, let us call thee devil!

**Iago.** What was he that you followed with your sword? What hath he done to you?

**Cassio.** I know not.

**Iago.** Is 't possible?

**Cassio.** I remember a mass of things, but nothing distinctly; a quarrel, but nothing wherefore. O God! that men should put an enemy in their mouths to steal away their brains; that we should, with joy, pleasance,[293] revel, and applause, transform ourselves into beasts. 260

**Iago.** Why, but you are now well enough; how came you thus recovered?

**Cassio.** It hath pleased the devil drunkenness to give place to the devil wrath; one unperfectness shows me another, to make me frankly despise myself.

**Iago.** Come, you are too severe a moraler. As the time, the place, and the condition of this country stands, I could heartily wish this had not befallen, but since it is as it is, mend it for your own good.

**Cassio.** I will ask him for my place again; he shall tell me I am a drunkard! Had I as many mouths as Hydra,[294] such an answer would stop them all. To be now a sensible man, by and by a fool, and presently a beast! O strange! Every inordinate cup is unblessed and the ingredient[295] is a devil. 270

**Iago.** Come, come; good wine is a good familiar creature if it be well used; exclaim no more against it. And, good lieutenant, I think you think I love you.

**Cassio.** I have well approved it, sir. I drunk!

**Iago.** You or any man living may be drunk at some time, man. I'll tell you what you shall do. Our general's wife is now the general; I may say so in this respect, for that he hath devoted and given up himself to the contemplation, mark, and denotement of her parts and graces: confess yourself freely to her; importune her; she'll help to put you in your place again. She is of so free, so kind, so apt, so blessed a disposition, that she holds it a vice in her goodness not to do more than she is requested. This broken joint between you and her husband entreat her to splinter;[296] and, my fortunes against any lay[297] worth naming, this crack of your love shall grow stronger than it was before. 282

**Cassio.** You advise me well.

**Iago.** I protest, in the sincerity of love and honest kindness.

**Cassio.** I think it freely; and betimes in the morning I will beseech the virtuous Desdemona to undertake for me. I am desperate of my fortunes if they check me here.

**Iago.** You are in the right. Good-night, lieutenant; I must to the watch.

**Cassio.** Good-night, honest Iago! *(Exit.)*

**Iago.** And what's he then that says I play the villain? 290
When this advice is free I give and honest,
Probal[298] to thinking and indeed the course

---

[292] I.e., nonsense.   [293] Pleasure.   [294] Many-headed snake in Greek mythology.   [295] Contents.
[296] Bind up with splints.   [297] Wager.   [298] Provable.

To win the Moor again? For 'tis most easy
The inclining Desdemona to subdue
In any honest suit; she's fram'd as fruitful[299]
As the free elements. And then for her
To win the Moor, were 't to renounce his baptism,
All seals and symbols of redeemed sin,
His soul is so enfetter'd to her love,
That she may make, unmake, do what she list, 300
Even as her appetite shall play the god
With his weak function.[300] How am I then a villain
To counsel Cassio to this parallel[301] course,
Directly to his good? Divinity of hell!
When devils will the blackest sins put on,
They do suggest at first with heavenly shows,
As I do now; for while this honest fool
Plies Desdemona to repair his fortunes,
And she for him pleads strongly to the Moor,
I'll pour this pestilence into his ear 310
That she repeals[302] him for her body's lust;
And, by how much she strives to do him good,
She shall undo her credit with the Moor.
So will I turn her virtue into pitch,
And out of her own goodness make the net
That shall enmesh them all.

*(Re-enter Roderigo.)*

**Iago.**                    How now, Roderigo!
**Roderigo.**  I do follow here in the chase, not like a hound that hunts, but one that
fills up the cry.[303] My money is almost spent; I have been to-night exceedingly
well cudgelled; and I think the issue will be, I shall have so much experience for
my pains; and so, with no money at all and a little more wit, return again to
Venice.
**Iago.**  How poor are they that have not patience!
What wound did ever heal but by degrees?
Thou know'st we work by wit and not by witchcraft,
And wit depends on dilatory time.
Does 't not go well? Cassio hath beaten thee,
And thou by that small hurt hast cashiered Cassio.
Though other things grow fair against the sun,
Yet fruits that blossom first will first be ripe:
Content thyself awhile. By the mass, 'tis morning; 330
Pleasure and action make the hours seem short.

---

[299] Generous.    [300] Faculties.    [301] Purposeful.    [302] I.e., seeks to recall.    [303] Pack (hunting term).

Retire thee; go where thou art billeted:
Away, I say; thou shalt know more hereafter:
Nay, get thee gone. *(Exit Roderigo.)* Two things are to be done,
My wife must move for Cassio to her mistress;
I'll set her on;
Myself the while to draw the Moor apart,
And bring him jump[304] when he may Cassio find
Soliciting his wife: ay, that's the way:
Dull not device by coldness and delay.                                    *(Exit.)*

## ACT III

**Scene 1.**    Cyprus. Before the Castle.

*(Enter Cassio, and some Musicians.)*

**Cassio.**  Masters, play here, I will content your pains;[305]
 Something that's brief; and bid 'Good-morrow, general.'        *(Music.)*

*(Enter Clown.)*

**Clown.**  Why, masters, have your instruments been in Naples, that they speak i'
 the nose[306] thus?
**First Musician.**  How, sir, how?
**Clown.**  Are these, I pray you, wind-instruments?
**First Musician.**  Ay, marry, are they, sir.
**Clown.**  O! thereby hangs a tale.
**First Musician.**  Whereby hangs a tale, sir?
**Clown.**  Marry, sir, by many a wind-instrument that I know. But, masters, here's
 money for you; and the general so likes your music, that he desires you, for love's
 sake, to make no more noise with it.                                        12
**First Musician.**  Well, sir, we will not.
**Clown.**  If you have any music that may not be heard, to 't again; but, as they say, to
 hear music the general does not greatly care.
**First Musician.**  We have none such, sir.
**Clown.**  Then put up your pipes in your bag, for I'll away.
 Go; vanish into air; away!                                    *(Exeunt Musicians.)*
**Cassio.**  Dost thou hear, mine honest friend?
**Clown.**  No, I hear not your honest friend; I hear you.                    20
**Cassio.**  Prithee, keep up thy quillets.[307] There's a poor piece of gold for thee. If the
 gentlewoman that attends the general's wife be stirring, tell her there's one Cas-
 sio entreats her a little favour of speech: wilt thou do this?

---

[304] At the exact moment.    [305] Reward your efforts.    [306] Naples was notorious for venereal disease, and syphilis was believed to affect the nose.    [307] Quibbles.

**Clown.** She is stirring, sir: if she will stir hither, I shall seem to notify unto her.

**Cassio.** Do, good my friend. *(Exit Clown.)*

*(Enter Iago.)*

In happy time, Iago.

**Iago.** You have not been a-bed, then?

**Cassio.** Why, no; the day had broke
Before we parted. I have made bold, Iago,
To send in to your wife; my suit to her
Is, that she will to virtuous Desdemona    30
Procure me some access.

**Iago.**           I'll send her to you presently;
And I'll devise a mean to draw the Moor
Out of the way, that your converse and business
May be more free.

**Cassio.** I humbly thank you for 't. *(Exit Iago.)*
         I never knew
A Florentine more kind and honest.[308]

*(Enter Emilia.)*

**Emilia.** Good-morrow, good lieutenant: I am sorry
For your displeasure,[309] but all will soon be well.
The general and his wife are talking of it,
And she speaks for you stoutly: the Moor replies    40
That he you hurt is of great fame in Cyprus
And great affinity,[310] and that in wholesome wisdom
He might not but refuse you; but he protests he loves you,
And needs no other suitor but his likings
To take the safest occasion by the front[311]
To bring you in again.[312]

**Cassio.**         Yet, I beseech you,
If you think fit, or that it may be done,
Give me advantage of some brief discourse
With Desdemona alone.

**Emilia.**         Pray you, come in:
I will bestow you where you shall have time    50
To speak your bosom[313] freely.

**Cassio.**         I am much bound to you. *(Exeunt.)*

**Scene 2.** A Room in the Castle.

*(Enter Othello, Iago, and Gentlemen.)*

---

[308] Cassio means that not even a fellow Florentine could behave to him in a friendlier fashion than does Iago.   [309] Disgrace.   [310] Family connection.   [311] Forelock.   [312] Restore you (to Othello's favor).   [313] Heart, inmost thoughts.

**Othello.**  These letters give, Iago, to the pilot,
  And by him do my duties to the senate;
  That done, I will be walking on the works;
  Repair there to me.
**Iago.**                      Well, my good lord, I'll do 't.
**Othello.**  This fortification, gentlemen, shall we see 't?
**Gentlemen.**  We'll wait upon your lordship.                           *(Exeunt.)*

**Scene 3.**   Before the Castle.

*(Enter Desdemona, Cassio, and Emilia.)*

**Desdemona.**  Be thou assur'd, good Cassio, I will do
  All my abilities in thy behalf.
**Emilia.**  Good madam, do: I warrant it grieves my husband,
  As if the case were his.
**Desdemona.**  O! that's an honest fellow. Do not doubt, Cassio,
  But I will have my lord and you again
  As friendly as you were.
**Cassio.**                      Bounteous madam,
  Whatever shall become of Michael Cassio,
  He's never any thing but your true servant.
**Desdemona.**  I know 't; I thank you. You do love my lord;                    10
  You have known him long; and be you well assur'd
  He shall in strangeness[314] stand no further off
  Than in a politic[315] distance.
**Cassio.**                      Ay, but, lady,
  That policy may either last so long,
  Or feed upon such nice[316] and waterish diet,
  Or breed itself so out of circumstance,
  That, I being absent and my place supplied,
  My general will forget my love and service.
**Desdemona.**  Do not doubt[317] that; before Emilia here
  I give thee warrant of thy place. Assure thee,                    20
  If I do vow a friendship, I'll perform it
  To the last article; my lord shall never rest;
  I'll watch him tame,[318] and talk him out of patience;
  His bed shall seem a school, his board a shrift;[319]
  I'll intermingle every thing he does
  With Cassio's suit. Therefore be merry, Cassio;
  For thy solicitor shall rather die
  Than give thy cause away.[320]

*(Enter Othello and Iago, at a distance.)*

---

[314] Aloofness.    [315] I.e., dictated by policy.    [316] Slight, trivial.    [317] Fear.    [318] Outwatch him (i.e., keep him awake) till he submits.    [319] Confessional.    [320] Abandon your cause.

**Emilia.**  Madam, here comes my lord.

**Cassio.**  Madam, I'll take my leave.                                      30

**Desdemona.**  Why, stay, and hear me speak.

**Cassio.**  Madam, not now; I am very ill at ease,
  Unfit for mine own purposes.

**Desdemona.**  Well, do your discretion.                *(Exit Cassio.)*

**Iago.**  Ha! I like not that.

**Othello.**                    What dost thou say?

**Iago.**  Nothing, my lord: or if — I know not what.

**Othello.**  Was not that Cassio parted from my wife?

**Iago.**  Cassio, my lord? No, sure, I cannot think it,
  That he would steal away so guilty-like,
  Seeing you coming.

**Othello.**                    I do believe 'twas he.               40

**Desdemona.**  How now, my lord!
  I have been talking with a suitor here,
  A man that languishes in your displeasure.

**Othello.**  Who is 't you mean?

**Desdemona.**  Why, your lieutenant, Cassio. Good my lord,
  If I have any grace or power to move you,
  His present[321] reconciliation take;
  For if he be not one that truly loves you,
  That errs in ignorance and not in cunning,
  I have no judgment in an honest face.               50
  I prithee[322] call him back.

**Othello.**                    Went he hence now?

**Desdemona.**  Ay, sooth; so humbled,
  That he hath left part of his grief with me,
  To suffer with him. Good love, call him back.

**Othello.**  Not now, sweet Desdemona; some other time.

**Desdemona.**  But shall 't be shortly?

**Othello.**                              The sooner, sweet, for you.

**Desdemona.**  Shall 't be to-night at supper?

**Othello.**                              No, not to-night.

**Desdemona.**  To-morrow dinner, then?

**Othello.**                              I shall not dine at home;
  I meet the captains at the citadel.

**Desdemona.**  Why, then, to-morrow night; or Tuesday morn;     60
  Or Tuesday noon, or night; or Wednesday morn:
  I prithee name the time, but let it not
  Exceed three days: in faith, he's penitent;
  And yet his trespass, in our common reason, —
  Save that they say, the wars must make examples
  Out of their best, — is not almost[323] a fault

---

[321] Immediate.    [322] Pray thee.    [323] Hardly.

To incur a private check.[324] When shall he come?
Tell me, Othello: I wonder in my soul,
What you could ask me, that I should deny,
Or stand so mammering[325] on. What! Michael Cassio,        70
That came a wooing with you, and so many a time,
When I have spoke of you dispraisingly,
Hath ta'en your part; to have so much to do
To bring him in! Trust me, I could do much, —

**Othello.** Prithee, no more; let him come when he will;
I deny thee nothing.

**Desdemona.**        Why, this is not a boon;
'Tis as I should entreat you wear your gloves,
Or feed on nourishing dishes, or keep you warm,
Or sue to you to do a peculiar profit
To your own person: nay, when I have a suit        80
Wherein I mean to touch your love indeed,
It shall be full of poise[326] and difficult weight,
And fearful to be granted.

**Othello.**        I will deny thee nothing:
Whereon, I do beseech thee, grant me this,
To leave me but a little to myself.

**Desdemona.** Shall I deny you? no: farewell, my lord.

**Othello.** Farewell, my Desdemona: I'll come to thee straight.

**Desdemona.** Emilia, come. Be as your fancies teach you;
Whate'er you be, I am obedient.        *(Exit, with Emilia.)*

**Othello.** Excellent wretch![327] Perdition catch my soul,        90
But I do love thee! and when I love thee not,
Chaos is[328] come again.

**Iago.** My noble lord, —

**Othello.**        What dost thou say, Iago?

**Iago.** Did Michael Cassio, when you woo'd my lady,
Know of your love?

**Othello.** He did, from first to last: why dost thou ask?

**Iago.** But for a satisfaction of my thought;
No further harm.

**Othello.**        Why of thy thought, Iago?

**Iago.** I did not think he had been acquainted with her.

**Othello.** O! yes; and went between us very oft.        100

**Iago.** Indeed!

**Othello.** Indeed! ay, indeed; discern'st thou aught in that?
Is he not honest?

**Iago.**        Honest, my lord?

**Othello.**        Honest! ay, honest.

---

[324] (Even) a private reprimand.   [325] Shilly-shallying.   [326] Weight.   [327] Here, a term of endearment.
[328] Will have.

**Iago.** My lord, for aught I know.

**Othello.** What dost thou think?

**Iago.** Think, my lord!

**Othello.** Think, my lord!
By heaven, he echoes me,
As if there were some monster in his thought
Too hideous to be shown. Thou dost mean something:
I heard thee say but now, thou lik'dst not that,
When Cassio left my wife; what didst not like? 110
And when I told thee he was of my counsel
In my whole course of wooing, thou criedst, 'Indeed!'
And didst contract and purse thy brow together,
As if thou then hadst shut up in thy brain
Some horrible conceit.[329] If thou dost love me,
Show me thy thought.

**Iago.** My lord, you know I love you.

**Othello.** I think thou dost;
And, for[330] I know thou art full of love and honesty,
And weigh'st thy words before thou givest them breath,
Therefore these stops[331] of thine fright me the more; 120
For such things in a false disloyal knave
Are tricks of custom, but in a man that's just
They are close dilations,[332] working from the heart
That passion cannot rule.

**Iago.** For Michael Cassio,
I dare be sworn I think that he is honest.

**Othello.** I think so too.

**Iago.** Men should be what they seem;
Or those that be not, would they might seem none!

**Othello.** Certain men should be what they seem.

**Iago.** Why then, I think Cassio's an honest man.

**Othello.** Nay, yet there's more in this. 130
I pray thee, speak to me as to thy thinkings,
As thou dost ruminate, and give thy worst of thoughts
The worst of words.

**Iago.** Good my lord, pardon me;
Though I am bound to every act of duty,
I am not bound to[333] that all slaves are free to.
Utter my thoughts? Why, say they are vile and false;
As where's that palace whereinto foul things
Sometimes intrude not? who has a breast so pure
But some uncleanly apprehensions[334]
Keep leets and law-days,[335] and in session sit 140
With meditations lawful?

---

[329] Fancy.    [330] Because.    [331] Interruptions, hesitations.    [332] Secret (i.e., involuntary, unconscious)
revelations.    [333] Bound with regard to.    [334] Conceptions.    [335] Sittings of the local courts.

**Othello.**  Thou dost conspire against thy friend, Iago,
If thou but think'st him wrong'd, and mak'st his ear
A stranger to thy thoughts.
**Iago.**                    I do beseech you,
Though I perchance am vicious in my guess, —
As, I confess, it is my nature's plague
To spy into abuses, and oft my jealousy[336]
Shapes faults that are not, — that your wisdom yet,
From one that so imperfectly conceits,
Would take no notice, nor build yourself a trouble                    150
Out of his scattering and unsure observance.
It were not for your quiet nor your good,
Nor for my manhood, honesty, or wisdom,
To let you know my thoughts.
**Othello.**                    What dost thou mean?
**Iago.**  Good name in man and woman, dear my lord,
Is the immediate jewel of[337] their souls:
Who steals my purse steals trash; 'tis something, nothing;
'Twas mine, 'tis his, and has been slave to thousands;
But he that filches from me my good name
Robs me of that which not enriches him,                    160
And makes me poor indeed.
**Othello.**  By heaven, I'll know thy thoughts.
**Iago.**  You cannot, if my heart were in your hand;
Nor shall not, whilst 'tis in my custody.
**Othello.**  Ha!
**Iago.**          O! beware, my lord, of jealousy;
It is the green-ey'd monster which doth mock
The meat it feeds on: that cuckold[338] lives in bliss
Who, certain of his fate, loves not his wronger;
But, O! what damned minutes tells[339] he o'er
Who dotes, yet doubts; suspects, yet soundly loves!                    170
**Othello.**  O misery!
**Iago.**  Poor and content is rich, and rich enough,
But riches fineless[340] is as poor as winter
To him that ever fears he shall be poor.
Good heaven, the souls of all my tribe defend
From jealousy!
**Othello.**          Why, why is this?
Think'st thou I'd make a life of jealousy,
To follow still the changes of the moon
With fresh suspicions? No; to be once in doubt
Is once to be resolved. Exchange me for a goat                    180

---

[336] Suspicion.    [337] Jewel closest to.    [338] Husband of an adulterous woman.    [339] Counts.
[340] Boundless.

When I shall turn the business of my soul
To such exsufflicate[341] and blown[342] surmises,
Matching thy inference. 'Tis not to make me jealous
To say my wife is fair, feeds well, loves company,
Is free of speech, sings, plays, and dances well;
Where virtue is, these are more virtuous:
Nor from mine own weak merits will I draw
The smallest fear, or doubt of her revolt;
For she had eyes, and chose me. No, Iago;
I'll see before I doubt; when I doubt, prove;                      190
And, on the proof, there is no more but this,
Away at once with love or jealousy!

**Iago.** I am glad of it; for now I shall have reason
To show the love and duty that I bear you
With franker spirit; therefore, as I am bound,
Receive it from me; I speak not yet of proof.
Look to your wife; observe her well with Cassio;
Wear your eye thus, not jealous nor secure:
I would not have your free and noble nature
Out of self-bounty[343] be abus'd; look to 't:                    200
I know our country disposition[344] well;
In Venice they do let heaven see the pranks
They dare not show their husbands; their best conscience
Is not to leave 't undone, but keep 't unknown.

**Othello.** Dost thou say so?

**Iago.** She did deceive her father, marrying you;
And when she seem'd to shake and fear your looks,
She lov'd them most.

**Othello.**             And so she did.

**Iago.**                         Why, go to,[345] then;
She that so young could give out such a seeming,
To seel her father's eyes up close as oak,                        210
He thought 'twas witchcraft; but I am much to blame;
I humbly do beseech you of your pardon
For too much loving you.

**Othello.**             I am bound to thee for ever.

**Iago.** I see, this hath a little dash'd your spirits.

**Othello.** Not a jot, not a jot.

**Iago.**                   I' faith, I fear it has.
I hope you will consider what is spoke
Comes from my love. But I do see you're mov'd;
I am to pray you not to strain my speech
To grosser issues nor to larger reach
Than to suspicion.                                                220

---

[341] Spat out (?).   [342] Fly-blown.   [343] Innate generosity.   [344] I.e., that of Venice.   [345] Colloquialism; here, something like "all right."

**Othello.** I will not.

**Iago.**                        Should you do so, my lord,
My speech should fall into such vile success
As my thoughts aim not at. Cassio's my worthy friend —
My lord, I see you're mov'd.

**Othello.**                        No, not much mov'd:
I do not think but Desdemona's honest.[346]

**Iago.** Long live she so! and long live you to think so!

**Othello.** And yet, how nature erring from itself, —

**Iago.** Ay, there's the point: as, to be bold with you,
Not to affect many proposed matches
Of her own clime,[347] complexion, and degree,[348]                    230
Whereto, we see, in all things nature tends;
Foh! one may smell in such, a will most rank,
Foul disproportion, thoughts unnatural.
But pardon me; I do not in position[349]
Distinctly[350] speak of her, though I may fear
Her will, recoiling[351] to her better judgment,
May fall to match you with her country forms
And happily[352] repent.

**Othello.**                        Farewell, farewell:
If more thou dost perceive, let me know more;
Set on thy wife to observe. Leave me, Iago.                    240

**Iago.** My lord, I take my leave.                        *(Going.)*

**Othello.** Why did I marry? This honest creature, doubtless,
Sees and knows more, much more, than he unfolds.

**Iago** *(returning).* My lord, I would I might entreat your honour
To scan this thing no further; leave it to time.
Although 'tis fit that Cassio have his place,
For, sure he fills it up with great ability,
Yet, if you please to hold him off awhile,
You shall by that perceive him and his means:
Note if your lady strain his entertainment[353]                    250
With any strong or vehement importunity;
Much will be seen in that. In the mean time,
Let me be thought too busy[354] in my fears,
As worthy cause I have to fear I am,
And hold her free, I do beseech your honour.

**Othello.** Fear not my government.

**Iago.** I once more take my leave.                        *(Exit.)*

**Othello.** This fellow's of exceeding honesty,
And knows all qualities, with a learned spirit,
Of human dealings; if I do prove her haggard,[355]                    260

---

[346] Chaste.    [347] Country.    [348] Social rank.    [349] In definite assertion.    [350] Specifically.    [351] Reverting.
[352] Perhaps.    [353] Urge his re-welcome (i.e., to Othello's trust and favor).    [354] Meddlesome.    [355] Wild hawk.

Though that her jesses[356] were my dear heart-strings,
I'd whistle her off and let her down the wind,[357]
To prey at fortune. Haply, for I am black,
And have not those soft parts of conversation
That chamberers[358] have, or, for I am declin'd
Into the vale of years — yet that's not much —
She's gone, I am abus'd;[359] and my relief
Must be to loathe her. O curse of marriage!
That we can call these delicate creatures ours,
And not their appetites. I had rather be a toad,                              270
And live upon the vapour of a dungeon,
Than keep a corner in the thing I love
For others' uses. Yet, 'tis the plague of great ones;
Prerogativ'd[360] are they less than the base;
'Tis destiny unshunnable, like death:
Even then this forked plague[361] is fated to us
When we do quicken.[362]
                          Look! where she comes.
If she be false, O! then heaven mocks itself.
I'll not believe it.

*(Re-enter Desdemona and Emilia.)*

**Desdemona.**          How now, my dear Othello!
   Your dinner and the generous[363] islanders                                 280
   By you invited, do attend your presence.
**Othello.**  I am to blame.
**Desdemona.**          Why do you speak so faintly?
   Are you not well?
**Othello.**  I have a pain upon my forehead here.[364]
**Desdemona.**  Faith, that's with watching; 'twill away again:
   Let me but bind it hard, within this hour
   It will be well.
**Othello.**          Your napkin[365] is too little:

*(She drops her handkerchief.)*

   Let it alone. Come, I'll go in with you.
**Desdemona.**  I am very sorry that you are not well.

                          *(Exeunt Othello and Desdemona.)*

---

[356] Leather thongs by which the hawk's legs were strapped to the trainer's wrist.     [357] I'd let her go and take care of herself.     [358] Courtiers; or (more specifically) gallants, frequenters of bed chambers.     [359] Deceived.     [360] Privileged.     [361] I.e., the cuckold's proverbial horns.     [362] Are conceived, come alive.     [363] Noble.     [364] Othello again refers to his cuckoldom.     [365] Handkerchief.

**Emilia.**  I am glad I have found this napkin;                                    290
This was her first remembrance from the Moor;
My wayward husband hath a hundred times
Woo'd me to steal it, but she so loves the token,
For he conjur'd her she should ever keep it,
That she reserves it evermore about her
To kiss and talk to. I'll have the work ta'en out,[366]
And giv 't Iago:
What he will do with it heaven knows, not I;
I nothing but[367] to please his fantasy.[368]

*(Enter Iago.)*

**Iago.**  How now! what do you here alone?                                300
**Emilia.**  Do not you chide; I have a thing for you.
**Iago.**  A thing for me? It is a common thing —
**Emilia.**  Ha!
**Iago.**  To have a foolish wife.
**Emilia.**  O! is that all? What will you give me now
For that same handkerchief?
**Iago.**                              What handkerchief?
**Emilia.**  What handkerchief!
Why, that the Moor first gave to Desdemona:
That which so often you did bid me steal.
**Iago.**  Hath stol'n it from her?                                       310
**Emilia.**  No, faith; she let it drop by negligence,
And, to the advantage, I, being there, took 't up.
Look, here it is.
**Iago.**              A good wench; give it me.
**Emilia.**  What will you do with 't, that you have been so earnest
To have me filch it?
**Iago.**                  Why, what's that to you?                *(Snatches it.)*
**Emilia.**  If it be not for some purpose of import
Give 't me again; poor lady! she'll run mad
When she shall lack it.
**Iago.**  Be not acknown on 't;[369] I have use for it.
Go, leave me.                                              *(Exit Emilia.)*
I will in Cassio's lodging lose this napkin,
And let him find it; trifles light as air
Are to the jealous confirmations strong
As proofs of holy writ; this may do something.
The Moor already changes with my poison:
Dangerous conceits are in their natures poisons,

---

[366] Pattern copied.    [367] I.e., only want.    [368] Whim.    [369] You know nothing about it.

Which at the first are scarce found to distaste,[370]
But with a little act upon the blood,
Burn like the mines of sulphur. I did say so:
Look! where he comes!

*(Enter Othello.)*

Not poppy,[371] nor mandragora,[372]                                                     330
Nor all the drowsy syrups[373] of the world,
Shall ever medicine thee to that sweet sleep
Which thou ow'dst yesterday.
**Othello.**                              Ha! ha! false to me?
**Iago.** Why, how now, general! no more of that.
**Othello.** Avaunt! be gone! thou hast set me on the rack;
I swear 'tis better to be much abus'd
Than but to know 't a little.
**Iago.**                            How now, my lord!
**Othello.** What sense had I of her stol'n hours of lust?
I saw 't not, thought it not, it harm'd not me;
I slept the next night well, was free and merry;                                      340
I found not Cassio's kisses on her lips;
He that is robb'd, not wanting what is stol'n,
Let him not know 't, and he's not robb'd at all.
**Iago.** I am sorry to hear this.
**Othello.** I had been happy, if the general camp,[374]
Pioners[375] and all, had tasted her sweet body,
So[376] I had nothing known. O! now, for ever
Farewell the tranquil mind; farewell content!
Farewell the plumed troop and the big wars
That make ambition virtue! O, farewell!                                               350
Farewell the neighing steed, and the shrill trump,
The spirit-stirring drum, the ear-piercing fife,
The royal banner, and all quality,
Pride, pomp, and circumstance[377] of glorious war!
And, O you mortal engines,[378] whose rude throats
The immortal Jove's dread clamours counterfeit,
Farewell! Othello's occupation's gone!
**Iago.** Is it possible, my lord?
**Othello.** Villain, be sure thou prove my love a whore,
Be sure of it; give me the ocular proof;                                               360
Or, by the worth of mine eternal soul,
Thou hadst been better have been born a dog
Than answer my wak'd wrath.

---

[370] Scarce can be tasted.   [371] Opium.   [372] A soporific.   [373] I.e., soporifics.   [374] Whole army.
[375] Lowest rank of manual laborers in the army.   [376] As long as.   [377] Pageantry.   [378] Deadly artillery.

**Iago.**                              Is 't come to this?

**Othello.**  Make me to see 't; or, at the least, so prove it,
That the probation[379] bear no hinge nor loop
To hang a doubt on; or woe upon thy life!

**Iago.**  My noble lord —

**Othello.**  If thou dost slander her and torture me,
Never pray more; abandon all remorse;
On horror's head horrors accumulate;                              370
Do deeds to make heaven weep, all earth amaz'd;
For nothing canst thou to damnation add
Greater than that.

**Iago.**                    O grace! O heaven forgive me!
Are you a man! have you a soul or sense?
God be wi' you; take mine office. O wretched fool!
That liv'st to make thine honesty a vice.
O monstrous world! Take note, take note, O world!
To be direct and honest is not safe.
I thank you for this profit,[380] and, from hence
I'll love no friend, sith[381] love breeds such offence.                              380

**Othello.**  Nay, stay; thou shouldst be honest.

**Iago.**  I should be wise; for honesty's a fool,
And loses that it works for.

**Othello.**                    By the world,
I think my wife be honest and think she is not;
I think that thou art just and think thou art not.
I'll have some proof. Her name, that was as fresh
As Dian's[382] visage, is now begrim'd and black
As mine own face. If there be cords or knives,
Poison or fire or suffocating streams,
I'll not endure it. Would I were satisfied!                              390

**Iago.**  I see, sir, you are eaten up with passion.
I do repent me that I put it to you.
You would be satisfied?

**Othello.**                    Would! nay, I will.

**Iago.**  And may; but how? how satisfied, my lord?
Would you, the supervisor,[383] grossly gape on;
Behold her tupp'd?

**Othello.**                    Death and damnation! O!

**Iago.**  It were a tedious[384] difficulty, I think,
To bring them to that prospect; damn them then,
If ever mortal eyes do see them bolster[385]
More[386] than their own! What then? how then?                              400
What shall I say? Where's satisfaction?

---

[379] Proof.    [380] Lesson.    [381] Since.    [382] Diana's, the goddess of the moon.    [383] Observer.    [384] Laborious.
[385] Lie together.    [386] Other.

It is impossible you should see this,
Were they as prime[387] as goats, as hot as monkeys,
As salt as wolves in pride,[388] and fools as gross
As ignorance made drunk; but yet, I say,
If imputation, and strong circumstances,
Which lead directly to the door of truth,
Will give you satisfaction, you may have it.

**Othello.** Give me a living reason she's disloyal.

**Iago.** I do not like the office;                                         410
But, sith I am enter'd in this cause so far,
Prick'd to 't by foolish honesty and love,
I will go on. I lay with Cassio lately;
And, being troubled with a raging tooth,
I could not sleep.
There are a kind of men so loose of soul
That in their sleeps will mutter their affairs;
One of this kind is Cassio.
In sleep I heard him say, 'Sweet Desdemona,
Let us be wary, let us hide our loves!'                                     420
And then, sir, would he gripe[389] and wring my hand,
Cry, 'O, sweet creature!' and then kiss me hard,
As if he pluck'd up kisses by the roots,
That grew upon my lips; then laid his leg
Over my thigh, and sigh'd, and kiss'd; and then
Cried, 'Cursed fate, that gave thee to the Moor!'

**Othello.** O monstrous! monstrous!

**Iago.**                                         Nay, this was but his dream.

**Othello.** But this denoted a foregone conclusion:[390]
'Tis a shrewd doubt,[391] though it be but a dream.

**Iago.** And this may help to thicken other proofs                         430
That do demonstrate thinly.

**Othello.**                                         I'll tear her all to pieces.

**Iago.** Nay, but be wise; yet we see nothing done;
She may be honest yet. Tell me but this:
Have you not sometimes seen a handkerchief
Spotted with strawberries in your wife's hand?

**Othello.** I gave her such a one; 'twas my first gift.

**Iago.** I know not that; but such a handkerchief—
I am sure it was your wife's — did I to-day
See Cassio wipe his beard with.

**Othello.**                                         If it be that, —

**Iago.** If it be that, or any that was hers,                              440
It speaks against her with the other proofs.

---

[387] Lustful.     [388] Heat.     [389] Seize.     [390] Previous consummation.     [391] (1) Cursed, (2) Acute, suspicion.

**Othello.** O! that the slave had forty thousand lives;
    One is too poor, too weak for my revenge.
    Now do I see 'tis true. Look here, Iago;
    All my fond love thus do I blow to heaven:
    'Tis gone.
    Arise, black vengeance, from the hollow hell!
    Yield up, O love! thy crown and hearted throne
    To tyrannous hate. Swell, bosom, with thy fraught,[392]
    For 'tis of aspics'[393] tongues!
**Iago.**                     Yet be content.[394]                 450
**Othello.** O! blood, blood, blood!
**Iago.** Patience, I say; your mind, perhaps, may change.
**Othello.** Never, Iago. Like to the Pontic sea,[395]
    Whose icy current and compulsive course
    Ne'er feels retiring ebb, but keeps due on
    To the Propontic and the Hellespont,[396]
    Even so my bloody thoughts, with violent pace,
    Shall ne'er look back, ne'er ebb to humble love,
    Till that a capable[397] and wide revenge
    Swallow them up.                          *(Kneels.)*
                Now, by yond marble heaven,        460
    In the due reverence of a sacred vow
    I here engage my words.
**Iago.**                   Do not rise yet.               *(Kneels.)*
    Witness, you ever-burning lights above!
    You elements that clip[398] us round about!
    Witness, that here Iago doth give up
    The execution of his wit, hands, heart,
    To wrong'd Othello's service! Let him command,
    And to obey shall be in me remorse,[399]
    What bloody business ever.[400]             *(They rise.)*
**Othello.**               I greet thy love,
    Not with vain thanks, but with acceptance bounteous,     470
    And will upon the instant put thee to 't:
    Within these three days let me hear thee say
    That Cassio 's not alive.
**Iago.** My friend is dead; 'tis done at your request:
    But let her live.
**Othello.**         Damn her, lewd minx! O, damn her!
    Come, go with me apart; I will withdraw.
    To furnish me with some swift means of death
    For the fair devil. Now art thou my lieutenant.
**Iago.** I am your own for ever.              *(Exeunt.)*

---

[392] Burden.   [393] Poisonous snakes.   [394] Patient.   [395] The Black Sea.   [396] The Sea of Marmara, the Dardanelles.   [397] Comprehensive.   [398] Encompass.   [399] Probably a corrupt line; the meaning appears to be: "to obey shall be my solemn obligation."   [400] Soever.

**Scene 4.**  Before the Castle.

*(Enter Desdemona, Emilia, and Clown.)*

**Desdemona.**  Do you know, sirrah,[401] where Lieutenant Cassio lies?[402]
**Clown.**  I dare not say he lies any where.
**Desdemona.**  Why, man?
**Clown.**  He is a soldier; and for one to say a soldier lies, is stabbing.[403]
**Desdemona.**  Go to;[404] where lodges he?
**Clown.**  To tell you where he lodges is to tell you where I lie.
**Desdemona.**  Can anything be made of this?
**Clown.**  I know not where he lodges, and for me to devise[405] a lodging, and say he lies here or he lies there, were to lie in mine own throat.
**Desdemona.**  Can you inquire him out, and be edified by report?                    10
**Clown.**  I will catechize the world for him; that is, make questions, and by them answer.
**Desdemona.**  Seek him, bid him come hither; tell him I have moved my lord in his behalf, and hope all will be well.
**Clown.**  To do this is within the compass of man's wit, and therefore I will attempt the doing it.                    *(Exit.)*
**Desdemona.**  Where should I lose that handkerchief, Emilia?
**Emilia.**  I know not, madam.
**Desdemona.**  Believe me, I had rather have lost my purse
  Full of cruzadoes;[406] and, but my noble Moor                    20
  Is true of mind, and made of no such baseness
  As jealous creatures are, it were enough
  To put him to ill thinking.
**Emilia.**                    Is he not jealous?
**Desdemona.**  Who! he? I think the sun where he was born
  Drew all such humours from him.
**Emilia.**                    Look! where he comes.
**Desdemona.**  I will not leave him now till Cassio
  Be call'd to him.

*(Enter Othello.)*

**Desdemona.**        How is 't with you, my lord?
**Othello.**  Well, my good lady. *(Aside.)* O! hardness to dissemble.
  How do you, Desdemona?
**Desdemona.**                    Well, my good lord.
**Othello.**  Give me your hand. This hand is moist,[407] my lady.                    30
**Desdemona.**  It yet has felt no age nor known no sorrow.
**Othello.**  This argues fruitfulness and liberal[408] heart;
  Hot, hot, and moist; this hand of yours requires

---

[401] Common form of address to inferiors.    [402] Lives.    [403] I.e., is cause for stabbing.    [404] Here apparently: "Come on!"    [405] Invent.    [406] Portuguese gold coins.    [407] A supposed symptom of a lustful nature.    [408] With overtones of: too free, loose.

A sequester[409] from liberty, fasting and prayer,
Much castigation, exercise devout;
For here 's a young and sweating devil here,
That commonly rebels. 'Tis a good hand,
A frank one.

**Desdemona.** You may, indeed, say so;
For 'twas that hand that gave away my heart.                                        40

**Othello.** A liberal hand; the hearts of old gave hands,
But our new heraldry[410] is hands not hearts.

**Desdemona.** I cannot speak of this. Come now, your promise.

**Othello.** What promise, chuck?[411]

**Desdemona.** I have sent to bid Cassio come speak with you.

**Othello.** I have a salt and sorry rheum offends me.
Lend me thy handkerchief.

**Desdemona.**                          Here, my lord.

**Othello.** That which I gave you.

**Desdemona.**                          I have it not about me.

**Othello.** Not?

**Desdemona.** No, indeed, my lord.

**Othello.**                          That is a fault.
That handkerchief                                                                    50
Did an Egyptian[412] to my mother give;
She was a charmer,[413] and could almost read
The thoughts of people; she told her, while she kept it,
'Twould make her amiable[414] and subdue my father
Entirely to her love, but if she lost it
Or made a gift of it, my father's eye
Should hold her loathed, and his spirits should hunt
After new fancies.[415] She dying gave it me;
And bid me, when my fate would have me wive,
To give it her. I did so; and take heed on 't;                                       60
Make it a darling like your precious eye;
To lose 't or give 't away, were such perdition
As nothing else could match.

**Desdemona.**                          Is 't possible?

**Othello.** 'Tis true; there 's magic in the web of it;
A sibyl,[416] that had number'd in the world
The sun to course two hundred compasses,
In her prophetic fury sew'd the work;
The worms were hallow'd that did breed the silk,
And it was dy'd in mummy[417] which the skilful
Conserv'd of maidens' hearts.

---

[409] Separation.    [410] I.e., new heraldic symbolism (Othello means that the new way is not to give
the heart together with the hand).    [411] Common term of endearment.    [412] Gypsy.    [413] Sorceress.
[414] Lovable, desirable.    [415] Loves.    [416] Prophetess.    [417] Drug (medicinal or magic) derived from
embalmed bodies.

**Desdemona.** Indeed! is 't true? 70
**Othello.** Most veritable; therefore look to 't well.
**Desdemona.** Then would to heaven that I had never seen it!
**Othello.** Ha! wherefore?
**Desdemona.** Why do you speak so startingly and rash?
**Othello.** Is 't lost? is 't gone? speak, is it out o' the way?
**Desdemona.** Heaven bless us!
**Othello.** Say you?
**Desdemona.** It is not lost; but what an if[418] it were?
**Othello.** How!
**Desdemona.** I say, it is not lost.
**Othello.** Fetch 't, let me see 't! 80
**Desdemona.** Why, so I can, sir, but I will not now.
This is a trick to put me from my suit:
Pray you let Cassio be receiv'd again.
**Othello.** Fetch me the handkerchief; my mind misgives.
**Desdemona.** Come, come;
You'll never meet a more sufficient[419] man.
**Othello.** The handkerchief!
**Desdemona.** I pray, talk[420] me of Cassio.
**Othello.** The handkerchief!
**Desdemona.** A man that all his time
Hath founded his good fortunes on your love,
Shar'd dangers with you, — 90
**Othello.** The handkerchief!
**Desdemona.** In sooth, you are to blame.
**Othello.** Away! *(Exit.)*
**Emilia.** Is not this man jealous?
**Desdemona.** I ne'er saw this before.
Sure, there's some wonder in this handkerchief;
I am most unhappy in the loss of it.
**Emilia.** 'Tis not a year or two shows us a man;
They are all but stomachs, and we all but[421] food;
They eat us hungrily, and when they are full 100
They belch us. Look you! Cassio and my husband.

*(Enter Iago and Cassio.)*

**Iago.** There is no other way; 'tis she must do 't:
And, lo! the happiness;[422] go and importune her.
**Desdemona.** How now, good Cassio! what 's the news with you?
**Cassio.** Madam, my former suit: I do beseech you
That by your virtuous means I may again
Exist, and be a member of his love

---

[418] If.   [419] Adequate.   [420] Talk to.   [421] Only . . . only.   [422] "What luck!"

Whom I with all the office[423] of my heart
Entirely honour; I would not be delay'd.
If my offence be of such mortal kind                                          110
That nor my service past, nor present sorrows,
Nor purpos'd merit in futurity,
Can ransom me into his love again,
But to know so must be my benefit;
So shall I clothe me in a forc'd content,
And shut myself up in some other course
To fortune's alms.

**Desdemona.**          Alas! thrice-gentle Cassio!
My advocation is not now in tune;
My lord is not my lord, nor should I know him,
Were he in favour[424] as in humour alter'd.                                  120
So help me every spirit sanctified,
As I have spoken for you all my best
And stood within the blank of[425] his displeasure
For my free speech. You must awhile be patient;
What I can do I will, and more I will
Than for myself I dare: let that suffice you.

**Iago.**  Is my lord angry?

**Emilia.**                    He went hence but now,
And certainly in strange unquietness.

**Iago.**  Can he be angry? I have seen the cannon,
When it hath blown his ranks[426] into the air,                              130
And, like the devil, from his very arm
Puff'd his own brother; and can he be angry?
Something of moment[427] then; I will go meet him;
There's matter in 't indeed, if he be angry.

**Desdemona.**  I prithee, do so. *(Exit Iago.)* Something, sure, of state,[428]
Either from Venice, or some unhatch'd[429] practice
Made demonstrable here in Cyprus to him,
Hath puddled[430] his clear spirit; and, in such cases
Men's natures wrangle with inferior things,
Though great ones are their object. 'Tis even so;                           140
For let our finger ache, and it indues[431]
Our other healthful members even to that sense
Of pain. Nay, we must think men are not gods,
Nor of them look for such observancy[432]
As fits the bridal.[433] Beshrew me much, Emilia,
I was — unhandsome warrior as I am —
Arraigning his unkindness with[434] my soul;

---

[423] Duty.    [424] Appearance.    [425] As the target for.    [426] I.e., his soldiers.    [427] Important.    [428] Public affairs.
[429] Abortive or budding plot.    [430] Muddied.    [431] Brings, leads.    [432] Attention.    [433] Wedding.    [434] To.

But now I find I had suborn'd the witness,[435]
And he's indicted falsely.

**Emilia.** Pray heaven it be state matters, as you think, 150
And no conception,[436] nor no jealous toy[437]
Concerning you.

**Desdemona.** Alas the day! I never gave him cause.

**Emilia.** But jealous souls will not be answer'd so;
They are not ever jealous for the cause,
But jealous for they are jealous; 'tis a monster
Begot upon itself, born on itself.

**Desdemona.** Heaven keep that monster from Othello's mind!

**Emilia.** Lady, amen.

**Desdemona.** I will go seek him. Cassio, walk hereabout; 160
If I do find him fit, I'll move your suit
And seek to effect it to my uttermost.

**Cassio.** I humbly thank your ladyship.

*(Exeunt Desdemona and Emilia.)*

*(Enter Bianca.)*

**Bianca.** Save you, friend Cassio!

**Cassio.**                          What make you from home?
How is it with you, my most fair Bianca?
I' faith, sweet love, I was coming to your house.

**Bianca.** And I was going to your lodging, Cassio.
What! keep a week away? seven days and nights?
Eight score eight hours? and lovers' absent hours,
More tedious than the dial eight score times? 170
O weary reckoning!

**Cassio.**                Pardon me, Bianca,
I have this while with leaden thoughts been press'd;
But I shall, in a more continuate[438] time,
Strike off[439] this score of absence. Sweet Bianca,

*(Giving her Desdemona's handkerchief.)*

Take me this work out.

**Bianca.**                O Cassio! whence came this?
This is some token from a newer friend;
To the felt absence now I feel a cause;
Is 't come to this? Well, well.

**Cassio.**                Go to, woman!
Throw your vile guesses in the devil's teeth,

---

[435] I.e., caused my soul to bring in wrong charges.   [436] Fancy, supposition.   [437] Fancy.   [438] Uninterrupted.
[439] Cancel (i.e., make up for).

From whence you have them. You are jealous now    180
That this is from some mistress, some remembrance:
No, in good troth, Bianca.

**Bianca.** Why, whose is it?

**Cassio.** I know not, sweet; I found it in my chamber.
I like the work well; ere it be demanded, — [440]
As like enough it will, — I'd have it copied;
Take it and do 't; and leave me for this time.

**Bianca.** Leave you! wherefore?

**Cassio.** I do attend here on[441] the general,
And think it no addition,[442] nor my wish,
To have him see me woman'd.

**Bianca.** Why, I pray you?    190

**Cassio.** Not that I love you not.

**Bianca.** But that you do not love me.
I pray you, bring me on the way a little
And say if I shall see you soon at night.

**Cassio.** 'Tis but a little way that I can bring you,
For I attend here; but I'll see you soon.

**Bianca.** 'Tis very good; I must be circumstanc'd.[443]    *(Exeunt.)*

## ACT IV

Scene 1.   Cyprus. Before the Castle.

*(Enter Othello and Iago.)*

**Iago.** Will you think so?

**Othello.** Think so, Iago!

**Iago.** What!
To kiss in private?

**Othello.** An unauthoriz'd kiss.

**Iago.** Or to be naked with her friend a-bed
An hour or more, not meaning any harm?

**Othello.** Naked a-bed, Iago, and not mean harm?
It is hypocrisy against the devil:[444]
They that mean virtuously, and yet do so,
The devil their virtue tempts, and they tempt heaven.

**Iago.** If they do nothing, 'tis a venial slip;
But if I give my wife a handkerchief, —    10

**Othello.** What then?

---

[440] Asked for.    [441] Wait for.    [442] Advantage, credit.    [443] Governed by circumstances.    [444] I.e., by not committing the sin which the situation invites.

**Iago.** Why, then, 'tis hers, my lord; and, being hers,
　She may, I think, bestow 't on any man.
**Othello.** She is protectress of her honour too;
　May she give that?
**Iago.** Her honour is an essence that 's not seen;
　They have it very oft that have it not:[445]
　But for the handkerchief, —
**Othello.** By heaven, I would most gladly have forgot it: —
　Thou said'st, — O! it comes o'er my memory,　　　　　　　　　20
　As doth the raven[446] o'er the infected house,
　Boding to all, — he had my handkerchief.
**Iago.** Ay, what of that?
**Othello.**　　　　　　　That's not so good now.
**Iago.**　　　　　　　　　　　　　　　What,
　If I had said I had seen him do you wrong?
　Or heard him say, as knaves be such abroad,[447]
　Who having, by their own importunate suit,
　Or voluntary dotage[448] of some mistress,
　Convinced or supplied them,[449] cannot choose
　But they must blab.
**Othello.**　　　　　　Hath he said any thing?
**Iago.** He hath, my lord; but be you well assur'd,　　　　　　30
　No more than he'll unswear.
**Othello.**　　　　　　　　What hath he said?
**Iago.** Faith, that he did — I know not what he did.
**Othello.** What? what?
**Iago.** Lie —
**Othello.** With her?
**Iago.**　　　　　　With her, on her; what you will.
**Othello.** Lie with her; lie on her! We say, lie on her, when they belie her. Lie with her! that's fulsome. Handkerchief, — confessions, — handkerchief! To confess, and be hanged for his labour. First, to be hanged, and then to confess: I tremble at it. Nature would not invest herself in such shadowing passion without some instruction.[450] It is not words that shake me thus. Pish! Noses, ears, and lips. Is it possible? — Confess! — Handkerchief! — O devil!　　　　　　41

*(Falls in a trance.)*

**Iago.** Work on,
　My medicine, work! Thus credulous fools are caught;
　And many worthy and chaste dames even thus,

---

[445] I.e., some unchaste women are thought chaste.　[446] (1) A bad omen, (2) A carrier of the plague.　[447] As there are some such in the world.　[448] Foolish affection.　[449] Overcome (their reluctance) or satisfied (their desires).　[450] I would not fall into such passion unless there were some real grounds for it.

All guiltless, meet reproach. What, ho! my lord!
My lord, I say! Othello!

*(Enter Cassio.)*

How now, Cassio!
**Cassio.**  What's the matter?
**Iago.**  My lord is fallen into an epilepsy;[451]
  This is his second fit; he had one yesterday.
**Cassio.**  Rub him about the temples.
**Iago.**                                      No, forbear;                                      50
  The lethargy[452] must have his quiet course,
  If not, he foams at mouth, and by and by
  Breaks out to savage madness. Look! he stirs;
  Do you withdraw yourself a little while,
  He will recover straight; when he is gone,
  I would on great occasion[453] speak with you.          *(Exit Cassio.)*
  How is it, general? have you not hurt your head?
**Othello.**  Dost thou mock me?[454]
**Iago.**                                 I mock you! no, by heaven.
  Would you would bear your fortune like a man!
**Othello.**  A horned man's a monster and a beast.          60
**Iago.**  There's many a beast then, in a populous city,
  And many a civil[455] monster.
**Othello.**  Did he confess it?
**Iago.**                             Good sir, be a man;
  Think every bearded fellow that's but yok'd
  May draw[456] with you; there's millions now alive
  That nightly lie in those unproper[457] beds
  Which they dare swear peculiar;[458] your case is better.
  O! 'tis the spite of hell, the fiend's arch-mock,
  To lip[459] a wanton in a secure[460] couch,
  And to suppose her chaste. No, let me know;          70
  And knowing what I am, I know what she shall be.
**Othello.**  O! thou art wise; 'tis certain.
**Iago.**                                 Stand you awhile apart;
  Confine yourself but in a patient list.[461]
  Whilst you were here o'erwhelmed with your grief, —
  A passion most unsuiting such a man, —
  Cassio came hither; I shifted him away,
  And laid good 'scuse upon your ecstasy;[462]
  Bade him anon return and here speak with me;

---

[451] Seizure, fit.    [452] Coma.    [453] Important matter.    [454] Another allusion to the cuckold's horns.
[455] Citizen.    [456] I.e., pull the burden of cuckoldom.    [457] Not exclusively their own.    [458] Exclusively
their own.    [459] Kiss.    [460] I.e., without suspicion of having a rival.    [461] Bounds of patience.
[462] Derangement, trance.

The which he promis'd. Do but encave yourself,
And mark the fleers, the gibes, and notable scorns,                    80
That dwell in every region of his face;
For I will make him tell the tale anew,
Where, how, how oft, how long ago, and when
He hath, and is again to cope[463] your wife:
I say, but mark his gesture. Marry, patience;
Or I shall say you are all in all in spleen,[464]
And nothing of a man.
**Othello.**                    Dost thou hear, Iago?
I will be found most cunning in my patience;
But — dost thou hear? — most bloody.
**Iago.**                         That's not amiss:
But yet keep time[465] in all. Will you withdraw?        *(Othello goes apart.)*
Now will I question Cassio of Bianca,
A housewife[466] that by selling her desires
Buys herself bread and clothes; it is a creature
That dotes on Cassio; as 'tis the strumpet's plague
To beguile many and be beguil'd by one.
He, when he hears of her, cannot refrain
From the excess of laughter. Here he comes:

*(Re-enter Cassio.)*

As he shall smile, Othello shall go mad;
And his unbookish[467] jealousy must construe
Poor Cassio's smiles, gestures, and light behaviour        100
Quite in the wrong. How do you now, lieutenant?
**Cassio.** The worser that you give me the addition[468]
Whose want[469] even kills me.
**Iago.** Ply Desdemona well, and you are sure on 't.
*(Speaking lower.)* Now, if this suit lay in Bianca's power,
How quickly should you speed!
**Cassio.**                         Alas! poor caitiff![470]
**Othello.** Look! how he laughs already!
**Iago.** I never knew woman love man so.
**Cassio.** Alas! poor rogue, I think i' faith, she loves me.
**Othello.** Now he denies it faintly, and laughs it out.        110
**Iago.** Do you hear, Cassio?
**Othello.**                    Now he importunes him
To tell it o'er: go to; well said, well said.
**Iago.** She gives it out that you shall marry her;
Do you intend it?
**Cassio.** Ha, ha, ha!

---

[463] Close with.    [464] Completely overcome by passion.    [465] Maintain control.    [466] Hussy.
[467] Unpracticed, naive.    [468] Title.    [469] The want of which.    [470] Wretch.

**Othello.**  Do you triumph, Roman?[471] do you triumph?

**Cassio.**  I marry her! what? a customer?[472] I prithee, bear some charity to my wit;[473] do not think it so unwholesome. Ha, ha, ha!

**Othello.**  So, so, so, so. They laugh that win.[474]

**Iago.**  Faith, the cry goes that you shall marry her.                                                     120

**Cassio.**  Prithee, say true.

**Iago.**  I am a very villain else.

**Othello.**  Have you scored me?[475] Well.

**Cassio.**  This is the monkey's own giving out: she is persuaded I will marry her, out of her own love and flattery, not out of my promise.

**Othello.**  Iago beckons me;[476] now he begins the story.

**Cassio.**  She was here even now; she haunts me in every place. I was the other day talking on the sea-bank with certain Venetians, and thither comes this bauble,[477] and, by this hand, she falls me thus about my neck; —

**Othello.**  Crying, 'O dear Cassio!' as it were; his gesture imports it.      130

**Cassio.**  So hangs and lolls and weeps upon me; so hales[478] and pulls me; ha, ha, ha!

**Othello.**  Now he tells how she plucked him to my chamber. O! I see that nose of yours, but not the dog I shall throw it to.

**Cassio.**  Well, I must leave her company.

**Iago.**  Before me![479] look, where she comes.

**Cassio.**  'Tis such another fitchew![480] marry, a perfumed one.

*(Enter Bianca.)*

What do you mean by this haunting of me?                                                   138

**Bianca.**  Let the devil and his dam haunt you! What did you mean by that same handkerchief you gave me even now? I was a fine fool to take it. I must take out the work! A likely piece of work, that you should find it in your chamber, and not know who left it there! This is some minx's token, and I must take out the work! There, give it your hobby-horse;[481] wheresoever you had it I'll take out no work on 't.

**Cassio.**  How now, my sweet Bianca! how now, how now!

**Othello.**  By heaven, that should be[482] my handkerchief!

**Bianca.**  An you'll come to supper to-night, you may; an you will not, come when you are next prepared[483] for.                                                          *(Exit.)*

**Iago.**  After her, after her.

**Cassio.**  Faith, I must; she'll rail in the street else.                                              150

**Iago.**  Will you sup there?

**Cassio.**  Faith, I intend so.

**Iago.**  Well, I may chance to see you, for I would very fain[484] speak with you.

---

[471] I.e., one who triumphs (?).    [472] Courtesan, prostitute.    [473] Give me credit for some sense.
[474] "He who laughs last laughs longest" (?).    [475] Wounded, defaced (?); or: settled my account (?).
[476] Signals.    [477] Plaything.    [478] Hauls.    [479] An exclamation of surprise.    [480] Polecat, noted both for its strong smell and for its lechery.    [481] Harlot.    [482] I.e., I think that is.    [483] Expected (Bianca means that if he does not come that night, she will never want to see him again).    [484] Gladly.

**Cassio.** Prithee come; will you?

**Iago.** Go to; say no more. *(Exit Cassio.)*

**Othello** *(advancing).* How shall I murder him, Iago?

**Iago.** Did you perceive how he laughed at his vice?

**Othello.** O! Iago!

**Iago.** And did you see the handkerchief?

**Othello.** Was that mine? 160

**Iago.** Yours, by this hand; and to see how he prizes the foolish woman your wife!
She gave it him, and he hath given it his whore.

**Othello.** I would have him nine years a-killing. A fine woman! a fair woman! a
sweet woman!

**Iago.** Nay, you must forget that.

**Othello.** Ay, let her rot, and perish, and be damned to-night; for she shall not live.
No, my heart is turned to stone; I strike it, and it hurts my hand. O! the world
hath not a sweeter creature; she might lie by an emperor's side and command
him tasks.

**Iago.** Nay, that's not your way.[485] 170

**Othello.** Hang her! I do but say what she is. So delicate with her needle! An
admirable musician! O, she will sing the savageness out of a bear. Of so high
and plenteous wit and invention!

**Iago.** She's the worse for all this.

**Othello.** O! a thousand, a thousand times. And then, of so gentle a condition![486]

**Iago.** Ay, too gentle.[487]

**Othello.** Nay, that's certain; — but yet the pity of it, Iago!
O! Iago, the pity of it, Iago!

**Iago.** If you are so fond over her iniquity, give her patent to offend; for, if it touch
not you, it comes near nobody.

**Othello.** I will chop her into messes.[488] Cuckold me!

**Iago.** O! 'tis foul in her.

**Othello.** With mine officer!

**Iago.** That's fouler.

**Othello.** Get me some poison, Iago; this night: I'll not expostulate with her, lest
her body and beauty unprovide my mind again.[489] This night, Iago.

**Iago.** Do it not with poison, strangle her in her bed, even the bed she hath
contaminated.

**Othello.** Good, good; the justice of it pleases; very good. 190

**Iago.** And for Cassio, let me be his undertaker;[490] you shall hear more by
midnight.

**Othello.** Excellent good. *(A trumpet within.)* What trumpet is that same?

**Iago.** Something from Venice, sure. 'Tis Lodovico,
Come from the duke; and see, your wife is with him.

*(Enter Lodovico, Desdemona, and Attendants.)*

---

[485] Proper course. [486] So much the high-born lady. [487] I.e., yielding. [488] Bits. [489] Unsettle my
intention. [490] Dispatcher.

**Lodovico.** God save you, worthy general!
**Othello.** With all my heart, sir.
**Lodovico.** The duke and senators of Venice greet you.

*(Gives him a packet.)*

**Othello.** I kiss the instrument of their pleasures.

*(Opens the packet, and reads.)*

**Desdemona.** And what's the news, good cousin Lodovico?
**Iago.** I am very glad to see you, signior;                          200
 Welcome to Cyprus.
**Lodovico.** I thank you. How does Lieutenant Cassio?
**Iago.** Lives, sir.
**Desdemona.** Cousin, there's fall'n between him and my lord
 An unkind[491] breach; but you shall make all well.
**Othello.** Are you sure of that?
**Desdemona.** My lord?
**Othello** *(reads).* 'This fail you not to do, as you will' —
**Lodovico.** He did not call; he's busy in the paper.
 Is there division[492] twixt my lord and Cassio?                  210
**Desdemona.** A most unhappy one; I would do much
 To atone[493] them, for the love I bear to Cassio.
**Othello.** Fire and brimstone!
**Desdemona.** My lord?
**Othello.** Are you wise?
**Desdemona.** What! is he angry?
**Lodovico.** May be the letter mov'd him;
 For, as I think, they do command him home,
 Deputing Cassio in his government.
**Desdemona.** Trust me, I am glad on 't.
**Othello.** Indeed!
**Desdemona.** My lord?
**Othello.** I am glad to see you mad.
**Desdemona.** Why, sweet Othello?
**Othello.** Devil!                                                *(Strikes her.)*
**Desdemona.** I have not deserved this.                             220
**Lodovico.** My lord, this would not be believ'd in Venice,
 Though I should swear I saw 't; 'tis very much;
 Make her amends, she weeps.
**Othello.** O devil, devil!
 If that the earth could teem with woman's tears,
 Each drop she falls[494] would prove a crocodile.[495]

---

[491] Unnatural.   [492] Estrangement.   [493] Reconcile.   [494] Lets fall.   [495] The crocodile's tears were supposed to be hypocritical.

Out of my sight!
**Desdemona.** I will not stay to offend you. *(Going.)*
**Lodovico.** Truly, an obedient lady;
I do beseech your lordship, call her back.
**Othello.** Mistress!
**Desdemona.** My lord?
**Othello.** What would you with her, sir? 230
**Lodovico.** Why, I, my lord?
**Othello.** Ay; you did wish that I would make her turn:
Sir, she can turn, and turn, and yet go on,
And turn again; and she can weep, sir, weep;
And she's obedient, as you say, obedient,
Very obedient. Proceed you in your tears.
Concerning this, sir — O well-painted passion! —
I am commanded home. Get you away;
I'll send for you anon. Sir, I obey the mandate,
And will return to Venice. Hence! avaunt!⁴⁹⁶ *(Exit Desdemona.)*
Cassio shall have my place. And, sir, to-night,
I do entreat that we may sup together;
You are welcome, sir, to Cyprus. Goats and monkeys! *(Exit.)*
**Lodovico.** Is this the noble Moor whom our full senate
Call all-in-all sufficient? is this the noble nature
Whom passion could not shake? whose solid virtue
The shot of accident nor dart of chance
Could neither graze nor pierce?
**Iago.** He is much chang'd.
**Lodovico.** Are his wits safe? is he not light of brain?
**Iago.** He's that he is; I may not breathe my censure. 250
What he might be, if, what he might, he is not,
I would to heaven he were!⁴⁹⁷
**Lodovico.** What! strike his wife!
**Iago.** Faith, that was not so well; yet would I knew
That stroke would prove the worst!
**Lodovico.** Is it his use?
Or did the letters work upon his blood,
And new-create this fault?
**Iago.** Alas, alas!
It is not honesty in me to speak
What I have seen and known. You shall observe him,
And his own courses⁴⁹⁸ will denote him so
That I may save my speech. Do but go after 260
And mark how he continues.
**Lodovico.** I am sorry that I am deceiv'd in him. *(Exeunt.)*

---

⁴⁹⁶ Begone! ⁴⁹⁷ Another of Iago's gnomic speeches; perhaps approximately: "If now he is not himself, I wish he would be what he could be!" ⁴⁹⁸ Actions.

**Scene 2.**   A Room in the Castle.

*(Enter Othello and Emilia.)*

**Othello.**  You have seen nothing, then?
**Emilia.**  Nor ever heard, nor ever did suspect.
**Othello.**  Yes, you have seen Cassio and her together.
**Emilia.**  But then I saw no harm, and then I heard
    Each syllable that breath made up between them.
**Othello.**  What! did they never whisper?
**Emilia.**                                        Never, my lord.
**Othello.**  Nor send you out o' the way?
**Emilia.**  Never.
**Othello.**  To fetch her fan, her gloves, her mask, nor nothing?[499]
**Emilia.**  Never, my lord.                                        10
**Othello.**  That's strange.
**Emilia.**  I durst, my lord, to wager she is honest,
    Lay down my soul at stake: if you think other,
    Remove your thought; it doth abuse your bosom.
    If any wretch have put this in your head,
    Let heaven requite it with the serpent's curse!
    For, if she be not honest, chaste, and true,
    There's no man happy; the purest of their wives
    Is foul as slander.
**Othello.**                  Bid her come hither; go.                *(Exit Emilia.)*
    She says enough; yet she 's a simple[500] bawd                20
    That cannot say as much. This is a subtle whore,
    A closet lock and key of villainous secrets;
    And yet she 'll kneel and pray; I have seen her do 't.

*(Re-enter Emilia with Desdemona.)*

**Desdemona.**  My lord, what is your will?
**Othello.**                                        Pray, chuck, come hither.
**Desdemona.**  What is your pleasure?
**Othello.**                                Let me see your eyes;
    Look in my face.
**Desdemona.**          What horrible fancy 's this?
**Othello** *(to Emilia).*  Some of your function,[501] mistress;
    Leave procreants alone and shut the door;
    Cough or cry 'hem' if any body come;
    Your mystery,[502] your mystery; nay, dispatch.                *(Exit Emilia.)*
**Desdemona.**  Upon my knees, what doth your speech import?
    I understand a fury in your words.
    But not the words.

[499] Anything.    [500] Simpleminded.    [501] To your duty, business.    [502] Trade.

**Othello.** Why, what art thou?

**Desdemona.**                          Your wife, my lord; your true
And loyal wife.

**Othello.**           Come, swear it, damn thyself;
Lest, being like one of heaven, the devils themselves
Should fear to seize thee; therefore be double-damn'd;
Swear thou art honest.

**Desdemona.**                 Heaven doth truly know it.

**Othello.** Heaven truly knows that thou art false as hell.

**Desdemona.** To whom, my lord? with whom? how am I false?                    40

**Othello.** Ah! Desdemona; away, away, away!

**Desdemona.** Alas, the heavy day! — Why do you weep?
Am I the motive of these tears, my lord?
If haply you my father do suspect
An instrument of this your calling back,
Lay not your blame on me; if you have lost him,
Why, I have lost him too.

**Othello.**                          Had it pleas'd heaven
To try me with affliction, had he rain'd
All kinds of sores and shames on my bare head,
Steep'd me in poverty to the very lips,                    50
Given to captivity me and my utmost hopes,
I should have found in some part of my soul
A drop of patience; but, alas! to make me
The fixed figure for the time of scorn[503]
To point his slow and moving finger at;
Yet could I bear that too; well, very well:
But there, where I have garner'd[504] up my heart,
Where either I must live or bear no life,
The fountain from the which my current runs
Or else dries up; to be discarded thence!                    60
Or keep it as a cistern for foul toads
To knot and gender in![505] Turn thy complexion there,[506]
Patience, thou young and rose-lipp'd cherubin;
Ay, there, look grim as hell!

**Desdemona.** I hope my noble lord esteems me honest.

**Othello.** O! ay; as summer flies are in the shambles,[507]
That quicken even with blowing. O thou weed!
Who art so lovely fair and smell'st so sweet
That the sense aches at thee, would thou hadst ne'er been born.

**Desdemona.** Alas! what ignorant sin have I committed?                    70

**Othello.** Was this fair paper, this most goodly book,
Made to write 'whore' upon? What committed!
Committed! O thou public commoner![508]

---

[503] I.e., the scornful world.    [504] Stored.    [505] Bunch up and procreate.    [506] I.e., change your color
to suit the "cistern for foul toads."    [507] Slaughterhouse.    [508] Harlot.

I should make very forges of my cheeks,
That would to cinders burn up modesty,
Did I but speak thy deeds. What committed!
Heaven stops the nose at it and the moon winks,[509]
The bawdy wind that kisses all it meets
Is hush'd within the hollow mine of earth,
And will not hear it. What committed!                                80
Impudent strumpet!

**Desdemona.**          By heaven, you do me wrong.
**Othello.**  Are not you a strumpet?
**Desdemona.**                    No, as I am a Christian.
    If to preserve this vessel for my lord
    From any other foul unlawful touch
    Be not to be a strumpet, I am none.
**Othello.**  What! not a whore?
**Desdemona.**                No, as I shall be sav'd.
**Othello.**  Is it possible?
**Desdemona.**  O! heaven forgive us.
**Othello.**                    I cry you mercy,[510] then;
    I took you for that cunning whore of Venice
    That married with Othello. You, mistress,                        90
    That have the office opposite to Saint Peter,
    And keep the gate of hell!


*(Re-enter Emilia.)*


                    You, you, ay, you!
    We have done our course; there's money for your pains.
    I pray you, turn the key and keep our counsel.                *(Exit.)*
**Emilia.**  Alas! what does this gentleman conceive?[511]
    How do you, madam? how do you, my good lady?
**Desdemona.**  Faith, half asleep.
**Emilia.**  Good madam, what 's the matter with my lord?
**Desdemona.**  With who?
**Emilia.**  Why, with my lord, madam.                              100
**Desdemona.**  Who is thy lord?
**Emilia.**                He that is yours, sweet lady.
**Desdemona.**  I have none; do not talk to me, Emilia;
    I cannot weep, nor answer have I none,
    But what should go by water.[512] Prithee, to-night
    Lay on my bed my wedding sheets: remember:
    And call thy husband hither.
**Emilia.**                Here is a change indeed!                *(Exit.)*


[509] Closes her eyes.    [510] Beg your pardon.    [511] Imagine.    [512] Be conveyed by means of tears.

**Desdemona.** 'Tis meet I should be us'd so, very meet.
How have I been behav'd, that he might stick
The small'st opinion on my least misuse?[513]

*(Re-enter Emilia, with Iago.)*

**Iago.** What is your pleasure, madam? How is it with you?    110
**Desdemona.** I cannot tell. Those that do teach young babes
Do it with gentle means and easy tasks;
He might have chid me so; for, in good faith,
I am a child to chiding.
**Iago.**                    What 's the matter, lady?
**Emilia.** Alas, Iago, my lord hath so bewhor'd her,
Thrown such despite[514] and heavy terms upon her,
As true hearts cannot bear.
**Desdemona.** Am I that name, Iago?
**Iago.**                    What name, fair lady?
**Desdemona.** Such as she says my lord did say I was.
**Emilia.** He call'd her whore; a beggar in his drink    120
Could not have laid such terms upon his callat.[515]
**Iago.** Why did he so?
**Desdemona.** I do not know; I am sure I am none such.
**Iago.** Do not weep, do not weep. Alas the day!
**Emilia.** Has she forsook so many noble matches,
Her father and her country and her friends,
To be call'd whore? would it not make one weep?
**Desdemona.** It is my wretched fortune.
**Iago.**                    Beshrew[516] him for it!
How comes this trick upon him?
**Desdemona.**                    Nay, heaven doth know.
**Emilia.** I will be hang'd, if some eternal villain,    130
Some busy and insinuating rogue,
Some cogging[517] cozening slave, to get some office,
Have not devis'd this slander; I'll be hang'd else.
**Iago.** Fie! there is no such man; it is impossible.
**Desdemona.** If any such there be, heaven pardon him!
**Emilia.** A halter pardon him, and hell gnaw his bones!
Why should he call her whore? who keeps her company?
What place? what time? what form? what likelihood?
The Moor 's abus'd by some most villainous knave,
Some base notorious knave, some scurvy fellow.    140
O heaven! that such companions[518] thou'dst unfold,

---

[513] The least suspicion on my slightest misconduct.    [514] Abuse.    [515] Slut.    [516] Curse.    [517] Cheating.
[518] Fellows (derogatory).

And put in every honest hand a whip
To lash the rascals naked through the world,
Even from the east to west!

**Iago.**                              Speak within door.

**Emilia.**  O! fie upon them. Some such squire he was
That turn'd your wit the seamy side without,[519]
And made you to suspect me with the Moor.

**Iago.**  You are a fool; go to.

**Desdemona.**              O good Iago,
What shall I do to win my lord again?
Good friend, go to him; for, by this light of heaven,                    150
I know not how I lost him. Here I kneel:
If e'er my will did trespass 'gainst his love,
Either in discourse of thought or actual deed,
Or that mine eyes, mine ears, or any sense,
Delighted them[520] in any other form;
Or that I do not yet,[521] and ever did,
And ever will, though he do shake me off
To beggarly divorcement, love him dearly,
Comfort forswear me! Unkindness may do much;
And his unkindness may defeat[522] my life,                              160
But never taint my love. I cannot say 'whore':
It does abhor me now I speak the word;
To do the act that might the addition earn
Not the world's mass of vanity could make me.

**Iago.**  I pray you be content, 'tis but his humour;
The business of the state does him offence,
And he does chide with you.

**Desdemona.**              If 'twere no other, —

**Iago.**  'Tis but so, I warrant.                           *(Trumpets.)*
Hark! how these instruments summon to supper;
The messengers of Venice stay the meat:                                 170
Go in, and weep not; all things shall be well.

                                        *(Exeunt Desdemona and Emilia.)*

*(Enter Roderigo.)*

How now, Roderigo!

**Roderigo.**  I do not find that thou dealest justly with me.

**Iago.**  What in the contrary?[523]

**Roderigo.**  Every day thou daffest me[524] with some device, Iago; and rather, as
it seems to me now, keepest from me all conveniency,[525] than suppliest me
with the least advantage of hope. I will indeed no longer endure it, nor am I yet
persuaded to put up[526] in peace what already I have foolishly suffered.

---

[519] Outward.    [520] Found delight.    [521] Still.    [522] Destroy.    [523] I.e., what reason do you have for
saying that?    [524] You put me off.    [525] Favorable circumstances.    [526] Put up with.

**Iago.** Will you hear me, Roderigo?

**Roderigo.** Faith, I have heard too much, for your words and performances are no kin together. 181

**Iago.** You charge me most unjustly.

**Roderigo.** With nought but truth. I have wasted myself out of my means. The jewels you have had from me to deliver to Desdemona would half have corrupted a votarist;[527] you have told me she has received them, and returned me expectations and comforts of sudden respect[528] and acquaintance, but I find none.

**Iago.** Well; go to; very well.

**Roderigo.** Very well! go to! I cannot go to, man; nor 'tis not very well: by this hand, I say, it is very scurvy, and begin to find myself fobbed[529] in it. 190

**Iago.** Very well.

**Roderigo.** I tell you 'tis not very well. I will make myself known to Desdemona; if she will return me my jewels, I will give over my suit and repent my unlawful solicitation; if not, assure yourself I will seek satisfaction of you.

**Iago.** You have said now.[530]

**Roderigo.** Ay, and said nothing, but what I protest intendment of doing.

**Iago.** Why, now I see there's mettle in thee, and even from this instant do build on thee a better opinion than ever before. Give me thy hand, Roderigo; thou hast taken against me a most just exception; but yet, I protest, I have dealt most directly in thy affair. 200

**Roderigo.** It hath not appeared.

**Iago.** I grant indeed it hath not appeared, and your suspicion is not without wit and judgment. But, Roderigo, if thou hast that in thee indeed, which I have greater reason to believe now than ever, I mean purpose, courage, and valour, this night show it: if thou the next night following enjoy not Desdemona, take me from this world with treachery and devise engines for[531] my life.

**Roderigo.** Well, what is it? is it within reason and compass?

**Iago.** Sir, there is especial commission come from Venice to depute Cassio in Othello's place. 210

**Roderigo.** Is that true? why, then Othello and Desdemona return again to Venice.

**Iago.** O, no! he goes into Mauritania, and takes away with him the fair Desdemona, unless his abode be lingered here by some accident; wherein none can be so determinate[532] as the removing of Cassio.

**Roderigo.** How do you mean, removing of him?

**Iago.** Why, by making him uncapable of Othello's place; knocking out his brains.

**Roderigo.** And that you would have me do? 219

**Iago.** Ay; if you dare do yourself a profit and a right. He sups to-night with a harlotry,[533] and thither will I go to him; he knows not yet of his honourable fortune. If you will watch his going thence, — which I will fashion to fall out between

---

[527] Nun.   [528] Immediate consideration.   [529] Cheated.   [530] I.e., "I suppose you're through?" (?); or: "Now you're talking" (?).   [531] Devices against.   [532] Effective.   [533] Harlot.

twelve and one, — you may take him at your pleasure; I will be near to second your attempt, and he shall fall between us. Come, stand not amazed at it, but go along with me; I will show you such a necessity in his death that you shall think yourself bound to put it on him. It is now high supper-time, and the night grows to waste; about it.

**Roderigo.** I will hear further reason for this.

**Iago.** And you shall be satisfied.                                    (*Exeunt.*)

**Scene 3.**   Another Room in the Castle.

(*Enter Othello, Lodovico, Desdemona, Emilia, and Attendants.*)

**Lodovico.** I do beseech you, sir, trouble yourself no further.

**Othello.** O! pardon me; 'twill do me good to walk.

**Lodovico.** Madam, good-night; I humbly thank your ladyship.

**Desdemona.** Your honour is most welcome.

**Othello.**                                    Will you walk, sir?
    O! Desdemona, —

**Desdemona.** My lord?

**Othello.** Get you to bed on the instant; I will be returned forthwith; dismiss your attendant there; look it be done.

**Desdemona.** I will, my lord.          (*Exeunt Othello, Lodovico, and Attendants.*)

**Emilia.** How goes it now? He looks gentler than he did.                    10

**Desdemona.** He says he will return incontinent;[534]
    He hath commanded me to go to bed,
    And bade me to dismiss you.

**Emilia.**                         Dismiss me!

**Desdemona.** It was his bidding; therefore, good Emilia,
    Give me my nightly wearing, and adieu:
    We must not now displease him.

**Emilia.** I would you had never seen him.

**Desdemona.** So would not I; my love doth so approve him,
    That even his stubbornness,[535] his checks[536] and frowns, —
    Prithee, unpin me, — have grace and favour in them.                    20

**Emilia.** I have laid those sheets you bade me on the bed.

**Desdemona.** All's one.[537] Good faith! how foolish are our minds!
    If I do die before thee, prithee, shroud me
    In one of those same sheets.

**Emilia.**                         Come, come, you talk.

**Desdemona.** My mother had a maid call'd Barbara;
    She was in love, and he she lov'd prov'd mad[538]
    And did forsake her; she had a song of 'willow';

---

[534] At once.    [535] Roughness.    [536] Rebukes.    [537] I.e., it doesn't matter.    [538] Wild.

An old thing 'twas, but it express'd her fortune,
And she died singing it; that song to-night
Will not go from my mind; I have much to do 30
But to go hang my head all at one side,
And sing it like poor Barbara. Prithee, dispatch.

**Emilia.** Shall I go fetch your night-gown?

**Desdemona.** No, unpin me here.
This Lodovico is a proper man.

**Emilia.** A very handsome man.

**Desdemona.** He speaks well.

**Emilia.** I know a lady in Venice would have walked barefoot to Palestine for a touch of his nether lip.

**Desdemona** *(sings).*

The poor soul sat sighing by a sycamore tree,
    Sing all a green willow; 40
Her hand on her bosom, her head on her knee,
    Sing willow, willow, willow:
The fresh streams ran by her, and murmur'd her moans;
    Sing willow, willow, willow:
Her salt tears fell from her and soften'd the stones; —

Lay by these: —
    Sing willow, willow, willow:

Prithee, hie thee;[539] he 'll come anon. —

Sing all a green willow must be my garland.
    Let nobody blame him, his scorn I approve, — 50
Nay, that's not next. Hark! who is it that knocks?

**Emilia.** It is the wind.

**Desdemona.**

I call'd my love false love; but what said he then?
    Sing willow, willow, willow:
If I court moe[540] women, you 'll couch with moe men.

So, get thee gone; good-night. Mine eyes do itch;
Doth that bode weeping?

**Emilia.** 'Tis neither here nor there.

**Desdemona.** I have heard it said so. O! these men, these men!
Dost thou in conscience think, tell me, Emilia,
That there be women do abuse their husbands 60
In such gross kind?

---

[539] Hurry.    [540] More.

**Emilia.**                    There be some such, no question.

**Desdemona.**  Wouldst thou do such a deed for all the world?

**Emilia.**  Why, would not you?

**Desdemona.**                    No, by this heavenly light!

**Emilia.**  Nor I neither by this heavenly light;
I might do 't as well i' the dark.

**Desdemona.**  Wouldst thou do such a deed for all the world?

**Emilia.**  The world is a huge thing; 'tis a great price
For a small vice.

**Desdemona.**      In troth, I think thou wouldst not.

**Emilia.**  In troth, I think I should, and undo 't when I had done. Marry, I would
not do such a thing for a joint-ring,[541] nor measures of lawn,[542] nor for gowns,
petticoats, nor caps, nor any petty exhibition;[543] but for the whole world, who
would not make her husband a cuckold to make him a monarch? I should
venture purgatory for 't.

**Desdemona.**  Beshrew me, if I would do such a wrong
For the whole world.

**Emilia.**  Why, the wrong is but a wrong i' the world; and having the world for
your labour, 'tis a wrong in your own world, and you might quickly make it
right.

**Desdemona.**  I do not think there is any such woman.

**Emilia.**  Yes, a dozen; and as many to the vantage,[544] as                    80
Would store[545] the world they played for.
But I do think it is their husbands' faults
If wives do fall. Say that they slack their duties,
And pour our treasures into foreign laps,
Or else break out in peevish jealousies,
Throwing restraint upon us; or say they strike us,
Or scant[546] our former having[547] in despite;
Why, we have galls;[548] and though we have some grace,
Yet have we some revenge. Let husbands know
Their wives have sense like them; they see and smell,                    90
And have their palates both for sweet and sour,
As husbands have. What is it that they do
When they change us for others? Is it sport?[549]
I think it is; and doth affection breed it?
I think it doth; is 't frailty that thus errs?
It is so too; and have not we affections,
Desires for sport, and frailty, as men have?
Then, let them use us well; else let them know,
The ills we do, their ills instruct us so.

**Desdemona.**  Good-night, good night; heaven me such usage[550] send,                    100
Not to pick bad from bad, but by bad mend!                    (*Exeunt.*)

---

[541] Ring made in separable halves.      [542] Fine linen.      [543] Offer, gift.      [544] Over and above.
[545] Populate.      [546] Reduce.      [547] Allowance.      [548] Spirits, temper.      [549] Lust, sexual enjoyment.
[550] Habits (?), treatment (?).

## ACT V

**Scene 1.** Cyprus. A Street.

*(Enter Iago and Roderigo.)*

**Iago.** Here, stand behind this bulk,[551] straight will he come:
   Wear thy good rapier bare, and put it home.
   Quick, quick; fear nothing; I 'll be at thy elbow.
   It makes us, or it mars us; think on that,
   And fix most firm thy resolution.
**Roderigo.** Be near at hand; I may miscarry in 't.
**Iago.** Here, at thy hand: be bold, and take thy stand.     *(Retires.)*
**Roderigo.** I have no great devotion to the deed;
   And yet he has given me satisfying reasons:
   'Tis but a man gone: forth, my sword; he dies.     10
**Iago.** I have rubb'd this young quat[552] almost to the sense,[553]
   And he grows angry. Now, whether he kill Cassio,
   Or Cassio him, or each do kill the other,
   Every way makes my gain: live Roderigo,
   He calls me to a restitution large
   Of gold and jewels that I bobb'd[554] from him,
   As gifts to Desdemona;
   It must not be: if Cassio do remain,
   He hath a daily beauty in his life
   That makes me ugly: and, besides, the Moor     20
   May unfold me to him; there stand I in much peril.
   No, he must die. But so;[555] I hear him coming.

*(Enter Cassio.)*

**Roderigo.** I know his gait; 'tis he. Villain, thou diest!

*(Makes a pass at Cassio.)*

**Cassio.** That thrust had been mine enemy indeed
   But that my coat is better than thou know'st;
   I will make proof of thine.

*(Draws, and wounds Roderigo.)*

**Roderigo.**               O! I am slain.

*(Iago from behind wounds Cassio in the leg, and exit.)*

---

[551] Jutting part of a wall.    [552] Pimple.    [553] To the quick.    [554] Swindled.    [555] I.e., that's the only way.

**Cassio.** I am maim'd for ever. Help, ho! murder! murder!          *(Falls.)*

*(Enter Othello, at a distance.)*

**Othello.** The voice of Cassio: Iago keeps his word.
**Roderigo.** O! villain that I am!
**Othello.**                              It is e'en so.
**Cassio.** O, help, ho! light! a surgeon!                          30
**Othello.** 'Tis he: O brave Iago, honest and just!
    That hast such noble sense of thy friend's wrong;
    Thou teachest me. Minion,[556] your dear lies dead,
    And your unblest fate hies; strumpet, I come!
    Forth of my heart those charms, thine eyes, are blotted;
    Thy bed lust-stain'd shall with lust's blood be spotted.          *(Exit.)*

*(Enter Lodovico and Gratiano, at a distance.)*

**Cassio.** What ho! no watch? no passage?[557] murder! murder!
**Gratiano.** 'Tis some mischance; the cry is very direful.
**Cassio.** O, help!
**Lodovico.** Hark!
**Roderigo.** O wretched villain!                                   40
**Lodovico.** Two or three groans: it is a heavy[558] night;
    These may be counterfeits; let 's think 't unsafe
    To come in to the cry[559] without more help.
**Roderigo.** Nobody come? then shall I bleed to death.
**Lodovico.** Hark!

*(Re-enter Iago, with a light.)*

**Gratiano.** Here 's one comes in his shirt, with light and weapons.
**Iago.** Who 's there? whose noise is this that cries on murder?
**Lodovico.** We do not know.
**Iago.**                              Did not you hear a cry?
**Cassio.** Here, here! for heaven's sake, help me.
**Iago.**                                             What's the matter?          50
**Gratiano.** This is Othello's ancient, as I take it.
**Lodovico.** The same indeed; a very valiant fellow.
**Iago.** What are you here that cry so grievously?
**Cassio.** Iago? O! I am spoil'd, undone by villains!
    Give me some help.
**Iago.** O me, lieutenant! what villains have done this?
**Cassio.** I think that one of them is hereabout,
    And cannot make away.

---

[556] (Cassio's) darling, i.e., Desdemona.    [557] Passer-by.    [558] Dark.    [559] Where the cry comes from.

**Iago.**                     O treacherous villains!
  *(To Lodovico and Gratiano.)* What are you there? come in, and
  give some help.                                                            60
**Roderigo.**  O! help me here.
**Cassio.**  That's one of them.
**Iago.**                     O murderous slave! O villain!

*(Stabs Roderigo.)*

**Roderigo.**  O damn'd Iago! O inhuman dog!
**Iago.**  Kill men i' the dark! Where be these bloody thieves?
  How silent is this town! Ho! murder! murder!
  What may you be? are you of good or evil?
**Lodovico.**  As you shall prove us, praise us.
**Iago.**  Signior Lodovico?
**Lodovico.**  He, sir.
**Iago.**  I cry you mercy. Here 's Cassio hurt by villains.                 70
**Gratiano.**  Cassio!
**Iago.**  How is it, brother?
**Cassio.**  My leg is cut in two.
**Iago.**                     Marry, heaven forbid.
  Light, gentlemen; I 'll bind it with my shirt.

*(Enter Bianca.)*

**Bianca.**  What is the matter, ho? who is 't that cried?
**Iago.**  Who is 't that cried!
**Bianca.**  O my dear Cassio! my sweet Cassio!
  O Cassio, Cassio, Cassio!
**Iago.**  O notable strumpet! Cassio, may you suspect
  Who they should be that have thus mangled you?                             80
**Cassio.**  No.
**Gratiano.**  I am sorry to find you thus; I have been to seek you.
**Iago.**  Lend me a garter. So. O! for a chair,
  To bear him easily hence!
**Bianca.**  Alas; he faints! O Cassio, Cassio, Cassio!
**Iago.**  Gentlemen all, I do suspect this trash[560]
  To be a party in this injury.
  Patience awhile, good Cassio. Come, come.
  Lend me a light. Know we this face, or no?
  Alas! my friend and my dear countryman,                                   90
  Roderigo? no: yes, sure, O heaven! Roderigo.
**Gratiano.**  What! of Venice?
**Iago.**  Even he, sir, did you know him?

[560] I.e., Bianca.

**Gratiano.**                              Know him! ay.
**Iago.**  Signior Gratiano? I cry you gentle pardon;
  These bloody accidents must excuse my manners,
  That so neglected you.
**Gratiano.**              I am glad to see you.
**Iago.**  How do you, Cassio? O! a chair, a chair!
**Gratiano.**  Roderigo!

*(A chair brought in.)*

**Iago.**  He, he, 'tis he, — O! that 's well said; the chair:
  Some good men bear him carefully from hence;                              100
  I 'll fetch the general's surgeon. *(To Bianca.)* For you, mistress,
  Save you your labour. He that lies slain here, Cassio,
  Was my dear friend. What malice was between you?
**Cassio.**  None in the world; nor do I know that man.
**Iago** *(to Bianca).*  What! look you pale? O! bear him out o' the air —

*(Cassio and Roderigo are borne off.)*

  Stay you, good gentlemen. Look you pale, mistress? —
  Do you perceive the gastness[561] of her eye?
  Nay, if you stare, we shall hear more anon.
  Behold her well; I pray you, look upon her.
  Do you see, gentlemen? nay, guiltiness will speak                              110
  Though tongues were out of use.

*(Enter Emilia.)*

**Emilia.**  'Las! what 's the matter? what 's the matter, husband?
**Iago.**  Cassio hath here been set on in the dark
  By Roderigo and fellows that are 'scaped:
  He 's almost slain, and Roderigo dead.
**Emilia.**  Alas! good gentleman; alas! good Cassio!
**Iago.**  This is the fruit of whoring. Prithee, Emilia,
  Go know of Cassio where he supp'd to-night.
  *(To Bianca.)* What! do you shake at that?
**Bianca.**  He supp'd at my house; but I therefore shake not.                              120
**Iago.**  O! did he so? I charge you, go with me.
**Emilia.**  Fie, fie, upon thee, strumpet!
**Bianca.**  I am no strumpet, but of life as honest
  As you that thus abuse me.
**Emilia.**                              As I! foh! fie upon thee!
**Iago.**  Kind gentlemen, let 's go see poor Cassio dress'd.[562]

---

[561] Terror.     [562] Bandaged.

Come, mistress, you must tell 's another tale.
Emilia, run you to the citadel,
And tell my lord and lady what hath happ'd.
Will you go on afore? *(Aside.)* This is the night
That either makes me or fordoes[563] me quite. *(Exeunt.)*

**Scene 2.** A Bedchamber in the Castle. Desdemona in bed asleep. A light burning.

*(Enter Othello.)*

**Othello.** It is the cause,[564] it is the cause, my soul;
Let me not name it to you, you chaste stars!
It is the cause. Yet I 'll not shed her blood,
Nor scar that whiter skin of hers than snow,
And smooth as monumental alabaster.
Yet she must die, else she 'll betray more men.
Put out the light, and then put out the light:
If I quench thee, thou flaming minister,[565]
I can again thy former light restore,
Should I repent me; but once put out thy light,                    10
Thou cunning'st[566] pattern of excelling nature,
I know not where is that Promethean[567] heat
That can thy light relume.[568] When I have pluck'd the rose,
I cannot give it vital growth again,
It needs must wither: I 'll smell it on the tree. *(Kisses her.)*
O balmy breath, that dost almost persuade
Justice to break her sword! One more, one more.
Be thus when thou art dead, and I will kill thee,
And love thee after. One more, and this the last:
So sweet was ne'er so fatal. I must weep,                    20
But they are cruel tears; this sorrow 's heavenly,
It strikes where it doth love. She wakes.
**Desdemona.** Who 's there? Othello?
**Othello.**                                   Ay, Desdemona.
**Desdemona.** Will you come to bed, my lord?
**Othello.** Have you pray'd to-night, Desdemona?
**Desdemona.**                                   Ay, my lord.
**Othello.** If you bethink yourself of any crime
   Unreconcil'd as yet to heaven and grace,
   Solicit for it straight.
**Desdemona.** Alas! my lord, what may you mean by that?

---

[563] Ruins.   [564] I.e., Desdemona's unchastity (Othello means that the severity of the punishment is required by the nature of her sin).   [565] I.e., the candle.   [566] Most intricately wrought.   [567] In Greek mythology the demigod Prometheus stole fire from the gods and gave it to man.   [568] Relight.

**Othello.** Well, do it, and be brief; I will walk by:[569]          30
  I would not kill thy unprepared spirit;
  No; heaven forfend![570] I would not kill thy soul.
**Desdemona.** Talk you of killing?
**Othello.**                                   Ay, I do.
**Desdemona.**                                        Then heaven
  Have mercy on me!
**Othello.**            Amen! with all my heart.
**Desdemona.** If you say so, I hope you will not kill me.
**Othello.** Hum!
**Desdemona.** And yet I fear you; for you are fatal then
  When your eyes roll so. Why I should fear I know not,
  Since guiltiness I know not; but yet I feel I fear.
**Othello.** Think on thy sins.
**Desdemona.**                        They are loves I bear to you.          40
**Othello.** Ay, and for that thou diest.
**Desdemona.** That death's unnatural that kills for loving.
  Alas! why gnaw you so your nether lip?
  Some bloody passion shakes your very frame;
  These are portents,[571] but yet, I hope, I hope
  They do not point on me.
**Othello.**                          Peace, and be still!
**Desdemona.** I will so. What's the matter?
**Othello.** That handkerchief which I so lov'd and gave thee
  Thou gav'st to Cassio.
**Desdemona.**              No, by my life and soul!
  Send for the man and ask him.
**Othello.**                              Sweet soul, take heed,          50
  Take heed of perjury; thou 'rt on thy death-bed.
**Desdemona.** Ay, but not yet to die.
**Othello.**                              Yes, presently;[572]
  Therefore confess thee freely of thy sin;
  For to deny each article with oath
  Cannot remove nor choke the strong conception[573]
  That I do groan withal. Thou art to die.
**Desdemona.** Then Lord have mercy on me!
**Othello.**                                  I say, amen.
**Desdemona.** And have you mercy too! I never did
  Offend you in my life; never lov'd Cassio
  But with such general warranty[574] of heaven          60
  As I might love; I never gave him token.
**Othello.** By heaven, I saw my handkerchief in 's hand.
  O perjur'd woman! thou dost stone[575] my heart,
  And mak'st me call what I intend to do

---

[569] Nearby.   [570] Forbid.   [571] Omens.   [572] At once.   [573] Belief.   [574] Permission.   [575] Turn to stone.

A murder, which I thought a sacrifice:
I saw the handkerchief.
**Desdemona.**              He found it then;
I never gave it him. Send for him hither;
Let him confess a truth.
**Othello.**            He had confessed.
**Desdemona.** What, my lord?
**Othello.** That he hath us'd thee.
**Desdemona.**            How? Unlawfully?
**Othello.**                   Ay.          70
**Desdemona.** He will not say so.
**Othello.**            No; his mouth is stopp'd:
Honest Iago hath ta'en order for 't.[576]
**Desdemona.** O! my fear interprets. What! is he dead?
**Othello.** Had all his hairs been lives, my great revenge
Had stomach[577] for them all.
**Desdemona.** Alas! he is betray'd and I undone.
**Othello.** Out, strumpet! Weep'st thou for him to my face?
**Desdemona.** O! banish me, my lord, but kill me not!
**Othello.** Down, strumpet!
**Desdemona.** Kill me to-morrow; let me live to-night!      80
**Othello.** Nay, if you strive, —
**Desdemona.** But half an hour!
**Othello.**            Being done, there is no pause.
**Desdemona.** But while I say one prayer!
**Othello.**            It is too late.       *(He smothers her.)*
**Emilia** *(within)*. My lord, my lord! what, ho! my lord, my lord!
**Othello.** What noise is this? Not dead? Not yet quite dead?
I that am cruel am yet merciful;
I would not have thee linger in thy pain.
So, so.
**Emilia** *(within)*. What, ho! my lord, my lord!
**Othello.**            Who's there?
**Emilia** *(within)*. O! good my lord, I would speak a word with you!    90
**Othello.** Yes; 'tis Emilia: by and by.[578] She's dead.
'Tis like[579] she comes to speak of Cassio's death;
The noise was high. Ha! no more moving?
Still as the grave. Shall she come in? were 't good?[580]
I think she stirs again: no. What 's best to do?
If she come in she'll sure speak to my wife:
My wife! my wife! what wife? I have no wife;
O, insupportable! O heavy hour!
Methinks it should be now a huge eclipse
Of sun and moon, and that the affrighted globe      100

---

[576] Taken steps.     [577] Appetite.     [578] I.e., "just a moment."     [579] Likely.     [580] Would that be wise.

Should yawn[581] at alteration.

**Emilia** *(within).*           I do beseech you
That I may speak with you, O! good my lord.

**Othello.** I had forgot thee: O! come in, Emilia:
Soft, by and by: let me the curtains draw.
Where art thou?                               *(Unlocks the door.)*

*(Enter Emilia.)*

                    What 's the matter with thee now?

**Emilia.** O! my good lord, yonder 's foul murder done.

**Othello.** What! now?

**Emilia.** But now, my lord.

**Othello.** It is the very error[582] of the moon;
She comes more near the earth than she was wont,                    110
And makes men mad.

**Emilia.** Cassio, my lord, has kill'd a young Venetian
Call'd Roderigo.

**Othello.**           Roderigo kill'd!
And Cassio kill'd?

**Emilia.**           No, Cassio is not kill'd.

**Othello.** Not Cassio kill'd! then murder 's out of tune,
And sweet revenge grows harsh.

**Desdemona.** O! falsely, falsely murder'd.

**Emilia.**                     Alas! what cry is that?

**Othello.** That! what?

**Emilia.** Out, and alas! that was my lady's voice:
Help! Help, ho! help! O lady, speak again!                    120
Sweet Desdemona! O! sweet mistress, speak.

**Desdemona.** A guiltless death I die.

**Emilia.** O! who hath done this deed?

**Desdemona.** Nobody; I myself; farewell:
Commend me to my kind lord. O! farewell!                    *(Dies.)*

**Othello.** Why, how should she be murder'd?

**Emilia.**                     Alas! who knows?

**Othello.** You heard her say herself it was not I.

**Emilia.** She said so; I must needs report the truth.

**Othello.** She 's like a liar gone to burning hell;
'Twas I that kill'd her.

**Emilia.**                 O! the more angel she,                    130
And you the blacker devil.

**Othello.** She turn'd to folly, and she was a whore.

**Emilia.** Thou dost belie her, and thou art a devil.

**Othello.** She was false as water.

---

[581] Open up (as in an earthquake).     [582] Straying.

**Emilia.** Thou art rash as fire to say
That she was false! O! she was heavenly true.
**Othello.** Cassio did tup her; ask thy husband else.
O! I were damn'd beneath all depth in hell
But that I did proceed[583] upon just grounds
To this extremity. Thy husband knew it all.
**Emilia.** My husband! 140
**Othello.** Thy husband.
**Emilia.** That she was false to wedlock?
**Othello.** Ay, with Cassio. Nay, had she been true,
If heaven would make me such another world
Of one entire and perfect chrysolite,[584]
I'd not have sold her for it.
**Emilia.** My husband!
**Othello.** Ay, 'twas he that told me first:
An honest man he is, and hates the slime
That sticks on filthy deeds.
**Emilia.** My husband!
**Othello.** What needs this iterance,[585] woman? I say thy husband. 150
**Emilia.** O mistress! villany hath made mocks with love.
My husband say that she was false!
**Othello.** He, woman;
I say, thy husband: dost understand the word?
My friend, thy husband, honest, honest Iago.
**Emilia.** If he say so, may his pernicious soul
Rot half a grain a day! he lies to the heart:
She was too fond of her most filthy bargain.[586]
**Othello.** Ha!
**Emilia.** Do thy worst:
This deed of thine is no more worthy heaven 160
Than thou wast worthy her.
**Othello.** Peace! you were best.[587]
**Emilia.** Thou hast not half the power to do me harm
As I have to be hurt. O gull! O dolt!
As ignorant as dirt! thou hast done a deed, —
I care not for thy sword; I'll make thee known,
Though I lost twenty lives. Help! help, ho! help!
The Moor has kill'd my mistress! murder! murder!

*(Enter Montano, Gratiano, Iago, and others.)*

**Montano.** What is the matter? How now, general!
**Emilia.** O! are you come, Iago? you have done well,
That men must lay their murders on your neck. 170

---

[583] Had I not proceeded.    [584] Topaz.    [585] Repetition.    [586] I.e., Othello.    [587] You'd better be quiet.

**Gratiano.** What is the matter?

**Emilia.** Disprove this villain if thou be'st a man:
He says thou told'st him that his wife was false.
I know thou didst not, thou 'rt not such a villain.
Speak, for my heart is full.

**Iago.** I told him what I thought, and told no more
Than what he found himself was apt and true.

**Emilia.** But did you ever tell him she was false?

**Iago.** I did.

**Emilia.** You told a lie, an odious damned lie;                     180
Upon my soul, a lie, a wicked lie;
She false with Cassio! Did you say with Cassio?

**Iago.** With Cassio, mistress. Go to, charm[588] your tongue.

**Emilia.** I will not charm my tongue; I am bound to speak.
My mistress here lies murder'd in her bed.

**All.** O heavens forfend!

**Emilia.** And your reports have set the murder on.

**Othello.** Nay, stare not, masters; it is true, indeed.

**Gratiano.** 'Tis a strange truth.

**Montano.** O monstrous act!

**Emilia.**                      Villany! villany! villany!          190
I think upon 't, I think, I smell 't; O villany!
I thought so then;[589] I'll kill myself for grief.
O! villany, villany!

**Iago.** What! are you mad? I charge you, get you home.

**Emilia.** Good gentlemen, let me have leave to speak:
'Tis proper I obey him, but not now.
Perchance, Iago, I will ne'er go home.

**Othello.** O! O! O!                                   *(Falls on the bed.)*

**Emilia.**                 Nay, lay thee down and roar,
For thou hast kill'd the sweetest innocent
That e'er did lift up eye.

**Othello.**                  O! she was foul.                       *(Rises.)*
I scarce did know you, uncle. There lies your niece,
Whose breath, indeed, these hands have newly stopp'd:
I know this act shows terrible and grim.

**Gratiano.** Poor Desdemona! I am glad thy father 's dead.
Thy match was mortal to him, and pure grief
Shore[590] his old thread in twain: did he live now,
This sight would make him do a desperate turn,
Yea, curse his better angel from his side,
And fall to reprobation.[591]

---

[588] I.e., into silence.   [589] *Cf.* "I will be hang'd, if some eternal villain, / Some busy and insinuating rogue, / Some cogging cozening slave, to get some office, / Have not devis'd this slander; . . ." (IV, 2, 130 ff.). Emilia means not that she guessed Iago's guilt but that she rightly guessed the slanderer's motive.   [590] Cut.   [591] Damnation.

**Othello.** 'Tis pitiful; but yet Iago knows                                    210
    That she with Cassio hath the act of shame
    A thousand times committed; Cassio confess'd it:
    And she did gratify[592] his amorous works
    With that recognizance and pledge of love
    Which I first gave her. I saw it in his hand:
    It was a handkerchief, an antique token
    My father gave my mother.
**Emilia.** O heaven! O heavenly powers!
**Iago.**                                    Come, hold your peace.
**Emilia.** 'Twill out, 'twill out; I hold my peace, sir? no;
    No, I will speak as liberal as the north;[593]                                    220
    Let heaven and men and devils, let them all,
    All, all, cry shame against me, yet I'll speak.
**Iago.** Be wise, and get you home.
**Emilia.**                                    I will not.

*(Iago threatens to stab Emilia.)*

**Gratiano.**                                    Fie!
    Your sword upon a woman!
**Emilia.** O thou dull Moor! that handkerchief thou speak'st of
    I found by fortune and did give my husband;
    For often, with a solemn earnestness,
    More than, indeed, belong'd to such a trifle,
    He begg'd of me to steal it.
**Iago.**                                    Villainous whore!
**Emilia.** She give it Cassio! no, alas! I found it,                                    230
    And I did give 't my husband.
**Iago.**                                    Filth, thou liest!
**Emilia.** By heaven, I do not, I do not, gentlemen.
    O murderous coxcomb![594] what should such a fool
    Do with so good a wife?
**Othello.**                                    Are there no stones[595] in heaven
    But what serve for the thunder? Precious villain!

*(He runs at Iago. Iago stabs Emilia.)*

**Gratiano.** The woman falls; sure, he has kill'd his wife.                                    *(Exit Iago.)*
**Emilia.** Ay, ay; O! lay me by my mistress' side.
**Gratiano.** He 's gone; but his wife 's kill'd.
**Montano.** 'Tis a notorious[596] villain. Take you this weapon,
    Which I have here recover'd from the Moor.                                    240

---

[592] Reward.    [593] I.e., the north wind (?), the supposedly free-spoken people of north England (?).
[594] Idiot.    [595] I.e., thunderbolts (to strike Iago down).    [596] Notable.

Come, guard the door without; let him not pass,
But kill him rather. I'll after that same villain,
For 'tis a damned slave.                    *(Exeunt Montano and Gratiano.)*

**Othello.**                    I am not valiant neither,
But every puny whipster[597] gets my sword.
But why should honour outlive honesty?
Let it go all.

**Emilia.**          What did thy song bode, lady?
Hark, canst thou hear me? I will play the swan,
And die in music: —
*(Sings.)*                    Willow, willow, willow.
Moor, she was chaste; she lov'd thee, cruel Moor;
So come my soul to bliss as I speak true;                    250
So speaking as I think, I die, I die.                    *(Dies.)*

**Othello.** I have another weapon in this chamber;
It is a sword of Spain, the ice-brook's temper.[598]
O! here it is. Uncle, I must come forth.

**Gratiano** *(within).* If thou attempt it, it will cost thee dear:
Thou hast no weapon, and perforce must suffer.

**Othello.** Look in upon me then, and speak with me,
Or, naked[599] as I am, I will assault thee.


*(Re-enter Gratiano.)*


**Gratiano.** What is the matter?
**Othello.**                              Behold! I have a weapon;
A better never did itself sustain                    260
Upon a soldier's thigh: I have seen the day,
That with this little arm, and this good sword,
I have made my way through more impediments
Than twenty times your stop: but, O vain boast!
Who can control his fate? 'tis not so now.
Be not afraid, though you do see me weapon'd;
Here is my journey's end, here is my butt,[600]
And very sea-mark of my utmost sail.[601]
Do you go back dismay'd? 'tis a lost fear;
Man but a rush[602] against Othello's breast,                    270
And he retires. Where should Othello go?
Now how dost thou look now? O ill-starr'd wench!
Pale as thy smock! when we shall meet at compt,[603]
This look of thine will hurl my soul from heaven,
And fiends will snatch at it. Cold, cold, my girl!

---

[597] I.e., a small boy whipping a top.    [598] Tempered in icy water (or the reference may be to Innsbruck, famed for the quality of its steel, but this hardly fits "a sword of Spain"). [599] Unarmed.    [600] Goal, end, limit.    [601] Destination of my farthest journey.    [602] Wield but a reed. [603] On the day of judgment.

Even like thy chastity.
O! cursed, cursed slave. Whip me, ye devils,
From the possession of this heavenly sight!
Blow me about in winds! roast me in sulphur!
Wash me in steep-down gulfs of liquid fire!                                    280
O Desdemona! Desdemona! dead!
Oh! Oh! Oh!

*(Enter Lodovico, Montano, Cassio carried in a chair, and Officers with Iago, prisoner.)*

**Lodovico.**  Where is this rash and most unfortunate man?
**Othello.**  That's he that was Othello; here I am.
**Lodovico.**  Where is that viper? bring the villain forth.
**Othello.**  I look down towards his feet;[604] but that's a fable.
    If that thou be'st a devil, I cannot kill thee.                   *(Wounds Iago.)*
**Lodovico.**  Wrench his sword from him.                    *(Othello is disarmed.)*
**Iago.**                              I bleed, sir; but not kill'd.
**Othello.**  I am not sorry neither; I'd have thee live;
    For, in my sense,[605] 'tis happiness to die.                               290
**Lodovico.**  O thou Othello! that wert once so good,
    Fall'n in the practice[606] of a damned slave,[607]
    What shall be said to thee?
**Othello.**                    Why, any thing:
    An honourable murderer, if you will;
    For nought did I in hate, but all in honour.
**Lodovico.**  This wretch hath part confess'd his villany:
    Did you and he consent in Cassio's death?
**Othello.**  Ay.
**Cassio.**  Dear general, I never gave you cause.
**Othello.**  I do believe it, and I ask your pardon.                            300
    Will you, I pray, demand that demi-devil
    Why he hath thus ensnar'd my soul and body?
**Iago.**  Demand me nothing: what you know, you know:
    From this time forth I never will speak word.
**Lodovico.**  What! not to pray?
**Gratiano.**                    Torments will ope[608] your lips.
**Othello.**  Well, thou dost best.
**Lodovico.**  Sir, you shall understand what hath befall'n,
    Which, as I think, you know not. Here is a letter
    Found in the pocket of the slain Roderigo,
    And here another; the one of them imports                               310
    The death of Cassio to be undertook
    By Roderigo.

---

[604] I.e., for the Devil's cloven hoof.    [605] The way I feel.    [606] Plot, machination.    [607] I.e., Iago.    [608] Open.

**Othello.** O villain!

**Cassio.**                 Most heathenish and most gross!

**Lodovico.** Now here's another discontented paper,
Found in his pocket too; and this, it seems,
Roderigo meant to have sent this damned villain,
But that, belike,[609] Iago in the interim[610]
Came in and satisfied him.

**Othello.**                     O the pernicious caitiff!
How came you, Cassio, by that handkerchief
That was my wife's?

**Cassio.**             I found it in my chamber;                    320
And he himself confess'd but even now
That there he dropp'd it for a special purpose
Which wrought to his desire.

**Othello.**                 O fool! fool! fool!

**Cassio.** There is besides in Roderigo's letter
How he upbraids Iago that he made him
Brave me upon the watch; whereon it came
That I was cast:[611] and even but now he spake,
After long seeming dead, Iago hurt him,
Iago set him on.

**Lodovico.** You must forsake this room and go with us;          330
Your power and your command is taken off,
And Cassio rules in Cyprus. For this slave,
If there be any cunning cruelty
That can torment him much and hold him long,
It shall be his. You shall close prisoner rest,
Till that the nature of your fault be known
To the Venetian state. Come, bring him away.

**Othello.** Soft you; a word or two before you go.
I have done the state some service, and they know 't;
No more of that. I pray you, in your letters,                    340
When you shall these unlucky deeds relate,
Speak of me as I am; nothing extenuate,
Nor set down aught[612] in malice: then, must you speak
Of one that lov'd not wisely but too well;
Of one not easily jealous, but, being wrought,
Perplex'd[613] in the extreme; of one whose hand
Like the base Indian,[614] threw a pearl away
Richer than all his tribe; of one whose subdu'd[615] eyes
Albeit unused to the melting mood,

---

[609] Most likely.    [610] In the meantime.    [611] Dismissed.    [612] Anything.    [613] Distracted.    [614] The Folio reads "Iudean." Both readings denote the foolish infidel who fails to appreciate the treasure he possesses.    [615] Overcome (by grief).

Drop tears as fast as the Arabian trees                                          350
Their med'cinable gum. Set you down this;
And say besides, that in Aleppo once,
Where a malignant and a turban'd Turk
Beat a Venetian and traduc'd the state,
I took by the throat the circumcised dog,
And smote him, thus.                                        *(Stabs himself.)*
**Lodovico.**  O bloody period![616]
**Gratiano.**                        All that's spoke is marr'd.
**Othello.**  I kiss'd thee ere I killed thee; no way but this.
                                                    *(Falling upon Desdemona.)*
Killing myself to die upon a kiss.                              *(Dies.)*
**Cassio.**  This did I fear, but thought he had no weapon;              360
For he was great of heart.
**Lodovico** *(to Iago).*        O Spartan dog!
More fell[617] than anguish, hunger, or the sea.
Look on the tragic loading of this bed;
This is thy work; the object poisons sight;
Let it be hid. Gratiano, keep the house,
And seize upon the fortunes of the Moor,
For they succeed on you. To you, lord governor,
Remains the censure of this hellish villain,
The time, the place, the torture; O! enforce it.
Myself will straight aboard, and to the state                    370
This heavy act with heavy heart relate.                        *(Exeunt.)*

## FOR ANALYSIS

**1.**  In what sense might it be said that Othello is responsible for his own downfall?

**2.**  Discuss the functions of the minor **characters**, such as Roderigo, Bianca, and Emilia.

**3.**  Is the rapidity of Othello's emotional collapse (act III, scene 3) plausible? Does his race contribute to his emotional turmoil? Explain.

**4.**  The first part of act IV, scene 2 (until Othello exits), is sometimes called the "brothel" scene. What features of Othello's language and behavior justify this designation?

**5.**  Why does Iago kill Roderigo?

**6.**  What are the benefits of moving the main characters to Cyprus rather than setting the drama in Venice?

**7.**  Compare the speeches of Cassio and Iago in act II, scene 1. What do the differences in language and **style** reveal about their characters?

**8.**  Carefully review the play to determine how much time elapses between the arrival in Cyprus and the end of the action. Can you find narrated events that could not possibly have occurred within that time frame? What effect do the chronological inconsistencies have on you? Explain.

[616] Ending.    [617] Grim, cruel.

## MAKING ARGUMENTS

In a note that Romantic poet Samuel Taylor Coleridge wrote in his copy of Shakespeare's play, Iago is described in a now-famous phrase as possessing a "motiveless malignity," that is, a desire to do evil for evil's sake, and for no other reason. Do you find the reasons that Iago gives for his actions consistent and convincing, or do you agree with Coleridge? Why?

## WRITING TOPICS

**1.** Write an analysis of the **figurative language** in Iago's soliloquies at the end of act I and at the end of act II, scene 1.

**2.** Choose a minor **character**, such as Roderigo, Emilia, or Bianca, and in a carefully reasoned essay, explain how the character contributes to the design of the play.

**3.** Discuss the relationship between love and hate in this **tragedy**.

## MAKING CONNECTIONS

**1.** Place yourself in Othello's position. How would you respond to Iago's machinations? If you were in Desdemona's position, how would you deal with Othello's apparently bizarre behavior?

**2.** Compare Desdemona's hope that her virtue will win out to the hope (or cynicism) of the wife Terri in Carver's "What We Talk About When We Talk About Love" (p. 598). Why do you think Desdemona remains submissive?

## SUSAN GLASPELL   (1876–1948)

# TRIFLES   1916

CHARACTERS

**George Henderson,** county
   attorney
**Henry Peters,** sheriff

**Lewis Hale,** a neighboring farmer
**Mrs. Peters**
**Mrs. Hale**

**Scene**

*The kitchen in the now abandoned farmhouse of John Wright, a gloomy kitchen, and left without having been put in order — the walls covered with a faded wall paper. Down right is a door leading to the parlor. On the right wall above this door is a built-in kitchen cupboard with shelves in the upper portion and drawers below. In the rear wall at right, up two steps is a door opening onto stairs leading to the second floor. In the rear wall at left is a door to the shed and from there to the outside. Between these two doors is an old-fashioned black iron stove. Running along the left wall from the shed door is an old iron sink and sink shelf, in which is set a hand pump. Downstage of the sink is an uncurtained window. Near the window is an old wooden rocker. Center stage is an unpainted wooden kitchen table with straight chairs on either side. There is a small chair down right. Unwashed pans under the sink, a loaf of bread outside the breadbox, a dish towel on the table — other signs of incompleted work. At the rear the shed door opens and the Sheriff comes in followed by the County Attorney and Hale. The Sheriff and Hale are men in middle life, the County Attorney is a young man; all are much bundled up and go at once to the stove. They are followed by the two women — the Sheriff's wife, Mrs. Peters, first; she is a slightly wiry woman, with a thin nervous face. Mrs. Hale is larger and would ordinarily be called more comfortable looking, but she is disturbed now and looks fearfully about as she enters. The women have come in slowly, and stand close together near the door.*

**County Attorney** *(at stove rubbing his hands).* This feels good. Come up to the
   fire, ladies.
**Mrs. Peters** *(after taking a step forward).* I'm not — cold.
**Sheriff** *(unbuttoning his overcoat and stepping away from the stove to right of table
   as if to mark the beginning of official business).* Now, Mr. Hale, before we move
   things about, you explain to Mr. Henderson just what you saw when you came
   here yesterday morning.
**County Attorney** *(crossing down to left of the table).* By the way, has anything
   been moved? Are things just as you left them yesterday?
**Sheriff** *(looking about).* It's just about the same. When it dropped below zero
   last night I thought I'd better send Frank out this morning to make a fire for

us — *(sits right of center table)* no use getting pneumonia with a big case on, but I told him not to touch anything except the stove — and you know Frank.

**County Attorney.** Somebody should have been left here yesterday.

**Sheriff.** Oh — yesterday. When I had to send Frank to Morris Center for that man who went crazy — I want you to know I had my hands full yesterday. I knew you could get back from Omaha by today and as long as I went over everything here myself —

**County Attorney.** Well, Mr. Hale, tell just what happened when you came here yesterday morning.

**Hale** *(crossing down to above table).* Harry and I started to town with a load of potatoes. We came along the road from my place and as I got here I said, "I'm going to see if I can't get John Wright to go in with me on a party telephone." I spoke to Wright about it once before and he put me off, saying folks talked too much anyway, and all he asked was peace and quiet — I guess you know about how much he talked himself; but I thought maybe if I went to the house and talked about it before his wife, though I said to Harry that I didn't know as what his wife wanted made much difference to John————

**County Attorney.** Let's talk about that later, Mr. Hale. I do want to talk about that, but tell now just what happened when you got to the house.

**Hale.** I didn't hear or see anything; I knocked at the door, and still it was all quiet inside. I knew they must be up, it was past eight o'clock. So I knocked again, and I thought I heard somebody say, "Come in." I wasn't sure. I'm not sure yet, but I opened the door — this door *(indicating the door by which the two women are still standing)* and there in that rocker — *(pointing at it)* sat Mrs. Wright. *(They all look at the rocker down left.)*

**County Attorney.** What — was she doing?

**Hale.** She was rockin' back and forth. She had her apron in her hand and was kind of — pleating it.

**County Attorney.** And how did she — look?

**Hale.** Well, she looked queer.

**County Attorney.** How do you mean — queer?

**Hale.** Well, as if she didn't know what she was going to do next. And kind of done up.

**County Attorney** *(takes out notebook and pencil and sits left of center table).* How did she seem to feel about your coming?

**Hale.** Why, I don't think she minded — one way or another. She didn't pay much attention. I said, "How do, Mrs. Wright, it's cold, ain't it?" And she said, "Is it?" — and went on kind of pleating at her apron. Well, I was surprised; she didn't ask me to come up to the stove, or to set down, but just sat there, not even looking at me, so I said, "I want to see John." And then she — laughed. I guess you would call it a laugh. I thought of Harry and the team outside, so I said a little sharp: "Can't I see John?" "No," she says, kind o' dull like. "Ain't he home?" says I. "Yes," says she, "he's home." "Then why can't I see him?" I asked her, out of patience. " 'Cause he's dead," says she. *Dead?* says I. She just nodded her head, not getting a bit excited, but rockin' back and forth. "Why — where is he?" says I, not knowing what to say. She just pointed upstairs — like that. *(Himself pointing to the room above.)* I started for the stairs, with the idea of going up there. I walked from there to here — then I says, "Why, what did he die of?" "He died of a rope round his neck," says she, and just went on, pleatin' at her apron. Well, I went out and called Harry. I thought I might — need help. We went upstairs and there he was lyin'———

County Attorney. I think I'd rather have you go into that upstairs, where you can point it all out. Just go on now with the rest of the story.

Hale. Well, my first thought was to get that rope off. It looked . . . *(stops; his face twitches)* . . . but Harry, he went up to him, and he said, "No, he's dead all right, and we'd better not touch anything." So we went back downstairs. She was still sitting that same way. "Has anybody been notified?" I asked. "No," says she, unconcerned. "Who did this, Mrs. Wright?" said Harry. He said it business-like — and she stopped pleatin' of her apron. "I don't know," she says. "You don't *know*?" says Harry. "No," says she. "Weren't you sleepin' in the bed with him?" says Harry. "Yes," says she, "but I was on the inside." "Somebody slipped a rope round his neck and strangled him and you didn't wake up?" says Harry. "I didn't wake up," she said after him. We must 'a' looked as if we didn't see how that could be, for after a minute she said, "I sleep sound." Harry was going to ask her more questions but I said maybe we ought to let her tell her story first to the coroner, or the sheriff, so Harry went fast as he could to Rivers' place, where there's a telephone.

County Attorney. And what did Mrs. Wright do when she knew that you had gone for the coroner?

Hale. She moved from the rocker to that chair over there *(pointing to a small chair in the down right corner)* and just sat there with her hands held together and looking down. I got a feeling that I ought to make some conversation, so I said I had come in to see if John wanted to put in a telephone, and at that she started to laugh, and then she stopped and looked at me — scared. *(The County Attorney, who has had his notebook out, makes a note.)* I dunno, maybe it wasn't scared. I wouldn't like to say it was. Soon Harry got back, and then Dr. Lloyd came and you, Mr. Peters, and so I guess that's all I know that you don't.

County Attorney *(rising and looking around)*. I guess we'll go upstairs first — and then out to the barn and around there. *(To the Sheriff.)* You're convinced that there was nothing important here — nothing that would point to any motive?

Sheriff. Nothing here but kitchen things.

*(The County Attorney, after again looking around the kitchen, opens the door of a cupboard closet in right wall. He brings a small chair from right — gets on it and looks on a shelf. Pulls his hand away, sticky.)*

County Attorney. Here's a nice mess. *(The women draw nearer up center.)*

**Mrs. Peters** *(to the other woman)*. Oh, her fruit; it did freeze. *(To the Lawyer.)* She worried about that when it turned so cold. She said the fire'd go out and her jars would break.

**Sheriff** *(rises)*. Well, can you beat the woman! Held for murder and worryin' about her preserves.

**County Attorney** *(getting down from chair)*. I guess before we're through she may have something more serious than preserves to worry about. *(Crosses down right center.)*

**Hale.** Well, women are used to worrying over trifles. *(The two women move a little closer together.)*

**County Attorney** *(with the gallantry of a young politician)*. And yet, for all their worries, what would we do without the ladies? *(The women do not unbend. He goes below the center table to the sink, takes a dipperful of water from the pail, and pouring it into a basin, washes his hands. While he is doing this the Sheriff and Hale cross to cupboard, which they inspect. The County Attorney starts to wipe his hands on the roller towel, turns it for a cleaner place.)* Dirty towels! *(Kicks his foot against the pans under the sink.)* Not much of a housekeeper, would you say, ladies?

**Mrs. Hale** *(stiffly)*. There's a great deal of work to be done on a farm.

**County Attorney.** To be sure. And yet *(with a little bow to her)* I know there are some Dickson County farmhouses which do not have such roller towels.

*(He gives it a pull to expose its full length again.)*

**Mrs. Hale.** Those towels get dirty awful quick. Men's hands aren't always as clean as they might be.

**County Attorney.** Ah, loyal to your sex, I see. But you and Mrs. Wright were neighbors. I suppose you were friends, too.

**Mrs. Hale** *(shaking her head)*. I've not seen much of her of late years. I've not been in this house — it's more than a year.

**County Attorney** *(crossing to women up center)*. And why was that? You didn't like her?

**Mrs. Hale.** I liked her all well enough. Farmers' wives have their hands full, Mr. Henderson. And then————

**County Attorney.** Yes————?

**Mrs. Hale** *(looking about)*. It never seemed a very cheerful place.

**County Attorney.** No — it's not cheerful. I shouldn't say she had the homemaking instinct.

**Mrs. Hale.** Well, I don't know as Wright had, either.

**County Attorney.** You mean that they didn't get on very well?

**Mrs. Hale.** No, I don't mean anything. But I don't think a place'd be any cheerfuller for John Wright's being in it.

**County Attorney.** I'd like to talk more of that a little later. I want to get the lay of things upstairs now.

*(He goes past the women to up right where steps lead to a stair door.)*

**Sheriff.** I suppose anything Mrs. Peters does'll be all right. She was to take in some clothes for her, you know, and a few little things. We left in such a hurry, yesterday.

**County Attorney.** Yes, but I would like to see what you take, Mrs. Peters, and keep an eye out for anything that might be of use to us.

**Mrs. Peters.** Yes, Mr. Henderson.

*(The men leave by up right door to stairs. The women listen to the men's steps on the stairs, then look about the kitchen.)*

**Mrs. Hale** *(crossing left to sink)*. I'd hate to have men coming into my kitchen, snooping around and criticizing.

*(She arranges the pans under sink which the Lawyer had shoved out of place.)*

**Mrs. Peters.** Of course it's no more than their duty.

*(Crosses to cupboard up right.)*

**Mrs. Hale.** Duty's all right, but I guess that deputy sheriff that came out to make the fire might have got a little of this on. *(Gives the roller towel a pull.)* Wish I'd thought of that sooner. Seems mean to talk about her for not having things slicked up when she had to come away in such a hurry.

*(Crosses right to Mrs. Peters at cupboard.)*

**Mrs. Peters** *(who has been looking through cupboard, lifts one end of towel that covers a pan)*. She had bread set.

*(Stands still.)*

**Mrs. Hale** *(eyes fixed on a loaf of bread beside the breadbox, which is on a low shelf of the cupboard)*. She was going to put this in there. *(Picks up a loaf, abruptly drops it. In a manner of returning to familiar things.)* It's a shame about her fruit. I wonder if it's all gone. *(Gets up on the chair and looks.)* I think there's some here that's all right, Mrs. Peters. Yes — here; *(holding it toward the window)* this is cherries, too. *(Looking again.)* I declare I believe that's the only one. *(Gets down, jar in her hand. Goes to the sink and wipes it off on the outside.)* She'll feel awful bad after all her hard work in the hot weather. I remember the afternoon I put up my cherries last summer.

*(She puts the jar on the big kitchen table, center of the room. With a sigh, is about to sit down in the rocking chair. Before she is seated realizes what chair it is; with a slow*

*look at it, steps back. The chair which she has touched rocks back and forth. Mrs. Peters moves to center table and they both watch the chair rock for a moment or two.)*

**Mrs. Peters** *(shaking off the mood which the empty rocking chair has evoked. Now in a businesslike manner she speaks).* Well I must get those things from the front room closet. *(She goes to the door at the right but, after looking into the other room, steps back.)* You coming with me, Mrs. Hale? You could help me carry them. *(They go in the other room; reappear, Mrs. Peters carrying a dress, petticoat, and skirt, Mrs. Hale following with a pair of shoes.)* My, it's cold in there.

*(She puts the clothes on the big table and hurries to the stove.)*

**Mrs. Hale** *(right of center table examining the skirt).* Wright was close. I think maybe that's why she kept so much to herself. She didn't even belong to the Ladies' Aid. I suppose she felt she couldn't do her part, and then you don't enjoy things when you feel shabby. I heard she used to wear pretty clothes and be lively, when she was Minnie Foster, one of the town girls singing in the choir. But that — oh, that was thirty years ago. This all you want to take in?

**Mrs. Peters.** She said she wanted an apron. Funny thing to want, for there isn't much to get you dirty in jail, goodness knows. But I suppose just to make her feel more natural. *(Crosses to cupboard.)* She said they was in the top drawer in this cupboard. Yes, here. And then her little shawl that always hung behind the door. *(Opens stair door and looks.)* Yes, here it is.

*(Quickly shuts door leading upstairs.)*

**Mrs. Hale** *(abruptly moving toward her).* Mrs. Peters?

**Mrs. Peters.** Yes, Mrs. Hale?

*(At up right door.)*

**Mrs. Hale.** Do you think she did it?

**Mrs. Peters** *(in a frightened voice).* Oh, I don't know.

**Mrs. Hale.** Well, I don't think she did. Asking for an apron and her little shawl. Worrying about her fruit.

**Mrs. Peters** *(starts to speak, glances up, where footsteps are heard in the room above. In a low voice).* Mr. Peters says it looks bad for her. Mr. Henderson is awful sarcastic in a speech and he'll make fun of her sayin' she didn't wake up.

**Mrs. Hale.** Well, I guess John Wright didn't wake when they was slipping that rope under his neck.

**Mrs. Peters** *(crossing slowly to table and placing shawl and apron on table with other clothing).* No, it's strange. It must have been done awful crafty and still. They say it was such a — funny way to kill a man, rigging it all up like that.

**Mrs. Hale** *(crossing to left of Mrs. Peters at table).* That's just what Mr. Hale said. There was a gun in the house. He says that's what he can't understand.

**Mrs. Peters.** Mr. Henderson said coming out that what was needed for the case was a motive; something to show anger, or — sudden feeling.

**Mrs. Hale** *(who is standing by the table).* Well, I don't see any signs of anger around here. *(She puts her hand on the dish towel, which lies on the table, stands looking down at table, one-half of which is clean, the other half messy.)* It's wiped to here. *(Makes a move as if to finish work, then turns and looks at loaf of bread outside the breadbox. Drops towel. In that voice of coming back to familiar things.)* Wonder how they are finding things upstairs. *(Crossing below table to down right.)* I hope she had it a little more red-up[1] up there. You know, it seems kind of *sneaking.* Locking her up in town and then coming out here and trying to get her own house to turn against her!

**Mrs. Peters.** But, Mrs. Hale, the law is the law.

**Mrs. Hale.** I s'pose 'tis. *(Unbuttoning her coat.)* Better loosen up your things, Mrs. Peters. You won't feel them when you go out.

*(Mrs. Peters takes off her fur tippet, goes to hang it on chair back left of table, stands looking at the work basket on floor near down left window.)*

**Mrs. Peters.** She was piecing a quilt.

*(She brings the large sewing basket to the center table and they look at the bright pieces, Mrs. Hale above the table and Mrs. Peters left of it.)*

**Mrs. Hale.** It's a log cabin pattern. Pretty, isn't it? I wonder if she was goin' to quilt it or just knot it?

*(Footsteps have been heard coming down the stairs. The Sheriff enters followed by Hale and the County Attorney.)*

**Sheriff.** They wonder if she was going to quilt it or just knot it!

*(The men laugh, the women look abashed.)*

**County Attorney** *(rubbing his hands over the stove).* Frank's fire didn't do much up there, did it? Well, let's go out to the barn and get that cleared up.

*(The men go outside by up left door.)*

**Mrs. Hale** *(resentfully).* I don't know as there's anything so strange, our takin' up our time with little things while we're waiting for them to get the evidence.

---

[1] A slang expression for "make attractive."

*(She sits in chair right of table smoothing out a block with decision.)* I don't see as it's anything to laugh about.

**Mrs. Peters** *(apologetically).* Of course they've got awful important things on their minds.

*(Pulls up a chair and joins Mrs. Hale at the left of the table.)*

**Mrs. Hale** *(examining another block).* Mrs. Peters, look at this one. Here, this is the one she was working on, and look at the sewing! All the rest of it has been so nice and even. And look at this! It's all over the place! Why, it looks as if she didn't know what she was about!

*(After she has said this they look at each other, then start to glance back at the door. After an instant Mrs. Hale has pulled at a knot and ripped the sewing.)*

**Mrs. Peters.** Oh, what are you doing, Mrs. Hale?

**Mrs. Hale** *(mildly).* Just pulling out a stitch or two that's not sewed very good. *(Threading a needle.)* Bad sewing always made me fidgety.

**Mrs. Peters** *(with a glance at door, nervously).* I don't think we ought to touch things.

**Mrs. Hale.** I'll just finish up this end. *(Suddenly stopping and leaning forward.)* Mrs. Peters?

**Mrs. Peters.** Yes, Mrs. Hale?

**Mrs. Hale.** What do you suppose she was so nervous about?

**Mrs. Peters.** Oh — I don't know. I don't know as she was nervous. I sometimes sew awful queer when I'm just tired. *(Mrs. Hale starts to say something, looks at Mrs. Peters, then goes on sewing.)* Well, I must get these things wrapped up. They may be through sooner than we think. *(Putting apron and other things together.)* I wonder where I can find a piece of paper, and string.

*(Rises.)*

**Mrs. Hale.** In that cupboard, maybe.

**Mrs. Peters** *(crosses right looking in cupboard).* Why, here's a bird-cage. *(Holds it up.)* Did she have a bird, Mrs. Hale?

**Mrs. Hale.** Why, I don't know whether she did or not — I've not been here for so long. There was a man around last year selling canaries cheap, but I don't know as she took one; maybe she did. She used to sing real pretty herself.

**Mrs. Peters** *(glancing around).* Seems funny to think of a bird here. But she must have had one, or why would she have a cage? I wonder what happened to it?

**Mrs. Hale.** I s'pose maybe the cat got it.

**Mrs. Peters.** No, she didn't have a cat. She's got that feeling some people have about cats — being afraid of them. My cat got in her room and she was real upset and asked me to take it out.

**Mrs. Hale.** My sister Bessie was like that. Queer, ain't it?

**Mrs. Peters** *(examining the cage).* Why, look at this door. It's broke. One hinge is pulled apart.

*(Takes a step down to Mrs. Hale's right.)*

**Mrs. Hale** *(looking too).* Looks as if someone must have been rough with it.

**Mrs. Peters.** Why, yes.

*(She brings the cage forward and puts it on the table.)*

**Mrs. Hale** *(glancing toward up left door).* I wish if they're going to find any evidence they'd be about it. I don't like this place.

**Mrs. Peters.** But I'm awful glad you came with me, Mrs. Hale. It would be lonesome for me sitting here alone.

**Mrs. Hale.** It would, wouldn't it? *(Dropping her sewing.)* But I tell you what I do wish, Mrs. Peters. I wish I had come over sometimes when *she* was here. I — *(looking around the room)* — wish I had.

**Mrs. Peters.** But of course you were awful busy, Mrs. Hale — your house and your children.

**Mrs. Hale** *(rises and crosses left).* I could've come. I stayed away because it weren't cheerful — and that's why I ought to have come. I — *(looking out left window)* — I've never liked this place. Maybe because it's down in a hollow and you don't see the road. I dunno what it is, but it's a lonesome place and always was. I wish I had come over to see Minnie Foster sometimes. I can see now —

*(Shakes her head.)*

**Mrs. Peters** *(left of table and above it).* Well, you mustn't reproach yourself, Mrs. Hale. Somehow we just don't see how it is with other folks until — something turns up.

**Mrs. Hale.** Not having children makes less work — but it makes a quiet house, and Wright out to work all day, and no company when he did come in. *(Turning from window.)* Did you know John Wright, Mrs. Peters?

**Mrs. Peters.** Not to know him; I've seen him in town. They say he was a good man.

**Mrs. Hale.** Yes — good; he didn't drink, and kept his word as well as most, I guess, and paid his debts. But he was a hard man, Mrs. Peters. Just to pass the time of day with him — *(Shivers.)* Like a raw wind that gets to the bone. *(Pauses, her eye falling on the cage.)* I should think she would 'a' wanted a bird. But what do you suppose went with it?

**Mrs. Peters.** I don't know, unless it got sick and died.

*(She reaches over and swings the broken door, swings it again, both women watch it.)*

**Mrs. Hale.** You weren't raised round here, were you? *(Mrs. Peters shakes her head.)* You didn't know — her?

**Mrs. Peters.** Not till they brought her yesterday.

**Mrs. Hale.** She — come to think of it, she was kind of like a bird herself — real sweet and pretty, but kind of timid and — fluttery. How — she — did — change. *(Silence: then as if struck by a happy thought and relieved to get back to everyday things. Crosses right above Mrs. Peters to cupboard, replaces small chair used to stand on to its original place down right.)* Tell you what, Mrs. Peters, why don't you take the quilt in with you? It might take up her mind.

**Mrs. Peters.** Why, I think that's a real nice idea, Mrs. Hale. There couldn't possibly be any objection to it could there? Now, just what would I take? I wonder if her patches are in here — and her things.

*(They look in the sewing basket.)*

**Mrs. Hale** *(crosses to right of table).* Here's some red. I expect this has got sewing things in it. *(Brings out a fancy box.)* What a pretty box. Looks like something somebody would give you. Maybe her scissors are in here. *(Opens box. Suddenly puts her hand to her nose.)* Why———*(Mrs. Peters bends nearer, then turns her face away.)* There's something wrapped up in this piece of silk.

**Mrs. Peters.** Why, this isn't her scissors.

**Mrs. Hale** *(lifting the silk).* Oh, Mrs. Peters — it's———

*(Mrs. Peters bends closer.)*

**Mrs. Peters.** It's the bird.

**Mrs. Hale.** But, Mrs. Peters — look at it! Its neck! Look at its neck! It's all — other side *to.*

**Mrs. Peters.** Somebody — wrung — its — neck.

*(Their eyes meet. A look of growing comprehension, of horror. Steps are heard outside. Mrs. Hale slips box under quilt pieces, and sinks into her chair. Enter Sheriff and County Attorney. Mrs. Peters steps down left and stands looking out of window.)*

**County Attorney** *(as one turning from serious things to little pleasantries).* Well, ladies, have you decided whether she was going to quilt it or knot it?

*(Crosses to center above table.)*

**Mrs. Peters.** We think she was going to — knot it.

*(Sheriff crosses to right of stove, lifts stove lid, and glances at fire, then stands warming hands at stove.)*

**County Attorney.** Well, that's interesting, I'm sure. *(Seeing the bird-cage.)* Has the bird flown?

**Mrs. Hale** *(putting more quilt pieces over the box)*. We think the — cat got it.

**County Attorney** *(preoccupied)*. Is there a cat?

*(Mrs. Hale glances in a quick covert way at Mrs. Peters.)*

**Mrs. Peters** *(turning from window takes a step in)*. Well, not *now*. They're superstitious, you know. They leave.

**County Attorney** *(to Sheriff Peters, continuing an interrupted conversation)*. No sign at all of anyone having come from the outside. Their own rope. Now let's go up again and go over it piece by piece. *(They start upstairs.)* It would have to have been someone who knew just the————

*(Mrs. Peters sits down left of table. The two women sit there not looking at one another, but as if peering into something and at the same time holding back. When they talk now it is in the manner of feeling their way over strange ground, as if afraid of what they are saying, but as if they cannot help saying it.)*

**Mrs. Hale** *(hesitatively and in hushed voice)*. She liked the bird. She was going to bury it in that pretty box.

**Mrs. Peters** *(in a whisper)*. When I was a girl — my kitten — there was a boy took a hatchet, and before my eyes — and before I could get there————*(Covers her face an instant.)* If they hadn't held me back I would have — *(catches herself, looks upstairs where steps are heard, falters weakly)* — hurt him.

**Mrs. Hale** *(with a slow look around her)*. I wonder how it would seem never to have had any children around. *(Pause.)* No, Wright wouldn't like the bird — a thing that sang. She used to sing. He killed that, too.

**Mrs. Peters** *(moving uneasily)*. We don't know who killed the bird.

**Mrs. Hale.** I knew John Wright.

**Mrs. Peters.** It was an awful thing was done in this house that night, Mrs. Hale. Killing a man while he slept, slipping a rope around his neck that choked the life out of him.

**Mrs. Hale.** His neck. Choked the life out of him.

*(Her hand goes out and rests on the bird-cage.)*

**Mrs. Peters** *(with rising voice)*. We don't know who killed him. We don't know.

**Mrs. Hale** *(her own feeling not interrupted)*. If there'd been years and years of nothing, then a bird to sing to you, it would be awful — still, after the bird was still.

**Mrs. Peters** *(something within her speaking)*. I know what stillness is. When we homesteaded in Dakota, and my first baby died — after he was two years old, and me with no other then————

**Mrs. Hale** *(moving)*. How soon do you suppose they'll be through looking for the evidence?

**Mrs. Peters.** I know what stillness is. *(Pulling herself back.)* The law has got to punish crime, Mrs. Hale.

**Mrs. Hale** *(not as if answering that).* I wish you'd seen Minnie Foster when she wore a white dress with blue ribbons and stood up there in the choir and sang. *(A look around the room.)* Oh, I *wish* I'd come over here once in a while! That was a crime! That was a crime! Who's going to punish that?

**Mrs. Peters** *(looking upstairs).* We mustn't — take on.

**Mrs. Hale.** I might have known she needed help! I know how things can be — for women. I tell you, it's queer, Mrs. Peters. We live close together and we live far apart. We all go through the same things — it's all just a different kind of the same thing. *(Brushes her eyes, noticing the jar of fruit, reaches out for it.)* If I was you I wouldn't tell her her fruit was gone. Tell her it *ain't*. Tell her it's all right. Take this in to prove it to her. She — she may never know whether it was broke or not.

**Mrs. Peters** *(takes the jar, looks about for something to wrap it in; takes petticoat from the clothes brought from the other room, very nervously begins winding this around the jar. In a false voice).* My, it's a good thing the men couldn't hear us. Wouldn't they just laugh! Getting all stirred up over a little thing like a — dead canary. As if that could have anything to do with — with — wouldn't they *laugh!*

*(The men are heard coming downstairs.)*

**Mrs. Hale** *(under her breath).* Maybe they would — maybe they wouldn't.

**County Attorney.** No, Peters, it's all perfectly clear except a reason for doing it. But you know juries when it comes to women. If there was some definite thing. *(Crosses slowly to above table. Sheriff crosses down right. Mrs. Hale and Mrs. Peters remain seated at either side of table.)* Something to show — something to make a story about — a thing that would connect up with this strange way of doing it———

*(The women's eyes meet for an instant. Enter Hale from outer door.)*

**Hale** *(remaining by door).* Well, I've got the team around. Pretty cold out there.

**County Attorney.** I'm going to stay awhile by myself. *(To the Sheriff.)* You can send Frank out for me, can't you? I want to go over everything. I'm not satisfied that we can't do better.

**Sheriff.** Do you want to see what Mrs. Peters is going to take in?

*(The Lawyer picks up the apron, laughs.)*

**County Attorney.** Oh, I guess they're not very dangerous things the ladies have picked out. *(Moves a few things about, disturbing the quilt pieces which cover the box. Steps back.)* No, Mrs. Peters doesn't need supervising. For that matter a sheriff's wife is married to the law. Ever think of it that way, Mrs. Peters?

**Mrs. Peters.** Not — just that way.

**Sheriff** *(chuckling).* Married to the law. *(Moves to down right door to the other room.)* I just want you to come in here a minute, George. We ought to take a look at these windows.

**County Attorney** *(scoffingly).* Oh, windows!

**Sheriff.** We'll be right out, Mr. Hale.

*(Hale goes outside. The Sheriff follows the County Attorney into the room. Then Mrs. Hale rises, hands tight together, looking intensely at Mrs. Peters, whose eyes make a slow turn, finally meeting Mrs. Hale's. A moment Mrs. Hale holds her, then her own eyes point the way to where the box is concealed. Suddenly Mrs. Peters throws back quilt pieces and tries to put the box in the bag she is carrying. It is too big. She opens box, starts to take bird out, cannot touch it, goes to pieces, stands there helpless. Sound of a knob turning in the other room. Mrs. Hale snatches the box and puts it in the pocket of her big coat. Enter County Attorney and Sheriff, who remain down right.)*

**County Attorney** *(crosses to up left door facetiously).* Well, Henry, at least we found out that she was not going to quilt it. She was going to — what is it you call it, ladies?

**Mrs. Hale** *(standing center below table facing front, her hand against her pocket).* We call it — knot it, Mr. Henderson.

*Curtain.*

### FOR ANALYSIS

**1.** What is the meaning of the title? Glaspell titled a short-story version of the play "A Jury of Her Peers." Is that a better title than *Trifles*? Explain.

**2.** What are the major differences between Mrs. Hale and Mrs. Peters?

**3.** At one point, Mrs. Peters tells Mrs. Hale a childhood story about a boy who killed her kitten. Why is she reminded of this event? What does it tell us about her reaction to the Wrights' marriage?

**4.** Which of the two women undergoes the most noticeable character development? Explain.

**5.** In what ways do the relationships between the two couples — Mrs. Hale and Mrs. Peters, and Henry Peters and Lewis Hale — change by the end of the play?

**6.** Do Henry Peters and Lewis Hale change in the course of the play?

**7.** Why are the men unable to see the clues that become obvious to the women?

**8.** Can you suggest why Mrs. Wright is the only one identified by her birth name?

### MAKING ARGUMENTS

Argue for or against the proposition that Mrs. Hale and Mrs. Peters are morally obligated to tell the county attorney what they know about the murder.

**WRITING TOPIC**

Show how the discussion of Mrs. Wright's quilt embodies the major **themes** of *Trifles*.

**MAKING CONNECTIONS**

**1.** What similarities in attitudes toward women do you find in this play and in Ibsen's *A Doll's House* (p. 194)?

**2.** Do you think it is fair to say that Mrs. Wright in this play and the **narrator** in Gilman's "The Yellow Wallpaper" (p. 442) are people whose lives have been blighted by a patriarchal society that confines women to narrow, stereotypical roles? Explain.

# NONFICTION

**PAUL**  (D. CA. 64 CE)

## 1 CORINTHIANS 13    CA.56

I f I speak in the tongues of men° and of angels, but have not love, I am a noisy gong or a clanging cymbal.² And if I have prophetic powers, and understand all mysteries and all knowledge, and if I have all faith, so as to remove mountains, but have not love, I am nothing.³ If I give away all I have, and if I deliver my body to be burned, but have not love, I gain nothing.

⁴Love is patient and kind; love is not jealous or boastful;⁵ it is not arrogant or rude. Love does not insist on its own way; it is not irritable or resentful;⁶ it does not rejoice at wrong, but rejoices in the right.⁷ Love bears all things, believes all things, hopes all things, endures all things.

⁸Love never ends; as for prophesies, they will pass away; as for tongues, they will cease; as for knowledge, it will pass away.⁹ For our knowledge is imperfect and our prophecy is imperfect;¹⁰ but when the perfect comes, the imperfect will pass away.¹¹ When I was a child, I spoke like a child, I thought like a child, I reasoned like a child; when I became a man, I gave up childish ways.¹² For now we see in a mirror dimly, but then face to face. Now I know in part; then I shall understand fully, even as I have been fully understood.¹³ So faith, hope, love abide, these three; but the greatest of these is love.

## FOR ANALYSIS

**1.** How does Paul emphasize the significance of love in verses 1–3?

**2.** What does Paul mean by "now" and "then" in verse 12?

**3.** In verse 13, Paul mentions "faith, hope, love" as abiding values. What do you understand by "faith" and "hope"? What do you think "love" means to Paul? Why does he rank it above the others?

---

°Glossolalia, the ecstatic uttering of unintelligible sounds that some interpret as a deeply religious experience.

## MAKING ARGUMENTS

This passage is often chosen as a reading at weddings. Just to be contrary, and regardless of your opinion, make the argument that it offers bad advice about love.

## WRITING TOPICS

**1.** Read Paul's First Epistle to the Corinthians (preferably in a well-annotated study Bible), and analyze the relationship of chapter 13 to the rest of the epistle.

**2.** This text, translated from the original Greek, is taken from the Revised Standard Version of the Bible. Read the same passage in two or three other versions (for example, the King James Version, the Douay Version, the New American Bible), and compare the translations in terms of **style** and effectiveness.

## MAKING CONNECTIONS

How do you think the **characters** in Carver's "What We Talk About When We Talk About Love" (p. 598) would respond to Paul's definition of *love* or the absence of love?

## MAXINE HONG KINGSTON (B. 1940)

# NO NAME WOMAN 1970

Y ou must not tell anyone," my mother said, "what I am about to tell you. In China your father had a sister who killed herself. She jumped into the family well. We say that your father has all brothers because it is as if she had never been born.

"In 1924 just a few days after our village celebrated seventeen hurry-up weddings — to make sure that every young man who went 'out on the road' would responsibly come home — your father and his brothers and your grandfather and his brothers and your aunt's new husband sailed for America, the Gold Mountain. It was your grandfather's last trip. Those lucky enough to get contracts waved good-bye from the decks. They fed and guarded the stowaways and helped them off in Cuba, New York, Bali, Hawaii. 'We'll meet in California next year,' they said. All of them sent money home.

"I remember looking at your aunt one day when she and I were dressing; I had not noticed before that she had such a protruding melon of a stomach. But I did not think, 'She's pregnant,' until she began to look like other pregnant women, her shirt pulling and the white tops of her black pants showing. She could not have been pregnant, you see, because her husband had been gone for years. No one said anything. We did not discuss it. In early summer she was ready to have the child, long after the time when it could have been possible.

"The village had also been counting. On the night the baby was to be born the villagers raided our house. Some were crying. Like a great saw, teeth strung with lights, files of people walked zigzag across our land, tearing the rice. Their lanterns doubled in the disturbed black water, which drained away through the broken bunds. As the villagers closed in, we could see that some of them, probably men and women we knew well, wore white masks. The people with long hair hung it over their faces. Women with short hair made it stand up on end. Some had tied white bands around their foreheads, arms, and legs.

"At first they threw mud and rocks at the house. Then they threw eggs 5 and began slaughtering our stock. We could hear the animals scream their deaths — the roosters, the pigs, a last great roar from the ox. Familiar wild heads flared in our night windows; the villagers encircled us. Some of the faces stopped to peer at us, their eyes rushing like searchlights. The hands flattened against the panes, framed heads, and left red prints.

"The villagers broke in the front and the back doors at the same time, even though we had not locked the doors against them. Their knives dripped with the blood of our animals. They smeared blood on the doors and walls. One woman swung a chicken, whose throat she had slit, splattering blood in red arcs about her. We stood together in the middle of our house, in the family hall with the pictures and tables of the ancestors around us, and looked straight ahead.

"At that time the house had only two wings. When the men came back, we would build two more to enclose our courtyard and a third one to begin a second courtyard. The villagers pushed through both wings, even your grandparents' rooms, to find your aunt's, which was also mine until the men returned. From this room a new wing for one of the younger families would grow. They ripped up her clothes and shoes and broke her combs, grinding them underfoot. They tore her work from the loom. They scattered the cooking fire and rolled the new weaving in it. We could hear them in the kitchen breaking our bowls and banging the pots. They overturned the great waist-high earthenware jugs; duck eggs, pickled fruits, vegetables burst out and mixed in acrid torrents. The old woman from the next field swept a broom through the air and loosed the spirits-of-the-broom over our heads. 'Pig.' 'Ghost.' 'Pig,' they sobbed and scolded while they ruined our house.

"When they left, they took sugar and oranges to bless themselves. They cut pieces from the dead animals. Some of them took bowls that were not broken and clothes that were not torn. Afterward we swept up the rice and sewed it back up into sacks. But the smells from the spilled preserves lasted. Your aunt gave birth in the pigsty that night. The next morning when I went for the water, I found her and the baby plugging up the family well.

"Don't let your father know that I told you. He denies her. Now that you have started to menstruate, what happened to her could happen to you. Don't humiliate us. You wouldn't like to be forgotten as if you had never been born. The villagers are watchful."

Whenever she had to warn us about life, my mother told stories that ran 10 like this one, a story to grow up on. She tested our strength to establish realities. Those in the emigrant generations who could not reassert brute survival died young and far from home. Those of us in the first American generations have had to figure out how the invisible world the emigrants built around our childhoods fit in solid America.

The emigrants confused the gods by diverting their curses, misleading them with crooked streets and false names. They must try to confuse their offspring as well, who, I suppose, threaten them in similar ways — always trying to get things straight, always trying to name the unspeakable. The Chinese I know hide their names; sojourners take new names when their lives change and guard their real names with silence.

Chinese Americans, when you try to understand what things in you are Chinese, how do you separate what is peculiar to childhood, to poverty, insanities, one family, your mother who marked your growing with stories, from what is Chinese? What is Chinese tradition and what is the movies?

If I want to learn what clothes my aunt wore, whether flashy or ordinary, I would have to begin, "Remember Father's drowned-in-the-well sister?"

I cannot ask that. My mother has told me once and for all the useful parts. She will add nothing unless powered by Necessity, a riverbank that guides her life. She plants vegetable gardens rather than lawns; she carries the odd-shaped tomatoes home from the fields and eats food left for the gods.

Whenever we did frivolous things, we used up energy; we flew high kites. We children came up off the ground over the melting cones our parents brought home from work and the American movie on New Year's Day — *Oh, You Beautiful Doll* with Betty Grable one year, and *She Wore a Yellow Ribbon* with John Wayne another year. After the one carnival ride each, we paid in guilt; our tired father counted his change on the dark walk home.

Adultery is extravagance. Could people who hatch their own chicks and eat the embryos and the heads for delicacies and boil the feet in vinegar for party food, leaving only the gravel, eating even the gizzard lining — could such people engender a prodigal aunt? To be a woman, to have a daughter in starvation time was a waste enough. My aunt could not have been the lone romantic who gave up everything for sex. Women in the old China did not choose. Some man had commanded her to lie with him and be his secret evil. I wonder whether he masked himself when he joined the raid on her family.

Perhaps she had encountered him in the fields or on the mountain where the daughters-in-law collected fuel. Or perhaps he first noticed her in the marketplace. He was not a stranger because the village housed no strangers. She had to have dealings with him other than sex. Perhaps he worked an adjoining field, or he sold her the cloth for the dress she sewed and wore. His demand must have surprised, then terrified her. She obeyed him; she always did as she was told.

When the family found a young man in the next village to be her husband, she had stood tractably beside the best rooster, his proxy, and promised before they met that she would be his forever. She was lucky that he was her age and she would be the first wife, an advantage secure now. The night she first saw him, he had sex with her. Then he left for America. She had almost forgotten what he looked like. When she tried to envision him, she only saw the black and white face in the group photograph the men had had taken before leaving.

The other man was not, after all, much different from her husband. They both gave orders: she followed. "If you tell your family, I'll beat you. I'll kill you. Be here again next week." No one talked sex, ever. And she might have separated the rapes from the rest of living if only she did not have to buy her oil from him or gather wood in the same forest. I want her fear to have lasted just as long as rape lasted so that the fear could have been contained. No drawn-out fear. But women at sex hazarded birth and hence lifetimes. The fear did not stop but permeated everywhere. She told the man, "I think I'm pregnant." He organized the raid against her.

On nights when my mother and father talked about their life back home, sometimes they mentioned an "outcast table" whose business they still seemed to be settling, their voices tight. In a commensal tradition, where food is precious, the powerful older people made wrongdoers eat alone. Instead of letting them start separate new lives like the Japanese, who could become samurais and geishas, the Chinese family, faces averted but eyes glowering sideways, hung on to the offenders and fed them leftovers. My aunt must have lived in the same house as my parents and eaten at an outcast table. My mother spoke about the raid as if she had seen it, when she and my aunt, a daughter-in-law to a different household, should not have been living together at all. Daughters-in-law lived with their husbands' parents, not their own; a synonym for marriage in Chinese is "taking a daughter-in-law." Her husband's parents could have sold her, mortgaged her, stoned her. But they had sent her back to her own mother and father, a mysterious act hinting at disgraces not told me. Perhaps they had thrown her out to deflect the avengers.

She was the only daughter; her four brothers went with her father, husband, and uncles "out on the road" and for some years became Western men. When the goods were divided among the family, three of the brothers took land, and the youngest, my father, chose an education. After my grandparents gave their daughter away to her husband's family, they had dispensed all the adventure and all the property. They expected her alone to keep the traditional ways, which her brothers, now among the barbarians, could fumble without detection. The heavy, deep-rooted women were to maintain the past against the flood, safe for returning. But the rare urge west had fixed upon our family, and so my aunt crossed boundaries not delineated in space. 20

The work of preservation demands that the feelings playing about in one's guts not be turned into action. Just watch their passing like cherry blossoms. But perhaps my aunt, my forerunner, caught in a slow life, let dreams grow and fade and after some months or years went toward what persisted. Fear at the enormities of the forbidden kept her desires delicate, wire and bone. She looked at a man because she liked the way the hair was tucked behind his ears, or she liked the question-mark line of a long torso curving at the shoulder and straight at the hip. For warm eyes or a soft voice or a slow walk — that's all — a few hairs, a line, a brightness, a sound, a pace, she gave up family. She offered us up for a charm that vanished with tiredness, a pigtail that didn't toss when the wind died. Why, the wrong lighting could erase the dearest thing about him.

It could very well have been, however, that my aunt did not take subtle enjoyment of her friend, but, a wild woman, kept rollicking company. Imagining her free with sex doesn't fit, though. I don't know any women like that, or men either. Unless I see her life branching into mine, she gives me no ancestral help.

To sustain her being in love, she often worked at herself in the mirror, guessing at the colors and shapes that would interest him, changing them frequently in order to hit on the right combination. She wanted him to look back.

On a farm near the sea, a woman who tended her appearance reaped a reputation for eccentricity. All the married women blunt-cut their hair in flaps about their ears or pulled it back in tight buns. No nonsense. Neither style blew easily into heart-catching tangles. And at their weddings they displayed themselves in their long hair for the last time. "It brushed the backs of my knees," my mother tells me. "It was braided, and even so, it brushed the backs of my knees."

At the mirror my aunt combined individuality into her bob. A bun could   25
have been contrived to escape into black streamers blowing in the wind or in quiet wisps about her face, but only the older women in our picture album wear buns. She brushed her hair back from her forehead, tucking the flaps behind her ears. She looped a piece of thread, knotted into a circle between her index fingers and thumbs, and ran the double strand across her forehead. When she closed her fingers as if she were making a pair of shadow geese bite, the string twisted together catching the little hairs. Then she pulled the thread away from her skin, ripping the hairs out neatly, her eyes watering from the needles of pain. Opening her fingers, she cleaned the thread, then rolled it along her hairline and the tops of her eyebrows. My mother did the same to me and my sisters and herself. I used to believe that the expression "caught by the short hairs" meant a captive held with a depilatory string. It especially hurt at the temples, but my mother said we were lucky we didn't have to have our feet bound when we were seven. Sisters used to sit on their beds and cry together, she said, as their mothers or their slave removed the bandages for a few minutes each night and let the blood gush back into their veins. I hope that the man my aunt loved appreciated a smooth brow, that he wasn't just a tits-and-ass man.

Once my aunt found a freckle on her chin, at a spot that the almanac said predestined her for unhappiness. She dug it out with a hot needle and washed the wound with peroxide.

More attention to her looks than these pullings of hairs and pickings at spots would have caused gossip among the villagers. They owned work clothes and good clothes, and they wore good clothes for feasting the new seasons. But since a woman combing her hair hexes beginnings, my aunt rarely found an occasion to look her best. Women looked like great sea snails—the corded wood, babies, and laundry they carried were the whorls on their backs. The Chinese did not admire a bent back; goddesses and warriors stood straight. Still there must have been a marvelous freeing of beauty when a worker laid down her burden and stretched and arched.

Such commonplace loveliness, however, was not enough for my aunt. She dreamed of a lover for the fifteen days of New Year's, the time for families to exchange visits, money, and food. She plied her secret comb. And sure enough she cursed the year, the family, the village, and herself.

Even as her hair lured her imminent lover, many other men looked at her. Uncles, cousins, nephews, brothers would have looked, too, had they been home between journeys. Perhaps they had already been restraining their curiosity, and they left, fearful that their glances, like a field of nesting birds, might be startled and caught. Poverty hurt, and that was their first reason for leaving. But another, final reason for leaving the crowded house was the never-said.

She may have been unusually beloved, the precious only daughter, spoiled and mirror-gazing because of the affection the family lavished on her. When her husband left, they welcomed the chance to take her back from the in-laws; she could live like the little daughter for just a while longer. There are stories that my grandfather was different from other people, "crazy ever since the little Jap bayoneted him in the head." He used to put his naked penis on the dinner table, laughing. And one day he brought home a baby girl, wrapped up inside his brown Western-style greatcoat. He had traded one of his sons, probably my father, the youngest, for her. My grandmother made him trade back. When he finally got a daughter of his own, he doted on her. They must have all loved her, except perhaps my father, the only brother who never went back to China, having once been traded for a girl.

Brothers and sisters, newly men and women, had to efface their sexual color and present plain miens. Disturbing hair and eyes, a smile like no other, threatened the ideal of five generations living under one roof. To focus blurs, people shouted face to face and yelled from room to room. The immigrants I know have loud voices, unmodulated to American tones even after years away from the village where they called their friendships out across the fields. I have not been able to stop my mother's screams in public libraries or over telephones. Walking erect (knees straight, toes pointed forward, not pigeon-toed, which is Chinese-feminine) and speaking in an inaudible voice, I have tried to turn myself American-feminine. Chinese communication was loud, public. Only sick people had to whisper. But at the dinner table, where the family members came nearest one another, no one could talk, not the outcasts nor any eaters. Every word that falls from the mouth is a coin lost. Silently they gave and accepted food with both hands. A preoccupied child who took his bowl with one hand got a sideways glare. A complete moment of total attention is due everyone alike. Children and lovers have no singularity here, but my aunt used a secret voice, a separate attentiveness.

She kept the man's name to herself throughout her labor and dying; she did not accuse him that he be punished with her. To save her inseminator's name she gave silent birth.

He may have been somebody in her own household, but intercourse with a man outside the family would have been no less abhorrent. All the village were kinsmen, and the titles shouted in loud country voices never let kinship be forgotten. Any man within visiting distance would have been neutralized as a lover — "brother," "younger brother," "older brother" — 115 relationship titles. Parents researched birth charts probably not so much to assure good fortune as to circumvent incest in a population that has but one hundred surnames. Everybody has eight million relatives. How useless then sexual mannerisms, how dangerous.

As if it came from an atavism deeper than fear, I used to add "brother" silently to boys' names. It hexed the boys, who would or would not ask me to dance, and made them less scary and as familiar and deserving of benevolence as girls.

But, of course, I hexed myself also — no dates. I should have stood up, both 35 arms waving, and shouted out across libraries, "Hey, you! Love me back." I had no idea, though, how to make attraction selective, how to control its direction and magnitude. If I made myself American-pretty so that the five or six Chinese boys in the class fell in love with me, everyone else — the Caucasian, Negro, and Japanese boys — would too. Sisterliness, dignified and honorable, made much more sense.

Attraction eludes control so stubbornly that whole societies designed to organize relationships among people cannot keep order, not even when they bind people to one another from childhood and raise them together. Among the very poor and the wealthy, brothers married their adopted sisters, like doves. Our family allowed some romance, paying adult brides' prices and providing dowries so that their sons and daughters could marry strangers. Marriage promises to turn strangers into friendly relatives — a nation of siblings.

In the village structure, spirits shimmered among the live creatures, balanced and held in equilibrium by time and land. But one human being flaring up into violence could open up a black hole, a maelstrom that pulled in the sky. The frightened villagers, who depended on one another to maintain the real, went to my aunt to show her a personal, physical representation of the break she had made in the "roundness." Misallying couples snapped off the future, which was to be embodied in true offspring. The villagers punished her for acting as if she could have a private life, secret and apart from them.

If my aunt had betrayed the family at a time of large grain yields and peace, when many boys were born, and wings were being built on many houses, perhaps she might have escaped such severe punishment. But the men — hungry, greedy, tired of planting in dry soil, cuckolded — had been forced to leave the village in order to send food-money home. There were ghost plagues, bandit plagues, wars with the Japanese, floods. My Chinese brother and sister had died of an unknown sickness. Adultery, perhaps only a mistake during good times, became a crime when the village needed food.

The round moon cakes and round doorways, the round tables of graduated size that fit one roundness inside another, round windows and rice bowls — these talismans had lost their power to warn this family of the law: a family must be whole, faithfully keeping the descent line by having sons to feed the old and the dead, who in turn look after the family. The villagers came to show my aunt and her lover-in-hiding a broken house. The villagers were speeding up the circling of events because she was too shortsighted to see that her infidelity had already harmed the village, that waves of consequences would return unpredictably, sometimes in disguise, as now, to hurt her. This roundness had to be made coin-sized so that she would see its circumference: punish her at the birth of her baby. Awaken her to the inexorable. People who refused fatalism because they could invent small resources insisted on culpability. Deny accidents and wrest fault from the stars.

After the villagers left, their lanterns now scattering in various directions 40
toward home, the family broke their silence and cursed her. "Aiaa, we're going
to die. Death is coming. Death is coming. Look what you've done. You've
killed us. Ghost! Dead ghost! Ghost! You've never been born." She ran out
into the fields, far enough from the house so that she could no longer hear
their voices, and pressed herself against the earth, her own land no more.
When she felt the birth coming, she thought that she had been hurt. Her body
seized together. "They've hurt me too much," she thought. "This is gall, and it
will kill me." With forehead and knees against the earth, her body convulsed
and then relaxed. She turned on her back, lay on the ground. The black well of
sky and stars went out and out and out forever; her body and her complexity
seemed to disappear. She was one of the stars, a bright dot in blackness, without home, without a companion, in eternal cold and silence. An agoraphobia
rose in her, speeding higher and higher, bigger and bigger; she would not be
able to contain it; there would be no end to fear.

Flayed, unprotected against space, she felt pain return, focusing her body.
This pain chilled her — a cold, steady kind of surface pain. Inside, spasmodically, the other pain, the pain of the child, heated her. For hours she lay on
the ground, alternately body and space. Sometimes a vision of normal comfort obliterated reality: she saw the family in the evening gambling at the
dinner table, the young people massaging their elders' backs. She saw them
congratulating one another, high joy on the mornings the rice shoots came
up. When these pictures burst, the stars drew yet further apart. Black space
opened.

She got to her feet to fight better and remembered that old-fashioned
women gave birth in their pigsties to fool the jealous, pain-dealing gods, who
do not snatch piglets. Before the next spasms could stop her, she ran to the
pigsty, each step a rushing out into emptiness. She climbed over the fence and
knelt in the dirt. It was good to have a fence enclosing her, a tribal person
alone.

Laboring, this woman who had carried her child as a foreign growth that
sickened her every day, expelled it at last. She reached down to touch the hot,
wet, moving mass, surely smaller than anything human, and could feel that
it was human after all — fingers, toes, nails, nose. She pulled it up on to her
belly, and it lay curled there, butt in the air, feet precisely tucked one under
the other. She opened her loose shirt and buttoned the child inside. After resting, it squirmed and thrashed and she pushed it up to her breast. It turned its
head this way and that until it found her nipple. There, it made little snuffling
noises. She clenched her teeth at its preciousness, lovely as a young calf, a pig-
let, a little dog.

She may have gone to the pigsty as a last act of responsibility: she would
protect this child as she had protected its father. It would look after her soul,
leaving supplies on her grave. But how would this tiny child without family
find her grave when there would be no marker for her anywhere, neither in the
earth nor the family hall? No one would give her a family hall name. She had

taken the child with her into the wastes. At its birth the two of them had felt the same raw pain of separation, a wound that only the family pressing tight could close. A child with no descent line would not soften her life but only trail after her, ghostlike, begging her to give it purpose. At dawn the villagers on their way to the fields would stand around the fence and look.

Full of milk, the little ghost slept. When it awoke, she hardened her breasts 45 against the milk that crying loosens. Toward morning she picked up the baby and walked to the well.

Carrying the baby to the well shows loving. Otherwise abandon it. Turn its face into the mud. Mothers who love their children take them along. It was probably a girl; there is some hope of forgiveness for boys.

"Don't tell anyone you had an aunt. Your father does not want to hear her name. She has never been born." I have believed that sex was unspeakable and words so strong and fathers so frail that "aunt" would do my father mysterious harm. I have thought that my family, having settled among immigrants who had also been their neighbors in the ancestral land, needed to clean their name, and a wrong word would incite the kinspeople even here. But there is more to this silence: they want me to participate in her punishment. And I have.

In the twenty years since I heard this story I have not asked for details nor said my aunt's name; I do not know it. People who can comfort the dead can also chase after them to hurt them further — a reverse ancestor worship. The real punishment was not the raid swiftly inflicted by the villagers, but the family's deliberately forgetting her. Her betrayal so maddened them, they saw to it that she would suffer forever, even after death. Always hungry, always needing, she would have to beg food from other ghosts, snatch and steal it from those whose living descendants give them gifts. She would have to fight the ghosts massed at crossroads for the buns a few thoughtful citizens leave to decoy her away from village and home so that the ancestral spirits could feast unharassed. At peace, they could act like gods, not ghosts, their descent lines providing them with paper suits and dresses, spirit money, paper houses, paper automobiles, chicken, meat, and rice into eternity — essences delivered up in smoke and flames, steam and incense rising from each rice bowl. In an attempt to make the Chinese care for people outside the family, Chairman Mao encourages us now to give our paper replicas to the spirits of outstanding soldiers and workers, no matter whose ancestors they may be. My aunt remains forever hungry. Goods are not distributed evenly among the dead.

My aunt haunts me — her ghost drawn to me because now, after fifty years of neglect, I alone devote pages of paper to her, though not origamied into houses and clothes. I do not think she always means me well. I am telling on her, and she was a spite suicide, drowning herself in the drinking water. The Chinese are always very frightened of the drowned one, whose weeping ghost, wet hair hanging and skin bloated, waits silently by the water to pull down a substitute.

## FOR ANALYSIS

**1.** In what sense did the **narrator** participate in her aunt's punishment?

**2.** Given the Chinese belief system, what is the No Name Woman's most significant punishment?

**3.** What evidence in the essay supports the view that the Chinese villagers favored males over females?

**4.** Why does the woman enter the pigsty to give birth?

**5.** What factors intensify the ferocity of the villagers' attack on the house?

**6.** Discuss the significance of the assertion in paragraph 49: "I alone devote pages of paper to her, though not origamied into houses and clothes."

**7.** Reread the essay, noting scenes the speaker seems to invent. What reasons might Kingston have for imagining the events that she could not have known?

## MAKING ARGUMENTS

The final sentence of this essay is haunting, both literally and **figuratively**. Make an argument about the significance of its final image — the threat of the ghost of the drowned pulling down a substitute — to the essay as a whole.

## WRITING TOPIC

Describe the No Name Woman's sin. Was it a sin against the absent husband of her hastily arranged marriage, against her extended family, against the village, against the gods?

## MAKING CONNECTIONS

Some authors, such as Chopin in "The Storm" (p. 579), seem to treat sexual infidelity casually; others, such as Shakespeare in *Othello* (p. 664), treat it murderously. Give reasons to support each view.

## SONYA CHUNG  (B. 1973)

# GETTING IT RIGHT  1999

M y mother called today from the other coast asking if I got the package she sent. I said no, and then the buzzer buzzed, and the UPS man
knocked on the door with the package. "Call me back after you've opened it,"
my mother said.

Inside the big brown box, I find another flat, rectangular box, covered with
a lime-green rice paper — very thin, textured, fibrous. In the center of the box
top, some kind of Asian graphic: purple lines forming what looks to me like
a stick figure sitting cross-legged, but is probably a Chinese character. I open
the box. Underneath pink tissue paper, a hand mirror. Octagonal, technically,
but wider at the top, narrowing towards the bottom. A beautiful dark wood,
mahogany perhaps, but lighter. Koa? A large tassle of bright colors — red, neon
pink, lime green, royal blue, electric yellow — trailing down from the handle.
A Korean giveaway. The backside of the mirror proper: embroidered flowers,
pale pink, and small leaves in all shades of green, red veins accenting. Another
Chinese character in the left-hand corner. Buried in the tissue paper, the note
says: *from Jagunummah, youngest aunt. In Korea, mother gives to daughter on
wedding day. I think it means "happiness" but not sure. Be sure to send thank
you note.*

Back to the big brown box, I find 50 lavender packages of birth control pills,
floating in foam peanuts. The note reads: *thought you running low.* I notice the
expiration date on all of them: 10/93. Next, a mouse pad bearing the snow-
capped mountains of Yosemite National Park —*from our trip last year. I keep
forget to send to you.* Finally, an envelope: photos from Christmas day, my
family minus my husband and me. My father smiling wide, wearing the wool
zipper-front vest we sent him, my mother's corduroy floral backside to the
camera as she bends over to pick up crumpled wrapping paper, my sisters both
with eyes blinking shut (who took the photo? I wonder). Double prints.

Last night, in the silence after the ugly argument, I lay in bed thinking, in
a Jimmy Stewart-esque way, what would happen if I were to disappear. If I
simply ceased to exist.

I call my mother back and thank her for everything. I ask what's new, and   5
she says she wants to buy a computer, she's been researching. "What about
all those megahertz of memory?" she asks, mixing up computer terms. "Do I
need all that? I want one of those big screens and big sound systems; you know,
for music and for old people." I tell her to go with mail order, so she can get the
800-number help desk. "You think?" she says. "What about zip drive? You have
a zip drive?"

My mother used to rummage through piles of papers around the house, asking, "Where is that L.L. Crew J. catalogue?"

Today, we talk about the rain, my father's business, his secretary who is suicidal *again*. All the while, I'm carefully laying out the contents of the package on my bedroom floor: the mirror from my aunt that my mother forgot to give me when I got married, the expired pills, the mouse pad for my mouseless ergonomic keyboard, the terribly shot photos. And as my mother tells me about the latest deal between Microsoft and Sony, about how despite Sony's reputation for unreliability Microsoft is forging some kind of partnership based on mutual interest, I find myself covering the mouthpiece on the telephone, blubbering uncontrollably, dripping tears onto lime-green rice paper. I am remembering what it is to feel the largeness of love, the relief of simple gifts, given in earnest. I am thinking of my first week of college, of the package of crumbled cookies my mother sent me, the note enclosed boldly saying: *Hope your first day is as smooth as a sail.*

## FOR ANALYSIS

1. What is the significance to the essay of the event recounted in the fourth paragraph?

2. Why does the author cry as she talks to her mother on the phone?

3. To what does the title refer?

## MAKING ARGUMENTS

The photographs mentioned in Chung's essay capture the **narrator's** complicated feelings of love, embarrassment, and separation — geographic and emotional — from her birth family. Are these the most important objects described in this essay? Make an argument that they are, or that some other object is more important, explaining its significance.

## WRITING TOPIC

While Chung makes fun of her mother's errors in idiomatic English and other things she sees as shortcomings, she does so with fondness. Do you have similar things you could note about a parent or caregiver? If you are a parent or caregiver yourself, how would a child of yours answer this question?

## MAKING CONNECTIONS

1. Select a poem in this book that considers immigrant experience in America and compare it to this essay. How does the author's treatment of assimilation compare to Chung's?

2. Read this essay alongside Lee's "Eating Alone" (p. 657) and compare the ways in which the two treat the combinations of traditional and adopted cultures to immigrant experience. How is filial love expressed at the point where the two cross?

It is hard to imagine two more different pieces of nonfiction. As you will see, these two authors approach the subject of love from different angles and with different strategies. That both arrive at compelling and similar places is testament to the literary version of the truism that there's more than one way to skin a cat. As you read, think about the way these two writers approach their subjects, and how both are able to tell affecting, complicated stories about the ways we look for love.

**DAGOBERTO GILB**   (B. 1950)

# I KNEW SHE WAS BEAUTIFUL   2000

I was holding her hand at a train depot. I can still feel my arm in the air, limp and soft with trust. It must have been Union Station, Los Angeles, and I don't know where we were going or why. I was thrilled. I was small, probably just walking, and looking up at her I swear I knew then that she was beautiful. She was wearing a hat, one of those brimless hats women wore in the fifties that matched the rest of the outfit. There was a red rose in the hat, I'm sure. It wasn't a real rose but a lacy decorative one. Almost all my other early images of her are from the department stores we used to go to together. She's trying clothes on, everybody paying attention to her, or standing at a cosmetics counter, my mommy and the women around talking fast and unashamed, giggling, playing with the silver and gold and glass tubes, the jars and sprays, the smallest brushes, the colored powders. The train depot on that trip was the black-and-white of a dream, and the indoors had the faraway feel of the outdoors, its expanse as dusty as a memory.

I think it was La Cienega. It was a Spanish name, and the other stores where she modelled — downtown or on Wilshire Boulevard, department stores like the Broadway and Robinson's — didn't have Spanish names. The store didn't seem large. Just elegant. Racks of women's clothes with beads and jewels, collars and sleeves, strings and straps and bows, low in the front, low in the back. I went into the dressing room, where all the models were changing from one thing into another for the show that day. I watched them, breathing the cool mist of perfume, as they hurried through the step-throughs and pull-offs of dress and undress — the zippers and snaps, the gritty static or smooth wisp of on and off. Skin that was legs and arms, and round hips that cut into small waists; bras, even a breast, and panties that showed that darkened mystery hair. The piccolo of women's voices. I was a good boy, they said. I would be such a handsome man. I remember the warmth of their touch, like that of my favorite blanket. I used to scissor my fingers onto its nylon end seam to go to sleep, my thumb in my mouth, sucking. Even then I knew it was women, their attraction and allure, that I loved, *mi* mommy and her friends, her best friend, the woman from Puerto Rico who she could whisper to in Spanish. But it was this day I remember because on the other side of the store there was an old man in a uniform tinting a display window that faced the street. There were mannequins behind him and he let me go through a half door to sit between him and them. He brushed on the tint, the glass becoming a yellow brown, that biting, tart odor, and I looked out at the people and cars passing by on the other side of the window. I would run from him back to the dressing room, from one scent to the other, back and forth, the fumes subliminal and intoxicating as I ran from the old man with the paintbrush and can in the room no one got to sit in to the beautiful women in their underwear.

She loved to go to Hollywood Park, and we went to the last race because admission was free. I loved to go, too, and not just because of the horses, the earth shuddering under me as they left the gate and pounded across the finish line. I liked to collect the bet stubs like baseball cards, the losers thrown down, a trail of litter that began in the parking lot until it carpeted the grandstands. I collected fives and tens, win, place, or show. Win stubs were the hardest to find. Wandering the track was like walking on a beach looking for unbroken shells. We'd go down to the general-admission area, at track level, or we'd walk right over to a nicer area, where there were chairs and tables and drinks, and sometimes we were invited to sit in a private glass-enclosed clubhouse. A man would offer to buy us drinks, and I'd get a Roy Rogers — grenadine and Coke. She gave me the green olives on toothpicks from her drink to eat. The man who bought the drinks might say something at a distance first, and then approach. Usually, she just told a waiter, or the man himself, thank you so much, polite, generously happy about the drinks, but that would be it, and there we'd be, her and me at the races. I was her date. I was her man. Those men, in their suits and their blazers, snugged or loosened ties, stinking in their colognes, snapping bills off silver money clips, they were obvious, stupid, easy even for me to figure out. She might light a cigarette. She didn't smoke, though, for the taste. It was a look she wanted. I'd complain that I couldn't find betting stubs. She'd tell me to look around where we were sitting, and I'd search the tops of the starched tablecloths, the ashtrays, hunting the big losers. One time, I found four hundred-dollar tickets to win, creased the long way.

She was seeing this one man. Years later, I learned that she'd been seeing him for some time, even before she and my father divorced, which was soon after I was born. His voice was loud by design, the way a horn is loud. She used to ask me, Do you like him? He took us to baseball games. The Tigers and Angels and Yankees, the Dodgers and Giants and Pirates. The year Roger Maris hit sixty-one home runs I caught one of his B.P. homers. The loud man let me hang around after the games and get autographs. He was a big man, a fireman, and sometimes we visited him at his station. I was too scared to slide down the pole. It was too fat, too thick. I played handball alone in a white room beside the red trucks. He wasn't a bad man, but I didn't like him very much. I couldn't explain why, except that he was loud when he talked, and even though he bought me ice cream anytime I wanted it, he was no fun. And so I would answer her. No, I would say.

We were in the kitchen. I was sitting in one of those heavy metal chairs with glossy vinyl covering — we had two of them — and my mom got mad at me. I was used to this. She had a job now in a dental office, and things like this happened because she was tired when she came home. But this time he was there. They were always going out, and I was left at home alone with our knobless television and a TV dinner, sometimes two, because I was getting taller, flexing muscles I could see in my arms. He only came inside our house once in a while, and she must have told me to go away, to get out of the kitchen. In that loud voice he told me to do what she said. I sat there. Then he was louder, really yelling. I sat there. And so he grabbed me and I held onto the metal rails under the chair and he picked it up along with me. I'm not leaving! I told him. You don't tell me! He was furious, and my mom was yelling now, too, and she told him to leave me alone, and he stopped, dropping the chair and me in it. I went into the bedroom and I was crying, waiting for her to come. She hit me sometimes, and when she got there that's what I was expecting. Instead she held me and she was smiling. She was proud of me. She said, You're such a man already.

At school the kids said things. I knew it. I was bigger than they were and more athletic, and angry all the time, and it wasn't like they were going to say anything much to my face. My mom was a Mexican and my mom was divorced, and one time a girl told me her mom didn't like mine and she didn't like me, either. I didn't hang out with too many kids. There was this one boy — he had his own bedroom, with toys everywhere. He had a basketball, and a hoop on the garage. I would want to play, but he was soft, blubbery, and I'd shoot alone for as long as his mom would let me. She was always smoking and drinking coffee in a stained white mug and talking on the phone, and once I came over and she took me into their clean bathroom and got a washcloth and washed my neck and behind my ears, scrubbed so hard it hurt. She was supposed to be a friend of my mom's, but I knew she wasn't, not really, because whenever my mom came to collect me only my mom talked.

Sometimes my mom would take me to the Food Giant and buy me a chili dog with finely grated cheese on the top that would melt in a minute. When she went out, which was a lot, she left me some money and I'd ride a bike down to the Thrifty and buy a half-gallon square of chocolate ice cream. She didn't cook, except on my birthday, when she made *chile verde* that stewed for hours. She'd buy tamales from a bakery on Whittier Boulevard. In the morning, before she went to work and I went to school, we had breakfast at a coffee shop, and she'd give me her hash-brown potatoes. Even then, at that hour, men looked at her. Even then, men would come up to our table, squat so that they could talk to her. Introduce themselves. I was starting junior high, I had touched a girl, looked at nudie magazines, and I knew what these men wanted. I was such a good-looking boy, they would tell her. When they guessed at my age, they missed by years, and then the talk would be about her beauty — how could such a young woman have a son so old? She was too polite to them, and one time I remember this man's eyes looking at my mom. I wanted us to be alone. I didn't want her to be polite. I was so mad at her. I was so mad then that I think I never got over it.

She'd stopped modelling, but when she and her Puerto Rican friend got together they talked about the other models' getting fat butts and saggy *chiches*, girdles and falsies. Her Puerto Rican friend was marrying a man who owned the biggest sailboat ever and they were going around the world in it. He was so rich he didn't have to work. My mom had to work. It made her tired. She was going out on more dates, too, so she was always busy. She talked wistfully about Pancho Gonzalez, the tennis star. Another friend of hers was supposed to be his cousin. She was a woman who talked too fast and too much, and she drank, and she laughed wrong. She and my mom both bleached their hair platinum, but this friend's was ugly and cheap looking. She was a *fea*, short and plump and pimply, but she thought she was as pretty as my mom. She was bad news, I knew, because by then I was smarter than my mom seemed to be. This "cousin" did not help my mom win Pancho Gonzalez, but they got drunk a lot together. My mom's Puerto Rican friend stopped coming around. Maybe she was sailing on the Pacific Ocean, maybe not yet, but she was married, and she was rich, and we weren't.

Though the modelling jobs weren't around anymore, the pretty clothes were. Bills came in the mail daily. I answered the phone and a bill collector would ask for her and I'd say she wasn't home even if she was. She was working for a dentist who was a Mormon, and she was dating him, too, and two old biddies started coming to our door lecturing my mom, and I listened to them with her. I answered their questions because she didn't know the answers. She wanted to become a Mormon, she didn't care how. We went to the dentist's house for Thanksgiving, my first Thanksgiving dinner. His mother had a bun of white and gray hair and a frilly apron just like one of those grandmothers on a TV show. We had to sit at a long dinner table, crowded with people. It was a feast of full bowls and platters, and I ate so much turkey and mashed potatoes that I got sick, but I didn't think it was because I overate. It was because they didn't like my mom. Well, I didn't like these people from the start. My mom and I spoke to each other, and they looked at us as if we were being secretive, as if we were talking in Spanish, not in English. After dinner we were taking a walk around the neighborhood with the dentist — it was green with overgrown trees and grass, and there weren't always sidewalks, and the idea was that he should get to know me a little — when my mom said that something was wrong, she was bleeding. She assured me it wasn't that kind of bleeding, teased me for not understanding immediately, but he didn't laugh. He didn't like this, didn't want to have to find an open store, couldn't believe she wouldn't be prepared. She sloughed that off, wanting to be cheerful. She wanted to make him happy.

But he didn't laugh. This was the man I'd been lying about to new junior-high friends. Before I met him, my mom had told me that she was going to marry him. My dad, I'd tell these guys, snooty, was a dentist. I wanted us to be richer than them. After that day I don't remember ever hearing her talk about him again, and I never asked.

Two or three times my mom took me to an old lady's house. It was an old 10 house, with old things, and I had to have good manners and eat boring food. The woman thought I was a bright boy and liked it when I visited, my mom told me, and I might be getting an inheritance from her. When the old lady died, I went to the funeral parlor with my mom to pay last respects. There were no other people there, and still I felt as though we were being watched like thieves. The casket was open, but I didn't look close. It was like a church, with wooden pews and crosses and Jesuses, though no Virgins. My mom's knees went onto the padded kneel board, and as they did she made a loud *pedo*. I don't think I'd ever heard that from her before. She looked at me and I looked at her and we both tried to hold back from laughing. The more we did, the worse it hurt, and the stronger was the desire to laugh. She kept kneeling there, her hands folded and her head down as though she were praying, but really she was giggling and then we both started laughing too hard. There was no inheritance for either of us.

One night I was watching TV when a man who my mom worked for, someone I think she'd also gone out with, came to the door screaming about her. She was out on a date. He was wailing about money, what had she done with his money. He was drunk and howling and cussing. I knew about drunk because sometimes there were bottles in the house, broken glasses, laughter. I knew who this man was because he'd shot someone. Mom had told me about him, and I'd heard her tell her friends. He kept beating on the door, and it finally blew open right in front of me just as a cop neighbor I'd called came running up. A week later she married a man raised near Lancaster. I'd never heard of him, I'd never met him before. He was the cousin of a woman she'd worked with. He had the stupidest grin, as stupid as his hick name. He asked me if there was one thing he could do for me. I said I wanted him to take me to see Washington, D.C., and he grinned that dumb grin and said he would. I actually believed him. He and my mom went to Arizona for a week for their honeymoon, and after that we moved in. He wore a different clean green uniform every day for his job, and most of the rest of the time, too. There were deer heads and birds and fish on the walls. Maple furniture, a family table with matching chairs. He had a son who was a taxidermist, and he was proud of him. My mom's new husband was an electrician and a couple of times I worked for him and that's when I heard him tell his working friends he just felt so lucky to be married to such a pretty Mexican gal. A few weeks later she went on the TV show "Let's Make a Deal" and she was chosen. When Monty Hall asked her name, she told him her new name without a flinch. But she didn't win anything big — twenty or forty bucks, that was all — and she didn't get to pick a door.

Not too long afterward, she asked me to go to lunch with her. We hadn't gone out together, the two of us, for some time because she was so busy with her new husband. They were beginning to have arguments about bills and money, and they raced to get the mail first. The lunch wasn't only with my mom. It was with the loud man, the fireman, she'd dated before. He took us to a restaurant. I don't remember the food, only that when he pulled into the driveway of the apartment building where we lived, she jumped out of the car and rushed to the front door, and I was stuck in the back seat and this old boyfriend leaned over to talk to me. He told me he loved my mom and he was sorry and he wished something or other, I don't know. It was a speech, and it seemed as if he might cry or already was crying, but I told him I had to go. Maybe this was why I didn't like him. Big as he was, he was too loud, and yet he would cry. I think the car was a Thunderbird coupe, and I didn't even enjoy that. Things weren't good between my mom and her husband, and I knew she wasn't happy — I figured that she'd been sneaking out for these lunches with the fireman for a while — but I started avoiding my mom and her husband as much as possible. I never liked the deer meat or the maple furniture or the Hank Snow music, and I ate with my new neighborhood friends, stayed as late as I could. Then my mom and her husband separated, and we moved to an apartment complex on the south side of town. She would just lie on the couch, half awake, half asleep, depressed. We didn't talk too much. I had a job, and even though I was getting in fights at school and she was getting calls from the vice-principal about suspensions and swats and the rest, she didn't really care, and I didn't think it was such a big deal, either.

She married the loud fireman, who was almost ten years younger than she was — though nobody ever thought so — and who loved her after all this time. He bought her a brand-new house and everything that went in it, and it was as if we were rich, though I didn't feel as though anything was mine. It was all theirs. His and hers. He wasn't there very much. He worked hard at two jobs — he drove a Brink's truck, too — and she had all the money she'd ever dreamed of because he gave her his paychecks as if she were a financial wizard. When we were alone, or when she was joking in front of the women who would visit, she would say that he could be boring and dull, and that if he wasn't gone most of the time, if she didn't keep him working two jobs . . . Then she'd laugh, and everyone laughed with her. She always had food, and always a drink. There were jugs of wine and there was beer and liquor. There was a new blender, the best. He loved to drink with her, too. He loved everything she did, everything she bought, and she bought everything. She was the best thing that he could ever imagine happening to him, his life was full of sunlight and colors he'd never seen. I wasn't around much, going back to my old friends in my old high school, going to a new job to have my own money, partying myself now, playing with drugs and liquor and girlfriends, but I was happy that she wasn't worried anymore. Since she didn't have to do anything but please him, she pleased him. He didn't like "spicy" food, so she learned to cook potatoes and roasts. She babied him when he got home, made him feel like he ran the world. They drank together. They talked to each other and had fun when they drank. When she was around him, she became like him. When he thought he should be serious, he droned philosophically about black people and illegal aliens. My mom was an illegal alien, born out of wedlock in Mexico City and baptized at the Basilica Santa María de Guadalupe. She often tried to stop him when he went off on a long editorial, but it wasn't always worth it to her.

My mother was becoming a person I wouldn't want to know, and sometimes, especially when I was reminding her of a past that she didn't want to remember, she'd get mad. Once I told a neighbor that her husband wasn't my real father. I didn't know that I wasn't supposed to say this. I was sorry I embarrassed her. I didn't even care about my real father much, I only saw him a couple of days a year, but the only times my mother's husbands were fathers were when others made that assumption. They were just men to me, part of her life, not mine. Another time, after a year of living in this new house, with this new husband, I made her so angry by something I'd said or done, she told me she didn't know where I'd come from. She meant it, too, looking at me like I was an utter stranger, a lousy tenant.

On a Tuesday morning, just before dawn, I jerked myself out of a dream. It 15 was so vivid I turned on a light and wrote it down. In the dream, a voice was talking to me, asking me if I wanted to talk to my mother. Why wouldn't I? Because we never did anymore, hadn't really talked in decades. When we did, there was nothing but awkwardness and mutual disapproval between us, and for several years there was nothing at all. I'd moved far away, to El Paso. The voice in the dream was asking me questions from my mother, and I started responding to the dream, to the voice, and straight to my mom. I answered the voice, yes, I always loved her. She had to know that I didn't care about whatever it was that had come between us, that I would remember only how much I loved her. I was always proud of her. I thought she was the best mommy, the most beautiful woman. I said I understood everything she'd gone through. Of course I didn't think only about the past, our troubles. Of course I forgave her, and I told her I wanted her to forgive me, too. And then I was overcome by a sob that wasn't in my dream but in my body and my mouth and my eyes.

Two days later, her husband called me. He was calm and positive. My mom, he said, had been taken to the hospital Tuesday. She was found unconscious. There was a problem with her liver. She was in intensive care, but he was convinced she'd be home soon. He just thought I should know. I thought this sounded much more serious, and I called the hospital. A nurse there said I was right, usually it was only a matter of time, it could be at any moment, though it could also take days or even a few weeks. I asked about the liver, whether it was the usual reason a liver goes. She asked, Well, was she always the life of the party? I got a plane ticket. I remembered a previous visit, and finding an empty vodka bottle — plastic, the cheapest brand you could buy — in the corner of the bedroom where I was sleeping, and where she kept a mountain of purses and shoes and wallets. I found another, most of it gone, behind a closet door.

I rented a car at the airport and went to the hospital. She was bloated, her hair a tousle — a woman who never missed a hairdresser's appointment — an unappealing white gown tied around her. Tubes needled into her hand and arm, a clear mask was over her mouth and nose. When she heard me, her eyes opened. She had no voice. I talked. Years had passed, she knew little about my life. She knew that I did construction work, thought it was all I did, ever, didn't know anything about the other life I led, the one as a writer. I never told her. I was afraid that she would only be his wife, not my mom, and she wouldn't care in the appropriate way. Or that she would be too relieved, and that all those other years I'd been struggling, when she disapproved of me, even thought I deserved whatever misery befell me, would be forgotten. I didn't want to give that up so easily. These were the reasons I had told her nothing. But I knew my mom would be proud. I knew she would be happy for me. I told her that I was a writer, and that I'd had a book published, another one just out. I had been going to New York City and Washington, D.C. I'd gone there more than once, and I never paid. Her eyes smiled so big. I knew she would like this the most. She always wanted to travel the world. Can you believe they even give me money? I asked her. She was proud of me, and she was as surprised as I was about it. And then I told her why I had to come. I told her about the dream I'd had two nights before, on the first night she spent in the hospital. My mom's eyes stopped moving. I said, I talked to you, you were talking to me, we were talking. She nodded — her whole weakened body squirmed while she was nodding. I knew it, and yet I wouldn't believe this story if I'd heard it. It was such a *telenovela* deathbed scene, mother and son, both weeping about a psychic conversation routed hundreds of miles through the smog and traffic and over the mountains and across three deserts, from one dream to another, so that we wouldn't miss telling each other for the last time before she died. She was as stunned as I was, as happy. You know? She kept nodding, looking at me, crying. Oh, Mom, I said.

## For Analysis

**1.** What else does Gilb know about his mother, other than that she was beautiful?

**2.** How does Gilb relate to the men in his mother's life? What do they have in common with each other? How does he see them?

**3.** What does Gilb's mother value? How does that contrast with what Gilb thinks is important? How do you read the final scene in relation to this difference?

## Making Arguments

**1.** Some readers of this essay will object to the story of the dream. If you are one of them, how would you argue that such a thing could not happen? If you are not, how would you argue that it could?

**2.** Do you think the difficulty of Gilb's mother's life — her trouble with men, with responsibility, with alcohol — are of her own making or the result of circumstance? Make an argument in response to this question using the essay and any ideas and facts about individual psychology, social forces, or anything else you find relevant as evidence.

## WRITING TOPIC

Do you think Gilb's mother was a good parent? A bad parent? Reflect on Gilb's portrayal of her — what does he think of her parenting? Does he judge her? Should we?

## PABLO PIÑERO STILLMANN (B. 1982)

# LIFE, LOVE, HAPPINESS: A FOUND ESSAY FROM THE TWITTERVERSE[1]  2013

#Pisces often wonder what the meaning of #Life truly is. The meaning of life is to give life meaning. #WorkHard. For an example: Me: "Mom you look skinnier." Mom: "Thanks, now what do you want?" About to take my son up on the mountain and show him the meaning of life by having him kill a bear. YOLO. We tell our kids it's not about winning, it's about having fun. But all they see on TV are the biggest games: politics and war. What about love!??? I value a good friendship. I'm craving spontaneity, change, and maybe just something different to look forward to. Because that's what life is all about! We live in a World where losing your phone is more dramatic than losing your virginity. We live in a world full of people who are pretending to be something they're not. We live in a world where entertainers make way more money than people who save lives. We live in a really messed up world so appreciate the little bit of good you do see in people. If you think faking an orgasm is bad, wait until you meet someone who fakes a relationship. If you meet someone off OKC and the next day they delete their profile, that's good right? Or maybe you sucked so bad they gave up. Hmm. I want someone who'll save my texts just to look at them when they missed me . . . Ugh, I just want someone I can bake and cook for all the time. THE ONLY THING I WANT IN LIFE IS A FOLLOW FROM THE BOYS OK. IS THAT TOO MUCH TO ASK FOR, GOD? WHY DO YOU HATE ME ☹ I'm sorry that I am not good enough. I'm sorry that I am annoying. I'm sorry that I am lame. I'm sorry that I am not pretty enough. I have so much fun being single in the daylight or when I'm with friends, but when I'm all by myself I instantly become bored & depressed. Slowly dying with

---

[1] Contributors, in order of appearance: @PiscesAreUs, @Swiperboy, @YoDaddyAsia, @LeeBLVD, @patrickptomey, @PablodaJunkie, ©AsianPersuashin, @Narioo, ©mirzsunshine, @WeKnowComedy, @NiceTweets_, @Ask_Ricky, @Beauty_OMG, @sierranickellxo, @saraelizabethW, @MrEpicMind, @RaqNavaXO, @YumOneDirection, @RuzanaLah, @Khvlen, @wohlaa, @NCs_Finesttt, @caioschelege, @ohyescokyes, @iCanBUrDestiny_, @GirlDictionary, @gloriacharper, @bayorwheezy, @cOndoms, @Thebieberjunkie, @OliviaDresher.

boredom and loneliness. WOO YEAH! I'm so unhappy with my life. No one understands. When will you realize? Baby, I'm not like the rest . . . Bitch, I'm special! I'm not odd, just different. You may not understand me 'cause maybe I don't want you to. I'm not to be like everyone else. I'm unique. If you ignore me, I will ignore you. If you don't start the conversation, we won't talk. If you don't put in the effort, why should I? I just bought a whole bunch of new cute clothes. I deserve to be taken out on a date. I just wanna hold you and never let go! If I could kill myself without affecting anyone else's life, I'd be gone tonight. Suicide is stupid? You wanna know what is stupid? Hurting someone so much emotionally, that they think suicide is the only answer. That feeling of waves crashing over me, the waves as helpless as myself.

### FOR ANALYSIS

**1.** What kind of essay is this? Who wrote these words? What's with the hashtags?

**2.** How would you characterize the **tone** of this essay? Is it uniform or does it shift, and if the latter, where and how?

**3.** Many of these found sentences are clichés, but not all of them. How would you characterize the kinds of statements the author has collected here? Do you think they comment on the ideas of cliché and common wisdom?

### MAKING ARGUMENTS

Some people think that different forms of social media make people write in different ways, that the sentences on one social medium are different from the sentences on another, for various reasons. Do you believe this? Construct an argument on this topic, in support of or refuting this idea or changing the terms of the discussion entirely.

### WRITING TOPICS

**1.** The author, in a blog post on the origins of this essay, wrote that it came out of his anxieties about the waning of interest in literature and a resulting determination to confront its biggest competition — what he calls "the screen" — rather than running from it, and the form this confrontation took was a series of found essays composed of others' tweets. Reflect on this strategy. What is the result of this confrontation? What does it tell us about all the screens that distract us from books? Are they only a distraction or are there points of commonality?

**2.** Compose your own found essay from tweets or Facebook posts or any other social media. Be careful to respect the privacy of others while doing so.

### MAKING CONNECTIONS

**1.** How are the people in Gilb's essay — perhaps including Gilb himself — looking for love in all the wrong places? How are those in Stillmann's essay doing the same thing? What commonalities do you find in the way they do this?

**2.** Gilb sees his mother as focused on love — of a lover, a husband, sexual or romantic — at the expense of other things, including perhaps care of her son. Compare the way Gilb reveals this side of his mother to the way Stillmann chooses and arranges his tweets. When does love and the search for love become the essays' subjects — from the start? Sometime later? How does it happen?

## FURTHER QUESTIONS
## FOR THINKING AND WRITING

**1.** How do the works in this section support the contention that love and hate are closely related emotions? **Writing Topic:** Discuss the relationship between love and hate in Raymond Carver's "What We Talk About When We Talk About Love" and William Shakespeare's *Othello*.

**2.** What images are characteristically associated with love in the prose and poetry of this section? What images are associated with hate? **Writing Topic:** Compare the image patterns in William Shakespeare's Sonnets 18 and 130 or the image patterns in John Donne's "A Valediction: Forbidding Mourning" and Robert Burns's "A Red, Red Rose."

**3.** The Greeks have three words that can be translated by the English word *love*: *eros*, *agape*, and *philia*. Describe the differences among these three types of love. **Writing Topic:** Find a story or poem that is representative of each type of love. In analyzing each work, discuss the extent to which the primary notion of love being addressed or celebrated is tempered by the other two types.

**4.** William Blake's "A Poison Tree," Carolyn Kizer's "Bitch," and Sylvia Plath's "Daddy" all seem to describe aspects of hate. Distinguish among the different varieties of hatred expressed in each poem. **Writing Topic:** Compare and contrast the source of the speaker's hatred in two of these poems.

**5.** Which works in this section treat love and/or hate in a way that corresponds most closely with your own experience or conception of those emotional states? Which contradict your experience? **Writing Topic:** For each case, isolate the elements in the work that provoke your response, and discuss them in terms of their "truth" or "falsity."

# LIFE AND DEATH

*Death and Life*, Gustav Klimt. Before 1911, finished 1915. Oil on canvas, 178 × 198 cm.

The inevitability of death is not implied in the biblical story of creation; it required an act of disobedience before an angry God passed a sentence of hard labor and mortality on humankind: "In the sweat of your face you shall eat bread till you return to the ground, for out of it you were taken; you are dust and to dust you shall return." These words, written down some 2,800 years ago, preserve one ancient explanation for a persistently enigmatic condition of life and a persistent awareness of the implications of our actions. From earliest times men and women have attempted to characterize death, to cultivate beliefs about it, and to let it inform how they spend their time among the living. The mystery and certainty of death, in every age, make it an important theme for literary art.

Beliefs about the nature of death vary widely. The ancient Jews of the Pentateuch reveal no conception of immortality. Ancient Buddhist writings describe death as a mere translation from one painful life to another in an ongoing process of atonement that only the purest can avoid. The Christians conceive of a soul, separate from the body, which at the body's death is freed for a disembodied eternal life. The speaker in Robert Frost's "Stopping by Woods on a Snowy Evening" gazes into the dark woods filling up with snow, momentarily drawn toward the peace it represents; but Frost's is a secular poem, and the speaker turns back to life. In much religious poetry—John Donne's sonnet "Death, Be Not Proud" is an outstanding example—death is celebrated as a release from a burdensome existence into the eternal happiness of the afterlife. More recently, attitudes about death have reflected the great intellectual revolutions that affected all thought. For example, the Darwinian revolution replaced humans, the greatest glory of God's creation, with upright primates whose days are likely to be numbered by the flux between the fire and ice of geological history; and the Freudian revolution robbed men and women of their proudest certainty—the conviction that they possessed a dependable and controlling rational mind. In the context of Western tradition, these ideas serve to diminish us, to mock our self-importance. And, inevitably, these shifts lead us to alter our conception of death.

The view that establishes death as the great leveler, bringing citizens and emperors to the selfsame dust, is apparent in such poems as Percy Bysshe Shelley's "Ozymandias" and A. E. Housman's "To an Athlete Dying Young." This leveling view of death leads easily to the tradition wherein life itself is made absurd by the fact of death. Shakespeare's Macbeth finally declares that life is "a tale / Told by an idiot, full of sound and fury, / Signifying nothing." And the contemplation of suicide, which the pain and absurdity of life would seem to commend, provokes responses such as Edwin Arlington Robinson's ironic "Richard Cory." Some rage against death, as Dylan Thomas does in "Do Not Go Gentle into That Good Night"; others caution a quiet resignation, like Frost in "After Apple-Picking." Much fine poetry on death is elegiac—it speaks the melancholy response of the living to the fact of death. And reminders of this fact do not arise only from the death of a solitary person or within a grieving community: we are faced with it when we recognize the lives and deaths of the animals with whom we share the planet, as we see in the "Animal Fates" cluster. These writers urge us to see that the animal world is an inextricable part of the human experience; it isn't there simply to help us think about our own deaths and lives, but exists in its own right as a world worthy of attention, one whose own cycle of life and death can be shaped, sometimes quite harmfully, by human actions.

In short, literary treatments of death and how it shapes life display immense diversity. In Leo Tolstoy's "The Death of Iván Ilých," dying leads to a redemptive awareness. Leslie Marmon Silko's "The Man to Send Rain Clouds" explores sacrificial death as a means to control nature. In Victor Hernández Cruz's "Problems with Hurricanes," the comic lightens the weight of death. The inevitability of death and the way one confronts it paradoxically give life its meaning and its value.

## QUESTIONS FOR THINKING AND WRITING

As you read the selections in this section, consider the following questions. You may want to write out your thoughts informally in a journal as a way of preparing to respond to the selections, or you may wish to make one of these questions the basis for a formal essay.

**1.** Has a close relative or friend of yours died? Was the person young or old, vigorous or in poor health? How did you feel? How might the circumstances of death alter one's feelings toward death or toward the person who died?

**2.** Do you believe that some essential part of you will survive the death of your body? On what do you base the belief? How does this belief alter your feelings about the death of people close to you? How does it alter your own behavior?

**3.** Are there any circumstances that justify suicide? Explain. If you believe that some suicides are justifiable, would it also be justifiable to help someone end his or her life? Explain.

**4.** Are there any circumstances that justify killing someone? Explain.

**5.** Imagine as best you can the circumstances of your own death. Describe them.

**6.** Write your own obituary. How would you like to be remembered? If you want, instead of the reserved, respectful tone characteristic of the genre, write something funny or satirical, but still take the exercise seriously. What are the important things you want people to remember about you, that you did or said? What kind of person were you really?

# FICTION

**EDGAR ALLAN POE**   (1809–1849)

## THE CASK OF AMONTILLADO   1846

The thousand injuries of Fortunato I had borne as I best could, but when he ventured upon insult, I vowed revenge. You, who so well know the nature of my soul, will not suppose, however, that I gave utterance to a threat. At *length* I would be avenged; this was a point definitely settled—but the very definitiveness with which it was resolved precluded the idea of risk. I must not only punish, but punish with impunity. A wrong is unredressed when retribution overtakes its redresser. It is equally unredressed when the avenger fails to make himself felt as such to him who has done the wrong.

It must be understood that neither by word nor deed had I given Fortunato cause to doubt my good will. I continued, as was my wont, to smile in his face, and he did not perceive that my smile *now* was at the thought of his immolation.

He had a weak point—this Fortunato—although in other regards he was a man to be respected and even feared. He prided himself on his connoisseurship in wine. Few Italians have the true virtuoso spirit. For the most part their enthusiasm is adopted to suit the time and opportunity to practise imposture upon the British and Austrian *millionnaires*. In painting and gemmary Fortunato, like his countrymen, was a quack, but in the matter of old wines he was sincere. In this respect I did not differ from him materially;—I was skillful in the Italian vintages myself, and bought largely whenever I could.

It was about dusk, one evening during the supreme madness of the carnival season, that I encountered my friend. He accosted me with excessive warmth, for he had been drinking much. The man wore motley. He had on a tight-fitting parti-striped dress, and his head was surmounted by the conical cap and bells. I was so pleased to see him, that I thought I should never have done wringing his hand.

I said to him—"My dear Fortunato, you are luckily met. How remarkably 5 well you are looking to-day! But I have received a pipe[1] of what passes for Amontillado, and I have my doubts."

"How?" said he, "Amontillado? A pipe? Impossible! And in the middle of the carnival!"

[1] Large wine cask.

"I have my doubts," I replied; "and I was silly enough to pay the full Amontillado price without consulting you in the matter. You were not to be found, and I was fearful of losing a bargain."

"Amontillado!"

"I have my doubts."

"Amontillado!" 10

"And I must satisfy them."

"Amontillado!"

"As you are engaged, I am on my way to Luchesi. If any one has a critical turn, it is he. He will tell me—"

"Luchesi cannot tell Amontillado from Sherry."

"And yet some fools will have it that his taste is a match for your own." 15

"Come, let us go."

"Whither?"

"To your vaults."

"My friend, no; I will not impose upon your good nature. I perceive you have an engagement. Luchesi—"

"I have no engagement;—come." 20

"My friend, no. It is not the engagement, but the severe cold with which I perceive you are afflicted. The vaults are insufferably damp. They are encrusted with nitre."

"Let us go, nevertheless. The cold is merely nothing. Amontillado! You have been imposed upon; and as for Luchesi, he cannot distinguish Sherry from Amontillado."

Thus speaking, Fortunato possessed himself of my arm. Putting on a mask of black silk, and drawing a *roquelaure*[2] closely about my person, I suffered him to hurry me to my palazzo.

There were no attendants at home; they had absconded to make merry in honor of the time. I had told them that I should not return until the morning, and had given them explicit orders not to stir from the house. These orders were sufficient, I well knew, to insure their immediate disappearance, one and all, as soon as my back was turned.

I took from their sconces two flambeaux, and giving one to Fortunato, 25 bowed him through several suites of rooms to the archway that led into the vaults. I passed down a long and winding staircase, requesting him to be cautious as he followed. We came at length to the foot of the descent, and stood together on the damp ground of the catacombs of the Montresors.

The gait of my friend was unsteady, and the bells upon his cap jingled as he strode.

"The pipe," said he.

"It is farther on," said I; "but observe the white web-work which gleams from these cavern walls."

He turned towards me, and looked into my eyes with two filmy orbs that distilled the rheum of intoxication.

---

[2] Short cloak.

"Nitre?" he asked, at length.                                                    30

"Nitre," I replied. "How long have you had that cough?"

"Ugh! ugh! ugh!—ugh! ugh! ugh!—ugh! ugh! ugh!—ugh! ugh! ugh!—ugh! ugh! ugh!"

My poor friend found it impossible to reply for many minutes.

"It is nothing," he said, at last.

"Come," I said, with decision, "we will go back; your health is precious. You   35
are rich, respected, admired, beloved; you are happy, as once I was. You are a
man to be missed. For me it is no matter. We will go back; you will be ill, and I
cannot be responsible. Besides, there is Luchesi—"

"Enough," he said; "the cough is a mere nothing: it will not kill me. I shall
not die of a cough."

"True—true," I replied; "and, indeed, I had no intention of alarming you
unnecessarily—but you should use all proper caution. A draught of this
Medoc will defend us from the damps."

Here I knocked off the neck of a bottle which I drew from a long row of its
fellows that lay upon the mould.

"Drink," I said, presenting him the wine.

He raised it to his lips with a leer. He paused and nodded to me familiarly,   40
while his bells jingled.

"I drink," he said, "to the buried that repose around us."

"And I to your long life."

He again took my arm, and we proceeded.

"These vaults," he said, "are extensive."

"The Montresors," I replied, "were a great and numerous family."             45

"I forget your arms."

"A huge human foot d'or, in a field azure; the foot crushes a serpent rampant
whose fangs are imbedded in the heel."

"And the motto?"

"*Nemo me impune lacessit.*"[3]

"Good!" he said.                                                                50

The wine sparkled in his eyes and the bells jingled. My own fancy grew
warm with the Medoc. We had passed through walls of piled bones, with
casks and puncheons intermingling, into the inmost recesses of the catacombs. I paused again, and this time I made bold to seize Fortunato by an
arm above the elbow.

"The nitre!" I said; "see, it increases. It hangs like moss upon the vaults.
We are below the river's bed. The drops of moisture trickle among the bones.
Come, we will go back ere it is too late. Your cough—"

"It is nothing," he said; "let us go on. But first, another draught of the Medoc."

---

[3] No one provokes me with impunity (the motto of Scotland).

I broke and reached him a flagon of De Grâve. He emptied it at a breath. His eyes flashed with a fierce light. He laughed and threw the bottle upwards with a gesticulation I did not understand.

I looked at him in surprise. He repeated the movement—a grotesque one.   55

"You do not comprehend?" he said.

"Not I," I replied.

"Then you are not of the brotherhood."

"How?"

"You are not of the masons."[4]   60

"Yes, yes," I said; "yes, yes."

"You? Impossible! A mason?"

"A mason," I replied.

"A sign," he said.

"It is this," I answered, producing a trowel from beneath the folds of my   65
*roquelaure.*

"You jest," he exclaimed, recoiling a few paces. "But let us proceed to the Amontillado."

"Be it so," I said, replacing the tool beneath the cloak, and again offering him my arm. He leaned upon it heavily. We continued our route in search of the Amontillado. We passed through a range of low arches, descended, passed on, and descending again, arrived at a deep crypt, in which the foulness of the air caused our flambeaux rather to glow than flame.

At the most remote end of the crypt there appeared another less spacious. Its walls had been lined with human remains piled to the vault overhead, in the fashion of the great catacombs of Paris. Three sides of this interior crypt were still ornamented in this manner. From the fourth the bones had been thrown down, and lay promiscuously upon the earth, forming at one point a mound of some size. Within the wall thus exposed by the displacing of the bones, we perceived a still interior recess, in depth about four feet, in width three, in height six or seven. It seemed to have been constructed for no especial use within itself, but formed merely the interval between two of the colossal supports of the roof of the catacombs, and was backed by one of their circumscribing walls of solid granite.

It was in vain that Fortunato, uplifting his dull torch, endeavored to pry into the depths of the recess. Its termination the feeble light did not enable us to see.

"Proceed," I said; "herein is the Amontillado. As for Luchesi—"   70

"He is an ignoramus," interrupted my friend, as he stepped unsteadily forward, while I followed immediately at his heels. In an instant he had reached the extremity of the niche, and finding his progress arrested by the rock, stood stupidly bewildered. A moment more and I had fettered him to the granite. In its surface were two iron staples, distant from each other about two feet, horizontally. From one of these depended a short chain, from the other a

---

[4] A member of the Freemasons, an international secretive mutual aid society.

padlock. Throwing the links about his waist, it was but the work of a few seconds to secure it. He was too much astounded to resist. Withdrawing the key I stepped back from the recess.

"Pass your hand," I said, "over the wall; you cannot help feeling the nitre. Indeed it is *very* damp. Once more let me *implore* you to return. No? Then I must positively leave you. But I must first render you all the little attentions in my power."

"The Amontillado!" ejaculated my friend, not yet recovered from his astonishment.

"True," I replied; "the Amontillado."

As I said these words I busied myself among the pile of bones of which I have before spoken. Throwing them aside, I soon uncovered a quantity of building-stone and mortar. With these materials and with the aid of my trowel, I began vigorously to wall up the entrance of the niche.

I had scarcely laid the first tier of the masonry when I discovered that the intoxication of Fortunato had in a great measure worn off. The earliest indication I had of this was a low moaning cry from the depth of the recess. It was *not* the cry of a drunken man. There was then a long and obstinate silence. I laid the second tier, and the third, and the fourth; and then I heard the furious vibrations of the chain. The noise lasted for several minutes, during which, that I might hearken to it with the more satisfaction, I ceased my labors and sat down upon the bones. When at last the clanking subsided, I resumed the trowel, and finished without interruption the fifth, the sixth, and the seventh tier. The wall was now nearly upon a level with my breast. I again paused, and holding the flambeaux over the masonwork, threw a few feeble rays upon the figure within.

A succession of loud and shrill screams, bursting suddenly from the throat of the chained form, seemed to thrust me violently back. For a brief moment I hesitated—I trembled. Unsheathing my rapier, I began to grope with it about the recess; but the thought of an instant reassured me. I placed my hand upon the solid fabric of the catacombs, and felt satisfied. I reapproached the wall. I replied to the yells of him who clamored. I re-echoed—I aided—I surpassed them in volume and in strength. I did this, and the clamorer grew still.

It was now midnight, and my task was drawing to a close. I had completed the eighth, the ninth, and the tenth tier. I had finished a portion of the last and the eleventh; there remained but a single stone to be fitted and plastered in. I struggled with its weight; I placed it partially in its destined position. But now there came from out the niche a low laugh that erected the hairs upon my head. It was succeeded by a sad voice, which I had difficulty in recognizing as that of the noble Fortunato. The voice said—

"Ha! ha! ha!—he! he! he!—a very good joke indeed—an excellent jest. We will have many a rich laugh about it at the palazzo—he! he! he!—over our wine—he! he! he!"

"The Amontillado!" I said.                                                                        80

"He! he! he!—he! he! he!—yes, the Amontillado. But is it not getting late? Will not they be awaiting us at the palazzo, the Lady Fortunato and the rest? Let us be gone."

"Yes," I said, "let us be gone."

*"For the love of God, Montresor!"*

"Yes," I said, "for the love of God!"

But to these words I hearkened in vain for a reply. I grew impatient. I called     85 aloud;

"Fortunato!"

No answer. I called again;

"Fortunato!"

No answer still, I thrust a torch through the remaining aperture and let it fall within. There came forth in return only a jingling of the bells. My heart grew sick—on account of the dampness of the catacombs. I hastened to make an end of my labor. I forced the last stone into its position; I plastered it up. Against the new masonry I reerected the old rampart of bones. For the half of a century no mortal has disturbed them. *In pace requiescat!*[5]

### FOR ANALYSIS

**1.** We are not told how Fortunato insulted Montresor. Would the story be more effective if we knew? Explain.

**2.** Are there any clues that suggest when and to whom Montresor tells his tale? Explain.

**3.** How is Montresor able to lure Fortunato into the catacombs?

**4.** Describe the qualities that Montresor insists on as the characteristics of a successful vengeance.

**5.** Describe the **style** of this story, particularly the speech of the characters. What effect does the archaic flavor contribute to the tale?

### MAKING ARGUMENTS

Choose a short section of the story—say, three or four paragraphs—and carefully analyze the language line by line (particularly as it differs from ordinary colloquial English). Make an argument for or against this change, using as evidence your story of how this story works or doesn't work and of how stories work generally.

### WRITING TOPIC

In an essay, imagine and describe the circumstances and the nature of Fortunato's insult.

### MAKING CONNECTIONS

Compare this story with Jackson's "The Lottery" (p. 315), which also ends with an unexpected and horrible murder. What similarities do you find? What differences?

---

[5] May he rest in peace.

**LEO TOLSTOY**   (1828–1910)

# THE DEATH OF IVÁN ILÝCH[1]   1886

### CHAPTER I

During an interval in the Melvínski trial in the large building of the Law Courts the members and public prosecutor met in Iván Egórovich Shébek's private room, where the conversation turned on the celebrated Krasóvski case. Fëdor Vasílievich warmly maintained that it was not subject to their jurisdiction, Iván Egórovich maintained the contrary, while Peter Ivánovich, not having entered into the discussion at the start, took no part in it but looked through the *Gazette* which had just been handed in.

"Gentlemen," he said, "Iván Ilých has died!"

"You don't say so!"

"Here, read it yourself," replied Peter Ivánovich, handing Fëdor Vasílievich the paper still damp from the press. Surrounded by a black border were the words: "Praskóvya Fëdorovna Gol* viná, with profound sorrow, informs relatives and friends of the demise of her beloved husband Iván Ilých Golovín, Member of the Court of Justice, which occurred on February the 4th of this year 1882. The funeral will take place on Friday at one o'clock in the afternoon."

Iván Ilých had been a colleague of the gentlemen present and was liked by 5 them all. He had been ill for some weeks with an illness said to be incurable. His post had been kept open for him, but there had been conjectures that in case of his death Alexéev might receive his appointment, and that either Vínnikov or Shtábel would succeed Alexéev. So on receiving the news of Iván Ilých's death the first thought of each of the gentlemen in that private room was of the changes and promotions it might occasion among themselves or their acquaintances.

"I shall be sure to get Shtábel's place or Vínnikov's," thought Fëdor Vasílievich. "I was promised that long ago, and the promotion means an extra eight hundred rubles a year for me besides the allowance."

"Now I must apply for my brother-in-law's transfer from Kalúga," thought Peter Ivánovich. "My wife will be very glad, and then she won't be able to say that I never do anything for her relations."

"I thought he would never leave his bed again," said Peter Ivánovich aloud. "It's very sad."

"But what really was the matter with him?"

"The doctors couldn't say—at least they could, but each of them said some- 10 thing different. When last I saw him I thought he was getting better."

[1] Translated by Aylmer Maude.

"And I haven't been to see him since the holidays. I always meant to go."

"Had he any property?"

"I think his wife had a little—but something quite trifling."

"We shall have to go to see her, but they live so terribly far away."

"Far away from you, you mean. Everything's far away from your place."    15

"You see, he never can forgive my living on the other side of the river," said Peter Ivánovich, smiling at Shébek. Then, still talking of the distances between different parts of the city, they returned to the Court.

Besides considerations as to the possible transfers and promotions likely to result from Iván Ilých's death, the mere fact of the death of a near acquaintance aroused, as usual, in all who heard of it the complacent feeling that, "it is he who is dead and not I."

Each one thought or felt, "Well, he's dead but I'm alive!" But the more intimate of Iván Ilých's acquaintances, his so-called friends, could not help thinking also that they would now have to fulfill the very tiresome demands of propriety by attending the funeral service and paying a visit of condolence to the widow.

Fëdor Vasílievich and Peter Ivánovich had been his nearest acquaintances. Peter Ivánovich had studied law with Iván Ilých and had considered himself to be under obligations to him.

Having told his wife at dinner-time of Iván Ilých's death, and of his conjec-    20
ture that it might be possible to get her brother transferred to their circuit, Peter Ivánovich sacrificed his usual nap, put on his evening clothes, and drove to Iván Ilých's house.

At the entrance stood a carriage and two cabs. Leaning against the wall in the hall downstairs near the cloak-stand was a coffin-lid covered with cloth of gold, ornamented with gold cord and tassels, that had been polished up with metal powder. Two ladies in black were taking off their fur cloaks. Peter Ivánovich recognized one of them as Iván Ilých's sister, but the other was a stranger to him. His colleague Schwartz was just coming downstairs, but on seeing Peter Ivánovich enter he stopped and winked at him, as if to say: "Iván Ilých has made a mess of things—not like you and me."

Schwartz's face with his Piccadilly whiskers, and his slim figure in evening dress, had as usual an air of elegant solemnity which contrasted with the playfulness of his character and had a special piquancy here, or so it seemed to Peter Ivánovich.

Peter Ivánovich allowed the ladies to precede him and slowly followed them upstairs. Schwartz did not come down but remained where he was, and Peter Ivánovich understood that he wanted to arrange where they should play bridge that evening. The ladies went upstairs to the widow's room, and Schwartz with seriously compressed lips but a playful look in his eyes, indicated by a twist of his eyebrows the room to the right where the body lay.

Peter Ivánovich, like everyone else on such occasions, entered feeling uncertain what he would have to do. All he knew was that at such times it is always safe to cross oneself. But he was not quite sure whether one should make obeisances while doing so. He therefore adopted a middle course. On entering the room he began crossing himself and made a slight movement resembling a bow. At the same time, as far as the motion of his head and arm allowed, he surveyed the room. Two young men—apparently nephews, one of whom was a high-school pupil—were leaving the room, crossing themselves as they did so. An old woman was standing motionless, and a lady with strangely arched eyebrows was saying something to her in a whisper. A vigorous, resolute Church Reader, in a frock-coat, was reading something in a loud voice with an expression that precluded any contradiction. The butler's assistant, Gerásim, stepping lightly in front of Peter Ivánovich, was strewing something on the floor. Noticing this, Peter Ivánovich was immediately aware of a faint odour of a decomposing body.

The last time he had called on Iván Ilých, Peter Ivánovich had seen Gerásim  25 in the study. Iván Ilých had been particularly fond of him and he was perform-ing the duty of a sick nurse.

Peter Ivánovich continued to make the sign of the cross slightly inclining his head in an intermediate direction between the coffin, the Reader, and the icons on the table in a corner of the room. Afterwards, when it seemed to him that this movement of his arm in crossing himself had gone on too long, he stopped and began to look at the corpse.

The dead man lay, as dead men always lie, in a specially heavy way, his rigid limbs sunk in the soft cushions of the coffin, with the head forever bowed on the pillow. His yellow waxen brow with bald patches over his sunken temples was thrust up in the way peculiar to the dead, the protruding nose seeming to press on the upper lip. He was much changed and had grown even thin-ner since Peter Ivánovich had last seen him, but, as is always the case with the dead, his face was handsomer and above all more dignified than when he was alive. The expression on the face said that what was necessary had been accom-plished, and accomplished rightly. Besides this there was in that expression a reproach and a warning to the living. This warning seemed to Peter Ivánovich out of place, or at least not applicable to him. He felt a certain discomfort and so he hurriedly crossed himself once more and turned and went out of the door—too hurriedly and too regardless of propriety, as he himself was aware.

Schwartz was waiting for him in the adjoining room with legs spread wide apart and both hands toying with his top-hat behind his back. The mere sight of that playful, well-groomed, and elegant figure refreshed Peter Ivánovich. He felt that Schwartz was above all these happenings and would not surrender to any depressing influences. His very look said that this incident of a church service for Iván Ilých could not be a sufficient reason for infringing the order of the session—in other words, that it would certainly not prevent his unwrap-ping a new pack of cards and shuffling them that evening while a footman placed four fresh candles on the table: in fact, there was no reason for sup-posing that this incident would hinder their spending the evening agreeably. Indeed he said this in a whisper as Peter Ivánovich passed him, proposing that they should meet for a game at Fëdor Vasílievich's. But apparently Peter Ivánovich was not destined to play bridge that evening. Praskóvya Fëdorovna (a short, fat woman who despite all efforts to the contrary had continued to broaden steadily from her shoulders downwards and who had the same extraordinarily arched eyebrows as the lady who had been standing by the coffin), dressed all in black, her head covered with lace, came out of her own room with some other ladies, conducted them to the room where the dead body lay, and said: "The service will begin immediately. Please go in."

Schwartz, making an indefinite bow, stood still, evidently neither accepting nor declining this invitation. Praskóvya Fëdorovna recognizing Peter Ivánovich, sighed, went close up to him, took his hand, and said: "I know you were a true friend to Iván Ilých . . ." and looked at him awaiting some suitable response. And Peter Ivánovich knew that, just as it had been the right thing to cross himself in that room, so what he had to do here was to press her hand, sigh, and say, "Believe me . . ." So he did all this and as he did it felt that the desired result had been achieved: that both he and she were touched.

"Come with me. I want to speak to you before it begins," said the widow. 30 "Give me your arm."

Peter Ivánovich gave her his arm and they went to the inner rooms, passing Schwartz who winked at Peter Ivánovich compassionately.

"That does for our bridge! Don't object if we find another player. Perhaps you can cut in when you do escape," said his playful look.

Peter Ivánovich sighed still more deeply and despondently, and Praskóvya Fëdorovna pressed his arm gratefully. When they reached the drawing-room, upholstered in pink cretonne and lighted by a dim lamp, they sat down at the table—she on a sofa and Peter Ivánovich on a low pouffe, the springs of which yielded spasmodically under his weight. Praskóvya Fëdorovna had been on the point of warning him to take another seat, but felt that such a warning was out of keeping with her present condition and so changed her mind. As he sat down on the pouffe Peter Ivánovich recalled how Iván Ilých had arranged this room and had consulted him regarding this pink cretonne with green leaves. The whole room was full of furniture and knick-knacks, and on her way to the sofa the lace of the widow's black shawl caught on the carved edge of the table. Peter Ivánovich rose to detach it, and the springs of the pouffe, relieved of his weight, rose also and gave him a push. The widow began detaching her shawl herself, and Peter Ivánovich again sat down, suppressing the rebellious springs of the pouffe under him. But the widow had not quite freed herself and Peter Ivánovich got up again, and again the pouffe rebelled and even creaked. When this was all over she took out a clean cambric handkerchief and began to weep. The episode with the shawl and the struggle with the pouffe had cooled Peter Ivánovich's emotions and he sat there with a sullen look on his face. This awkward situation was interrupted by Sokolóv, Iván Ilých's butler, who came to report that the plot in the cemetery that Praskóvya Fëdorovna had chosen would cost two hundred rubles. She stopped weeping and, looking at Peter Ivánovich with the air of a victim, remarked in French that it was very hard for her. Peter Ivánovich made a silent gesture signifying his full conviction that it must indeed be so.

"Please smoke," she said in a magnanimous yet crushed voice, and turned to discuss with Sokolóv the price of the plot for the grave.

Peter Ivánovich while lighting his cigarette heard her inquiring very circum- 35 stantially into the price of different plots in the cemetery and finally decide which she would take. When that was done she gave instructions about engaging the choir. Sokolóv then left the room.

"I look after everything myself," she told Peter Ivánovich, shifting the albums that lay on the table; and noticing that the table was endangered by his cigarette-ash, she immediately passed him an ashtray, saying as she did so: "I consider it an affectation to say that my grief prevents my attending to practical affairs. On the contrary, if anything can—I won't say console me, but— distract me, it is seeing to everything concerning him." She again took out her handkerchief as if preparing to cry, but suddenly, as if mastering her feeling, she shook herself and began to speak calmly. "But there is something I want to talk to you about."

Peter Ivánovich bowed, keeping control of the springs of the pouffe, which immediately began quivering under him.

"He suffered terribly the last few days."

"Did he?" said Peter Ivánovich.

"Oh, terribly! He screamed unceasingly, not for minutes but for hours. For the 40 last three days he screamed incessantly. It was unendurable. I cannot understand how I bore it; you could hear him three rooms off. Oh, what I have suffered!"

"Is it possible that he was conscious all that time?" asked Peter Ivánovich.

"Yes," she whispered. "To the last moment. He took leave of us a quarter of an hour before he died, and asked us to take Volódya away."

The thought of the sufferings of this man he had known so intimately, first as a merry little boy, then as a school-mate, and later as a grown-up colleague, suddenly struck Peter Ivánovich with horror, despite an unpleasant consciousness of his own and this woman's dissimulation. He again saw that brow, and that nose pressing down on the lip, and felt afraid for himself.

"Three days of frightful suffering and then death! Why, that might suddenly, at any time, happen to me," he thought, and for a moment felt terrified. But— he did not himself know how—the customary reflection at once occurred to him that this had happened to Iván Ilých and not to him, and that it should not and could not happen to him, and that to think that it could would be yielding to depression which he ought not to do, as Schwartz's expression plainly showed. After which reflection Peter Ivánovich felt reassured, and began to ask with interest about the details of Iván Ilých's death, as though death was an accident natural to Iván Ilých but certainly not to himself.

After many details of the really dreadful physical sufferings Iván Ilých 45 had endured (which details he learnt only from the effect those sufferings had produced on Praskóvya Fëdorovna's nerves) the widow apparently found it necessary to get to business.

"Oh, Peter Ivánovich, how hard it is! How terribly, terribly hard!" and she again began to weep.

Peter Ivánovich sighed and waited for her to finish blowing her nose. When she had done so he said, "Believe me . . ." and she again began talking and brought out what was evidently her chief concern with him—namely, to question him as to how she could obtain a grant of money from the government on the occasion of her husband's death. She made it appear that she was asking Peter Ivánovich's advice about her pension, but he soon saw that she already knew about that to the minutest detail, more even than he did himself. She knew how much could be got out of the government in consequence of her husband's death, but wanted to find out whether she could not possibly extract something more. Peter Ivánovich tried to think of some means of doing so, but after reflecting for a while and, out of propriety, condemning the government for its niggardliness, he said he thought that nothing more could be got. Then she sighed and evidently began to devise means of getting rid of her visitor. Noticing this, he put out his cigarette, rose, pressed her hand, and went out into the anteroom.

In the dining-room where the clock stood that Iván Ilých had liked so much and had bought at an antique shop, Peter Ivánovich met a priest and a few acquaintances who had come to attend the service, and he recognized Iván Ilých's daughter, a handsome young woman. She was in black and her slim figure appeared slimmer than ever. She had a gloomy, determined, almost angry expression, and bowed to Peter Ivánovich as though he were in some way to blame. Behind her, with the same offended look, stood a wealthy young man, an examining magistrate, whom Peter Ivánovich also knew and who was her fiancé, as he had heard. He bowed mournfully to them and was about to pass into the death-chamber, when from under the stairs appeared the figure of Iván Ilých's schoolboy son, who was extremely like his father. He seemed a little Iván Ilých, such as Peter Ivánovich remembered when they studied law together. His tear-stained eyes had in them the look that is seen in the eyes of boys of thirteen or fourteen who are not pure-minded. When he saw Peter Ivánovich he scowled morosely and shamefacedly. Peter Ivánovich nodded to him and entered the death-chamber. The service began: candles, groans, incense, tears, and sobs. Peter Ivánovich stood looking gloomily down at his feet. He did not look once at the dead man, did not yield to any depressing influence, and was one of the first to leave the room. There was no one in the anteroom, but Gerásim darted out of the dead man's room, rummaged with his strong hands among the fur coats to find Peter Ivánovich's and helped him on with it.

"Well, friend Gerásim," said Peter Ivánovich, so as to say something. "It's a sad affair, isn't it?"

"It's God's will. We shall all come to it some day," said Gerásim, displaying 50 his teeth—the even, white teeth of a healthy peasant—and, like a man in the thick of urgent work, he briskly opened the front door, called the coachman, helped Peter Ivánovich into the sledge, and sprang back to the porch as if in readiness for what he had to do next.

Peter Ivánovich found the fresh air particularly pleasant after the smell of incense, the dead body, and carbolic acid.

"Where to, sir?" asked the coachman.

"It's not too late even now. . . . I'll call round on Fëdor Vasílievich."

He accordingly drove there and found them just finishing the first rubber, so that it was quite convenient for him to cut in.

## CHAPTER II

Iván Ilých's life had been most simple and most ordinary and therefore most terrible.

He had been a member of the Court of Justice, and died at the age of forty-five. His father had been an official who after serving in various ministries and departments in Petersburg had made the sort of career which brings men to positions from which by reason of their long service they cannot be dismissed, though they are obviously unfit to hold any responsible position, and for whom therefore posts are specially created, which though fictitious carry salaries of from six to ten thousand rubles that are not fictitious, and in receipt of which they live on to a great age.

Such was the Privy Councillor and superfluous member of various superfluous institutions, Ilyá Epímovich Golovín.

He had three sons, of whom Iván Ilých was the second. The eldest son was following in his father's footsteps only in another department, and was already approaching that stage in the service at which a similar sinecure would be reached. The third son was a failure. He had ruined his prospects in a number of positions and was now serving in the railway department. His father and brothers, and still more their wives, not merely disliked meeting him, but avoided remembering his existence unless compelled to do so. His sister had married Baron Greff, a Petersburg official of her father's type. Iván Ilých was *le phénix de la famille*[2] as people said. He was neither as cold and formal as his elder brother nor as wild as the younger, but was a happy mean between them—an intelligent, polished, lively and agreeable man. He had studied with his younger brother at the School of Law, but the latter had failed to complete the course and was expelled when he was in the fifth class. Iván Ilých finished the course well. Even when he was at the School of Law he was just what he remained for the rest of his life: a capable, cheerful, good-natured, and sociable man, though strict in the fulfilment of what he considered to be his duty: and he considered his duty to be what was so considered by those in authority. Neither as a boy nor as a man was he a toady, but from early youth was by nature attracted to people of high station as a fly is drawn to the light, assimilating their ways and views of life and establishing friendly relations with them. All the enthusiasms of childhood and youth passed without leaving much trace on him; he succumbed to sensuality, to vanity, and latterly among the highest classes to liberalism, but always within limits which his instinct unfailingly indicated to him as correct.

---

[2] The phoenix of the family, here meaning "rare bird" or "prodigy."

At school he had done things which had formerly seemed to him very horrid and made him feel disgusted with himself when he did them; but when later on he saw that such actions were done by people of good position and that they did not regard them as wrong, he was able not exactly to regard them as right, but to forget about them entirely or not be at all troubled at remembering them.

Having graduated from the School of Law and qualified for the tenth rank 60 of the civil service, and having received money from his father for his equipment, Iván Ilých ordered himself clothes at Scharmer's, the fashionable tailor, hung a medallion inscribed *respice finem*[3] on his watch-chain, took leave of his professor and the prince who was patron of the school, had a farewell dinner with his comrades at Donon's first-class restaurant, and with his new and fashionable portmanteau, linen, clothes, shaving and other toilet appliances, and a travelling rug, all purchased at the best shops, he set off for one of the provinces where, through his father's influence, he had been attached to the Governor as an official for special service.

In the province Iván Ilých soon arranged as easy and agreeable a position for himself as he had had at the School of Law. He performed his official tasks, made his career, and at the same time amused himself pleasantly and decorously. Occasionally he paid official visits to country districts, where he behaved with dignity both to his superiors and inferiors, and performed the duties entrusted to him, which related chiefly to the sectarians,[4] with an exactness and incorruptible honesty of which he could not but feel proud.

In official matters, despite his youth and taste for frivolous gaiety, he was exceedingly reserved, punctilious, and even severe; but in society he was often amusing and witty, and always good-natured, correct in his manner, and *bon enfant*, as the governor and his wife—with whom he was like one of the family—used to say of him.

In the provinces he had an affair with a lady who made advances to the elegant young lawyer, and there was also a milliner; and there were carousals with aides-de-camp who visited the district, and after-supper visits to a certain outlying street of doubtful reputation; and there was too some obsequiousness to his chief and even to his chief's wife, but all this was done with such a tone of good breeding that no hard names could be applied to it. It all came under the heading of the French saying: "Il faut que jeunesse se passe."[5] It was all done with clean hands, in clean linen, with French phrases, and above all among people of the best society and consequently with the approval of people of rank.

So Iván Ilých served for five years and then came a change in his official life. The new and reformed judicial institutions were introduced, and new men were needed. Iván Ilých became such a new man. He was offered the post

---

[3] Regard the end.
[4] A large sect, whose members were placed under many legal restrictions, which broke away from the Orthodox Church in the seventeenth century.
[5] Youth must have its fling.

of Examining Magistrate, and he accepted it though the post was in another province and obliged him to give up the connections he had formed and to make new ones. His friends met to give him a send-off; they had a group-photograph taken and presented him with a silver cigarette-case, and he set off to his new post.

As examining magistrate Iván Ilých was just as *comme il faut*[6] and deco- 65 rous a man, inspiring general respect and capable of separating his official duties from his private life, as he had been when acting as an official on special service. His duties now as examining magistrate were far more interesting and attractive than before. In his former position it had been pleasant to wear an undress uniform made by Scharmer, and to pass through the crowd of petitioners and officials who were timorously awaiting an audience with the governor, and who envied him as with free and easy gait he went straight into his chief's private room to have a cup of tea and a cigarette with him. But not many people had then been directly dependent on him—only police officials and the sectarians when he went on special missions—and he liked to treat them politely, almost as comrades, as if he were letting them feel that he who had the power to crush them was treating them in this simple, friendly way. There were then but few such people. But now, as an examining magistrate, Iván Ilých felt that everyone without exception, even the most important and self-satisfied, was in his power, and that he need only write a few words on a sheet of paper with a certain heading, and this or that important, self-satisfied person would be brought before him in the role of an accused person or a witness, and if he did not choose to allow him to sit down, would have to stand before him and answer his questions. Iván Ilých never abused his power; he tried on the contrary to soften its expression, but the consciousness of it and of the possibility of softening its effect, supplied the chief interest and attraction of his office. In his work itself, especially in his examinations, he very soon acquired a method of eliminating all considerations irrelevant to the legal aspect of the case, and reducing even the most complicated case to a form in which it would be presented on paper only in its externals, completely excluding his personal opinion of the matter, while above all observing every prescribed formality. The work was new and Iván Ilých was one of the first men to apply the new Code of 1864.[7]

On taking up the post of examining magistrate in a new town, he made new acquaintances and connections, placed himself on a new footing, and assumed a somewhat different tone. He took up an attitude of rather dignified aloofness towards the provincial authorities, but picked out the best circle of legal gentlemen and wealthy gentry living in the town and assumed a tone of slight dissatisfaction with the government, of moderate liberalism, and of enlightened citizenship. At the same time, without at all altering the elegance of his toilet, he ceased shaving his chin and allowed his beard to grow as it pleased.

[6] Proper.
[7] Judicial procedures were reformed after the emancipation of the serfs in 1861.

Iván Ilých settled down very pleasantly in this new town. The society there, which inclined towards opposition to the Governor, was friendly, his salary was larger, and he began to play *vint*,[8] which he found added not a little to the pleasure of life, for he had a capacity for cards, played good-humouredly, and calculated rapidly and astutely, so that he usually won.

After living there for two years he met his future wife, Praskóvya Fëdorovna Míkhel, who was the most attractive, clever, and brilliant girl of the set in which he moved, and among other amusements and relaxations from his labours as examining magistrate, Iván Ilých established light and playful relations with her.

While he had been an official on special service he had been accustomed to dance, but now as an examining magistrate it was exceptional for him to do so. If he danced now, he did it as if to show that though he served under the reformed order of things, and had reached the fifth official rank, yet when it came to dancing he could do it better than most people. So at the end of an evening he sometimes danced with Praskóvya Fëdorovna, and it was chiefly during these dances that he captivated her. She fell in love with him. Iván Ilých had at first no definite intention of marrying, but when the girl fell in love with him he said to himself: "Really, why shouldn't I marry?"

Praskóvya Fëdorovna came of a good family, was not bad looking and had 70 some little property. Iván Ilých might have aspired to a more brilliant match, but even this was good. He had his salary, and she, he hoped, would have an equal income. She was well connected, and was a sweet, pretty, and thoroughly correct young woman. To say that Iván Ilých married because he fell in love with Praskóvya Fëdorovna and found that she sympathized with his views of life would be as incorrect as to say that he married because his social circle approved of the match. He was swayed by both these considerations: the marriage gave him personal satisfaction, and at the same time it was considered the right thing by the most highly placed of his associates.

So Iván Ilých got married.

The preparations for marriage and the beginning of married life, with its conjugal caresses, the new furniture, new crockery, and new linen, were very pleasant until his wife became pregnant—so that Iván Ilých had begun to think that marriage would not impair the easy, agreeable, gay and always decorous character of his life, approved of by society and regarded by himself as natural, but would even improve it. But from the first months of his wife's pregnancy, something new, unpleasant, depressing, and unseemly, and from which there was no way of escape, unexpectedly showed itself.

His wife, without any reason—*de gaieté de coeur*[9] as Iván Ilých expressed it to himself—began to disturb the pleasure and propriety of their life. She began to be jealous without any cause, expected him to devote his whole attention to her, found fault with everything, and made coarse and ill-mannered scenes.

---

[8] A card game similar to bridge.
[9] Of a joyous heart. Iván uses the expression ironically.

At first Iván Ilých hoped to escape from the unpleasantness of this state of affairs by the same easy and decorous relation to life that had served him heretofore: he tried to ignore his wife's disagreeable moods, continued to live in his usual easy and pleasant way, invited friends to his house for a game of cards, and also tried going out to his club or spending his evenings with friends. But one day his wife began upbraiding him so vigorously, using such coarse words, and continued to abuse him every time he did not fulfil her demands, so resolutely and with such evident determination not to give way till he submitted—that is, till he stayed at home and was bored just as she was—that he became alarmed. He now realized that matrimony—at any rate with Praskóvya Fëdorovna—was not always conducive to the pleasures and amenities of life but on the contrary often infringed both comfort and propriety, and that he must therefore entrench himself against such infringement. And Iván Ilých began to seek for means of doing so. His official duties were the one thing that imposed upon Praskóvya Fëdorovna, and by means of his official work and the duties attached to it he began struggling with his wife to secure his own independence.

With the birth of their child, the attempts to feed it and the various failures 75 in doing so, and with the real and imaginary illnesses of mother and child, in which Iván Ilých's sympathy was demanded but about which he understood nothing, the need of securing for himself an existence outside his family life became still more imperative.

As his wife grew more irritable and exacting and Iván Ilých transferred the centre of gravity of his life more and more to his official work, so did he grow to like his work better and became more ambitious than before.

Very soon, within a year of his wedding, Iván Ilých had realized that marriage, though it may add some comforts to life, is in fact a very intricate and difficult affair towards which in order to perform one's duty, that is, to lead a decorous life approved of by society, one must adopt a definite attitude just as towards one's official duties.

And Iván Ilých evolved such an attitude towards married life. He only required of it those conveniences—dinner at home, housewife, and bed—which it could give him, and above all that propriety of external forms required by public opinion. For the rest he looked for lighthearted pleasure and propriety, and was very thankful when he found them, but if he met with antagonism and querulousness he at once retired into his separate fenced-off world of official duties, where he found satisfaction.

Iván Ilých was esteemed a good official, and after three years was made Assistant Public Prosecutor. His new duties, their importance, the possibility of indicting and imprisoning anyone he chose, the publicity his speeches received, and the success he had in all these things, made his work still more attractive.

More children came. His wife became more and more querulous and 80 ill-tempered, but the attitude Iván Ilých had adopted towards his home life rendered him almost impervious to her grumbling.

After seven years' service in that town he was transferred to another province as Public Prosecutor. They moved, but were short of money and his wife did not like the place they moved to. Though the salary was higher the cost of living was greater, besides which two of their children died and family life became still more unpleasant for him.

Praskóvya Fëdorovna blamed her husband for every inconvenience they encountered in their new home. Most of the conversations between husband and wife, especially as to the children's education, led to topics which recalled former disputes, and those disputes were apt to flare up again at any moment. There remained only those rare periods of amorousness which still came to them at times but did not last long. These were islets at which they anchored for a while and then again set out upon that ocean of veiled hostility which showed itself in their aloofness from one another. This aloofness might have grieved Iván Ilých had he considered that it ought not to exist, but he now regarded the position as normal, and even made it the goal at which he aimed in family life. His aim was to free himself more and more from those unpleasantnesses and to give them a semblance of harmlessness and propriety. He attained this by spending less and less time with his family, and when obliged to be at home he tried to safeguard his position by the presence of outsiders. The chief thing however was that he had his official duties. The whole interest of his life now centered in the official world and that interest absorbed him. The consciousness of his power, being able to ruin anybody he wished to ruin, the importance, even the external dignity of his entry into court, or meetings with his subordinates, his success with superiors and inferiors, and above all his masterly handling of cases, of which he was conscious—all this gave him pleasure and filled his life, together with chats with his colleagues, dinners, and bridge. So that on the whole Iván Ilých's life continued to flow as he considered it should do—pleasantly and properly.

So things continued for another seven years. His eldest daughter was already sixteen, another child had died, and only one son was left, a schoolboy and a subject of dissension. Iván Ilých wanted to put him in the School of Law, but to spite him Praskóvya Fëdorovna entered him at the High School. The daughter had been educated at home and had turned out well: the boy did not learn badly either.

## CHAPTER III

So Iván Ilých lived for seventeen years after his marriage. He was already a Public Prosecutor of long standing, and had declined several proposed transfers while awaiting a more desirable post, when an unanticipated and unpleasant occurrence quite upset the peaceful course of his life. He was expecting to be offered the post of presiding judge in a University town, but Happe somehow came to the front and obtained the appointment instead. Iván Ilých became irritable, reproached Happe, and quarreled both with him and with his immediate superiors—who became colder to him and again passed him over when other appointments were made.

This was in 1880, the hardest year of Iván Ilých's life. It was then that it became evident on the one hand that his salary was insufficient for them to live on, and on the other that he had been forgotten, and not only this, but that what was for him the greatest and most cruel injustice appeared to others a quite ordinary occurrence. Even his father did not consider it his duty to help him. Iván Ilých felt himself abandoned by everyone, and that they regarded his position with a salary of 3,500 rubles as quite normal and even fortunate. He alone knew that with the consciousness of the injustices done him, with his wife's incessant nagging, and with the debts he had contracted by living beyond his means, his position was far from normal.

In order to save money that summer he obtained leave of absence and went with his wife to live in the country at her brother's place.

In the country, without his work, he experienced *ennui* for the first time in his life, and not only *ennui* but intolerable depression, and he decided that it was impossible to go on living like that, and that it was necessary to take energetic measures.

Having passed a sleepless night pacing up and down the veranda, he decided to go to Petersburg and bestir himself, in order to punish those who had failed to appreciate him and to get transferred to another ministry.

Next day, despite many protests from his wife and her brother, he started for Petersburg with the sole object of obtaining a post with a salary of five thousand rubles a year. He was no longer bent on any particular department, or tendency, or kind of activity. All he now wanted was an appointment to another post with a salary of five thousand rubles, either in the administration, in the banks, with the railways, in one of the Empress Márya's Institutions,[10] or even in the customs—but it had to carry with it a salary of five thousand rubles and be in a ministry other than that in which they had failed to appreciate him.

And this quest of Iván Ilých's was crowned with remarkable and unexpected success. At Kursk an acquaintance of his, F. I. Ilyín, got into the first-class carriage, sat down beside Iván Ilých, and told him of a telegram just received by the Governor of Kursk announcing that a change was about to take place in the ministry: Peter Ivánovich was to be superseded by Iván Semënovich.

The proposed change, apart from its significance for Russia, had a special significance for Iván Ilých, because by bringing forward a new man, Peter Petróvich, and consequently his friend Zachár Ivánovich, it was highly favourable for Iván Ilých, since Zachár Ivánovich was a friend and colleague of his.

In Moscow this news was confirmed, and on reaching Petersburg Iván Ilých found Zachár Ivánovich and received a definite promise of an appointment in his former Department of Justice.

A week later he telegraphed to his wife: "Zachár in Miller's place. I shall receive appointment on presentation of report."

Thanks to this change of personnel, Iván Ilých had unexpectedly obtained an appointment in his former ministry which placed him two stages above

---

[10] A charitable organization founded in the late eighteenth century by the empress Márya.

his former colleagues besides giving him five thousand rubles salary and three thousand five hundred rubles for expenses connected with his removal. All his ill humour towards his former enemies and the whole department vanished, and Iván Ilých was completely happy.

He returned to the country more cheerful and contented than he had been for a long time. Praskóvya Fëdorovna also cheered up and a truce was arranged between them. Iván Ilých told of how he had been fêted by everybody in Petersburg, how all those who had been his enemies were put to shame and now fawned on him, how envious they were of his appointment, and how much everybody in Petersburg had liked him. 95

Praskóvya Fëdorovna listened to all this and appeared to believe it. She did not contradict anything, but only made plans for their life in the town to which they were going. Iván Ilých saw with delight that these plans were his plans, that he and his wife agreed, and that, after a stumble, his life was regaining its due and natural character of pleasant lightheartedness and decorum.

Iván Ilých had come back for a short time only, for he had to take up his new duties on the 10th of September. Moreover, he needed time to settle into the new place, to move all his belongings from the province, and to buy and order many additional things: in a word, to make such arrangements as he had resolved on, which were almost exactly what Praskóvya Fëdorovna too had decided on.

Now that everything had happened so fortunately, and that he and his wife were at one in their aims and moreover saw so little of one another, they got on together better than they had done since the first years of marriage. Iván Ilých had thought of taking his family away with him at once, but the insistence of his wife's brother and her sister-in-law, who had suddenly become particularly amiable and friendly to him and his family, induced him to depart alone.

So he departed, and the cheerful state of mind induced by his success and by the harmony between his wife and himself, the one intensifying the other, did not leave him. He found a delightful house, just the thing both he and his wife had dreamt of. Spacious, lofty reception rooms in the old style, a convenient and dignified study, rooms for his wife and daughter, a study for his son—it might have been specially built for them. Iván Ilých himself superintended the arrangements, chose the wallpapers, supplemented the furniture (preferably with antiques which he considered particularly *comme il faut*), and supervised the upholstering. Everything progressed and progressed and approached the ideal he had set himself: even when things were only half completed they exceeded his expectations. He saw what a refined and elegant character, free from vulgarity, it would all have when it was ready. On falling asleep he pictured to himself how the reception-room would look. Looking at the yet unfinished drawing-room he could see the fireplace, the screen, the what-not, the little chairs dotted here and there, the dishes and plates on the walls, and the bronzes, as they would be when everything was in place. He was pleased by the thought of how his wife and daughter, who shared his taste in this matter, would be impressed by it. They were certainly not expecting as much.

He had been particularly successful in finding, and buying cheaply, antiques which gave a particularly aristocratic character to the whole place. But in his letters he intentionally understated everything in order to be able to surprise them. All this so absorbed him that his new duties—though he liked his official work—interested him less than he had expected. Sometimes he even had moments of absent-mindedness during the Court Sessions, and would consider whether he should have straight or curved cornices for his curtains. He was so interested in it all that he often did things himself, rearranging the furniture, or rehanging the curtains. Once when mounting a step-ladder to show the upholsterer, who did not understand, how he wanted the hangings draped, he made a false step and slipped, but being a strong and agile man he clung on and only knocked his side against the knob of the window frame. The bruised place was painful but the pain soon passed, and he felt particularly bright and well just then. He wrote: "I feel fifteen years younger." He thought he would have everything ready by September, but it dragged on till mid-October. But the result was charming not only in his eyes but to everyone who saw it.

In reality it was just what is usually seen in the houses of people of moder- 100 ate means who want to appear rich, and therefore succeed only in resembling others like themselves: there were damasks, dark wood, plants, rugs, and dull and polished bronzes—all the things people of a certain class have in order to resemble other people of that class. His house was so like the others that it would never have been noticed, but to him it all seemed to be quite exceptional. He was very happy when he met his family at the station and brought them to the newly furnished house all lit up, where a footman in a white tie opened the door into the hall decorated with plants, and when they went on into the drawing room and the study uttering exclamations of delight. He conducted them everywhere, drank in their praises eagerly, and beamed with pleasure. At tea that evening, when Praskóvya Fëdorovna among other things asked him about his fall, he laughed and showed them how he had gone flying and had frightened the upholsterer.

"It's a good thing I'm a bit of an athlete. Another man might have been killed, but I merely knocked myself, just here; it hurts when it's touched, but it's passing off already—it's only a bruise."

So they began living in their new home—in which, as always happens, when they got thoroughly settled in they found they were just one room short—and with the increased income, which as always was just a little (some five hundred rubles) too little, but it was all very nice.

Things went particularly well at first, before everything was finally arranged and while something had still to be done: this thing bought, that thing ordered, another thing moved, and something else adjusted. Though there were some disputes between husband and wife, they were both so well satisfied and had so much to do that it all passed off without any serious quarrels. When nothing was left to arrange it became rather dull and something seemed to be lacking, but they were then making acquaintances, forming habits, and life was growing fuller.

Iván Ilých spent his mornings at the law court and came home to dinner, and at first he was generally in a good humour, though he occasionally became irritable just on account of his house. (Every spot on the tablecloth or the upholstery, and every broken window-blind string, irritated him. He had devoted so much trouble to arranging it all that every disturbance of it distressed him.) But on the whole his life ran its course as he believed life should do: easily, pleasantly, and decorously.

He got up at nine, drank his coffee, read the paper, and then put on his 105 undress uniform and went to the law courts. There the harness in which he worked had already been stretched to fit him and he donned it without a hitch: petitioners, inquiries at the chancery, the chancery itself, and the sittings public and administrative. In all this the thing was to exclude everything fresh and vital, which always disturbs the regular course of official business, and to admit only official relations with people, and then only on official grounds. A man would come, for instance, wanting some information. Iván Ilých, as one in whose sphere the matter did not lie, would have nothing to do with him: but if the man had some business with him in his official capacity, something that could be expressed on officially stamped paper, he would do everything, positively everything he could within the limits of such relations, and in doing so would maintain the semblance of friendly human relations, that is, would observe the courtesies of life. As soon as the official relations ended, so did everything else. Iván Ilých possessed this capacity to separate his real life from the official side of affairs and not mix the two, in the highest degree, and by long practice and natural aptitude had brought it to such a pitch that sometimes, in the manner of a virtuoso, he would even allow himself to let the human and official relations mingle. He let himself do this just because he felt that he could at any time he chose resume the strictly official attitude again and drop the human relation. And he did it all easily, pleasantly, correctly, and even artistically. In the intervals between the sessions he smoked, drank tea, chatted a little about politics, a little about general topics, a little about cards, but most of all about official appointments. Tired, but with the feelings of a virtuoso—one of the first violins who has played his part in an orchestra with precision—he would return home to find that his wife and daughter had been out paying calls, or had a visitor, and that his son had been to school, had done his homework with his tutor, and was duly learning what is taught at High Schools. Everything was as it should be. After dinner, if they had no visitors, Iván Ilých sometimes read a book that was being much discussed at the time, and in the evening settled down to work, that is, read official papers, compared the depositions of witnesses, and noted paragraphs of the Code applying to them. This was neither dull nor amusing. It was dull when he might have been playing bridge, but if no bridge was available it was at any rate better than doing nothing or sitting with his wife. Iván Ilých's chief pleasure was giving little dinners to which he invited men and women of good social position, and just as his drawing-room resembled all other drawing-rooms so did his enjoyable little parties resemble all other such parties.

Once they even gave a dance. Iván Ilých enjoyed it and everything went off well, except that it led to a violent quarrel with his wife about the cakes and sweets. Praskóvya Fëdorovna had made her own plans, but Iván Ilých insisted on getting everything from an expensive confectioner and ordered too many cakes, and the quarrel occurred because some of those cakes were left over and the confectioner's bill came to forty-five rubles. It was a great and disagreeable quarrel. Praskóvya Fëdorovna called him "a fool and an imbecile," and he clutched at his head and made angry allusions to divorce.

But the dance itself had been enjoyable. The best people were there, and Iván Ilých had danced with Princess Trúfonova, a sister of the distinguished founder of the Society "Bear My Burden."

The pleasures connected with his work were pleasures of ambition; his social pleasures were those of vanity; but Iván Ilých's greatest pleasure was playing bridge. He acknowledged that whatever disagreeable incident happened in his life, the pleasure that beamed like a ray of light above everything else was to sit down to bridge with good players, not noisy partners, and of course to four-handed bridge (with five players it was annoying to have to stand out, though one pretended not to mind), to play a clever and serious game (when the cards allowed it) and then to have supper and drink a glass of wine. After a game of bridge, especially if he had won a little (to win a large sum was unpleasant), Iván Ilých went to bed in specially good humour.

So they lived. They formed a circle of acquaintances among the best people and were visited by people of importance and by young folk. In their views as to their acquaintances, husband, wife and daughter were entirely agreed, and tacitly and unanimously kept at arm's length and shook off the various shabby friends and relations who, with much show of affection, gushed into the drawing-room with its Japanese plates on the walls. Soon these shabby friends ceased to obtrude themselves and only the best people remained in the Golovíns' set.

Young men made up to Lisa, and Petríshchev, an examining magistrate and 110 Dmítri Ivanovich Petríshchev's son and sole heir, began to be so attentive to her that Iván Ilých had already spoken to Praskóvya Fëdorovna about it, and considered whether they should not arrange a party for them or get up some private theatricals.

So they lived, and all went well, without change, and life flowed pleasantly.

### CHAPTER IV

They were all in good health. It could not be called ill health if Iván Ilých sometimes said that he had a queer taste in his mouth and felt some discomfort in his left side.

But this discomfort increased and, though not exactly painful, grew into a sense of pressure in his side accompanied by ill humour. And his irritability became worse and worse and began to mar the agreeable, easy, and correct life that had established itself in the Golovín family. Quarrels between husband

and wife became more and more frequent, and soon the ease and amenity disappeared and even the decorum was barely maintained. Scenes again became frequent, and very few of those islets remained on which husband and wife could meet without explosion. Praskóvya Fëdorovna now had good reason to say that her husband's temper was trying. With characteristic exaggeration she said he had always had a dreadful temper, and that it had needed all her good nature to put up with it for twenty years. It was true that now the quarrels were started by him. His bursts of temper always came just before dinner, often just as he began to eat his soup. Sometimes he noticed that a plate or dish was chipped, or the food was not right, or his son put his elbow on the table, or his daughter's hair was not done as he liked it, and for all this he blamed Praskóvya Fëdorovna. At first she retorted and said disagreeable things to him, but once or twice he fell into such a rage at the beginning of dinner that she realized it was due to some physical derangement brought on by taking food, and so she restrained herself and did not answer, but only hurried to get the dinner over. She regarded this self-restraint as highly praiseworthy. Having come to the conclusion that her husband had a dreadful temper and made her life miserable, she began to feel sorry for herself, and the more she pitied herself the more she hated her husband. She began to wish he would die; yet she did not want him to die because then his salary would cease. And this irritated her against him still more. She considered herself dreadfully unhappy just because not even his death could save her, and though she concealed her exasperation, that hidden exasperation of hers increased his irritation also.

After one scene in which Iván Ilých had been particularly unfair and after which he had said in explanation that he certainly was irritable but that it was due to his not being well, she said that if he was ill it should be attended to, and insisted on his going to see a celebrated doctor.

He went. Everything took place as he had expected and as it always does. 115 There was the usual waiting and the important air assumed by the doctor, with which he was so familiar (resembling that which he himself assumed in court), and the sounding and listening, and the questions which called for answers that were foregone conclusions and were evidently unnecessary, and the look of importance which implied that "if only you put yourself in our hands we will arrange everything—we know indubitably how it has to be done, always in the same way for everybody alike." It was all just as it was in the law courts. The doctor put on just the same air towards him as he himself put on towards an accused person.

The doctor said that so-and-so indicated that there was so-and-so inside the patient, but if the investigation of so-and-so did not confirm this, then he must assume that and that. If he assumed that and that, then . . . and so on. To Iván Ilých only one question was important: was his case serious or not? But the doctor ignored that inappropriate question. From his point of view it was not the one under consideration, the real question was to decide between a floating kidney, chronic catarrh, or appendicitis. It was not a question of Iván Ilých's life or death, but one between a floating kidney and appendicitis. And that question the doctor solved brilliantly, as it seemed to Iván Ilých, in favour of the appendix, with the reservation that should an examination of the urine give fresh indications the matter would be reconsidered. All this was just what Iván Ilých had himself brilliantly accomplished a thousand times in dealing with men on trial. The doctor summed up just as brilliantly, looking over his spectacles triumphantly and even gaily at the accused. From the doctor's summing up Iván Ilých concluded that things were bad, but that for the doctor, and perhaps for everybody else, it was a matter of indifference, though for him it was bad. And this conclusion struck him painfully, arousing in him a great feeling of pity for himself and of bitterness towards the doctor's indifference to a matter of such importance.

He said nothing of this, but rose, placed the doctor's fee on the table, and remarked with a sigh: "We sick people probably often put inappropriate questions. But tell me, in general, is this complaint dangerous, or not? . . ."

The doctor looked at him sternly over his spectacles with one eye, as if to say: "Prisoner, if you will not keep to the questions put to you, I shall be obliged to have you removed from the court."

"I have already told you what I consider necessary and proper. The analysis may show something more." And the doctor bowed.

Iván Ilých went out slowly, seated himself disconsolately in his sledge, and 120 drove home. All the way home he was going over what the doctor had said, trying to translate those complicated, obscure, scientific phrases into plain language and find in them an answer to the question: "Is my condition bad? Is it very bad? Or is there as yet nothing much wrong?" And it seemed to him that the meaning of what the doctor had said was that it was very bad. Everything in the streets seemed depressing. The cabmen, the houses, the passersby, and the shops, were dismal. His ache, this dull gnawing ache that never ceased for a moment, seemed to have acquired a new and more serious significance from the doctor's dubious remarks. Iván Ilých now watched it with a new and oppressive feeling.

He reached home and began to tell his wife about it. She listened, but in the middle of his account his daughter came in with her hat on, ready to go out with her mother. She sat down reluctantly to listen to this tedious story, but could not stand it long, and her mother too did not hear him to the end.

"Well, I am very glad," she said. "Mind now to take your medicine regularly. Give me the prescription and I'll send Gerásim to the chemist's." And she went to get ready to go out.

While she was in the room Iván Ilých had hardly taken time to breathe, but he sighed deeply when she left it.

"Well," he thought, "perhaps it isn't so bad after all."

He began taking his medicine and following the doctor's directions, which 125 had been altered after the examination of the urine. But then it happened that there was a contradiction between the indications drawn from the examination of the urine and the symptoms that showed themselves. It turned out that what was happening differed from what the doctor had told him, and that he had either forgotten, or blundered, or hidden something from him. He could not, however, be blamed for that, and Iván Ilých still obeyed his orders implicitly and at first derived some comfort from doing so.

From the time of his visit to the doctor, Iván Ilých's chief occupation was the exact fulfilment of the doctor's instructions regarding hygiene and the taking of medicine, and the observation of his pain and his excretions. His chief interests came to be people's ailments and people's health. When sickness, deaths, or recoveries were mentioned in his presence, especially when the illness resembled his own, he listened with agitation which he tried to hide, asked questions, and applied what he heard to his own case.

The pain did not grow less, but Iván Ilých made efforts to force himself to think that he was better. And he could do this so long as nothing agitated him. But as soon as he had any unpleasantness with his wife, any lack of success in his official work, or held bad cards at bridge, he was at once acutely sensible of his disease. He had formerly borne such mischances, hoping soon to adjust what was wrong, to master it and attain success, or make a grand slam. But now every mischance upset him and plunged him into despair. He would say to himself: "There now, just as I was beginning to get better and the medicine had begun to take effect, comes this accursed misfortune, or unpleasantness. . . ." And he was furious with the mishap, or with the people who were causing the unpleasantness and killing him, for he felt that this fury was killing him but could not restrain it. One would have thought that it should have been clear to him that this exasperation with circumstances and people aggravated his illness, and that he ought therefore to ignore unpleasant occurrences. But he drew the very opposite conclusion: he said that he needed peace, and he watched for everything that might disturb it and became irritable at the slightest infringement of it. His condition was rendered worse by the fact that he read medical books and consulted doctors. The progress of his disease was so gradual that he could deceive himself when comparing one day with another—the difference was so slight. But when he consulted the doctors it seemed to him that he was getting worse, and even very rapidly. Yet despite this he was continually consulting them.

That month he went to see another celebrity, who told him almost the same as the first had done but put his questions rather differently, and the interview with this celebrity only increased Iván Ilých's doubts and fears. A friend of a friend of his, a very good doctor, diagnosed his illness again quite differently from the others, and though he predicted recovery, his questions and suppositions bewildered Iván Ilých still more and increased his doubts. A homeopathist diagnosed the disease in yet another way, and prescribed medicine which Iván Ilých took secretly for a week. But after a week, not feeling any improvement and having lost confidence both in the former doctor's treatment and in this one's, he became still more despondent. One day a lady acquaintance mentioned a cure effected by a wonder-working icon. Iván Ilých caught himself listening attentively and beginning to believe that it had occurred. This incident alarmed him. "Has my mind really weakened to such an extent?" he asked himself. "Nonsense! It's all rubbish. I mustn't give way to nervous fears but having chosen a doctor must keep strictly to his treatment. That is what I will do. Now it's all settled. I won't think about it, but will follow the treatment seriously till summer, and then we shall see. From now there must be no more of this wavering!" This was easy to say but impossible to carry out. The pain in his side oppressed him and seemed to grow worse and more incessant, while the taste in his mouth grew stranger and stranger. It seemed to him that his breath had a disgusting smell, and he was conscious of a loss of appetite and strength. There was no deceiving himself: something terrible, new, and more important than anything before in his life, was taking place within him of which he alone was aware. Those about him did not understand or would not understand it, but thought everything in the world was going on as usual. That tormented Iván Ilých more than anything. He saw that his household, especially his wife and daughter who were in a perfect whirl of visiting, did not understand anything of it and were annoyed that he was so depressed and so exacting, as if he were to blame for it. Though they tried to disguise it he saw that he was an obstacle in their path, and that his wife had adopted a definite line in regard to his illness and kept to it regardless of anything he said or did. Her attitude was this: "You know," she would say to her friends, "Iván Ilých can't do as other people do, and keep to the treatment prescribed for him. One day he'll take his drops and keep strictly to his diet and go to bed in good time, but the next day unless I watch him he'll suddenly forget his medicine, eat sturgeon—which is forbidden—and sit up playing cards till one o'clock in the morning."

"Oh, come, when was that?" Iván Ilých would ask in vexation. "Only once at Peter Ivánovich's."

"And yesterday with Shébek." 130

"Well, even if I hadn't stayed up, this pain would have kept me awake."

"Be that as it may you'll never get well like that, but will always make us wretched."

Praskóvya Fëdorovna's attitude to Iván Ilých's illness, as she expressed it both to others and to him, was that it was his own fault and was another of the annoyances he caused her. Iván Ilých felt that this opinion escaped her involuntarily—but that did not make it easier for him.

At the law courts too, Iván Ilých noticed, or thought he noticed, a strange attitude towards himself. It sometimes seemed to him that people were watching him inquisitively as a man whose place might soon be vacant. Then again, his friends would suddenly begin to chaff him in a friendly way about his low spirits, as if the awful, horrible, and unheard-of thing that was going on within him, incessantly gnawing at him and irresistibly drawing him away, was a very agreeable subject for jests. Schwartz in particular irritated him by his jocularity, vivacity, and *savoir-faire*, which reminded him of what he himself had been ten years ago.

Friends came to make up a set and they sat down to cards. They dealt, bend- 135 ing the new cards to soften them, and he sorted the diamonds in his hand and found he had seven. His partner said "No trumps" and supported him with two diamonds. What more could be wished for? It ought to be jolly and lively. They would make a grand slam. But suddenly Iván Ilých was conscious of that gnawing pain, that taste in his mouth, and it seemed ridiculous that in such circumstances he should be pleased to make a grand slam.

He looked at his partner Mikháil Mikháylovich, who rapped the table with his strong hand and instead of snatching up the tricks pushed the cards courteously and indulgently towards Iván Ilých that he might have the pleasure of gathering them up without the trouble of stretching out his hand for them. "Does he think I am too weak to stretch out my arm?" thought Iván Ilých, and forgetting what he was doing he over-trumped his partner, missing the grand slam by three tricks. And what was most awful of all was that he saw how upset Mikháil Mikháylovich was about it but did not himself care. And it was dreadful to realize why he did not care.

They all saw that he was suffering and said: "We can stop if you are tired. Take a rest." Lie down? No, he was not at all tired, and he finished the rubber. All were gloomy and silent. Iván Ilých felt that he had diffused this gloom over them and could not dispel it. They had supper and went away, and Iván Ilých was left alone with the consciousness that his life was poisoned and was poisoning the lives of others, and that this poison did not weaken but penetrated more and more deeply into his whole being.

With this consciousness, and with physical pain besides the terror, he must go to bed, often to lie awake the greater part of the night. Next morning he had to get up again, dress, go to the law courts, speak, and write; or if he did not go out, spend at home those twenty-four hours a day each of which was a torture. And he had to live thus all alone on the brink of an abyss, with no one who understood or pitied him.

## CHAPTER V

So one month passed and then another. Just before the New Year his brother-in-law came to town and stayed at their house. Iván Ilých was at the law courts and Praskóvya Fëdorovna had gone shopping. When Iván Ilých came home and entered his study he found his brother-in-law there—a healthy, florid man—unpacking his portmanteau himself. He raised his head on hearing Iván Ilých's footsteps and looked up at him for a moment without a word. That stare told Iván Ilých everything. His brother-in-law opened his mouth to utter an exclamation of surprise but checked himself, and that action confirmed it all.

"I have changed, eh?"

"Yes, there is a change."

And after that, try as he would to get his brother-in-law to return to the subject of his looks, the latter would say nothing about it. Praskóvya Fëdorovna came home and her brother went out to her. Iván Ilých locked the door and began to examine himself in the glass, first full face, then in profile. He took

140

up a portrait of himself taken with his wife, and compared it with what he saw in the glass. The change in him was immense. Then he bared his arms to the elbow, looked at them, drew the sleeves down again, sat down on an ottoman, and grew blacker than night.

"No, no, this won't do!" he said to himself, and jumped up, went to the table, took up some law papers and began to read them, but could not continue. He unlocked the door and went into the reception-room. The door leading to the drawing room was shut. He approached it on tiptoe and listened.

"No, you are exaggerating!" Praskóvya Fëdorovna was saying.

"Exaggerating! Don't you see it? Why, he's a dead man! Look at his eyes—   145
there's no light in them. But what is it that is wrong with him?"

"No one knows. Nikoláevich (that was another doctor) said something, but I don't know what. And Leshchetítsky (this was the celebrated specialist) said quite the contrary . . ."

Iván Ilých walked away, went to his own room, lay down, and began musing: "The kidney, a floating kidney." He recalled all the doctors had told him of how it detached itself and swayed about. And by an effort of imagination he tried to catch that kidney and arrest it and support it. So little was needed for this, it seemed to him. "No, I'll go to see Peter Ivánovich again." (That was the friend whose friend was a doctor.) He rang, ordered the carriage, and got ready to go.

"Where are you going, Jean?" asked his wife, with a specially sad and exceptionally kind look.

This exceptionally kind look irritated him. He looked morosely at her.

"I must go to see Peter Ivánovich."   150

He went to see Peter Ivánovich, and together they went to see his friend, the doctor. He was in, and Iván Ilých had a long talk with him.

Reviewing the anatomical and physiological details of what in the doctor's opinion was going on inside him, he understood it all.

There was something, a small thing, in the vermiform appendix. It might all come right. Only stimulate the energy of one organ and check the activity of another, then absorption would take place and everything would come right. He got home rather late for dinner, ate his dinner, and conversed cheerfully, but could not for a long time bring himself to go back to work in his room. At last, however, he went to his study and did what was necessary, but the consciousness that he had put something aside—an important, intimate matter which he would revert to when his work was done—never left him. When he had finished his work he remembered that this intimate matter was the thought of his vermiform appendix. But he did not give himself up to it, and went to the drawing-room for tea. There were callers there, including the examining magistrate who was a desirable match for his daughter, and they were conversing, playing the piano and singing. Iván Ilých, as Praskóvya Fëdorovna remarked, spent that evening more cheerfully than usual, but he never for a moment forgot that he had postponed the important matter of the appendix. At eleven o'clock he said good-night and went to his bedroom. Since his illness he had slept alone in a small room next to his study.

He undressed and took up a novel by Zola, but instead of reading it he fell into thought, and in his imagination that desired improvement in the vermiform appendix occurred. There was the absorption and evacuation and the reestablishment of normal activity. "Yes, that's it!" he said to himself. "One need only assist nature, that's all." He remembered his medicine, rose, took it, and lay down on his back watching for the beneficent action of the medicine and for it to lessen the pain. "I need only take it regularly and avoid all injurious influences. I am already feeling better, much better." He began touching his side: it was not painful to the touch. "There, I really don't feel it. It's much better already." He put out the light and turned on his side . . . "The appendix is getting better, absorption is occurring." Suddenly he felt the old, familiar, dull, gnawing pain, stubborn and serious. There was the same familiar loathsome taste in his mouth. His heart sank and he felt dazed. "My God! My God!" he muttered. "Again, again! and it will never cease." And suddenly the matter presented itself in a quite different aspect. "Vermiform appendix! Kidney!" he said to himself. "It's not a question of appendix or kidney, but of life and . . . death. Yes, life was there and now it is going, going and I cannot stop it. Yes. Why deceive myself? Isn't it obvious to everyone but me that I'm dying, and that it's only a question of weeks, days . . . it may happen this moment. There was light and now there is darkness. I was here and now I'm going there! Where?" A chill came over him, his breathing ceased, and he felt only the throbbing of his heart.

"When I am not, what will there be? There will be nothing. Then where shall I be when I am no more? Can this be dying? No, I don't want to!" He jumped up and tried to light the candle, felt for it with trembling hands, dropped candle and candlestick on the floor, and fell back on his pillow.

"What's the use? It makes no difference," he said to himself, staring with 155 wide-open eyes into the darkness. "Death. Yes, death. And none of them know or wish to know it, and they have no pity for me. Now they are playing." (He heard through the door the distant sound of a song and its accompaniment.) "It's all the same to them, but they will die too! Fools! I first, and they later, but it will be the same for them. And now they are merry . . . the beasts!"

Anger choked him and he was agonizingly, unbearably miserable. "It is impossible that all men have been doomed to suffer this awful horror!" He raised himself.

"Something must be wrong. I must calm myself—must think it all over from the beginning." And he again began thinking. "Yes, the beginning of my illness: I knocked my side, but I was still quite well that day and the next. It hurt a little, then rather more. I saw the doctors, then followed despondency and anguish, more doctors, and I drew nearer to the abyss. My strength grew less and I kept coming nearer and nearer, and now I have wasted away and there is no light in my eyes. I think of the appendix—but this is death! I think of mending the appendix, and all the while here is death! Can it really be death?" Again terror seized him and he gasped for breath. He leant down and began feeling for the matches, pressing with his elbow on the stand beside the bed.

It was in his way and hurt him, he grew furious with it, pressed on it still harder, and upset it. Breathless and in despair he fell on his back, expecting death to come immediately.

Meanwhile the visitors were leaving. Praskóvya Fëdorovna was seeing them off. She heard something fall and came in.

"What has happened?"

"Nothing. I knocked it over accidentally." 160

She went out and returned with a candle. He lay there panting heavily, like a man who has run a thousand yards, and stared upwards at her with a fixed look.

"What is it, Jean?"

"No . . . o . . . thing. I upset it." ("Why speak of it? She won't understand," he thought.)

And in truth she did not understand. She picked up the stand, lit his candle, and hurried away to see another visitor off. When she came back he still lay on his back, looking upwards.

"What is it? Do you feel worse?" 165

"Yes."

She shook her head and sat down.

"Do you know, Jean, I think we must ask Leshchetítsky to come and see you here."

This meant calling in the famous specialist, regardless of expense. He smiled malignantly and said "No." She remained a little longer and then went up to him and kissed his forehead.

While she was kissing him he hated her from the bottom of his soul and 170 with difficulty refrained from pushing her away.

"Good-night. Please God you'll sleep."

"Yes."

## CHAPTER VI

Iván Ilých saw that he was dying, and he was in continual despair.

In the depth of his heart he knew he was dying, but not only was he not accustomed to the thought, he simply did not and could not grasp it.

The syllogism he had learnt from Kiezewetter's Logic:[11] "Caius is a man, 175 men are mortal, therefore Caius is mortal," had always seemed to him correct as applied to Caius, but certainly not as applied to himself. That Caius—man in the abstract—was mortal, was perfectly correct, but he was not Caius, not an abstract man, but a creature quite, quite separate from all others. He had been little Ványa, with a mamma and a papa; with Mitya and Volódya, and the toys, a coachman and a nurse, afterwards with Kátenka and with all the joys, griefs, and delights of childhood, boyhood, and youth. What did Caius know of the smell of that striped leather ball Ványa had been so fond of? Had Caius kissed his mother's hand like that, and did the silk of her dress rustle so for Caius? Had he rioted like that at school when the pastry was bad? Had Caius

[11] Karl Kiezewetter (1766–1819), author of an outline of logic widely used in Russian schools at the time.

been in love like that? Could Caius preside at a session as he did? "Caius really was mortal, and it was right for him to die; but for me, little Ványa, Iván Ilých, with all my thoughts and emotions, it's altogether a different matter. It cannot be that I ought to die. That would be too terrible."

Such was his feeling.

"If I had to die like Caius I should have known it was so. An inner voice would have told me so, but there was nothing of the sort in me and I and all my friends felt that our case was quite different from that of Caius. And now here it is!" he said to himself. "It can't be. It's impossible! But here it is. How is this? How is one to understand it?"

He could not understand it, and tried to drive this false, incorrect, morbid thought away and to replace it by other proper and healthy thoughts. But that thought, and not the thought only but the reality itself, seemed to come and confront him.

And to replace that thought he called up a succession of others, hoping to find in them some support. He tried to get back into the former current of thoughts that had once screened the thought of death from him. But strange to say, all that had formerly shut off, hidden, and destroyed, his consciousness of death, no longer had that effect. Iván Ilých now spent most of his time in attempting to re-establish that old current. He would say to himself: "I will take up my duties again—after all I used to live by them." And banishing all doubts he would go to the law courts, enter into conversation with his colleagues, and sit carelessly as was his wont, scanning the crowd with a thoughtful look and leaning both his emaciated arms on the arms of his oak chair; bending over as usual to a colleague and drawing his papers nearer he would interchange whispers with him, and then suddenly raising his eyes and sitting erect would pronounce certain words and open the proceedings. But suddenly in the midst of those proceedings the pain in his side, regardless of the stage the proceedings had reached, would begin its own gnawing work. Iván Ilých would turn his attention to it and try to drive the thought of it away, but without success. *It* would come and stand before him and look at him, and he would be petrified and the light would die out of his eyes, and he would again begin asking himself whether *It* alone was true. And his colleagues and subordinates would see with surprise and distress that he, the brilliant and subtle judge, was becoming confused and making mistakes. He would shake himself, try to pull himself together, manage somehow to bring the sitting to a close, and return home with the sorrowful consciousness that his judicial labours could not as formerly hide from him what he wanted them to hide, and could not deliver him from *It*. And what was worst of all was that *It* drew his attention to itself not in order to make him take some action but only that he should look at *It*, look it straight in the face: look at it and without doing anything, suffer inexpressibly.

And to save himself from this condition Iván Ilých looked for consolations— 180
new screens—and new screens were found and for a while seemed to save him,
but then they immediately fell to pieces or rather became transparent, as if *It*
penetrated them and nothing could veil *It*.

In these latter days he would go into the drawing-room he had arranged—
that drawing-room where he had fallen and for the sake of which (how bitterly ridiculous it seemed) he had sacrificed his life—for he knew that his
illness originated with that knock. He would enter and see that something had
scratched the polished table. He would look for the cause of this and find that
it was the bronze ornamentation of an album, that had got bent. He would
take up the expensive album which he had lovingly arranged, and feel vexed
with his daughter and her friends for their untidiness—for the album was torn
here and there and some of the photographs turned upside down. He would
put it carefully in order and bend the ornamentation back into position. Then
it would occur to him to place all those things in another corner of the room,
near the plants. He could call the footman, but his daughter or wife would
come to help him. They would not agree, and his wife would contradict him,
and he would dispute and grow angry. But that was all right, for then he did
not think about *It*. *It* was invisible.

But then, when he was moving something himself, his wife would say: "Let
the servants do it. You will hurt yourself again." And suddenly *It* would flash
through the screen and he would see it. It was just a flash, and he hoped it would
disappear, but he would involuntarily pay attention to his side. "It sits there as
before, gnawing just the same!" And he could no longer forget *It*, but could distinctly see it looking at him from behind the flowers. "What is it all for?"

"It really is so! I lost my life over that curtain as I might have done when
storming a fort. Is that possible? How terrible and how stupid. It can't be true!
It can't, but it is."

He would go to his study, lie down, and again be alone with *It*: face to face
with *It*. And nothing could be done with *It* except to look at it and shudder.

## CHAPTER VII

How it happened it is impossible to say because it came about step by step, 185
unnoticed, but in the third month of Iván Ilých's illness, his wife, his daughter,
his son, his acquaintances, the doctors, the servants, and above all he himself,
were aware that the whole interest he had for other people was whether he
would soon vacate his place, and at last release the living from the discomfort
caused by his presence and be himself released from his sufferings.

He slept less and less. He was given opium and hypodermic injections of
morphine, but this did not relieve him. The dull depression he experienced
in a somnolent condition at first gave him a little relief, but only as something
new, afterwards it became as distressing as the pain itself or even more so.

Special foods were prepared for him by the doctors' orders, but all those
foods became increasingly distasteful and disgusting to him.

For his excretions also special arrangements had to be made, and this was a torment to him every time—a torment from the uncleanliness, the unseemliness, and the smell, and from knowing that another person had to take part in it.

But just through this most unpleasant matter Iván Ilých obtained comfort. Gerásim, the butler's young assistant, always came in to carry the things out. Gerásim was a clean, fresh peasant lad, grown stout on town food and always cheerful and bright. At first the sight of him, in his clean Russian peasant costume, engaged on that disgusting task embarrassed Iván Ilých.

Once when he got up from the commode too weak to draw up his trousers, he dropped into a soft armchair and looked with horror at his bare, enfeebled thighs with the muscles so sharply marked on them. 190

Gerásim with a firm light tread, his heavy boots emitting a pleasant smell of tar and fresh winter air, came in wearing a clean Hessian apron, the sleeves of his print shirt tucked up over his strong bare young arms; and refraining from looking at his sick master out of consideration for his feelings, and restraining the joy of life that beamed from his face, he went up to the commode.

"Gerásim!" said Iván Ilých in a weak voice.

Gerásim started, evidently afraid he might have committed some blunder, and with a rapid movement turned his fresh, kind, simple young face which just showed the first downy signs of a beard.

"Yes, sir?"

"That must be very unpleasant for you. You must forgive me. I am helpless." 195

"Oh, why, sir," and Gerásim's eyes beamed and he showed his glistening white teeth, "what's a little trouble? It's a case of illness with you, sir."

And his deft strong hands did their accustomed task, and he went out of the room stepping lightly. Five minutes later he as lightly returned.

Iván Ilých was still sitting in the same position in the armchair.

"Gerásim," he said when the latter had replaced the freshly-washed utensil. "Please come here and help me." Gerásim went up to him. "Lift me up. It is hard for me to get up, and I have sent Dmítri away."

Gerásim went up to him, grasped his master with his strong arms deftly but gently, in the same way that he stepped—lifted him, supported him with one hand, and with the other drew up his trousers and would have set him down again, but Iván Ilých asked to be led to the sofa. Gerásim, without an effort and without apparent pressure, led him, almost lifting him, to the sofa and placed him on it. 200

"Thank you. How easily and well you do it all!"

Gerásim smiled again and turned to leave the room. But Iván Ilých felt his presence such a comfort that he did not want to let him go.

"One thing more, please move up that chair. No, the other one—under my feet. It is easier for me when my feet are raised."

Gerásim brought the chair, set it down gently in place, and raised Iván Ilých's legs on to it. It seemed to Iván Ilých that he felt better while Gerásim was holding up his legs.

"It's better when my legs are higher," he said. "Place that cushion under  205
them."

Gerásim did so. He again lifted the legs and placed them, and again Iván
Ilých felt better while Gerásim held his legs. When he set them down Iván
Ilých fancied he felt worse.

"Gerásim," he said. "Are you busy now?"

"Not at all, sir," said Gerásim, who had learnt from the townsfolk how to
speak to gentlefolk.

"What have you still to do?"

"What have I to do? I've done everything except chopping the logs for  210
tomorrow."

"Then hold my legs up a bit higher, can you?"

"Of course I can. Why not?" And Gerásim raised his master's legs higher
and Iván Ilých thought that in that position he did not feel any pain at all.

"And how about the logs?"

"Don't trouble about that, sir. There's plenty of time."

Iván Ilých told Gerásim to sit down and hold his legs, and began to talk to  215
him. And strange to say it seemed to him that he felt better while Gerásim held
his legs up.

After that Iván Ilých would sometimes call Gerásim and get him to hold
his legs on his shoulders, and he liked talking to him. Gerásim did it all easily,
willingly, simply, and with a good nature that touched Iván Ilých. Health,
strength, and vitality in other people were offensive to him, but Gerásim's
strength and vitality did not mortify but soothed him.

What tormented Iván Ilých most was the deception, the lie, which for some
reason they all accepted, that he was not dying but was simply ill, and that
he only need keep quiet and undergo a treatment and then something very
good would result. He however knew that do what they would nothing would
come of it, only still more agonizing suffering and death. This deception tortured him—their not wishing to admit what they all knew and what he knew,
but wanting to lie to him concerning his terrible condition, and wishing and
forcing him to participate in that lie. Those lies—lies enacted over him on the
eve of his death and destined to degrade this awful, solemn act to the level
of their visitings, their curtains, their sturgeon for dinner—were a terrible
agony for Iván Ilých. And strangely enough, many times when they were going
through their antics over him he had been within a hairbreadth of calling out
to them: "Stop lying! You know and I know that I am dying. Then at least stop
lying about it!" But he had never had the spirit to do it. The awful, terrible act
of his dying was, he could see, reduced by those about him to the level of a
casual, unpleasant, and almost indecorous incident (as if someone entered a
drawing-room diffusing an unpleasant odour) and this was done by that very
decorum which he had served all his life long. He saw that no one felt for him,
because no one even wished to grasp his position. Only Gerásim recognized it
and pitied him. And so Iván Ilých felt at ease only with him. He felt comforted
when Gerásim supported his legs (sometimes all night long) and refused to go

to bed, saying, "Don't you worry, Iván Ilých. I'll get sleep enough later on," or when he suddenly became familiar and exclaimed: "If you weren't sick it would be another matter, but as it is, why should I grudge a little trouble?" Gerásim alone did not lie; everything showed that he alone understood the facts of the case and did not consider it necessary to disguise them, but simply felt sorry for his emaciated and enfeebled master. Once when Iván Ilých was sending him away he even said straight out: "We shall all of us die, so why should I grudge a little trouble?"—expressing the fact that he did not think his work burdensome, because he was doing it for a dying man and hoped someone would do the same for him when his time came.

Apart from this lying, or because of it, what most tormented Iván Ilých was that no one pitied him as he wished to be pitied. At certain moments after prolonged suffering he wished most of all (though he would have been ashamed to confess it) for someone to pity him as a sick child is pitied. He longed to be petted and comforted. He knew he was an important functionary, that he had a beard turning grey, and that therefore what he longed for was impossible, but still he longed for it. And in Gerásim's attitude towards him there was something akin to what he wished for, and so that attitude comforted him. Iván Ilých wanted to weep, wanted to be petted and cried over, and then his colleague Shébek would come, and instead of weeping and being petted, Iván Ilých would assume a serious, severe, and profound air, and by force of habit would express his opinion on a decision of the Court of Cassation and would stubbornly insist on that view. This falsity around him and within him did more than anything else to poison his last days.

## CHAPTER VIII

It was morning. He knew it was morning because Gerásim had gone, and Peter the footman had come and put out the candles, drawn back one of the curtains, and begun quietly to tidy up. Whether it was morning or evening, Friday or Sunday, made no difference, it was all just the same: the gnawing, unmitigated, agonizing pain, never ceasing for an instant, the consciousness of life inexorably waning but not yet extinguished, that approach of that ever dreaded and hateful Death which was the only reality, and always the same falsity. What were days, weeks, hours, in such a case?

"Will you have some tea, sir?"                                           220

"He wants things to be regular, and wishes the gentlefolk to drink tea in the morning," thought Iván Ilých, and only said "No."

"Wouldn't you like to move onto the sofa, sir?"

"He wants to tidy up the room, and I'm in the way. I am uncleanliness and disorder," he thought, and said only:

"No, leave me alone."

The man went on bustling about. Iván Ilých stretched out his hand. Peter   225
came up, ready to help.

"What is it, sir?"

"My watch."

Peter took the watch which was close at hand and gave it to his master.

"Half-past eight. Are they up?"

"No, sir, except Vladímir Ivánich" (the son) "who has gone to school. 230 Praskóvya Fëdorovna ordered me to wake her if you asked for her. Shall I do so?"

"No, there's no need to." "Perhaps I'd better have some tea," he thought, and added aloud: "Yes, bring me some tea."

Peter went to the door but Iván Ilých dreaded being left alone. "How can I keep him here? Oh yes, my medicine." "Peter, give me my medicine." "Why not? Perhaps it may still do me some good." He took a spoonful and swallowed it. "No, it won't help. It's all tomfoolery, all deception," he decided as soon as he became aware of the familiar, sickly, hopeless taste. "No, I can't believe in it any longer. But the pain, why this pain? If it would only cease just for a moment!" And he moaned. Peter turned towards him. "It's all right. Go and fetch me some tea."

Peter went out. Left alone Iván Ilých groaned not so much with pain, terrible though that was, as from mental anguish. Always and for ever the same, always these endless days and nights. If only it would come quicker! If only *what* would come quicker? Death, darkness? . . . No, no! Anything rather than death!

When Peter returned with the tea on a tray, Iván Ilých stared at him for a time in perplexity, not realizing who and what he was. Peter was disconcerted by that look and his embarrassment brought Iván Ilých to himself.

"Oh, tea! All right, put it down. Only help me to wash and put on a clean shirt." 235

And Iván Ilých began to wash. With pauses for rest, he washed his hands and then his face, cleaned his teeth, brushed his hair, and looked in the glass. He was terrified by what he saw, especially by the limp way in which his hair clung to his pallid forehead.

While his shirt was being changed he knew that he would be still more frightened at the sight of his body, so he avoided looking at it. Finally he was ready. He drew on a dressing-gown, wrapped himself in a plaid, and sat down in the armchair to take his tea. For a moment he felt refreshed, but as soon as he began to drink the tea he was again aware of the same taste, and the pain also returned. He finished it with an effort, and then lay down stretching out his legs, and dismissed Peter.

Always the same. Now a spark of hope flashes up, then a sea of despair rages, and always pain; always pain, always despair, and always the same. When alone he had a dreadful and distressing desire to call someone, but he knew beforehand that with others present it would be still worse. "Another dose of morphine—to lose consciousness. I will tell him, the doctor, that he must think of something else. It's impossible, impossible, to go on like this."

An hour and another pass like that. But now there is a ring at the door bell. Perhaps it's the doctor? It is. He comes in fresh, hearty, plump, and cheerful, with that look on his face that seems to say: "There now, you're in a panic about something, but we'll arrange it all for you directly!" The doctor knows this expression is out of place here, but he has put it on once for all and can't take it off—like a man who has put on a frock-coat in the morning to pay a round of calls.

The doctor rubs his hands vigorously and reassuringly.                                    240

"Brr! How cold it is! There's such a sharp frost; just let me warm myself!" he says, as if it were only a matter of waiting till he was warm, and then he would put everything right.

"Well now, how are you?"

Iván Ilých feels that the doctor would like to say: "Well, how are our affairs?" but that even he feels that this would not do, and says instead: "What sort of a night have you had?"

Iván Ilých looks at him as much as to say: "Are you really never ashamed of lying?" But the doctor does not wish to understand this question, and Iván Ilých says: "Just as terrible as ever. The pain never leaves me and never subsides. If only something . . ."

"Yes, you sick people are always like that. . . . There, now I think I am warm   245 enough. Even Praskóvya Fëdorovna, who is so particular, could find no fault with my temperature. Well, now I can say good-morning," and the doctor presses his patient's hand.

Then, dropping his former playfulness, he begins with a most serious face to examine the patient, feeling his pulse and taking his temperature, and then begins the sounding and auscultation.

Iván Ilých knows quite well and definitely that all this is nonsense and pure deception, but when the doctor, getting down on his knee, leans over him, putting his ear first higher then lower, and performs various gymnastic movements over him with a significant expression on his face, Iván Ilých submits to it all as he used to submit to the speeches of the lawyers, though he knew very well that they were all lying and why they were lying.

The doctor, kneeling on the sofa, is still sounding him when Praskóvya Fëdorovna's silk dress rustles at the door and she is heard scolding Peter for not having let her know of the doctor's arrival.

She comes in, kisses her husband, and at once proceeds to prove that she has been up a long time already, and only owing to a misunderstanding failed to be there when the doctor arrived.

Iván Ilých looks at her, scans her all over, sets against her the whiteness and   250 plumpness and cleanness of her hands and neck, the gloss of her hair, and the sparkle of her vivacious eyes. He hates her with his whole soul. And the thrill of hatred he feels for her makes him suffer from her touch.

Her attitude towards him and his disease is still the same. Just as the doctor had adopted a certain relation to his patient which he could not abandon, so had she formed one towards him—that he was not doing something he ought to do and was himself to blame, and that she reproached him lovingly for this—and she could not now change that attitude.

"You see he doesn't listen to me and doesn't take his medicine at the proper time. And above all he lies in a position that is no doubt bad for him—with his legs up."

She described how he made Gerásim hold his legs up.

The doctor smiled with a contemptuous affability that said: "What's to be done? These sick people do have foolish fancies of that kind, but we must forgive them."

When the examination was over the doctor looked at his watch, and then 255
Praskóvya Fëdorovna announced to Iván Ilých that it was of course as he pleased, but she had sent to-day for a celebrated specialist who would examine him and have a consultation with Michael Danílovich (their regular doctor).

"Please don't raise any objections. I am doing this for my own sake," she said ironically, letting it be felt that she was doing it all for his sake and only said this to leave him no right to refuse. He remained silent, knitting his brows. He felt that he was so surrounded and involved in a mesh of falsity that it was hard to unravel anything.

Everything she did for him was entirely for her own sake, and she told him she was doing for herself what she actually was doing for herself, as if that was so incredible that he must understand the opposite.

At half-past eleven the celebrated specialist arrived. Again the sounding began and the significant conversations in his presence and in another room, about the kidneys and the appendix, and the questions and answers, with such an air of importance that again, instead of the real question of life and death which now alone confronted him, the question arose of the kidney and appendix which were not behaving as they ought to and would now be attacked by Michael Danílovich and the specialist and forced to amend their ways.

The celebrated specialist took leave of him with a serious though not hopeless look, and in reply to the timid question Iván Ilých, with eyes glistening with fear and hope, put to him as to whether there was a chance of recovery, said that he could not vouch for it but there was a possibility. The look of hope with which Iván Ilých watched the doctor out was so pathetic that Praskóvya Fëdorovna, seeing it, even wept as she left the room to hand the doctor his fee.

The gleam of hope kindled by the doctor's encouragement did not last long. 260
The same room, the same pictures, curtains, wall-paper, medicine bottles, were all there, and the same aching suffering body, and Iván Ilých began to moan. They gave him a subcutaneous injection and he sank into oblivion.

It was twilight when he came to. They brought him his dinner and he swallowed some beef tea with difficulty, and then everything was the same again and night was coming on.

After dinner, at seven o'clock, Praskóvya Fëdorovna came into the room in evening dress, her full bosom pushed up by her corset, and with traces of powder on her face. She had reminded him in the morning that they were going to the theater. Sarah Bernhardt was visiting the town and they had a box, which he had insisted on their taking. Now he had forgotten about it and her toilet offended him, but he concealed his vexation when he remembered that he had himself insisted on their securing a box and going because it would be an instructive and aesthetic pleasure for the children.

Praskóvya Fëdorovna came in, self-satisfied but yet with a rather guilty air. She sat down and asked how he was, but, as he saw, only for the sake of asking and not in order to learn about it, knowing that there was nothing to learn—and then went on to what she really wanted to say: that she would not on any account have gone but that the box had been taken and Helen and their daughter were going, as well as Petríshchev (the examining magistrate, their daughter's fiancé) and that it was out of the question to let them go alone; but that she would have much preferred to sit with him for a while; and he must be sure to follow the doctor's orders while she was away.

"Oh, and Fëdor Petróvich" (the fiancé) "would like to come in. May he? And Lisa?"

"All right." 265

Their daughter came in in full evening dress, her fresh young flesh exposed (making a show of that very flesh which in his own case caused so much suffering), strong, healthy, evidently in love, and impatient with illness, suffering, and death, because they interfered with her happiness.

Fëdor Petróvich came in too, in evening dress, his hair curled *á la Capoul*, a tight stiff collar round his long sinewy neck, an enormous white shirt-front and narrow black trousers tightly stretched over his strong thighs. He had one white glove tightly drawn on, and was holding his opera hat in his hand.

Following him the schoolboy crept in unnoticed, in a new uniform, poor little fellow, and wearing gloves. Terribly dark shadows showed under his eyes, the meaning of which Iván Ilých knew well.

His son had always seemed pathetic to him, and now it was dreadful to see the boy's frightened look of pity. It seemed to Iván Ilých that Vásya was the only one besides Gerásim who understood and pitied him.

They all sat down and again asked how he was. A silence followed. Lisa asked 270 her mother about the opera-glasses, and there was an altercation between mother and daughter as to who had taken them and where they had been put. This occasioned some unpleasantness.

Fëdor Petróvich inquired of Iván Ilých whether he had ever seen Sarah Bernhardt. Iván Ilých did not at first catch the question, but then replied: "No, have you seen her before?"

"Yes, in *Adrienne Lecouvreur*."[12]

Praskóvya Fëdorovna mentioned some roles in which Sarah Bernhardt was particularly good. Her daughter disagreed. Conversation sprang up as to the elegance and realism of her acting—the sort of conversation that is always repeated and is always the same.

In the midst of the conversation Fëdor Petróvich glanced at Iván Ilých and became silent. The others also looked at him and grew silent. Iván Ilých was staring with glittering eyes straight before him, evidently indignant with them. This had to be rectified, but it was impossible to do so. The silence had to be

---

[12] A play by the French dramatist Eugène Scribe (1791–1861).

broken, but for a time no one dared to break it and they all became afraid that the conventional deception would suddenly become obvious and the truth become plain to all. Lisa was the first to pluck up courage and break that silence, but by trying to hide what everybody was feeling, she betrayed it.

"Well, if we are going it's time to start," she said, looking at her watch, 275 a present from her father, and with a faint and significant smile at Fëdor Petróvich relating to something known only to them. She got up with a rustle of her dress.

They all rose, said good-night, and went away.

When they had gone it seemed to Iván Ilých that he felt better; the falsity had gone with them. But the pain remained—that same pain and that same fear that made everything monotonously alike, nothing harder and nothing easier. Everything was worse.

Again minute followed minute and hour followed hour. Everything remained the same and there was no cessation. And the inevitable end of it all became more and more terrible.

"Yes, send Gerásim here," he replied to a question Peter asked.

## CHAPTER IX

His wife returned late at night. She came in on tiptoe, but he heard her, opened 280 his eyes, and made haste to close them again. She wished to send Gerásim away and to sit with him herself, but he opened his eyes and said: "No, go away."

"Are you in great pain?"

"Always the same."

"Take some opium."

He agreed and took some. She went away.

Till about three in the morning he was in a state of stupefied misery. It seemed 285 to him that he and his pain were being thrust into a narrow, deep black sack, but though they were pushed further and further in they could not be pushed to the bottom. And this, terrible enough in itself, was accompanied by suffering. He was frightened yet wanted to fall through the sack, he struggled but yet co-operated. And suddenly he broke through, fell, and regained consciousness. Gerásim was sitting at the foot of the bed dozing quietly and patiently, while he himself lay with his emaciated stockinged legs resting on Gerásim's shoulders; the same shaded candle was there and the same unceasing pain.

"Go away, Gerásim," he whispered.

"It's all right, sir. I'll stay a while."

"No. Go away."

He removed his legs from Gerásim's shoulders, turned sideways onto his arm, and felt sorry for himself. He only waited till Gerásim had gone into the next room and then restrained himself no longer but wept like a child. He wept on account of his helplessness, his terrible loneliness, the cruelty of man, the cruelty of God, and the absence of God.

"Why hast Thou done all this? Why hast Thou brought me here? Why, why 290 dost Thou torment me so terribly?"

He did not expect an answer and yet wept because there was no answer and could be none. The pain again grew more acute, but he did not stir and did not call. He said to himself: "Go on! Strike me! But what is it for? What have I done to Thee? What is it for?"

Then he grew quiet and not only ceased weeping but even held his breath and became all attention. It was as though he were listening not to an audible voice but to the voice of his soul, to the current of thoughts arising within him.

"What is it you want?" was the first clear conception capable of expression in words, that he heard.

"What do you want? What do you want?" he repeated to himself.

"What do I want? To live and not to suffer," he answered. 295

And again he listened with such concentrated attention that even his pain did not distract him.

"To live? How?" asked his inner voice.

"Why, to live as I used to—well and pleasantly."

"As you lived before, well and pleasantly?" the voice repeated.

And in imagination he began to recall the best moments of his pleasant life. 300 But strange to say none of those best moments of his pleasant life now seemed at all what they had then seemed—none of them except the first recollections of childhood. There, in childhood, there had been something really pleasant with which it would be possible to live if it could return. But the child who had experienced that happiness existed no longer, it was like a reminiscence of somebody else.

As soon as the period began which had produced the present Iván Ilých, all that had then seemed joys now melted before his sight and turned into something trivial and often nasty.

And the further he departed from childhood and the nearer he came to the present the more worthless and doubtful were the joys. This began with the School of Law. A little that was really good was still found there—there was lightheartedness, friendship, and hope. But in the upper classes there had already been fewer of such good moments. Then during the first years of his official career, when he was in the service of the Governor, some pleasant moments again occurred: they were the memories of love for a woman. Then all became confused and there was still less of what was good; later on again there was still less that was good, and the further he went the less there was. His marriage, a mere accident, then the disenchantment that followed it, his wife's bad breath and the sensuality and hypocrisy: then that deadly official life and those preoccupations about money, a year of it, and two, and ten, and twenty, and always the same thing. And the longer it lasted the more deadly it became. "It is as if I had been going downhill while I imagined I was going up. And that is really what it was. I was going up in public opinion, but to the same extent life was ebbing away from me. And now it is all done and there is only death."

"Then what does it mean? Why? It can't be that life is so senseless and horrible. But if it really has been so horrible and senseless, why must I die and die in agony? There is something wrong!"

"Maybe I did not live as I ought to have done," it suddenly occurred to him. "But how could that be, when I did everything properly?" he replied, and immediately dismissed from his mind this, the sole solution of all the riddles of life and death, as something quite impossible.

"Then what do you want now? To live? Live how? Live as you lived in the 305 law courts when the usher proclaimed 'The judge is coming!'" "The judge is coming, the judge!" he repeated to himself. "Here he is, the judge. But I am not guilty!" he exclaimed angrily. "What is it for?" And he ceased crying, but turning his face to the wall continued to ponder on the same question: Why, and for what purpose, is there all this horror? But however much he pondered he found no answer. And whenever the thought occurred to him, as it often did, that it all resulted from his not having lived as he ought to have done, he at once recalled the correctness of his whole life and dismissed so strange an idea.

## CHAPTER X

Another fortnight passed. Iván Ilých now no longer left his sofa. He would not lie in bed but lay on the sofa, facing the wall nearly all the time. He suffered ever the same unceasing agonies and in his loneliness pondered always on the same insoluble question: "What is this? Can it be that it is Death?" And the inner voice answered: "Yes, it is Death."

"Why these sufferings?" And the voice answered, "For no reason—they just are so." Beyond and besides this there was nothing.

From the very beginning of his illness, ever since he had first been to see the doctor, Iván Ilých's life had been divided between two contrary and alternating moods: now it was despair and the expectation of this uncomprehended and terrible death, and now hope and an intently interested observation of the functioning of his organs. Now before his eyes there was only a kidney or an intestine that temporarily evaded its duty, and now only that incomprehensible and dreadful death from which it was impossible to escape.

These two states of mind had alternated from the very beginning of his illness, but the further it progressed the more doubtful and fantastic became the conception of the kidney, and the more real the sense of impending death.

He had but to call to mind what he had been three months before and what 310 he was now, to call to mind with what regularity he had been going downhill, for every possibility of hope to be shattered.

Latterly during that loneliness in which he found himself as he lay facing the back of the sofa, a loneliness in the midst of a populous town and surrounded by numerous acquaintances and relations but that yet could not have been more complete anywhere—either at the bottom of the sea or under the earth—during that terrible loneliness Iván Ilých had lived only in memories of the past. Pictures of his past rose before him one after another. They always began with what was nearest in time and then went back to what was most remote—to his childhood—and rested there. If he thought of the stewed prunes that had been offered him that day, his mind went back to the raw shrivelled French plums of his childhood, their peculiar flavor and the flow of saliva when he sucked their stones, and along with the memory of that taste came a whole series of memories of those days: his nurse, his brother, and their toys. "No, I mustn't think of that. . . . It is too painful," Iván Ilých said to himself, and brought himself back to the present—to the button on the back of the sofa and the creases in its morocco. "Morocco is expensive, but it does not wear well: there had been a quarrel about it. It was a different kind of quarrel and a different kind of morocco that time when we tore father's portfolio and were punished, and mamma brought us some tarts. . . ." And again his thoughts dwelt on his childhood, and again it was painful and he tried to banish them and fix his mind on something else.

Then again together with that chain of memories another series passed through his mind—of how his illness had progressed and grown worse. There also the further back he looked the more life there had been. There had been more of what was good in life and more of life itself. The two merged together. "Just as the pain went on getting worse and worse so my life grew worse and worse," he thought. "There is one bright spot there at the back, at the beginning of life, and afterwards all becomes blacker and blacker and proceeds more and more rapidly—in inverse ratio to the square of the distance from death," thought Iván Ilých. And the example of a stone falling downwards with increasing velocity entered his mind. Life, a series of increasing sufferings, flies, further and further towards its end—the most terrible suffering. "I am flying. . . ." He shuddered, shifted himself, and tried to resist, but was already aware that resistance was impossible, and again with eyes weary of gazing but unable to cease seeing what was before them, he stared at the back of the sofa and waited—awaiting that dreadful fall and shock and destruction.

"Resistance is impossible!" he said to himself. "If I could only understand what it is all for! But that too is impossible. An explanation would be possible if it could be said that I have not lived as I ought to. But it is impossible to say that," and he remembered all the legality, correctitude, and propriety of his life. "That at any rate can certainly not be admitted," he thought, and his lips smiled ironically as if someone could see that smile and be taken in by it. "There is no explanation! Agony, death. . . . What for?"

## CHAPTER XI

Another two weeks went by in this way and during that fortnight an event occurred that Iván Ilých and his wife had desired. Petríshchev formally proposed. It happened in the evening. The next day Praskóvya Fëdorovna came into her husband's room considering how best to inform him of it, but that very night there had been a fresh change for the worse in his condition. She found him still lying on the sofa but in a different position. He lay on his back, groaning and staring fixedly straight in front of him.

She began to remind him of his medicines, but he turned his eyes towards her with such a look that she did not finish what she was saying; so great an animosity, to her in particular, did that look express.

"For Christ's sake, let me die in peace!" he said.

She would have gone away, but just then their daughter came in and went up to say good morning. He looked at her as he had done at his wife, and in reply to her inquiry about his health said dryly that he would soon free them all of himself. They were both silent and after sitting with him for a while went away.

"Is it our fault?" Lisa said to her mother. "It's as if we were to blame! I am sorry for papa, but why should we be tortured?"

The doctor came at his usual time. Iván Ilých answered "Yes" and "No," never taking his angry eyes from him, and at last said: "You know you can do nothing for me, so leave me alone."

"We can ease your sufferings."

"You can't even do that. Let me be."

The doctor went into the drawing-room and told Praskóvya Fëdorovna that the case was very serious and that the only resource left was opium to allay her husband's sufferings, which must be terrible.

It was true, as the doctor said, that Iván Ilých's physical sufferings were terrible, but worse than the physical sufferings were his mental sufferings which were his chief torture.

His mental sufferings were due to the fact that that night, as he looked at Gerásim's sleepy, good-natured face with its prominent cheek-bones, the question suddenly occurred to him: "What if my whole life has really been wrong?"

It occurred to him that what had appeared perfectly impossible before, namely that he had not spent his life as he should have done, might after all be true. It occurred to him that his scarcely perceptible attempts to struggle against what was considered good by the most highly placed people, those scarcely noticeable impulses which he had immediately suppressed, might have been the real thing, and all the rest false. And his professional duties and the whole arrangement of his life and of his family, and all his social and official interests, might all have been false. He tried to defend all those things to himself and suddenly felt the weakness of what he was defending. There was nothing to defend.

"But if that is so," he said to himself, "and I am leaving this life with the consciousness that I have lost all that was given me and it is impossible to rectify it—what then?"

He lay on his back and began to pass his life in review in quite a new way. In the morning when he saw first his footman, then his wife, then his daughter, and then the doctor, their every word and movement confirmed to him the awful truth that had been revealed to him during the night. In them he saw himself—all that for which he had lived—and saw clearly that it was not real at all, but a terrible and huge deception which had hidden both life and death.

This consciousness intensified his physical suffering tenfold. He groaned and tossed about, and pulled at his clothing which choked and stifled him. And he hated them on that account.

He was given a large dose of opium and became unconscious, but at noon his sufferings began again. He drove everybody away and tossed from side to side.

His wife came to him and said:

"Jean, my dear, do this for me. It can't do any harm and often helps. Healthy   330
people often do it."

He opened his eyes wide.

"What? Take communion? Why? It's unnecessary! However. . . ."

She began to cry.

"Yes, do, my dear. I'll send for our priest. He is such a nice man."

"All right. Very well," he muttered.                                                335

When the priest came and heard his confession, Iván Ilých was softened and seemed to feel a relief from his doubts and consequently from his sufferings, and for a moment there came a ray of hope. He again began to think of the vermiform appendix and the possibility of correcting it. He received the sacrament with tears in his eyes.

When they laid him down again afterwards he felt a moment's ease, and the hope that he might live awoke in him again. He began to think of the operation that had been suggested to him. "To live! I want to live!" he said to himself.

His wife came in to congratulate him after his communion, and when uttering the usual conventional words she added:

"You feel better, don't you?"

Without looking at her he said "Yes."                                              340

Her dress, her figure, the expression of her face, the tone of her voice, all revealed the same thing. "This is wrong, it is not as it should be. All you have lived for and still live for is falsehood and deception, hiding life and death from you." And as soon as he admitted that thought, his hatred and his agonizing physical suffering again sprang up, and with that suffering a consciousness of the unavoidable, approaching end. And to this was added a new sensation of grinding shooting pain and a feeling of suffocation.

The expression of his face when he uttered that "yes" was dreadful. Having uttered it, he looked her straight in the eyes, turned on his face with a rapidity extraordinary in his weak state and shouted:

"Go away! Go away and leave me alone!"

## CHAPTER XII

From that moment the screaming began that continued for three days, and was so terrible that one could not hear it through two closed doors without horror. At the moment he answered his wife he realized that he was lost, that there was no return, that the end had come, the very end, and his doubts were still unsolved and remained doubts.

"Oh! Oh! Oh!" he cried in various intonations. He had begun by screaming 345 "I won't!" and continued screaming on the letter "o."

For three whole days, during which time did not exist for him, he struggled in that black sack into which he was being thrust by an invisible, resistless force. He struggled as a man condemned to death struggles in the hands of the executioner, knowing that he cannot save himself. And every moment he felt that despite all his efforts he was drawing nearer and nearer to what terrified him. He felt that his agony was due to his being thrust into that black hole and still more to his not being able to get right into it. He was hindered from getting into it by his conviction that his life had been a good one. That very justification of his life held him fast and prevented his moving forward, and it caused him most torment of all.

Suddenly some force struck him in the chest and side, making it still harder to breathe, and he fell through the hole and there at the bottom was a light. What had happened to him was like the sensation one sometimes experiences in a railway carriage when one thinks one is going backwards while one is really going forwards and suddenly becomes aware of the real direction.

"Yes, it was all not the right thing," he said to himself, "but that's no matter. It can be done. But what *is* the right thing?" he asked himself, and suddenly grew quiet.

This occurred at the end of the third day, two hours before his death. Just then his schoolboy son had crept softly in and gone up to the bedside. The dying man was still screaming desperately and waving his arms. His hand fell on the boy's head, and the boy caught it, pressed it to his lips, and began to cry.

At that very moment Iván Ilých fell through and caught sight of the light, 350 and it was revealed to him that though his life had not been what it should have been, this could still be rectified. He asked himself, "What *is* the right thing?" and grew still, listening. Then he felt that someone was kissing his hand. He opened his eyes, looked at his son, and felt sorry for him. His wife came up to him and he glanced at her. She was gazing at him open-mouthed, with undried tears on her nose and cheek and a despairing look on her face. He felt sorry for her too.

"Yes, I am making them wretched," he thought. "They are sorry, but it will be better for them when I die." He wished to say this but had not the strength to utter it. "Besides, why speak? I must act," he thought. With a look at his wife he indicated his son and said: "Take him away . . . sorry for him . . . sorry for you too. . . ." He tried to add, "forgive me," but said "forego" and waved his hand, knowing that He whose understanding mattered would understand.

And suddenly it grew clear to him that what had been oppressing him and would not leave him was all dropping away at once from two sides, from ten sides, and from all sides. He was sorry for them, he must act so as not to hurt them: release them and free himself from these sufferings. "How good and how simple!" he thought. "And the pain?" he asked himself. "What has become of it? Where are you, pain?"

He turned his attention to it.

"Yes, here it is. Well, what of it? Let the pain be."

"And death . . . where is it?"                                                                    355

He sought his former accustomed fear of death and did not find it. "Where is it? What death?" There was no fear because there was no death.

In place of death there was light.

"So that's what it is!" he suddenly exclaimed aloud. "What joy!"

To him all this happened in a single instant, and the meaning of that instant did not change. For those present his agony continued for another two hours. Something rattled in his throat, his emaciated body twitched, then the gasping and rattle became less and less frequent.

"It is finished!" said someone near him.                                                          360

He heard these words and repeated them in his soul.

"Death is finished," he said to himself. "It is no more!"

He drew in a breath, stopped in the midst of a sigh, stretched out, and died.

## FOR ANALYSIS

**1.** Discuss the evidence that Ilých's death is a moral judgment—that is, a punishment for his life.

**2.** Discuss "The Death of Iván Ilých" from Paul's perspective revealed in 1 Corinthians 13 (p. 767). What accounts for the change in Ilých's attitude toward his approaching death?

**3.** Discuss the fact that Gerásim, Ilých's peasant servant, is more sympathetic to his condition than Ilých's family is.

**4.** Suggest a reason for Tolstoy's decision to begin the story immediately after Ilých's death and then move back to recount the significant episodes of his life.

## MAKING ARGUMENTS

Ilých's life is described as "most simple and most ordinary and therefore most terrible" (para. 55). What is it exactly about his life that makes it so terrible? Would any life that was simple and ordinary be terrible? Make an argument for your answer to this question, with close reference to the text as support.

## WRITING TOPICS

**1.** At the conclusion of the story, Ilých achieves peace and understanding, and the questions that have been torturing him are resolved. He realizes that "though his life had not been what it should have been, this could still be rectified" (para. 350). What does this mean?

**2.** In an essay, compare and contrast the attitudes of various **characters** to Ilých's mortal illness. How do his colleagues respond? His wife? His children? His servant Gerásim?

## MAKING CONNECTIONS

Compare the significance of death to the **characters** in this story with the significance of death to the characters in Allegra Goodman's "Apple Cake" (p. 869).

# KATE CHOPIN   (1850–1904)

# THE STORY OF AN HOUR   1894

Knowing that Mrs. Mallard was afflicted with a heart trouble, great care was taken to break to her as gently as possible the news of her husband's death.

It was her sister Josephine who told her, in broken sentences; veiled hints that revealed in half concealing. Her husband's friend Richards was there, too, near her. It was he who had been in the newspaper office when intelligence of the railroad disaster was received, with Brently Mallard's name leading the list of "killed." He had only taken the time to assure himself of its truth by a second telegram, and had hastened to forestall any less careful, less tender friend in bearing the sad message.

She did not hear the story as many women have heard the same, with a paralyzed inability to accept its significance. She wept at once, with sudden, wild abandonment, in her sister's arms. When the storm of grief had spent itself she went away to her room alone. She would have no one follow her.

There stood, facing the open window, a comfortable, roomy armchair. Into this she sank, pressed down by a physical exhaustion that haunted her body and seemed to reach into her soul.

She could see in the open square before her house the tops of trees that were 5 all aquiver with the new spring life. The delicious breath of rain was in the air. In the street below a peddler was crying his wares. The notes of a distant song which some one was singing reached her faintly, and countless sparrows were twittering in the eaves.

There were patches of blue sky showing here and there through the clouds that had met and piled one above the other in the west facing her window.

She sat with her head thrown back upon the cushion of the chair, quite motionless, except when a sob came up into her throat and shook her, as a child who had cried itself to sleep continues to sob in its dreams.

She was young, with a fair, calm face, whose lines bespoke repression and even a certain strength. But now there was a dull stare in her eyes, whose gaze was fixed away off yonder on one of those patches of blue sky. It was not a glance of reflection, but rather indicated a suspension of intelligent thought.

There was something coming to her and she was waiting for it, fearfully. What was it? She did not know; it was too subtle and elusive to name. But she felt it, creeping out of the sky, reaching toward her through the sounds, the scents, and the color that filled the air.

Now her bosom rose and fell tumultuously. She was beginning to recognize 10 this thing that was approaching to possess her, and she was striving to beat

843

it back with her will—as powerless as her two white slender hands would have been.

When she abandoned herself a little whispered word escaped her slightly parted lips. She said it over and over under her breath: "free, free, free!" The vacant stare and the look of terror that had followed it went from her eyes. They stayed keen and bright. Her pulses beat fast, and the coursing blood warmed and relaxed every inch of her body.

She did not stop to ask if it were or were not a monstrous joy that held her. A clear and exalted perception enabled her to dismiss the suggestion as trivial.

She knew that she would weep again when she saw the kind, tender hands folded in death; the face that had never looked save with love upon her, fixed and gray and dead. But she saw beyond that bitter moment a long procession of years to come that would belong to her absolutely. And she opened and spread her arms out to them in welcome.

There would be no one to live for her during those coming years: she would live for herself. There would be no powerful will bending hers in that blind persistence with which men and women believe they have a right to impose a private will upon a fellow-creature. A kind intention or a cruel intention made the act seem no less a crime as she looked upon it in that brief moment of illumination.

And yet she had loved him—sometimes. Often she had not. What did it mat- 15 ter! What could love, the unsolved mystery, count for in face of this possession of self-assertion which she suddenly recognized as the strongest impulse of her being!

"Free! Body and soul free!" she kept whispering.

Josephine was kneeling before the closed door with her lips to the keyhole, imploring for admission. "Louise, open the door! I beg; open the door—you will make yourself ill. What are you doing, Louise? For heaven's sake open the door."

"Go away. I am not making myself ill." No; she was drinking in a very elixir of life through that open window.

Her fancy was running riot along those days ahead of her. Spring days, and summer days, and all sorts of days that would be her own. She breathed a quick prayer that life might be long. It was only yesterday she had thought with a shudder that life might be long.

She arose at length and opened the door to her sister's importunities. There 20 was a feverish triumph in her eyes, and she carried herself unwittingly like a goddess of Victory. She clasped her sister's waist, and together they descended the stairs. Richards stood waiting for them at the bottom.

Some one was opening the front door with a latchkey. It was Brently Mallard who entered, a little travel-stained, composedly carrying his gripsack and umbrella. He had been far from the scene of accident, and did not even know there had been one. He stood amazed at Josephine's piercing cry; at Richards' quick motion to screen him from the view of his wife.

But Richards was too late.

When the doctors came they said she had died of heart disease—of joy that kills.

## FOR ANALYSIS

**1.** How does Chopin's story begin? Are we introduced to **character**, **setting**, and **plot** first, or do we find things out gradually? Does all the important action happen in the story's present, or has some already happened? What are the effects of beginning the story this way?

**2.** How did you feel as you read of Mrs. Mallard's reactions to the news? Did your feelings change as hers did? How did all of this make you feel about her as a person?

**3.** How would you describe **point of view** in this story? From what perspective is the story told? How do we know what we know? What are the effects of this use of point of view?

## MAKING ARGUMENTS

Argue for or against the proposition that "The Story of an Hour" is informed by feminism. What makes Mrs. Mallard unexpectedly joyful at the initial bad news? What is it that seems to kill her? Use as evidence your observations about the text and your knowledge/research about feminist thought.

## WRITING TOPIC

Write about a time in your own life when your reaction to an event was not what others might have expected it to be. What did this situation feel like? How did you deal with the fact that you were not meeting expectations? Were these expectations fair?

## MAKING CONNECTIONS

What do Mrs. Mallard and the main character in Gilman's "The Yellow Wallpaper" (p. 442) have in common? How are the two **characters** different in terms of their situations and their reactions to them?

## TIM O'BRIEN (B. 1946)

# THE THINGS THEY CARRIED 1986

First Lieutenant Jimmy Cross carried letters from a girl named Martha, a junior at Mount Sebastian College in New Jersey. They were not love letters, but Lieutenant Cross was hoping, so he kept them folded in plastic at the bottom of his rucksack. In the late afternoon, after a day's march, he would dig his foxhole, wash his hands under a canteen, unwrap the letters, hold them with the tips of his fingers, and spend the last hour of light pretending. He would imagine romantic camping trips into the White Mountains in New Hampshire. He would sometimes taste the envelope flaps, knowing her tongue had been there. More than anything, he wanted Martha to love him as he loved her, but the letters were mostly chatty, elusive on the matter of love. She was a virgin, he was almost sure. She was an English major at Mount Sebastian, and she wrote beautifully about her professors and roommates and midterm exams, about her respect for Chaucer and her great affection for Virginia Woolf. She often quoted lines of poetry; she never mentioned the war, except to say, Jimmy, take care of yourself. The letters weighed ten ounces. They were signed "Love, Martha," but Lieutenant Cross understood that "Love" was only a way of signing and did not mean what he sometimes pretended it meant. At dusk, he would carefully return the letters to his rucksack. Slowly, a bit distracted, he would get up and move among his men, checking the perimeter, then at full dark he would return to his hole and watch the night and wonder if Martha was a virgin.

The things they carried were largely determined by necessity. Among the necessities or near necessities were P-38 can openers, pocket knives, heat tabs, wrist watches, dog tags, mosquito repellent, chewing gum, candy, cigarettes, salt tablets, packets of Kool-Aid, lighters, matches, sewing kits, Military Payment Certificates, C rations, and two or three canteens of water. Together, these items weighed between fifteen and twenty pounds, depending upon a man's habits or rate of metabolism. Henry Dobbins, who was a big man, carried extra rations; he was especially fond of canned peaches in heavy syrup over pound cake. Dave Jensen, who practiced field hygiene, carried a toothbrush, dental floss, and several hotel-size bars of soap he'd stolen on R&R[1] in Sydney, Australia. Ted Lavender, who was scared, carried tranquilizers until he was shot in the head outside the village of Than Khe in mid-April. By necessity, and because it was SOP,[2] they all carried steel helmets that weighed five pounds including the liner and camouflage cover. They carried the standard

[1] Rest and recreation.
[2] Standard operating procedure.

fatigue jackets and trousers. Very few carried underwear. On their feet they carried jungle boots—2.1 pounds—and Dave Jensen carried three pairs of socks and a can of Dr. Scholl's foot powder as a precaution against trench foot. Until he was shot, Ted Lavender carried six or seven ounces of premium dope, which for him was a necessity. Mitchell Sanders, the RTO, carried condoms. Norman Bowker carried a diary. Rat Kiley carried comic books. Kiowa, a devout Baptist, carried an illustrated New Testament that had been presented to him by his father, who taught Sunday school in Oklahoma City, Oklahoma. As a hedge against bad times, however, Kiowa also carried his grandmother's distrust of the white man, his grandfather's old hunting hatchet. Necessity dictated. Because the land was mined and booby-trapped, it was SOP for each man to carry a steel-centered, nylon-covered flak jacket, which weighed 6.7 pounds, but which on hot days seemed much heavier. Because you could die so quickly, each man carried at least one large compress bandage, usually in the helmet band for easy access. Because the nights were cold, and because the monsoons were wet, each carried a green plastic poncho that could be used as a raincoat or ground sheet or makeshift tent. With its quilted liner, the poncho weighed almost two pounds, but it was worth every ounce. In April, for instance, when Ted Lavender was shot, they used his poncho to wrap him up, then to carry him across the paddy, then to lift him into the chopper that took him away.

They were called legs or grunts.

To carry something was to "hump" it, as when Lieutenant Jimmy Cross humped his love for Martha up the hills and through the swamps. In its intransitive form, "to hump" meant "to walk," or "to march," but it implied burdens far beyond the intransitive.

Almost everyone humped photographs. In his wallet, Lieutenant Cross carried two photographs of Martha. The first was a Kodachrome snapshot signed "Love," though he knew better. She stood against a brick wall. Her eyes were gray and neutral, her lips slightly open as she stared straight-on at the camera. At night, sometimes, Lieutenant Cross wondered who had taken the picture, because he knew she had boyfriends, because he loved her so much, and because he could see the shadow of the picture taker spreading out against the brick wall. The second photograph had been clipped from the 1968 Mount Sebastian yearbook. It was an action shot—women's volleyball—and Martha was bent horizontal to the floor, reaching, the palms of her hands in sharp focus, the tongue taut, the expression frank and competitive. There was no visible sweat. She wore white gym shorts. Her legs, he thought, were almost certainly the legs of a virgin, dry and without hair, the left knee cocked and carrying her entire weight, which was just over one hundred pounds. Lieutenant Cross remembered touching that left knee. A dark theater, he remembered, and the movie was *Bonnie and Clyde*, and Martha wore a tweed skirt, and during the final scene, when he touched her knee, she turned and looked at him in a sad, sober way that made him pull his hand back, but he would always remember the feel of the tweed skirt and the knee beneath it and the sound of the gunfire that killed Bonnie and Clyde, how embarrassing it was, how slow and oppressive. He remembered kissing her good night at the dorm door. Right then, he thought, he should've done something brave. He should've carried her up the stairs to her room and tied her to the bed and touched that left knee all night long. He should've risked it. Whenever he looked at the photographs, he thought of new things he should've done.

What they carried was partly a function of rank, partly of field specialty.

As a first lieutenant and platoon leader, Jimmy Cross carried a compass, maps, code books, binoculars, and a .45-caliber pistol that weighed 2.9 pounds fully loaded. He carried a strobe light and the responsibility for the lives of his men.

As an RTO, Mitchell Sanders carried the PRC-25 radio, a killer, twenty-six pounds with its battery.

As a medic, Rat Kiley carried a canvas satchel filled with morphine and plasma and malaria tablets and surgical tape and comic books and all the things a medic must carry, including M&M's for especially bad wounds, for a total weight of nearly twenty pounds.

As a big man, therefore a machine gunner, Henry Dobbins carried the 10 M-60, which weighed twenty-three pounds unloaded, but which was almost always loaded. In addition, Dobbins carried between ten and fifteen pounds of ammunition draped in belts across his chest and shoulders.

As PFCs or Spec 4s, most of them were common grunts and carried the standard M-16 gas-operated assault rifle. The weapon weighed 7.5 pounds unloaded, 8.2 pounds with its full twenty-round magazine. Depending on numerous factors, such as topography and psychology, the riflemen carried anywhere from twelve to twenty magazines, usually in cloth bandoliers, adding on another 8.4 pounds at minimum, fourteen pounds at maximum. When it was available, they also carried M-16 maintenance gear—rods and steel brushes and swabs and tubes of LSA oil—all of which weighed about a pound. Among the grunts, some carried the M-79 grenade launcher, 5.9 pounds unloaded, a reasonably light weapon except for the ammunition, which was heavy. A single round weighed ten ounces. The typical load was twenty-five rounds. But Ted Lavender, who was scared, carried thirty-four rounds when he was shot and killed outside Than Khe, and he went down under an exceptional burden, more than twenty pounds of ammunition, plus the flak jacket and helmet and rations and water and toilet paper and tranquilizers and all the rest, plus the unweighed fear. He was dead weight. There was no twitching or flopping. Kiowa, who saw it happen, said it was like watching a rock fall, or a big sandbag or something—just boom, then down—not like the movies where the dead guy rolls around and does fancy spins and goes ass over teakettle—not like that, Kiowa said, the poor bastard just flat-fuck fell. Boom. Down. Nothing else. It was a bright morning in mid-April. Lieutenant Cross felt the pain. He blamed himself. They stripped off Lavender's canteens and ammo, all the heavy things, and Rat Kiley said the obvious, the guy's dead, and Mitchell Sanders used his radio to report one U.S. KIA and to request a chopper. Then they wrapped Lavender in his poncho. They carried him out to a dry paddy, established security, and sat smoking the dead man's dope until the chopper came. Lieutenant Cross kept to himself. He pictured Martha's smooth young face, thinking he loved her more than anything, more than his men, and now Ted Lavender was dead because he loved her so much and could not stop thinking about her. When the dust-off arrived, they carried Lavender aboard. Afterward they burned Than Khe. They marched until dusk, then dug their holes, and that night Kiowa kept explaining how you had to be there, how fast it was, how the poor guy just dropped like so much concrete. Boom-down, he said. Like cement.

In addition to the three standard weapons—the M-60, M-16, and M-79— they carried whatever presented itself, or whatever seemed appropriate as a means of killing or staying alive. They carried catch-as-catch-can. At various times, in various situations, they carried M-14s and CAR-15s and Swedish Ks and grease guns and captured AK-47s and Chi-Coms and RPGs and Simonov carbines and black-market Uzis and .38-caliber Smith & Wesson handguns and 66 mm LAWs and shotguns and silencers and blackjacks and bayonets and C-4 plastic explosives. Lee Strunk carried a slingshot; a weapon of last resort, he called it. Mitchell Sanders carried brass knuckles. Kiowa carried his grandfather's feathered hatchet. Every third or fourth man carried a Claymore antipersonnel mine—3.5 pounds with its firing device. They all carried fragmentation grenades—fourteen ounces each. They all carried at least one M-18 colored smoke grenade—twenty-four ounces. Some carried CS or tear-gas grenades. Some carried white-phosphorus grenades. They carried all they could bear, and then some, including a silent awe for the terrible power of the things they carried.

In the first week of April, before Lavender died, Lieutenant Jimmy Cross received a good-luck charm from Martha. It was a simple pebble, an ounce at most. Smooth to the touch, it was a milky-white color with flecks of orange and violet, oval-shaped, like a miniature egg. In the accompanying letter, Martha wrote that she had found the pebble on the Jersey shoreline, precisely where the land touched water at high tide, where things came together but also separated. It was this separate-but-together quality, she wrote, that had inspired her to pick up the pebble and to carry it in her breast pocket for several days, where it seemed weightless, and then to send it through the mail, by air, as a token of her truest feelings for him. Lieutenant Cross found this romantic. But he wondered what her truest feelings were, exactly, and what she meant by separate-but-together. He wondered how the tides and waves had come into play on that afternoon along the Jersey shoreline when Martha saw the pebble and bent down to rescue it from geology. He imagined bare feet. Martha was a poet, with the poet's sensibilities, and her feet would be brown and bare, the toenails unpainted, the eyes chilly and somber like the ocean in March, and though it was painful, he wondered who had been with her that afternoon. He imagined a pair of shadows moving along the strip of sand where things came together but also separated. It was phantom jealousy, he knew, but he couldn't help himself. He loved her so much. On the march, through the hot days of early April, he carried the pebble in his mouth, turning it with his tongue, tasting sea salts and moisture. His mind wandered. He had difficulty keeping his attention on the war. On occasion he would yell at his men to spread out the column, to keep their eyes open, but then he would slip away into daydreams, just pretending, walking barefoot along the Jersey shore, with Martha, carrying nothing. He would feel himself rising. Sun and waves and gentle winds, all love and lightness.

What they carried varied by mission.

When a mission took them to the mountains, they carried mosquito net- 15 ting, machetes, canvas tarps, and extra bug juice.

If a mission seemed especially hazardous, or if it involved a place they knew to be bad, they carried everything they could. In certain heavily mined AOs, where the land was dense with Toe Poppers and Bouncing Betties, they took turns humping a twenty-eight-pound mine detector. With its headphones and big sensing plate, the equipment was a stress on the lower back and shoulders, awkward to handle, often useless because of the shrapnel in the earth, but they carried it anyway, partly for safety, partly for the illusion of safety.

On ambush, or other night missions, they carried peculiar little odds and ends. Kiowa always took along his New Testament and a pair of moccasins for silence. Dave Jensen carried night-sight vitamins high in carotin. Lee Strunk carried his slingshot; ammo, he claimed, would never be a problem. Rat Kiley carried brandy and M&M's. Until he was shot, Ted Lavender carried the starlight scope, which weighed 6.3 pounds with its aluminum carrying case. Henry Dobbins carried his girlfriend's pantyhose wrapped around his neck as a comforter. They all carried ghosts. When dark came, they would move out single file across the meadows and paddies to their ambush coordinates, where they would quietly set up the Claymores and lie down and spend the night waiting.

Other missions were more complicated and required special equipment. In mid-April, it was their mission to search out and destroy the elaborate tunnel complexes in the Than Khe area south of Chu Lai. To blow the tunnels, they carried one-pound blocks of pentrite high explosives, four blocks to a man, sixty-eight pounds in all. They carried wiring, detonators, and battery-powered clackers. Dave Jensen carried earplugs. Most often, before blowing the tunnels, they were ordered by higher command to search them, which was considered bad news, but by and large they just shrugged and carried out orders. Because he was a big man, Henry Dobbins was excused from tunnel duty. The others would draw numbers. Before Lavender died there were seventeen men in the platoon, and whoever drew the number seventeen would strip off his gear and crawl in head first with a flashlight and Lieutenant Cross's

.45-caliber pistol. The rest of them would fan out as security. They would sit down or kneel, not facing the hole, listening to the ground beneath them, imagining cobwebs and ghosts, whatever was down there—the tunnel walls squeezing in—how the flashlight seemed impossibly heavy in the hand and how it was tunnel vision in the very strictest sense, compression in all ways, even time, and how you had to wiggle in—ass and elbows—a swallowed-up feeling—and how you found yourself worrying about odd things—will your flashlight go dead? Do rats carry rabies? If you screamed, how far would the sound carry? Would your buddies hear it? Would they have the courage to drag you out? In some respects, though not many, the waiting was worse than the tunnel itself. Imagination was a killer.

On April 16, when Lee Strunk drew the number seventeen, he laughed and muttered something and went down quickly. The morning was hot and very still. Not good, Kiowa said. He looked at the tunnel opening, then out across a dry paddy toward the village of Than Khe. Nothing moved. No clouds or birds or people. As they waited, the men smoked and drank Kool-Aid, not talking much, feeling sympathy for Lee Strunk but also feeling the luck of the draw. You win some, you lose some, said Mitchell Sanders, and sometimes you settle for a rain check. It was a tired line and no one laughed.

Henry Dobbins ate a tropical chocolate bar. Ted Lavender popped a tran- 20 quilizer and went off to pee.

After five minutes, Lieutenant Jimmy Cross moved to the tunnel, leaned down, and examined the darkness. Trouble, he thought—a cave-in maybe. And then suddenly, without willing it, he was thinking about Martha. The stresses and fractures, the quick collapse, the two of them buried alive under all that weight. Dense, crushing love. Kneeling, watching the hole, he tried to concentrate on Lee Strunk and the war, all the dangers, but his love was too much for him, he felt paralyzed, he wanted to sleep inside her lungs and breathe her blood and be smothered. He wanted her to be a virgin and not a virgin, all at once. He wanted to know her. Intimate secrets—why poetry? Why so sad? Why the grayness in her eyes? Why so alone? Not lonely, just alone—riding her bike across campus or sitting off by herself in the cafeteria. Even dancing, she danced alone—and it was the aloneness that filled him with love. He remembered telling her that one evening. How she nodded and looked away. And how, later, when he kissed her, she received the kiss without returning it, her eyes wide open, not afraid, not a virgin's eyes, just flat and uninvolved.

Lieutenant Cross gazed at the tunnel. But he was not there. He was buried with Martha under the white sand at the Jersey shore. They were pressed together, and the pebble in his mouth was her tongue. He was smiling. Vaguely, he was aware of how quiet the day was, the sullen paddies, yet he could not bring himself to worry about matters of security. He was beyond that. He was just a kid at war, in love. He was twenty-two years old. He couldn't help it.

A few moments later Lee Strunk crawled out of the tunnel. He came up grinning, filthy but alive. Lieutenant Cross nodded and closed his eyes while the others clapped Strunk on the back and made jokes about rising from the dead.

Worms, Rat Kiley said. Right out of the grave. Fuckin' zombie.

The men laughed. They all felt great relief. 25

Spook City, said Mitchell Sanders.

Lee Strunk made a funny ghost sound, a kind of moaning, yet very happy, and right then, when Strunk made that high happy moaning sound, when he went *Ahhooooo*, right then Ted Lavender was shot in the head on his way back from peeing. He lay with his mouth open. The teeth were broken. There was a swollen black bruise under his left eye. The cheekbone was gone. Oh shit, Rat Kiley said, the guy's dead. The guy's dead, he kept saying, which seemed profound—the guy's dead. I mean really.

The things they carried were determined to some extent by superstition. Lieutenant Cross carried his good-luck pebble. Dave Jensen carried a rabbit's foot. Norman Bowker, otherwise a very gentle person, carried a thumb that had been presented to him as a gift by Mitchell Sanders. The thumb was dark brown, rubbery to the touch, and weighed four ounces at most. It had been cut from a VC[3] corpse, a boy of fifteen or sixteen. They'd found him at the bottom of an irrigation ditch, badly burned, flies in his mouth and eyes. The boy wore black shorts and sandals. At the time of his death he had been carrying a pouch of rice, a rifle, and three magazines of ammunition.

You want my opinion, Mitchell Sanders said, there's a definite moral here.

He put his hand on the dead boy's wrist. He was quiet for a time, as if count- 30 ing a pulse, then he patted the stomach, almost affectionately, and used Kiowa's hunting hatchet to remove the thumb.

Henry Dobbins asked what the moral was.

Moral?

You know. *Moral.*

Sanders wrapped the thumb in toilet paper and handed it across to Norman Bowker. There was no blood. Smiling, he kicked the boy's head, watched the flies scatter, and said, It's like with that old TV show—Paladin. Have gun, will travel.

Henry Dobbins thought about it. 35

Yeah, well, he finally said. I don't see no moral.

There it *is*, man.

Fuck off.

They carried USO stationery and pencils and pens. They carried Sterno, safety pins, trip flares, signal flares, spools of wire, razor blades, chewing tobacco, liberated joss sticks and statuettes of the smiling Buddha, candles, grease pencils, *The Stars and Stripes*,[4] fingernail clippers, Psy Ops leaflets, bush hats, bolos, and much more. Twice a week, when the resupply choppers came in, they carried hot chow in green Mermite cans and large canvas

---

[3] Vietcong.

[4] The military's officially sanctioned overseas newspaper.

bags filled with iced beer and soda pop. They carried plastic water containers, each with a two-gallon capacity. Mitchell Sanders carried a set of starched tiger fatigues for special occasions. Henry Dobbins carried Black Flag insecticide. Dave Jensen carried empty sandbags that could be filled at night for added protection. Lee Strunk carried tanning lotion. Some things they carried in common. Taking turns, they carried the big PRC-77 scrambler radio, which weighed thirty pounds with its battery. They shared the weight of memory. They took up what others could no longer bear. Often, they carried each other, the wounded or weak. They carried infections. They carried chess sets, basketballs, Vietnamese-English dictionaries, insignia of rank, Bronze Stars and Purple Hearts, plastic cards imprinted with the Code of Conduct. They carried diseases, among them malaria and dysentery. They carried lice and ringworm and leeches and paddy algae and various rots and molds. They carried the land itself—Vietnam, the place, the soil—a powdery orange-red dust that covered their boots and fatigues and faces. They carried the sky. The whole atmosphere, they carried it, the humidity, the monsoons, the stink of fungus and decay, all of it, they carried gravity. They moved like mules. By daylight they took sniper fire, at night they were mortared, but it was not battle, it was just the endless march, village to village, without purpose, nothing won or lost. They marched for the sake of the march. They plodded along slowly, dumbly, leaning forward against the heat, unthinking, all blood and bone, simple grunts, soldiering with their legs, toiling up the hills and down into the paddies and across the rivers and up again and down, just humping, one step and then the next and then another, but no volition, no will, because it was automatic, it was anatomy, and the war was entirely a matter of posture and carriage, the hump was everything, a kind of inertia, a kind of emptiness, a dullness of desire and intellect and conscience and hope and human sensibility. Their principles were in their feet. Their calculations were biological. They had no sense of strategy or mission. They searched the villages without knowing what to look for, not caring, kicking over jars of rice, frisking children and old men, blowing tunnels, sometimes setting fires and sometimes not, then forming up and moving on to the next village, then other villages, where it would always be the same. They carried their own lives. The pressures were enormous. In the heat of early afternoon, they would remove their helmets and flak jackets, walking bare, which was dangerous but which helped ease the strain. They would often discard things along the route of march. Purely for comfort, they would throw away rations, blow their Claymores and grenades, no matter, because by nightfall the resupply choppers would arrive with more of the same, then a day or two later still more, fresh watermelons and crates of ammunition and sunglasses and woolen sweaters—the resources were stunning—sparklers for the Fourth of July, colored eggs for Easter. It was the great American war chest—the fruits of science, the smokestacks, the canneries, the arsenals at Hartford, the Minnesota forests, the machine shops, the vast fields of corn and wheat—they carried like freight trains; they carried it on their backs and shoulders—and for all the ambiguities of Vietnam, all the mysteries and unknowns, there was at least the single abiding certainty that they would never be at a loss for things to carry.

After the chopper took Lavender away, Lieutenant Jimmy Cross led his men 40 into the village of Than Khe. They burned everything. They shot chickens and dogs, they trashed the village well, they called in artillery and watched the wreckage, then they marched for several hours through the hot afternoon, and then at dusk, while Kiowa explained how Lavender died, Lieutenant Cross found himself trembling.

He tried not to cry. With his entrenching tool, which weighed five pounds, he began digging a hole in the earth.

He felt shame. He hated himself. He had loved Martha more than his men, and as a consequence Lavender was now dead, and this was something he would have to carry like a stone in his stomach for the rest of the war.

All he could do was dig. He used his entrenching tool like an ax, slashing, feeling both love and hate, and then later, when it was full dark, he sat at the bottom of his foxhole and wept. It went on for a long while. In part, he was grieving for Ted Lavender, but mostly it was for Martha, and for himself, because she belonged to another world, which was not quite real, and because she was a junior at Mount Sebastian College in New Jersey, a poet and a virgin and uninvolved, and because he realized she did not love him and never would.

Like cement, Kiowa whispered in the dark. I swear to God—boom-down. Not a word.

I've heard this, said Norman Bowker.                                                    45

A pisser, you know? Still zipping himself up. Zapped while zipping.

All right, fine. That's enough.

Yeah, but you had to see it, the guy just—

I *heard*, man. Cement. So why not shut the fuck *up*?

Kiowa shook his head sadly and glanced over at the hole where Lieutenant 50 Jimmy Cross sat watching the night. The air was thick and wet. A warm, dense fog had settled over the paddies and there was the stillness that precedes rain.

After a time Kiowa sighed.

One thing for sure, he said. The Lieutenant's in some deep hurt. I mean that crying jag—the way he was carrying on—it wasn't fake or anything, it was real heavy-duty hurt. The man cares.

Sure, Norman Bowker said.

Say what you want, the man does care.

We all got problems.                                                                  55

Not Lavender.

No, I guess not, Bowker said. Do me a favor, though.

Shut up?

That's a smart Indian. Shut up.

Shrugging, Kiowa pulled off his boots. He wanted to say more, just to 60 lighten up his sleep, but instead he opened his New Testament and arranged it beneath his head as a pillow. The fog made things seem hollow and unattached. He tried not to think about Ted Lavender, but then he was thinking how fast it was, no drama, down and dead, and how it was hard to feel anything except surprise. It seemed un-Christian. He wished he could find some great sadness, or even anger, but the emotion wasn't there and he couldn't make it happen. Mostly he felt pleased to be alive. He liked the smell of the New Testament under his cheek, the leather and ink and paper and glue, whatever the chemicals were. He liked hearing the sounds of night. Even his fatigue, it felt fine, the stiff muscles and the prickly awareness of his own body, a floating feeling. He enjoyed not being dead. Lying there, Kiowa admired Lieutenant Jimmy Cross's capacity for grief. He wanted to share the man's pain, he wanted to care as Jimmy Cross cared. And yet when he closed his eyes, all he could think was Boom-down, and all he could feel was the pleasure of having his boots off and the fog curling in around him and the damp soil and the Bible smells and the plush comfort of night.

After a moment Norman Bowker sat up in the dark.

What the hell, he said. You want to talk, *talk*. Tell it to me.

Forget it.

No, man, go on. One thing I hate, it's a silent Indian.

For the most part they carried themselves with poise, a kind of dignity. 65 Now and then, however, there were times of panic, when they squealed or wanted to squeal but couldn't, when they twitched and made moaning sounds and covered their heads and said Dear Jesus and flopped around on the earth and fired their weapons blindly and cringed and sobbed and begged for the noise to stop and went wild and made stupid promises to themselves and to God and to their mothers and fathers, hoping not to die. In different ways, it happened to all of them. Afterward, when the firing ended, they would blink and peek up. They would touch their bodies, feeling shame, then quickly hiding it. They would force themselves to stand. As if in slow motion, frame by frame, the world would take on the old logic—absolute silence, then the wind, then sunlight, then voices. It was the burden of being alive. Awkwardly, the men would reassemble themselves, first in private, then in groups, becoming soldiers again. They would repair the leaks in their eyes. They would check for casualties, call in dust-offs, light cigarettes, try to smile, clear their throats and spit and begin cleaning their weapons. After a time someone would shake his head and say, No lie, I almost shit my pants, and someone else would laugh, which meant it was bad, yes, but the guy had obviously not shit his pants, it wasn't that bad, and in any case nobody would ever do such a thing and then go ahead and talk about it. They would squint into the dense, oppressive sunlight. For a few moments, perhaps, they would fall silent, lighting a joint and tracking its passage from man to man, inhaling, holding in the humiliation. Scary stuff, one of them might say. But then someone else would grin or flick his eyebrows and say, Roger-dodger, almost cut me a new asshole, *almost*.

There were numerous such poses. Some carried themselves with a sort of wistful resignation, others with pride or stiff soldierly discipline or good humor or macho zeal. They were afraid of dying but they were even more afraid to show it.

They found jokes to tell.

They used a hard vocabulary to contain the terrible softness. *Greased*, they'd say. *Offed, lit up, zapped while zipping*. It wasn't cruelty, just stage presence. They were actors and the war came at them in 3-D. When someone died, it wasn't quite dying, because in a curious way it seemed scripted, and because they had their lines mostly memorized, irony mixed with tragedy, and because they called it by other names, as if to encyst and destroy the reality of death itself. They kicked corpses. They cut off thumbs. They talked grunt lingo. They told stories about Ted Lavender's supply of tranquilizers, how the poor guy didn't feel a thing, how incredibly tranquil he was.

There's a moral here, said Mitchell Sanders.

They were waiting for Lavender's chopper, smoking the dead man's dope.    70

The moral's pretty obvious, Sanders said, and winked. Stay away from drugs. No joke, they'll ruin your day every time.

Cute, said Henry Dobbins.

Mind-blower, get it? Talk about wiggy—nothing left, just blood and brains.

They made themselves laugh.

There it is, they'd say, over and over, as if the repetition itself were an act 75 of poise, a balance between crazy and almost crazy, knowing without going. There it is, which meant be cool, let it ride, because oh yeah, man, you can't change what can't be changed, there it is, there it absolutely and positively and fucking well *is*.

They were tough.

They carried all the emotional baggage of men who might die. Grief, terror, love, longing—these were intangibles, but the intangibles had their own mass and specific gravity, they had tangible weight. They carried shameful memories. They carried the common secret of cowardice barely restrained, the instinct to run or freeze or hide, and in many respects this was the heaviest burden of all, for it could never be put down, it required perfect balance and perfect posture. They carried their reputations. They carried the soldier's greatest fear, which was the fear of blushing. Men killed, and died, because they were embarrassed not to. It was what had brought them to the war in the first place, nothing positive, no dreams of glory or honor, just to avoid the blush of dishonor. They died so as not to die of embarrassment. They crawled into tunnels and walked point and advanced under fire. Each morning, despite the unknowns, they made their legs move. They endured. They kept humping. They did not submit to the obvious alternative, which was simply to close the eyes and fall. So easy, really. Go limp and tumble to the ground and let the muscles unwind and not speak and not budge until your buddies picked you up and lifted you into the chopper that would roar and dip its nose and carry you off to the world. A mere matter of falling, yet no one ever fell. It was not courage, exactly; the object was not valor. Rather, they were too frightened to be cowards.

By and large they carried these things inside, maintaining the masks of composure. They sneered at sick call. They spoke bitterly about guys who had found release by shooting off their own toes or fingers. Pussies, they'd say. Candyasses. It was fierce, mocking talk, with only a trace of envy or awe, but even so, the image played itself out behind their eyes.

They imagined the muzzle against flesh. They imagined the quick, sweet pain, then the evacuation to Japan, then a hospital with warm beds and cute geisha nurses.

They dreamed of freedom birds.

At night, on guard, staring into the dark, they were carried away by jumbo jets. They felt the rush of takeoff. *Gone!* they yelled. And then velocity, wings and engines, a smiling stewardess—but it was more than a plane, it was a real bird, a big sleek silver bird with feathers and talons and high screeching. They were flying. The weights fell off, there was nothing to bear. They laughed and held on tight, feeling the cold slap of wind and altitude, soaring, thinking *It's over, I'm gone!*—they were naked, they were light and free—it was all lightness, bright and fast and buoyant, light as light, a helium buzz in the brain, a giddy bubbling in the lungs as they were taken up over the clouds and the war, beyond duty, beyond gravity and mortification and global entanglements—*Sin loi!* they yelled, *I'm sorry, motherfuckers, but I'm out of it, I'm goofed, I'm on a space cruise, I'm gone!*—and it was a restful, disencumbered sensation, just riding the light waves, sailing that big silver freedom bird over the mountains and oceans, over America, over the farms and great sleeping cities and cemeteries and highways and the golden arches of McDonald's. It was flight, a kind of fleeing, a kind of falling, falling higher and higher, spinning off the edge of the earth and beyond the sun and through the vast, silent vacuum where there were no burdens and where everything weighed exactly nothing. *Gone!* they screamed, *I'm sorry but I'm gone!* And so at night, not quite dreaming, they gave themselves over to lightness, they were carried, they were purely borne. 80

On the morning after Ted Lavender died, First Lieutenant Jimmy Cross crouched at the bottom of his foxhole and burned Martha's letters. Then he burned the two photographs. There was a steady rain falling, which made it difficult, but he used heat tabs and Sterno to build a small fire, screening it with his body, holding the photographs over the tight blue flame with the tips of his fingers.

He realized it was only a gesture. Stupid, he thought. Sentimental, too, but mostly just stupid.

Lavender was dead. You couldn't burn the blame.

Besides, the letters were in his head. And even now, without photographs, Lieutenant Cross could see Martha playing volleyball in her white gym shorts and yellow T-shirt. He could see her moving in the rain. 85

When the fire died out, Lieutenant Cross pulled his poncho over his shoulders and ate breakfast from a can.

There was no great mystery, he decided.

In those burned letters Martha had never mentioned the war, except to say, Jimmy, take care of yourself. She wasn't involved. She signed the letters "Love," but it wasn't love, and all the fine lines and technicalities did not matter.

The morning came up wet and blurry. Everything seemed part of everything else, the fog and Martha and the deepening rain.

It was a war, after all.                                                                                  90

Half smiling, Lieutenant Jimmy Cross took out his maps. He shook his head hard, as if to clear it, then bent forward and began planning the day's march. In ten minutes, or maybe twenty, he would rouse the men and they would pack up and head west, where the maps showed the country to be green and inviting. They would do what they had always done. The rain might add some weight, but otherwise it would be one more day layered upon all the other days.

He was realistic about it. There was that new hardness in his stomach.

No more fantasies, he told himself.

Henceforth, when he thought about Martha, it would be only to think that she belonged elsewhere. He would shut down the daydreams. This was not Mount Sebastian, it was another world, where there were no pretty poems or midterm exams, a place where men died because of carelessness and gross stupidity. Kiowa was right. Boom-down, and you were dead, never partly dead.

Briefly, in the rain, Lieutenant Cross saw Martha's gray eyes gazing back    95
at him.

He understood.

It was very sad, he thought. The things men carried inside. The things men did or felt they had to do.

He almost nodded at her, but didn't.

Instead he went back to his maps. He was now determined to perform his duties firmly and without negligence. It wouldn't help Lavender, he knew that, but from this point on he would comport himself as a soldier. He would dispose of his good-luck pebble. Swallow it, maybe, or use Lee Strunk's slingshot, or just drop it along the trail. On the march he would impose strict field discipline. He would be careful to send out flank security, to prevent straggling or bunching up, to keep his troops moving at the proper pace and at the proper interval. He would insist on clean weapons. He would confiscate the remainder of Lavender's dope. Later in the day, perhaps, he would call the men together and speak to them plainly. He would accept the blame for what had happened to Ted Lavender. He would be a man about it. He would look them in the eyes, keeping his chin level, and he would issue the new SOPs in a calm, impersonal tone of voice, an officer's voice, leaving no room for argument or discussion. Commencing immediately, he'd tell them, they would no longer abandon equipment along the route of march. They would police up their acts. They would get their shit together, and keep it together, and maintain it neatly and in good working order.

He would not tolerate laxity. He would show strength, distancing himself. 100

Among the men there would be grumbling, of course, and maybe worse, because their days would seem longer and their loads heavier, but Lieutenant Cross reminded himself that his obligation was not to be loved but to lead. He would dispense with love; it was not now a factor. And if anyone quarreled or complained, he would simply tighten his lips and arrange his shoulders in the correct command posture. He might give a curt little nod. Or he might not. He might just shrug and say Carry on, then they would saddle up and form into a column and move out toward the villages of Than Khe.

## FOR ANALYSIS

**1.** What are the various meanings of "Things" in the title?

**2.** What is the **narrator's** attitude toward war? Does his attitude differ from the attitudes of the soldiers he is describing? Explain.

**3.** How do Lieutenant Cross's thoughts about Martha fit into the overall **thematic** pattern of the story?

**4.** What is the attitude of the men toward the enemy?

**5.** How effective do you find the cataloging of things as a way to tell this story? Explain.

## MAKING ARGUMENTS

Another story in *The Things They Carried*, the book this story comes from, is entitled "How to Tell a True War Story." In it, the implicit argument is that there are different kinds of truth, and that reporting factual truth isn't always as instructive—doesn't always impart what an event or situation was like—as fiction can be. Does it matter to you if the wealth of detail in this story is accurate? Construct an argument about truth and fiction, making reference to both the story and larger ideas about these issues.

## WRITING TOPIC

Discuss the meaning of heroism in this story.

## MAKING CONNECTIONS

Compare and contrast O'Brien's perspective on war with Thomas Hardy's in "The Man He Killed" (p. 351). Which do you find to be a more effective antiwar statement? Explain.

## HELENA MARÍA VIRAMONTES   (B. 1954)

# THE MOTHS    1985

I was fourteen years old when Abuelita requested my help. And it seemed only fair. Abuelita had pulled me through the rages of scarlet fever by placing, removing, and replacing potato slices on the temples of my forehead; she had seen me through several whippings, an arm broken by a dare jump off Tío Enrique's toolshed, puberty, and my first lie. Really, I told Amá, it was only fair.

Not that I was her favorite granddaughter or anything special. I wasn't even pretty or nice like my older sisters and I just couldn't do the girl things they could do. My hands were too big to handle the fineries of crocheting or embroidery and I always pricked my fingers or knotted my colored threads time and time again while my sisters laughed and called me bull hands with their cute waterlike voices. So I began keeping a piece of jagged brick in my sock to bash my sisters or anyone who called me bull hands. Once, while we all sat in the bedroom, I hit Teresa on the forehead, right above her eyebrow and she ran to Amá with her mouth open, her hand over her eye while blood seeped between her fingers. I was used to the whippings by then.

I wasn't respectful either. I even went so far as to doubt the power of Abuelita's slices, the slices she said absorbed my fever. "You're still alive, aren't you?" Abuelita snapped back, her pasty gray eye beaming at me and burning holes in my suspicions. Regretful that I had let secret questions drop out of my mouth, I couldn't look into her eyes. My hands began to fan out, grow like a liar's nose until they hung by my side like low weights. Abuelita made a balm out of dried moth wings and Vicks and rubbed my hands, shaped them back to size and it was the strangest feeling. Like bones melting. Like sun shining through the darkness of your eyelids. I didn't mind helping Abuelita after that, so Amá would always send me over to her.

In the early afternoon Amá would push her hair back, hand me my sweater and shoes, and tell me to go to Mama Luna's. This was to avoid another fight and another whipping, I knew. I would deliver one last direct shot on Marisela's arm and jump out of our house, the slam of the screen door burying her cries of anger, and I'd gladly go help Abuelita plant her wild lilies or jasmine or heliotrope or cilantro or hierbabuena in red Hills Brothers coffee cans. Abuelita would wait for me at the top step of her porch holding a hammer and nail and empty coffee cans. And although we hardly spoke, hardly looked at each other as we worked over root transplants, I always felt her gray eye on me. It made me feel, in a strange sort of way, safe and guarded and not alone. Like God was supposed to make you feel.

On Abuelita's porch, I would puncture holes in the bottom of the coffee cans with a nail and a precise hit of a hammer. This completed, my job was to fill them with red clay mud from beneath her rose bushes, packing it softly, then making a perfect hole, four fingers round, to nest a sprouting avocado pit, or the spidery sweet potatoes that Abuelita rooted in mayonnaise jars with toothpicks and daily water, or prickly chayotes that produced vines that twisted and wound all over her porch pillars, crawling to the roof, up and over the roof, and down the other side, making her small brick house look like it was cradled within the vines that grew pear-shaped squashes ready for the pick, ready to be steamed with onions and cheese and butter. The roots would burst out of the rusted coffee cans and search for a place to connect. I would then feed the seedlings with water.

But this was a different kind of help, Amá said, because Abuelita was dying. Looking into her gray eye, then into her brown one, the doctor said it was just a matter of days. And so it seemed only fair that these hands she had melted and formed found use in rubbing her caving body with alcohol and marihuana, rubbing her arms and legs, turning her face to the window so that she could watch the Bird of Paradise blooming or smell the scent of clove in the air. I toweled her face frequently and held her hand for hours. Her gray wiry hair hung over the mattress. Since I could remember, she'd kept her long hair in braids. Her mouth was vacant and when she slept, her eyelids never closed all the way. Up close, you could see her gray eye beaming out the window, staring hard as if to remember everything. I never kissed her. I left the window open when I went to the market.

Across the street from Jay's Market there was a chapel. I never knew its denomination, but I went in just the same to search for candles. I sat down on one of the pews because there were none. After I cleaned my fingernails, I looked up at the high ceiling. I had forgotten the vastness of these places, the coolness of the marble pillars and the frozen statues with blank eyes. I was alone. I knew why I had never returned.

That was one of Apá's biggest complaints. He would pound his hands on the table, rocking the sugar dish or spilling a cup of coffee and scream that if I didn't go to mass every Sunday to save my goddamn sinning soul, then I had no reason to go out of the house, period. Punto final. He would grab my arm and dig his nails into me to make sure I understood the importance of catechism. Did he make himself clear? Then he strategically directed his anger at Amá for her lousy ways of bringing up daughters, being disrespectful and unbelieving, and my older sisters would pull me aside and tell me if I didn't get to mass right this minute, they were all going to kick the holy shit out of me. Why am I so selfish? Can't you see what it's doing to Amá, you idiot? So I would wash my feet and stuff them in my black Easter shoes that shone with Vaseline, grab a missal and veil, and wave good-bye to Amá.

I would walk slowly down Lorena to First to Evergreen, counting the cracks on the cement. On Evergreen I would turn left and walk to Abuelita's. I liked her porch because it was shielded by the vines of the chayotes and I could get a good look at the people and car traffic on Evergreen without them knowing. I would jump up the porch steps, knock on the screen door as I wiped my feet and call Abuelita? mi Abuelita? As I opened the door and stuck my head in, I would catch the gagging scent of toasting chile on the placa. When I entered the sala, she would greet me from the kitchen, wringing her hands in her apron. I'd sit at the corner of the table to keep from being in her way. The chiles made my eyes water. Am I crying? No, Mama Luna, I'm sure not crying. I don't like going to mass, but my eyes watered anyway, the tears dropping on the tablecloth like candle wax. Abuelita lifted the burnt chiles from the fire and sprinkled water on them until the skins began to separate. Placing them in front of me, she turned to check the menudo. I peeled the skins off and put the flimsy, limp looking green and yellow chiles in the molcajete and began to crush and crush and twist and crush the heart out of the tomato, the clove of garlic, the stupid chiles that made me cry, crushed them until they turned into liquid under my bull hand. With a wooden spoon, I scraped hard to destroy the guilt, and my tears were gone. I put the bowl of chile next to a vase filled with freshly cut roses. Abuelita touched my hand and pointed to the bowl of menudo that steamed in front of me. I spooned some chile into the menudo and rolled a corn tortilla thin with the palms of my hands. As I ate, a fine Sunday breeze entered the kitchen and a rose petal calmly feathered down to the table.

I left the chapel without blessing myself and walked to Jay's. Most of the 10 time Jay didn't have much of anything. The tomatoes were always soft and the cans of Campbell soups had rusted spots on them. There was dust on the tops of cereal boxes. I picked up what I needed: rubbing alcohol, five cans of chicken broth, a big bottle of Pine Sol. At first Jay got mad because I thought I had forgotten the money. But it was there all the time, in my back pocket.

When I returned from the market, I heard Amá crying in Abuelita's kitchen. She looked up at me with puffy eyes. I placed the bags of groceries on the table and began putting the cans of soup away. Amá sobbed quietly. I never kissed her. After a while, I patted her on the back for comfort. Finally: "¿Y mi Amá?" she asked in a whisper, then choked again and cried into her apron.

Abuelita fell off the bed twice yesterday, I said, knowing that I shouldn't have said it and wondering why I wanted to say it because it only made Amá cry harder. I guess I became angry and just so tired of the quarrels and beatings and unanswered prayers and my hands just there hanging helplessly by my side. Amá looked at me again, confused, angry, and her eyes were filled with sorrow. I went outside and sat on the porch swing and watched the people pass. I sat there until she left. I dozed off repeating the words to myself like rosary prayers: when do you stop giving when do you start giving when do you. . . . and when my hands fell from my lap, I awoke to catch them. The sun was setting, an orange glow, and I knew Abuelita was hungry.

There comes a time when the sun is defiant. Just about the time when moods change, inevitable seasons of a day, transitions from one color to another, that hour or minute or second when the sun is finally defeated, finally sinks into the realization that it cannot with all its power to heal or burn, exist forever, there comes an illumination where the sun and earth meet, a final burst of burning red orange fury reminding us that although endings are inevitable, they are necessary for rebirths, and when that time came, just when I switched on the light in the kitchen to open Abuelita's can of soup, it was probably then that she died.

The room smelled of Pine Sol and vomit and Abuelita had defecated the remains of her cancerous stomach. She had turned to the window and tried to speak, but her mouth remained open and speechless. I heard you, Abuelita, I said, stroking her cheek, I heard you. I opened the windows of the house and let the soup simmer and overboil on the stove. I turned the stove off and poured the soup down the sink. From the cabinet I got a tin basin, filled it with lukewarm water and carried it carefully to the room. I went to the linen closet and took out some modest bleached white towels. With the sacredness of a priest preparing his vestments, I unfolded the towels one by one on my shoulders. I removed the sheets and blankets from her bed and peeled off her thick flannel nightgown. I toweled her puzzled face, stretching out the wrinkles, removing the coils of her neck, toweled her shoulders and breasts. Then I changed the water. I returned to towel the creases of her stretch-marked stomach, her sporadic vaginal hairs, and her sagging thighs. I removed the lint from between her toes and noticed a mapped birthmark on the fold of her buttock. The scars on her back which were as thin as the life lines on the palms of her hands made me realize how little I really knew of Abuelita. I covered her with a thin blanket and went into the bathroom. I washed my hands, and turned on the tub faucets and watched the water pour into the tub with vitality and steam. When it was full, I turned off the water and undressed. Then, I went to get Abuelita.

She was not as heavy as I thought and when I carried her in my arms, her body fell into a V, and yet my legs were tired, shaky, and I felt as if the distance between the bedroom and bathroom was miles and years away. Amá, where are you?

I stepped into the bathtub one leg first, then the other. I bent my knees slowly to descend into the water slowly so I wouldn't scald her skin. There, there, Abuelita, I said, cradling her, smoothing her as we descended, I heard you. Her hair fell back and spread across the water like eagle's wings. The water in the tub overflowed and poured onto the tile of the floor. Then the moths came. Small, gray ones that came from her soul and out through her mouth fluttering to light, circling the single dull light bulb of the bathroom. Dying is lonely and I wanted to go to where the moths were, stay with her and plant chayotes whose vines would crawl up her fingers and into the clouds; I wanted to rest my head on her chest with her stroking my hair, telling me about the moths that lay within the soul and slowly eat the spirit up; I wanted to return to the waters of the womb with her so that we would never be alone again. I wanted. I wanted my Amá. I removed a few strands of hair from Abuelita's face and held her small light head within the hollow of my neck. The bathroom was filled with moths, and for the first time in a long time I cried, rocking us, crying for her, for me, for Amá, the sobs emerging from the depths of anguish, the misery of feeling half born, sobbing until finally the sobs rippled into circles and circles of sadness and relief. There, there, I said to Abuelita, rocking us gently, there, there.

### FOR ANALYSIS

**1.** Why do you think the observation that the **narrator** does not kiss people is repeated?

**2.** Why is it important that the old person with whom the narrator connects is a woman and not a man?

**3.** In what ways is the grandmother's death important to the narrator? Why, when the narrator holds her body at the end of the story, does she say that she rocks "us"?

### MAKING ARGUMENTS

Does the story read significantly differently if you do or don't believe that the moths at the end actually exist? How so? Make an argument one way or the other. What do you choose to believe?

### WRITING TOPIC

Reread "The Moths" and keep a reading log, tracking your emotions as you go. Then reflect on what elements of the story made you feel these ways.

### MAKING CONNECTIONS

**1.** Compare the relationships between the two elderly women and their caregivers in "The Moths" and Allegra Goodman's "Apple Cake" (p. 869). How are they similar? How are they different?

**2.** How does telling the story of an older woman's death from her **point of view** differ from telling it from the younger woman's point of view? What effects does each have? Why do you think the authors chose to tell their stories the way they did?

It is hard (though not impossible) to imagine two more different stories about the same thing, but Leslie Marmon Silko's and Allegra Goodman's stories manage to cover a lot of the same terrain while walking quite divergent paths. As you read these stories, consider how the characters in them think about death and mourning, how the rest of their lives are inextricably tied to their thoughts, and how the significance of death trumps both everything and nothing at the same time.

## LESLIE MARMON SILKO   (B. 1948)

# THE MAN TO SEND
# RAIN CLOUDS   1981

They found him under a big cottonwood tree. His Levi jacket and pants were faded light blue so that he had been easy to find. The big cottonwood tree stood apart from a small grove of winterbare cottonwoods which grew in the wide, sandy arroyo. He had been dead for a day or more, and the sheep had wandered and scattered up and down the arroyo. Leon and his brother-in-law, Ken, gathered the sheep and left them in the pen at the sheep camp before they returned to the cottonwood tree. Leon waited under the tree while Ken drove the truck through the deep sand to the edge of the arroyo. He squinted up at the sun and unzipped his jacket—it sure was hot for this time of year. But high and northwest the blue mountains were still in snow. Ken came sliding down the low, crumbling bank about fifty yards down, and he was bringing the red blanket.

Before they wrapped the old man, Leon took a piece of string out of his pocket and tied a small gray feather in the old man's long white hair. Ken gave him the paint. Across the brown wrinkled forehead he drew a streak of white and along the high cheekbones he drew a strip of blue paint. He paused and watched Ken throw pinches of corn meal and pollen into the wind that fluttered the small gray feather. Then Leon painted with yellow under the old man's broad nose, and finally, when he had painted green across the chin, he smiled.

"Send us rain clouds, Grandfather." They laid the bundle in the back of the pickup and covered it with a heavy tarp before they started back to the pueblo.

They turned off the highway onto the sandy pueblo road. Not long after they passed the store and post office they saw Father Paul's car coming toward them. When he recognized their faces he slowed his car and waved them to stop. The young priest rolled down the car window.

"Did you find old Teofilo?" he asked loudly.                                                                                 5

Leon stopped the truck. "Good morning, Father. We were just out to the sheep camp. Everything is O.K. now."

"Thank God for that. Teofilo is a very old man. You really shouldn't allow him to stay at the sheep camp alone."

"No, he won't do that any more now."

"Well, I'm glad you understand. I hope I'll be seeing you at Mass this week— we missed you last Sunday. See if you can get old Teofilo to come with you." The priest smiled and waved at them as they drove away.

Louise and Teresa were waiting. The table was set for lunch, and the coffee 10 was boiling on the black iron stove. Leon looked at Louise and then at Teresa.

"We found him under a cottonwood tree in the big arroyo near sheep camp. I guess he sat down to rest in the shade and never got up again." Leon walked toward the old man's bed. The red plaid shawl had been shaken and spread carefully over the bed, and a new brown flannel shirt and pair of stiff new Levi's were arranged neatly beside the pillow. Louise held the screen door open while Leon and Ken carried in the red blanket. He looked small and shriveled, and after they dressed him in the new shirt and pants he seemed more shrunken.

It was noontime now because the church bells rang the Angelus. They ate the beans with hot bread, and nobody said anything until after Teresa poured the coffee.

Ken stood up and put on his jacket. "I'll see about the gravediggers. Only the top layer of soil is frozen. I think it can be ready before dark."

Leon nodded his head and finished his coffee. After Ken had been gone for a while, the neighbors and clanspeople came quietly to embrace Teofilo's family and to leave food on the table because the gravediggers would come to eat when they were finished.

The sky in the west was full of pale yellow light. Louise stood outside with 15 her hands in the pockets of Leon's green army jacket that was too big for her. The funeral was over, and the old men had taken their candles and medicine bags and were gone. She waited until the body was laid into the pickup before she said anything to Leon. She touched his arm, and he noticed that her hands were still dusty from the corn meal that she had sprinkled around the old man. When she spoke, Leon could not hear her.

"What did you say? I didn't hear you."

"I said that I had been thinking about something."

"About what?"

"About the priest sprinkling holy water for Grandpa. So he won't be thirsty."

Leon stared at the new moccasins that Teofilo had made for the ceremo- 20 nial dances in the summer. They were nearly hidden by the red blanket. It was getting colder, and the wind pushed gray dust down the narrow pueblo road. The sun was approaching the long mesa where it disappeared during the winter. Louise stood there shivering and watching his face. Then he zipped up his jacket and opened the truck door. "I'll see if he's there."

Ken stopped the pickup at the church, and Leon got out; and then Ken drove down the hill to the graveyard where people were waiting. Leon knocked at the old carved door with its symbols of the Lamb. While he waited he looked up at the twin bells from the king of Spain with the last sunlight pouring around them in their tower.

The priest opened the door and smiled when he saw who it was. "Come in! What brings you here this evening?"

The priest walked toward the kitchen, and Leon stood with his cap in his hand, playing with the earflaps and examining the living room—the brown sofa, the green armchair, and the brass lamp that hung down from the ceiling by links of chain. The priest dragged a chair out of the kitchen and offered it to Leon.

"No thank you, Father. I only came to ask you if you would bring your holy water to the graveyard."

The priest turned away from Leon and looked out the window at the patio 25 full of shadows and the dining-room windows of the nuns' cloister across the patio. The curtains were heavy, and the light from within faintly penetrated; it was impossible to see the nuns inside eating supper. "Why didn't you tell me he was dead? I could have brought the Last Rites anyway."

Leon smiled. "It wasn't necessary, Father."

The priest stared down at his scuffed brown loafers and the worn hem of his cassock. "For a Christian burial it was necessary."

His voice was distant, and Leon thought that his blue eyes looked tired.

"It's O.K. Father, we just want him to have plenty of water."

The priest sank down into the green chair and picked up a glossy missionary 30 magazine. He turned the colored pages full of lepers and pagans without looking at them.

"You know I can't do that, Leon. There should have been the Last Rites and a funeral Mass at the very least."

Leon put on his green cap and pulled the flaps down over his ears. "It's getting late, Father. I've got to go."

When Leon opened the door Father Paul stood up and said, "Wait." He left the room and came back wearing a long brown overcoat. He followed Leon out the door and across the dim churchyard to the adobe steps in front of the church. They both stooped to fit through the low adobe entrance. And when they started down the hill to the graveyard only half of the sun was visible above the mesa.

The priest approached the grave slowly, wondering how they had managed to dig into the frozen ground, and then he remembered that this was New Mexico, and saw the pile of cold loose sand beside the hole. The people stood close to each other with little clouds of steam puffing from their faces. The priest looked at them and saw a pile of jackets, gloves, and scarves in the yellow, dry tumbleweeds that grew in the graveyard. He looked at the red blanket, not sure that Teofilo was so small, wondering if it wasn't some perverse Indian trick—something they did in March to ensure a good harvest—wondering if maybe old Teofilo was actually at sheep camp corraling the sheep for the night. But there he was, facing into a cold dry wind and squinting at the last sunlight, ready to bury a red wool blanket while the faces of his parishioners were in shadow with the last warmth of the sun on their backs.

His fingers were stiff, and it took him a long time to twist the lid off the holy water. Drops of water fell on the red blanket and soaked into dark icy spots. He sprinkled the grave and the water disappeared almost before it touched the dim, cold sand; it reminded him of something—he tried to remember what it was, because he thought if he could remember he might understand this. He sprinkled more water; he shook the container until it was empty, and the water fell through the light from sundown like August rain that fell while the sun was still shining, almost disappearing before it touched the wilted squash flowers.

The wind pulled at the priest's brown Franciscan robe and swirled away the corn meal and pollen that had been sprinkled on the blanket. They lowered the bundle into the ground, and they didn't bother to untie the stiff pieces of new rope that were tied around the ends of the blanket. The sun was gone, and over on the highway the eastbound lane was full of headlights. The priest walked away slowly. Leon watched him climb the hill, and when he had disappeared within the tall, thick walls, Leon turned to look up at the high blue mountains in the deep snow that reflected a faint red light from the west. He felt good because it was finished, and he was happy about the sprinkling of the holy water; now the old man could send them big thunderclouds for sure.

## FOR ANALYSIS

**1.** Why do Leon and Ken not tell Father Paul that Teofilo is dead? Why do they later ask Father Paul to bring holy water to the funeral?

**2.** Two rituals associated with death—the Native American and the Roman Catholic— seem to conflict. Why does Teofilo's family seek the priest's help? Why does Father Paul agree to help them?

**3.** Although the story is mostly told from the **point of view** of an omniscient narrator, at one point we share two characters' thoughts. What effect does this shift generate?

**4.** Why do you think Silko included the detail (in the last paragraph) about the automobile lights on the highway?

**5.** Why does Leon feel good at the end of the story?

## MAKING ARGUMENTS

Why do so many if not all cultures have elaborate, codified rituals for handling death? Make an argument based on research, the story, and your own thoughts on what death means to people and to communities and on how rituals and processes plug into those meanings.

## WRITING TOPIC

"The Man to Send Rain Clouds" remains silent about the characters' spirituality: there is no **narrator** commenting on whether their rituals and beliefs are effective or true. How did you respond to the different **points of view** on death and the natural world presented in the story? How might the characters respond to your points of view about the world? Where did you get them?

**ALLEGRA GOODMAN**   (B. 1967)

# APPLE CAKE   2014

Her sisters flinched because she was the youngest, but she looked so old. Jeanne was just seventy-four, and no one had ever thought . . . They didn't speak of it. They would not allow themselves, but Helen was eighty, Sylvia seventy-eight. They'd married first, been mothers first. They were older. They should have been frailer. How could Jeanne be first to go?

Their baby sister lay propped up on pillows. Jeanne, who had celebrated her first birthday in eyelet lace, a slice of cake on the tray of her high chair, and her sisters on either side. Their living doll, with her blond curls and round blue eyes. They'd pulled her in their wagon over grass bumpy with apples from the apple tree. It was dreadful to approach her now—her hair just wisps, her voice nearly gone, her cough breaking every sentence. Horror, pity, shame. They felt all that at once, to see her now and to remember her as she had been. They were sorry and they were glad to feel so alive, their steps firm in their low-heeled shoes. Their own bodies sound, rejoicing with each breath. What a terrible thing to say! They would never have admitted it. Their own strength, their own good fortune and their guilt—they could never put it into words. No one should!

"How are you, darling?" Helen asked.

Jeanne didn't answer.

"Did you see the orchid Richard sent?" Sylvia turned a tall white orchid  5 toward Jeanne's chair.

Jeanne glanced at her nephew's gift. There were so many. Blossoms filled the first-floor music studio where Jeanne had to live because she couldn't take the stairs. The orchid from Richard, the sunflowers from her daughter-in-law, Melanie, the roses from the Auerbachs next door. Wherever she looked, she saw arrangements from neighbors, nieces, grandchildren. The piano tuner had sent a basket of mums, which were losing petals, shedding everywhere. The cards said, "All our love," and "Thinking of you," and even "Healing light." This from her niece Wendy, the music therapist.

"Look how beautiful they are," Sylvia said. She meant, Do you see how much everybody loves you?

Jeanne made a face. The flowers depressed her, especially those that were already wilting. When she looked at the mums, she felt she wasn't dying fast enough.

Her sisters sat chattering about the heat, the traffic, and the rain. They were afraid to leave her alone—she had lived by herself for fifteen years, a widow. She lived alone because she liked it. Her late husband had been difficult, to say the least.

According to Jeanne's sons, her Tudor home was much too big. According to  10 Phoebe, her twenty-year-old granddaughter, Jeanne's house wasted energy. For years, everybody had been telling Jeanne to move. Now nobody mentioned it.

These were the privileges of hospice. You didn't have to blow insulation into your walls. No one suggested assisted living or criticized your carbon footprint, which would disappear entirely in weeks, or even days. On the other hand, everyone came to see you and confide in you. Jeanne didn't believe in God or any kind of afterlife, but lung cancer made believers of her family, so that she, who despised superstition, became a touchstone and talisman to the rest of them. Her sisters were always pressing her cold hands.

Helen told Jeanne, "Pam and Wendy are coming up this weekend."

Jeanne nodded.

"Richard's coming, too," Sylvia said. Her only child was having a terrible time, switching jobs, divorcing, and she felt he deserved credit for dropping everything to see his aunt. Pam was coming up from Providence, and Wendy lived in Brooklyn, but Richard had to drive all the way from Philly.

Jeanne closed her eyes and listened to her sisters say, She's tired. She's 15 exhausted. She heard them echo and repeat each other. She has to rest. Yes, she has to rest. She was looking at the sun, red through her closed eyelids.

The autumn sun felt good, but darkness was better, because everybody left except Shawn, the night nurse. Then Jeanne lay awake in her rented hospital bed and listened to symphonies and choral rhapsodies, quartets, and concertos on WGBH, Boston's classical radio. When she heard a solo violin, her fingers curled reflexively; her left hand knew.

Her sons had pushed away her music stands and moved the piano to make room for Shawn, now dozing in his straight-backed chair. Jeanne assumed he had another job during the day, and she saw that he was trying to study as well. He was always reading a textbook, but he never got very far. Just before dawn, the book slipped off his lap onto the floor.

Shawn started up and saw Jeanne staring at him from her bed. "I'm sorry. I'm sorry. Ma'am." He bent down for the book.

She said, "You rest."

"No, I'm here if you need something."                                               20

"Sleep."

His eyes widened. There was no way he was going back to sleep. He'd lose his job.

"I'll let you know if anything happens," Jeanne said.

Her sons and their wives came to see her every afternoon. First, Steve and Andrea would sit by her side. Andrea showed videos on her phone of their huge boys, born just eighteen months apart, lion cubs who played high-school soccer. They were coming to see Jeanne right after regionals. Andrea was going to drive them straight from the field, cleats and all.

Next came Dan and Melanie. They had just the one daughter, Phoebe. Melanie 25 had gained fifty pounds when she was pregnant. She never had another child, and she never lost the weight. "Phoebe sends her love," Melanie said.

Dan explained, "She wants to be here, but she won't fly."

Jeanne tried to picture her ecological granddaughter biking from Ann Arbor. She imagined Phoebe's long blond hair streaming out from under her helmet. "Her schoolwork is more important."

"Actually, she's taking the semester off," Melanie said.

"What was that?"

Dan frowned, upset with Melanie for mentioning this. "She says she wants 30 to work with her hands."

"Preferably in the dirt," Melanie said. "She wants to be a farmer and write poetry."

Jeanne couldn't help laughing. Her breath came short and quick. For a few moments, she couldn't breathe at all, and then she couldn't see. With help from her day nurse, Lorraine, Jeanne sat up, and wiped the tears from her eyes.

"I don't think dropping out is funny," Dan said.

"She isn't dropping out," Melanie said. "She just needs a little time."

Jeanne croaked, "Let her do what she wants." 35

Dan and Melanie looked crushed, and Jeanne felt sorry for them—but why did everyone expect her to be so concerned?

Illness did not bring out the angel in her. At first, she'd appreciated visitors, but as she lingered on they didn't leave. Her sisters kept bringing in their middle-aged children—for what? Good-byes? Advice? Some final blessing? Sylvia begged, "Tell Richard to stop smoking!"

Oh, really, Jeanne thought. That's what I am. Exhibit A. She studied her ruddy nephew. His wife had just won custody of the children, and the dog. "I enjoyed smoking," Jeanne said. "Your mother did, too."

Sylvia shrank back as though Jeanne had struck her, but she said nothing. It was too late, apparently, to retaliate.

Jeanne's sons appeared, and they looked terrible, both of them. Dan wore 40 wire-rimmed glasses. He was thick in the middle and he had hardly any hair. It amused and saddened Jeanne to see him look so much like his late father. As for Steve, he had a bad back, so he had to walk around the room. He made Jeanne dizzy, pacing up and down.

Her daughters-in-law got emotional—especially Melanie, herself a doctor. Please, Jeanne thought. I lost my parents when I was half your age. We're all over fifty here.

She pretended to sleep, and then she really did drop off. When she woke, her sisters were hovering over her. Some of us have overstayed our welcome, Jeanne thought. And then, with sudden shock, No: I'm the one. That would be me.

Sardonic as she was, husk that she was, she shuddered at the thought of disappearing, of losing consciousness and irony, her music, her unrenovated house, her sun. Cancer had consumed her body, drugs clouded her mind. Even so, Jeanne held on. Barely eating, scarcely speaking, she endured. Her nieces and her nephew sat with her. Wendy sang and strummed her battered guitar. Jeanne's soccer-playing grandsons arrived. Zach cracked his knuckles. Nate jiggled his right leg. The boys were like a pair of jackrabbits, all ears and feet.

The hospice nurses said that Jeanne would drift away in a day or two, but four days passed, and then a fifth. It was awkward, because her sons had to take off work, and her grandchildren could miss only so many days of school. Should they stay or should they go? Did it make sense to return home and then come right back for the funeral?

Helen said, "We need a plan." Oldest and bossiest, she told Jeanne, "We need 45
to know your wishes."

"To get up," Jeanne said immediately.

Later, in the hall, Sylvia turned on Helen. "How can you speak to her like that?"

Helen was amazed at the question. "Well, we can't ask her when she's gone!"

Sylvia began to cry.

"Don't get hysterical," Helen snapped. 50

"I'm not hysterical. I have feelings. Be considerate."

"I am considerate," Helen said. "I'm doing for Jeanne what I hope someone
would do for me. If I didn't have a living will."

Weeping, Sylvia retreated to the dining room to criticize her husband, Lew.

That afternoon, at Jeanne's bedside, Helen appealed to her daughter Pam, a
tax attorney. "She left no instructions."

At the word "instructions," Jeanne opened her eyes. It was disconcerting the 55
way she did that. Just as Helen slipped into the past tense, Jeanne roused herself.
Then everyone hurried to her side again.

Sons and daughters-in-law watched Jeanne's face.

"Melanie," Jeanne whispered.

"What is it?" Melanie asked. Already the tears. Always the tears.

"Half a bagel," Jeanne said.

That sent them off again, scrambling to Rosenfeld's. The two couples took 60
Dan's Volvo to Newton Centre, even as they told each other there was no way.
Melanie, the doctor, said, "She'll never eat a whole half a bagel."

"Does that matter?" Dan demanded, as he drove.

"No," Melanie said. "Of course not."

"If my mother wants half a bagel, she's getting half a bagel."

Melanie said, "No poppy. She could aspirate the seeds."

"Get her an egg bagel," Steve suggested from the back seat. 65

Andrea corrected him. "She doesn't like egg. She likes plain."

By the time they returned with a dozen bagels, two large containers of whipped
cream cheese, a side of lox, and a chocolate babka, Jeanne was sleeping again.

The nurses stopped predicting when she would drift away. Now they said
that only Jeanne would know when it was time. Lorraine suggested that everybody share a moment. Was there unfinished business in the family? Sometimes people had to forgive each other before they could let go.

Tremulous, angelic, Sylvia told Helen, "I forgive you."

"Oh, for God's sake," Helen said. There was nothing to forgive. There was 70
simply the great divide between them: Helen told the truth, while Sylvia tried
to paper over everything.

"She never listens to me," Sylvia told the family assembled at Jeanne's bedside.
"I'm invisible to her."

Amazed at this mixed metaphor, Helen said, "Obviously I see you."

At this point, Dan spoke up. "I think we need to focus on the time we have
together."

"Amen," Lorraine said, and everyone was jealous, because she liked Dan best.

Look at you, Jeanne thought. All vying for attention! Even so, she forgave 75 everybody. Good night, she told them silently. Farewell. She wished that she could send a blanket dispensation. After which she could stay and they would leave.

In fact, she looked a little better. She drank some juice and tried a bite of toast. She asked for her violin. She couldn't play it. She couldn't even open the case, but she kept it near her on the window ledge next to her bed. She wanted her instrument where she could see it.

Like a cat, Jeanne slept most of the day, but, waking, she seemed a heightened, sharper version of herself. When Pam drove up from Providence for the second time, Jeanne asked why she'd never married. When Melanie sniffled, Jeanne said, "Stop feeling sorry for yourself."

Obviously, Melanie was sad because she was afraid of her own death. Jeanne could see it in her eyes. Jeanne's sisters were even worse. They looked at her and thought only of their mortality.

But this was cruel! Not just unkind. Untrue. Jeanne's sisters thought nothing of themselves. Sylvia berated Lew all the way home to Weston. Helen stayed up late in Brookline, baking. Lemon squares, and brownies, pecan bars, apple cake, sandy almond cookies. Alone in her kitchen, she wrapped these offerings in waxed paper and froze them in tight-lipped containers.

Her husband, Charles, ventured, "You should get some rest." 80

What a thing to say! How could anybody rest? Helen had not pursued a career like Jeanne, the music teacher, or three successive husbands, like Sylvia. No, Helen had always been a homemaker. Now her family needed sustenance, so she doubled every recipe and froze half. After all, there would be a memorial service, and shivah afterward. Helen could already picture Jeanne's students descending with their parents. Sylvia hadn't baked in years, because Lew was diabetic. As for Melanie and Andrea—what would they throw together? A box of doughnut holes? No. Helen was the baker of the family. What she felt could not be purchased. She grieved from scratch.

And yet Jeanne kept on living. Her sisters held vigil; her sons came up on weekends. In the kitchen, her family nibbled Helen's lemon squares. Melanie urged brownies on the nurses. "Take these," she told Lorraine. "We can't eat them all, but Helen won't stop baking."

"Sweetheart," Lorraine said, "everybody mourns in her own way."

Helen mourned her sister deeply. She arrived each day with shopping bags. Her cake was tender with sliced apples, but her almond cookies crumbled at the touch. Her pecan bars were awful, sticky-sweet and hard enough to break your teeth. They remained untouched in the dining room, because Helen never threw good food away.

Sometimes Jeanne asked in a confused voice why everyone had come. And 85 then there were moments when she remembered and took charge. She ordered Melanie to take all the plants and flowers to Newton-Wellesley Hospital. She told Wendy to put her guitar away. After this, she asked to speak to her sons alone. She lay in bed and watched Dan and Steve approach. This is it, the two of them were thinking. "We'll see," Jeanne said.

Guilty, nervous, Steve asked, "What did you say?"

"These are my wishes," Jeanne said.

Dan pulled up a chair, but Steve paced up and down.

"Stop that."

"What are your wishes? "Dan asked.                                                    90

"First of all"—Jeanne looked at Steve—"don't pace. Second of all . . ."

They waited.

"No funeral."

"A private burial?" Dan ventured.

"No burial."                                                                          95

Astonished, Steve said, "You have the plot." He might as well have added, And it's paid for.

"I don't want it."

Steve protested, "But it's next to Dad."

"Yes, I am aware of that."

Dan's glasses were fogging up. He took them off and wiped them on the bottom   100
of his sweater. "You shared your life with Dad for thirty-eight years."

"Exactly."

If Jeanne had another plan, she did not reveal it to her sons. If she had a good word to say about their father, she did not say it. Fiercely, she insisted that there would be no burial. No memorial. Privately, she decided not to die.

Jeanne's voice grew stronger as she kept living. Outside, the leaves were turning. AAA Sparkling Windows and Gutters called to schedule a cleaning. Still, she endured.

Uneasily, the family dispersed. Jeanne's grandsons returned to school. Jeanne's sons and their wives went back to work. Even Melanie stopped crying. Her mother-in-law was a medical miracle. She was going to outlast them all. Only the nurses kept the faith. Lorraine said that sometimes older people held on for an occasion. They willed themselves to stay alive for one final milestone. A wedding. A grandchild's graduation.

No one could think of a milestone, apart from Richard's divorce. Nobody   105
was marrying or graduating. The next family birthday was in May. Everyone had shared a moment. Nieces and nephew and grandchildren had . . . Wait! They'd forgotten Phoebe, writing poetry in Michigan, working with her hands, refusing to fly.

Melanie and Dan spoke to Phoebe on the phone. They called her from Jeanne's house, and then Melanie called again from the car as Dan drove home. She talked to Phoebe about respect and compassion—thinking about others, not just about the earth.

Meanwhile, Helen and Sylvia kept coming every day, baleful, fearful, sorry for their lot. Helen wanted to bring her rabbi to the house.

"No rabbis," Jeanne said. "No members of the clergy."

"Well, what would you suggest?" Helen demanded.

Sylvia cried, "How dare you scream at her?"  110

"Only one of us is screaming," Helen said.

Sylvia left the room, and then she left the house. Maybe she raised her voice at times. Maybe she felt overwhelmed. The situation was overwhelming. Jeanne's death unimaginable, and now—even worse—postponed. There was nothing to be done, and yet Helen managed to do it. As usual, she took over everything. Sylvia was up all night, she was so upset. "It's all about Helen," Sylvia told Lew. "Her plan, her rabbi, her stale old pecan bars."

Columbus Day, when the family gathered at the house, Sylvia arrived with fresh-baked apple cake, warm from her oven, fragrant in its pan.

Heads up, suddenly alert, Jeanne's huge grandsons sniffed the cake. Can I have a piece? Can I have some?

In the kitchen, Sylvia turned the cake out on a plate and sliced big wedges  115 for the boys. Then Dan and Melanie had pieces, as did Steve and Andrea. In the dining room, Helen's defrosted brownies, pecan bars, and almond cookies sat undisturbed. Charles did take a brownie out of loyalty, but he slipped into the kitchen for Sylvia's cake.

"I smell baked apples," Jeanne whispered in the studio. The bed seemed to swallow her up, and yet she spoke.

"It's my recipe," Helen said. "I gave that recipe to Sylvia twenty years ago."

"Yes, I remember," Jeanne said. "She bakes a very good apple cake."

"I bake the same one! I brought you apple cake last week!"

"I know, but I like hers better," Jeanne said.  120

Helen marched into the kitchen and gazed at the last crumbs of Sylvia's cake. Zach and Nate were eating standing up. Melanie and Dan, Steve and Andrea, were eating at the table. Then Helen caught her own husband throwing away a paper plate.

"*Et tu*, Charles," Lew said.

"You used my recipe," Helen told Sylvia.

"Yes, I did," Sylvia replied, with such an air that even Zach and Nate knew she meant, What's it to you?

The next day, Sylvia brought her homemade jelly rolls, soft sponges rolled  125 with tangy apricot, dusted on top with coconut flakes. She had not baked jelly rolls in fifteen years, and the whole family fell upon them. Even Lew, so careful with his diet, took a tiny piece. Only Helen and Jeanne abstained. Helen would not, and Jeanne could not partake.

She was sick of visitors, but she made an effort to say a few words to each one. She advised her younger son, Dan, to look into hair-replacement therapy. She told Melanie to try antidepressants. Maybe they would help her lose some weight. As for Steve and Andrea, they were neglecting music. Neither of their boys played an instrument. Jeanne told Andrea to look into marching band, since the boys loved sports so much. Or, if they refused to practice, there were youth choirs. With some ear training, they might learn to sing.

Andrea was speechless for a moment. Then she said slowly, "I realize that music is important to you."

"My life," Jeanne whispered.

"Would you like to see your students?" Steve asked.

Jeanne thought of her young violinists—George, with his sweet tone and his 130 tendency to rush. Sophie, who forgot to count. Wyatt had a good ear but didn't work at all. Emma would not relax her tight goat-trill vibrato.

Andrea said, "Would you like some of them to come and play for you?"

"God, no," Jeanne said.

Sisters, sons, daughters-in-law were always begging to know what they could do. Jeanne gazed out the window at her sugar maple, and she told them what she wanted, since they asked.

They carried her into the garden, where she could see the trees. Tethered to her wheelchair and to her oxygen, she turned her face up to the fiery maples, the gold oaks, the breezy sky. How good the world smelled, the fresh damp grass.

She leaned back and she smiled, and her family thought she was at peace. 135 They were wrong. She was not at peace; quite the opposite. She was happy. Full of plans.

She told Helen she would see the rabbi. She would have a conversation with him. "Thank you," Helen said.

Rabbi Lieberman, when he arrived the next day, looked about twelve. He could have come for lessons. He wore a suit, but he seemed to Jeanne not much bigger than a child.

"Jeanne wanted to have a conversation with you," Helen said.

Jeanne told the rabbi, "You should know that I'm an atheist."

The rabbi nodded. "Yes, I understand."                                                   140

Jeanne added, "I don't have time for organized religion."

"You're in good company," the rabbi said.

Jeanne frowned to find him so accommodating. Didn't rabbis believe anything anymore? "But you believe in God," she said.

"I do."

Jeanne looked at Helen. "That's a relief," she said.                                       145

"You see?" Helen told her sister, and she meant, You see, it's a relief, a comfort to think of the Creator. "You see?"

"Belief is very personal," the rabbi said.

"I agree," Jeanne said. "That's why we should keep it to ourselves."

The rabbi smiled.

"My family would like to bury me."                                                        150

Helen broke in. "You know that's not true."

"They want to bury me next to my late husband," Jeanne said. "I would like to go somewhere else."

"Where would you like to go?"

"I'd like to be scattered," Jeanne said.

"Cremated?" Rabbi Lieberman asked delicately.                                             155

"That's not Jewish," Helen declared.

Jeanne looked at the rabbi, who seemed reluctant to speak.

"It's not our tradition," the rabbi said at last.

"Good."

"And how will we visit you?" Helen demanded. 160

Jeanne said, "Why do you assume that I want visitors?"

Helen's tears startled Jeanne. Not you, she thought. Helen never cried.

"I would visit," Helen said.

"Oh, fine," Jeanne said. "Go ahead and bury me. I won't mind."

"Thank you," Helen whispered. 165

After all, Jeanne reasoned, she would never feel it. She wouldn't even know. "Do what you want," she told her sister. "Cover me with rocks."

They wore her down. They came in shifts. Jeanne closed her eyes and listened to the house. Doors closing. Water running. The crackle of crumbs flying up the vacuum cleaner. Raised voices. Furious words. Helen baked mandelbrot from their mother Esther's recipe. Sylvia countered with Esther's honey cake.

Jeanne tasted none of it, but she remained the cause, the crux of the matter, the still fixed point of the entire family. How long had she been sleeping? When would she wake? She was as surprised as anyone to find herself alive each morning. She opened her eyes and everyone turned to her as to an oracle. She did her best to keep them busy. "Take a day off," she told Helen. "Serve on a committee." She turned to Sylvia. "Bring me another apple cake."

"You're angry at me," Helen told Jeanne later when they were alone.

Jeanne shook her head. 170

"You're angry because I have beliefs."

Jeanne said, "I don't hold any of your beliefs against you." She said this, but she added silently, I do think less of you.

"Sylvia covers her apples with brown sugar," Helen said. "She sugars everything."

"Of course she does," Jeanne said. After all, people liked sweet things. Anything sweet and easy. The bitter, dark, and complicated could not compete. This had always pained her before, but she enjoyed the injustice of it now. Joy mixed with fear as she looked out the window and saw scarlet trees. How dazzling the world was. How strange.

She heard voices at her door and saw a beautiful girl, dressed all in rags. At 175 last, her granddaughter, Phoebe, had arrived with her gold hair trailing down her back. She'd come on the bus from Michigan, and she'd brought a young man, a huntsman in a rough leather shirt.

Jeanne clasped her granddaughter's hand, but Phoebe started back, shocked by Jeanne's ghastly face.

Oh, you're afraid of me, Jeanne thought. Grandmother, what big eyes you have, what withered cheeks.

"Sharp nails," Phoebe murmured, looking down at Jeanne's claws.

The wolf inside Jeanne whispered, The better to eat you with, my dear. But Jeanne said, "Introduce me."

Phoebe didn't understand. 180

Jeanne turned to Phoebe's deerslayer. "What's your name?"

"I'm Christian."

Jeanne had no breath, but laughter racked her body anyway. She held on to Phoebe, and she began to shake.

Dan and Melanie did not find Phoebe's boyfriend funny, nor did they laugh about his name. He was twenty-eight years old, without a full-time job. He said he wanted to raise blueberries. They did not appreciate meeting him like this. They did not appreciate meeting him at all. He sat on the couch with his arms wrapped around Phoebe, as though she belonged to him. They couldn't even have a conversation with their daughter. And yet Christian withstood every hint and every disapproving look. He nuzzled their only child, and he ate. Unblinking, he finished off Helen's pecan bars. He devoured Sylvia's apple cake.

Now that Phoebe had arrived, Jeanne was supposed to let go, but she stayed 185 alive to gaze at Phoebe's lovely face. "Where's your violin?" she asked.

Phoebe looked down at her hiking boots.

"You sold it, didn't you?"

Phoebe began to cry.

"It doesn't matter. In the grand scheme of things . . ."

Phoebe waited for Jeanne. Then she said, "What is it?" 190

Oh, who can remember, Jeanne thought. Maybe she was sleeping. It was hard to tell. She could have been dreaming, or talking in her sleep. "You played well, but other people play much better."

"Thanks, Grandma," Phoebe said, and suddenly Jeanne saw her as a little child, golden-haired, sitting on the beach. She could see Phoebe sand-dusted in her bathing suit. The rippling tide around her, deep-blue waves, white foam.

Jeanne lost consciousness the next day. Dan and Steve kissed their mother's forehead. Once more, everybody said goodbye, but another day passed, and then a third. Finally, at night, when she was all alone except for Shawn, Jeanne cried out.

"Mrs. Rubinstein!" He tried to make her comfortable, but she fought him. She didn't want help. She wanted to open her eyes, to rise up from her bed. She wanted music and she wanted apples. She wanted to touch the sandy beach, to feel summer's heat. She wanted all this, but she couldn't have it. She died because she couldn't breathe.

In the morning, Jeanne's sons tried to make arrangements. Everybody sat in 195 the dining room, and Helen insisted that her rabbi lead prayers.

Sylvia turned on her. "She said no memorial service. You know she hated organized religion!"

"Stop shrieking at me," Helen said.

"We are honoring Jeanne's life, not yours."

Dan intervened. "A simple burial."

"No service," Steve added. 200

"But she didn't want a burial," Sylvia reminded them.

Helen drew herself up. "She said fine."

"Because you pressured her!"

"I would never pressure anyone," Helen said.

"Oh, really!"                                                                          205

"She told me fine."

"Nobody else heard her."

"The rabbi heard."

"Because the two of you were pressuring her into it."

"For the last time, she wasn't pressured. She said yes. Bury me."          210

"Because she was dying! That's why she agreed."

Even as they argued in the dining room, the rental company came to collect Jeanne's cannisters of oxygen. Someone was on the phone about the hospital bed, now stripped bare.

"She wanted to be scattered," Sylvia declared.

"She said, Bury me. She told the rabbi."

"She didn't believe in rabbis!"                                                       215

"Does that mean he never existed?" Helen shot back. "Does that mean the conversation never happened?"

"Stop," Dan begged them, but they would not stop.

"As far as you're concerned," Sylvia said, "the only conversations that happen are the ones happening to you."

Now Helen lost her temper entirely. "I asked her to make plans, and you accused me of having no feelings! I talked about instructions, because I knew this was going to happen!"

"She stated her wishes a thousand times." Sylvia spoke with resolve. "She said    220
she wanted to be scattered."

"That is what she said," Dan admitted.

"She never wavered," Sylvia told Helen.

"She changed her mind!" Helen cried out, but no one believed her. Once, Helen had been the sane one. Now they treated her as though she were delusional. Sylvia had begun the insurrection. She'd waged this war for weeks. Helen's voice broke, even as she appealed to them all. "Jeanne talked to the rabbi and she said, Bury me, and that's the truth!"

Sylvia fixed her eyes on Helen. "Don't get hysterical."

But of course it wasn't up to them. Dan and Steve made all the plans. They    225
interpreted their mother's wishes. There would be no burial, just a celebration of Jeanne's life.

Privately, their wives spoke to Sylvia and Helen. They said that the reception after the service would be catered, and for the sake of the family they requested no homemade desserts. They asked Jeanne's sisters to promise. No cookies, no pecan bars. Absolutely no cake.

"I will do whatever you decide," Helen said with dignity.

"And so will I," Sylvia said.

Helen added, "I would never use an occasion like this to call attention to myself."

No rabbi spoke at the celebration of Jeanne's life. Jeanne's student Emma    230
Kantor played Bach, and Dan spoke about how Jeanne's music had filled the

house. Steve talked about what he had learned from his mother: "Don't quit. Don't feel sorry for yourself. Don't just stand there, do something." These were the lessons he remembered, although Jeanne's actual words had been "Don't pace."

In the front row of the funeral chapel, Sylvia sat wearing tinted glasses. She didn't think that she could speak. However, when the time came she walked up to the lectern and the words began to come. She'd written them all down on college-ruled paper.

"All my friends were jealous when she was born," Sylvia said. "But I didn't even let them touch her. She was a perfect baby and an angel. From the time she was born, she was my special charge. I used to dress her and play with her. I was her teacher when we played school on the porch. And this is why . . . this is why it's so difficult . . . impossible to . . ."

Sylvia broke down, and her son rushed to the lectern to comfort her, which made her cry even more. How could he keep smoking after all this? How could his wife, his college sweetheart, leave him?

Lew was standing. He helped her take her seat, and she sat between the two of them, her husband and her son, and the tears kept coming—until Helen began to speak.

"It is perhaps appropriate that I speak last, because I am the oldest," Helen 235 said. "And yet I have no monopoly on my sister. Like every human, she belonged to many people, not just one. She had parents." Helen stared straight at Sylvia. "She had two older sisters. She was a beloved member of our family. Daughter, sister, mother, cousin, friend. She was a musician. She was a teacher who spent countless hours instructing children. She was not sentimental, but she was giving."

Now Sylvia took off her glasses. Now she wiped the last tears from her eyes.

"She did not love tradition," Helen said, "but in her final days she spoke of God."

"Not true!" Sylvia whispered to Lew.

"She talked about belief."

Louder, Sylvia whispered to her husband, "That's just not true!" 240

As Helen spoke, Sylvia rattled her notes, her own words left unsaid. She wanted to stand up and finish her eulogy. She wanted to deliver her bright version of Jeanne's life, the true picture, unvarnished with religion, but it was too late. Already Helen was speaking about eternity. Already she was reciting Kaddish.

Sylvia wanted to cry out and stop the prayer. She whispered loud enough for those around her to hear, "This is not what Jeanne wanted!" Apart from that, she suffered in silence. She would not ruin the memorial. She would never make a scene.

To close the service Jeanne's twelve-year-old student, George Leong, played the Meditation on a Theme from "Thaïs." He didn't rush until the last cascading phrases at the end. Horse knows the way, Jeanne would have said.

After the celebration, the family convened at Jeanne's house to sit shivah for one day. No one could take off another week. Silent, staring, Helen watched the caterers serve quiche and crudités and sweet noodle kugel in a silver chafing dish.

Fresh-fruit platters stood in for dessert, along with factory-made cookies and weak coffee.

In the living room, Melanie and Andrea tried to comfort friends and neigh- 245 bors who were shaken by Jeanne's passing. Several confided that Jeanne's sudden death had prompted them to enjoy life while they could. The Auerbachs next door had decided to tour the Galápagos Islands. After that, they hoped to see the northern lights. They had a list.

In Jeanne's studio, Dan and Steve and their cousins, Pam, Wendy, and Richard, talked about how they used to play Wiffle ball together in the back yard. Someone asked Helen to look for the photo albums, but she sat in a daze. As for Sylvia, she was nowhere to be seen.

Late in the day, just as the guests began to leave, Sylvia slipped into the house. Sober, Lew followed, carrying a tube pan.

"Lew?" Andrea said in a warning voice. "What is that?"

Lew kept moving. He knew that this was the nuclear option, and he felt culpable, but he loved his wife.

In the dining room, Sylvia sliced her fresh-baked apple cake. The caterers 250 were still packing up. Their chafing dishes were hardly cold when the house filled with the cake's fragrance. Jeanne's grandsons ran straight to the table. Christian appeared with Phoebe right behind him.

The scent of apples woke Helen from her trance. She marched into the dining room and saw the family eating; she saw what Sylvia had done, and her eyes brightened; her whole body tensed with indignation.

That was the end.

Melanie tried. Everybody tried. Nobody could reconcile Jeanne's sisters. This was all a misunderstanding, their children said. Don't be stubborn, their children pleaded. Andrea said that they only had each other now, but they refused to listen. Dan said life was short. They didn't care. In fact, they knew it wasn't true. Their lives were long.

Lorraine was right. Everybody mourned in his or her own way. Phoebe wrote a poem, and Melanie did in fact start taking antidepressants. Richard began dating a woman he'd met at a bar. Pam adopted a shelter dog. As for Jeanne's sisters, they would not forgive each other for Jeanne's death. They would not reconcile, not even when the whole family gathered at Singing Beach in the spring to scatter Jeanne's ashes in the ocean. Wendy stood on the sand and asked the sisters, in Jeanne's memory, to open their hearts and to embrace each other so that they might begin to heal, but no, not even then.

## FOR ANALYSIS

**1.** How would you characterize **point of view** in this story? Whose point of view do we see from for most of the story? What other points of view are we granted access to? What is the effect of this splitting?

**2.** What is your reaction to this sentence: "When she looked at the mums, she felt she wasn't dying fast enough" (para. 8)? Does it strike you as the kind of thing you tend to hear in narratives about death? What is its significance in the story?

**3.** Why do Melanie and Dan call Phoebe?

## MAKING ARGUMENTS

Make an argument about Helen and Sylvia. How are we supposed to feel about them? How are we to judge their actions and reactions? What purpose do these **characters** serve in the story?

## WRITING TOPICS

**Irony** is an important device in this story. Reread the story and note instances of irony, and how they work in themselves and in the larger story. What do you think the larger function of irony is in "Apple Cake"?

## MAKING CONNECTIONS

As a rule, elderly women do not tend to be a staple of fiction. Think about this story alongside "The Moths" by Helena María Viramontes (p. 860). What do these stories have in common, and where do they part ways? On the evidence of this small sample, what would you say about fiction about older women?

# POETRY

## ANONYMOUS

## EDWARD

### 1

"Why does your sword so drip with blood
    Edward, Edward?
Why does your sword so drip with blood
  And why so sad go ye, O?"
"O I have killed my hawk so good,
    Mother, mother,
O I have killed my hawk so good,
  And I had no more but he, O."

### 2

"Your hawk's blood was never so red,
    Edward, Edward;                         10
Your hawk's blood was never so red,
  My dear son I tell thee, O."
"O I have killed my red-roan steed,
    Mother, mother,
O I have killed my red-roan steed,
  That once was so fair and free, O."

### 3

"Your steed was old, and ye have got more,
    Edward, Edward;
Your steed was old, and ye have got more,
  Some other grief ye dree,° O."          suffer  20
"O I have killed my father dear,
    Mother, mother,

O I have killed my father dear,
    Alas, and woe is me, O!"


### 4

"And what penance will ye dree for that,
      Edward, Edward?
And what penance will ye dree for that,
    My dear son, now tell me, O?"
"I'll set my feet in yonder boat,
      Mother, mother,                30
I'll set my feet in yonder boat,
    And I'll travel o'er the sea, O."


### 5

"And what will ye do with your towers and your hall,
      Edward, Edward?
And what will ye do with your towers and your hall,
    That were so fair to see, O?"
"I'll let them stand 'til they down fall,
      Mother, mother,
I'll let them stand 'til they down fall,
    For here never more must I be, O."        40


### 6

"And what will ye leave to your children and your wife,
      Edward, Edward?
And what will ye leave to your children and your wife,
    When ye travel o'er the sea, O?"
"The world has room, let them beg through life,
      Mother, mother,
The world has room, let them beg through life,
    For them never more will I see, O."


### 7

"And what will ye leave to your own mother dear,
      Edward, Edward?          50
And what will ye leave to your own mother dear,
    My dear son, now tell me, O?"

"The curse of hell from me shall ye bear,
    Mother, mother,
The curse of hell from me shall ye bear,
  Such counsels ye gave to me, O."

## FOR ANALYSIS

**1.** Why does the mother reject Edward's answers to her first two questions?

**2.** Does the poem provide any clues to the murderer's motive?

**3.** Edward has murdered his father and then bitterly turns away from his mother, wife, and children. What basis is there in the poem for nevertheless sympathizing with Edward?

## MAKING ARGUMENTS

Do a little research on murder **ballads**, and make an argument based on that evidence and on your reading of "Edward" for why murder ballads exist. Why do people write them? Why do people like to hear them? What need(s) do they meet? What purpose do they serve?

## WRITING TOPIC

What effects are achieved through the question-and-answer technique and the repetition of lines?

## WILLIAM SHAKESPEARE (1564-1616)

# SONNET 1609

### 73

That time of year thou mayst in me behold
When yellow leaves, or none, or few, do hang
Upon those boughs which shake against the cold,
Bare ruined choirs, where late the sweet birds sang.
In me thou see'st the twilight of such day
As after sunset fadeth in the west;
Which by and by black night doth take away,
Death's second self, that seals up all in rest.
In me thou see'st the glowing of such fire,
That on the ashes of his youth doth lie,          10

As the deathbed whereon it must expire,
Consumed with that which it was nourished by.
This thou perceiv'st, which makes thy love more strong,
To love that well which thou must leave ere long.

# FEAR NO MORE
# THE HEAT O' THE SUN   1623

Fear no more the heat o' the sun,[1]
   Nor the furious winter's rages;
Thou thy worldly task hast done,
   Home art gone, and ta'en thy wages:
Golden lads and girls all must,
As chimney-sweepers, come to dust.

Fear no more the frown o' the great;
   Thou art past the tyrant's stroke;
Care no more to clothe and eat;
   To thee the reed is as the oak:                          10
The scepter, learning, physic,° must[2]                      medicine
All follow this, and come to dust.

Fear no more the lightning flash,
   Nor the all-dreaded thunder stone;[3]
Fear not slander, censure rash;
   Thou hast finished joy and moan:
All lovers young, all lovers must
Consign to° thee, and come to dust.                          agree with

No exorciser harm thee!
Nor no witchcraft charm thee!                                20
Ghost unlaid forbear thee!
Nothing ill come near thee!
Quiet consummation have;
And renownéd be thy grave!

*Fear No More the Heat o' the Sun*
  [1] From Cymbeline, act IV, scene 2.
  [2] I.e., kings, scholars, and physicians.
  [3] It was believed that thunder was caused by falling meteorites.

## John Donne   (1572–1631)

# Death, Be Not Proud   1633

Death be not proud, though some have calléd thee
Mighty and dreadful, for thou art not so;
For those whom thou think'st thou dost overthrow
Die not, poor Death, nor yet canst thou kill me.
From rest and sleep, which but thy pictures be,
Much pleasure; then from thee much more must flow,
And soonest our best men with thee do go,
Rest of their bones, and soul's delivery.
Thou art slave to fate, chance, kings, and desperate men,
And dost with poison, war, and sickness dwell,                    10
And poppy or charms can make us sleep as well
And better than thy stroke; why swell'st thou then?
One short sleep past, we wake eternally
And death shall be no more; Death, thou shalt die.


## Jonathan Swift   (1667–1745)

# A Satirical Elegy on the Death
# of a Late Famous General   1722

His Grace! impossible! what dead!
Of old age too, and in his bed!
And could that mighty warrior fall?
And so inglorious, after all!
Well, since he's gone, no matter how,
The last loud trump must wake him now:
And, trust me, as the noise grows stronger,
He'd wish to sleep a little longer.
And could he be indeed so old
As by the newspapers we're told?                    10
Threescore, I think, is pretty high;
'Twas time in conscience he should die
This world he cumbered long enough;
He burnt his candle to the snuff;
And that's the reason, some folks think,
He left behind so great a stink.
Behold his funeral appears,
Nor widow's sighs, nor orphan's tears,

Wont at such times each heart to pierce,
Attend the progress of his hearse.                                    20
But what of that, his friends may say,
He had those honours in his day.
True to his profit and his pride,
He made them weep before he died.

   Come hither, all ye empty things,
Ye bubbles raised by breath of kings;
Who float upon the tide of state,
Come hither, and behold your fate.
Let pride be taught by this rebuke,
How very mean a thing's a Duke;                                       30
From all his ill-got honours flung,
Turned to that dirt from whence he sprung.

### FOR ANALYSIS

**1.** How would you describe the **tone** of this poem? Give examples.

**2.** How does the speaker feel about the general? How does he feel about the general's death?

**3.** What about the poem changes in its second **stanza**?

**4.** To where is the speaker asking "ye empty things" (l. 25) to come in the second stanza? Why?

### MAKING ARGUMENTS

Swift wrote this poem about a contemporary of his, John Churchill, Duke of Marlborough, whom Swift believed was a war profiteer. Do a little reading on this subject and make an argument about whether knowing this information makes you read the poem differently, or if it has no effect. As you construct your argument, think about methods of literary criticism, about whether historical context is crucial or extraneous to interpretation.

### WRITING TOPIC

Write a **satirical elegy** for a deceased public figure. Don't get personal or ad hominem, but criticize him or her on the basis of important public acts you find worthy of criticism (that is, think about why you don't like what this person did in his or her career). Make sure to have your facts as straight as you can get them, with outside help, and try to be creative; don't copy Swift, but be inspired by him to find your own way to say good-bye.

### MAKING CONNECTIONS

Compare Swift's tone with the tone of W. H. Auden's "The Unknown Citizen" (p. 360). What does each poem ultimately say about war? Do they treat the topic similarly? How are they different?

## PERCY BYSSHE SHELLEY (1792–1822)

# OZYMANDIAS[1]  1818

I met a traveller from an antique land
Who said: Two vast and trunkless legs of stone
Stand in the desert . . . Near them, on the sand,
Half sunk, a shattered visage lies, whose frown,
And wrinkled lip, and sneer of cold command,
Tell that its sculptor well those passions read
Which yet survive, stamped on these lifeless things,
The hand that mocked them, and the heart that fed:
And on the pedestal these words appear:
"My name is Ozymandias, king of kings:                    10
Look on my works, ye Mighty, and despair!"
Nothing beside remains. Round the decay
Of that colossal wreck, boundless and bare
The lone and level sands stretch far away.


## JOHN KEATS (1795–1821)

# ODE ON A GRECIAN URN  1820

### I

Thou still unravished bride of quietness,
    Thou foster child of silence and slow time,
Sylvan historian, who canst thus express
    A flowery tale more sweetly than our rhyme:
What leaf-fringed legend haunts about thy shape
    Of deities or mortals, or of both,
        In Tempe or the dales of Arcady?[1]
    What men or gods are these? What maidens loath?
What mad pursuit? What struggle to escape?
        What pipes and timbrels? What wild ecstasy?       10

### II

Heard melodies are sweet, but those unheard
    Are sweeter; therefore, ye soft pipes, play on;
Not to the sensual ear, but, more endeared,

*Ozymandias*
  [1] Egyptian monarch of the thirteenth century BCE, said to have erected a huge statue of himself.

*Ode on a Grecian Urn*
  [1] Tempe and Arcady are valleys in Greece famous for their beauty. In ancient times, Tempe was regarded as sacred to Apollo.

Pipe to the spirit ditties of no tone:
Fair youth, beneath the trees, thou canst not leave
    Thy song, nor ever can those trees be bare;
        Bold Lover, never, never canst thou kiss,
Though winning near the goal—yet, do not grieve;
        She cannot fade, though thou hast not thy bliss,
    Forever wilt thou love, and she be fair!           20

### III

Ah, happy, happy boughs! that cannot shed
    Your leaves, nor ever bid the Spring adieu;
And, happy melodist, unweariéd,
    Forever piping songs forever new;
More happy love! more happy, happy love!
    Forever warm and still to be enjoyed,
        Forever panting, and forever young;
All breathing human passion far above,[2]
    That leaves a heart high-sorrowful and cloyed,
        A burning forehead, and a parching tongue.      30

### IV

Who are these coming to the sacrifice?
    To what green altar, O mysterious priest,
Lead'st thou that heifer lowing at the skies,
    And all her silken flanks with garlands dressed?
What little town by river or sea shore,
    Or mountain-built with peaceful citadel,
        Is emptied of this folk, this pious morn?
And, little town, thy streets forevermore
    Will silent be; and not a soul to tell
        Why thou art desolate, can e'er return.        40

### V

O Attic[3] shape! Fair attitude! with brede
    Of marble men and maidens overwrought,
With forest branches and the trodden weed;
    Thou, silent form, dost tease us out of thought
As doth eternity: Cold Pastoral!
    When old age shall this generation waste,

---

[2] I.e., far above all breathing human passion.
[3] Athenian, thus simple and graceful.

Thou shalt remain, in midst of other woe
  Than ours, a friend to man, to whom thou say'st,
"Beauty is truth, truth beauty,—that is all
    Ye know on earth, and all ye need to know." 50

## FOR ANALYSIS

**1.** Describe the scene the poet sees depicted on the urn. Describe the scene the poet imagines as a consequence of the scene on the urn.

**2.** Why are the boughs, the piper, and the lovers happy in **stanza** III?

**3.** Explain the assertion of stanza II: "Heard melodies are sweet, but those unheard / Are sweeter."

**4.** Does the poem support the assertion of the last two lines? What do they mean?

## MAKING ARGUMENTS

Perhaps the most famous lines of this poem—which is filled with well-known lines—come at the poem's close, ending with "Beauty is truth," and so on (l. 49). They are also the source of the greatest critical disagreements, as some readers find these lines define the poem, while others feel they nearly ruin it. Make an argument concerning these lines; if it helps, do a bit of reading on what the critics have said (for example, I. A. Richards, T. S. Eliot), and think about who voices these lines, whether they are endorsed or the speech of a "**character**," and whether they are critiqued or championed.

## WRITING TOPIC

Discuss Keats's view of the connection between art and life. With this in mind, consider the meaning of the phrase "Cold Pastoral!" (l. 45).


## EMILY DICKINSON   (1830–1886)

# AFTER GREAT PAIN,
# A FORMAL FEELING COMES   CA. 1863

After great pain, a formal feeling comes—
The Nerves sit ceremonious, like Tombs—
The stiff Heart questions was it He, that bore,
And Yesterday, or Centuries before?

The Feet, mechanical, go round—
Of Ground, or Air, or Ought—
A Wooden way
Regardless grown,
A Quartz contentment, like a stone—

This is the Hour of Lead— 10
Remembered, if outlived,

As Freezing persons, recollect the Snow—
First—Chill—then Stupor—then the letting go—

**FOR ANALYSIS**

Is this poem about physical or psychic pain? Explain.

**WRITING TOPIC**

What is the meaning of "stiff Heart" (l. 3) and "Quartz contentment" (l. 9)? What part
do they play in the larger pattern of **images** in this poem?

## I HEARD A FLY BUZZ— WHEN I DIED    CA. 1862

I heard a Fly buzz—when I died—
The Stillness in the Room
Was like the Stillness in the Air—
Between the Heaves of Storm—

The Eyes around—had wrung them dry—
And Breaths were gathering firm
For that last Onset—when the King
Be witnessed—in the Room—

I willed my Keepsakes—Signed away
What portion of me be                                          10
Assignable—and then it was
There interposed a Fly—

With Blue—uncertain stumbling Buzz—
Between the light—and me—
And then the Windows failed—and then
I could not see to see—

## APPARENTLY WITH NO SURPRISE    CA. 1884

Apparently with no surprise
To any happy Flower,
The Frost beheads it at its play
In accidental power.
The blond Assassin passes on,
The Sun proceeds unmoved
To measure off another Day
For an Approving God.

# BECAUSE I COULD NOT STOP
# FOR DEATH   CA. 1863

Because I could not stop for Death—
He kindly stopped for me—
The Carriage held but just Ourselves—
And Immortality.

We slowly drove—He knew no haste
And I had put away
My labor and my leisure too,
For his Civility—

We passed the School, where Children strove
At Recess—in the Ring—                                                    10
We passed the Fields of Gazing Grain—
We passed the Setting Sun—

Or rather—He passed Us—
The Dews drew quivering and chill—
For only Gossamer, my Gown—
My Tippet—only Tulle—

We paused before a House that seemed
A Swelling of the Ground—
The Roof was scarcely visible—
The Cornice—in the Ground—                                                20

Since then—'tis Centuries—and yet
Feels shorter than the Day
I first surmised the Horses' Heads
Were toward Eternity—

## GERARD MANLEY HOPKINS   (1844–1889)

# GOD'S GRANDEUR   1918

The world is charged with the grandeur of God.
    It will flame out, like shining from shook foil°                       metal foil
    It gathers to a greatness, like the ooze of oil
Crushed. Why do men then now not reck° his rod?                             heed
Generations have trod, have trod, have trod;
    And all is seared with trade; bleared, smeared with toil;

And wears man's smudge and shares man's smell: the soil
Is bare now, nor can foot feel, being shod.

And for all this, nature is never spent;
   There lives the dearest freshness deep down things;                    10
And though the last lights off the black West went
   Oh, morning, at the brown brink eastward, springs—
Because the Holy Ghost over the bent
   World broods with warm breast and with ah! bright wings.


## A. E. HOUSMAN   (1859–1936)

# TO AN ATHLETE DYING YOUNG   1896

The time you won your town the race
We chaired you through the market place;
Man and boy stood cheering by,
And home we brought you shoulder-high.

Today, the road all runners come,
Shoulder-high we bring you home,
And set you at your threshold down,
Townsman of a stiller town.

Smart lad, to slip betimes away
From fields where glory does not stay,                                            10
And early though the laurel grows
It withers quicker than the rose.

Eyes the shady night has shut
Cannot see the record cut,
And silence sounds no worse than cheers
After earth has stopped the ears:

Now you will not swell the rout
Of lads that wore their honors out,
Runners whom renown outran
And the name died before the man.                                                20

So set, before its echoes fade,
The fleet foot on the sill of shade,
And hold to the low lintel up
The still-defended challenge cup.

And round that early-laureled head
Will flock to gaze the strengthless dead
And find unwithered on its curls
The garland briefer than a girl's.

## WILLIAM BUTLER YEATS  (1865–1939)

# SAILING TO BYZANTIUM[1]  1927

### 1

That is no country for old men. The young
In one another's arms, birds in the trees
—Those dying generations—at their song,
The salmon-falls, the mackerel-crowded seas,
Fish, flesh, or fowl, commend all summer long
Whatever is begotten, born, and dies.
Caught in that sensual music all neglect
Monuments of unaging intellect.

### 2

An aged man is but a paltry thing,
A tattered coat upon a stick, unless                    10
Soul clap its hands and sing, and louder sing
For every tatter in its mortal dress,
Nor is there singing school but studying
Monuments of its own magnificence;
And therefore I have sailed the seas and come
To the holy city of Byzantium.

### 3

O sages standing in God's holy fire
As in the gold mosaic of a wall,

---

*Sailing to Byzantium*
    [1] Capital of the ancient Eastern Roman Empire, Byzantium (modern Istanbul) is celebrated for its great art, including mosaics (in ll. 17–18, Yeats addresses the figures in one of these mosaics). In *A Vision*, Yeats cites Byzantium as possibly the only civilization that had achieved what he called "Unity of Being"—a state where "religious, aesthetic, and practical life were one."

Come from the holy fire, perne in a gyre,[2]
And be the singing-masters of my soul.                    20
Consume my heart away; sick with desire
And fastened to a dying animal
It knows not what it is; and gather me
Into the artifice of eternity.

### 4

Once out of nature I shall never take
My bodily form from any natural thing,
But such a form as Grecian goldsmiths make
Of hammered gold and gold enameling
To keep a drowsy Emperor awake;[3]
Or set upon a golden bough to sing                        30
To lords and ladies of Byzantium
Of what is past, or passing, or to come.

## FOR ANALYSIS

**1.** This poem incorporates a series of contrasts, among them "that" country and Byzantium, and the real birds of the first **stanza** and the artificial bird of the final stanza. What others do you find?

**2.** What are the meanings of "generations" (l. 3)?

**3.** For what is the poet "sick with desire" (l. 21)?

**4.** In what sense is eternity an "artifice" (l. 24)?

## MAKING ARGUMENTS

Do some reading on Yeats, in particular on his idiosyncratic view of human history but also on his other poems, for example "The Second Coming" (p. 354). Make an argument concerning the final line of "Sailing to Byzantium." What is past? What is passing? Most importantly, what would you argue Yeats sees coming, and how does he feel about it?

## WRITING TOPIC

In what ways are the **images** of bird and song used throughout this poem?

---

[2] I.e., whirl in a spiral motion. Yeats associated this motion with the cycles of history and the fate of the individual. Here he entreats the sages represented in the mosaic to take him out of the natural world described in the first stanza and into the eternal world of art.

[3] "I have read somewhere," Yeats wrote, "that in the Emperor's palace at Byzantium was a tree made of gold and silver, and artificial birds that sang." The poet wishes to become an artificial bird (a work of art) in contrast to the real birds of the first stanza.

## EDWIN ARLINGTON ROBINSON   (1869–1935)

# RICHARD CORY   1897

Whenever Richard Cory went down town,
We people on the pavement looked at him:
He was a gentleman from sole to crown,
Clean favored, and imperially slim.

And he was always quietly arrayed,
And he was always human when he talked;
But still he fluttered pulses when he said,
"Good-morning," and he glittered when he walked.

And he was rich—yes, richer than a king—
And admirably schooled in every grace:                    10
In fine, we thought that he was everything
To make us wish that we were in his place.

So on we worked, and waited for the light,
And went without the meat, and cursed the bread;
And Richard Cory, one calm summer night,
Went home and put a bullet through his head.

## ROBERT FROST   (1874–1963)

# AFTER APPLE-PICKING   1914

My long two-pointed ladder's sticking through a tree
Toward heaven still,
And there's a barrel that I didn't fill
Beside it, and there may be two or three
Apples I didn't pick upon some bough.
But I am done with apple-picking now.
Essence of winter sleep is on the night,
The scent of apples: I am drowsing off.
I cannot rub the strangeness from my sight
I got from looking through a pane of glass                 10
I skimmed this morning from the drinking trough
And held against the world of hoary grass.
It melted, and I let it fall and break.
But I was well
Upon my way to sleep before it fell,
And I could tell
What form my dreaming was about to take.

Magnified apples appear and disappear,
Stem end and blossom end,
And every fleck of russet showing clear.                    20
My instep arch not only keeps the ache,
It keeps the pressure of a ladder-round.
I feel the ladder sway as the boughs bend.
And I keep hearing from the cellar bin
The rumbling sound
Of load on load of apples coming in.
For I have had too much
Of apple-picking: I am overtired
Of the great harvest I myself desired.
There were ten thousand thousand fruit to touch,      30
Cherish in hand, lift down, and not let fall.
For all
That struck the earth,
No matter if not bruised or spiked with stubble,
Went surely to the cider-apple heap
As of no worth.
One can see what will trouble
This sleep of mine, whatever sleep it is.
Were he not gone,
The woodchuck could say whether it's like his            40
Long sleep, as I describe its coming on,
Or just some human sleep.

### FOR ANALYSIS

**1.** What does apple-picking **symbolize**?

**2.** At the end of the poem, why is the speaker uncertain about what kind of sleep is coming on him?

### MAKING ARGUMENTS

Do you think the speaker's "sleep" will be troubled? What does the poem seem to think the future holds for him, after life? Make an argument in response to these questions, supporting your claim with specific textual observations.

## 'OUT, OUT—'[1]   1916

The buzz-saw snarled and rattled in the yard
And made dust and dropped stove-length sticks of wood,
Sweet-scented stuff when the breeze drew across it.

---

[1]The title is taken from the famous speech of Macbeth upon hearing that his wife has died (*Macbeth*, act v, scene 5).

And from there those that lifted eyes could count
Five mountain ranges one behind the other
Under the sunset far into Vermont.
And the saw snarled and rattled, snarled and rattled,
As it ran light, or had to bear a load.
And nothing happened: day was all but done.
Call it a day, I wish they might have said                      10
To please the boy by giving him the half hour
That a boy counts so much when saved from work.
His sister stood beside them in her apron
To tell them 'Supper.' At the word, the saw,
As if to prove saws knew what supper meant,
Leaped out at the boy's hand, or seemed to leap—
He must have given the hand. However it was,
Neither refused the meeting. But the hand!
The boy's first outcry was a rueful laugh,
As he swung toward them holding up the hand            20
Half in appeal, but half as if to keep
The life from spilling. Then the boy saw all—
Since he was old enough to know, big boy
Doing a man's work, though a child at heart—
He saw all spoiled. 'Don't let him cut my hand off—
The doctor, when he comes. Don't let him, sister!'
So. But the hand was gone already.
The doctor put him in the dark of ether.
He lay and puffed his lips out with his breath.
And then—the watcher at his pulse took fright.         30
No one believed. They listened at his heart.
Little—less—nothing!—and that ended it.
No more to build on there. And they, since they
Were not the one dead, turned to their affairs.


# NOTHING GOLD CAN STAY   1923

Nature's first green is gold,
Her hardest hue to hold.
Her early leaf's a flower;
But only so an hour.
Then leaf subsides to leaf.
So Eden sank to grief,
So dawn goes down to day.
Nothing gold can stay.

**1.** Does this poem protest or accept the transitoriness of things?

**2.** Why does Frost use the word *subsides* in line 5 rather than a word like *expands* or *grows*?

**3.** How are "Nature's first green" (l. 1), "Eden" (l. 6), and "dawn" (l. 7) linked together?

# STOPPING BY WOODS
# ON A SNOWY EVENING  1923

Whose woods these are I think I know.
His house is in the village though;
He will not see me stopping here
To watch his woods fill up with snow.

My little horse must think it queer
To stop without a farmhouse near
Between the woods and frozen lake
The darkest evening of the year.

He gives his harness bells a shake
To ask if there is some mistake.                              10
The only other sound's the sweep
Of easy wind and downy flake.

The woods are lovely, dark and deep,
But I have promises to keep,
And miles to go before I sleep,
And miles to go before I sleep.

### FOR ANALYSIS

**1.** What does the description of the horse tell us about the speaker?

**2.** What function does the repetition in the last two lines of the poem serve?

**3.** Why does the speaker refer to the owner of the woods in the opening **stanza**?

### MAKING ARGUMENTS

Like many of Frost's poems, this one seems simple. Argue for the idea that, behind its simple, even lovely surface, this poem is (to continue borrowing from l. 13) "dark and deep." Build your argument from observations of the poem's specifics, both to demonstrate the simplicity and argue that it possesses dark depths.

# DESIGN 1936

I found a dimpled spider, fat and white,
On a white heal-all, holding up a moth
Like a white piece of rigid satin cloth—
Assorted characters of death and blight
Mixed ready to begin the morning right,
Like the ingredients of a witches' broth—
A snow-drop spider, a flower like a froth,
And dead wings carried like a paper kite.

What had that flower to do with being white,
The wayside blue and innocent heal-all?                    10
What brought the kindred spider to that height,
Then steered the white moth thither in the night?
What but design of darkness to appall?—
If design govern in a thing so small.

**WRITING TOPIC**

Compare this poem with Dickinson's "Apparently with no surprise" (p. 892).

## PABLO NERUDA  (1904–1973)

# THE DEAD WOMAN  1972

If suddenly you do not exist,
if suddenly you are not living,
I shall go on living.

I do not dare,
I do not dare to write it,
if you die.

I shall go on living.

Because where a man has no voice,
there, my voice.

Where blacks are beaten,                                    10
I can not be dead.
When my brothers go to jail
I shall go with them.

When victory,
not my victory
but the great victory
arrives,
even though I am mute I must speak:
I shall see it come even though I am blind.

No, forgive me.                                          20
If you are not living,
if you, beloved, my love,
if you
have died,
all the leaves will fall on my breast,
it will rain upon my soul night and day,
the snow will burn my heart,
I shall walk with cold and fire and death and snow,
my feet will want to march toward where you sleep,
but                                                      30
I shall go on living,
because you wanted me to be, above all things,
untamable,
and, love, because you know that I am not just one man
but all men.

## CZESŁAW MIŁOSZ  (1911–2004)

# A SONG ON THE END OF THE WORLD[1]  1944

On the day the world ends
A bee circles a clover,
A fisherman mends a glimmering net.
Happy porpoises jump in the sea,
By the rainspout young sparrows are playing
And the snake is gold-skinned as it should always be.

On the day the world ends
Women walk through the fields under their umbrellas,
A drunkard grows sleepy at the edge of a lawn,
Vegetable peddlers shout in the street                   10
And a yellow-sailed boat comes nearer the island,
The voice of a violin lasts in the air
And leads into a starry night.

[1] Translated by Anthony Milosz.

And those who expected lightning and thunder
Are disappointed.
And those who expected signs and archangels' trumps
Do not believe it is happening now.
As long as the sun and the moon are above,
As long as the bumblebee visits a rose,
As long as rosy infants are born                 20
No one believes it is happening now.

Only a white-haired old man, who would be a prophet
Yet is not a prophet, for he's much too busy,
Repeats while he binds his tomatoes:
There will be no other end of the world,
There will be no other end of the world.

## FOR ANALYSIS

**1.** How would you describe the **tone** of this poem? Is it sad? Foreboding? Does it feel more positive than negative?

**2.** Think again about the title of the poem. How is this a song about the end of the world? How is it not? What else is it about? How do these two things relate?

## MAKING ARGUMENTS

The poem was written in 1944 in Warsaw. Based on a bit of research, make an argument for the importance of the place and time of its creation to the poem.

## DYLAN THOMAS   (1914–1953)

# DO NOT GO GENTLE INTO THAT GOOD NIGHT   1952

Do not go gentle into that good night,
Old age should burn and rave at close of day;
Rage, rage against the dying of the light.

Though wise men at their end know dark is right,
Because their words had forked no lightning they
Do not go gentle into that good night.

Good men, the last wave by, crying how bright
Their frail deeds might have danced in a green bay,
Rage, rage against the dying of the light.

Wild men who caught and sang the sun in flight,          10
And learn, too late, they grieved it on its way,
Do not go gentle into that good night.

Grave men, near death, who see with blinding sight
Blind eyes could blaze like meteors and be gay,
Rage, rage against the dying of the light.

And you, my father, there on the sad height,
Curse, bless, me now with your fierce tears, I pray.
Do not go gentle into that good night.
Rage, rage against the dying of the light.

### For Analysis

**1.** What do wise, good, wild, and grave men have in common?

**2.** Why does the poet use the adjective *gentle* rather than the adverb *gently* in the title?

**3.** What is the "sad height" (l. 16)?

### Making Arguments

"Do Not Go Gentle into That Good Night" is filled with paradoxes, even before it starts, in its title (which is really just its first line). How would you construct an argument for the importance of **paradox** not formally but thematically? Build your argument from observations about how Thomas uses paradox and from claims for paradox as a way to think about his subject.

### Writing Topic

This poem is a **villanelle**, which means that it contains only two rhymes and that the first and third lines alternate as the third lines in each **stanza** following and form a final **couplet**. Why do you think Thomas chose this form for his poem? How does it relate to the poem's subject and its treatment of that subject?

### James Wright   (1927–1980)

## Lying in a Hammock at William Duffy's Farm in Pine Island, Minnesota   1990

Over my head, I see the bronze butterfly,
Asleep on the black trunk,
Blowing like a leaf in green shadow.
Down the ravine behind the empty house,
The cowbells follow one another
Into the distances of the afternoon.
To my right,
In a field of sunlight between two pines,
The droppings of last year's horses

Blaze up into golden stones.  10
I lean back, as the evening darkens and comes on.
A chicken hawk floats over, looking for home.
I have wasted my life.

## FOR ANALYSIS

**1.** What is the speaker doing as he sees the things he describes in this poem?

**2.** What unites the different things the speaker sees? Is there anything more than the fact that he can see them from where he lies?

**3.** What might the last line mean? Does what the speaker has been doing constitute the wasting of his life, or has he wasted his life not doing more of it? Defend your answer.

**4.** Do you think there might be any special significance to the fact that the day is ending at the end of the poem? What might it be?

## MAKING ARGUMENTS

Argue either that the speaker's realization is one of regret at having spent too much time in hammocks, or that the speaker's realization is one of regret at not having spent enough time in hammocks. If a hammock is available, spend some time in it considering this question first.

## WRITING TOPIC

Poets sit around a lot, thinking and looking at things. Write an essay in which you honestly consider the writing of poetry as an activity, calling, or profession. Is it a noble profession? A necessary one? Is it a nice thing to have people doing? Is it a waste of time? Explain your answer(s).

## MARVIN KLOTZ  (1930-2014)

# REQUIEM  2007

**FOR S.S.**

Inside the skin's where it happens.
Amazing what that space contains—
Interstices, the roads, all mapped
By what we've done—our lives' refrain,

A song within the skin. Childhood
Anxieties, first love, the rough
And tumble scars, ecstatic good—
All melt, and cool—become one tough

Amalgam: our unburnished selves.
There reside affections, taste, pain,  10

And politics. And there we delve
Among the crystal cracks, to gain
That sense of who we are, to find,
Among inchoate parts, a center.

Sometimes, inside the skin, the mind
Demurs, sweeps out all debris—vents,
And leaves that arid space within
Where plain grief abides, untarnished
By our lives' complex and foolish
Stuff—just empty, inside the skin.                           20

## ALICIA OSTRIKER   (B. 1937)

# DAFFODILS   2005

### FOR DAVID LEHMAN

> Ten thousand saw I at a glance
> Tossing their heads in sprightly dance.
>        —WILLIAM WORDSWORTH

> Going to hell so many times tears it
> Which explains poetry.
>        —JACK SPICER

The day the war against Iraq begins
I'm photographing the yellow daffodils
With their outstretched arms and ruffled cups
Blowing in the wind of Jesus Green

Edging the lush grassy moving river
Along with the swans and ducks
Under a soft March Cambridge sky
Embellishing the earth like a hand

Starting to illustrate a children's book
Where people in light clothes come out                       10
To play, to frisk and run about
With their lovers, friends, animals, and children

As down every stony back road of history
They've always done in the peaceful springs
—Which in a sense is also hell because
The daffodils do look as if they dance

And make some of us in the park want to dance
And breathe deeply and I know that
Being able to eat and incorporate beauty like this
I am privileged and by that token can                                    20

Taste pain, roll it on my tongue, it's good
The cruel wars are good the stupidity is good,
The primates hiding in their caves are very good,
They do their best, which explains poetry.

What explains poetry is that life is hard
But better than the alternatives,
The no and the nothing. Look at this light
And color, a splash of brilliant yellow

Punctuating an emerald text, white swans
And mottled brown ducks floating quietly along                           30
Whole and alive, like an untorn language
That lacks nothing, that excludes

Nothing. Period. Don't you think
It is our business to defend it
Even the day our masters start a war?
To defend the day we see the daffodils?

## FOR ANALYSIS

**1.** How does the physical **setting** of the poem and the way it is described contrast with the day on which it is set?

**2.** What is the effect of ending the poem with questions? What kind of questions are they?

**3.** By the end of the poem, it is clear what the speaker thinks "explains poetry." What is it? How does it explain poetry?

## MAKING ARGUMENTS

Arguments over whether literature should be political are as old as literature and politics themselves. Critic Lionel Trilling described their intersection as "the dark and bloody crossroads where literature and politics meet," "bloody" in the sense that they are argued over violently. Using this poem as evidence, but also relying on your thoughts about this issue and anything you can learn from others' statements on the matter, make your own argument about politics in poetry.

**WRITING TOPIC**

As the first **epigraph** makes plain, this poem alludes to William Wordsworth's 1807 poem "I Wandered Lonely as a Cloud" (often referred to as "Daffodils"). Find a copy of Wordsworth's poem and write a short essay explaining Ostriker's **allusion**. Why does she point to that poem in particular? What about the subject and spirit of her poem is illuminated by bringing to mind Wordsworth's?

## SEAMUS HEANEY    (B. 1939–2013)

# MID-TERM BREAK    1966

I sat all morning in the college sick bay
Counting bells knelling classes to a close.
At two o'clock our neighbors drove me home.

In the porch I met my father crying—
He had always taken funerals in his stride—
And Big Jim Evans saying it was a hard blow.

The baby cooed and laughed and rocked the pram
When I came in, and I was embarrassed
By old men standing up to shake my hand

And tell me they were "sorry for my trouble,"                    10
Whispers informed strangers I was the eldest,
Away at school, as my mother held my hand

In hers and coughed out angry tearless sighs.
At ten o'clock the ambulance arrived
With the corpse, stanched and bandaged by the nurses.

Next morning I went up into the room. Snowdrops
And candles soothed the bedside; I saw him
For the first time in six weeks. Paler now,

Wearing a poppy bruise on his left temple,
He lay in the four foot box as in his cot.                        20
No gaudy scars, the bumper knocked him clear.

A four foot box, a foot for every year.

## FOR ANALYSIS

**1.** Although it contains little **rhyme**, this poem is remarkably musical. Identify the **assonance** and **alliteration** that permeate the poem.

**2.** What event does the poem describe?

**3.** How is the poem's title relevant?

## MAKING ARGUMENTS

Different poems depend on different effects. "Mid-term Break" depends in large measure on the timing of the disclosure of information. Make an argument about the use of this surprise ending—do you find it powerful? Will its power persist through multiple readings? Do you find it gimmicky, like the twist at the end of an O. Henry story?

## WRITING TOPIC

Describe the family and the society revealed in this short poem.

## JANE KENYON   (1947–1995)

# LET EVENING COME   1996

Let the light of late afternoon
shine through chinks in the barn, moving
up the bales as the sun moves down.

Let the cricket take up chafing
as a woman takes up her needles
and her yarn. Let evening come.

Let dew collect on the hoe abandoned
in long grass. Let the stars appear
and the moon disclose her silver horn.

Let the fox go back to its sandy den.          10
Let the wind die down. Let the shed
go black inside. Let evening come.

To the bottle in the ditch, to the scoop
in the oats, to air in the lung
let evening come.

Let it come, as it will, and don't
be afraid. God does not leave us
comfortless, so let evening come.

## FOR ANALYSIS

**1.** What does evening signify in this poem?

**2.** Why do you think Kenyon includes "air in the lung" (l. 14) as one of the things that evening should be allowed to come to?

**3.** How would you characterize the sounds and **rhythms** of this poem? How do they serve the subject?

## MAKING ARGUMENTS

"Let Evening Come" was published shortly after the death of its author. Reflect on how knowing this might change your reading experience or interpretation of the poem. Does it change your sense of what the poem is about? Does it change its emotional **tone**? Should it? Should knowing something about the life of a writer change how you read that writer's work?

## WRITING TOPIC

Do you have an opinion on the poem's assertion that "God does not leave us / comfortless" (ll. 17–18)? What does it mean? Does your agreement or disagreement with that assertion change how you feel about the poem?

## YUSEF KOMUNYAKAA  (B. 1947)

# FACING IT  1988

My black face fades,
hiding inside the black granite.
I said I wouldn't,
dammit: No tears.
I'm stone. I'm flesh.
My clouded reflection eyes me
like a bird of prey, the profile of night
slanted against morning. I turn
this way—the stone lets me go.
I turn that way—I'm inside                         10
the Vietnam Veterans Memorial
again, depending on the light
to make a difference.
I go down the 58,022 names,
half-expecting to find
my own in letters like smoke.
I touch the name Andrew Johnson;
I see the booby trap's white flash.
Names shimmer on a woman's blouse

but when she walks away                                            20
the names stay on the wall.
Brushstrokes flash, a red bird's
wings cutting across my stare.
The sky. A plane in the sky.
A white vet's image floats
closer to me, then his pale eyes
look through mine. I'm a window.
He's lost his right arm
inside the stone. In the black mirror
a woman's trying to erase names:                                   30
No, she's brushing a boy's hair.

## FOR ANALYSIS

**1.** What is the speaker in "Facing It" facing? Is it one thing? More than one thing? If more than one, does "facing" mean the same thing for each "it"?

**2.** In what ways does the poem refer to the war itself? Does it include direct representation of the violence or the participants? Indirect representation? Why do you think Komunyakaa chose to refer to it in these ways?

## MAKING ARGUMENTS

With the support of research into other memorials—restricting yourself to those in Washington, DC, would make sense—make an argument about the Vietnam Veterans Memorial. Is it appropriate? Inappropriate? Does it or does it not comport with your sense of what these kinds of memorials should be and do?

## WRITING TOPIC

The Vietnam Veterans Memorial was controversial when it first opened. (If you are not familiar with the memorial, refer to a picture of it.) How does "Facing It" engage how the memorial is experienced by people? What might it have to say to those who criticize the memorial as unpatriotic or disrespectful?

## VICTOR HERNÁNDEZ CRUZ    (B. 1949)

# PROBLEMS WITH HURRICANES    1991

A campesino looked at the air
And told me:
With hurricanes it's not the wind
or the noise or the water.
I'll tell you he said:
it's the mangoes, avocados
Green plantains and bananas
flying into town like projectiles.

How would your family
feel if they had to tell          10
The generations that you
got killed by a flying
Banana.

Death by drowning has honor
If the wind picked you up
and slammed you
Against a mountain boulder
This would not carry shame
But
to suffer a mango smashing          20
Your skull
or a plantain hitting your
Temple at 70 miles per hour
is the ultimate disgrace.

The campesino takes off his hat—
As a sign of respect
towards the fury of the wind
and says:
Don't worry about the noise
Don't worry about the water          30
Don't worry about the wind—
If you are going out
beware of mangoes
And all such beautiful
sweet things.


## MARK HALLIDAY   (B. 1949)

## CHICKEN SALAD   2007

Three hours before he died,
my father felt he should have an answer
when I asked what he might like to eat.
He remembered a kind of chicken salad he liked
weeks ago when living was more possible
and he said, "Maybe that chicken salad"
but because of the blood in his mouth
and because of his shortness of breath
he had to say it several times before I understood.

So I went out and bought a container of chicken salad,                    10
grateful for the illusion of helping,
but when I brought it back to the apartment
my father studied it for thirty seconds
and set it aside on the bed. I wasn't ready
to know what the eyes of the nurse at the hospice
had tried to tell me before dawn, so I said,
"Don't you want your chicken salad, Daddy?"
He glanced at it from a distance of many miles—
little tub of chicken salad down on the planet of
slaughtered birds and mastication, digestion, excretion—            20
and murmured. "Maybe later." He was in
the final austerity
which I was too frazzled to quite recognize
but ever since his death I see with stony clarity
the solitary dignity of
the totality of his knowing
how far beyond the pleasure of chicken salad
he had gone already and would go.


## MARIE HOWE   (B. 1950)

# WHAT THE LIVING DO   1998

Johnny, the kitchen sink has been clogged for days, some utensil
        probably fell down there.
And the Drano won't work but smells dangerous, and the crusty
        dishes have piled up

waiting for the plumber I still haven't called. This is the everyday
        we spoke of.
It's winter again: the sky's a deep, headstrong blue, and the sunlight
        pours through

the open living-room windows because the heat's on too high in
        here and I can't turn it off.
For weeks now, driving, or dropping a bag of groceries in the
        street, the bag breaking,

I've been thinking: This is what the living do. And yesterday,
        hurrying along those
wobbly bricks in the Cambridge sidewalk, spilling my coffee
        down my wrist and sleeve,

I thought it again, and again later, when buying a hairbrush:
        This is it.

Parking. Slamming the car door shut in the cold. What you
    called that yearning.                                     10

What you finally gave up. We want the spring to come and the
    winter to pass. We want
whoever to call or not call, a letter, a kiss—we want
    more and more and then more of it.

But there are moments, walking, when I catch a glimpse of myself
    in the window glass,
say, the window of the corner video store, and I'm gripped by a
    cherishing so deep

for my own blowing hair, chapped face, and unbuttoned coat
    that I'm speechless:
I am living. I remember you.

### FOR ANALYSIS

**1.** Who do you think Johnny might be?

**2.** What is it that Johnny "finally gave up" (l. 11)?

**3.** What kinds of things make the speaker stop and think about Johnny? How does she characterize these thoughts?

### MAKING ARGUMENTS

The situation of "What the Living Do," its subject, is not unfamiliar to us. What makes this poem is not the idea—that one shape grief can take is this one—but the way in which that shape is realized in the shape of the poem. Make an argument for this claim, using the poem's structure and **rhythm** as evidence.

### WRITING TOPIC

Often we think of the dead in terms of loss—of who they were, of what they meant to us, of how they are gone. The speaker in "What the Living Do" thinks of them in terms of what the title names—what those of us still here do in our everyday lives. Write an essay in which you describe the ways in which you think of those who are no longer with us.

### DILRUBA AHMED   (B. 1973)

# SNAKE OIL, SNAKE BITE   2013

They staunched the wound with a stone.
They drew blue venom from his blood
    until there was none.
When his veins ran true his face remained
lifeless and all the mothers of the village
wept and pounded their chests until the sky
    had little choice

but to grant their supplications. God made
      the boy breathe again.

God breathes life into us, it is said,
only once. But this case was an exception.
God drew back in a giant gust and blew life into the boy
and like a stranded fish, he shuddered, oceanless.          10

It was true: the boy lived.
He lived for a very long time. The toxins
were an oil slick: contaminated, cleaned.
But just as soon as the women
kissed redness back into his cheeks
the boy began to die again.
He continued to die for the rest of his life.
The dying took place slowly, sweetly.
The dying took a very long time.

## FOR ANALYSIS

**1.** Who saves the boy's life?

**2.** What is the **tone** at the poem's end?

## MAKING ARGUMENTS

Make an argument about the presence of the divine in this poem. Is this a religious poem? Does the speaker endorse the mothers' opinion that God saves the boy? If so, does the poem endorse the speaker?

## WRITING TOPIC

Reread the poem and annotate it by speaker. That is, note who is responsible for each line of the poem (beyond the poet herself, who of course is ultimately responsible for all of it). Reflect on your observations. Is this poem more complicated than it at first seems? Does recognizing possible shifts in **point of view** complicate your understanding of the poem? How?

**CONNECTING POEMS:**
**ANIMAL FATES**

The poems in this unit focus on the ways in which our own reflections on mortality can involve the animal world beyond the human. They consider the decisions people must make when faced with the death of animals, the way such deaths can make us think about our own lives, and the thoughts about the mysteries of life itself that as innocent a gesture as playing with a cat can prompt.

**ELIZABETH BISHOP**   (1911–1979)

# THE FISH   1946

I caught a tremendous fish
and held him beside the boat
half out of water, with my hook
fast in a corner of his mouth.
He didn't fight.
He hadn't fought at all.
He hung a grunting weight,
battered and venerable
and homely. Here and there
his brown skin hung in strips                               10
like ancient wallpaper,
and its pattern of darker brown
was like wallpaper:
shapes like full-blown roses
stained and lost through age.
He was speckled with barnacles,
fine rosettes of lime,
and infested
with tiny white sea-lice,
and underneath two or three                               20
rags of green weed hung down.
While his gills were breathing in
the terrible oxygen
—the frightening gills,
fresh and crisp with blood,
that can cut so badly—
I thought of the coarse white flesh
packed in like feathers,

the big bones and the little bones,
the dramatic reds and blacks                                          30
of his shiny entrails,
and the pink swim-bladder
like a big peony.
I looked into his eyes
which were far larger than mine
but shallower, and yellowed,
the irises backed and packed
with tarnished tinfoil
seen through the lenses
of old scratched isinglass.                                          40
They shifted a little, but not
to return my stare.
—It was more like the tipping
of an object toward the light.
I admired his sullen face,
the mechanism of his jaw,
and then I saw
that from his lower lip
—if you could call it a lip—
grim, wet, and weaponlike,                                           50
hung five old pieces of fish-line,
or four and a wire leader
with the swivel still attached,
with all their five big hooks
grown firmly in his mouth.
A green line, frayed at the end
where he broke it, two heavier lines,
and a fine black thread
still crimped from the strain and snap
when it broke and he got away.                                       60
Like medals with their ribbons
frayed and wavering,
a five-haired beard of wisdom
trailing from his aching jaw.
I stared and stared
and victory filled up
the little rented boat,
from the pool of bilge
where oil had spread a rainbow
around the rusted engine                                             70
to the bailer rusted orange,
the sun-cracked thwarts,
the oarlocks on their strings,

the gunnels—until everything
was rainbow, rainbow, rainbow!
And I let the fish go.

### FOR ANALYSIS

**1.** What is the nature of the speaker's "victory" (l. 66)?

**2.** Where does the poem turn—that is, where does the poem shift its attention to something that changes what it is about and what it means?

### MAKING ARGUMENTS

Bishop's poem hinges on the decision to let the fish go. While this is not really the poem's subject, it could be taken as a commentary on sportfishing and hunting, a pastime enjoyed by millions but also criticized by many. Make an argument defending or attacking this pastime based on whatever evidence and support you think will help you make your case.

### WRITING TOPIC

"The Fish" is packed with details. List the details Bishop includes, breaking them down into the groups in which they appear (e.g., those describing the fish's skin, those describing the boat). Then reflect on how the poem uses these details. How do they create pictures, set moods, imply thoughts and feelings?

## WILLIAM STAFFORD   (1914–1993)

# TRAVELING THROUGH THE DARK   1962

Traveling through the dark I found a deer
dead on the edge of the Wilson River road.
It is usually best to roll them into the canyon:
that road is narrow; to swerve might make more dead.

By glow of the tail-light I stumbled back of the car
and stood by the heap, a doe, a recent killing;
she had stiffened already, almost cold.
I dragged her off; she was large in the belly.

My fingers touching her side brought me the reason—
her side was warm; her fawn lay there waiting,                    10
alive, still, never to be born.
Beside that mountain road I hesitated.

The car aimed ahead its lowered parking lights;
under the hood purred the steady engine.
I stood in the glare of the warm exhaust turning red;
around our group I could hear the wilderness listen.

I thought hard for us all—my only swerving—,
then pushed her over the edge into the river.

## FOR ANALYSIS

**1.** Why is it best to clear the dead deer off the road? Why does the speaker hesitate?

**2.** How is the speaker's car described? Why do you think Stafford describes it this way?

**3.** Stafford uses versions of the word *swerve* twice. Why do you think he uses them?

## MAKING ARGUMENTS

There are estimates that 350,000 deer are killed by cars each year. For some, this is a tragedy for the animals; for others, it is more concerning because of the danger to drivers and passengers. Where do you stand on this situation? Could it be avoided? Is it a necessary evil given the modern world's car-based way of life?

## WRITING TOPIC

Stafford chose not to explain how the deer came to be dead, perhaps in part because it is obvious that cars kill deer on this road often. Why else might he not have mentioned it? What could this poem be saying about this unnamed cause?

## JOHN UPDIKE  (1932–2009)

# DOG'S DEATH  1993

She must have been kicked unseen or brushed by a car.
Too young to know much, she was beginning to learn
To use the newspapers spread on the kitchen floor
And to win, wetting there, the words, "Good dog! Good dog!"

We thought her shy malaise was a shot reaction.
The autopsy disclosed a rupture in her liver.
As we teased her with play, blood was filling her skin
And her heart was learning to lie down forever.

. . .

Monday morning, as the children were noisily fed
And sent to school, she crawled beneath the youngest's bed.    10
We found her twisted and limp but still alive.
In the car to the vet's, on my lap, she tried

To bite my hand and died. I stroked her warm fur
And my wife called in a voice imperious with tears.
Though surrounded by love that would have upheld her,
Nevertheless she sank and, stiffening, disappeared.

Back home, we found that in the night her frame,
Drawing near to dissolution, had endured the shame
Of diarrhea and had dragged across the floor
To a newspaper carelessly left there. *Good dog.*                    20

### FOR ANALYSIS

**1.** Why is the dog's dying described the way it is in line 8?

**2.** Are the speaker and his family to blame for the dog's death? Do they feel they are?

**3.** Why do you think Updike ends the poem the way he does—in particular, why with that sentence?

### MAKING ARGUMENTS

There is a difference between sentiment and sentimentality. Argue that Updike's poem is characterized by the former or the latter.

### WRITING TOPIC

Many of us are very attached to our pets and think of them as members of the family. There are some people who find this very odd, even indulgent and irrational. What do you think about the way people feel about their pets? Write a reflection on this question, using as material not only your own feelings and experiences but your observations and knowledge of relevant issues.

## WILLIAM GREENWAY   (B. 1947)

# PIT PONY   1987

There are only a few left, he says,
kept by old Welsh miners, souvenirs, like
gallstones or gold teeth, torn
from this "pit," so cold and wet my
breath comes out a soul up
into my helmet's lantern
beam, anthracite walls running,
gleaming, and the floors iron-rutted
with tram tracks, the almost pure
rust that grows and waves like                                       10
orange moss in the gutters of water
that used to rise and drown.
He makes us turn all lights off, almost

a mile down. While children scream
I try to see anything, my hand touching
my nose, my wife beside me—darkness palpable,
a velvet sack over our heads, even the glow
of watches left behind. This is where
they were born, into this nothing, felt
first with their cold noses for the shaggy                      20
side and warm bag of black
milk, pulled their trams for twenty
years through pitch, past birds
that didn't sing, through doors
opened by five-year-olds who sat
in the cheap, complete blackness listening
for steps, a knock. And they
died down here, generation after
generation. The last one, when it
dies in the hills, not quite blind, the mines               30
closed forever, will it die strangely? Will it
wonder dimly why it was exiled from the rest
of its race, from the dark flanks of the soft
mother, what these timbers are that hold up
nothing but blue? If this is the beginning
of death, this wind, these stars?

## FOR ANALYSIS

**1.** What are there only a few of left in the poem's first line?

**2.** While down in the mine, the speaker imagines life for the ponies that worked there. How might the speaker's act of imagination be affected by the fact that he is touring the mine with his family?

**3.** What is the **tone** of the poem's description of the pony's lives in the pits? How about the tone of the description of life aboveground? Is it what you might expect? Why or why not?

## MAKING ARGUMENTS

We anthropomorphize animals. But that doesn't mean that they don't have consciousness—emotions, attachments, self-awareness—according to many people. Others think they are far more different from us and that we shouldn't pretend to know what could be going on in their heads, if anything. Make an argument about "Pit Pony" in this context. Can a poet attempt to empathize with a nonhuman subject? Does our having sympathy for them depend on what we imagine their feelings are?

## WRITING TOPIC

Write (or describe) a poem written in whole or in part from the **point of view** of an animal, and reflect on what you've written. How is the animal's life like and unlike human life? Can our imagination of an animal's interior life ever approach what it's actually like?

## MAKING CONNECTIONS

**1.** How do these poems create moments in which the speakers think of animals as individual beings? How do they create personal (or emotional) connections with animals?

**2.** Some of these poems confront humans with a dilemma about killing animals. How does each resolve its dilemma? How does each poem present the decision that is made? Do any of them judge the decision?

**3.** What do humans do for animals in these poems? What do animals do for humans? Reflect on what these poems as a group say about the relationship between humans and nonhuman animals.

# DRAMA

**EDWARD ALBEE**   (1928–2016)

## THE SANDBOX   1959

CHARACTERS

**The Young Man**, Twenty-five. A good-looking, well-built boy in a bathing suit.
**Mommy**, Fifty-five. A well-dressed, imposing woman.
**Daddy**, Sixty. A small man; gray, thin.

**Grandma**, Eighty-six. A tiny, wizened woman with bright eyes.
**The Musician**, No particular age, but young would be nice.

*Note:* When, in the course of the play, Mommy and Daddy call each other by these names, there should be no suggestion of regionalism. These names are of empty affection and point up the pre-senility and vacuity of their characters.

**Scene**
*A bare stage, with only the following: Near the footlights, far stage-right, two simple chairs set side by side, facing the audience; near the footlights, far stage-left, a chair facing stage-right with a music stand before it; farther back, and stage-center, slightly elevated and raked, a large child's sandbox with a toy pail and shovel; the background is the sky, which alters from brightest day to deepest night.*

*At the beginning, it is brightest day; the Young Man is alone on stage, to the rear of the sandbox, and to one side. He is doing calisthenics; he does calisthenics until quite at the very end of the play. These calisthenics, employing the arms only, should suggest the beating and fluttering of wings. The Young Man is, after all, the Angel of Death.*

*(Mommy and Daddy enter from stage-left, Mommy first.)*

**Mommy** *(Motioning to Daddy).*   Well, here we are; this is the beach.
**Daddy** *(Whining).*   I'm cold.
**Mommy** *(Dismissing him with a little laugh).*   Don't be silly; it's as warm as toast. Look at that nice young man over there: *he* doesn't think it's cold. *(Waves to the Young Man)* Hello.

**Young Man** *(With an endearing smile).* Hi!

**Mommy** *(Looking about).* This will do perfectly . . . don't you think so, Daddy? There's sand there . . . and the water beyond. What do you think, Daddy?

**Daddy** *(Vaguely).* Whatever you say, Mommy.

**Mommy** *(With the same little laugh).* Well, of course . . . whatever I say. Then, it's settled, is it?

**Daddy** *(Shrugs).* She's *your* mother, not mine.

**Mommy.** *I* know she's my mother. What do you take me for? *(A pause)* All right, now; let's get on with it. *(She shouts into the wings, stage-left)* You! Out there! You can come in now.

*(The Musician enters, seats himself in the chair, stage-left, places music on the music stand, is ready to play. Mommy nods approvingly)*

**Mommy.** Very nice; very nice. Are you ready, Daddy? Let's go get Grandma.

**Daddy.** Whatever you say, Mommy.

**Mommy** *(Leading the way out, stage-left).* Of course, whatever I say. *(To the Musician)* You can begin now.

*(The Musician begins playing; Mommy and Daddy exit; the Musician, all the while playing, nods to the Young Man)*

**Young Man** *(With the same endearing smile).* Hi!

*(After a moment, Mommy and Daddy re-enter, carrying Grandma. She is borne in by their hands under her armpits; she is quite rigid; her legs are drawn up; her feet do not touch the ground; the expression on her ancient face is that of puzzlement and fear)*

**Daddy.** Where do we put her?

**Mommy** *(The same little laugh).* Wherever I say, of course. Let me see . . . well . . . all right, over there . . . in the sandbox. *(Pause)* Well, what are you waiting for, Daddy? . . . The sandbox!

*(Together they carry Grandma over to the sandbox and more or less dump her in)*

**Grandma** *(Righting herself to a sitting position; her voice a cross between a baby's laugh and cry).* Ahhhhhh! Graaaaa!

**Daddy** *(Dusting himself).* What do we do now?

**Mommy** *(To the Musician).* You can stop now.

*(The Musician stops)*

*(Back to Daddy)* What do you mean, what do we do now? We go over there and sit down, of course. *(To the Young Man)* Hello there.

**Young Man** *(Again smiling).*  Hi!

*(Mommy and Daddy move to the chairs, stage-right, and sit down. A pause)*

**Grandma** *(Same as before).*  Ahhhhhh! Ah-haaaaaa! Graaaaaa!
**Daddy.**  Do you think . . . do you think she's . . . comfortable?
**Mommy** *(Impatiently).*  How would I know?
**Daddy** *(Pause).*  What do we do now?
**Mommy** *(As if remembering).*  We . . . wait. We . . . sit here . . . and we wait . . . that's what we do.
**Daddy** *(After a pause).*  Shall we talk to each other?
**Mommy** *(With that little laugh; picking something off her dress).*  Well, *you* can talk, if you want to . . . if you can think of anything to *say* . . . if you can think of anything *new*.
**Daddy** *(Thinks).*  No . . . I suppose not.
**Mommy** *(With a triumphant laugh).*  Of course not!
**Grandma** *(Banging the toy shovel against the pail).*  Haaaaaa! Ahhaaaaaa!
**Mommy** *(Out over the audience).*  Be quiet, Grandma . . . just be quiet, and wait.

*(Grandma throws a shovelful of sand at Mommy)*

**Mommy** *(Still out over the audience).*  She's throwing sand at me! You stop that, Grandma; you stop throwing sand at Mommy! *(To Daddy)* She's throwing sand at me.

*(Daddy looks around at Grandma, who screams at him)*

**Grandma.**  GRAAAAAA!
**Mommy.**  Don't look at her. Just . . . sit here . . . be very still . . . and wait. *(To the Musician)* You . . . uh . . . you go ahead and do whatever it is you do.

*(The Musician plays)*

*(Mommy and Daddy are fixed, staring out beyond the audience. Grandma looks at them, looks at the Musician, looks at the sandbox, throws down the shovel)*

**Grandma.**  Ah-haaaaaa! Graaaaaa! *(Looks for reaction; gets none. Now . . . directly to the audience)* Honestly! What a way to treat an old woman! Drag her out of the house . . . stick her in a car . . . bring her out here from the city . . . dump her in a pile of sand . . . and leave her here to set. I'm eighty-six years old! I was married when I was seventeen. To a farmer. He died when I was thirty. *(To the Musician)* Will you stop that, please?

*(The Musician stops playing).*

I'm a feeble old woman . . . how do you expect anybody to hear me over that peep! peep! peep! *(To herself)* There's no respect around here. *(To the Young Man)* There's no respect around here!

**Young Man** *(Same smile)*. Hi!

**Grandma** *(After a pause, a mild double-take, continues, to the audience)*. My husband died when I was thirty *(indicates Mommy)*, and I had to raise that big cow over there all by my lonesome. You can imagine what *that* was like. Lordy! *(To the Young Man)* Where'd they get *you*?

**Young Man.** Oh . . . I've been around for a while.

**Grandma.** I'll bet you have! Heh, heh, heh. Will you look at you!

**Young Man** *(Flexing his muscles)*. Isn't that something? *(Continues his calisthenics)*

**Grandma.** Boy, oh boy; I'll say. Pretty good.

**Young Man** *(Sweetly)*. I'll say.

**Grandma.** Where ya from?

**Young Man.** Southern California.

**Grandma** *(Nodding)*. Figgers, figgers. What's your name, honey?

**Young Man.** I don't know. . . .

**Grandma** *(To the audience)*. Bright, too!

**Young Man.** I mean . . . I mean, they haven't given me one yet . . . the studio . . .

**Grandma** *(Giving him the once-over)*. You don't say . . . you don't say. Well . . . uh, I've got to talk some more . . . don't you go 'way.

**Young Man.** Oh, no.

**Grandma** *(Turning her attention back to the audience)*. Fine; fine. *(Then, once more, back to the Young Man)* You're . . . you're an actor, hunh?

**Young Man** *(Beaming)*. Yes. I am.

**Grandma.** *(To the audience again; shrugs)*. I'm smart that way. *Anyhow*, I had to raise . . . *that* over there all by my lonesome; and what's next to her there . . . that's what she married. Rich? I tell you . . . money, money, money. They took me off the *farm* . . . which was real decent of them . . . and they moved me into the big town house with *them* . . . fixed a nice place for me under the stove . . . gave me an army blanket . . . and my own dish . . . my very own dish! So, what have I got to complain about? Nothing, of course. I'm not complaining. *(She looks up at the sky, shouts to someone offstage)* Shouldn't it be getting dark now, dear?

*(The lights dim; night comes on. The Musician begins to play; it becomes deepest night. There are spots on all the players, including the Young Man, who is, of course, continuing his calisthenics)*

**Daddy** *(Stirring)*. It's nighttime.

**Mommy.** Shhhh. Be still . . . wait.

**Daddy** *(Whining)*. It's so hot.

**Mommy.** Shhhhhh. Be still . . . wait.

**Grandma** *(To herself)*. That's better. Night. *(To the Musician)* Honey, do you play all through this part?

*(The Musician nods)*

Well, keep it nice and soft; that's a good boy.

*(The Musician nods again; plays softly)*

That's nice.

*(There is an off-stage rumble)*

**Daddy** *(Starting)*. What was that?
**Mommy** *(Beginning to weep)*. It was nothing.
**Daddy.** It was . . . it was . . . thunder . . . or a wave breaking . . . or something.
**Mommy** *(Whispering, through her tears)*. It was an off-stage rumble and you know
what *that* means. . . .
**Daddy.** I forget. . . .
**Mommy** *(Barely able to talk)*. It means the time has come for poor Grandma . . .
and I can't bear it!
**Daddy** *(Vacantly)*. I . . . I suppose you've got to be brave.
**Grandma** *(Mocking)*. That's right, kid; be brave. You'll bear up; you'll get over it.

*(Another off-stage rumble . . . louder)*

**Mommy.** Ohhhhhhhhhh . . . poor Grandma . . . poor Grandma. . . .
**Grandma** *(To Mommy)*. I'm fine! I'm all right! It hasn't happened yet!

*(A violent off-stage rumble. All the lights go out, save the spot on the Young Man; the
Musician stops playing)*

**Mommy.** Ohhhhhhhhhh . . . Ohhhhhhhhhh. . . .

*(Silence)*

**Grandma.** Don't put the lights up yet . . . I'm not ready; I'm not quite ready.
*(Silence)* All right, dear . . . I'm about done.

*(The lights come up again, to brightest day; the Musician begins to play. Grandma
is discovered, still in the sandbox, lying on her side, propped up on an elbow, half
covered, busily shoveling sand over herself)*

**Grandma** *(Muttering)*. I don't know how I'm supposed to do anything with this
goddamn toy shovel. . . .
**Daddy.** Mommy! It's daylight!
**Mommy** *(Brightly)*. So it is! Well! Our long night is over. We must put away our
tears, take off our mourning . . . and face the future. It's our duty.
**Grandma** *(Still shoveling; mimicking)* . . . take off our mourning . . . face the
future. . . . Lordy!

*(Mommy and Daddy rise, stretch. Mommy waves to the Young Man)*

**Young Man** *(With that smile)*. Hi!

*(Grandma plays dead. (!) Mommy and Daddy go over to look at her; she is a little
more than half buried in the sand; the toy shovel is in her hands, which are crossed
on her breast)*

**Mommy** *(Before the sandbox; shaking her head)*. Lovely! It's . . . it's hard to be sad . . . she looks . . . so happy. *(With pride and conviction)* It pays to do things well. *(To the Musician)* All right, you can stop now, if you want to. I mean, stay around for a swim, or something; it's all right with us. *(She sighs heavily)* Well, Daddy . . . off we go.

**Daddy.** Brave Mommy!

**Mommy.** Brave Daddy!

*(They exit, stage-left)*

**Grandma.** *(After they leave; lying quite still).* It pays to do things well . . . Boy, oh boy! *(She tries to sit up)* . . . well, kids . . . *(but she finds she can't)* . . . I . . . I can't get up. I . . . I can't move. . . .

*(The Young Man stops his calisthenics, nods to the Musician, walks over to Grandma, kneels down by the sandbox)*

**Grandma.** I . . . can't move. . . .

**Young Man.** Shhhhh . . . be very still. . . .

**Grandma.** I . . . I can't move. . . .

**Young Man.** Uh . . . ma'am; I . . . I have a line here.

**Grandma.** Oh, I'm sorry, sweetie; you go right ahead.

**Young Man.** I am . . . uh . . . I am . . .

**Grandma.** Take your time, dear.

**Young Man** *(Prepares; delivers the line like a real amateur).* I am the Angel of Death. I am . . . uh . . . I am come for you.

**Grandma.** What . . . wha . . . *(Then, with resignation)* . . . ohhhh . . . ohhhh . . . I see.

*(The Young Man bends over, kisses Grandma gently on the forehead)*

**Grandma** *(Her eyes closed, her hands folded on her breast again, the shovel between her hands, a sweet smile on her face).* Well . . . that was very nice, dear . . .

**Young Man** *(Still kneeling).* Shhhhhh . . . be still. . . .

**Grandma.** What I meant was . . . you did that very well, dear. . . .

**Young Man** *(Blushing).* . . . oh . . .

**Grandma.** No; I mean it. You've got that . . . you've got a quality.

**Young Man** *(With his endearing smile).* Oh . . . thank you; thank you very much . . . ma'am.

**Grandma** *(Slowly; softly—as the Young Man puts his hands on top of Grandma's).* You're . . . you're welcome . . . dear.

*(Tableau. The Musician continues to play as the curtain slowly comes down)*

*Curtain*

## FOR ANALYSIS

1. How would you characterize the relationship between Mommy and Daddy on the one hand and Grandma on the other? How do they treat her? What can you tell about them and their feelings?

2. What are Mommy and Daddy waiting for?

3. Is this a realistic play? How so, and/or how not?

4. As odd as this play is, do you still feel emotion by its end? If so, what causes it?

## MAKING ARGUMENTS

While Albee is a giant of American theater and this is one of his better-known works, not every critic loved this play when it first appeared. Make an argument in defense of the play against these critics. What do you imagine their criticisms might have been? How would you counter them?

## WRITING TOPIC

Think about the absurdism of this play. Describe how it is absurdist (defining what that means—research is fine here) and reflect on what it means to write about this subject in this way.

## MAKING CONNECTIONS

Revisit Allegra Goodman's "Apple Cake" (p. 869) and think about it in the light of this (very different) play. Do they share observations about the relationship between adult children and their parents and the nature of the moment when elderly parents die?

# Nonfiction

**John Donne**   (1572–1631)

## Meditation XVII, from Devotions upon Emergent Occasions   1623

Nunc lento sonitu dicunt morieris.
   Now this bell tolling softly for another says to me, Thou must die.

Perchance he for whom this bell tolls may be so ill as that he knows not it tolls for him; and perchance I may think myself so much better than I am, as that they who are about me and see my state may have caused it to toll for me, and I know not that. The church is catholic, universal, so are all her actions; all that she does belongs to all. When she baptizes a child, that action 5 concerns me; for that child is thereby connected to that head which is my head too, and ingrafted into that body whereof I am a member. And when she buries a man, that action concerns me: all mankind is of one author and is one volume; when one man dies, one chapter is not torn out of the book, but translated into a better language; and every chapter must be so translated. God employs sev- 10 eral translators; some pieces are translated by age, some by sickness, some by war, some by justice; but God's hand is in every translation, and his hand shall bind up all our scattered leaves again for that library where every book shall lie open to one another. As therefore the bell that rings to a sermon calls not upon the preacher only, but upon the congregation to come, so this bell calls us all; 15 but how much more me, who am brought so near the door by this sickness. There was a contention as far as a suit[1] (in which piety and dignity, religion and estimation, were mingled) which of the religious orders should ring to prayers first in the morning; and it was determined that they should ring first that rose earliest. If we understand aright the dignity of this bell that tolls for our evening 20 prayer, we would be glad to make it ours by rising early, in that application, that it might be ours as well as his whose indeed it is. The bell doth toll for him that

[1] An argument settled by a lawsuit.

thinks it doth, and though it intermit again, yet from that minute that that occasion wrought upon him, he is united to God. Who casts not up his eye to the sun when it rises? but who takes off his eye from a comet when that breaks out? 25 Who bends not his ear to any bell which upon any occasion rings? but who can remove it from that bell which is passing a piece of himself out of this world? No man is an island, entire of itself; every man is a piece of the continent, a part of the main. If a clod be washed away by the sea, Europe is the less, as well as if a promontory were, as well as if a manor of thy friend's or of thine own were. Any 30 man's death diminishes me, because I am involved in mankind; and therefore never send to know for whom the bell tolls; it tolls for thee. Neither can we call this a begging of misery or a borrowing of misery, as though we were not miserable enough of ourselves but must fetch in more from the next house, in taking upon us the misery of our neighbors. Truly it were an excusable covetousness 35 if we did; for affliction is a treasure, and scarce any man hath enough of it. No man hath affliction enough that is not matured and ripened by it, and made fit for God by that affliction. If a man carry treasure in bullion, or in a wedge of gold, and have none coined into current moneys, his treasure will not defray him as he travels. Tribulation is treasure in the nature of it, but it is not current 40 money in the use of it, except we get nearer and nearer our home, heaven, by it. Another man may be sick too, and sick to death, and this affliction may lie in his bowels as gold in a mine and be of no use to him; but this bell that tells me of his affliction digs out and applies that gold to me, if by this consideration of another's danger I take mine own into contemplation and so secure myself by 45 making my recourse to my God, who is our only security.

## FOR ANALYSIS

**1.** What does Donne mean when he says that the death bell "tolls for thee" (l. 32)?

**2.** Toward the end of his meditation, Donne states that "tribulation is treasure" (l. 40). What does he mean? What will that treasure purchase?

**3.** Donne is justly admired for his use of **figurative language**. What extended **metaphors** does he use to characterize humankind and death?

## MAKING ARGUMENTS

Look up the larger work from which this meditation is drawn. Make an argument concerning the relation to the biographical and theological in this work. How does one relate to the other? How does this relation manifest in the work?

## WRITING TOPICS

**1.** What does Donne mean by "affliction is a treasure" (l. 36)? Do you agree? Explain.

**2.** Identify and analyze the **figurative language** Donne uses to illuminate the human condition and his attitude toward death.

## MAKING CONNECTIONS

Read this meditation with Donne's "Death, Be Not Proud" (p. 887). What attitude does each have toward death? How does each offer alternatives to fear of death and sadness about death?

CONNECTING NONFICTION:
MISSING MOTHERS

These two fantastic new essays are among the saddest in this book, and among the most interesting. They are about the same subject, generally, but approach that subject in very different ways and with very different goals in mind. As you read, notice how both manage to be intensely personal, yet do so in different ways.

## JONATHAN LETHEM    (B. 1964)

# 13, 1977, 21    2006

1. In the summer of 1977 I saw *Star Wars*—the original, which is all I want to discuss here—twenty-one times. Better to blurt this at the start so I'm less tempted to retreat from what still seems to me a sort of raw, howling confession, one I've long hidden in shame. Again, to pin myself like a Nabokovian butterfly (no high-lit reference is going to bail me out here, I know) to my page in geek history: I watched *Star Wars* twenty-one times in the space of four months. I was that kid alone in the ticket line, slipping past ushers who'd begun to recognize me, muttering in impatience at a urinal before finding my favorite seat. That was me, occult as a porn customer, yes, though I've sometimes denied it. Now, a quarter-century later, I'm ready for my close-up. Sort of.

2. That year I was thirteen, and likely as ideal an audience member as any mogul could have drooled for. Say every kid in the United States with even the passingest fondness for comic books or adventure fiction, *any kid with a television, even,* had bought a ticket for the same film in a single summer: blah, blah, right, that's what happened. So figure that for every hundred kids who traveled an ordinary path (*Cool movie, wouldn't mind seeing it again with my friends*) there might be one who'd make himself ill returning to the cookie jar five or six times (*It's really still good the fourth time, I swear!*) before copping to a tummy ache. Next figure that for each *five* hundred, one or two would slip into some brain-warped identificatory obsession (*I am* Star Wars, Star Wars *am me, goo goo ga joob*) and return to the primal site often enough to push into the realm of trance and memorization. That's me, with my gaudy *twenty-one,* like DiMaggio's *fifty-six.* But what actually occurred within the secret brackets of that experience? What emotions lurk within that ludicrous temple of hours? *What the fuck was I thinking?*

3. Every one of those twenty-one viewings took place at the Loew's Astor Plaza on Forty-fourth Street, just off Times Square. I'd never seen a movie there before (and unless you count *The Empire Strikes Back*, I didn't again until

1999—*The Matrix*). And I've still never seen *Star Wars* anywhere else. The Astor Plaza was a low, deep-stretched hall with a massive screen and state-of-the-art sound, and newly enough renovated to be free of too much soda-rotted carpet, a plague among New York theaters those days. Though architecturally undistinguished, it was a superior place to see anything, I suppose. But for me it was a shrine meant for just one purpose—I took it as weirdly significant that "Astor" could be rearranged into "astro"—and in a very *New Yorker*-coverish way I believed it to be the only real and right place to see *Star Wars*, the very ground zero of the phenomenon. I felt a definite but not at all urgent pity for any benighted fools stuck watching it elsewhere. I think I associated the Astor Plaza with the Death Star, in a way. Getting in always felt like an accomplishment, both elevating and slightly dangerous.

4. Along those lines I should say it was vaguely unnerving to be a white kid in spectacles routinely visiting Times Square by subway in the middle of the 1970s. Nobody ever said anything clearly about what was wrong or fascinating about that part of the city we lived in—the information was absorbed in hints and mutterings from a polyphony of sources. In fact, though I was conscious of a certain seamy energy in those acres of sex shows and drug dealers and their furtive sidewalk customers, I was never once hassled (and this was a time when my home neighborhood, in Brooklyn, was a minefield for me personally). But the zone's reputation ensured I'd always plan my visits to fall wholly within summer's long daylight hours.

5. Problem: it doesn't seem at all likely that I went to the movie alone the first time, but I can't remember who I was with. I've polled a few of my likeliest friends from that period, but they're unable to help. In truth I can't recall a "first time" in any real sense, though I do retain a flash memory of the moment the prologue first began to crawl in tilted perspective up the screen, an Alice-in-Wonderland doorway to dream. I'd been so primed, so attuned and ready to love it (I remember mocking my friend Evan for his thinking that the title meant it was going to be some kind of all-star cavalcade of a comedy, like *It's a Mad Mad Mad Mad World* or *Smokey and the Bandit*) that my first time was gulped impatiently, then covered quickly in the memory of return visits. From the first I was "seeing it again." I think this memory glitch is significant. I associate it with my practice of bluffing familiarity with various drug experiences, later (not much later). My refusal to recall or admit to a first time was an assertion of maturity: I was *always already* a *Star Wars* fanatic.

6. I didn't buy twenty-one tickets. My count was amassed by seeing the movie twice in a day over and over again. And one famous day (famous to myself) I sat through it three times. That practice of seeing a film twice through originated earlier. Somebody—my mother?—had floated the idea that it wasn't important to be on time for a movie, or even to check the screening times before going. Instead, moviegoing in Brooklyn Heights or on Fulton Street with my brother or with friends, we'd pop in at any point in the story, watch to the end, then sit through the break and watch the beginning. Which led

naturally, if the film was any good, to staying past the original point of entry to see the end twice. Which itself led to routinely twice-watching a movie we liked, even if we hadn't been late. This was encouraged, partly according to a general *Steal This Book*–ish anticapitalist imperative for taking freebies in my parents' circle in the seventies. Of course somebody—my mother?—had also figured out a convenient way to get the kids out of the house for long stretches.

7. I hate arriving late for movies now and would never watch one in this broken fashion. (It seems to me, though, that I probably learned something about the construction of narratives from the practice.) The lifelong moviegoing habit which does originate for me with *Star Wars* is that of sitting in movie theaters alone. I probably only had company in the Loew's Astor Plaza four or five times. The rest of my visits were solitary, which is certainly central to any guesses I'd make about the emotional meaning of the ritual viewings.

8. I still go to the movies alone, all the time. In the absenting of self which results—so different from the quality of solitude at my writing desk—this seems to me as near as I come in my life to any reverent or worshipful or meditational practice. That's not to say it isn't also indulgent, with a frisson of guilt, of stolen privilege, every time. I'm acutely conscious of this joyous guilt in the fact that when as a solitary moviegoer I take a break to go to the bathroom *I can return to another part of the theater and watch from a different seat.* I first discovered this thrill during my *Star Wars* summer, and it's one which never diminishes. The rupture of the spectator's contract with perspective feels as transgressive as wife-swapping.

9. The function or dysfunction of my *Star Wars* obsession was paradoxical. I was using the movie as a place to hide, sure. That's obvious. At the same time, this activity of hiding inside the Loew's Astor Plaza, and inside my private, *deeper-than-yours, deeper-than-anyone's* communion with the film itself, was something I boasted widely about. By building my lamebrain World Record for screenings (fat chance, I learned later) I was teaching myself to package my own craving for solitude, and my own obsessive tendencies, as something to be admired. *You can't join me inside this box where I hide,* I was saying, *but you sure can praise the box. You're permitted to marvel at me for going inside.*

10. What I was hiding from is easy, though. My parents had separated a couple of years earlier. Then my mother had begun having seizures, been diagnosed with a brain tumor, and had had the first of two surgeries. The summer of *Star Wars* she was five or six months from the second, unsuccessful surgery, and a year from dying.

11. I took my brother, and he stayed through it twice. We may have done that together more than once—neither of us clearly remembers. I took a girl, on a quasi-date: Alissa, the sister of my best friend, Joel. I took my mother. I tried to take my grandmother.

12. That same summer I once followed Alissa to a ballet class at Carnegie Hall and hung around the studio, expressing a polite curiosity which was cover for another, less polite curiosity. The instructor was misled or chose to misunderstand—a thirteen-year-old boy willing to set foot inside a ballet studio was a commodity, a raw material. I was offered free classes, and the teacher called my house and strong-armed my parents. I remember vividly my mother's pleasure in refusing on my behalf—I was too much of a coward—and how strongly she fastened on the fact that my visit had had nothing to do with any interest in ballet. For years this seemed to me an inexplicable cruelty in my mother toward the ballet teacher. Later I understood that in those first years of adolescence I was giving off a lot of signals to my parents that I might be gay. I was a delicate, obedient, and bookish kid, a constant teacher's pet. Earlier that year my father had questioned me regarding a series of distended cartoon noses I'd drawn in ballpoint on my loose-leaf binder—they had come out looking a lot like penises. And my proclaimed favorite *Star Wars* character was the tweaking English robot, C-3P0.

13. I did and do find C-3P0 sexy. It's as if a strand of DNA from Fritz Lang's fetishized girl robot in *Metropolis* has carried forward to the bland world of *Star Wars*. Also, whereas Carrie Fisher's robes went to her ankles, C-3PO is obviously naked, and ashamed of it.

14. Alissa thought the movie was okay (my overstated claims generally cued a compensating shrug in others) and that was our last date, if it was a date. We're friends now.

15. I don't know how much of an effort it was for my mother to travel by subway to a movie theater in Manhattan by the summer of '77, but I do know it was unusual, and that she was certainly doing it to oblige me. It might have been one of our last ventures out together, before it was impossible for her. I remember fussing over rituals inside the theater, showing her my favorite seat, and straining not to watch her watch it throughout, not to hang on her every reaction. Afterward she too found the movie just okay. It wasn't her kind of thing, but she could understand why I liked it so much. Those were pretty close to her exact words. Maybe with her characteristic Queens hard-boiled tone: *I see why you like it, kiddo.* Then, in a turn I find painful to relate, she left me there to watch it a second time, and took the subway home alone. What a heartbreaking rehearsal! I was saying, in effect: *Come and see my future, post-mom self. Enact with me your parting from it. Here's the world of cinema and stories and obsessive identification I'm using to survive your going—now go.* How generous of her to play in this masquerade, if she knew.

16. I spent a certain amount of time that year trying hopelessly to distract my grandmother from the coming loss of her only child—it would mostly wreck her—by pushing my new enthusiasms at her. For instance she and I had a recurrent argument about rock and roll, one which it now strikes me was probably a faint echo, for her, of struggles over my mother's dropping out of Queens

College in favor of a Greenwich Village beatnik-folk lifestyle. I worked to find a hit song she couldn't quibble with, and thought I'd found one in Wings' "Mull of Kintyre," which is really just a strummy faux-Irish folk song. I played it for her at top volume and she grimaced, her displeasure not at the music but at the apparent trump card I'd played. Then, on the fade, Paul McCartney gave out a kind *of whoop-whoop* holler and my grandmother seized on this, with relish: "You hear that? He had to go and scream. It wasn't good enough just to sing, he had to scream like an animal!" Her will was too much for me. So when she resisted being dragged to *Star Wars* I probably didn't mind, being uninterested in having her trample on my secret sand castle. She and I were ultimately in a kind of argument about whether or not our family was a site of tragedy, and I probably sensed I was on the losing end of that one.

17. My father lived in a commune for part of that summer, though my mother's illness sometimes drew him back into the house. There was a man in the commune—call him George Lucas—whose married life, which included two young children, was coming apart. George Lucas was the person I knew who'd seen *Star Wars* the most times, apart from me, and we had a ritualized bond over it. He'd ask me how many times I'd seen the film and I'd report, like an emissary with good news from the front. George Lucas had a copy of the soundtrack and we'd sit in the commune's living room and play it on the stereo, which I seem to remember being somewhat unpopular with the commune's larger membership. George Lucas, who played piano and had some classical training, would always proclaim that the score was *really pretty good symphonic composition*—he'd also play me Gustav Holst's *Planets Suite* as a kind of primer, and to show me how the Death Star theme came from Holst's Jupiter—and I would dutifully parrot this for my friends, with great severity: John Williams's score was *really pretty good symphonic composition*.

18. The movie itself, right: of course, I must have enjoyed it immensely the first few times. That's what I least recall. Instead I recall now how as I memorized scenes I fought my impatience, and yet fought not to know I was fighting impatience—all that mattered were the winnowed satisfactions of crucial moments occurring once again, like stations of the cross: "Help me, Obi-Wan Kenobi, you're my only hope," "These aren't the droids you're looking for," "If you strike me down, I'll become more powerful than you can possibly imagine," and the dunk shot of Luke's missiles entering the Death Star's duct. I hated, absolutely, the scene in the Death Star's sewers. I hated Han Solo and Princess Leia's flirtation, after a while, feeling I was being manipulated, that it was too mannered and rote: of course they're grumbling now, that's how it *always* goes. I hated the triumphalist ceremony at the end, though the spiffing-up of the robots was a consolation, a necessary relief. I think I came to hate a lot of the film, but I couldn't permit myself to know it. I even came, within a year or so, to hate the fact that I'd seen the movie twenty-one times.

19. Why that number? Probably I thought it was safely ridiculous and extreme to get my record into the twenties, yet stopping at only twenty seemed too

mechanically round. Adding one more felt plausibly arbitrary, more *realistic*. That was likely all I could stand. Perhaps at twenty-one I'd also attained the symbolic number of adulthood, of maturity. By bringing together *thirteen* and *twenty-one* I'd made *Star Wars* my Bar Mitzvah, a ritual I didn't have and probably could have used that year. Now I was a man.

20. By the time I was fifteen, not only had I long since quit boasting about my love of *Star Wars* but it had become privately crucial to have another favorite movie inscribed in its place. I decided Kubrick's *2001: A Space Odyssey* was a suitably noble and alienated choice, but that in order to make it official I'd have to see it more times than *Star Wars*. An exhausting proposition, but I went right at it. One day at the Thalia on West Ninety-fifth Street I sat alone through *2001* three times in a row in a nearly empty theater, a commitment of some nine hours. That day I brought along a tape recorder in order to whisper notes on this immersion experience to my friend Eliot—I also taped *Also sprach Zarathustra* all six times. If *Star Wars* was my Bar Mitzvah then *2001* was getting laid, an experience requiring a more persuasive maturity, and one which I more honestly enjoyed, especially fifteen or twenty showings in. Oddly enough, though, I never did completely overwrite *Star Wars* with *2001*. Instead I stuck at precisely twenty-one viewings of the second movie as well, leaving the two in a dead heat. Even that number was only attained years later, at the University Theater in Berkeley, California, two days after the 1989 Loma Prieta earthquake. There was a mild aftershock which rumbled the old theater during the Star Gate sequence, a nice touch.

21. I'll never see another film so many times, though I still count. I've seen *The Searchers* twelve times—a cheat, since it was partly research. Otherwise, I usually peak out at six or seven viewings, as with *Bringing Up Baby* and *Three Women* and *Love Streams* and *Vertigo*, all films I believe I love more than either *Star Wars* or *2001*. But that kid who still can't decide which of the two futuristic epics to let win the struggle for his mortal soul, the kid who left the question hanging, the kid who partly invented himself in the vacuum collision of *Star Wars* and real loss—that kid is me.

## FOR ANALYSIS

**1.** Explain the title. Why is it an unusual title? Why do you think the author might have decided to use it?

**2.** Number 18 begins, "The movie itself, right." Is this essay about *Star Wars* at all? If so, how? If not, what is it really about?

**3.** Although she is mentioned in number 6, Lethem's mother's illness isn't brought up until number 10. Why do you think he waits so long?

## MAKING ARGUMENTS

Culture criticism—reviews of specific works of literature, film, music, and theater, and longer pieces about these fields—is an important and ever-changing branch of writing.

Where such work is available changes, and how it is written changes. Argue that Lethem's brand of personal criticism as shown here is better, worse, or just different from more traditional, objective criticism.

## WRITING TOPIC

Reread the essay and keep a reading log. At multiple points, reflect on what you thought the essay was about then and where you thought it was going. When you are done, write a reflection on the essay's structure. Consider difficulty, linearity or the lack thereof, and anything else that jumps out at you.

## RUTH MARGALIT  (B. 1983)

# THE UNMOTHERED  2014

When I was growing up in Israel, there was a short-lived show on television called "*Hahaverim Shel Yael*" ("Yael's Friends"), which featured a peppy girl who introduced short clips acted out by puppets. The actress who played Yael was probably in her twenties, but she was dressed up to look like a child, in flowery dresses and pigtails. I loved that program, in which the puppets occasionally crossed into real life and made a mess of Yael's studio. Right before the opening music came on, Yael would look into the camera and fake-whisper to the viewers, "Tell your mother to turn up the volume!" Once, as my twin sister and I were settling down on the sofa to watch, my mother overheard this opening bit. "And what about those who don't have a mother?" she asked.

I must have been seven or eight at the time. I was irritated with her for asking that question, forever ruining the show for me. But I shouldn't have been surprised. It summed up, I now realize, her parenting philosophy. The way she didn't baby us, but treated us like thoughtful people, capable of empathy. The way she was always fully there—registering, questioning. But mostly, I think, it showed her unyielding belief in fairness, which, years later, I would hear her define as justice played out in the private sphere. (She was a philosophy professor, preoccupied with definitions.) It was a particular kind of fairness, one that centered on a child's sensibility. Once, when I asked her whom she loved more, my sister or me, she answered, simply, "You." Incredulous, my sister posed the same question. "Who do you love more, *Ima*? Ruth or me?" "You," my mother said. We tried again. Each time, my mother invariably told whoever asked that she loved her more. "This doesn't make any sense," we finally said. She smiled and told us, "Sure it does. Don't you see? I love *you* more and I love *you* more." This was her sense of fairness: no kid wants to hear that they are loved the *same* as their sister.

This Mother's Day, three and a half years after she died, I find myself turning over her question in my mind. *And what about those who don't have a mother?*

"CALL MOM" said a sign the other day, and something inside me clenched. In my inbox, at work, an email waited from the New York *Times*: a limited offer to "treat Mom" to a free gift. It's nothing, I tell myself. A day for advertisers. So I shrug off the sales and the offers, the cards and the flowers. I press delete. Still, I now mark Mother's Day on my private calendar of grief. Anyone who has experienced a loss must have one of those. There's August 29th, my mother's birthday—forever stopped at sixty-four. September 17th, my parents' anniversary—a day on which I now make a point of calling my father, and we both make a point of talking about anything but. There's June 6th, the day she was diagnosed—when a cough that she had told us was "annoying" her and a leg that she had been dragging, thinking she must have pulled a muscle, turned out to be symptoms of Stage IV lung cancer. And then there's October 16th: the day she died, four months and ten days after the diagnosis. The year becomes a landscape filled with little mines.

Trust me, I'm too aware of the fact that my mother is gone to wish her here 5 in any serious way on Mother's Day. But does the holiday have to be in May, when the lilacs are in full bloom? When a gentle breeze stirs—the kind of breeze that reminds me of days when she would recline on a deck chair on our Jerusalem porch, head tilted back, urging me to "sit a while"?

Meghan O'Rourke has a wonderful word for the club of those without mothers. She calls us not motherless but unmothered. It feels right—an ontological word rather than a descriptive one. I had a mother, and now I don't. This is not a characteristic one can affix, like being paperless, or odorless. The emphasis should be on absence.


I remember driving back to my apartment in Tel Aviv for the first time after those first agitated days in the hospital. A man was out on the street walking his dog. I stared at him, waiting for some sign of acknowledgment that the fundamentals of life had changed. He kept on strolling, of course. How stupid of me, to think that everyone knew.

They say time heals. It's true that the pain wears off, slightly, around the edge, like a knife in need of whetting. But here's what they're missing: It gets harder to explain to myself why I haven't seen her. A month can make sense. (*I took a trip; she was busy with work.*) Even six months is excusable. (*I moved; she's on sabbatical.*) But how to make sense of more than three years worth of distance? How to comprehend that time will only drive my mother and me farther and farther apart?

I've learned that some mourners experience anticipatory grief, mourning their loved ones before they have died, while others experience delayed grief— a postponed reaction to the loss. It might sound strange, but I used to think that I experienced both.

I fully grieved the day we were given the diagnosis. My mother was told that 10 she would be admitted overnight to the cardiology department, because there were no available beds yet to take her in oncology. I heard that phrase—no beds "yet" in oncology—and knew that we were entering a new universe, with its own set of rules. That night, when I finally had a moment to myself, I stood in the hospital's darkened hallway, stared out a sullied window, and wailed in a way I never have before or since. A passing nurse, seeing me keen, brought me a tiny cup of water and made me sit down. I never told my parents or my siblings about this. I simply wiped my eyes and dutifully returned to my mother's bedside. Every now and then, I try to recall what went through my mind as I was standing in that hallway, crying my heart out. (And if you think that the cliché can't be real—well, then, you're lucky.) The truth is, I was thinking, selfishly, about myself. That my mother would never see me marry. That she would not know my children. That the following summer I would turn twenty-eight—her lucky number—and she might not be there.

But there was also what I experienced as a delayed state of grief. I had begun graduate school at Columbia that August—my mother was by then on a targeted drug treatment called Tarceva that had somewhat stabilized her tumor, and she insisted that I go—when I got a call from my sister telling me that things were deteriorating rapidly, and that I should get on a plane back. I had been lying on a lawn in Central Park, reading, when she called. I hung up and couldn't feel anything.

When I returned to New York in late October, only two days after the Shiva, I threw myself right back into school as though nothing had happened. The trees were undressing for winter, and I walked down the chilly streets of Morningside Heights squinting against a nonexistent sun. What I kept hearing from friends during that time was that I looked "good" and "strong." That I seemed "fine." I didn't *feel* fine, but I also had no idea what to do except carry on. "I don't know how you manage," an old friend told me. "If it had been *my* mother, I wouldn't be able to get out of bed in the morning." She thought she was paying me a compliment, not realizing that that's about the worst thing you can say to someone in mourning—as though by merely starting my days I was betraying my mother. *Am I?* I started to panic. But then I came across Roland Barthes's "Mourning Diary," which he kept immediately following the death of his mother. In it, he writes, "No sooner has she departed than the world deafens me with its *continuance*." I remember reading this and experiencing a physical spasm of recognition. He adds, "I seem to have a kind of ease of control that makes other people think I'm suffering less than they would have imagined. But it comes over me when our love for each other is torn apart once again. The most painful moment at the most abstract moment."

Yes, I remember thinking. Yes, yes, yes. This wasn't delayed grief, after all. It was simply this: grief keeps odd hours, *the most painful moment at the most abstract moment.* Strangely, I began to think of Barthes (whose relationship with his mother famously bordered on the Oedipal) as my grief buddy. Largely preferring books to people around that time, I discovered that he wasn't the only one.

In my journal from that period, instead of writing how I felt, I sought out and copied everything that seemed to express what to me was inexpressible. From Proust, I took: "For henceforth you will always keep something broken about you." From C. S. Lewis: "No one ever told me that grief felt so like fear. I am not afraid but the sensation is like being afraid. The same fluttering in the stomach, the same restlessness, the yawning. I keep on swallowing." From Joan Didion: "A single person is missing for you, and the whole world is empty." From O'Rourke: "Am I really she who has woken up again without a mother? Yes, I am." From a short story by Alice Munro: "What he carried with him, all he carried with him, was a lack, something like a lack of air, of proper behavior in his lungs, a difficulty that he supposed would go on forever." From one by David Long: "Eventually, a truck would come rattling down . . . a car door would chuff, and the world would go on—not where it had left off but on the other side of this nothing time. And when it did, though she couldn't quite see it yet, [she] would begin the never-ending task of not forgetting her mother."

Or this, from my mother's favorite Hebrew poem, in which the poet, Natan   15
Alterman, describes his beloved as "sudden forever." Those two words, as well as the poem's title—"A Meeting for Eternity"—are oxymorons that spell out the contradictions inherent in loss. What is the death of a loved one if not an oxymoron? My mother isn't here, and yet I see her everywhere. I kept on look-ing for hints of her on the page, as though by retracing her beloved books and poems I would get to reclaim a part of her that was already slipping away.

Two days before she died, my father walked into the hospital room and told me to time a minute. I looked at my watch. When the minute was up, I told him. He said, "Twenty-three. Very good." He had been counting her breaths, I realized. Willing her to stay. And she did—she waited until we were all there, flanking her bed—before letting go.

We buried her just outside of Jerusalem, on a kibbutz, facing the mountains of her youth. She adored her hometown, and ached over what it had become. The growing zealotry, the flickering lights of peace. The news coming out of Israel today—another botched round of negotiations—would have depressed her terribly. Instead, I like to think of what is immutable. The warm wind whis-tling past those hills. The pine needles crackling underfoot. And on the other side of the mountains, down by the coastal plain—hidden—the sea. Another memory floats by without warning: my mother and me, after a dip in the water. My teeth are chattering. My fingers are raisins. I want to rush toward my towel. But my mother tells me softly, "We don't run to our towels; we walk." That moment distills her essence for me: a hint of old-fashioned formality—a proper woman should know how to carry herself—combined with an implicit imperative. *Hold your head high*, was what she was really telling me. *Take your time. Soon it won't be this cold.*

About two weeks after her death, I wrote in my diary: "The finality of it. When she was sick, at least things kept changing. She felt better, or worse. It was a good time to talk, or it wasn't. *Things happened.* Now nothing is happen-ing. This is it."

A year later, my diary reads: "Hardest thing: overhearing colleagues tell their mothers 'Love you' on the phone. So *casually*."

If, in the first months after losing my mother, I searched for books that   20
made my grief echo and reverberate—that rendered it as shocking as I felt it to be—after a while I found my reading diet largely unsustainable. Part of moving

on, I realized, was learning to let my grief buddies go, or at least putting them back on the shelf. That is, until I read Cheryl Strayed's "Wild." No, read isn't quite right. More like ravaged. For some time after the book came out, I purposely avoided it. Something in its subhead—"From Lost to Found"— put me off, as did a few of the reviews praising the book for being "uplifting" and "spiritual." I knew it was about the author's hike through the Pacific Crest Trail, on which she had embarked a few years after the death of her mother, but I expected it to be an Oprahfied memoir—hopelessly positive, sentimental, diluted. I didn't expect to gulp it down in one reading. Nor did I expect that Strayed's experience—of watching her healthy, dominant mother beset by advanced lung cancer—would so closely mirror my own.

Strayed serves her material raw. Of receiving her mother's diagnosis, she writes: "We went to the women's restroom. Each of us locked in separate stalls, weeping. We didn't exchange a word. Not because we felt so alone in our grief, but because we were so together in it, as if we were one body instead of two." Strayed's writing is so piercing and precise that I found myself nodding along as I was reading, as though it were a hymn. (Maybe "spiritual" wasn't far-fetched, after all.) Her mother's death, she writes, "had cut me short at the very height of my youthful arrogance. It had forced me to instantly grow up and forgive her every motherly fault at the same time that it kept me forever a child, my life both ended and begun in that premature place where we'd left off." Nothing I've read has managed to describe that exact point in time, that "place where we'd left off," as accurately as those few lines have. I always thought that literature's draw lay in making me identify with people and situations that were as different from my lived experience as possible. But my mother's death changed that. It made me seek out my own kind—the left-behind and the heartbroken. The unmothered.

There's a word in Hebrew—*malkosh*—that means "last rain." It's a word that only means something in places like Israel, where there's a clear distinction between winter and the long, dry stretch of summer. It's a word, too, that can only be applied in retrospect. When it's raining, you have no way of knowing that the falling drops would be the last ones of the year. But then time goes by, the clouds clear, and you realize that *that* rain shower was the one. Having a mother—being mothered—is similar, in a way. It's a term that I only fully grasp now, with the thirst of hindsight: who she was, who I was for her, what she has equipped me with.

Like a last rain, my mother left behind an earthy scent that lingered long after she was gone. Like a last rain, for a fleeting moment, everything she touched seemed to glow.

### FOR ANALYSIS

1. What is the occasion for the author's writing of this essay?

2. What is an **oxymoron**? What is the oxymoron Margalit identifies in her essay?

3. What does the author say literature does for her? Has its usefulness or importance to her changed?

## MAKING ARGUMENTS

Make an argument about the much-discussed topic of sensitivity in speech and writing, using as a jumping-off point Margalit's observations about what she sees as unthinking references to mothers. How much should people think about who they might offend or sadden when they make an utterance, spoken or written? How much is the offense people take or the sadness they feel their own responsibility?

## WRITING TOPICS

Reflect on your own state of motheredness or unmotheredness (and/or your state with regard to a father or guardian) and on Margalit's use of her reading of literature to deal with her feelings. How does your reading of her essay compare to her reading of Barthes and Proust and Strayed? Do you recognize yourself, or learn about different kinds of experiences, or both?

## MAKING CONNECTIONS

**1.** How do Lethem's use of movies and Margalit's of literature compare? How do they use them? When? What do they get out of them?

**2.** While neither Lethem nor Margalit hide their feelings about the mother's deaths in these essays, they do deal with explicit statements about grief and mourning differently. How would you characterize that difference? Do they seem appropriate to the circumstances they write about, or to the kind of thing they are writing? Do you find one more congenial?

**3.** Both of these essays focus much more on self-examination than **character** portrait—that is, they are more about the authors' dealing with their mothers' deaths than about the mothers themselves. Yet the mothers still emerge as figures. How does each author make this happen? What do the outlines of the figures that emerge tell you about each of the authors, as writers and as people?

## FURTHER QUESTIONS
## FOR THINKING AND WRITING

**1.** Although A. E. Housman's "To an Athlete Dying Young" and Pablo Neruda's "The Dead Woman" employ different poetic forms, they both embody a poetic mode called **elegy**. Define *elegy* in terms of the characteristic **tone** of these poems. Compare the elegiac tone of these poems. **Writing Topic:** Compare the elegiac tone of one of these poems with the tone of Dylan Thomas's "Do Not Go Gentle into That Good Night."

**2.** What **figurative language** in the prose and poetry of this section is commonly associated with death? With dying? Contrast the characteristic **imagery** of this section with the characteristic imagery of love poetry. **Writing Topic:** Compare the imagery in Shakespeare's Sonnet 18 with the imagery in Sonnet 73.

**3.** In Leo Tolstoy's "The Death of Iván Ilých" and John Donne's **sonnet** "Death, Be Not Proud," death and dying are considered from a religious viewpoint. **Writing Topic:** Discuss whether these works develop a similar attitude toward death or whether the attitudes they develop differ.

**4.** Helena María Viramontes, a Mexican American, and Leslie Marmon Silko, a Native American Indian, both treat death as a ritualistic event. How are their stories similar? How do they differ? **Writing Topic:** Contrast the ritualistic elements in these stories with the religious elements in Tolstoy's "The Death of Iván Ilých."

**5.** Which works in this section treat death and dying in a way that corresponds most closely to your own attitude toward mortality? Which contradict your attitude? **Writing Topic:** Choose two works, each of which affects you differently, and discuss the elements responsible for your response.

# APPENDIXES

# GLOSSARY OF CRITICAL APPROACHES

## INTRODUCTION

This glossary attempts to define, briefly and in general terms, some major critical approaches to literature. Because literary criticism has to do with the value of literature — not with its history — judgments tend to be subjective, and disagreements frequent and even acrimonious. The truth of a work of art is very different from the truth of a mathematical formula. Certainly one's attitudes toward war, religion, sex, and politics are irrelevant to the truth of a formula but quite relevant to one's judgment of a literary work.

Most critical approaches can, in a general sense, be placed into one of three categories:

**1.** those that focus exclusively on the work itself, including the internal connections between its various parts and elements,

**2.** those that approach a work with certain preconceived assumptions against which the work is evaluated, and

**3.** those that reject any "pure" approach and instead encourage an eclecticism that draws from whatever sources seem best suited to the work and the predilections of the critic.

Most of us are likely to find the third approach most congenial.

Yet any examination of the broad range of literary criticism reveals that groups of critics (and all readers are ultimately critics) share certain assumptions about literature. These assumptions govern the way critics approach a work, the elements they tend to look for and emphasize, the details they find significant or insignificant, and finally, the overall value they place on the work.

We do not suggest that one approach is more valid than another or that the lines dividing the various approaches are always clear and distinct. Readers will perhaps discover one approach more congenial to their temperament, more "true" to their sense of the world, than another. More likely, they will find themselves using more than one approach in dealing with a single work. Many of the diverse approaches described here actually overlap, and even those critics who champion a single abstract theory often draw on a variety of useful approaches when they write about a particular work.

*Formalist* critics assume that a literary text remains independent of the writer who created it. The function of the critic, then, is to discover how the author has deployed language to create (or perhaps failed to create) a formal and aesthetically satisfying structure. The influential American formalists of the 1940s and 1950s (the New Critics) were fond of describing literary texts as "autonomous," meaning that political, historical, biographical, and other considerations were always secondary if not irrelevant to any discussion of their merits.

Furthermore, formalist critics argue that the various elements of a "great" work interweave to create a seamless whole that embodies "universal" values. Unsurprisingly, the "universal" values formalist critics praise, on close analysis, tend to parallel the moral, political, and cultural ideals of the critics' social class. This tendency becomes even more problematic and complex in dealing with the literature of formerly colonized people.

But the formalist point of view, cherishing the artwork's structure, spawned its own antithesis — a group of theorists called *deconstructionists*. These writers argued that language itself was too shifty to support the expectations of formalist criticism. One reader might read a sentence literally, while another might read it ironically. Hence, their "understanding" of the text would be diametrically opposed.

The deconstructionists believe that intelligent readers cannot be expected to ignore those responses that interfere with some "correct" or "desirable" reading of the piece. Given what they see as the notoriously ambiguous and unstable nature of language, deconstructionist critics argue that a literary text can never have a fixed meaning.

While the formalists and deconstructionists wrestle over the philosophy of language and its implications for the nature of literary texts, other critics pursue quite different primary interests. The term *ethical criticism* describes a variety of approaches, all of which argue that literature, like any other human activity, connects to the real world and, consequently, influences real people. If that is so, our appraisal of a work must take into account the ethical and moral values it embodies. Though it sounds simple enough, in reality the task is difficult and often quite controversial. Ethical criticism is the very opposite of the "art for art's sake" approach, best represented by formalist criticism. The formalist critic tries to isolate the work in a timeless world of universal aesthetic considerations; the ethical critic insists on making judgments about whether a work serves values that are "good" or encourages values that are "bad."

Other critical approaches analyze literary works from still other perspectives. *Reader-response* critics assert that a work of art is created as much by its audience as by the artist. For these critics, art has no significant abstract existence: a reader's experience of the work gives birth to it and contributes crucially to its power and value. Further, since each reader embodies a unique set of experiences and values, each reader's response to the work will in some respects be uniquely personal. *Psychoanalytic* criticism, similar to reader-response, is nevertheless distinctive in its application of psychoanalytic principles to works of art. Those principles, originally derived from the work of Sigmund Freud (1856–1939), now often reflect the views of more recent theorists such as Jacques Lacan (1901–1981). There is, finally, the recently emergent approach called *new historical* criticism, which brings historical knowledge to bear on the analysis of literary works in new and sophisticated ways. The result is a some-times dizzying proliferation of analyses that argue for the relationship between literature and life.

The glossary that follows reveals the widely diverse and often contradictory views expressed by professional theorists and critics.

**Deconstruction**  This approach grew out of the work of certain twentieth-century European philosophers, notably Jacques Derrida (1930–2004), whose study of language led to the conclusion that since we can know only through the medium of language, and lan-guage is unstable and ambiguous, it is impossible to talk about truth and knowledge and meaning in any absolute sense. Verbal structures, these critics maintained, inevitably con-tained within themselves oppositions. Derrida asserted that in the Western world, language leads us to think in terms of opposites (for example, soul/body, man/woman, master/slave) that imply what he called "a violent hierarchy," with one of the terms (the first) always being superior to the other (the second). The aim of deconstruction is to show that this hierarchy of values cannot be permanent and absolute.

Readers therefore cannot be expected to ignore the oppositions and contradictions in a text just because they do not contribute to some "correct" or "desirable" reading of the piece that might uphold a particular political, social, or cultural view.

Formalism assures us that the successful artist is the master of language and that he or she consciously deploys all its resources to achieve a rich and unified work. Sensitive read-ers can aspire to a complete understanding of a work undistorted by their own idiosyncra-sies, subjective states, or ideological biases.

Rejecting the formalist assumption about authorial control and conscious design, decon-struction attempts to show that by its very nature, language is constantly "saying" more than the writer can control or even know. Thus, a close study of any text (literary or otherwise) will reveal contradictory and irreconcilable elements.

Deconstructionist critics do not necessarily reject the validity of feminist, Marxist, for-malist, and other critical approaches. In fact, they often draw on the insights furnished by them. But the deconstructionist critic says that any discourse or critical approach that fails to recognize the inherently shifting and unstable nature of language is bound to produce only a partial if not misleading interpretation. For example, in his study *America the Scriv-ener: Deconstruction and the Subject of Literary Studies* (1990), Gregory S. Jay finds Emily Grierson, the protagonist of William Faulkner's famous story "A Rose for Emily," a "puzzle" and warns against simplistic interpretations:

> As feminist subject, her story speaks of a revolutionary subversion of patriarchy; as herself, a figure of racial and class power, Emily also enacts the love affair of patriarchy with its own past, despite all the signs of decline and degradation. She is a split subject, crossed by rival discourses. What the text forces us to think, then, is the complex and ironic alliances between modes of possession and subjection, desire and ownership, identity and position.

Like Marxism and feminism, deconstruction defines itself both as a critical theory of literature and as a philosophy of human values. Hence, it is applicable not only to literature but also to an understanding of the power relations among humans and the societies they create. In insisting that we recognize the way language embodies and supports class, gender, and other biases, deconstruction challenges both the ethnocentrism of political structures and the idea of "universal values" in literary works.

**Ethical Criticism**   Ethical criticism may range from a casual appraisal of a work's moral content to the more rigorous and systematic analysis driven by a coherent set of stated beliefs and assumptions. A *religious* critic (committed to certain moral positions) might attack a work (regardless of its artfulness or brilliance) because it does not condemn adultery. A *feminist* critic might focus on the way literary works devalue women; a *black* critic, on the way they stereotype blacks; a *Marxist* critic, on the way they support class divisions; and a *new historicist* critic, on the way a dominant class interprets history to protect its own interests. But all of them agree that literary works invite ethical judgments. Most of them also agree that literary works must be judged as another means by which a society both defines and perpetuates its political institutions and cultural values. The feminist critic, the black critic, and the Marxist critic would also agree that the political institutions and cultural values of most Western societies have been carefully designed to serve the interests of a dominant class: white, male, and wealthy.

Ethical criticism takes us out of the comparatively calm, academic world of aesthetic values into the larger world of moral judgments. If a literary work's capacity to promote good or bad behavior becomes the criterion for judging its value, then surely some people will try to suppress works they perceive as morally threatening. It is here that ethical criticism encounters its most vexing and dangerous problem: censorship. The literary critic Wayne Booth, who advocates ethical criticism in his book *The Company We Keep: An Ethics of Fiction* (1988), concedes the danger but notes that teaching itself is a form of censorship in that "we impose our ethical choices on our students when we choose our reading lists."

**Feminist Criticism**   Feminist critics hold that literature is merely one of many expressions of a patriarchal society with a vested interest in keeping women subordinate to men. Thus literature, in the way it portrays gender roles, helps to condition women to accept as normal a society that directs them to become nurses rather than doctors, secretaries rather than attorneys or corporate executives, sex symbols rather than thinkers, elementary school teachers rather than university professors. Beyond this general critique of patriarchy, feminists differ in their detailed analyses. Some have re-examined history to show that a literary canon created by males has slighted and ignored female authors. Others, studying canonical works from a feminist perspective, have come up with fresh readings that challenge conventional interpretations, focusing on how women are empowered in literary texts or through writing literary texts. Some, believing that language itself allows men to impose their power, use literary analyses to expose the gender bias of language. Why, they ask, is the English language so rich in words to describe a quarrelsome, abusive woman (*shrew, harridan, termagant*) but so lacking in comparable terms for men? Some feminists believe that the male bias of language, far deeper than mere words, is actually structural. The constellation of qualities connoted by *masculine* and *feminine*, they say, reveals how deeply the positive (male) and negative (female) values are embedded in the language.

While a psychoanalytic critic might use Freud's Oedipal theories to explain female protagonists' relationships to men, such as in Kate Chopin's "The Storm" (p. 579) or Zora Neale Hurston's "Sweat" (p. 584), the feminist critic Judith Fetterley maintains that the explanation is to be found in the fact that a patriarchal culture instills in us the notion "that men and women are made for each other" and that "'masculinity' and 'femininity' are the natural reflection of that divinely ordained complement." In a society where there is "a massive differentiation of everything according to sex, one sees that in reality a sexist culture is one in which men and women are not simply incompatible but murderously so (*The Resisting Reader: A Feminist Approach to American Fiction*, 1978).

**Formalist Criticism**   Like deconstruction, formalism focuses on the ambiguous and multilayered nature of language but does so to achieve the precisely opposite effect. Formalism assures us that the successful artist is the master of language and consciously deploys all its resources to achieve a rich and unified work. Careful readers can aspire to a complete understanding of a work undistorted by their own idiosyncrasies or subjective states or ideological biases. The formalist rejects the central tenet of the reader-response critic — that a work comes into existence, so to speak, through the interaction of the reader with the work. For the formalist, the work exists independent of any particular reader. The work is a structured and formal aesthetic object comprising such elements as symbol, image, and sound patterns. Political, biographical, or historical considerations not embodied in the work itself are irrelevant.

The formalist sees literature as a sort of Platonic ideal form — immutable and objective. Works close to that ideal are praised for their aesthetic energy and their universality (a characteristic of the greatest literature). Works that do not exhibit this prized formal coherence are dispraised and often dismissed as neither universal nor important. Because formalism focuses on the internal structure of literature above all else, it rejects didactic works — those intended to teach or convey moral observations. During the 1940s and 1950s, when the New Critics (as the formalists were called) dominated academic literary criticism, social protest writing was generally dismissed as subliterary because it lacked the "universality" of great literature. What was important in a work of art was not that it might change people's behavior but that its parts coalesced into a beautiful whole. Consider the following comment by two formalist critics (Caroline Gordon and Allen Tate, *The House of Fiction*, 1950) on Nathaniel Hawthorne's "Young Goodman Brown" (p. 79):

> *The dramatic impact would have been stronger if Hawthorne had let the incidents tell their own story: Goodman Brown's behavior to his neighbors and finally to his wife show us that he is a changed man. Since fiction is a kind of shorthand of human behavior and one moment may represent years in a man's life, we would have concluded that the change was to last his entire life. But Hawthorne's weakness for moralizing and his insufficient technical equipment betray him into the anticlimax of the last paragraph.*

African American writers and critics, for example, complained that the criterion of universality was merely a way of protecting white, conservative social and political dominance. The New Critics dismissed African American literature that sought to deal with racism and the struggle for equality as mere didacticism or agitprop, not to be compared with the great white literary productions that achieved universal import. In a major work of New Criticism published in 1952, the influential critic R. P. Blackmur dismissed *Native Son*, a powerful and now classic novel about white racism, as "one of those books in which everything is undertaken with seriousness except the writing."

**Marxist Criticism**   The Marxist critic sees literature as one activity among many to be studied and judged in terms of a larger and all-encompassing ideology derived from the economic and political doctrines of Karl Marx (1818–1883). Marxism offers a comprehensive theory about the nature of humans and the way in which a few of them manage to seize control of the means of production and thereby exploit the masses of working people. But Marxism is about more than analysis. As Karl Marx himself said, "It is not enough to analyze society; we must also change it."

The Marxist critic analyzes literary works to show how, wittingly or unwittingly, they support the dominant social class or how they, in some way, contribute to the struggle against oppression and exploitation. And since the Marxist critic views literature as just one among the variety of human activities that reflect power relations and class divisions, he or she is likely to be more interested in what a work says than in its formal structure.

The Marxist argues that one cannot properly understand a literary work unless one understands how it reflects the relationship between economic production and social class. Further, this relationship cannot be explored adequately without examining a range of questions that other critical approaches, notably formalism, deem irrelevant. How does the work relate to the profit-driven enterprise of publishing? What does the author's biography reveal about his or her class biases? Does the work accurately portray the class divisions of society? Does the work expose the economic bases of oppression and advance the cause of liberation?

And since Marxist critics see their duty — indeed, the duty of all responsible and humane people — as not merely to describe the world but to change it, they judge literature by the contribution it makes to bringing about revolution or in some way enlightening its readers about oppression and the necessity for class struggle.

For example, a Marxist critic's analysis of Matthew Arnold's poem "Dover Beach" (p. 639) might see it not as a brilliantly structured pattern of images and sounds but as the predictable end product of a dehumanizing capitalist economy in which a small class of oligarchs is willing, at whatever cost, to protect its wealth and power. The Marxist critic, as a materialist who believes that humans make their own history, would find Arnold's reference to the "eternal note of sadness" (l. 14) a mystic evasion of the real sources of his alienation and pain: Arnold's misery can be clearly and unmystically explained by his fearful responses to the socioeconomic conditions of his time.

Arnold's refusal to face this fact leads him to the conclusion typical of a bourgeois artist-intellectual who cannot discern the truth. But the cure for Arnold's pain, the Marxist would argue, cannot be found in a love relationship because relations between people are determined crucially by socioeconomic conditions. The cure for the pain he describes so well will be found in the world of action, in the struggle to create a society that is just and humane. "Dover Beach," the Marxist critic would conclude, is both a brilliant evocation of the alienation and misery caused by a capitalist economy and a testimony to the inability of a bourgeois intellectual to understand what is responsible for his feelings.

**New Historical Criticism**   There is nothing "new" about historians drawing on literary works as significant documents to support and illuminate historical analysis; nor is there anything "new" about literary critics drawing on history to illuminate literary works. For the historian, Sophocles' *Antigonê* (p. 371) tells us much about the conflict between the old-time religion and the new secularism in fifth-century BCE Athens. The literary critic of *Othello* (p. 664) goes to the historian to understand the way in which Shakespeare and his contemporaries viewed black Africans. But until recently, the provinces of the historian and of the literary critics were pretty much mutually exclusive.

The new historians (influenced by modern theories of language and literature) began to question the very idea of history as it had been practiced. The historians of the past tended, for the most part, to think of history in terms of overarching themes and theses, and attempted to understand it in terms of some perceived Zeitgeist, or "spirit of the times." This kind of history was often linked to nationalism. Hence (for one example), nineteenth-century Americans created the idea of manifest destiny and then used it to explain and justify eastern settlers' movement west and their attendant atrocities against the Native Americans who resided there. When the Nazis came to power in Germany, they developed the idea that true Germans were descended from a superior Aryan race and then used that idea to deprive "inferior races" of civil rights, of property, and finally, of life.

More abstractly, the purpose of writing history was to articulate and reinforce the values and beliefs that gave a culture unity. By that means, some new historians note, history became the story (and the ideas and beliefs and culture) of the rich, the powerful, the privileged, the victorious. The new historians see history not as the search for some grand, unifying thesis but as the articulation of the various kinds of discourse that compete with, contradict, overlap, and modify one another in the constant struggle for dominance. Indeed, the new historians, influenced by deconstructionist views of language, came to question the very idea of historical truth.

The new historians also reject the traditional division between history and other disciplines, appropriating to historical studies many kinds of texts — including literary texts — that traditional historians left to others. These critics assert that without an understanding of the historical context that produced it, no work of literature can really be understood; therefore, in their eyes, literature belongs as much to the historian as to the literary critic. Such critics aim at what they call a "thick" description of a literary work, one that applies to a text as much information as can be gathered about every aspect of the author, his work, and his times. While its practitioners generally share the fundamental ideas outlined here, they can differ widely in the tools and methodologies they use to analyze a literary text. That is to say, a new historian may also be a Marxist, feminist, or deconstructionist.

**Postcolonial Criticism**    Postcolonial criticism belongs to the larger field of postcolonial studies, which evolved in the wake of the liberation of many nations from the domination of the European powers of the nineteenth century. It is distinguished not so much by any singular approach as by its subject: the examination of postcolonial writings that explore the way in which the colonizers imposed their culture and values on native peoples and thus distorted or suppressed their past.

One prominent purpose of postcolonial criticism is to explain and expose the mechanisms the colonizer used — from brute force to subtle psychological techniques — to gain and maintain control. It becomes, in effect, a new lens through which the literature of the colonizing culture can be examined in order to expose its biased judgments about the society it has dominated, its distortions of native culture as compared with the colonizing culture. This kind of analysis will lead the critic away from narrowly defined literary concerns to examine the colonized culture's past, including its precolonial past. Thus postcolonial critics (and historians), by uncovering the past, may give their newly liberated compatriots the means of re-creating an identity and may give its imaginative writers the material for a national literature.

Because postcolonial criticism is a relatively new field, it is still developing its distinctive areas of interest and techniques of analysis. By its nature it is eclectic, drawing on any other literary approach (as well as academic discipline) that seems relevant to a critic's purpose.

**Psychoanalytic Criticism**    Psychoanalytic criticism always proceeds from a set of principles that describes the inner life of men and women. Though differing psychological theorists argue for diverse views, all analysts and all psychoanalytic critics assume that the development of the psyche is analogous to the development of the body. Doctors can provide charts indicating physical growth stages; analysts can supply similar charts indicating stages in the growth of the psyche. Sigmund Freud, for all practical purposes, invented psychoanalysis by creating a theoretical model for the (mostly male) human psyche.

The Oedipus complex is a significant element in that model. Freud contends that everyone moves through a childhood stage of erotic attachment to the parent of the opposite sex and an accompanying hostility and aggression against the parent of the same sex, who is seen as a rival. Such feelings, part of the natural biography of the psyche, pass or are effectively controlled in most cases. But sometimes the child grown to adulthood is still strongly gripped by the Oedipal mode, which then may result in neurotic or even psychotic behavior. Freud did not invent the Oedipus complex — he simply described it. It was always there, especially noticeable in the work of great literary artists who, in every era, demonstrate a special insight into the human condition.

Along with Oedipal feelings, the psyche inevitably embodies aggressive feelings — the urge to attack those who exercise authority, who deny us our primal desires. For the young, the authority figure is frequently a parent. Adults must deal with police, government officials, the boss. As far back as the Hebrew Bible story of the tower of Babel and the old Greek myths in which the giant Titans, led by Cronus, overthrow their father, and Zeus and the Olympians subsequently overthrow Cronus, there is evidence of the rebellion against the parent-authority figure. Freud views that aggressive hostility as another component of the developing psyche. But, in the interest of civilization, society has developed ways to control that aggressiveness.

Freud saw us as divided selves. An unconscious *id* struggles to gratify aggressive and erotic primal urges, while a *superego* (roughly what society calls *conscience*), by producing guilt feelings, struggles to control the id. The *ego* (the self) is defined by the struggle. Thus the Freudian psychoanalytic critic is constantly aware that authors and their characters suffer and resuffer a primal tension that results from the conflict between psychic aggressions and social obligations.

Freud has been succeeded by a number of psychological theorists who present quite different models of the psyche, and recent literary theory has responded to these post-Freudian views. Among the most important are Carl Gustav Jung (1875–1961), who argued that there exists a collective (as well as a racial and individual) unconscious. Residing there are archetypes — original patterns — that emerge into our consciousness in the form of shadowy images that persistently appear and reappear in such literary themes as the search for the father, death and resurrection, the quest, and the double.

The psychoanalytic critic understands literature in terms of the psychic models that Freud and others defined. Originally, such critics tended to analyze literature in an attempt to identify the author's neuroses. More recently, psychoanalytic critics have argued that the patterns they discover in works allow us to tap into and, perhaps, resolve our own neuroses.

**Reader-Response Criticism** Reader-response criticism (also called *transactional theory*) emerged in the 1970s as one of the many challenges to formalist principles. Reader-response critics focus on the interaction between the work and the reader, holding that, in a sense, a work exists only when it is experienced by the reader. If the work exists only in the mind of the reader, the reader becomes an active participant in the creative process rather than a passive receptacle for an autonomous work. The creation of a work thus becomes a dynamic enterprise between the reader and the text, each acting on the other. The study of the affective power of a work becomes not a fallacy, as formalism holds, but the central focus of criticism. The task of the critic is to investigate this dynamic relationship between reader and text in order to discover how it works.

We know that various readers respond differently to the same text. In fact, the same reader might respond to the text quite differently at a different time. The reader-response critic wants to know why. In what ways do such conditions as age, gender, upbringing, and race account for differing responses? Does the reader's mood at the time of reading make a difference? If you accept the principles of reader-response criticism, the inevitable conclusion — *reductio ad absurdum*, its critics would say — is that there is no limit to the possible readings of any text. Consequently, many reader-response critics qualify the intense subjectivity of their approach by admitting that an "informed" or "educated" reader is likely to produce a more "valid" reading than an "uninformed" or "uneducated" one.

Gaps or blanks in literary texts provide particular opportunities to readers. Every narrative work omits, for example, periods of time that the reader must fill in. In Nathaniel Hawthorne's "Young Goodman Brown" (p. 79), the author omits all the years of Brown's life between his emergence from the forest and his death. The reader is free to imagine that history. The filling in of these blanks enables readers to participate in "creating" a text and reinforces the arguments of reader-response theorists.

# BIOGRAPHICAL NOTES ON THE AUTHORS

**CHRIS ABANI** (b. 1966)   Born in Nigeria to an Igbo father and an English mother, Abani wrote his first novel at age sixteen. A political thriller about a foiled government take-over, the book landed Abani in prison for insurrection when a real-life coup was attempted shortly after his novel's publication. Abani has since written three novels: *GraceLand* (2004), which won the PEN/Hemingway Book Prize, *The Virgin of Flames* (2007), and *The Secret History of Las Vegas* (2014). He has also received recognition for his shorter works of fiction *Becoming Abigail* (2006) and *Song for Night* (2007) and for his poetry, including *Dog Woman* (2004) and *Sanctificum* (2010). A graduate of Imo State University, Nigeria, Abani received his MA from the University of London and his PhD from the University of Southern California. Currently a professor of English at Northwestern University, Abani's varied research interests include the living architecture of cities, West African music, and Yoruba and Igbo philosophy and religion. His critical and personal essays on humanitarianism, art, ethics, and our shared political responsibility have appeared in numerous sources, including the *New York Times* and *O* magazine. On being named a United States Artists Ford Fellow in 2014, Abani remarked on the importance of imagination: "The world as we know it is a product of human imagination. Without imagination there is no invention, there are no tools, there is nothing but a more instinctual place of being."

**DILRUBA AHMED** (b. 1973)   Ahmed won the Bread Loaf Writers' Conference Bakeless Prize for her book *Dhaka Dust* (2011), and her poetry has appeared in several literary reviews as well as *Indivisible: An Anthology of Contemporary South Asian Poetry* (2010). A writer, editor, and educator with roots in Pennsylvania, Ohio, and Bangladesh, Ahmed received her undergraduate and master's degrees from the University of Pittsburgh and her MFA from Warren Wilson College. Reflecting on why she became a poet, Ahmed credits her literature-loving Bangladeshi parents and her status as an outsider who moved a lot as a child. Poet and critic Vijay Seshadri said of Ahmed's poems, "On the surface, . . . they'd probably seem as exotic to a citizen of Dhaka as they would to a citizen of Duluth. In their depths, though, they seem anything but exotic; they seem to be our own impossible, loving, intimate, bereaved thoughts restored to us transformed and ennobled."

**EDWARD ALBEE** (1928–2016)   Award-winning playwright Edward Albee was born in Washington, DC, and adopted by a wealthy couple with ties to powerful New York theater companies. Albee later rebelled against the snobbery and prejudice he detected amid his affluent upbringing. After being kicked out of Trinity College for skipping classes and compulsory chapel attendance, Albee broke from his parents and moved to New York City in the 1940s. There, he mingled with the avant-garde Greenwich Village circle of artists, musicians, and intellectuals, and his long-term romantic partner and mentor, William Flanagan. Although he was determined to be a writer, Albee's many works of fiction, poetry, and drama were mostly rejected by publishers and producers until he wrote *The Zoo Story* (1958) just before his thirtieth birthday. This critical and commercial success launched Albee's playwriting career. He went on to write several notable plays, including *The American Dream* (1960), before the enormously successful *Who's Afraid of Virginia Woolf?* (1961–62), which won five Tony Awards including best play. Albee continued to produce plays in the decades that followed, often to great critical acclaim. Some of his most successful plays since *Who's Afraid of Virginia Woolf?* include the Pulitzer Prize-winning *Three Tall Women* (1991) and *The Goat, or Who Is Sylvia* (2002), which won the Tony Award for best new play and was well-received at the box office despite its controversial plot, which features a man who falls in love with a goat. Known for pushing the limits with their experimental use of absurd elements and raw dialogue, Albee's plays unsympathetically examine modern conventions. Albee received the Tony Lifetime Achievement Award in 2005.

**SHERMAN ALEXIE** (b. 1966)  A Spokane/Coeur d'Alene Indian, Sherman Alexie was born on the Spokane Indian Reservation in Wellpinit, Washington. In 1981 he left the reservation school and enrolled in a predominantly white high school, where, according to Alexie, he "kept [his] mouth shut and became a good white Indian." He enrolled at Gonzaga University in Spokane and began to discover his love for literature and his talent for writing. After two years at Gonzaga, he transferred to Washington State University in Pullman, where he began to write seriously. A year after he received his degree, he published two collections of poetry, *The Business of Fancydancing* (1992) and *I Would Steal Horses* (1992), followed the next year by another poetry collection, *First Indian on the Moon* (1993). Alexie then turned to prose, publishing a volume of loosely related stories dealing with life on the reservation, *The Lone Ranger and Tonto Fistfight in Heaven* (1993). One of the stories in this collection, "This Is What It Means to Say Phoenix, Arizona," provided the basis for the film *Smoke Signals* (1998), which Alexie produced and for which he wrote the screenplay. He went on to write two more films: *The Business of Fancydancing* (2002), which he also directed, and *49?* (2003). He has published two other collections of short stories, *The Toughest Indian in the World* (2000) and *Ten Little Indians* (2003), along with a number of collections of poetry, including *Dangerous Astronomy* (2005). Alexie has also penned several novels, among them *Reservation Blues* (1995), *Indian Killer* (1996), and *Flight* (2007). His novel for young adults, *The Absolutely True Diary of a Part-Time Indian* (2007), won the National Book Award for Young People's Literature. Alexie received the PEN/Faulkner Award for his book *War Dances* (2009), a collection of stories, poems, and question-and-answer sequences that explore generational and artistic complexities. About the criticism he has received from members of his reservation, who find his portrayals of Native Americans and reservation life demeaning, Alexie replied, "I write what I know, and I don't try to mythologize myself, which is what some seem to want, and which some Indian women and men writers are doing, this Earth Mother and Shaman Man thing, trying to create these 'authentic, traditional' Indians. We don't live our lives that way."

**MATTHEW ARNOLD** (1822–1888)  Born in Middlesex, England, Arnold attended Rugby School, where his father was headmaster, and studied classics at Oxford University. Following his graduation in 1844, he became a fellow at Oxford and a master at Rugby. In 1851 he was appointed inspector of schools in England and was sent by the government to observe educational systems in Europe. He remained in that post for some thirty-five years. As a poet, Arnold took inspiration from Greek tragedies, Keats, and Wordsworth. His collections include *Empedocles on Etna and Other Poems* (1852). An eminent social and literary critic in his later years, Arnold lectured in the United States in 1883 and 1886. His essay "The Function of Criticism" sheds light on his transition from poet to critic. Much of his work is collected in *Complete Prose Works* (eleven volumes, 1960–1977).

**W. H. AUDEN** (1907–1973)   A poet, playwright, translator, librettist, critic, and editor, Wystan Hugh Auden was born in York, England, the son of a medical officer and a nurse. He attended Oxford University from 1925 to 1928, then taught, traveled, and moved from faculty to faculty of several universities in the United States, becoming a naturalized citizen in 1946. He won the Pulitzer Prize in 1948 for his collection *The Age of Anxiety*, an expression he coined to describe the 1930s. While his early writing exhibited Marxist sympathies and reflected the excitement of new Freudian psychoanalytic thought, he later embraced Christianity and produced sharply honed verse in the rhyme and meter of traditional forms.

**KOFI AWOONOR** (1935–2013)   Born to Ewe parents in Ghana, Awoonor was a writer, a diplomat, and a professor of comparative literature at numerous universities, including State University of New York at Stony Brook, where he received his PhD. Author of literary criticism, political essays, novels, and plays, Awoonor is best-known for his works of poetry, including *Rediscovery and Other Poems* (1964), *Night of My Blood* (1971), *Ride Me, Memory* (1973), *The House by the Sea* (1978), and *The Latin American and Caribbean Notebook* (1992). Awoonor's early poems are notable for drawing on the Ewe oral tradition of his ancestors. While serving as head of the English Department at the University of Cape Coast in Ghana in the mid-1970s, Awoonor was imprisoned without trial for his alleged role in an attempt to overthrow the government. He wrote his book *The House by the Sea* about the time he spent in jail. Kwame Dawes, Awoonor's nephew and editor of the literary journal *Prairie Schooner*, categorized his uncle as one of those "artists and writers . . . who felt themselves deeply engaged in the political realities of the world." In September 2013, while visiting Nairobi, Kenya, Awoonor was killed in the Westgate shopping mall attack by the militant group al-Shabaab. He had been in Nairobi for a literary festival to celebrate and promote his forthcoming book, *The Promise of Hope: New and Selected Poems, 1964–2013* (2014), which was published posthumously.

**JAMES BALDWIN** (1924–1987)   Born in New York City, the son of a Harlem minister, Baldwin began preaching as a young teenager. Some years later, he experienced a religious crisis, left the church, and moved to New York City's bohemian Greenwich Village, where he began his career as a writer, supporting himself with menial jobs and publishing occasional articles in journals such as the *Nation* and *Commentary*. By the end of the 1940s, Baldwin's anger over the treatment of African Americans led him into exile in France. There, Baldwin completed his acclaimed first novel, *Go Tell It on the Mountain* (1953), a work focusing on a minister's son for which he drew heavily on his own childhood. His next work, *Notes of a Native Son* (1955), a collection of personal, literary, and social essays, secured Baldwin's reputation as a major American writer. Two later collections of essays, *Nobody Knows My Name* (1961) and *The Fire Next Time* (1963), established Baldwin as one of the most powerful voices of the turbulent civil rights movement of the 1960s. But as riots, bombings, and other violence grew more frequent, Baldwin grew increasingly pessimistic over the prospect that white America could ever overcome its racism. That pessimism was deepened by two traumatic events: the 1963 bombing of the Sixteenth Street Baptist Church in Birmingham, Alabama, that killed four young girls attending a Sunday school class, and the assassination of the Reverend Martin Luther King Jr. in 1968. Baldwin began making periodic trips to France, settling there permanently in 1974.

**TONI CADE BAMBARA** (1939–1995)   Born in New York City, Bambara was educated there as well as in Italy and Paris. Early in her career she worked as an investigator for the New York State Department of Social Welfare, but she later devoted herself to teaching and writing. One of the best representatives of a group of African American writers who emerged in the 1960s, Bambara was a consistent civil rights activist, involved both politically and culturally in African American life. Much of her writing focuses on African American women, particularly as they confront experiences that force them to new awareness. She authored several collections of short stories, including *Gorilla, My Love* (1972) and *The Sea Birds Are Still Alive: Collected Stories* (1977), and two novels, *The Salt Eaters* (1980) and *If Blessing Comes* (1987). She also edited a groundbreaking collection of African American women's writing, *The Black Woman: An Anthology* (1970). Two works, *Deep Sightings and Rescue Missions: Fiction, Essays, and Conversations* (1996) and the novel *These Bones Are Not My Child* (1999), were published posthumously.

**APHRA BEHN** (ca. 1640–1689)   Little is known for certain about the early life of Aphra Behn, but it is generally believed that she sailed with her parents and brother from England to Surinam in 1663. Behn's best-known work, the short novel *Oroonoko* (1688), grew out of her experience in the South American colony, particularly her friendship with an enslaved African prince. Most likely married to a Dutch man sometime after 1664, Behn was forced to make her own living after her husband died in 1665. Hired to spy on the Dutch for the British Crown, Behn traveled to Antwerp but was left broke and in debt when the king would not reimburse her for her work and expenses. She was sent to debtor's prison in 1668 and later began writing plays, vowing never again to rely on others for money. Although her writing was viewed as too masculine and was criticized as indecent by some contemporaries, "Mrs. Behn" went on to become one of the first professional English writers. In *A Room of One's Own*, Virginia Woolf wrote, "All women together ought to let flowers fall upon the tomb of Aphra Behn, . . . for it was she who earned them the right to speak their minds." Behn's prose continues to be highly regarded for its wit and satirical commentary; her poetry is admired for its distinctive voice. Behn's published works of poetry include *Poems upon Several Occasions: With A Voyage to the Island of Love* (1684) and *Lycidus: Or The Lover in Fashion* (1688).

**ELIZABETH BISHOP** (1911–1979)   Bishop was born in Worcester, Massachusetts. Her father died before she was a year old; four years later, when her mother suffered a mental breakdown, Bishop was taken to live with her grandmother in Nova Scotia. Although her mother lived until 1934, Bishop saw her for the last time in 1916, a visit recalled in one of her rare autobiographical stories, "In the Village." Bishop planned to enter Cornell Medical School after graduating from Vassar, but was persuaded by poet Marianne Moore to become a writer. For the next fifteen years, she was a virtual nomad, traveling in Canada, Europe, and North and South America. In 1951 she finally settled in Rio de Janeiro, where she lived for almost twenty years. During the final decade of her life, Bishop continued to travel, but she resumed living in the United States and taught frequently at Harvard University. She was an austere writer, publishing only four slim volumes of poetry: *North and South* (1946); *A Cold Spring* (1955), which won the Pulitzer Prize; *Questions of Travel* (1965); and *Geography III* (1976), which won the National Book Critics Circle Award. *The Complete Poems, 1927–1979* (1984) was published after her death, as was a collection of her prose. Despite her modest output, she has earned an enduring place of respect among twentieth-century poets.

**EULA BISS** (b. 1977)   Nonfiction writer Eula Biss received her BA from Hampshire College and her MFA from the University of Iowa. A senior lecturer at Northwestern University, she has written three books, and her essays have appeared in numerous publications. In an interview, Biss said, "One essential element of the personal essay tradition is self-scrutiny." Her book of essays on race and identity, *Notes from No Man's Land: American Essays* (2009), won the National Book Critics Circle Award for criticism. Her most recent book, *On Immunity: An Inoculation* (2014), a National Book Critics Circle Award finalist, examines the history, motivations, politics, and fears surrounding the modern vaccination debate.

**WILLIAM BLAKE** (1757–1827)   Born in London to an obscure family, Blake was educated at home until he was ten and then enrolled in a drawing school, advancing ultimately to a formal apprenticeship as an engraver. At an early age, Blake exhibited talent as both an artist and a poet. Throughout his life, he read widely among modern philosophers and poets and experienced mystical visions that provided him with the inspiration for many of his poems. Blake devised a process he called illuminated printing, which involved the preparation of drawings and decorative frames to complement his poems. He published *Songs of Innocence* (1789) and *Songs of Experience* (1794) in this fashion. These books, as well as the many subsequent works he wrote and illustrated, earned him a reputation as one of the most important artists of his day. Many of Blake's works assert his conviction that the established church and state hinder rather than nurture human freedom and the sense of divine love.

**ANNE BRADSTREET** (1612–1672)   The first notable poet in American literature, Bradstreet was born in England, where her father, a Puritan, managed the business affairs of the estate of the Earl of Lincoln. Unlike most women of her time, Bradstreet received a good deal of formal education. At age sixteen she married Simon Bradstreet, a graduate of Cambridge University, who, like her father, was a Puritan. Two years later, Bradstreet, her husband, and her parents set sail for the Massachusetts Bay Colony, where her father and husband became governors. Anne and Simon Bradstreet settled on a farm near Andover, on the Merrimac River, where the primitive conditions of life left her unhappy and unsatisfied for a period. Ultimately, she reconciled to this new life and her role as a wife, giving birth to eight children. But despite the demands of domestic life in a frontier village, she read a great deal and wrote poetry, which she circulated among family and friends. One of her relatives, who preserved copies of her poems without her knowledge, took them to England, where they were published in 1650 under the title *The Tenth Muse Lately Sprung Up in America . . . By a Gentlewoman of Those Parts*. The first volume of poetry by an English colonist, it was to be the only volume of Bradstreet's poetry published during her lifetime. She continued to write new poems and to revise her older ones; these later poems were included in the second edition of *The Tenth Muse*, published posthumously in 1678.

**GWENDOLYN BROOKS** (1917–2000)   Brooks, who was born in Topeka, Kansas, attended public schools in Chicago and graduated from Wilson Junior College in 1936. She received early recognition for her talent when she attended a poetry workshop at Chicago's Southside Community Art Center. Shortly after, she published her first book of poems, *A Street in Bronzeville* (1945). She quickly established her reputation as a major poet with *Annie Allen* (1949), which received the Pulitzer Prize for Poetry, making Brooks the first African American to receive this distinction. Her many honors include her designation as poet laureate of Illinois (1968) and as poetry consultant to Congress (1985–86). Although her poetry always focused on the hardships and joys of being poor and black, she steadily moved away from the apolitical integrationist views of her early years. By the 1960s, she had become a passionate advocate of African American consciousness and activism. In addition to reworking traditional forms such as the ballad and sonnet, Brooks achieved greater power in many poems by juxtaposing formal speech with black vernacular. Her other collections of poems include *The Bean Eaters* (1960), *In the Mecca* (1968), *To Disembark* (1981), and *Children Coming Home* (1992). She also published a novel, *Maude Martha* (1953), and an autobiography, *Report from Part One* (1972). Her final volume of poetry, *Montgomery and Other Poems*, was published posthumously in 2003. Its title is taken from the Alabama city that one critic describes as "one of those iconic sites of the Civil Rights Movement, in large part because of the yearlong bus boycotts from 1955 to 1956."

**ROBERT BROWNING** (1812–1889)   Born in London, Browning attended a private school and was later tutored at home. After one year as a student of Greek at the University of London, he moved with his family to Hatcham, where he studied, wrote poetry, and practiced writing for the theater. In 1845 he began exchanging poems and letters with the already famous poet Elizabeth Barrett; they eloped in 1846. They moved to Italy, where Browning completed most of his work. When Elizabeth died in 1861, he returned to England and began to establish his own reputation. He is noted especially for his fine dramatic monologues in which a wide range of characters reveal the complexity of human belief and passion. His many volumes include *Dramatis Personae* (1864) and *The Ring and the Book* (1868–1869).

**HALLMAN B. BRYANT** (b. 1936)   Bryant's literary criticism has appeared in *Literature/ Film Quarterly* and *Studies in Short Fiction* as well as many edited collections. His article "Reading the Map in 'A Good Man Is Hard to Find'" is among the most famous essays on Flannery O'Connor's renowned short story.

**ROBERT BURNS** (1759–1796)   Born in Scotland to a family of poor tenant farmers, Burns was working in the fields with his father by age twelve. During these early years, the family moved often, in fruitless attempts to improve their lot. Although Burns received formal education only intermittently, he read widely on his own. After the death of his father, Burns and his brother worked vainly to make their farm pay, an effort Burns was able to abandon when his first volume of poetry, *Poems, Chiefly in the Scottish Dialect* (1786) brought him overnight fame. One result of this fame was his appointment as an excise officer, a position that gave him some financial security while he continued to write poetry. Burns's humble origins instilled in him a lifelong sympathy for the poor and downtrodden, the rebels and iconoclasts, as well as a disdain for religion, particularly Calvinism and what he considered the hypocrisy of its "devout" ministers.

**RAYMOND CARVER** (1938–1988)   Carver was born in Clatskanie, Oregon, the son of a sawmill worker and a mother who did odd jobs. He graduated from high school at age eighteen, and was married and the father of two children before he was twenty. The following years were difficult as he struggled to develop a writing career while supporting a family. While at Chico State College (now California State University at Chico), Carver took a creative writing course that profoundly affected him. He went on to earn a BA (1963) from Humboldt State College in Eureka and spent the following year studying writing at the University of Iowa. As he became known, he began to lecture on English and creative writing at various universities, including the University of Iowa's Writers' Workshop. He taught at Goddard College in Vermont and was professor of English at Syracuse University from 1980 to 1983. In 1983 he received the Mildred and Harold Strauss Living Award, which allowed him to devote the next five years to writing. His first collection of short stories, *Will You Please Be Quiet, Please?* (1976), was nominated for the National Book Award. Other short-story collections include *What We Talk About When We Talk About Love* (1981) and *Cathedral* (1984). He also published five volumes of poems, among them *Near Klamath* (1968), *Ultramarine* (1986), and *A New Path to the Waterfall* (1989); *No Heroics, Please* (1992) was published posthumously. During the last ten years of his life, Carver lived with the poet and short-story writer Tess Gallagher, whom he married shortly before his death.

**SANDRA M. CASTILLO** (b. 1962)  Castillo was born in Havana, Cuba, and moved to Miami, Florida, with her family in 1970. Her poetry draws heavily from her early experience of emigrating to the United States as well as from her family's relationships, frequently looking back on the life her family left behind when they fled Cuba. Castillo received both her BA and MA in creative writing from Florida State University. Her first published collection was the chapbook *Red Letters* (1991), and her first full-length collection was *My Father Sings to My Embarrassment* (2002), which Cornelius Eady selected for the White Pine Press Poetry Prize. Her poems have been published in *Cimarron Review, Midway Journal, Borderlands: Texas Poetry Review, PALABRA: A Magazine of Chicano & Latino Literary Art,* and the anthology *Cool Salsa: Bilingual Poems on Growing Up Latino in the United States* (1994). In 2012 she received a grant from the National Endowment for the Humanities. She currently teaches at Miami Dade College in Florida.

**CATULLUS** (ca. 84–ca. 54 BCE)  Relatively little is known about the Latin poet Gaius Valerius Catullus. He is believed to have been born into an influential family in Verona, and his father was said to be a friend to Julius Caesar. The Roman philosopher Cicero described Catullus as a "neoteric" poet who rejected the epic poems characteristic of his time, opting instead to compose poems in plain language mainly about personal experiences. All knowledge of Catullus's poetry has been gleaned from a single extant manuscript of 116 poems, or *carmina*, and the majority of what is known about Catullus's short life has been gathered from the experiences and observations presented in these poems.

**MARILYN CHIN** (b. 1955)  Chin emigrated with her family from Hong Kong, grew up in Portland, Oregon, and earned degrees from the University of Massachusetts and the University of Iowa. She is the author of four volumes of poetry — *Dwarf Bamboo* (1987), *The Phoenix Gone, the Terrace Empty* (1994), *Rhapsody in Plain Yellow* (2002), and *Hard Love Province* (2014) — as well as a novel, *Revenge of the Mooncake Vixen* (2009). She has received two grants from the National Endowment for the Arts as well as a Stegner Fellowship, the PEN/Josephine Miles Award, four Pushcart Prizes, and a Fulbright scholarship. She is codirector of the MFA program at San Diego State University. About her work, Chin says, "My poetry both laments and celebrates my 'hyphenated' identity. . . . I am an American poet, a hyphenated American poet, to be precise; and what is American about my poetry is my muse's indomitable conviction to hammer the rich virtues and contradictions of my adopted country into a fusionist's delight."

**KATE CHOPIN** (1850–1904)   Born Kate O'Flaherty in St. Louis, Missouri, Chopin was raised by her mother, grandmother, and great-grandmother, all widows, after her father's death when she was four. In 1870, following her graduation from Sacred Heart Convent, she married Oscar Chopin and moved to New Orleans, where she became a housewife and eventually had six children. After her husband's death in 1882, she returned to her mother's home in St. Louis and began her career as a writer. Her first novel, *At Fault* (1890), and her stories, collected in *Bayou Folk* (1894) and *A Night in Acadie* (1897), gained her a reputation as a vivid chronicler of the lives of Creoles and Acadians (Cajuns) in Louisiana. Many of these stories explore a female protagonist's attempts to achieve self-fulfillment. Her novel *The Awakening* (1899) is probably her most ambitious exploration of this theme. It is the story of a woman whose awakening to her passion and inner self leads her to adultery and suicide. The storm of controversy with which this work was met virtually ended Chopin's literary career.

**SONYA CHUNG** (b. 1973)   Korean American writer Sonya Chung received her BA from Columbia University and her MFA from the University of Washington. She currently teaches fiction writing at Skidmore College. Her stories, reviews, and essays have appeared in periodicals such as the *Threepenny Review* and the *Huffington Post* as well as in books such as *The Late American Novel: Writers on the Future of Books*. She has also published a novel, *Long for This World* (2010), about a family divided between America and a small town in South Korea. Paraphrasing Anne Tyler, Chung says, "I write fiction so I can live many lives." She is a staff writer for the online literature and culture magazine *The Millions*, and the founding editor of *Bloom*, a literary site focused on authors whose first major work was published when they were age forty or older.

**SANDRA CISNEROS** (b. 1954)   Cisneros, the daughter of a Mexican father and a Mexican American mother, grew up in poor neighborhoods of Chicago, where she attended public schools. The only daughter among seven children, Cisneros recalled that because her brothers attempted to control her and expected her to assume a traditional female role, she grew up feeling as if she had "seven fathers." The family's frequent moves, many of them between the United States and Mexico to visit a grandmother, left Cisneros feeling alone and displaced. She found refuge both in reading and in writing poems and stories. In the late 1970s, Cisneros's writing talent earned her admission to the University of Iowa's Writers' Workshop. There, Cisneros observed, "Everyone seemed to have some communal knowledge which I did not have. . . . My classmates were from the best schools in the country. They had been bred as fine hothouse flowers. I was a yellow weed among the city's cracks." This realization led Cisneros to focus her writing on the conflicts and yearnings of her own life and culture. Her writings include four volumes of poetry — *Bad Boys* (1980), *The Rodrigo Poems* (1985), *My Wicked, Wicked Ways* (1987), and *Loose Woman* (1994) — and three volumes of fiction — *The House on Mango Street* (1983), *Woman Hollering Creek and Other Stories* (1991), and *Caramelo* (2002). She is also the author of a bilingual children's book, *Hairs = Pelitos* (1994). She received a prestigious MacArthur Fellowship in 1995. Her most recent works include the children's book *Bravo Bruno!* (2011) and the adult fable *Have You Seen Marie?* (2012).

**MICHAEL CLARK** (1946–1999)   After earning his PhD in American literature from the University of Wisconsin–Madison in 1981, Michael Clark taught creative writing, composition, and American literature at Widener University in Pennsylvania. He published short stories, poems, and essays in numerous magazines. His articles on major American authors such as Herman Melville and James Baldwin appeared in a variety of scholarly journals.

**LUCILLE CLIFTON** (b. 1936–2010)   Born in Depew, New York, Clifton attended Howard University (1953–55) and Fredonia State Teachers College. She worked as a claims clerk in the New York State Division of Employment in Buffalo (1958–60), and as literature assistant in the Office of Education in Washington, DC (1960–71). In 1969 she received the YM-YWHA Poetry Center Discovery Award, and her first collection, *Good Times*, was selected as one of the ten best books of 1969 by the *New York Times*. From 1971 to 1974 she was poet-in-residence at Coppin State College in Baltimore, and in 1979 she was named poet laureate of the state of Maryland. She wrote many collections for children and a free-verse chronicle of five generations of her family, *Generations: A Memoir* (1976). Her final publication was *Voices* (2008). In 2007 Clifton was awarded the Ruth Lilly Poetry Prize, a prestigious honor given to living U.S. poets "whose lifetime accomplishments warrant extraordinary recognition." Noted for celebrating ordinary people and everyday things, Clifton was quoted as saying, "I am a black woman poet, and I sound like one."

**JUDITH ORTIZ COFER** (1952–2016)   Cofer was born in Hormigueros, Puerto Rico. She earned a BA (1974) from Augusta College and an MA (1977) from Florida Atlantic University and briefly attended Oxford University. She began her teaching career as a bilingual instructor in Florida public schools and taught at a number of schools, including the University of Miami and the University of Georgia. Her first volume of poems, *Latin Women Pray*, appeared in 1981, and she published many subsequent poetry collections, and essays about coming of age in the barrio, including *The Year of Our Revolution: New and Selected Stories and Poems* (1998), *Woman in Front of the Sun: On Becoming a Writer* (2000), and *A Love Story Beginning in Spanish* (2005). She also published two young adult novels — *Call Me María* (2004) and *If I Could Fly* (2011) — as well as several children's books. Cofer pointed to her family as an important source for her writing: "The place of birth itself becomes a metaphor for the things we must all leave behind; the assimilation of a new culture is the coming into maturity by accepting the terms necessary for survival."

**BILLY COLLINS** (b. 1941)   Collins was born in New York City and earned a BA (1963) from the College of the Holy Cross and a PhD (1971) from the University of California, Riverside. He has been teaching at the City University of New York since 1971. *Pokerface*, the first of his several books of poetry, was published in 1977. Collins's later work attracted so much attention that his early poetry books became economically valuable. Consequently, the University of Pittsburgh Press, publisher of *The Art of Drowning* (1995) and *Picnic, Lightning* (1998), at first withheld permission from Random House to reprint earlier poems in Collins's *Sailing around the Room: New and Selected Poems* (2000). The matter was settled, and Random House published his next collection of poems, *Nine Horses* (2002). The struggle between Random House and the University of Pittsburgh Press over the rights to Collins's work made him sufficiently notorious. He has since published *The Trouble with Poetry and Other Poems* (2005), *Ballistics: Poems* (2008), *Horoscopes for the Dead: Poems* (2012), and *Aimless Love* (2013). He has won several poetry prizes as well as fellowships from the New York Foundation for the Arts, the National Endowment for the Arts, and the Guggenheim Foundation. Collins was the poet laureate of the United States from 2001 to 2003 and the poet laureate for New York State from 2004 to 2006. In 2005 he was the first recipient of the Mark Twain Prize for Humor in Poetry. He commented to one journalist: "I think my work has to do with a sense that we are attempting, all the time, to create a logical, rational path through the day. To the left and right there are an amazing set of distractions that we usually can't afford to follow. But the poet is willing to stop anywhere."

**RICHARD CRASHAW** (1612–1649)   Crashaw was the only son of William Crashaw, a fervently anti-Catholic preacher. Crashaw did not share his father's religious views, however; he was a Catholic sympathizer. He attended Pembroke College, Cambridge, where he earned his BA in 1634. He went to Peterhouse in 1636 and became a fellow of the college in 1637, earning his MA there in 1638. However, in 1644 he was ejected from the college for his religious leanings, after which he fled to France and became a Catholic sometime around 1645. His friend Abraham Cowley later found him destitute in Paris and helped him regain his footing, introducing Crashaw to Charles I's queen, Henrietta Maria, who sent Crashaw to Rome with a recommendation to the pope. Crashaw died in 1649 while serving in the Cathedral of Santa Casa in Loreto. He wrote throughout his life, and his poetry came to be known for its brilliant use of extravagant baroque imagery. His works were first collected by an anonymous friend and published as *Steps to the Temple* in 1646.

**VICTOR HERNÁNDEZ CRUZ** (b. 1949)   Cruz was born in Aguas Buenas, Puerto Rico, and immigrated with his family to New York City in 1954. He recalls, "My family life was full of music, guitars and conga drums, maracas and songs.... Even when it was five below zero in New York [my mother] sang warm tropical ballads." By 1966, he had already completed a collection of verse, *Papa Got His Gun, and Other Poems*, and in 1969 he published *Snaps*. He has edited *Umbra* magazine in New York, lectured at the University of California, Berkeley, and taught at San Francisco State University. Cruz says he writes in three languages: Spanish, English, and bilingual. "From the mixture a totally new language emerges, an intense collision, not just of words, but of attitudes." His other works include *Mainland* (1973), *Tropicalizations* (1976), *Red Beans: Poems* (1991), *Panoramas* (1997), *Maraca: New and Selected Poems, 1965–2000* (2001), *The Mountain in the Sea* (2006), and, most recently, *In the Shadow of Al-Andalus* (2011). Cruz is also coeditor of the poetry anthology *Paper Dance: 55 Latino Poets* (2008).

**COUNTEE CULLEN** (1903–1946)   Born Countee L. Porter in New York City, Cullen was adopted by the Reverend and Mrs. Cullen in 1918 and raised in Harlem. He was extraordinarily precocious, and by 1920 his poems had been published in *Poetry*, the *Nation*, and *Harper's*. He published his famous poem "Heritage" in 1925, the year he graduated from New York University. After earning an MA in English from Harvard in 1926, he taught French in a junior high school and was assistant editor of the National Urban League's *Opportunity: Journal of Negro Life*. Cullen, along with Langston Hughes and Jean Toomer, was a central figure in the Harlem Renaissance of the 1920s. He received a Guggenheim Fellowship in 1929. In addition to five volumes of poetry, he published a novel, *One Way to Heaven* (1932), which deals with the interaction between upper- and lower-class African Americans in Harlem in the 1920s.

**E. E. CUMMINGS** (1894–1962)   Born in Cambridge, Massachusetts, Edward Estlin Cummings attended Harvard University (BA, 1915; MA, 1916), served as a volunteer ambulance driver in France during World War I, was imprisoned for three months in a French detention camp, served in the U.S. Army (1918–19), and then studied art and painting in Paris (1920–24). His prose narrative *The Enormous Room* (1922), a recollection of his imprisonment, brought instant acclaim. Several volumes of poetry followed. His experiments with punctuation, line division, and capitalization make his work immediately recognizable. In a letter to young poets published in a high school newspaper, Cummings said, "[N]othing is quite so easy as using words like somebody else. We all of us do exactly this nearly all the time — and whenever we do it, we're not poets."

**EMILY DICKINSON** (1830–1886)   Dickinson, one of three children, was born in Amherst, Massachusetts. Her father was a prominent lawyer. Except for one year away at a nearby college and a trip with her sister to Washington, DC, to visit her father when he was serving in Congress, she lived out her life, unmarried, in her parents' home. During her trip to Washington, she met the Reverend Charles Wadsworth, a married man, whom she came to characterize as her "dearest earthly friend." Little is known of this relationship except that Dickinson's feelings for Wadsworth were strong. In 1862 Wadsworth moved to San Francisco, an event that coincided with a period of Dickinson's intense poetic creativity. Also in that year, she initiated a literary correspondence with the critic T. W. Higginson, to whom she sent some of her poems for his opinion. Higginson, although he recognized her talent, was puzzled by her startling originality and urged her to write more conventionally, advice she was unable to follow. Only seven of her poems were published while she was alive, none of them with her consent. After her death, the extraordinary richness of her imaginative life came to light with the discovery of her more than 1,000 poems.

**GREGORY DJANIKIAN** (b. 1949)   Born in Egypt of Armenian parentage, Djanikian came to the United States at age eight. He is a graduate of the Syracuse University writing program and is director of creative writing at the University of Pennsylvania, where he received his undergraduate degree. Djanikian is the author of several collections of poetry that explore, among other things, family, history, culture, and language. His books include *The Man in the Middle* (1984), *Falling Deeply into America* (1989), *Years Later* (2000), *So I Will Till the Ground* (2007), and, most recently, *Dear Gravity* (2014). His poems have appeared in numerous periodicals, including the *American Scholar*, the *Iowa Review*, *Poetry*, and the *Nation*. His work has also appeared in several anthologies, including *Best American Poetry* (2000) and *Becoming Americans: Four Centuries of Immigrant Writing* (2009).

**JOHN DONNE** (1572–1631)   Born in London into a prosperous Roman Catholic family of tradespeople at a time when England was staunchly anti-Catholic, Donne was forced to leave Oxford University without a degree because of his religion. He studied law and at the same time read widely in theology in an attempt to decide whether the Roman or the Anglican Church was the true Catholic Church, a decision he was not able to make for many years. In the meantime, he became known as a witty man of the world and the author of original, often dense, erotic poems. Donne left his law studies, participated in two naval expeditions, and then became secretary to a powerful noble, a job he lost when he was briefly sent to prison for secretly marrying his patron's niece. In 1615, at the age of forty-two, Donne accepted ordination in the Anglican Church. He quickly earned a reputation as one of the greatest preachers of his time. He was dean of St. Paul's from 1621 until his death. In his later years, Donne repudiated the poetry of his youth.

**TISHANI DOSHI** (b. 1975)   Born in India to a Welsh mother and a Gujarati father, Doshi has published five books of fiction, nonfiction, and poetry. She is also a dancer. When asked about the connection between writing and dance in a 2013 interview for *Port* magazine, Doshi said, "There's the sense that if you're working with words, whether it's fiction or poetry, you're working with the body." Her essays, poems, and short stories have been widely anthologized. She is the recipient of an Eric Gregory Award for Poetry, winner of the All-India Poetry Competition, and her first book of poems, *Countries of the Body* (2006), won the prestigious Forward Prize for Best First Collection. Doshi's debut novel, *The Pleasure Seekers* (2010), was shortlisted for the Hindu Literary Prize. Her most recent works include the poetry collection *Everything Begins Elsewhere* (2013) and *Fountainville* (2013), a retelling of a Welsh legend.

**BOB DOWELL** (b. 1932)   Born and raised in East Texas, Dowell earned his PhD in 1962, at which point he embarked on a teaching career. He taught college English and did stints as academic dean for more than thirty years. In 1999 Dowell retired from college teaching in order to write about the Bible, a subject he knew well from years of teaching a Bible as literature course. He also created a church Bible study forum for understanding Christian doctrine through the use of prose (for the head) and poetry (for the heart). The success of that program led to the publication of *Understanding the Bible: Head and Heart* in three parts: *The Old Testament* (2010), *Matthew through Acts* (2011), and *Romans through Revelations* (2012). In addition to writing, Dowell continues to raise cattle on the family farm where he was born.

**BRIAN DOYLE** (1956–2017)   Doyle, the son of a journalist and a teacher, was born in New York City and graduated from the University of Notre Dame. He was an editor at *U.S. Catholic* magazine and a writer at *Boston College Magazine* before becoming the editor of *Portland Magazine* at the University of Portland. He authored several books, among them *Credo: Essays on Grace, Altar Boys, Bees, Kneeling, Saints, the Mass, Priests, Strong Women, Epiphanies, a Wake, and the Haunting Thin Energetic Dusty Figure of Jesus the Christ* (1999); *The Wet Engine: Exploring the Mad Wild Miracle of the Heart* (2005); *Epiphanies and Elegies: Very Short Stories* (2006); *Mink River* (2010); and *The Plover* (2014). His work has also appeared in anthologies, such as *The Best Spiritual Writing* and *The Best American Essays*, and a number of periodicals, among them *Atlantic Monthly*, *American Scholar*, *Harper's*, *Gourmet*, and the *London Times*. Doyle served as editor of the Best Catholic Writing series from Loyola Press from 2004 to 2006. He passed away in 2017 from complications related to a brain tumor.

**T. S. ELIOT** (1888–1965)   Thomas Stearns Eliot was born in St. Louis, Missouri. His father was president of the Hydraulic Press Brick Company, and his mother was a teacher, social worker, and writer. Educated at private academies, Eliot earned two philosophy degrees at Harvard University (BA, 1909; MA, 1910). After graduate study in Paris and England, he worked for eight years as a clerk in Lloyd's Bank in London and became a naturalized British citizen in 1927. He was editor, then director, of Faber & Gwyer Publishers (later Faber & Faber) from 1925 to 1965 and spent time in the United States as a visiting lecturer and scholar. Admirers and detractors alike agree that Eliot was the most imposing and influential poet writing between the world wars. His poems "The Love Song of J. Alfred Prufrock" (1917) and *The Waste Land* (1922) are among his earliest and most famous. Acknowledging his dependence on a preexisting cultural tradition, Eliot explained: "The existing order is complete before the new work arrives; for order to persist after the supervention of novelty, the whole existing order must be altered." Eliot also wrote plays, including *Murder in the Cathedral* (1935) and *The Cocktail Party* (1950). The long-running Broadway musical *Cats* is based on his 1939 verse collection, *Old Possum's Book of Practical Cats*. He won the Nobel Prize in Literature in 1948.

**HARLAN ELLISON®** (b. 1934)   Born in Cleveland, Ohio, Ellison published his first story when he was thirteen. He left Ohio State University after two years and worked at a variety of odd jobs while establishing himself as a writer. In a career spanning over sixty years, he has written or edited a hundred books and more than 1,700 stories, essays, reviews, articles, motion picture scripts, and teleplays. He has won the Hugo Award ten and a half times; the Nebula Award five times, as well as a Grandmaster Nebula Award (basically a lifetime achievement award); the Edgar Allan Poe Award of the Mystery Writers of America twice; the Bram Stoker Award from the Horror Writers Association six times, including the Lifetime Achievement Award in 1996; the Georges Méliès fantasy film award twice; the World Fantasy Award twice, the second time for lifetime achievement; two Audie Awards (for the best in audio recordings); the British Fantasy Award; and the Silver Pen for journalism from PEN. He was presented with the first Living Legend award by the International Horror Critics at the 1995 World Horror Convention, and in March 1998, the National Women's Committee of Brandeis University honored him with their Words, Wit, Wisdom Award. He is the only scenarist in Hollywood ever to have won the Writers Guild of America award for Most Outstanding Teleplay four times for solo work. His latest books are *Bugf#ck: The Useless Wit & Wisdom of Harlan Ellison* (2011) and a new series with the Publishing 180 program. These books are a mixture of classic stories and essays and original never-before-available teleplays: *Brain Movies: The Original Teleplays of Harlan Ellison* (Volumes One and Two), *Harlan 101: Encountering Ellison*, and *Harlan 101: The Sound of a Scythe Plus Three Classic Novellas*. For the first time, Ellison's collections of essays on television, *The Glass Teat* and *The Other Glass Teat*, have been published in one volume as the complete *Omnibus*. He has also written numerous short stories for various magazines, most recently "How Interesting: A Tiny Man," which garnered Ellison his fourth Nebula Award. In celebration of Ellison's seventy-fifth birthday, documentarian Erik Nelson produced a feature-length film that looks at Ellison's life and work. The documentary, *Dreams with Sharp Teeth*, was released on DVD in May 2009. Ellison currently lives with his wife, Susan, in the Los Angeles area.

**RALPH ELLISON** (1914–1994)   Ellison was born in Oklahoma City, Oklahoma. He studied music, specifically trumpet and piano, and sculpture before embarking on a writing career. In New York City, encouraged by his friend and fellow writer Richard Wright, Ellison began writing book reviews, essays, and short stories. He also earned money as a freelance photographer. His first novel, *Invisible Man* (1952), for which he is best known, won the National Book Award in 1953. He published two collections of essays, *Shadow and Act* (1964) and *Going to the Territory* (1986). He taught at Bard College, Rutgers University, the University of Chicago, and New York University before dying of pancreatic cancer in 1994. His short stories were collected and published posthumously in *Flying Home and Other Stories* (1996). Ellison wrote more than 2,000 pages for a second novel, *Juneteenth*, over the span of forty years; it was edited down to 368 pages and published in 1999, five years after his death.

**LOUISE ERDRICH** (b. 1954)   Erdrich was born in Little Falls, Minnesota, and grew up in North Dakota. Her father was German American and her mother was French and Anishinaabe; Erdrich is a member of the Native American Anishinaabe Nation. She earned degrees from Dartmouth College and Johns Hopkins University. Before fully embarking on her writing career, she worked as a lifeguard, waitress, prison poetry teacher, construction flagger, and newspaper editor. She began by publishing poems and short fiction and won the Nelson Algren Prize for her short story "The World's Greatest Fisherman" in 1982. Her first novel, *Love Medicine* (1984), won the National Book Critics Circle Award. She went on to write more than ten other novels, notably *The Beet Queen* (1986), *Tracks* (1988), *The Antelope Wife* (1998), and *The Painted Drum* (2005). In addition to having written five novels for adolescents and three works of nonfiction, Erdrich has published three books of poetry: *Jacklight* (1984), *Baptism of Desire* (1989), and *Original Fire: Selected and New Poems* (2003). Her most recent works include the novels *The Plague of Doves* (2008), *Shadow Tag* (2010), and *The Round House* (2012), which won the National Book Award. She has won several other awards including an O. Henry Award, a Pushcart Prize, the Dayton Literary Peace Prize, and the PEN/Saul Bellow Award for Achievement in American Fiction. Erdrich owns a bookstore in Minneapolis, Minnesota, and hosts annual writing workshops on the Turtle Mountain Indian Reservation in North Dakota.

**FAIZ AHMED FAIZ** (1911–1984)    Often referred to as Pakistan's greatest poet, Faiz was also known for his political ideology. Born to wealthy and educated Muslim parents, Faiz was brought up in a secular tradition of Islam. After his college and postcollege studies, he taught literature and economics courses at universities in India. He served in the British Army during World War II, earning the rank of Lieutenant-Colonel in 1944. He resigned from the military in 1947, the same year he cofounded the Communist Party of Pakistan and became editor of the socialist newspaper the *Pakistan Times*. In 1951 he was arrested for his alleged role in plotting a coup against the right-wing government, and he spent four years in prison. In the 1960s he returned to teaching, held prominent positions in the Pakistan Arts Council, and took on several advisory roles in the culture and education departments of the Pakistani government, which had by that time shifted to the left. A humanist and internationalist committed to global peace, Faiz was awarded the Lenin Peace Prize (the Soviet equivalent of the Nobel Peace Prize) in 1962. His major works include *Naqsh-e-Faryadi* (1943) and *Dast-e-Tah-e-Sung* (1965). Many of his poems have been translated into English and published in collections such as *The Rebel's Silhouette: Selected Poems* (1995) and *The True Subject: Selected Poems of Faiz Ahmed Faiz* (2012).

**ALAN FELDMAN** (b. 1945)    Feldman's poetry has appeared in many top literary publications throughout his career, including the *Atlantic*, the *New Yorker, Nation, Poetry, Kenyon Review, Southern Review, Ploughshares, Iowa Review, Threepenny Review, Virginia Quarterly Review*, and others. His work has also been included in many anthologies, including *To Woo and To Wed: Poets on Love and Marriage* (1992), *The Best American Erotic Poems 1800–Present*, and *The Best American Poetry 2001 and 2011*, and Feldman has also been honored with poetry fellowships from the National Endowment for the Arts and the Massachusetts Artists Foundation. In 1979 his collection *The Happy Genius* (1978) won the Elliston Book Award, and his full-length collection *A Sail to Great Island* (2004) won the 2004 Felix Pollak Prize in Poetry. His most recent collection, *Immortality* (2015), was awarded the Four Lakes Prize. Feldman lives in Framingham, Massachusetts, and is married to Nan Hass Feldman, an artist.

**LAWRENCE FERLINGHETTI** (b. 1919)    Born Lawrence Ferling, this irreverent writer assumed his original family name in 1954. He earned a BA in journalism from the University of North Carolina in 1941, served as lieutenant commander in the U.S. Naval

Reserve during World War II, and then received graduate degrees from Columbia University and the University of Paris. He worked briefly as a translator of French before rising to prominence in the San Francisco–based Beat literary movement of the 1950s, composed of a group of writers who felt strongly that art should be accessible to all, not just to a small group of intellectuals. Ferlinghetti received great praise from many readers and some critics for his attempts to incorporate American vernacular speech and the rhythms of modern jazz into his writings, while he was roundly attacked by defenders of the status quo. Ferlinghetti has been a prolific writer in all genres. In addition, he cofounded the San Francisco bookstore City Lights and two publishing enterprises, City Lights Books and the Pocket Book Series. In 1998 Ferlinghetti was named San Francisco's first poet laureate. He won the Poetry Society of America's Robert Frost Medal and the Authors Guild Lifetime Achievement Award, and was elected to the American Academy of Arts and Letters in 2003. In 2005 he received the National Book Foundation's first Literarian Award for outstanding service to the American literary community. He has published two novels, many plays, and over two dozen volumes of poetry including *Americus, Book I* (2004) and *Poetry as Insurgent Art* (2007). His early work *A Coney Island of the Mind* (1958) remains his most popular and best-selling poetry collection.

**DONALD FINKEL** (1929–2008)   Donald Finkel was born in New York City, the son of an attorney. He earned a BS (1952) and an MA (1953) from Columbia University. In 1956 he married the writer Constance Urdang. Shortly thereafter, Finkel began a university teaching career at the University of Iowa and in 1960 moved to Washington University in St. Louis where he became poet-in-residence. His interest in Antarctica and exploration produced *Endurance: An Antarctic Idyll* and *Going Under* (1978). The first describes the shipwreck and rescue of Ernest Shackleton's 1914 expedition. The second examines two men who explored Kentucky's Mammoth Cave. His many books, including *Selected Shorter Poems* (1987), *A Splintered Mirror: Chinese Poetry from the Democracy Movement* (1991), and *A Question of Seeing: Poems* (1998), have earned him abundant awards and honors, among them a Guggenheim Fellowship (1967), nomination for a National Book Award (1970), and two nominations for the National Book Critics Circle Award (1975, 1981). His final volume was *Not So the Chairs: Selected and New Poems* (2003).

**CAROLYN FORCHÉ** (b. 1950)   Born in Detroit, Forché earned a BA in international relations and creative writing at Michigan State University in 1972. After graduate study at Bowling Green State University in 1975, she taught at a number of schools, including the University of Arkansas, Vassar College, Columbia University, and George Mason University. She won the Yale Series of Younger Poets Award in 1976 for her first collection, *Gathering the Tribes*. Other honors include a Guggenheim Fellowship and the Lamont Award (1981). Forché was a journalist for Amnesty International in El Salvador in 1983 and Beirut correspondent for the National Public Radio program *All Things Considered*. Her works include the collections of poetry *The Country between Us* (1981) and *The Angel of History* (1994), both embodying her passionate preoccupation with the dehumanizing effects of political repression. Among her most recent publications are a memoir, *The Horse on Our Balcony* (2009), and the poetry collections *Blue Hour* (2003) and *In the Lateness of the World* (2015). In 2013 Forché received the Academy of American Poets Fellowship, given for distinguished poetic achievement. She currently is director of the Lannan Center for Poetics and Social Practice at Georgetown University.

**DAISY FRIED** (b. 1967)   Fried has taught creative writing at Villanova University, Haverford College, the University of Pennsylvania, in Warren Wilson College's low-residency MFA program, and as the Grace Hazard Conkling Writer-in-Residence at Smith College. She has been the recipient of Guggenheim, Hodder, and Pew Fellowships, a Pushcart Prize, and the Cohen Award from *Ploughshares*. Her poetry has been featured in such publications as the *Nation, Poetry, New Republic, American Poetry Review, Antioch Review, Threepenny Review, Ploughshares*, and elsewhere. She has published three books of poetry: *She Didn't Mean to Do It* (2000), which won the Agnes Lynch Starrett Prize, *My Brother Is Getting Arrested Again* (2006), a finalist for the National Book Critics Circle Award, and *Women's Poetry: Poems and Advice* (2013), which was named one of the five best poetry books of the year by *Library Journal*. In 2009 she was awarded *Poetry's* Editors Prize for Feature Article for her essay "Sing, God-Awful Muse," which discusses *Paradise Lost* and breastfeeding. She lives in Philadelphia with her husband and daughter.

**ROBERT FROST** (1874–1963)   Frost was born in San Francisco but from the age of ten lived in New England. He attended Dartmouth College briefly and then became a teacher, but soon decided to resume his formal training and enrolled at Harvard University. He left Harvard after two years without a degree and for several years supported himself and his growing family by tending a farm his grandfather bought for him. When he was not farming, he read and wrote intensively, though he received little recognition. Discouraged by his lack of success, he sold the farm and moved his family to England, where he published his first volumes of poetry, *A Boy's Will* (1913) and *North of Boston* (1914). After three years in England, Frost returned to the United States a recognized poet. Later volumes, notably *Mountain Interval* (1916), *New Hampshire* (1923), *West-Running Brook* (1928), and *A Further Range* (1936), won Frost wide popularity and numerous awards, including two Pulitzer Prizes. By the time he delivered his poem "The Gift Outright" at the inauguration of President John F. Kennedy in 1961, Frost had achieved the status of unofficial poet laureate of the United States, widely revered and beloved for his folksy manner and seemingly artless, accessible poems.

**RIVKA GALCHEN** (b. 1976)   Galchen was born in Toronto, though she moved with her parents to the United States when she was just a baby. She entered Princeton University in 1994 to study English, but during her sophomore year she applied to an early admissions program at the Mount Sinai School of Medicine. She received her MD from Mount Sinai in 2003 and went on to earn an MFA from Columbia University. Her work has appeared in the *New Yorker, Harper's*, the *New York Times*, the *Believer*, and elsewhere. She has received many literary honors, including the 2006 Rona Jaffe Foundation Writers' Award, and she was included in the *New Yorker's* 2010 "20 Under 40" list. She was also the 2011 Mary Ellen von der Heyden Fiction Fellow at the American Academy in Berlin. Her first novel, *Atmospheric Disturbances* (2008), has been translated into over twenty languages and won the William J. Saroyan International Prize for Fiction. Her collection of short stories, *American Innovations* was published in 2014. Galchen currently teaches writing at Columbia University and is a contributing editor for *Harper's Magazine*.

**DAGOBERTO GILB** (b. 1950)   Gilb was raised by his mother in Los Angeles. He graduated from the University of California, Santa Barbara, in 1974 with a double major in philosophy and religious studies, and went on to earn his MA in religious studies in 1976. His work has appeared in many magazines, most recently *Harper's*, the *New Yorker*, and *Callaloo*, and has been widely anthologized and translated. Gilb also received a Guggenheim

Fellowship and has been a finalist for the National Book Critics Circle Award. Some of his publications include *The Magic of Blood* (1993), which won the PEN/Hemingway Award and was a finalist for the PEN/Faulkner Award; *The Last Known Residence of Mickey Acuña* (1994), a New York Times Notable Book; *Woodcuts of Women* (2001); *Gritos* (2003), a finalist for the 2004 National Book Critics Circle Award; and *The Flowers* (2008). His most recent work is *Before the End, After the Beginning* (2011), a collection of stories that Gilb wrote while recovering from a stroke in 2009. He is currently writer-in-residence and executive director of Centro Victoria: Center for Mexican American Literature and Culture at University of Houston–Victoria.

**CHARLOTTE PERKINS GILMAN** (1860–1935)   Gilman was born in Hartford, Connecticut. Shortly after her birth, her father deserted the family. Left with two children to support and scant help from their father, her mother was unable to provide her children with a secure and stable childhood. Gilman attended the Rhode Island School of Design for a time and went on to work as a commercial artist and teacher. In 1884 she married Charles Stetson, an artist. Following the birth of her only child the next year, Gilman was immobilized by a deep depression. At the urging of her husband, she became the patient of S. Weir Mitchell, a physician celebrated for his treatment of female nervous disorders. Gilman found the treatment intolerable and finally abandoned it. In 1888, convinced that her marriage threatened her sanity, she moved with her daughter to California and began her productive career as writer and feminist. In 1900, after her divorce, she married her first cousin George Houghton Gilman, enjoying a happy relationship that lasted until his sudden death thirty-four years later. Among Gilman's many works are *Women and Economics* (1899), *The Home: Its Work and Influence* (1903), and *The Man-Made World* (1911), whose thesis is that war and injustice will be eliminated only when women assume a larger role in national and international affairs. Gilman's fiction includes the novels *Moving the Mountain* (1911), *Herland* (1915), and *With Her in Ourland* (1916). Her autobiography, *The Living of Charlotte Perkins Gilman*, was published posthumously in 1935, the year she committed suicide to avoid suffering the final stages of breast cancer.

**ALLEN GINSBERG** (1926–1997)   Born in Newark, New Jersey, Ginsberg was among the foremost members of the Beat Generation. He matriculated to Columbia University in 1943, where he met Lucien Carr — the man who introduced him to William S. Burroughs, Neal Cassady, John Clellon Holmes, and Jack Kerouac, who would all eventually become renowned Beat poets: writers whose poetry conveyed a sense of spiritual exhaustion and rebellion against the hypocrisy and unprecedented materialism that overtook America in the wake of World War II. In his journal, Ginsberg described the "new vision" to which the Beats led him: "Since art is merely and ultimately self-expressive, we conclude that the fullest art, the most individual, uninfluenced, unrepressed, uninhibited expression of art is true expression and the true art." In 1954 Ginsberg moved to San Francisco where his mentor, William Carlos Williams, introduced him to Kenneth Rexroth, a prominent figure in the San Francisco Renaissance. Rexroth helped to establish Ginsberg as part of the San Francisco poetry scene, a task that came to a head when Ginsberg organized a reading for the Six Gallery on October 7, 1955. This was the first public reading of Ginsberg's "Howl" — a poem that attracted worldwide attention for the poet and his colleagues — and came to be known as the birth of the Beat Generation. Ginsberg labored tirelessly thereafter to promote his work and that of his peers, traveling throughout America and Europe to give readings. Ginsberg's first full-length poetry collection, *Howl and Other Poems* (1956), was widely banned for obscenity when it was first published, but over time "Howl" became one of the most read poems of the century. Ginsberg published nearly two dozen other poetry collections, including *Kaddish and Other Poems* (1961), *Planet News* (1968), *Iron Horse* (1972), and *The Fall of America: Poems of These States* (1973), which won the National Book Award. Ginsberg was also involved in many political activities throughout the 1960s and 1970s, including Vietnam War protests and speaking out in defense of the North American Man/Boy Love Association (NAMBLA). In 1973 he cofounded and directed the Jack Kerouac School of Disembodied Poetics at the Naropa Institute in Colorado. In his later years, Ginsberg became a distinguished professor at Brooklyn College, and in 1993 he was named a *Chevalier des Arts et des Lettres* (Knight of the Order of Arts and Letters) by the French Minister of Culture. He continued to travel throughout his life despite developing both diabetes and Reynaud's disease and suffering two minor strokes in the 1970s. He died in New York in 1997 after a battle with liver cancer.

**MALCOLM GLADWELL** (b. 1963)   Journalist Malcolm Gladwell was born in England and grew up in rural Ontario. In 1984 he received his undergraduate degree in history from the University of Ontario. He was a reporter covering business and science at the *Washington Post* from 1987 until 1996, when he began working as a staff writer at the *New Yorker*. Most of Gladwell's works center around sociological and psychological phenomena that he finds interesting or unexpected, such as the underlying causes of crime rates and the evolution of racism and sexism. He has written five books, all of them on the *New York Times* best-seller list: *The Tipping Point: How Little Things Can Make a Big Difference* (2000), *Blink: The Power of Thinking Without Thinking* (2005), *Outliers: The Story of Success* (2008), *What the Dog Saw: And Other Adventures* (2009), and *David and Goliath: Underdogs, Misfits, and the Art of Battling Giants* (2013). In *Outliers*, Gladwell contends that the key to success in any field lies mostly in practicing a given task for 10,000 hours. In his own experience at the *Washington Post*, he spent 10,000 hours — over the course of ten years — developing his expertise as a journalist.

**SUSAN GLASPELL** (1876–1948)   Born and raised in Davenport, Iowa, Glaspell began her career as a novelist and author of sentimental short stories for popular magazines. By 1915, she had turned her energies to the theater, becoming one of the founders of the Provincetown Players, a group devoted to experimental drama. In 1916 Glaspell moved with the company, now called the Playwright's Theatre, to Greenwich Village in New York, where for two seasons — as writer, director, and actor — she played an important role in a group that came to have a major influence on the development of American drama. *Trifles* was written to be performed with a group of one-act plays by Eugene O'Neill at the company's summer playhouse on Cape Cod. Among her longer plays that embody a feminist perspective are *The Verge* (1921) and *Allison's House* (1931), a Pulitzer Prize–winning drama based on the life of Emily Dickinson. Among more than forty short stories, some twenty plays, and ten novels, Glaspell's best works deal with the theme of the new woman, presenting a protagonist who embodies the American pioneer spirit of independence and freedom.

**LOUISE GLÜCK** (b. 1943)   Glück was born in New York City and raised on Long Island. She attended Sarah Lawrence College and Columbia University and has taught at over a dozen institutions, among them the University of Iowa, Columbia University, the University of California, Berkeley, and Harvard University; she currently teaches at Yale University and lives in Cambridge, Massachusetts. Her numerous awards include an Academy of

American Poets Prize, a National Book Critics Circle Award, a Pulitzer Prize, and a Wallace Stevens Award. She is also the recipient of fellowships from the Guggenheim Foundation, the Rockefeller Foundation, and the National Endowment for the Arts. Glück was poet laureate of the United States from 2003 to 2004. She is the author of one nonfiction book, *Proofs and Theories: Essays on Poetry* (1994), and a dozen volumes of poetry, including *Firstborn* (1968), *The Triumph of Achilles* (1985), *Ararat* (1990), *The Wild Iris* (1992), *Vita Nova* (1999), *Averno* (2006), and *A Village Life: Poems* (2009). Her most recent works include *Poems 1962–2012* (2012), which won the Los Angeles Times Book Prize, and *Faithful and Virtuous Night* (2014), which won the National Book Award.

**ALLEGRA GOODMAN** (b. 1967)   Born in Brooklyn, New York, Goodman grew up in Honolulu, where both her parents taught at the University of Hawaii. She began writing fiction at a young age, and her first short story was published in the literary journal *Commentary* during her first semester of college. Her first collection of short stories, *Total Immersion* (1989), was published the day she received her undergraduate degree from Harvard University. She did postgraduate work at Stanford, where she earned a PhD in English literature. Goodman has published five novels: *Kaaterskill Falls* (1998), *Paradise Park* (2001), *Intuition* (2006), *The Other Side of the Island* (2008), and *The Cookbook Collector* (2010). She has taught a writing workshop that focused mainly on revision at Boston University's graduate program in creative writing. On being a writer, Goodman says, "I love my job. Each book teaches me something new about character and plot and structure. I am dedicating my life to learning how to tell a story."

**WILLIAM GREENWAY** (b. 1947)   Greenway was born and raised in Atlanta, Georgia, and earned his BA from Georgia State University in 1970. After being drafted by the U.S. Navy as an electronics technician in New Orleans, he went on to earn his PhD in modern literature and poetry from Tulane University. Greenway has taught English at Youngstown State University since 1986, where he has been awarded three distinguished professorships in both teaching and scholarship. Greenway has also been honored with the Larry Levis Editors' Prize from *Missouri Review*, the Open Voice Poetry Award from the *Writer's Voice*, the Helen and Laura Krout Memorial Poetry Award, an Academy of American Poets Prize, and an Ohio Arts Council Grant, and he was named the 1994 Georgia Author of the Year. In addition to having published over 600 poems in various top literary journals, Greenway has written nine full-length poetry collections, including *Ascending Order* (2003), winner of the 2004 Ohioana Poetry Book of the Year Award; *Fishing at the End of the World* (2005); and *Everywhere at Once* (2008), which was nominated for the 2008 Ohioana Poetry Book of the Year Award. In a 2010 interview with the YSU Student Literary Arts Association, Greenway said that though his poems "are often set in a real and particular place, the place is changed, almost surrealistically, as in a dream, to a place which, though still recognizable as a particular place, is now universal, an Everywhere which I hope is accessible to everyone."

**MARK HALLIDAY** (b. 1949)   Halliday earned bachelor's and master's degrees from Brown University before earning a doctorate in English literature from Brandeis University. He taught at Wellesley College, the University of Pennsylvania, Western Michigan University, and Indiana University before joining the faculty at Ohio University. He is the author of six volumes of poems: *Little Star* (1987), *Tasker Street* (1992), *Selfwolf* (1999), *Jab* (2002), *Keep This Forever* (2008), and *Thresherphobe* (2013). He was awarded the Rome Prize of the American Academy of Arts and Letters in 2001 and a fellowship from the Guggenheim Foundation in 2006. About the colloquial style of his poetry, Halliday has said, "I love the analogy between a poem and a speech that you might actually hear in real life. . . . People do, over a few beers, let's say, if they're having trouble in their marriage or they're trying to change their lives, they do go from anecdote to meditation to comic speculation and then back to the beer, back to a joke — the movement of thought has those different levels. I love poems that show a speaker living through those moves."

**THOMAS HARDY** (1840–1928)   Hardy was born near Dorchester in southeastern England, on which he based the Wessex of many of his novels and poems. Hardy worked for the ecclesiastical architect John Hicks from 1856 to 1861. He then moved to London to practice architecture and took evening classes at King's College for six years. In 1867 he gave up architecture to become a full-time writer, and after writing short stories and poems, he found success as a novelist. *The Mayor of Casterbridge* (1886) and *Tess of the d'Urbervilles* (1891) reveal Hardy's concern for victims of circumstance and his appeal to humanitarian sympathy in readers. After his novel *Jude the Obscure* (1896) was strongly criticized, Hardy set aside prose fiction and returned to poetry — a genre in which he was most prolific and successful after he reached the age of seventy.

**NATHANIEL HAWTHORNE** (1804–1864)   The son of a merchant sea captain who died in a distant port when Nathaniel was four, Hawthorne grew up in genteel poverty in Massachusetts and Maine. His earliest American ancestor, the magistrate William Hathorne, ordered the whipping of a Quaker woman in Salem. William's son John was one of the three judges at the Salem witch trials of 1692. Aware of his family's role in colonial America, Hawthorne returned to Salem after graduating from Bowdoin College (where future president Franklin Pierce was a friend and classmate), determined to be a writer. He recalled and destroyed copies of his first novel, the mediocre *Fanshawe* (1828). His short stories, often set in Puritan America, revealed a moral complexity that had not troubled his righteous ancestors William and John. His success as an author allowed him to marry Sophia Peabody in 1842, after a four-year engagement. Though his stories were critically praised, they did not earn much money, and in 1846 he used his political connections with the Democratic Party to obtain a job at the U.S. Custom House in Salem. His dismissal in 1849 (when the Democrats lost) produced both anger and resolve. The result was a great American novel, *The Scarlet Letter* (1850), which made him famous and improved his fortune. Although he was friendly with Emerson and his circle of optimistic transcendentalists, some of whom established the utopian socialist community at Brook Farm, Hawthorne's vision of the human condition was considerably darker. Herman Melville dedicated *Moby-Dick* to Hawthorne and characterized him as a man who could say "No! in thunder."

**ROBERT HAYDEN** (1913–1980)   Born in Detroit, Hayden studied at Wayne State University and the University of Michigan (MA, 1944). In 1946 he joined the faculty of Fisk University. He left Fisk in 1968 for a professorship at the University of Michigan, where he remained until his death. He produced some ten volumes of poetry but did not receive the acclaim many thought he deserved until late in life, with the publication of *Words in the Mourning Time: Poems* (1971). In the 1960s, he aroused some hostility from African Americans who wanted him to express more militancy. But Hayden did not want to be part of what he called a "kind of literary ghetto." He considered his own work "a form of prayer — a prayer for illumination, perfection."

**TERRANCE HAYES** (b. 1971)   Hayes was born in Columbia, South Carolina. He studied at Coker College and later earned his MFA from the University of Pittsburgh. He has received many literary honors including a Whiting Award, three *Best American Poetry* selections, a Pushcart Prize, and fellowships from the National Endowment for the Arts, the Guggenheim Foundation, and the MacArthur Foundation. His collections of poetry include *Muscular Music* (1999), winner of the Kate Tufts Discovery Award; *Hip Logic* (2002), which won the 2001 National Poetry Series and was a finalist for the Los Angeles Times Book Award; *Wind in a Box* (2006); *Lighthead* (2010), which won the National Book Award for Poetry; and *How to Be Drawn* (2015). In praise of Hayes's work, Cornelius Eady has said, "First you'll marvel at his skill, his near-perfect pitch, his disarming humor, his brilliant turns of phrase. Then you'll notice the grace, the tenderness, the unblinking truth-telling just beneath his lines, the open and generous way he takes in our world." Hayes is a professor of creative writing at the University of Pittsburgh and lives in Pittsburgh with his wife, the poet Yona Harvey, and their children.

**SEAMUS HEANEY** (1939–2013)   Heaney, the eldest of nine children, was born on his family's farm near Belfast in County Derry, Northern Ireland. He attended local schools, earned a degree in English with first-class honors from Queen's University, Belfast, and received a teacher's certificate in English from St. Joseph's College in Belfast. He published his first writings while a student at St. Joseph's and began a career as a teacher. His first volume of poetry, *Death of a Naturalist* (1966), won several prizes and launched Heaney's distinguished career as a poet. He produced several volumes of essays, including *Finders Keepers: Selected Prose 1971–2001* (2002). Among his numerous volumes of poetry are *The Spirit Level* (1996), *Opened Ground: Poems 1966–1996* (1998), *The Riverbank Field* (2007), and *Articulations* (2008). His 2006 volume, *District and Circle*, won the T. S. Eliot Prize, and his final volume, *Human Chain* (2010), won the Forward Poetry Prize Best Collection 2010 award and the Irish Times Poetry Now Award for 2011. Other publications include *Beowulf: A New Verse Translation* (2002) and *The Burial at Thebes: A Version of Sophocles' Antigone* (2004). He taught at Oxford University, the University of California, Berkeley, and Harvard University. In 1995 Heaney was awarded the Nobel Prize in Literature, and several modern critics have characterized him as "the most important Irish poet since Yeats." An immensely popular poet, he enjoyed the support of a host of "Heaneyboppers" who attended his readings. On the day after he died in 2013, over 80,000 people attending an Irish football match in Dublin cheered for Heaney for three minutes.

**ERNEST HEMINGWAY** (1899–1961)   Born in Oak Park, Illinois, Hemingway became a cub reporter after high school. After World War I — during which he was seriously wounded while serving as an ambulance driver — he lived in Paris, a member of a lively and productive expatriate community characterized by Gertrude Stein as "a lost generation." He lived an active life, not only as a writer but also as a war correspondent, big-game hunter, and fisherman. In such novels as *The Sun Also Rises* (1926), *A Farewell to Arms* (1929), and *For Whom the Bell Tolls* (1940), his fictional characters exhibit a passion for courage and integrity, for grace under pressure. Hemingway's spare, unembellished style reinforced his central theme that one must confront danger and live honorably. He won the Nobel Prize in Literature in 1954. In 1961, unable to write because treatment for mental instability affected his memory, he killed himself with the shotgun he had so often used when hunting.

**JUAN FELIPE HERRERA** (b. 1948)   Herrera was born in Fowler, California, to Mexican migrant farmworkers. He earned a bachelor's degree in social anthropology at the University of California, Los Angeles, a master's degree in social anthropology from Stanford University, and an MFA from the University of Iowa. He taught at California State University at Fresno before assuming his current role as the Tomás Rivera Endowed Chair in the Creative Writing Department at the University of California, Riverside. Herrera describes himself as an educator, poet, writer, artist, performer, and musician. In addition to writing children's books, novels for young adults, prose, and short stories, he is the author of more than a dozen volumes of poetry. Among his most recent publications are *Cinnamon Girl: Letters Found Inside a Cereal Box* (2005), *Downtown Boy* (2005), *187 Reasons Mexicanos Can't Cross the Border: Undocuments 1971–2007* (2007), and *Half of the World in Light: New and Selected Poems* (2008), which won the National Book Critics Circle Award. In 2009 he won the PEN/Beyond Margins Award, and in 2010 he received a Guggenheim Fellowship. Herrera served as California's poet laureate from 2012 to 2014.

**ROBERT HERRICK** (1591–1674)   Born in London, Herrick was apprenticed to his uncle, a goldsmith, for ten years until at age twenty-two he was sent to Cambridge University in recognition of his academic talents. Little is known of the decade following his graduation from Cambridge, although it seems certain that he associated with a circle of literary artists. In 1629, he was appointed vicar at Dean Prior, Devonshire, a rural parish that the sophisticated and cosmopolitan Herrick viewed as a kind of exile. Yet, he was fascinated by the pagan elements of local songs and dances, and often drew upon pre-Christian writers for inspiration. His chief work, *Hesperides* (1648), is a collection of some 1,200 poems — mostly written in Devonshire — about local scenery, customs, and people.

**TONY HOAGLAND** (b. 1953)   Hoagland was born in Fort Bragg, North Carolina, and educated at the University of Iowa and the University of Arizona. He has taught at many institutions, including Kalamazoo College, University of Michigan, Warren Wilson College, and Colby College. He now teaches in the creative writing program at the University of Houston. His poems and critical writings have appeared in such publications as *Ploughshares*, *American Poetry Review*, and the *Pushcart Prize Anthology* (1991). Hoagland's first three collections of poems were chapbooks: *A Change in Plans* (1985), *Talking to Stay Warm* (1986), and *History of Desire* (1990). His first full-length volume of poetry, *Sweet Ruin* (1992), won the Brittingham Prize in poetry as well as the Zacharas Award from Emerson College. His most recent collections of poetry are *What Narcissism Means to Me* (2003), *Hard Rain* (2005), *Unincorporated Persons in the Late Honda Dynasty: Poems* (2010), and the chapbook *Don't Tell Anyone* (2014). Hoagland has also published two essay collections: *Real Sofistikashun: Essays on Poetry and Craft* (2006) and *Twenty Poems That Could Save America and Other Essays* (2014). In 2005 he won the Poetry Foundation's Mark Twain Award and the Folger Shakespeare Library's O. B. Hardison Jr. Poetry Prize, which honors excellence in teaching as well as in writing. He is also the recipient of fellowships from the National Endowment for the Arts and the Guggenheim Foundation.

**ANDREA HOLLANDER** (b. 1947)   Born to American parents in Berlin, Germany, and raised in the United States, Hollander is the author of several full-length poetry collections: *House Without a Dreamer* (1995), *The Other Life* (2001), and *Woman in the Painting* (2006). Her most recent work, *Landscape with Female Figure: New & Selected Poems, 1982–2012* (2014) was a finalist for the Oregon Book Award in Poetry. Other honors include a Pushcart Prize for prose memoir, the Runes Poetry Prize, and two poetry fellowships from the National Endowment for the Arts. In 2008 she received the Subiaco Award for Literary Excellence in the Writing and Teaching of Poetry. Her poems and essays have appeared in numerous anthologies including *Writing Poems, The Poets' Grimm,* and *The Autumn House Anthology of Contemporary American Poetry.* Her work also appears regularly in such literary journals as *Poetry, Georgia Review,* and *Gettysburg Review.* For more than twenty-two years, Hollander served as writer-in-residence at Lyon College, which awarded her the Lamar Williamson Prize for Excellence in Teaching. In 2011 she moved to Portland, Oregon, where she teaches writing workshops in poetry and the personal essay.

**GERARD MANLEY HOPKINS** (1844–1889)   Raised in London, Hopkins won a scholarship to Balliol College, Oxford University, where he studied classical literature. He converted to Roman Catholicism in 1866 and two years later entered the Jesuit novitiate. In 1877 he was ordained a Jesuit priest and served in missions in London, Liverpool, Oxford, and Glasgow until 1882. From 1884 to his death in 1889, he was professor of Greek at University College, Dublin. A technically innovative poet, Hopkins saw only three of his poems published during his lifetime. He gained posthumous recognition in 1918 when a friend, the poet laureate Robert Bridges, published Hopkins's complete works. His early poems celebrate the beauty of God's world, but later works reflect his poor health and depression.

**A. E. HOUSMAN** (1859–1936)   Born in Fockbury, England, and an outstanding student, Alfred Edward Housman nonetheless failed his final examinations at Oxford University in 1881, possibly due to emotional chaos caused by his love for a male classmate. Working as a clerk in the patent office in London, he pursued classical studies on his own, earned an MA, and was appointed chair of Latin at University College, London. In 1910 he became professor of Latin at Cambridge, where he remained until his death in 1936. As a poet, Housman was concerned primarily with the fleetingness of love and the decay of youth. After his first collection, *A Shropshire Lad,* was rejected by several publishers, Housman published it at his own expense in 1896. It gained popularity during World War I, and his 1922 collection, *Last Poems,* was well received. In his lecture "The Name and Nature of Poetry" (1933), Housman argued that poetry should appeal to emotions rather than intellect. *More Poems* (1936) was published posthumously.

**MARIE HOWE** (b. 1950)   Howe was born in Rochester, New York, and received her MFA from Columbia University in 1983. Her first poetry collection, *The Good Thief* (1988), was selected by Margaret Atwood for the National Poetry Series, and that same year, Stanley Kunitz also selected Howe for a Lavan Younger Poets Award from the Academy of American Poets. Kunitz called Howe's poetry "luminous, intense, and eloquent, rooted in an abundant inner life." Howe's second collection of poetry was *What the Living Do* (1998), which she wrote as something of an elegy for her brother John, who died of AIDS in 1989. Howe was coeditor of the anthology *In the Company of My Solitude: American Writing from the AIDS Pandemic* (1995). Her most recent poetry collection, *The Kingdom of Ordinary Time: Poems* (2008), was a finalist for the Los Angeles Times Book Prize. Among Howe's other honors are grants from the Guggenheim Foundation, the Bunting Institute, and the National Endowment for the Arts. She served as poet laureate for the state of New York from 2012 to 2014. Howe currently lives in New York City and teaches at Sarah Lawrence College, New York University, and Columbia University.

**LANGSTON HUGHES** (1902–1967)   Hughes was born in Joplin, Missouri. His father was a businessman and lawyer; his mother, a teacher. Hughes attended Columbia University, graduated from Lincoln University in 1929, traveled throughout the world, and held many odd jobs as a young man. While Hughes had a long and prolific career as a writer in all genres, he is still remembered as the central figure of the Harlem Renaissance of the 1920s, a movement that committed itself to the examination and celebration of black life in America and its African heritage. He was the Madrid correspondent for the Baltimore *Afro-American* (1937) and a columnist for the Chicago *Defender* (1943–67) and the New York *Post* (1962–67). His poems of racial affirmation and protest are often infused with the rhythms of blues and jazz music. He wrote over two dozen plays (many musicalized) and founded the Suitcase Theater (Harlem, 1938), the New Negro Theater (Los Angeles, 1939), and the Skyloft Players (Chicago, 1941). His works include *The Weary Blues* (1926), *Montage of a Dream Deferred* (1951), and *The Panther and the Lash: Poems of Our Times* (1969).

**ZORA NEALE HURSTON** (1891–1960)   Born in Eatonville, Florida, an African American town, Hurston enjoyed a happy early childhood in a town that spared her from racism and with a mother who instilled a strong sense of self-worth in her. With the death of her mother, she was sent off to boarding school but was forced to give up her formal education when her father remarried and refused to give her further financial help. She supported herself with odd jobs, managing to earn a high school diploma and enter Howard University in Washington, DC. Unable to support herself as a full-time student, Hurston quit college after five years, having earned only a year and a half of college credits. She moved to Harlem, determined to pursue a writing career. In New York, she was hired as a personal secretary by the novelist Fannie Hurst, who arranged a scholarship for her at Barnard College. There, she studied with the famous anthropologist Franz Boas and became interested in black folk traditions. She earned her degree from Barnard in 1927 and received a fellowship to study the oral traditions of her hometown. She wrote her first novel, *Jonah's Gourd Vine* (1934), while doing fieldwork in Eatonville. *Mules and Men* (1935), based on the material her fieldwork had produced, was attacked by African American intellectuals and writers for its refusal to acknowledge and confront racism. Nevertheless, Hurston was awarded a Guggenheim Fellowship to study voodoo in the Caribbean, which gave her the material for her second and most celebrated novel, *Their Eyes Were Watching God* (1937). During the last two decades of her life, she continued to write novels, plays, and an autobiography, *Dust Tracks on the Road* (1942), but drew increasing criticism from the African American press for her refusal to publicly condemn segregation. In 1950 she was the subject of a *Miami Herald* news story that carried the headline: "Famous Negro Author Working as a Maid Here 'Just to Live a Little.'" She claimed that she needed a break from writing and that she was busy making plans for writing projects and for a national magazine devoted to domestics. Her last years were troubled by poor health, emotional fatigue, and lack of money. She died of a stroke, penniless, in a welfare home in Fort Pierce, Florida.

**DAVID HENRY HWANG** (b. 1957)   Hwang was born in Los Angeles, earned a degree from Stanford University, and attended the Yale University School of Drama for one year. His first play, *F.O.B.* (for "fresh off the boat") won an OBIE for best New American Off-Broadway Play of 1980. Hwang has written a number of plays, musicals, operas, and screenplays but is best known for *M. Butterfly*, for which he won a Tony Award in 1988 and received a Pulitzer Prize nomination in 1989. His other awards include fellowships from the

Guggenheim Foundation and the National Endowment for the Arts; an OBIE for best playwriting in 1997 and a Tony Award nomination for best Broadway play in 1998 for *Golden Child*; and a Tony Award nomination for his adaptation of the musical *Flower Drum Song* in 2003. Although Hwang once called his Chinese American heritage "a minor detail, like having red hair," cultural conflict and Asian themes are hallmarks of his most acclaimed works. In 2014 he received the Doris Duke Artist Award and became the director of Columbia University's Playwrighting Concentration.

**HENRIK IBSEN** (1828–1906)  Ibsen was born in the seaport of Skien, Norway, the son of a wealthy merchant. When Ibsen was eight, his father's business failed, and at fifteen he was apprenticed to an apothecary in the tiny town of Grimstad. He hated this profession. To solace himself, he read poetry and theology and began to write. When he was twenty-two, he became a student in Christiania (now Oslo) and published his first play. In 1851 his diligent though unremarkable writing earned him an appointment as theater-poet at a new theater in Bergen, where he remained until 1857, learning both the business and the art of drama. He wrote several plays based on Scandinavian folklore, held positions at two theaters in Christiania, and married. When he was thirty-six, he applied to the government for a poet's pension — a stipend that would have permitted him to devote himself to writing. The stipend was refused. Enraged, he left Norway and, though he was granted the stipend two years later, spent the next twenty-seven years in Italy and Germany, where he wrote the realistic social dramas that established his reputation as the founder of modern theater. Such plays as *Ghosts* (1881), *An Enemy of the People* (1882), and *A Doll's House* (1878) inevitably generated controversy as Ibsen explored venereal disease, the stupidity and greed of the "compact majority," and the position of women in society. In 1891 he returned to live in Christiania, where he was recognized and honored as one of Norway's (and Europe's) finest writers.

**SHIRLEY JACKSON** (1916–1965)  Born in San Francisco, Jackson moved with her family to Rochester, New York, in her teens. An episode of severe depression (a recurrent problem during her life) forced her out of the University of Rochester, but she later graduated from Syracuse University. She married the eminent critic Stanley Edgar Hyman, had four children, and kept to a rigid writing schedule. Although her major work tends toward the ominous, she contributed humorous pieces to popular magazines on the problems of housekeeping and raising children. These were collected in *Life among the Savages* (1953) and *Raising Demons* (1957). She wrote four novels, and her short stories are collected in three volumes: *The Lottery* (1949), *The Magic of Shirley Jackson* (1966), and *Come Along with Me* (1968).

**JAMES WELDON JOHNSON** (1871–1938)  Johnson was born in Jacksonville, Florida, where from a young age he was encouraged by his parents to study English literature and the European musical tradition — an exception for most African Americans at the time. He later attended Atlanta University, during which time he taught for two summers in the poor, rural town of Hampton, Georgia. This experience exposed him to hardships from which he had been previously sheltered and ignited what became an enduring desire to help the black community. In 1901 Johnson and his brother Rosamond — a talented composer — moved to New York City to pursue a life writing songs for the musical theater. The brothers collaborated on the song "Lift Ev'ry Voice and Sing," which swiftly gained popularity and was adopted by the NAACP as the "Negro National Anthem." Johnson also studied creative literature at Columbia University for three years and became an active member of the Republican Party.

He served as treasurer of New York's Colored Republican Club and helped compose songs for Republican candidate Theodore Roosevelt's presidential campaign. In 1906 Johnson was appointed to a job as U.S. consul to Venezuela, where he had poems published in the *Century Magazine* and the *Independent*. In 1912 he pseudonymously published *The Autobiography of an Ex-Colored Man*, the story of a biracial musician who rejects his African American heritage in favor of living a life of leisure among whites. In 1916 Johnson became the national organizer for the NAACP and served as its executive secretary for ten years starting in 1920. He also remained an active literary figure, editing *The Book of American Negro Poetry* (1922), which is to this day a landmark text in African American literature; *The Book of American Negro Spirituals* (1925); and *The Second Book of American Negro Spirituals* (1926). He also published *God's Trombones* (1927), a book of poetry that was greatly influenced by his time spent in Hampton, and *Black Manhattan* (1930), a survey of African American contributions to the artistic scene in New York. In 1934 he published *Negro Americans, What Now?*, an extended political argument in favor of racial integration. Of the adversities that he and other African Americans had faced, he declared, "I will not allow one prejudiced person or one million or one hundred million to blight my life. I will not let prejudice or any of its attendant humiliations and injustices bear me down to spiritual defeat. My inner life is mine, and I shall defend and maintain its integrity against all the powers of hell."

**LACY M. JOHNSON** (b. 1978)    Johnson earned her PhD from the University of Houston's Creative Writing Program. Her work has appeared in *Sentence, Nimrod, Memoir (and), Gulf Coast, Pebble Lake Review*, and *Irish Studies Review*. Her first book, *Trespasses: A Memoir* (2012), explores identity as it is associated with region, and region as it is experienced through memory, history, and theory. Author and critic Nick Flynn said of *Trespasses*: "Utterly hip, while at the same time a voice from another era, *Trespasses* is about 'growing up in a poor farming town in the Great Plains,' an examination of the term 'white trash' through interviews, research, and memory, and an evocation of a place many of us will never see. Yet, at its heart, it is a lyric evocation of self. Plainspoken, tattooed, and brilliant, Lacy Johnson pushes the boundaries of what memoir — and, perhaps more importantly, what any of us — can be." Her most recent book is *The Other Side* (2014), a National Book Critics Circle Award finalist that chronicles her kidnapping and rape by an abusive ex-boyfriend. On writing about this painful event, she says, "When I set out to write this book, it wasn't to 'fix' myself, or to make myself 'whole' again, but to change that story I told myself about who I am, who I was, and who I could still be." Johnson teaches interdisciplinary art at University of Houston.

**BEN JONSON** (1572–1637)    Jonson was born in Westminster, England, and after leaving school, began earning his living as a bricklayer, the trade of his stepfather. Though he never attended college, he taught himself enough to be considered learned. He soon abandoned construction work and earned his reputation as one of the preeminent playwrights of his period. A contemporary of Shakespeare, he also wrote poetry and translations of classical Roman authors for his English Renaissance audience. Among other works, Jonson is the author of the satirical plays *Volpone, The Alchemist*, and *Bartholemew Fair*; his best known poems include "On My First Sonne," "To Celia," and "To Penshurst."

**CAMDEN JOY** (b. 1964)    Writer and musician Tom Adelman adopted the pen name Camden Joy around 1994 when he finished writing his first novel, in which the narrator bears the same name as the pseudonymous author. "My writing felt curiously liberated under a pseudonym," he says, and as Joy, he attempted to blur the lines between music criticism, memoir, and fiction in various underground "guerilla" formats such as street posters and pamphlets. He gained some notoriety as an impassioned writer who focused mainly on the indie rock scene of the early 1990s, and his writing was featured in the *Village Voice*, *Boston Phoenix*, and other alternative weeklies. After Joy's first novel, *The Last Rock Star Book, or, Liz Phair: a Rant*, came out in 1998, he went on to publish other works including the novel *Boy Island* (2000), the novella *Palm Tree 13* (2001), and *Lost Joy* (2002), a collection of his writing from the 1990s. Using his legal name, Tom Adelman, he has also written two nonfiction books on baseball: the best-selling *Long Ball: The Summer of '75 — Spaceman, Catfish, Charlie Hustle, and the Greatest World Series Ever Played* (2003) and *Black and Blue: The Golden Arm, the Robinson Boys, and the World Series That Stunned America* (2006). Joy currently produces a podcast about alternative music, "Real Good Music with Camden Joy." In 2015, all books published under the name Camden Joy will be reissued by Verse Chorus Press.

**JAMES JOYCE** (1882–1941)   Though educated in Jesuit schools, Joyce came to reject Catholicism; and though an expatriate living in Paris, Trieste, and Zurich for most of his adult life, he wrote almost exclusively about his native Dublin. Joyce's rebelliousness, which surfaced during his university career, generated a revolution in modern literature. His novels *Ulysses* (1922) and *Finnegan's Wake* (1939) introduced radically new narrative techniques. "Araby" — from his first collection of short stories, *Dubliners* (1914) — is one of a series of sharply realized vignettes based on Joyce's experiences in Ireland, the homeland he later characterized as "a sow that eats its own farrow." Joyce lived precariously on earnings as a language teacher and also modest contributions from wealthy patrons, support that he justified by becoming one of the most influential novelists of the twentieth century. Because *Ulysses* dealt frankly with sexuality and used coarse language, the U.S. Post Office charged that the novel was obscene and forbade its importation. A celebrated 1933 court decision lifted the ban.

**FRANZ KAFKA** (1883–1924)   Born into a middle-class, German-speaking Jewish family in Prague, Kafka earned a law degree in 1906 and worked as a claims investigator for an insurance company for most of his adult life. He remained in constant conflict with his domineering father, who belittled his literary aims. He became engaged to a woman in 1912 but broke with her after five years. In 1917 he contracted the tuberculosis that was to kill him at age forty-one. Despite the deadening monotony of his job and his personal anguish, he created a remarkable and original body of work during his short life, including the masterful novels *The Trial* (1925) and *The Castle* (1926). His starkly realistic stories and novels take place in nightmarish dreamworlds where stifling bureaucracy chokes his protagonists and diminishes their dignity and their lives. A fierce perfectionist, Kafka published little during his life and left written instructions to his friend and executor, Max Brod, to destroy his unpublished manuscripts. Fortunately, Brod could not bring himself to comply.

**JOHN KEATS** (1795–1821)   Keats was born in London, the eldest son of a stable keeper who died in an accident in 1804. His mother died of tuberculosis shortly after remarrying, and the grandmother who raised Keats and his siblings died in 1814. At eighteen, Keats wrote his first poem, "Imitation of Spenser," inspired by Edmund Spenser's long narrative poem *The Faerie Queene*. The thirty-three poems he wrote while training to be a surgeon were published in a collection in 1817, and Keats then gave up medicine for writing. After more traumatic losses in 1818, including the departure of one brother for the United States and the death of his other brother of tuberculosis, Keats wrote his second collection, *Lamia*,

*Isabella, The Eve of St. Agnes, and Other Poems* (1820). Ill with tuberculosis himself, Keats was sent to Rome to recover. He died at twenty-six, but despite his short career he is a major figure of the romantic period.

**JANE KENYON** (1947–1995)   Kenyon was born in Ann Arbor, Michigan, and attended the University of Michigan, where she received a BA (1970) and MA (1972). While at Michigan she studied under Donald Hall, the eminent poet and teacher, whom she married in the year she received her master's. The couple moved to Eagle Pond Farm in rural New Hampshire, living a quiet life that Kenyon celebrated in many of her early poems. They became well known not only through her poems but also through the books Hall wrote about life on their farm. In her last poems, Kenyon wrote about her struggle with leukemia, which claimed her life at age forty-seven. At the time of her death, she was New Hampshire's poet laureate. During her lifetime, she published four collections of poems, *From Room to Room* (1978), *The Boat of Quiet Hours* (1986), *Let Evening Come* (1990), and *Constance* (1993). Since her death, two additional volumes have been published, *Otherwise: New and Selected Poems* (1996) and *A Hundred White Daffodils: Essays, Interviews, the Akhmatova Translations, Newspaper Columns, and One Poem* (1999). In 1998, on the third anniversary of Kenyon's death, Donald Hall published *Without: Poems*, a volume *Publishers Weekly* called "a heartbreaking portrait of a marriage that has not quite ended."

**JAMAICA KINCAID** (b. 1949)   Kincaid was born Elaine Potter Richardson in St. Johns, Antigua, in the West Indies, then a British colony. At age seventeen, she left home to become an au pair in New York. Determined to make something of her life, Kincaid took night classes and ultimately earned a high school diploma. She went on to take classes at the New School for Social Research in New York, and attended college in New Hampshire on a scholarship. When she returned to New York, she changed her name to Jamaica Kincaid and began writing. Of her life up to this point, Kincaid told a reporter: "Everyone thought I had a way with words, but it came out as a sharp tongue. No one expected anything from me at all. Had I just sunk in the cracks it would not have been noted. I would have been lucky to be a secretary somewhere." Her first publication, a collection of short stories titled *At the Bottom of the River* (1983), earned her wide critical praise and recognition as a new voice in American fiction. That was followed by three novels, including *The Autobiography of My Mother* (1995). *My Brother* (1997) deals with the death of her brother from AIDS. Her most recent novel is *See Now Then* (2013) and her most recent nonfiction work is *Among Flowers: A Walk in the Himalaya* (2005). The recipient of many literary honors, Kincaid served as a staff writer for the *New Yorker* (1976–95) and visiting professor at Harvard University. She is currently a professor of literature at Claremont McKenna College in California.

**MAXINE HONG KINGSTON** (b. 1940)   Kingston was born in Stockton, California. She earned a bachelor's degree from the University of California, Berkeley (1962), and a teaching certificate (1965). After teaching English and mathematics at a California high school, she moved to Hawaii and taught language arts and English as a second language at a number of schools. She became a visiting associate professor of English at the University of Hawaii after winning the National Book Critics Circle Award for *The Woman Warrior: Memoirs of a Girlhood among Ghosts* (1976). In that volume, she fashioned a new sort of genre — essays with substantial fictive elements. Her next book, *China Men* (1980), further developed that form and received the National Book Award for Nonfiction. Her most recent works include *To Be the Poet* (2002), *The Fifth Book of Peace* (2003), and *I Love a Broad*

*Margin to My Life* (2011), a free-verse memoir informed by the wide page margins in the Chinese editions of her work. An early critic characterized Kingston's work as the blending of "myth, legend, history, and autobiography into a genre of her own invention." Another argued that though Kingston's works are classified as nonfiction, "in a deeper sense, they are fiction at its best — novels, fairy tales, epic poems." In 1993 Kingston founded the Veteran's Writing Group; she compiled and edited a collection of the group's writings in *Veterans of War, Veterans of Peace* (2006). In 2013 Kingston was awarded the National Medal of Arts.

**GALWAY KINNELL** (1927–2014)   Born in Providence, Rhode Island, Kinnell graduated summa cum laude from Princeton University, served in the navy during World War II, and returned to earn a master's degree from the University of Rochester. He traveled extensively and lectured in France and Iran before returning to the United States. In 1963 he was a fieldworker for the Congress of Racial Equality (CORE) and his involvement in the American civil rights movement informed what is perhaps his most famous collection of poetry, *Body Rags* (1968). Another of his prominent works, *The Book of Nightmares* (1971), is a book-length poem about the Vietnam War. He was the author of more than twenty additional volumes of poetry, the last one being *Strong Is Your Hold* (2006). Kinnell taught at a large number of institutions and earned numerous awards and honors including a MacArthur Fellowship and a Wallace Stevens Award. He served as chancellor of the Academy of American Poets from 2001 to 2007 before retiring to his home in Vermont, where he died at age eighty-seven.

**CAROLYN KIZER** (1925–2014)   Kizer was born in Spokane, Washington. Her father was a lawyer, her mother a biologist and professor. After graduating from Sarah Lawrence College in 1945, Kizer pursued graduate study at Columbia University and the University of Washington. From 1959 to 1965, she was editor of *Poetry Northwest* (which she founded in 1959 in Seattle) and spent 1964 and 1965 as a State Department specialist in Pakistan, where she taught at a women's college and translated poems from Urdu into English. She chose to leave early, after the U.S. decision to bomb North Vietnam in 1965. Later, she joined archaeological tours in Afghanistan and Iran. She worked as director of literary programs for the National Endowment for the Arts in Washington, DC; taught at several universities; and was poet-in-residence at the University of North Carolina and Ohio University. Her volumes of poetry include *Yin* (1984), which won a Pulitzer Prize the following year; *Mermaids in the Basement: Poems for Women* (1984); *The Nearness of You* (1986); *Harping On: Poems 1985–1995* (1996); *Pro Femina: A Poem* (2000); and *Cool, Calm & Collected: Poems 1960–2000* (2001). She also published two collections of essays — *Proses: On Poems and Poets* (1993) and *Picking and Choosing: Essays on Prose* (1995) — and edited *100 Great Poems by Women: A Golden Ecco Anthology* (1995). Kizer's many awards and honors include the Frost Medal, the Theodore Roethke Memorial Poetry Award, three Pushcart Prizes, and an American Academy of Arts and Letters Award.

**MARVIN KLOTZ** (1930–2014)   Born in New York City, Klotz earned a PhD from New York University and, in 1959, joined the faculty at what later became California State University, Northridge, where he taught for thirty-three years and won Northridge's distinguished teaching award in 1983. He also won two Fulbright professorships (in Vietnam and Iran) and was a National Endowment for the Arts Summer Fellow twice. Klotz was one of the original authors of this textbook. After retiring in 1992, he began writing verse about fractured neighborhoods and a bipolar world.

**ETHERIDGE KNIGHT** (1931–1991)  Knight was born in Corinth, Mississippi, attended two years of public high school in Kentucky, and served in the U.S. Army from 1948 to 1951. After being convicted on a robbery charge and sentenced in 1960 to twenty years in Indiana State Prison, he discovered poetry; his first collection is entitled *Poems from Prison* (1968). Knight was paroled after eight years. From 1968 to 1971 he was poet-in-residence at several universities. An important African American voice in the 1960s and 1970s, Knight rejected the American and European aesthetic tradition, arguing that "the red of this esthetic rose got its color from the blood of black slaves, exterminated Indians, napalmed Vietnamese children." His collection *Belly Song and Other Poems* was nominated for the National Book Award and the Pulitzer Prize in 1973. His awards include National Endowment for the Arts and Guggenheim grants and the 1987 American Book Award for *The Essential Etheridge Knight* (1986).

**YUSEF KOMUNYAKAA** (b. 1947)  Born and raised in Bogalusa, Louisiana, James Willie Brown Jr. later took the surname of his great grandparents who had come from Trinidad on a slave ship. His work often explores themes related to his life in the American South, the civil rights movement in America, and his tour of duty as a soldier during the Vietnam War. He began composing poetry even before he earned degrees from the University of Colorado, Colorado State University, and the University of California, Irvine. He taught at the University of New Orleans, Indiana University at Bloomington, and Princeton University before assuming his current role as a professor in the Creative Writing Program at New York University. He is the author of over a dozen books of poetry but gained attention for *Copacetic* (1984), *I Apologize for the Eyes in My Head* (1986), and *Dien Cai Dau* (1988). His most recent collection is *The Chameleon Couch: Poems* (2012), which was shortlisted for the 2012 International Griffin Poetry Prize. He is best known for *Neon Vernacular: New and Selected Poems* (1993), for which he won the Kingsley Tufts Poetry Award and a Pulitzer Prize. He also received the 2001 Ruth Lilly Poetry Prize, a prestigious honor given to living U.S. poets "whose lifetime accomplishments warrant extraordinary recognition." From 1999 to 2005, Komunyakaa served as chancellor of the American Academy of Poets.

**PHILIP LARKIN** (1922–1985)  Born in Coventry, Larkin attended St. John's College, Oxford University (BA, 1943; MA, 1947). He was appointed librarian at the University of Hull in 1955, wrote jazz feature articles for the London *Daily Telegraph* from 1961 to 1971, and won numerous poetry awards, including the Queens Gold Medal (1965) and the Benson Medal (1975). His first collection, *The North Ship* (1945), was not well received, but he gained recognition after publication of *The Less Deceived* (1960). Larkin once said, "Form holds little interest for me. Content is everything."

**EVELYN LAU** (b. 1971)  Lau was born in Vancouver, Canada, to Chinese Canadian parents. Driven by an unhappy family life, she ran away from home and wound up living on the streets of Vancouver working as a prostitute to support her drug addiction. During these turbulent early years, Lau kept a diary, and she published poems in Canadian and American journals even before she ran away. Throughout the years of living on the edge, during which she made a number of suicide attempts and was confined in a psychiatric ward, Lau continued to write. With the help of a sympathetic psychiatrist and her commitment to writing, she managed to pull herself out of the chaos and turn herself into a very successful professional writer. Her first published work was an autobiographical account of her early years, *Runaway: Diary of a Street Kid* (1989). An immediate success, it was filmed as *The Diary of Evelyn Lau* and aired on the Canadian Broadcasting Corporation in 1994. *Runaway* was followed by three volumes of poems, *You Are Not Who You Claim* (1990); *Oedipal Dreams*, nominated for the prestigious Governor General's Award for poetry (1993); and *In the House of Slaves* (1993). Lau is also the author of a novel, *Other Women* (1995), two collections of short stories, and a second memoir, *Inside Out: Reflections on a Life So Far* (2001). Her most recent poetry collections are *Treble* (2005), *Living Under Plastic* (2010), and *A Grain of Rice* (2012). Asked by an interviewer if she had acquired her "beautiful, clear" writing style in school, Lau replied, "Nope. All self-taught. In my teens I took some one-day writers' workshops and things like that. But I've never gone properly back to school."

**EMMA LAZARUS** (1849–1887)  American poet Emma Lazarus was born in New York City and is best known for her sonnet "The New Colossus" (1883), which appears on a plaque at the base of the Statue of Liberty and features the familiar lines "Give me your tired, your poor, / Your huddled masses yearning to breathe free." One of seven children in a well-established family, she was educated by private tutors and became part of the literary elite in late-nineteenth-century New York, capturing the attention of Ralph Waldo Emerson with her writing. One of the first successful Jewish American authors, she wrote poetry, plays, and a novel, and she edited German poems, including some by Johann Wolfgang von Goethe and Heinrich Heine. In the early 1880s, when anti-Semitic violence swept through Russia, thousands of Jews immigrated to New York. In response, Lazarus became an important activist on the refugees' behalf. She penned articles and a book on Jewish issues, organized relief efforts for the poor, and helped establish a vocational training institute for newcomers. An early advocate for the creation of a Jewish homeland, Lazarus died shortly after her second trip to Europe at the age of thirty-eight.

**LI-YOUNG LEE** (b. 1957)  Lee was born in Jakarta, Indonesia, to Chinese parents. While there, his father was imprisoned for his religious beliefs, and further anti-Chinese sentiment caused the entire family to flee the country. They traveled in exile for six years before finally settling in the United States. Lee earned a degree from the University of Pittsburgh and attended the University of Arizona and the State University of New York College at Brockport for brief periods. He began writing in earnest in college and is the author of four books of poetry: *Rose* (1986), *The City in Which I Love You* (1990), *Book of My Nights* (2001), and *Behind My Eyes* (2008). He also penned a memoir, *The Winged Seed: A Remembrance* (1995), in which he recounts his family's troubled history and his turbulent youth. Lee has received awards from the Lannan and Whiting Foundations, as well as fellowships from the Guggenheim Foundation and the National Endowment for the Arts.

**JONATHAN LETHEM** (b. 1964)  Born in Brooklyn, New York, Lethem attended Bennington College in Vermont, dropped out during sophomore year, hitchhiked across the country, and landed in California, where he worked as a clerk in a bookstore for over a decade. He published his first short story in 1989. A prolific writer of novels, short stories, and essays, Lethem's work straddles genres. A profile about Lethem in *Publishers Weekly* noted that his writing "exists somewhere in the previously uncharted interstices between science fiction, western, and coming-of-age novels." His notable novels include his first book, *Gun, with Occasional Music*, published in 1994; *Motherless Brooklyn* (1999), which won a National Book Critics Circle Award; and *The Fortress of Solitude* (2003), which was a *New York Times* best seller. His most recent publications include the collections *The Ecstasy of Influence: Nonfictions, Etc.* (2011) and *Wastelands: Stories of the Apocalypse* (2015), and the novel *Dissident Gardens* (2013). His work has appeared in numerous periodicals, among them *Entertainment Weekly*, *Esquire*, *GQ*, *Harper's*, the *New York Times*, the *New Yorker*, *Rolling Stone*, *Salon*, and the *Village Voice*. In 2010 he was named Disney Professor of Writing at Pomona College in Claremont, California.

**SHIRLEY GEOK-LIN LIM** (b. 1944)  Lim was born in Malacca, Malaysia, and received her PhD from Brandeis University in 1973. Lim's first collection of poems, *Crossing the Peninsula* (1980), won the Commonwealth Poetry Prize, a first both for an Asian author and a female author. She has written four other books of poetry; three books of short stories; a novel, *Joss and Gold* (2001); and two books of criticism: *Nationalism and Literature* (1993) and *Writing South/East Asia in English: Against the Grain* (1994). Her memoir *Among the White Moon Faces: An Asian-American Memoir of Homelands* (1996) received the 1997 American Book Award. She has edited and coedited several scholarly collections, including *The Forbidden Stitch: An Asian American Women's Anthology* (1989), *Power, Race, and Gender in Academe: Strangers in the Tower?* (1999), and *The Columbia Companion to the Twentieth-Century American Short Story* (2001). She has taught abroad at the National University of Singapore, NIE of Nanyang Technological University, and the University of Hong Kong, and she currently teaches English at the University of California, Santa Barbara.

**SAM LIPSYTE** (b. 1968)  Fiction writer Sam Lipsyte grew up in New Jersey and attended Brown University, where he received his BA in English. His most recent novel is *The Fun Parts* (2012). He is also the author of *The Ask* (2010) and *Home Land* (2004), both of which were named New York Times Notable Books. His first book, *Venus Drive* (2000), a collection of short stories, was named one of the Twenty-Five Best Books of the year by the *Village Voice Literary Supplement*. Known for his black humor and self-deprecating narrators, his fiction has appeared in the *New Yorker*, *Paris Review*, *Harper's*, and *McSweeney's*, among other publications. His essays and reviews have appeared in the *New York Times Book Review*, *Esquire*, *GQ*, and the *Washington Post Book World*. A 2008 Guggenheim Fellow, Lipsyte currently teaches at Columbia University's School of the Arts, where he also directs the undergraduate fiction program.

**AUDRE LORDE** (1934–1992)  Born to middle-class West Indian immigrant parents in New York City, Lorde grew up in Harlem and attended the National University of Mexico (1954), Hunter College (BA, 1959), and Columbia University (MLS, 1961). Her marriage in 1962, which produced two children, ended in divorce in 1970. During these early years, she worked as a librarian, but in 1968 her growing reputation as a writer led to her appointment as lecturer in creative writing at City College of New York. The following year, she was named lecturer in the education department at Herbert H. Lehman College. In 1970 she joined the English department at John Jay College of Criminal Justice, and in 1980 returned to Hunter College as professor of English. Besides teaching, Lorde raised a son and a daughter in an interracial lesbian relationship and was involved in political organizing of other black feminists and lesbians. In the early 1980s, Lorde helped to start Kitchen Table: Women of Color Press, and in 1991 she was named New York State Poet. Lorde is probably best known for her prose writings, among them two collections of essays, *Sister Outsider* (1984) and *Burst of Light* (1988), and the autobiographical *Zami: The Cancer Journals* (1980), a chronicle of her struggle with the breast cancer that ultimately claimed her life. Her poetry publications include *The First Cities* (1968), *The Black Unicorn* (1978), and *Undersong: Chosen Poems Old and New* (1993). Near the end of her life, Lorde made her home on St. Croix, U.S. Virgin Islands, and adopted the African name Gamba Adisa (Warrior — She Who Makes Her Meaning Known).

**NAGUIB MAHFOUZ** (1911–2006)   Egyptian writer Mahfouz was born and raised in Cairo in a devout Muslim family. Watching from his window as a child, he witnessed British soldiers firing on demonstrators during the Egyptian Revolution of 1919, an event he says had a profound effect on him. He received a BA (1934) in philosophy from what is now Cairo University, and he immediately began working as a civil servant. Although he began writing at a young age, he maintained various positions in the Egyptian civil service until he retired in 1971. His first novel, *Khufu's Wisdom* (1939), began his long and prolific writing career, in which he produced more than thirty-five novels, hundreds of short stories (collected in fifteen volumes), dozens of movie scripts, and five plays. He also produced a weekly newspaper column for over three decades and wrote *Echoes of an Autobiography* in 1994. In 1988 he became the only Arab writer to win the Nobel Prize in Literature, bringing him international fame and introducing his many works to the Western world. Mahfouz's earliest books were mainly historical fiction set in ancient Egypt, but after World War II, he began focusing more on the impact of society on the lives of individuals. One of his most famous works from this period, *The Cairo Trilogy* (1956, 1957), centers around the lives of three generations of fictional families in Cairo from World War I until the overthrow of King Farouk in 1952. His fiction tackles a broad range of topics, some of which were banned in Egypt, such as socialism, homosexuality, and religion. His works and political views also rattled some Islamic fundamentalists, who called for Mahfouz's death. In a 1994 assassination attempt, Mahfouz was stabbed in the neck by an Islamic militant, an event that caused nerve damage to his right arm, greatly hindering his ability to write for the remainder of his life. Widely praised around the world for his contributions to literature, Mahfouz was elected to the American Academy of Arts and Sciences in 2002.

**RUTH MARGALIT** (b. 1983)   Margalit is an Israeli writer living in New York. Her writing has appeared in the *New Yorker, Slate, Tablet, Bookforum*, and *Haaretz*, where she was a staff writer, among other publications. Her fiction was included in the anthology *Tel Aviv Short Stories*, and her poetry in *Maayan Magazine* (in Hebrew). A graduate of the Columbia Journalism School and of Tel Aviv University, Margalit works on the editorial staff of the *New Yorker*.

**ANDREW MARVELL** (1621–1678)   Born in Yorkshire and educated at Cambridge University, Marvell received an inheritance on his father's death that allowed him to spend four years traveling the Continent. Though not a Puritan himself, Marvell supported the Puritans' cause during the English Civil War and held a number of posts during the Puritan regime, including that of assistant to the blind John Milton, Oliver Cromwell's Latin secretary. In 1659, a year before the Restoration, Marvell was elected to Parliament, where he served until his death. Soon after the Restoration, Marvell expressed strong disagreements with the government in a series of outspoken and anonymously printed satires. It was for these satires, rather than for his many love poems, that he was primarily known in his own day.

**CLAUDE MCKAY** (1890–1948)   Born in Sunny Ville, Jamaica, McKay had already completed two volumes of poetry before coming to the United States in 1912 at the age of twenty-three (the two volumes earned him awards, which paid his way). The racism he encountered as a black immigrant brought a militant tone to his writing. His popular poem "If We Must Die" (1919) helped to initiate the Harlem Renaissance of the 1920s. Between 1922 and 1934 he lived in Great Britain, Russia, Germany, France, Spain, and Morocco. His writings include four volumes of poems, many essays, the autobiography *A Long Way from Home* (1937), the novel *Home to Harlem* (1928), and a sociological study of Harlem. His conversion to Roman Catholicism in the 1940s struck his audience as an ideological retreat. McKay wrote in a letter to a friend: "[T]o have a religion is very much like falling in love with a woman. You love her for her . . . beauty, which cannot be defined."

**BILL MCKIBBEN** (b. 1960)   Born and raised in the Boston suburb of Lexington, Massachusetts, McKibben attended Harvard University and served as editor of its student newspaper. After graduating from college, he worked as a staff writer for the *New Yorker* for five years before becoming a freelance writer. His debut publication, *The End of Nature* (1989), is regarded as the first book for a general audience about climate change, and has appeared in twenty-four languages. He has since written more than ten books about environmental issues, most recently *Deep Economy: The Wealth of Communities and the Durable Future* (2007), *Eaarth: Making a Life on a Tough New Planet* (2010), and *Oil and Honey: The Education of an Unlikely Activist* (2013). The Schumann Distinguished Scholar in Environmental Studies at Middlebury College and a fellow of the American Academy of Arts and Sciences, he has received numerous awards and honors, including a Guggenheim Fellowship and a Gandhi Peace Award. Called "probably America's most important environmentalist" by the *Boston Globe* and one of the world's 100 most important global thinkers by *Foreign Policy*, he was arrested and jailed in Washington, DC, in 2011 for protesting the proposed Keystone XL pipeline project. He writes frequently for a wide variety of publications around the world, including the *New York Review of Books*, *National Geographic*, and *Rolling Stone*.

**PETER MEINKE** (b. 1932)   Born in Brooklyn, New York, the son of a salesman, Meinke served in the U.S. Army from 1955 to 1957, attended Hamilton College (BA, 1955) and the University of Michigan (MA, 1961), and earned his PhD at the University of Minnesota (1965). He taught English at a New Jersey high school, Hamline University, Presbyterian College (now Eckerd College), and Old Dominion University, where he held the Darden Chair in Creative Writing. His reviews, poems, and stories have appeared in periodicals such as the *Atlantic*, the *New Yorker*, and the *New Republic*. The latest of his published books include *Zinc Fingers: Poems A to Z* (2000), *The Contracted World: New & More Selected Poems* (2006), *Unheard Music: Stories* (2007), and the poetry collection *Lucky Bones* (2014). His collection of stories, *The Piano Tuner*, won the 1986 Flannery O'Connor Award. He has also been the recipient of a National Endowment for the Arts Fellowship in poetry.

**HERMAN MELVILLE** (1819–1891)   The death of his merchant father when Melville was twelve shattered the economic security of his family. The financial panic of 1837 reduced the Melvilles to the edge of poverty, and at age nineteen, Melville went to sea. Economic conditions on his return were still grim, and after a frustrating stint as a country schoolteacher, he again went to sea — this time on a four-year whaling voyage. He deserted the whaler in the South Pacific, lived for some time with cannibals, made his way to Tahiti and Hawaii, and finally joined the navy for a return voyage. He mined his experiences for two successful South Sea adventure books, *Typee* (1846) and *Omoo* (1847). On the strength of these successes he married, but his next novel, *Mardi* (1849), was too heavy-handed an allegory to succeed. Driven by the obligation to support his growing family, Melville returned to sea-adventure stories, with moderate success. But neither his masterpiece, *Moby-Dick* (1851), nor his subsequent short stories and novels found much of an audience, and in 1886 he accepted an appointment as customs inspector in Manhattan, a job he held until retirement. He continued to write, mostly poetry, and lived to see himself forgotten as an author. *Billy Budd*, found among his papers after his death and published in 1924, led to a revival of interest in Melville, now recognized as one of America's greatest writers.

**ROBERT MEZEY** (b. 1935)    Born in Philadelphia, Mezey attended Kenyon College and served a troubled hitch in the U.S. Army before earning his BA from the University of Iowa in 1959. He worked as a probation officer, advertising copywriter, and social worker; did graduate study at Stanford University; and began teaching English at Case Western Reserve University in 1963. After a year as poet-in-residence at Franklin and Marshall College, he joined the English department of California State University, Fresno, spent three years at the University of Utah, and settled in 1976 at Pomona College in Claremont, California. Mezey won the Lamont Award for *The Lovemaker* in 1960 and has published many other poetry collections. In addition, he coedited *Naked Poetry* (1969) and was one of several translators for *Poems from the Hebrew* (1973). His recent work includes *Collected Poems: 1952–1999* (2000), for which he was awarded the 2002 Poet's Prize.

**EDNA ST. VINCENT MILLAY** (1892–1950)    Born in Rockland, Maine, in 1892, Edna St. Vincent Millay was raised by her divorced mother who imbued a strong cultural and literary sensibility in her children. At age nineteen, Millay won a literary contest for her poem "Renascence," which attracted the attention of a wealthy benefactor who paid for her education at Vassar College. Following her 1917 graduation, Millay emerged as a major figure in the cultural life of Greenwich Village, which at the time served as an incubator of important American literary, artistic, and political movements. As part of this milieu, Millay's work and life came to represent the modern, liberated woman of the Jazz Age. Although she was married for over twenty-five years, Millay was openly bisexual, and both she and her husband carried on extramarital affairs. Her first published work, *Renascence, and Other Poems* (1917), was followed by *A Few Figs from Thistles: Poems and Sonnets* (1920), which was considered controversial for its feminist themes and its exploration of female sexuality. In 1921 she published two dramatic works: *The Lamp and the Bell*, about love between women, and the pacifist play *Aria da Capo*. Her 1922 book, *The Harp-Weaver, and Other Poems*, won the Pulitzer Prize. Subsequent publications by Millay include *The Buck in the Snow, and Other Poems* (1928), *Fatal Interview* (1931), *Wine from These Grapes* (1934), *There Are No Islands, Any More: Lines Written in Passion and in Deep Concern for England, France, and My Own Country* (1940), *Make Bright the Arrows: 1940 Notebook* (1940), and *The Murder of Lidice* (1942). In 1943 Millay was awarded the Frost Medal for her lifetime contribution to American poetry.

**LYDIA MILLET** (b. 1969)    Millet was born in Boston, Massachusetts, and raised in Toronto. She received her BA in creative writing from the University of North Carolina at Chapel Hill and her MA in environmental policy from Duke University. Her short story collection *Love in Infant Monkeys* (2009) was a finalist for the Pulitzer Prize. She has also written nine novels: *Omnivores* (1996); *George Bush: Dark Prince of Love* (2000); *My Happy Life* (2002), the 2003 winner of the PEN/USA Award for Fiction; *Everyone's Pretty* (2005); *Oh Pure and Radiant Heart* (2005); the trilogy *How the Dead Dream* (2008), *Ghost Lights* (2011), and *Magnificence* (2012), which was a finalist for the National Book Critics Circle Award and the Los Angeles Times Book Prize; and her most recent novel, *Mermaids in Paradise* (2014). Millet has also written several young adult novels including the Dissenters series books *The Fires Beneath the Sea* (2011) and *The Shimmers in the Night* (2012), as well as *Pills and Starships* (2014). She received a Guggenheim Fellowship in 2012 and currently works as a staff writer at the Center for Biological Diversity in Tucson.

**CZESŁAW MIŁOSZ** (1911–2004)    Born in a Lithuanian-Polish province in pre-revolutionary Russia, Milosz began writing poetry and became active in leftist politics while studying law at the University of Vilnius. He began producing poetry in the 1930s, although much of it would be banned from publication in his home country for half a century. During World War II, he worked as a writer and translator for the Polish resistance, and he helped support Jews seeking to evade Nazi persecution. After the war he became a diplomat for Poland's new communist government, but he soon found the repressiveness of Stalin's Soviet regime to be too restrictive for his writing. He defected to the West in 1951, moving to the United States in 1960. His best-known work of nonfiction, *The Captive Mind* (1953), grew out of his experience of living under totalitarianism and explains why he defected. It begins with the sentence, "Like many of my generation, I could have wished that my life had been a more simple affair." In 1961 Milosz became a professor of Slavic languages and literature at the University of California, Berkeley, where he taught until 1998. In 1980 he received the Nobel Prize in Literature, earning him some fame in his home country where his work had been banned, and many had never heard of him. Some of the most notable collections among his many volumes of poetry and prose include *The World* (1953, trans. 1989), a sequence of twenty "naïve" poems composed in an intentionally rudimentary style during World War II, and *Legends of Modernity: Essays and Letters from Occupied Poland 1942–1943* (1996, trans. 2005). Milosz was awarded the U.S. National Medal of Arts in 1989.

**LISEL MUELLER** (b. 1924)   Born in Hamburg, Germany, to parents who were both teachers, Mueller moved to the United States in 1939 and became a citizen in 1945. Shortly before earning a BA from the University of Evansville (1944), she married. Later, she bore two children, pursued graduate studies at Indiana University, and held a number of positions, among them receptionist, caseworker, and library assistant. She served as an instructor in poetry writing at Elmhurst College (1969–72) and later as an instructor in the MFA Writing Program at Goddard College, Vermont. She has received numerous awards, including the Robert M. Ferguson Memorial Award for her first book of poems, *Dependencies* (1965), the Pulitzer Prize for Poetry (1997) for *Alive Together: New and Selected Poems*, and a National Book Award for *The Need to Hold Still* (1980). Commenting on the nature of her verse in *The Private Life* (1976), one critic noted that "she goes after our secrets, this poet; often she finds them." In 2002 Mueller was awarded the Ruth Lilly Poetry Prize, a prestigious honor given to living U.S. poets "whose lifetime accomplishments warrant extraordinary recognition."

**BHARATI MUKHERJEE** (1940–2017)   Born in Calcutta, India, Mukherjee attended the University of Calcutta (BA, 1959), the University of Baroda (MA, 1961), and the University of Iowa, where she earned an MFA (1963) and a PhD (1969). In 1963 she married Clark Blaise, a Canadian writer and professor, and joined the faculty at McGill University in Montreal. In 1973 Mukherjee and her husband visited India and kept separate diaries of the trip, published as *Days and Nights in Calcutta* (1977). The diaries reveal marked differences in their responses: Mukherjee found her home environs, especially the status of women, worse than she remembered, while Blaise, after an initial revulsion at the squalor and poverty, found India a fascinating and attractive culture compared to the West. Mukherjee "left Canada after fifteen years due to the persistent effects of racial prejudice against people of my national origin." Her fiction frequently explores the tensions inevitable in intercultural relationships. Her first novel, *The Tiger's Daughter* (1972), deals with the disappointment of an expatriate's return to India. In her second novel, *Wife* (1975), a psychologically abused woman finally kills her husband. *The Middleman and Other Stories* (1988) won the National Book Critics Circle Award. Her trilogy *Desirable Daughters* (2003), *The Tree Bride* (2004), and *Miss New India* (2011) explore the lives of Indian expatriates in America. Mukherjee noted that while she had changed during her 30 years in America, "[America] has also had to change because of the hundreds of thousands of people like me, forcing the culture, moment by moment, into something new."

**TASLIMA NASRIN** (b. 1962)   Born and educated in Mymensingh, Bangladesh, Nasrin began writing poetry in her childhood, her earliest works appearing in a literary journal edited by her eldest brother. Following in the footsteps of her father, a doctor, she earned a degree in medicine from Mymensingh Medical College and for a few years practiced as a government doctor. Her study of modern science, Nasrin has written, "made me a rationalist." While practicing medicine, she continued her writing, publishing poems and novels. These works, along with the essays she penned as a syndicated columnist in Bangladesh, earned her a number of important literary prizes in 1992 and 1993. However, her rationalism and her feminism, as well as her 1993 novel *Shame*, enraged Islamic fundamentalists. Forced into hiding by death threats, Nasrin fled to Europe in 1994; she returned to India in 2007 only to flee again after facing further threats and physical violence. She entered India once again in 2008 and lives in hiding under tight security. Nasrin has won several humanitarian awards, among them the UNESCO-Madanjeet Singh Prize in 2004 for the promotion of tolerance and nonviolence and the Simone de Beauvoir feminist award in 2008 in recognition of her writing on women's rights. In an essay titled "Women's Rights," Nasrin writes, "My poetry, my prose, my entire output expresses the deprivation of women who have been exploited for centuries." She has written a multivolume autobiography which includes *Meyebela, My Bengali Girlhood: A Memoir of Growing Up Female in a Muslim World* (2002); *Ka* (*Speak Up*, 2003), which was banned in Bangladesh; *Nei, Kichu Nei* (*Nothing Is There*, 2010); and *Nirbasan* (*Exile*, 2012). Among her other publications are an essay collection, *Narir Kono Desh Nei* (*A Woman Has No Country*, 2007), and several volumes of poetry, most recently *Bondini* (*Prisoner*, 2008).

**HOWARD NEMEROV** (1920–1991)   Born to well-off Russian Jewish immigrants in New York City, Nemerov was raised in a culturally sophisticated atmosphere and was drawn to the arts at a young age. He received his bachelor's degree from Harvard University (1941), served as a pilot in World War II, and published his first book, the poetry collection *The Image of the Law*, in 1947. He taught at several small colleges in the Northeast before becoming professor of English and Distinguished Poet in Residence at Washington University in St. Louis in 1969. Nemerov published numerous additional collections of poetry, including *The Salt Garden* (1955), *Mirrors and Windows* (1958), and *The Winter Lightning: Selected Poems* (1968). His 1977 publication, *The Collected Poems of Howard Nemerov*, won the Pulitzer Prize, the National Book Award, and the Bollingen Prize. *Trying Conclusions: New and Selected Poems, 1961–1991* (1991) was published the year he died. His well-received novels include *The Melodramatists* (1949), *Federigo: Or the Power of Love* (1954), and *The Homecoming Game* (1957). Of Nemerov, author Joyce Carol Oates wrote, "Romantic, realist, comedian, satirist, relentless and indefatigable brooder upon the most ancient mysteries — Nemerov is not to be classified." His many awards and honors include fellowships from the Academy of American Poets and the Guggenheim Foundation, a National Endowment for the Arts grant, and the National Medal of Arts. He served as poet laureate of the United States from 1988 to 1990, and as chancellor of the American Academy of Poets from 1976 to 1991.

**PABLO NERUDA** (1904–1973)    Neruda was born in Parral, Chile, the son of a railroad worker. Shortly after leaving college, he joined the Chilean foreign service to begin a distinguished career as consul and ambassador at a variety of posts around the world, including Burma, Ceylon, Indonesia, Siam, Cambodia, Spain, France, and Mexico. He was elected to the Chilean senate as a communist. But when he published letters attacking the policies of Gabriel González Videla, the president of Chile, he was forced into exile. He returned to Chile after the victory of anti-Videla forces and rejoined the foreign service. His vast literary output won many prizes and honors. And, although American readers found it difficult to separate his poetry from his politics, he was, at his prime, generally considered to be the greatest poet writing in Spanish. One critic pointed out that Neruda "never bothered his head about the state of poetry. He has just gone on exuding it as he draws breath." In an essay on impure poetry, Neruda wrote: "Let [this] be the poetry we search for: worn with the hand's obligations, as by acids, steeped in sweat and in smoke, smelling of lilies and urine, spattered diversely by the trades that we love by, inside the law or beyond it. A poetry impure as the clothing we wear, or our bodies, soup-stained, soiled with our shameful behavior, our wrinkles and vigils and dreams, observations and prophecies, declarations of loathing and love, idylls and beasts, the shocks of encounter, political loyalties, denials and doubts, affirmation and taxes." *Five Decades, a Selection: Poems, 1925–1970* appeared in 1974. He was awarded the Nobel Prize in Literature in 1971.

**JOYCE CAROL OATES** (b. 1938)    Born in Lockport, New York, Oates majored in English at Syracuse University (BA, 1960) as a scholarship student and earned an MA in English (1961) from the University of Wisconsin. While still an undergraduate, she won the *Mademoiselle* college fiction award (1959), beginning an enormously prolific career as a writer and editor. She publishes an average of two books a year, to date well over fifty volumes including novels, short story collections, poetry, drama, and critical essays. Her numerous awards and honors include the 1970 fiction National Book Award for her novel *Them* (1969). She has also won two O. Henry Awards, the National Humanities Medal, a Norman Mailer Prize for Lifetime Achievement, and multiple Pulitzer Prize nominations. She taught at the universities of Detroit and Windsor (Canada) before joining the faculty at Princeton University. Among her many recent publications are the short story collection *Lovely, Dark, Deep* (2014), the memoir *A Widow's Story* (2012), and the novels *The Accursed* (2013), *Carthage* (2014), and *The Sacrifice* (2015). Oates retired from full-time teaching in 2015.

**TIM O'BRIEN** (b. 1946)    O'Brien was born in Austin, Minnesota, attended public schools, and received a BA summa cum laude from Macalester College. Immediately following graduation, he was drafted into the U.S. Army (1968–70), earning a Purple Heart. On his return to civilian life, he pursued graduate work at Harvard University and worked as a national affairs reporter for the *Washington Post*. His first novel, *If I Die in a Combat Zone, Box Me Up and Ship Me Home* (1973), is a semi-fictionalized account of his own Vietnam experiences. Many of O'Brien's novels either are set in Vietnam or focus on characters haunted by the war: *Northern Lights* (1975); *Going After Cacciato* (1978), which won a National Book Award; *The Nuclear Age* (1985); *The Things They Carried* (1990); and *In the Lake of the Woods* (1994). In an interview, O'Brien explained that his preoccupation with the Vietnam War was part of his need to write with "passion." Writing "good" stories, he went on to say, "requires a sense of passion, and my passion as a human being and as a writer intersect in Vietnam, not in the physical stuff but in the issues of Vietnam — of courage, rectitude, enlightenment, holiness, trying to do the right thing in the world." O'Brien wrote a comic novel, *Tomcat in Love* (1998), about a womanizing professor's midlife crisis, before returning to his earlier themes in his most recent book, *July, July* (2002). He has received several literary awards and fellowships from institutions including the American Academy of Arts and Letters, the Guggenheim Foundation, the National Endowment for the Arts, and the Dayton Literary Peace Prize Foundation. O'Brien is currently professor of creative writing at Texas State University in Austin.

**FLANNERY O'CONNOR** (1925–1964)   O'Connor, afflicted with lupus erythematosus, spent most of her short life in Milledgeville, Georgia. She began writing while a student at Georgia State College for Women in her hometown, and in 1947 earned an MFA from the University of Iowa. Back in Milledgeville, she lived on a farm with her mother, raised peacocks, and endured constant treatment for her progressive and incurable disease. She traveled and lectured when she could. She wrote two novels, *Wise Blood* (1952) and *The Violent Bear It Away* (1960), and two collections of stories, *A Good Man Is Hard to Find* (1955) and *Everything That Rises Must Converge* (1965).

**GEORGE ORWELL** (1903–1950)   Born Eric Blair in India, the son of a minor British colonial officer, Orwell was raised in England. His education at good grammar schools, culminating with a stay at Eton College, introduced him to what he later called the snobbish world of England's middle and upper classes. Denied a university scholarship, he joined the Indian Imperial Police in 1922 and served in Burma until he resigned in 1927, disgusted with the injustice of British imperialism in India and Burma. He was determined to be a writer and, living at the edge of poverty, deliberately mingled with social outcasts and impoverished laborers. These experiences produced *Down and Out in Paris and London* (1933). Although he was a socialist, his experiences while fighting alongside the leftists during the Spanish Civil War disillusioned him, and he embodied his distaste for any totalitarian system in *Animal Farm* (1945) — a satirical attack on the leadership of the Soviet Union. In his pessimistic novel *1984* (1949), he imagined a social order shaped by a propagandistic perversion of language, in which the government, an extension of "Big Brother," uses two-way television to control the citizenry. Orwell succumbed to tuberculosis at the age of forty-seven, but not before he produced six novels, three documentary works, over 700 newspaper articles and reviews, and a volume of essays.

**ALICIA OSTRIKER** (b. 1937)   Ostriker is a professor emerita of Rutgers University and a faculty member of the New England College Low-Residency Poetry MFA Program. A major American poet and critic for decades, her poems have appeared in the *New Yorker*, *Paris Review*, *Antaeus*, *Nation*, *Poetry*, *American Poetry Review*, *Kenyon Review*, *Atlantic*, *MS*, *Tikkun*, and many other literary journals, and have been translated into French, German, Italian, Chinese, Japanese, Hebrew, and Arabic. She has lectured and given performances of her work throughout the United States as well as in Europe, Australia, Israel, Japan, and China. In recognition of her tremendous contribution to the world of poetry, Ostriker has received awards from the National Endowment for the Arts, the Poetry Society of America, the San Francisco State Poetry Center, the Judah Magnes Museum, the New Jersey Arts Council, the Rockefeller Foundation, and the Guggenheim Foundation. She has written twelve volumes of poetry, most recently *The Book of Seventy* (2009), which won the Jewish Book Award for Poetry, and *At the Revelation Restaurant and Other Poems* (2010). She has also authored two seminal critical volumes on women's poetry: *Writing Like* *a Woman* (1983) and *Stealing the Language: The Emergence of Women's Poetry in America* (1987). Her most recent book of criticism is *Dancing at the Devil's Party: Essays on Poetry, Politics, and the Erotic* (2000). She lives in Princeton, New Jersey, with her husband.

**DOROTHY PARKER** (1893–1967)  Parker was born in West End, New Jersey, to a Scottish Presbyterian mother and a Jewish father as "a late unexpected arrival in a loveless family." She was educated in private schools and moved in 1911 to New York, where she lived in a boardinghouse and earned her living by playing piano at a dancing school. In 1915 one of the verses she sent around was accepted by *Vogue* magazine, and the editor later hired her to write captions for fashion illustrations. Her native wit captivated the editor, and he persuaded her to join *Vanity Fair* as drama critic, although she was fired when she wrote unfavorable reviews of several plays. She became the first woman among the regulars of the Algonquin Round Table — a group of writers who met regularly at the Algonquin Hotel in New York City that included Alexander Woollcott, George S. Kaufman, Robert Benchley, and Edna Ferber, among others. A master of irony and scathing wit, Parker, despite a troubled personal life that led to suicide attempts, flourished as a humorist, poet, short-story writer, playwright, and screenwriter.

**PAUL** (d. ca. 64 CE)  Paul was born Saul in Tarsus of Cilicia (located near the Mediterranean Sea in south-central Turkey, near Syria). He was an important Jerusalem Pharisee who, according to the Acts of the Apostles (Chapter 9), vigorously attacked both intellectually and physically those who proclaimed the deity of Jesus. The same source provides an account of Saul's conversion. Traveling to Damascus to arrest followers of Jesus, he experienced an intense light that blinded him and heard a voice that declared, "I am Jesus, whom you are persecuting." In Tarsus, his blindness was cured by Ananias, a follower of Jesus, and Paul became, arguably, the most important disciple of Jesus in the early church: his letters, and those attributed to him, constitute a quarter of the New Testament. His attempts to preach the new Way in the synagogues of the region were rebuffed, sometimes violently, and Paul was frequently jailed. He became the apostle to the Gentiles, traveling throughout the Mediterranean region to establish churches. His epistles to those young and fragile congregations helped formulate the political, legal, and spiritual institutions of the early church. His final arrest brought him to Rome to answer charges, and after two years of imprisonment, he died about 64 CE.

**OMAR PÉREZ** (b. 1964)  Pérez was born and raised in Havana, earning a degree in English from the University of Havana and a degree in Italian from the Università per Straniere di Siena. At the age of 25, Pérez discovered that his father was the Marxist revolutionary Ernesto "Che" Guevara; Pérez has remained largely mum on the subject since discovering his lineage, preferring to let his own work speak for itself. Pérez has worked as an editor for the magazines *La naranja dulce* and *Mantis*, as a journalist for *El Caimán Barbudo*, and as a translator, boasting notable translations of the Italian-Cuban novelist Alba de Céspedes's *Nadie vuelve atrás* (2003) and William Shakespeare's *As You Like It* (as *Como Les Guste*, 2000). Pérez is also a poet and an ordained Zen Buddhist monk. His poetry collections include *Lingua Franca* (2010), *Oíste hablar del gato de pelea?* (1999, translated as *Did You Hear about the Fighting Cat?* by Kristin Dykstra, 2010), and *Algo de lo Sagrado* (1996, translated as *Something of the Sacred* by Kristin Dykstra and Robert Tejada, 2007). Pérez's poetry explores the intersections of human experience, often intertwining his Zen beliefs with political and cultural messages. In an interview with *Jacket* magazine in 2008, Pérez said that "Poetry is a natural function, like god, or DNA, or rain. The fact that we can give notice of it does not mean that we make it."

**MARGE PIERCY** (b. 1936)    Born in Detroit, Piercy was the first of her family to attend college. In 1957 she graduated from the University of Michigan (where she won prizes for poetry and fiction) and earned an MA from Northwestern University (1958). She was active in social and political causes and fought for equal treatment of women and minorities while opposing the Vietnam War. She supported herself with odd jobs in Chicago as she pursued a writing career, but her first novel was not published until after her 1969 move to Wellfleet, Massachusetts, where she still lives. She is an extraordinarily prolific writer. Among her more than a dozen novels are *He, She and It* (1991), *The Longings of Women* (1994), and *City of Darkness, City of Lights* (1996). Her many volumes of poetry include *My Mother's Body* (1985), *Available Light* (1988), *The Earth Shines Secretly: A Book of Days* (1990), and *Mars and Her Children* (1992). She has also written plays and several volumes of nonfiction and has edited the anthology *Early Ripening: American Women's Poetry Now* (1987). In the introduction to a volume of selected poems, *Circles on the Water* (1982), Piercy asserted that she wanted her poems to be "useful," saying, "What I mean by useful is simply that readers will find poems that speak to and for them, will take those poems into their lives and say them to each other and put them up on the bathroom wall and remember bits and pieces of them in stressful or quiet moments. . . . To find ourselves spoken for in art gives dignity to our pain, our anger, our lust, our losses." Most recently, she has published two novels, *The Third Child* (2003) and *Sex Wars: A Novel of Gilded Age in New York* (2005); three collections of poetry, *Colors Passing through Us* (2003), *The Crooked Inheritance* (2006), and *The Hunger Moon: New and Selected Poems, 1980–2010* (2011); and a collection of short stories, *The Cost of Lunch, Etc.* (2014).

**SYLVIA PLATH** (1932–1963)    Plath was born in Boston, Massachusetts, where her parents taught at Boston University. She graduated summa cum laude in English from Smith College (1955); earned an MA as a Fulbright Scholar at Newnham College, Cambridge (1955–57); and married British poet Ted Hughes (1956). Plath's poetry reveals the anger and anxiety that would eventually lead to her suicide. Her view that all relationships were in some way destructive and predatory surely darkened her life. Yet in 1963, during the month between the publication of her only novel, *The Bell Jar* (about a suicidal college student), and her death, Plath was extraordinarily productive; she produced finished poems every day. Her *Collected Poems* was published in 1981.

**EDGAR ALLAN POE** (1809–1849)    Poe, the son of traveling actors, was born in Boston. Within a year, his alcoholic father deserted his mother and their three infant children. When his mother died of tuberculosis in Richmond, Virginia, three-year-old Edgar was adopted by John Allan and his wife. Allan, a prosperous businessman, spent time in England, where Poe began his education at private schools. Back in the United States, Allan forced Poe to leave the University of Virginia in 1826, when Poe incurred gambling debts he could not pay. Poe served in the U.S. Army from 1827 to 1829, eventually attaining the rank of sergeant major, and then attended West Point, hoping for further military advancement. Shortly thereafter, Mrs. Allan died of tuberculosis. Poe angrily confronted his foster father about his extramarital affairs, and for this candor he was disowned. Believing that Allan would never reinstate him as heir, Poe deliberately violated rules to provoke his dismissal from the academy. In 1835 Poe began his career as editor, columnist, and reviewer, earning a living he could not make as a writer of stories and poems. He married his thirteen-year-old cousin, Virginia Clemm, in 1836, and lived with her and her mother during a period marked by illness and poverty. Virginia died of tuberculosis in 1847. Poe died, delirious and under mysterious circumstances, in 1849. He perfected the gothic horror story ("Fall of the House of Usher") and originated the modern detective story ("The Gold Bug," "The

Murders in the Rue Morgue"). Poe's work fascinated the French poet Baudelaire, who translated it into French.

**WYATT PRUNTY** (b. 1947)   Prunty was born in Humboldt, Tennessee. After earning a BA from the University of the South in Sewanee, he went on to earn an MA from Johns Hopkins University and a PhD (1979) from Louisiana State University. His poetry chapbook, *Domestic of the Outer Banks*, was published in 1980. Several volumes followed, among them *Since the Noon Mail Stopped* (1997) and *Unarmed and Dangerous* (2000). His poetry has been anthologized in *Anthology of Magazine Verse and Yearbook of American Poetry* for both 1979 and 1980. He was awarded a poetry prize by *Sewanee Review* (1969) and has been a fellow at the Bread Loaf Writers' Conference. He has taught in the graduate program of the Johns Hopkins Writing Seminars, where he was Elliott Coleman Professor of Poetry. Currently, he serves as Carlton Professor of English at the University of the South, where he teaches poetry, and where he founded and now directs the Sewanee Writers' Conference. His most recent work is a collection of poetry and fiction, *The Lover's Guide to Trapping* (2009).

**DUDLEY RANDALL** (1914–2000)   Born in Washington, DC, Randall worked during the Depression in the Ford Motor Company foundry in Dearborn, Michigan, and then as a carrier and clerk for the U.S. Post Office in Detroit. He served in the U.S. Army Signal Corps (1942–46) and graduated from Wayne State University (BA, 1949) and the University of Michigan (MALS, 1951). He was a librarian at several universities and founded the Broadside Press in 1965 "so black people could speak to and for their people." Randall told *Negro Digest*, "Precision and accuracy are necessary for both white and black writers. . . . 'A black aesthetic' should not be an excuse for sloppy writing." He urged African American writers to reject what was false in white poetry but not to forsake universal concerns in favor of a racial agenda. His works include *On Getting a Natural* (1969) and *A Litany of Friends: New and Selected Poems* (1981). He edited *For Malcolm: Poems on the Life and Death of Malcolm X* (1969) and *The Black Poets* (1971), an extensive anthology of poetry, from slave songs to the present.

**ADRIENNE RICH** (1929–2012)   Born to a middle-class family, Rich was educated by her parents until she entered public school in the fourth grade. She graduated Phi Beta Kappa from Radcliffe College in 1951, the same year her first book of poems, *A Change of World*, appeared. That volume, chosen by W. H. Auden for the Yale Series of Younger Poets Award, and her next, *The Diamond Cutters and Other Poems* (1955), earned her a reputation as an elegant, controlled stylist. In the 1960s, however, Rich began a dramatic shift away from her earlier mode as she took up political and feminist themes and stylistic experimentation in such works as *Snapshots of a Daughter-in-Law* (1963), *The Necessities of Life* (1966), *Leaflets* (1969), and *The Will to Change* (1971). In *Diving into the Wreck* (1973) and *The Dream of a Common Language* (1978), she continued to experiment with form and to deal with the experiences and aspirations of women from a feminist perspective. In addition to her poetry, Rich published many essays on poetry, feminism, motherhood, and lesbianism. She also won numerous awards, most recently the National Book Foundation's Medal for Distinguished Contribution to American Letters in 2006 and the Lifetime Recognition Award from the Griffin Poetry Prize in 2010. Her recent collections include *Telephone Ringing in the Labyrinth: Poems: 2004–2006* (2007), *A Human Eye: Essays on Art in Society, 1997–2008* (2009), and, her final publication, *Tonight No Poetry Will Serve: Poems 2007–2010* (2011).

**EDWIN ARLINGTON ROBINSON** (1869–1935)  Robinson grew up in Gardiner, Maine; attended Harvard University; returned to Gardiner as a freelance writer; and then settled in New York City in 1896. His various odd jobs included a one-year stint as subway-construction inspector. President Theodore Roosevelt, a fan of his poetry, had him appointed to the U.S. Custom House in New York, where he worked from 1905 to 1909. Robinson wrote about people rather than nature, particularly New England characters remembered from his early years. Describing his first volume of poems, *The Torrent and the Night Before* (1896), he told a friend there was not "a single red-breasted robin in the whole collection." Popular throughout his career, Robinson won three Pulitzer Prizes (1921, 1924, and 1927).

**THEODORE ROETHKE** (1908–1963)  Born in Saginaw, Michigan, Roethke was the son of a greenhouse owner, and greenhouses figure prominently in the imagery of his poems. He graduated magna cum laude from the University of Michigan in 1929, where he also earned an MA in 1936 after graduate study at Harvard University. He taught at several universities, coached two varsity tennis teams, and settled at the University of Washington in 1947. Intensely introspective and demanding of himself, Roethke was renowned as a great teacher, though he was sometimes incapacitated by bipolar disorder. His collection *The Waking: Poems 1933–1953* won the Pulitzer Prize in 1954. Other awards include Guggenheim Fellowships in 1945 and 1950, and a National Book Award and the Bollingen Prize in 1959 for *Words for the Wind* (1958).

**KAY RYAN** (b. 1945)  Ryan was born in San Jose and grew up in central and southern California. She attended Antelope Valley College in Lancaster, California, before earning two degrees from University of California, Los Angeles. For over thirty-five years, she was a part-time instructor of English at the College of Marin. Ryan is the author of eight volumes of poetry: *Dragon Acts to Dragon Ends* (1983), *Strangely Marked Metal* (1985), *Flamingo Watching* (1994), *Elephant Rocks* (1997), *Say Uncle* (2000), *The Niagara River* (2005), *The Jam Jar Lifeboat and Other Novelties Exposed* (2008), and *The Best of It: New and Selected Poems* (2010), for which she won the Pulitzer Prize. Her poems have also appeared in a number of periodicals, including *American Scholar*, *Atlantic*, the *New Yorker*, *Paris Review*, and *Poetry* magazine. Among her many awards are fellowships from the Guggenheim Foundation and the National Endowment for the Arts, and the 2004 Ruth Lilly Poetry Prize, a prestigious honor given to living U.S. poets "whose lifetime accomplishments warrant extraordinary recognition." Ryan served two terms as poet laureate of the United States, from 2008 through 2010. In 2011 she was named a MacArthur Fellow, and in 2012 she received the National Humanities Medal.

**CARL SANDBURG** (1878–1967)  H. L. Mencken once described Carl Sandburg as "indubitably an American in every pulse-beat." Sandburg came from humble beginnings in Galesburg, Illinois. His parents had emigrated to America from northern Sweden and were very poor. Sandburg spent much of his youth working odd jobs to earn money, from driving a milk truck to bricklaying. In 1898 he voluntarily joined the military, serving eight months in Puerto Rico during the Spanish-American War. After leaving the military, he returned to his hometown and enrolled in Lombard College, though he dropped out in 1903 before receiving his degree. He then moved to Milwaukee, and joined the Socialist Party of America, where he met his future wife, Lilian Steichen. The couple moved around frequently in their early years together, eventually settling in Elmhurst in 1919. During that time, Sandburg became an editor for the *Chicago Daily News* and came to be known as a part of the Chicago literary renaissance. In 1919 he won the Pulitzer Prize for Poetry for his collection *Cornhuskers* (1918), which celebrated the ordinary working people of the Midwest. The celebration of America became a trademark of Sandburg's poetry and was reflected in his subsequent poetry collections, some of which include *Smoke and Steel* (1920), *Slabs of the Sunburnt West* (1922), *Good Morning, America* (1928), *The People, Yes* (1936), *Harvest Poems* (1950), *Sandburg's Complete Poems* (1951, which also won a Pulitzer Prize), and *Honey and Salt* (1963). The 1920s also saw Sandburg tap into American folklore. He made brief yearly tours across America with a banjo or guitar, singing folk songs and reciting poems, and thereafter put those uniquely American experiences into songbooks: *The American Songbag* (1927) and *The New American Songbag* (1950). He also wrote a series of children's books called *Rootabaga Stories* (1922), *Rootabaga Pigeons* (1923), and *Potato Face* (1930), which grew out of his desire to have "American fairy tales" match actual American childhood. Sandburg spent years researching and writing a definitive, two-volume biography of Abraham Lincoln, the second volume of which — *Abraham Lincoln: The War Years* (1939) — also earned Sandburg a Pulitzer Prize. He recorded excerpts from the biography for Caedmon Records in New York City in 1957 and made a recording of Aaron Copland's *Lincoln Portrait* with the New York Philharmonic, for which he won a 1959 Grammy Award. In 1945 Sandburg and his wife moved to an estate in Flat Rock, North Carolina, where they lived until Sandburg's death in 1967.

**SAPPHO** (ca. 610–ca. 580 BCE)   Almost nothing certain is known of the finest woman lyric poet of the ancient world. Sappho was born to an aristocratic family and had three brothers, one of whom was a court cupbearer, a position limited to the sons of good families. She is associated with the island of Lesbos, set in the Aegean Sea. She married and had a daughter. For over 2,000 years, her reputation depended on fragments of her work quoted by other ancient authors. However, in the late nineteenth century a cache of papyrus and vellum codices, dating from the second to the sixth centuries CE and containing authentic transcriptions of a few of her lyrical poems, was discovered in Egypt. Unlike other ancient Greek poets, she wrote in ordinary Greek rather than in an exalted literary dialect; her lyrics, despite their simple language, conveyed women's concerns with intense emotion.

**GEORGE SAUNDERS** (b. 1958)   Born in Amarillo, Texas, Saunders grew up in the Chicago suburb of Oak Forest. He received a BS in geophysical engineering from Colorado School of Mines in 1981, and an MA in creative writing from Syracuse University in 1988. His writing, which has been compared to that of Kurt Vonnegut, has appeared in the *New Yorker*, *Harper's*, the *Guardian*, *McSweeney's*, and *GQ*, as well as *Best American* anthologies for short stories, travel writing, and science fiction. Saunders, who has won the National Magazine Award for fiction four times, was a finalist for the PEN/Hemingway Award for his first story collection, *CivilWarLand in Bad Decline* (1996). In 2006 Saunders received a MacArthur Fellowship as well as a Guggenheim Fellowship, and he won the World Fantasy Award for his short story "CommComm." His collection *In Persuasion Nation* (2006) was a finalist for the Story Prize, an award he won for his later collection *Tenth of December* (2013), which was also a finalist for the National Book Award. Among his many other honors, he received an award from the American Academy of Arts and Letters in 2009, and the PEN/Malamud Award in 2013. Saunders has taught at the Syracuse MFA program since 1996.

**LÉOPOLD SÉDAR SENGHOR** (1906–2001)   Regarded by many as one of the most important African intellectuals of the twentieth century, Senghor was born to a prosperous family and raised in the French colony of Senegal. He was drawn to French literature from a young age, and after receiving his bachelor's degree in Senegal, he continued his studies in France and began a teaching career there. He served in the French army during World War II and spent two years in German prison camps, where he devoted much of his time to writing poetry. Upon his release from prison in 1942, he returned to his teaching career and worked for the French resistance during the Nazi occupation. After the war, Senghor became active in politics and was elected to represent his colonial homeland in the French National Assembly. An early proponent of the Négritude movement, Senghor used his political influence to advocate for a revival of African pride and to argue against colonial rule. In 1960 he became the first democratically elected president of the newly independent Senegal, a position he held until voluntarily resigning in 1980. Throughout his political career, Senghor maintained his cultural and literary activities, helping to found the journal *Presence Africaine* in 1947, and publishing several works of his own including the English translations *Selected Poems* (1964), *On African Socialism* (1964), *Nocturnes* (1971), *Prose and Poetry* (1976), and *The Collected Poetry* (1991). Senghor won numerous international awards both as a writer and political thinker, and in 1984 he was inducted into the French Academy, becoming the first African member in that body's history.

**ANNE SEXTON** (1928–1974)   Born in Newton, Massachusetts, Sexton attended Garland Junior College and Boston University, where she studied under Robert Lowell. She worked for a year as a fashion model in Boston and later wrote her first poetry collection, *To Bedlam and Part Way Back* (1960), while recovering from a nervous breakdown. Writing a poem almost every day was successful therapy for her. From 1961 to 1963, Sexton was a scholar at the Radcliffe Institute for Independent Study. A confessional poet, Sexton acknowledged her debt to W. D. Snodgrass, whose collection of poetry *Heart's Needle* (1959) influenced her profoundly. Her second collection, *All My Pretty Ones* (1962), includes a quote from a letter by Franz Kafka that expresses her own literary philosophy: "A book should serve as the axe for the frozen sea within us." *Live or Die* (1967), her third collection of poems, won a Pulitzer Prize. She committed suicide in 1974.

**WILLIAM SHAKESPEARE** (1564–1616)   Shakespeare was born at Stratford-on-Avon in April 1564. His father became an important public figure, rising to the position of high bailiff (equivalent to mayor) of Stratford. Although we know practically nothing of Shakespeare's personal life, we may assume that he received a decent grammar school education in literature, logic, and Latin (though not in mathematics or natural science). When he was eighteen he married Anne Hathaway, eight years his senior; six months later their son was born. Two years later, Anne bore twins. We do not know how the young Shakespeare supported his family, and we do not hear of him again until 1592, when a rival London playwright sarcastically refers to him as an "upstart crow." Shakespeare seems to have prospered in the London theater world. He probably began as an actor and earned enough as author and part owner of his company's theaters to acquire property. His sonnets, which were written during the 1590s, reveal rich and varied interests. Some are addressed to an attractive young man (whom the poet urges to marry); others to the mysterious dark lady; still others suggest a love triangle of two men and a woman. His dramas include historical plays based on English dynastic struggles; comedies, both festive and dark; romances such as *Pericles* (1608) and *Cymbeline* (1611) that cover decades in the lives of their characters; and the great tragedies *Hamlet* (1602), *Othello* (1604), *King Lear* (1605), and *Macbeth* (1606). About 1611, at age forty-seven, he retired to the second largest house in Stratford.

He died in 1616, leaving behind a body of work that still stands as a pinnacle in world literature.

**PERCY BYSSHE SHELLEY** (1792–1822)   Born near Horsham, England, Shelley was the son of a wealthy landowner who sat in Parliament. At University College, Oxford University, he befriended Thomas Jefferson Hogg. Both became interested in radical philosophy and quickly became inseparable. After one year at Oxford they were both expelled for writing and circulating a pamphlet entitled "The Necessity of Atheism." Shelley married Harriet Westbrook soon after leaving Oxford. Though they had two children, the marriage was unsuccessful, and in 1814, Shelley left Harriet for Mary Wollstonecraft Godwin, the author of *Frankenstein*. After Harriet's apparent suicide, Shelley and Godwin were married. Escaping legal problems in England, he settled in Pisa, Italy, in 1820, and died in a sailing accident before his thirtieth birthday. A playwright and essayist as well as a romantic poet, Shelley is admired for his dramatic poem "Prometheus Unbound" (1820).

**LESLIE MARMON SILKO** (b. 1948)   Born in Albuquerque, New Mexico, Silko grew up on the Laguna Pueblo Reservation. She was educated in Bureau of Indian Affairs schools and at the University of New Mexico, where she graduated with highest honors. After three semesters in the American Indian Law program, Silko decided to devote her talents to writing about Native Americans. Her short stories quickly earned her a reputation; in 1974 she published a volume of poems, *Laguna Woman*. Her novel *Ceremony* (1977) was widely acclaimed and revived interest in her earlier short stories. *Storyteller* (1981) is a semiautobiographical collection of stories and poems. In 1991 the novel *Almanac of the Dead* appeared, and a collection of essays on contemporary Native American life, *Yellow Woman and a Beauty of the Spirit,* followed in 1996. Silko has taught at the University of Arizona and the University of New Mexico, but with a large award from the prestigious MacArthur Foundation, she has been, in her words, "a little less beholden to the everyday world." Her other work includes the novel *Gardens in the Dunes* (1999) and *The Turquoise Ledge* (2010), a memoir that was the first book Silko had published in ten years.

**STEVIE SMITH** (1902–1971)   Born Florence Margaret Smith in Hull, England, Stevie Smith was a secretary at Newnes Publishing Company in London from 1923 to 1953 and occasionally worked as a writer and broadcaster for the BBC. Though in the 1930s she began publishing verse, which she often illustrated herself, Smith did not reach a wide audience until 1962, with the publication of *Selected Poems* and her appearance in the Penguin Modern Poets series. She is noted for her eccentricity and mischievous humor, often involving an acerbic twist on nursery rhymes, common songs, or hymns. Force-fed with what she considered lifeless language in the New English Bible, she often aimed satirical barbs at religion. Smith won the Queen's Gold Medal for poetry in 1969, two years before her death. She published three novels in addition to her eight volumes of poetry.

**REBECCA SOLNIT** (b. 1961)   A product of the California public education system from kindergarten through graduate school, writer, historian, and activist Rebecca Solnit is the author of more than a dozen books about environment, landscape, community, art, and politics. Her most recent work, *Men Explain Things to Me* (2014), is a collection of essays focused on the presumption that men know (or think they know) more than women, which "keeps women from speaking up and from being heard when they dare," she writes.

"It trains us in self-doubt and self-limitation just as it exercises men's unsupported over-confidence." Solnit's other recent works include the New York Times Notable Books *The Faraway Nearby* (2013) and *A Paradise Built in Hell: The Extraordinary Communities That Arise in Disaster* (2009); *A Field Guide to Getting Lost* (2005); *Hope in the Dark: Untold Histories, Wild Possibilities* (2004); and *Wanderlust: A History of Walking* (1999). She received the National Book Critics Circle Award in criticism for *River of Shadows, Eadweard Muybridge and the Technological Wild West* (2003). A recipient of fellowships from the National Endowment for the Arts and the Guggenheim Foundation, Solnit is a contributing editor to *Harper's* and regular contributor to the political site Tomdispatch.com. When asked in an interview how to change people's minds about an issue without alienating them, Solnit advises, "Know what motivates you. Love does a lot more, and keeps you going in a much better way, than hate. It connects you to people."

**SOPHOCLES** (496?–406 BCE)    Born into a wealthy family at Colonus, a village just outside Athens, Sophocles distinguished himself early in life as a performer, musician, and athlete. Our knowledge of him is based on a very few ancient laudatory notices, but he certainly had a brilliant career as one of the three great Greek classical tragedians (the other two are Aeschylus, an older contemporary, and Euripides, a younger contemporary). He won the drama competition associated with the Dionysian festival (entries consisted of a tragic trilogy and a farce) at least twenty times, far more often than his two principal rivals. However, *Oedipus Rex*, his most famous tragedy, and the three other plays it was grouped with, took second place (ca. 429 BCE). He lived during the golden age of Athens, when architecture, philosophy, and the arts flourished under Pericles. In 440 BCE Sophocles was elected as one of the ten *strategoi* (military commanders), an indication of his stature in Athens. But his long life ended in sadder times, when the Peloponnesian War (431–404 BCE), between the Athenian empire and an alliance led by Sparta, darkened the region. Though Sophocles wrote some 123 plays, only seven have survived; nonetheless, these few works establish him as the greatest of the ancient Western tragedians.

**GARY SOTO** (b. 1952)    Soto was born in Fresno, California, to working-class Mexican American parents. He grew up in the San Joaquin Valley and worked as a migrant laborer in California's rich agricultural regions. Uncertain of his abilities, he began his academic career at Fresno City College, moving on to California State University at Fresno and the University of California, Irvine, where he earned an MFA (1976). In 1975 he married Carolyn Oda, a woman of Japanese ancestry. Although his work earned him recognition as early as 1975 (an Academy of American Poets Prize), his first book of poems — *The Elements of San Joaquin*, portraying grim pictures of Mexican American life in California's central valley — didn't appear until 1977. In 1985 he joined the faculty at the University of California, Berkeley, where he taught in both the English and Chicano studies departments. He gave up teaching in 1993 to become a full-time writer but returned to teaching in 2003, at the University of California, Riverside. His prolific output of poetry, memoirs, essays, and fiction continues unabated and has earned him numerous prizes, including an American Book Award from the Before Columbus Foundation for *Living up the Street* (1985). Soto's novel *Buried Onions* (1999) deals with the struggle and discomfort of a teenage boy's life in Fresno, California. *Nickel and Dime* (2000) is a fictional exploration of the interlocking lives of three Mexican American men in California. His latest publications are a novel for teenagers, *Accidental Love* (2006); a collection of stories for adolescents, *Facts of Life: Stories* (2008); two collections of poems, *Partly Cloudy: Poems of Love and Longing* (2009) and *Human Nature* (2010); and a memoir, *What Poets Are Like: Up and Down with the*

*Writing Life* (2013). One critic points out that Soto has transcended the social commentary of his early work and shifted to "a more personal, less politically motivated poetry." Another argues that "Gary Soto has become not an important Chicano poet but an important American poet."

**WILLIAM STAFFORD** (1914–1993)    Born in Hutchinson, Kansas, Stafford earned his bachelor's and master's degrees from the University of Kansas and his doctorate from the University of Iowa. Drafted during World War II, he declared himself a pacifist and conscientious objector and spent several years doing forestry and soil-conservation work instead. He taught at a small number of institutions around the country before settling on Lewis & Clark College and the Pacific Northwest. Stafford did not publish a collection of poetry until he was forty-eight years old; his first volume, *Traveling through the Dark* (1962), won the National Book Award in 1963. An astonishingly prolific writer, he kept a journal for fifty years and composed almost 22,000 poems, 3,000 of which were published in nearly 60 volumes of poetry. Among his many titles are *The Rescued Year* (1966), *Stories That Could Be True: New and Collected Poems* (1977), *Writing the Australian Crawl: Views on the Writer's Vocation* (1978), and *An Oregon Message* (1987). Stafford also contributed to numerous periodicals; authored a memoir, essays, reviews, and a children's book; and edited and translated the works of others. His many awards include a Guggenheim Fellowship, a grant from the National Endowment for the Arts, a Shelley Memorial Award, and a Western States Lifetime Achievement Award in Poetry.

**WALLACE STEVENS** (1879–1955)    Born in Reading, Pennsylvania, Stevens graduated from Harvard University in 1900, worked for a year as a reporter for the New York *Herald Tribune*, graduated from New York University Law School in 1903, and practiced law in New York for twelve years. From 1916 to 1955, Stevens worked for the Hartford Accident and Indemnity Company, where he was appointed vice president in 1934. He was in his forties when he published his first book of poetry, *Harmonium, Ideas of Order* (1923). Stevens argued that poetry is a "supreme fiction" that shapes chaos and provides order to both nature and human relationships. He illuminates his philosophy in *Ideas of Order* (1935) and *Notes toward a Supreme Fiction* (1942). His *Collected Poems* (1954) won the Pulitzer Prize and established him as a major American poet.

**PABLO PIÑERO STILLMANN** (b. 1982)    Stillmann moved from Mexico City to the Midwest in 2009 to attend graduate school. He has received fellowships from the Foundation for Mexican Literature and Indiana University. His work has appeared or is forthcoming in the *Normal School*, *Rumpus*, *Cream City Review*, *Brevity*, *Bodega*, and other journals. He lives and writes in Indianapolis.

**JONATHAN SWIFT** (1667–1745)    Born in Dublin, Ireland, of English parents, Swift moved to England following his graduation from Trinity College, Dublin. In 1695 he was ordained minister of the Anglican Church of Ireland and five years later became a parish priest in Laracor, Ireland. The conduct of church business took Swift to England frequently, where his wit and skill in defense of Tory politics made him many influential friends. He was rewarded for his efforts in 1713, when Queen Anne appointed him dean of St. Patrick's Cathedral in Dublin. The accession of George I to the throne in the following year, followed by the Tory's loss of the government to Whig control, ended the political power of Swift and his friends. He spent the rest of his life as dean of St. Patrick's, writing during this period his most celebrated satirical narrative, *Gulliver's Travels* (1726), and his most savage essay, "A Modest Proposal" (1729). Among his many other works are *A Tale of a Tub* and *The Battle of the Books* (both 1704), and many poems.

**AMY TAN** (b. 1952)   Tan's parents emigrated from China to Oakland, California, before she was born, and she grew up in a rather traditional Chinese household. She earned a BA (1973) and an MA (1974) from San Jose State University and spent an additional two years in postgraduate study at the University of California at Berkeley. Her shift from a premed program to English and linguistics caused a serious break with her mother, and they didn't speak for two years. She was a writer from the outset and earned her living for several years as a medical and freelance technical writer. But her interest in fiction led her to the Squaw Valley Community of Writers, and shortly after returning from a trip to China, she published her first novel, *The Joy Luck Club* (1989), consisting of sixteen interwoven stories that reveal the struggles of four Chinese mothers with their sometimes rebellious daughters. Four more novels followed: *The Kitchen God's Wife* (1991), *The Hundred Secret Senses* (1995), *The Year of No Flood* (1995), and *The Bonesetter's Daughter* (2001). Her most recent publications are the collection of essays *The Opposite of Fate* (2003), as well as the novels *Saving Fish from Drowning* (2005), *Rules for Virgins* (2012), and *The Valley of Amazement* (2013).

**ALFRED, LORD TENNYSON** (1809–1892)   Tennyson was born in Lincolnshire and attended Trinity College, Cambridge (1828–31), where he won the Chancellor's Medal for poetry in 1829. His 1842 collection, *Poems*, was not well received, but he gained prominence and Queen Victoria's favor with the 1850 publication of *In Memoriam*, an elegy written over seventeen years and inspired by the untimely death of his friend Arthur Hallam in 1833. That same year he married Emily Sellwood, after what had been a fourteen-year engagement. In 1850 he was named poet laureate of England after Wordsworth's death. His works include *Maud and Other Poems* (1855) and *Idylls of the King* (1859), based on the legendary exploits of King Arthur and the knights of the Round Table.

**DYLAN THOMAS** (1914–1953)   Born in Swansea, Wales, Thomas decided to pursue a writing career directly after grammar school. At age twenty he published his first collection, *Eighteen Poems* (1934), but his lack of a university degree deprived him of most opportunities to earn a living as a writer in England. Consequently, his early life (as well as the lives of his wife and children) was darkened by a poverty compounded by his free spending and heavy drinking. A self-proclaimed romanticist, Thomas called his poetry a "record of [his] struggle from darkness towards some measure of light." *The Map of Love* appeared in 1939 and *Deaths and Entrances* in 1946. Later, as a radio playwright and screenwriter, Thomas delighted in the sounds of words, sometimes at the expense of sense. *Under Milk Wood* (produced in 1953) is filled with his private, onomatopoetic language. He suffered from alcoholism and lung ailments and died in a New York hospital in 1953. Earlier that year, he noted in his *Collected Poems*: "These poems, with all their crudities, doubts and confusions are written for the love of man and in Praise of God, and I'd be a damn fool if they weren't."

**LEO TOLSTOY** (1828–1910)   Born in Russia into a family of aristocratic landowners, Tolstoy cut short his university education and joined the army, serving among the primitive Cossacks, who became the subject of his first novel, *The Cossacks* (1863). Tolstoy left the army and traveled abroad, but was disappointed by Western materialism and returned home. After a brief period in St. Petersburg, he became bored with the life of literary celebrity and returned to his family estate. There he wrote his two greatest novels, *War and Peace* (1869) and *Anna Karenina* (1877). Around 1876, Tolstoy experienced a spiritual crisis that ultimately led him to reject his former beliefs, way of life, and literary works. He adopted the simple life of the Russian peasants, rejecting orthodoxy in favor of a rational Christianity that disavowed private property, class divisions, secular and institutional religious authority, as well as all art (including his own) that failed to teach the simple principles he espoused.

**NATASHA TRETHEWEY** (b. 1966)   Trethewey was born in Gulfport, Mississippi. She earned a BA in English from the University of Georgia, an MA in English and creative writing from Hollins University, and an MFA in poetry from the University of Massachusetts. She has published four collections of poetry: *Domestic Work* (2000), *Bellocq's Ophelia* (2002), *Native Guard* (2006), for which she won the 2007 Pulitzer Prize for Poetry, and *Thrall* (2012). Trethewey has also written a book of creative nonfiction, *Beyond Katrina: A Meditation on the Mississippi Gulf Coast* (2010). In addition to several fellowships from the Guggenheim Foundation, the Rockefeller Foundation, and elsewhere, she was awarded the 2008 Mississippi Governor's Award for Excellence in the Arts and named the 2008 Georgia Woman of the Year. She was inducted into the Fellowship of Southern Writers in 2009 and into the Georgia Writers Hall of Fame in 2011. In 2012 she was named poet laureate both for Mississippi and the United States. She is currently the director of the creative writing program at Emory University.

**JOHN UPDIKE** (1932–2009)   Updike was born in Shillington, Pennsylvania, and graduated from Harvard University before attending the Ruskin School of Drawing and Fine Arts in Oxford. In England, he made the acquaintance of E. B. White, who offered Updike a job at the *New Yorker*. After two years at the magazine, he left to pursue his writing. His first book of poetry, *The Carpentered Hen and Other Tame Creatures*, was published in 1958. Updike was a prolific short-story writer, poet, novelist, and critic, having written over sixty books, among them *A & P* (short stories, 1961), *Self-Consciousness: Memoirs* (1989), *Collected Poems 1953–1993* (1993), *Still Looking: Essays on American Art* (2005), and the novels *The Poorhouse Fair* (1959), *Rabbit, Run* (1960), *The Centaur* (1963), *The Witches of Eastwick* (1984), and *In the Beauty of the Lilies* (1996). His recent works include *Terrorist* (2006), *Due Considerations: Essays and Criticism* (2007), and *The Widows of Eastwick* (2008). Until he lost his battle with cancer in 2009, he was a regular contributor to the *New Yorker* and the *New York Review of Books*. His countless awards include a Guggenheim Fellowship, a National Book Award, an O. Henry Prize, a Fulbright Fellowship, a Pulitzer Prize, a National Book Critics Circle Award, a PEN/Faulkner Award, a National Medal of Arts, and a Caldecott Medal. Updike said that it was his aim to "give the mundane its beautiful due."

**HELENA MARÍA VIRAMONTES** (b. 1954)   Viramontes was one of nine children born to a construction worker and a homemaker in East Los Angeles, California. She earned degrees from Immaculate Heart College and the University of California, Irvine, and currently teaches at Cornell University. Her work has appeared in a number of anthologies; in addition, she coedited *Chicana Creativity and Criticism: Charting New Frontiers in American Literature* (1988) and *Chicana (w)rites: On Word and Film* (1995). She received a first prize for fiction from *Statement Magazine* and a fellowship from the National Endowment for the Arts. Viramontes, who writes about Chicano culture and women, is the author of three books: *The Moths and Other Stories* (1985), *Under the Feet of Jesus* (1995), and *Their Dogs Came with Them* (2007), which took her seventeen years to complete.

**ALICE WALKER** (b. 1944)   Born in Eatonton, Georgia, the eighth child of sharecroppers, Walker was educated at Spelman College and Sarah Lawrence College. She has been deeply involved in the civil rights movement, working to register voters in Georgia and on behalf of welfare rights and Head Start in Mississippi. She also worked for the Welfare Department of New York City. She has taught at Wellesley College and Yale University and been an editor of *Ms.* Her nonfiction works include a biography for children, *Langston Hughes: American Poet* (1973); numerous contributions to anthologies about African American writers; and a collection of essays, *In Search of Our Mothers' Gardens: Womanist Prose* (1983). Her novels, all dealing with the African American experience, include *The Third Life of Grange Copeland* (1973); *Meridian* (1976); *The Color Purple* (1982), which won both the Pulitzer Prize and the National Book Award; *The Temple of My Familiar* (1989); and *Possessing the Secret of Joy* (1992). Her short stories are collected in three volumes, *In Love and Trouble: Stories of Black Women* (1973), *You Can't Keep a Good Woman Down* (1981), and *The Way Forward Is with a Broken Heart* (2000). Her recent publications include the memoir *The Chicken Chronicles: Sitting with the Angels Who Have Returned with My Memories: Glorious, Rufus, Gertrude Stein, Splendor, Hortensia, Agnes of God, The Gladyses, & Babe* (2011), the poetry collection *The World Will Follow Joy: Turning Madness into Flowers* (2013), and *The Cushion in the Road: Meditation and Wandering as the Whole World Awakens to Being in Harm's Way* (2013).

**PHILLIS WHEATLEY** (1753–1784)   Wheatley was abducted from her home in Africa by slave traders and brought to Boston. There, according to an advertisement on August 3, 1761, in the *Boston Evening Post*, "A parcel of likely Negroes, imported from Africa" was offered "cheap for cash." One of them, a seven- or eight-year-old child, was bought as a house servant for Susannah Wheatley, the wife of a prosperous Boston tailor. The Wheatley family, impressed by the young African's quickness of intellect, taught her English and Christianity as well as Latin, ancient history, and classical literature. As Phillis's formidable talents developed, the family allowed her time to study and to write. Her early poems, the first of them published when she was a young teenager, appeared in local broadside sheets sold on the streets of Boston. In 1773, her fame as a poet growing, she was taken by the Wheatleys' son to London, where thirty-nine of her poems were published as *Poems on Various Subjects Religious and Moral*. The book was an instant success, and Phillis was widely honored and lionized. The "Sable Muse," as the English dubbed her, received a visit from Benjamin Franklin, America's colonial agent in Britain; the Lord Mayor of London honored her with a gift; and even Voltaire praised her poems. As arrangements were being made to present her to George III, she was recalled to America to tend to her ailing mistress. In the following years, upon the deaths of the Wheatleys, she gained her freedom; married another freed slave, John Peters; and bore three children, all of whom died in childhood. During her final years, which were marked by failing health and the burdens of menial work, she did not publish any poems. Her attempt to revive her fortunes by advertising a 300-page volume titled "Poems & Letters on various subjects dedicated to the Right Hon. Benjamin Franklin, Esq." failed to attract enough subscribers. She died, obscure and destitute, when she was about thirty.

**WALT WHITMAN** (1819–1892)  One of nine children, Whitman was born in Huntington, Long Island, in New York, and grew up in Brooklyn, where his father worked as a carpenter. At age eleven, after five years of public school, Whitman took a job as a printer's assistant. He learned the printing trade and, before his twentieth birthday, became editor of the *Long Islander*, a Huntington newspaper. He edited several newspapers in the New York area and one in New Orleans before leaving the newspaper business in 1848. He then lived with his parents, worked as a part-time carpenter, and began writing *Leaves of Grass*, which he first published at his own expense in 1855. After the Civil War (during which he was a devoted volunteer, ministering to the wounded), Whitman was fired from his job in the Department of the Interior by Secretary James Harlan, who considered *Leaves of Grass* obscene. Soon, however, he was rehired in the attorney general's office, where he remained until 1874. In 1881, after many editions, *Leaves of Grass* finally found a publisher willing to print it uncensored. Translations were enthusiastically received in Europe, but Whitman remained relatively unappreciated in the United States; not until after his death would a large audience come to admire his original and innovative expression of American individualism.

**VIRGINIA WOOLF** (1882–1941)  Woolf was born in London, where she spent most of her life. Because of her frail health and her father's Victorian attitudes about the proper role of women, she received little formal education. Nevertheless, the advantages of an upper-class family (her father, Sir Leslie Stephen, was a distinguished scholar and man of letters who hired tutors for her) and an extraordinarily powerful and inquiring mind allowed Woolf to educate herself. She began keeping a regular diary in her early teens. After moderate success with her first novels, the publication of *To the Lighthouse* (1927) and *Orlando* (1929) established her as a major novelist. While Woolf's reputation rests primarily on her novels, which helped revolutionize fictional technique, she was also a distinguished literary and social critic. A strong supporter of women's rights, she expressed her views on the subject in a series of lectures published as *A Room of One's Own* (1929) and in a collection of essays, *Three Guineas* (1938). Her reputation grew with the publication of her letters and diaries following her suicide by drowning.

**WILLIAM WORDSWORTH** (1770–1850)  Born in Cockermouth in the Lake District of England, Wordsworth was educated at Cambridge University. During a summer tour in France in 1790, Wordsworth had an affair with Annette Vallon that resulted in the birth of a daughter. The tour also made Wordsworth an ardent defender of the French Revolution of 1789 and kindled his sympathies for the plight of the common person. Wordsworth's acquaintance with Samuel Taylor Coleridge in 1795 began a close friendship that led to the collaborative publication of *Lyrical Ballads* in 1798. Wordsworth supplied a celebrated preface to the second edition in 1800, in which he announced himself a nature poet of pantheistic leanings, committed to democratic equality and the language of common people. He finished *The Prelude* in 1805, but it was not published until after his death. As he grew older, Wordsworth grew increasingly conservative, and though he continued to write prolifically, little that he wrote during the last decades of his life attained the heights of his earlier work. In 1843 he was appointed poet laureate.

**JAMES WRIGHT** (1927–1980)  Wright was born in Martins Ferry, Ohio, into a family afflicted by poverty and misfortune. His parents had never attended school beyond the eighth grade, and Wright himself graduated from high school a year late due to a nervous breakdown that forced him to take time off. After high school he joined the army and was stationed in Japan during the American occupation. After serving, he attended Kenyon College on the GI Bill, from where he graduated cum laude and Phi Beta Kappa in 1952. Wright went on to earn his MA and PhD at the University of Washington, where he studied with Theodore Roethke and Stanley Kunitz. While Wright was a graduate student, W. H. Auden selected Wright's manuscript *The Green Wall* (1957) for publication in the Yale Younger Poets Series. Wright also contributed to many literary journals during this time, such as the *Sewanee Review*, the *New Yorker*, and *New Orleans Poetry Review*. He went on to teach at the University of Minnesota, Macalester College, and New York City's Hunter College. The subjects of Wright's earlier books, *The Green Wall* and *Saint Judas* (1959), focus on profound, isolating human issues such as lost love and marginalization from society, which Wright had witnessed firsthand during his childhood. Whereas his earlier work is mostly conventional in form, Wright's later works are more open and looser in structure, as seen in *The Branch Will Not Break* (1963) and *Shall We Gather at the River* (1968). In 1971 Wright was elected a fellow of the Academy of American Poets, and his *Collected Poems* (1972) received the Pulitzer Prize for Poetry the following year. He wrote actively during this period, publishing the collections *Two Citizens* (1973), *I See the Wind* (1974), *Old Booksellers and Other Poems* (1976), *Moments of the Italian Summer* (1976), and *To a Blossoming Pear Tree* (1978). He died in New York City in 1980. Three posthumous collections of his work have been published: *This Journey* (1982), *The Temple in Nîmes* (1982), and *Above the River: The Complete Poems* (1992).

**WILLIAM BUTLER YEATS** (1865–1939)   Yeats was born in Ireland and educated in both Ireland and London. Much of his poetry and many of his plays reflect his fascination with the history of Ireland—particularly the myths and legends of its ancient, pagan past—as well as his interest in the occult. As Yeats matured, he turned increasingly to contemporary subjects, expressing his nationalism in poems about the Irish struggle for independence from England. In 1891 he became one of the founders of an Irish literary society in London, the Rhymers' Club, and of another in Dublin the following year. Already a recognized poet, Yeats helped to establish the Irish National Theater in 1899; its first production was his play *The Countess Cathleen*, written in 1892. His contribution to Irish cultural and political nationalism led to his appointment as a senator when the Irish Free State was formed in 1922. Yeats's preeminence as a poet was recognized in 1923, when he received the Nobel Prize in Literature. Among his works are *The Wanderings of Oisin and Other Poems* (1889), *The Wind among the Reeds* (1899), *The Green Helmet and Other Poems* (1910), *Responsibilities: Poems and a Play* (1914), *The Tower* (1928), and *Last Poems and Two Plays* (1939).

**KEVIN YOUNG** (b. 1970)   Young was born in Lincoln, Nebraska, and earned degrees from Harvard University and Brown University. He was a Stegner Fellow at Stanford University in the interim. He taught at the University of Georgia and Indiana University, before becoming professor of English and creative writing at Emory University. He has edited two collections in the Everyman's Library, *Blues Poems* (2003) and *Jazz Poems* (2006), and has published several volumes of his own poetry, including *Most Way Home* (1998), *To Repel Ghosts: Five Sides in B Minor* (2002), *Jelly Roll: A Blues* (2003), *Black Maria: Poems Produced and Directed* (2005), *For the Confederate Dead* (2007), and *Dear Darkness* (2008). His work has also appeared in a number of periodicals, including the *New Yorker*, the *Paris Review*, *Ploughshares*, and *Poetry*. His most recent works include the poetry collections *Ardency: A Chronicle of the Amistad Rebels* (2011), which won the Before Columbus Foundation American Book Award, and *Book of Hours* (2014), as well as the essay collection *The Gray Album: On the Blackness of Blackness* (2012), a New York Times Notable Book.

**LU XUN** (1881–1936)   Born into a prosperous Chinese family, Lu Xun was educated in the Confucian classics of poetry, history, and philosophy from a young age. His preference, however, was for the folk tales and traditional stories related to him by Ah Chang, the illiterate servant woman who raised him. Because of his family's declining fortune as he got older, Lu was forced to continue his secondary studies at government-funded military schools that specialized in Western education. In 1902 he moved to Japan and began attending a Western-style medical school, but he abandoned this track in 1906 to become a writer. He returned to China in 1909, taking on some teaching positions and working on traditional Chinese scholarship, which he considered beneath his intellect. After the revolution, which overthrew imperial rule in 1912, Lu began working for the Ministry of Education in Beijing, where he was highly regarded for renovating and expanding the Beijing Library, establishing a Natural History Museum, and establishing the Library of Popular Literature. In 1918 he published "Diary of a Madman," which was praised for being antitraditional; it earned him recognition as one of the leading writers of China's New Culture Movement. In 1920 Lu began teaching fiction and literary theory at colleges including Peking University, Beijing Normal University, and Beijing Women's College. In the 1920s he published two collections of short stories: *A Call to Arms* (1923) and *Wandering* (1926), classics that are often considered to mark the beginning of modern Chinese literature. He also published a volume of prose poetry, *Wild Grass* (1927), and an autobiographical collection of essays about his youth, *Morning Blossoms Plucked at Dusk* (1932). After developing an interest in Marxism, Lu cofounded the League of Left-Wing Writers in 1930. A year later, when the right-wing government passed strict censorship laws, he went into hiding and used a pseudonym to write essays critical of the ruling party. Described by Nobel laureate Kenzaburō Ōe as "The greatest writer Asia produced in the twentieth century," Lu published his final collection of fiction, *Old Tales Retold*, in 1935.

# Glossary of Literary Terms

**Abstract language**    Language that describes ideas, concepts, or qualities, rather than particular or specific persons, places, or things. *Beauty, courage, love* are abstract terms, as opposed to such concrete terms as *man, stone, woman.* George Washington, the Rosetta stone, and Helen of Troy are particular concrete terms. Characteristically, literature uses *concrete* language to animate *abstract* ideas and principles. When Robert Frost, in "Provide, Provide," describes the pain of impoverished and lonely old age, he doesn't speak of an old, no longer beautiful female. He writes: "The witch that came (the withered hag) / To wash the steps with pail and rag, / Was once the beauty Abishag."

**Alexandrine**    In poetry, a line containing six iambic feet (iambic hexameter). Alexander Pope, in "An Essay on Criticism," reveals his distaste for the forms in a couplet: "A needless Alexandrine ends the song, / That, like a wounded snake, drags its slow length along." *See* Meter.

**Allegory**    A narrative in verse or prose, in which abstract qualities (*death, pride, greed,* for example) are personified as characters. In Nathaniel Hawthorne's story "Young Goodman Brown" (p. 79), Brown's wife personifies faith and the old man in the forest personifies Satan.

**Alliteration**    The repetition of the same consonant sounds, usually at the beginning of words in close proximity. The *w* sounds in these lines from Robert Frost's "Provide, Provide" alliterate: "The witch that came (the withered hag) / To wash the steps with pail and rag, / Was once the beauty Abishag."

**Allusion**    A reference in a literary work to something outside the work, usually to some famous person, place, thing, event, or other literary work.

**Ambiguity**    A phrase, statement, or situation that may be understood in two or more ways. In literature, ambiguity is used to enrich meaning or achieve irony by forcing readers to consider alternative possibilities. When the duke in Robert Browning's "My Last Duchess" (p. 168) says that he "gave commands; / Then all smiles stopped together. There she stands / As if alive," the reader cannot know exactly what those commands were or whether the last words refer to the commands (as a result of which she is no longer alive) or merely refer to the skill of the painter (the painting is extraordinarily lifelike).

**Analogy**    A comparison that uses a known thing or concept to explain something unfamiliar. *See* Metaphor; Simile.

**Anapest**    A three-syllable metrical foot consisting of two unaccented syllables followed by an accented syllable. *See* Meter.

**Antagonist**    A character in a story, play, or narrative poem who stands in opposition to the hero (*see* Protagonist). The conflict between antagonist and protagonist often generates the action or plot of the story.

**Antistrophe**    *See* Strophe.

**Apostrophe**    A direct address to a person who is absent or to an abstract or inanimate entity. In one of his sonnets (p. 887), John Donne admonishes: "Death, be not proud!" And in "Lines Composed a Few Miles above Tintern Abbey," Wordsworth speaks to a river in Wales: "How oft, in spirit, have I turned to thee, / O sylvan Wye! thou wanderer through the woods."

**Archaism**   The literary use of obsolete language. When Keats, in "Ode on a Grecian Urn" (p. 889), writes: "with brede / Of marble men and maidens overwrought," he uses an archaic word for *braid* and intends an obsolete definition, "worked all over" (that is, "ornamented"), for *overwrought*.

**Archetype**   Themes, images, and narrative patterns that are universal and thus embody some enduring aspects of human experience. Some of these themes are the death and rebirth of the hero, the underground journey, and the search for the father.

**Assonance**   The repetition of vowel sounds in a line, stanza, or sentence: *road nowhere*. By using assonance that occurs at the end of words — *my, pie* — or a combination of assonance and consonance (the repetition of final consonant sounds — *fish, wish*), poets create rhyme. Some poets use assonantial and consonantial off rhymes (*see* Near rhyme). W. H. Auden, in a celebrated verse from "Five Songs," writes: "That night when joy began / Our narrowest veins to flush, / We waited for the flash / Of morning's levelled gun." *Flush* and *gun* are assonantial, *flush* and *flash* are consonantial (and, of course, alliterative).

**Atmosphere**   The general feeling or mood created in the reader by a work. *See* Mood.

**Aubade**   A love song or lyric to be performed at sunrise.

**Ballad**   A narrative poem, originally of folk origin, usually focusing on a climactic episode and told without comment. The most common ballad form consists of quatrains of alternating four- and three-stress iambic lines, with the second and fourth lines rhyming. Often, the ballad will employ a *refrain* — that is, the last line of each stanza will be identical or similar. Dudley Randall's "Ballad of Birmingham" is a twentieth-century example of the ballad tradition.

**Blank verse**   Lines of unrhymed iambic pentameter. Shakespeare's dramatic poetry is written principally in blank verse. *See* Meter.

**Caesura**   A strong pause within a line of poetry. Note the caesuras indicated by a double vertical line (‖) in these lines from Robert Browning's "My Last Duchess" (p. 168): "That's my last Duchess painted on the wall, / Looking as if she were alive, ‖ I call / That piece a wonder, now: ‖ Frà Pandolf's hands / Worked busily a day, ‖ and there she stands."

***Carpe diem***   Latin, meaning "seize the day." A work, usually a lyric poem, in which the speaker calls the attention of the auditor (often a young woman) to the shortness of youth and life and then urges the auditor to enjoy life while there is time. Andrew Marvell's "To His Coy Mistress" (p. 636) is among the best of the *carpe diem* tradition in English. The opening stanza of a famous Robert Herrick poem nicely illustrates *carpe diem* principles: "Gather ye rosebuds while ye may, / Old Time is still a-flying / And this same flower that smiles today, / Tomorrow will be dying."

**Catharsis**   A key concept in the *Poetics* of Aristotle that attempts to explain why representations of suffering and death in drama paradoxically leave the audience feeling relieved rather than depressed. According to Aristotle, the fall of a tragic hero arouses in the viewer feelings of "pity" and "terror" — pity because the hero is an individual of great moral worth and terror because the viewer identifies with and, consequently, feels vulnerable to the hero's tragic fate. Ideally, the circumstances within the drama allow viewers to experience a catharsis that purges those feelings of pity and terror and leaves them emotionally purified.

**Central intelligence**   *See* Point of view.

**Character**   A person or figure in a literary work, sometimes classified as either *flat* (quickly describable) or *round* (more developed, complex). *See* Protagonist *and* Antagonist.

**Characterization**   The means of presenting and developing a character, shown through the author's description, the character's actions or thoughts, or other characters' actions or thoughts.

**Chorus**   Originally, a group of masked dancers who chanted lyric hymns at religious festivals in ancient Greece. In the plays of Sophocles, the chorus, while circling around the altar to Dionysus, chants the odes that separate the episodes. These odes, in some respects, represented an audience's reaction to, and comment on, the action in the episodes. In Elizabethan drama, and even, on occasion, in modern drama, the chorus appears, usually as a single person who comments on the action.

**Comedy**   In drama, the representation of situations that are designed to delight and amuse and that end happily. Comedy often deals with ordinary people in their human condition, while tragedy deals with the ideal and heroic and, until recently, embodied only the high born as tragic heroes. *Compare* Tragedy.

**Conceit**   A figure of speech that establishes an elaborate parallel between unlike things. The *Petrarchan conceit* (named for the fourteenth-century Italian writer of love lyrics) was often imitated by Elizabethan sonneteers until the device became so hackneyed that Shakespeare mocked the tendency in Sonnet 130 (p. 630): "My mistress' eyes are nothing like the sun; / Coral is far more red than her lips' red; / If snow be white, why then her breasts are dun; / If hairs be wires, black wires grow on her head." The *metaphysical conceit* employs strange, even bizarre, comparisons to heighten the wit of the poem. Perhaps the most famous metaphysical conceit is John Donne's elaborate and extended parallel of a drawing compass to the souls of the couple in "A Valediction: Forbidding Mourning" (p. 632).

**Concrete language**   *See* Abstract language.

**Conflict**   The struggle of a protagonist, or main character, with forces that threaten to destroy him or her. The struggle creates suspense and is usually resolved at the end of the narrative. The force opposing the main character may be another person — the antagonist — or society (as in Harlan Ellison's "'Repent, Harlequin!' Said the Ticktockman," p. 322), or natural forces. A fourth type of conflict reflects the struggle of opposing tendencies within an individual (as in Tolstoy's "The Death of Iván Ilých," p. 801).

**Connotation**   The associative and suggestive meanings of a word, in contrast to its literal or *denotative* meaning. One might speak of an *elected official*, a relatively neutral term without connotative implications. Others might call the same person a *politician*, a more negative term; still others might call him or her a *statesman*, a more laudatory term. *Compare* Denotation.

**Consonance**   Repetition of the final consonant sounds in stressed syllables. In the second poem of W. H. Auden's "Five Songs," lines 1 and 4 illustrate consonance, as do lines 2 and 3. "That night when joy began / Our narrowest veins to flush, / We waited for the flash / Of morning's levelled gun."

**Couplet**   A pair of rhymed lines — for example, these from Andrew Marvell's "To His Coy Mistress" (p. 636): "Thus, though we cannot make our sun / Stand still, yet we will make him run."

**Dactyl**   A three-syllable metrical foot consisting of an accented syllable followed by two unaccented syllables. *See* Meter.

**Denotation**   The literal dictionary definition of a word, without associative and suggestive meanings. *See* Connotation.

**Denouement**   The final revelations that occur after the main conflict is resolved; literally, the "untying" of the plot following the climax.

**Deus ex machina**   Latin for "god from a machine." Difficulties were sometimes resolved in ancient Greek and Roman plays by a god, who was lowered to the stage by means of machinery. The term is now used to indicate unconvincing or improbable coincidences that are used to advance or resolve a plot.

**Dialect**   A variety of a language distinguished by its pronunciation, vocabulary, rhetoric, and grammar. When used in dialogue, dialect reveals a character's membership in certain groups or communities.

**Dialogue**   The exchange of words between characters in a drama or narrative.

**Diction**   The choice of words in a work of literature and hence an element of style crucial to the work's effectiveness. The diction of a story told from the point of view of an inner-city child (as in Toni Cade Bambara's "The Lesson," p. 100) will differ markedly from a similar story told from the point of view of a mature and educated adult, like the narrator of James Joyce's "Araby" (p. 121).

**Didactic**   A term applied to works with the primary and avowed purpose of persuading the reader that some philosophical, religious, or moral doctrine is true.

**Dimeter**   A line of poetry consisting of two metrical feet. *See* Meter.

**Distance**   The property that separates an author or a narrator from the actions of the characters he or she creates, thus allowing a disinterested, or aloof, narration of events. Similarly, distance allows the reader or audience to view the characters and events in a narrative dispassionately.

**Dramatic irony**   *See* Irony.

**Dramatic monologue**   A type of poem in which the speaker addresses another person (or persons) whose presence is known only from the speaker's words. During the course of the monologue, the speaker (often unintentionally) reveals his or her own character. Such poems are dramatic because the speaker interacts with another character at a specific time and place; they are monologues because the entire poem is uttered by the speaker. Robert Browning's "My Last Duchess" (p. 168), Matthew Arnold's "Dover Beach" (p. 639), and T. S. Eliot's "The Love Song of J. Alfred Prufrock" (p. 505) are dramatic monologues.

**Elegy**   Usually, a poem that laments the death of a particular person. The term often is used to describe meditative poems on the subject of human mortality. A. E. Housman's "To an Athlete Dying Young" (p. 894) is an elegy.

**End-rhyme**   *See* Rhyme.

**End-stopped line**   A line of verse that embodies a complete logical and grammatical unit. A line of verse that does not constitute a complete syntactic unit is called *run-on*. For example, in the opening lines of Robert Browning's "My Last Duchess" (p. 168): "That's my last Duchess painted on the wall, / Looking as if she were alive. I call / That piece a wonder, now . . . ," the opening line is end-stopped while the second line is run-on, because the direct object of *call* runs on to the third line.

**English sonnet**   Also called *Shakespearean sonnet*. *See* Sonnet.

**Enjambment**   The use of run-on lines. *See* End-stopped line.

**Epigraph**   In literature, a short quotation or observation related to the theme and placed at the head of the work. T. S. Eliot's "The Love Song of J. Alfred Prufrock" (p. 505) has an epigraph.

**Epiphany**   In literature, a showing forth, or sudden manifestation. James Joyce used the term to indicate a sudden illumination that enables a character (and, presumably, the reader) to understand his situation. The narrator of Joyce's "Araby" (p. 121) experiences an epiphany toward the end of the story, as does Leo Tolstoy's Iván Ilých (p. 801).

**Epode**  *See* Strophe.

**Euphony**  Language embodying sounds pleasing to the ear.

**Exposition**  Information supplied to readers and audiences that enables them to understand narrative action. Often, exposition establishes what has occurred before the narrative begins, or informs the audience about relationships among principal characters. The absence of exposition from some modern literature, particularly modern drama, contributes to the unsettling feelings sometimes experienced by the audience.

**Farce**  A type of comedy, usually satiric, that relies on exaggerated character types, ridiculous situations, and often horseplay.

**Feminine rhyme**  A two-syllable rhyme in which the second syllable is unstressed, as in the second and fourth lines of these verses from James Fenton's "God, A Poem": "A nasty surprise in a sandwich, / A drawing-pin caught in your sock, / The limpest of shakes from a hand which / You'd thought would be firm as a rock."

**Figurative language**  A general term covering the many ways in which language is used nonliterally. *See* Hyperbole, Irony, Metaphor, Metonymy, Paradox, Simile, Symbol, Synecdoche, Understatement.

**First-person narrator**  *See* Point of view.

**Foot**  *See* Meter.

**Free verse**  Poetry, usually unrhymed, that does not adhere to the metrical regularity of traditional verse. Although free verse is not metrically regular, it is nonetheless clearly more rhythmic than prose and makes use of other aspects of poetic discourse to achieve its effects.

**Heroic couplet**  Iambic pentameter lines that rhyme *aa*, *bb*, *cc*, and so on. Usually, heroic couplets are *closed*—that is, the couplet's end coincides with a major syntactic unit so that the line is end-stopped. These lines from Alexander Pope's "Essay on Man" illustrate the form: "And, spite of pride, in erring reason's spite, / One truth is clear; Whatever IS, IS RIGHT."

**Hexameter**  A line of verse consisting of six metrical feet. *See* Meter.

**Hubris**  In Greek tragedy, arrogance resulting from excessive pride.

**Hyperbole**  Figurative language that embodies overstatement or exaggeration. The boast of the speaker in Robert Burns's "A Red, Red Rose" (p. 638) is hyperbolic: "And I will luve thee still, my dear, / Til a' the seas gang dry."

**Iamb**  A metrical foot consisting of an unstressed syllable followed by a stressed syllable. *See* Meter.

**Imagery**  Language that embodies an appeal to a physical sense, usually sight, although the words may invoke sound, smell, taste, and touch as well. The term is often applied to all figurative language. *Images* illustrate a concept, thing, or process by appealing to the senses.

**Internal rhyme**  *See* Rhyme.

**Irony**  Figurative language in which the intended meaning differs from the literal meaning. *Verbal irony* includes overstatement (hyperbole), understatement, and opposite statement. The following lines from Robert Burns's "A Red, Red Rose" (p. 638) embody overstatement: "As fair art thou, my bonnie lass, / So deep in luve am I; / And I will luve thee still, my dear, / Til a' the seas gang dry." These lines from Andrew Marvell's "To His Coy Mistress" (p. 636) understate: "The grave's a fine and private place, / But none, I think, do there embrace." W. H. Auden's ironic conclusion to "The Unknown Citizen" (p. 360) reveals opposite statement: "Was he free? Was he happy? The question is absurd: / Had anything been wrong, we should certainly have heard." *Dramatic irony* occurs when a reader or an audience knows things a character does not and, consequently, hears things differently. For example, in Shakespeare's *Othello* (p. 664), the audience knows that Iago is Othello's enemy, but Othello doesn't. Hence, the audience's understanding of Iago's speeches to Othello differs markedly from Othello's.

**Italian sonnet**   Also called *Petrarchan sonnet*. *See* Sonnet.

**Lyric**   Originally, a song accompanied by lyre music. Now, a relatively short poem expressing the thought or feeling of a single speaker. Almost all the nondramatic poetry in this anthology is lyric poetry.

**Metaphor**   A figurative expression consisting of two elements in which one element is provided with special attributes by being equated with a second, unlike element. *See* Simile.

**Meter**   Refers to recurrent patterns of accented and unaccented syllables in verse. A metrical unit is called a *foot*, and there are four basic accented patterns. An *iamb*, or *iambic foot*, consists of an unaccented syllable followed by an accented syllable (bĕfóre, tŏdáy). A *trochee*, or *trochaic foot*, consists of an accented syllable followed by an unaccented syllable (fúnnў, phántŏm). An *anapest*, or *anapestic foot*, consists of two unaccented syllables followed by an accented syllable (in the line "If év ‖ erўthĭng háp ‖ pĕns thăt cán't ‖ bĕ dóne," the second and third metrical feet are anapests). A *dactyl*, or *dactylic foot*, consists of a stressed syllable followed by two unstressed syllables (sýllăblĕ, métrĭcăl). One common variant, consisting of two stressed syllables, is called a *spondee*, or *spondaic foot* (dáybréak, moónshíne).

Lines are classified according to the number of metrical feet they contain (an iambic hexameter line is an *alexandrine*):

| | |
|---|---|
| one foot | monometer |
| two feet | dimeter |
| three feet | trimeter |
| four feet | tetrameter |
| five feet | pentameter |
| six feet | hexameter |

Here are some examples of various metrical patterns:

| | |
|---|---|
| Tŏ eách ‖ hĭs súff ‖ erĭngs: áll ‖ ăre mén, | *iambic tetrameter* |
| Cŏndemnéd ‖ ălíkĕ ‖ tŏ groán; | *iambic trimeter* |
| Ónce ŭp ‖ ón ă ‖ mídnĭght ‖ dréarў, ‖ whíle Ĭ ‖ | |
| póndĕred ‖ wéak ănd ‖ wéarў | *trochaic octameter* |
| Thĕ Ăssýr ‖ iăn căme dówn ‖ líkĕ ă wólf ‖ ŏn thĕ fóld | *anapestic tetrameter* |
| Iš thís ‖ thĕ rég ‖ iŏn, thís ‖ thĕ soíl, ‖ thĕ clíme, | *iambic pentameter* |
| Fóllŏw ĭt ‖ úttĕrlў, | *dactylic dimeter* |
| Hópe bĕ ‖ yónd hópe: | *dimeter line — trochee and spondee* |

**Metonymy**   A figure of speech in which a word stands for a closely related idea. In the expression "The pen is mightier than the sword," *pen* and *sword* are metonyms for written ideas and physical force.

**Monologue**   A long, uninterrupted speech by a character.

**Mood**   The atmosphere or general feeling of a work. *See* Atmosphere.

**Muses**   The nine daughters of Zeus and Mnemosyne (memory) who preside over various humanities. Although there are some variations, generally they may be assigned as follows: Calliope, epic poetry; Clio, history; Erato, lyric poetry; Euterpe, music; Melpomene, tragedy; Polyhymnia, sacred poetry; Terpsichore, dance; Thalia, comedy; and Urania, astronomy.

**Narrator**   The speaker of the story, not to be confused with the author. For kinds of narrators, *see* Point of view.

**Near rhyme**   Also called *off rhyme, slant rhyme,* or *oblique rhyme.* Usually the occurrence of consonance where rhyme is expected, as in *pearl, alcohol,* or *heaven, given. See* Rhyme.

**Octave**   An eight-line stanza. More often, the opening eight-line section of an Italian sonnet, rhymed *abbaabba,* followed by the sestet that concludes the poem. *See* Sonnet.

**Ode**   Usually, a long, serious poem on exalted subjects, often in the form of an address. Keats's "Ode on a Grecian Urn" (p. 889) is representative. In Greek dramatic poetry, odes consisting of three parts — the *strophe,* the *antistrophe,* and the *epode* — were sung by the chorus between the episodes of the play. *See* Strophe.

**Off rhyme**   *See* Near rhyme.

**Omniscient narrator**   *See* Point of view.

**Onomatopoeia**   Language that sounds like what it means. Words like *buzz, bark,* and *hiss* are onomatopoetic. Also, sound patterns that reinforce the meaning may be designated onomatopoetic. Alexander Pope illustrates such onomatopoeia in this passage from "An Essay on Criticism":

> 'Tis not enough no harshness gives offense,
> The sound must seem an echo to the sense:
> Soft is the strain when Zephyr gently blows,
> And the smooth stream in smoother numbers flows;
> But when loud surges lash the sounding shore,
> The hoarse, rough verse should like the torrent roar:
> When Ajax strives some rock's vast weight to throw,
> The line too labors, and the words move slow;
> Not so, when swift Camilla scours the plain,
> Flies o'er the unbending corn, and skims along the main.

**Opposite statement**   *See* Irony.

**Ottava rima**   An eight-line, iambic pentameter stanza rhymed *abababcc.* Originating with the Italian poet Boccaccio, the form was made popular in English poetry by Milton, Keats, and Byron, among others.

**Oxymoron**   Literally, "acutely silly." A figure of speech in which contradictory ideas are combined to create a condensed paradox: *thunderous silence, sweet sorrow, wise fool.*

**Paean**   In classical Greek drama, a hymn of praise, usually honoring Apollo. Now, any lyric that joyously celebrates its subject.

**Paradox**   A statement that seems self-contradictory or absurd but is, somehow, valid. The conclusion of Donne's "Death, Be Not Proud" (p. 887) illustrates: "One short sleep past, we wake eternally / And death shall be no more; Death, thou shalt die." In Holy Sonnet 14, Donne, speaking of his relationship with God, writes: "Take me to You, imprison me, for I, / Except You enthrall me, never shall be free, / Nor ever chaste, except You ravish me."

**Parody**   An imitation of a work using the original's form or content as a model, meant to criticize or create a humorous effect.

**Pastoral**   *Pastor* is Latin for "shepherd," and the pastoral is a poetic form invented by ancient Roman writers that deals with the complexities of the human condition as if they exist in a world peopled by idealized rustic shepherds. Pastoral poetry suggests that country life is superior to urban life. In the hands of such English poets as Marlowe and Milton, the pastoral embodies highly conventionalized and artificial language and situations.

**Pentameter**    A line containing five metrical feet. *See* Meter.

**Persona**    Literally, "actor's mask." The term is applied to a first-person narrator in fiction or poetry. The persona's views may differ from the author's.

**Personification**    The attribution of human qualities to nonhuman things, such as animals, aspects of nature, or even ideas and processes. When Donne exclaims in "Death, Be Not Proud" (p. 887), "Death, thou shalt die," he uses personification.

**Petrarchan sonnet**    Also called *Italian sonnet*. *See* Sonnet.

**Plot**    A series of events in a story or drama that bear a significant relationship to each other. E. M. Forster illuminates the definition: " 'The King died, and then the Queen died,' is a story. 'The King died, and then the Queen died of grief,' is a plot."

**Poetic license**    Variation from standard word order to satisfy the demands of rhyme and meter.

**Point of view**    The person or intelligence a writer of fiction creates to tell the story to the reader. The major techniques are: (1) *first person*, where the story is told by someone (often, though not necessarily, the principal character) who identifies himself or herself as "I," as in James Joyce's "Araby" (p. 121); (2) *third person*, where the story is told by someone (not identified as "I") who is not a participant in the action and who refers to the characters by name or as "he," "she," and "they," as in Harlan Ellison's " 'Repent, Harlequin!' Said the Ticktockman" (p. 322); (3) *omniscient*, a variation on the third person, where the narrator knows everything about the characters and events, can move about in time and place as well as from character to character at will, and can, whenever he or she wishes, enter the mind of any character, as in Tolstoy's "The Death of Iván Ilých" (p. 801); (4) *central intelligence*, another variation on the third person, where narrative elements are limited to what a single character sees, thinks, and hears, as in Toni Cade Bambara's "The Lesson" (p. 100). *See also* Unreliable narrator.

**Prose**    Ordinary written or spoken expression, resembling everyday language or speech.

**Prosody**    The study of the elements of versification, such as *rhyme, meter, stanzaic patterns*, and so on.

**Protagonist**    Originally, the first actor in a Greek drama. In Greek, *agon* means "contest." Hence, the protagonist is the hero, the main character in a narrative, in conflict either with his or her situation or with another character. *See* Antagonist.

**Quatrain**    A four-line stanza.

**Refrain**    The repetition within a poem of a group of words, often at the end of ballad stanzas.

**Rhyme**    The repetition of the final stressed vowel sound and any sounds following (*cat, rat; debate, relate; pelican, belly can*) produces perfect rhyme. When the last stressed syllable rhymes, the rhyme is called masculine (*cat, rat*). Two-syllable rhymes with unstressed last syllables are called feminine (*ending, bending*). When rhyming words appear at the end of lines, the poem is *end-rhymed*. When rhyming words appear within one line, the line contains *internal rhyme*. When the correspondence in sounds is imperfect (*heaven, given; began, gun*), *off rhyme, slant rhyme*, or *near rhyme* is produced.

**Rhythm**    The quality created by the relationship between stressed and unstressed syllables. A regular pattern of alternation between stressed and unstressed syllables produces *meter*. Irregular alternation of stressed and unstressed syllables produces *free verse*. Compare the rhythm of the following verses from Robert Frost's "Stopping by

Woods on a Snowy Evening" (p. 900) and Walt Whitman's "Out of the Cradle Endlessly Rocking":

> Whose woods these are I think I know.
> His house is in the village though;
> He will not see me stopping here
> To watch his woods fill up with snow.

> Out of the cradle endlessly rocking,
> Out of the mocking-bird's throat, the musical shuttle,
> Out of the Ninth-month midnight,
> Over the sterile sands and the fields beyond, where the child leaving his bed
>     wander'd alone, bareheaded, barefoot,
> Down from the shower'd halo.

**Run-on line**   *See* End-stopped line.

**Satire**   Writing in a comic mode that holds a subject up to scorn and ridicule, often with the purpose of correcting human vice and folly. Harlan Ellison's "'Repent, Harlequin!' Said the Ticktockman" (p. 322) satirizes a society obsessed with time and order.

**Scansion**   The analysis of patterns of stressed and unstressed syllables to establish the metrical or rhythmical pattern of a poem.

**Sestet**   The six-line resolution of a Petrarchan sonnet. *See* Sonnet.

**Setting**   The place, time, and social context in which a work occurs. Often the setting contributes significantly to the story; for example, the tawdry gloom at the fair in James Joyce's "Araby" (p. 121) destroys the narrator's expectations.

**Shakespearean sonnet**   Also called *English sonnet*. *See* Sonnet.

**Simile**   Similar to metaphor, the simile is a comparison of unlike things introduced by the words *like* or *as*. For example, Robert Burns, in "A Red, Red Rose" (p. 638), exclaims, "O My Luve's like a red, red rose," and Shakespeare mocks extravagant similes when he admits in Sonnet 130, "My mistress' eyes are nothing like the sun" (p. 630).

**Slant rhyme**   *See* Rhyme.

**Soliloquy**   A dramatic convention in which an actor, alone on the stage, speaks his or her thoughts aloud. Iago's speech that closes act I of Shakespeare's *Othello* (p. 664) is a soliloquy, as is Othello's speech in act III, scene 3, lines 258–79.

**Sonnet**   A lyric poem of fourteen lines, usually of iambic pentameter. The two major types are the Petrarchan (or Italian) and Shakespearean (or English). The Petrarchan sonnet is divided into an octave (the first eight lines, rhymed *abbaabba*) and sestet (the final six lines, usually rhymed *cdecde* or *cdcdcd*). The Shakespearean sonnet consists of three quatrains and a concluding couplet, rhymed *abab cdcd efef gg*. In general, the sonnet establishes some issue in the octave or three quatrains and then resolves it in the sestet or final couplet. Robert Frost's "Design" (p. 901) is a Petrarchan sonnet; several Shakespearean sonnets appear in the text.

**Spondee**   A metrical foot consisting of two stressed syllables, usually a variation within a metrical line. *See* Meter.

**Stanza**   The grouping of a fixed number of verse lines in a recurring metrical and rhyme pattern. Keats's "Ode on a Grecian Urn" (p. 889), for example, employs ten-line stanzas rhymed *ababcdecde*.

**Stream-of-consciousness technique**   The narrative technique that attempts to reproduce the full and uninterrupted flow of a character's mental process, in which ideas, memories, and sense impressions may intermingle without logical transitions. Writers using this technique sometimes abandon conventional rules of syntax and punctuation.

**Strophe**   In Greek tragedy, the unit of verse the chorus chanted as it moved to the left in a dance rhythm. The chorus sang the *antistrophe* as it moved to the right and the *epode* while standing still.

**Style**   The way an author expresses his or her matter. Style embodies, and depends upon, all the choices an author makes — the diction, syntax, figurative language, and sound patterns of the piece.

**Subplot**   A second plot, usually involving minor characters. The subplot is subordinate to the principal plot but is often resolved by events that figure in the main plot. For example, Iago's manipulation of Roderigo in Shakespeare's *Othello* (p. 664) is a subplot that enters the main plot and figures prominently in the play's climax.

**Symbol**   An object, an action, or a person that represents more than itself. The urn in Keats's "Ode on a Grecian Urn" (p. 889) symbolizes the cold immortality of art. The symbolism arises from the *context*. *Public symbols*, in contrast to these *contextual symbols*, are objects, actions, or persons that history, myth, or legend has invested with meaning — the cross, Helen of Troy, a national flag.

**Synecdoche**   A figure of speech in which a part is used to signify the whole. In "Elegy Written in a Country Churchyard," Thomas Gray writes of "Some heart once pregnant with celestial fire; / Hands that the rod of empire might have swayed." That heart, and those hands, of course, refer to whole persons who are figuratively represented by significant parts.

**Synesthesia**   An image that uses a second sensory impression to modify the primary sense impression. When one speaks of a "cool green," for example, the primary *visual* evocation of green is combined with the *tactile* sensation of coolness. Keats, in "Ode to a Nightingale," asks for a drink of wine "Tasting of Flora and the country green, / Dance, and Provençal song, and sunburnt mirth!" Here, the *taste* of wine is synesthetically extended to the sight of flowers and meadows, the movement of dance, the sound of song, and the heat of the sun.

**Tetrameter**   A verse line containing four metrical feet. *See* Meter.

**Theme**   The statement or underlying idea of a literary work, advanced through the concrete elements of character, action, and setting. The theme of Harlan Ellison's "'Repent, Harlequin!' Said the Ticktockman" (p. 322), in which an ordinary person defies an oppressive system, might be that to struggle against dehumanizing authority is obligatory.

**Third-person narrator**   A voice telling a story who refers to characters by name or as "he," "she," or "they." *See* Point of view.

**Tone**   The attitude embodied in the language a writer chooses. The tone authors take in a work toward readers, the subject matter, or themselves might be sad, joyful, ironic, solemn, playful. Notice, for example, the somber tone of Matthew Arnold's "Dover Beach" (p. 639).

**Tragedy**   The dramatic representation of serious and important actions that culminate in catastrophe for the protagonist, or chief actor, in the play. Aristotle saw tragedy as the fall of a noble figure from a high position and happiness to defeat and misery as a result of *hamartia*, some misjudgment or frailty of character. *Compare* Comedy.

**Trimeter**   A verse line consisting of three metrical feet. *See* Meter.

**Triplet**   A sequence of three verse lines that rhyme.

**Trochee**   A metrical foot consisting of a stressed syllable followed by an unstressed syllable. *See* Meter.

**Understatement**   A figure of speech that represents something as less important than it really is — hence, a form of irony. When in Robert Browning's "My Last Duchess" (p. 168) the duke asserts, "This grew; I gave commands; / Then all smiles stopped together," the words ironically understate what was likely an order for his wife's execution.

**Unreliable narrator**   The speaker or voice of a work who is not able to accurately or objectively report events, as in Charlotte Perkins Gilman's "The Yellow Wallpaper" (p. 442).

**Verse**   A stanza of a poem. More generally, verse can be used interchangeably with the term *poetry*.

**Villanelle**   A French verse form of nineteen lines (of any length) divided into six stanzas — five tercets and a final quatrain — employing two rhymes and two refrains. The refrains consist of lines 1 (repeated as lines 6, 12, and 18) and 3 (repeated as lines 9, 15, and 19). Dylan Thomas's "Do Not Go Gentle into That Good Night" (p. 903) is a villanelle.

**Michael Clark.** From "Flannery O'Connor's 'A Good Man Is Hard to Find': The Moment of Grace." From *English Language Notes.* Used with permission of the Board of Regents, University of Colorado.

**Lucille Clifton.** "There Is a Girl Inside." Copyright © 1977, 1980 by Lucille Clifton. First appeared in *American Poetry Review.* Now appears in *The Collected Poems of Lucille Clifton 1965–2010,* published BOA Editions, Ltd. Reprinted by permission of Curtis Brown, Ltd.

**Judith Ortiz Cofer.** "American History" from *The Latin Deli: Prose and Poetry.* Copyright © 1993 by Judith Ortiz Cofer. Reprinted with the permission of the University of Georgia Press. "Latin Women Pray" from *Reaching for the Mainland and Selected New Poems* by Judith Ortiz Cofer; Bilingual Press/Editorial Bilingüe, 1995, Tempe, AZ. Reprinted by permission of Bilingual Press/Editorial Bilinque.

**Victor Hernández Cruz.** "Problems with Hurricanes" from *Maraca: New and Selected Poems 1965–2000.* Copyright © 2001 by Victor Hernández Cruz. Reprinted with the permission of The Permissions Company, Inc., on behalf of Coffee House Press, www.coffeehousepress.org.

**Countee Cullen.** "Incident," from *On These I Stand* by Countee Cullen. Copyright © 1947 by Harper & Bros., NY, renewed 1975 by Ida M. Cullen. Copyrights held by Amistad Research Center, Tulane University, administered by Thompson and Thompson, Brooklyn, NY.

**Gregory Djanikian.** "Sailing to America" from *Falling Deeply into America.* Copyright © 1989 by Gregory Djanikian. Reprinted with the permission of The Permissions Company, Inc., on behalf of Carnegie Mellon University Press. www.cmu.edu/university press.

**Tishani Doshi.** "Lament I" and "The Immigrant's Song" from *Everything Begins Elsewhere.* Copyright © 2013 by Tishani Doshi. Used with the permissions of The Permission Company, Inc., on behalf of Copper Canyon Press, www.coppercanyonpress.org.

**Brian Doyle.** "Pop Art." From *Brevity,* Issue 10, Fall 2001. Used with permission from the author.

**T. S. Eliot.** "The Love Song of J. Alfred Prufrock" from *Collected Poems 1909–1962* by T. S. Eliot. Copyright © 1936 by Houghton Mifflin Harcourt Publishing Company. Copyright © renewed 1964 by Thomas Stearns Eliot. Reprinted by permission of Houghton Mifflin Harcourt Publishing Company and Faber & Faber Ltd. All rights reserved.

**Harlan Ellison\*.** "'Repent, Harlequin!' Said the Tictockman." Copyright © 1965 by Harlan Ellison. Renewed, 1993 by The Kilimanjaro Corporation. Reprinted by arrangement with, and permission of, the Author and the Author's agent, Richard Curtis Associates, Inc., New York. All rights reserved. Harlan Ellison is a registered trademark of The Kilimanjaro Corporation.

**Ralph Ellison.** "Battle Royal" copyright © 1948 and renewed 1976 by Ralph Ellison; from *Invisible Man* by Ralph Ellison. Used by permission of Random House, an imprint and division of Penguin Random House LLC. All rights reserved.

**Louise Erdrich.** "Dear John Wayne" copyright © originally published in *Jacklight,* currently collected in *Original Fire: New and Selected Poems.* Copyright © 1984 by Louise Erdrich, used by permission of The Wylie Agency LLC.

**Faiz Ahmed Faiz.** "Be Near Me" from *The True Subject,* translated by Naomi Lazard. © 1987 Princeton University Press. Reprinted by permission of the publisher via Rightslink.

**Alan Feldman.** "My Century" from *A Sail to Great Island* © 2004 by the Board of Regents of the University of Wisconsin System. Reprinted by permission of The University of Wisconsin Press.

**Lawrence Ferlinghetti.** "In Goya's Greatest scenes we seem to see" from *A Coney Island of the Mind,* copyright © 1958 by Lawrence Ferlilnghetti. Reprinted by permission of New Directions Publishing Corp.

**Carolyn Forche.** "The Colonel" from *The Country Between Us* by Carolyn Forche. Copyright © 1981 by Carolyn Forche. Originally appeared in *Women's International Resource Exchange.* Reprinted by permission of HarperCollins Publishers.

**Daisy Fried.** "Econo Motel, Ocean City" from *Women's Poetry: Poems and Advice* by Daisy Fried © 2013. Reprinted by permission of the University of Pittsburgh Press.

**Robert Frost.** "The Road Not Taken," "Birches," "Fire and Ice," "After Apple-Picking," "Out, Out," "Nothing Gold Can Stay," "Stopping by Woods on a Snowy Evening," and "Design," from the book *The Poetry of Robert Frost* edited by Edward Connery Lathem. Copyright © 1923, 1930, 1939, 1969 by Henry Holt and Company, copyright © 1936, 1944, 1951, 1958 by Robert Frost, copyright © 1964, 1967 by Lesley Frost Ballantine. Permission granted by Henry Holt and Company. All rights reserved.

**Rivka Galchen.** "Wild Berry Blue" from *American Innovations* by Rivka Galchen. Copyright © 2014 by Rivka Galchen. Reprinted by permission of Farrar, Straus and Giroux.

**Shirley Geok-lin Lim.** "Learning to Love America" from *What the Fortune Teller Didn't Say*. Copyright © 1998 by Shirley Geok-lin Lim. Reprinted with the permission of The Permissions Company, Inc., on behalf of West End Press, Albuquerque, New Mexico, http://www.westendpress.org.

**Dagoberto Gilb.** "I Knew She Was Beautiful" first published in *The New Yorker*. Reprinted by permission of the author.

**Allen Ginsberg.** "A Supermarket In California" from *Collected Poems 1947–1980* by Allen Ginsberg. Copyright © 1955 by Allen Ginsberg. Reprinted by permission of HarperCollins Publishers.

**Malcolm Gladwell.** "Small Change: Why the Revolution Will Not Be Tweeted," *The New Yorker*, October 4, 2010. Copyright © 2010 by Malcom Gladwell. Used with permission from the author.

**Louise Glück.** "The School Children" from *The First Four Books of Poems* by Louise Glück. Copyright © 1968, 1971, 1972, 1973, 1974, 1975, 1976, 1977, 1978, 1979, 1980, 1985, 1995 by Louise Glück. Reprinted by permission of HarperCollins Publishers. "A Myth of Innocence" from *Poems 1962–2012* by Louise Glück. Copyright © 2012 by Louise Glück. Reprinted by permission of Farrar, Straus & Giroux, LLC.

**Allegra Goodman.** "Apple Cake" from *The New Yorker*, July 7, 2014. Copyright © 2014. Reprinted by permission of Irene Skolnick Literary Agency.

**William Greenway.** "Pit Pony" from *Where We've Been* by William Greenway. Reprinted by permission of the author.

**Mark Halliday.** "Chicken Salad" from *Keep This Forever*. Published by Tupelo Press, Copyright 2008 by Mark Halliday.

**Robert Hayden.** "Those Winter Sundays." Copyright © 1966 by Robert Hayden, from *Collected Poems of Robert Hayden* by Robert Hayden, edited by Frederick Glaysher. Used by permission of Liveright Publishing Corporation.

**Terrance Hayes.** "Root" from *Wind in a Box* by Terrance Hayes, copyright © 2006 by Terrance Hayes. Used by permission of Penguin Books, an imprint of Penguin Publishing Group, a division of Penguin Random House LLC.

**Seamus Heaney.** "Mid-Term Break" and "Valediction" from *Opened Ground: Selected Poems 1966–1996* by Seamus Heaney. Copyright © 1998 by Seamus Heaney. Reprinted by permission of Farrar, Straus and Giroux.

**Anthony Hecht.** "After the Rain" from *Collected Earlier Poems* by Anthony Hecht, copyright © 1990 by Anthony E. Hecht. Used by permission of Alfred A. Knopf, an imprint of the Knopf Doubleday Publishing Group, a division of Penguin Random House LLC. All rights reserved.

**Ernest Hemingway.** "Hills Like White Elephants" from *The Short Stories of Ernest Hemingway* by Ernest Hemingway. Copyright © 1927 by Charles Scribner's Sons. Copyright renewed © 1955 by Ernest Hemingway. Reprinted with the permission of Scribner, a division of Simon & Schuster, Inc. All rights reserved.

**Juan Filipe Herrera.** "187 Reasons Why Mexicans Can't Cross the Border" from *187 Reasons Why Mexicans Can't Cross the Border:Undocuments 1971–2007*. Copyright © 2007 by Juan Filipe Herrera. Reprinted with the permission of The Permissions Company, Inc., on behalf of City Lights, www.citylights.com.

**Andrea Hollander.** "Betrayal" © 2009 by Andrea Hollander. Reprinted by permission of the author.

**Marie Howe.** "What the Living Do" from *What the Living Do* by Marie Howe. Copyright © 1997 by Marie Howe. Used by permission of W. W. Norton & Company, Inc.

**Langston Hughes.** "I, Too" and "Harlem" from *The Collected Poems of Langston Hughes* by Langston Hughes, edited by Arnold Rampersad with David Roessel, Associate Editor, copyright © 1994 by the Estate of Langston Hughes. Used by permission of Alfred A. Knopf, an imprint of the Knopf Doubleday Publishing Group, a division of Penguin Random Hosue LLC. All rights reserved. "Salvation" from *The Big Sea* by Langston Hughes. Copyright © 1940 by Langston Hughes. Copyright renewed 1968 by Arna Bontemps and George Houston Bass.

**David Henry Hwang.** *Trying to Find Chinatown*. Published in *Trying to Find Chinatown: The Selected Plays of David Henry Hwang*. Copyright © 2000 by David Henry Hwang. Published by Theatre Communications Group. Used by permission of Theatre Communications Group.

**Shirley Jackson.** "The Lottery" from *The Lottery* by Shirley Jackson. Copyright © 1948, 1949 by Shirley Jackson. Coyright renewed 1976, 1977 by Laurence Hyman, Barry Hyman, Mrs. Sarah Webster and Mrs. Joanne Schnurer. Reprinted by permission of Farrar, Straus and Giroux.

**James Weldon Johnson.** "A Poet to His Baby Son," from *Saint Peter Relates an Incident: Selected Poems* by James Weldon Johnson, copyright 1935 by James Weldon Johnson; copyright renewed © 1963 by Grace Nail Johnson. Used by permission of Viking Books, an imprint of Penguin Publishing Group, a division of Penguin Random House LLC. All rights reserved.

**Lacy M. Johnson.** "White Trash Primer" first appeared in *Memoir Journal*; adapted for inclusion in *Trespasses: A Memoir.* Copyright © 2012 University of Iowa Press. Reprinted by permission of Lacy M. Johnson.

**Camden Joy.** "Dum Dum Boys" from *Lost Joy.* Reprinted by permission of Tom Adelman.

**Franz Kafka.** "A Hunger Artist." Translated by Ann Charters. Used by permission of Ann Charters.

**Jane Kenyon.** "Let Evening Come" from *Collected Poems.* Copyright © 2005 by The Estate of Jane Kenyon. Reprinted with the permission of The Permissions Company, Inc., on behalf of Graywolf Press, Minneapolis, Minnesota, www.graywolfpress.org.

**Jamaica Kincaid.** "Girl" from *At the Bottom of the River* by Jamaica Kincaid. Copyright © 1983 by Jamaica Kincaid. Reprinted by permission of Farrar, Straus and Giroux.

**Maxine Hong Kingston.** "No Name Woman" from *The Woman Warrior: Memoirs of a Girlhood Among Ghosts* by Maxine Hong Kingston, copyright © 1975, 1976 by Maxine Hong Kingston. Used by permission of Alfred A. Knopf, an imprint of the Knopf Doubleday Publishing Group, a division of Penguin Random House LLC. All rights reserved.

**Galway Kinnell.** "After Making Love We Hear Footsteps" from *Mortal Acts, Mortal Words* by Galway Kinnell. Copyright © 1980 by Galway Kinnell, renewed 2008 by Galway Kinnell. Reprinted by permission of Houghton Mifflin Harcourt Publishing Company. All rights reserved.

**Carolyn Kizer.** "Bitch" from *Cool, Calm and Collected: Poems 1960–2000.* Copyright © 2001 by Carolyn Kizer. Reprinted with the permission of The Permissions Company, Inc., on behalf of Copper Canyon Press, www.coppercanyonpress.org. "Afternoon Happiness" from *Yin: New Poems.* Copyright © 1984 by Carolyn Kizer. Reprinted with the permission of The Permissions Company, Inc., on behalf of BOA Editions, Ltd., www.boaeditions.org.

**Marvin Klotz.** "Requiem" is reprinted by permission of the Klotz family.

**Etheridge Knight.** "Hard Rock Returns to Prison From The Hospital For The Criminal Insane" from *The Essential Etheridge Knight* by Etheridge Knight © 1986. Reprinted by permission of the University of Pittsburgh Press.

**Yusef Komunyakaa.** "Facing It" from *Pleasure Dome: New and Collected Poems.* © 2001 by Yusef Komunyakaa. Published by Wesleyan University Press. Used by permission.

**Philip Larkin.** "This be the verse" from *The Complete Poems of Philip Larkin* by Philip Larkin, edited by Archie Burnett. Copyright © 2012 by The Estate of Philip Larkin. Introduction copyright © 2012 by Archie Burnett. Reprinted by permission of Farrar, Straus and Giroux, LLC.

**Evelyn Lau.** "Solipsism" is reprinted by permission of the author.

**Li-Young Lee.** "Eating Alone" from *Rose.* Copyright © 1986 by Li-Young Lee. Reprinted with the permission of The Permissions Company, Inc., on behalf of BOA Editions, Ltd. www.boaeditions.org.

**Jonathan Lethem.** "13, 1977, 21" from *The Disappointment Artist: Essays* by Jonathan Lethem, copyright © 2005 by Jonathan Lethem. Used by permission of Doubleday, an imprint of the Knopf Doubleday Publishing Group, a division of Penguin Random House LLC. All rights reserved.

**Audre Lorde.** "Hanging Fire" from *The Black Unicorn* by Audre Lorde. Copyright © 1978 by Audre Lorde. Used by permission of W. W. Norton & Company, Inc.

**Naguib Mahfouz.** "Half a Day." Used with permission of the Estate of Naguib Mahfouz and The University of Cairo Press.

**Ruth Margalit.** "The Unmothered." Ruth Margalit/*The New Yorker.* © Conde Nast. *The New Yorker*, web, May 2015.

**Bill McKibben.** "A Call to Arms: An Invitation to Demand Action on Climate Change" by Bill McKibben, *Rolling Stone*, Issue 1210, June 5, 2014. Copyright © Rolling Stone LLC 2014. All Rights Reserved. Used by Permission.

**Peter Meinke.** "Advice to My Son" from *Liquid Paper: New and Selected Poems*, by Peter Meinke, © 1991. Reprinted by permission of the University of Pittsburgh Press.

**Robert Mezey.** "My Mother" from *Collected Poems 1952–1999.* Copyright © 2000 by Robert Mezey. Reprinted with the permission of The Permissions Company, Inc, on behalf of the University of Arkansas Press, www.aupress.com.

**Lydia Millet.** "Love in Infant Monkeys" from *Love in Infant Monkeys.* Copyright © 2009 by Lydia Millet. Reprinted by permission of Counterpoint.

**Czeslaw Milosz.** "A Song on the End of the World" from *The Collected Poems 1931–1987* by Czeslaw Milosz. Copyright © 1988 by Czeslaw Milosz Royalties, Inc. Reprinted by permission of HarperCollins Publishers.

**Lisel Mueller.** "Happy and Unhappy Families" from *Alive Together* by Liesel Mueller. Copyright © 1996 by Lisel Mueller. Reprinted with permission of Louisiana State University Press.

**Bharati Mukherjee.** "Two Ways to Belong in America" by Bharati Mukherjee. Copyright © 1996 by Bharati Mukherjee. Originally published in *The New York Times.* Reprinted by permission of the author.

**Taslima Nasrin.** "Things Cheaply Had" from *The New Yorker*, October 9, 1995. Translated from the Bengali by Carolyne Wright, with Mohammad Nurul Huda and the author. Copyright © 1995 by Carolyne Wright. Reprinted with permission of Carolyne Wright.

**Howard Nemerov.** "Money" from *The Collected Poems of Howard Nemerov*, Copyright © 1977 by Howard Nemerov. Reprinted by permission of The University of Chicago Press.

**Pablo Neruda.** "The Dead Woman" by Pablo Neruda from *The Captain's Verses*, copyright © 1972 by Pablo Neruda and Donald D. Walsh. Reprinted by permission of New Directions Publishing Corp. "A Dog has Died" (*"Un perro ha muerto"*), translated by William O'Daly, from *Winter Garden.* Copyright © 1986, 2002 by William O'Daly. *"Un perro ha muerto"* from *Jardín de invierno* by Pablo Neruda, copyright Fundación Pablo Neruda, 1974. Reprinted with the permission of The Permissions Company, Inc., on behalf of Copper Canyon Press, www.coppercanyonpress.org, and with the permission of Agencia Literaria Carmen Balcells, S.A.

**Joyce Carol Oates.** "Where Are You Going, Where Have You Been?" [pp. 249–66] from *High Lonesome: New and Selected Stories 1968–2006* by Joyce Carol Oates. Copyright © 1970 Ontario Review, Inc. Reprinted by permission of HarperCollins Publishers.

**Tim O'Brien.** "The Things They Carried" from *The Things They Carried* by Tim O'Brien. Copyright © 1990 by Tim O'Brien. Reprinted by permission of Houghton Mifflin Harcourt Publishing Company. All rights reserved.

**Flannery O'Connor.** "A Good Man is Hard to Find" from *A Good Man Is Hard To Find and Other Stories* by Flannery O'Connor. Copyright 1953 by Flannery O'Connor and renewed 1981 by Regina O'Connor. Reprinted by permission of Houghton Mifflin Harcourt Publishing Company. All rights reserved. Excerpt from *Mystery and Manners* by Flannery O'Connor, edited by Sally and Robert Fitzgerald. Copyright © 1969 by the Estate of Mary Flannery O'Connor. Reprinted by permission of Farrar, Straus and Giroux, LLC.

**George Orwell.** "Shooting an Elephant" from *A Collection of Essays* by George Orwell. Copyright © 1950 by Sonia Brownell Orwell and renewed 1978 by Sonia Pitt-Rivers. Reprinted by permission of Houghton Mifflin Harcourt Publishing Company. All rights reserved.

**Alicia Suskin Ostriker.** "Daffodils" from *No Heaven* by Alicia Suskin Ostriker, © 2005. Reprinted by permission of the University of Pittsburgh Press. "The Dogs at Live Oak Beach, Santa Cruz" from *The Little Space: Poems Selected and New, 1968–1998* by Alicia Suskin Ostriker, © 1998. Reprinted by permission of the University of Pittsburgh Press.

**Dorothy Parker.** "One Perfect Rose" copyright 1926, renewed © 1954 by Dorothy Parker, from *The Portable Dorothy Parker* by Dorothy Parker, edited by Marion Meade. Used by permission of Viking Books, an imprint of Penguin Publishing Group, a division of Penguin Random House LLC. All rights reserved.

**Omar Pérez.** "Contributions to a Rudimentary Concept of Nation" from *Something of the Sacred.* Copyright © 2007 by Omar Pérez, translated by Roberto Tejada. Reprinted by permission of the author and translator from *Something of the Sacred* (Factory School, 2007).

**Marge Piercy.** "Barbie Doll," and "The Market Economy" from *Circles on the Water* by Marge Piercy, copyright © 1982 by Middlemarsh, Inc. Used by permission of Alfred A. Knopf, an imprint of the Knopf Doubleday Publishing Group, a division of Penguin Random House LLC. All rights reserved.

**Sylvia Plath.** All lines from "Daddy" from *The Collected Poems of Sylvia Plath, Edited by Ted Hughes* by Ted Hughes. Copyright © 1960, 1965, 1971, 1981 by The Estate of Sylvia Plath. Reprinted by permission of HarperCollins Publishers.

**Wyatt Prunty.** "Learning the Bicycle" from *The American Scholar*, Vol. 58, No. 1, Winter 1989. Copyright © 1988 by Wyatt Prunty. Used with permission.

**Dudley Randall.** "Ballad of Birmingham" reprinted by permission of the Dudley Randall Literary Estate, from *Roses and Revolutions: The Selected Writings of Dudley Randall*, Melba Joyce Boyd. Ed. (Detroit: Wayne State University Press, 2009).

**Adrienne Rich.** "Living In Sin" from *Collected Poems: 1950–2012* by Adrienne Rich. Copyright © 2016 by the Adrienne Rich Literary Trust. Copyright © 1955 by Adrienne Rich. Used by permission of W. W. Norton & Company, Inc.

**Theodore Roethke.** "My Papa's Waltz" copyright © 1942 by Hearst Magazines, Inc.; and "I Knew a Woman," copyright © 1954 by Theodore Roethke; from *Collected Poems* by Theodore Roethke. Used by permission of Doubleday, an imprint of the Knopf Doubleday Publishing Group, a division of Penguin Random House LLC. All rights reserved.

**Kay Ryan.** "All Shall Be Restored." Excerpts from *Elephant Rocks*, copyright © 1996 by Kay Ryan. Used by permission of Grove/Atlantic, Inc. Any third party use of this material, outside of this publication, is prohibited.

**Sappho.** "With His Venom" from *Sappho: A New Translation*, translated by Mary Barnard. Copyright © 1986 by Mary Barnard. Published by the University of California Press and reprinted via Rightslink.

**George Saunders.** "The End of Firpo in the World" from *Pastoralia* by George Saunders, copyright © 2000 by George Saunders. Used by permission of Riverhead, an imprint of Penguin Publishing Group, a division of Penguin Random House LLC. All rights reserved.

**Léopold Sédar Senghor.** "To New York" from *The Collected Poetry*. Translated by Melvin Dixon pp. 87–89. Copyright © 1991 by the Rector and Visitors of the University. Reprinted by permission of the University of Virginia Press.

**Leslie Marmon Silko.** "The Man to Send Rain Clouds" from *Storyteller* by Leslie Marmon Siko, copyright © 1981, 2012 by Leslie Marmon Silko. Used by permission of Viking Books, an imprint of Penguin Publishing Group, a division of Penguin Random House LLC. All rights reserved.

**Stevie Smith.** "Not Waving But Drowning." By Stevie Smith, from *Collected Poems of Stevie Smith*, copyright © 1957 by Stevie Smith. Reprinted by permission of New Directions Publishing Corp.

**Rebecca Solnit.** "Revolutions per Minute." Copyright 2008, Rebecca Solnit. Used by permission of the author.

**Sophocles.** "Antigonê" from *Sophocles, The Oedipus Cycle: An English Version* by Dudley Fitts and Robert Fitzgerald. Copyright 1939 by Houghton Mifflin Harcourt Publishing Company. Copyright © Renewed 1967 by Dudley Fitts and Robert Fitzgerald. Reprinted by permission of Houghton Mifflin Harcourt Publishing Company. All rights reserved.

**Gary Soto.** "Behind Grandma's House." From *New and Selected Poems*. © 1995 by Gary Soto. Used with permission of Chronicle Books LLC, San Francisco. Visit ChronicleBooks.com.

**William Stafford.** "Traveling through the Dark" from *The Way It Is: New and Selected Poems*. Copyright © 1962, 1998 by William Stafford and the Estate of William Stafford. Reprinted with the permission of The Permissions Company, Inc. on behalf of Graywolf Press, Minneapolis, Minnesota, www.graywolfpress.org.

**Pablo Piñero Stillmann.** "Life, Love, Happiness: A Found Essay on the Twitterverse" from *Brevity*, March 2, 2013. Reprinted by permission of the author.

**Wisława Szymborska.** "A Happy Love" Magnus J. Kryzski, translator, from *Sounds, Feelings, Thought*. Copyright © 1981 Princeton University Press. Reprinted by permission of Princeton University Press via Copyright Clearance Center.

**Amy Tan.** "Two Kinds" from *The Joy Luck Club* by Amy Tan, copyright © 1989 by Amy Tan. Used by permission of G. P. Putnam's Sons, an imprint of Penguin Publishing Group, a division of Penguin Random House LLC.

**Dylan Thomas.** "Do Not Go Gentle Into That Good Night." By Dylan Thomas, from *Collected Poems of Dylan Thomas*, copyright © 1952 by Dylan Thomas. Reprinted by permission of New Directions Publishing Corp.

**Natasha Trethewey.** "Flounder" from *Domestic Work*. Copyright © 2000 by Natasha Trethewey Reprinted with the permission of The Permissions Company, Inc., on behalf of Graywolf Press, Minneapolis, Minnesota, www.graywolfpress.org.

**John Updike.** "A & P" from *Pigeon Feathers and Other Stories* by John Updike, copyright © 1962, copyright renewed 1990 by John Updike. Used by permission of Alfred A. Knopf, an imprint of the Knopf Doubleday Publishing Group, a division of Penguin Random House LLC. All rights reserved. "Dog's Death" from *Collected Poems, 1953–1993* by John Updike, copyright © 1993 by John Updike. Used by permission of Alfred A. Knopf, an imprint of the Knopf Doubleday Publishing Group, a division of Penguin Random House LLC. All rights reserved.

**Helena María Viramontes.** "The Moths" is reprinted with permission from the publishers of *The Moths and Other Stories* by Helena María Viramontes (© 1995 Arte Público Press—University of Houston).

**Alice Walker.** "Everyday Use"; "Everyday Use" from *In Love & Trouble: Stories of Black Women* by Alice Walker. Copyright © 1973 by Alice Walker. Reprinted by permission of Houghton Mifflin Harcourt Publishing Company and The Joy Harris Literary Agency. All rights reserved.

**Virginia Woolf.** "Shakespeare's Sister" from *A Room of One's Own* by Virginia Woolf. Copyright 1929 by Houghton Mifflin Harcourt Publishing Company and renewed 1957 by Leonard Woolf. Reprinted by permission of Houghton Mifflin Harcourt Publishing Company and The Society of Authors. All rights reserved.

**James Wright.** "Lying in a Hammock at William Duffy's Farm in Pine Island, MN" in *Collected Poems* by James Wright © 1971. Reprinted by permission of Wesleyan University Press.

**Kevin Young.** "Negative." Reprinted from *To Repel Ghosts* by permission of Steerforth Press L.L.C.

**Lu Xun.** "Diary of a Madman" from *Diary of a Madman and Other Stories*, by Lu Xun, translated by William A. Lyell. Copyright © 1990 University of Hawaii Press. Reprinted by permission of the University of Hawaii Press.

# INDEX OF AUTHORS AND TITLES